THE DOCTRINE OF GOD

CHURCH DOGMATICS

BY

KARL BARTH

VOLUME II

THE DOCTRINE OF GOD

SECOND HALF-VOLUME

EDITORS
Rev. G. W. BROMILEY, Ph.D., D.Litt.
Rev. Prof. T. F. TORRANCE, D.D., D.Theol.

Edinburgh: T. & T. CLARK, 36 George Street

THE DOCTRINE OF GOD

(Being Volume II, Part 2 of Church Dogmatics)

BY

KARL BARTH, Dr.Theol., D.D., LL.D.

TRANSLATORS

Rev. G. W. BROMILEY, Ph.D., D.Litt.
Rev. J. C. CAMPBELL, B.D.
Rev. Prof. IAIN WILSON, B.D., Ph.D.
Rev. J. STRATHEARN McNAB, M.A.
Rev. HAROLD KNIGHT, M.A., D.Phil.
Rev. R. A. STEWART, B.D., M.Litt.

EDINBURGH: T. & T. CLARK, 36 George Street

Authorised English Translation from
DIE KIRCHLICHE DOGMATIK, II:
Die Lehre von Gott, 2
Published by
EVANGELISCHER VERLAG A.G.
ZOLLIKON—ZÜRICH

©

KARL BARTH
27th September 1957

PRINTED IN GREAT BRITAIN BY
CLARK CONSTABLE (1982) LIMITED
FOR
T. & T. CLARK, EDINBURGH

ISBN 0 567 09022 1

FIRST PRINTED 1957
LATEST IMPRESSION 1983

EDITORS' PREFACE

IN the first half-volume of his doctrine of God, Barth expounded God as the One He is in the act of His revelation and the freedom of His love. He showed that God cannot be known *in abstracto*, but only in the overflow of the divine life to His creature, and therefore in His eternal decision. But this eternal decision demands separate treatment and therefore brings us to this second half-volume. It is God's decision to elect Himself for fellowship with man, and man for fellowship with Himself. Hence Barth is impelled to consider the doctrine of the divine election and its implied command within the context of the doctrine of God. The election is God's gracious decision in Jesus Christ to bestow His love on man (ch. 7), and thus to take man into a responsible relation to His own will (ch. 8).

In his doctrine of election Barth emphasises the freedom, mystery and righteousness of God's predestinating will, but he refuses to find its ultimate ground in a dark and unknown area of the divine will. The election is essentially God's gracious will to choose us for Himself as revealed and fulfilled in Jesus Christ. His eternal decree and His eternal Word are one and the same, and therefore the ultimate ground of election is identical with the reality of Jesus Christ. In Jesus Christ, electing and elect, God has eternally willed to lay hold of man, and fulfilled His will, reconciling man to Himself. Thus election includes the atoning work of Christ as the Elect who bore our rejection, and the doctrine of election is regarded not merely as a part but as the very sum of the Gospel. The sustained exposition of this theme, with its constant reference to Jesus Christ as the basis of the election of the community and the individual, is one of the most original, profound and moving in the whole history of theology.

The chapter on the divine command follows naturally from that on election, for the predestinating will of God is necessarily His will for the object of His love. Here then, in his doctrine of God, Barth lays the foundation for a theological ethics covering the whole area of man's freedom and self-determination as one called to be a covenant-partner of God. In virtue of the election of grace, his existence is not left to itself, but adopted and assumed into the existence of God in Jesus Christ. A general ethics is impossible, because it attempts to ignore the election of grace. It can be attempted only in a sinful self-isolation from God. A true ethics will protest against all abstraction, whether in relation to God or in relation to man and his existence,

vii

and it will thus be a theological ethics, and fundamentally an ethics of grace. But grace, as we have seen, means the gracious will and action of God in Jesus Christ, in whom the will of God is not merely declared to us but obediently fulfilled for us and in us. Thus ethics, too, belongs to the proclamation of the Gospel.

The originality of the treatment, especially in relation to election, means that there is a correspondingly high proportion of dogmatic and especially exegetical material. Indeed, some of the central sections consist almost exclusively of biblical exposition. Yet the basic affirmations are made with the majestic power and simplicity which characterise the mature Barth of the *Dogmatics*. And the discerning reader will be well-advised not to shirk the serious demands made by the passages in small print, whether for the information which is imparted or for the insights which are opened up.

The size and nature of the volume have naturally made similar demands in the preparation of the English rendering. The translators have carried the main burden, Dr. G. W. Bromiley being responsible for pp. 3–194, the Rev. J. C. Campbell for pp. 195–305, Prof. Iain Wilson for pp. 306–506, the Rev. J. Strathearn McNab for pp. 507–630, Dr. Harold Knight for pp. 631–732 and the Rev. R. A. Stewart for pp. 731 to the end. A good deal of editorial work has also been necessitated in the scrutiny of the translation, the standardising of terminology and style, the checking of references and the adjustment (and improvement) of the Indexes. At the proof-stage we have enjoyed the valuable help of our assistant editor, Prof. J. K. S. Reid. And finally the printers are to be congratulated on the high level of accuracy which they have maintained with such formidable material.

EDINBURGH. *Trinity*, 1957.

PREFACE

In the Preface to the first half-volume of my *Church Dogmatics* I made some observations on the plan of the work as a whole. I concluded with the words of Jas. 4[15] : " If the Lord will, and we live." That was almost ten years ago. I did not then suspect how very appropriate it was to speak in that way. A year later we were plunged into the Third Reich and the German Church-conflict. From that time the affairs of Europe and finally of the whole world hurtled with ever increasing violence into the crisis which still engulfs us. By the very nature of things I have not been able to devote the last ten years solely to dogmatics, as was my intention in 1932. Yet dogmatics has been ever with me, giving me a constant awareness of what should be my central and basic theme as a thinker. Some of the proofs of the present volume were corrected by night in a Federal guard-room. It might well be told how one of my comrades there in the friendliest fashion asked me whether I had brought my carnival-paper. The significance of the question will be appreciated in Basel. I am truly thankful that *per varios casus, per tot discrimina rerum*, I have already found it possible to write and publish the fourth of a series which will probably run to nine or ten half-volumes.

A good deal has already been said about the size both of the work as a whole and also of each of its constituent parts. It may be conceded that the Bible itself can put things more concisely. But if dogmatics is to serve its purpose, then I cannot see how either I myself, or any contemporaries known to me, can properly estimate the more concise statements of the Bible except in penetrating expositions which will necessarily demand both time and space. In the last analysis I ask of my readers no greater patience than that already demanded of myself. For our mutual consolation I offer a historical reminiscence. When Schleiermacher was struggling to finish the first draft of his *Christian Faith*, on September 7, 1822 he wrote to his friend Twesten : " Every time I see this book, I sigh at its bulk." I know that my own *Dogmatics* is already a good deal bulkier than Schleiermacher's *Christian Faith*. Yet Twesten's reply on March 9, 1823 might equally well be applied to my own book : " You complain about the size of your book, but do not worry ; for most of us the size is indispensable to understanding, and the few who would perhaps have understood you from a lesser work will certainly accept with gratitude all the elucidations you want to give " (cf. G. Heinrici, *D. August Twesten nach Tagebüchern und Briefen*, 1899, p. 377, 379 f.). Yes, for a right understanding and exposition there is need of a thorough elucidation. May it not be that I have been too short and not too long at some important points ?

The specific subject-matter of this half-volume made it necessary for me to set out more fully than in previous sections the exegetical background to the dogmatic exposition. For this purpose there has

been a great increase in both the number and the size of the passages
in small print. The disadvantages are obvious, but I had no option.
By way of appeasement I offer a story about the Dutch theologian,
Petrus van Mastricht (1630–1710). In 1698 Mastricht published the
whole second edition of his *Theoretica-Practica Theologia* in even smaller
print than that of the small-type passages of the present book. And
in the *Praefatio* he had the coolness to tell his readers : *si hoc officiat
oculorum perspicaciae, cogitabam hoc facili negotio compensaturum
iuvenum quidem oculorum acumen, senilium vero perspicillos.*

To think of the contents of this volume gives me much pleasure,
but even greater anxiety. The work has this peculiarity, that in it I
have had to leave the framework of theological tradition to a far
greater extent than in the first part on the doctrine of God. I would
have preferred to follow Calvin's doctrine of predestination much more
closely, instead of departing from it so radically. I would have preferred, too, to keep to the beaten tracks when considering the basis
of ethics. But I could not and cannot do so. As I let the Bible itself
speak to me on these matters, as I meditated upon what I seemed to
hear, I was driven irresistibly to reconstruction. And now I cannot
but be anxious to see whether I shall be alone in this work, or whether
there will be others who will find enlightenment in the basis and scope
suggested. It is because of the rather critical nature of the case that
I have had to introduce into this half-volume such long expositions
of some Old and New Testament passages. For the rest, I have
grounds for thinking that to some my meaning will be clearer in these
passages than in the main body of the text.

It is an excellent thing that I can place this volume alongside the
books of my two friends, Eduard Thurneysen (*Der Jacobusbrief in
Predigten*) and Wilhelm Vischer (*Das Christuszeugnis des Alten Testaments*, Vol. II), both of which appeared some six months ago. The
three books are of independent growth and quite different in form,
but at the same time they belong closely together in purpose and
content. I gratefully recognise it to be an excellent thing, for we may
not take it for granted, that to-day there is again the possibility of a
serious theological unity even where there can be no question of a
school in any meaningful sense—for who in the present case would be the
teacher ?—and that even in these evil times we are able to set forward
that unity without let or hindrance in our forward post at ancient Basel.

In the meantime I have already set in hand the continuation of
my *Dogmatics* (treating of the doctrine of creation). In the light
of what world events may still have in store, and in the light, too, of
my own more advanced age, it will be even more fitting if once again,
and this time more seriously, I lay all my plans for the future under
the *conditio Jacobea.*

BASEL. *Whitsuntide*, 1942.

CONTENTS

CHAPTER VII

THE ELECTION OF GOD

CHAPTER VII

THE ELECTION OF GOD

§ 32

THE PROBLEM OF A CORRECT DOCTRINE OF THE ELECTION OF GRACE

The doctrine of election is the sum of the Gospel because of all words that can be said or heard it is the best : that God elects man; that God is for man too the One who loves in freedom. It is grounded in the knowledge of Jesus Christ because He is both the electing God and elected man in One. It is part of the doctrine of God because originally God's election of man is a predestination not merely of man but of Himself. Its function is to bear basic testimony to eternal, free and unchanging grace as the beginning of all the ways and works of God.

1. THE ORIENTATION OF THE DOCTRINE

The time has now come to leave the doctrine of the knowledge of God and the reality of God. We have tried to learn the lofty but simple lesson that it is by God that God is known, and that He is the living God as the One who loves in freedom; living both in the unity and also in the wealth of His perfections. Our starting-point in that first part of the doctrine of God was neither an axiom of reason nor a datum of experience. In the measure that a doctrine of God draws on these sources, it betrays the fact that its subject is not really God but a hypostatised reflection of man. At more than one stage in our consideration of the earlier history of the doctrine we have had to guard steadfastly against the temptation of this type of doctrine. We took as our starting-point what God Himself said and still says concerning God, and concerning the knowledge and reality of God, by way of the self-testimony which is accessible and comprehensible because it has been given human form in Holy Scripture, the document which is the very essence and basis of the Church. As strictly as possible we have confined ourselves to the appropriation and repetition of that self-testimony as such. As strictly as possible we have let our questions be dictated by the answers which are already present in the revelation of God attested in Holy Scripture. In so doing

3

we have listened gratefully to the voices of the Church as well, both old and new. But we have continually measured those voices by the only voice which can reign in the Church. Whether we could follow them or not, we allowed ourselves to use them only in order that we might learn the better to hear and understand that voice which reigns in the Church as the source and norm of all truth. It was in that way that we came to perceive the lofty but simple truth concerning the knowledge and reality of God. It was in that way that we rendered our account of what is pure and correct doctrine in this matter.

But the voice which reigns, the voice by which we were taught by God Himself concerning God, was the voice of Jesus Christ. Along all the path now behind us we could not take a single step without stumbling again and again across that name. And " across that name " does not mean across an empty title. It does not mean across a form or figure in which God could declare Himself to us or exist for us and yet be quite different in and by Himself. It does not mean across a name which is only a means or medium, and which God could ultimately discard, because ultimately it is not the real name of God, but only of a divine arrangement which in the last analysis is quite different from God Himself. The truth is that we continuously stumbled across that name in matter and substance. We stumbled across it necessarily. For as we proceeded along that path, we found that that name was the very subject, the very matter, with which we had to deal. In avoiding the different sources of error, we saw that they had one feature in common : the negligence or arbitrariness with which even in the Church the attempt was made to go past or to go beyond Jesus Christ in the consideration and conception and definition of God, and in speech about God. But when theology allows itself on any pretext to be jostled away from that name, God is inevitably crowded out by a hypostatised image of man. Theology must begin with Jesus Christ, and not with general principles, however better, or, at any rate, more relevant and illuminating, they may appear to be : as though He were a continuation of the knowledge and Word of God, and not its root and origin, not indeed the very Word of God itself. Theology must also end with Him, and not with supposedly self-evident general conclusions from what is particularly enclosed and disclosed in Him : as though the fruits could be shaken from this tree ; as though in the things of God there were anything general which we could know and designate in addition to and even independently of this particular. The obscurities and ambiguities of our way were illuminated in the measure that we held fast to that name and in the measure that we let Him be the first and the last, according to the testimony of Holy Scripture. Against all the imaginations and errors in which we seem to be so hopelessly entangled when we try to speak of God, God will indeed maintain Himself if we will only allow the name of Jesus Christ to be maintained in our thinking as the beginning and the end of all our thoughts. We recall how in our consideration of the divine perfections everything became clear and orderly when He, Jesus Christ, emerged as the perfect One, the fulness of the love and freedom of God Himself, the love and freedom of God in which all the divine perfections are neither more nor less than God Himself. So long as we remained true to the witness of Holy Scripture there was no alternative but to follow this line and to hold fast by it. For witnessing to God, the Old and New Testament Scriptures also witness to this name, and to the fulness of God which it encloses and represents, which cannot be separated from it, which cannot precede or follow it, but in it begins and continues and ends.

This is the decisive result of all our previous discussion. This is the sum and substance of the whole doctrine of the knowledge and reality of God. But that means that the Christian doctrine of God cannot end with the matter which we have treated so far. In a Christian doctrine of God our concern is to define and expound the Subject of all that the Christian Church receives and proclaims. If it is true, then, that this Subject is disclosed only in the name of Jesus Christ, that it is wholly and entirely enclosed in Him, then we cannot stop at this point, defining and expounding the Subject only in and for itself. We tried to do that on the earlier part of our way. But we should be overlooking and suppressing something essential, and a serious gap would be left in our reflection on the Word of God as the norm of Christian proclamation, if we now tried to proceed without treating of what the Church must receive and proclaim as the work of this Subject, the activity of God as Creator, Reconciler and Redeemer. We should still not have learned to say " God " correctly (i.e., as understood in the Christian Church on the basis of Holy Scripture) if we thought it enough simply to say " God." However well-grounded or critical our utterance, if it has a logical exclusiveness, if it is only " God," it will not suffice. For if it is true that in Jesus Christ there dwells the fulness of the Godhead bodily (Col. 2^9), then in all the perfection with which it is differentiated from everything that is not God, and thus exists for itself, the Subject God still cannot, as it were, be envisaged, established and described only in and for itself. We must not be so exact, so clever, so literal, that our doctrine of God remains only a doctrine of God. We must demonstrate its Christian character by avoiding such abstraction. In virtue of the truth of its specific content it must burst through the frame which apparently—but only apparently—surrounds it. Otherwise the highest reality can, and inevitably will, be reduced to the flattest unreality. All that we have previously said concerning this Subject will be enveloped again in darkness. From the very outset a new obscurity will, in fact, extend over all that we have still to say concerning the work of this Subject. To be truly Christian, the doctrine of God must carry forward and complete the definition and exposition of the Subject God. It must do this in such a way that quite apart from what must be said about the knowledge and the reality of God as such, it makes the Subject known as One which in virtue of its innermost being, willing and nature does not stand outside all relationships, but stands in a definite relationship *ad extra* to another. It is not as though the object of this relationship, the other, constitutes a part of the reality of God outside of God. It is not as though it is in any other way comparable with God. It is not as though God is forced into this relationship. It is not as though He is in any way constrained or compelled by this other. As we have often enough seen and asserted, there can be no question of any such compulsion coming upon God from without. God is love. But He is also perfect freedom. Even if there were no such relationship, even if there were no other outside of Him, He would still be love. But positively, in the free decision of His love, God is God in the very fact, and in such a way, that He does stand in this relation, in a definite relationship with the other. We cannot go back on this decision if we would know God and speak accurately of God. If we did, we should be betrayed into a false abstraction which sought to speak only of God, not recognising that, when we speak of God, then in consideration of His freedom, and of His free decision, we must speak also of this relationship. This relationship belongs to the Subject God, and to the doctrine of God in the narrower sense, to the extent that it rests upon a definite attitude of God which, when we speak of God, we must always and in all respects take into consideration. And that we have never so far failed to do. For how could we have said anything about the knowledge and reality of God had we not considered this positive attitude, learning from it how God gives Himself to be known, and what He is both in Himself and in all His works? But this fact, that God is God only in this way and not in any other, must now be made explicit. We move onto solid ground when we seek to learn from this positive attitude that which can be learned concerning the knowledge and reality of God, considering Him and conceiving of Him in the constant light of His revelation and all His works. For the divine attitude is not a matter of chance. It is not revocable or transitory. God lays upon us the obligation of this attitude because first of all He lays it upon Himself. In dealing with this attitude, we have to do with His free but definitive decision. We cannot abstract from it without falling into arbitrary speculation. But we cannot ignore it. Once made, it belongs definitively to God Himself, not in His being in and for Himself, but in His being within this relationship. It belongs to the reality of God which is a reality not apart from but in this decision. It is so adjoined to this reality that we must not allow any objectivity of logic to prevent us from introducing the adjunct as an element in our knowledge of God. We cannot speak correctly of God in His being in and for Himself without considering Him always in this attitude, without allowing both our questions and answers to be dictated by it. We cannot speak accurately or confidently of the work of God unless first we see clearly that the attitude which God has taken up, and by which His work is determined, belongs to God Himself, and cannot in any way be isolated from Him. For that reason, the question of this attitude must be raised specifically and independently within the framework of the doctrine of God. In a Christian doctrine of God, if God is to be exhaustively described and represented as the Subject who governs and determines everything else, there must be an advance beyond the immediate logical sense of the concept to the actual relationship in which God has placed Himself; a relationship outside of which God no longer wills to be and no longer is God, and within which alone He can be truly honoured and worshipped as God. If it is true that it pleased the fulness of God to dwell in Jesus Christ (Col. 1[19]), then in a Christian doctrine of God this further step is unavoidable. And it is immediately apparent in which direction the step must be taken.

Jesus Christ is indeed God in His movement towards man, or, more exactly, in His movement towards the people represented in the one man Jesus of Nazareth, in His covenant with this people, in His being and activity amongst and towards this people. Jesus Christ is the decision of God in favour of this attitude or relation. He is Himself the relation. It is a relation *ad extra*, undoubtedly; for both the man and the people represented in Him are creatures and not God. But it is a relation which is irrevocable, so that once God has willed to enter into it, and has in fact entered into it, He could not be God without it. It is a relation in which God is self-determined, so that the determination belongs no less to Him than all that He is in and for Himself. Without the Son sitting at the right hand of the Father, God would not be God. But the Son is not only very God. He is also called Jesus of Nazareth. He is also very man, and as such He is the Representative of the people which in Him and through Him is united as He is with God, being with Him the object of the divine movement. That we know God and have God only in Jesus Christ means that we can know Him and have Him only with the man Jesus of Nazareth and with the people which He represents. Apart from this man and apart from this people God would be a different, an alien God. According to the Christian perception He would not be God at all. According to the Christian perception the true God is what He is only in this movement, in the movement towards this man, and in Him and through Him towards other men in their unity as His people.

That other to which God stands in relationship, in an actuality which can neither be suspended nor dissolved, is not simply and directly the created world as such. There is, too, a relationship of God to the world. There is a work of God towards it and with it. There is a history between God and the world. But this history has no independent signification. It takes place in the interests of the primal history which is played out between God and this one man and His people. It is the sphere in which this primal history is played out. It attains its goal as this primal history attains its goal. And the same is true both of man as such and also of the human race as a whole. The partner of God which cannot now be thought away is neither " man " as an idea, nor " humanity," nor indeed a large or small total of individual men. It is the one man Jesus and the people represented in Him. Only secondarily, and for His sake, is it " man," and " humanity " and the whole remaining cosmos. Even human nature and human history in general have no independent signification. They point to the primal history played out within them between God and the one man, and all other men as His people. The general (the world or man) exists for the sake of the particular. In the particular the general has its meaning and fulfilment. The particular is that other over against God which cannot be thought away, which is outside of God, which is the object of the divine movement, which is so adjoined now to the reality of God that we cannot and should not say the word " God " without at once thinking of it. We must think at once, then, of Jesus of Nazareth and of His people. The attitude or relation for which God has once and for all decided, to which He has committed us and wills to be committed by us, is the relation or attitude to Jesus Christ. In the person of His eternal Son He has united Himself with the man Jesus of Nazareth, and in Him and through Him with this people. He is the Father of Jesus Christ. He is not only the Father of the eternal Son, but as such He is the eternal Father of this temporal man. He is, then, the eternal Father, the Possessor, the Lord and the Saviour of the people which this man represents as King and Head. In this determination, as carried through by His own decision, God is, therefore, the Subject of everything that is to be received and proclaimed in the Christian Church. All His work takes place according to this plan and under this sign. As such it has, of course, a wider reach. The other towards which God moves in this wider sphere is, of course, the created world as a whole. It is, of course, " man " and " humanity." But everything which comes from God takes place according to this plan and under this sign. Everything is from this beginning and to this end. Everything is in this order and has this meaning. Everything happens according to this basic and determinative pattern, model and system. Everything which comes from God takes place " in Jesus Christ," i.e., in the establishment of the covenant which, in the union of His Son with Jesus of Nazareth, God has instituted and maintains and directs between Himself and His people, the people consisting of those who belong to Him, who have become His in this One. The primal history which underlies and is the goal of the whole history of His relationship *ad extra*, with the creation and man in general, is the history of this covenant. The primal history, and with it the covenant, are, then, the attitude and relation in which by virtue of the decision of His free love God wills to be and is God. And this relation cannot be separated from the Christian conception of God as such. The two must go together if this conception is to be truly Christian. For that reason, this relation must form the subject of a second part of our doctrine of God.

But as we approach this particular subject, two aspects of the one truth must be considered and two spheres of investigation are disclosed.

It is at once apparent that in the decision by which He institutes, maintains and directs this covenant, in His decision " in Jesus Christ," God on His side does accomplish something quite definite. He executes this decision in His movement towards man, towards the man Jesus Christ and the people which He represents. And this movement is an act of divine sovereignty. To characterise it as such we must select from the fulness of His essential attributes, We must say : This act demonstrates His mercy and righteousness, His constancy and omnipotence. It is as the Lord who lives in the fulness of these perfections that God acts when He institutes and directs this covenant. He constitutes Himself the Lord of the covenant. He is, therefore, its free author. He gives it its content and determines its order. He maintains it. He directs it to its goal. He governs it in every respect. It is His decision that there is a covenant-partner. It is also His decision who this partner is, and what must befall him. It is only as He wills it that the covenant arises at all. The covenant-member is the one whom He ordains. It is what He wills that takes place within the covenant. All that we have to say concerning this aspect of the divine movement may be summed up in the concept which is the title of this chapter : that of the election in the sense of the election of divine grace, the choice which God makes in His grace, thus making this movement, and instituting, maintaining and directing this covenant. In accordance with the theological tradition of the Reformed Churches (and especially the German-speaking), what we have in mind is the election of grace (in translation of ἐκλογὴ χάριτος, Rom. 11⁵) ; and it may be noted how the term reflects the being of God as we have hitherto sought to understand and explain it. It is a question of grace, and that means the love of God. It is a question of election, and that means the freedom of God.

Here, again, we must deal first with grace. The fact that God makes this movement, the institution of the covenant, the primal decision " in Jesus Christ," which is the basis and goal of all His works—that is grace. Speaking generally, it is the demonstration, the overflowing of the love which is the being of God, that He who is entirely self-sufficient, who even within Himself cannot know isolation, willed even in all His divine glory to share His life with another, and

to have that other as the witness of His glory. This love of God is
His grace. It is love in the form of the deepest condescension. It
occurs even where there is no question of claim or merit on the part
of the other. It is love which is overflowing, free, unconstrained,
unconditioned. And we must add at once : It is love which is merciful,
making this movement, this act of condescension, in such a way that,
in taking to itself this other, it identifies itself with its need, and meets
its plight by making it its own concern. And we must add at once :
It is love which is patient, not consuming this other, but giving it
place, willing its existence for its own sake and for the sake of the goal
appointed for it. For the moment, however, it is important to stop
at the first concept, the concept of grace. God's decision in Jesus
Christ is a gracious decision. In making it, God stoops down from
above. In it He does something which He has no need to do, which
He is not constrained to do. He does something which He alone can
constrain Himself, and has in fact constrained Himself, to do. In
entering into this covenant, He freely makes Himself both benefactor
and benefit. It will be seen that the whole sovereignty of this act is
contained already in the concept of grace. Because grace is here the
Alpha and Omega, it cannot be otherwise than that, in the total
manner already indicated, God should be the Lord " in Jesus Christ."
But with this concept the other aspect forces itself to the forefront,
and must there remain—that " in Jesus Christ " we have to do with
a divine benefit or favour. It is a matter of God's love. If in His
majesty He establishes fellowship with the other which does not
partake of His majesty, but in its otherness stands in the very depths
over against Him, that means favour. In showing His grace, God
proves Himself both Saviour and Helper. He does so freely as the
Lord. But this exercise of lordship is kind as well as good, communicating and sharing its goods. The doctrine of the divine election
of grace is the sum of the Gospel. It is the content of the good news
which is Jesus Christ.

The other part of the concept cannot and should not alter this
fact in the least. Election should serve at once to emphasise and
explain what we have already said in the word grace. God in His
love elects another to fellowship with Himself. First and foremost
this means that God makes a self-election in favour of this other. He
ordains that He should not be entirely self-sufficient as He might be.
He determines for Himself that overflowing, that movement, that
condescension. He constitutes Himself as benefit or favour. And in
so doing He elects another as the object of His love. He draws it
upwards to Himself, so as never again to be without it, but to be
who He is in covenant with it. In this concept of election there is
reflected more clearly, of course, the other element in the being of
God : the freedom in which He is the One who eternally loves. The
concept election means that grace is truly grace. It means that God

owes His grace to no one, and that no one can deserve it. It means that grace cannot be the subject of a claim or a right on the part of the one upon whom it is directed. It means that it is the determination and decision of the will of God. Again, God elects that He shall be the covenant-God. He does so in order not to be alone in His divine glory, but to let heaven and earth, and between them man, be the witnesses of His glory. He elects the way in which His love shall be shown and the witness to His glory established. He elects creation, man, the human race, as the sphere in which He wills to be gracious. But the existence of creation and of the human race does not constrain Him in the future exercise of grace. He elects even within this sphere. He elects the man of Nazareth, that He should be essentially one with Himself in His Son. Through Him and in Him He elects His people, thus electing the whole basis and meaning of all His works. He elects, i.e., He is free, and He remains free, both in what He does and in what He permits. He does what He does, but without any claim arising that He must do it, or that He must do it in this or that way. Over against Him no claim can ever arise. Nothing can precede His grace, whether in eternity or time, whether from the beginning or in the process of development. In all its manifestations, in all its activity, His grace is free grace. It is the Lord who is the Saviour and Helper. His taking to Himself of that other is an act of unconditioned sovereignty. This is what the word " election " tells us as the second component of the concept " election of grace." It cannot possibly mean any restriction of the evangelical character of the concept. It reminds us emphatically, however, that the good news summarised in this concept is good news only because it proclaims to us the salvation which is the will of the real Lord both of our life and of all life. The truth to which the whole concept points is the specific subject to which we must address ourselves in this seventh chapter.

The doctrine of God's covenant-relation with the people represented in the man Jesus is the fulfilment of the doctrine of God in the narrower sense of the term. But it is not exhausted by the doctrine of the election of grace. God acts in His free grace, but He also wills and expects and demands something from His covenant-partner. To the majesty of that activity which no claim can condition, there corresponds the unconditional nature of the very definite claim which He Himself must advance. Encountering man in His free love, God becomes the companion of man. That is what He determined to do " in Jesus Christ." That is the foundation-plan and sign of all His works. But in virtue of His absolute ascendancy, in virtue of the fact that in this relationship He must have both the first and the last word concerning His partner, He is of necessity the Judge. We use the expression here in its most comprehensive sense. God is for His covenant-partner both the One by whom he will be judged and also the One according to whom he must judge himself. God is for him the criterion, the standard, the question of the good or the evil, the rightness or the wrongness, of his being and activity. God ordained and created him as partner in this covenant ; God elected and called him to that position ; and in that position He makes him responsible. How could God draw him to Himself, as He does, without making him responsible ? God constitutes this " being responsible " the whole meaning of his existence. He shows him His own way as the only one which he can tread. He calls him to order and keeps him in order, revealing to him His own order and seeing that he keeps to it. Even this He does in genuine fulfilment of His love and grace. Here too, then, we have to do with the Gospel. But we have to do with the Gospel in so far as it has always the form of the Law. The practical significance of the freedom of grace, of the sovereignty in which God elects, is this : that in his very election the one elected finds a Master and Lord. Grace does not will only to be received and known. As it is truly received and known, as it works itself out as the favour which it is, it wills also to rule. But it rules by offering God to His covenant-partner as Lord of the covenant. That is the second basic point which we must make concerning the life of God " in Jesus Christ," in and with His people. We must be constantly aware of this point as we consider all the divine work grounded upon the grace of God and the divine election of grace. There is no grace without the lordship and claim of grace. There is no dogmatics which is not also and necessarily ethics. The basic points in the inter-relationship between divine grace and the divine claim will occupy us in the next chapter (which will also serve as a foundation for " theological ethics ") under the title " The Command of God." The theme which first confronts us (and it is most intimately connected with the second) is the divine election of grace.

As we take up this theme, we enter the field of theology which is known in the history of dogma as the doctrine of predestination. Before we do anything more, it is essential that we should make emphatically the first affirmation inscribed in the synopsis at the head of this section. The truth which must now occupy us, the truth of the doctrine of predestination, is first and last and in all circumstances the sum of the Gospel, no matter how it may be understood in detail, no matter what apparently contradictory aspects or moments it may present to us. It is itself evangel : glad tidings ; news which uplifts and comforts and sustains. Once and for all, then, it is not a truth which is neutral in face of the antithesis of fear and terror, of need and danger, which the term itself suggests. It is not a mere theorem whose content does not amount to anything more than instruction in, or the elucidation of, something which is quite unaffected by the distinction between right and wrong or good and evil. Its content is instruction and elucidation, but instruction and elucidation which are to us a proclamation of joy. It is not a mixed message of joy and terror, salvation and damnation. Originally and finally it is not dialectical but non-dialectical. It does not proclaim in the same breath both good and evil, both help and destruction, both life and death. It does, of course, throw a shadow. We cannot overlook or ignore this aspect of the matter. In itself, however, it is light and not darkness. We cannot, therefore, speak of the latter aspect in the same breath. In any case, even under this aspect, the final word is never that of warning, of judgment, of punishment, of a barrier erected, of a grave opened. We cannot speak of it without mentioning all these things. The Yes cannot be heard unless the No is also heard. But the No is said for the sake of the Yes and not for its own sake. In substance, therefore, the first and last word is Yes and not No.

We must establish this at the outset because, as the " doctrine of predestination," the doctrine of the divine election of grace has fallen under something of a shadow during the course of its history. The shadow has become so pronounced that when one mentions the terms " election of grace " or " predestination " one must expect to awaken in one's hearers or readers associations which necessarily confuse and thus make impossible the necessary recognition of the great truth with which we have to do at this point. The association may be resentment against the " pathetic inhumanity " of the doctrine (as in Max Weber, *Ges. Aufs. z. Rel. Soz.*, I, 1922, p. 93), or perhaps against the danger of dialectical ambiguity, or worse than both these, against what we mentioned earlier : the idea that in this matter we are dealing only with an abstract and neutral theorem. If we glance at the history of the doctrine, even as presented by its greatest and profoundest exponents, we cannot simply dismiss these associations as completely without foundation. Everywhere this shadow is in the ascendancy. A good deal has, in fact, been said in such a way as to give rise to confusion, to savage hostility, to well-meant but fatal misrepresentations of what ought to be received, indeed to a whole mass of misunderstanding and indifference with regard to the doctrine. " I may go to hell, but such a God (as that of the Calvinistic teaching) will never command my respect "—that was the cry of John Milton (according to M. Weber, *op. cit.*, p. 91), and openly or secretly how many others have made some similar utterance. For that reason it cannot be our present task simply to take one of the classical forms of the traditional doctrine and to present it as integrally as possible—as, in the case of the Calvinistic form, Loraine Boettner has recently attempted to do in his book, *The Reformed Doctrine of Predestination*, 1932. The task which confronts us is rather a critical one, even in face of the very best tradition. The task is imposed by the nature of the matter, as was the case, although rather differently, in the first part of our doctrine of God. If the doctrine is to shed forth its light, then the shadow must be dispersed. The dispersing of this shadow will be our definite objective in the polemical discussions throughout this whole chapter. We cannot be too soon, or too radical, in the opposition which we must offer to the classical tradition, or rather in the attempt to do justice to the particular and justifiable and necessary intention which underlies that tradition. And we introduce the first and most radical point with our thesis that the doctrine of election must be understood quite definitely and unequivocally as Gospel ; that it is not something neutral on the yonder side of Yes and No ; that it is not No but Yes ; that it is not Yes and No, but in its substance, in the origin and scope of its utterance, it is altogether Yes.

The election of grace is the sum of the Gospel—we must put it as pointedly as that. But more, the election of grace is the whole of the Gospel, the Gospel *in nuce*. It is the very essence of all good news. It is as such that it must be understood and evaluated in the Christian Church. God is God in His being as the One who loves in freedom. This is revealed as a benefit conferred upon us in the fact which corresponds to the truth of God's being, the fact that God elects in His grace, that He moves towards man, in his dealings within this covenant with the one man Jesus, and the people represented by Him. All the joy and the benefit of His whole work as Creator, Reconciler and Redeemer, all the blessings which are divine and therefore real blessings, all the promise of the Gospel which has been declared : all these are grounded and determined in the fact that God is the God of the eternal election of His grace. In the light of this election the whole of the Gospel is light. Yes is said here, and all the promises of God are Yea and Amen (2 Cor. 1[20]). Confirmation and comfort and help are promised us at this point, and they are promised us at every point. Whatever problems or contradictions we may encounter elsewhere, they all cease to be such, they become the very opposite, when we see them in their connexion with the real truth which we must receive and proclaim here. On the other hand, if it is the shadow which really predominates, if we must still fear, or if we can only half rejoice and half fear, if we have no truth at all to receive or proclaim but only the neutral elucidation of a neutral subject, then it is quite certain that we can never again receive or proclaim as such the Gospel previously declared. In this sphere, too, the shadow will necessarily predominate.

Many of the great exponents of the doctrine of predestination in the history of the Church have clearly expressed the basic character of the doctrine of the divine election of grace even from the positive standpoint, at any rate in some leading passages. We may note the definition of Augustine : *Haec est praedestinatio sanctorum, nihil aliud : praescientia sc. et praeparatio beneficiorum Dei, quibus certissime liberantur quicumque liberantur* (*De dono persev.* 14, 35). Predestination, according to Luther, is *voluntas Dei ordinantis suo consilio, quos et quales praedicatae et oblatae misericordiae capaces et participes esse velit* (*De servo arb. W.A.* 18, 684, 35). Even Calvin assures us that here it is not a question of an *arguta vel spinosa speculatio, quae absque fructa ingenia fatiget,* but of a *disputatio solida et ad pietatis usum maxime accommoda ; nempe, quae et fidem probe aedificet et nos ad humilitatem erudiat et in admirationem extollat immensae erga nos Dei bonitatis et ad hanc celebrandam excitet. Nulla aedificandae fidei aptior est ratio, quam dum audimus electionem illam, quam spiritus Dei cordibus nostris obsignat, in aeterno et inflexibili Dei beneplacito consistere, ut nullis mundi procellis, nullis satanae insultibus, nulli carnis vacillationi sit obnoxia. Tunc enim demum nobis certa est nostra salus, quum in Dei pectore causam reperimus. Sic enim vitam in Christo manifestatam fide apprehendimus, ut eadem fide duce procul intueri liceat, ex quo fonte vita prodierit* (*De aet. Dei praed.*, 1552, *C.R.* 8, 260). even if they do also make specific mention of a *decretum horribile* (*Instit.* III, 23, 7) : *In ipsa quae terret caligine non modo utilitas huius doctrinae, sed suavissimus quoque fructus se profert. Nunquam liquido ut decet persuasi erimus salutem nostram ex fonte gratuitae misericordiae Dei fluere, donec innotuerit nobis aeterna eius electio* (*Instit.* III, 21, 1). Intentionally, I have quoted only what these passages say positively about the doctrine of election as such. In the same context all of them do speak of the non-election or rejection which accompanies election. But in face and in spite of this second and accompanying aspect, they ascribe to the doctrine as such and in its entirety this redemptive and evangelical character. "The godlike consideration of Predestination, and our Election in Christ, is full of sweet, pleasant and unspeakable comfort to godly persons" (The *Irish Articles* of 1615, cf. E. F. Karl Müller, p. 528). Always and in all circumstances the doctrine must be understood according to this character, even in the detailed exposition of the second aspect. The Lutheran *Formula of Concord* is undoubtedly right when it finds in such understanding a criterion of correctness of doctrine in this matter : *Haec nequaquam erit vera et sana sententia aut legitimus usus doctrinae de aeterna praedestinatione Dei quibus vel impoenitentia vel desperatio in hominum mentibus excitatur aut confirmatur. Neque vero nobis scriptura hanc doctrinam aliter quam hoc modo proponit, ut nos ad verbum Dei revelatum fide amplectendum ableget, ad poenitentiam agendam hortetur, ad pie vivendum invitet (Sol. decl. XI, 12). Doctrina illa amplissimam consolationis verae materiam nobis suppeditabit* (43). If the preaching of the Gospel brings with it instead of consolation either despair or a false assurance, then it is certain *quod articulus de electione non ad normam et iuxta voluntatem Dei sed secundum humanae rationis caecae iudicium et ex impulsu atque instinctu diaboli male et perverse doceatur* (91). *Quodsi nobis per scripturam consolatio illa vel enervatur vel eripitur, certo certius est scripturam contra sententiam et mentem Spiritus Sancti explicari et intelligi* (92). This could not be said against Calvin and the Calvinists except through misunderstanding, or with reference to certain inferences which seriously embarrass their teaching. The Calvinists themselves might well have spoken, and did in fact speak, in the very same way. One can only wish that they had done so more emphatically in order that misunderstanding might have been avoided.

In this matter the real source and goal of all thought and utterance must be the Gospel itself, and that in a comprehensive, and to a certain extent compendious, sense. This will at once be apparent when we cast a first and general glance at the part played by the concept of election in the testimony of Holy Scripture. In the Old Testament it is the basic category used to describe the relationship between Yahweh and His people Israel. From its election, and as a result of the elections which constitute its history, there follow all the blessings visited upon this people by its God. In some degree the election is the fundamental blessing with which it has been and in detail continues to be visited. It is true that the rejection of Israel was determined when it stubbornly resisted the Gospel. Yet in face and in spite of that rejection, the fundamental blessing, the election, is still confirmed. Its confirmation is both the starting-point and the goal even of the crooked path of the chief New Testament passage in this matter : Rom. 9–11. In these chapters there are many apparent hesitations and contradictions which we shall have to consider and reckon with ; and yet we cannot overlook the fact that their final word is one of testimony to the divine Yes to Israel (to the Israel which had crucified Christ). Only when they are understood in the light of this final word can they be understood aright. So, too, the content and purpose of the other New Testament passages which touch on the election is always testimony to divine favour ; or, more exactly, to the one ultimate and decisive presupposition of all divine favour. The fact that they are elected should make clear to Christians the fact that they are the new and the true Israel, the people of God partaking of all the promises (I Pet. 2⁹). It should make clear to them the fact that they are called unto salvation in sanctification (2 Thess. 2¹³) ; that they are called of God, justified and already glorified (Rom. 8³⁰) ; that unto them is given the mystery of the kingdom of God (Mk. 4¹¹) ; that they are blessed by God, the Father of Jesus Christ (Eph. 1³f·). It is grace itself which visits them, and it does so because they have been appointed thereto by the divine election of grace—by grace to grace. In the

New Testament election is the divine ordination to discipleship, to the apostolate, to the community : to the apostolate in so far as this constitutes the community and to the community in so far as this is constituted by the apostolate ; but either one way or the other, the divine ordination to participation in the salvation of the Messianic future. The " book " spoken of by God in Ex. 32³² has always, and quite rightly, been connected with the election of grace. In Ps. 69²⁹ it is called unequivocally the " book of the living " (Prayer Book Version),[1] and it is described as the " book of life " in the New Testament (Phil. 4³ ; Rev. 3⁵, 17⁸, 20¹², ¹⁵). One's name may not be in this book. It can be blotted out from it. And yet there are not two columns, but only one. Similarly, the concept of the divine πρόθεσις used in Rom. 8²⁸ and 9¹¹ and Eph. 1¹¹ etc. relates to the divine election to salvation, but only to that election as such, and not to the accompanying non-election, or rejection. The problem began to be obscured when the " book of life " came to be spoken of as though it had in it a death-column ; when the divine election and the divine rejection came to be spoken of as inter-connected divine acts similar in character and determination ; when they came to be regarded and understood as though they could both be grouped under the one over-ruling concept.

When we look at the matter, it is here that there is a movement away from the biblical testimony even in Augustine. Augustine wanted to know why some believe and are saved, and others do not believe and are damned. He found the answer (supposedly in relation to certain texts in Rom. 9) in the fact of a double divine decision from all eternity, i.e., a decision with two parallel sides : *Multi audiunt verbum veritatis ; sed alii credunt, alii contradicunt. Volunt ergo isti credere, nolunt autem illi. Quis hoc ignoret ? Quis hoc neget ? Sed cum aliis praeparetur, aliis non praeparetur voluntas a Domino ; discernendum est utique, quid veniat de misericordia eius, quid de iudicio (De praed. sanct.* 6, 11). *Cur ergo non omnes docet, ut veniant ad Christum, nisi quia omnes quos docet, misericordia docet, quos autem non docet, iudicio non docet ? (ib.,* 8, 14). *Scimus iis quibus datur misericordia Dei gratuita dari. Scimus iis, quibus non datur, iusto iudicio non dari (Ep.* 217, 5, 16). It is certainly true that God's mercy and righteousness are both active in God's dealings with believers and unbelievers. But in view of the unity of the divine essence, we must at once ask whether it is possible to allocate the two attributes to different dealings of God, as though only His mercy were at work in the one case and only His righteousness in the other. Above all, we must ask what biblical or inherent authority Augustine has for relating God's dealings in this way, as though we had only to look at God's work here and His work there and to understand them as a unity in order to find the premiss for this inter-relationship. At any rate, in Holy Scripture there is no parallelism of this kind in the treatment and proclamation of the divine election and rejection.

Augustine himself did receive here a salutary check, as is shown by the fact that on the whole he avoided reducing God's twofold dealings to one common denominator, even in concept. By *praedestinatio* he always (or almost always) understood *praedestinatio ad gratiam* (a definition taken over by Peter Lombard, *Sent.* I, *dist.* 40 A) and therefore *praedestinatio ad vitam*. Predestination consists positively in *electio*, and does not include *reprobatio*. Thomas Aquinas held a similar concept. For him predestination was *ratio transmissionis vitae aeternae praeexistens in Deo (S. th.* I, *qu.* 23, *art.* 1 *c*), or, according to a later definition : *quaedam praeordinatio ab aeterno de his quae per gratiam Dei sunt fienda in tempore (S. th.* III, *qu.* 24, *art.* 1 *c*). Thomas, like Augustine, does set the two alongside : *voluit Deus in hominibus quantum ad aliquos, quos praedestinavit, suam bonitatem repraesentare per modum misericordiae, parcendo—et quantum ad aliquos, quos reprobat, per modum iustitiae, puniendo (qu.* 23, *art.* 5 *ad.* 3). But more clearly

---

[1] In the A.V. and R.V. " the book of life," Ps. 69²⁸ (R.V. margin " the living "). Trans.

than Augustine he regards *reprobatio* as in fact a separate genus, quite apart from and standing to some extent only in the shadow of *praedestinatio*. A similar view was held in the 14th century even by such strong " predestinarians " as Gregory of Rimini and John Wyclif.

Already, however, Isidore of Seville in the 7th and Gottschalk in the 9th century had taught a doctrine which differed formally from that of Augustine : *Gemina est praedestinatio, sive electorum ad requiem, sive reproborum ad mortem* (Isidore, *sent.* 2, 6, 1). *Sicut electos omnes (Deus) praedestinavit ad vitam per gratuitum solius gratiae suae beneficium, . . . sic omnino et reprobos quosque ad aeternae mortis praedestinavit supplicium per iustissimum videlicet iustitiae suae iudicium* (Gottschalk, according to Hinkmar, *De praed.* 5). In this case predestination is an over-ruling concept, including both election and rejection. This was the usage adopted by the Reformers. In Luther's *De servo arbitrio*, in Zwingli's *De providentia* and in the writings of Calvin, predestination means quite unequivocally double predestination : double in the sense that election and rejection are now two species within the one genus designated by the term predestination. It is true that not only in Luther but in Calvin too there are passages in which the matter is expounded with the same disproportion, the same over-emphasis upon the positively evangelical element, as had obviously appeared necessary to Thomas. Yet of Calvin it must be said that at any rate in his stricter teaching he did not think it possible to dispense with this fatal parallelism of the concepts election and rejection : *Fateri necesse est, Deum aeterno suo beneplacito, cuius aliunde causa non pendet, quos illi visum est, destinasse ad salutem, aliis relictis et quos gratuita adoptione dignatus est, spiritu suo illuminare, ut vitam in Christo oblatam recipiant, alios ita sponte esse incredulos, ut fidei luce destituti in tenebris maneant* (*De aet. Dei praed. C.R.* 8, 261 f.). So, too, in the famous definition in the *Institutio* (III, 21, 5) : *Praedestinationem vocamus aeternum Dei decretum, quo apud se constitutum habuit, quid de unoquoque homine fieri vellet. Non enim pari conditione creantur omnes : sed aliis vita aeterna, aliis damnatio aeterna praeordinatur. Itaque prout in alterutrum finem quisque conditus est, ita vel ad vitam vel ad mortem praedestinatum dicimus.* It was quite in the spirit of Calvin, and yet quite fatal, when many of the older Reformed dogmaticians thought that they ought to balance against the concept of the election of grace that of an election of wrath. Although they attempted to amend the doctrine, it is noteworthy that even the Arminians could not escape the concept of a " double " predestination in this sense : *Est praedestinatio Dei decretum divinum, quo pro voluntatis suae beneplacito constituit ante tempora saecularia fideles in Jesum Christum Filium suum eligere, in filios adoptare, iustificare, et, si in fide perseverent, aeternum glorificare—infideles vero ac contumaces reprobare, excoecare, indurare, et, si in contumacia sua perseverent, in aeternum damnare* (P. a Limborch, *Theol. chr.*, 1686, IV, 1, 5).

As against that, it is one of the merits of the *Canones* of the Synod of Dort (1619) that a definition of predestination was there given (I, 7) which, although it did not, of course, exclude the divine reprobation, did not include or append it as an autonomous truth, being content rather to state positively what *electio* is : the *immutabile Dei propositum, quo ante iacta mundi fundamenta e universo genere humano, ex primaeva integritate in peccatum et exitium sua culpa prolapso, secundum liberrimum voluntatis suae beneplacitum, ex mera gratia, certam quorundam hominum multitudinem, aliis nec meliorum, nec digniorum, sed in communi miseria cum aliis iacentium, ad salutem elegit in Christo, quem etiam ab aeterno mediatorem et omnium electorum caput, salutisque fundamentum constituit, atque ita eos ipsi salvandos dare, et ad eius communionem per verbum et spiritum suum efficaciter vocare ac trahere seu vera in ipsum fide donare, iustificare, sanctificare et potenter in Filii sui communione custoditos tandem glorificare decrevit, ac demonstrationem suae misericordiae et laudem divitiarum gloriosae suae gratiae.* Whatever else one may think of the formula, in this form the doctrine of predestination certainly did take on again the character of evangelical proclamation which it had lost in the definitions in which it referred simultaneously and equally to grace and non-grace, salvation and reprobation.

While they could not evade the importance of the content of his doctrine, some of Calvin's more timid contemporaries were much exercised about the danger of misunderstanding. They expressed the view that the doctrine of predestination ought to be reserved as a kind of secret wisdom for theologians of sobriety and discretion, and not published abroad amongst the people. Calvin made the forceful answer that true discretion cannot consist in burying away a truth to which all true servants of God testify, but only in the sober and reverent yet quite open confession of what is learned in the school of the heavenly Teacher (*De aet. Dei praed. C.R.* 8, 347). It would not be a true Christian simplicity, *eorum, quae Deus ostendit scientiam noxiam refugere* (*ib.*, 264). What is revealed to us in Scripture is as such necessary and useful and worthy to be known by all. On no account, then, must the doctrine of predestination be withheld from believers (*Instit.* III, 21, 3). *Sicut enim praedicanda est pietas ut rite colatur Deus, ita et praedestinatio, ut, qui habet aures audiendi, de gratia Dei, in Deo, non in se glorietur* (*De aet. Dei praed. ib.*, 327). Calvin was right. But although his point was right, he could have made it more emphatically and impressively if his understanding of predestination had been less speculative and more in accordance with the biblical testimony; if it had been a strictly evangelical understanding. And with its *parallelismus membrorum*, with that balanced assertion of the twofold dealings of God, as a doctrine of double predestination, this is precisely what it is not. The balance gives to the doctrine a neutrality which is almost scientific. It does not differentiate between the divine Yes and the divine No. It does not come down on the side of the divine Yes. On the very same level as the Yes it registers an equally definitive divine No concerning man. In such a form it is inevitable that the No should become much the stronger and ultimately the exclusive note. It is inevitable that the doctrine should in the last resort be understood as δυσαγγέλιον, and that as such it should be repudiated with horror (and not without inward cause). It is not surprising, then, that the same miserable counsel once defeated by Calvin could 150 years later be reintroduced by Samuel Werenfels as the latest wisdom—just as though nothing had happened—and that since that time it has achieved something of the dignity of an *opinio communis* amongst the half-hearted.

The basic demand by which any presentation of the doctrine must be measured, and to which we ourselves must also conform, is this : that (negatively) the doctrine must not speak of the divine election and rejection as though God's electing and rejecting were not quite different, as though these divine dealings did not stand in a definite hierarchical relationship the one with the other ; and that (positively) the supremacy of the one and subordination of the other must be brought out so radically that the Gospel enclosed and proclaimed even in this doctrine is introduced and revealed as the tenor of the whole, so that in some way or other the Word of the free grace of God stands out even at this point as the dominating theme and the specific meaning of the whole utterance. It is along these lines that it will be proved whether or not the doctrine is understood in conformity with the Bible and therefore with divine revelation. Only if understood in this way can it lay claim to the full publicity within the Church rightly defended by Calvin. If not understood in this way, then even as a secret wisdom for theologians it can have no real significance, or rather it can have only a very dangerous significance.

The specific proof of this thesis can be introduced connectedly only in and with the doctrine of predestination grounded upon it. Our preliminary concern is to show how right and necessary it is to set up this thesis at the very outset as a kind of working hypothesis.

We may establish first a point which all serious conceptions of the doctrine have in common. They all find the nerve of the doctrine, the peculiar concern which forces them to present and assert it, in the fact that it characterises the grace of God as absolutely free and thereby divine. In electing, God decides according to His good-pleasure, which as such is holy and righteous. And because He who elects is constant and omnipotent and eternal, the good-pleasure by which He decides, and the decision itself, are independent of all other decisions, of all creaturely decisions. His decision precedes every creaturely decision. Over against all creaturely self-determination it is pre-determination—*prae-destinatio.* Grace is the divine movement and condescension on the basis of which men belong to God and God to men. Whether offered or received, whether self-revealing and reconciling or apprehended and active in faith, it is God's dealing, God's will and God's work, God's lordship, God Himself in all His sovereignty. Grace cannot be called forth or constrained by any claim or merit, by any existing or future condition, on the part of the creature. Nor can it be held up or rendered nugatory and ineffective by any contradiction or opposition on the part of the creature. Both in its being and in its operation its necessity is within itself. In face of it there is no place for the self-glorying or the self-praise of the creature. It comes upon the creature as absolute miracle, and with absolute power and certainty. It can be received by the creature only where there is a recognition of utter weakness and unworthiness, an utter confidence in its might and dignity, and an utter renunciation of wilful self-despair. What the creature cannot claim or appropriate for itself, it cannot of itself renounce when it does partake of it, nor can it even will to deprive itself of it. The decision by which it receives and affirms grace takes place in fulfilment of the prior divine decision. It cannot, then, be asserted over against God as a purely creaturely achievement, nor can it be revoked. As the fulfilment of that prior divine decision, it redounds *per se* to the praise of the freedom of grace : of its independence both of the majesty and of the misery of our human volition and achievement ; of the sovereignty in which it precedes and thus fully over-rules our human volition and achievement. All serious conceptions of the doctrine (more or less exactly and successfully, and with more or less consistency in detail) do at least aim at this recognition ; at the freedom of the grace of God. We can put it more simply : They aim at an understanding of grace as grace. For what kind of grace is it that is conditioned and constrained, and not free grace and freely electing grace ? What kind of a God is it who in any sense of the term has to be gracious, whose grace is not His own most personal and free good-pleasure.

Quidquid est in homine ordinans ipsum in salutem, totum comprehenditur sub effectu praedestinationis, etiam ipsa praeparatio ad gratiam : neque enim hoc fit nisi per auxilium divinum (Thomas Aqu. *S. th.* I, *qu.* 23, *art.* 5 c). It is certain *que Dieu nous a esleus, voire non seulement devant que nous le cogneussions, mais devant que nous fussions nais, et avant que le monde fut creé ; et qu'il nous a esleus par sa bonté gratuite, et qu'il n'a point cerché la cause ailleurs ; qu'il a deliberé ce propos en soy-mesme, et qu'il faut que nous cognoissions cela, afin qu'il soit glorifié de nous comme il appartient. Or la gloire telle qu'elle luy est deue, ne luy peut estre rendue sans cela* . . . (Calvin, *Congrég. sur l'Election ét.*, 1562, *C.R.* 8, 103). We must *Deo reddere, quod suum est* (*De aet. Dei praed.*, 1552, *C.R.* 8, 261). *Proprio cordis motu* we are just as little ordained (*ordinati*) for fellowship with God as the world is self-created (*ib.*, 299). *Ut Deus cultores suos diligat, necesse est, ut, dum adhuc omni bono vacui sunt, gratuito amore praeveniat indignos et illis donet, quod postea amore prosequatur. Hanc vero primam gratiam dat quibus vult* (*ib.*, 306). *Quand il dit que Dieu a deliberé en soy-mesme ce propos, c'est à dire, qu'il n'est point sorty hors de soy, qu'il n'a point ietté les yeux çà ne là, pour dire : Je serai esmeu à ce faire* (*Congrég.*, 1562, *ib.*, 95). *Clarissime Dominus pronuntiat, nullam hominibus benefaciendi rationem in ipsis se habere, sed a sola sua misericordia sumere ; ideoque suum esse opus suorum salutem. Quum tuam in se uno salutem Deus statuat, cur ad teipsum descendes ? Quum unam tibi suam misericordiam assignet, cur ad propria merita decurres ? Quum tuam cogitationem in sua miseratione contineat, cur ad operum tuorum intuitum partem reflectes ?* (*Instit.* III, 22, 6). This note is still sounded in the older Reformed dogmatics : *Deus est liberrimae potestatis et solus vere* ἀνυπεύθυνος. *Deus igitur de suo fecit, quod sibi placuit, ac proinde creaturas suas praedestinavit quo voluit.* . . . *Nihil est in ulla creatura rationali, quod ei gratiam apud Deum conciliet ; sed Deus ipse sibi gratos et acceptos in Filio suo fecit quos voluit. Nec Deus est cuiquam obligatus, ut ei teneatur quicquam dare* (Polanus, *Synt. Theol. chr.*, 1609, *col.* 1561 f.). But the teaching of the *Formula of Concord* has the same emphasis : It is an error *quod non sola Dei misericordia et sanctissimum Christi meritum, sed etiam in nobis ipsis aliqua causa sit electionis divinae, cuius causae ratione Deus nos ad vitam aeternam elegerit* (*Ep.* XI, 20, cf. *Sol. decl.* XI, 88). *Electio nostra ad vitam aeternam non virtutibus aut iustitia nostra sed solo Christi merito et benigna coelestis patris voluntate nitatur, qui seipsum negare non potest* (*Sol. decl.* XI, 75). For Quenstedt, too, the *causa agens* of election is *Dei unitrini voluntas libere decernens* (*Theol. did. pol.*, 1685, III, *c.* 2, *sect.* 1, *th.* 9) ; its *causa movens interna : gratia Dei mere gratuita, excludens omne omnino operum humanorum meritum sive omne id, quod nomine operis vel actionis, sive per gratiam Dei, sive ex viribus naturae factae venit. Elegit enim nos Deus non secundum opera, sed ex mera sua gratia. Etiam fides ipsa huc non pertinet, si spectatur tanquam conditio, magis vel minus digna, sive per se, sive ex aestimio per voluntatem Dei, fidei superaddito, quod nihil horum decretum electionis ingrediatur tanquam causa movens aut impellens Deum ad tale decretum faciendum, sed id purae putae gratiae Dei est adscribendum* (*ib.*, *th.* 10).

All serious conceptions of the doctrine also agree that in this free decision of God we have to do with the mystery of God, i.e., with the divine resolve and decree whose basis is hidden and inscrutable. We were not admitted to the counsel of God as He made His election, nor can we subsequently call Him to give account or to make answer in respect of it. The will of God knows no Wherefore ? It is an absolute Therefore, the ultimate Therefore of all. And it is as such that it wills to be known and honoured and obeyed. We resist the very being of this election as an election of grace, as a decision in accordance with the good-pleasure of the holy and righteous, the constant and omnipotent and eternal God ; we resist the very being and existence of God Himself, if we raise even a question concerning the purpose and validity of this election, if we do not recognise that any such question is already answered by the fact that it is God who here decides and elects.

Sic inquirenda est ratio praedestinationis, sicut inquiritur ratio divinae voluntatis (Thomas Aqu., *S. th.*, I, *qu.* 23, *art.* 5 *c*). It was in recognition of this fact that Luther gave full vent to his wrath against Erasmus : *Quid quaeritur ? Voluntati eius quis resistet ? Hoc est illud, quod ratio neque capere, neque ferre potest, hoc offendit tot viros excellentes ingenio tot saeculis receptos. Hic expostulant ut Deus agat iure humano et faciat quod ipsis rectum videtur, aut Deus esse desinat. Nihil illi profuerint secreta maiestatis, rationem reddat, quare sit Deus, aut quare vellit aut faciat, quod nullam speciem iustitiae habeat, ac si sutorem aut zonarium roges iudicio se sistere. Non dignatur Deum caro gloria tanta, ut credat iustum esse et bonum, dum supra et ultra dicit et facit, quam definivit Codex Justiniani vel quintus liber Ethicorum Aristotelis. Cedat maiestas creatrix omnium feci uni creaturae suae et Coricius ille specus metuat versa vice spectatores suos. Igitur absurdum est, ut damnet eum, qui vitare non potest meritum damnationis. Et propter hanc absurditatem falsum esse oportet, quod Deus, cuius vult, miseretur, quem vult indurat, sed redigendus est in ordinem et praescribendae illi leges, ut non damnet quenquam nisi qui nostro iudicio id meruerit* (De servo arb. W.A. 18, 729, 13). Calvin likewise drew attention to the mystery of the election of grace : *Il est donc ici question d'adorer les secrets de Dieu qui nous sont incomprehensibles. Et sans cela iamais nous ne gousterons les principes de la foy. Car nous sçavons que nostre sagesse doit commencer touisours par humilité ; et ceste humilité-là emporte que nous ne venions point avec nostre balance pour peser les iugemens de Dieu, que nous n'en vueillions point estre iuges ni arbitres : mais que nous soyons sobres, voyant la petitesse de nostre Esprit, voyant que nous sommes grossiers et lours, que nous magnifions Dieu, et que nous disions (comme nous sommes enseignez par l'Escriture saincte), Seigneur, c'est un abysme trop profond que ton conseil, nul ne le peut raconter* (Serm. on Eph. 1³ᵗ· C.R. 51, 260 f.). *Non alia nos cognitio iuvet, quam quae admiratione claudatur. Rideant nos qui volent : modo stupori nostro Deus e çoelo annuat et angeli applaudant* (De aet. Dei praed. C.R. 8, 292). We might also bring in as an instructive indirect confirmation some words of Kant on this subject : " That there should be at work in man a heavenly grace which not by any merit of works but by an unconditioned decree grants its aid to one and refuses it to another, predestinating one part of our race to salvation and the other to eternal perdition, does not give us any concept of divine righteousness, but must necessarily be referred to a wisdom whose canon is to us an absolute mystery. Concerning such mysteries, in so far as they touch on the moral history of every individual—how it comes about, for instance, that there is good and evil in the world at all, or (if the latter is in all and at all times) how the former can arise out of it and be restored in any man, or why, if this does take place in some, others are excluded therefrom—God has not revealed anything to us, nor indeed can He, for we would not understand it even if He did " (*Rel. innerh. d. Grenzen d. blossen Vernunft*, 1793, ed. K. Vorländer, p. 166). And elsewhere rather less morosely : " If we represented this faith itself as having such mystical (or magical) power that, although so far as we know it ought to be regarded as merely historical, it could yet radically improve a man (make of him a new man) if accepted with all its attendant emotions, then we should have to regard the faith itself as mediated and given directly from heaven (with and under historical faith), in which case everything that has to do with the moral activity of man would come back ultimately to an unconditioned decree of God : He hath mercy on whom He will, and whom He will He hardeneth ; a sentence which, taken literally, is the *salto mortale* of human reason " (*op. cit.*, p. 139).

And now we can mention a third point which unites all serious conceptions of the doctrine. To the confession of the mystery of

God's freedom in the election of grace they all quite definitely relate, in some sense as a basis, the confession that in the mystery of His freedom God always does that which is worthy of Himself, i.e., the confession of His righteousness. As we regard the work of God in the election of grace we must always remember Rom. 9^{20} : " Nay but, O man, who art thou that repliest against God ? " We must recognise the sovereignty of God and the inscrutability of His election, respecting the Therefore of it which no Wherefore can circumvent. Yet in so doing—if we really have God before us as the Subject of this work—we honour the source and citadel of all equity and judgment : not merely the wisdom which *must* silence the objections of our thinking and feeling, as though we were confronted by a *brutum factum*—as though all discussion were terminated at this point by force—by a " higher " force, but still by force ; but the wisdom before which we *can* only be silent. We are not bowing before the caprice of a tyrant. Our submission cannot be such that it is accompanied by a still-remaining and ever-increasing inward complaint and resistance. Rather, of ourselves, of our own better knowledge, we will to be silent. It is not that our mouth is stopped—for then our silence would not be a voluntary act of obedience, but an act of disobedience which has been prevented and suppressed. It is rather because our ears have heard the Therefore which is the truly satisfying and convincing answer to every Wherefore. We are persuaded, and have no more questions to put. God Himself, and in Him wisdom itself and righteousness itself, has communicated Himself to us and given us Himself as the answer. What God does in freedom is in order. And in that it is done in freedom, we can and must perceive and recognise that it is in order without first measuring it by our own conceptions of order and only then recognising it to be such. It belongs to God that He should teach us what order is. It belongs to us to measure our conceptions of order by His decision, and to learn from Him what order is. In so doing we do not make any *sacrificium intellectus*, but we become and are truly wise : so assuredly is the fear of the Lord the beginning of wisdom. " O man, who art thou that repliest against God ? " And the answer is : " Thou art a fool. It is high time to learn wisdom and to leave off thy disputing. In the mystery of God's freedom in His election thou mayest contemplate and adore the only and true righteousness, and in such contemplation and adoration thou mayest be truly wise."

In the history of the doctrine the justifiable concern to bring out this aspect of the matter has inspired innumerable efforts which have done further violence to the only possible form of such an acknowledgment as we have here tried to sketch it. It was not thought sufficient simply to assert that in the freedom of His decision God Himself is as such righteousness and the Teacher of righteousness, and that the sum of all wisdom consists in listening to Him as such a Teacher. There was a desire to be wise in respect of God before learning wisdom from God Himself. Thus there sprang up within the sphere of this doctrine all those attempts which resulted in violence being done to the freedom of God by the indication of certain external conditions of God's work in the light of which the validity and order of His election could again be measured by our conceptions of order, and thus acknowledged as righteous and worthy of God without that silence, without that listening to God Himself. It is self-evident that in greater or lesser degree all such attempts must call in question the divine mystery which Kant found so strange and repugnant but the denial of which could provoke a Luther to such great indignation. Attempts of this kind have been made again and again since the Gottschalk controversy of the 9th century. We do not take part in them, but we can and must appreciate that their appearance points to an underlying concern which must be vindicated in some form or other. It is all the more interesting to hear Calvin on this point, for he did not wish the slightest diminution of the freedom of the divine election, but the preservation in all circumstances of the divine mystery. And yet he showed the righteousness of this election, and the need for us to do justice to it as an act, as *the* act, of the only and true wisdom, with an impressiveness hardly surpassed by any other writer. It is true that when any question was raised concerning the basis or ground of the divine decision Calvin loved—and rightly—to quash it at once simply along the line of Rom. 9^{20} : *Il y en a qui trouvent estrange quand on ne leur donne point de resolution qui soit facile. Et je voudroye qu'on me dit les choses plus clairement, que j'aperceusse pourquoy telle chose se fait. Mon amy, il te faut aller cercher une autre escole, puis que tu es si presomptueux, que tu ne veux point donner gloire à Dieu, sinon que tu voyes les enseignes. Or va cercher une autre escole que celle du sainct Esprit* (Congrég. *C.R.* 8, 108). *Nous savons quelle est l'audace des hommes ; et il n'y a celuy qui n'en ait l'experience en soy, qu'il est bien difficile de dompter nos esprits, tellement que nous recevions en paix et humilité tout ce qu'on nous declare. Il faut qu'un homme soit bien matté de Dieu devant qu'il se reigle là.* . . . . *Ces objections qui se font, doivent estre repoussés par ce mot seulement de l'autorité de Dieu : assavoir quelle maistrise et préeminence est-ce qu'il doit avoir par dessus nous* (*op. cit.*, 104). *Iniquum est calculo nostro subiici profunda illa iudicia, quae sensus omnes nostros absorbent* (*Instit.* III, 23, 1). *In sola eius voluntate quiescendum est : ut quod illic placere intelligimus, cuius nos causa fugit instar mille rationum sufficiat* (*De aet. Dei praed. C.R.* 8, 312). *Adeo enim summa est iustitiae regula Dei voluntas, ut quicquid vult, iustum habendum sit. Ubi ergo quaeritur, cur ita fecerit Dominus, respondendum est : Quia voluit.* . . . *Quod si ultra pergas rogando cur voluerit, maius aliquid quaeris et sublimius Dei voluntate, quod inveniri non potest* (*Instit.* III, 23, 2). But Calvin did not rest content with that. He followed the line of Rom. 9^{20} to its conclusion : *Quod tibi sonat Dei nomen ?* he demanded of those to whom it appeared *molestum ac odiosum* that God should have been able to do and should have done more than their reason could comprehend (*De aet. Dei praed. C.R.* 8, 262). The very name of God is our guarantee that it is sensible to be silent at this point : *Quavis enim sapientia praestantior est sobrietas, quae Dei timore subacta intra praescriptum ab eo intelligendi modum se continet* (*ib.*, 8, 263). But we must say too, and just as definitely, that in God we are not dealing with a tyrant, or a God of caprice : *Non fingimus Deum exlegem, qui sibi ipsi lex est.* . . . *Dei voluntas non modo ab omni vitio pura, sed summa perfectionis regula, etiam legum omnium lex est* (*Instit.* III, 23, 2). *Nous disons, que ceste volonté de Dieu est ordonnée et tellement ordonnée que c'est la source de tout équité et iustice* (Congrég. *C.R.* 8, 115). *Si velle se ac iubere pronuntiet mortalis homo ut pro ratione sit sua voluntas, tyrannicam esse vocem fateor : sed id ad Deum transferre sacrilegi est furoris. Neque enim quidquam Deo immoderatum affingere licet, ut in eo sicut in hominibus exsultet libido : sed merito hoc honoris defertur eius voluntati, ut pro ratione valeat ; quando omnis iustitiae fons est ac regula.* To distinguish between a *voluntas Dei ordinata* and *absoluta* is a blasphemy from which we can only recoil in horror. *Ego autem ex adverso contendo, adeo nihil esse in Deo inordinatum, ut inde potius fluat, quidquid est in coelo et in terra ordinis. Quum ergo in summum gradum evehimus Dei voluntatem, ut sit omni ratione superior, absit ut eum quidquam nisi summa ratione velle imaginemur ; sed simpliciter sentimus, eum iure suo tantum habere potestatis, ut solo eius nutu contento esse nos oporteat. . . . An mihi portentum hoc unquam venit in mentem, nullam Deo consilii sui rationem constare ? Dum ego Deum praesidem totius mundi statuo, qui incomprehensibili et mirifico consilio gubernet modereturque omnia : an illum fortuito huc illuc raptari, vel caeca temeritate eum facere quod facit, quisquam ex verbis meis colliget ? . . . Gloriae suae rationem in actis suis omnibus habet Dominus. Nempe hic universalis est finis . . . (De aet. Dei praed. C.R. 8, 310 f.).* And finally therefore : *Praedestinatio nihil aliud est quam iustitiae occultae quidem sed inculpatae dispensatio (Instit. III, 23, 8).*

We have emphasised three points (we shall have to treat them more fully in detail) common to all conceptions of the doctrine : the freedom of God, the mystery of God, and the righteousness of God in His election of grace. We have done this because as we consider these three points we cannot refrain from asking a question of the exponents of the dogma (no matter how they may interpret it in detail). This question will occupy us in different forms as we proceed. We now put it for the first time in this way : Are we at liberty to accuse or blame these exponents because as Christian theologians they did speak in this way of the freedom, the mystery and the righteousness of God in His election of grace ; because they did speak of the freedom, the mystery and the righteousness of the triune God, the Father revealed in the Son by the Holy Ghost, as testified in Holy Scripture ; because they did not wander off and speak of a " supreme being " posited by human invention and, as the absolutised image of man, endowed with certain pre-eminent qualities ; because they did not speak of the ostensible freedom, the ostensible mystery and the ostensible righteousness of this being ? There can be no doubt that when we consider the serious exponents of the doctrine we have reason on the whole to return a favourable answer to the question, unconditionally so when we take into account their intention. The theologians we have in mind did wish to be Christian theologians, and in the particular form in which it was presented their doctrine of predestination was meant to be the exposition of Scripture, and therefore a testimony to the revelation of the triune God. There was, then, no question of arbitrary speculation concerning an arbitrarily conceived absolute, but rather an obedient reckoning with the One whom Jesus Christ called His Father, and who called Jesus Christ His Son. In so far as we hold fast by their intention, we think we shall still be in agreement with them when we add at once that the freedom, mystery and righteousness of God in the election of grace must be understood in terms of Christian theology. Only as understood in this way are they the truth which must be received and proclaimed in the Church. But if this is the case, it is settled once and for all that in the doctrine of election we have to do with the sum of the Gospel. This is the theme which we must now finally develop.

We did not form at random the concept of the election of grace. In it we described the choice of God which, preceding all His other choices, is fulfilled in His eternal willing of the existence of the man Jesus and of the people represented in Him. If we are to understand and explain the nature of this primal and basic act of God, we cannot stop, then, at the formal characteristic that it is a choice. We must resist the temptation to absolutise in some degree the concept choosing or electing. We must not interpret the freedom, the mystery and the righteousness of the election of grace merely as the definitions and attributes of a supreme form of electing posited as absolute. We must not find in this supreme form as such the reality of God. Otherwise we shall be doing what we ought not to do. We shall be forging and constructing (out of this very characteristic) a supreme being. And it is difficult to imagine how the description of the activity of this being can ever become a Gospel. If the distinctive and ultimate feature in God is absolute freedom of choice, or an absolutely free choice, then it will be hard to distinguish His freedom from caprice or His mystery from the blindness of such caprice. It will be no less hard to maintain His righteousness in any form except that of mere assertion. It will then be difficult to make it clear that God is not merely a tyrant living by His whims, that He is not merely blind fate, that He is something other than the essential inscrutability of all being. It cannot well be denied that there has taken place such an absolutising of the concept of electing, or of its freedom, with the accompanying influence of a non-Christian conception of God, in the history of the doctrine. Nor can it be denied that as a result the utterances on the subject have to a greater or lesser extent been obscured, and in any case fairly generally distorted. As against that, we must take as our starting-point the fact that this divine choice or election is the decision of the divine will which was fulfilled in Jesus Christ, and which had as its goal the sending of the Son of God. As such, it has always in God Himself, as a spontaneous *opus internum ad extra* of the trinitarian God, and to that extent originally and properly, the character of grace. Its freedom is indeed divine and therefore absolute. It is not, however, an abstract freedom as such, but the freedom of the One who loves in freedom. It is He Himself, and not an essence of the freedom of choice, or of free choice, who is the divine Subject of the electing which takes place at this point. We must not seek the ground of this election anywhere but in the love of God, in His free love—otherwise it would not be His—but still in His love. If we seek it elsewhere, then we are no longer talking about this election. We are no longer talking about the decision of the divine will which was fulfilled in Jesus Christ. We are looking beyond these to a supposedly greater depth in God (and that undoubtedly means nothingness, or rather the depth of Satan). What takes place in this election is always that God is for us ; for us, and therefore for the world which was created by Him, which is distinct from Him, but which is yet maintained by Him. The election is made with a view to the sending of His Son. And this means always that in Him and through Him God moves towards the world. It means not merely that He creates and sustains the world, but that He works on it and in it by (miracle of all miracles) giving Himself to it. It means that the will for fellowship, which is His very being and to which the world owes its existence, is actively demonstrated to the world in a way which surpasses anything that could be expected or claimed. If we describe this movement as election, then it is only because we would thereby emphasise that it is the active demonstration of His love. Would it be love—the love of the personal God, and as such real love—if it were not an electing? As electing love it can never be hatred or indifference, but always love. And the active demonstration of that love is this : " God so loved the world, that he gave his only begotten Son, that whosoever believeth in him should not perish, but have everlasting life " (Jn. 3[16]). Whatever may be the inner link in God's election between that giving of His only-begotten Son and the faith in Him by which the intended salvation is effected, this much is certain, that in this election (in giving Himself to this work, and in electing as the object of this work the man Jesus from among the world of men, and in Him the whole race) God loved the world. It is certain that this election is a work in which God meets the world neither in indifference nor in enmity, but in which at the very highest and lowest levels (in the giving of His only-begotten Son) He is for this man Jesus, and in Him for the whole race, and therefore for the world. That God wills neither to be without the world nor against it can never be stated more clearly or forcibly than when we speak of His election. At bottom, then, to speak of the election means necessarily to speak of the Gospel. In our teaching concerning the election we must always bring in the fact, definitely and basically and as the meaning and substance of all our assertions, that of and from Himself God has decided for this loftiest and most radical movement towards His creation, ordaining and constituting Himself its Friend and Benefactor. It is in this way, in the form of this election, that God has made His decision. And the tidings of the divine decision in this form are glad tidings. It is as such and in such a sense that they must be delivered : without any concealment of the fact that God does elect (for what need is there of concealment ?) ; without any transmutation of God's way of loving the world into some other way, a general " loving " which involves no election and which is not really love ; without any suppression or obfuscation of the fact that in this way and in the form of this election God has truly loved the world. In this form and this form alone the tidings of the divine decision made in Jesus Christ are glad tidings directed to all men, directed indeed to the whole world. It is also true that in the world there is opposition to the love of God, indeed that this opposition constitutes the being of the world as such. The text itself points indirectly but quite definitely to this fact when it says : " Whosoever believeth in him should not perish." But the will and the power of God smash this opposition. Where the opposition does not break down in faith in the Son given, even the love of God must itself be destructive. To an opposing world the election must of the same force and necessity become non-election, or rejection. And it is for this reason, and to this extent, that there does exist a definite sphere of damnation ordained and determined by God as the negation of the divine affirmation, the work of the almighty non-willing which accompanies God's willing. But the divine affirmation, the divine willing as such, is salvation and not damnation. The divine election as such does not negate creation but affirms it. The message of God's election means always the message of the Yes determined and pronounced by God. Another message can, of course, be given apart from that of God's election, e.g., the message of the blind election of fate, or of the supposedly most enlightened election of our own judgment. Here we shall be told something quite different from the divine affirmation. But we cannot hear of God's election without also hearing God's Yes. If we truly hear, then in face of this election and its meaning it is not possible for us not to be able to hear or obey that Yes, not to will to be amongst those who are affirmed by God. This is not a possibility but an impossibility. It is a turning of the sense of that election into nonsense. It is a descent into the abyss of the divine non-willing and the divine non-electing. Even in such a descent the creature cannot escape God. Even in this abyss it is still in the hands of God, the object of His decision. Yet that does not mean that it has been flung, or even allowed to fall, into the abyss by God Himself. God is and God remains the One who has decided for the creature and not against it. It is by love itself that the creature is confounded. Even there, in the midst of hell, when it thinks of God and His election it can think only of the love and grace of God. The resolve and power of our opposition cannot put any limit to the power and resolve of God. Even in our opposition there comes upon us that which God has foreordained for us. But that means that what comes upon us cannot alter in the slightest the nature and character of the foreordination which is God's decree. In that decree as such we find only the decree of His love. In the proclaiming and teaching of His election we can hear only the proclaiming of the Gospel.

With this in mind we may now take up again the three points on which we found agreement amongst the different exponents of the doctrine.

In the light of an evangelical understanding of the election of grace, what is the meaning of the freedom of God in this His work ? In His grace God is the One who unconditionally precedes the creature. Man with his decision can only follow. He cannot forestall God with any claim, or condition, or ground of action. But this fact carries within itself the final and severest humiliation of the creature. If it is really the case, then over against God the creature cannot produce or proclaim any inherent dignity, anything that is good within itself. It is obviously the creature's destiny to owe all that is good in its nature and existence as a creature to God alone. On account of that good it has no claim to be elected by God. But it seems evident, too, that before God even the good of its creatureliness as such is null and void. Before God the creature has lost and forfeited that good. It stands accused because it has misused that good, because it has not been thankful in respect of it. Even out of its gratitude there cannot arise, then, any expectation of divine election. The freedom of the divine election means that over against God the creature finds itself within the cordon not merely of its creatureliness but of its sin. It is not only little before God but blameworthy. Against the love of God it is in a state of opposition in which that love turns to its destruction and in which fellowship with God can result only in judgment and perdition. That is what the freedom of grace means for the creature towards whom it is directed. That is the self-knowledge which is demanded of the creature side by side with the knowledge of God's freedom. In the depth of its plight there is reflected the fore-ordination under which it stands when God is gracious to it on the basis of His free election. With the radicalness therein implied it must renounce everything which might be regarded as earning or even partially meriting its election. But that is not all that God's freedom in this work means for the creature, for this freedom is His freedom in respect of this particular work, the freedom of His grace. Grace is the Nevertheless of the divine love to the creature. The election consists in this Nevertheless. It is indeed election. It is indeed grace, and for that reason it is free. How could the divine love to the creature be really love, how could it be divine, unless it were free ? But it is grace, loving-kindness, favour. In it God says Yes to the creature and not No. He says it of Himself. He says it without the creature having any right or claim to it. He says it, then, in freedom. But what He says, He says as the One who loves in freedom. He does not say No but Yes. Against our No He places His own Nevertheless. He is free in the very fact that the creature's opposition to His love cannot be any obstacle to Him. He is free, too, in the fact that He cannot be satisfied merely with smashing this opposition, and thus allowing the creature to be confounded by His love. He could have been satisfied with that. But He need not. And in His free grace He will not and is not. He is not free, then, merely in the fulfilling of His will for fellowship with the creature by allowing it to perish beneath the hand which it has rejected but still cannot escape. He is free rather, and His hand is almighty, in the fact that He can rescue the creature from the destruction into which it has plunged itself by its opposition. He is free in the fact that He can turn it in spite of itself to the salvation and life which are the positive and distinctive meaning and goal of His love. And it is that which God elects. It is that which He does in the election of His grace. He chooses the Yes and not the No, inevitable as the latter seems in face of the attitude of the creature. He elects grace as grace and not as judgment, which the attitude of the creature seems inevitably to have made it. He elects the fulfilment and not the non-fulfilment of the purpose and meaning of love, even though the creature seems as though it must inevitably be confounded by that love, even though His will seemingly can only take its course in the non-fulfilment, in the damnation of the creature, in its destruction and perdition. There is nothing inevitable against which the love of God must for its part be shattered. God elects, then, not the punishment but the undeserved rewarding of the creature, not its death but the life which it had forfeited, not its non-being but its impossible being. He elects. Neither to the creature nor to Himself is He under an obligation to elect in this way. But He does elect in this way. This means the freedom of God for His creature. And if it means the final and severest humiliation of the creature, it does not mean that it is driven to despair. It means that despair of self, which appears to be its only remaining portion, is forbidden as mere wilfulness. It means that such despair loses its point because it is unnecessary. It means that it is made quite impossible because it is deprived of its object. Where God does not despair, the creature cannot despair. And grace, the freedom of the election of grace, means that God does not despair of the creature. Not only does He not despair of it, but in all the riches of His own glory He moves towards it and interests Himself in it. The sovereignty of God is not only confirmed by the fact that the creature cannot escape Him, that it must fulfil the divine will even in its condemnation. It is also confirmed by the fact that God's last word to it and the positive goal of His will is always one of blessedness. It is confirmed in the Nevertheless with which He rescues the creature from condemnation and ordains it to blessedness, notwithstanding the decision of the creature, in opposition to it, in reversal of that mistaken decision, in the reconstitution of it by His own prior decision. The sovereignty of God is thus confirmed by the freedom of the election of grace, and that means for the creature not simply humiliation, but the humiliation which is really and in the same moment exaltation. If a man has not been allowed to fall by God, then He cannot fall at all, and least of all can he cause himself to fall. God Himself in His freedom has decided that he shall stand, that he shall be saved and not lost, that he shall live and not die. He cannot take these things, but they are given to him in the freedom of God. He himself has no freedom for God. He cannot assert any such freedom over against God. He has no freedom in which he may will to help himself. But God in His freedom stands substitute for him. And in that very fact he has his own real freedom for God and for the purpose of the will of God ; the freedom to obey Him and to live by Him. That he is elected by the grace of God means also, then, that he too becomes free : free from the threat of the accusation laid against him, free from the curse of his own proven guilt, free from the bondage in which the curse works itself out, free from death, in which its end is finally attained ; free for the thankfulness which he can never again deny to God now that his ingratitude has been passed over, free for the service of which he is now made worthy without any merit of his own, free for a joy which only now can live again and which is unfathomable in its depths. And all this means the freedom of the grace of God for the humiliated who has no help apart from God, who even now can only cling to the grace of God as such. This is the incomparable and inexhaustible blessing visited upon him in the election of God. This is the blessing held out to every man who hears ; the blessing which must always be proclaimed as the final word whenever we make mention of the doctrine of the divine election of grace.

We ask further : In the light of an evangelical understanding of the election of grace, what is the meaning of the mystery of the freedom of this divine work ? The will of God in His grace knows no Wherefore. God's decision is grounded in His good-pleasure, and for that reason it is inexplicable to us. If we tried to call God to account for His decision we should be questioning and indeed denying God Himself. But if this is the case, then it means that the creature must bow before the gracious God and submit itself to Him. Confronted with the mystery of God, the creature must be silent : not merely for the sake of being silent, but for the sake of hearing. Only to the extent that it attains to silence, can it attain to hearing. But, again, it must be silent not merely for the sake of hearing, but for that of obeying. For obedience is the purpose and goal of hearing. Our return to obedience is indeed the aim of free grace. It is for this that it makes us free. It is for this that it confronts us as a mystery, as a supreme court, as a verdict against which there can be no appeal, as a decision the rightness of which cannot be tested by the standards of other decisions because, on account of the One who made it, it is inherently right. In its very character as unsearchable the election of God demands as such our obedience. It is not proclaimed to us, nor does it reach us, but as an election of the creature it is the mere imagination of the creature, if in and with that election there is no summons to obedience—quite irrespective of the accusation laid against us, the curse resting upon us, the death shadowing our whole life. From these very things the election of grace has, in fact, released us. And in so doing it has undermined the pretence and subterfuge that we had no power to obey, that the demand laid upon us by God was too great. In the demand He makes God does not ask us concerning ourselves :

He asks us rather concerning our acknowledgment of that which He in His grace has determined and adjudged concerning us. We are not summoned to an active demonstration of our own powers. We are summoned to live in the power of His grace. But to that we are summoned, being confronted by the omnipotent and unsearchable Therefore of God, which in its unsearchability both cuts off our retreat and drives us forward. Drives us forward : for no longer can we sustain ourselves with anything but the positive meaning and purpose of the will of God, in the power of which we are saved and ought to live, to whose pre-determination our own self-determination is subject. Everything else is the old past of which we can never again lay hold. The mystery of grace is the middle-point in our lives, divisive and disturbing. And by this fact it is decided that God's will is our salvation. This is what the mystery means for the creature. But there is more to it than that. It was necessary to point out that the mystery of the election of God summons to obedience. It does so because it is the mystery of the living and life-giving God, and not of an enthroned but lifeless idol beside which we could only sit in an equally lifeless fear or confidence. But now we must maintain, and, if possible, emphasise even more strongly, the other side of the matter : that when the mystery of God in election comes into the life of the creature, demanding, compelling and disturbing, it is really grace and loving-kindness and favour which visits the creature. When this happens, God is in fact saying Yes to it. And it is God who says Yes. It is, therefore, a Yes which is unconditional in its certainty, preceding all self-determination and outlasting any change in self-determination on the part of the creature. It is the foreordination under which the creature must always live. It disturbs us but does not disquiet us. The sphere of disquiet is the sphere outside the divine election of grace, the sphere of the creature resisting the love of God. The creature is restless, and necessarily so, having brought about its own fall by this resistance. Once it has left its only possible and real resting-place, it seeks another in vain. It has no rest because that resistance has made it completely untrustworthy and yet it would trust in itself. By the divine election of grace, however, it is removed from this sphere of unrest. And the mystery of this election means for the creature that it is set at rest. The rest of decision and obedience : for it is the mystery of the living and the life-giving God. But truly at rest : for it is the mystery of the constant God, who gives to the creature whose interests He espouses a part in His own constancy. When God says Yes to the creature, He does say Yes ; without any if or but, without any afterthought or reservation, not temporarily but definitively, with a fidelity which is not partial and temporal, but total and eternal. Once the election has taken place, there is no further question as to the validity or non-validity of this Yes. There is no further anxiety as to how such a Yes can be fashioned or maintained. There is no further despair in face of the ever-present and total impossibility of living by one's own strength in the light of this Yes. All this lies behind the creature—as the old past. As truly as God has said Yes, as truly as God is God, the creature is affirmed, and it has no other life than life in the light of this Yes. The obedience demanded of it by the divine election of grace, what else is it but the self-evident authorisation of the creature elected and therefore affirmed by God ? And so the decision which in this election is made concerning the creature cannot mean that it is placed under the alien law of an all-powerful destiny, which it must restlessly fulfil, tormented by the consciousness of its own insufficiency in the face of its greatness and demand. What indeed is there to fulfil when by the divine Yes the law of its life has not merely been established but fulfilled ? All that is left for it to do is simply to live the life ordained for it, and to live therefore at peace. All that is left to it is wonder, reverent astonishment, at the fact of the mystery that it can live this life affirmed by God : not an idle wonder, but not one which could lead to new unrest ; wonder at the God who in advance has answered all our questions, removed all our anxiety and taken away the object of all our self-despair, by Himself, i.e., by His intervention for us, in which account is already taken of our insufficiency, and by which He has created a perfect sufficiency for us. Inasmuch as He does not allow Himself to be called to account for His election, God permits and commands the creature to surrender to Him the responsibility for its existence. Inasmuch as in the election He disposes of us without allowing any questions as to the grounds of His action, we can and must reckon with the fact that the dispositions concerning our conduct have already been made, and need not be made again by us, but need only be recognised as already made. Inasmuch as in the election He has made Himself the object of our worship, all the demand now made of us consists in the one thing—that we should really offer Him this worship. This is the rest which is signified by God's election of grace even for the creature which is rigorously and inexorably claimed for service. Thus claimed, it has no longer any need to justify itself, to defend itself, or to save itself. It may be silent and still before this mystery. Even as it runs, it may wait for the joyous revelation of this mystery. In God's election of grace it is visited by an incomparable and inexhaustible blessing even from this second standpoint ; even in the very fact that it is always God's mystery, that in it God disposes of us, not allowing us to approve of the disposition made, but only to acknowledge it as something already accomplished. And that is the blessing held out to every man who hears ; the blessing which must always be proclaimed as the final word whenever we make mention of the doctrine of the divine election of grace.

And now, thirdly, we ask : In the light of an evangelical understanding of the election of grace, what is the meaning of the divine righteousness of this event ? Undoubtedly the first meaning is this, that in this work God exercises judgment on the creature—He who has and alone has the right and the discernment for such a task. It means that in this work God creates order—He who is the source and norm of all order, who is Himself the order by whose standard all other order is still, or yet again, disorder. It means that God maintains His own worth over against the creature—He who in His wisdom knows, and alone knows, what is worthy of Himself. And so again the knowledge of the righteousness of the divine election means that we are made aware of our own limitations. Who is there can come before the judgment-seat of God with the consciousness that he has a good case and nothing therefore to fear ? Who is there can discuss or argue with God as to what constitutes order ? Who can anticipate God's wisdom with his own judgment, or even wish to find it confirmed thereby ? Before the mystery of His freedom we not only must, but can only be silent. And when we know this, and will to be really silent, then this willing becomes the confession of those who acknowledge themselves to be in the wrong before Him, who find in themselves no grounds either of justification or even excuse, no grounds, therefore, for a divine pardon, no grounds which could move God to elect them. It is inevitable that the righteousness of the divine election, when recognisable by us as such, should remind us that of ourselves we must stand outside in the realm of non-election, and therefore perdition. It is inevitable that the known righteousness of God in His election should constantly lead the creature to the fact that it is in opposition to the love of God directed towards it in that election, thus making itself unworthy of it. The known righteousness of the divine election of grace has for the creature the significance of a glimpse into the abyss into which it has caused itself to fall and from which it has no power to save itself. But, again, that is not all. The righteousness of God utterly crushes us. In it God asserts and vindicates His own worth over against the creature. Yet in the election of the creature even this righteousness reveals itself as the grace and loving-kindness and favour of God directed towards it. It is not out of negligence or procrastination, not out of any kind of weakness, but in the relentless vindication and exercise of His righteousness that God, in electing, is merciful towards the creature, espousing its cause, giving to it in its poverty, need and suffering His own substance, creating its righteousness, guaranteeing its future. For, according to the judgment of His wisdom, it is His substance and righteousness which comes upon it. It is arrested in that self-caused fall, it is kept and delivered from the abyss, it is allowed to live by the ordination and power of God, quite irrespective and even in spite of its deserts, and with a clear indication of its limitations. And it is this which God regards as worthy of Himself, which is therefore truly worthy of Himself. It is in this way that He wills to maintain and vindicate Himself over against the creature. This is the righteous order which He creates and establishes. He opposes to the creature the fact of His loving-kindness. He avenges sin not by regarding but by forgiving it. He attacks and overcomes the unreason of our opposition by His peace, which is higher than all reason of ours, and which is therefore revealed as the true, divine wisdom. The righteousness of God in His election means, then, that as a righteous Judge God perceives and estimates as such the lost case of the creature, and that in spite of its opposition He gives sentence in its favour, fashioning for it His own righteousness. It means that God does not acquiesce in the creature's self-destruction as its own enemy. He sees to it that His own prior claim on the creature, and its own true claim to life, is not rendered null and void. He cares for the creature as for His own possession. And in seeking its highest good, He magnifies His own glory. We cannot distinguish God's kingly righteousness from His mercy. We need not deny it for the sake of His mercy. It is in that righteousness that He says Yes to the creature in the mystery of His freedom. And that is what makes the Yes so stirring as a challenge and so firm as a basis of the sure confidence in which the creature can live. It lifts the accusation from us and yet it does not expose God Himself to accusation. It is rather the revelation of the reasonableness of His work, in which we may recognise that work as well-founded, and accept it, and allow it to come upon us as a blessing—the great blessing with which He has visited us. Once again, it is a question of the incomparable and inexhaustible blessing which is for all those who may hear. And from this third standpoint, too, this blessing must always be proclaimed as the final word if we are to speak rightly and evangelically of the doctrine of the divine election of grace.

Such, then, are the stipulations of an understanding of the three basic concepts of the doctrine of predestination—stipulations which we had to bring out at once with a view to the further investigation and exposition of the doctrine. The doctrine of election is the sum of the Gospel.

2. THE FOUNDATION OF THE DOCTRINE

What is the source of the doctrine of predestination ? This is the second preliminary question to which we must now turn. What we mean by it is this : What are the truths and realities thereby presented to us ? What is the specific knowledge which compels us to think and speak about this matter, and to think and speak about it in this particular way ? What impression is it that will and must find in this doctrine its expression ? What is the particular concern which has the power, a power at once stimulating, dynamic and formative,

an authorising and commanding and directive power, to make this
doctrine both possible and necessary, and to give to it this or that
specific form ?

There is reason to ask ourselves this question with particular care
and candour at this specific juncture. Consciously or unconsciously,
all conceptions of the doctrine must, of course, glance in this direction.
But we may glance at many different aspects of the matter. And
ever after our doctrine of predestination will assume a different form,
and with it our whole dogmatic system, and the Church proclamation
informed by that system. In the first part of our discussion it has
become clear that we have reached a point in Christian doctrine which
is vital for the whole, and yet also very vulnerable. And the most
common failure has been an insufficient notice or investigation of the
question which is the real starting-point for what we have to think
and say in this connexion. On the basis of presupposedly self-evident
answers to the question, courses have been adopted—and very definite
courses in spite of the untested nature of the answers—which can lead
to the most momentous decisions and statements. And such decisions
and statements have then established themselves by their own natural
weight, and have thus been able to characterise and even dominate
the whole of Christian doctrine. It is only natural that in spite of all
the accompanying good intentions and moments of truth, such statements and decisions are endangered by their doubtful and possibly
erroneous starting-point. It is only natural that they can themselves
become a danger, perhaps inevitably so. We must at this point recall
the basic rule of all Church dogmatics : that no single item of Christian
doctrine is legitimately grounded, or rightly developed or expounded,
unless it can of itself be understood and explained as a part of the
responsibility laid upon the hearing and teaching Church towards the
self-revelation of God attested in Holy Scripture. Thus the doctrine
of election cannot legitimately be understood or represented except
in the form of an exposition of what God Himself has said and still
says concerning Himself. It cannot and must not look to anything
but the Word of God, nor set before it anything but the truth and
reality of that Word. It can seek its basis and necessity only in the
knowledge of the God self-manifested there. It can seek to give expression only to the impression of that Word. It can seek to meet
only the one concern, receiving its stimulus and dynamic and form
only from the fact that this Word must always be heard and validated
in the Christian Church because this Word has constituted itself its
basis and the nourishment by which it must live. Before we seek to
discuss generally the implications of this basic principle, it is necessary,
as matters stand, to execute certain specific defensive movements.

1. To begin with something apparently self-evident, yet not generally recognised to-day, it is not simply a matter of proceeding to develop
the doctrine along lines which allow the tradition of the Church to

prescribe and lay down in advance the theme and programme of its exposition. In the matter of election the best ecclesiastical tradition can indeed serve both as an occasion and an ancillary. But it cannot be the subject and norm of dogmatic effort. On the contrary, in this matter we must ask even of the best ecclesiastical tradition what is its true origin, and to what extent it may or may not be properly adapted in this respect to serve as an ancillary.

It is remarkable enough that in the question of the election this warning must today be addressed to a certain movement in Reformed theology. It is a well-known historical fact that more than any other doctrine the doctrine of predestination stamped itself upon the face of the Reformed Church, or rather of 16th and 17th century Reformed theology, thus distinguishing it from others. This fact can and ought to stimulate Reformed theology to concern itself especially seriously with this doctrine. But it cannot serve as a basis for the doctrine. We cannot regard any doctrine of election as Reformed, or prove it Reformed (let alone Christian), merely in virtue of the fact that it maintains as such the historical characteristics of the Reformed confession and theology, seeking, if possible, to resurrect the doctrine in its historical form, or in the form of the most accurate possible repetition of the Reformed teaching. The book of Loraine Boettner already mentioned begins with the words : " The purpose of this book is . . . to give a re-statement to that great system, which is known as the Reformed faith or Calvinism, and to show that this is beyond all doubt the teaching of the Bible and of reason." And directly afterwards the author thinks it necessary to commend himself by saying that he is a " Calvinist without reserve." But this is simply to say that he has set himself a task which is scholastic in the wrong sense of the word, and completely at variance with the basic principle even of Reformed dogmatics. The reproduction of the Calvinistic system is a necessary, rewarding and instructive exercise within the sphere of ecclesiastical or dogmatic history. But we cannot substitute it for, or confuse it with, the task of presenting Christian, and even Reformed Christian doctrine. Nor can such doctrine be presented in the form of a reproduction of " Calvinism." Consultation of the Bible must mean something more than simply giving a supplementary proof—side by side with the consultation of reason—that the doctrine of the Bible is identical with that of Calvin. Calvinism may be a good and praiseworthy thing from the human standpoint, even if we give to the concept more than its historical sense. But from the standpoint of a strict Christian theology there is no such thing as " Calvinism," just as there ought never to have been any such thing as " Lutheranism." Calvinism does not exist as a subject and norm of Christian doctrine. Calvin and the older Reformed Church did present in all seriousness the doctrine of predestination. They did so in a specific form. We may accept their work, and always keep it in mind, as a penetrating approach to the question, as a contribution to its treatment which we must respect and value. But we shall be doing Calvin the most fitting honour if we go the way that he went and start where he started. And according to his own most earnest protestations, he did not start with himself, nor with his system, but with Holy Scripture as interpreted in his system. It is to Scripture that we must again address ourselves, not refusing to learn from that system, but never as " Calvinists without reserve." And it is to Scripture alone that we must ultimately be responsible. Modern Neo-Calvinism involves at once, on its formal side, a mistaken re-introduction of the Catholic principle of tradition repudiated by all the Reformers, and most sharply of all by Calvin. Out of loyalty to Calvin himself we must never begin by treating the doctrine of predestination as a kind of *palladium* of the older Reformed Church. Our point of departure must never be the particular form of the doctrine as there presented.

2. If we are to understand the doctrine of election rightly, we may not substitute for its foundation what we think must in any case be acknowledged as its didactic value, or its pedagogic usefulness in the cure of souls. We may not set before us this value and usefulness, only, and inevitably, to construct and expound the doctrine in accordance with the usefulness and value which we think ought to be ascribed to it. The order of procedure must be the very opposite. We must enquire into the foundation of the doctrine in the divine revelation quite independently of its value and usefulness, and the doctrine must then be constructed and expounded in accordance with that foundation. Only as that is done will the fact and the extent of its didactic and pedagogic value and usefulness really emerge.

At the very beginning of his exposition in the *Institutio* (III, 21, 1) Calvin maintained the *utilitas*, indeed the *suavissimus fructus huius doctrinae*, along three lines : first, that it teaches us to put our trust wholly in the mercy of God ; second, that it demonstrates to us the glory of God in its full grandeur ; and third, that it inclines us to a true humility (*humilitas*). There is no doubt that factually we can only agree with him on these points. Heinz Otten (*Calvins theol. Anschauung von der Praedestination*, 1938, p. 34) writes in this regard : " When we treat of these impulses towards edification, we introduce the particular concern or interest of Calvin in the matter of predestination." But it is precisely in this kind of " particular concern or interest " that there lurk the main sources of dogmatic error. For such " particular interests " have it within themselves to shift quite remarkably both in purpose and emphasis as the years pass. It needed only the gradual disappearance of respect for the Word of God as such which characterised the age which followed ; it needed only the increased prevalence of arbitrariness in systematisation, to transform the *utilitates* of Calvin into formally didactic and pedagogic axioms which as such claimed a permanent importance and the value of basic principles. Once that was done, it was these axioms which inevitably gave to the doctrine its shape and form. Already with Beza and Gomarus the glory of God had given rise to the concept of His comprehensive and exclusive action and efficacy. In the *Westminster Confession* the sure confidence in God's mercy had become the absolute assurance of the elect. Throughout the Reformed world *humilitas* had become the highly practical and in time all too practical sense of the Christian world-citizen, whom Max Weber and others have described as the specific outcome and result of the Reformed doctrine of election ; a world-citizen lowly indeed before God but for that reason all the more self-assured in his conduct upon earth. If from the very first the doctrine was worked out with a view to such results it was inevitable that it should develop in this direction. But it can also happen that many Christians and theologians have a natural sympathy with particularly hard and mysterious and high-soaring teachings which stand in the sharpest possible antithesis to ordinary human thought, and for that reason they are inclined to have a positive interest in this very doctrine. It cannot be denied that the doctrine may also commend itself from what is to some extent an æsthetic standpoint. But what if this aspect, and the formal pleasure which it awakens, become the dominating motif in its development ? Again, L. Boettner seems quite prepared to accept it as a recommendation—presumably in an apologetic interest—" that among non-Christian religions Mohammedanism has so many millions who believe in some kind (!) of predestination, that the doctrine of Fatalism has been held in some form or other in several heathen countries, and that the mechanistic and deterministic philosophies have exerted such great influence in England, Germany and America " (p. 2). However that may be, it is always a serious matter when, on his own confession, a theologian approaches this matter with so wishful a picture in his mind. What is certain about all bases of this type is that they always leave us at a point where the Yes only too easily becomes a No and the confirmation a denial. Very different judgments can be passed on the value and usefulness of the doctrine, as history has in fact demonstrated. Where Calvin and his followers saw nothing but *suavissimum fructum*, the Lutherans of the 16th and 17th centuries, and many others too, saw only an endangering of assurance of salvation, the sense of responsibility, etc., or even an open relapse into Stoicism, Manicheism, Quietism and Libertinism. Boettner appears to rejoice at the supposed kinship between the doctrine of predestination, as understood Calvinistically, and the teaching of Islam. But this supposed kinship was the very reason why the older Lutherans sought to discredit the Calvinists by describing them as secret adherents of the Eastern Antichrist. While the one can never cease to find æsthetic edification in the paradox of the doctrine, the other will find in that paradox the reason for an angry repudiation of it. It is impossible to build upon the foundation of such value-judgments or predilections, and it is as well to maintain a radical and consistent reserve in such matters, grounding the doctrine first in the Word of God, and then letting its value and usefulness speak for themselves.

3. There is a third possibility, more serious than the first two and the more decidedly to be rejected. This is the possibility of basing the doctrine of election upon a datum of experience, presumed or actual. On this view our concern is with what we observe to be the evident contrast between those who through the Church hear the Gospel and those who never have the opportunity to hear it at all ; or, again, between those who hear it obediently and with profit, and so to salvation, and those who hear with open hostility, or without any result at all, and so finally to condemnation. How—it is asked— are these facts to be explained ? And how especially is it to be explained that there seem to be those who either outwardly or inwardly cannot hear the Gospel ? And if this is a fact, what is its bearing on our understanding of the other observation, that there are some who do seem actually to hear the Gospel ? To answer this question the Bible is consulted (although only in a secondary capacity), and it is shown that some are elected by God and some rejected. But this raises the further question : Is it right to go to the Bible with a question dictated to us by experience, i.e., with a presupposition which has only an empirical basis, in order then to understand the statements of the Bible as an answer to this question, which means chiefly as a confirmation of the presupposition which underlies the question ? Ought our observation and judgment in regard to the external and internal relationship of men to the Gospel really to force us to the position where we may recognise in this distinction between men the divine decision of the election of grace to which the Bible testifies ? Can this observation impress itself upon us as all that significant ? Can the standards by which we judge be as accurate and serviceable as that ? After all, the resultant judgment is ours and not God's. And we have no right to proceed at once to understand the divine

judgment of the election to which Scripture testifies simply from this external judgment, and to some extent as the divine ratification of it. If it is to be a question of the divine judgment, as it must be in dealing with the doctrine of election, then Scripture must not be brought in simply as an interpretation of the facts of the case as given by our own judgment. The very facts which we consider must be sought not in the realm of our experience but in Scripture, or rather in the self-revelation of God attested in Scripture.

We have already seen how Augustine began quite expressly with the question of a would-be experience. And after him Calvin in particular demands careful watching. I could not say that he made the experience in question the basis of his doctrine of predestination. But he did buttress his doctrine so emphatically by the appeal to it that we can hardly fail to recognise that much of the pathos and emotional power with which he defended it, and to an even greater extent the form in which he did so, were determined by this experience, the effects of which were inevitably serious from the point of view of the purity of the doctrine. This is particularly the case in the work *De aet. Dei praed.*, 1552, in which there is a constant appeal (e.g., *C.R.* 8, 261, 275, 292, 298, 317) to the *convincere* or *docere* or *demonstrare* of *experientia*, to *palam apparet* or *palam constat*, whenever the question arises of the basis of the assertion that from the very first men stand in a different relationship to the Gospel ; a difference which can be explained only by a difference in the divine decree made concerning them. But in the *Institutio*, too, we read : *Apud centum eadem fere habetur concio, viginti prompta fidei oboedientia suscipiunt ; alii vel nullius pensi habent, vel rident, vel explodunt, vel abominantur* (III, 24, 12). *Experientia docet, ita (Deum) velle resipiscere quos ad se invitat, ut non tangat omnium corda* (III, 24, 15). Indeed, the whole exposition begins with the methodologically only too revealing words : *Quod non apud omnes peraeque homines foedus vitae praedicatur et apud eos, quibus praedicatur, non eundem locum vel aequaliter vel perpetuo reperit : in ea diversitate mirabilis divini iudicii altitudo se profert. Nec enim dubium quin aeternae Dei electionis arbitrio haec quoque varietas serviat. Quod si palam est Dei nutu fieri ut aliis ultro offeratur salus, alii ab eius aditu arceantur : hic magnae et arduae protinus emergunt quaestiones, quae aliter explicari nequeunt, quam si de electione ac praedestinatione constitutum habeant piae mentes quod tenere convenit* (III, 21, 1). The answer to these questions is then strikingly given in the famous definition : *Non pari conditione creantur omnes, sed aliis vita aeterna, aliis damnatio aeterna praeordinatur* (III, 21, 5). According to the tenor of all these statements the fact which above all others inspired Calvin, and was thus decisive for the formation of his doctrine, was not at all the contrast between the Church on the one hand, and on the other the heathen world entirely unreached by the Gospel. It could not be said that Calvin particularly concerned himself with this aspect of the problem within the context of the doctrine of predestination. Again, it was not the positive observation that at all times the Gospel has both reached so many externally and also seemed to prevail over them internally. Of course, this aspect of the matter does enter in strongly—the thankfulness of the Church which hears and receives God's Word. And obviously Calvin might very well have put this aspect in the foreground, and begun his thinking at this point. But because in this connexion he already thought of this positive aspect as a fact of experience, it was inevitable that he should regard it as limited by that other fact of experience which excites both pain and anger, the fact of the opposition, the indifference, the hypocrisy and the self-deception with which the Word of God is received by so many of those who hear it (80 per cent. according to the estimate there given). And it is this limiting experience, the negative in conjunction with the positive, which is obviously the decisive factor as Calvin thought he must see it. It was out of this presupposition, laid down with axiomatic certainty, that there arose for him the *magnae et arduae quaestiones* for which he saw an answer in what he found to be the teaching of Scripture concerning the election ; questions which he thought he himself ought to answer in his doctrine of election supposedly gathered from Scripture. Within the sphere of the Church he saw men in whose being, words and actions when confronted by the Gospel proclaimed to them he thought he could recognise only that which Scripture describes as the divine rejection, and therefore the hardening accompanying the divine election. It is true that he saw in these men and their like only a foil to what, on the other hand, he thought he could gratefully recognise as the positive result of the divine election in the living faith of the Church and also, of course, in his own personal faith. He knew, too, with a perfect clarity that it was not of his own or of any other believer's merit that he did not belong equally well to the number of those rejected and hardened by God : *Si quis respondeat, diversitatem ex eorum provenire malitia et perversitate, nondum satisfactum fuerit : quia et illorum* (of believers) *ingenium eadem malitia occuparetur, nisi Deus sua bonitate corrigeret. Ideoque semper implicabimur, nisi succurrat illud Pauli : Quis te discernit ?* (1 Cor. 4[7]). *Quo significat non propria virtute, sed sola Dei gratia alios aliis praecellere* (III, 24, 12). And he also knew that there are no absolutely unequivocal marks of the divine rejection of certain men, and that there can be no absolutely unequivocal perception of the reprobate state of this or that individual. He knew, too, that the election of a man cannot be gathered with absolute certainty from a fact of experience. He recognised with Augustine (*De corr. et gratia* 14, 45) : *Nescimus quis ad praedestinatorum numerum pertineat vel non pertineat* (III, 23, 14). He knew and constantly acknowledged that the Lord knoweth them that are His. And yet it is only too evident that Calvin thought himself competent to recognise very well, if not the reprobate, at least the stupid and deceived and wicked who in that age formed so distressingly large a majority of men. He thought himself competent to distinguish all kinds of fools, scoundrels and wretches, both the crass and the subtle. He thought that he could recognise the *canaille* in all its forms. He thought that he could know those who must at any rate be suspected of the divine rejection and hardening, especially in the case of theological opponents, in whom such a characteristic might be noted with a sureness which bordered on absolute certainty. Both in word and deed he obviously dealt with such people in accordance with that knowledge. It would be petty to seek to dispute with Calvin on this issue. Unless we can see what he saw, and for similar reasons, we have no right whatever to do so. One of the characteristic traits of this Reformer was a torturing exposedness and sensitiveness to all that mass of most radical wrongdoing which just at that period, and in direct opposition to the whole preaching of the Gospel, extended itself quite shamelessly over every section of human life (acutely so in the ecclesiastical, and most acutely of all in the theological world). And even if it were partly conditioned by his spleen, who is there would not really maintain that this was one of his great characteristics ? It should be remembered, too, that the age of Calvin was that of the Counter-Reformation : a time which saw the harassing resurgence of temporal and spiritual powers against the but newly attempted renovation of the Church ; a time which exposed the painful weaknesses, negligences and perversities of the supposedly renovated Church itself ; a time which knew all the self-willed and ill-conceived and dangerous parallel movements within that renovation ; a time, then, which might very well cause a clever and determined man to keep and turn away himself with grief and horror from the majority of his contemporaries. The fact which Calvin believed he experienced so definitely was that of the contrast and the appalling numerical discrepancy between the multitude of those who were useless in one way or another, the 80 per cent. whom one could meet only with a 100 per cent. aversion, and the tiny company of those who were " right."

And when and where did that fact not obtrude itself, even in the sphere of the Church ? Calvin was, indeed, comparatively tolerant when he believed that he could estimate the strength of the latter group as 20 per cent. of the whole. Yet even when we grant him that, even when we agree that the experience which claimed his attention was and is solidly founded, and does in some way obtrude itself, it must still be held against him that such experience can never claim more than human value and relevance. No matter what practical or theoretical results it may have, according to Calvin's own presuppositions it could not and cannot ever claim the character of a revelation. It could not and cannot be adapted as an axiom in accordance with which Scripture itself must be interrogated and expounded. We may already ask, and we cannot simply presuppose that it is decided in advance, whether a doctrine of election which is obedient to Scripture is required without further ado to answer the questions—no matter how pressing—forced upon us by the contrast either between the Church and the world or between the true Church and the false. We may ask whether in Scripture the divine electing and rejecting are related to one another in the same way as are Christendom and heathendom according to the construct of our experience, or as the small company of the righteous and the great multitude of *canaille* within the Church itself according to the construct which Calvin found so particularly impressive. If the undoubted statistics of this construct are taken as the point of departure for reflection on the divine election of grace, strengthened by the influence of so clever and determined a perception as that of Calvin, then quite obviously Scripture is no longer able to say freely what it wills to say. It can only answer the questions put to it by man. What it wills to do first is to give us with its answers the right questions. " At the very outset, before he consulted the Bible," Calvin had " reached a decision which—quite independently of the answer of Scripture—determined the character of his outlook on predestination in accordance with the question put by experience " (H. Otten, *op. cit.* p. 29). But that is the very thing which should not happen. If it does, then there is a pressing danger—which Calvin himself did not escape—that the divine election which it is our task to explore and expound will take on far too great a similarity with the perhaps very well grounded and very praiseworthy but still human electing of the outstanding theological thinker, and that the electing God there revealed will come to resemble far too closely the electing, and more particularly the rejecting theologian. Whether and how far the work and being of God in this matter have anything to do with the positive and negative constructs of our experience can only be discovered, like the generally admitted usefulness of the doctrine, when without any reference to such constructs, indeed with a setting aside so far as possible of all existing constructs, the doctrine has been grounded upon God's own Word and has already taken shape. Not before !

We must go on at once to give to this delimitation greater precision and content.

If the doctrine of election is grounded upon supposed or real facts of experience, materially that obviously means that it is grounded with reference to man in general. In one way or another the election is thought of as the description of a differing and differentiating attitude of God towards the totality of individual men as such ; an attitude in which God (according to some, more or less completely in accordance with His own mysterious good-pleasure ; according to others, with more or less regard to the attitude of men towards Himself) divides this totality of individuals into two sections or groups, electing here and not electing or rejecting there, with the aim and result of salvation and blessedness in the case of the former, perdition and damnation in the case of the latter. The divine electing and human election (and the negative counterpart of both) are thus understood in some sense as the ordaining of a private relationship between God and each individual man as such. Thus it is possible and necessary on the one side to consider God in His private relationship with each individual, and on the other side to consider each individual in his private relationship with God. The action of God in the plenitude of these private relationships cannot as such, of course, become the subject of our experience. Yet the individuals in their election or non-election can enter in as such a subject of experience. The differences between them in relation to the Gospel, the difference between heathen and Christians, or between good Christians and bad, may be taken as a cause for enquiry concerning their private relationship with God, or at least for the assertion of the existence of such a relationship (which by its very nature cannot perhaps be defined in detail with any certainty). Upon the basis of that assertion it is then possible to speak of the divine electing and human election (and the negative counterpart of both). Even where great caution is exercised in the foundation of the doctrine in accordance with experience, it is naturally presupposed that there is at all events a connexion between the doctrine of election and these private relationships between God and each individual as such ; between the doctrine of election and the positive or negative character of the decision made between God and every individual man. In such circumstances the first and final purpose of the doctrine is to denote and describe what the relationship with God determines, as grace or as non-grace, for the totality of these individuals, each of whom exists and must be considered equally in and for himself. In some measure it is the first and final word of a doctrine of man as the creature of God subjected to the divine decision, of his exodus and entry to salvation or perdition, to life or death, as determined by his relationship with God. It is the first and final word of a rightly conceived anthropology, i.e., an anthropology which takes into account the relationship with God.

It cannot be denied that such private relationships between God and each individual do exist, and that in these relationships there is in fact a first and final divine decision. How can God be God, how can He be in every respect the Lord of the creature, unless He is sovereign as the Lord and God of each individual as such, unless for the individual as such the first and final decision is in fact made in his relationship with God ? It also cannot be denied that the divine election stands in a radically necessary connexion with the ordination of the plenitude of these relationships between God and the individual, and with the decisions made in these relationships. How can it be otherwise ? As we concluded in our first sub-section, the election is always God's decision over against man as His creature, a decision which was fulfilled in Jesus Christ, and in virtue of which God wills to be, not without this creature, but with it, as the One who in His free love has bound Himself to it. But this creature, man, exists concretely in the plenitude of individual men. Thus the divine election does indeed determine and ordain the plenitude of the private relationships between God and every individual. What they may or may not be is decided in God's election. That is not to say, however, that God's election as such is identical with the determination of these private relationships as already made. This is a presupposition which has been taken too much for granted. What we ought rather to ask in this connexion is whether the electing God as such, as self-revealed, and attested in Holy Scripture, is in fact simply this counterpart of the individual as such, fixed and rigid in His decision one way or the other. Is it practicable, therefore, to consider Him merely with reference to individuals, asking whether He has perhaps elected these or not elected those ? And, on the other hand, is it practicable to consider individuals as such in relation to Him, enquiring whether they are elected or rejected ? Is there any justification for such a conception when we have regard to the electing God as self-revealed and attested in Holy Scripture ? It cannot be questioned that the election of God does concern all men, and that in it the will of God is determined concerning all men. The question is, however, whether the divine election is for this reason to be understood as an already made and existent determination of all men ; whether it is meaningful or possible to understand each man as such as already either " elected " or " rejected," i.e., in the light of this determination. *For* this determination—yes. To be determined by God's election is the final—but really the final mystery of every human life. But this does not mean that the mystery as such derives from the " determining " in the sense that every human life has already received the determination corresponding to it. The election is decisively important for each individual, but it does not follow that it is for the individual a character already imparted to him, immanent in him from the very first. It does not follow that it is bound up with his very existence. It is still the activity of the free love of God. As such, it is intended for every man, and it concerns and determines every man. But it does so without necessitating that he should be elected or rejected immediately and in advance. According to Scripture, the divine election of grace is an activity of God which has a definite goal and limit. Its direct and proper object is not individuals generally, but one individual—and only in Him the people called and united by Him, and only in that people individuals in general in their private relationships with God. It is only in that one man that a human determination corresponds to the divine determining. In the strict sense only He can be understood and described as " elected " (and " rejected "). All others are so in Him, and not as individuals. It is not right, therefore, to take it as self-evident, as has so frequently been the case, that the doctrine of predestination may be understood and presented as the first and final word of a general anthropology. On the contrary, it is right and necessary to get back from things supposedly self-evident to the true sources, the self-revelation of God and the testimony of Holy Scripture, and to discover the definite form in which the electing God encounters and confronts humanity as a whole, and in which humanity also confronts and encounters the electing God. Without a reference to the specific form of this encounter, it would be premature to attempt an investigation of man as such and in general, and of the private relationships between God and the individual. In such an investigation we should remain completely blind to what election is and what it really means both for all men and also for each of those private relationships.

This question takes us deep into the main problem of the doctrine. We had to raise it here because the dubious basing of the doctrine on certain experiences has its root in the supposedly self-evident pre-supposition that the divine election is a direct determination of human existence as such. Once we are freed from this presupposition, there is no further point in attempting in some way or other to derive the divine election of grace from the existence of heathen and Christians, or of good Christians and bad. There is no further point in attempting to understand and fashion the doctrine of election as an answer to questions raised by the facts of experience.

4. Another foundation which must be taken seriously, but all the more carefully avoided, is that which begins with the concept of God as omnipotent Will, governing and irresistibly directing each and every creature according to His own law, and thus disposing also of the salvation and perdition of men. The concept *praedestinatio* (foreordination or pre-decision) is not unequivocal, nor are the biblical concepts πρόθεσις, πρόγνωσις and προορισμός if once divorced from their contexts. Who and what is it that in authority, time and logic is " prior " to everything else—" prior," then, to human decision, whether to the right hand or to the left ? It cannot be denied that it is God who even in this sense is " prior " to everything else, that He is the absolute *prius*. He is so even in His election. Otherwise He would not be God. He is the Almighty, and in His almightiness He is free. There can be no question of any diminution of this fact. But here error can also arise : the error of supposing that God is irresistibly efficacious power *in abstracto*, naked freedom and sovereignty as it were ; and in respect of the election, the error of supposing that this is a manifestation of this free sovereignty, and that the doctrine of election is only a matter of deducing and asserting, in relation to the positive or negative destiny of men, the logical consequences of the notion of a being who is sovereign over the whole world and whose operations are therefore necessary, as though the eternal salvation or perdition of men, like anything and everything else that takes place in the

created order, could be traced back to the righteous decision of the will of this most necessary being. On such a view predestination is only one moment within the world-order established and executed by the principle of freedom and necessity proclaimed under the name of God. The doctrine of predestination is only one moment in a deterministic scheme. When we oppose this view we must beware of coming down on the side of indeterminacy. But we must also assert that we do not exhaustively define or describe God when we identify Him with irresistible omnipotence. Indeed, if we make this identification *in abstracto*, we do not define or describe God at all. Irresistible omnipotence cannot be made the beginning and end of the being of God. And even if we do not make or intend this abstraction, we must still ask whether we understand the election aright if we understand it from the very first within the framework of the presumably superior reality of the divine government of the world, as one specific act of this general divine activity. That it is logically convenient to do this is quite evident. But what we must enquire is whether it is in fact correct to do it ; whether we ought not rather to understand the divine government of the world in the light of the divine election of grace. May it not be that we can believe and understand, not merely the election itself, but the fact that God and not a blindly determining and deciding something rules the world, and that the world is really ruled by Him, only when we recognise and proclaim in God the electing God, and as such the Lord, the Subject of that all-comprehensive activity ? May it not be that it is as the electing God that He is the Almighty, and not *vice versa* ?

A classical statement of the position which we must oppose is that of Thomas Aquinas. It is so because in content it is certainly not deterministic. For that reason, its critical character for the methodological question which here concerns us is all the more evident. According to Thomas, the doctrine of predestination belongs directly to that of the divine providence. Providence is God's ordering and directing of all things to their appointed end in virtue of His knowledge and will. To the knowledge and will of God, and therefore to His providence, all things are subordinate : *non* (*tantum*) *in universali, sed etiam in particulari* (*S. theol.* I, *qu.* 22, *art.* 2 *c*). And this includes man with his free will and his own human *providentia* in matters of good and evil (*ib.*, *ad* 4). Predestination is *quaedam pars providentiae.* Its specific concern is with the ordering and directing of man to eternal life, which he cannot as such attain by his own powers. He must be dispatched (*transmittitur*) towards this mark like the archer's arrow. And as for every event, so for this event in particular, there is a pre-existent *ratio* in God Himself. This *ratio transmissionis creaturae rationalis in finem vitae aeternae,* this particular instance of general providence, is predestination (*qu.* 23, *art.* 1 *c*). From this standpoint—it is a matter of the execution of one specific purpose of the Creator in respect of one of His creatures, but a purpose which basically and formally is in line with all His purposes—Thomas then attempted to treat and to solve all the problems of predestination in detail. He carried this so far that sometimes he could say quite expressly that the concept grace does not in itself belong to the definition of predestination. It does so only in so far as it is here the specific effect and purpose of the divine work (*qu.* 23, *art.* 3 *ad.* 4). Bonaventura, too (*Breviloq.* I 9), spoke of predestination entirely from the standpoint of the divine omnipotence and free will : *Est enim voluntas Dei prima et summa causa omnium specierum et motionum. Nihil enim fit visibile aut intelligibile in ista totius creaturae amplissima quadam universaque republica, quod non de illa imperiali aula summi imperatoris aut iubeatur aut permittatur.* That is the major : the general divine world-government. And : *Quia (voluntas Dei) efficassima est, nullo modo potest aliquis aliquid efficere nisi ipsa cooperante et coefficiente ; nullus deficere vel peccare potest, nisi ipsa iuste deserente.* That is the minor : predestination, as Bonaventura sees it. Zwingli's teaching was exactly the same : *Ex providentiae loco praedestinationis, liberi arbitrii meritique universum negotium pendet (Comm. de vera et falsa relig.*, 1525, ed. Schuler u. Schulth., Vol. 3, p. 163). *Est autem providentia praedestinationis veluti parens (ib.,* p. 282). *Nascitur praedestinatio (quae nihil aliud est, quum si tu dicas praeordinatio) ex providentia, imo est ipsa providentia (ib.,* p. 283).

We must count it highly in Calvin's favour that methodologically at least he broke with this tradition, treating the doctrine of providence (*Instit.* I, 16–18) in conjunction with that of creation, and the doctrine of predestination (III, 21–24) as the climax of that of the communication of the grace of God manifested and active in Jesus Christ. Of course, when we come to his arguments and statements at this latter point, we must constantly ask whether in matters of detail he does justice to the movement which this separation rightly indicates. Is it not the case that some of the decisive insights which dominate his doctrine of predestination derive from the generally acquired conception of the governance of God's omnipotence and will in the world at large ? At the former point, too, we must ask whether it is not the case that predestination is already asserted in a different way—but still predestination according to the peculiar understanding of the term ? That predestination should not only be subordinate to providence but superior to it was apparently not what Calvin intended, although in the second draft of the *Institutio* (1539 f *cap.* 14, 1) it is noteworthy that it is at least given the precedence over it (cf. Heinz Otten, *op. cit.*, p. 99 f.).

It is not surprising, then, that amongst the very orthodox, amongst those who thought that they were following Calvin most faithfully, there took place the converse of a quite distinct subordination of the doctrine of predestination to that of providence. It is true that many of these placed the doctrine of predestination in some sense at the very head of the dogmatic system, immediately after the doctrine of God. But a closer inspection reveals at once (as with Polanus, *Synt. Theol. chr.*, 1609, *col.* 1559, and Wolleb, *Chr. Theol. Comp.*, 1626, I, *cap.* 4) that, although general providence is only named and developed as such later, it is already presupposed in fact under the title *decretum generale*, forming the pattern for an understanding of predestination. Even as early as Polanus (*col.* 1560) there is a distinct reappearance of the Thomistic statement : *praedestinatio pars est providentiae.* On the other hand, with him too we see the tendency towards that broadening of the concept of predestination as such which made possible the understanding of the doctrine of predestination as the comprehensive doctrine of the divine world-governance, which includes as a specific application God's dealings with those elected or rejected by Him. That is how the Supralapsarian F. Gomarus put it : There is a *praedestinatio universalis, quae res omnes spectat totumque Dei decretum est* and a *praedestinatio particularis, quae ad quasdam earum tantum pertinet et pars aeterni atque universalis illius decreti existit (Disp. de div. hom. praed., th.* 15, *op.* III, 1644). By *praedestinare* (and indeed by the προορίζειν of Rom. 8[29] and Eph. 1[5]) Gomarus did not mean to understand the divine *eligere* in particular, but generally and abstractly the divine *decernere* as such (*ib., coroll.* 1). Into the doctrine of predestination there was now brought as a ruling concept that of the general, absolutely free divine disposing. Fundamentally, the thought was the same even where the doctrine was treated at a later stage, ostensibly as a basis for the atoning work of Jesus Christ, as in the Infralapsarian *Synopsis purior. Theol.* of Leiden (1624). Here, too, we read : *Sumitur haec praedestinationis vox vel generalius de actionibus divinae providentiae tam in bono quam in malo . . . vel de ordinatione personarum ad certum et supernaturalem finem* (*Disp.* 24, 4). And it is one of the peculiar features of the latest defence of the older Reformed doctrine by L. Boettner that he begins, as though there were no alternative, with the assertion that the doctrine of predestination is the representation of the absolute and unconditional purpose of the divine will, which is independent of all creation and grounded solely in God's eternal counsel. Everything outside of God is enclosed by this decree. All creatures owe their creation and preservation to the divine will and power (*The Ref. Doctr. of Pred.*, 1932, p. 13). Everything which exists does so only as a medium through which God in some way manifests His glory. The doctrine of predestination is no more than the application of this perception to the doctrine of the salvation of man (p. 14). When He created the world, God had a plan, like any " rational and intelligent man," like Napoleon before his Russian campaign (!). It is this plan which He executes. To confess that is to confess predestination, and the true and Calvinistic confession of predestination is the confession that God does everything, whether great or small, in accordance with this plan. To put it more exactly, predestination is the choice of this plan, now to be executed unquestioningly and unalterably. The whole history of the world is nothing other than the execution of it (p. 20 f.). " What can give the Christian more satisfaction and joy than to know that the whole course of the world is ordered with reference to the establishment of the kingdom of heaven and the manifestation of the divine glory ; and that he is one of the objects upon which infinite love and mercy is to be lavished ? " (p. 25). When with all thinking men we confess that our lives are overruled—we were not asked whether we wished to enter the world or not, or when, or where, or in what capacity we should be born, whether in the 20th century or before the Flood, whether as white men or black, whether in America or China—we confess as Christians that it is God who rules and determines all these things, as He does everything else in the world ; and if we hold fast by the perception of this truth, then we are already adopting the Calvinistic position (p. 30). It befits the sovereignty of God to be able to do everything consonant with His nature. He can dispose of the creature as of His property. He can overrule man in every aspect of his being, and He does so according to His own good-pleasure : whether in what he is or is not, in what he has or has not, in what he ought to become or ought not to become (p. 36). Like everything else, these things all happen as they are definitely ordained by God for the attainment of the end which God has set for Himself and for all things : " Every raindrop and every snowflake which falls from the clouds, every insect which moves, every plant which grows, every grain of dust which floats in the air, has had certain definite causes and will have certain definite effects. Each is a link in the chain of events, and many of the great events of history have turned on these apparently insignificant things " (p. 37). In this connexion God deals with each creature according to its own nature, and therefore according to His own most proper will (p. 38). And if we remember that all that God foreordained and infallibly executes He equally infallibly foresaw, that is only to say that everything which happens does so exactly as God has prescribed (p. 42 f.). This is the basis upon which Boettner undertakes to present the doctrine of predestination. He can hardly have imagined that he stood in the succession of Calvin in so doing, for the context at least of Calvin's doctrine points only too clearly in a different direction. What we can say, however, is that with a painful fidelity Boettner has reproduced the older Reformed method as used by Gomarus. In so doing he has brought new credit to the method of Thomas. Now naturally there can be no question of casting doubt upon all these statements about the freedom and omnipotence of God and the sovereignty of his ruling and disposing.

Boettner has said something which has to be said concerning the divine government of the world and its definitiveness as a sovereign act of power. His statements are rather trite, but they are correct in content, and finely put. What is missing is the answer to two questions : (1) On what basis and with reference to what subject should these statements be made ? How are they to be distinguished from what a Jew or Mohammedan or Stoic might say in this respect ? What is the role of divine grace in the designation and description of the divine government of the world ? Can it and should it play a purely supplementary and subordinate role, as one mode of divine action side by side with others ? And if it can, do these utterances really bring us within the sphere of the Christian confession, and if so, to what extent ? And (2) if we accept all this, what has it to do with predestination ? There may be a formal interconnexion, consisting in the fact that in the one as in the other we are concerned with the sovereign will of God, in the one case with that will in general, in the other with a particular application of it. But is that interconnexion really sufficient to justify the deducing of the doctrine of predestination from that of providence, like a species from a genus ?—the more so when the Christian character of that doctrine of providence has not yet been shown, and the doctrine is in all likelihood incomplete. Is it not the case that when God elects (in the sense in which He proclaims Himself the electing One and is attested as such in Holy Scripture) something more takes place than simply one manifestation among others of His willing and working ? Do we not here find ourselves at the beginning of all God's ways and works, which as such must be considered in and for itself, and in the light of which the divine world-government is alone real or recognisable ? Once again we must say that use has been made here of a presupposition which is not so self-evident as it makes itself out to be. Recourse has been had here to an apparent movement in formal logic from the general to the particular, without any demonstration whether or not such a procedure corresponds to the specific logic of this subject. As an obtrusive experience was followed in respect of the object of election, an obtrusive logical necessity is here followed in respect of its Subject. The one was and is just as arbitrary as the other, and just as little adapted to the theme. In this respect, too, we shall have to open up afresh certain matters which have been all too self-evidently closed.

At this point the necessary delimitation must take on a definite character in respect of its content. We have already seen that if the doctrine of election is grounded upon the facts of experience this means that it is abstractly grounded as far as concerns elected man. If it is grounded upon the logical necessity of the free and omnipotent divine will active both in general matters and in particular, both in the world as a whole and also in relation to the salvation or damnation of man, this means that it is just as abstractly grounded so far as concerns the electing God. On the one hand, regard is had to man in general and to the differences between individuals, and the phenomenon is then explained by the fact that individuals are what they are because they are elected or rejected by God. On the other hand, there is the thought of God in general, the concept of one Individual absolutely controlling everything else, of a *summus imperator*, and from that concept it is most logically deduced that amongst all the other things it belongs to the free power of God either to elect man and to bring him to salvation or to reject him and allow him to be lost.

Latet periculum in generalibus : we were forced to say this of the first error, and we must now repeat it with reference to the second. In the first case we were forced to challenge the general character of the presupposed view of humanity. In the second, we must challenge the general character of the presupposed concept of God. When we deal with what is called God's electing in God's self-revelation and the testimony of Holy Scripture, what authority have we to seek its meaning simply and solely in the alleged definitiveness of the private relationship between God and the individual as such ? And now further : What authority have we to interpret this electing as the act of a God alleged to be divine merely in His naked sovereignty ? When we do such things, do we not misunderstand at the very outset, in the one case the view of elected man, and in the other the concept of the electing God, as these should be normative for a Christian doctrine of election and therefore for the doctrine of election in Church dogmatics ? And supposing there develops a friendly rivalry between the two misapprehensions, as was very largely the case in the traditional teaching ? Supposing it becomes impossible to correct the mistaken view by the correct concept, and the mistaken concept by the correct view—a thing not impossible in itself ? Supposing the one misapprehension almost necessarily gives rise to the other ? Supposing the same fundamental error is at work in both ? In such circumstances, will it be at all surprising if the doctrine of election becomes, as Calvin himself once described it (*Comm. on Rom.* 9[14], *C.R.* 49, 180), a "labyrinth," in which only the very humblest may at a pinch detect any great part of the way, and from which even many of the cleverest and greatest—let alone the great majority whether in the world or the Church—will prefer to remain in perplexed aloofness ? Will it be at all surprising if the doctrine cannot at any rate shed that light which properly it could and should shed if grounded upon a true view of man and a true concept of God ? There is, indeed, every reason to proceed critically at this point.

If we allow God's self-revelation and the testimony of Scripture to prescribe our concept, then the Subject of election, the electing God, is not at all the absolute World-ruler as such and in general. We cannot, therefore, understand the election as one of the many functions of world-government exercised by Him, nor can we deduce it from, or establish it as a consequence and application of, that one basic principle. The Subject of the election, of this election, the Subject with which the Christian doctrine of election must reckon, is not in the least a " God in general," as he may be conceived and systematically constructed from the standpoint of sovereignty, of omnipotence, of a first cause, of absolute necessity. It is always unconditioned thinking which undertakes to construct such a " God in general," and (notwithstanding all the theoretical protestation against *potentia absoluta*) the result of such unconditioned thinking must always be an unconditioned God, a God who is free *in abstracto*. Even if the concept freedom is filled out by that of love, it makes no essential difference, unless by both concepts we understand the one decisive thing : that the true God is the One whose freedom and love have nothing to do with abstract absoluteness or naked sovereignty, but who in His love and freedom has determined and limited Himself to be God in particular and not in general, and only as such to be omnipotent and sovereign and the possessor of all other perfections. The true God (true according to His self-revelation and the biblical testimony), the God who is the object of thinking which is conditioned in a way conformable with

His self-revelation, is, of course, the sovereign Lord and Ruler of all things and all events, from the greatest to the smallest. Naturally, then, there is nothing outside of Him. There is nothing which is efficacious or significant or even existent except only by His will. There is nothing which in respect both of its being and its nature is not predetermined by Him. But from that it does not at all follow that to conceive of God Himself we need only conceive of a being which rules absolutely. On the contrary, such a concept in itself might well and indeed must be the concept of a false god, an idol, the exact opposite of the true God. If we are to lay hold of the concept of the true God, we shall do so only as we conceive of Him in His *dominium*, in His actuality as Lord and Ruler. We shall do so only as we conceive of Him in the determination and limitation which are peculiar to Him, which He has not taken upon Himself as something additional, in His relationship with the world or as an accommodation to it, but which are the characteristics of His presence and activity in the world because they are the determination and limitation proper to His own eternal being, so assuredly has He decided for them by the decree of His eternal will. God does rule. Yet it is not the fact that He rules that makes Him the divine Ruler, for false gods and idols also rule. The mere fact of ruling with infinite power in an infinite sphere does not make God the divine Ruler, for that is the very thing which He does not do. Infinite power in an infinite sphere is rather the characteristic of the government of ungodly and anti-godly courts. God Himself rules in a definite sphere and with a definite power. What makes Him the divine Ruler is the very fact that His rule is determined and limited : self-determined and self-limited, but determined and limited none the less ; and not in the sense that His caprice as such constitutes His divine being and therefore the principle of His world-government, but in such a way that He has concretely determined and limited Himself after the manner of a true king (and not of a tyrant) ; in such a way, then, that we can never expect any decisions from God except those which rest upon this concrete determination and limitation of His being, upon this primal decision made in His eternal being ; decisions, then, which are always in direct line with this primal decision, and not somewhere to right or left of it in an infinite sphere. If we begin quite simply with the divine world-government which holds sway in and over all things, if we think that the election should be subordinated to this world-government as one specific instance of it, then it is difficult to escape a twofold danger : first, that of losing sight of the primal decision which is identical with the basis of the election, and therefore of the eternal divine being in the determination and limitation in which it is the divine being ; and second, and in consequence, that of missing the line or succession of the later divine decisions which derive from this primal decision. If we do that, then ultimately and in effect we can describe the divine world-government, and with it the overruling of divine providence, only as the sequence and inter-relation of the actions of absolute caprice. And we can present the divine predestination only as one of such capricious actions. It is necessary then, as we consider predestination and form our concept of it, to consider and to form a concept of the deity of God which is true deity because it is self-determined and self-limited. In so doing we shall perceive both the fact and the extent that the true God is as such the true Ruler of the world, the omnipotent sovereign over all things both great and small, and to that extent "God in general." He is that, and He wills to be acknowledged and worshipped as such. And it is for that reason, and to attain that end, that our thinking on the subject of the election cannot begin arbitrarily with the concept of a World-ruler as such. We must know first who this Ruler is and what He wills and does in that rule. But this concrete aspect of His rule results from our consideration and concept of the election. It is there that God is (and is self-revealed as) who and what He is, in contrast with all false gods and idols. It is there, in the election itself so to speak, and not in an underlying higher principle from which it must be deduced, that its true basis must be sought. It is there, in the singularity of this activity itself, and not in what it has in common with all God's other activities. It is there ; so that only from that point can we perceive and understand the divine providence and world-government, and not only that, but creation too, and not only creation, but the totality of all God's other activities.

It is easy to see the link between the correction necessary here and that which we made earlier. In the doctrine of predestination we have to do with the understanding both of God and of man in particular ; in the particular relationship in which God is the true God and man true man. In itself, and as such, the particular leads us to the general, which it includes within itself. For finally, of course, the election has to do with the whole of humanity and therefore with each individual, although materially it has to do first and exclusively only with the one man, and then with specific members of the people which belongs to Him, which is called by Him and which is gathered around Him ; a people which as such is not identical either with the whole of humanity or with an aggregate of individuals. Finally, then, the election has to do with the sovereign rule of God and His omnipotent world-government, although materially it has to do with the specific being and activity of God in His relationship with this particular man and the people represented in Him. It is a matter of the specific attitude of God in which He fulfils the primal decision which as such is the basic law of His lordship and sovereign rule as a whole. The doctrine of election is rightly grounded when in respect of elected man as well as the electing God it does not deal with a generality or abstraction in God or man, but with the particularity and concretion of the true God and true man. It is rightly grounded when only from that starting-point it goes on to perceive and to understand whatever there is of consequence about God or man in general ; from that starting-point alone, and not *vice versa*.

We can now make an attempt to give a positive answer to the question of the origin of the doctrine of election. The two answers just mentioned and rejected have been and have to be taken seriously because they do contain decisive moments of truth. It is undoubtedly the case (and considerations advanced in the first sub-section have prepared us for this conclusion) that the election does in some sense denote the basis of all the relationships between God and man, between God in His very earliest movement towards man and man in his very earliest determination by this divine movement. It is in the decision in favour of this movement, in God's self-determination and the resultant determination of man, in the basic relationship which is enclosed and fulfilled within Himself, that God is who He is. The primal relationship belongs, therefore, to the doctrine of God. The doctrine of God would be incomplete without the extension necessitated by this relationship, without the inclusion of the decision which precedes and characterises and gives rise to all God's work *ad extra* ; the decision in which God gives Himself to another, to man, and on the basis of which He is the One who has willed and done this, who has indeed given Himself to man. If their incorrect form is ignored, and they are taken together, the two answers just mentioned and rejected do have the merit of indicating the real problem of the doctrine : God as the Subject of the election and man as its object. In so doing, they point to the fact that they, too, in their own way derive from the perception which is basic and normative in this matter; that they, too, in their own way, have been presented within the sphere of the Christian Church. Because of their incorrect form we must reject them as answers to the question of the basis of the doctrine, but we must keep their substance in so far as it indicates the two poles of the problem, God on the one side and man on the other. They fail because prematurely, and with serious consequences for the purity of the doctrine from the Christian standpoint, they think that the two poles are to be found, not in their particularity, but in a general view of man and a general concept of God. It is with this point that we must begin as we seek to be taught by the self-revelation of God attested by Holy Scripture.

When Holy Scripture speaks of God, it does not permit us to let our attention or thoughts wander at random until at this or that level they set up a being which is furnished with utter sovereignty and all other perfections, and which as such is the Lord, the Law-giver, the Judge and the Saviour of man and men. When Holy Scripture speaks of God it concentrates our attention and thoughts upon one single point and what is to be known at that point. And what is to be known there is quite simple. It is the God who in the first person singular addressed the patriarchs and Moses, the prophets and later the apostles. It is the God who in this " I " is and has and reveals sovereignty and all other perfections. It is the God who wills to be known and worshipped and reverenced as such. It is the God who created His people Israel by His Word, and separated them from all other peoples, and later separated the Church from Israel. It is the

God who exercises His rule in what He wills and does with this people, the people first called Israel and later the Church. It is He, this God, who as the Lord and Shepherd of that people is also, of course, the World-ruler, the Creator of all things, the Controller of all events, both great and small. But in every way His government of the world is only the extension, the application and the development of His government in this one particular sphere. He does the general for the sake of the particular. Or to put it in another way, He does the general through the particular, and in and with it. That is God according to His self-revelation.

We may look closer and ask : Who and what is the God who is to be known at the point upon which Holy Scripture concentrates our attention and thoughts ? Who and what is the God who rules and feeds His people, creating and maintaining the whole world for its benefit, and guiding it according to His own good-pleasure—according to the good-pleasure of His will as it is directed towards this people ? If in this way we ask further concerning the one point upon which, according to Scripture, our attention and thoughts should and must be concentrated, then from first to last the Bible directs us to the name of Jesus Christ. It is in this name that we discern the divine decision in favour of the movement towards this people, the self-determination of God as Lord and Shepherd of this people, and the determination of this people as " his people, and the sheep of his pasture " (Ps. 100³). And in this name we may now discern the divine decision as an event in human history and therefore as the substance of all the preceding history of Israel and the hope of all the succeeding history of the Church. What happened was this, that under this name God Himself became man, that He became this particular man, and as such the Representative of the whole people that hastens towards this man and derives from Him. What happened was this, that under this name God Himself realised in time, and therefore as an object of human perception, the self-giving of Himself as the Covenant-partner of the people determined by Him from and to all eternity. What happened was this, that it became a true fact that under this name God Himself possesses this people : possesses it no less than He does Himself ; swears towards it the same fidelity as He exercises with Himself ; directs upon it a love no less than that with which in the person of the Son He loves Himself ; fulfilling His will upon earth as in the eternal decree which precedes everything temporal it is already fulfilled in heaven. What happened was this, that under this name God Himself established and equipped the people which bears the name to be " a light of the Gentiles," the hope, the promise, the invitation and the summoning of all peoples, and at the same time, of course, the question, the demand and the judgment set over the whole of humanity and every individual man. As all these things happened under this name, the will of God was done. And according to God's self-revelation attested in Scripture, it is wholly and utterly in these happenings that we are to know what really is the good-pleasure of His will, what is, therefore, His being, and the purpose and orientation of His work, as Creator of the world and Controller of history. There is no greater depth in God's being and work than that revealed in these happenings and under this name. For in these happenings and under this name He has revealed Himself. According to Scripture the One who bears this name is the One who in His own " I " introduces the concept of sovereignty and every perfection. When the bearer of this name becomes the object of our attention and thoughts, when they are directed to Jesus Christ, then we see God, and our thoughts are fixed on Him.

As we have to do with Jesus Christ, we have to do with the electing God. For election is obviously the first and basic and decisive thing which we have always to say concerning this revelation, this activity, this presence of God in the world, and therefore concerning the eternal decree and the eternal self-determination of God which bursts through and is manifested at this point. Already this self-determination, as a confirmation of the free love of God, is itself the election or choice of God. It is God's choice that He wills to be God in this determination and not otherwise. It is God's choice that He moves towards man, that He wills to be and is the Covenant-partner of man. It is God's choice that under the name of Jesus Christ He wills to give life to the substance of His people's history and to that people itself, constituting Himself its Lord and Shepherd. It is God's choice that in this specific form, in one age, in the very midst of that people's history, He acts on behalf of all ages, thus giving to all created time, becoming indeed, its meaning and content. It is God's choice that for the sake of the Head whose name it bears He has created and established this particular body, this people, to be the sign of blessing and judgment, the instrument of His love and the sacrament of His movement towards men and each individual man. It is God's choice that at every stage in its history He deals with this people with that purpose in view. It is in the utter particularity of His activity, and therefore of His volition, and to that extent of His self-determined being, that He is the electing God. He is so at that one point upon which Scripture concentrates our attention and thoughts. He is so in that He is the Lord and Shepherd of His people. He is so in Jesus Christ, in His only-begotten Son, and therefore from all eternity in Himself. To put it the other way round : If we would know who God is, and what is the meaning and purpose of His election, and in what respect He is the electing God, then we must look away from all others, and excluding all side-glances or secondary thoughts, we must look only upon and to the name of Jesus Christ, and the existence and history of the people of God enclosed within Him. We must look only upon the divine mystery of this name and this history, of this Head and this body.

It is exactly of a piece with this that when Scripture speaks of man it does not allow our attention or thoughts to lose themselves in any self-selected generalities. In the Bible we are not concerned with the abstract concept of man, or with the human race as a whole, or with the being and destiny of the individual man as such.

It is true that in the beginning Scripture does tell us about Adam, the progenitor and representative of the whole race. But the further course of the record makes it clear that the object of the story is not universal history and its problems. After Adam there are a few almost incidental side-glances at the further propagation and extension of the race, and then we pass directly to Noah, and from Noah to Abraham, and from Abraham to Jacob-Israel. We are led most firmly and definitely from the general to the particular. Here and always it is in the sphere of the particular that the events are played out which it is the purpose of the Bible to record concerning man. It is for the sake of the particular that the Bible is interested and seeks to interest its readers in man. In this series the individual man is not important because he is a particular specimen in the propagation and extension of the race, or because in some way this propagation and extension is set forward by him. On the contrary, he is interesting because within this succession of events, as one of the many sons or grandsons of the one father, he is always a special case, and because there will always be similar special cases amongst his own sons and grandsons. The whole history from Adam onwards aims ultimately at the emergence of the particular man Jacob-Israel, the ancestor of the twelve tribes of the chosen people. It is in this most narrowed future that the meaning and necessity of the history is to be found, so that looking backward even Adam is ultimately or primarily important (and is thought of) as *the* man in the Old and New Testaments, not because he is the father of the human race, but because he is the first of these special cases, the first in this succession of particular men— and more expecially because this succession was to make possible the existence of Jacob-Israel. See above.

And the narrowing down does not cease with the man Jacob-Israel and his descendants. It is not the case that from his time onwards there existed in the form of the people named after him a kind of lesser humanity within the whole ; a race which as such, in all its members, constitutes the particular envisaged in the whole. What is attained, or rather manifested, from Jacob-Israel (better, from the succession Abraham-Isaac-Jacob) onwards is simply the existence of a specific people as such. It is revealed that each of the special cases had its meaning only in the existence of a whole. In the narrowing down which took place from the very first it was not and is not simply a question of the individual as an individual, but of the many in the individual. It is a question, indeed, of a definite aggregate, of the necessary and intimate connexion, the obvious coherence and unity of the many, as it has all been realised in this one people. But only in this way. For "the people Israel" as such, as a community of blood and speech and history, is still only a sign of this definite aggregate within humanity as a whole. Israel is self-deceived when it thinks that in itself, as the people Jacob, as the community of blood and race and history, it can recognise this particular humanity within humanity in general. It had, in fact, hardly existed as a people in this sense before there began a further narrowing down within itself, the cutting off of whole generations and whole sections of the people (already foreshadowed in the cutting away of Ishmael and Esau, and impressively declared by the covenant sign of circumcision). And this process constantly gained ground, constantly diminishing what was left of the particularity imparted to this people in its forefather ; a process which was apparently a vast retrogression to the narrowing down which was involved in and commenced with the existence of the one man Adam. The people still lived, but it lived only as a sign of the people obviously envisaged. The specific purpose of its history approximated more and more to that of the preceding history of the propagation and extension of the race from the time of Adam to that of the patriarchs. It lived on as a people, but, like the race in that earlier period, it did so only as it prepared and made possible the existence of a special case. Its life was directed towards one individual figure. Whose is that figure ? If we take the Old Testament, the record of its history, only in and for itself, then without doubt we must return at once the answer : the figure of King David. In the powerful and righteous kindom of David the promise given to the descendants of Jacob, that they should possess the land of Canaan, found fulfilment in a way which apparently cannot be, and (in the direct sense) never has been, surpassed. When this man was brought forth and attained to the kingship, Israel reached the end of all its ways. It was towards this king, and to become his people, subject to him as such, that all its life had been directed during the whole of this second Old Testament period. Even in the establishment of the people, which was the specific aim of the first period, this king had been intended ; for the people established was the people which should have David as its powerful and righteous sovereign.

But now, surprisingly, a new period began. It lasted from David to the Exile. Its peculiar feature was this. The dissolution of the historical existence of the people as such, a dissolution already proclaimed clearly at such turning-points as the journey through the wilderness and the conquest of Canaan, and in the very personal climax of the rejection of Saul, now became the true and proper subject of the history and its record. The promise to Israel had been conclusively fulfilled in the figure of David, but it now became clear that that fulfilment was only a repetition of the promise. Even the reign of David as such was only a sign. Indeed, it was upon the Son of David that David himself fixed all his hopes, as though he himself were not the end of all Israel's ways thus far. And Solomon did, in fact, mount the throne of David. He reigned on that throne with a wisdom and glory which overshadowed all that David was and did. He could do what even David was not permitted to do—build the temple. To that extent it did seem as though the promise had at last found its true fulfilment. By its rapid appearance, however, this supposedly true fulfilment, the *regnum gloriae* which only followed the Davidic *regnum gratiae*, served merely to emphasise the fact that David himself was the purpose of the previous existence of Israel : not, of course, as an end, but for his son's sake ; as the beginning of a new way. And by its equally rapid disappearance it served merely to emphasise the fact that while Solomon did, of course, represent and declare the wisdom and glory of the Son of David, he could not himself be the Son promised and awaited, but could only act as another of His representatives. And then there began irresistibly the dissolution which the prophets did not arrest but step by step announced and proclaimed to be inevitable. Its result was the manifestation of yet another son of David ; the Jehoiachin or Jeconiah who reigned only three months as next to the last king in Jerusalem and was then overthrown by Nebuchadnezzar and led away captive to Babylon. This son was in everything the direct opposite of David—we need only read what is written about him in Jer. 22$^{24-30}$—and in him the goal of Israel seemed to have become its end, the gracious separation a wrathful rejection. And yet, even in his function as a powerless, dethroned and exiled king, he belonged no less to the Davidic monarchy than his forefather David himself. In his own way he represented the promised Son of David no less than Solomon. According to the likeliest interpretation, the Suffering Servant of Is. 49 ff. is not merely Israel as such, not merely Jeremiah seen as a monumental figure, not merely an unknown prophet of the Exile, not merely the quintessence of all the prophets, but (together with all these) it is in the first instance this pitiful ex-king and

shadow-ruler Jeconiah, of whom, significantly enough, the record of 2 K. 25²⁷ᶠ·
tells us that not only was he graciously favoured and kindly spoken to by Evil-
Merodach in Babylon, but that his throne was set above the thrones of all the
kings that were there with him.

But this figure is found only at the very beginning of the Exile. He is the
Son of David who represents the people punished and cast off for their sin.
Obviously he is not the One who is to come, the expected Son. But then a
fourth Old Testament period began. Punished and cast off, Israel was not
allowed to fall from God. In the second part of the Book of Isaiah the promise
was made yet again and still more comprehensively. Israel was to return.
And another Davidic line was raised up, with Zerubbabel, the grandson of
Jehoiachin, at its head. He was not king, of course, for Israel would never again
be a kingdom. Those signs had been given and would not recur. There is
always a similarity in this history, but there is never simple recurrence. The
commission given this new David by the prophet Haggai was rather that he should
build again the ruined temple, " not by might, nor by power, but by my spirit "
(Zech. 4⁶). For the rest, he was only a deputy-ruler, standing side by side with
the high-priest Joshua as one of the two olive-trees beside the seven-branched
candlestick. It seemed that Israel had now become a people without a king.
Was it a people at all ? Was not this the end of all that had been promised ?
But the question we ought really to put is quite different : Was not this son of
David, Zerubbabel, the clearest of all the signs, just because he was only a deputy-
ruler who stood side by side with the high-priest, not having any proper office
but only the non-political task of directing the restoration of the temple ? Did
he not bear the highest political testimony to something which David and
Solomon had also to attest, but as holders of direct political power could not
do so as clearly, something which the political rulers of the succeeding house of
David had denied, namely, that God Himself is (both in word and deed) the King
of this people and that his human representative is summoned only to make
good the destruction of His earthly sanctuary ? Is it not perhaps the case that
in this way and at this time, by becoming no more than Jewry inhabiting the
land of Palestine, Israel achieved visible unity under this King as the true people
of God ? That it should become such a people was the promise and the offer
with which this fourth period began—and ended. It ended with the birth of
the promised Son of David Himself, the one who in His own person was David
and Solomon, Jeconiah and Zerubbabel, and more than they all. After all that
had gone before, none but God Himself could take the throne as David's Son,
fulfilling all the promises at one blow. The Word—that Word which created
Israel, and accompanied and directed it as prophetic judge and comforter—
the Word itself became flesh. The Word Himself became the Son of David.
Now at last there had come the special case for which there had had to be all
those others from Adam to Zerubbabel, and for which Israel had had to be separated out from the whole race, and Judah from Israel. This coming was to the
detriment of Israel. Face to face with its Messiah, the Son of David who was
also the Son of God, Israel knew no better than to give Him up to the Gentiles
to be put to death on the cross. In so doing, they confirmed the rightness of
God's dealings with them from the very first, when He cut them off and destroyed
them. And yet because the righteousness of God stands fast like the mountains
against the unrighteousness of man, this coming was also to the benefit of Israel,
and of the Gentiles, and of the world. In the crucifixion of Jesus Christ the
world was shown to be a co-partner in guilt with Israel, but only in order that
it might be shown a co-partner in the promise with Israel. The promise could
not be destroyed or overthrown. Only now was it completely fulfilled. And its
fulfilment was made manifest in the resurrection of Jesus Christ. Jews and
Gentiles were in the same guilt of disobedience. But now they could hear the
same words : You, my people ; I, God, in the person of David's Son, your King.

Those who are called by this King, and hear this King, whether they are Jews or Gentiles, constitute the people whose existence was envisaged throughout the whole of that long history. In the person of this King there enters the man as whose type Adam had already been *the* man. In Adam's case, it was man the creature of God, and forthwith the sinful creature. In this case it is man the Son of God, more powerful and righteous than David, more wise and glorious than Solomon. It is also, of course, the man who has to suffer shame and insult, although quite differently from Jeconiah. It is also the man who rebuilds the temple, although quite differently from Zerubbabel. This man is the Holy One who in His suffering and triumph gathers the sinner under His wings and by Himself covers and saves him. This is the man who is the fulfilment of the promise and hope of His people, and the meaning and purpose of its existence and history. As such He is very man.

This man, who as God's Son is the King of His people, is elected man. In Him and through Him those who are His subjects and the members of His people are elected. Even under this aspect it is obviously a question of God's choice. None of the figures mentioned appointed itself a special case, a link in that chain, and in its particular function a sign of the special case to which they must all point and for which they must all prepare. From the standpoint of the general it must always be demanded : Why this one and that one ? Why not this other, or that other ? And always there is only one answer to such a demand, and that is the event as a fact, the existence of the cases as such. But that means a choice which was not made by the men themselves, but which came upon them, and which cannot, therefore, be explained by anything in the men themselves. Obviously, then, it is wholly because of a choice of which man himself is not the subject that within the sphere of humanity, and not some other sphere, there should take place this sequence of events, these special cases. Obviously the people whose establishment was at once the goal and the new starting-point in this sequence did not choose for itself this position and function. If it had regarded it as a matter of its own choosing, and fulfilled it accordingly, it would already have forfeited it. The extent, the completeness, with which God is the electing One in all these happenings is revealed by the continual cutting and falling away of countless numbers—something which does not make the promise null and void as given to the whole, but which indirectly confirms it, because the whole must be always the whole which is elected by God and the bearer and recipient of His promise. The extent to which God is the electing One in these happenings is revealed in the remarkable way in which the promise is constantly fulfilled only to be renewed, until at last the fulfilment is before us in all its singularity, itself the true promise unequivocally revealed. Even the fulfilment, even the purpose and meaning of these happenings, has still to be God's choice. And it is only really God's choice when this sequence of special cases, the sign of the coming One, their goal, is shown not to be infinite, but to be bounded by the one special case in which their goal is revealed, by the one case which is also a sign—it is so as the true fulfilment, as the promise unequivocally revealed— but which as a sign is also and at the same time the thing signified.

If we listen to what Scripture says concerning man, then at the point where our attention and thoughts are allowed to rest there is revealed an elect man, *the* elect man, and united in Him and repre- sented by Him an elect people. But just as truly there is revealed at that same point the electing God. The elect One is true man according to God's self-revelation, and that revelation, being God's, has the decisive word concerning man too. And once again we must put it the other way : If we would know what election is, what it is to be elected by God, then we must look away from all others, and excluding all side-glances or secondary thoughts we must look only upon the name of Jesus Christ and upon the actual existence and history of the people whose beginning and end are enclosed in the mystery of His name.

We perceive that the statements of Scripture concerning God and those concerning man converge at this point. And it is as statements concerning what takes place at this point that the statements concerning God's election of man must be formulated and understood. For it is at this point that election takes place. If this perception is right, and if we feel bound always to base the doctrine of election upon the self-revelation of God according to the witness of Scripture, then we have answered positively the question of the basis of the doctrine and the standpoint which we ought to take up in relation to it. If our perception has been fundamentally correct in this preparatory survey, then the necessity of the doctrine has been decided once and for all. We are not free either to give ourselves to this matter or not to give ourselves to it, either to take seriously the knowledge of divine predestination or not to take it seriously. Election is that which takes place at the very centre of the divine self-revelation. In the light of this fact we can understand the emphasis with which the doctrine of predestination has been presented by all the great doctors of the Church. And in particular, we need feel no shame at the witness of the Reformed Church, in which from the outset this doctrine has played so outstanding a role. We must admit rather (not out of mere conservatism or the impulse to imitate, but out of inner necessity) that our forefathers were right. And we shall regard ourselves as bound to follow in their footsteps. But if in this survey our perception has been a right one, then it is also the case that the form in which we must take up and present the doctrine has been radically decided. In face of the whole history, even the Reformed history, of the doctrine, a corrective has been inserted and a standard brought to light. It is the name of Jesus Christ which, according to the divine self-revelation, forms the focus at which the two decisive beams of the truth forced upon us converge and unite : on the one hand the electing God and on the other elected man. It is to this name, then, that all Christian teaching of this truth must look, from this name that it must derive, and to this name that it must strive. Like all Christian teaching, it must always testify to this name. On the way now before us we must never allow this name to fade or to be blurred in favour of abstract presuppositions concerning God or man, or of the abstract consequences of such abstract presuppositions. We can advance on this way only if in conformity with our attempted survey we confirm and develop the presuppositions which in respect of the divine election of man are contained in the name of Jesus Christ. In the measure that we hold fast to this principle, we shall find ourselves on solid ground as we advance into this as into every other sphere of dogmatic enquiry and presentation. It will not be the ground of arbitrary speculation. It will be that of the responsibility and stewardship laid upon the Church (and upon theology in particular) with regard to the theme of its proclamation, the theme which is also the basis of its existence and the standard of its truth.

It is not as though we are really making an innovation when we describe the name of Jesus Christ as the basis of the doctrine of election. There has been much regrettable deviation at this point in the way of the abstractions mentioned, but even so the Church and theology have always kept before their eyes certain utterances in the New Testament witness which reminded them clearly enough, and not altogether ineffectively, that knowledge of the election is only a distinctive form of the knowledge of Jesus Christ. Chief amongst such utterances is Eph. 1⁴ᶠ·, where we read that God " has chosen us (the Church) in him (ἐν αὐτῷ) that we should be holy and without blame before him," that " before the foundation of the world " (πρὸ καταβολῆς κόσμου), " according to the good pleasure of his will " (κατὰ τὴν εὐδοκίαν τοῦ θελήματος αὐτοῦ), " that in him we might be predestinated unto the adoption of children by Jesus Christ to himself " (διὰ Ἰησοῦ Χριστοῦ εἰς αὐτόν). And again : " In him (ἐν αὐτῷ, ἐν ᾧ) we have obtained an inheritance, being predestinated according to the purpose of him who worketh all things after the counsel (βουλή) of his will, that we should be to the praise of his glory, who had before first trusted in him " (τοὺς προηλπικότας ἐν Χριστῷ, Eph. 1¹¹). And again : " To the intent that now unto the principalities and powers in the heavenly places might be known by the existence of the church (ἐκκλησία) the manifold wisdom of God, according to the eternal purpose (κατὰ πρόθεσιν τῶν αἰώνων) which He purposed (ἣν ἐποίησεν) in Christ Jesus our Lord, in whom we have (therefore) boldness and access with confidence by the faith of him " (Eph. 3¹⁰). Another passage is Rom. 8²⁹ᶠ·, where we read : " For whom he did foreknow (i.e., the called according to his purpose), he also did predestinate " — προέγνω and προώρισεν are not two different and consecutive acts, but, according to Paul's consistent usage of the connecting καὶ, they are one and the same divine act described with additional distinctness—" to be conformed to the image of his Son " (i.e., according to Col. 1¹⁵, to that image which His own Son is), that " he might be the first-born among many brethren." And " whom he did predestinate, them he also called, them he also justified, them he also glorified." Now all these statements show us quite plainly that when we have to do with the reality indicated by the concept of election or predestination we are not outside the sphere of the name of Jesus Christ but within it and within the sphere of the unity of very God and very man indicated by this name. Indeed, the great exponents of the doctrine have not hesitated to point most emphatically to Jesus Christ when speaking of the knowledge of election. The only exception is Thomas Aquinas. He did quote Eph. 1⁴ (*S. th.* I, *qu.* 23), but in his interpretation he succeeded in not paying any attention to the *in ipso*. Only in a much later context did he treat *De praedestinatione Christi* (*S. th.* III, *qu.* 24).

Quite different was Augustine before him, and to Augustine we owe a christological explanation of predestination to which we must return more penetratingly at the appropriate place. Quite different, above all, was the older Luther, who declared with the greatest possible emphasis that there is only one way which our thinking can take with the text : " Many are called, few are chosen " : " We must leave the predestinating God undisturbed in His majesty. For He is incomprehensible. And it is not possible for man not to be offended at such thoughts, whether by falling into despair, or by sinking into utter godlessness and recklessness. To know God and the way of God rightly, we must follow the right way, and then we shall be edified and not offended. But the right way is the Lord Christ, as He Himself says, ' No man cometh unto the Father but by me.' To know the Father rightly and to come to Him, you must come first to Christ and learn to know Him, thus : Christ is the Son of God, and the almighty eternal God. What does the Son of God do ? He becomes man for our sakes ; He becomes obedient to the law to redeem us from the law. He lets Himself be crucified and dies on the cross to pay the price for our sins, and He rises again from the dead to open up for us by His resurrection a way to eternal life, and to help us against eternal death, and He sits now at the right hand of God to represent us, and to send us the Holy Ghost, and by the Holy Ghost to rule and guide believers and to guard them against all the assaults of the devil and temptation. To know that is to know Christ rightly. When that know-ledge is well and truly in your heart, then set forth and climb up into heaven, and make reckoning with yourself what must be the heart of God towards us men, seeing the Son of God did all that for our sakes, and seeing He did it of the will and commandment of the Father. Is it not so that your reason will constrain you, so that you have to say : Since God has thus given His only-begotten Son for our sakes, He can never intend evil towards men, He never wills that they should perish, seeing that He seeks and uses the very highest means to help them to life " (*Serm. on Matt.* 20¹⁻¹⁶ *W.A.* 52, 140, 28). And with the older Luther we may number Melanchthon : *Nec ex ratione nec ex lege iudicandum est de electione, sed ex evangelio. Totus numerus salvandorum proper Christum electus est. Quare nisi complectamur agnitionem Christi, non potest de electione dici. Non aliam iustificationis, aliam electionis causam quaeramus. . . . Quaeramus ergo promissionem, in qua voluntatem suam expressit Deus et sciamus non esse aliam voluntatem quaerendam de gratia extra verbum, sed mandatum Dei immutabile esse, ut audiamus Filium* (*Loci,* 1559, *C.R.* 21, 914). Following Melanchthon, the *Formula of Concord* gave the truth in symbolical form : *Praedestinatio non in arcano Dei consilio est scrutanda, sed in verbo Dei* (*Ep.* XI, 6). The Word of God, however, *deducit nos ad Christum, is est liber vitae* (*ib.,* 7). *Vera igitur sententia de praedestinatione ex evangelio Christi discenda est* (*ib.,* 10). *Aeterna Dei praedestinatio in Christo et nequaquam extra mediatorem Christum consideranda est* (*Sol. decl.* XI, 65).

The Lutherans thought that they had to maintain this thesis against Calvin and the Calvinists. But in Calvin himself they might have read the following : *Neque ego sane ad arcanam Dei electionem homines ablego, ut inde salutem hiantes expectent, sed recta ad Christum pergere iubeo, in quo nobis proposita est salus : quae alioqui in Deo absondita lateret. Nam quisquis plana fidei via non ingreditur, illi Dei electio nihil quam exitialis erit labyrinthus. Itaque ut certa sit nobis pecca-torum remissio, ut in vitae aeternae fiducia conscientiae nostrae acquiescant, ut Deum intrepide patrem invocemus, hinc minime faciendum est exordium, quid de nobis ante mundum conditum Deus statuerit, sed quid de paterno eius amore nobis in Christo sit patefactum et quotidie per evangelium Christus ipse praedicet. . . . Fateor. . . . Christum unicam esse ianuam, qua in regnum coelorum omnes ingredi opportet . . . quicunque inde vel minimum deflectunt, nihil quam per flexuosas ambages errare, et quo quisque in profunda illa divini consilii adyta confidentius irrumpere et penetrare conatur, eo longius a Deo recedere* (*De aet. Dei praed.,* 1552, *C.R.* 8, 306 f.). *Quum nobis in Christo proposita sit salutis certitudo, per-peram, nec sine Christi ipsius iniuria, facere qui praeterito hoc vitae fonte, ex quo haurire promptum erat, ex reconditis Dei abyssis vitam eruere moliuntur. . . . Ne quis ergo aliunde electionis suae fiduciam petat, nisi librum vitae, in quo scriptus est, delere velit. . . . Christus aeternae et absconditae Dei electionis tum luculentum nobis speculum est, tum arra quoque et pignus. Fide autem, quam Deus in hoc speculo nobis repraesentat, vitam contemplamur : fide pignus hoc arramque amplec-timur* (*ib.,* 318). *Ideo manifestare nobis Christus patris nomen dicitur, quia electionis nostrae scientiam, evangelii sui voce testatam, spiritu quoque suo in cordibus nostris obsignat* (*ib.,* 319). *Quod si in Christo sumus electi, non in nobis ipsis reperiemus electionis nostrae certitudinem ac ne in Deo quidem patre, si nudum illum absque filio imaginamur. Christus ergo speculum est, in quo electionem nostram contemplari convenit, et sine fraude licet* (*Instit.* III, 24, 5). Bullinger, too, declares most definitely : *Improbamus illos, qui extra Christum quaerunt : An sint electi ? Et quid ante omnem aeternitatem de ipsis statuerit Deus ? Audienda est enim praedicatio evangelii, eique credendum est et pro indubitato habendum : si credis et sis in Christo electum te esse. Pater enim praedestinationis suae aeternam sententiam . . . in Christo nobis aperuit. Docendum ergo et considerandum ante omnia, quantus amor patris erga nos in Christo nobis sit revelatus. . . . Christus itaque sit speculum, in quo praedestinationem nostram contemplemur. Satis perspicuum et firmum habebimus testimonium nos in libro vitae inscriptos esse, si communicaverimus cum Christo et is in vera fide noster sit, nos eius simus* (*Conf. Helv. post.*, 1566, *art.* 10).

In view of these texts it can hardly be said that the Reformed theology deserved to be reprimanded by Luther and the Lutherans in this respect. The Reformed school knew just as well as the Lutheran what was that biblical centre which must form the object of genuinely theological knowledge in matters of predestination. Indeed, Calvin was not content simply to maintain this line. Following the suggestions of Augustine—to which we will return in their proper context—he tried to show that Christ is the *speculum electionis* to the extent that in the incarnation of the divine Word in the man Jesus of Nazareth we have to do with the prototype and essence of, as it were, all divine electing and human election. And in this respect the *Confessio Scotica* (1561) went so far that first of all, in articles 7 and 8, the question *Cur Deus homo ?* was answered by a reference to the eternal and immutable divine decree, i.e., predestination, and then later, and most surprisingly, under the title *De electione* there was simply presented the doctrine of the true Godhead and the true manhood of Jesus Christ, and the necessity and reality of both in the unity of the person of the Mediator. In spite of their zealous protestations that predestination is to be known only in Christ, the Lutherans exerted themselves far less for a christological understanding of predestination than did the Reformed school against which they thought themselves bound to make a polemical assertion of that very thesis. However that may be, the Augustinian-Reformed allusion to Christ as the mirror of election does make one thing clear beyond all possible doubt—and its merit in this respect can never be rated too highly. It emphasises in most drastic fashion the singularity of the election, and of the freedom in which God as Elector stands over against the elect. The elect must look always to Jesus Christ in matters of the election because whoever is elected is elected in Christ and only in Christ. But if this is so, then it is settled conclusively that no one can ever seek the basis of election in himself, because no one is ever elected in himself or for the sake of himself or finally of himself. There is no basis for the divine election in man as such, and no such basis may be found in man. When they pointed to our election in Christ, Augustine and the Reformers were undoubtedly right, and faithful to the teaching of the Bible on this matter. But such a reference carries with it an unmistakable call always to magnify in this matter the grace of God, the grace which appeared concretely in the person of the Mediator between God and man. It is not in man himself or in the work of man that the basis of election must be sought. It is in this other person who is the person of God Himself in the flesh. It is in the work of this other person : a work which comes to man and comes upon man from without ; a work which is quite different from anything that he himself is or does. Man and his decision follow the decision which is already made before him, without him and against him ; the decision which is not made in himself at all, but is made concerning him in this wholly other person. And as he recognises this, he recognises in truth the meaning and nature of the divine election : that it is the essence of divine favour. He recognises, too, the meaning and nature of the doctrine of election : that it is the sum of the Gospel. In the last resort this was how Augustine and Calvin would have it understood. It is good for man and his decision to stand so wholly and utterly under the prior decision of God, as is actually the case according to the doctrine of election. To that extent that christological reference asserts the very thing which we have stated with regard to the biblical basis of the doctrine : *Quos Deus sibi filios assumpsit, non in ipsis eos dicitur elegisse sed in Christo suo, quia nonnisi in eo amare illos poterat, nec regni sui haereditate honorare nisi eius consortes ante factos. Quod si in eo sumus electi, non in nobis ipsis reperiemus electionis nostrae certitudinem* (Calvin, *Instit.* III, 24, 5). *En nous-mesmes nous sommes hays et dignes que Dieu nous ait en abomination ; mais il nous regarde en sons Fils, et lors il nous aime* (*Congr. sur l'élection éternelle*, 1562, *C.R.* 8, 95). *Sachons donc que nostre salut est certain. Et pourquoy cela ? Pource qu'il est en la main de Dieu. Et comment en sommes-nous assurez ? Pource qu'il l'a mis en la main de nostre Seigneur Jesus, qui nous manifeste que le Pere, qui nous a esleus, veut avancer son conseil à plein effect et perfection* (*ib.*, 100). *Apprenons que nous ne pouvons pas nous asseurer de nostre salut que par la foy. Car si un homme dit : Et que say-ie si ie suis sauvé ou damné ? par cela il demonstre que iamais il n'a cognu que c'est de foy ne de l'asseurance que nous devons avoir en Dieu, par Jesus Christ. Veux-tu donc bien savoir si tu es esleu ? Regarde-toy en Jesus Christ. Car ceux qui, par foy, communiquent vraye-ment en Jesus Christ, se peuvent bien asseurer, qu'ils appartiennent à l'élection éternelle de Dieu, et qu'ils sont de ses enfans. Quiconque donc se trouve en Jesus Christ, et est membre de son corps par foy, celuy-là est asseuré de son salut, et quand nous le voudrions savoir, il ne faut pas que nous montions là-haut pour nous enquerir de ce qui nous doit à ceste heure estre caché. Mais voilà Dieu qui s'abaisse à nous ; il nous monstre dequoy en son Fils ; comme s'il disoit : Me voicy : contemplez-moy, et cognoissez comment ie vous ay adoptez pour mes enfans. Quand donc nous recevons ce tesmoignage de salut qui nous est rendu par l'Evangile, de là nous congnoissons et sommes asseurez que Dieu nous a esleu. Et ainsi il ne faut point que les fideles doutent de leur election, mais qu'ils ayent cela pour tout resolu, que depuis qu'ils sont appelez à la foy par la predication de l'Evangile, ils sont participans de ceste grace de nostre Seigneur Jesus Christ, et de la promesse qu'il leur a faite en son Nom. Car nostre Seigneur Jesus Christ est le fondement de ces deux : c'est assavoir, des promesses de salut et de nostre election gratuite, qui a ésté faite dès la creation du monde* (*ib.*, 114).

In all these texts, however, (even those of Luther and the Lutherans) there is something unsatisfactory about the christological reference, factually important though it undoubtedly is. The reason for this is that notwithstanding all these earnest protestations the following question still remains unanswered : Is it the intention of these thinkers that serious theological attention should be paid to the assertion that the election is to be known in Jesus Christ ? Does this assertion contain the first and last word on this matter, the word by which we must hold conclusively, and beyond which we must not conceive of any further word ? Is it a fact that there is no other basis of election outside Jesus Christ ? Must the doctrine as such be related to this basis and this basis only ? Must it take account only of this basis ? In this matter of election are we noetically to hold by Christ and Christ alone because ontically there is no election and no electing God outside Him ? Or is it rather the case that we are to understand this assertion merely as an impressively stated pastoral rule, a practical direction regarding the attitude which, *rebus sic stantibus*, we ought to adopt towards this matter if we are not to be plunged into doubt or despair ? Is it the case, in fact, that behind the pastoral (and in some measure the historico-psychological) truth that God's election meets us and is revealed to us in Jesus Christ, there stands a higher truth which, for the sake of prudence and charity, must be withdrawn from the practical usage of the Church, a truth which cannot be denied or entirely suppressed, but which is so dangerous that it must be covered over and kept out of the reach of the curious like a kind of poison ? Is it the case that, according to this higher and dangerous truth concealed for practical purposes in the background, while Christ is indeed the medium and instrument of the divine activity at the basis of the election, and to that extent He is the revelation of the election by which factually we must hold fast, yet the electing God Himself is not Christ but God the Father, or the triune God, in a decision which precedes the being and will and word of Christ, a hidden God, who as such made, as it were, the actual resolve and decree to save such and such men and to bring them to blessedness, and then later made, as it were, the formal or technical decree and resolve to call the elect and to bring them to that end by means of His Son, by means of His Word and Spirit ? Is it the case, then, that in the divine election as such we have to do ultimately, not with a divine decision made in Jesus Christ, but with one which is independent of Jesus Christ and only executed by Him ? Is it the case that that decision made in Jesus Christ by which we must hold fast is, in fact, only another and a later and subordinate decision, while the first and true decision of election is to be sought—or if we follow the pastoral direction had better not be sought—in the mystery of the self-existent being of God, and of a decree made in the absolute freedom of this divine being ?

If in any sense we are forced to accept this second interpretation, it is inevitable that there should be tension between the theological truth and the pastoral direction which would have us hold fast by Christ. And in this tension it is the latter which will feel the strain the more seriously. It is only those who accidentally have not experienced or suspected the existence of the hidden truth who can really be satisfied with the advice simply to hold fast by the incarnate Son of God and the Word and Spirit of God and not enquire concerning the hidden will of the Father or of the eternal Godhead. For why should they not enquire concerning it, if it is true, and if they know that we have here two very different things and that the decisive word for salvation is spoken at that hidden and secret place ? If there does exist something like an absolute decree of this nature concerning the salvation and blessedness of individuals, a decree which is independent of and precedes the decision made in Jesus Christ, and if we have to take account of a decree which is absolute in this sense, even if only theoretically, then what right has anyone to suppress the question concerning such a decree as the basis of election ? By the power of what *sic volo sic iubeo* can this question actually be quashed ? In spite of all pastoral intentions, however excellent, is it not a highly relevant and highly necessary question ? Is it not a question to which we must pay heed and which in some way we must answer ? But of course, when this happens, when the question of the decree which is absolute in this sense crops up again, what an abyss of uncertainty is opened up! The thought of the election becomes necessarily the thought of the will and decision of God which are hidden somewhere in the heights or depths behind Jesus Christ and behind God's revelation. The first and last question in respect of the relationship between God and man brings us face to face with a God who is above and beyond Jesus Christ and with a relationship which is independent of Jesus Christ. How, then, can we attain to any sure knowledge of God or ourselves ? How, then, can we have any sure knowledge of this relationship ? How can we be certain that it is good to be so fully in the hands of God as we are proclaimed to be when we assert that God elects ? Such an uncertainty is almost inevitably imposed by a presentation like that of Thomas Aquinas. It was against this uncertainty that Reformation theology sought to protect itself by its thesis that Jesus Christ is the *speculum electionis*. The reference to the person of the Mediator and the Word and self-revelation of God was intended to liberate reflection on this subject from the inevitable tendency to lose itself in a sphere inaccessible by its very nature to human effort, a sphere which allows only of assertions which cannot sustain us because they are never more than our own assertions and are as such hopelessly dialectical. What can sustain us is the declaration which God Himself as Creator and Lord of life and death has made in our favour in Jesus Christ. When we let ourselves be taught by the Word of God and the Spirit of God, then we can and should be sure of the divine election. We can and should be sure of the fact that it is good for us to have an electing God. We can and should rejoice in God and in ourselves because we can see God's electing and our election at the place where God Himself has revealed it, in the Word of God made flesh. By this christological reference Reformation theology did assert and defend the honour and dignity of the divine self-revelation as such against all the attempts of man to be his own instructor in the things concerning God and himself. It did this in a way which had very obviously not been the case with Thomas Aquinas, with detriment to the purity and the power of the Church's doctrine. Reformation theology did have a proper regard for the fact of the biblical witness which must always be the proper starting-point for thinking on the divine election.

If only it could be said that it had so adhered to this line (as correctly perceived) that it had not only combated but completely banished all the uncertainty, and with it the compromising of the honour and dignity of the divine self-revelation in Jesus Christ. But while we may gratefully acknowledge the right intention expressed in the Reformation allusion to Christ, this is the very thing which we cannot say. The christological reference was warmly and impressively made, but it is left standing in the air. It cannot be carried through theologically, and for this reason. It does forbid in practice any glancing away at an absolute decree of God, i.e., a decree which is different from the eternal saving decision of God as made in Jesus Christ. Yet it does not exclude any such glancing away in theory, but more or less expressly permits it. This fact appears incidentally in a passage like *Conf. helv. post.* 10. In his sober ecclesiastical fashion, Bullinger had been content simply to lay down what it is that the Church must ask and hear and consider and teach, and he had stated that this is Jesus Christ Himself, and that we ought not to enquire concerning any other basis of election outside of and beyond Christ. *Vestrum non est, de his curiosius inquirere, sed magis anniti, ut per rectam viam coelum ingrediamini.* But then his first and decisive statement on the subject ran as follows : *Deus ab aeterno praedestinavit vel elegit libere et mera sua gratia nullo hominum respectu sanctos, quos vult salvos facere in Christo.* Even with him, then, it is evident that the *velle salvos facere in Christo* is preceded by a *praedestinare vel eligere quos* . . . and thus by the election itself and as such. It is evident that to Christ must be ascribed not the function of the electing God Himself, but only that of the organ which serves the electing will of God, as a means towards the attainment of the end foreordained for the elect. Now, according to John's Gospel, the electing of the Father and that of the Son are one and the same. And according to Ephesians 1[4] we are not only called and redeemed in Christ, but are already elected to calling and salvation in Him. Bullinger not only says nothing of all this, but in the formula mentioned he expressly denies it, although he never returns later to this background truth. What, then, is the value of the most praiseworthy pastoral zeal with which he refers us to Christ as the *speculum electionis* ? Whatever else Christ may be, *speculum electionis* is the very thing which on this presupposition He obviously is not. In respect of our election, and therefore of our calling and redemption, all that remains according to Bullinger's formula is secret speculation of quite a different kind, and contrary to Bullinger's own prohibition. That which the pastoral prudence of Bullinger to a large extent conceals is, however, quite palpably revealed elsewhere. And because Luther and the later Lutherans thought that this was one of the matters which they ought particularly to hold against Calvin and the Calvinists, it is very much to the point to recall that, long before Calvin, Luther himself had been foremost in adding to the christological reference the equally definite reference to a divine decision which took place apart from Christ, a decision hidden and unsearchable, but not on that account any the less real. It is to the point to recall that in this hidden and unsearchable but nevertheless real decision Luther had found the true and ultimate reality of the divine election. In his old age Luther, as a rule, made no mention of this side of the matter. In the fragments of his preaching which have come down to us it is impossible to find any further trace of this background. The christological reference became for Luther the one and only thing that mattered. Yet it should not be forgotten that the older Luther ranked the *De servo arbitrio* (1525) as one of his best works. Thus there had not been any theoretical abandonment of the earlier position. And in that work we find already (*W.A.* 18, 689, 18) the most impressive warning : *de secreta illa voluntate maiestatis non esse disputandum et temeritatem humanam, quae perpetua perversitate relictis necessariis illa semper impetit et tentat, esse avocandam et retrahendam, ne occupet sese scrutandis illis secretis maiestatis, quae impossibile est attingere, ut quae habitet lucem inaccessibilem.* On the positive side, too, Luther tells the thinking man quite definitely that his concern must be *cum Deo incarnato, cum Jesu crucifixo.* It is this *Deus incarnatus* whom we find weeping over Jerusalem. It is He whom we hear saying : " Ye would not." It is He whom we see offering to all men everything that they need for salvation . . . *cum voluntas maiestatis ex proposito aliquos relinquat et reprobet, ut pereant.* Luther would reject and suppress the question concerning the nature and content of this *voluntas maiestatis : Nec nobis quaerendum, cur ita faciat sed reverendus Deus, qui talia et possit et velit.* But how can this question possibly be rejected, how can there be any confident turning to the *Deus incarnatus*, when behind Him and above Him another and different *voluntas maiestatis* is always laid down and maintained ? (And it was to the presentation of the omnipotent rule of this *voluntas maiestatis* that Luther devoted the whole work in his controversy with Erasmus.) No matter what warnings or prohibitions may accompany it, does not the establishment of such a *voluntas* mean that the revelation of God is only a relative truth about God ? In defiance of all such warnings and prohibitions, will not the question of the hidden God emerge one day as the question of the true God ? Even where in conformity with the warnings and prohibitions there is still an adherence to the *Deus revelatus*, will not the question of the electing of this true God always lurk in the background ? Is there not something necessarily spasmodic and artificial about the reference to Jesus Christ when in fact it is accompanied by the assertion of a quite different *voluntas maiestatis* ? And we must ask the same question of Calvin. What are we to think when on one occasion he makes use of this formula : *videmus, ut a se ipso incipiat Deus, quum nos eligere dignatur ; sed nos a Christo incipere velit, ut nos sciamus in sacro illo peculio censere* (*De aet. Dei praed.*, 1552, *C.R.* 8, 319) ? It is obvious what Calvin means by the latter part : Christ is *sic toti mundo ordinatus ad salutem, ut eos servet, qui a Patre illi dati sunt—eorum sit vita, quorum est caput—eos in bonorum suorum societatem recipit, quos sibi Deus gratuito beneplacito haeredes adoptavit* (*ib.*, 298). It is in the being and work of Christ accomplished on the basis of the election and for the attainment of its end—that He ministers to certain men, that He is their life, that He adopts them into the fellowship of the benefits which He Himself has and is—it is here that we must know the electing God. And to that extent God wills that in respect of the election we, at any rate, should begin with Christ. But what does Calvin mean when he says that on His side God begins *a se ipso* (in contradistinction to *a Christo*) when He elects us, i.e., when the Father gives us the Son, when He predestinates us members of the body of this Head and partakers of His inheritance ? And what is this *gratuitum beneplacitum* which plainly here precedes and is superior to the being and work of Christ ? The question of the election is really the question of this *gratuitum beneplacitum* as such. And the reference to Christ as the One who executed the *beneplacitum* is only an answer to the question of the *beneplacitum* if the *beneplacitum* as such is understood to be Christ's, if Christ is already thought of not merely as the executive instrument of the divine dealings with man ordained in the election but as the Subject of the election itself. But Calvin was not prepared to think of Him in this way. He did come appreciably near to such an understanding in his exposition of the passages in John (13⁸, 15¹⁹) which speak of Christ's own election of His disciples. We do find there the words: *Sibi ius eligendi communiter vindicat cum Patre. . . . Se Christus electionis facit autorem.* But the thought is not followed to its conclusion. From other passages in John, however, whose tenor was apparently different, the unequivocal deduction is drawn: *Electi dicuntur ante fuisse Patris, quam eos donaret unigenito Filio* (*Instit.* III, 22, 7). The fact that according to Eph. 1⁴ the *electio Patris* which preceded the *donatio* is to be thought of as taking place *in Christo* is something which Calvin will not acknowledge. He says the direct opposite: *Qui ad Christum accedunt, iam filii Dei erant in eius corde . . . et quia praeordinati erant ad vitam, Christo dati sunt* (*De praed. C.R.* 8, 292). It was inevitable, then, that in spite of the christological reference the main emphasis in Calvinistic doctrine should come to rest in effect upon this reference to the secret *electio Patris*. But how, then, could the first reference have any force ? Assent might be given to it, but it was inevitable that a secret dissatisfaction should lead to its supersession by the real truth to be found *in Deo incipiente a se ipso*, in the *beneplacitum gratuitum* which was before Christ and behind Him and above Him. It was inevitable, then, that little store should be set by the revelation when there was no need to adhere strictly to it. It was inevitable that even within the revelation the main concern should be, not with a relative truth, but quite unreservedly and unhesitatingly with this real and inward truth concerning God.

As is known, at the end of the 16th and beginning of the 17th centuries there arose a lively opposition to the Calvinistic doctrine of the *decretum absolutum*.

On the one hand, there was the opposition within the Reformed Church itself. This was made by the Dutch Remonstrants named after Jacob Arminius.

This party drew up a series of Articles on the whole complex of questions relating to predestination. These Articles were discussed and condemned at the Synod of Dordrecht (Dort). The fifth of them contains (I, 3) the striking sentence: *Christus mediator non est solum executor electionis, sed ipsius decreti electionis fundamentum.* But because of the context in which it was presented, and the intention which obviously underlay it, we unfortunately cannot find much cause for pleasure in such a statement. We can say only that it would have been good if the orthodox majority at Dort had let the (in any case) remarkable wording remind them of the problem to which the Calvinistic and in particular the Reformation conception of the doctrine had returned so unsatisfactory an answer. But the general tenor of the Remonstrant theology laid down in the Five Articles was so bad that in effect they failed to give the stimulus which they might have given in this respect. The only result was a hardening of the conception inherited from the Reformers. There can be no doubt that the Remonstrants were, in fact, the last exponents of an understanding of the Reformation which Erasmus had once represented against Luther and later Castellio against Calvin ; an understanding which can and should be interpreted in the light of the persistence of mediæval semi-Pelagianism no less than in that of the Renaissance. And as the last exponents of that understanding they were also the first exponents of a modern Christianity which is characterised by the very same ambiguity. They were the first Neo-Protestants of the Church, and it was their basic decision which gave unity to all subsequent developments along this line (from the end of the 17th century onwards). The basic decision which they made was this— that in the understanding of God and His relationship with man, in the question of the formulation of Christian doctrine, the criterion or measure of all things must always be man, i.e., man's conception of that which is right, and rational, and worthy, therefore, of God and man. It was in the light of this basic decision that the Remonstrants opposed to the Calvinistic doctrine of the *decretum absolutum* the assertion that we cannot and must not state that God elects (and rejects) whom He wills solely upon the basis of His own free *beneplacitum* and without reference to conduct, and particularly to belief or unbelief, obedience or disobedience. On the contrary, the divine election is made with due consideration of the conduct of men as foreseen by God from all eternity, i.e., of the use which, according to God's foreknowledge, they make of their freedom, whether in belief or unbelief, whether in obedience or disobedience. It is to this context, unfortunately, that there belongs the intrinsically so remarkable statement of the Remonstrants that Christ is the *fundamentum electionis*, a statement which was obviously meant to outbid and correct the Calvinist statement that Christ is the *speculum electionis*. We cannot take the statement to mean that as Christ is the Subject of the saving decree of God, so, too, He is the Subject of the free election which underlies it, an election independent of and preceding and predetermining absolutely all creaturely decisions. It is simply a polemical assertion in the battle against the *servum* and for the *liberum arbitrium*. It does not mean, unfortunately, what in itself the wording might well mean : that *in concreto* the Calvinistic and Reformation magnifying of the freedom of the election of grace must consist in the magnifying of the sovereignty of Jesus Christ, who in His own person is Himself the God who freely elects and then acts towards the creature, the One behind and above whom there is no other God and no other election. As directed against the *decretum absolutum* the statement does not contend for the dignity of Jesus Christ, but for the dignity of man standing over against Jesus Christ in an autonomous freedom of decision. Read in the context of the general teaching of the Five Remonstrant Articles it unfortunately means nothing more than that Christ is the essence of the divine order of salvation. It is in Him that the grace of God is offered to men. It is by their belief or unbelief in Him that the decision is made—according to God's foreknowledge, but independently—whether the grace of God profits or does not profit them. The Remonstrants did not say that Christ is the electing God. They can never have wanted to say that. What they did want to say, and what they actually did say in this statement, was that in the distinctive sense of the word there is no divine decision at all. There is only the establishment of a just and reasonable order of salvation, of which Christ must be regarded as the content and the decisive instrument. Above and beyond that, there is no more than a divine foreknowledge of what individuals will become as measured by this order of salvation and on the basis of the use which they make of their creaturely freedom. It might almost be called fate that a statement which is so interesting in its wording should engage the attention of Calvinistic orthodoxy, and the Synod of Dort in particular, only in the form of an argument for so revolutionary an error, and that in the mouth of the Remonstrants it should not be a more accurate or Christian definition of the mystery of the election of grace, but an attempt to deny it altogether ; an attempt to make of divine predestination something more akin to a religious world-order.

It was not that the importance of the statement was simply not recognised at Dort. It was not that there was no attempt made to come to grips with it. In the 65th session (Jan. 22, 1619) it was the occasion of a clash between the most resolute champion of Calvinistic orthodoxy, Franz Gomarus, and the leader of the Bremen delegation, Matthias Martini—a clash which nearly assumed dangerous proportions. In modification of the orthodox Calvinistic thesis that the decree of salvation follows the decree of election, and is brought into effect only in Christ, the English expounded Eph. 1[4] to mean that after this human nature Christ is the first of the elect, and the Swiss that He is the basis of those blessings of which the elect are made partakers. But Martini wished to go further, and to say that Christ is the basis of the election itself, on the ground that He is its principal author : the *causa meritoria eligibilitatis*, i.e., the cause of the election of anyone at all—although we have still to seek elsewhere than in Christ the *causa electionis* as such, i.e., the election of this or that particular individual. On this point, the following statement is still to be found amongst the final resolutions of the Bremen delegation : *Hoc decretum est liberrimum, quatenus Deus miseretur cuius vult ; est iustissimum utpote factum in Christo mediatore, irae Dei placatore et hominum reconciliatore ; benignissimum ut simul dandae salutiferae gratiae et gloriae propositum.* It was sheer narrow-mindedness when the Palatinate delegates indignantly rejected the Bremen position simply on the ground that it was out of place to attempt in any way to improve upon the teaching of Calvin. And it rested upon a more adequate but even more malicious recognition of the actual facts of the case when the anti-Remonstrants accused the Bremen party of Arminian tendencies. Unfortunately, it cannot be stated positively that the Bremen delegates were impelled to the point at which their conception, while clearly avoiding the Arminian error, might have taken on the character of a real correction of the Calvinistic teaching. In such a form it might perhaps have struck the Synod as really necessary. The Canons of the Synod did aim, indeed, to take account of the Bremen conception (in the main definition I, 7 often quoted in this connexion). The divine *propositum* of the election is there defined as that *quo Deus . . . certam hominum multitudinem . . . ad salutem elegit in Christo, quem etiam ab aeterno mediatorem . . . constituit.* But the rulings of other foreign delegations and the Dutch provincial synods show that now as ever this passage from Canon I, 7 was, on the whole, to be taken as implying the superiority of a genuine decree of election, which was independent of Christ, over a decree of salvation which was subordinate to it and had Christ as its content. In the last analysis, the English would speak of Christ as the *fundamentum electionis* (I, 2) only in the sense that all the benefits ordained in election are conferred upon us *non nisi propter Christum, per Christum et in Christo* ; the Hessians (I, 3) only in the sense, *quatenus electio accipitur pro ordinatione mediorum ad vitam aeternam tendentium ;* the Nassau delegates (I, 2) only in so far as *in mediis istis (ad vitam aeternam) primum locum obtinet adeoque reliquorum mediorum fundamentum est Christus mediator, cui Deus electos dedit ;* the Emden representatives (I, 11) only in so far as Christ is the way *inter electionis decretum et decreti finem,* etc. And the Swiss delegation (which consisted of J. J. Breitinger of Zurich, Markus Rütimeyer of Berne, Sebastian Beck and Wolfgang Meyer of Basel and J. C. Koch of Schaffhausen) unfortunately had the temerity to reject the phrase altogether : *etsi electio respectum habeat ad Christum mediatorem, in quo omnes ad salutem et gratiam eligimur, tamen nos elegit Deus non velut existentes in illo priusquam eligeremur, sed elegit ut essemus in illo, perque eum servaremur* (I, 4). It was fatal that in all these expositions of Eph. 1⁴, or understandings of the concept *fundamentum*, there was too close an agreement with the Remonstrants in seeking to relate the ἐν αὐτῷ only to the pre-existent decree of salvation as such, and not to the election properly speaking. This was done by maintaining against the Remonstrants a decree of election different from the decree of salvation. On the one hand, then, the decree of salvation was emptied of meaning, for quite unintentionally it was rendered inevitable that the true divine decision should be sought elsewhere than in the Saviour, Jesus Christ. And, on the other hand, the decree of election was also emptied of meaning, for it was removed to the divine sphere above and behind Christ where it could not in fact be known as Christian truth. And that meant that there could be no sure knowledge of it at all, and that it was set in the light of a purely speculative axiom. Thus the way was made all too easy for future Neo-Protestants some day to set aside the decree of election as too obscure and uncertain, and to understand the decree of salvation, now deprived of its mysterious background, only after the semi-Pelagian fashion of the Remonstrants. Our consideration of the interaction between Calvinism and the Remonstrant thesis that Christ is the *fundamentum electionis* can lead us to only one conclusion, that here, too, we stand at one of those points where unwittingly and unwillingly the older Protestant orthodoxy helped to dig its own grave.

From our present standpoint, the opposition brought against the doctrine of the *decretum absolutum* by 17th century Lutheran theology is far more significant. The motive of the opposition was not in this case the mediæval and humanistic axiom that man is the measure of all things, although it must be asked whether it, too, did not ultimately work itself out in the sense of this axiom. It must be recognised that at least in aim and tendency we have to do here with a genuine and necessary concern to take the common Reformation assertion that the basis of the election is to be found in Jesus Christ (as we are most impressively reminded in the utterances of the later Luther), and so to confirm it that, unlike a direction intended merely for pastoral understanding, it has to be reckoned with quite seriously from the theological standpoint. In this way an attempt was made to intercept the fatal glancing aside at an election which takes place behind and above Christ in the hiddenness of God. The direction was no longer to be construed merely as a prohibition. It was to be understood as a pointer to the real and ultimate truth of the matter, a truth which cannot be supplemented in any other quarter. Yet at this point the Lutheranism of the *Formula of Concord* obviously found itself in the dilemma of not being able to do more than to make mere assertions along these lines, or rather simply to negate the Calvinistic *decretum absolutum* (which involved, of course, an abandonment of the 1525 Luther!). At a decisive point (*Sol. decl.* XI 23) we find this statement : *Deus illo suo consilio, proposito et ordinatione . . . omnes et singulas personas electorum (qui per Christum salvandi sunt) clementer praescivit, elegit et decrevit.* It will be noted that *praescrivit* is given the emphasis of precedence, and that *elegit* and *descrevit* must obviously be explained largely in the light of it. This shows us at once the direction in which it was intended to move (in the steps of the mediating theologians of the 9th century). It will be seen, however, that if the *electi* are defined as those *qui per Christum salvandi sunt*, there has not been any true or genuine overthrowal of the Calvinistic conception of Christ as merely the *medium salutis* or *executor decreti.* So long as these terms were used, what advance was there at Kloster Bergen in 1577 upon the position which Dort showed itself determined to maintain in 1619 ? Was there here any real grounding of the election as such in Jesus Christ ? This was clearly the question which rightly disturbed Lutheran theologians even after that great codification of Lutheran belief. Much of their further effort in this matter was devoted to its further elucidation. And whether (in pursuing this legitimate question) it did to any extent attain its object is the standard by which we must measure this activity. In what follows we will confine ourselves to J. Gerhard at the beginning and A. Quenstedt at the end of the " orthodox " period in Lutheran theology.

An outstanding characteristic of the orthodox Lutheran teaching on predestination is that in its initial stages the concept of predestination or election as such is usually replaced by a general heading under which it is introduced later. The common setting in which it is put by the Lutherans is a doctrine *De universali Dei misericordia et benefica erga omnes voluntate* (as with J. Gerhard, *Loci theol.*, 1610 f. VII, *cap.* 4), or, more briefly (as with Quenstedt, *Theol. did. pol.*, 1685, III, *cap.* 1), *De benevolentia Dei universali.* There is a *catholicismus paternae miserationis* (Quenstedt, *ib.*, *sect.* 1, *th.* 9). Its subject is God the Father, *non tamen excluso Filio et Spiritu Sancto, quorum Trium unus erga nos amor est* (*th.* 8). Its object is the whole of fallen humanity as such : *homines per lapsum miseri facti, illique in universum omnes, ne unico quidem excluso, nemine excepto* (*th.* 9). Its basis within the Godhead is the *interventio Filii Dei . . . qui ab aeterno in arcano S.S. Trinitatis consilio ad perfectissimam satisfactionem . . . vice et loco omnium hominum . . . sese obtulit et spopondit* (*th.* 10). It is as such God's *voluntas antecedens* (*th.* 5). It is meant in all seriousness, i.e., it wills the salvation of men not in appearance only but with an ultimate sincerity and urgency (*th.* 12). It is not a mere wish, not *velleitas*, not *voluntas inefficax*, but *voluntas efficax, qua Deus salutem hominum ardentissime desideratam etiam efficere ac per media suffi-cientia et efficacia consequi et procurare serio intendit : . . . quantum in se est, omnes homines ex aequo vult salvi* (*th.* 6). It is not, of course, *absoluta* but *ordinata : fundatur enim in Christo et determinatur ad finem et media, quibus illa accenditur* (*th.* 12). *Benignissima haec Dei voluntas primum salutis humanae principium* (*th.* 13). In the exposition of this basic doctrine appeal could be made to certain passages of Scripture ; as 1 Tim. 2⁴ : " God willeth that all men should be saved, and come unto the knowledge of the truth " ; Rom. 11³² : " For God hath shut up all unto disobedience, that he might have mercy upon all " ; 2 Pet. 3⁹ : " He does not will that any should perish, but that all should come to repentance." J. Gerhard (*cap.* 5) further enlarges it by laying down that all men are as such created in the divine image.

It is only on the ground of this basic doctrine that the Lutherans arrive at the doctrine of predestination properly speaking. By this time it has naturally been decided that the basis and essence of the divine election is not to be sought in any *propositum Dei absolutum*. The will of God is wholly and utterly the will which in Jesus Christ is directed to the salvation of all men. Yet God elects whom He elects in view of the twofold fact present to His foreknowledge from all eternity—the fact of the work of Christ, and the fact of faith directed towards that work : *intuitu satisfactionis in Christo praestandae et per fidem acceptandae* (J. Gerhard, *cap.* 8, 148). The divine election corresponds exactly with the temporal event in which salvation is provided for men and appropriated by them : *Quae enim in tempore Deus agit, sunt manifestatio eorum quae ab aeterno agere decrevit ; quod et quomodo Deus in tempore agit, illud et non aliud, illo et non alio modo ab aeterno agere decrevit*. God's consideration of the work of Christ in time belongs, then, to the divine decree of election itself, so certain is it that that decree is identical with God's eternal resolution to provide salvation for man in that work (*ib.*, 151). But to the divine decree of election there belongs equally God's consideration of the faith in which man meets that work and in which he makes right use of it : the *intuitus fidei*. For : *Christi meritum nemini prodest absque fide* (*ib.*, *cap.* 9, 161). It is in view of this twofold reality fulfilled in time that God elects from all eternity. We saw that God's *benevolentia* is indeed *universalis, seria* and *efficax*, but it is not for that reason *absoluta*. As God's *benevolentia* it is *ordinata*. And the *ordinatio* in which God's *benevolentia* is made real and effective for all men is this—that in His answering of the question which men should profit by it, God keeps to the way which He Himself has appointed : the work of Christ, and the faith which meets that work, and in which it becomes profitable to this or that man. According to the Lutheran teaching, the elect from all eternity are those who in faith—by this is meant, of course, a serious and persevering faith (*ib.*, 176)—make a right and proper use of that work, according to the divine foreknowledge. In the characteristic expression of Quenstedt (*cap.* 2, *sect.* 2, *qu.* 4, *Thesis*) there is a *circulus electionis*. God's eternal will to save all men is directed *in concreto* to those who are called to faith in Jesus Christ and who are obedient to this calling. To that extent it is an electing will. The more detailed statement (*cap.* 2, *sect.* 1) runs as follows. Concretely the gracious will of God to all men is the divine will as determined by the *meritum Christi* and its appropriation in faith. As such it is an electing will, distinguishing and separating within the totality of men (*th.* 9–11). But God's electing, His πρόθεσις, is determined by His πρόγνωσις, by His *praevisio individuorum finaliter crediturorum* (*th.* 12). These individuals : *quicunque finaliter in Christum, mundi redemptorem credituri sunt, illi electi sunt ad vitam aeternam* (*th.* 13). The divine will in its election is directed, therefore, by the divine knowledge, and to that extent by the actuality of an object which is distinct from God. But this object is on the one side Christ, and on the other faith wrought by the Holy Spirit. It is still true, then, that in the words of Rom. 9[16] " it is not of him that willeth nor of him that runneth, but of God that sheweth mercy " (*th.* 10). It is still true that we have to do with an eternal, specific, unalterable election of divine grace (*th.* 20). But we do not have to do with an absolute decree. For it is in the *meritum Christi praevisum et praedefinitum* which He Himself has established that God, its author, finds the good-pleasure in which He elects whom He wills (*sect.* 2, *qu.* 3). And His electing is partly determined by the consideration of the faith which He Himself gives man and in which the *meritum Christi* is appropriated by man (*sect.* 2, *qu.* 4). In this way Quenstedt (*qu.* 4, *ekth.* 5) hopes to be able to avoid Pelagianism as well as " Absolutism."

We must recognise at once and unreservedly the seriousness of this effort to reach an understanding of the thought of election which at all points takes account of the ἐν αὐτῷ of Eph. 1[4]. The basic concern of the Lutheran teaching was to remove the useless blemish of an absolute and meaningless divine freedom behind and above the divine decree of salvation, a blemish which marred all Reformation teaching, and especially the, in this respect, far too orthodo.· predestinarian doctrine of the Reformed Church. Its aim was to make the reference to the primal decision of God a genuine christological reference. In the accomplishment of this task it was concerned just as basically with the establishment of the fact that the primal decision is really God's grace. Looking back at the predestinarian teaching of the *Formula of Concord*, we must say that in it the problem was at least taken up and advanced energetically. Looking away from it to the doctrine of the Synod of Dort, we are obliged to confess that it compares favourably with it. It does so in virtue of its initial concern for a Christian conception of this article of faith. We can only regret that on the Reformed side this teaching failed to give rise to any effort to make place for such a concern even if in very different fashion. It must always be a matter for surprise that the Reformed Church and Reformed theology so obstinately forbade any following of the Lutherans along this path, preferring to cling to the unsatisfactory and dangerous doctrinal forms of the earlier 16th century rather than to allow of the correction which had been so zealously and carefully made in Lutheranism. And if this is a matter for surprise, then there is certainly cause to regret that the Reformed school never reached the point of attempting what might perhaps have been a better correction. For it must be recognised in any case that the Lutheran solution for its part was not so satisfactory that its success was inevitable or even possible. There are, in fact, reasons which help to explain why the Reformed party, faced with the choice, could still believe that the doctrine of the *decretum absolutum* offered a relatively better safeguard for Reformed and Christian interests in this whole matter.

The first consideration arises at once in respect of the Lutheran point of departure. We, too, had to understand the doctrine of election at the very outset as the sum of the Gospel. It is the first and decisive expression, belonging to the doctrine of God as such, of the knowledge of the *benevolentia divina erga omnes homines*. But it is one thing to interpret the doctrine in advance from this starting-point and quite another to try to deduce it in advance from this starting-point. And it was the latter which the older Lutherans obviously did. For with them is not that fine *benevolentia Dei universalis*, that *catholicismus paternae miserationis*, simply another general truth, another systematic principle which must be developed and carried through in the doctrine of predestination as such ? And such being the case, we cannot but allow to the older Reformed and Calvinistic *decretum absolutum* at least the merit that it was designed to prevent any over-rash assumption that we can always know the will of God (theology's over-confident control of its subject). For it referred away even from the *paterna miseratio* of God to God Himself and to the freedom of the divine mercy. We are not overlooking the fact that the Lutherans found the *fundamentum* of this general redemptive will of God in Jesus Christ, in the self-offering of the Son of God for man's salvation which was determined and made from all eternity in the bosom of the Trinity. But can we take this fact at its face value ? Is it really a question of Jesus Christ, and not rather of the divine *benevolentia* as such understood as a systematic principle ? If in this basic doctrine it really is a question of Jesus Christ and of the eternal and temporal reality of His self-offering for man's salvation, then what place is there in the Lutheran presentation for the judicial character of this self-offering of the Son of God ? If it is true that He came to seek and to save that which was lost, and that from all eternity He was destined and empowered to do so, then it is equally true that even in this activity foreordained from all eternity and fulfilled in time He is the One before whom the spirits divide, and that even in this capacity He is no less the One who fulfils the divine will and the divine *benevolentia*. The question of the nature of this *benevolentia*, of this love of God for all men, is, of course, a question which is raised and answered in the reality of Jesus Christ. But the question must not be dissolved in this reality. There must not be any systematisation, or setting up of a principle. There must not be any delimitation by the assertion of the *benevolentia Dei universalis* as an assertion which binds God in advance and thus anticipates and secretly controls the reality. The Gospel is the one thing which does not lend itself to be translated or transformed into such a principle. *Quantum in se est, omnes homines ex aequo vult salvi*— that is the Gospel translated and transformed into a principle. Yet the Gospel does not permit itself to be translated or transformed even into a principle so excellent in itself as this one. For the Gospel is what it is in the divine-human person of Jesus Christ Himself. And this person does not permit Himself to be translated into a proposition. It is not our task to understand this person in the light of a Gospel abstractly formulated and presupposed. Our task is to understand the concrete Gospel in the light of this person. And this being the case, under the main heading—if there ought to be such a heading at all—the concept of the election in which the Gospel is revealed as person must be considered and prepared and grounded quite otherwise than was the case in the Lutheran constructions. When we have heard that basic doctrine of the Lutherans, there is nothing we expect less than to be told that there is still an election even within the *catholicismus paternae miserationis*. Has not the general redemptive will of God already been described as *voluntas universalis, seria et efficax* ? How, then, can it be an electing will ? Is it not bound in advance, and in itself, to its object, and therefore to the totality of men ? Where, then, is its freedom ? Where, then, is its character as free grace ? The Lutherans answer that it is not *voluntas absoluta* but *ordinata*. That is correct. But when we say that it sets up an order, and itself adheres to that order, and deals with the totality of men within the sphere of that order, we have obviously hardly attained to, let alone exhausted, the concept of divine election, of a differentiation within the totality of men freely controlled and executed by God. The Lutherans, however, imagine that by saying this we actually do exhaust the concept of election as such. This is the great *quid pro quo* of their predestinarian doctrine. If we inspect it closely, their teaching has nothing whatever to say about the fact that God elects. It says only that God has determined to actualise, and has actualised, His general redemptive purpose in such a form that in its operation it does necessarily give rise to a selection from amongst men. Naturally God knows about this selection from all eternity. He also affirms it by fulfilling His purpose in this particular form. But He affirms it only secondarily, and the fact that He affirms it does not mean that it is His selection in the strict sense of the word. This construction excludes the initiative of a free divine election. And at this point, in spite of all other differences, in spite of its intended and avowed anti-Pelagianism, the Lutheran teaching occupies common ground with the Arminian doctrine rejected at Dort. For this reason, and quite decisively, it can never be acceptable to

Calvinists. The divine salvation revealed in Jesus Christ is the place where the basis of the election is to be found. But according to the Lutheran construction this means that the decree of election merges into the decree of salvation and there disappears. What apparently remains, but only apparently, is the idea of the divine foreknowledge : that everything in time is fulfilled in accordance with the eternal redemptive decree by which God gives specific form to His general redemptive will. It is in this way (properly speaking, without any initiative on the part of God) that there arises the question of a selection. From all eternity God has had the *intuitus meriti Christi* and the *intuitus fidei*. On the basis of this twofold *intuitus* He wills from all eternity the salvation of those who present this twofold aspect : that in faith the *meritum Christi* avails for them, and that in faith they allow the *meritum Christi* to avail for them. This will of His is the divine election of such men. Between the general benevolence of God towards all on the one hand, and, on the other the *ordinatio* by which it is joined with the work of Christ and with faith, it is useless to ask what is the true meaning of the will of God by which He wills to save some. At all events, that will cannot be a free and electing will which differentiates between men. Once we have denied the *decretum absolutum*, and substituted for it that *catholicismus paternae miserationis*, we can no longer attribute to God the capacity for such a will. In Lutheran teaching the fact that God elects can mean no more and no less than that God wills and affirms in advance that which He knows will take place within the sphere of His ordained redemptive will. But obviously this is not a free electing on the part of God. Of course the Lutherans did maintain most emphatically that not merely the foreseen work of Christ but also the *praevisa fides* in which this work is made available and effective to man must be derived wholly and utterly from the free decision and the personal work of God. But at this point, especially in the concept of *praevisa fides*, a dangerous dilemma was bound to arise. On the one hand, we may take in all seriousness this deriving of *praevisa fides* from the grace of the Holy Spirit and therefore from the will of God. In this case a free electing of God will emerge as the foundation of the whole process. It will be decided that it was altogether of God that in faith the work of Christ availed for some men and that in faith they allowed it to avail for them. We shall then have to understand such men as truly elected by God and not as self-elected to that status. But this being the case, how can we avoid the Calvinistic *decretum absolutum*, as originally intended ? On the other hand, we may have doubts about the freedom of the grace of the Holy Spirit, supposing that the gift of faith may be conditioned and circumscribed on the human side, at least so far as the lack of opposition to it is concerned. In this case we shall avoid " Absolutism," but what about Pelagianism ? The Lutherans did not openly maintain any such circumscribing or conditioning. On the contrary, they rejected it as a scholastic and papistical heresy (Quenstedt, *sect*. 2, *qu*. 4, *antith*. II). But to say that they did not intend to maintain it was the very last thing they could really say in this context. How could they help maintaining it when they would not state the opposite view, that of the unconditioned nature of the divine will over against man, and when they intended by that refusal to steer clear of " Absolutism." The deduction may not be explicit and it may be involuntary, but is it not inevitable that God knows from all eternity that in certain men there will not be any opposition, and that because He knows these men He elects them ? The deduction was denied, but it could hardly be evaded, and it was on account of this undeclared deduction that the Calvinists decisively rejected the tenet of *praevisa fides*, and with it the whole Lutheran doctrine of predestination. As they saw it, it is at this decisive point in the whole relationship of God with man that the complete freedom of grace should always be maintained. They thought it better to cling to the *decretum absolutum* than in attempting to avoid it to enter on a path which seemed as though it must ultimately endanger the basic interest of the Reformation. Why was it, they asked, that at this decisive point the Lutherans allowed the will of God to be conditioned by the knowledge or prescience of God, why was it that they thought it necessary to introduce the concept of *praevisa fides*, if they had no wish to compromise this basic interest, the defence of the free grace of God against every form of Pelagianism ? Since the Lutherans could not clearly explain this to the Reformed school, the result was that the latter determined to choose Charybdis rather than Scylla, holding fast by the *decretum absolutum*. And the further result was that the Lutheran teaching did not become the effective stimulus which in virtue of its intention it well deserved to be. It cannot be maintained that there was no foundation for the mistrust with which the Reformed party persisted in their views as against the Lutheran effort, or, indeed, for the defiance with which they clung to the opposing solution of the older Reformation theology. The Lutheran doctrine of predestination was, in fact, a doubtful experiment. The purity of its intention was compromised at least by the fact that the whole of Lutheran orthodoxy thought it justifiable to appropriate the Jesuit doctrine of the divine *scientia media*. It did this partly for the express reason that that doctrine could be of service in combating the Calvinistic *decretum absolutum*, and partly and more positively in order that it might explain the decisive point in Lutheran teaching, the concept of *fides praevisa*. Yet when the Jesuit doctrine deals with the specific form of the divine foreknowledge in which it has as its object the free acts of the creature as such, it does so in a way which allows those acts virtually to precede the decision of the divine will, and thus to limit and determine the divine will itself. If there was any possibility or intention of the divine foreknowledge or its specific object the *fides praevisa* being understood in this way, then it was indeed all up with the basic interest of the Reformation. The Lutheran doctrine could very well become the entrance-gate for a new Pelagianism. And it cannot be denied that the heritage of orthodox Lutheranism on this side—a heritage which dates from as early as Melanchthon—did later work itself out in this direction.

On the other hand, we must not conceal the fact that some risk had to be taken to improve on the older Reformation solution. We must adopt at least the intention of the Lutheran doctrine in so far as it aimed to establish the christological basis of the election. We must not identify this basis quite so rashly or systematically with the general redemptive will of God. Nor must we reduce God's will concerning individuals to a mere ratification of what He knows from all eternity concerning their salvation in Christ and their faith. On behalf of a truly electing and free will of God we must claim boldly the place maintained for it in the Reformed doctrine of the *decretum absolutum*. The assertion of the christological basis should not lead to an ultimate denial of the election as such and therefore of the free grace of God. It must be shown, then, that it is Jesus Christ Himself who occupies this place. It must be shown that in Him we have to do not only with very man but with very God. It must be shown that in Him we have to do not only with elected man but with the electing, the truly and freely electing God. This is the point which must be made clear if in accordance with the correct intention of the Lutherans we are to find in the revealed decree of salvation as such the divine decree of election. The most serious objection to the Lutheran doctrine is that ultimately it does not succeed in making this point clear, any more than does the Calvinistic doctrine. It deduced the election from the basic concept of the *paterna miseratio*. True, it did maintain that the eternal self-offering of the Son of God was the basis of this divine attitude. But it hesitated to understand this self-offering of the Son of God as the act of eternal election. It failed to point to the person of the Son, Jesus Christ, as the Subject of that act. If it had done this, it would have overcome the Reformed doctrine of the *decretum absolutum* and really improved on the older Reformation solution. And it could then have represented that act quite genuinely as election, the free election of God, the decision of the gracious and merciful Judge, Jesus Christ. In this way it would not of itself have approached so closely the Scylla of Pelagianism. When we stand unequivocally and definitively before Jesus Christ, when we stand before the electing God, all longings of this kind are at an end.

The historical survey leads us, then, to the following conclusion. We found previously that the doctrine of election must not begin *in abstracto* either with the concept of an electing God or with that of elected man. It must begin concretely with the acknowledgment of Jesus Christ as both the electing God and elected man. But, generally speaking, this finding is not really an innovation. It is the confirmation and readoption of something which Reformation theology has always said, and said most emphatically, in this connexion. Unfortunately, it did not say it in a way which stamped it as a tenet for serious theological study rather than a purely pastoral direction. Notwithstanding the Reformation statements, then, there has always lurked in the background the doctrine of a God who elects *in abstracto*. The Arminians and Lutherans saw the blemish and attempted to remove it. But what happened was that the concept of the election as such was thereby attacked and set aside. And the result was a fresh approximation to the doctrine of man elected *in abstracto*, or of man's electing of God. This was palpably the case with the Arminians and implicitly with the Lutherans. The historical survey clearly reveals to us again our own task. We must adopt the Reformation thesis. But we must ground and formulate it in such a way that on both sides it is treated with the seriousness which it deserves. We must do so in such a way that when we utter the name of Jesus Christ we really do speak the first and final word not only about the electing God but also about elected man.

3. THE PLACE OF THE DOCTRINE IN DOGMATICS

It is not at all self-evident that the doctrine of election should occupy in dogmatic enquiry the place here accorded to it. We have given it precedence over all the other individual tenets of the Christian faith relating to the work of God, and placed it in the context of the doctrine of God itself. As far as I know, no previous dogmatician has adopted such a course. We must ask then: Is it really the case that the doctrine of election forms a part of the definition of the Subject of all Christian doctrine? May we and must we deal with it before we deal even with the creation of the world and of man, or before we deal with the work of reconciliation and the end of that work in eternal redemption?

We answer this question affirmatively when we maintain of God that in Himself, in the primal and basic decision in which He wills to be and actually is God, in the mystery of what takes place from and to all eternity within Himself, within His triune being, God is none other than the One who in His Son or Word elects Himself, and in and with Himself elects His people. In so far as God not only is love, but loves, in the act of love which determines His whole being God elects. And in so far as this act of love is an election, it is at the same time and as such the act of His freedom. There can be no subsequent knowledge of God, whether from His revelation or from His work as disclosed in that revelation, which is not as such knowledge of this election. There can be no Christian truth which does not from the very first contain within itself as its basis the fact that from and to all eternity God is the electing God. There can be no tenet of Christian doctrine which if it is to be a Christian tenet does not necessarily reflect both in form and content this divine electing—the eternal electing in which and in virtue of which God does not will to be God, and is not God, apart from those who are His, apart from His people. Because this is the case, the doctrine of election occupies a place at the head of all other Christian dogmas. And it belongs to the doctrine of God Himself because God Himself does not will to be God, and is not God, except as the One who elects. There is no height or depth in which God can be God in any other way. We have not perceived or understood aright the Subject of all Christian doctrine if in our doctrine of God there is lacking the moment which is the specific content of the doctrine of election.

It was and is for these reasons that we introduced the matter at this point, and this point particularly. But this involves us in an innovation for which we must give account in the face of dogmatic tradition. Tradition itself, of course, is not quite so unanimous in this matter as it was for the most part in relation to the doctrine of the Trinity. But it is at least unanimous to this degree, that all the arrangements attempted differ from that planned and carried out in the present work. For this reason it is just and necessary that we should at least mention these other arrangements. By defining our attitude towards them from the standpoint of the considerations we have in mind, we shall defend our own arrangement from any taint of arbitrariness.

1. At a first glance it might seem as though we are in agreement with, or approximate very closely to, the arrangement which became to some extent classical in the Reformed orthodoxy of the 17th century. According to that scheme, the doctrine of predestination followed closely upon the doctrine of God, preceding directly the doctrine of creation and the whole remaining content of confession and dogmatics.

We find this arrangement in the *Irish Articles of Religion* (1615) and the *Westminster Confession* (1647). Amongst dogmaticians we find it in Polanus, Wolleb, Wendelin, H. Alting, A. Heidanus, F. Burmann, F. Turrettini, P. van Mastricht, S. van Til and others. It is in the light of this striking branch of the Reformed tradition, especially as concerns the dogmaticians, that in the modern period the doctrine of predestination has often been called the " central dogma " of Reformed theology. Even some of the older Reformed writers themselves did occasionally speak of it in that way. In this connexion we must draw attention to the fact that the arrangement was not that of Zwingli, or Bullinger, or even Calvin himself. Nor was it the arrangement followed by most of the Reformed confessions. And not quite all the Reformed dogmaticians of the 17th century adopted it. In any case there can be no historical justification for taking the concept " central dogma " to mean that the doctrine of predestination was for the older Reformed theologians a kind of speculative key—a basic tenet from which they could deduce all other dogmas. Not even the famous schema of T. Beza (cf. Heppe. *Dogm. d. ev. ref. Kirche*, ed. 1935, p. 119) was intended in such a sense. Its aim was rather (rightly or wrongly) to show the systematic interconnexion of all other dogmas with that of predestination in the then popular graphic fashion. There was no question of making the latter doctrine a derivative principle for all the rest. And even in the *Westminster Confession* and the theologians mentioned, it was not a matter of deducing all dogmatics from the doctrine of predestination. They did bring the doctrine into direct relationship with the doctrine of God. They placed it at the head of all other doctrines. And this meant, of course, but meant only, that in it they found the first and decisive word which we have to receive and proclaim in respect of the will of God in relation to creation ; the word of which we have always to take account in everything that follows. If we read their expositions connectedly we are more likely to get the impression that from the standpoint of its systematic range and importance they gave to the doctrine too little consideration rather than too much.

Our present procedure, however, cannot be identified simply with that followed in this branch of the Reformed tradition. One reason for this is that according to that tradition the main confessional and and dogmatic tenet was not strictly speaking the doctrine of election. It was rather the tenet which took precedence over that of the election— the tenet of the decrees of God in general.

Decretum Dei est interna voluntatis divinae actio, qua de iis, quae in tempore fieri debebant, ab aeterno liberrime et certissime statuit (Wolleb, *Chr. Theol. comp.*, 1626, I, 3, 3). It was the assertion of this general divine decree which formed the starting-point once the doctrine of God had been completed. And it was explained that the purpose of God in this general *decretum* was to set forth the glory of His power, wisdom and goodness. Only within the context of this general decree could there be any mention of the *speciale decretum*, the purpose of which was defined as the same self-glorification of God *in creaturis rationalibus eligendis aut reprobandis*. And even here the predestination of angels had the precedence over that of men (*ib.*, I, 4, 1 f.). After the model of Thomas Aquinas the doctrine of election was understood as *pars providentiae*. It is a sign of the sure instinct of these theologians that they did not follow out the systematic logic of this view to the point of beginning with the doctrine of providence as such. Consistently and explicitly they introduced the doctrine of providence only in the context of that of creation. Even so, in the doctrine *De decretis in genere* the doctrine of providence had already been anticipated *in nuce*, and it was under this specific aspect, the absolute world-governance of God, that the doctrine of predestination arose as the specific doctrine of God's purposes with respect to the salvation of men.

We have already stated the reasons why we cannot adopt this line of approach. It takes God in His general relationship with the world as its first datum and understands His electing as one function in this general relationship. As against that, we are commanded by the Bible and our Christian profession to take and to understand first the living God in His electing, in the specific relationship which He has established with man in Jesus Christ. Only from this point can we go on to consider His general relationship with the world and His *decretum generale*. A further difference between us is that with these theologians, so far as I can see, the doctrine of election was never regarded or treated as an integral part of the doctrine of God.

There is a link here with the particular conception of the fathers and scholastics frequently touched on in the first part of our doctrine of God—a conception now appropriated afresh by the older Protestant orthodoxy. According to this conception God is everything in the way of aseity, simplicity, immutability, infinity, etc., but He is not the living God, that is to say, He is not the God who lives in concrete decision. God lives in this sense only figuratively. It is not something which belongs to His proper and essential life, but only to His relationship with the world. Basically, then, it may only be " ascribed " to Him, while it is believed that His true being and likewise His true Godhead are to be sought in the impassibility which is above and behind His living activity within the universe. It was illogical, but most fortunate, that theologians still dared to speak not only of the *opera Dei ad extra externa* but also, with reference to the divine decrees, of the *opera Dei ad extra interna*. They could speak, then, of the concrete forms and directions and aims of the divine will and the divine being. They could define the concept of the decree as *interna voluntatis divinae actio*, in spite of the fact that God, as *ens simplex et infinitum*, was not properly or by definition capable of such *opera ad extra interna*, of such *interna actio*. It was surprising enough that this being should be capable of any such *opera ad extra* at all. But how could it be capable of such a concrete decision within itself ? It was the Bible which plainly enforced the latter concession not less than the former. But what these theologians did not dare to do was this. From the fact that God is the living God, that He is the living God inwardly as well as outwardly, a quality expressed and attested in concrete decision, they did not dare to deduce the further fact that clearly God does not exist otherwise, and that He does not will to be understood otherwise, than in the concreteness of life, in the determination of His will, which is as such a determination of His being. Strangely enough, they did not feel driven to make such a deduction even by their doctrine of the Trinity. They spoke of the three persons, of their inter-relationship, of their common work *ad extra*, without ever realising the implications of the fact that this triune being does not exist and cannot be known as a being which rests or moves purely within itself. God is not *in abstracto* Father, Son and Holy Ghost, the triune God. He is so with a definite purpose and reference ; in virtue of the love and freedom in which in the bosom of His triune being He has foreordained Himself from and to all eternity. And when we treat of the doctrine of election, we have to do with this determination of His will, and *eo ipso* of His being and all His perfections. For how can we speak of the being of God without at once speaking of this *interna actio* of His being, i.e., the election ? And how can we speak of the election without speaking of the concrete life of the very being of God ? It is this unity which we would honour by thinking and treating of the doctrine of election as a constituent part of the doctrine of God. Yet at this point even the representatives of the Reformed tradition now under consideration put asunder what ought not to be put asunder —to the detriment of the doctrine of God, and to the detriment of the doctrine of election. For in the case of the doctrine of the being of God the result of this separation was to confirm the fatal picture of a God not living in Himself. And in the case of the doctrine of election there resulted a fatal forgetfulness of the fact that the task of this doctrine is to speak of the election whose Subject is the person of God Himself.

Our intention, then, is to recapture a concern which underlay this particular Reformed tradition. With the tradition, we acknowledge the importance of the doctrine of predestination, not as a derivative principle for all that follows, not as a basic tenet, of which all the rest is only interpretation—we are dealing with much more than a development of the thought of election when we treat later of creation, reconciliation and redemption—but as the Word which together with the revealed and eternal being of God we must accept as the determination of the decision in which God is God. To do justice to this concern we must follow up the two lines indicated, but we must do so far more radically than was the case in this very important Reformed tradition. To that extent, even in relation to this tradition, we shall find ourselves on a path which is characteristically different.

2. All the other methods of arrangement which may now be mentioned have one feature in common. As against the Reformed scheme already referred to, they speak first of creation and providence, and only then, in greater or lesser proximity, of the election. It is plain that with these arrangements we depart increasingly from the order which we ourselves believe to be correct. It will be useful, however, to consider in detail how things worked out in such cases. At the outset, we must notice a small but interesting group in which the Christology followed directly upon the doctrine of God, being succeeded by creation and then predestination.

To this class there belongs Zwingli in his *Fidei ratio* (1530). With him the doctrine of election (III) forms the crown and completion of the doctrine of providence (II). This in turn is preceded by the Christology, which is included in the doctrine of God and of the Trinity (I). Among the older Lutherans, L. Hutterus (*Comp. Loc. theol.*, 1610) and J. Gerhard (*Loci theol.*, 1610 f.) belong to the same group. The latter in particular brings out remarkably well the direct sequence God-Christ-providence-predestination. In the case of Hutterus, the arrangement betrays the influence of another tradition which we have yet to mention, for between the doctrines of creation and predestination he has interjected those of sin, the Law, the Gospel and justification. Finally, one of the Reformed Confessions is to be found in this class, the *Consensus Bremensis* (1595), which introduced the polemical articles against Lutheranism in the same sequence, Christ-providence-election (-sacraments).

If we could allow that this arrangement had been determined by some objective consideration, then, as in the case of the classical Reformed sequence, we should have to see in it the correct insight that the work of God (the work of all works!) is not creation, but that which precedes creation both eternally and in effect temporally, the incarnate Word of God, Christ. We ourselves attempted to do justice to this truth by treating the doctrine of the incarnation even earlier, as the central part of the doctrine of the Word of God which introduces all dogmatics. But we must repeat that Christology is more than the doctrine of the incarnation or person of Christ. It is also the doctrine of the work of Christ, His humiliation, His exaltation, His threefold office. And as such it forms the presupposition and substance of our whole doctrine of reconciliation and faith, of justification and sanctification, of the Church and the sacraments. To that extent those who would introduce their Christology at this point might have showed greater perspicacity in their thinking. It is obvious that the doctrine must also be asserted in the place reverently enough allotted to it in this second form of arrangement, i.e., in direct connexion with the doctrine of God and therefore with that of creation. But it can be asserted here only in the form of the doctrine of election, which, if we comprehend it aright, must from its very roots be thought of and developed christologically. Those who advocated this arrangement, however, allowed the Christology to displace the doctrine of election, instead of filling it out and giving it form. The precedence given to Christology might have been justified and illuminating in its effects if the doctrine of election had been grounded upon it and the transition to the doctrine of creation and providence made in that way. But its advocates did not do that. With them the doctrine of election seems to be co-ordinated with that of creation and providence, and even subordinated to it, according to the well-known Thomistic *schema*. In this decisive relationship the precedence given to Christology was thus rendered ineffective. For this reason, although the arrangement is interesting in itself, it is not one which we are tempted to follow.

In view of the fact that the arrangement was never applied effectively, it is probable that its adoption was not based upon any material consideration, but solely upon a regard for the teaching of the Early Church, i.e., the Niceno-Chalcedonian sequence. The main intention was to bring out the ecumenical orthodoxy of Protestant doctrine. That is no doubt an interesting consideration. But materially the arrangement was very unsatisfactory and its exponents did not ground or apply it in a very illuminating way. It might surely have bee turned to much better account.

3. The specific characteristic of all remaining arrangements is that now the election of grace is quite clearly detached from the doctrine of God and treated after the doctrine of creation and even after that of sin. The result is that it is detached equally clearly from the doctrine of providence, and instead brought into direct connexion with the doctrine of reconciliation. To this doctrine it is in some sort the key, and at every point in its discussion it has to be taken into account. We have this arrangement in its original and basic form when predestination is dealt with quite simply within the context of the doctrine of the Church.

At this point we must again mention Zwingli's *Fidei ratio*, for Zwingli re-introduced the election when he came (VI) to speak of the Church, i.e., of the Church of true believers concealed in the Church visible and as such known only to God and to itself. According to Zwingli, the Church in this most inward sense is identical with the totality of the *electi*, *qui Dei voluntate destinati sunt ad vitam aeternam*. This view is chiefly important because it was also that of the younger Calvin. Thus in the first edition of the *Institutio* (1536), which was openly modelled on the *schema* of Luther's *Smaller Catechism*, the election of grace appeared in the second chapter : *De fide*, and it came in there in the discussion of the fourth article of the Creed (according to Calvin's reckoning) : *Credo ecclesiam.* According to Calvin this *ecclesia sancta et catholica* of faith is identical with the *universus electorum numerus, sive angeli sint, sive homines, ex hominibus ; sive mortui sive adhuc vivant, ex viventibus : quibuscumque in terris agant aut ubivis gentium dispersi sint.* It is so because it is undoubtedly identical with the Pauline *ordo misericordiae Dei* (Rom. 8[30]) : " Whom he did predestinate, them he also called : and whom he called, them he also justified : and whom he justified, them he also glorified." Where there are the called and justified and glorified—and the place where they are is, in fact, the Church—there God proclaims (*declarat*) His eternal election, in which He foreordained them even before they were born. Already, then, Calvin declares quite expressly that this is not a question of the *una illa et incommutabilis Dei providentia*, but of the basic determination of the existence of those who may be known—at any rate by certain signs—as the children of God, in that they are impelled by the Spirit of God along this course from *vocatio* to *glorificatio*. We must take account of the fact that within the visible Church there are also the non-elect, those who belong to this place only in appearance. And this is a warning to us to be circumspect. But it should not prevent us from hoping the best for everyone. Above all, it should not prevent us from holding to the unity of election, faith, and the true Church, which is always true and valid. Calvin has expressed in unforgettable terms the Christian assurance which has its basis in this unity : *Cum autem ecclesia sit populus electorum Dei, fieri non potest, ut qui vere eius sunt membra tandem pereant, aut malo exitio perdantur. Nititur enim eorum salus tam certis solidisque fulcris, ut, etiamsi tota orbis machina labefactetur, concidere ipsa et corruere non possit. Primum, stat cum Dei electione, nec nisi cum aeterna illa sapientia variare aut deficere potest. Titubare ergo et fluctuari, cadere etiam possunt, sed non colliduntur, quia Dominus supponit manum suam ; id est quod ait Paulus* (Rom. 11[29]) : *sine poenitentia esse dona et vocationem Dei. Deinde, quos Dominus elegit, eos Christo filio suo in fidem ac custodiam tradidit, ut neminem ex illis perderet, sed resuscitaret omnes in novissimo die* (Jn. 6[39]). *Sub tam bono custode et errare et labi possunt, perdi certe non possunt.* In the *Instruction et confession de foi* of 1537 (the first form of his *Catechism*), and also in the later drafts of the *Institutio*, Calvin abandoned this arrangement in favour of others which we shall consider later. In the final (1542) form of the *Catechism*, however, he did return to it. But now the Lutheran arrangement as a whole had been replaced by one which was more consistent with the Calvinistic conception, for faith was put first and the Law second. Even here, however, predestination appeared in the context of an exposition of the 4th (or 3rd) article of the Creed : *Qu'est ce que l'Eglise catholique ? C'est la compagnie des fidèles, que Dieu a ordonné et éleu à la vie éternelle.* Rom. 8[30] was again quoted and expounded, and it was again stated that there is also a visible Church of God which may be known by certain marks or notes. But the Church *proprement parlé*, the Church in which we believe, is the *compagnie de ceux, que Dieu a eleu pour les sauver : laquelle ne se peut pas pleinement voir à l'œil.* There is an echo of this teaching in *Qu.* 54 of the *Heidelberg Catechism* (the only place in this document, apart from *Qu.* 52, in which the doctrine of election is expressly dealt with) : " What dost thou believe concerning the Holy Catholic Church ? Answer : That out of the whole human race, from the beginning to the end of the world, the Son of God, by His Spirit and Word, gathers, defends, and preserves for Himself unto everlasting life, a chosen communion in the unity of the true faith ; and that I am, and forever shall remain, a living member of the same." At a more distant remove, this conception seems most surprisingly to have engaged and satisfied the older Melanchthon. At any rate in the final edition of the *Loci* (1559, and departing from the 1521 scheme) he let the article on predestination follow immediately that on the Church. And even if after his manner he softened the contours, and under the heading *praedestinatio* spoke in effect only of *vocatio*, to which we must and ought to restrict ourselves in matters of the election, yet it does emerge to some extent that he, too, would base both belief in the Church and the Church itself on the fact that in reality it is the *ecclesia electorum semper mansura, quam Deus mirabiliter etiam in hac vita servat, defendit et gubernat*. It may be said, then, that there can be no radical development of the doctrine of the Church which does not at least introduce more or less definitely the concept of election.

In favour of this third arrangement we certainly can and should say this. It is marked out from all others by its direct relationship with the Bible. As we stated in our own introductory observations, in the Bible the concept of election stands decidedly in a direct and indissoluble union with that of the people of God, the people which is called Israel in the Old Testament and the Church in the New. The divine election is the election of and to this people. All the consequences of this election as they concern the relationship between God and man, indeed the relationship itself and as such, are worked out within the framework of the life of this people which is twofold but one and the same. The connexion between the election and the Church is both close and comprehensive, and for this reason constitutive for the whole of Christian doctrine. But because this is so, it is advisable, at any rate when we are attempting a coherent understanding of the whole of Christian doctrine, to consider the election, not when we treat directly and specifically of the Church, but much earlier, when our theme is God Himself as the Creator, Lord and Ruler of this people. It is obvious that before the *populus electus* there comes the *Deus elector*. Before the assurance of election, described so finely by Calvin and proper to the true Church or the true humanity gathered into the body of Christ, there stand the mercy and righteousness of the true God who has created and who preserves this true humanity as such, and in whom its assurance has both its ground and Subject. There is no such thing as an assurance of faith apart from the electing God. Assurance of faith is only in the knowledge of the electing God. And it is this fact which at the very least this conception can only too easily obscure.

Self-evidently, this was not Calvin's own intention. But something of it does appear in the rather jejune presentation of Melanchthon. It seems there as if the concept of election is ultimately only a kind of reflection of the comfort which we may have in faith. It seems as if it is enough to give to the *ecclesia senescens* "in these last and tragic days" the assurance that in the last resort it will always be preserved and sustained by God Himself. The other aspect, that of His free grace God has foreordained it from all eternity to that which it possesses, and that the claim which He has upon it corresponds to this fact, in a word, the transcendence of the electing God in and over His Church—all this remains strangely in the background. When we realise the tenuous nature of Melanchthon's perception of the relationship between predestination and the Church, we shall readily understand why it was that Calvin for his part was impelled in the meantime to move forward to a more comprehensive consideration of the question. We shall also understand why this later consideration could subsequently be given an even more radical turn by the Reformed school (as described under the first heading).

If, in our later treatment of the doctrine of the Church, we are to stand on the firm ground which is none other than the Church's eternal divine election, and if we are to do full justice to the aim and intention of this third arrangement, then we must begin our consideration of the divine election at a much earlier point, in the doctrine of God Himself as the Lord and foundation of the Church.

4. Three other arrangements have still to be mentioned. They have this in common, that in different ways they all seek to present predestination as the principle and key to the whole doctrine of reconciliation, or soteriology. This was naturally the opinion of those who related predestination more particularly to the Church as the place where atonement between God and man is actualised. But, of course, there could be many ways of bringing this out. A first possibility was to let predestination follow immediately after Christology. From this point one could then proceed to the work of the Holy Spirit both in individual believers and in the Church as such.

This was the method chosen by Calvin in the first draft of his *Catechism* (1537), and later by Peter Martyr in his *Loci communes* (1576). According to this presentation the doctrine of election brings us, as it were, to the climax of that activity which begins with the gracious God and is completed in sinful man. In it we look backwards from God's electing and man's election to Christ Himself, the basis of the salvation which God has wrought. And in it we look forward to the status of the Christian and to the Church where this salvation is applied to and avails for us. I am aware of only one later presentation in which this conception recurs—the dogmatics of a later disciple of Coccejus, Hermann Witsius, *De oeconomia foederum* (1693). In the second book of this work Witsius develops the doctrine of the divine origin and the person and work of Christ. In the third he then deals with the doctrine of the economy of personal salvation under the title *De foedere Dei cum electis*. This is a more extended and detailed treatment of the concepts of Rom. 8[30] and therefore of the election.

5. A second possibility within the sphere of this particular outlook is that of either directly or indirectly conjoining the doctrine of election with that of sin. In this case it will be given precedence over Christology as well as soteriology, occupying the same position in relation to the full doctrine of reconciliation as in the arrangement mentioned under (1) it does in relation to dogmatics as a whole.

Here, again, we must first mention Calvin, this time as the author of the basic text of the *Conf. Gallicana* (1559). The order in this confession became a standard and model for a whole series of Reformed statements: for the *Conf. Scotica* (1560), which was substantially the work of John Knox, and which brought together the doctrines of election and of Christ in the original manner already indicated ; for the *Conf. Belgica* (1561) ; for H. Bullinger's *Conf. Helv. post.* (1562) ; for the confession of the Markgraf Ernst Friedrich von Baden-Durlach usually known as the *Staffort Book* (1599) ; and also for the *Waldensian Confession* of 1655. Amongst the Reformed dogmatics the *Leidener Synopsis pur. Theol.* (1642) belongs to this group, although in this case the doctrine of sin was followed by that of the Law and the Gospel and of the relationship between the Old and the New Testament, this doctrine being given the precedence over that of election. Also under this heading we must put the *Loci communes* of Anton Waläus (1640), who, without any explanation, without any attempt even to show its reasonableness or value, adopted a highly original and capricious order. From the doctrine of sin he proceeded at once to that of providence, and only then (it is almost incredible), at the farthest possible remove from the doctrine of God, did he move forward to the doctrine of the Trinity, the Trinity being followed by Christology and Soteriology. To this same group there belongs above all the *Summa Theologiae* of J. Coccejus (1662). In this work *Locus* 14 : *De consilio gratiae et irae*, forms the point of transition from the doctrine of sin to that of grace. And yet here, too, Christology and the doctrine of election seem to be most closely inter-related. The same arrangement was also adopted by a group of Lutheran theologians, e.g., by F. J. König in his *Theologia positiva* (1664.) The order of this work, like everything else, was most closely followed by Quenstedt in his *Theol. did. Pol.* (1685), and in the final stages of Lutheran orthodoxy by D. Hollaz in his *Examen theol. acroam.* (1707). These Lutherans followed J. Gerhard in putting their specific doctrine of the *benevolentia Dei universalis* at the head of the doctrine of predestination, but this did not alter the fact that in respect of the place of the doctrine within the *schema* as a whole —and certainly in the avoidance of the federal theology of Coccejus, which was most influential on the Lutheran side—they appropriated the plan of the *Conf. Gallicana*, and therefore one of the plans of the theologian whom, in other respects, they so consistently opposed, Calvin himself.

6. The third possibility within this understanding of the doctrine of election as the key to that of reconciliation is to make the doctrine of election in some degree the consummation of that of reconciliation, introducing it not in the middle or at the beginning, but as the ultimate and decisive word which sheds additional light upon all that has gone before.

This was the function of the doctrine as Melanchthon obviously meant it to be understood in the *schema* of *res theologicae* which he put at the head of the first draft of the *Loci communes* (1521), a *schema* to which, of course, he did not himself adhere in the actual work. But, above all, this was the place and function of the doctrine in the editions of Calvin's *Institutio* which appeared between 1539 and 1554, and ultimately in the definitive redaction itself. Here Christology had become the climax and culmination of the second book *De Deo redemptore*, which dealt earlier with sin, the Law and the distinction and unity between the Old Testament and the New. In the third book, *De modo percipiendae Christi gratiae*, we are led from the work of the Holy Ghost actualised in faith to repentance and the Christian life, the latter being seen from the standpoint both of its outlook on eternity and also of its conditioning in time. We then proceed to the basis of this life in the justification given by God, to its character as Christian freedom, to its maintenance by prayer, and only finally to its eternal root in the divine election of grace, against which there is counter-balanced in a most effective conclusion its eternal end and purpose in the resurrection of the dead. The doctrine of the Church forms the content of the fourth book, and in relation to the rest it has something of the same self-sufficiency as the first book at the beginning of the work : *De Deo creatore*. We must confess, however, that the very *caesurae* serve to bring out more clearly the inter-connexion both of the end and the beginning with the main body of the work in the second and third books and with the doctrine of election in which that central section culminates.

In order to appreciate Calvin's own position, we must establish first the following points. It is true that Calvin did partly share and partly inaugurate four different conceptions of the place and function of the doctrine of election. But it is also true that we do not find amongst these the conception which is usually described as classical in Reformed dogmatics. Calvin never connected the doctrine of predestination with that of God, whether directly or indirectly. And we can describe only as a complete and evident delusion the *opinio communis*, expressed even by serious dogmatic historians, which attributes to Calvin something which even the later Reformed dogmaticians did not do—the establishment of this doctrine as a basic tenet from which all other doctrines may be deduced. W. Niesel (*Die Theologie Calvins*, 1938, p. 159) is quite right when he says : " If anyone does maintain such a view, then here, as elsewhere, he is constructing the theology of Calvin as for one reason or another best suits himself." But we must still ask whether in combating this traditional error some recent writers have not underestimated the function of the doctrine in Calvin's theology (e.g., P. Barth, " Die Erwählungslehre in Calvins Institutio, 1536," in *Theol. Aufsätze*, 1936, p. 432 f. ; Heinz Otten, *Calvins theol. Anschauung von d. Praed.*, 1938, p. 26 ; and even W. Niesel). Can we really say that Calvin spoke of the election at the proper place, " but not more fully than of other matters " (Niesel, *op. cit.*) ? Is not the proper place where he does speak of it, and what he says concerning it, far too important and far too prominent for us to be able to say that this doctrine should not be used, and Calvin did not mean it to be used, to shed a decisive light on all that precedes and follows ? Undoubtedly Calvin did not understand or handle the doctrine as a basic tenet. But this does not mean that he placed it on the same level as all the rest. Between these two views there is a third. What Calvin did appear to find in the doctrine of election was this—a final (and therefore a first) word on the whole reality of the Christian life, the word which tells us that the existence and the continuance and the future of that life are wholly and utterly of the free grace of God. But all Christian doctrine, even that of God at the beginning and that of the Church at the end, deals substantially with this reality of the Christian life, with the life of the man whom God has claimed for Himself in Jesus Christ. And if this is the case, then how can we help thinking of the doctrine of election as the last or first word of all Christian doctrine ? When we consider the place given to the doctrine of election in the later forms of Calvin's *Institutio* and especially in the definitive redaction, it seems that the total picture presented by that work drives us irresistibly to the conclusion that at this point Calvin did intend to find and to say something particularly and appropriately significant both in its substance and also in its consequences.

It is a matter for surprise that the pattern set in the definitive redaction of the *Institutio* did not gain a greater following than was actually the case. It was obviously under its influence, or under that of one of the earlier post-1539 editions, which followed the same plan, that this arrangement passed both into the *Forty-Two Articles* (later *Thirty-Nine*) which in 1553 became the confessional basis of the Church of England, and also into the *Conf. Rhaetica* (1562). The only Reformed dogmatician to adopt it was W. Bucanus in his *Institutiones theol.* (1602). Bucanus also followed Calvin in the inter-connexion of predestination with eschatology. As against that, we may again mention a whole series of important Lutherans. Thus in the great *Systema loc. theol.* (1655 f.) of A. Calov, the doctrine of predestination forms the conclusion of the great sequence Christ-Church-sacraments-personal salvation according to Rom. 8[30] (the content of this sequence should be studied as well as the order). At the head of this sequence, apparently far removed from the doctrine of predestination, but in reality most impressively balanced against it from an architectonic standpoint, Calov introduces the peculiar Lutheran doctrine of the divine *misericordia generalis*. In his *Comp. Theol. pos.* (1686), J. W. Baier has a similar arrangement : Christ-personal salvation-sacraments-predestination, but he differs from Calov by removing the Church from this sequence and treating of it independently. With a similar modification J. F. Buddeus, who was of the so-called " rationalist orthodoxy," took up the same arrangement in his *Institutiones theol. dogm.* (1723). It is quite singular to see how in the constructions of later Lutheranism the doctrine of predestination seems to move more and more to the end of the whole dogmatic sequence. In the talented plan of Calov it is followed only by a special doctrine of the cross in Christian life and by the doctrine of the Law and eschatology, while with Baier and Buddeus it is followed only by the doctrine of Church and state. Even with these theologians we are forced to ask whether their intention would not have been realised just as well, and perhaps better, if they had put the doctrine at the very beginning.

It is obvious that one and the same systematic purpose underlies the three attempts last mentioned. In different ways they understand the divine election as the divine reality which controls the particular activity of salvation between God and man. In a developed and comprehensive form they say the very same thing as was already intended when the election was introduced in connexion with the Church. The point must be made that all three of the possibilities which here present themselves were exploited—the doctrine of election was put at the beginning of the full doctrine of reconciliation, in the middle of that doctrine, and at the end. The point must also be made that we meet with Calvin on each of these paths (and also at their point of departure, the inter-connexion of election with the Church). To establish these facts is far more important than to decide along which of the three paths the common intention is best fulfilled, or which of the three ways is best adapted to the matter in hand. Equally good reasons may be adduced in favour (and also against) all three of these possibilities.

The doctrine of election is indeed " the final and necessary expression of the evangelical doctrine of grace " (W. Niesel, *op. cit.* p. 161). This fact would seem to favour the third way. In presenting the doctrine of election we look back, characterising again the mystery, and the meaning and purpose of the mystery, of all the reality which is between Christ and the Christian. The necessity of this third way is exclusively upheld and argued by Buddeus : *nec enim aliter quam ex eventu de decretis divinis nobis iudicare licet* (*op. cit.*, V, 2, 1). Yet in spite of that, we cannot come to such a decision. At the very place where the doctrine of election may be understood as the final word, it is borne in upon us that it may also be understood as the first word, and that it must indeed be understood in this way. And in the passage so frequently appealed to, Rom. 8³⁰, the election is actually the first word. There can be no doubt that the doctrine of election is more than a mere underlining of the remaining content of the doctrine of grace. There can be no doubt that it is more than a mere heightening of the awareness that grace is free and eternal and divine grace. It does contribute to such a heightening and underlining, but it does far more. And it should never be regarded as a result of our awareness and experience of grace, as a postulate consequent upon such awareness and experience. Here, at any rate, the concept of a *iudicium ex eventu* must always be suspect. Some such suspicion might rest even upon Calvin's arrangement in the *Institutio* of 1559, but it is dispersed by the fact that in that same year, in the *Conf. Gallicana*, he adopted the second and opposite arrangement whereby the doctrine of election forms the beginning of the whole sequence. There can be no doubt that Calvin, too, regarded that last word as also the first. If this fact ought to find expression in the ordering of the material, then it might be asked whether Calvin's first attempt at a solution (1537) was not the best (cf. 4). There the doctrine of the election was placed between Christology and the doctrine of personal salvation. This helped to bring out more clearly than any of the other works both the connexion of the election with Christ and also the order of Rom. 8[30]. But in the light of this we have to reinterpret the solution of the *Conf. Gallicana* (1559) and all the other solutions which, obviously following the thought of Eph. 1[4], aim at a proper introduction, substantiation and effective application of Christology, and also aim to set the doctrine of reconciliation in clear relief against the preceding doctrines of sin, original sin and the *servum arbitrium*, to that end giving precedence to the doctrine of election over every other doctrine except Christology itself (cf. 5). Along all three paths, however, there is a clear recognition of the outstanding character of the doctrine of election in relation to all other aspects of the doctrine of reconciliation. If we had to choose between them, then we should prefer the first solution advocated by Calvin in 1537, on the ground that this solution best expresses the intention underlying all these attempts : to understand the decision of the divine election as an event which works itself out between Christ and the Christian.

But we do not need to choose between these three possibilities. The doctrine of election is the last or first or central word in the whole doctrine of reconciliation, as all of them rightly perceive. But the doctrine of reconciliation is itself the first or last or central word in the whole Christian confession or the whole of Christian dogma. Dogmatics has no more exalted or profound word—essentially, indeed, it has no other word—than this : that God was in Christ reconciling the world unto Himself (2 Cor. 5[19]). As the doctrine of the Word of God it can describe the Christian knowledge of God upon the basis of God's self-revelation only with a constant and wholehearted reference to the event which as such is both the source of truth and the truth itself. It can understand and present the divine work revealed to us in God's Word, whether creation or redemption, only in the light of the mystery of this event. It must already have dealt with the mystery of this event, and only with the mystery of this event, at the very outset, if it is ever to treat of it directly and in detail at its real centre, in the specific doctrine of grace. How, indeed, could we ever speak of God at all, as the Subject of the whole divine work, the Creator, Reconciler and Redeemer, if in our teaching about His being and perfections we were not ready to acknowledge that which is the centre of this work, which contains within itself its beginning and end, which alone makes possible the knowledge of it ? It is here that we make the decisive step, the transition from the knowledge of God to the knowledge of all His work. Is it not necessary, then, that first of all we should show what is the centre, and as such the beginning and end of this work ? Is it not necessary that we should first show who and what God is in His dealings with His creation, who and what the God is whose dealings correspond to what does actually take place and is made known at this centre ? How can we speak rightly of God unless we deal first with this word of decision, unless we point first to the mystery of this doctrine of reconciliation? Does not this word of decision belong necessarily at this point? Must not this mystery be considered at the very outset? How can we possibly take cognisance of this word and this mystery in a merely secondary and supplementary capacity? But, according to the right insight of all the theologians who advocated the three (or four) solutions last mentioned, it is the doctrine of election itself which is this decisive word, this mystery of the doctrine of reconciliation. And all the attempts based upon these arrangements suffer from the fact that their order necessarily gives to the doctrine of election the character of teaching which is purely supplementary and secondary.

This means that when we come to treat of Christ and the Christian (or the Church), it may well appear as though we suddenly remember something which hitherto we have for the most part forgotten. We make amends by enlarging upon what for some reason has hitherto been suppressed, i.e., the fact that in all His work as the One who reconciles the world to Himself, God is the One who acts in Jesus Christ; and not only the One who acts in Jesus Christ, but the One who from all eternity has willed and ordained that He should act in Jesus Christ. In this whole conception the discussion of the eternity, freedom and immutability of God as the basis, meaning and dynamic of what takes place between Christ and His people, between Christ and the Church, comes in a sense too late. And when it is a matter of God's eternity, we obviously cannot afford to let the discussion come too late. The happening which is the meaning and purpose of all the divine work is grounded in God's election and decision. It is, therefore, glorious beyond measure. It is absolutely different from all other happenings. For this reason, we can never speak of it too soon. We cannot be too insistent in the recognition and introduction of it as the presupposition of all God's perfect work (as that which is truly and properly perfect in its perfection). It is because of this that we put the doctrine of election—meaning, of course, this decisive word, this mystery of the doctrine of reconciliation, the doctrine of the election which took place in Jesus Christ—at the very beginning, and indeed before the beginning, of what we have to say concerning God's dealings with His creation. It is for this reason that we understand the election as ordination, as God's self-ordaining of Himself. And it is for this reason, then, that we regard the doctrine of election as a constituent part of the doctrine of God.

Again, if the doctrine of election is treated as something secondary and supplementary along the lines of the three possibilities mentioned, this means that it may well appear as if we could deal at least with creation and sin without any previous consideration of this decisive word, this mystery of the doctrine of reconciliation. But in this case creation takes on the character of a presupposition relatively independent of reconciliation and redemption. It becomes self-sufficient. It has its own reality and must be considered in and for itself. But this makes it appear as if the universe and man might well have been created and sustained without any inner necessity of the continuation and completion of the divine work in reconciliation and redemption. They may, then, be considered directly, apart from the divine election and decision, apart from the kingdom of Christ. But in this case there arises the concept of a realm whose existence allows us at least to question the infinity and divinity of this kingdom, opposing to it the parallel kingdom of nature. But this means that sin, the mishap which takes place in this separate kingdom of nature, acquires the character of an unforeseen incident which suddenly transforms the good creation of God into something problematical, breaking and shattering it in such a way that only a few traces of the original remain and what virtually amounts to a different world is brought into being. On this view God Himself appears in a sense to be halted and baffled by sin, being pressed back into a kind of special " world of God." From this it might easily appear as if reconciliation is the corresponding escape from this dilemma, a mysterious wrestling with what is almost a rival God, a reaction against a different power, something not at all in keeping with the unity and omnipotence of God. In the whole of the divine work, however, it is really a question of only a single act of divine rule. This act is, of course, differentiated and flexible within itself. But it is not arrested or broken. It fulfils itself step by step, and at each step it is irresistible. We can and should recognise that in His unbroken grace and truth the one and omnipotent God is the One in whom there is neither error nor mistake, neither weakness nor compromise, but who in and through everything lets His own good-will be done. We can and should recognise that the *regnum Christi* is not one kingdom with others, for in that case it might well be merely hypothetical. On the contrary, it is the kingdom of all kingdoms. We can and should recognise the fact that however we regard man, as creature, sinner or Christian, we must always regard him and understand him as one who is sustained by the hand of God. Neither in the height of creation nor in the depth of sin is he outside the sphere of the divine decision. And if we see in this decision the divine election, this means that he is not outside the sphere of the election of grace. At no time and in no way is he neutral in the face of the resolve and determination which are proper to the will of God in virtue of the decision made between Father and Son from all eternity. For this reason we must see the election at the beginning of all the ways of God, and treat of the doctrine accordingly. We believe that in so doing we shall not be disloyal to the intention which activated Calvin especially as he drew up those different outlines. We shall rather be taking up and realising this very same intention.

When we give to the doctrine the position suggested, it assumes

in Church dogmatics its necessary function ; the function proper to
the concept of election in the biblical testimony to God and to the
work and revelation of God. That God elects man, that He determines man for Himself, having first determined Himself for man, is
not one moment with others in the prophetic and apostolic testimony.
Enclosed within the testimony to God Himself, it is the moment which
is the substance and basis of all other moments in that testimony.
The biblical witness to God is itself wholly characterised by the fact
that this God has determined Himself the Lord of Israel and the
Church, and as such the Lord of the universe and man in general. It
is for this reason and to this end that He wills the calling of Israel
and the Church and the creation of the universe and man. It is only
in this self-determination, and in the indestructible order which results
from it, that the Bible bears witness to God, and that according to
that biblical witness God can be truly known as God. It is, then,
only upon the basis of this divine self-determination that, according
to this witness, all the works of God are what they are. In this self-
determination and only in this self-determination does God will to
be known, to be loved and feard, to be believed in and worshipped
as Creator, Reconciler and Redeemer. There is no single moment in
the biblical witness that must not be understood in the light of it.
There is no single moment in this witness that can be understood in
the light of anything else, whether out of religious or philosophical
caprice or perversity. It is in virtue of this self-determination that
God wills to be God solely in Jesus Christ. And it is as such that He
is the Lord of Israel and the Church, and as such, and not otherwise,
that He is the Creator, Reconciler and Redeemer of the universe and
man. But it is with this primal decision of God that the doctrine of
election deals.

In the first sub-section we established the fact that inasmuch as
the doctrine does deal with this decision it contains and expresses
the sum of the Gospel. It does so because it is the good news, the
best news, the wholly redemptive news, that from all eternity God
has decided to be God only in this way, and in the movement towards
man which takes on this form. Then in the second sub-section we
established the fact that the basis of our knowledge of this doctrine
cannot be any other than its basis in actuality, i.e., Jesus Christ
Himself, who because He is the Head of Israel and the Church is the
content of this primal decision of God, and as such the authentic
revelation of it. We treat of the doctrine as understood in this way
within the context of the doctrine of God. And as an integral part of
this doctrine we put it at the head of all other doctrines. Thus placed,
it is in relation to all that follows a necessary witness to the fact that
all God's works and ways have their origin in His grace. In virtue
of this self-determination of His, God is from the very first the gracious
God. For this self-determination is identical with the decree of His

movement towards man. This movement is always the very best thing that could happen to man. The reality and revelation of this movement is Jesus Christ Himself. This movement is an eternal movement, and therefore one which encloses man in his finitude and temporality. It is free, and therefore it is entirely grounded in the good-pleasure and the will of God. It is constant, and therefore it cannot deceive, nor can it be withdrawn or rejected. In virtue of the self-determination which is to be presented in the doctrine of election, God is, as the gracious God, the constantly self-asserting Subject which calls always for renewed thought and consideration. He is *Deus ipse* at the beginning of all His ways and works. From the standpoint of this beginning and this Subject these ways and works are *per se*, in all circumstances and in all forms and stages, the ways and works of grace. Since it is the divine self-determination, the primal decision from which they derive cannot be over-ridden, abrogated, weakened or altered by any other decision. Always and from every point of view they derive from the fact that from and to all eternity God has moved towards man freely and therefore definitively. Always and from every point of view they derive from Jesus Christ, the One who in the will of God was to be, was, is, and will be both very man and very God. Always and from every point of view they are what from all eternity they were necessarily foreordained to be. And that applies to all God's works without exception. There is no such thing as a created nature which has its purpose, being or continuance apart from grace, or which may be known in this purpose, being and continuance except through grace. Even sin, death, the devil and hell—works of God's permissive will which are negative in their effects—even these works do not constitute any exception to the general rule. For even in these God's knowing and willing are gracious, even though they take effect as negation (and in that sense are permissive). Even the enemies of God are the servants of God and the servants of His grace. Thus God and the enemies of God cannot be known at all unless both they and their negative character and whole work of negation are known in the service which they render as instruments of the eternal, free and immutable grace of God. God is gracious and continues gracious even where there is no grace. And it is only by grace that the lack of grace can be recognised as such. For in the beginning, in His primal decision, in Jesus Christ, at the place where alone He can be known as God, where alone He can be known at all, known as the *Deus ipse* which He is still even in His permitting of sin and the devil, even in the terrors of death and hell, God is gracious and not ungracious. To know Him always means to know the gracious God, even in sin and death, even under the dominion of the devil, even in the abyss of hell. And conversely, where can there be any true or serious knowledge of sin and the devil, of death and hell, if there is not also a knowledge of the gracious God? But, above all, the blessings and triumphs of His work as Creator, Reconciler and Redeemer do not constitute any exception to this general rule. For except with grace, and through grace, and to the glory of grace, there can be no rejoicing and praise of creation, no receiving of the Holy Spirit and of the enlightenment and guidance of the Holy Spirit, no glory of saints and angels in the consummation of His kingdom, no height and no depth. Church doctrine must speak not only of God Himself, but also of all His ways and works, of all the ways and works of God. But in so doing it must be aware that in their very origin these ways and works have been determined, and at all times and in all places it must make mention of their determination. It must never speak as though it had to do with someone other than the gracious God. It must always give glory to God and bear witness to God as the gracious God. But the gracious God is the One who is God in the beginning, and therefore in the self-determination which is the specific concern of the doctrine of election. This doctrine is the basic witness to the fact that the gracious God is the beginning of all the ways and works of God. It defines grace as the starting-point for all reflection and utterance, the common denominator which should never be omitted in any statements which follow, and which should, if possible, be asserted in some form in these statements. The specific function of the doctrine is, in fact, to bear this basic witness. It is to enable it to fulfil this function that we have given to it its present position. To do this we have had to part company with tradition to a more or less noticeable degree. Yet we have also taken up the concern or aim of tradition, doing justice to it in a very different form.

THE ELECTION OF JESUS CHRIST

The election of grace is the eternal beginning of all the ways and works of God in Jesus Christ. In Jesus Christ God in His free grace determines Himself for sinful man and sinful man for Himself. He therefore takes upon Himself the rejection of man with all its consequences, and elects man to participation in His own glory.

1. JESUS CHRIST, ELECTING AND ELECTED

Between God and man there stands the person of Jesus Christ, Himself God and Himself man, and so mediating between the two. In Him God reveals Himself to man. In Him man sees and knows God. In Him God stands before man and man stands before God, as is the eternal will of God, and the eternal ordination of man in accordance with this will. In Him God's plan for man is disclosed, God's judgment on man fulfilled, God's deliverance of man accomplished, God's gift to man present in fulness, God's claim and promise to man declared. In Him God has joined Himself to man. And so man exists for His sake. It is by Him, Jesus Christ, and for Him and to Him, that the universe is created as a theatre for God's dealings with man and man's dealings with God. The being of God is His being, and similarly the being of man is originally His being. And there is nothing that is not from Him and by Him and to Him. He is the Word of God in whose truth everything is disclosed and whose truth cannot be over-reached or conditioned by any other word. He is the decree of God behind and above which there can be no earlier or higher decree and beside which there can be no other, since all others serve only the fulfilment of this decree. He is the beginning of God before which there is no other beginning apart from that of God within Himself. Except, then, for God Himself, nothing can derive from any other source or look back to any other starting-point. He is the election of God before which and without which and beside which God cannot make any other choices. Before Him and without Him and beside Him God does not, then, elect or will anything. And He is the election (and on that account the beginning and the decree and the Word) of the free grace of God. For it is God's free grace that in Him He elects to be man and to have dealings with man and to join

94

Himself to man. He, Jesus Christ, is the free grace of God as not content simply to remain identical with the inward and eternal being of God, but operating *ad extra* in the ways and works of God. And for this reason, before Him and above Him and beside Him and apart from Him there is no election, no beginning, no decree, no Word of God. Free grace is the only basis and meaning of all God's ways and works *ad extra*. For what *extra* is there that the ways and works could serve, or necessitate, or evoke ? There is no *extra* except that which is first willed and posited by God in the presupposing of all His ways and works. There is no *extra* except that which has its basis and meaning as such in the divine election of grace. But Jesus Christ is Himself the divine election of grace. For this reason He is God's Word, God's decree and God's beginning. He is so all-inclusively, comprehending absolutely within Himself all things and everything, enclosing within Himself the autonomy of all other words, decrees and beginnings.

We shall elucidate these statements by a short exegesis of the passage Jn. 1^{1-2}:
Ἐν ἀρχῇ ἦν ὁ λόγος, καὶ ὁ λόγος ἦν πρὸς τὸν θεόν, καὶ θεὸς ἦν ὁ λόγος. οὗτος ἦν ἐν ἀρχῇ πρὸς τὸν θεόν.
" *In the beginning* was the Word "—this is the emphasis according to the order of the sentence. The sentence does tell us, of course, what was in the beginning. But it does so in the form of a declaration about the Word. The Word was in the beginning. It did not arise later. It did not enter in as one moment with others in the totality of the world created by God and differentiated from Him. Again, it was not merely the first and original link in the development of this totality. It was not merely (as Philo said of his Logos); πρεσβύτατος τῶν γένεσιν εἰληφότων. And we certainly must not understand in this sense what Prov. 8^{22} says concerning wisdom : " The Lord possessed me in the beginning of his way, before his works of old ; " for the continuation in v. 23 tells us : " I was set up from everlasting, from the beginning, or ever the earth was." Again we cannot understand in this sense the statement in Col. 1^{15}, πρωτότοκος τῆς κτίσεως, for it continues : ὅτι ἐν αὐτῷ ἐκτίσθη τὰ πάντα. The First-begotten is thus clearly removed from the series of created realities. What is said in these passages, and in the Johannine ἐν ἀρχῇ (or ἀπ᾽ ἀρχῆς, 1 Jn. 1^1) is this. The Word as such is before and above all created realities. It stands completely outside the series of created things. It precedes all being and all time. It is like God Himself. As was rightly said concerning it in the expositions of the 4th century : " There was no time when it was not." And this Word was in the beginning and at the beginning of all that which, being created by Him, is distinct from God. Within the sphere of this creation there is, then, no time which is not enclosed by the eternity of this Word, no space which does not have its origin in its omnipresence and which is not for this reason conditioned by it. There is, in fact, no possibility of escaping or avoiding this Word. But the question arises, where, except in or with God, can there be any being which is " in the beginning " in this sense.

The answer to this question is given in the second statement. " And the Word was *with God*." Here the emphasis falls beyond all doubt upon the two final words. This statement too, then, constitutes an assertion concerning the Word. It declares that there was, in fact, no being " in the beginning " in this sense except in and with God. But the Word itself was in and with God. Πρὸς θεόν does not mean " for God," as in the famous saying of Augustine : *Ad te me creasti* ; nor does it mean " in communication with God " (T. Zahn). These statements could both be made of a being which was not " in the beginning " in this sense. Strictly speaking, they could be made only of such a being. If the second assertion is to elucidate and not to contradict the first, then the πρός must be understood quite plainly and simply to mean this : That He could be " in the beginning " who was with God, who is beyond all created reality, because He belongs to God, because His being is as the being of God Himself. It was because the Word was " with God " in this sense that it could also be " in the beginning." But how could it be " with God " in this sense ? What do we mean when we say that it belongs to God, or that its being is as the being of God Himself ?

The answer to this question is given in the third statement ; and as in the first two, we must again find our subject in " the Word " : " And the Word was *God*." The sentence tells us, then, that the Word was itself God ; it participated absolutely in the divine mode of being, in the divine being itself. The fact that there is no article before " God " does not mean that deity is not ascribed to the Word in the strictest and most proper sense. What is done is simply this. The mode of being, and being, of a second " He," the Logos, is identified with the mode of being and being of the first " He," God. Thus the deity of ὁ θεός is also ascribed to ὁ λόγος. In saying this, we are at once pre-supposing that in view of the definite article " the Word " ought to be character-ised as a " He " in exactly the same way as " the God." That this presupposition is correct is forcibly demonstrated by what follows. And if it is correct, then here, too, the exegesis of the 4th century must have been on the right track with its doctrine of the *homoousion*, or unity of substance of the three distinctive divine persons, prosopa or hypostases. The step taken in the third sentence is this—that the Word can be with God, and it can be " in the beginning," because as person (that of the Son) it participates in its own way with the person of " God " (the Father) in the same dignity and perfection of the one divine being. It must be conceded that read in this way, after the manner of so-called " orthodoxy," the verse is at any rate meaningful within itself, each word being intelligible in its own place.

But who or what is the Word whose predicates are declared in Jn. 1[1] ? As is well known, in the Johannine Prologue the concept recurs only once (v. 14), and in the rest of the Gospel it does not recur at all in this sense. In the presenta-tion as a whole its character is obviously that of a stop-gap. It is a preliminary indication of the place where later something or someone quite different will be disclosed. The same is true of the only other place in the whole of the New Testament where the concept is unequivocally used in the same sense as in Jn. 1[1]. In Rev. 19[13] it is said of the Rider on the white horse that one of the diadems on His head bears a name which no one knows (i.e., understands) but He Himself. And this name, which can be read but which only He can understand, this ideogram which only He can decipher, is as follows : ὁ λόγος τοῦ θεοῦ. Here, too, the concept is used as a stop-gap. It is a preliminary and veiling concept for that other and true concept which the Rider on the white horse has of Him-self, which, as it were, consists and is expressed in His very existence. In Jn. 1[1] the reference is very clear : ὁ λόγος is unmistakably substituted for Jesus. His is the place which the predicates attributed to the Logos are meant at once to mark off, to clear and to reserve. It is He, Jesus, who is in the beginning with God. It is He who by nature is God. This is what is guaranteed in Jn. 1[1]. But why specifically by means of this concept ? If we ask this as a question in historical genetics, we are faced by a whole host of possibilities, ranging from the Logos of Philo to the personal, semi-personal and impersonal essences of Man-daistic theory. Within this medley it will probably always be a waste of time to look for that unknown quantity, the source used by the writer of the Fourth Gospel ; for we do not know in what form the author took over this widespread and variously used concept, nor do we know in what way he transformed this concept, nor finally can we be absolutely certain of the fact that he did take over the concept from some other source. What is certain is that he had no intention of honouring Jesus by investing Him with the title of Logos, but rather that he honoured the title itself by applying it a few lines later as a predicate of Jesus. He offered no other exegesis of the concept apart from that in which he made this predication. We can only say that by offering this exegesis he rejects all other possible interpretations of the concept in this context, interpretations which would define it primarily and essentially as the principle of an epistemology or of a metaphysical explanation of the universe. There is no doubt that in Jn. 1³ (and 1¹⁰) a cosmogenic function is ascribed to the Logos. But there is also no doubt that the Evangelist did not adopt the concept for the sake of this interpretation of it. It is rather that in vv. 3 and 10 he recalls this interpretation in order to emphasise and elucidate what he has said in vv. 1 and 2. And he leaves it at once without construing anything more out of it. Having touched lightly on this aspect of the concept he moves forward quickly to his own conclusion : the Word was the bearer of life (v. 4), the life which was the light of men in their age-long battle with darkness (vv. 5, 9) ; the Word became flesh ; the Word is the μονογενὴς θεός, which was in the bosom of the Father ; and as such the Word has made known to us the unknown God (v. 18). Such is the Johannine Logos so far as we can define it at all apart from the recognition that the Logos is Jesus. It is the principle, the intrinsically divine basis of God's revelation, God's supernatural communication to man. And this was what the author of the Fourth Gospel found in Jesus. Jesus was the life which was light, the revelation of God, the saying, or address, or communication in which God declares Himself to us. But as this revelation He was not something other outside and alongside God. He was God Himself within the revelation. He was not revelation alone, then, but in the revelation He was the principle, the intrinsically divine basis of revelation. He was revelation in its complete and absolute form. It was to show this that the Evangelist—no matter where he derived the concept, or what else it conveyed to him—made use of the term Logos. We can be satisfied with the translation " Word." In German the word *Spruch* (saying) might be better, since it would proclaim the contents of v. 2 in the masculine as is done in the Greek. As is well known, Goethe's *Faust* found it difficult to rate the concept "word" so highly, and he thought that the term should be translated differently. " Suddenly I see the way and boldly write : In the beginning was the deed." But the moment he had boldly written it, the devil appeared ! " Word " or " saying " is the simple but genuine form in which person communicates with person. It is by the Word that God communicates with man. Because it is God's Word it is not called " a " word but " the " Word, the Word of all words. There is no need to import into this Word reason, signification, power, etc., for it contains all these within itself in virtue of the fact that it is Word, the divine self-communication proceeding from person to person and uniting God and man. It may be noticed that the Evangelist presupposes that the Word is there, that it has been given or spoken. This is not something which must be proved, or inferred from anything else. The force of the threefold ἦν in Jn. 1¹ is more than axiomatic. It points to an eternal happening and to a temporal : to an eternal in the form of time, and to a temporal with the content of eternity. For this reason no stress is laid upon the threefold ὁ λόγος, and there can be no point in attaching oneself to this or that signification of the concept as authenticated elsewhere. It is there as an ideogram, like the inscription on the diadem of the Rider of the Apocalypse. It is something which we can read but not comprehend. It is the *x* in an equation whose value we can know only when the equation has been solved. Of this solution Jn. 1¹⁹ is the beginning. But the Prologue states the equation, giving the unknown factor its place in relation to those which are known, God, the universe, man, the testimony (of John the Baptist) and the believer. The beginning of this presentation is Jn. 1¹: Where God is, that is, in the beginning, there is the Word. It must, therefore, belong to God, and by nature it must itself be God. If the Word of God is to be there in the beginning, then God Himself is required, no more and no less. But the Word is there, and therefore God Himself must be there with it. Thus far v. 1.

The Prologue continues : "The same was in the beginning with God." The supposition that these words are a recapitulation of v. 1 is quite unconvincing. For one thing, v. 1 does not stand in need of any such recapitulation. For another, there is no clear reason why it should be given in v. 2. And since the third assertion in v. 1 is itself the elucidation of the first two, we can hardly hold (with T. Zahn) that the repetition of the first two in v. 2 is meant, for its part, to be an elucidation of the third. We ought rather to follow A. Schlatter on this point : that the οὗτος must be understood as a reference forward and not backward. The expression οὗτος ἦν occurs again in the Prologue, at the climax of the most important record of the witness of the Baptist (v. 15 f.) : "This was he of whom I said, He that cometh after me is preferred before me : for he was before me. And of his fulness have all we received, and grace for grace." The remaining contents of the Prologue all show clearly enough that the Evangelist has appropriated this attestation of the Baptist, and that he has identified himself with the testimony which he bore. This first becomes apparent in the significant anticipation in v. 2. The Evangelist himself (also a " John ") points to οὗτος ἦν. And this reference in v. 2 shows us that v. 1 is meant as the marking off or reservation of a place, for it points us to that which fills the place indicated by the concept Logos. The statement tells us, then, that " the same," the One who no more needs to be made known as a person than the One described as ὁ θεός, the One whom we all know because He has come forth to all of us, " the same " was in the beginning with God, and " the same " was Jesus. For this reason, when we think of the Word which was in the beginning with God and which belongs to God, we may count upon the fact that it has been spoken with a certitude which is far more than axiomatic. And for this reason, too, we have no need to project anything into eternity, for at this point eternity is time, i.e., the eternal name has become a temporal name, and the divine name a human. It is of this name that we speak. V. 2 is, then, a part of the third assertion of v. 1, but it is not a repetition of it. What v. 2 does tell us, with backward reference to v. 1, is that " the same," Jesus, is the Word which partakes of the divine essence. What it tells us is that " the same," Jesus, was in the beginning because as this same divine Word he belongs legitimately to God. Thus this witness of the Evangelist, this οὗτος ἦν, answers two of our questions at the same time : Who was in the beginning with God, sharing His divine nature ? and : Is it true that there was anyone in the beginning with God, sharing the divine essence ? The answer to both questions is that it was He, Jesus. The naming of this name (and for the moment it is only indicated) is at once a thesis and a proof in relation to that which was in the beginning with God. And as v. 2 is to be understood in this way, as a reference to the name and person of Jesus, we are forced to the following exposition of the third statement in v. 1, with its identification of two distinctive persons in respect of their divine essence : that side by side with the One described as ὁ θεός, and itself partaker of the same θεότης, there has entered in the Word (that Word which is " the same," οὗτος).

It is to Him, then, " the same," that the αὐτοῦ refers in vv. 3 and 10, where we are told that τὰ πάντα, the κόσμος, was made by Him, and that without Him was not anything made that was made. And here the unique statement of Jn. 1¹⁻² issues in a reflection which is quite familiar in the witness of the New Testament. Thus in Col. 1¹⁷ we read that the Son of God—the Son *in concreto* and not *in abstracto*, Jesus Christ, who is the Head of His body, the Church—this Son is " before all things," and " in Him all things consist." It was, in fact,

" the good pleasure of the fulness of the Godhead " (and here the concept of election is quite clear) to take form, or to take up residence in Him (κατοικῆσαι . . . σωματικῶς, Col. 1¹⁹, 2⁹). For this reason we must understand the passages 2 Cor. 4⁴, Col. 1¹⁵ and Hebrews 1³ exclusively : He is the one " image of God," " the effulgence of his glory," " the image of his substance," and therefore " before all things " He is " the mystery of God . . . in whom are hid all the treasures of wisdom and knowledge," " the mystery which from the beginning of the world hath been hid in God, who created all things " (Eph. 3⁹). For this reason He Himself is categorical and exclusive : He is " the first-born of every creature " (Col. 1¹⁵), and in order " that in all things he might have the pre-eminence " He is affirmed to be such by the fact that " he is the beginning, the first-born from the dead " (1 Cor. 15²⁰, Col. 1¹⁸). For this reason He is the κεφαλή of all principality and power (Col. 2¹⁰), so that in the revelation and reconciliation which He has accomplished there can be only an ἀνακεφαλαιοῦσθαι of all things, " both which are in heavens, and which are on the earth " (Eph. 1¹⁰). For this reason He is " the fulness of him that filleth all in all " (Eph. 1²³), so that His temporal manifestation and work must necessarily be called " the fulness of time(s) " (Gal. 4⁴, Eph. 1¹⁰). It is, then, only by way of explanation of His being as the God who is conceived of in this primal, original and basic movement towards man that Heb. 1² (like Jn. 1³, ¹⁰) says concerning Him that He whom God " appointed heir of all things " is the one " by whom also he made the worlds," and Heb. 1³ that He " upholds all things (φέρων) by the word of his power," and Col. 1¹⁶ that " by him were all things created, that are in heavens, and that are in earth, visible and invisible . . . all things were created by him and for him."

If that is true, then in the name and person of Jesus Christ we are called upon to recognise the Word of God, the decree of God and the election of God at the beginning of all things, at the beginning of our own being and thinking, at the basis of our faith in the ways and works of God. Or, to put it the other way, in this person we are called upon to recognise the beginning of the Word and decree and election of God, the conclusive and absolute authority in respect of the aim and origin of all things. And this authority we must acknowledge not merely as something which is like God, but as God Himself, since God Himself in all His ways and works willed wholly and utterly to bear this name, and actually does bear it : the Father of our Lord Jesus Christ, the Son of the Father, the Holy Spirit of the Father and the Son. There is given to man under heaven no ἕτερον ὄνομα . . . ἐν ᾧ δεῖ σωθῆναι ἡμᾶς (Ac. 4¹²), and if this is the case, it is decided even more comprehensively that " at the name of Jesus every knee should bow, of things in heaven, and things in earth, and things under the earth " (Phil. 2¹⁰). If this is so, then there is no higher place at which our thinking and speaking of the works of God can begin than this name. We are not thinking or speaking rightly of God Himself if we do not take as our starting-point the fact which should be both " first and last " : that from all eternity God elected to bear this name. Over against all that is really outside God, Jesus Christ is the eternal will of God, the eternal decree of God and the eternal beginning of God.

It is as God's election that we must understand the Word and decree and beginning of God over against the reality which is distinct from Himself. When we say this, we say that in His decision all God's works, both " inward " and " outward," rest upon His freedom. We say, too, that in so far as these works are done in time, they rest upon the eternal decision of God by which time is founded and governed. God elects. It is this that precedes absolutely all other being and happening. And at this point both subject and predicate clearly lead us beyond time and beyond the nexus of the created world and its history. They lead us to the sphere where God is with Himself, the sphere of His free will and pleasure. And this sphere is His eternity, which gives to the world and time and all that is in them their origin, their direction and their destiny.

But there is a temptation here, and we have already seen something of the part played by it in the history of the doctrine. It is the temptation to think of this sphere as at once empty and undetermined. It is the temptation to think of God the Father, Son and Holy Spirit merely as a Subject which can and does elect, a Subject which is furnished, of course, with supereminent divine attributes, but which differs from other such subjects only by the fact that in its election it is absolutely free. It is not responsible to any other being for the nature or direction of this election. It must be acknowledged, then, as the Subject whose election is always absolutely right. And it follows that its election is absolutely unconditioned, or is conditioned only by the Subject in and for itself and as such. And this means that the choice actually made must be regarded as a *decretum absolutum*. This construction has been very influential in the history of the doctrine. And it can still actually be a temptation, and a temptation which we must recognise and resist. And first, we must ask a question of its exponents. In respect of the whole attitude and being of God *ad extra*, in His relationship with the order created by Him, can there be anything higher or more distinctive and essential in God than His electing ? Must we not say that in His confrontation of the creature, in His relationship with everything which is outside Himself, God is God absolutely in the fact that from all eternity He elects, He decides one way or the other concerning the being and nature of the creature (with all that this involves) ? And if so, how are we to distinguish God's electing from His Word and decree in the beginning ? Are we not forced to say that the electing consists in this Word and decree in the beginning ; and conversely, that this Word and decree in the beginning are God's electing, His free, subjective self-determination, the primal act of lordship over everything else, independently of all outward constraint, conditioning or compulsion ? And if we agree in this with the exponents of the construction referred to, we must ask further whether we can agree in saying that God's Word and decree in the beginning consist in the fact that He has assumed and bears the name of Jesus Christ, that this name itself is God's Word and decree in the beginning. But if this is so, how can we avoid the all-important assertion that in its origin, in its real truth and power as that which is decisive for all that follows, the election of God consists in the fact that from all eternity, in an act of unconditional self-determination, He has ordained Himself the bearer of this name ? If this is not God's election, then what else can it be ? What choice can precede the choice by which God has of Himself

chosen to have with Himself in the beginning of all things the Word
which is Jesus ? What *decretum absolutum* is there that secretly or
openly can over-ride or challenge this *decretum absolutum* ? What
room is there even for the notion of a *decretum absolutum* ? In
face of this choice, how can we regard as absolute and autonomous
the choice by which God decides for the existence and nature of the
creature ? How can we even understand this choice except as it is
included in the choice by which God (obviously first) decides for Himself, i.e., for this self-ordination, this being under the name of Jesus,
this being in Jesus Christ ?

The choice or election of God is basically and properly God's
decision that as described in Jn. 1$^{1-2}$ the Word which is " the same,"
and is called Jesus, should really be in the beginning, with Himself,
like Himself, one with Himself in His deity. And for this reason
it is *per se* an election of grace. This is not, of course, self-evidently
the case. God would not be God, He would not be free, if this had
to be so. " What is man, that thou art mindful of him? and the
son of man, that thou visitest him ? " (Ps. 8^5). The eternal God
was not under an obligation to man to be in Himself the God whose
nature and property it is to bear this name. That He is, in fact, such
a God is grace, something which is not merited by man but can only
be given to him. And that God is gracious, that in assuming this
name He gives Himself to the man who has not merited it, is His
election, His free decree. It is the divine election of grace. In a free
act of determination God has ordained concerning Himself ; He has
determined Himself. Without any obligation, God has put Himself
under an obligation to man, willing that that should be so which according to Jn. 1$^{1-2}$ actually is so. It is grace that it is so, and it is grace
that God willed it to be so.

In the beginning, before time and space as we know them, before
creation, before there was any reality distinct from God which could
be the object of the love of God or the setting for His acts of freedom,
God anticipated and determined within Himself (in the power of His
love and freedom, of His knowing and willing) that the goal and
meaning of all His dealings with the as yet non-existent universe
should be the fact that in His Son He would be gracious towards
man, uniting Himself with him. In the beginning it was the choice
of the Father Himself to establish this covenant with man by giving
up His Son for him, that He Himself might become man in the fulfilment of His grace. In the beginning it was the choice of the Son to
be obedient to grace, and therefore to offer up Himself and to become
man in order that this covenant might be made a reality. In the
beginning it was the resolve of the Holy Spirit that the unity of God, of
Father and Son should not be disturbed or rent by this covenant with
man, but that it should be made the more glorious, the deity of God,
the divinity of His love and freedom, being confirmed and demonstrated

by this offering of the Father and this self-offering of the Son. This choice was in the beginning. As the subject and object of this choice, Jesus Christ was at the beginning. He was not at the beginning of God, for God has indeed no beginning. But He was at the beginning of all things, at the beginning of God's dealings with the reality which is distinct from Himself. Jesus Christ was the choice or election of God in respect of this reality. He was the election of God's grace as directed towards man. He was the election of God's covenant with man.

We are following an important insight of J. Coccejus (*S. Theol.*, 1662, *c.* 37, 2) when we trace back the concept of predestination to the biblical concept of the covenant or testament, the self-committal first revealed to Noah (Gen. 9¹⁴) as God's covenant with " every living creature of all flesh that is upon the earth," then (Gen. 17⁷ᶠ·) as His covenant with Abraham and his posterity, and later (Is. 55³, Jer. 32⁴⁰, Ezek. 16⁶⁰, 37²⁶ and cf. Jer. 50⁵) as His covenant with Israel. By its definition as *bᵉrith 'olam* this self-committal is characterised (no matter what time-concepts may be presupposed) as a relationship which is not haphazard and transitory, but which derives its necessity from God Himself. It is more steadfast than the hills (Is. 54¹⁰). God has sworn it by Himself (Gen. 22¹⁶, Ex. 32¹³, Is. 45²³, 54⁹, 62⁸, Ps. 110⁴, Heb. 6¹³). In Mic. 5² (cf., too, Is. 9⁷, Dan. 7¹³ᶠ·) it can be said of the Messiah that " his goings forth have been from of old, from everlasting." As the Jews are aware in Jn. 12³⁴, He " abideth " for ever. According to Heb.7¹⁶ᶠ· (cf. Ps. 110⁴), He " is a priest for ever " " after the power of an endless life." " Through the eternal Spirit he offered himself without spot to God " (Heb. 9¹⁴). " Before Abraham was," He was, and " Abraham rejoiced to see his day " (Jn. 8⁵⁶ᶠ·). We also find references to this divine past in the εὐδόκησα of Mt. 3¹⁷, the εὐδόκησεν of Col. 1¹⁹, the διέθετο of Lk. 22²⁹, and the προέθετο of Eph. 1⁹. Now it is quite impossible to distinguish all these from the reality which is treated of in the New Testament passages which speak of the election in express connexion with the name and person of Jesus. In Eph. 1³⁻⁵ the one follows directly on the other : there is a general mention of the blessings with which we have been blessed " in heavenly places " in Christ εὐλογήσας ἡμᾶς . . . ἐν Χριστῷ, and then there is the particular statement : ἐξελέξατο ἡμᾶς ἐν αὐτῷ πρὸ καταβολῆς κόσμου . . . προορίσας ἡμᾶς εἰς υἱοθεσίαν διὰ Ἰησοῦ Χριστοῦ εἰς αὐτόν, κατὰ τὴν εὐδοκίαν τοῦ θελήματος αὐτοῦ. Again, in Eph. 1⁹⁻¹¹ there is the general : προέθετο εὐδοκίαν . . . ἀνακεφαλαιώσασθαι τὰ πάντα ἐν τῷ Χριστῷ, and the particular ἐν αὐτῷ, ἐν ᾧ καὶ ἐκληρώθημεν προορισθέντες κατὰ πρόθεσιν τοῦ τὰ πάντα ἐνεργοῦντος κατὰ τὴν βουλὴν τοῦ θελήματος αὐτοῦ. From these passages, and from Eph. 3¹, we gather that the concrete form of the divine εὐλογία, and of the εὐδοκία of the eternal πρόθεσις is in fact that προορίζειν which will be made known by the existence of the Church (Eph. 3¹⁰), so assuredly did God " purpose his eternal πρόθεσις in Jesus Christ our Lord." And conversely, what we now experience as our deliverance and calling takes place only because it is gifted to us as God's own purpose (πρόθεσις) and grace : ἐν τῷ Χριστῷ Ἰησοῦ πρὸ χρόνων αἰωνίων (2 Tim. 1¹⁹) ; because Christ as the Lamb without blemish and without spot was προεγνωσμένος πρὸ καταβολῆς κόσμου (1 Pet. 1²⁰, cf. Rev. 13⁸) ; because ἀπὸ καταβολῆς κόσμου His high-priestly suffering was necessary (ἔδει) (Heb. 9²⁶). " Him, being delivered by the determinate counsel and foreknowledge (πρόγνωσις) of God, ye have taken, and by wicked hands have crucified and slain " (Ac. 2²³). " For to do whatsoever thy hand and thy counsel determined before to come to pass," both Herod and Pilate, with the Gentiles and the peoples of Israel, were gathered together against thy holy servant Jesus (Ac. 4²⁷ᶠ·). Again, the glory with which Jesus prayed that He might be glorified (in

Jn. 17⁵) is none other than that glory which He had with the Father before the
world was. In these texts it is not of any importance whether the mention of
God's will and purpose preceding the history, or more specifically the expressions
πρὸ χρόνων αἰωνίων and πρὸ or ἀπὸ καταβολῆς κόσμου, are meant to refer to the
eternity of God in itself, or " only " to the beginning of the creation, and therefore of the universe and time. What is certain is that in all the passages the
reference is to the beginning of all God's ways and works *ad extra*. And it is
also certain that all these passages describe this beginning under the name of
Jesus Christ, whose person is that of the executor within the universe and time
of the primal decision of divine grace, the person itself being obviously the
content of this decision.

In its simplest and most comprehensive form the dogma of predestination consists, then, in the assertion that the divine predestination
is the election of Jesus Christ. But the concept of election has a double
reference—to the elector and to the elected. And so, too, the name
of Jesus Christ has within itself the double reference : the One called
by this name is both very God and very man. Thus the simplest
form of the dogma may be divided at once into the two assertions
that Jesus Christ is the electing God, and that He is also elected man.

In so far as He is the electing God, we must obviously—and above
all—ascribe to Him the active determination of electing. It is not
that He does not also elect as man, i.e., elect God in faith. But this
election can only follow His prior election, and that means that it
follows the divine electing which is the basic and proper determination
of His existence.

In so far as He is man, the passive determination of election is
also and necessarily proper to Him. It is true, of course, that even
as God He is elected ; the Elected of His Father. But because as the
Son of the Father He has no need of any special election, we must
add at once that He is the Son of God elected in His oneness with
man, and in fulfilment of God's covenant with man. Primarily, then,
electing is the divine determination of the existence of Jesus Christ,
and election (being elected) the human.

Jesus Christ is the electing God. We must begin with this assertion
because by its content it has the character and dignity of a basic
principle, and because the other assertion, that Jesus Christ is elected
man, can be understood only in the light of it.

We may notice at once the critical significance of this first assertion
in its relation to the traditional understanding of the doctrine. In
particular, it crowds out and replaces the idea of a *decretum absolutum*.
That idea does, of course, give us an answer to the question about the
electing God. It speaks of a good-pleasure of God which in basis and
direction is unknown to man and to all beings outside God Himself.
This good-pleasure is omnipotent and incontrovertible in its decisions.
If we are asked concerning its nature, then ultimately no more can
be said than that it is divine, and therefore absolutely supreme and
authoritative. But now in the place of this blank, this unknown

quantity, we are to put the name of Jesus Christ. According to the witness of the Bible, when we are called upon to define and name the first and decisive decision which transcends and includes all others, it is definitely not in order to answer with a mysterious shrug of the shoulders. How can the doctrine of predestination be anything but " dark " and obscure if in its very first tenet, the tenet which determines all the rest, it can speak only of a *decretum absolutum* ? In trying to understand Jesus Christ as the electing God we abandon this tradition, but we hold fast by Jn. 1¹⁻².

Jesus Christ was in the beginning with God. He was so not merely in the sense that in view of God's eternal knowing and willing all things may be said to have been in the beginning with God, in His plan and decree. For these are two separate things : the Son of God in His oneness with the Son of Man, as foreordained from all eternity ; and the universe which was created, and universal history which was willed for the sake of this oneness, in their communion with God, as foreordained from all eternity. On the one hand, there is the Word of God by which all things were made, and, on the other, the things fashioned by that Word. On the one hand, there is God's eternal election of grace, and, on the other, God's creation, reconciliation and redemption grounded in that election and ordained with reference to it. On the one hand, there is the eternal election which as it concerns man God made within Himself in His pre-temporal eternity, and, on the other, the covenant of grace between God and man whose establishment and fulfilment in time were determined by that election. We can and must say that Jesus Christ was in the beginning with God in the sense that all creation and its history was in God's plan and decree with God. But He was so not merely in that way. He was also in the beginning with God as " the first-born of every creature " (Col. 1¹⁵), Himself the plan and decree of God, Himself the divine decision with respect to all creation and its history whose content is already determined. All that is embraced and signified in God's election of grace as His movement towards man, all that results from that election and all that is presupposed in such results— all these are determined and conditioned by the fact that that election is the divine decision whose content is already determined, that Jesus Christ is the divine election of grace.

Thus Jesus Christ is not merely one object of the divine good-pleasure side by side with others. On the contrary, He is the sole object of this good-pleasure, for in the first instance He Himself is this good-pleasure, the will of God in action. He is not merely the standard or instrument of the divine freedom. He is Himself primarily and properly the divine freedom itself in its operation *ad extra*. He is not merely the revelation of the mystery of God. He is the thing concealed within this mystery, and the revelation of it is the revelation of Himself and not of something else. He is not merely the Reconciler between God and man. First, He is Himself the reconciliation between them. And so He is not only the Elected. He is also Himself the Elector, and in the first instance His election must be understood as active. It is true that as the Son of God given by the Father to be one with man, and to take to Himself the form of man, He is elected. It is also true that He does not elect alone, but in company with the electing of the Father and the Holy Spirit. But He does elect. The obedience which He renders as the Son of God is, as genuine obedience, His own decision and electing, a decision and electing no less divinely free than the electing and decision of the Father and the Holy Spirit. Even the fact that He is elected corresponds as closely as possible to His own electing. In the harmony of the triune God He is no less the original Subject of this electing than He is its original object. And only in this harmony can He really be its object, i.e., completely fulfil not His own will but the will of the Father, and thus confirm and to some extent repeat as elected man the election of God. This all rests on the fact that from the very first He participates in the divine election ; that that election is also His election ; that it is He Himself who posits this beginning of all things ; that it is He Himself who executes the decision which issues in the establishment of the covenant between God and man ; that He too, with the Father and the Holy Spirit, is the electing God. If this is not the case, then in respect of the election, in respect of this primal and basic decision of God, we shall have to pass by Jesus Christ, asking of God the Father, or perhaps of the Holy Spirit, how there can be any disclosure of this decision at all. For where can it ever be disclosed to us except where it is executed ? The result will be, of course, that we shall be driven to speculating about a *decretum absolutum* instead of grasping and affirming in God's electing the manifest grace of God. And that means that we shall not know into whose hands we are committing ourselves when we believe in the divine predestination. So much depends upon our acknowledgment of the Son, of the Son of God, as the Subject of this predestination, because it is only in the Son that it is revealed to us as the predestination of God, and therefore of the Father and the Holy Spirit, because it is only as we believe in the Son that we can also believe in the Father and the Holy Spirit, and therefore in the one divine election. If Jesus Christ is only elected, and not also and primarily the Elector, what shall we really know at all of a divine electing and our election ? But of Jesus Christ we know nothing more surely and definitely than this—that in free obedience to His Father He elected to be man, and as man, to do the will of God. If God elects us too, then it is in and with this election of Jesus Christ, in and with this free act of obedience on the part of His Son. It is He who is manifestly the concrete and manifest form of the divine decision—the decision of Father, Son and Holy Spirit—in favour of the covenant to be established between Him and us. It is in Him that the eternal election becomes immediately and directly the promise of our own election as it is enacted in time, our calling, our summoning to faith, our assent to the divine intervention on our behalf, the revelation of ourselves as the sons of God and of God as our Father, the communication of the Holy Spirit who is none other than the Spirit of this act of obedience, the Spirit of obedience itself, and for us the Spirit of adoption. When we ask concerning the reality of the divine election, what can we do but look at the One who performs this act of obedience, who is Himself this act of obedience, who is Himself in the first instance the Subject of this election.

The passages in Jn. 13[18] and 15[16, 19], in which Jesus points to Himself as the One who elects His disciples, are not to be understood loosely but in their strictest and most proper sense. It is clear that at this point John knows nothing of a rivalry which can and should be dissolved by subordination. If Jesus does nothing " of himself" (ἀφ' ἑαυτοῦ, Jn. 5[19, 30]), there is the closely corresponding verse : " Without me ye can do nothing " (Jn. 15[5]). The statement : " All mine are thine," is balanced by the further statement : " Thine are mine " (Jn. 17[10]). Jesus was " sent," but He also " came." As He is in the Father, the Father is also in Him (Jn. 14[10]). " As the Father hath life in himself, so hath he given to the Son to have life in himself " (Jn. 5[26]). The Father glorifies Him, but He, too, glorifies the Father (Jn. 17[1-5]). It is Jesus' " meat to do the will of him that sent him " (Jn. 4[34]), but the Father abiding in Him doeth His works (Jn. 14[10]). The Father is greater than He (Jn. 14[28]), but " he hath given all things into his hand " (Jn. 3[35]), and " hath given him power over all flesh " (Jn. 17[2]). In the same breath He says : " Believe in God, and believe also in me " (Jn. 14[1]). No man can come unto Jesus except it be given unto him of the Father (Jn. 6[65]). He who comes must have " heard and learned of the Father " (Jn. 6[45]). He must have been " drawn " by the Father (Jn. 6[44]). He must have been given Jesus by the Father (Jn. 6[37], 17[6, 9, 24]). But again, He, Jesus, is the way, the truth and the life, and no one cometh unto the Father but by Him (Jn. 14[6]). The Father is the husbandman, but He, Jesus, is the true vine (Jn. 15[1f.]). And for this reason He prays (!) : " Father, I will that they also, whom thou hast given me, be with me where I am ; that they may behold my glory, which thou hast given me " (Jn. 17[24]). In the light of these passages the electing of the disciples ascribed to Jesus must be understood not merely as a function undertaken by Him in an instrumental and representative capacity, but rather as an act of divine sovereignty, in which there is seen in a particular way the primal and basic decision of God which is also that of Jesus Christ. And so, too, behind that summons to " discipleship " which is so frequent in the Synoptics, there stands the statement of Mt. 11[27] : " Neither knoweth any man the Father, save . . . he to whomsoever the Son will reveal him." And that other statement in Mt. 16[17], that the Son may be known only by revelation of the Father, does not in any way restrict this truth, but rather expounds it according to its true sense. Even in those places where it is said of Christ that He " emptied " Himself and " humbled " Himself (Phil. 2[7f.]), or that He " gave " Himself (Gal. 1[4], 1 Tim. 2[6]), or that He " offered " Himself (Gal. 2[20], Eph. 5[2]), or that He " sacrificed " Himself (Heb. 7[27], 9[14]) ; even in those passages which treat of His obedience (Phil. 2[8], Heb. 5[8]), we cannot but see the reflection of the divine spontaneity and activity in which His own existence is grounded, and together with it the covenant between God and man.

It is not sufficient, then, to say with Thomas Aquinas : *ipsa unio naturarum in persona Christi cadit sub aeterna Dei praedestinatione : et ratione huius Christus dicitur esse praedestinatus* (S. *Theol.* III, *qu.* 24, *art.* 1, *c*). It is also true, of course, that in His divinity, as in His humanity, Jesus Christ is indeed *praedestinatus*, the first of the elect. But Thomas would restrict the election of Christ to this passive relationship, and thus to His human nature : *Praedestinatio attribuitur personae Christi non quidem secundum se vel secundum quod subsistit in divina natura sed secundum quod subsistit in humana natura (ib., ad. 2). Solum ratione humanae naturae praedestinatio competit Christo (ib., art. 2 c). Dicitur lumen praedestinationis et gratiae, in quantum per eius praedestinationem et gratiam manifestatur nostra praedestinatio (ib., art. 3 s.c.).* The limitation implied in these sentences is one which cannot be sustained, especially in the light of the Johannine relationship between the Father and the Son. Of course, the fact that Jesus Christ is the Son of God does not rest on the election. What does rest on it is the fact that as such He also becomes man, that as such (to use the Johannine concept) He is "sent," that as such He is the bearer of the divine name of the Father in the world. Between the eternal Godhead of Christ which needs no election and His elected humanity, there is a third possibility which was over-looked by Thomas. And that is the being of Christ in the beginning with God, the act of the good-pleasure of God by which the fulness of the Godhead is allowed to dwell in Him, the covenant which God made with Himself and which is for that reason eternal, the oath which God sware by Himself in the interests of man. But this third possibility does not belong only passively to the *aeterna Dei praedestinatio.* That is, of course, one side of the truth, for the man Jesus can only suffer, receive and accept the divine election, and in that act of the good-pleasure of God, in that covenant of God with Himself, even the eternal Son is elected, ordained and sent by the Father to be its executor. But if He and the Father are one in this unity of the divine name and glory, a unity in which there can be no question of rivalry, then it is clear that the Son, too, is an active Subject of the *aeterna Dei praedestinatio* as Son of Man, that He is Himself the electing God, and that only in this way, and therefore in an unlimited divine sovereignty, is He the Elect, the One who is subjected to the divine pre-destination, the Son who is voluntarily obedient to the Father ; that only in this way and for this reason is He the Son of Man establishing and fulfilling the will of God in the world. If we say only what Thomas would say, then we have knowledge only of the election of the man Jesus as such, and not of the election and personal electing of the Son of God which precedes this election. And once again we make the election of grace a divine mystery detached from the person of Jesus Christ. And of the reality of that mystery we know nothing. We cannot even believe it. In face of it we can only attempt to create the necessary knowledge by constructing a *decretum absolutum.* In such circumstances pre-destination is not only a higher something behind and above the covenant effected and revealed in the divine-human person of Jesus Christ. In its very essence it is something quite different from this person. It is a hidden decree which we can never recognise as divine and to which we cannot possibly be required or advised to entrust ourselves. For trust in the divine decision depends upon whether that decision can be and actually is manifested to us as God's decision. And this is impossible unless it can be and actually is manifested to us as the decision of Jesus Christ. But how can it really be manifested to us as the decision of Jesus Christ if this is not actually the case, as according to the doctrine of Thomas and many others it is not ? How can it really be manifested to us as the decision of Jesus Christ if we can think of the reality of the divine-human person of Jesus Christ only as one of those divine works which come about under the divine foreordination, and not as the work of works, not as the content of the Word and decree of God at the beginning of all things, not as the revelation of the mystery of predestination itself ? Our own election by the grace of God directed towards us is revealed in the election of Jesus Christ. The election of that man is for us the *lumen praedestinationis.* But we can only believe this if we can find in that election the eternal election (both passive and also active)

of the Son of God Himself, if we can be absolutely certain that in Jesus Christ
we have to do immediately and directly with the electing God. If this is not the
case, we are exposed always to the doubt that in the election we have to do
perhaps with the will of a God who has not bound Himself in covenant with us
and who is not gracious towards us. If our own election is truly revealed to us
in the election of the man Jesus—and that is the meaning of the New Testament
when it speaks of this man's election as our Saviour, Head and Priest, and of
the foreordination of His passion and death—it is because in Him we have to
do not merely with elected man, but with the electing God, with the Word and
decree which was in the beginning with God ; not, then, with a messenger or
angel (Is. 63⁹), but with God Himself, with our Saviour, with the One who alone
can be a true and faithful witness to our election.

Thomas, and many others after him, spoke of the election of Jesus Christ
only in this second and passive sense, and with reference only to the man Jesus.
Augustine, too, had spoken of it in this way, and we ourselves must do the same.
But Augustine—and in this we must at once follow him—also looked upwards
to the place where the incarnation, the reality of the divine-human person of
Jesus Christ before the foundation of the world and all other reality, is identical
with the eternal purpose of the good-pleasure of God, and where the eternal
purpose of the good-pleasure of God which precedes all created reality is identical
with the reality of the divine-human person of Jesus Christ. He looked upwards
to the place where the eternal God not only foresees and foreordains this person,
but where He Himself, as the presupposition of its revelation in time, actually
is this person. The text Tit. 1² speaks of " the hope of eternal life, which God,
that cannot lie, promised before times eternal." And in face of this text Augustine
asks how God can make a promise " before times eternal " to men who did not
exist " before times eternal." He answers : *In (Dei) ipsius aeternitate atque in
Verbo eius coaeterno iam praedestinatione fixum erat, quod suo tempore futurum
erat (De civ. Dei* XII, 16). When he described it as an ultimate authority in
which there is established already what was later to be in time, Augustine can
hardly have been thinking of the eternal Word of God in itself and as such. If
he had been, he would have been doing something very far from his purpose
(and expressly contested by him at a later point in the passage), i.e., defining
temporal existence as something externally pre-existent in God. His statement
is, however, understandable, and valid and important, if by the eternal Word
he understands the Word and decree which was in the beginning with God as
maintained in Jn. 1¹⁻², and if he identifies this Word with Jesus, and regards
in Verbo eius coaeterno as an equivalent of *in Verbo eius incarnando*. It is in
this Word that before times eternal life eternal could be and actually was promised
to man, even before man himself existed at all.

But Augustine was not the only father whose witness should be summoned
and heard on this point. Nor was he the first. Before Augustine, and much
more fully, Athanasius had expressed himself as follows (*Or. II c. Arianos, cap.*
75–77) : " As the apostle has said (Tit. 2¹¹), the grace of God brought by the
Saviour hath appeared, and hath been conveyed to us by His coming ; but it
was prepared long before we ourselves or even the world was in being. And the
reason is indeed good and admirable. For it would be unworthy of God to think
of Him as taking counsel to provide for us only later, lest it should appear as
though our circumstances were not previously known to Him. The God of all
things, who created us by His Word, knew what should befall us better than we
ourselves, and He foreknew that after our first righteousness we should transgress
His commandment, and that because of our disobedience we should be expelled
from paradise. For that reason in His loving-kindness and goodness He prepared
beforehand in His Word by whom He created us a provision for our salvation
(προετοιμάζει ἐν τῷ ἰδίῳ λόγῳ, δι᾽ οὗ καὶ ἔκτισεν ἡμᾶς τὴν περὶ τῆς σωτηρίας ἡμῶν οἰκονομίαν).
He did this so that even if we fell, deceived by the serpent, we should not finally

be destroyed, but possessing the redemption and salvation prepared beforehand in the Word, should rise again and live for ever. For the Word Himself was created for our sakes 'the beginning of His ways,' and 'the First-born of the brethren,' and He Himself rose again as the first-fruits from the dead. . . . How, then, has He chosen us before we came into existence, unless, as He Himself says, we were typified and represented in Him ? And how could He have pre-destined us to sonship before man was created, unless the Son Himself had been laid as a foundation before time was, and had undertaken to provide a way of salvation for us (πρὸ τοῦ αἰῶνος τεθεμελίωτο, ἀναδεξάμενος τὴν ὑπὲρ ἡμῶν οἰκονομίαν) ? Or how could we, as the Apostle goes on to say, 'have an inheritance being predestinated' (Eph. 1¹¹), unless the Lord Himself had been laid as a foundation before time was, and had thus been able to purpose in Himself (πρὸ τοῦ αἰῶνος ἦν θεμελιωθείς, ὥστε αὐτὸν πρόθεσιν ἔχειν ὑπὲρ ἡμῶν) to take upon Himself in His flesh the sentence decreed against Him, so that in Him we might finally attain to sonship ? And how could we receive anything before times eternal, we, the creatures of time, who did not then exist, unless the grace appointed for us had already been deposited in Christ (εἰ μὴ ἐν τῷ Χριστῷ ἦν ἀποκειμένη ἡ εἰς ἡμᾶς φθάνουσα χάρις). For that reason, on the day of judgment, when everyone re-ceives according to his works, He says : ' Come, ye blessed of my Father, inherit the kingdom prepared for you from the foundation of the world ' (Mt. 25³⁴). But how, or in whom, could this kingdom be prepared for us before our exist-ence, unless it were in the Lord who was laid as the foundation of it before the world (ἐν τῷ κυρίῳ τῷ πρὸ αἰῶνος εἰς τοῦτο θεμελιωθέντι), in order that built up upon Him we might be the partakers of His life and grace as stones fitly framed together ? And all this happened . . . that, as has been said before, we may rise again shortly after our death and live for ever. For this would be impossible for us as men formed of earth unless before time there had been prepared for us in Christ the hope of life and salvation (εἰ μὴ πρὸ τοῦ αἰῶνος ἦν προετοιμασθεῖσα ἡμῖν ἐν Χριστῷ ἡ τῆς ζωῆς καὶ σωτηρίας ἐλπίς). Obviously the Word which dwelt in our flesh, set there as a beginning of God's ways for His works, was Himself laid as a foundation even as the will of the Father fulfilled in Him . . . that is to say, ' before time,' ' before the earth was,' ' before the mountains were settled ' and ' before the fountains burst forth,' so that when the earth and the moun-tains and the forms of the phenomenal world pass at the end of the present age, we should not decay as they do, but live on, possessing the life and spiritual blessings prepared for us in the Word Himself according to the election even before these things were. And thus it is granted to us not to live only for the moment, but to live for ever in Christ, our life having been grounded and pre-pared in Christ Jesus long before (ἐπειδὴ καὶ πρὸ τούτων ἡ ζωὴ ἡμῶν τεθεμελίωτο καὶ ἡτοίμαστο ἐν Χριστῷ Ἰησοῦ). Nor was it possible for our life to be grounded in any other, but only in the Lord who was before all time and by whom time was, in order that we might inherit eternal life as it was in Him ; for God is good. And being always good, He willed this, He who saw that our weak nature stood in need of His help and salvation. Now a wise master-builder, when he undertakes to build a house, considers at the same time how he may repair that house should it fall into decay after its erection, and weighs up what prepara-tions must be made for that purpose, supplying the foreman with the materials necessary for such repair, and thus making all the preparations for renovation even before the house is built. In like manner, the renewing of our salvation is grounded in Christ even before we were created (τὸν αὐτὸν τρόπον πρὸ ἡμῶν ἡ τῆς ἡμετέρας σωτηρίας ἀνανέωσις θεμελιοῦται ἐν τῷ Χριστῷ), in order that it might be possible for us to be created afresh in Him. The decree and purpose of this fresh creation was formed before time was, but it was only as the need required it that the work was executed and the Saviour came. For in heaven the Lord Himself will represent us all, receiving us to everlasting life." It should be quite clear that Athanasius had a very powerful perception of the third possibility which lies between the being of the eternal Word or Son as such and the reality of the elected man Jesus, together with the election of those who believe in Him as this election is bound up with His election. He saw that the election of the man Jesus and our election, with all the grace and gifts of grace which this includes, have their " foundation," as he himself says, in the eternity of the Word or Son, an eternity which differs not at all from that of the Father. Without prejudice to His eternity, then, he ascribed to the eternal Word or Son of God a determination towards the elected man Jesus and towards the election of believers in Him as they are enclosed in Him. As against Thomas, he not only had a conception of the pure being of the triune God on the one hand, and a conception of the concrete temporal history of salvation willed and fulfilled by God on the other, but over and above that he had also a conception of the concrete decree of salvation made in the bosom of the triune Godhead, and a conception of the Johannine Logos which was identical with Jesus and which was in the beginning with God. He had, then, a truly Christian conception of the divine decree. With Athanasius the decree, or predestination, or election, was, in fact, the decision reached at the beginning of all things, at the beginning of the relationship between God and the reality which is distinct from Him. The Subject of this decision is the triune God—the Son of God no less than the Father and the Holy Spirit. And the specific object of it is the Son of God in His determination as the Son of Man, the God-Man, Jesus Christ, who is as such the eternal basis of the whole divine election.

We can conclude only that in spite of its great richness this insight had little or no influence upon the later development of the doctrine of predestination, to which it might well have given a completely different aspect. Not only Thomas, but the Reformers too, ignored it altogether. They did state that Jesus Christ is for us the *lumen* or *speculum electionis*. But they thought it sufficient to base this belief upon the reference to Jesus Christ as the first of the elect according to His human nature. They restricted themselves to this basis with the same exclusiveness as Thomas. They missed the fact that this basis is quite insufficient to explain the ἐν αὐτῷ of Eph. 1⁴. And they also missed the fact that to establish the certainty of a belief in our own salvation it is not sufficient merely to say that in respect of our election we must cleave only to Jesus Christ on the ground that He must be regarded as the first of the elect, the Head of all others, the means chosen by the electing God for the execution of that which He determined concerning those elected by Him. A statement of this kind will hardly serve even as a truly effective or penetrating pastoral admonition. For when we tackle that question which is no mere quibble, but decisive for each of us, the question whether we ourselves belong to those who profit by what God has ordained to be of benefit to His elect in and through the means which He first elected, in other words, whether we ourselves are of the number of the elect, what is the value of an answer of this type ? If in regard to the decisive factor, the election itself, or the electing God, we cannot fix our gaze and keep it fixed on Jesus Christ, because the electing God is not identical with Christ but behind and above Him, because in the beginning with God we have to reckon with someone or something other than the οὗτος of Jn. 1², a decision of the divine good-pleasure quite unrelated to and not determined by Him, what useful purpose can such an answer serve ? Of what avail is it to exhort us, as did the Reformers, and after them orthodox Protestants of both confessions, that we must acquiesce in the hidden decision of that ultimate authority, respecting it as a secret ? Of what avail is it for the Calvinists to protest that as God's decision it is based on grounds which are just and adequate although beyond our comprehension, or for the Lutherans to assist us with the comforting assurance that this decision is determined by the general loving-kindness of God towards us ? If it is not true that Jesus Christ Himself is for us the electing God, then all these attempts at consolation point us elsewhere than to the Word of God. We are directed to a different mystery from that of the cradle and cross of Christ, a different revelation from that of His resurrection. And all the earnest statements concerning the majesty and mystery of God, all the well-meaning protestations of His fatherly loving-kindness, cannot in any way alter the fact that we necessarily remain anxious in respect of our election. For with statements of this kind we neither can nor ought to let ourselves be appeased. How can we have assurance in respect of our own election except by the Word of God ? And how can even the Word of God give us assurance on this point if this Word, if Jesus Christ, is not really the electing God, not the election itself, not our election, but only an elected means whereby the electing God—electing elsewhere and in some other way—executes that which He has decreed concerning those whom He has—elsewhere and in some other way—elected ? The fact that Calvin in particular not only did not answer but did not even perceive this question is the decisive objection which we have to bring against his whole doctrine of predestination. The electing God of Calvin is a *Deus nudus absconditus*. It is not the *Deus revelatus* who is as such the *Deus absconditus*, the eternal God. All the dubious features of Calvin's doctrine result from the basic failing that in the last analysis he separates God and Jesus Christ, thinking that what was in the beginning with God must be sought elsewhere than in Jesus Christ. Thus with all his forceful and impressive acknowledgment of the divine election of grace, ultimately he still passes by the grace of God as it has appeared in Jesus Christ. We have seen already how the Synod of Dort failed to answer this same question. It merely repeated, more harshly if anything, the unsatisfactory answer already given by Calvin. We have shown, too, that the Dutch Remonstrants on the one hand and the Lutherans on the other, while they did perceive and answer the question, unfortunately answered it in such a way as to alter the concept of the divine election, of the free and eternal decision of God, replacing it by the quite different concept of a divinely established religious world-order. In the last resort, then, they denied that the election of grace was God's election ; and with the Remonstrants there was the quite unmistakeable introduction of a new and humanistic Pelagianism from which Neo-Protestantism was later to derive. In general, the theology of 17th century Protestantism could find no escape from this dilemma, apart from the attempt made in Coccejus.

Amongst the orthodox dogmaticians known to me I can think of only one in whom we find passages which point a way past the dilemma, and that is Polanus. With reference to Eph. 1[4], he sees first : *Elegit nos Pater non ut Pater, quia electio non est opus personae Patris proprium, sed ut Deus, quandoquidem electio est totius sacrosanctae Trinitatis commune opus, cuius principium est Pater* (*Synt. Theol. chr.*, 1609, *col.* 1574). To this statement he adds the further statement : *Electionis subiectum ἐν ᾧ in quo electi sumus, est Christus, non quatenus Deus, nec quatenus nudus homo, sed quatenus θεάνθρωπος et mediator noster. Medio enim, in quo eligeremur, opus erat, quia sine illo non poterat fieri unio inter Deum eligentem et homines electos. Ita Christus est vinculum, quo Deus et electi coniunguntur* (*col.* 1596). For this reason, Polanus accepts as self-evident the assertion which Dort in part contested and in part blatantly reinterpreted : *Electio Christi est fundamentum et firmamentum electionis angelorum et hominum* (*col.* 1570). His main definition can then read as follows : *Aeterna electio Christi est praedestinatio qua Deus Filium suum unigenitum designavit ab aeterno, ut etiam quoad suam humanam naturam esset Filius Dei et caput angelorum et hominum et mediator inter Deum et angelos hominesque* (*col.* 1568 f.). We cannot say quite simply that in these passages the loftiness of Athanasius' teaching has again been attained. They are too general and indeterminate for that. Yet at the same time Polanus did know the passage of Athanasius. Indeed, he expressly reproduced it (*col.* 1596 f.). And in Jesus Christ the Mediator (with characteristic boldness he contrasted this concept with that of Redeemer, *col.* 1596 f.) he found the true and primary object of the divine election (which he characterised expressly as the work of the whole Trinity). In view of these facts we are forced to the conclusion that he was at least aware of the loftiness of Athanasius' conception, and that he did make some effort to direct his own thinking into similar channels.

If we except the doubtful efforts of the Lutherans and Coccejus and his school, the same cannot be said of the doctrine as held and taught by other orthodox dogmaticians, any more than it can of that of Thomas and the Reformers. The Reformed party were right to safeguard against the Remonstrants and Lutherans the tenet that the *causa efficiens impulsiva electionis*, that which motivates the will of God, is not to be sought outside of God Himself, but solely in His free good-pleasure. Thus it is not to be sought in a created reality foreseen by God. Nor is it to be sought in the good will of man, or the use which he makes of divine grace, or the meritorious work of faith, or even faith itself, or prayer, or perseverance, or the dignity and worth of the race. Nor is it to be sought even in the *meritum Christi* ; the obedience as such which was rendered by the man Jesus. All that is an effect and result of the divine election, but not its basis. The election itself is grace, free grace, having its origin and basis in God alone and not elsewhere : *Itaque electionis nostrae omniumque beneficiorum, quae cum ea coniuncta sunt, causam in Deo solum ab aeterno exsistere necesse est* (as Polanus clearly has it, *ib. col.* 1575 f.). What was not seen, however, was that the correctness of this necessary thesis, and the power of the proclamation of free grace, are bound up with the fact that grace in its origin is concretely determined and fulfilled in God. Thus when we think of the origin of grace and the beginning of all things, we cannot and must not think either of divine caprice or divine loving-kindness, for these are both general and therefore without real content. What we must think of is Jesus Christ. To define and explain the election as free grace, it is not enough simply to keep on speaking of it as the unique work of God. Yet when the Reformed doctrine comes to speak of that which motivates the will of the electing God, all that it can tell us is this : *antecessit voluntas in Patre quosdam eligendi antequam Filium elegit* (Walaeus, *Loci comm.*, 1640, p. 381, cf. *Syn. pur. Theol.* of Leiden, 1624, *Disp.* 24, 25). It is only because this *voluntas antecedens per iustitiam suam impediebatur* (!) *quoniam illis actu completo salutem aeternam destinaret, ideo illis destinavit mediatorem, qui iustitiae Dei satisfaceret*, and only in so far as our election is in fact determined by the election of this Mediator, that our election follows His and we are elected " in Christ." It is true that these theologians did speak of a *certus aliquis respectus*, a *mutua relatio inter Christum tanquam caput et electos* (*Leiden Synopsis*, 25, 27). But they made, too, the express distinction : *Decretum de nobis servandis est praedestinatio ad finem, decretum vero de Christo tanquam capite nobis dando est praedestinatio ad media* (Wolleb, *Theol. chr. comp.*, 1626, I *cap.* 4, 9). It could even be said : *Christum substratum esse electioni tanquam fundamentum conferendae salutis, ad quam electi eramus, adeo ut Christus demum electus consideretur post nostram electionem* (Walaeus, *ib.*, p. 380). *Electi erant Patris, antequam Christi erant* (p. 381). Of what avail was it, then, to append the philosophical observation that this was merely a question of a *prioritas ordinis, non temporis : nam et electi Christo et Christus electis datus in caput eodem eligendi actu* (*ib.*, p. 382) ? If in this order the higher authority is the general choice of the Father, and the election of Jesus Christ is only His election in execution of the decree of the Father, if the order is not to be understood as meaning that the divine election is as such the election of Jesus Christ, the passive and active election of the Son of God to be the Son of Man, and in Him the election of those who believe in Him, then it is inevitable that we should enquire concerning the decision of this higher authority, and certainly we cannot be described as elected " in Christ," but at very best only " for Christ." Jesus Christ is not in any sense, then, the *fundamentum electionis*—at the Synod of Dort this was disputed on all sides and in all kinds of ways, with the exception of the timid and easily quashed suggestion of the Bremen delegation—but at very best He is only the *fundamentum salutis*. And the question is whether this " very best " is actually the case, i.e., whether it is the case with us. Is Christ really the *fundamentum salutis* for us, because we belong to those whom the Father has given Him in fulfilment of the decree of election, and who now have Him as their Head ? This question is absolutely decisive for the whole relationship between God and man, but there is no answer to it in the Reformed dogma of predestination. On the contrary, the question is raised there in its most acute form, raised in such a way as apparently to exclude all possibility of a positive answer unless recourse is had either to a pretended knowledge of the secret divine decree, or to personal faith, some inward testimony of the Spirit, or indeed (with the assistance of the much misunderstood *syllogismus practicus*) to certain works of faith whose existence is supposed to give direct confirmation of faith and indirect confirmation of election. Certainly in this matter, in regard to the election and the electing God Himself, recourse cannot be had to Jesus Christ, of whom we are necessarily told that He is only the *primum medium electionis*. A zeal for the free divinity of the *causa efficiens impulsiva electionis* has led to the obscuring of the election itself (and the electing God) by the clouds of a divine good-pleasure which does not yield to more exact definition. And in proportion to the growing secrecy which was demanded in the face of this unknown factor, and the ever greater impressiveness and mysteriousness with which the name of God came to be uttered, the danger became ever more acute that in one way or another the emphasis would and could be laid again upon " man," with theologians concerning themselves more and more with the affairs of the very enemy that they had set out to fight—semi-Pelagianism both old and new. The refusal to speak of Christ in order to speak rightly of grace prevented any proper discernment of the fact that the complement of election is faith. And the inevitable result was an experimenting with those other " complements " which are always in the offing when it is thought that there can be dealings with God apart from Jesus Christ, and consequently the call to faith cannot be heard. On the one hand, it was only to be expected that in the shadow of such a Christless doctrine of predestination there should develop a Reformed mysticism. G. Tersteegen bore classical witness to this trend when in his last words he could glorify God as " omnipresent " and " all-sufficient being " without even so much as an allusion to the name of Jesus Christ. On the other hand, it was quite understandable that in the shadow of this same doctrine there should develop a Reformed ethic of " secular " asceticism and industry, an ethic which did for a time—as embodied to some extent in a Benjamin Franklin—enable Calvinism to play so triumphant a part in world affairs. What there was of goodness and greatness in these developments, from the Christian standpoint, did not in any case derive from the orthodox Reformed doctrine of predestination as such, but from those elements of a Christian and biblical doctrine of predestination which were suppressed and yet in spite of the suppression still lived on in the orthodox teaching. There can be no doubt that even in the abbreviated form of a doctrine of the elected Mediator the Pauline ἐν αὐτῷ could in practice be presented in such a way as, in fact, to cover over the mysterious background of the *decretum absolutum*. To that extent men would be constrained to cleave directly to Christ in respect of their election and salvation, and thus headed off—or at any rate many of them—from the flight into mysticism or moralism which is apparently an unavoidable consequence of the doctrine of the *decretum absolutum*. But for this happy inconsistency, there is no telling what fate might not have overtaken the Reformed Church. But this Church has no cause to pride itself on manifestations which can be explained only as the results of a false start, i.e., the results of the doctrine of a *decretum absolutum*. And the possibility of such a happy inconsistency should not prevent us from recognising this false start for what it was. Nor must it encourage us to perpetuate the error. It must encourage us rather to correct it, replacing the doctrine of the *decretum absolutum* by that of the Word which was in the beginning with God.

As early as the beginning of the 17th century an important attempt was made in this direction even within the older Reformed dogmatics. This attempt was by J. Coccejus and his disciples. It is no mere accident that Coccejus came from the theological school of Bremen, from which there had already originated at Dort a protest which was at first quite ineffective. The merit of Coccejus consists primarily in something which we have already mentioned—that he reunites two things which would never have been separated if the Bible had been properly studied : the eternal election of grace and the eternal decree of salvation, the testament or covenant-decree of God which is His *voluntas ultima, qua apud se ipsum designavit haeredes iustitiae et salutis per fidem non sine mediatore testamenti* (*S. Theol.*, 1662, *cap.* 33, 7). Coccejus thought of that decree as identical with the decree of predestination (*ib.*, 37, 2). So, too, did F. Burmann, *Syn. Theol.*, 1678, I, 38, 23 : *Consilium exercendae gratiae a Deo dispositum est per modum testamenti. Testamentum autem de haeredibus Deo sine mediatore et sponsore testamenti factum non est, cui primo dispositum est regnum.* It is true that at a first glance these statements seem to leave the question open whether the direct object of salvation is not sought in the elect themselves predestinated the heirs of righteousness and salvation ; whether it is not held that the election of Jesus Christ belongs to this primary election with a necessity which is only relative and not absolute : *non sine mediatore testamenti. Simul constituit Christum caput et primogenitum et illos membra et fratres Christi* (Coccejus 37, 31). Later writers like F. Burmann (*op. cit.*) and P. van Mastricht (*Theor. Pract. Theol.*, 1698, III, 3, 8) identified the *obiectum electionis* with the *totus Christus mysticus, h. e. Christus cum omnibus suis.* In reality the true sequence of thought is quite plain both with Coccejus and his disciples : *primum Christum electum fuisse ut caput, deinde nos ut membra in ipso* (Burmann, *op. cit.*). Coccejus himself (*ib.*, 33, 16 f.) developed the doctrine of the covenant under three heads. *Prima pars testamenti est, quod Deus decrevit Filium suum unigenitum dare, eumque mittere in carne ut esset caro, semen Abrahae et mulieris, frater servandorum, atque ita sanctificans et qui sanctificantur ex uno essent omnes* (Jn. 3¹⁶, Heb. 2¹¹). The second part of the covenant is the divine *voluntas iustificandi per fidem in sponsorem*, i.e., the dispensation indicated in Jn. 3¹⁶, that those that believe in Him should not perish but have everlasting life, the *communio peccatoris et sponsoris per spiritum sponsoris, qui peccatorem unit sponsori* and whose first work is faith. It is only in the third part of the covenant that we come to the *designatio haeredum iustitiae*, the eternal separating out of those who according to Jn. 3¹⁷ are to be saved by the coming into the world of the Son of God, and who according to Rom. 8²⁹ are to belong to the brethren of the first-born, and according to Gal. 3⁸ to the Gentiles justified by faith. At the decisive point, then, Coccejus can say quite unequivocally : *Patet, hoc consilio introductam esse illam plenam ut consolationis et amabilitatis ita gloriae oeconomiam, qua Pater se constituit vindicem sanctitatis et nominis divini, regnumque ac iudicium Filio dedit, Filius autem ut Sapientia (h. e. in quo sapientia Dei creatoris, volentis glorificari in homine, potuit explicari) unctus est et designatus princeps salutis, sacerdos populi sui, eiusque rex et dominus et uno verbo, angelus Jehovae assertor, Patris gloriae restitutor et manifestator* (*ib.*, 34, 22). According to Coccejus (37, 31), then, the ἐν αὐτῷ of Eph. 1⁴ must be understood in a twofold sense : *cum Christo ut praecognito* and *per Christum et cum Christo ut eligente : quod est sponsoris.* The same applies to the ἐποίησεν πρόθεσιν ἐν τῷ Χριστῷ Ἰησοῦ of Eph. 3¹¹ ; to the passages in John which relate to the election of Jesus ; to Ps. 2⁸ : " Ask of me, and I shall give thee the heathen for thine inheritance, and the uttermost parts of the earth for thy possession " ; to Jn. 5²¹ : " For as the Father raiseth up the dead and quickeneth them ; even so the Son quickeneth whom he will " ; and strangely enough to Mt. 11¹⁷: " We have piped unto you, and ye have not danced. . . ." To sum up, Coccejus saw three things : (1) that the decree of election is identical with that of salvation ; (2) that the decree of salvation relates primarily to the mission and people of the Son ; and (3) that, like the Father and the Holy Spirit, the Son participates in the decree as divine Subject, so that He is both *electus* and *eligens*. These three things enable us to overcome and set aside the Calvinistic *decretum absolutum* (the notion that the true basis of election is an indeterminate and abstract good-pleasure of God), and to attain to a genuinely Christian understanding of the doctrine of predestination. This is especially the case if the first assertion in particular is meant and carried through with all strictness. The defect of Coccejus and his followers consists in the fact that while they did maintain the identity of the two decrees they did not exploit this identity as they might have done in relation to the whole doctrine of election. The discovery which they made is like a light shining above the doctrine of this particular school, but not interpenetrating it in such a way as to mark off its outlines clearly and effectively from those of the older Calvinistic teaching held by the other orthodox dogmaticians of the Reformed Church. The result is that in the development of theology Coccejus has gained a name and played his part as a pioneer of the so-called soteriological understanding of the divine covenant of grace actualised in time, but not as a pioneer of this important correction of the Reformed doctrine of predestination. Hence it is possible and even understandable that on the one hand a Coccejus specialist like G. Schrenk (*Gottesreich und Bund im älteren Protestantismus*, 1923) should hardly have been aware of the scope of Coccejus' reflections on the doctrine of predestination, and that on the other a specialist on the history of the doctrine like A. Schweitzer should completely overlook and ignore Coccejus and his disciples. It is true that the suggestions of the school did not, in fact, change the aspect of 17th century Reformed theology in this respect, but we must conclude that within those suggestions there was always present at least the possibility of such a change.

The election of Jesus Christ is the eternal choice and decision of God. And our first assertion tells us that Jesus Christ is the electing God. We must not ask concerning any other but Him. In no depth of the Godhead shall we encounter any other but Him. There is no such thing as Godhead in itself. Godhead is always the Godhead of the Father, the Son and the Holy Spirit. But the Father is the Father of Jesus Christ and the Holy Spirit is the Spirit of the Father and the Spirit of Jesus Christ. There is no such thing as a *decretum absolutum*. There is no such thing as a will of God apart from the will of Jesus Christ. Thus Jesus Christ is not only the *manifestatio* and *speculum nostrae praedestinationis*. And He is this not simply in the sense that our election can be known to us and contemplated by us only through His election, as an election which, like His and with His, is made (or not made) by a secret and hidden will of God. On the contrary, Jesus Christ reveals to us our election as an election which is made by Him, by His will which is also the will of God. He tells us that He Himself is the One who elects us. In the very foreground of our existence in history we can and should cleave wholly and with full assurance to Him because in the eternal background of history, in the beginning with God, the only decree which was passed, the only Word which was spoken and which prevails, was the decision which was executed by Him. As we believe in Him and hear His Word and hold fast by

His decision, we can know with a certainty which nothing can ever shake that we are the elect of God.

Jesus Christ is elected man. In making this second assertion we are again at one with the traditional teaching. But the christological assertion of tradition tells us no more than that in His humanity Jesus Christ was one of the elect. It was in virtue of His divinity that He was ordained and appointed Lord and Head of all others, the organ and instrument of the whole election of God and the revelation and reflection of the election of those who were elected with Him.

Now without our first assertion we cannot maintain such a position. For where can Jesus Christ derive the authority and power to be Lord and Head of all others, and how can these others be elected " in Him," and how can they see their election in Him the first of the elect, and how can they find in His election the assurance of their own, if He is only the object of election and not Himself its Subject, if He is only an elect creature and not primarily and supremely the electing Creator ? Obviously in a strict and serious sense we can never say of any creature that other creatures are elect " in it," that it is their Lord and Head, and that in its election they can and should have assurance of their own. How can a mere creature ever come to the point of standing in this way before God, above and on behalf of others ? If the testimony of Holy Scripture concerning the man Jesus Christ is true, that this man does stand before God above and on behalf of others, then this man is no mere creature but He is also the Creator, and His own electing as Creator must have preceded His election as creature. In one and the same person He must be both elected man and the electing God. Thus the second assertion rests on the first, and for the sake of the second the first ought never to be denied or passed over.

Because of this interconnexion we must now formulate the second statement with rather more precision. It tells us that before all created reality, before all being and becoming in time, before time itself, in the pre-temporal eternity of God, the eternal divine decision as such has as its object and content the existence of this one created being, the man Jesus of Nazareth, and the work of this man in His life and death, His humiliation and exaltation, His obedience and merit. It tells us further that in and with the existence of this man the eternal divine decision has as its object and content the execution of the divine covenant with man, the salvation of all men. In this function this man is the object of the eternal divine decision and foreordination. Jesus Christ, then, is not merely one of the elect but *the* elect of God. From the very beginning (from eternity itself), as elected man He does not stand alongside the rest of the elect, but before and above them as the One who is originally and properly the Elect. From the very beginning (from eternity itself), there are no other elect together with or apart from Him, but, as Eph. 1⁴ tells us, only " in " Him. " In Him " does not simply mean with Him, together with Him, in His

company. Nor does it mean only through Him, by means of that
which He as elected man can be and do for them. "In Him" means
in His person, in His will, in His own divine choice, in the basic decision
of God which He fulfils over against every man. What singles Him
out from the rest of the elect, and yet also, and for the first time,
unites Him with them, is the fact that as elected man He is also the
electing God, electing them in His own humanity. In that He (as
God) wills Himself (as man), He also wills them. And so they are
elect "in Him," in and with His own election. And so, too, His
election must be distinguished from theirs. It must not be distinguished from theirs merely as the example and type, the revelation
and reflection of their election. All this can, of course, be said quite
truly of the election of Jesus Christ. But it must be said further that
His election is the original and all-inclusive election ; the election
which is absolutely unique, but which in this very uniqueness is
universally meaningful and efficacious, because it is the election of
Him who Himself elects. Of none other of the elect can it be said
that his election carries in it and with it the election of the rest. But
that is what we must say of Jesus Christ when we think of Him in
relation to the rest. And for this reason, as elected man, He is the
Lord and Head of all the elect, the revelation and reflection of their
election, and the organ and instrument of all divine electing. For
this reason His election is indeed the type of all election. For this
reason we must now learn really to recognise in Him not only the
electing God but also elected man.

The basic passage in Jn. 1¹⁻² speaks of the man Jesus. In so doing, it contains self-evidently this second assertion, that Jesus Christ is elected man. All
the Johannine passages which speak of His mission, of His doing the will and
works of His Father, of His submission, and of the submission of His people to
the rule of the Father, really point to this aspect of the matter. Indeed, all
the New Testament passages so far quoted find in Jesus Christ this elected man
and therefore in a creature distinct from God the divine decree in the very beginning. To that extent do they not all testify to a second and passive meaning
of the election of Jesus Christ ? More specific testimony is given in the words
of Jn. 17²⁴ : " Thou lovedst me before the foundation of the world " ; and quite
expressly in Lk. 9³⁵ and 23³⁵. It is common to the verses from Luke " that Jesus
is identified as the Christ in the immediate context of His sufferings. He was
declared υἱός μου ὁ ἐκλελεγμένος at the transfiguration, just before His entry on
the way of suffering. His declaration as ὁ Χριστὸς τοῦ θεοῦ ὁ ἐκλεκτός came when
He had already taken the form of the crucified. He is elected man not only in
His passion and in spite of His passion, but for His passion " (G. Schrenk in
Theol. W.B. zum N.T. IV 194, 11 f.). There is little room for doubt that in
Jn. 17²⁴, too, there is a specific reference to the story of the passion. If we
compare with it Ac. 2²³, 4²⁷ᶠ·, 1 Pet. 1²⁰, Heb. 9¹⁴ and Rev. 13⁸, we can hardly
make too much of this aspect of it. Deutero-Isaiah speaks of the Servant whom
Yahweh upholds ; of the Elect in whom His soul delighteth and upon whom He
has set His Spirit, that he may bring forth judgment to the Gentiles (Is. 42¹) ;
of the One who was given as a covenant for the people, for a light of the Gentiles
(Is. 42⁶, 49⁸). And it is of this One that he tells us, at the very climax of his
presentation, that " they made his grave with the wicked, and with the rich in

his death ; although he had done no violence, neither was any deceit in his mouth. Yet it pleased the Lord to bruise him ; he hath put him to grief : when thou shalt make his soul an offering for sin, he shall see his seed, he shall prolong his days, and the pleasure of the Lord shall prosper in his hand '' (Is. 53[9f.]). And it is in the light of this climax—election for suffering—that the relevant passage in Heb. 2[11f.] must certainly be understood : '' For both he that sanctifieth and they that are sanctified are all of one : for which cause he is not ashamed to call them brethren, saying, I will declare thy name unto my brethren, in the midst of the church will I sing praise unto thee. And again, I will put my trust in him. And again, Behold I and the children which God hath given me. Forasmuch then the children are partakers in flesh and blood, he also himself likewise took part of the same ; that through death he might destroy him that had the power of death, that is, the devil.'' Ἰδοὺ ὁ ἄνθρωπος (Jn. 19[5]).

In relation to this passive election of Jesus Christ the great exponents of the traditional doctrine of predestination developed an insight which we too must take as our starting-point, because, rightly understood, it contains within itself everything else that must be noted and said in this connexion. The insight is this : that in the predestination of the man Jesus we see what predestination is always and everywhere—the acceptance and reception of man only by the free grace of God. Even in the man Jesus there is indeed no merit, no prior and self-sufficient goodness, which can precede His election to divine sonship. Neither prayer nor the life of faith can command or compel His election. It is by the work of the Word of God, by the Holy Spirit, that He is conceived and born without sin, that He is what He is, the Son of God ; by grace alone. And as He became Christ, so we become Christians. As He became our Head, so we become His body and members. As He became the object of our faith, so we become believers in Him. What we have to consider in the elected man Jesus is, then, the destiny of human nature, its exaltation to fellowship with God, and the manner of its participation in this exaltation by the free grace of God. But more, it is in this man that the exaltation itself is revealed and proclaimed. For with His decree concerning this man, God decreed too that this man should be the cause and the instrument of our exaltation.

It was along this line that Augustine (De praed. sanct. 15) made his second important contribution to the christological understanding of predestination. The praeclarissimum lumen praedestinationis et gratiae is ipse salvator, ipse mediator Dei et hominum homo Jesus Christus. What works of His own, what prior faith, could ever have given this man, as man, the right to be the Son of God, our Mediator and Redeemer ? Respondeatur quaeso : ille homo, ut a Verbo Patri coaeterno in unitatem personae assumptus Filius Dei esset, unde hoc meruit ? Quod eius bonum qualecumque praecessit ? Quid egit ante, quid credidit, quid petivit, ut ad hanc ineffabilem excellentiam perveniret ? Nonne faciente ac suscipiente Verbo ipse homo ex quo esse coepit, Filius Dei unicus esse coepit ? At this point we are forced to ask in all seriousness : '' O man, who art thou that repliest against God ? '' (Rom. 9[20]) and we receive the answer : '' Thou art man as He, Jesus, is man.'' At enim gratia ille talis ac tantus est. Appareat itaque nobis in nostro capite ipse fons gratiae, unde secundum unius cuiusque mensuram se per cuncta eius membra diffundit. Ea gratia fit ab initio fidei suae homo quicumque *christianus, qua gratia homo ille ab initio suo factus est Christus : de ipso Spiritu et hic renatus, de quo est ille natus ; eodem Spiritu fit in nobis remissio peccatorum, quo Spiritu factum est, ut nullum haberet ille peccatum . . . ipsa est igitur prae-destinatio sanctorum quae in Sancto sanctorum maxime claruit : quam negare quis potest recte intelligentium eloquia veritatis ? Nam et ipsum dominum gloriae, in quantum homo factus est Dei Filius, praedestinatum esse didicimus.* Augustine's reference here to Rom. 1[14] is not a very happy one, for he relied upon the Vulgate translation of ὁρισθέντος υἱοῦ θεοῦ as *qui praedestinatus est Filius Dei*, which can hardly be the correct rendering. But in the light of those passages of Scripture which are really relevant he is quite right when he continues : *Preadestinatus est ergo Jesus, ut qui futurus erat secundum carnem Filius David, esset tamen in virtute Filius Dei secundum Spiritum sanctificationis. . . . Praedestinata est ista naturae humanae tanta et tam celsa et summa subvectio, ut quo attolleretur altius non haberet, sicut pro nobis ipsa divinitas quo usque se deponeret humilius non habuit quam suscepta natura hominis cum infirmitate carnis usque ad mortem crucis.* When we consider Jesus, how else can we understand the grace which comes to us except as grace and therefore as predestination ? *Sicut ergo praedestinatus est ille unus, ut caput nostrum esset, ita multi praedestinati sumus, ut membra eius essemus. . . . Ille quippe nos fecit credere in Christum, qui nobis fecit in quem cred-imus Christum ; ille facit in hominibus principium et perfectionem in Jesum, qui fecit hominem principem fidei et perfectorem Jesum* (Heb. 12[2]). Augustine ex-pressed himself to the same effect in *De dono persev.* 24, 67 (cf. too *Tract. in Joann.* 105, 5–7, and *Sermo* 175, 2) : *Nullum est illustrius praedestinationis exemplum quam ipse Jesus . . . ipse mediator. Quisquis fidelis vult eam bene intelligere, attendat ipsum, atque in illo inveniat et seipsum : fidelis, inquam, qui in eo veram naturam credit et confitetur humanam, id est nostram quamvis singulariter suscipiente Deo Verbo in unicum Filium Dei sublimatam. . . . Et illum ergo et nos praedestinavit ; quia et in illo, ut esset caput nostrum et in nobis, ut eius corpus essemus, non prae-cessura merita nostra sed opera sua futura praescivit.*

All this was said by Augustine against Pelagius and the Pelagians. It is of a piece, then, that as he saw it the significance of the predestination of Jesus Christ for us should lie essentially in the fact that in it we are forced to see clearly the freedom of grace as against all human claims to merit. Yet it was not an inversion of the teaching of Augustine, but only a making explicit of what was already implicit within it, when Thomas Aquinas gave to this thought a positive turn : *Dicitur (Christus) lumen praedestinationis et gratiae in quantum per eius praedestinationem et gratiam manifestatur nostra praedestinatio* (*S. theol.* III, *qu.* 24, *art.* 3 *s.c.*). We have had occasion to contest Thomas' qualifying of this statement, but even as qualified by Thomas it is still correct, and as an expansion of the polemical teaching of Augustine it is most important. The election of Jesus Christ is, in fact, the revelation of our election. In His election we can and should recognise our own. *Praedestinatio Christi est exemplum nostrae praedestinationis secundum illud ad quod aliquis praedestinatur. . . . Ipse enim est praedestinatus ad hoc quod esset Dei Filius naturalis ; nos autem praedestinamur ad filiationem adoptionis, quae est quaedam participata similitudo filiationis natur-alis* (*ib.*, *qu.* 24, *art.* 3 *c.*). And if it might be asked whether the words *manifestatio* and *exemplum* are not inadequate in this connexion, we are taught in *qu.* 24, *art.* 4 that the *praedestinatio Christi* may indeed be called the *causa nostrae prae-destinationis* to the extent that God did decree our salvation from all eternity together with the attainment of it through Jesus Christ and therefore with the incarnation of Jesus Christ. It was because God decreed the incarnation of Christ that He also and at the same time (*simul*) decreed *ut esset nostrae salutis causa*. But that, too, is surely inadequate. Thomas rests, unfortunately, upon a basic assertion which he made in due form and with complete clarity : *prae-destinatio nostra ex simplici voluntate Dei dependet* (*qu.* 24, *vid.* 2). And this means that he rests like Calvin upon the *decretum absolutum*. He can even hazard the outrageous statement : *Si Christus non fuisset incarnandus, Deus praeordinasset homines salvari per aliam causam* (*ib.*, *ad.* 3). As against that, we reaffirm the necessity of our first assertion, that only if Jesus Christ is the true and incontestable basis of our election can He be the basis of our knowledge of the election according to the second assertion, and only then can we have any assurance of our own election. But once again, within these limits Thomas did perceive and state quite correctly that the election of Jesus Christ, understood as the election of the man Jesus, has for us the positive significance that it carried with it (we should say, in it) from all eternity the reality and discernible truth of our own election.

On the same line as Augustine and Thomas, we now arrive at Calvin. *Jesus Christ est le miroir et le patron où Dieu a déclaré les thresors infinis de sa bonté ; car il est le chef de l'Eglise. Aussi nous faudra il commencer par luy, quand nous voudrons cognoistre comment Dieu besongne en ses membres inferieurs. Voila Jesus Christ, vray Dieu et vray homme. Or ceste nature humaine a esté exaltée en une dignité merveilleuse ; car Jesus Christ estant Dieu et homme, est toutesfois Fils de Dieu : je dy, Fils unique, Fils naturel. Qu'est-ce qu'a merité la nature humaine qui est en Jesus Christ ? Car elle procede de la race d'Adam ; il falloit qu'il fust de la semence de David, ou autrement il n'eust point esté nostre Sauveur. Il a esté conceu de sa mere d'une façon miraculeuse, mais tant y a qu'il est venu de la race de David, d'Abraham et d'Adam. Ce qu'il a esté sanctifié et qu'il n'a point esté subiet à mesme corruption que nous, cela est venu de la grace admirable de Dieu et excellente. Mais tant y a, que si nous considerons la nature humaine de Jesus Christ, elle n'avoit point merité d'estre exaltée en ce degré d'honneur, pour dire : Voila celuy qui dominera par dessus les Anges, devant lequel tout genouil se ployera. Quand nous considerons une telle grace de Dieu en nostre Chef, ne faut-il pas qu'un chacun de nous entre en soy-mesme pour cognoistre : Dieu m'a esleu, moy qui estoye banny et rejetté de son Royaume. Je n'avoye aucune chose en moy qui luy peust estre agreable, et neantmoins il m'a choisi pour estre des siens. Ne faut-il pas bien que nous cognoissions une telle grace, pour la magnifier ?* (*Congrég. sur l'élect. ét.*, 1562, *C.R.* 8, 108 f. ; cf. *De aet. Dei praed.*, 1552, *ib.*, 306 f. ; *Instit.* III, 22, 1).

This insight is a true and important one. Yet we cannot say that in the form given to it by the great exponents of the doctrine of election it exhausts or embraces everything that is to be perceived and remembered in relation to this topic. Even as the object of predestination, even as elected man, Jesus Christ must still be understood as truly the beginning of all God's ways and works. That is the first thing which we have to bring out more clearly in this connexion. The second is that the election of the man Jesus is specifically His election to suffering, and that it is for this reason and in this form that it is the basic act of the divine election of grace. And the third is that we have to see our own election in that of the man Jesus because His election includes ours within itself and because ours is grounded in His. We are elected together with Him in so far as we are elected " in Him," i.e., through Him who is not merely the object but also and primarily the Subject of the divine election. We must attempt so to think of the reality of the passive election of Christ, of Jesus Christ as the object of the divine predestination, that in all our further discussion of this topic we may turn to good account the insight handed down to us by tradition.

Augustine and his followers emphasised quite rightly that the man Jesus as such has nothing to bring before the electing God which would make Him worthy of the divine election or make His election necessary. He is the Son of God only by the grace of God. That this is indeed the case may be proved conclusively by the absoluteness of the gratitude and obedience with which this man stands before God and submits Himself to Him. It is thus that the creature lives before God, its freedom consisting in the fact that in its autonomy it recognises and acknowledges that it is wholly and utterly responsible to God. And so this man Jesus, as the object of the divine decree, is the beginning of all God's ways and works, the first-born of all creation. In Him it comes to pass for the first time that God wills and posits another being different from Himself, His creature. Be it noted that this determination of the will of God, this content of predestination, is already grace, for God did not stand in need of any particular ways or works *ad extra*. He had no need of a creation. He might well have been satisfied with the inner glory of His threefold being, His freedom, and His love. The fact that He is not satisfied, but that His inner glory overflows and becomes outward, the fact that He wills the creation, and the man Jesus as the first-born of all creation, is grace, sovereign grace, a condescension inconceivably tender. But this determination of the will of God is eminently grace to the extent that in relation to this other, the creation of God, God's first thought and decree consists in the fact that in His Son He makes the being of this other His own being, that He allows the Son of Man Jesus to be called and actually to be His own Son. In and with His lordship over this other, in and with the creaturely autonomy of this other—and even that is grace— God wills and decrees and posits in the beginning both His own fatherhood and also the sonship of the creature. This is more than mere kindness and condescension. It is self-giving. And that is how the inner glory of God overflows. From all eternity it purports and wills its own impartation to the creature, the closest possible union with it, a fellowship which is not to its own advantage but to that of the creature. It is in being gracious in this way that God sets forth His own glory. It is in the election of the man Jesus that His decision to be gracious is made. " God so loved the world, that he gave his only begotten Son " (Jn. 3[16]). In a first and most important way we can now understand the extent to which, in the light of the election of the man Jesus, all election can be described only as free grace. The man Jesus is the elect of God. Those whom God elects He elects " in Him," not merely " like Him," but in His person, by His will, and by His election. Those whom God elects, the One blessed of God elects also. What can this election be, then, but more grace, a participation in the grace of the One who elects, a participation in His creatureliness (which is already grace), and a participation in His sonship (which is eminently grace) ? From its very source the election derives from the man Jesus. And as election by Him it is indirectly identical with that beginning willed and posited by the condescension and self-suffering of God. It is " the grace of our Lord Jesus Christ."

But the elected man Jesus was foreordained to suffer and to die. That is how His selection, and sending, and, as we have seen, His election, are understood in the New Testament. The free grace of God directed in Him towards the creature took on this form from the very first (from all eternity). According to Phil. $2^{6f.}$ it is obedience unto death, even unto the death of the cross, to which the Son of God predestines Himself when He empties Himself of His divine form of being. And this predestining is the content of the divine decree at the beginning of all things. " The Word became flesh " (Jn. 1^{14}). This formulation of the message of Christmas already includes within itself the message of Good Friday. For " all flesh is as grass." The election of the man Jesus means, then, that a wrath is kindled, a sentence pronounced and finally executed, a rejection actualised. It has been determined thus from all eternity. From all eternity judgment has been foreseen—even in the overflowing of God's inner glory, even in the ineffable condescension of God's embracing of the creature, even in the fulness of self-giving by which God Himself wills to become a creature. For teleologically the election of the man Jesus carries within itself the election of a creation which is good according to the positive will of God and of man as fashioned after the divine image and foreordained to the divine likeness (reflection). But this involves necessarily the rejection of Satan, the rebel angel who is the very sum and substance of the possibility which is not chosen by God (and which exists only in virtue of this negation) ; the very essence of the creature in its misunderstanding and misuse of its creation and destiny and in its desire to be as God, to be itself a god. Satan (and the whole kingdom of evil, i.e., the demonic, which has its basis in him) is the shadow which accompanies the light of the election of Jesus Christ (and in Him of the good creation in which man is in the divine image). And in the divine counsel the shadow itself is necessary as the object of rejection. To the reality of its existence and might and activity (only, of course, in the power of the divine negation, but to that extent grounded in the divine will and counsel) testimony is given by the fall of man, in which man appropriates to himself the satanic desire. When confronted by Satan and his kingdom, man in himself and as such has in his creaturely freedom no power to reject that which in His divine freedom God rejects. Face to face with temptation he cannot maintain the goodness of his creation in the divine image and foreordination to the divine likeness. This is done by the elected man Jesus (Mt. 4^{1-11}). In himself and as such man will always do as Adam did in Gen. 3. And for this reason, according to the will and counsel of God, man in himself and as such incurs the rejection which rests upon his temptation and corruption. He stands under the wrath which is God's only answer to the creature which abuses and dishonours its creatureliness. Exposed to the power of the divine negation, he is guilty of death. But it is this very man in himself and as such who in and with the election of the man Jesus is loved of God from all eternity and elected to fellowship with Him : he who was powerless against the insinuations of the tempter and seducer ; he who in his actual temptation and seduction became the enemy of God ; he who incurred rejection and became guilty of death. In this one man Jesus, God puts at the head and in the place of all other men the One who has the same power as Himself to reject Satan and to maintain and not surrender the goodness of man's divine creation and destiny ; the One who according to Mt. 4 actually does this, and does it for all who are elected in Him, for man in himself and as such who does not and cannot do it of himself. The rejection which all men incurred, the wrath of God under which all men lie, the death which all men must die, God in His love for men transfers from all eternity to Him in whom He loves and elects them, and whom He elects at their head and in their place. God from all eternity ordains this obedient One in order that He might bear the suffering which the disobedient have deserved and which for the sake of God's righteousness must necessarily be borne. Indeed, the very obedience which was exacted of Him and attained by Him was His willingness to take upon Himself the divine rejection of all others and to suffer that which they ought to have suffered. He is elected, and He maintains the goodness of man's divine creation and destiny, not for His own sake but for their sake, for the sake of man in himself and as such. He, the Elect, is appointed to check and defeat Satan on behalf of all those that are elected " in Him," on behalf of the descendants and confederates of Adam now beloved of God. And this checking and defeating of Satan must consist in His allowing the righteousness of God to proceed against Himself instead of them. For this reason, He is the Lamb slain, and the Lamb slain from the foundation of the world. For this reason, the *crucified* Jesus is the " image of the invisible God." If, then, there is an election of others on the basis of the election of this man Jesus, we can see that that election is to be understood only as free grace, and we can also see why this is so. The ones who " in Him," i.e., through Him, are elected and made partakers of His grace are those who could see in themselves only lost sinners " oppressed of the devil " (Ac. 10[38]). If He did not stand at their head, if they were not elected " in Him," without Him and outside Him they would be for ever rejected. They have nothing which they can call their own except their transgression. Yet these transgressors are the ones on whose behalf the eternal love of God for Jesus Christ is willed and extended. They knew nothing of this love. They did not even desire it. But for His part the Elect who stands at the head of the rejected elects only the rejected. The Gospel tells us unequivocally in this connexion that " the Son of man is come to seek and to save that which is lost " (Lk. 19[10]), that the sick have need of Him and not the whole (Mk. 2[17]), and that in heaven there is more joy over one sinner that repenteth than over ninety and nine just persons which have no need of repentance (Lk. 15[7]). Who is the Elect ? He is always the one who " was dead and is alive again," who " was lost and is found " (Lk. 15[24]). That the elected man Jesus had to suffer and die means no more and no less than that in becoming man God makes Himself responsible for man who became His enemy, and that He takes upon Himself all the consequences of man's action—his rejection and his death. This is what is involved in the self-giving of God. This is the radicalness of His grace. God must let righteousness reign, and He wills to do so. Against the aggression of the shadow-world of Satan which is negated by Him and which exists only in virtue of this negation, God must and will maintain the honour of His creation, the honour of man as created and ordained for Him, and His own honour. God cannot and will not acquiesce in the encroachment of this shadow-world upon the sphere of His positive will, an encroachment made with the fall of man. On the contrary, it must be His pleasure to see that Satan and all that has its source and origin in him are rejected. But this means that God must and will reject man as he is in himself. And He does so. But He does it in the person of the elected man Jesus. And in Him He loves man as he is in himself. He elects Jesus, then, at the head and in the place of all others. The wrath of God, the judgment and the penalty, fall, then, upon Him. And this means upon His own Son, upon Himself : upon Him, and not upon those whom He loves and elects " in Him ; " upon Him, and not upon the disobedient. Why not upon the disobedient ? Why this interposition of the just for the unjust by which in some incomprehensible manner the eternal Judge becomes Himself the judged ? Because His justice is a merciful and for this reason a perfect justice. Because the sin of the disobedient is also their need, and even while it affronts Him it also moves Him to pity. Because He knows quite well the basis of Satan's existence and the might and force with which sinners were overthrown and fell in the negative power of His own counsel and will. Because in the powerlessness of sinners against Satan He sees their guilt, but in their guilt He sees also their powerlessness. Because He knows quite well that those who had no strength to resist Satan are even less able to bear and suffer the rejection which those who hear Satan and obey him merit together with him. Because from all eternity He knows " whereof we are made " (Ps. 103[14]). That is why He intervened on our behalf in His Son. That is why He did no less. He did not owe it to us to do it. For it was not He but we ourselves in our culpable weakness who delivered us up to Satan and to the divine wrath and rejection. And yet God does it because from all eternity He loves and elects us in His Son, because from all eternity He sees us in His Son as sinners to whom He is gracious.   For all those, then, whom God elects in His Son, the essence of the free grace of God consists in the fact that in this same Jesus God who is the Judge takes the place of the judged, and they are fully acquitted, therefore, from sin and its guilt and penalty.   Thus the wrath of God and the rejection of Satan and his kingdom no longer have any relevance for them. On the contrary, the wrath of God and the rejection of Satan, the free course of divine justice to which God Himself has subjected Himself on their behalf, has brought them to freedom.   In the One in whom they are elected, that is to say, in the death which the Son of God has died for them, they themselves have died as sinners.   And that means their radical sanctification, separation and purification for participation in a true creaturely independence, and more than that, for the divine sonship of the creature which is the grace for which from all eternity they are elected in the election of the man Jesus.

And now we must say, too, of the elected man Jesus (apart from the fact that He is what He is by grace, and that His grace consists in bringing many to freedom) that in His mercy God remains just as faithful to Him as He in His readiness to do God's will remains faithful to God.   There is steadfastness on both sides.   On God's side, it is the steadfastness of grace even in the judgment to which He condemns the Elect.   It is the constancy of love even in the fire of the wrath which consumes Him.   It is the steadfastness of election even in the midst of the rejection which overtakes Him.   And on the side of the Elect, it is the steadfastness of obedience to God, and of calling only upon Him, and of confidence in the righteousness of His will.   It is in the unity of this steadfastness both divine and human that we shall find the peculiar secret of the election of the man Jesus.   In this twofold steadfastness there is to be seen both the glorifying of God and also the salvation of men, the two things which together constitute the aim and meaning of the covenant willed by God and the election of this man.   In this steadfastness Satan is resisted, defied and defeated both by the God against whom he revolted and also by the man against whom he had triumphed.   In this steadfastness the Word of God is spoken and the answer of man is given, and together the Word and the answer represent the decision willed by God in all His ways and works, and therefore constitute the content of the will and counsel of God in the beginning.   The Word of the divine steadfastness is the resurrection of Jesus from the dead, His exaltation, His session at the right hand of the Father.   By these events God confirms the fact that the Elect is the only-begotten Son of God who can suffer death but cannot be holden of death, who by His death must destroy death.   By these events God makes manifest the vindication of His positive will as Creator against the assault of Satan, a vindication which He made by the offering up of His Elect.   There takes place here the decisive act of history, which is the actualisation of the overflowing of the

inner glory of God. The kingdom of God is here set up as the consummation towards which all God's ways and works are moving. And
the answer of human steadfastness is the prayer which is the assent
of Jesus to the will of God as it confronts His own will. This prayer
is His intercession with God on behalf of His people. And yet it is
also a prayer which He teaches His people and places on the lips of
His people. With this prayer He proves Himself to be the Son of
God who is rejected for their sakes and yet who is still the Elect of
God even in His rejection. With this prayer He undertakes to be
both priest and victim, thus affirming for His part the salutariness of
the holy wrath of God. In this prayer He fulfils His creaturely office
in the history of creation as it was determined and prepared by God.
In this prayer He affirms the fact that He is the King who was appointed
by God to be at the head and in the place of the elect as their Lord
and Head. In this prayer He affirms that He Himself in His own
person is the kingdom of God. This divine and human steadfastness
(reflected in the resurrection and the prayer of Jesus) constitutes the
meaning and purpose of the election of Jesus. And so, too, this
election itself is the content of the divine decree which obviously
precedes not only creation but that whole complex of problems which
accompany and threaten creation. The real concern in the resurrection and prayer of the man Jesus is that those problems should be
overcome and solved, the divine lordship over Satan actualised and
the positive will of God as Creator vindicated and enthroned. Looking
at it from that standpoint, we can never be too comprehensive as we
attempt to understand the election of Jesus as the beginning of all
things. If it is true that this man is the Elect of God, if it is true that
the free grace which is the basis of all election is the reality of the
divine and human steadfastness determined and actualised in this
man, the reality of the resurrection and the prayer of Jesus, then in
respect of those who are elected " in Him " it follows that their election consists concretely in their faith in Him. The mystery of the
elected man Jesus is the divine and human steadfastness which is the
end of all God's ways and works and therefore the object and content
of the divine predestination. And the fact that it is actualised in
Him and on their behalf is the fact to which those who are elected
" in Him " must cling, the fact in which their confidence must repose,
the fact from which their joy and consolation must be derived. And
this fact is one which is ever new, and one which is their strength and
wisdom in all circumstances. Being elected " in Him," they are
elected only to believe in Him, i.e., to love in Him the Son of God
who died and rose again for them, to laud in Him the priest and
victim of their reconciliation with God, to recognise in Him the justification of God (which is also their own justification), to honour in Him
their Leader and Representative, their Lord and Head, and the kingdom
of God which is a kingdom above all other kingdoms. It is as they

love Him and laud Him and recognise Him and honour Him in this way that they can have their own life, their rejection being put behind them and beneath them, rejected with His rejection. To believe in Jesus means to have His resurrection and prayer both in the mind and in the heart. And this means to be elected. For it is the man that does this who " in Him " is the object of the divine election of grace.

This is perhaps the place to make a statement and to come to some decision on a notable controversy which took place within the orthodox Reformed theology of the 17th century : the so-called Supralapsarian-Infralapsarian controversy. It has been recognised and accepted fairly generally, and quite correctly, that this controversy was not fundamental and not therefore a controversy which (like that between the Calvinists and Arminians) disrupted the Church. It was rather a difference which could form the subject of purely academic disputation *sine ullo mutuae caritatis et fraternitatis dispendio* (as A. Heidanus put it, *Corp. Theol. chr.*, 1686, I, p. 217). And as such it was left an open question at the Synod of Dort (although with a clear bias towards Infralapsarianism). Later it found gradual settlement in the form of various compromises. At a first glance it does not seem to have anything to do with the specific question of the election of Jesus Christ. But to recall it may well shed light upon the path which we have to tread, and it will itself be illuminated by the conclusions which result from our own sequence of thought. There is good reason, then, to introduce it at this juncture.

In the controversy between the 17th century Supralapsarians and Infralapsarians the point at issue is the *obiectum praedestinationis* (for what follows, cf. H. Heppe : *Dogm. d. ev. ref. Kirche*, 1935, p. 129 f. ; A. Schweizer, *Protest. Centraldogmen*, 1856, II, p. 43 f., 181 f.). The question is put in this way : What do we mean when we say that from all eternity man was elected by God, or, as we should have to say with equal emphasis according to the presuppositions of their theology, rejected by God ? Is it that in His eternal election God was thinking simply of man, man as not yet created but still to be created, man as not yet fallen but still to fall by divine permission and human action ? Or is it that He was thinking of man as already created and already fallen in virtue of this divine permission and human action ? In other words, is the one elected or rejected *homo creabilis et labilis*, or is he *homo creatus et lapsus ?* The whole difference of opinion narrows down ultimately to this formula.

We will consider first the Supralapsarian position. Its best known exponents were Beza, Bucanus, Gomarus, Maccovius, Heidanus and Burmann. About the turn of the 17th century it was readopted most forcefully by the mathematician Philip Naudaeus. It is difficult to prove whether Calvin himself can be claimed as a Supralapsarian (cf. on this point Heinz Otten, *op. cit.*, p. 91 f.). To be sure, his basic definition (*Instit*. III, 21, 5) can be understood in this sense : *Non enim pari conditione creantur omnes ; sed aliis vita aeterna, aliis damnatio aeterna praeordinatur. Itaque prout in alterutrum finem quisque conditus est, ita vel ad vitam vel ad mortem praedestinatum dicimus.* And the passage in *Instit.* III, 23, 7 seems to point even more clearly in the same direction : *Inficiari nemo potest, quin praesciverit Deus quem exitum esset habiturus homo antequam ipsum conderet et ideo praesciverit quia decreto suo sic ordinarat.* But it is difficult and even impossible to judge whether he had clearly in mind the alternatives as formulated in the later controversy. The same is true of Zwingli, who is usually cited in this connexion, especially in view of the opening section of Chapter 5 of his *De providentia*. The probability of consequence supports the view that if they could have been questioned further on the matter Zwingli and Calvin (but also the Luther of the *De servo arbitrio*) would have been found on the Supralapsarian side. The thesis of the genuine 17th century Supralapsarian is stated by W. Bucanus (*Instit. theol.*, 1605, *Loc.* 36, 8 f.) in the following way : *Quid est praedestinationis decretum ? Quo Deus homines a se creandos, antequam eos conderet, iam tum quorsum eos conderet constituens, sic ipsius gloriae inservire pro suo iure et mera voluntate decrevit, ut eorum alii essent vasa et exempla ipsius bonitatis et misericordiae, alii autem vasa et ὑποκείμενα ipsius irae, iustae in scelera ultionis atque potentiae. . . . Estque hoc decretum eiusmodi, quod ipsas exequutionis causas disponit, nedum ut ab iis pendeat.* But the only cause is *quod sic velit glorificari Dominus summe misericors et summe iustus.* The sequence of thought in the Supralapsarian scheme is this. God had and has a primal and basic purpose which has to be considered and taken into account quite apart from all His other specific purposes, and therefore quite apart from His purpose to create the world and quite apart from the further purpose to permit the fall of man. The original and proper purpose of God consists quite simply in this : that He Himself, and His glory, and more particularly His mercy and justice, should be revealed among men and to men by means of the salvation of some and the damnation of others. To this proper divine will and decree of God everything else that God wills is subordinate, as an interrelated means to its accomplishment. Because He has decreed this self-revelation, and in decreeing it, God has also decreed that man should be created to serve this end. It was also necessary that man should be created in such a way that by his own fault but with unfailing certainty he should fall into sin, thus arriving at the status and situation which would be a means to reveal the mercy of God in the salvation of some men and the justice of God in the damnation of others. For the purpose of executing the one divine decree it was necessary, then, that Adam, and all men in Adam, should in actual fact be brought to this situation and status. It was necessary, then, that they should in actual fact fall into sin. And for the purpose of executing this one divine decree it was also necessary that individual men should be willed either to salvation or to damnation and thus for one possibility or the other of divine self-revelation—as already predestinated thereto by God even before He decided to allow the fall of all men in the one man Adam, even before He decided on the original being of Adam in a state of innocence, even before He decided on the creation of Adam and the universe and all men. *Quod primum est in intentione, ultimum est in executione.* And conversely : *Quod ultimum est in executione, primum est in intentione.* The revelation of the mercy of God in the salvation of the elect and the justice of God in the damnation of the reprobate is last in execution. But for this reason it must have been first in the decree and purpose of God. What the Supralapsarian says, then, is that the fall had inevitably to take place, not apart from but in accordance with the will of God. But he also knows why it was that the fall and even creation had to take place. He tells us that the fall and creation had to have a place in God's plan and purpose, and that they had to take place, because God willed to reveal His mercy and justice. He knows that in God's primal and basic will as such there was decreed all that was necessary to such a revelation : the election of some men and the reprobation of others ; the creation and the fall. He knows, in fact, that for the sake of His own glory God from all eternity predestinated each individual man either to the one alternative or to the other, either to election or to reprobation. And he knows that God created man, and each individual man, and allowed him to sin in the person of Adam, in order that he might fulfil either the one destiny or the other, and therefore be a means to the revelation of God's glory, whether of His mercy or of His justice.

It must be noted that on the Supralapsarian view evil does not cease to be evil, sin does not cease to be sin, and the guilt of man does not cease to be real guilt. But the Supralapsarian does know why it is that God has allowed these things, and why it is that He has to that extent willed these things. As he sees it, God's overruling of evil is not to be presented or explained as a later and additional struggle in which God is dealing with a new and to some extent disruptive feature in His original plan. On the contrary, it must be thought of as an element in that original plan itself. As the Supralapsarian considers the details of the execution of the divine plan, i.e., in the course of created history as controlled by God, and as he considers the corresponding details in the whole eternal purpose of God, he does not regard these details individually or even in their relationships the one to the other. He regards them wholly and utterly in the light of the one divine plan which is the plan of all plans. In all the details it is the one basic plan which the Supralapsarian would have known and honoured. According to him, we cannot say simply that God created man to allow him to fall into sin. Nor can we say that He allowed him to fall into sin in order to damn him, or in His mercy to save some. Rather, all these individual *media* combine to form one single *medium*. And to know this *medium* as such, and the basis and meaning of all individual *media*, we must see them in the light of their ultimate purpose : that God created the universe and man, that He allowed the fall of man, that He allowed a general condemnation of sin to follow, and that in mercy He delivered some men from the general condemnation, in order that in and through this whole process He Himself might be glorified as the God of mercy and justice. Not one of the details is an end in itself—not even the eternal salvation or damnation of individuals which is the final link in the chain. On the contrary : *Omnia fecit propter se ipsum,* a much quoted verse in Prov. 16[14] which was understood to mean that God made all things, and from all eternity He willed all things for Himself. *Est enim Deus ipse summum et amabile bonum, in quod fertur necessitate naturae. Ita Deus fertur non nisi in seipsum et gloriam suam. Qua cum voluerit misericordiam et iustitiam suam effulgere, non potuit id effectum dare, nisi in salute vel damnatione peccatoris* (Heidan, *op. cit.,* p. 221). That is the function and the only function of the eternal salvation or damnation of men in the counsel of God. And it was because his eternal salvation or damnation had this necessary function (but only this function) in the counsel of God that man had to become *peccator.* And it was because he had to become *peccator* that he had to be created *homo.* The *obiectum praedestinationis* is, then, man as he is seen by God in His eternal election, i.e., *homo creabilis et labilis.*

Such are the main features of Supralapsarianism. At the outset we may characterise it as a system of consistent theistic monism. In view of its bold consistency and outstanding clarity we surely cannot withhold our admiration from this system.

Against it we may set the position of the Infralapsarians. Amongst strict Calvinists, at the furthest possible remove from any concessions to Arminianism and Lutheranism, this has always been the dominant view right up to our own day. At the Synod of Dort in particular, Supralapsarianism, while not rejected, was accepted only as a private opinion over against and distinct from the orthodox teaching. The Infralapsarian, too, knows of a primal and basic plan of God. God's eternal purpose is to reveal and to glorify Himself. According to him, too, creation and evil do not enter into this plan by chance, but by the efficient will of God in the one case, and by His permissive will in the other. For him, too, the fall is inevitable because it is an event decreed by God. Unlike the Supralapsarian, however, the Infralapsarian does not think that he has any exact knowledge either of the content of God's primal and basic plan or of the reasons for the divine decree in respect of creation and the fall. On the contrary, he holds that the reasons for this decree are ultimately unknown and unknowable. And, in any case, he does not say that creation and the fall were necessary in order to reveal the divine mercy and justice. He does not explain the creation of man and the universe in relation to this twofold revelation, but more generally as *communicatio et velut* ἔκστασις *potentiae, sapientiae et bonitatis creatoris* (F. Turrettini, *Instit. Theol. el.,* 1679, L. IV, qu. 9, 22). And he would have the decree of predestination as such subordinated as a decree of creation and the fall which has its basis elsewhere (and not in this specific plan). Only in the decree of predestination as such does he come across the particular divine purpose to reveal God's mercy and justice by the salvation of some and the damnation of others. But the existence of sin, and the existence of man as a sinner, and his existence at all, cannot be explained by this purpose. We cannot say that because God willed to reveal His mercy and justice by election and reprobation, therefore He willed creation and the fall. All that we can say is that the same God who willed men who would necessarily fall into sin, and who as Creator willed the existence of men at all, wills also that of those men some should of His mercy be saved, and the rest abandoned to the punishment which all have merited. It is true that God is absolutely free in His choice of the elect and reprobate. It is true that there can be no question of grounding this choice in the greater or lesser sins of the one group or the other. It is true that it is not a matter of the merit of good works which the one group has earned and the other has not earned. Elect and reprobate, they are all sinners, and they are such by the will and counsel of God. But the fact that they are sinners and the fact that they are created ought not to be connected with the decree of predestination as such, nor deduced from that decree. We must understand the decree of predestination as an independent entity, related to the decree of creation and the fall only to the extent that in an inconceivable unity they are both the eternal decree of God. And in order, although not of course in time, the decree of predestination must be thought of as subsequent to that of creation and the fall. It must be thought of, then, as referring to and presupposing that prior decree. The revelation of the *misericordia Dei* presupposes an already existent *miser*, and the revelation of the *iustitia Dei* presupposes an already existent *iniustitia*. And both these presuppose an existent creature to whom that twofold revelation can apply, and also the creation of this creature. We may say that the revelation is made by a means already appointed, Christ Himself, and that it takes place by way of a calling and justification and sanctification which are efficacious either to life or to death. But the means already presuppose the existence of sin and the existence of sinful, guilty and wicked men. Creation and sin are then *conditiones in obiecto praerequisitae. Nisi enim homo conditus esset et lapsus praedestinatio non posset venire in executionem* (F. Turrettini, *op. cit.,* IV, *qu.* 9, 20 f.). Against the Supralapsarian application of the assertion : *Quod ultimum est in executione, debet esse primum in intentione,* it is objected that the *illustratio misericordiae et iustitiae in hominum salute vel damnatione* is not absolutely the *finis ultimus, quoad hominis gubernationem in genere,* but only *secundum quid et relate, quoad gubernationem hominis lapsi. Finis ultimus fuit manifestatio gloriae Dei in communi per hominis creationem et lapsum.* The decree of election is the first and chief of those decrees which relate to the destiny of sinful man, but it is not the first and chief of all the divine decrees. Between creation and the fall on the one hand and salvation on the other there is no *necessaria connexio et subordinatio.* For : *Nemo non videt hiatum et* μέγα χάσμα *propter peccatum quod creationis ordinem abrupit et redemptionis oeconomiae locum dedit : peccatum est contra naturam, nec medium vel respectu salutis, nisi per accidens* (F. Turrettini, *op., cit.* IV, *qu.* 9, 23). Only to this extent do one or two think that they may speak of the unity of the divine purpose in respect of both dispensations—that God willed first to show *quid in homine possit liberum arbitrium,* and then *quid possit suae gratiae beneficium* (*Syn. pur. Theol.,* 1624, *Disp.* 24, 23). Or else, it is a question of the revelation of the twofold majesty of God, first in the Law and then in the Gospel (H. Heidegger, *Corp. Theol.,* 1700, V, 34, as quoted by Heppe, p. 130).

The attack on the Supralapsarians was conducted along the following lines (cf. F. Turrettini, *op. cit.,* IV, *qu.* 9, 9–14). (1) *Homo creabilis et labilis* is a *Non-ens.* But predestination has to do with a being which has already been raised from non-being to being. It has to do with an already existent being, and with a specific form of the existence of this being. (2) The concept *homo creabilis et labilis* would, in fact, include all men, even those who were never created and never fell. It would apply to all those whose existence was at least a possibility. But predestination has to do with men as really created and fallen. Its object, then, cannot be *homo creabilis et labilis*. (3) *Homo creabilis et labilis* is neither *eligibilis* nor *reprobabilis*. For to be a possible object of election or reprobation presupposes qualities corresponding to the electing mercy and reprobating justice of God. And such qualities belong only to *homo creatus et lapsus*. *Homo creabilis et labilis* cannot, then, be the *obiectum praedestinationis*. (4) If *homo creabilis et labilis* were indeed the object of predestination, then creation and the fall would be instruments of predestination. But they are not defined as such in Scripture. Man might well have been created and have fallen into sin without the question of election or reprobation ever arising. Creation and the fall belong to the *ordo naturalis providentiae*. Salvation and damnation form the specific content of the *ordo supernaturalis praedestinationis*. It is absurd to suppose that first of all God arranged the eternal salvation or damnation of men and only then arranged their actual existence and fall. Creation and the fall must be regarded as necessary from the standpoint of predestination not as a *medium per quod* but as a *conditio sine qua non*. Obviously the sick man cannot be cured unless he exists as a man and is sick. But obviously, too, his existence as a man and his sickness cannot be regarded as means to cure him. (5) The Supralapsarian view of *homo creabilis et labilis* is ἐνδιάβλητος and open to the severest criticism because it implies the impossible belief that God rejected some men even before they existed in His own consciousness as reprobates, and that He allowed them to become worthy of rejection simply in order that He might as such reject them.

As against this view the Infralapsarians advance positively the following propositions (cf. F. Turrettini, *op. cit.*, IV, *qu.* 9, 15-19). (1) Man is the object of the eternal predestination precisely in the situation in which God knows him as the one whom He will encounter in time. As Jn. 15[19] tells us : " I have chosen you out of the world." *Homo peccator*, the object of temporal calling, is also the object of eternal election. (2) The election of men takes place in Christ. The elect in Christ from all eternity are, however, the *redimendi et sanctificandi per ipsum*. Thus the elected man is *homo lapsus* as such. (3) In Rom. 9[21] Paul speaks of a φύραμα, the one lump from which the potter, according to his own pleasure, makes some vessels to honour and some to dishonour. Isaac and Ishmael, Jacob and Esau belonged equally to that one lump. And since God's varied dealings with them are determined by mercy and wrath, it is clear that they are a lump of sin and misery, a *massa corrupta*. It is also clear, then, that the object of God's twofold predestination is *homo lapsus*. Rom. 9[22] does not tell us that God created but that He prepared some to salvation and others to damnation. And that means that God's choice between men was made not according to a physical predetermination but according to an (admittedly inconceivable) ethical judgment. He made that choice from all eternity, but with reference to man as already created and fallen. (4) According to the common understanding of Rom. 9[22] the mercy and justice of God are the decisive motives in the divine predestination. But these must have fallen man as their object, not merely in temporal fulfilment, but in eternal purpose. Otherwise mercy would not be mercy, but *quaedam immensa bonitas*. And justice would not be justice, but *absoluta potestas*. As an act of mercy and justice predestination relates necessarily to *homo creatus et lapsus*.

Such, then, is the Infralapsarian view. At a first glance we cannot deny it one definite advantage—that even at the cost of a general systematic coherence and clarity in detail it does do greater justice than its Supralapsarian counterpart to the logical and moral difficulties of the common doctrine. If we consider the ever-recurring problem of the ecclesiastical utility of the doctrine we can readily understand why it was that the Infralapsarian and not the Supralapsarian view was adopted and retained as an official interpretation of the Calvinistic dogma. We can also understand why it was that the Supralapsarian view was more sharply attacked and repudiated by the Romanist, Lutheran, Arminian and other opponents of that dogma. And we can understand, too, why it was that the Infralapsarian arguments could be and actually were applied by these common enemies in their struggle against the particularly obnoxious Supralapsarian understanding. But this does not mean that the Infralapsarians did, in fact, approximate even in the slightest degree towards these common foes. The Infralapsarian interpretation did not involve the slightest concession to these enemies, and in relation to them we can regard it only as a variation which was based upon the same confessional position. Alongside the friendly words of the Supralapsarian A. Heidanus we may place the equally friendly statement of the Infralapsarian F. Turrettini : *Qualiscunque sit theologorum hac in parte diversitas, manet tamen apud utrosque salvum fidei fundamentum et ex aequo isti opponuntur exitiali Pelagianorum et Semipelagianorum errori. . . . In eo omnes conveniunt, quod homines Deo pares, non impares obiiciunt, et tales quorum discretio a solo Deo pendeat, a quo fundamento recedunt omnes sectarii* (*op. cit.*, IV, *qu.* 9, 4). Unfortunately we must add that from the standpoint of the present context the Supralapsarians and Infralapsarians had a further point in common. They were concerned—as we are—with the question of the *obiectum praedestinationis*, but they both of them missed the decisive insight into the heart of the matter.

It will be instructive, finally, to investigate one of the compromise theories which settled the controversy towards the end of the 17th century. For this purpose we will choose the presentation of P. van Mastricht (*Theor. Pract. Theol.*, 1699, III, *cap.* 2, 12 f.). As van Mastricht sees it, if we are to arrive at any true understanding and decision in this controversy, we must distinguish in our minds four different divine acts which characterise the one decree of God in relation to man. The first is the *propositum manifestandi gloriam misericordiae et iustitiae vindicantis*. In respect of this first act the object of predestination must undoubtedly be identified with *homo creabilis et labilis* as in the Supralapsarian scheme. For there can be no doubt that in this purpose the decree of creation and the fall is not yet presupposed. It is impossible then, that *homo creatus et lapsus* should be the object. The second is the *statutum creandi et in lapsum permittendi homines* which applies to all men equally. In respect of this second act the object of predestination must be identified as *homo creandus et lapsurus*—again in the Supralapsarian sense. For this second act is indeed identical with the decree of creation and the fall as such, but for that very reason we cannot think of *homo creatus et lapsus* as its object, but only of the future reality in time of *homo creatus et lapsus*. The third is the decree of election properly speaking, on the basis of which some are foreordained and separated to the glorifying of God's mercy and others to the glorifying of His justice. It is in respect of this third act that the Infralapsarians are in the right. Only *homo creatus et lapsus* can be the object of the divine will and purpose in the decree of election properly speaking and as such. The fourth is the divine purpose in respect of the ways and means appropriate to the *electio* of some and the *reprobatio* of others. In so far as these ways and means are intended and ordained for man, man as envisaged in this fourth act can only be *homo electus et reprobatus*, and as such, according to the third, he is *homo creatus et lapsus*. Here too, then, the Infralapsarians are in the right. In arriving at his decision van Mastricht presents the arguments of the two parties as follows. Against the Supralapsarians the Infralapsarians adduce Jn. 15[19] and Rom. 9[21] in proof of the assertion that it is *homo creatus et lapsus* who is elected or rejected. Against this it may be argued that while the assertion is true in relation to the third and fourth of the acts above mentioned, to which the texts quoted refer, and more particularly in relation to the narrower understanding of *electio* and *reprobatio*, yet this understanding of predestination is far too narrow, for predestination includes the first and second acts as well, and in relation to these the assertion is not true. As against that, the Supralapsarian complains that the Infralapsarian understanding of creation and the fall leaves no place for the divine purpose. It must be allowed that he is right when he speaks of the *manifestatio gratiae et iustitiae* as the divine purpose which lies behind predestination in its wider and more comprehensive sense. He is also right when he claims that *homo creabilis et labilis* is the object of this purpose. Nevertheless the object of election properly speaking, of *electio et reprobatio*, is not *homo creabilis et labilis* but *homo creatus et lapsus*, as the Infralapsarian rightly maintains. As an acute piece of work this compromise rightly deserves credit. Yet it must be asked whether the older and genuine exponents of the two trends could ever have accepted a judgment which reconciled and corrected them after this fashion. After all, both parties were proved wrong, the Supralapsarians in respect of the decisive concepts of election and reprobation, the Infralapsarians in respect of the equally decisive question of the distinction between the two dispensations. They were proved right, in fact, only by telling them that in their most important convictions they were wrong. In the light of this fact we must at least recognise that Mastricht was an honest mediator. He did not simplify the issue either for himself or for the two schools. And his proposal certainly has the merit that it brings out clearly and systematically the interrelatedness and indeed the unity of the two trends, a unity which was not challenged by either party. It proves, in fact, that there can be no question of finding any confessional difference between the two schools, or any disruptive significance in the controversy.

We may now attempt an estimate of the controversy. And first of all it will be well clearly to remind ourselves what were the common presuppositions underlying the two positions, and also the attempted compromise between them, as they are revealed in this attempted compromise. There can be no doubt that all the orthodox Reformed trends of that period shared the same earnest desire to serve the main interest of Calvinistic dogma—to extol the free grace of God and the sovereignty of the freely gracious God as the beginning of all Christian truth and of all Christian apprehension of truth. It should be noted in this respect that not only the Supralapsarians but such avowed Infralapsarians as Polanus and Wolleb, and at the end of the century F. Turrettini, gave to the doctrine of predestination a place immediately after the doctrine of God and before all the remaining *Loci*, although according to the Infralapsarian understanding of predestination it ought not to have been introduced prior to the doctrine of sin at the very earliest. Obviously they felt very strongly the need to treat this doctrine before everything else, so that all that followed could be set against the one background of the sovereignty of divine grace. But quite apart from this indisputably Christian kernel of Calvinistic dogma, there are other and equally unassailable presuppositions common to all the trends of the period.

Supralapsarians, Infralapsarians and mediators all agreed that the controverted *obiectum praedestinationis*, elected or rejected man, must be identified directly and independently with the partly elected and partly rejected individual descendants of Adam, both in the mass and also in detail. The interest of both parties, and of the older Reformed theology as a whole (and indeed of all the older theology), centred exclusively upon these individuals as such. It is in the election of some of these individuals that the man Jesus Christ plays a specific and indispensable part as the first of the elect. With the rejection of the others He has nothing whatever to do. Yet when the question of the *obiectum praedestinationis* arises, then in one way or another He is quickly passed over, and a proper solution is found in the individual *x* or *y*. It may be as *creabilis* or *creatus*, it may be as *labilis* or *lapsus*, but this *homo x* or *y* is always the *obiectum praedestinationis*.

Second, all parties were at one in thinking that in God's eternal decree predestination (and therefore the election or rejection of individuals) implies the setting up of a fixed system which the temporal life and history of individuals can only fulfil and affirm. The doctrine of predestination does not proclaim the free grace of God as glad tidings, but as the neutral impartation of the message that from all eternity God is gracious to whom He will be gracious, and whom He will He hardeneth, and that this constitutes the limit within which each individual must run his course. The Supralapsarian maintains that this system of the eternal election or reprobation of individuals is the system above every other system, being identical with the primal and basic plan of God besides which there is none other. The Infralapsarian allows the existence of another plan or system either alongside or prior to it, in the form of the decree of creation and the fall. But both parties presuppose and maintain that that system is in any case from all eternity, and that it is indeed fixed and unalterable, so that not merely individuals, but God Himself as its eternal author is bound by it in time, and (in relation to that pattern of all things, which is itself thought of as fixed) there can be nothing new under the sun, whether on man's part or on God's.

Third, all parties were agreed that when God set up this fixed system which anticipated the life-history and destiny of every individual as such, then in the same way, in the same sense, with the same emphasis, and in an exact equilibrium in every respect, God uttered both a Yes and a No, accepting some and rejecting others. In respect of the decree of creation the Infralapsarians do speak in some sense of a general purpose of God in the revelation of His glory, although without attempting to define this purpose more exactly. But when they come to the decree of predestination as such, they too speak of God's purpose in respect of created and fallen man in a way which is absolutely symmetrical. This purpose is to demonstrate His mercy to some and His justice to others. From the general mass of corruption the mercy of God infallibly inclines and guides a certain fixed number of individuals to election, and in the same way the justice of God infallibly inclines and guides a certain fixed number to perdition. There can be no more question of a disturbance or upsetting of the equilibrium of these two attitudes in God than there can be of any subsequent alteration within the system which has been established by the twofold will of God. The two attitudes together, the one balancing the other, constitute the divine will to self-glorification, and God is glorified equally in the eternal blessedness of the elect and the eternal damnation of the reprobate.

Fourth and above all—the hidden basis of all other agreement—all parties were agreed in their understanding of the divine good-pleasure which decided between election and rejection and thus determined the concrete structure of the system appointed from all eternity for time. They agreed, then, in thinking that this good-pleasure must be understood wholly and utterly as *decretum absolutum*. It is an act of divine freedom whose basis and meaning are completely hidden, and in their hiddenness must be regarded and reverenced as holy. This *decretum absolutum* is (according to the Infralapsarian view) the divine disposition in respect of *homo creatus et lapsus*, or (according to the Supralapsarian view) the divine disposition in respect of *homo creabilis et labilis*. Behind both these views (at a different point, but with the same effect in practice), there stands the picture of the absolute God in Himself who is neither conditioned nor self-conditioning, and not the picture of the Son of God who is self-conditioned and therefore conditioned in His union with the Son of David ; not the picture of God in Jesus Christ.

Such, then, are the common presuppositions of Supralapsarianism and Infralapsarianism, presuppositions which our earlier deliberations have shown to be not at all self-evident but most doubtful from a Christian standpoint. To do justice to the two trends we must take into account the doubtful presuppositions.

And the first question which we must ask in relation to them is to what extent, upon the basis and within the limits of these presuppositions, the two views did or did not serve the undoubtedly Christian interest or concern of Calvinistic dogma.

Now first it must be admitted that the Supralapsarian construction has a good deal to be said in its favour, for it puts the divine decision between mercy towards some and justice towards others—the free grace of God—so consistently and definitely at the head of all Christian knowledge and understanding. A clear light is shed upon all God's work—and indirectly upon all His being—when His will to reveal His glory is understood concretely as His will to reveal His mercy and justice, when we construe the *Omnia fecit propter seipsum* in the light of that understanding, when *Deus ipse* is thought of in advance as a God of mercy and justice. In its choice of this starting-point Supralapsarianism is not quite so speculative as a first and general glance would suggest. And we cannot but recognise that in its choice and unconditional assertion of this starting-point it did aim to treat of the God of Holy Scripture. To consider the eternally electing and rejecting One from the standpoint of the specific qualities of the God of Holy Scripture, to seek to understand the causative will of the Creator and the permissive will of the One who overrules even the fall as the will of this God of mercy and justice, is not an undertaking of speculative theology, but it is rather (and especially when we consider the conception of God dominant in the orthodoxy of the century) something in the nature of a sally against speculative theology in general. If we are to think of the Supralapsarians as theistic monists, we must at least admit that it was a biblical and Christian monism which they envisaged. Can we really blame them for wanting to know too much at this point? Should we not blame them rather because there was something more which they ought to have known in their obvious attempt to make the biblical conception of God their starting-point? They became speculative in the bad sense only in the abstract use which they permitted themselves to make of the biblical concepts of mercy and justice. They became speculative only when they looked for God Himself in the mysterious choice which governed the application of these two qualities. They were speculative in that they did not start with the concrete biblical form of these qualities and of God Himself. But when they chose this starting-point, when they sought to assert their *oeconomia supernaturalis praedestinationis*, and therefore the order of God's mercy and justice, as the first and chief order which is normative and decisive for all others and for the realisation of all others in time, there can be no doubt—and we must not forget this—that they were advancing in the direction of a penetration to the Christian understanding of the doctrine of predestination. As against that, the Infralapsarian isolation of a specific and prior *oeconomia naturalis providentiae* is undoubtedly weaker, redounding less to the credit of free grace, and relativising and contracting it in an unfortunate manner. Speaking of God, the Creator of heaven and earth, qu. 26 of the *Heidelberg Catechism* tells us that " the eternal Father of our Lord Jesus Christ . . . is my God and my Father for the sake of His Son Jesus Christ." Those who summarise and confess their faith in God in these words cannot isolate the dispensation of creation and providence from the later dispensation of grace and predestination. At any rate, they cannot hide the first dispensation in the obscurity which enfolds it in Infralapsarian teaching. The logico-empirical objections of the Infralapsarians sound well enough. Before God could decide in mercy and justice, there must have been a corresponding constitution of individuals and an actualisation of their existence. And there is a show of soundness and plausibility in their indignation at the very absurdity of the assumption that God could first arrange the salvation or damnation of men and only later their existence and fall. But we cannot deny that these are not spiritual objections. They are not the arguments of faith. They do not take into account the deity of the eternal God, and the possibility that with Him the last could actually be the first. Only too self-evidently they apply to God standards taken from the order of human reason. But the history of Israel and of Jesus Christ and of the Church is not played out within the framework of a prior and already preceding history of nature and the universe. That is not the picture of the world and history as it is given us in the Bible. According to the Bible, the framework and basis of all temporal occurrence is the history of the covenant between God and man, from Adam to Noah and Abraham, from Abraham and Jacob to David, from David to Jesus Christ and believers in Him. It is within this framework that the whole history of nature and the universe plays its specific role, and not the reverse, although logically and empirically the course of things ought to have been the reverse. At this point the Supralapsarians had the courage to draw from the biblical picture of the universe and history the logical deduction in respect of the eternal divine decree. The Infralapsarians did maintain the sequence of the biblical picture in respect of the realisation of salvation, but they shrank from the deduction. In respect of the eternal divine decree they maintained a supposedly more rational order, isolating the two dispensations and subordinating the order of predestination to that of providence. In so doing, they shrank from defining more closely the *oeconomia naturalis providentiae*. The result was that at a central point in their teaching, side by side with the still obscure *decretum absolutum*, there arose necessarily a further obscurity which overshadowed their whole doctrine of the second dispensation. This was the obscurity of the question with whom or with what we really have to do in the God who created man and the universe, and who permitted the fall of man. Where the distinction was thought of as a major one, and one that must be maintained, it was inevitable that a later age should ask for more information. And it was also inevitable that they should find such information in the belief that in the works of creation and providence (we may say, too, in nature and reason) there is a certain general goodness and power and wisdom of God which corresponds to the specific mercy and justice of God in the work of salvation. It was inevitable, then, that the Infralapsarian construction could at least help towards the later cleavage between natural and revealed theology. It is that which (within the framework of the common presuppositions) makes it appear the less happy of the two.

But within this framework we must not deny to the Infralapsarian view some particular advantages. Two things call for notice in this respect.

1. If we start with the position that predestination must be thought of as the decree of the free good-pleasure of God by which the election or rejection of individuals is foreordained with the fixity and equilibrium of the two systems, then from the standpoint first of God but also of man this means that on the Infralapsarian view there is a certain mitigation in the fact that this decree is not the first and primary decree, not the decree which is above all other decrees, not the absolute decree of God in respect of the distinct reality of the universe and man. We recall the affirmation made by the Supralapsarians on the basis of the same presupposition : that in so far as the divine concern is not self-concern, or a concern with the revelation of the divine glory, it is directed wholly and utterly to individuals as such, and to their eternal destiny of salvation or perdition, and to their progress towards this end. It is to serve this one end, the bringing of individual x to heaven and of individual y to hell, that there is brought into being the monstrous apparatus of the creation of heaven and earth, the sinister contrivance of a permitted fall and the resultant dominion of evil in the world, the appearance of Jesus Christ in the world, and His work, and the founding and maintaining of His Church, and all the operations of effectual calling and hardening which are involved in this redemptive work. This and this alone is the concern of the triune God (apart, of course, from His prior concern with Himself) in His movement towards the universe and man. But that means (with the constant proviso that the whole process and the end itself are

necessary and are made actual only for the self-glorification of God) that man, and indeed the individuals x and y are made the measure and centre of all things to a degree which could hardly be surpassed. What vistas open up and what extremes meet at this point! Is it an accident that A. Heidanus, and even so pronounced a disciple of Coccejus as his son-in-law F. Burmann, were at one and the same time Supralapsarians—and also Cartesians ? And supposing the theological basis of this whole outlook and system were shaken! Supposing an anthropological basis were disclosed, and openly or secretly it replaced the theological! Heidanus and Burmann were amongst the older Reformed theologians in whom we have advance warning of a movement in this direction. We can hardly deny that with its surprisingly direct relationship between the totality of the divine work and the individual, Supralapsarianism could, and in fact did, prepare the way for such a movement. As against that, Infralapsarianism—which in other ways contributed to the same development—could at least exercise a certain restraint by refusing to allow the divine rule over and in the world to be identified quite so dominantly or fully with the attainment of this one end. Its subordination of the decree of predestination to that of creation and the fall did at least achieve the negative result of preventing the individual's every possible thought about God from degenerating automatically into thought about himself. It prevented the reverence for the holy self-seeking whereby God is zealous for His own honour from carrying with it the immediate and direct stimulation of an equally holy self-seeking on the part of the predestinated man, whether in his desire to attain heaven or in his fear of being cast into hell. In such an understanding there lurks always the possibility of a reversal of the relationship. God may well come to be thought of as the One who is God for man's sake, for the sake of the individual x or y, and who is at the disposal of this individual in order that he may attain that which he desires and escape that which he fears. The Infralapsaraians could at least hold such a tendency in check, for they remembered that the decree of creation and the fall preceded that of predestination, thus leaving a place for thought about God and His lordship and work which does not stand in any direct relationship with thought about our own interests, which cannot be deduced from such thought, but which stands over against it as something independent and even superior. It is true that the way in which the Infralapsarians introduced this safeguard cannot be regarded as a happy one. In the long run the threat of anthropologism could not be warded off by a safeguard which consisted in the reference to a supposedly independent realm of creation and providence over and above that of redemption. On the contrary, the more strongly the autonomy of that realm was emphasised, the more surely was the foundation laid for a later proclamation of the self-glorification of the individual with divine help. Within the framework of the common presuppositions there is no effective safeguard against aberration in this direction. It must be allowed, however, that within these common presuppositions the Infralapsarian recollection of the first and independent divine decree, and the Infralapsarian loosening of the rigid relationship between God and the salvation or perdition of the individual, did exercise a retarding function in face of the threatened aberration. But such a loosening could also mean a certain mitigation in respect of man. According to Supralapsarian opinion man was nothing more than the elect or reprobate in whose whole existence there was only the one prospect of the fulfilment of a course already mapped out either one way or the other. But the Infralapsarians knew of another secret of God side by side with the decree of predestination. Theoretically at least, then, they knew of another secret of man apart from the fact that he is either elect or reprobate. For them man was also (and indeed primarily) the creature of God, and as such responsible to God. This view involved a softening in the understanding of God which is both dangerous and doubtful. And in the long run it could not have any really effective results. For practical purposes the

Infralapsarians knew of man only in his twofold destiny. But they needed only to let that slip, they needed only to let the theoretically possible modification take practical shape as a specific anthropology deriving from the first article, and they were well on the way to a naturalistic doctrine of man which would relativise and finally replace the Christian doctrine. For that reason the theoretically possible modification was never made in practice before the end of the 17th century. It can only be said that within the common presuppositions the Infralapsarians had the advantage of leaving open the question of how or in what respect man is elect or reprobate. They had, then, the advantage of pointing (although not from a very well-chosen standpoint) to something which lies beyond the determination of man as either the one thing or the other, thus calling in question the rigidity of the determination.

2. The second obvious advantage of Infralapsarianism consists naturally in its greater reserve with respect to the reality of the fall and the presence of evil in the world. The Infralapsarians, too, attributed this reality to God's eternal will and counsel. They could not be accused of dualism at this point. But they distinguished between the decree which permitted evil and the decree of predestination. The permitting of evil was not thought of as a means which God willed and posited in execution of His electing and rejecting, but rather as a means of which He actually made use in this activity. God's permitting of evil was a very different matter, as was His creating of the universe and man. But He then made use of the creation and the fall of man, acting on the man created by His will and fallen in accordance with it, according to the measure of this twofold predestination. In accordance with this fact the decrees of God must be considered and understood together in spite of the difference between them. In God they are one. But they must not be interfused the one with the other nor deduced the one from the other. On the Infralapsarian view the fact that these decrees stand alongside one another and together constitute the one holy will of God is—along with the freedom of the good-pleasure of God in respect of His decisions—the divine secret. The corresponding statements of the Supralapsarians were far bolder, but harsh and dangerous, giving occasion at least to the constant reproach made against the Calvinists that they think of God as the *auctor peccati*. The Supralapsarians so exalted the sovereignty of God above everything else that they did not sufficiently appreciate the danger of trying to solve the problem of evil and to rationalise the irrational by making it a constituent element in the divine world-order and therefore a necessity, a part of nature. In their eyes the more pressing danger was that of opening up the slightest chink to dualism. But the Infralapsarians obviously thought the other danger the more serious. That is why in their system evil (like creation itself) assumes a more enigmatical character, being enfolded in an impenetrable darkness. The enemy is the Evil One, and his power is a real power, and consequently our redemption is a real redemption. By separating instead of uniting the economies of evil and redemption the Infralapsarian can bring out these truths better, or at any rate more clearly. They can state much more decidedly that in our redemption a moral judgment is executed and a victory won for the almightiness of God. They can also state that God has not foreordained any one for evil, not even the reprobate. It must be conceded that within the common presuppositions Infralapsarianism is better able to show that that which takes place between God and man is not a natural, let alone a mechanical process. The Supralapsarians had no desire to maintain a view of this kind. But the Infralapsarians were better able to show why it ought not to be maintained. By leaving to God Himself a mystery which has nothing whatever to do with the revelation of His mercy and justice (the mystery of the divine permitting of evil), they were better able to safeguard the respect which is owed to God by the man who is enslaved to evil and does it. They were better able to avoid the temptation to find an excuse in the fact that the divine purpose includes

evil for the sake of election or reprobation. This legitimate interest was better safeguarded, although we cannot, of course, say more.

When we weigh the pros and contras together, our first inclination is to take up an attitude of radical neutrality or indifference. Within the presuppositions common to both parties the reasons and counter-reasons seem to be more or less equally balanced. We could, of course, concentrate upon the theological points which both parties held in common, as has been done since the end of the 17th century. This would leave us perfectly free to decide in favour of the one or the other according to taste or sentiment. It would also give the assurance that the two standpoints are not irreconcilable, as the compromise of van Mastricht has shown, but that at a pinch they can be fused into one. I do not think that this course is really possible. If the controversy is rightly understood, the indecision cannot be radical ; it cannot mean a renunciation of decision, but only the conclusion (inevitable, of course) that on the ground on which it was fought out the controversy was one which could not be decided, and one which we, too, cannot satisfactorily decide. But that does not mean that the controversy does not concern us and that we are not called at this point to decision. The question of the *obiectum praedestinationis*, the elect man, is still a question which we have to face, and we cannot very well maintain that it was satisfactorily answered in the 16th century. We are not in any position to dismiss the 17th century problem as superfluous, or to abandon the problem to merely capricious solution. Again, we are not in any position to concentrate upon what was common to both trends, for this common element has itself become a problem from the standpoint of the normative and central concern of Calvinistic dogma, and in the light of our own understanding of this concern. When on the basis of quite different presuppositions we are seeking an answer to the same question, we may not be able to accept the answers already given, but we cannot dismiss them as a matter of indifference. We are obliged to ask which side had relatively the greater truth at that age and within the now shattered theological unity of that age. We have no reason to assume that we can judge freely in this matter according to taste or sentiment, nor have we any reason to content ourselves with the fact that at a pinch some kind of compromise could be arranged. To know that at a pinch both standpoints could be accepted on the basis then adopted does not help us to learn from this tract of history. We are fully convinced that on that basis both standpoints were in their way necessary. But we are also convinced that it was only at a pinch, i.e., under all kinds of difficulties, that the two could be accepted and fused the one with the other. What we do really need to know is this : Granted the doubtful nature of the common presuppositions, which of the two standpoints has more in its favour in the sense of clearing the ground for the answer which, on quite different presuppositions, we ourselves must give to a question no less legitimate to-day than it was then ? In other words, when we adopt this quite different basis, to which of the two opposing standpoints can we attach ourselves, so that we not only reach a decision in the then controversy, but also think out the matter, not in an indifferent discontinuity, but in continuity with this section of the Church's theological history (not breaking off the threads but gathering them together) ?

When we put it in this way, the answer is unavoidable. The greater right (*praemissis praemittendis* and *omissis omittendis*) lay then on the side of the Supralapsarians. The objections against them, and our own objections against them (which constitute the relative correctness of Infralapsarianism), do not amount finally to anything more than a demonstration of the specific dangers in their position. Behind their rigid theocentricity there lurks somewhere the menace of a swing over to an equally rigid anthropocentricity. We may describe it as highly probable that Supralapsarianism did help to prepare the way for this swing over as it actually took place. Again, behind their consideration of creation, sin and redemption only from the standpoint of the revelation of God's glory, there lurks somewhere the relativisation of the problem of evil, the resolving of the whole relationship between God and man into a kind of natural process which admits of no contradictions. But the fact that a position is dangerous is not to say that it is wrong, even less that the contrary position is right. And when we examine more closely the undoubted and unavoidable dangers of Supralapsarianism, it becomes evident that they are real dangers, and that they could and did help to pave the way for the unfortunate developments later, only because Supralapsarianism rested on the fatal basis of the four common presuppositions. If the *obiectum praedestinationis* is the individual abstractly understood, then it is most dangerous to seek God's primal and basic purpose in election and reprobation. If predestination consists in the eternal setting up of that fixed system which governs all temporal reality, and if within that system election and reprobation are evenly balanced, then it is most dangerous so unconditionally to carry through the thought of the divine sovereignty that the fall and evil are understood as means foreseen and foreordained by God to the attainment of the finally good purpose which He has willed. If the *decretum absolutum* is the last possible word concerning the basis of divine predestination, then it is most dangerous to think of God as the One who sees and plans and achieves His own glory in the foreordaining of a certain number of individuals irresistibly to heaven and of a certain number of individuals no less irresistibly to hell. And it is most dangerous to believe that for this purpose God created the world, and permitted and to that extent willed the existence of sin and the devil, and then of course, in line as it were with these prior acts, accomplished the work of redemption. It is most dangerous to believe that, in virtue of His over-all determination, this redemptive work must itself mean both calling and also hardening, that it must be a means of election and also a means of rejection—and both with that unshakeable fixity, both in that indestructible equilibrium, both as the fulfilment of that secret good-pleasure of God which is wholly anonymous and completely closed in upon itself. It is quite true—and the relative truth of Infralapsarianism is based upon the fact—that if the presuppositions hold, the Supralapsarian God threatens to take on the appearance of a demon, and in the light of this fact we may well understand the horror with which Roman Catholics, Lutherans, Arminians and even many of the Reformed themselves recoiled from the doctrine. It must be made quite clear, however, that the danger and the corresponding horror arise only as Supralapsarianism is attempted on the basis of these presuppositions. On this basis Supralapsarianism is an enterprise which attracts and strikes us by what amounts almost to its intellectual audacity. It did, in fact, have something of this character and even more (as we see for example in the school of Maccovius). But the danger tells against Supralapsarianism as such only if the presuppositions are as necessary and unshakeable in themselves as they were for all the older theology and for the Supralapsarians of the 17th century.

Let us try for a moment to think of the Supralapsarian teaching as detached from this background and freed from all the influences which there affected it. Let us try to understand what happens in and to the universe and for and to man, the origin and purpose and meaning of the universe and man, in terms of the eternal counsel of a God who in His love is sovereign. The primal and basic purpose of this God in relation to the world is to impart and reveal Himself—and with Himself His glory, He Himself being the very essence of glory. And because all things are His creation, because He is the Lord of all things, this primal and basic purpose is the beginning of all things, the eternal reality in which everything future is already determined and comprehended. And in this purpose which is the beginning of all things God does not will at random. He wills man : not the idea of man, not humanity, not human individuals in the mass or in particular ; or rather all these, but *in concreto* and not *in abstracto*. He wills man, His man, elected man, man predestined as the witness to His glory and the object of His love. In this man, but only in him, He wills humanity and every individual man and what we may describe as the idea of humanity. But first and specifically and immediately He wills man, His man, man elected by Him. His intention is that this man should testify to His glory and thus reveal and confirm and verify both positively what He is and wills, and negatively what He is not and does not will. The latter part of the intention is not positive but negative ; a marking off, a separating, a setting aside. It is not a second Yes on God's part, but a No which is of God only to the extent that it corresponds and is opposed to the Yes, a No which forms the necessary boundary of the Yes : so assuredly is God God and not not God ; so assuredly does He live in eternal self-differentiation from all that is not God and is not willed by God. In this sense God is and is not ; He wills and does not will. And for this reason He intends and ordains that the object of His love and the witness to His glory in the universe which He has created should testify in a twofold manner— he should testify to His Yes and to what He wills, and he should also testify to His No and to what He does not will. In this way the witness can truly exist and live in covenant with God. In this way there may be manifest to him the fulness of the divine glory. It is not God's will that elected man should fall into sin. But it is His will that sin, that which God does not will, should be repudiated and rejected and excluded by him. It is God's will that elected man should repudiate what He repudiates, and that thereby the Yes of God should be revealed and proclaimed. God does not will and affirm evil and the fall and an act of sin on the part of this man (it will never come to that, so assuredly is he elected man), but for the sake of the fulness of His glory, for the sake of the completeness of His covenant with man, for the sake of the perfection of His love, He wills and affirms this man as sinful man, i.e., as man laden with sins and afflicted by their curse and misery, and He wills and affirms this man as one who stands like Himself in opposition to sin, as His companion in the necessity of repudiating it, as the one foreordained to utter the same No and thus to corroborate the divine Yes. But for this purpose it was necessary that this man should really be confronted with what God Himself repudiates, even as God Himself is confronted with it in that self-differentiation, in that disavowal of what He is not, and does not will. And it is inevitable that this confrontation with what God repudiates, with evil, should mean for man, who is certainly not God and not almighty, that evil confronts him as a hostile power, a power which is, in fact, greater than his own power. In his case, then, the defeat of this evil power cannot be so self-evident as it was in God's case. In his case it must take on the character of an event. It must become the content of a history : the history of an obstacle and its removing ; the history of a death and a resurrection ; the history of a judgment and a pardon ; the history of a defeat and a victory. In God Himself there is a simple and immediate victory of light over darkness, with the issue never for one moment in doubt. In the creaturely sphere and for man—as man is to be the witness to the divine glory—this victory must take on historical form, thus becoming an event in time. In willing man, His man, elected man, God wills that this should be the case. He wills the confrontation of man by the power of evil. He wills man as the one assailed by this power. He wills him as the one who, as man and not God, has not evolved this power of himself but is subjected to it. He wills Himself as the One who must and will come to the help of man in this subjection, who alone in this subjection can and will give to man the victory. He wills Himself as the One by whose grace alone man must live. He wills man as the one who is thrown wholly and utterly upon the resources of His grace. He does so in order that man should proclaim His glory as the one who is freed by Him from the dominion of sin, the one who is saved by Him from death the consequence of sin, the one for whom He Himself must and will and does act as Pledge and Substitute if he is really to take this path. God wills *homo labilis*, not in order that he may fall, but in order that when he has fallen he may testify to the fulness of God's glory. And His willing and election of *homo labilis*, not for the fall, but for uplifting and restitution by an act of divine power ; the demonstration in time, in the creaturely sphere, of His eternal self-differentiation : this foreordination of elected man is God's eternal election of grace, the content of all the blessings which from all eternity and before the work of creation was ever begun God intended and determined in Himself for man, for humanity, for each individual, and for all creation. The existence of this man, the predestined bearer and representative of the divine Yes and the divine No, foreordained to victory over sin and death but also to the bearing of the divine penalty, is the divine promise, the divine Word, in which the God who elects from all eternity confronts all humanity and each individual, in which His electing will encounters us and through which He Himself has dealings with us.

Such, then, is the Supralapsarian theory as detached and purified from the doubtful presuppositions of the older theology. For a moment, at least, we may picture it to ourselves as thus detached from its background. Its distinctive aims and tenets are brought into relief. No despite can be done to the sovereignty of God as the first and last Word in all matters concerning the relationship between Him and us. And this sovereignty is to be thought of as the sovereignty of the God of the Bible, the God who is Judge and yet also merciful, the God who is Judge just because He is merciful. The thought of this sovereignty should be our first and last and only and very real consolation and warning. Sinful man must, in fact, see himself as the object of God's love and witness to His glory. He must do so to the point of understanding that He must live wholly and utterly by the grace of God. And the life which is of grace should signify that God Himself represents him against the sin which he cannot overcome but which God has guaranteed to overcome in him by the existence of His Elect. He must live, then, by the promise which is given him in and with this Elect.

Of the Supralapsarian theory as detached from the doubtful presuppositions it must at least be said that in a positive way it does appropriate and respect the Calvinistic concern common to both trends. And it cannot be objected that it is exposed to the dangers which surround Supralapsarianism in its historical form. The God of this purified Supralapsarianism is not the God who in holy self-seeking is so preoccupied with Himself and the revelation of His own glory. He is not the God in face of whom man becomes no more than a means to accomplish the divine purpose. He is the God who loves man. He is the God who in love makes man a companion. He is the God who gives man a share in the divine Yes, and for the sake of the Yes in the divine No. He is the God who puts man in this antithesis and Himself overcomes it. The God of this Supralapsarianism does not demand a holy self-seeking on the part of man or of the individual, because there is no question of the individual as such ever being the final end of the revelation of the divine glory. It remains to the individual only to grasp the promise which is given in the one Elect, and to seek and find his salvation, not as a private end, but as a participation in the victory and blessedness of this other, the Elect of God. Again, we cannot accuse the God of this Supralapsarianism of having a demonic aspect. Indeed, in that His purpose and will aims at the negation of evil accomplished in elect man, and in that He gives to creation its meaning and goal in that man, there can be no question of His having abandoned creation or a part of creation to the dominion of evil. In the Elect He negated in advance the rule of evil, even in the sphere of creation. In the Elect He revealed evil only as a power already vanquished, a kingdom of darkness already destroyed. And, again, the God of this Supralapsarianism cannot give rise to the much feared levity of mind which in the face of evil committed finds comfort and excuse in the fact that even evil is willed by God. God did indeed will evil, but only in the just and holy non-willing to which His Elect is created and summoned to testify and which human history occurs in order to fulfil, in correspondence with the eternal self-determination by which God is God and not not God. And if this is how evil is willed, what excuse is there for doing it, whether consciously or unconsciously ? Who is not accused and judged by the existence, posited by God, of the One in whom evil is negated on our behalf ? Surely the grace of God that blots out our sin cannot permit us to continue in sin.

For these points to be valid, Supralapsarianism has to be understood in this way, and its historical form has to be drastically corrected and supplemented. We have to remove completely from our minds the thought of an individual purpose in predestination. We have to remove completely from our minds the thought of the foreordination of a rigid and balanced system of election and reprobation. Above all, we have to expunge completely the idolatrous concept of a *decretum absolutum*. In place of these we have to introduce the knowledge of the elect man Jesus Christ as the true object of the divine predestination. But the decisive advantage of Supralapsarianism as compared with Infralapsarianism is that these presuppositions can be removed without setting aside the basic thought. With no material alteration the thesis concerning *homo labilis* can be developed in a christological direction. Indeed, the thesis has to be corrected and supplemented in this way if the Supralapsarian position is to be established beyond all possibility of reproach. Supralapsarianism is itself a threat to these doubtful presuppositions because upon the basis of them it says something which we must admire for its boldness, which we must recognise as the logical vindication of the main interest and concern of Calvinism, but which —on this basis—we must reject as quite impossible by reason of its harsh and dangerous character. On this basis Supralapsarianism was bound to be at a disadvantage. It could have a place only as the private opinion of radicals and " outsiders " who were more feared than loved. Its success and recognition would have meant far too urgent a summons to the refounding of the whole structure. But this very fact could materially—and in the long run historically —work out in its favour. Its whole impulse was forwards, although in its then form, bound by those presuppositions, it could neither move nor lead in this forward direction.

The same cannot be said of Infralapsarianism. Infralapsarianism was an opposition fed by the dangers of Supralapsarianism. Its merit was to expose those dangers, and to that extent its opposition was justified. We have already noted, however, that its decisive arguments were not arguments of faith but of logic and morality. That is of a piece with the fact that what it says about *homo creatus et lapsus* does not emulate or improve but weakens what the Supralapsarians tried to say in their progressive representation of the common interest. By pointing to the dangers and rejecting their thesis, it defended against the Supralapsarians something which in the long run could not be defended. What Supralapsarianism was trying to say was that in the beginning of all things, in the eternal purpose of God before the world and before history, there was the electing God and elected man, the merciful and just God, and over against that God from all eternity *homo labilis*, man sinful and lost. It is true that it did not and, on the basis of those presuppositions, could not say what it can say when detached from those presuppositions—that Jesus Christ is the merciful and just God who elects from all eternity, and also *homo labilis* who is elected from all eternity. It cannot be denied, however, that Supralapsarianism can be understood as pointing in this direction, and can therefore be corrected and supplemented. It cannot be denied that it calls for correction and supplementation in this direction. The same cannot be said of Infralapsarianism. On the contrary, Infralapsarianism closes all doors which might open in this direction. It ordains another decree over and above that of predestination ; the decree of creation and providence, and then of the fall. It offers to see and to understand the two decrees in their inward relationships with each other. According to this view there were two divine decrees at the beginning of all things. In respect of the relationship later revealed as actually and definitely willed of God, these decrees are obscure and indeterminate and neutral. In them we must indeed respect God as God. But it is a mere assertion when we say that we recognise in them the God who is later manifested and revealed in this actual and definitive relationship as the true God. We remember from what we saw earlier how the understanding of predestination was constantly hampered by the placing of predestination within the framework of a general divine world-order. As Thomas Aquinas stated expressly, the aim was to understand predestination as *pars providentiae*. Now Calvinism, and Reformation theology in general, had certainly meant that side by side with the whole question of the appropriation of salvation, *this pars providentiae* (with its particular significance) had been given an emphasis which it had never had in mediæval theology. But Supralapsarianism meant that a hopeful attempt was at last made to burst out of the framework which had been a limiting concept from the time of Thomas onwards. It meant that an attempt was made to reverse the relationship between predestination and providence, to understand providence in the light of predestination and not *vice versa*. As against that, Infralapsarianism stood for the tradition which Reformation theology had questioned but not overcome. It canonised to some extent the statement of Thomas ; and in so doing it ceased to co-operate in the task of winning through to a deeper and more effective understanding of the Calvinistic dogma. It had, indeed, no contribution to make towards such a better understanding. All that it could do was to repeat the dogma in its traditional form. Fundamentally this was what happened at the Synod of Dort. It had plenty of apprehensions and warnings and assurances to put forward, but nothing of positive value in helping towards a better understanding of the common faith. It was conservative, and nothing more. And for that reason its arguments against Supralapsarianism could never truly be the arguments of faith. And while Supralapsarianism did at least give a jolt to the common theological presuppositions by involuntarily questioning and compromising them, Infralapsarianism could not, in fact, do more than confirm them. As we have seen, Infralapsarianism did soften the individualistic end of predestination, the rigidity of its system, the equilibrium of its twofold content, the mystery of its origin in the *decretum absolutum*. It did this by its reference to the *oeconomia naturalis providentiae* preceding the economy of predestination, a reference which theoretically at least made it possible to think of the will of God as something above the whole economy of predestination. Where it took practical effect this softening could only do harm, i.e., by leading to natural theology. As a theory, however, it could result only in a concealing of the questionable nature of the presuppositions, staying the outbreak of disease and rendering superfluous any further discussion of fundamentals. But that is not the best kind of medicine. Reformed theology was pacified, and it determined to hold on to these presuppositions until it could do so no longer. But when that time came it was too late, for here, as elsewhere, the Enlightenment had now shown that the conservative anxiety to hold on to the traditional form of the dogma had resulted in the forfeiture of its substance, concerning which there had for so long been a hesitation to think constructively. In other words, the dogma had now become so alien even to its exponents that in its theological form they could no longer take it seriously and did not dare attempt its defence. The whole process of rejecting Supralapsarianism must, in fact, be numbered as one of the signs of exhaustion which characterise 17th century theology—an exhaustion which made it powerless to resist the Enlightenment at the beginning of the 18th century, since it carried within it the seed of theological Enlightenment and its own dissolution. The theological Enlightenment was nothing more than the exhaustion of thinking upon a basis of faith, for in proportion as such thinking was exhausted it was inevitably replaced by thinking upon a basis of unbelief. Whatever objections we may have to bring against its assertions, in objective content Supralapsarianism provides us with thinking upon a basis of faith which was not yet exhausted, and in this respect the offer which it made was full of hope for the theology of the 17th century. Had it carried that theology with it then things might have been different at the beginning of the 18th century, and the dissolution of that theology might have been averted. But to do that the offer would have had to be pressed in a way which was not actually the case. In that it involuntarily shook the traditional presuppositions but did not consciously dispute or burst through them, Supralapsarianism itself shared in the general exhaustion. In the face of its enemies it could never be wholly convincing. It had to content itself with the position of one intellectual trend tolerated side by side with others. In the history of the doctrine of predestination it could never make an advance commensurate with its initial impetus. For theology as a whole it could never have the significance of a salutary stimulus as it might well have done in the light of that initial impetus. Yet it is still the case that in that initial impetus it did make some advance upon the substance of Calvinistic dogma, an advance which is instructive and which repays a closer acquaintance. The same cannot be said of the thinking of the Infralapsarians. In the long run the Infralapsarians have nothing to tell us which was not said just as well or better by Calvin and other theological masters of the 16th century. The Infralapsarians did nothing to answer the questions which still had to be asked in this matter. They did nothing to answer better the question of the *obiectum praedestinationis*. All that they did was to show that by holding fast the common presuppositions the Supralapsarian answer was too dangerous to be satisfying. They made no attempt to improve on it by producing a better answer.

2. THE ETERNAL WILL OF GOD IN THE ELECTION OF JESUS CHRIST

Starting from Jn. 1[1f.], we have laid down and developed two statements concerning the election of Jesus Christ. The first is that Jesus Christ is the electing God. This statement answers the question of the Subject of the eternal election of grace. And the second is that Jesus Christ is elected man. This statement answers the question of the object of the eternal election of grace. Strictly speaking, the whole dogma of predestination is contained in these two statements. Everything else that we have to say about it must consist in the development and application of what is said in these two statements taken together. The statements belong together in a unity which is indissoluble, for both of them speak of the one Jesus Christ, and God and man in Jesus Christ are both Elector and Elect, belonging together in a relationship which cannot be broken and the perfection of which can never be exhausted. In the beginning with God was this One, Jesus Christ. And that is predestination. All that this concept contains and comprehends is to be found originally in Him and must be understood in relation to Him. But already we have gone far enough from the traditional paths to make necessary a most careful explanation of the necessity and scope of the christological basis and starting-point for the doctrine as it is here expounded.

1. We may begin with an epistemological observation. Our thesis is that God's eternal will is the election of Jesus Christ. At this point we part company with all previous interpretations of the doctrine of predestination. In these the Subject and object of predestination (the electing God and elected man) are determined ultimately by the fact that both quantities are treated as unknown. We may say that the electing God is a supreme being who disposes freely according to His own omnipotence, righteousness and mercy. We may say that to Him may be ascribed the lordship over all things, and above all the absolute right and absolute power to determine the destiny of man. But when we say that, then ultimately and fundamentally the electing God is an unknown quantity. On the other hand, we may say that elected man is the man who has come under the eternal good-pleasure of God, the man whom from all eternity God has foreordained to fellowship with Himself. But when we say that, then ultimately and fundamentally elected man is also an unknown quantity. At this point obscurity has undoubtedly enveloped the theories of even the most prominent representatives and exponents of the doctrine of predestination. Indeed, in the most consistently developed forms of the dogma we are told openly that on both sides we have to do, necessarily, with a great mystery. In the sharpest contrast to this view our thesis that the eternal will of God is the election of Jesus Christ means that we deny the existence of any such twofold mystery.

In this antithesis it is not a matter of the mystery of God's freedom in His eternal will concerning man. We have to do with this mystery too—the mystery of God, and the mystery of man which arises as man is caught up by the eternal will of God into God's own mystery. But what matters here is really the nature of this one and twofold mystery, whether it is incomprehensible light or incomprehensible darkness. What matters is whether at this point we have to recognise and respect the majesty of a God who is known to us or whether we have to recognise and respect the majesty of a God who is not known to us. Again, what matters is whether the man confronted by the majesty of that God is known or not known to us. The history of the dogma is shot through with a great struggle for the affirmation of the fact that in the mystery of election we have to do with light and not darkness, that the electing God and elected man are known quantities and not unknown. But this affirmation could not and cannot be made as long as the step is not taken which we are now taking and have already taken in the present thesis; as long as it is not admitted that in the eternal predestination of God we have to do on both sides with only one name and one person, the same name and the same person, Jesus Christ. Unless this is done, either the Subject of the concept or its object, and in practice both, will be lost in the all-prevailing obscurity, and the assertion of the obscurity itself becomes necessarily the last and decisive word on the whole subject. For our part we can no longer agree to such a procedure. No doubt it does and often has kindled sensations of a fearful or pleasurable awe, but in the long run its effect is not to build up but to scatter and destroy. For as long as we are left in obscurity on the one side or the other, and in practice both, as long as we cannot ultimately know, and ought not to know, and ought not even to ask, who is the electing God and elected man, it does not avail us in the least to be assured and reassured that in face of this mystery we ought to be silent and to humble ourselves and to adore. For truly to be silent and to humble ourselves and to adore we must know with whom and with what we have to do. The mystery must be manifest to us as such, i.e., it must have a definite character. It must have the power and dignity to provoke in us an equally definite silence and humility and adoration. Otherwise it is inevitable that we ourselves should try to fill in the gap, that of ourselves we should try to make known the unknown. It is inevitable that we should arbitrarily ascribe to this unknown this or that name or concept. It is inevitable that we should seek in Him this or that reality. It is inevitable that we should humble ourselves before this or that self-projected image of God in a silence and adoration which is certainly not intended by those who plunge us into that obscurity, but from which we can hardly restrain ourselves so long as they refuse, like the traditional exponents of the dogma, to point us to the genuine form of the mystery which we could and should approach with genuine silence, humility and adoration.

It is one of the great puzzles of history that the step which we are now taking towards a true form of the electing God and elected man was not taken long ago, although, as we have seen, many thinkers did come near enough to taking it. It is no puzzle, of course, that in these circumstances the doctrine of predestination could not be asserted or carried through with the fundamental importance generally ascribed to it, but was the occasion of so many fatal developments to the right hand or to the left, and was even pushed on one side as a kind of offence— to the great detriment of thinking upon the basis of the Christian faith, which could never move radically enough in this matter, but was inevitably imperilled at the very roots as long as the only ultimate possibility was the mystification of an unknown God and unknown man.

But the fact that the step which we are taking is a step forward, an innovation, is sufficient to justify us in asking yet again whether such a step can be made, whether we are right to make it, or whether our thesis that the election of Jesus Christ is the substance of the dogma is not merely another arbitrary movement, an encroachment. The thesis does avoid this twofold obscurity. It does give a single and known form to the unknown God and unknown man. The two together acquire one name and the name of one person, so that we may know before whom and what we must be silent and humble ourselves and adore. But (as we look back over the history of the doctrine) this very fact sheds so clear a light that we must ask whether there is not something uncanny about it, whether we are not exceeding our prerogatives. How do we know that Jesus Christ is the electing God and elected man ? How do we know that all that is to be said concerning this mystery must be grounded in His name ? We may ask the older exponents of the doctrine how they on their side know about a God and man who in the last analysis are unknown. If we do, we shall be brought up against constructs which more closely resemble philosophical reflection on the origin and development of being than they do the confession of a Christian understanding of God and man. The older teachers think first of cause and effect, of the infinite and the finite, of eternity and time, of idea and phenomenon. And obviously such thinking, or the result and application of such thinking, leads them first and above all to the sovereignly determinative will of the unknown God, and then finally and at the very lowest level to the predestination of unknown man. We must not overlook the fact that these older theologians did read their Bibles carefully, and that in the teaching they did intend to comment as we do on Rom. 9–11 and other passages in the scriptural witness. We must not overlook the fact that the Bible did not impel or constrain them to take the step which we are now taking, but confirmed them rather (even Eph. 1[4] and similar passages) in their positing of a twofold obscurity in respect of God and man at the beginning of all things. The reasons why they did and could posit this obscurity, and the counter-reasons why we can no longer do so, must lie very deep. And they are not to be found, or at any rate not to be found decisively, merely in the fact that they, on the one hand, were committed to a definite *schema* of thought which did not derive from the Bible but with the help of which they read their Bibles, while we, on the other, have now freed ourselves from this *schema*. The decisive point is the reading of the Bible itself. It is the question where and how we find in the Bible itself the electing God and elected man, and therefore that reality of the divine election as a whole which must shape our thinking about the election and form the object of all our individual reflection and speech concerning it.

Proportionately the passages in the Bible which speak expressly and directly of the divine election and predestination are not very numerous. We must always take these as a starting-point. But what is it that these passages speak of, and in what direction do they constrain us to look ? Moreover, is it not the case that once we have recognised the subject with which they deal we have to take it into consideration as a necessary background to everything else that is said of the transactions between God and man ? Is it not the case that all God's dealings attested in the Bible can be understood only against this background, as the dealings of the elected God with elected man ? In exegetical considerations of this kind we may well be in full agreement with all the classical exponents of the doctrine. As regards the content of this concept it could hardly be otherwise : it is one of those comprehensive concepts which underlies all that the Bible says about God and man, and of which account must always and everywhere be taken even where it does not appear directly. In the Bible the eternal God is the electing God. It is as the electing God that He acts. This is so even when He passes over in wrath and rejection, even when He simply uses man to fulfil His own purposes. And (in one way or another) temporal man is man elected by God. Ishmael and Esau, Pharaoh, too, and Saul and Cyrus, even Judas Iscariot, and the heathen both far and near, all these are elected, at least potentially, at least as witnesses to God's electing and man's election. In their own way even the reprobate and those whom God merely uses are elected. Again, in respect of the divine work of creation, reconciliation and redemption as attested in the Bible, we are in agreement with the classical exponents of the doctrine in that to a greater or less degree of distinctness all of us understand the name and person of Jesus Christ as the keypoint and consummation, the true meaning of all that God says and does, and the true goal of all the divine purposes. In this respect it is hard to put Jesus Christ higher or to give greater prominence to His central and teleological office than did Calvin or in his own way Thomas Aquinas. Where the parting of the ways comes is in the question of the relationship between predestination and Christology. Is there any continuity between the two? Is there a continuity between the christological centre and *telos* of the temporal work of God which was so clearly recognised by the older theologians, and the eternal presupposing of that work in the divine election which was no less clearly recognised by them? Is there the continuity which would mean necessarily the expounding of predestination in the light of Christology and the understanding of Jesus Christ as the substance of predestination? If the witness of divine revelation is rightly received, is it possible to understand the eternal presupposing of God's temporal work in the light of the central point in that work? The older exponents of the doctrine did not see any such continuity and they had no desire to bring together the two doctrines in this way. The work of God which had its central point in Jesus Christ was one thing; the eternal presupposing of that work was quite another. Certainly in that eternal presupposing they did aim to acknowledge the true and triune God and none other. But they did not acknowledge Him as they saw Him in His work, or with the distinctness and form of His temporal activity. They separated Him from that one name and that one person. They did not acknowledge Him as the One who is identical with Jesus Christ. Quite naturally, too, they thought of man as the specific object of the eternal predestination. But it was man in general, or the race as a whole, or the sum total of individuals. It was not man as the one who is identical with Jesus Christ. Certainly they found a continuity between the eternal presupposing of the divine work and its centre and *telos* in Jesus Christ. But as they understood Scripture the relationship between the two was reversed. The eternal predestination was set up as a first and independent entity standing over against the centre and *telos* of the divine work and of time : a different encounter between God and man from that which became temporal event in Jesus Christ. As they saw it, the second decision and all that it involved followed on the first. Now clearly if this view is taken it is impossible to give a concrete answer to the question : Who is the electing God and elected man ? The twofold obscurity in the doctrine of predestination is thus made inevitable. The triune God neither appears nor speaks to us except in the form of Jesus Christ, but He is always the unknown God. And if we do not know the electing God, where can we turn when it is a question of elected man ? How can elected man be anything else but unknown ? However that may be, this was the actual state of affairs as the older theology thought to see it in the light of the testimony of Holy Scripture.

If we undertake to oppose this view, we do so because we believe that their exegesis in this matter was in line with a highly questionable general hermeneutical principle which we ourselves cannot follow. The very best of the older theologians have taught us that in the word which calls and justifies and sanctifies us, the word which forms the content of the biblical witness, we must recognise in all seriousness the Word of God. Beside and above and behind this Word there is none other. To this Word then we have good cause to hold fast both for time and eternity. This Word binds us to itself both for time and eternity, and in it all our confidence must be placed. This Word does not allow us to go beyond it. It allows us no other view of God or man that that which it reveals itself. It focusses all our thoughts upon this view and keeps them focussed there. It warns us against any distraction. This Word alone must satisfy all our questioning because it alone can do so. The work of God is revealed in this Word in its totality, being there revealed in such a way that there can be no depth of the knowledge of the divine work except in God's Word, and the knowledge of the divine work cannot lead us to any depth which is not that of God's Word. Again, the very best of the older theologians, who were also the classical exponents of the doctrine of predestination, have taught us that we must seek and will assuredly find (the in every respect) perfect and insurpassable Word of God in the name and person of Jesus Christ, in the unity of true deity and true humanity fulfilled in Him, and in the work accomplished by Him in that unity. Again, they have warned us most seriously that in respect of the knowledge of God and man we must not turn aside in the slightest degree from the knowledge of Jesus Christ, either to the right hand or to the left. We must not dream of any other God or any other man. We must not seek to know about God or man except as we look on Jesus Christ. The New Testament is full of statements about Jesus Christ which cast a penetrating light on the Old as well : that to Him is given all power in heaven and on earth ; that God has purposed in Him to gather up all things in heaven and on earth ; that in Him are hid all the treasures of knowledge and wisdom ; that outside of Him there is salvation in none other ; that none other name is given to men whereby they must be saved ; that He is the author and perfector of our faith. And we should find it difficult to take more seriously or to expound more impressively both the individual testimonies and the whole Messianic witness of the Old and New Testaments than did the older theologians when they applied themselves to texts of this kind.

Yet we must still ask whether they did apply themselves to these passages as constantly and continuously as they should have done, whether they were always as faithful to their own insights as we should expect, especially in this matter of predestination. And while we cannot be sufficiently grateful for these insights or pay sufficient attention to them, yet we must still answer these questions in the negative. When they came across the passages in the Bible which treat expressly of the electing God, or elected man, or both, when they read there of God's eternal and unshakable decree and of the fore-ordination of man by that decree, then in some inexplicable way there suddenly seemed to open up before them the vista of heights and depths beyond and behind the Word which calls and justifies and sanctifies us, the Word which they could never extol enough as the source and standard of all our knowledge of God and man. Suddenly there seemed to be some other eternity apart from the eternity of the eternal life whose revelation and promise and gift in the promised and temporally incarnate Word they elsewhere attest loudly and impressively enough. And in this eternity there seemed to be some other mystery apart from the mystery whose proclamation and disclosure they can confirm elsewhere with clear texts from the New Testament. In respect of the electing God and elected man there was supposed to be some other reality and knowledge apart from the reality and knowledge of which it could elsewhere be said that the Church is built upon it and wholly bound up with it. In the sphere of predestination there arose all at once a different order, even though it had appeared elsewhere that according to the biblical testimony upon which the Church is founded there can be no question of the recognition of any such order. And at this point the question was not merely an incidental question, as the older theologians knew only too well. It was the question of the beginning of all things. It was the question of the knowledge of God's absolutely decisive disposing which takes place in the eternity before time was, and which legislates for salvation or damnation, for life or death, both in time and in the eternity when time shall have ceased to be. It was the question of the knowledge of the specific order of the kingdom or rule of God, with all that that means for the existence, the preservation, the history and the destiny of creation and man. The question was in fact the actual and burning question : What is to become of us at the hand of God ? It was, and still is, immeasurably important that in answering this question the older theology thought itself dispensed, and let itself be forced away, from the hermeneutical principle which elsewhere it had so rigidly proclaimed and the application of which it had elsewhere so scrupulously regarded. But that is undoubtedly what took place. And it is astonishing how the older theologians thought it self-evident that there was no further need to adhere to the coherent whole of scriptural witness which they themselves had revealed and proclaimed, boldly taking it for granted that they could go beyond this whole and present as the doctrine of predestination a construction which was quite foreign to it and to their otherwise Christian witness, thus vitiating that witness at its most sensitive point, the point of departure. It can hardly be maintained that such a course was necessitated by the exegesis of the scriptural passages which speak directly of predestination. Like all other passages, these must be read in the context of the whole Bible, and that means with an understanding that the Word of God is the content of the Bible. The exegesis of these passages depends upon whether or not we have determined that our exposition should be true to the context in which they stand and are intended to be read. Even the attempt to philosophise did not compel the older theologians to take this course. At other points they resisted firmly enough. It was not necessary that they should be vanquished by it here. And even here the thought-scheme introduced could be dangerous only because a prior decision had already been made to depart from the whole meaning and context of Scripture.

From such a decision everything else results inevitably, and did in fact result. And that is the step which we cannot consent to take. At this juncture we cannot pursue further the reasons which led up to that decision. Nor do we need to discover its ultimate basis. We can only maintain that the decision was made, and that once made it was not altered, and that it passed unnoticed even by so large a company of penetrating thinkers. And we can only maintain that we for our part cannot approve that decision, but must decide differently. Against the general hermeneutical decision of the older theology we set up our own—that in the exegesis of the biblical passages which treat directly of the election we have to look in the same direction as we must always look in biblical exegesis. We must hold by the fact that the Word which calls us, the Word which forms the content of Scripture, is itself and as such the (in every respect) perfect and insurpassable Word of God, the Word which exhausts and reveals our whole knowledge of God, and from which we must not turn one step, because in itself it is the fulness of all the information that we either need or desire concerning God and man, and the relationship between them, and the ordering of that relationship. At no point, then, and on no pretext, can we afford either to dispense with, or to be turned aside from, the knowledge of Jesus Christ. And why indeed should we do so at this particular point ? We should be in full accord with the majority of those theologians if we were to defend the assertion that what the Bible calls the salvation of man is nothing other than the salvation once for all accomplished by Jesus Christ, or that what the Bible calls the Church is nothing other than the life of the earthly body which has in Jesus Christ its heavenly Head and Subject, or that what the Bible calls our hope can be nothing other than the return of Jesus Christ to the just judgment by which those who believe in Him will go to eternal life. We ask then : When it is a question of the understanding and exposition of what the Bible calls predestination or election, why and on what authority are we suddenly to formulate a statement which leaves out all mention of Jesus Christ ? How is it that at this point there suddenly arises the possibility of looking elsewhere ? How do we arrive at the position where we are able to do this, when we know that we cannot do it at any other point without parting company with the older theologians ? Is it that when we come to pre-temporal eternity, the sphere of predestination, that which was in the beginning with God, we are suddenly to think of these apart from Jesus Christ—something which quite rightly we are not allowed to do when we deal with supra-temporal and post-temporal eternity, with what is and will be ? Is Jesus Christ really the One who was, and is, and is to come, or is He not ? And if He is, what constraint or authority is there that we should not think through to the ultimate meaning of the " He was," not go back to the real beginning of all things in God, i.e., not think of the divine foreordination, the divine election of grace, as something which takes place in Him and through Him ? How is it that the concept of eternal election can be referred to some other reality and not Jesus Christ, who as our salvation and the Head of the Church and our hope must also be the electing God and elected man in one and the same person ? As presented to us in the Bible, what can the election be at all, and what can it mean, if it is divorced from the name and person to which the whole content of the Bible relates as to the exhaustive self-revelation of God, here with the forward look of expectation and there with the backward look of recollection ? Only in some other context than that of Holy Scripture can the concept of election, of foreordination, of the eternal divine decree, refer elsewhere, to the twofold mystery of an unknown God and unknown man. We cannot understand the hermeneutical decision which the older theologians made in relation to this question. But in arriving at a different decision we do not believe that we are doing anything out of the ordinary, but something obvious and straightforward. We believe, in fact, that we are doing the only possible thing in accordance with the method with which those theologians were conversant in other matters. And for this reason we do not accept the criticism that at this point we have been betrayed into an innovation which is purely capricious, wanting to know what by its very nature cannot be known. We know that Jesus Christ is the electing God and elected man from the same source which fed the older theology, and would have fed it at this point too, but obviously could not do so because the theologians themselves arbitrarily turned aside from it. The purpose of our thesis is to make good the arbitrary act of our predecessors. And if it is calculated to shed light upon a doctrine where obscurity has hitherto prevailed, the light is not one which we ourselves have arbitrarily kindled, but the same light as is given everywhere else. We have no cause to put that light under a bushel merely at this point.

In this thesis of ours we are taking up again the intention which was unequivocally disclosed but not developed by John Knox and his fellow-workers in the *Conf. Scotica* of 1560, Arts. 7–8. In this confession Christology and predestination were regarded as in some sort parallel, and for that reason were treated together. On the one hand, there is the miraculous union of Godhead and manhood in Jesus Christ, and, on the other, our redemption ; and both these have their origin and basis in the one eternal and unalterable decree of God. Thus in Art. 7 the answer to the question *Cur Deus homo ?* is a concise and simple reference to this decree. And Art. 8 shows to what extent the election of Jesus Christ dominates this reference, for under the heading " Of the Election " the remaining content of the Calvinistic doctrine of predestination, even to the election or rejection of individuals, is introduced only in the form of a citation of Eph. 1⁴. And in the place of a longer exposition there is a detailed development and explanation of the fact that to be our Head, our Brother and our Shepherd, to be the Messiah and Saviour, to bear the punishment which we had merited and to destroy death on our behalf, Jesus Christ had to become both very God and very man. According to the intention of this confession, what should have been said of our election or rejection as the second element in this eternal and unalterable decree has obviously been said already in the statement concerning the nature of Jesus Christ and His being as very God and very man as determined by that eternal and unalterable decree. It is surely no accident that in Arts. 2 and 3, instead of working out in the usual way an independent doctrine of sin, this same confession introduces the problem of the fall only as a postscript to the doctrine of the original foreordination of man, the problem of original sin only as a preface to the doctrine of faith in Jesus Christ as effected by the Holy Ghost. Obviously it is only in that context and not in and for itself that John Knox would have the fact of sin understood. That man is against God is important and must be taken seriously. But what is far more important and must be taken far more seriously is that in Jesus Christ God is for man. And it is only in the light of the second fact that the importance and seriousness of the first can be seen. It can hardly be denied that in the *Conf. Scotica* the specific conception of sin is intimately connected with the peculiar christological conception of predestination.

The christological meaning and basis of the doctrine of election have been brought out afresh in our own time, and with an impressive treatment of Jesus Christ as the original and decisive object of the divine election and rejection. This service has been rendered by Pierre Maury in the fine lecture which he gave on " Election et Foi " at the *Congrès international de théologie calviniste* in Geneva, 1936 (published in *Foi et Vie*, April–May 1936, and in German under the title

" Erwählung und Glaube " in *Theol. Studien, Heft* 8, 1940). That Congress dealt exclusively with the problem of predestination, and its records will easily show how instructive was Maury's contribution, and how it stood out from the other papers, which were interesting historically but in content moved entirely within the circle of the traditional formulations, and were almost hopelessly embarrassed by their difficulties.

Apart from these two voices, the one from the period of the Reformation and the other from our own, we can appeal in support of our thesis only (1) to the (in their own context highly significant) passages quoted in the first section from Athanasius and Augustine, together with occasional sentences from Coccejus ; (2) to the inevitability of such a solution in the light of the Supralapsarian controversy ; and (3) to the general Reformation assertion that Christ is the *speculum electionis,* an assertion which obviously stands in need of more profound and comprehensive treatment. Historically there are to hand all kinds of important materials which should encourage and even necessitate an adoption of this thesis, but it cannot be denied that in formulating it as we have done we have exposed ourselves to the risk of a certain isolation. And we may repeat that it is most singular that this should be the case, and that the obvious should have to be stated and defended in the apparent form of an innovation.

2. With the traditional teaching and the testimony of Scripture, we think of predestination as eternal, preceding time and all the contents of time. We also think of it as divine, a disposing of time and its contents which is based on the omnipotence of God and characterised by His constancy (or " immutability "). With the strict exponents of tradition, and especially with the Supralapsarians of the 17th century, we think of it as the beginning of all things, i.e., the beginning which has no beginning except in God's eternal being in Himself ; the beginning which in respect of God's relationship with the reality which is distinct from Himself is preceded by no other beginning ; the beginning which is itself the beginning of this relationship as such ; the beginning which everything else included or occurring within this relationship can only follow, proceeding from it and pointing back to it. We know God's will apart from predestination only as the act in which from all eternity and in all eternity God affirms and confirms Himself. We must guard against disputing the eternal will of God which precedes even predestination. We must not allow God to be submerged in His relationship to the universe or think of Him as tied in Himself to the universe. Under the concept of predestination, or the election of grace, we say that in freedom (its affirmation and not its loss) God tied Himself to the universe. Under the concept of predestination we confess the eternal will of the God who is free in Himself, even in the sense that originally and properly He wills and affirms and confirms Himself. But we can confess this will of God only under the concept of predestination. For it is only in the act of God which it denotes, only in the act by which God's relationship with the universe and ourselves is determined and ordered, that we can truly see this will and see God Himself in the sovereignty and glory which He has in Himself before all worlds. Under the concept of predestination, in full accord with tradition, we acknowledge the

unsearchable majesty of the good-pleasure with which God has from all eternity and in all eternity both the right and the power to dispose of the world and us, in which as God He has in fact disposed of us and the world, so that His eternal will is the Alpha and Omega with which all our thinking about the world and ourselves must begin and end.

But we depart from tradition when we say that for us there is no obscurity about this good-pleasure of the eternal will of God. It is not a good-pleasure which we have to admire and reverence as divine in virtue of such obscurity. For us it is not a question-mark to which we can make answer only with an empty and question-begging assertion. When we assert the wisdom and mercy and righteousness of this good-pleasure, we do not need to do so merely as a bald statement of fact. We negative this whole understanding because positively we must affirm that at the beginning of all things God's eternal plan and decree was identical with what is disclosed to us in time as the revelation of God and of the truth about all things. This is the light of the divine good-pleasure. This is the content of the statement which not only destroys the question-mark but answers the question. This is the wisdom and mercy and righteousness of God which not only asserts itself but discloses itself so fully and clearly that we may know what it is we do when we have to subordinate ourselves unreservedly to the good-pleasure of this wise and merciful and righteous God, and when in fact we can subordinate and surrender ourselves to this good-pleasure. As we understand the freedom of the predestinating God, it does not deny but opens up itself to our knowledge. And it is this positive understanding which constitutes our deviation from tradition, the " innovation " made in our thesis. The core of this thesis is to be found in the perception that in respect of predestination we must not and need not separate ourselves from the revelation of God as such, because in that revelation predestination is revealed as well, because predestination is not hidden but disclosed. God is the self-revealing God, and as such He is the electing God. The eternal will of God which is before time is the same as the eternal will of God which is above time, and which reveals itself as such and operates as such in time. In fact, we perceive the one in the other. For God's eternity is one. God Himself is one. He may only be known either altogether or not at all. When He is known He is known all at once and altogether. But these are secondary and derivative considerations which would have no force at all unless they were supported by the fact of the revelation of God. This fact has as such the character of completeness. Revealing to us the fulness of the one God, it discloses to us not only what the will of God is, but also what it was and what it will be. And it does so in such a way that we are satisfied as well as God. If we do not lazily close our eyes to this revelation, if we do not try to evade it, wantonly seeking instruction elsewhere, then there is nothing which is not told us concerning the meaning and direction and nature of God's will for us. Certainly, it is the secret of God's good-pleasure that it should take this form and not another, and that it should be revealed to us as such ; that in all its fulness it should have the character and form and content displayed to us in God's revelation, and that it should really be disclosed in this revelation and not hidden. Certainly, there corresponds to this secret the secret of faith, in the question whether we do know and know fully its character and form and content, whether the good-pleasure of God does find our confidence and obedience. This is, indeed, the secret of God's good-pleasure, and even in the secret of the decision of faith it is still a question of our relationship to this secret. It is a question of revelation. It is a question of the knowledge of the will of God ; of all His will, of His will which is before time, of His predestinating will. Even under this aspect it is still a matter of the intelligent reverence and worship and love of God. Even under this aspect it is still a matter of our being brought out of darkness into light, and not plunged into a new and ostensibly divine darkness. If we hold fast the revelation of God as the revelation of His eternal will and good-pleasure, if we acknowledge God's freedom in the revelation in which He has proclaimed and enacted it, then as the beginning of all things with God we find the decree that He Himself in person, in the person of His eternal Son, should give Himself to the son of man, the lost son of man, indeed that He Himself in the person of the eternal Son should *be* the lost Son of Man. In the beginning with God, i.e., in the resolve of God which precedes the existence, the possibility and the reality of all His creatures, the very first thing is the decree whose realisation means and is Jesus Christ. This decree is perfect both in subject and object. It is the electing God and also the elected man Jesus Christ, and both together in the unity the one with the other. It is the Son of God in His whole giving of Himself to the Son of Man, and the Son of Man in his utter oneness with the Son of God. This is the covenant of grace which is perfected and sealed in the power of God's free love, established openly and unconditionally by God Himself and confirmed with a faithfulness which has no reserve. And this decree is really the first of all things. It is the decision between God and the reality distinct from Himself. It is a decision which is the basis of all that follows. And this decree is itself the sum and substance of all the wisdom and power with which God has willed this reality and called it into being. It is the standard and source of all order and all authority within God's relationship to this reality. It is the fixing of an end for this reality, foreordained, valid without question, unfailing in efficacy. It is itself the eternal will of God. The will of God is Jesus Christ, and this will is known to us in the revelation of Jesus Christ. If we acknowledge this, if we seriously accept Jesus Christ as the content of this will, then we cannot seek any other will of God, either in heaven or earth, either in time or eternity. This will is God's will. We must abide by it because God Himself abides by it ; because God Himself allows us and commands us to abide by it. And this decree of God is not obscure, but clear. In this decree we do not have to assert a God of omnipotence and to cower down before Him. In all His incomprehensibility we may know Him and love Him and praise Him as the One who has truly revealed to us His wisdom and mercy and righteousness, and who has revealed Himself as the One who is Himself all these things. God's glory overflows in this the supreme act of His freedom : illuminating, and convincing, and glorifying itself ; not therefore demanding a *sacrificium intellectus* but awakening faith. The Son of God determined to give Himself from all eternity. With the Father and the Holy Spirit He chose to unite Himself with the lost Son of Man. This Son of Man was from all eternity the object of the election of Father, Son and Holy Spirit. And the reality of this eternal being together of God and man is a concrete decree. It has as its content one name and one person. This decree is Jesus Christ, and for this very reason it cannot be a *decretum absolutum*.

It cannot be said that this understanding of the divine election involves an illegitimate rationalisation and simplification of its mystery.

On the one hand, it is surely true that the idea of the unsearchable freedom of a predestinating God and of a man predestinated for unsearchable reasons cannot be that right conception of the mystery of the Christian life which we must be careful not to dissolve. On the contrary, we have to say that while such an idea of God and man is no doubt very mysterious and exciting and in its way consoling, it has nothing whatever to do with the Christian understanding. At bottom, it is an idea which belongs to natural theology, and is only too current in the history of non-Christian "religion." There is no difficulty in abandoning ourselves to the horror, or peace, of the thought of an unknown being disposing of and fixing our destiny in an unknown way. The thought is one which does so little to commit us, comfortably releasing our minds and wills from claims which might seriously tie us. For this reason it does to some extent commend itself as a background for the most diverse conceptions and modes of life as taste or inclination may direct. It is a thought which is so close to us all that to lay hold of it a divine revelation is not really necessary. At bottom, even to describe it as a secret or mystery is itself much too exaggerated if we take the word in its strictest sense. That this thought should take the position of a key-thought in the Christian doctrine of predestination and Christian theology in general is at root quite paradoxical, and that it should consistently be allowed to maintain this position, that it should be defended and honoured as something specifically sacred to Christianity, is a demand which cannot conceivably be represented as right and just. Ought we not, indeed, to expect and to demand the very opposite ? When we set this thought in the light of serious Christian reflection, is it not one which we ought to attack and destroy ? At root, can there ever be anything more unchristian or anti-christian than the horror or the peace which is given by the thought of the *decretum absolutum* as the first and last truth from which everything else proceeds ?

On the other hand, it is also true that what our thesis puts in the place of the *decretum absolutum*, the knowledge of God in Jesus Christ, is still a mystery, so that our proposal to correct and to give greater precision to the traditional teaching cannot be thought of as an attempt to rationalise that teaching. As we see it, our life is hid with Christ in God. In the beginning (the beginning of all things and our own beginning) we find only the one Jesus Christ as the electing God and elected man. The whole relationship between God and man (and the whole relationship between God and the reality which is distinct from Him) consists originally and properly in the relationship between God and man in Jesus Christ. We must seek and find our own part in this relationship only in Him. Our communion with God, God's choice of us, and our election by God, is faith in Jesus Christ. And that is a clear enough idea. It allows and even offers us some knowledge of the divine predestination : a knowledge of the electing God and elected man ; a knowledge of our own election and of the whole Whence ? and Whither ? of our life ; not merely the reflection of this knowledge but its substance ; not this knowledge with the menacing reservation that in some dark background everything is perhaps quite different, but with the certainty that in this matter background and foreground are one and the same, and that as the foreground may be known the background may also be known. And yet the light shed by this understanding is not a natural light. It is not the light of the logical or ethical deliberation of the human reason engaged in self-discussion. It is the light of revelation, the light of God. It is not something close to us but worlds removed It is not something given to man by his own capacities or energies. Of all ideas, it is the one which is in itself unthinkable, the one which is thinkable only in faith and by the miraculous power of the Holy Spirit : that God Himself should Himself become the Son of Man in His eternal Son ; that He should will to take up the cause of the Son of Man as His own cause ; that the will by which He did this should be the eternal will of God which constitutes the beginning of all things and our own beginning ; that we should stand under the foreordination of this will even before we were born and before the world was ; that from the very beginning in God's willing of the world the love of God should be God's rule over everything and all things. If there is any mystery of God, if there is any secret which, even as we know it and it is revealed to us and manifest before us, still proclaims and characterises itself more and more as a secret, then this is it. Here, if anywhere, good care is taken that we should not let slip this mystery in any attempt to rationalise. Here, if anywhere, we are challenged by this mystery itself in all our thinking and willing, so that there is no room for irresponsibility, and we are jolted out of all those conceptions or modes of life which we had freely selected or discovered for ourselves. Here, if anywhere, we can and must say that it is with the Christian mystery that we have to do ; not with a riddle of life or thought, but with the very core of the Christian Gospel and the Christian faith. We stand before the mystery to which worship and reverence belong because we know it, the mystery which is worthy to be regarded and treated as a mystery for this very reason. From this standpoint, too, there is no cause for anxiety if we adopt the view that where the traditional *decretum absolutum* used to stand there belongs the *decretum absolutum* of the election of Jesus Christ.

But if a footing can be gained for this view, if of the presuppositions which controlled the older doctrine the first and fundamental one is corrected—the specific doctrine of the character of the divine decree—then this means that at least we are not led into the void when we ask concerning the divine election, concerning that eternal will which predetermines and overrules both time and all that is in time. Fundamentally, this question is not unanswerable. It is not one of the questions which are destined always to remain questions. In face of it there is no place for that mysterious shaking of the head or shrugging of the shoulders or wringing of the hands which some perhaps regard as particularly pious in this connexion. Within the framework of the older theology it is the peculiarity and the peculiar scandal of the doctrine of the *decretum absolutum* that at the first and last and culminating point in all our thinking and reflection it confronts us with a factor—the unsearchable freedom of God as such—which can only put an end to our questioning, and in face of which our thinking loses itself and is reduced to mere wandering. Face to face with the absolute decree, if we would pursue the matter further, there remains only, as we have seen, the escape into mysticism or moralism, i.e., a self-chosen salvation, idolatry, the righteousness of works. The only fire which a knowledge of the *decretum absolutum* can kindle—if it does not extinguish all fires—is that of religion and not of faith. But the *decretum absolutum* of the election of Jesus Christ means directly that we are summoned to faith. As the content of the divine revelation itself, it makes of our questioning a questioning which is ordained and fulfilled and accomplished in advance. As the true and Christian mystery—compared with which the alleged mystery of the *decretum absolutum* is only a platitude, a truism of man's sound or not so sound understanding—it makes us begin to question and to question in good earnest. Those who come to rest in the *decretum absolutum* abandon all questioning. They think they know that we cannot know. But that knowledge, with the horror or peace that it brings, destroys all desire to know, all genuine and open questioning. Genuine and open questioning begins with the knowledge of the mystery of the election of Jesus Christ, for in this mystery we are confronted with an authority concerning which we cannot teach ourselves but must let ourselves be taught, and are taught, and can expect continually to be taught. The mystery of the election of Jesus Christ is the genuine answer ; and it is for this reason that it makes possible and indeed demands and kindles a genuine questioning, a genuine desire to know. When we say " genuine " we mean necessary, inescapable, claiming and controlling us wholly and utterly, so that we stand or fall by our questions, so that we are no longer free to question or not to question, to desire to know or not to desire to know. " Genuine " means non-academic. And questioning of that sort can arise only when we are confronted by the answer, only when we begin to ask in the light of an answer already given, only when the questioning, once begun, can never end. Ultimately only the election of Jesus Christ has the character of an answer which thus demands and kindles a genuine questioning. Only the election of Jesus Christ—for all the other mysteries which might provoke such questioning eventually lead back to the mystery of the *decretum absolutum*, the mystery of the unknown God and unknown man, and before this mystery our questioning can only wilt and die. The election of Jesus Christ is the one matter about which we always know and must always ask, for in this election an absolute decision is made in respect of all things, and not least ourselves. This election is the beginning from which everything else proceeds. Our being or non-being, our life or death, is foreordained in the light of it. It is the predestination which in one way or another we must all fulfil. Everything else that happens to us is openly or secretly characterised by the fact that first and fundamentally this election has already taken place. There is much we do not need to know, but one thing we must know is the basic nature and meaning of God's electing and our election. There is much we do not need to ask about, but about this one thing we must ask. This is indeed the one thing about which we are, in fact, always ignorant. This one thing is, in fact, the mystery which always confronts us as such and which we shall weary ourselves in attempting to reduce or to solve. In this matter no teaching can ever reach an end and then be dispensed with. If the teaching is successful, we need it all the more. When it ends, it brings us back again to the beginning. Again, the election of Jesus Christ is the subject about which we know and about which we can therefore ask. This election takes away the idle horror or peace of the knowledge that we cannot know. Notwithstanding its eternity, it is history. It stands in the midst of all history. It is one history with other histories. It is the self-attestation of eternity. And it is also a Word, a Word which is spoken, and can be heard and received and learned. It is not silent but vocal. It is not formless but has form. It is the eternal decree of God which bears one name and consists in the existence of one person. And for this reason it is an answer : not a dark and empty answer, but an eternal divine answer ; not a repetition of the question, but its fulfilment. Who and what was in the beginning with God ? This decree, this answer tells us. And in face of this answer our thoughts need not lose themselves or be reduced to mere wandering, and the escape into mysticism or moralism is rendered superfluous. This answer itself instructs us, and in so doing it automatically excludes all the self-instruction which we might otherwise inflict upon ourselves, and which could only result in the death of all our questioning.

The questioning and knowledge, the teaching and instruction of which we are now speaking is that of faith. It is the questioning of faith which is genuine questioning : the questioning which never ends and is never futile ; the questioning which from the very first, and again and again, is ordained and fulfilled and accomplished in terms of the answer already given. And the deepest and distinctive difference between the *decretum absolutum* and the election of Jesus Christ is the fact that we can believe in the latter. What the election of Jesus Christ necessarily demands and evokes is faith, a confidence in God which is itself obedience to God. We cannot believe in the *decretum absolutum*. We can only look at it and then forget it, turning elsewhere for the arbitrary satisfaction of religious needs. We cannot place any confidence at all in the *decretum absolutum*, and obedience to it is quite inconceivable. The substitution of the election of Jesus Christ for the *decretum absolutum* is, then, the decisive point in the amendment of the doctrine of predestination. It enables us for the first time to show and to say that we can really believe in the divine election. It will not be overlooked that if we presuppose the *decretum absolutum* the first and decisive link in the *catena aurea* of Rom. 8³⁰ᶠ· could only become even at the very best the object of a mystery-cult or mystery-drama, but certainly not the object of faith. The fact that election and faith belong together, or in Luther's phrase are jumbled together, in the same way as calling and faith, or justification and faith, or sanctification and faith, or God and faith, is made clear only when we understand the election originally and decisively as the election of Jesus Christ.

3. The eternal will of God in the election of Jesus Christ is His will to give Himself for the sake of man as created by Him and fallen from Him. According to the Bible this was what took place in the incarnation of the Son of God, in His death and passion, in His resurrection from the dead. We must think of this as the content of the eternal divine predestination. The election of grace in the beginning of all things is God's self-giving in His eternal purpose. His self-giving : God gave—not only as an actual event but as something eternally foreordained—God gave His only begotten Son. God sent forth His own Word. And in so doing He gave Himself. He gave Himself up. He hazarded Himself. He did not do this for nothing, but for man as created by Him and fallen away from Him. This is God's eternal will. And our next task is to arrive at a radical understanding of the fact and extent that this will, as recognised and expressed in the history of the doctrine, is a twofold will, containing within itself both a Yes and a No. We must consider how and how far the eternal divine predestination is a quality, a *praedestinatio gemina*.

What was it that God elected in the eternal election of Jesus Christ ? When we asked concerning the content of predestination in our previous expositions we could never give a single answer but only a double.

c.d.—6

Primarily God elected or predestinated Himself. God determined to give and to send forth His Son. God determined to speak His Word. The beginning in which the Son became obedient to the Father was with Himself. The form and concretion of His will, the determination of His whole being, was reached in Himself. All God's freedom and love were identical with this decree, with the election of Jesus Christ. That is the one side of the matter. And the other is that God elected man, this man. God's decision and ordination concerned this man. He predestinated His own Son to existence as the son of David. He decreed that His Word should be sounded forth in the world of man. And so it was this man, the same, Jesus Christ, who was in the beginning with God. The divine will took on a form and concretion in and with which God was no longer alone with Himself, but this man Jesus Christ was taken up into the will of God and made a new object of the divine decree, distinct from God. To the election of Jesus Christ there belongs, then, elected man as well as the electing God. There are two sides to the will of God in the election of Jesus Christ. And since this will is identical with predestination, from the very first and in itself it is a double predestination. We must return later to the distinction between the first and second aspects and the relationship between them. For the present we must be content with the simple assertion that there is already, in origin and from all eternity, this twofold reference, a double predestination. It is obvious that when we confess that God has elected fellowship with man for Himself we are stating one thing, and when we confess that God has elected fellowship with Himself for man we are stating quite another. Both things together are the divine election. But obviously if its object is twofold so too is its content. It is one thing for God to elect and predestinate Himself to fellowship with man, and quite another for God to predestinate man to fellowship with Himself. Both are God's self-giving to man. But if the latter means unequivocally that a gift is made to man, the former certainly does not mean that God gives or procures Himself anything—for what could God give or procure Himself in giving to man a share in His own being? What we have to consider under this aspect is simply God's hazarding of His Godhead and power and status. For man it means an infinite gain, an unheard of advancement, that God should give Himself to him as his own possession, that God should be his God. But for God it means inevitably a certain compromising of Himself that He should determine to enter into this covenant. Where man stands only to gain, God stands only to lose. And because the eternal divine predestination is identical with the election of Jesus Christ, its twofold content is that God wills to lose in order that man may gain. There is a sure and certain salvation for man, and a sure and certain risk for God.

If the teachers of predestination were right when they spoke always of a duality, of election and reprobation, of predestination to salvation or perdition, to life or death, then, we may say already that in the election of Jesus Christ which is the eternal will of God, God has ascribed to man the former, election, salvation and life ; and to Himself He has ascribed the latter, reprobation, perdition and death. If it is indeed the case that the divine good-pleasure which was the beginning of all things with God carries with it the risk and threat of negation, then it is so because the Son of God incarnate represents and Himself is this divine good-pleasure. The risk and threat is the portion which the Son of God, i.e., God Himself, has chosen for His own.

In the present connexion we must speak first of this negative side. For in the eternal predestination of God the first thing is that God has elected Himself as man's Friend and Partner, that He has elected fellowship with man for Himself. What was involved, then, when God elected to become the Son of Man in Jesus Christ ? In giving Himself to this act He ordained the surrender of something, i.e., of His own impassibility in face of the whole world which because it is not willed by Him can only be the world of evil. In Himself God cannot be affected either by the possibility or by the reality of that will which opposes Him. He cannot be affected by any potentiality of evil. In Him is light and no darkness at all. But when God of His own will raised up man to be a covenant-member with Himself, when from all eternity He elected to be one with man in Jesus Christ, He did it with a being which was not merely affected by evil but actually mastered by it. Man was tempted by evil. Man became guilty of evil. Man did evil. Man fell victim to all the consequences of evil. The very fact that man was not God but a creature, even though he was a good creature, had meant already a certain jeopardising of the honour of God as whose instrument man had been created. Would this good instrument extol God's honour as was meet, as God Himself extolled it, as a good instrument ought to extol it ? Man was in any case an extremely unreliable champion of this cause, an extremely compromised servant of the divine will, compromising even God Himself. What can it have meant for God to commit Himself to such a creature ? If for a moment we attempted the impossible task of picturing to ourselves man unfallen and sinless, we should at any rate have to say this concerning him. He is not God. The fulfilment of his calling to live to God's glory is in any case a matter of his creaturely freedom and decision. For he is quite different from God. He is at least challenged and not sovereign like God. And because of this, man stands on the frontier of that which is impossible, of that which is excluded, of that which is contradictory to the will of God. In so far as he can and should live by the Word of God, participation in this contradiction is impossible for him. It is excluded, forbidden. But will he live by the Word of God ? What a risk God ran when He willed to take up the cause of created man even in his original righteousness, when He constituted Himself his God and ordained Himself to solidarity with him! If even the man whose existence we cannot in the least imagine had everything to gain by such a covenant, God Himself had everything to lose by it. But the man with whom the eternal will of God has to do is not this man ; or rather, it is this man, not good as God created him, but fallen away from God. In fact, then, the risk taken by God was far greater. His partner in this covenant is not man on the brink of danger but man already overtaken by it ; man for whom the impossible has become possible, and the unreal real, and the fulfilment of evil an actual occurrence. It is the man who gave a hearing to Satan, who did not guard the frontier, who did not keep the divine commandment, who lived otherwise than by the will of God, who thus willed to surrender the whole meaning of his existence, who brought dishonour upon God instead of honour, who became a traitor to God, an enemy and an adversary, who could be visited only by the wrath of God. It was the man whose wife was Eve and first son Cain, who answered a long series of special visitations by an equally long series of fresh aggressions, who finally drove the Messiah of God to the cross, whose name is at very best Peter and at worst Judas. And God has chosen this man and fellowship with this man in the election of Jesus Christ. It is the lost son of man who is partner of the electing God in this covenant. We are not so far speaking of what this means for man. What is quite certain is that for God it means severe self-commitment. God does not merely give Himself up to the risk and menace, but He exposes Himself to the actual onslaught and grasp of evil. For if God Himself became man, this man, what else can this mean but that He declared Himself guilty of the contradiction against Himself in which man was involved ; that He submitted Himself to the law of creation by which such a contradiction could be accompanied only by loss and destruction ; that He made Himself the object of the wrath and judgment to which man had brought himself ; that He took upon Himself the rejection which man had deserved ; that He tasted Himself the damnation, death and hell which ought to have been the portion of fallen man ? What did God choose of glory or of joy or of triumph when in Jesus Christ He elected man ? What could this election bring except something of which God is free in Himself and for which He cannot truly have any desire : darkness, and the impossibility of our existence before Him as sinners, as those who have fallen victim to His penalties ? If we would know what it was that God elected for Himself when He elected fellowship with man, then we can answer only that He elected our rejection. He made it His own. He bore it and suffered it with all its most bitter consequences. For the sake of this choice and for the sake of man He hazarded Himself wholly and utterly. He elected our suffering (what we as sinners must suffer towards Him and before Him and from Him). He elected it as His own suffering. This is the extent to which His election is an election of grace, an election of love, an election to give Himself, an election to empty and abase Himself for the sake of the elect. Judas who betrays Him He elects as an apostle. The sentence of Pilate He elects as a revelation of His judgment on the world. He elects the cross of Golgotha as His kingly throne. He elects the tomb in the garden as the scene of His being as the living God. That is how God loved the world. That is how from all eternity His love was so selfless and genuine. And, conversely, if we would know what rejection is as determined in God's eternal counsel, the rejection of which we cannot but speak even in our doctrine of predestination, then we must look in the same direction. We must look to what God elected for Himself in His Son when in that Son He elected for Himself fellowship with man. We must look simply and solely to what God took upon Himself when He ordained His Son as Son of Man. We must look to His own portion in His Son, to what He Himself gained by this covenant between Himself and man. What could He expect to gain by this covenant, and what did He actually gain by it, except that there fell upon Him that which ought to have fallen upon man, except that He took to Himself shame and prepared for Himself distress ? In the very fact that He did this we must see what was willed by Him from all eternity. In the very fact that from all eternity He willed to suffer for us, we must consider the negative aspect of the divine predestination. Where else should we see it but here ? Where else should it be revealed to us but here ? For here we see it as God Himself determined it, as He determined it, indeed, from all eternity. Here it is revealed as it is grounded in God's good-pleasure itself, as it actually is from all eternity.

We may remark in passing that the fact that from all eternity God resolved to take to Himself and to bear man's rejection is a prior justification of God in respect of the risk to which He resolved to expose man by creation—and in respect of the far greater risk to which He committed him by His permitting of the fall. We cannot complain because God put a creaturely being on this frontier, a being unlike Himself in that it was subject to temptation. We cannot blame God for confronting man with evil, an evil which in His own case was excluded by the divine nature, but which in man's case could be excluded only by the divine Word and commandment. We cannot hold it against God that He did not prevent but permitted the fall of man, i.e., his succumbing to the temptation of the devil and his incurring of actual guilt. In God's eternal decree these things did not involve any injustice to the creature, for by this same decree God decided that the risk which He allowed to threaten the creature and the plight into which He allowed it to plunge itself should be His own risk and His own plight. God created man. In that sense He exposed him to the risk. Yet from all eternity God did not let him fall, but He upheld him even when Satan's temptation and his own culpability resulted in a fall into sin. Thus even when we think of man in this negative determination, we still think of him as the one whom God loved from all eternity in His Son, as the one to whom He gave Himself from all eternity in His Son, gave Himself that He might represent him, gave Himself that He might bear and suffer on his behalf what man himself had to suffer. We must insist upon man's responsibility for his failure to do on that frontier what he ought to have done as a creature of God and hearer of the Word of God. But much more, we must insist upon the responsibility which God Himself shouldered when He created man and permitted the fall of man. Man cannot evade his own responsibility by complaining that God required too much of him, for what God required of Himself on man's behalf is infinitely greater than what He required of man. In the last analysis what God required of man consists only in the demand that he should live as the one on whose behalf God required the very uttermost of Himself. " Thou wilt say then unto me, Why doth he yet find fault ? For who hath resisted his will ? Nay but, O man, who art thou that repliest against God ? " (Rom. 9$^{19f.}$). And the answer is : The man to whom God Himself turned from all eternity in His Son, even in the subordination to His will which is so strange to you ; the man at whose strange need and danger God estranged Himself from all eternity, making it His own ; the man who has no cause to reproach God, but if he will reproach anyone can reproach only himself ; the man who is justly reproached by God if he attempts to reply against Him, if he does not live as the one on whose behalf God has taken to Himself every reproach, if he does not live in a state of thankfulness towards God.

When we say that God elected as His own portion the negative side of the divine predestination, the reckoning with man's weakness and sin and inevitable punishment, we say implicitly that this portion is not man's portion. In so far, then, as predestination does contain a No, it is not a No spoken against man. In so far as it does involve exclusion and rejection, it is not the exclusion and rejection of man. In so far as it is directed to perdition and death, it is not directed to the perdition and death of man. All these things could come upon man and should come upon him, because by his unreliability as a creature, and more particularly by his demonstrated disloyalty as a sinful creature, he has clearly shown that he is quite unusable in the hands of God. He has clearly shown that he is not worthy of trust as a covenant-partner with God. From all eternity God could have excluded man from this covenant. He could have delivered him up to himself and allowed him to fall. He could have refused to will him at all. He could have avoided the compromising of His freedom by not willing to create him. He could have remained satisfied with Himself and with the impassible glory and blessedness of His own inner life. But He did not do so. He elected man as a covenant-partner. In His Son He elected Himself as the covenant-partner of man. This does not mean, of course, that He willed to overlook or to accept man's unreliability and disloyalty. It does not mean that He reconciled Himself to the outbreak of evil in the creaturely sphere as actualised in the existence of man. What it does mean is that He willed to make good this affronting and disturbing of His majesty, this devastating of His work, not by avenging Himself on its author, but by Himself bearing the inevitable wrath and perdition, by Himself mediating on behalf of the one who must necessarily be rejected, who had necessarily fallen victim to damnation and death, by allowing His own heart to be wounded by the wrath which, if it had fallen upon man, could only have obliterated and destroyed him.

God's eternal decree in the beginning was the decree of the just and merciful God, of the God who was merciful in His justice and just in His mercy. He was just in that He willed to treat evil seriously, to judge it and to sentence it, to reject and to condemn its author, delivering him over to death. But He was merciful in that He took the author of evil to His bosom, and willed that the rejection and condemnation and death should be His own. In this decree of the just and merciful God is grounded the justification of the sinner in Christ and the forgiveness of sins. It does not mean that God does not treat sins seriously, or that He does not summon man their author to render an account. What it does mean is that in doing this God declares His solidarity with their author, taking his place in respect of their necessary consequence, suffering in Himself what man ought to have suffered. It does not mean that God finds excuse. What it does mean is that God takes to Himself the torment that that which is inexcusable must inevitably carry with it. The justification of the sinner in Jesus Christ is the content of predestination in so far as predestination is a No and signifies rejection. On this side, too, it is eternal. It cannot be overthrown or reversed. Rejection cannot again become the portion or affair of man. The exchange which took place on Golgotha, when God chose as His throne the malefactor's cross, when the Son of God bore what the son of man ought to have borne, took place once and for all in fulfilment of God's eternal will, and it can never be reversed. There is no condemnation—literally none—for those that are in Christ Jesus. For this reason faith in the divine predestination as such and *per se* means faith in the non-rejection of man, or disbelief in his rejection. Man is not rejected. In God's eternal purpose it is God Himself who is rejected in His Son. The self-giving of God consists, the giving and sending of His Son is fulfilled, in the fact that He is rejected in order that we might not be rejected. Predestination means that from all eternity God has determined upon man's acquittal at His own cost. It means that God has ordained that in the place of the one acquitted He Himself should be perishing and abandoned and rejected—the Lamb slain from the foundation of the world. There is, then, no background, no *decretum absolutum*, no mystery of the divine good-pleasure, in which predestination might just as well be man's rejection. On the contrary, when we look into the innermost recesses of the divine good-pleasure, predestination is the non-rejection of man. It is so because it is the rejection of the Son of God. It is so because it is indeed a foreordination of the necessary revelation of divine wrath—but a revelation whose reality was God's own suffering in Jesus Christ. Only if we are unbelieving or disobedient or unthankful in face of what is ordained for us, only if we misunderstand completely the divine predestination, can we think of this revelation as something which has to do with our own suffering. If in face of the divine predestination we are believing and obedient and thankful, if we have a right understanding of its mystery, we shall never find there the decreed rejection either of ourselves or of any other men. This is not because we did not deserve rejection, but because God did not will it, because God willed the rejection of His Son in our stead.

That in faith it is impossible to believe in our rejection is an insight which we share with all the more penetrating exponents of the doctrine. Even Augustine, even Calvin and the Calvinists, always said that in faith we must and can hold by the fact that we are elected and not rejected. But it is hard to see how, or how far, there is any real basis for this insight, or any real possibility of carrying out the advice, unless it is quite clear that in believing in the divine predestination we have to believe in the election of Jesus Christ. We cannot believe in the *decretum absolutum*, and " faith " in it certainly cannot give or allow us the assurance that we are elected and not rejected. Even a general faith in God, or more concretely, in a God of mercy and justice, cannot be of any help in this matter. For by what logic or morality can we ascribe to God a justice and mercy which in their exercise would lead to the exclusion of rejection from the divine purpose ? We can maintain that this is the case only if the divine decree is identical with the divine self-giving in Jesus Christ, or, rather, if it is made and comprised wholly within this self-giving. And if this is so, then we must maintain it. For the confession of God and of God's justice and mercy results necessarily in the further confession that there is neither cause nor authorisation for the fear of possible rejection. For in God's self-giving in Jesus Christ it is clear that rejection does not concern us because God willed that it should concern Himself. We are not called upon to bear the suffering of rejection because God has taken this suffering upon Himself. And if it is the case that in believing in the divine self-giving in Jesus Christ we can and should believe in the divine predestination, then we can believe in our own non-rejection and the non-rejection of all men. We can think of the rejection of man only as the dark background of unbelief, or the objective correlative of false belief : belief in what God has not revealed because it is not true ; perverse belief in what God has not decreed but excluded by His decree. If, then, we would maintain what the older theologians rightly intended to maintain with regard to the necessarily positive character of predestination, and certainly not its negative character, then we must not attempt to separate the eternal will of God and the election of Jesus Christ. In this respect we differ from the older theology.

We now turn to the other aspect of this same reality. What did God elect in the election of Jesus Christ ? We have said already that not only did He elect fellowship with man for Himself, but He also elected fellowship with Himself for man. By the one decree of self-giving He decreed His own abandonment to rejection and also the wonderful exaltation and endowment of man to existence in covenant with Himself ; that man should be enriched and saved and glorified in the living fellowship of that covenant. In this primal decision God did not remain satisfied with His own being in Himself. He reached out to something beyond, willing something more than His own being. He willed and posited the beginning of all things with Himself. But this decision can mean only an overflowing of His glory. It can consist only in a revelation and communication of the good which God has and also is in Himself. If this were not so, God would not be

God. Because there is no darkness in God, there can be no darkness in what He chooses and wills. Nor is there anything midway, anything neutral, between light and darkness. In aim and purpose God is only light, unbroken light. What God does is well done. Our starting-point must always be that in all His willing and choosing what God ultimately wills is Himself. All God's willing is primarily a determination of the love of the Father and the Son in the fellowship of the Holy Ghost. How, then, can its content be otherwise than good ? How can it be anything else but glory—a glory which is new and distinctive and divine ? But in this primal decision God does not choose only Himself. In this choice of self He also chooses another, that other which is man. Man is the outward cause and object of this overflowing of the divine glory. God's goodness and favour are directed towards him. In this movement God has not chosen and willed a second god side by side with Himself, but a being distinct from Himself. And in all its otherness, as His creature and antithesis, this being has been ordained to participation in His own glory, the glory to which it owes its origin. It has been ordained to exist in the brightness of this glory and as the bearer of its image. In all its otherness it is predestined to receive the divine good which has been revealed and communicated. This is what is ordained for man in the primal decision of the divine decree. The portion which God willed and chose for him was an ordination to blessedness. For to be able to attest the overflowing glory of the Creator is blessedness. God willed man and elected man with the promise of eternal life. Life as a witness to the overflowing glory of God is eternal life. In this foreordination man exists in the beginning of all things, in the decree of God with God.

We state at once that we have to do here with the positive content, the Yes of predestination. We have to do with what is primary and proper to it, its meaning and end. For the fact that God willed and chose man with this ordination, the fact that He predestinated him to be a witness of His glory, and therefore to blessedness and eternal life, meant inevitably that he was foreordained to danger and trouble. Man was willed and chosen by God with his limitations, as a creature which could and would do harm to God by the application, or rather the misuse, of its freedom. The danger-point of man's susceptibility to temptation, and the zero-point of his fall, were thus included in the divine decree. In their own way they were even the object of the divine will and choice. This is also true. This second aspect accompanies the first like a shadow preceding and following. In ordaining the overflowing of His glory God also and necessarily ordains that this glory, which in Himself, in His inner life as Father, Son and Holy Spirit, cannot be subjected to attack or disturbance, which in Himself cannot be opposed, should enter the sphere of contradiction where light and darkness are marked off from each other, where what God wills, the good, stands out distinctively from what He does not will, the evil, where by the very existence of good there is conceded to evil and created for it a kind of possibility and reality of existence, where it can and does enter in as a kind of autonomous power, as Satan. The possibility of existence which evil can have is only that of the impossible, the reality of existence only that of the unreal, the autonomous power only that of impotence. But these as such it can and must have. How can God ordain the overflowing of His glory, how can He choose the creature man as witness to this glory, without also willing and choosing its shadow, without conceding to and creating for that shadow—not in Himself, but in the sphere of the outward overflowing of His glory—an existence as something yielding and defeated, without including the existence of that shadow in His decree ? Without evil as " permitted " in this sense there can be no universe or man, and without the inclusion of this " permission " God's decree would be something other than it actually is. It should be perfectly clear, however, that the overflowing and the shadow are the will of God at a completely different level and in a completely different sense. The positive will and choice of God is only the over-flowing of His glory and the blessedness and eternal life of man. Even in His permitting of man's liability to temptation and fall, even in His permitting of evil, this is always what God wills. The divine willing of evil has, then, no proper or autonomous basis in God. It is not, as it were, an independent light in God which shines or is suddenly kindled at this point. God wills evil only because He wills not to keep to Himself the light of His glory but to let it shine outside Himself, because He wills to ordain man the witness of this glory. There is nothing in God and nothing in His willing and choosing *ad extra* to which either evil or the doer of evil can appeal, as though evil too were divinely created, as though evil too had in God a divine origin and counterpart. God wills it only as a shadow which yields and flees. And He wills it only because He wills the shining of only the one true light, His own light, and because He wills to reveal and impart this light. Thus we cannot present as proportionate but only as disproportionate the relationship between the good which God in-tended for man and allotted to him from all eternity, and the danger and distress of the evil which He " permitted " and to that extent willed in the same eternal decree. We are saying too much and speak-ing inexactly even when we describe the one as primarily and properly God's will and the other as that will only secondarily and improperly ; for when we speak in this way evil can easily come to be thought of as having an autonomy and status within the divine economy which cannot be conceded to it. The only autonomy and status that evil can have is that of a being and essence excluded from the divine economy and rejected by it—the autonomy and status of the non-being which necessarily confronts and opposes being in the realm of creation, but which has its basis and meaning only in this confrontation and opposition, only as the spirit of constant negation. If we ask about the content of divine predestination, at no level do we come upon a foreordination of man which is a foreordination to evil, to the dominion of this spirit of negation, to the distress which results from this dominion. The real foreordination of man is to attestation of the divine glory, to blessedness and to eternal life. It is true that this foreordination cannot be fulfilled except on the brink of the abyss of foreordination to evil. But it is also true that evil can only be the abyss of negation in order at once to be opposed and overcome by the Yes of divine predestination. And the negation itself is revealed and is raised up to its own dreadful life by this Yes. When we say God we say Creator, Reconciler and Redeemer, not the opposite. We say the same and not the opposite even when we say Judge, even when we speak of the holiness and wrath of God. We cannot say that God ordains equally and symmetrically as man's end both good and evil, both life and death, both His own glory and the darkening of this glory. In fear and trembling we can and must and will speak of this abyss. We will take evil seriously for what in its own way—but only in its own way—it is allowed to be on the basis of the eternal divine decree. But we will not make of the twofold nature of this decree a dualism. Without overlooking or denying the accompanying shadow we will, in fact, speak of God only as Creator, Reconciler and Redeemer ; as the One from whom we can always expect good and only good. The concept which so hampered the traditional doctrine was that of an equilibrium or balance in which blessedness was ordained and declared on the right hand and perdition on the left. This concept we must oppose with all the emphasis of which we are capable.

But the emphatic nature of our opposition does not derive from any preconceived idea that the love of God prevents His equal willing of both, thus excluding any such symmetrical understanding of double predestination. What right have we to tell God that in His love, which is certainly quite different from ours, He cannot equally seriously, and from the very beginning, from all eternity, condemn as well as acquit, kill as well as make alive, reject as well as elect ? Even to-day we must still defend the older doctrine against this kind of objection. But we cannot defend it against the objection that while the will of God in the election of Jesus Christ is indeed double it is not dual. It is not a will directed equally towards man's life and man's death, towards salvation and its opposite. If we look at it from the standpoint of the election of Jesus Christ, and if we are consistent in finding the will and choice of God only in this election, then a " love " of God directed equally towards human salvation and human damnation would have to be described as a quite arbitrary construct—just as arbitrary, in fact, as that which would deny to God all right to a love of this kind. We must ask one thing of those who would ascribe to God this rather sinister type of love : What is their supposed source of information on this matter ? Certainly this source is not to be found in the consideration or the knowledge of Jesus Christ. Certainly it is not to be found in the knowledge of God's eternal will in the election of Jesus Christ. If we maintain the contrary we must oppose all those theories which presume an equilibrium of God's twofold will. For the only knowledge which we have of man's foreordination to evil and death is in the form in which God of His great mercy accepted it as His own portion and burden, removing it from us and refusing to let it be our foreordination in any form. That removing and refusing took place in Jesus Christ. On our behalf the Son of God took the form of a servant and became obedient unto death, even the death of the cross. In this fact we see the eternal will of God. We know nothing above or beyond the will of God as it is thus realised in time. And for this reason we do not find a proportion but a disproportion between the positive will of God which purposes the life and blessedness of man and the permissive will of God which ordains him to seduction by Satan and guilt before God. In this disproportion the first element is always predominant, the second subordinate. The first is an authoritative Yes, the second a No which is determined only by the Yes, thus losing its authority from the very outset. The first is the coming form of the divine work, the second the perishing. This would, indeed, be an arrogant and quite impossible presentation of the matter if we reached such a conclusion from an arbitrarily formed judgment of our own about God or man. But this presentation is the correct and indeed the only possible one, because all others are excluded by the judgment which God Himself has pronounced on man —excluded, that is to say, if we recognise in this judgment God's original and definitive decree, and if we acknowledge it as such. We are no longer free, then, to think of God's eternal election as bifurcating into a rightward and a leftward election. There is a leftward election. But God willed that the object of this election should be Himself and not man. God removed from man and took upon Himself the burden of the evil which unavoidably threatened and actually achieved and exercised dominion in the world that He had ordained as the theatre of His glory. God removed from man and took upon Himself the suffering which resulted from this dominion, including the condemnation of sinful man. For this reason we cannot ascribe any autonomy to the world of evil, or to the will of God as it is directed towards and assents to it in a permissive form. In Jesus Christ we can see and know this whole sphere of evil as something which has already been overcome, something which yields, something which has been destroyed by the positive will of God's overflowing glory. And what it is in Jesus Christ it is also in the beginning with God. And for this reason in God's decree at the beginning there is for man only a predestination which corresponds to the perfect being of God Himself; a predestination to His kingdom and to blessedness and life. Any other pre-destination is merely presumed and unreal : a predestination arising from sin and error and opposed by the revelation of God ; not the divine predestination fulfilled in God's eternal decree. Man takes upon him something which God has reserved for Himself if he tries to enter into this predestination or to think of himself as predestined to sin and death. If God has reserved for Himself the reckoning with evil, all that man can do is to take what is allotted to him by God. But this is nothing more or less than God's own glory. Unequivocally, and without reserve or diminution, God has elected and ordained man to bear the image of this glory. That and that alone is what we see and know in Jesus Christ in relation to man. The suffering borne on the cross of Golgotha by the son of man in unity with the Son of God, who is as such a sacrifice for the sins of the world, is a stage on the road, an unavoidable point of transition, to the glory of the resurrection, ascension and session. But it is not the Son of God who is glorified. He who humbled Himself according to the decree of God had no need of glorifying. He does not experience glorifying, but rather, in the power of His deity, He realises and accomplishes it. The glorification is of the Son of David. His is the justification, His the salvation from death, His the exaltation to fellowship with God, His the clothing upon with that form of existence predestined for Him, eternal life, His the foretaste of blessedness. This is man's portion in the amazing exchange between God and man as it was realised in time in Jesus Christ because already it was the beginning of all things. And we must recognise this as man's portion in the divine predestination if we trust that God's will revealed in Jesus Christ is the eternal will of God. It is evident that by an act of renunciation God diverts to man the portion which rightly belongs to Himself. If we may put it in this way, the glory and goodness and blessedness which we find in the sphere of creation is no longer God's own. He has given away what is His. He has given away Himself and all the prerogatives of His Godhead. He has given them to the man Jesus, and in Him to the creature. To put it more exactly, in the sphere of creation God has His glory and goodness and blessedness in what He reveals and communicates to the man Jesus and in Him to the creature. There can be no doubt that in His overflowing glory God is sacrificial love ; love which seeks not her own but the things of others. This corresponds to the humiliation which the Son of God accepted on behalf of the lost son of man, and to the whole exaltation conferred upon the son of man by this divine favour. And the latter is clearly the decisive element in the work of God accomplished in Jesus Christ and therefore in God's eternal decree. Obviously God wills the former : His own humiliation on man's behalf, that judgment might be taken away, all righteousness fulfilled, and the road trodden to the very end. But He wills the former only in connexion with and for the sake of the one thing : that by right man might be heir of His own glory, goodness and blessedness, entering into fellowship with Himself. The order proclaimed in the work of revelation and atonement must be regarded and respected as also the order of the divine predestination. Naturally we must know what it is that God wills to remove from us. But much more we must know what it is that He wills to give to us. And we can know this only in terms of what God has put behind us because He willed to take it from us and has in fact done so. We can know it only in terms of the abyss on whose brink we are held. We cannot look at this abyss as though it were still the place to which we belong. We know that our place is in heaven where Christ sits as our Representative on the right hand of God. We cannot balance the fact that Adam fell, or David sinned, or Peter denied, or Judas betrayed, against the resurrection of Jesus Christ. The facts are true, but it is also true that they are far outweighed by the resurrection of Jesus Christ and that as the result of this resurrection they belong already to the vanished past. The thought of God's predestination cannot, then, awaken in us the mixture of terror and joy which would be in order if we were confronted partly by promise and partly by threat. It can awaken only joy, pure joy. For this order is found in the divine predestination itself, and it cannot be revoked. It is not a system whose component parts must each be considered separately. It is a way willed by God Himself. At the end of this way God's glory is revealed in the fact that He Himself removed the threat and became our salvation. In the light of this end there is no place for anything but joy. And only the end affects us, only grace, not what God had to take away and willed to take away and did take away from us, taking it upon Himself. For this reason, in relation to the divine predestination we must look always to that end. This is not a matter of optimism. It is a matter of being obedient and not disobedient, of being thankful and not self-willed. In obedience and thankfulness we can only rejoice at the double predestination of God.

This interpretation of double predestination stands or falls, of course, with the view that the divine predestination is to be understood only within the election of Jesus Christ. It stands or falls with the view that in regard to the electing God and elected man we must look and continue to look neither to the right hand nor to the left but directly at Jesus Christ. In other words, the question is this : Is the electing God the Son beloved of the Father and Himself loving the Father, the Son who as such is the subject of the beginning and predestination of all things ? And is elected man, the object of this beginning and predestination of all things, the man Jesus of Nazareth who was born in the cradle of Bethlehem and died on the cross of Golgotha and on the third day rose again from the dead ? If this is so, then double predestination can be understood only in this order, only in this disproportionate relation between the divine taking away and the divine giving, between the humiliation of God and the exaltation of man, between rejection and election. It can hardly be questioned that, according to the witness of the New Testament, this is the relation as seen in the revelation and atonement made in Jesus Christ. But can we see and recognise in this relation the same relation as exists within the divine predestination itself? Or must we really look elsewhere at this point? The teaching of tradition has accustomed us to looking elsewhere. It did not see predestination or think of it as something held within the election of Jesus Christ. And on such a view it is self-evident that the relation between the decrees of election and rejection will take on quite a different character, that it will relapse more or less automatically into a relation of proportion or equilibrium. Now apart from our consideration of the revelation and atonement made in Jesus Christ we have no reason whatever to present the relation within God's double predestination in the form in which we have actually done so. But all we need ask is whether this one reason is not also a command, a command which we must obey regardless of all other considerations. We must ask what considerations can constitute a sufficient reason to release us from the stringency of the command of this one reason. If no satisfactory answer to this question is forthcoming, then for good or evil the above understanding of double predestination must be adopted.

4. Because it is identical with the election of Jesus Christ, the eternal will of God is a divine activity in the form of the history, encounter and decision between God and man. In God's eternal predestination we have to do already with the living God. From all eternity God is within Himself the living God. The fact that God is means that from all eternity God is active in His inner relationships as Father, Son and Holy Ghost, that He wills Himself and knows of Himself, that He loves, that He makes use of His sovereign freedom, that He maintains and exercises this freedom, and in so doing maintains and demonstrates Himself. In Himself God is rest, but this fact does not exclude but includes the fact that His being is decision. God does not, therefore, become the living God when He works or decides to work *ad extra*—in His being *ad extra* He is, of course, the living God in a different way—but His being and activity *ad extra* is merely an overflowing of His inward activity and being, of the inward vitality which He has in Himself. It is a proclamation of the decision in which in Himself He is who He is. The origin of this proclamation within God Himself is predestination. This is no less activity than in His own way God in Himself is activity and in a different way His whole work in the world is activity. It is the transition from the one to the other: from God's being in and for Himself to His being as Lord of creation. And what else can that be but activity and event? What right have we to think of God at this point except as the living God? The eternal will of God which is the predestination of all things is God's life in the form of the history, encounter and decision between Himself and man, a history, encounter and decision which are already willed and known from all eternity, and to that extent, prior to all external events, are already actual before Him and for Him.

If we are correct in saying this, we must say that the name and person of Jesus Christ was in the beginning with God. The will of God was His self-giving on behalf of man in the concrete form of the union of His own Son or Word with the man Jesus of Nazareth. And as such this beginning is life, the life of a history, encounter and decision. With God, in God's eternal will, a decision was made whose result is manifest to us in the existence of this man as attested by Holy Scripture. This man was the object of the divine good-pleasure. But why this man ? It is here surely that we come to the place where we must respect the freedom of the divine election. God's choice was made and fulfilled in such a way that its result confronts us as an unequivocal witness to the purpose and the holiness and the righteousness of this choice. What is demanded is respect for God's free disposing, but such respect is possible only if there is knowledge, not ignorance ; knowledge of the free will of God which is the subject of this choice. This is the respect for the divine good-pleasure which is demanded and authorised at this point. When we look at the content of the divine predestination, at once we can and must say that the divine life which was actively expressed in this predestination at the very beginning is the life of God's love. And the fact that God's love was there at the very beginning of all things, as the purpose and power of this overflowing of God's inward being as the living God, is not in any way limited or questioned but rather confirmed by the truth that the divine predestinating is done in freedom. What else can we say when the elect Son of Man is God's own Son, God Himself in His own self-giving ? The One elected testifies unequivocally to the nature and being of the One who elects. He speaks for that One : *a posteriori*, of course ; and only in virtue of the fact that that One first speaks for him, that the son of man is taken up into union with the Son of God. The Son of Man speaks, in fact, for the grace of God which stoops down to man and lifts up man to itself. He speaks not for Himself but for the mercy of God. He attests, therefore, the freedom of God's love, but obviously and far more the depth and uniqueness of that love. He testifies that what takes place between God and man according to God's predestination has its source wholly and utterly in the divine initiative. It is not that God and man begin to have dealings with each other, but that God begins to have dealings with man. Without any qualification the precedence is with God. There can be no question of any activity on man's part except upon the basis of the prior activity of God, and in the obvious form of a human response to this prior activity. God is the Lord both in His eternal decree and in all its execution. God decides, and the possibility and actuality of man's decision follow on this decision of God. But that does not mean that God's initiative is obscure even in its sovereignty. Its meaning and bearing are both clear. God does not need man, yet He wills not to be without him, to interest Himself in him. God is the presupposition both of Himself and of man. He has caught up man into the sovereign presupposing of Himself. This is the unqualified precedence of God's work, qualified only in so far as it is not a precedence over nothing—for how could it then be precedence ?—but over man. From all eternity God posits His whole majesty (and this is the meaning and purpose of the act of eternal predestination) in this particular relationship to this particular being over against Himself. God pledges and commits Himself to be the God of man.

Such is God's activity in predestination in so far as He is its Subject. But it is not the whole of this activity. In it there begins the history, encounter and decision between Himself and man. For the fulfilment of the election involves the affirmation of the existence of elected man and its counterpart in man's election, in which God's election evokes and awakens faith, and meets and answers that faith as human decision. The electing God creates for Himself as such man over against Himself. And this means that for his part man can and actually does elect God, thus attesting and activating himself as elected man. He can and actually does accept the self-giving of God in its twofold sense, and on the basis of this self-giving he has his true life. There is, then, a simple but comprehensive autonomy of the creature which is constituted originally by the act of eternal divine election and which has in this act its ultimate reality. We cannot over-emphasise God's freedom and sovereignty in this act. We cannot assert too strongly that in the election of grace it is a matter of the decision and initiative of the divine good-pleasure, that as the One who elects God has absolute precedence over the One who is elected. We can hardly go too far or say too much along these lines, more particularly when we remember that the theme of the divine election is primarily the relationship between God and man in the person of Jesus Christ. Who has the initiative in this relationship ? Who has the precedence ? Who decides ? Who rules ? God, always God. God founds and maintains the union between Himself and man. God awakens man to existence before Him and summons him to His service. God in His Son is Himself the person of man. God knows and confirms and blesses Him as His Son. God creates Him for His own Word. God vouchsafes to grant Him a part in His own suffering for man's frailty and sin and for the discord and judgment which inevitably result from them. God justifies Him, raises Him from the dead, gives Him a part in His own glory. All that man can and will do is to pray, to follow and to obey. The honour of the Son of Man adopted to union with the Son of God can and will consist only in promoting the honour of His heavenly Father. Only as the Son of Man is adopted into this union can He receive, receive His own task, receive the co-operation in suffering which is laid upon Him, receive finally the attestation from above and His own exaltation and glorification. " Not my will, but thine, be done." And this certainly means theonomy, the lordship of God at every point. Jesus Christ is Himself the established kingdom of God. And the establishment of this kingdom, the restoration of the relationship between Himself and the creature, was the will of God from the beginning, the content of divine predestination. Yet we must not emphasise any less strongly that the motive for this establishment of the kingdom is not in any sense an autocratic self-seeking, but a love which directs itself outwards, a self-giving to the creature. It is still true that God wills to be Himself even in His relationship with the reality distinct from Himself (and primarily in His relationship with man). It is still true that in this will it is His own glory which ordains for itself this overflowing as the predestination of all things. The goodness of God's will and work *ad extra* depends upon the fact that in the smallest things as in the greatest God wholly and utterly wills and fulfils and reveals Himself. But He wills and fulfils and reveals Himself not only in Himself but in giving Himself, in willing and recognising the distinct reality of the creature, granting and conceding to it an individual and autonomous place side by side with Himself. Naturally the individuality and autonomy are only of such a kind as His own goodness can concede and grant. God could not be God if He willed and permitted any other individuality or autonomy side by side with His own. An independent individuality or autonomy could be only devilish in character. It could belong only to evil. Evil as such does not and cannot receive any individuality or autonomy from God. From all eternity this gift is denied to evil. But to the creature God willed from all eternity to give, to communicate, and to reveal Himself. To the creature God determined, therefore, to give an individuality and autonomy, not that these gifts should be possessed outside Him, let alone against Him, but for Him, and within His kingdom; not in rivalry with His sovereignty but for its confirming and glorifying. But the sovereignty which was to be confirmed and glorified was the sovereignty of His love, which did not will to exercise mechanical force, to move the immobile from without, to rule over puppets or slaves, but willed rather to triumph in faithful servants and friends, not in their overthrow, but in their obedience, in their own free decision for Him. The purpose and meaning of the eternal divine election of grace consists in the fact that the one who is elected from all eternity can and does elect God in return. And on these lines, too, we cannot say too much or speak too definitely, especially when we remember that at the beginning of all God's ways and works, in the eternal decree of God, there stands the relationship between Himself and the creature which became event and revelation in Jesus Christ. In this event and revelation, what is it that takes place on God's side ? It is not a fatalistic overruling and disposing, but a deciding, a deciding which in a single and truly sovereign decision takes on the form and outward appearance of creation and the man Jesus. The man Jesus is not a mere puppet moved this way and that by God. He is not a mere reed used by God as the instrument of His Word. The man Jesus prays. He speaks and acts. And as He does so He makes an unheard of claim, a claim which makes Him appear the victim of delusion and finally brings down upon Him the charge of blasphemy.   He thinks of Himself as the Messiah, the Son of God. He allows Himself to be called *Kyrios*, and, in fact, conducts Himself as such.   He speaks of His suffering, not as a necessity laid upon Him from without, but as something which He Himself wills.   His glorifying is for Him not a matter of vague expectancy and hope, but the goal to which He strides with the same sober certainty as to the preceding fulfilment of His humiliation.   In His wholehearted obedience, in His electing of God alone, He is wholly free.   He is the witness to the kingdom of God whose establishment cannot be withheld.   And as such He, the man Jesus, can and should and must be the true King, hidden at first but later manifest, a King over men's hearts, but a King, too, over demons and sicknesses, over waves and storm, over death itself, always a King, even before Pilate, even and most of all on the cross.   The truly astounding feature about the person of Jesus Christ is this, that here is a man who not only testified to God's rule by His Word and deeds.   In the last analysis all the prophets had done that.   Jesus did that, too, but in doing it He did more.   He actually claimed and exercised lordship, even the lordship of God.   The perfection of God's giving of Himself to man in the person of Jesus Christ consists in the fact that far from merely playing with man, far from merely moving or using him, far from merely dealing with him as an object, this self-giving sets man up as a subject, awakens him to genuine individuality and autonomy, frees him, makes him a king, so that in his rule the kingly rule of God Himself attains form and revelation.   How can there be any possible rivalry here, let alone usurpation ?   How can there be any question of a conflict between theonomy and autonomy ? How can God be jealous or man self-assertive ?   It was in this light, of course, that the Jewish contemporaries of Jesus immediately saw the matter, and they charged and condemned Him in the name of the offended God.   They did so because in the King who stood before them they did not recognise the servant of God.   They did so because in the form of the servant they did not recognise the King.   They did so because they did not recognise in Jesus Christ either very God or very man.   They did so because the will of God was hidden from them. For what took place in Jesus Christ—and we shall have to take this further step if we are to see and confess in God's revelation God's eternal decree—was not merely a temporal event, but the eternal will of God temporally actualised and revealed in that event.   God's eternal will is man : man who is the wholehearted witness to God's kingdom and enjoys as such a kingly freedom—the Lamb of God which taketh away the sin of the world, but also the Lion of Judah which has gained the victory—man in a state of utter and most abject responsibility over against God, who even in this responsibility, even in the acknowledgment of the absolute pre-eminence of God Himself, is and become;

an individual, and autonomous, and in the sphere of creation a sovereign being, and as such the image of God. God's eternal will is the act of prayer (in which confidence in self gives way before confidence in God). This act is the birth of a genuine human self-awareness, in which knowledge and action can and must be attempted; in which there drops away all fear of what is above or beside or below man, of what might assault or threaten him; in which man becomes heir to a legitimate and necessary and therefore an effective and triumphant claim; in which man may rule in that he is willing to serve. If Jesus Christ was that man, if from the very beginning He was elected man, then we have to say that God's eternal will has as its end the life of this man of prayer. This is the man who was in the beginning with God. This is the man who was marked and sought out by God's love. This is the man to whom and to the existence of whom the whole work of God applied as it was predetermined from all eternity.

And if we consider God's eternal decree in its entirety, we see that as it is the decree of the living God it is itself divine and living. It is, in fact, the living God Himself in the beginning of all His ways. It is so in virtue of the fact that in the bosom of God it is itself this one event—the history, encounter and decision between God and man. God elects man. On man's side this election becomes actual in man's own electing of God, by which he is made free to do the will of God, and achieves and possesses individuality and autonomy before God. Everywhere we see the divine sovereignty and the divine initiative. This decree is wholly and utterly an election of grace. And yet the decision of the sovereign God, His election of grace (in the understanding of which we cannot be allowed to reverse or even to compare the two partners), has as its sole content the fact that God elects man in order that man may be awakened and summoned to elect God, and to pray that he may give himself to Him, and that in this act of electing and prayer he may exist in freedom before God : the reality *in nuce* which is distinct from God and yet united with Him in joy and peace ; man who is the meaning and purpose of the whole creation ; man who in his own sphere can and should have autonomy and a kingdom.

In this context we must stress the fact that the divine predestination as thus understood is a living act. We can only understand and describe it as an act because in itself it is solely and entirely an act : the theonomy of God which wills and decrees as such the autonomy of man; the electing of God and election of man which take on historical form as a human electing in which man can and should elect and affirm and activate himself. In this chain it is impossible to pick out any one link and to consider it in and for itself. But it is also impossible to make of it a single system and to consider it as such. We can view it as a whole only as we view the living person of Jesus Christ. We can understand it as a whole only if we understand it as an event which in its entirety is as such the will of God and encloses as such man and the will and decision of man and the autonomous existence of man. This divine will in its entirety was in the beginning with God. This divine act of will is predestination.

It is now possible and necessary for us to make the controversial assertion that predestination is the divine act of will itself and not an abstraction from or fixed and static result of it. It is not the case, then, that while the predetermined process of the world and life of man are living history, encounter and decision, predestination itself stands over against them as something unchanged and unchangeable. It is not the case that in the form of predestination a kind of death has become the divine law of creaturely life.

We are confronted at this point by a further limitation of the traditional teaching. On the basis of a doctrine of God which was pagan rather than Christian, it thought of predestination as an isolated and given enactment which God had decreed from all eternity and which to some extent pledged and committed even God Himself in time. Because of His immutability, even God could not alter this enactment once it had been determined. It is obvious that in the older Protestantism the reigning concept of the *decretum praedestinationis* could be and actually was misunderstood, with very serious consequences. The very concept " decree " reminds us inevitably of a military or political ordinance, a law, a statute, a rule which lays down in black and white and preserves and expresses in definitive form the will of a regnant power. Yet the decree of a human ruler has always the characteristic that notwithstanding respect to the letter, in its exposition and application regard is always and necessarily had, and can actually be had, to the living will of the lawgiver. And this decree has a further characteristic that it can always be corrected or suspended or replaced by another decree, and that sooner or later it will actually be corrected or suspended or replaced in this way. A human decree need not be a dead letter which kills. It can be a living organ of life. When we speak of a divine decree, however, it can easily happen that we conceive of it as our duty to deny to it the two characteristics in virtue of which a human decree can within certain limits be a living organ. The divinity of the decree is then sought in the fact that the will of God has in some measure taken on hard and fast form in that decree, so that there is no possibility of an appeal from the wording of the decree to the will of God, and all thought of an alteration or suspension of the decree is excluded. This could mean, however, that there was only one occasion when God willed, in the pre-temporal eternity when the decree was conceived and established. It was then that God elected. It was then that in the matter of salvation and perdition, of life and death, He decided either to the right or to the left according to His own good-pleasure. The living quality of this action is something *perfectum*, belonging to the eternal past. It is not an action, an electing and deciding, which is still continued in time. God's living action in the present consists only in the execution of this decree, the fulfilment of an election and decision already made. For us, then, who exist in time, the living God is perceptible and meaningful and active only in the execution and fulfilment of His predestination, not in predestination itself. What we may see in predestination itself and as such is in some degree the monument of the living God, of the God who is meaningful and active in practice. In it God is no longer for us the living God. He surrendered this quality by translating it into act. In His work in time He is the living God for us only to the extent that He is no longer the living God in that pre-temporal eternity. His speech and activity in the temporal present are only an echo of the note which was struck in His eternal decree. That note cannot ring out independently in time. It can only be repeated. As the eternally electing God, God was. He is and will be only in so far as the decree has been made by which He precedes all that is and will be, only in so far as all that is and will be is determined by that decree. God did predestinate. In time He predestinates no longer. In time there is only the predestination of all being and history by an act of predestinating which is past. There is no new or additional predestinating. On this view, then, it is the case that the law of creaturely life is a death which is absolutised in the form of a decision reached and an election made by God from all eternity. That which was in the beginning with God is an authoritative and all-powerful letter. The eternal God did all that was needed when He promulgated this letter and gave it authority and power over the whole realm of creaturely life in time. All that now lives derives its life from God only in the sense that it derives it from the authority and power of this letter. After that first and all-embracing act of life, God Himself, the living God, retired behind this letter, taking His rest and satisfying Himself again with His own inner life. He delivered up creaturely life to the rule of this letter. As far as concerned the creature He committed Himself by this letter. Such is the picture which might result, and has in fact resulted, from an application of the concept *decretum* to the divine predestination.

There can be no doubt that understood in this way the concept could and did help forward the cause of Deism. Deism separated the Creator of the world from the world-process. The Godhead was thought of as quite inactive in relation to this predetermined process. World development took place according to its own divinely established law. Now if God's will and decree in the beginning are regarded as an isolated and self-contained predestination, preceding the life of the creature but no longer present in it, then in the last resort it is hardly possible to maintain seriously that God is the Lord of all that evolves from that first decree. If predestination as such is no longer actual, then in fact God Himself is no longer actual. There is no point in asking us to believe in God at our stage in that development. We may still think of God as the principle of the mysterious authority and power which controls the stream of events in which we actually find ourselves. We may still recognise that at the beginning of that stream the letter must have been established under whose law the world and our own life continues. But we shall prefer to look within that development for other relative but at any rate actual quantities in which we may put the faith which we have no cause to put in that letter and its execution and Him who once perhaps conceived and elected it. Certainly the object of that faith cannot be a God who was once the electing and predestinating God, but is so no longer. Obviously, we can have faith only in a God who is present in His decision and election, who is actually the electing and deciding God. If He is not that, and we cannot have faith in Him, it is only a short step to the denial of the existence of God. Or, to put it better, if we do not have faith in God, if we do not know Him as actually the electing and deciding God, His existence is, in fact, already denied.

In face of this very real danger of misunderstanding it is not necessary, nor would it be wise, to erase or abandon altogether the concept *decretum*. The concept describes something which cannot be denied but must seriously be recognised and taken into account. It tells us, in fact, of God's constancy, the faithfulness, the reliability, the absoluteness, the definitiveness of the free love of God in which He elected and predestinated at the beginning of all things with Himself. In this election and predestination God at all events remains unchanged and unchangeably the same. And we cannot think of His will and predestinating without forming for ourselves the concept of an authoritative and all-powerful decree which is once and for all, far above time and all that is in time ; the concept of an ordinance. That notion of an eternal letter, posited once and for all and simply awaiting fulfilment in creaturely life, is one which we cannot dismiss hurriedly and lightly. There can be no doubt that God *has* taken upon Himself a committal, an obligation, and that in perfect freedom (in the freedom of His love) He has decided to abide by it. If we would think in non-legal terms in relation to this matter, we must see to it that in our fear of the concept *decretum* we do not fall into the error of the *decretum absolutum* which the older Protestant theology obviously thought that it could and should balance against a too pronounced legalism in the understanding of *decretum*. We must still allow that in predestination we have to confess the divine law, and not an arbitrary divine power overruling the life of the creature. It is for this reason that we have always spoken of God's eternal will as His decree, and must continue to do so.

We must remember however—and in so doing we part company with the older teaching—that God's decree is a living decree, a decree that is infinitely more living than any decree of man. It is the letter of God in the beginning in virtue of the fact that this letter is determined and posited with all the constancy, the faithfulness and the dependability of God Himself, enjoying an authority and power greater than that of the letter of any possible human law. But it is also spirit and life in a way impossible even for the very best of the written laws of man as best expounded or applied. The fact that from all eternity God has predestinated, elected and decided has, of course, all the weightiness of the eternal *perfectum*. It is something isolated and complete. It is the foreordination which precedes all creaturely life. It stands as hard as steel or granite before and above all things and all events. But in so doing, it has and is the life of God. It has really been predetermined from all eternity. It has the character not only of an unparalleled " perfect " but also of an unparalleled " present " and " future." And it remains because it is eternally before time. It is not left behind by time, but as that which is above time (for there is only one eternity with God) it accompanies time, and as that which is beyond time it outlasts it. It not only was but is and will be. It happened : never by any subversion can we weaken the fact that it happened, and happened once and for all. But it not only happened ; it does happen and will happen. For it is the principle and essence of all happening everywhere. How, then, can it be anything else but a happening ? How can it ever not happen ? How can it have a part in one perfection of happening and not another ? As God's foreordination, how can it happen only once and not continue to happen, giving place instead to that other happening, its execution and fulfilment, and itself becoming dead and obsolete, a happening which belongs only to the past ? What meaning can there be in the word " then " when we are speaking of God's eternity ? It is true, of course, that in that eternity there can be an " earlier " as there can be a " now " and a " later," for eternity is certainly not the negation but the boundary of time as such. But for this very reason "then " cannot mean only " earlier." When we speak of God's eternity we must recognise and accept what is " earlier " as something also present and future. God's predestination is a completed work of God, but for this very reason it is not an exhausted work, a work which is behind us. On the contrary, it is a work which still takes place in all its fulness to-day. Before time and above time and at every moment of time God is the predestinating God, positing this beginning of all things with Himself, willing and ordaining, electing and deciding, pledging and committing (us and first of all Himself), establishing the letter of the law which rules over all creaturely life. It is not the case, then, that God did will but that now He no longer wills, or wills only the effects of His willing. To speak in causal terms, God does will the effects, but in so doing He does not cease to will the cause. And He does not cease to be the living God in the cause. God is never an echo. He is and continues to be and always will be an independent note or sound. The predestination of God is unchanged and unchangeably God's activity. The point that we have to make against the older doctrine is this, that while in other respects it laid too great stress upon God's freedom, in this context it came very near to thinking of this freedom in such a way that in predestination God became His own prisoner.

As against this tendency we must remember that *praedestinatio*, like *creatio* and *reconciliatio*, like *vocatio, iustificatio, sanctificatio* and *glorificatio*, describes a divine activity, and that there is no reason whatever why we should suddenly substitute for this concept a concept of isolated and static being. What we have to see and understand here is that it is unchanged and unchangeably God's activity, and that as such it is in the beginning with God. When we speak of the divine predestination we speak of an eternal happening. And we do not say this merely on the basis of abstract recollection. We say it because an analysis of the reality designated by the concept predestination has shown us that it can, in fact, refer only to a happening. We say it because when we speak of the electing of God and election of man to which the concept refers, when we speak of the intimate connexion between theonomy and autonomy, between divine sovereignty and human faith, we are not dealing with a systematic relationship but with one which can be the object and content only of a law which is itself spirit and life, concrete history. The reality of predestination is not merely history's *schema* and programme, but history itself as once and for all determined in God's own will and decree. Only as concrete decree, only as an act of divine life in the Spirit, is it the law which precedes all creaturely life. In virtue of its character and content this decree can never be rigid and fixed. It can never belong only to the past. Because it is God's decree it must, of course, be constant, authoritative and powerful. But because it has pleased God to let it be a concrete decree, it never ceases to be event.

Thus the eternal history, encounter and decision between God and man, the content of the Gospel in which we have to acknowledge the concrete content of predestination, cannot be thought of as breaking off or concluding with an effect which we then have to describe as the presupposition of all other temporal histories, encounters and decisions within the sphere of creaturely reality. How can that history, encounter and decision be eternal if it ceases as such with the beginning of time, if it can to some extent be replaced or supplanted by temporal events? Since it is itself history, encounter and decision, since it is an act of divine life in the spirit, since it is the unbroken and lasting predetermining and decreeing of Him who as Lord of all things has both the authority and the power for such activity, it is the presupposition of all the movement of creaturely life. This presupposition is not merely static but moving. It has authority, and it also authorises. It is powerful, and it exercises power. It happened, and it also happens. Who then, and what then, is unchanged and unchangeable? God Himself in His triune being as free love. And not only God, but God's decree, God's electing of man according to His own good-pleasure, an electing which resulted in the election of man, and man's electing of God and finding of his good pleasure in God. All these are as unchanged and unchangeable as God Himself and God's eternal will. All these are the eternal predestination of temporal events. But what is truly unchangeable cannot simply be immovable. What is truly unchanged cannot be unmoved. It is that which moves everything and as such it is moved within itself. What is unchanged and unchangeable is that the beginning of all things with God is itself history, encounter and decision. This is predestination. In saying this we do not launch predestination upon the general stream of world-events in time. Nor do we launch it upon the particular stream of the saving events in which world-events as a whole find their meaning and end. This history, encounter and decision between God and man was in the beginning with God, and is identical neither with the one nor the other. It is, rather, the secret which is hidden in world-history as such and revealed in the history of salvation as such. The secret of all life is the existence of the living God as the One who has created life and who sustains and governs it. The secret of everything that takes place in this world is the decision of God which eternally precedes it. All other events culminate in the history of salvation and take place necessarily for the sake of it. In this history God's decision which precedes everything, and therefore the divine electing of man and man's election by God, is made visible and becomes operative in time in the form of the Word of God proclaimed and received, in the form of the people Israel and the Church, in the form of the calling, justification, sanctification and glorification of man, in the form of man's faith and hope and love. For this reason we must see in all these things quite literally the divine predestination, the eternal decision of God's free love. These things are not in any sense a law unto themselves. There is no separation of the temporal from the eternal. Man's work and experience, what he wins and possesses, cannot be asserted over against the divine disposing. There can be no praise of man, no boasting or arbitrary pretension on man's part, but only discipleship, thankfulness and adoration. But for the same reason there is also in this relationship a royal self-awareness on the part of the Elect. Because the eternal predestination is made manifest to us in that history of salvation, we accept it as the secret of everything else that takes place in the world. We have, if not to understand, at any rate to consider and weigh up all other events, both in general and in detail, as we are instructed by what we know of that history. In principle, then, predestination is not concealed from us. It would be so if it consisted in that letter set up in an inaccessibly distant past eternity. But it is an act of divine life in the spirit, an act which affects us, an act which occurs in the very midst of time no less than in that far distant pre-temporal eternity. It is the present secret, and in the history of salvation the revealed secret, of the whole history, encounter and decision between God and man. It takes place in time. It is revealed, and yet it still remains a secret, and is recognisable and recognised as such. It takes place in the proclamation of God's Word. It takes place in the foundation and existence and guidance of Israel and the Church. It takes place in the calling, justification, sanctification and glorification of man. It takes place in our awakening to faith and hope and love. What else are these things but the movement of the eternally electing God, the God who exercises His free love in the beginning ? But predestination also takes place even where we do not recognise it directly, even where we do not understand it, even where, knowing of it (and having directly recognised and understood it in the history of salvation), we can only confess it as a hidden reality in world-events as a whole. In principle, it is never concealed. But the perception of it depends upon our direct or indirect interest in its occurrence, i.e., whether we are amongst those to whom it applies. There is no knowledge of pre-destination except in the movement from the electing God to elected man, and back again from elected man to the electing God. There cannot be, for predestination is this movement. This movement is, in fact, God's eternal decree. God willed this movement, willed it from all eternity, and continues to will it. In face of this movement, in face of predestination, we cannot be spectators. If we stood without and not within, we should not be able to see anything at all in this matter. Each glimpse of predestination that we get, even the very slightest, we can understand only as a challenge and invitation to understand and to conduct ourselves more radically and more seriously as those who are already caught up in this movement. In proportion as we do this, we are then challenged and invited to see and to under-stand predestination with greater clarity and fulness, both directly and also indirectly.

The fundamental significance of the character of predestination as act ought to be clear without further discussion. If it is unchanged and unchangeably the history, encounter and decision between God and man, there is in time an electing by God and an election of man, as there is also a rejecting by God and a rejection of man, but not in the sense that God Himself is bound and imprisoned by it, not as though God's decree, the first step which He took, committed Him to take a corresponding second step, and the second a third. If it is true that the predestinating God not only is free but remains free, that He does not cease to make use of His freedom but continues to decide, then in the course of God's eternal deciding we have constantly to reckon with new decisions in time. As the Bible itself presents the matter, there is no election which cannot be followed by rejection, no rejection which cannot be followed by election. God continues always the Lord of all His works and ways. He is consistent with Himself. He is also consistent with the prearranged order of election and rejection. But He is always the living God. And since His life is the dynamic of that order, developments and alterations in it are always possible and do in fact take place. Neither in the history of Israel and the Church nor in the life of the individual can we dismiss these as mere appearance, a temporary obscuring of the inevitable outcome of things. On the contrary, it is in the developments and alterations as such, in their freshness, in their otherness, even in their conflicting nature as they succeed one another, that we must seek the inevitability of the divine predestination, the rule of the living God who is free to love where He was wroth and to be wroth where He loved, to bring death to the living and life to the dead, to repent Himself and to repent of His repenting. This is how predestination is described in the *locus classicus*, Rom. 9–11—a description which we cannot possibly reconcile with the understanding of predestination as a rigid and static law, but only with the understanding of it as a definition of God's eternal action in time.

But this activist understanding of predestination depends wholly and utterly upon the identifying of it with the election of Jesus Christ. Unless we start there, it is merely a case of one assertion against the other : the assertion of the divinity of static being as the beginning of all things against that of an activated history ; a static and in the last analysis perhaps a quietistic view of life against a dynamic and activist. And the question arises : Which of these is right ? How can we decide which of them is truly of God ? Ultimately there is only one reason that we can give for deciding in favour of an activist understanding, and that is that the predestination which we know in the person and work of Jesus Christ is undoubtedly event, the history, encounter and decision between God and man. God's electing and man's election ; God's self-humiliation and man's exaltation by God ; the self-giving as it is effected in the Son of God and the Son of Man Jesus Christ, and as it is made manifest in Him as the eternal divine decree ; the history of salvation in which we can see and understand predestination itself : all these are an act, or they are not what they are. They are an act, a definite act, concrete, completed. And this act does not contradict the being of God because in virtue of its definiteness it is letter as well as spirit, enjoying the authority and force of a law. At this point we must be very careful not to press the dynamic case against the static, or the activist case against the quietist. In different ways as much can be said against the former view as against the latter. In so far as we see the mystery of the divine decision in the concrete person of Jesus Christ we are against the activist view. And in so far as we think of Jesus Christ as the decision of the eternally living God we are opposed to the static. In the present context we are necessarily opposed to the latter. We could think of a *decretum absolutum* as a lifeless and timeless rule for temporal life. But we can think of Jesus Christ only as the living and eternal Lord of temporal life. The Father loves the Son and the Son is obedient to the Father. In this love and obedience God gives Himself to man. He takes upon Himself man's lowliness in order that man may be exalted. When this is done, man attains to freedom, electing the God who has already elected him. But all this is history. It cannot be interpreted as a static cause producing certain effects. As the content of eternity before time was, it cannot remain beyond time. *Per se* it is in time as well as before time. And in time it can only be history. Who and what Jesus Christ is, is something which can only be told, not a system which can be considered and described. If, then, we accept the presupposition that predestination is identical with the election of Jesus Christ, the assertion of its actuality cannot be disputed. And this being the case, we cannot give to the assertion the same meaning as it has in that conflict between two opposing outlooks. It attacks the one outlook without commending the other. It is opposed to both. If it is to be theologically correct, it can be understood only in the light of this presupposed identity.

At the *Congrès international de théologie calviniste* held at Geneva in 1936, Peter Barth advocated the activist understanding in his paper " The Biblical Basis of Calvin's Doctrine of Predestination " (" Die biblische Grundlage der Praedestinationslehre bei Calvin "). He did so with the express intention of correcting Calvin's interpretation. He claimed that God's freedom in His judgment and mercy ought to be thought of as " God Himself in the activity of His kingly work : God, whose hands are not bound, creating light and darkness, opening and closing, binding and loosing, according to His own righteous goodpleasure. . . . Does not Holy Scripture everywhere bring us before the face of the God who is free at every moment to make His decision, who marches on from one decision to another, the unchangeable Lord of life and death, in whose power it is both to elect and to reject, both to raise up and to cast down ? . . . The concept of God's repenting cannot be thought away from the biblical presentation of God's thinking and action. According to the testimony of Scripture, God always reserves to Himself the freedom to put forth His own superior power in unforeseen and astonishing developments. ' The Lord killeth, and maketh alive : he bringeth down to the grave, and bringeth up ' (1 Sam. 2⁶). At the same time Scripture shows us God the Lord—who can do what He wills—in a mysteriously living relation to us men. It speaks of God's earnest and urgent asking after us, of His seeking and knocking, of His patient waiting for our return. But this means that man is indeed put in the place of decision. The seriousness of our position cannot be altered by any foreordination of the outcome. ' Work out your own salvation with fear and trembling ' retains its full validity, just because the willing and working is God's doing. It is obviously fatal when the concept *causa* (cause) is introduced into descriptions of the relationship between the divine will and the human. In Holy Scripture the supremacy of God's grace meeting us is shown always as God's act towards us in the Spirit. We can never divest this act of its existential character, or reduce it to a relationship of causality." We should translate Ex. 3¹⁴ : " I will be that I will be " ; God unlimited and unsearchable in the freedom of His judgment and the freedom of His grace (*Transactions*, published under the title *De l'élection éternelle de Dieu*, Geneva, 1936, p. 21 f. ; cf. 70 f.).

In Geneva these ideas met partly with obvious evasion and partly with open opposition. It was evident from the first that the wholehearted Calvinists who formed the bulk of the Congress would not accept the proposed correction of Calvin. After a preliminary and rather futile protest, one of the first speakers declared that he was " displeased " at the closing section of the paper. *Mais voilà ; in cauda venenum* (G. Oorthuys, p. 58). In the course of the debate it always came back to the same fundamental issue. What is to be made of the concept of God's repenting, which a biblical theology such as the Calvinist claims to be cannot possibly evade ? Amongst other things, other very competent representatives of the ruling trend at that Congress said the following. First, we must distinguish in Calvin the standpoint of the exegete from that of the dogmatician, for in the two capacities Calvin had to tackle two very different problems. As an exegete (as in the exposition of Ezek. 18[23] : " Have I any pleasure at all that the wicked should die ? ") Calvin could oppose a mechanistic exposition of the divine will and frankly confess that God calls everyone without exception to repentance and that He allows definite threats of punishment to be followed by equally definite promises of grace. As a dogmatician, however, out of the same spirit of loyalty to Scripture and in the fight against error he could bring forward his asseveration of God's hidden decree to convert only the elect (R. Grob, p. 68). Or again, in His eternity God is just as immutable (*immuable*) as in time He is capable of repentance, change and alternation between wrath and forgiveness. How can we reconcile these two facts ? We cannot reconcile them, but it is *l'originalité de l'orthodoxie d'articuler ces confessions de foi avec un et tamen*, and yet, *und doch, et pourtant. . . . Oui Dieu se repent et puis oui il ne se repent pas ; oui son décret est éternel, oui Dieu change dans le temps. Et nous ne savons pas* (A. Lecerf, p. 66 f.). Statements like this can be described only as an evasion of the problem. In this matter it is of no value simply to separate the spheres of dogmatics and exegesis, or eternity and time, and then to assert comfortably that there is an insoluble tension between the contradictory statements relating to these spheres. If God's eternal decree is as such immutable, then it is not an idly academic question which can be dismissed with a wave of the hand but a serious question of faith why " a mechanistic exposition of the divine will " should not prevail first and last. To put it in another way, if the Scriptures make statements about the self-activated will of God which are valid only in the temporal sphere, in what sense are we to take these statements seriously when we set them against the eternal reality of God ? Have they any genuine seriousness with God, or have they not ? And how can they have if they have no seriousness in eternity ? We may reverse the question : On what authority, and from what loyalty to Scripture, may the dogmatician (even in the act of necessary confession against error) arrive at the point where he can use a quite different doctrine of God's eternal predestination to bracket and relativise and call in question his own exegetical findings as they relate to the manner of God's dealings with man in time ? Who has called us to seek God's eternal predestination anywhere but in God's temporal dealings as such, or to understand it except as it is revealed and active in these dealings ? Certainly the Bible does not invite us to do this. To create such contradictions artificially, and then to dismiss them as purely intellectual, and finally to leave them unexplained with a *nous ne savons pas*—that is not theology. At any rate it is hard to see what theological justification there is for making of the matter a riddle of this kind and then demanding that we should let it remain unsolved.

Other speakers in the discussion objected against the author that his asserting of an activist predestination would mean a return to the doctrine of the divine *potentia absoluta*, of a *Deus legibus solutus*, as held and taught in the later Middle Ages (M. J. Hommes, p. 63). *On assiste à une sorte de jeu : on est soulevé par la misericorde, on est précipité en bas par le jugement et l'on finit par ne pas très bien savoir où l'on en est* (J. Rilliet, p. 64). The author's only answer was to repeat his statement : We must be taught by Scripture that God has entered into a mysteriously living relation to us men. But in this ambiguous expression there lurks a dilemma which to some extent spoils the otherwise excellent paper of Peter Barth, or, at any rate, his intrinsically correct concluding thesis. This mysteriously living relation, including all that it is and means on man's part—in the free act of human faith—is the fulfilment of divine predestination, and it has been grounded and determined and ordained by God Himself. But can we really accept this as an end of the matter ? There can be no doubt that that is what the author intended to maintain, and he did maintain it in forcible terms. But the more forcibly we maintain it, the more effectively there may be used against this thesis of an activist predestination the consideration advanced by its opponents, that for the fixed enactment to which man was subject according to the older doctrine this view now substitutes a mere game which God plays with man, a game which is completely bewildering in its hiddenness and un-expectedness. And in this game of judgment and mercy, what chance is there, if any, of a final knowledge of how one stands with God ? To assert a mysteriously living relationship does not give us any answer to the difficulty if we really hold to the divine sovereignty in this relationship. We can thus understand rather better the objection of J. Rilliet (p. 64). As Rilliet saw it, the beauty and power of the Calvinistic doctrine of predestination consist in the idea of a pledged and static freedom of God in which He dominates the individual from all eternity in order *toujours et malgré lui* to save him in time. Rilliet felt that the doctrine would be stripped of these qualities if the thesis of an activist predestination were accepted. The author does not seem to have felt the force of the argument. In his paper, and more particularly in the conclusion, he could find only one way to meet it : that of transferring the mysteriousness and life of the relationship into the " existentiality " of the decision in or before which man is placed by God's decision. God does not treat us like puppets, but like living men, created as such by God Himself. He puts salvation and perdition before us " in the form of a question." The question of God is a matter of life and death. In our own life a decision must be made. The inner movement of divine predestination, the possibility and reality of God's repenting and the living character of the relationship, correspond to this decision. But this brings us to the other side of that dilemma which engulfs those who adopt the activist thesis. If predestination is not a divine game which God plays with man, if it is not the capricious vacillation of a *potentia absoluta*, the only other possibility is that it is an ordination of God which is wholly conditional upon God's insight into the decision for or against Him made in the life of man. In this case, however, it is not an amendment of Calvin but of the Lutheran doctrine of *fides praevisa*, or even of the (in its own way) very mysterious teaching of Thomas about the co-operation of God and man in the communicating and receiving of grace. Without doubt the predestinating God is the living God, but only in so far as He has to do with the living man which He has created. Predestination is still decision, but the specific nature of the actual decision made is determined by the fact that it is related to the existential decision of man. It is quite clear that P. Barth never intended to say that and could not have meant it. But it is also understandable that he could not convince the Congress of the correctness of his thesis by an attempt at explanation which tended in this direction. On the contrary, the attempt caused real anger (*Transactions*, 19, 28 f.), and for two hours they screamed and shouted that the immutable double decree is God's eternal will and that is an end of the matter.

The whole proceedings are extraordinarily instructive because they show that the thesis of an activist predestination is purely formal, and that as such it stands just as much in the air, and under the same twofold threat of determinism and synergism, as does the traditional counter-thesis. Peter Barth thought it sufficient to substitute for the rigid divine decree which is fixed and static from all eternity the idea of the Lord who not only is free but remains free and whose decrees are living and progressive. What is substituted is correct, but the correction of Calvin demands something more. The statement : *Idem est Deum praedestinare et praedestinasse et praedestinaturum esse* is a magnificent one, but it derives from Duns Scotus (quoted from Loof's *Dogmengeschichte*, 4th edit., 1906, p. 595). In opposition to the twofold subtlety of Scotus it must be shown that the Lord neither decrees arbitrarily nor allows Himself to be conditioned by His counterpart in that decree. And to do this it is not enough to refer generally to God and man and to the mysteriousness and life of the relationship between them. For if we confine ourselves to generalities, we cannot escape the clutches of that dilemma.

In the discussion at the Congress there was raised one voice (apart from the later contribution of P. Maury, who, unfortunately, did not take part in the discussion) in favour of an adoption of the thesis. The voice was that of Pastor R. Abramowski of Riga. But this delegate also wanted attention to be directed to the only possible and solid basis for such a thesis, a basis which seemed to have been overlooked not only by the genuine Calvinists but also by the speaker. He did not gain any support, but the point which he tried to make was this. Predestination as election and rejection is " a *modus* corresponding to God's redemptive work," and it is as such that it must be understood and proclaimed. In the Old Testament it stands in a strict relationship to the people Israel, and in the New Testament it stands in an equally strict relationship to Jesus Christ. It is impossible, then, to separate the doctrine of predestination from Christology and soteriology. Faith in the God of judgment and redemption has no direct connexion with the divine majesty, and must not be confused with an enthusiasm for God and for the glory of God. Together with our sins it must be " broken " by the cross of Christ. Now it is true that objections may be raised against this formulation. Predestination is not one *modus* but *the modus* of the divine work of redemption. It is not the *modus* merely of this work, but of all God's work *ad extra.* It not only corresponds to this work, but precedes it. Yet the direction indicated here is the direction in which we have to look. If it is presupposed that predestination is identical with the election of Jesus Christ the activist thesis is put on a basis against which no objection can be brought and is made secure from misunderstanding both on the one side and the other. Once we see this point it is settled that predestination does not antedate time, and all that is in it, and especially man and men in time, in the form of a letter, which, limited in this way, can mean only a dead letter. Predestination precedes time as a living act in the Spirit, similar to the cloud which went before Israel in the wilderness. It is settled, then, that predestination did indeed happen in the bosom of God before all time, but that for this very reason it happens and happens again before every moment of time. For the election of Jesus Christ is unchanged and unchangeably history. As such it is God's eternal will before all time, and also the eternal will of the living God in time. The fact that Calvin and the classical exponents of the doctrine failed to progress beyond a static understanding of God's eternal will was not due to their lack of a sufficiently " living " notion of God's working—in the last analysis Calvin could never be accused of that. We cannot help them, then, simply by placing a stronger emphasis upon the biblical doctrine of God's repenting and providing a new and better translation of Ex. 3[14]. Their failure was due rather to their nonadherence to the rule that the will of God as such, and therefore predestination, must be sought and found only in the work of God, i.e., in the core and purpose of that work, the name and person of Jesus Christ. Only by an adherence to this rule can we really know God's eternal will as the will of the living God. Only in this way can we expose the falsity of the view which would assert the fixity of that will and thus reduce it to a dead letter. The correction of the older doctrine in this matter must definitely consist in an attempt to adhere to a rule which the Reformers themselves did not keep—the rule that the eternal

God is to be known only in Jesus Christ and not elsewhere. If this is first done, the belief in an activist predestination is then self-evident.

And if this is first done, it is possible to avoid the dilemma which entangled the discussion at the 1936 Congress.

If predestination is identical with the election of Jesus Christ, there can be no question of any confusion between God's living predestinating, deciding and electing, and the vacillation of a *potentia absoluta* or a game capriciously played by the Deity with its creatures. That there is no such confusion was rightly maintained by P. Barth at Geneva, but he could only maintain it and not prove it (except by an imperceptible surrender of the sovereignty of the divine decision over against man). If God's eternal will is not found in the election of Jesus Christ, where is it to be found except in the unsearchable sovereign act of the *decretum absolutum* ? But if we accept God's sovereignty in this act, and yet think of this act as living and progressive, not something which happened once and for all but something which continues to happen, then unless we identify it with the election of Jesus Christ it is hard to see how this relationship of God to His creature can possibly be thought of except as the relationship of a player to his plaything, a relationship which takes on this or that form according to the whim of the moment. In these circumstances we can understand the inclination of the opposing faction to dispute a predestination in terms of act. We can understand their longing for the idea of a decree fixed before all time. In a decree of this kind the absoluteness of the act of freedom in which it arose does at least find rest. Even if in detail its content is always unknown, we do at least know that we have something definite to hold to. For it is quite impossible to see how a distinction can be made between predestination in terms of act and the *potentia absoluta* of the later Middle Ages. Only when we recognise that predestination is identical with the election of Jesus Christ does there arise at once a picture of God's will as it determined and ordered and to that extent limited itself even in its sovereignty. The history of this process is not any kind of history, but it has a definite content and it moves towards an appointed end. Its place cannot be taken by any other history moving perhaps towards some quite different end. In this history God's will is unequivocal. In Himself, God is free and He remains free. But in His freedom He decides in man's favour for the establishment and preservation of the covenant between Himself and man. He denies and hates the sin of fallen man with whom the covenant is to be made and maintained. But He wills an unequivocal affirmation and love of man himself, and it is in this affirmation and love that the covenant is willed and concluded. He decrees the rejection of the evil-doer, but in predestinating Himself to union with the Son of Man in His Son He decrees that this rejection should be lifted from man and laid upon Himself. In spite of man's unworthiness in himself, He wills and affirms and loves man, yet in so doing He does not will the continuance of man in his unworthiness. He wills rather that man should be exalted, and that (by the power of His grace) he should have a share in His own worthiness. He does not will the death of the sinner, but rather that he should be converted and live. The realisation of this foreordination of man is, of course, willed in such a way as to make man himself fulfil all the history which is the content of the divine will for him. From his supposed innocence he must be plunged into the depths of sin and misery, and from these depths he must be lifted up again to the heights of real innocence, righteousness and blessedness. But God treads the way with him. God knows the goal and will not swerve from it. For the man who will accompany God on this road there can be no uncertainty with regard to the outcome. It is God who elects man. Man's electing of God can come only second. But man's electing does follow necessarily on the divine electing. In this history, then, there is nothing wholly dark or obscure Even the mystery that it takes place at all, that God's will is in fact an affirmation and love of man, even this incomprehensible act of the divine freedom, is not as such dark but luminous; it is not obscure but clarity itself. This history is the sum and substance of all order, and for this reason it cannot be confused with the play of any actuality in itself and as such. It is not actuality in itself and as such, but one specific act. But if we say that this history does not end, if we say that God's eternal will is not left behind by time but precedes every moment of time, if we say that the God whose will is this history is not the prisoner either of Himself or of the historical process once and for all ordained by Him, it is utter folly to understand it to mean that man cannot know how he stands with God or what he may expect from Him, as though in and with the historical process God were merely playing a game with man. We arrive at its deep meaning from the fact that while the Bible does compare God's overruling will in creation with the will of a potter towards his work, while it does compare it, then, with the supreme will of a workman who plans, it does not compare it with the capricious will of a child at play, although the latter comparison would —apparently, but only apparently—be better calculated to bring out the sove- reignty of the divine good-pleasure. The sovereignty of God bears no relation whatever to the sovereignty of whim or chance or caprice. On the contrary, we learn from the revelation of this sovereignty that the power of whim and chance and caprice is not a sovereign power. It belongs to the sphere of evil, and evil, as that which is denied and repudiated by God, has only the power of impotence. The sovereignty of God and of God's good-pleasure consists in the fact that it is a sovereignty which orders history, the content of God's eternal will. We must think of that eternal and self-ordered will as the will of the living God, a progressive and constantly renewed act of the Spirit. But in so doing we must also think of it as law, as a letter which can neither be reinterpreted nor replaced. We cannot, then, think of ourselves as tossed hither and thither by an incalculable fluctuation of divine decisions. If we know this eternal and living will, we know a rule which is completely trustworthy, and no dark suspicions can assail us. In face of this will we can and should know how it stands with us. Beyond this will we cannot and need not go.

But if predestination is identified with the election of Jesus Christ, it follows, secondly, that there can be no question of a limiting and conditioning of the freedom of God in which this decision is made by the mystery of the existentiality of a complementary human decision. The relationship between God and man is constantly renewed and refashioned, but there can be no question of its having two sources—the one in God's decision and the other in the corresponding decision of man to which God's decision is itself related. We might connect such a view either with Lutheran or indeed Roman Catholic teaching. Certainly it was not what Peter Barth intended when at Geneva he tried to present his thesis of a predestination in action. It is worth noting, however, that as far as this side of his assertion was concerned the Calvinists assembled at Geneva appeared to be less perspicacious, for they seemed not to take any offence at his efforts from this standpoint. Yet it is not at all clear how this view can really be avoided if we assert the actuality of predestination merely as a general truth of Scripture and not in specific and concrete relation to the central point of biblical testimony. If we would think of the relationship between God and man as a living relationship, then in presenting it we are almost necessarily forced to the conclusion that in their dealings with each other the two partners stand on a footing which is equal basically, although not equal in practice. The life of this relationship cannot, therefore, be one-sided. Even if God has a powerful advantage over man, it is still necessarily two-sided, and its mystery must be thought of as the mystery of the human decision as well as the divine. Generally speaking, and even in the Bible, if we abstract from that central point, God and man appear as two partners with capabilities and competencies which are different but still autonomous. A subtle synergism—the kind which is never acknowledged, the reproach of which is always avoided, which is never quite

C.D.—7

clear even to those who hold it—will always result from the presentation of this relationship when it is regarded only as a generality, even as a biblical generality, as was the case at Geneva when Peter Barth aimed (and rightly aimed) to show that this relationship is not a deterministic but an intrinsically living relationship. From this view of the matter it is only a step to a compromise in which the living quality of this relationship derives not from God only but also from His human partner. But if we see the eternal will of the living God concretely in the election of Jesus Christ we avoid this side of the dilemma too. There is no synergism of any kind in the history of Jesus Christ's election, for in this history neither the sin of man nor the prayer of man can play the part of an autonomous mystery, as man's decision complementary to God's. There can be no co-operation or reciprocal action of any kind between any such mystery in man and the mystery of the predestinating God. Both sin and prayer are active in this history—but in what way ? Sin is active only as the ordination from which this man is released by God's grace, and which He does not, in fact, fulfil or accomplish. The rejection of this man is not, then, God's answer to His sin, but His rigorous answer to sin itself, to the sin of all other men. The rigour of the answer is thus borne by God Himself in the union of His Son with this man. But, again, the fact that this man does not commit sin, and positively, the prayer by which He for His part elects God, and the obedience in which He takes it upon Himself to bear the sin of all other men—these are no more than the confirmation of His election. It is not that His election is, as it were, the divine answer to His sinlessness and prayer. He has not ordained Himself to this decision but He is foreordained to it. By this decision He simply declares that He is this man, the Son of God who has become Son of Man. On this side, too, there is no autonomous or second mystery, the mystery of man, but only the revelation of the one divine mystery which is the mystery of God's omnipotence because it is the mystery of grace, of God's triumphant affirmation and love of man, and because it includes within itself the fact that man is allowed to be at all, and that in his rejection of sin and election of obedience he may in some degree be the image of the predestinating God. The glory and the life of all this history are God's. Certainly it is a history between God and man. Certainly there takes place within it a twofold human decision. But this decision takes place in such a way as to form, not the second point in an ellipse, but the circumference around the one central point of which it is the repetition and confirmation. If we think of predestination as identical with this history, there is no danger of the activist understanding leading us astray in the direction of synergism. In this history there is, of course, co-operation between God and man, but not of a kind which does not owe its origin entirely to the working of God. This history is a triumph only for God's grace and therefore for God's sovereignty. If we would do proper justice to the interests of predestination from this standpoint, we cannot do better than hold to the fact that its content is God's eternal will in the concrete form of this particular history. We must accept, then, the thesis which Peter Barth propounded at Geneva in 1936 : but not without providing its necessary and only possible basis, the christological ; not without safeguarding it in this way from the dilemma which opened up at Geneva. This is the lesson to be learned from the proceedings of that Congress.

§ 34

THE ELECTION OF THE COMMUNITY

The election of grace, as the election of Jesus Christ, is simultaneously the eternal election of the one community of God by the existence of which Jesus Christ is to be attested to the whole world and the whole world summoned to faith in Jesus Christ. This one community of God in its form as Israel has to serve the representation of the divine judgment, in its form as the Church the representation of the divine mercy. In its form as Israel it is determined for hearing, and in its form as the Church for believing the promise sent forth to man. To the one elected community of God is given in the one case its passing, and in the other its coming form.

1. ISRAEL AND THE CHURCH

The election of man is his election in Jesus Christ, for Jesus Christ is the eternally living beginning of man and of the whole creation. Electing means to elect " in Him." And election means to be elected " in Him." Yet there is " another " electing and election, not alongside or outside, but included in the election of Jesus Christ. Already we have found it impossible to speak of the latter in itself and as such without continually thinking of this " other " election. Materially, the self-giving of God determined in it concerns the man Jesus, but teleologically it concerns man in himself and as such created by and fallen away from God. It is to this man, to the plurality of these men, to each and all, that the eternal love of God is turned in Jesus Christ. And it is turned to them in such a way that in this name it is to be attested to everyone, and in this name it is to be believed by everyone. The way taken by the electing God is the way of witness to Jesus, the way of faith in Him. Included in His election there is, therefore, this " other " election, the election of the many (from whom none is excluded) whom the electing God meets on this way.

But if we keep to Holy Scripture, we find that unlike the classical doctrine of predestination it is in no hurry to busy itself with the " many " men elected in Jesus Christ, either in the singular or plural. It does do this, of course, and we shall have to do so. But starting from the election of Jesus Christ it does not immediately envisage the election of the individual believer (and in this too we shall have to follow it), but in the first place a mediate and mediating election. The Subject of this is indeed God in Jesus Christ, and its particular object is indeed men. But it is not men as private persons in the singular or plural. It is these men as a fellowship elected by God in Jesus Christ and determined from all eternity for a peculiar service, to be made capable of this service and to discharge it. According to Holy Scripture its life and function is the primary object of this " other " election which is included in the election of Jesus Christ. Only from the standpoint of this fellowship and with it in view is it possible to speak properly of the election of the individual believer (which tradition has been far too eager to treat as *the* problem of the doctrine of predestination). To designate the object of this " other " election we choose the concept of the community because it covers the reality both of Israel and of the Church. The meaning of the concept—given here only in outline—is as follows. The community is the human fellowship which in a particular way provisionally forms the natural and historical environment of the man Jesus Christ. Its particularity consists in the fact that by its existence it has to witness to Him in face of the whole world, to summon the whole world .to faith in Him. Its provisional character consists in the fact that in virtue of this office and commission it points beyond itself to the fellowship of all men in face of which it is a witness and herald. The community which has to be described in this way forms so to speak the inner circle of the " other " election which has taken place (and takes place) in and with the election of Jesus Christ. In so far as on the one hand it forms this special environment of the man Jesus, this inner circle, but on the other hand it is itself of the world or chosen from the world and composed of individual men, its election is to be described as mediate and mediating in respect of its mission and function. It is *mediate*, that is, in so far as it is the middle point between the election of Jesus Christ and (included in this) the election of those who have believed, and do and will believe, in Him. It is *mediating* in so far as the relation between the election of Jesus Christ and that of all believers (and *vice versa*) is mediated and conditioned by it.

There is, then, no independent election of the community. Only Jewish or clerical phantasy and arrogance can try to exalt the community above Jesus Christ into the beginning of all things. The honour of its election can never be anything but the honour of Jesus Christ, the selfless honour of witnessing to Him. If the community tries to be more than His environment, to do something more than mediate, it has forgotten and forfeited its election. Again, the existence of the community cannot be regarded as an end in itself with respect to the world. It has been chosen out of the world for the very purpose of performing for the world the service which it most needs and which consists simply in giving it the testimony of Jesus Christ and summoning it to faith in Him. It has forgotten and forfeited its election if it is found existing for itself only and omitting this service, if it is no longer really mediating. The inner circle is nothing apart from the relation to the outer circle of the election which has taken place (and takes place) in Jesus Christ.

But this outer circle, too, is in its turn nothing without the inner one ; all the election that has taken place and takes place in Jesus Christ is mediated, conditioned and bounded by the election of the community. It mirrors in its mediate and mediating character the existence of the one Mediator, Jesus Christ, Himself. In its particularity over against the world it reflects the freedom of the electing God, just as in its service to the world (that is, in the provisional nature of its particularity) it reflects His love. It is only in virtue of this reflection that witness to Jesus Christ, the summons to faith in Him and therefore the faith of the individual elect are achieved. Included in the election of the community—in the community, by the community (and then at once for it as well), these also are elected in and with the election of Jesus Christ. *Extra ecclesiam nulla salus.* This proposition has its place already in the doctrine of predestination, in the doctrine of God.

Now just as the electing God is one and elected man is one, i.e., Jesus, so also the community as the primary object of the election which has taken place and takes place in Jesus Christ is one. Everything that is to be said of it in the light of the divine predestination will necessarily result in an emphasising of this unity. But we had to regard the divine predestination that is to be equated with the election of Jesus Christ as a double predestination, as the primal act of the free love of God in which He chooses for Himself fellowship with man and therefore the endurance of judgment, but for man fellowship with Himself and therefore the glory of His mercy. According to the first aspect of this act He determines man for the hearing of His promise, and according to the second aspect of the same act for faith in it. In the one He determines him for an old and passing form of existence, in the other for a new and coming (and abiding) form. If the election of the community is included in the election of Jesus Christ, if in and with Jesus Christ it is the object of this primal act of the free love of God, then we must inevitably expect that in its election too we will encounter this twofold (and in its twofoldness single) direction of the eternal will of God. This is indeed the state of affairs with which, according to Holy Scripture, we have to do.

Who and what is Jesus Christ Himself in His relation to the community of God ? Here already we find unity and differentiation. He is the promised son of Abraham and David, the Messiah of Israel. And He is simultaneously the Head and Lord of the Church, called and gathered from Jews and Gentiles. In both these characters He is indissolubly one. And as the One He is ineffaceably both. As the

Lord of the Church He is the Messiah of Israel, and as the Messiah of Israel He is the Lord of the Church. This aspect of the matter is to be developed in what follows. To begin with, we may attempt a provisional survey.

Jesus Christ is the crucified Messiah of Israel. As such He is the authentic witness of the judgment that God takes upon Himself by choosing fellowship with man. As such He is the original hearer of the divine promise. As such He is the suffering inaugurator of the passing of the first human form of the community. But precisely as the crucified Messiah of Israel He is also the secret Lord of the Church which by His self-giving to live by His mercy and believe in His promise God founds as the graciously coming (and abiding) form of His community.

Jesus Christ is also the risen Lord of the Church. As such He is the authentic witness of the mercy in which God in choosing man for fellowship with Himself turns towards him His own glory. He is as such the original pattern of the believer. He is as such the triumphant inaugurator of the gracious coming of the new form of man. But precisely as the risen Lord of the Church He is also the revealed Messiah of Israel which by His self-giving God establishes as the scene of His judgment, but also as hearer of His promise, as the form of His community determined for a gracious passing.

To this unity and twofold form of Jesus Christ Himself there corresponds that of the community of God and its election. It exists according to God's eternal decree as the people of Israel (in the whole range of its history in past and future, *ante* and *post Christum natum*), and at the same time as the Church of Jews and Gentiles (from its revelation at Pentecost to its fulfilment by the second coming of Christ). In this its twofold (Old Testament and New Testament) form of existence there is reflected and repeated the twofold determination of Jesus Christ Himself. The community, too, is as Israel and as the Church indissolubly one. It, too, as the one is ineffaceably these two, Israel and the Church. It is as the Church indeed that it is Israel and as Israel indeed that it is the Church. This is the ecclesiological form of what we have previously described in christological terms. We shall now attempt a provisional survey of it in this form.

Israel is the people of the Jews which resists its divine election. It is the community of God in so far as this community has to exhibit also the unwillingness, incapacity and unworthiness of man with respect to the love of God directed to him. By delivering up its Messiah, Jesus, to the Gentiles for crucifixion, Israel attests the justice of the divine judgment on man borne by God Himself. Encountering the fulfilled promise in this way, it remains only its hearer without pressing on to faith in it. In its existence it can only reveal the passing of the old man who confronts God in this way. But Israel as the Jewish people resisting the divine election is at the same time the secret origin of the Church in which alone God's mercy can be praised only by faith in God alone, in which faith itself is simply obedience, the perfect hearing, in which the coming of the new man becomes true only in the passing of the old.

The Church is the gathering of Jews and Gentiles called on the ground of its election. It is the community of God in so far as this community has to set forth to sinful man the good-will, readiness and honour of God. As Jesus Christ the crucified Messiah of Israel shows Himself in His resurrection to be the Lord of the Church, the latter can recognise and confess the divine mercy shown to man. And as it recognises and confesses that the divine Word is in its fulfilment stronger than the contradiction of its hearers, it can believe and keep and do it. It can reveal in its existence the coming of the new man accepted and received of God. The Church, however, as the gathering of Jews and Gentiles, called on the ground of its election, is at the same time the revealed determination of Israel, which is established by it, as elected to bring forth Him in whose person God makes all human sin and need His own concern, as marked out by the hearing of His Word, which must in any case precede faith in it, as the form of the old man who in his passing makes room for the new and coming man.

Israel is the people of the Jews which resists its election ; the Church is the gathering of Jews and Gentiles called on the ground of its election. This is the formulation which we have adopted and this or a similar formulation is necessary if the unity of the election of the community (grounded in the election of the one Jesus Christ) is to remain visible. We cannot, therefore, call the Jews the " rejected " and the Church the " elected " community. The object of election is neither Israel for itself nor the Church for itself, but both together in their unity. (In speaking of elected Israel or of the elected Church, we must be clear that we are speaking " synecdochically.") What is elected in Jesus Christ (His " body ") is the community which has the twofold form of Israel and the Church. The glory of the election, the love of God to man as the basis of the election, the bow of the covenant that God in His love to man has from eternity purposed and established—all these are the same in the one case as in the other, for in both cases it is Jesus Christ who originally and properly is both Elector and Elected, and in both cases we find ourselves in His environment. Admittedly everything has a different form in the two cases. This difference is in the relation of election to the rejection which inevitably accompanies it. And it is in the twofold determination of Christ Himself that this difference has its basis. It consists in the fact that the Israelite form of the elected community reveals its essence in its Old Testament determination, as determined from the side of elected man as such, whilst its Church form, on the other hand, reveals the same essence of the elected community in its New Testament determination, as determined by the electing God as such. This ineffaceable differentiation of its essence is made plain by the fact that the people of the Jews (delivering up Jesus Christ to the Gentiles to be put to death) resists its divine election, whereas the gathering of Jews and Gentiles (believing in the same Jesus Christ) is called on the ground of its election. The decisive factor in the former case is human turning away from the electing God, and in the latter case the turning of the electing God towards man. These are the two forms of the elected community, the two poles between which its history moves (in a unilateral direction, from here to there), but in such a way that the bow of the one covenant arches over the whole. For all the necessary sharpness, therefore, restraint is also needed. The antithesis between the two cannot be formulated in exclusive terms. Behind and above the human obduracy characteristic of the Israelite form of the community there stands indeed the divine rejection, but there stands also God's election in which He has determined Himself to take upon Himself the rejection. And behind and above the divine calling characteristic of the Church form of the community there stands indeed the divine election, but for this same reason there stands also the rejection that God Himself has taken upon Him. The ineffaceable differentiation of the two forms of the community has certainly to be noted. But it has also to be noted that thereby its indissoluble unity is also brought to light.

It is, moreover, implicit in the nature of the case that only in the knowledge of Jesus Christ and of His election, i.e., in the faith of the Church, is the differentiation as well as the unity of the elect community knowable and actually known. The bow of the covenant over the two is not a neutral area and observation point between them but the history which takes place between Israel and the Church. The way of this history is, however, the way of the knowledge of Jesus Christ. It leads from Israel *to* the Church. Only in this movement, i.e., in practice only from the standpoint of the Church, can it be perceived, described and understood as the living way of the one elect community of God.

In the knowledge of Jesus Christ and His election Israel is revealed according to the interpretation of it given here. It is quite impossible that the Israel which resists its election, which fails to recognise and rejects its Messiah, can as such be in a position to apprehend itself along with the Church as the one community of God and at the same time, within this one community, to discern the special form of its own election in distinction from that of the Church. It is where Israel perceives in the risen Lord of the Church the God of its own election, i.e., where in the faith of the Church it becomes one with it, that in this very act there is revealed to it the unity of the whole elected community, and therefore its own position and function as the first form of this whole. It is there that Israel precedes the Church in confessing human unwillingness, incapacity and unworthiness in face of the divine love and in praising the sole sufficiency of the divine mercy. It is there that the Israel which delivered up its Messiah to be crucified attests to the Church the justice of the divine judgment, the suffering of which God has made His own concern. It is there that Israel reminds the Church that it can proclaim only what it has received. It is there that Israel as the passing form of the community makes room for the Church as its coming form. Where Israel apprehends and believes its own election in Jesus Christ it lives on in the Church and is maintained in it as its secret origin, as the hidden substance which makes the Church the community of God.

But it is in this same apprehension of Jesus Christ and of His election that the unity and differentiation of the elected community must be and are perceived and acknowledged on the part of the Church as well. Only unbelief with regard to Jesus Christ can try to separate here what God has joined together. Only where the calling that rests on election had not occurred is it possible to play off the special form of the Church within the one community against this unity with the people of the Jews, to forget and deny the unity of Israel and the Church. If this happens the Church is not the Church. Where the Church apprehends in the crucified Messiah of Israel its own election, where then in faith it knows itself to be one with Israel, there the unity of the whole elected community is revealed, and only in this unity the special position and function of the Church as the second form of this whole. There it is the Church which comforts Israel with the message of the good-will, readiness and honour of God with respect to sinful man, with the message of the reality of His mercy. There it is the Church which testifies to Israel that God has made good the evil that they, the Jews—in delivering up Jesus to the Gentiles— meant to do. There it is the Church which reminds Israel that the promise it received can be proclaimed to all the world. There the Church as the coming form of the community of God has taken up into itself and therefore saved from annihilation Israel as its passing form. Where the Church apprehends and believes in Jesus Christ its own election, there it will reveal the determination of Israel : its election as the people of the incarnate Son of God ; its distinction by the gift of the Word and promise of God ; its passing as a genuine and necessary prologue.

Thus with respect to the apprehension of this relation of unity and differentiation between Israel and the Church everything is based and depends on whether in both cases Jesus Christ and the election that has occurred in Him are believed and apprehended. To this extent it is self-evident that everything we have said can be said and understood only in the light of the Church as the New Testament form of the community of God.

Israel and the Church in this unity and differentiation are the mediate and mediating object of the divine election.

We accompany the points made in this section with a running exegesis of the chapters Rom. 9–11. Our examination and presentation has in view not only these chapters but all Holy Scripture as well. But in accordance with the theme of this section it has arisen particularly as a parallel to these chapters and is to be regarded as such. Hence it is not to be expected that a check will be provided for all our own statements by reference to this particular text, any more than that every point in this text can be discussed in our treatment. But our whole exposition, both in direction and content, is to be compared with Rom. 9–11 and checked by Rom. 9–11. The doctrine of predestination has only too often been presented without a coherent consideration of this *locus classicus*.

To begin with, we learn from Rom. $9^{1\cdot 5}$ that Paul is in a position to exercise the apostolic office committed to him by Jesus Christ only in the name and on behalf of both the Church and Israel. The verses show that it is constitutive for his work as an apostle, and necessary to him personally for his own salvation, always as a missionary to approach the Jews first, in the manner described in the Acts of the Apostles. Moreover the meaning and purpose of his summons to the Jews is not to confuse them about Israel's election but to call them to obedience to the election that is in the deepest sense their own. Further, when he is dismissed by the Jews and goes to the Gentiles and therefore issues his challenge to the Church, this does not mean that he has lost sight of the Jews, but rather that from the Church he will now summon them with all the greater emphasis to obedience to their own election. As the apostle of the Church, Paul can be, and means to be, more than ever a prophet of Israel—in the Old Testament meaning of the concept. Only in this unity of his office does he wish to gather the Church, and only in its unity with Israel does he wish to see the Church gathered.

He is not, as might be supposed, speaking out of nationalist emotion, but from the innermost core of his mission, when (vv. 1–2) he attests to the Church of Rome the " great heaviness," the " continual sorrow," by which—in view of that repulse—his " heart " is moved. What he says in these words is " the truth in Jesus Christ." The Holy Spirit shares with him the knowledge of his suffering. He is " lying " in this matter as little as in his proclamation of the Gospel. It is an integral part of this proclamation. The unbelief of his " kinsmen " (v. 3) seeks to separate him from them. But this cannot succeed. Even in their unbelief they are and remain his " brethren." His faith, the Church's faith in Jesus Christ, unites him with them. Whilst their unbelief creates this suffering for him his faith cannot let them go. Faith is possible for him only as he holds fast to them, only as he reaches out to them again and again, only as he prays for them (Rom. 10^1). Even the very suffering which he bears on their account can only unite him with them. It is the suffering of the Israelite (Rom. 11^1) who has recognised the Messiah of Israel in Him whom Israel has rejected, in whose rejection Israel seems resolved to persist. It is the suffering of the Israelite who sees Israel's election confirmed with a wonderful finality and now sees the dreadful denial of it by Israel itself. Who could be more of an Israelite than this same apostle of the Church in this suffering of his ? He is so much an Israelite, so united, according to v. 3, with the unbelieving Israel which causes him suffering—not in spite of his faith but by his faith, not in spite of his suffering but by his suffering—that for the sake of the conversion of Israel, for the sake of the completion of the unity between the Church and Israel, he is willing and ready even to be cut off from Christ, even to renounce his own portion in Christ (in the election of Jesus Christ). So dear to him—the parallel to Ex. 32^{32} inevitably suggests itself—is his apostolic office, dearer than his personal election, salvation and hope ! So utterly is his apostolic office a ministry in the name and on behalf of Israel ! So deeply is the standing and falling of the Church bound up with its brotherhood and solidarity in relation to unbelieving Israel !

But this brotherhood and solidarity has (vv. 4–5) its objective basis in the fact that these " kinsmen according to the flesh " have not ceased to be Israelites, and therefore bearers of the name given to Jacob (" wrestler with God "), and real wrestlers with God according to the meaning of this name, any more than Paul himself has with his faith. As in and with his faith—a believer and therefore a true Israelite—he is still united and bound to them, so they for their part, in spite of their unbelief, continue to be for him the elected community of God which as such has received for its possession no less than everything on which the faith of the Church is based, from which it draws sustenance, which makes it possible, necessary and real. " Behold, the heaven and the heaven of heavens is the Lord's thy God, the earth also with all that therein is. Only the Lord had a delight in thy fathers to love them, and he chose their seed after them, even you above all people, as it is this day " (Deut. 10¹⁴ᶠ·). The fact that the elected community of God has also the other form of Church, and that it has its consummation only in this second form, does not in the least alter the fact that these words still hold good to-day. The community has its basis and beginning there in unbelieving Israel. In its form as the Church it is, after all, only Israel as it has reached its determined goal. It lives, then, wholly and completely on what Israel has received in and with its determination as a wrestler with God. It lives, then, by Israel's " sonship " (Ex. 4²², Deut. 8⁵, Hos. 11¹, Jer. 31⁹), that is, by the divine promise which constitutes the stock of Abraham, of the coming Son of Man who arises from it. This promise is the blessing, a pledge of which every father in Israel may discern in his son. The Church knows that this promise has been kept and fulfilled because it is a witness to Jesus Christ. But Jesus Christ is the fulfilment of this promise given to Israel. The Church lives by the glory of God which goes before Israel and dwells in its midst, by God's own manifestation of His presence graciously occurring but also graciously concealed in the providences of its history (killing and making alive). Israel neither can nor is it meant to see this gracious presence. The Church lives as it sees it (Jn. 1¹⁴, 2 Cor. 4⁶). But it is not another glory which it beholds ; it beholds in the incarnate Word the glory bestowed and continually bestowing itself on Israel, and therefore the one, unique glory of God. The Church lives by the covenants made between God and Israel. Again and again new agreements and mutual obligations are made between God and the men of this people. The number of them shows how unilaterally they have been kept. And if there is a remarkable preponderance of divine warnings at the very making of them, even more so does their fulfilment seem to consist almost regularly and entirely in the occurrence of the corresponding penal judgments. The Church recognises the pure and full comfort of the one covenant of grace kept by man as by God. But what does it recognise in it but the meaning and the determined purpose of the many covenants made with Israel ? The Church lives by the " lawgiving " which took place in Israel, regulating the life of the people with a view to the holiness required by the holiness of its Lord. The law of the Church is the faith which it has been given in the Lord by whose holiness the holiness of His people is created. Yet when it is obedient in this faith, it is doing no more than what is really required by Israel's Law. The Church lives by the " worship " that is permitted and commanded Israel. The permission and the commandment consist in the priestly and sacrificial order which is given to the people and embraces its whole life. The Church exercises worship in spirit and in truth in view of the eternal High Priest and His sacrifice offered once for all. But it is the worship permitted and commanded Israel which is fulfilled in this way. The Church lives by the " promises " given to Israel according to which the people is to be blessed and numerous, to possess the land, to be rich and powerful and happy under its king, and finally to see all peoples united in Zion. The promises which the Church grasps by placing its hope in its risen Lord speak of the gift of the Holy Spirit, the forgiveness of sins, the overthrow of the might and powers of Satan, the resurrection of the dead, an eternal life in God's kingdom. But in them it is only grasping and apprehending the promises given to Israel. The Church lives by the " fathers " of Israel, by the fellowship of the spirit with Abraham, Isaac and Jacob, Moses, David and Elijah. They are the great witnesses to the divine calling, preservation and leading of this people. The Church knows that as such, and therefore in the concrete historical form in which they are presented in the tradition, they are witnesses of Jesus for whose sake this people was called, preserved and led by God. These fathers of Israel, and they alone, ought in strict justice to be called the " fathers of the Church." And now, in conclusion, the first and supreme and comprehensive and decisive thing : the Church lives by the existence of " Christ according to the flesh." It lives by Jesus Christ because and so far as He is, as man, the Son of Abraham and David, and is called Jesus of Nazareth : not in spite of this ; not under the incidental assumption that He is this too and not only the eternal Son of God ; but because and so far as He is an Israelite out of Israel. Paul does not here say ὧν but ἐξ ὧν. For although we can say of the Messiah that He is " given " to Israel, any idea suggesting that He " belonged " to Israel must be completely excluded. He does not " belong " to the Church either. On the contrary, the whole elected community of God belongs to Him. That is why Paul says that He has come out of Israel, that He has been snatched from it like a brand from the burning. But it is from Israel that this man has come and been snatched. Not from Greece, not from Rome, not from Germany, but from Israel ! This is simply a fact. It is independent either of Israel's unbelief or the faith of the Church. It cannot be destroyed by Israel's unbelief and therefore it is not to be denied in the faith of the Church but openly confessed : " Salvation is of the Jews " (Jn. 4²²). When the Church confesses in respect of the Jesus rejected by the Jews, it does, of course, disclose the obduracy of Israel with regard to its own election. In harmony with the Old Testament prophets, it contests the vaunting lie, the nationalist-legalistic Messiah-dream of the Synagogue, which has aroused the hatred and envy of every kind of Gentile arrogance, yet also been the subject of its own dilettante dreaming. But while this is true, the Church does not dispute, but asserts and teaches in defiance of all Gentile arrogance, the eternal election of Israel. Confessing Jesus Christ, it confesses the fulfilment of everything that is pledged to Israel as promise, the substance of all the hope of the fathers, of all the exhortations and threats of Moses and the prophets, of all the sacrifice in the tabernacle and the temple, of every letter in the sacred books of Israel. When it summons Israel to faith in Jesus Christ it can and will desire of it only that it should be obedient to its own election and repent, that it should become the thankful community of the Son of Man who came and was snatched out from it. This is how the matter is consistently presented in the sermons addressed to the Jews in the Acts of the Apostles written by (the Gentile Christian ?) Luke (Ac. 2¹⁴ᶠ·, 3¹²ᶠ, 4⁸ᶠ·, 7¹ᶠ·, 18⁵, 22¹ᶠ·, 28²³).

In thinking of Israel, there is only one thing which causes Paul to suffer and which (beneath the bow of the covenant that arches over both) the Church has to bring against it. This is that it is too little Israel. It refuses to confirm its own election by uniting with the Church—by abandoning, that is, its self-assertion with respect to it, and breaking out into the confession of Jesus as its own and promised Messiah. The antithesis which arises at this point (within the community of God) is, of course, in bitter earnest. " All manner of sin and blasphemy (the sin of the Gentiles) shall be forgiven unto men . . . but whosoever speaketh against the Holy Ghost (this is what Israel's unbelief does in relation to Him who is attested as Messiah by His resurrection), it shall not be forgiven unto him, neither in this world, neither in the world to come " (Mt. 12³¹ᶠ·). It is not, then, only the zeal of Paul, but that of the whole New Testament, which bursts into flame at this point. It is palpable, however, that this is a zeal which includes rather than excludes, which seeks rather than rejects, which loves rather than hates. It is the zeal for the house of the Lord grounded in Israel. An antisemitism which mistakes and disputes Israel's election from outside can have nothing to do with this zeal (to which indeed this mistaking and disputing is essentially foreign). It can only be the Gentile repetition of the same unforgivable sin from which Israel must at all costs be rescued. The Church cannot yield even a hair's breadth to it. The Church leads no life of its own beside and against Israel. It draws its life from Israel, and Israel itself lives in it. It is the realisation of the life of the community of God which is Israel's own destiny.

Therefore v. 5b: " Blessed be God, who is over all. Amen." (The conjecture ὧν ὁ ἐπὶ πάντων θεός which I formerly supported is unsatisfactory. If the connexion of ὁ ὢν . . . with ὁ Χριστός is not impossible, it is not probable; although it is self-evident that here as elsewhere in his use of such formulæ Paul is, in substance, speaking also of Jesus Christ.) The praise of the Church is for the God who is the God of all (Rom. 3[29]) and therefore over all, the God of the community which embraces Israel and the Church, and the Church and Israel. How can it be otherwise, seeing this community is itself the gathering of all believers: " of the Jews first and also of the Greeks " (Rom. 1[16], 2[9f.], 9[24]) ? If not all the Jews join in faith in this act of praise, the Church cannot reply by questioning the election of Israel as such or by acquiescence in the absence and aloofness of these unbelievers. The God who is over all is also—and indeed primarily—the God of those who are absent and aloof in unbelief. The only anwer the Church can give to the enigma of the Synagogue is this. As the living Israel, in and with its faith it must confront the unbelief of the Synagogue with the faith of elected Israel itself. In the name and on behalf of this dead Israel, it must confess the One who (as the Lord both of the dead and the living, Rom. 14[9]) does not even, in view of this form of death, cease to be the living Head of the whole community and therefore the hope even of these dead.

2. THE JUDGMENT AND THE MERCY OF GOD

In the eternal election of the one man Jesus of Nazareth, God makes Himself the covenant-partner of the sinful man who has fallen away from Him and therefore fallen a victim to death according to His just judgment. The purpose of the election of this one man is God's will to save this lost man and to make him a participant of the glory of eternal life in His kingdom by taking his place in the person of this one man, by taking to Himself man's misery in Him, by making it His own concern, by clothing him in return with His own righteousness, blessedness and power. Thus the election of this one man is His election for the execution of the judgment and mercy of God.

As the environment of the elected man, Jesus of Nazareth, the elected community of God is the place where God's honour dwells, i.e., where this Jesus as the Christ (Messiah) and Lord, and therefore in Him God's covenant purpose, His intervention for lost man, the execution of His judgment and mercy, is effective and visible among men. It is elected to serve the presentation (the self-presentation) of Jesus Christ and the act of God which took place in Him—as a testimony and summons to the whole world. The whole community of God—Israel and the Church—is elected for this as surely as it is

elected in Jesus Christ. The whole community exists in this service
as surely as Jesus Christ founds and constitutes it in both its forms, as
surely as He is its unity and in its midst. Wherever the community
is living, there—in the power and commission of Him who is in its
midst—it will at all events exist in the service of this presentation,
the presentation of the judgment and mercy of God.

The specific service for which Israel is determined within the whole
of the elected community is to reflect the judgment from which God
has rescued man and which He wills to endure Himself in the person
of Jesus of Nazareth. If in faith in Jesus Christ Israel is obedient to
its election, if it is given to it to come to the Church and rise to life
again in it, to attain in it the goal of its determination, the special
contribution which it will make within the whole of the community
to the work of the community will be this. It will express the awareness of the human basis of the divine suffering and therefore the
recognition of man's incapacity, unwillingness and unworthiness with
regard to the divine mercy purposed in Jesus Christ ; the recognition
of the justice of the judgment passed on man in the suffering of Jesus
Christ. The Church needs this contribution. It cannot voice its
witness to Jesus Christ and its summons to faith in Him without at
the same time expressing this testimony which is peculiarly Israel's.
Indeed there can be no witness borne to Jesus Christ without a confession of His saving passion, and therefore without a confession of
the human misery that in His passion He has taken upon Himself
and taken away. But the Church knows of man's misery only in so
far as Israel too lives in it—as a reflection of the divine judgment. If
this is lacking, if for any reason or in any form the Church has become
estranged from its Israelite origin, sooner or later this will inevitably
be seen and avenged in a loss of power in its witness to man's misery,
and therefore in a similar loss in its witness to the cross and saving
passion of Jesus Christ, so that in equal measure it will be a debtor
to the world for both of these. But what power at all will there then
be within it ? What will it *not* then owe to the world ? It will face
the threatened loss of its character and commission as the Church ;
its name " Church " may well be on the point of becoming sound and
fury. The Church has every reason to see that Israel's particular
service is rendered in the community of God.

The Israelite form of God's community reveals what God elects
for Himself when in His eternal election of grace He elects fellowship
with man. It is not an obedient but an obdurate people that He
chooses. He does not choose a people which has something to give
Him but one which has everything to receive from Him. He chooses
for Himself suffering under the obduracy of this people, and suffering
under the curse and shame and death which this inevitably brings
in its train. He burdens Himself with rebels and enemies and at the
same time with their merited fall. This is the twofold burden that

God chooses for Himself when He elects to make His fellowship with man radically true by becoming man Himself in the person of the Son of David, Jesus ; when He elects the people of Israel for the purpose of assuming its flesh and blood. What is really meant by the humanity of the whole elected community of God, what it costs God to make Himself one with it, to be its God, emerges in its Israelite form. Over and above this, there emerges what is really meant by the humanity of the man in general and as such to whom God's electing love is addressed—that the price which God pays for this great love of His is no less than to make Himself a curse. Judgment has overtaken man, and if it is borne and suffered by God Himself, this only emphasises its supreme reality and validity. What can we say, then, for man's good-will, his capacity and dignity, in view of the fact that he has been snatched from destruction only because God was pleased to take upon Himself this twofold burden, making Himself a curse ? One thing is sure : since this is God's good-will with him he will not pit himself a second time against God ; he will not suppose that he can abide in God's sight otherwise than by His mercy. One thing is sure : he will no longer be able to cast doubt upon the justice of the judgment that has overtaken him (just because it has been carried out in this way), nor on the truth of the verdict passed on him. The witness to all this is Israel's crucified Messiah (delivered up *by* and crucified *for* Israel). To testify to all this in His service is now also the duty of the whole community of God. It can and does do this in virtue of the fact that it is the community of Israel's Messiah and that accordingly it has also an Israelite form, so that Israel may and should come to life and live on even in its form as the Church. It acknowledges the misery of man for which God's mercy is the only help. By showing forth the mercy of God that passes understanding, it also shows to the world that on its own it can only plunge into ruin, that it cannot save itself from ruin. When Israel becomes obedient to its election—coming to life and living on in the Church—it then becomes the guarantee that this (the negative) side of the Church's message remains actual until the end of the world.

It is also God's aim that Israel should become obedient to its election, that it should enter the Church and perform this special office in the Church, in order that in this way the differentiation within the community should confirm its unity. But God does not wait till Israel is obedient before employing it in His service. This is settled and completed in and with its election as such, so that Israel cannot in any way evade it, whether it is obedient or disobedient. God does not make the purpose He has with Israel dependent on Israel's attitude to it. The situation is rather that Israel's attitude is itself dependent on God's purpose with it. Whatever its attitude, it necessarily takes place in the course of the fulfilment of the service assigned to and required of Israel in and with its election. It necessarily benefits the work of God's community as it is carried on in the Church. It necessarily witnesses to Jesus Christ. It necessarily confirms His election, and with His election the election of Israel, and with this the election of the Church as well.

If Israel were to be obedient to its election, this attitude would at once mean that its special witness about God's judgment would become the undertone to the Church's witness about God's mercy, and that sustained, covered and (in the best sense of the word) softened by the voice of the Church it would be taken up into the praise of the elected community. As a reminder of the settled dispute, the cancelled indictment, the forgiven sin, its witness would lend critical salt to the message of the accomplished reconciliation of the world with God without calling it in question. The special honour of Israel would then consist in continually consoling and exhorting the Church by magnifying to it the judgment which has overtaken man in and with the mercy of God, and therefore holding before it the cross of its Lord as its one and only hope, not to assail but to confirm the faith that the Church as such has to confess.

As things stand, however, Israel as such and as a whole is not obedient but disobedient to its election. What happens is that Israel's promised Messiah comes and in accordance with His election is delivered up by Israel and crucified for Israel. What happens further is that in His resurrection from the dead He is established as the promised One and believed on by many even of the Gentiles. What does not happen, however, is that Israel as such and as a whole puts its faith in Him. What happens, on the contrary, is that it resists its election at the very moment when the promise given with it passes into fulfilment. Israel refuses to join in the confession of the Church, refuses to enter upon its service in the one elected community of God. Israel forms and upholds the Synagogue (even though the conclusion of its history is confirmed by the fall of Jerusalem). It acts as if it had still another special determination and future beside and outwith the Church. It acts as if it could realise its true determination beside and outwith the Church. And in so doing it creates schism, a gulf, in the midst of the community of God.

But Israel's unbelief cannot in any way alter the fact that objectively, and effectively, even in this senseless attitude beside and outwith the Church, it is the people of its arrived and crucified Messiah, and therefore the people of the secret (concealed from it as yet) Lord of the Church. It cannot evade its electing God nor His elected community, and it cannot therefore escape its appointed service in it. It must now discharge it in a manner corresponding to its adopted attitude. Over against the witness of the Church it can set forth only the sheer, stark judgment of God, only the obduracy and consequent misery of man, only the sentence and punishment that God in His mercy has chosen to undergo Himself to prevent them from falling

on us, only the realm of darkness as covered and removed and destroyed by the saving passion of Jesus Christ, only the existence and
nature of fallen man in his futile revolt against God as completely
outmoded and superseded in virtue of the mercy of God in Jesus Christ.
This is how Israel punishes itself for its sectarian self-assertion. But
it cannot alter the fact that even in this way it discharges exactly the
service for which it is elected. Even in this way it really gives to the
world the very witness that is required of it. How it is with man,
the nature of the burden which God in His great love assumes, the
nature of the curse which God has made Himself for the good of man,
man himself by whom and for whom Jesus Christ was crucified—
these things and all that they mean it reveals even in this way, even
in and with its unbelief, even in the spectral form of the Synagogue.
The existence of the Jews, as is generally recognised, is an adequate
proof of the existence of God. It is an adequate demonstration of
the depths of human guilt and need and therefore of the inconceivable
greatness of God's love in the event in which God was in Christ reconciling the world to Himself. The Jews of the ghetto give this
demonstration involuntarily, joylessly and ingloriously, but they do
give it. They have nothing to attest to the world but the shadow
of the cross of Jesus Christ that falls upon them. But they, too, do
actually and necessarily attest Jesus Christ Himself.

But they cannot again reverse what for the sake of man and therefore for their sakes God has put right in this Jesus Christ. They
cannot restore to the sentence and punishment borne and taken away
by Jesus Christ, to the rule of Satan abolished by Him, to the existence
and condition of fallen man superseded by His saving passion, the
power which in God's eternal counsel these were allowed to hold only
at once to lose it again, which in God's eternal counsel is denied and
taken from them. They cannot give to the judgment willed and completed by God a meaning that runs counter to God's purpose. They
cannot give the lie to the mercy of God in this judgment. By their
resistance to their election they cannot create any fact that finally
turns the scale against their own election, separating them from the
love of God in Jesus Christ, cancelling the eternal decree of God.
They can put themselves in the wrong, but not God's offering of His
Son and the ordering of human affairs accomplished by it. They can
be unthankful, but they cannot efface the reason and occasion they
have for thanksgiving. They can disturb but not destroy the community of God of which they are the elected basis. They can assault
but not overthrow the Church elected in and with their own election.
They cannot prevent it from being called and gathered from among
themselves and the Gentiles. They cannot weaken the effectiveness
and truth of its message (the subject of which is their own Messiah
and therefore their own salvation). They can do nothing to hinder
the application and objective validity even for themselves of the

testimony of God's mercy in Jesus Christ. They can do nothing to alter the fact that Jesus Christ, delivered up by them, is crucified for their sakes too. They can continually ratify the sin of this betrayal by failing to recognise the hand of God which in this very sin was undeservedly over them and at work for them. But they cannot reduce to impotence this work of God's hand which by their very sin has procured and accomplished forgiveness for the whole world and therefore for them also. They cannot prevent the fact that even in and with their obduracy they stand in the realm of this work of God's power. They can, indeed, deny their only hope, but no denial that they can make can render it ineffective. They cannot deny that Jesus of Nazareth is—primarily and supremely—theirs. As the promise irrevocably given them with this fact is maintained 'their membership of the one elected community of God is confirmed and ratified. It is confirmed and ratified not only with respect to the service which they cannot evade, but also with respect to the grace of God addressed to them, which they can indeed resist but cannot nullify.

The service for which the Church as the perfect form of the one elected community is determined, whether Israel obeys its election or not, consists always in the fact that it is the reflection of the mercy in which God turns His glory to man. The community in the form of the Church is the community of the risen Lord Jesus Christ. As the Church is elected, called and gathered from among Jews and Gentiles, the task laid upon it consists in the proclamation of its knowledge of the divine meaning of the judgment that has overtaken man in the death of Jesus, in witness to the good-will, readiness and honour of God with respect to man accepted and received by Him in Jesus Christ. This knowledge and insight it owes to its Lord, the crucified Messiah of Israel. In distinction from that of Israel the service of the Church is not a specific service beside which there might yet be another in the community of God. On the contrary, it includes in itself the particular service of Israel as a necessary auxiliary service. It takes it up, using and applying it as a contribution. As the one service of God's community is really discharged by the Church in so far as Israel too lives in the Church, so it is also by Israel in so far as in and with the crucified Messiah the Church lives in Israel also ; in so far as in and with His resurrection the Church arises from Israel ; in so far as Israel's determined purpose is fulfilled in the form of the Church. Israel in itself and as such can have only the involuntary share in the service of God's community described above. Israel in itself and as such lives actually—to its hurt—by the fact that it cannot renounce this share in the life of the community, that it *must* serve as a witness to the divine judgment. It can live to its salvation only as its special witness to God's judgment becomes the undertone of the Church's witness, the witness to God's mercy.

The Church form of the community reveals what God chooses for man when He elects him for communion with Himself in His eternal election of grace. He chooses for man His whole selflessly self-giving love. He chooses out of the treasures of His own nature righteousness and holiness, peace and joy, life and blessedness. He chooses for man His own self as Brother but also as Leader, as Servant but also as Master, as Physician but also as King. He therefore chooses for man the reflection of His own glory. He does this by electing flesh and blood from Judah-Israel to be His tabernacle and the Church of Jews and Gentiles to be His sanctuary, to declare to the world His gracious turning. All this happens wholly for *our* benefit, for our *benefit*. All that is implied in the nature and will of the electing God, all that God has given and gives and will give, all that is in any circumstance to be expected from Him, is what the community of God reveals in its final form as the Church. It reveals that the primal, basic decision of God with regard to man is His mercy, the engagement of His heart, and therefore His most intimate and intensive involvement in the latter's existence and condition. It reveals that even God's judgment is sustained and surrounded by God's mercy, even His severity by His kindness, even His wrath by His love. If the judgment that has overtaken man (according to Israel's commission) forbids us to seek any refuge except in the mercy of God, even more strictly does the mercy of God laying hold of man (according to the Church's commission) forbid us to fear His judgment without loving Him as Judge, without looking for our justification from Him. All this is attested by the Lord of the Church ; the Lord who has created the Church by revealing Himself as such ; the Lord in whom the Church puts its faith as it has received it from Him. All this the community of God must attest in His service. It can and does so in virtue of the fact that it is the Church called and gathered by this Lord ; Israel gathered from Jews and Gentiles. In face of the great misery of man it acknowledges the still greater grace of God. It attests to the world its own misery by attesting to it first and foremost the divine mercy. The Church is the bearer of God's positive message to the world in which the negative is—necessarily, but still only subordinately—included.

The Church is the perfect form of the elected community of God. In this form the unity of the community is revealed in its differentiation. In this form it enters on its mediating function as the provisional environment of the man Jesus, on its mission in relation to the world. The Church form of the community stands in the same relation to its Israelite form as the resurrection of Jesus to His crucifixion, as God's mercy to God's judgment. But this means that the Church is older than its calling and gathering from among Jews and Gentiles which begins with the ascension or the miracle of Pentecost. It is manifested at this point, but it has already lived a hidden life in Israel. It is the goal and therefore the foundation of the election of the people of Israel too. Nor can Israel's obduracy do anything to alter the fact that His Church exists in its midst from the beginning—since it is from the first the natural root of the existence of Jesus of Nazareth—and that it is revealed over against Israel's own obduracy in the shape of a special revelation of the promise, special blessing, special calling, guidance, sanctification and claim, special faith and special service and obedience. If this pre-existence of the Church in Israel does not abrogate its peculiar determination for the setting forth of the divine judgment, the peculiar determination of Israel cannot and will not exclude the fact that in virtue of these special events occurring in its midst Israel too is already a witness to the divine mercy and therefore participates in advance in the definitive form of God's community, in its function and mission in relation to the world.

The election of Israel, then, is not only negatively confirmed by the fact that Israel as such and as a whole has in any case to fulfil its determination and to serve as a reflection of the divine judgment, but also positively by the fact that from the very first the Church pre-exists and is prefigured in its midst. With *Israel's* election in view God has, according to Scripture, acted among men from the beginning of the world in the form of election. And on the basis of Israel's *election*, in order continually to reveal and attest it, God proceeds to elect men in and from its midst for special appointment, mission and representative function, as exponents and instruments of the mercy in which He has made this people His own. Their existence does not alter in the very least the determination of Israel as such and on the whole. But it sets in relief what Israel has to reveal in reflection of the divine judgment : the misery of man, not as it is left to take its course, but as it is taken to heart by God and considered and limited from all eternity ; not the wrath of God raging for its own sake, but the fire of His love which consumes and yet does not destroy, but rather purifies and saves. It is, indeed, in this sense that the crucifixion of Christ is the fulfilment of the divine judgment. It is in this sense, too, that the negative side of the Church's message (as the Word of the cross of Jesus Christ) should and will retain its actuality until the end of the world. That it has been present with this meaning from the very first is shown by the existence of the elect from the foundation of the world, and within the elected people Israel by the pre-existence of the Church in Israel.

The existence of the elect in and from Israel does not alter at all the determination of Israel as such and as a whole because these elect are exceptions which as such do not suspend the rule that Israel has to serve the revelation of the divine judgment. Again, it is only partially that in their function and mission they point beyond this rule. Again, in Israel they are only too consistently opposed by " reprobates " in whom the rule appears to be expressly confirmed. And finally, the circle of the elect grows continually smaller, or at least continually less visible, in the course of Israel's history, until it is ultimately reduced to the person of one man, Jesus of Nazareth. Strictly speaking, the pre-existent life of the Church in Israel consists only in the light which, without changing its character, is provisionally cast on the history of Israel by this one man, who is Israel's future and goal, making visible within this history certain individual, fragmentary, contradictory and transitory prefigurations of the form of the community which will be revealed in and with the appearance, death and resurrection of Jesus Christ. The pre-existent life of the Church in Israel consists in the fact that again and again in its history there is revealed a contradiction against the sin of man, an illumination and clarification of the divine judgment, an obedience and faith which are disclosed and validated in their reality, not indeed by the course and character of this history in itself and as such, but by its future and goal in the person of Jesus of Nazareth and the existence of His Church. The pre-existent life of the Church in Israel consists, then, in what the fulfilment shows to be the real prevision and prophecy of the Church itself occurring in and with the existence of these elect in and from Israel and constituting the purpose of their special election.

But if, for its part, the Church as the perfect form of the elected community has as such and as a whole the universal, uncontradicted and constant determination to praise God's mercy, it will not refuse to recognise itself in the prototype, prevision and prophecy of the elect in and from Israel, and therefore to see its interrelationship with them. More than that, it will understand and acknowledge that in and with these elect the election of all Israel is established. It will thus regard itself as united and bound to all Israel—in spite of the very different form of its membership in the community of God. Even more, it will reckon it as a special honour to have in its midst living witnesses to the election of all Israel in the persons of Christian Israelites. And, finally, it will interpret its own existence, its calling and gathering from Jews and Gentiles, only in analogy to that of these elect in Israel. It can never by any chance fail to recognise that— in its Jewish and, above all, its Gentile members—it is snatched with them from the judgment to which (according to Israel's mission) the whole world as well as Israel is liable, and that it no less than they is called by special mercy to proclaim to the same world (and also to all Israel itself) the victorious mercy of God. To be sure, the Church waits for the conversion of Israel. But it cannot wait for the conversion of Israel to confess the unity of the mercy that embraces Israel as well as itself, the unity of the community of God.

Paul explains in Rom. 9[6a] that what was said in vv. 1–2 about his sorrow is not in any sense to be taken to mean that he sees cause to lament over a failure of God's Word (with regard to obdurate Judaism). It is "not as though the word of God hath taken none effect," i.e., has been disproved and given the lie by the stiff-necked obstinacy of the Jews. God makes no mistakes, suffers no reverses, and never has to withdraw. His Word is true and always in the right even when man meets it with deceit and puts himself in the wrong. Paul, therefore, (as a true Israelite) cannot lament over Israel without rejoicing (again as a true Israelite)—rejoicing for Israel's sake—in the steadfastness and faithfulness of Israel's God. Paul laments because, at the very moment when in Jesus Christ the perfect form of God's community and therefore Israel's own election is revealed to the whole world, Israel cuts itself off from God's community and goes into the ghetto. He cannot, however, avoid rejoicing that even in this there is effected a confirmation of its election, a fulfilment of the will of the God who elects Israel.

For it is (vv. 6b–7a) not at all the case that according to the Word and will of God all who belong to the race of Abraham, all bearers of the name Israel, were appointed to become members of the Church. They were certainly appointed members of the one elected community of God. This is something that none of this race can be deprived of ; this is something that not one of this race can decline, not even if his name is Caiaphas or indeed Judas Iscariot ; this is what Jews, one and all, are by birth. But they were not all appointed members of the Church hidden in Israel and revealed in Jesus Christ. This was always something different, and until the end of the world—no longer, but until the end of the world—it will be something different. " For they are not all Israel which are of Israel." That is, they are not the true Israel, i.e., the Israel which realises Israel's determination by accepting its proper place in the Church, which realises the mercy of God by joining in the Church's praise. Some of Israel are, of course, Israel. But not all who are " of Israel " are so in the way in which, according to v. 5, this is to be said of Jesus of Nazareth. Strictly speaking, He alone is Israel, and it is only in Him, as His prophets, witnesses, forerunners, that others are as well, those who are specially elected in Him, with Him and for His sake. Not one of them is so by nature ; not one in virtue of his Jewish blood ; not one as a self-evident consequence of his membership of this people : but each only on the ground of a special election in which the election of Israel as such is repeated and established. This special election—and this alone from the very beginning—constitutes the pre-existent Church in Israel, the true, spiritual Israel. " Neither because they are the seed of Abraham, are they all children." It is no small honour to be " Abraham's seed." There is no doubt that as such Abraham's seed is the elected people of God, determined in accordance with its election to be the mirror of the divine judgment, which is, for its part, the veil of the divine mercy. But Abraham's children, the hidden Church in Israel, appointed to announce in advance the one true Israelite coming by God's choice " out of Israel " and thus to show forth the praise of the divine mercy itself, are from the very beginning those of Abraham's seed who (like the coming Messiah Himself) are so by God's special choice. This is God's order in Israel just because Israel is the elected people. Election is its living order from the very beginning. Therefore the phenomenon which occupies Paul, Israel's resistance to the message of the Church, is nothing new according to God's order (revealed in His Word, v. 6a). On the contrary, however serious and painful it may be, it is a fresh occasion for praising the living God who has given Israel this order.

" In Isaac shall thy seed be called " (v. 7b), that is, by the special, sacred name of the children of Abraham, namely, of true Israelites. This saying is a quotation from Gen. 21[12], and thus expressly recalls the exclusion of Ishmael described there. It is in Isaac that there is a repetition and establishment of the election of Abraham, not in Ishmael, although he too is Abraham's son, and although he is not this for nothing. According to v. 8 the purport of this passage from Genesis is : " They which are the children of the flesh, these are not (as such) the children of God, but the children of the promise are counted for the seed." Both Isaac and Ishmael are " children of the flesh," begotten by man and born of woman ; and in the same way later both the elected and the rejected will be equally " children of the flesh." But it is not as such that they are prefigurations of the Son of God and Man coming from Israel, the proclamation of the divine mercy, the children of Abraham in the sense of v. 7b, the bearers of the spiritual name of his seed. It is as " children of the promise " that they are children of God and holy children of Abraham, i.e., as men whose existence (like that of the coming Messiah Himself) is the content and object of the promise given to Abraham with his election irrespective of their " carnal origin." Not the life arising from Abraham's flesh and blood as such but the life arising from the truth and power of the promise given to Abraham is the life of the children of God, the pre-existent Church in Israel. These children of the promise " are counted for seed." In them and them only does the seed receive its sacred name and character, and elected Israel is at the same time true Israel. In the provisional upbuilding of the Church in Israel the main issue in each case as it arises is the freedom of God to " count " as genuine, prefigurative and prophetic the seed which He has specially determined for this purpose (as according to Rom. 4[3] etc. He " counts " the faith of Abraham as righteousness in His sight). It is those who are introduced and have life by the truth and power of the divine promise that are the elect of the God who elected Abraham and who, before Abraham was, elected Jesus Christ ; it is they who are God's children and Abraham's children in the strict and proper sense, they alone and none beside them. Such a one is (v. 9) Isaac. He is so in a way that is made prominent and significant for the whole line after him, for as Paul emphasises in Rom. 4[19] (cf. Gen. 18[11]) he is the child of a miraculous begetting and a miraculous birth. " Isaac " means " one laughs." At the word spoken to Abraham : " I will certainly return unto thee according to the time of life ; and, lo, Sarah thy wife shall have a son " (cf. Gen. 18[10]), man calculating in human terms can only laugh (in sceptical enthusiasm) as in the explicit and extended account in Gen. 18[12f.] It is a divine word of promise corresponding—but in a much purer form—to the word by which, on the ground of his election, Abraham was called and led into the land. It can reach fulfilment either not at all or else only on the ground of its truth and power as a divine word of promise. In this very definite sense Isaac is the child of God and of Abraham. Since he, too, is a " child of the flesh," his existence is purely and simply the fulfilment of the divine word of promise. In this way the election of Abraham is repeated and established in him. In this way the pre-existent Church is built up in him. In this way, then, he is also, although indirectly, a witness to the election of all Israel.

The parallel in Gal. 4[21-31] is to be noted. There, too, we have two sons of the one Abraham, begotten and born, the one " after the flesh " of the bondwoman Hagar, the other on the ground of the promise, of the free woman Sarah. And now the point is expressly stated that in both cases we are concerned with " covenants," but with two covenants ($\delta \acute{v} o$ $\delta \iota a \theta \hat{\eta} \kappa a\iota$, v. 24). Hagar is the representation of the covenant made on Sinai and realised with its limitations in the present earthly Jerusalem. Sarah, " our mother," the one who became a mother miraculously, is the covenant adumbrated by the first, freed from its limitations and realised in the " Jerusalem which is above." " We, brethren, as Isaac was, are children of promise. . . . We are not children of the bondwoman, but of the free " (vv. 28, 31). Observe that it is from the Law itself (v. 21), from Scripture (vv. 22, 27, 30), that Paul derives the point that within what is common to them both ($\delta \iota a \theta \acute{\eta} \kappa \eta$) Israel and the Church are twofold—the Church being distinguished from Israel by the fact that it receives Abraham's promise anew and directly on the ground of special choice.

Attention should also be given to the parallel in Rom. 4[9-25]. Abraham believed before he was circumcised, before he was a " Jew." Circumcision too, the sign of the covenant between God and himself and his seed, he received as a " seal of the righteousness of the faith which he had while he was still a Gentile " in order that he might be simultaneously the father of all who believe, both from the Gentiles and the circumcision (v. 10 f.). That he is to become κληρονόμος κόσμου, i.e., that the world is to become his possession, is something which is not promised either to himself or his descendants διὰ νόμου, i.e., with the establishment of the Israelite Law and with a view to its fulfilment, but διὰ δικαιοσύνης πίστεως, i.e., in virtue of the judgment given by God which has equal validity before the establishment of this Law both in and even outside its sphere, and which Abraham trusted and obeyed (v. 13). Where the promise given to Abraham is assured to man through this judgment given by God, and is accepted accordingly by man in faith, there it is βεβαία, authenticating itself to its recipient, in virtue of the fact that its fulfilment is certain (v. 16). Where it is given and received only in the form of the Israelite Law in itself, where the fulfilment of this Law as such is intended to establish man's claim to this hope, faith loses its point (κεκένωται ἡ πίστις) and the promise itself is made impotent (κατήργηται ἡ ἐπαγγελία, v. 14). For to take one's stand under the Law of Israel means virtually the same thing as to stand in the sphere of the divine wrath. Where there is law there is transgression (discovered, condemned and threatened with punishment). It is only where there is no Law—that is, as a limitation of hope, as a substitute for the living promise—that there is no transgression, that transgression is forgiven (v. 15). But this is the case where the promise is given to man, as it was given to Abraham, through the sovereign judgment of God, and where this is accepted as Abraham accepted it, in faith. This can occur in the realm of circumcision and of the Israelite Law regarded as the sign of the covenant made with Abraham. But—in the track of this same Abraham's faith—it can also occur outside this realm. Abraham is the " father of us all " (as Sarah, according to Gal. 4²⁶, is in the same sense " our mother "). According to Gen. 17⁵ he is the father of many nations (vv. 16–17), as surely as in his faith in the promise he believes in the God who quickens the dead and calls the non-existent into being (v. 17). That he was strong in this faith contrary to all human calculations was, according to Gen. 15⁶, " counted " as his righteousness—corresponding to the righteous judgment of God (vv. 18–21). In saying this about Abraham, Scripture is obviously speaking not only of him but of us too, of the Church's faith in the One who awakened from the dead Jesus our Lord. As the father of Isaac Abraham is the father not only of Israel but also of the elected Church gathered from Jews and Gentiles.

Thus the Word of God (Rom. 9⁶) is not proved false but established by the phenomenon of the unbelieving Synagogue. According to the testimony of Scripture, God has from the first chosen, differentiated and divided in Israel. He has from the very beginning separated the Church and Israel, Israel and the Church. And in so doing He has confirmed the election of Israel.

This is the insight that is taken up in more acute form in vv. 10–13. It is more acute to the extent that we are now dealing not merely with the two sons of the one father (Isaac—it is he who is now called ὁ πατὴρ ἡμῶν like Abraham in Rom. 4¹, ¹⁶), but with the two sons of one mother as well (Rebecca), indeed with the twin fruits of one and the same begetting (v. 11). In relation to vv. 7–10 we might perhaps ask if Isaac was not after all chosen because of some merits of his own and Ishmael rejected because of some fault of his own. There was much to praise in the later nation Israel (and in Jacob too), and much to blame in Ishmael (and in Esau too). But whatever we may find to praise or blame, the election of the one and the rejection of the other certainly bear no relation to it. The issue is the separation of the Church in Israel. And what can that have to do with what may seem or may actually be praiseworthy or blameworthy in either the one or the other ? In the relationship of Jacob and Esau it becomes wholly clear that every explanation which takes this line can only go astray. For it is palpable there that the decision both ways is made before regard to the good or evil doings of the persons concerned can be considered at all as a ground of decision. " For the children being not yet born, neither having done any good or evil . . . it was (already) said, The elder (that is precisely the one who as firstborn could claim a natural prerogative) shall serve the younger " (vv. 11–12, Gen. 25²³) ; it had already come to pass : " Jacob have I loved, but Esau have I hated " (v. 13, Mal. 1²ᶠ·). The connexion between the determination of both is not to be mistaken in the formulation in v. 12, neither is it to be overlooked in the more trenchant saying of v. 13. The God of Jacob is also the God of Esau. He whose will elected Abraham and his whole race (to which both belong) unites the servant with the master, the hated with the loved one, the rejected with the elected. It is the one (albeit different) blessing of their father Jacob that both will receive. What occurs in both cases occurs within the community. But all the same the emphasis rests on the fact that it is something different which occurs, that the Church and Abraham's race are not identical, that the Church is founded and built by a separation which operates right from the beginning of the history of this race, and has as its principle, not the glory of good works done by man, but, as in the case of the election of the whole race of Abraham, the good-will of God. This separation must happen in order that the predetermination resting on election might stand, not on the ground of (human) works, but on the ground of (the will of) Him who calls (vv. 11–12). It is as the election stands in this elected race, as it continually takes place in this race, or is manifested in it in the form of calling, that the Church is founded and built up and the election of this race is established. But we must not lose sight of the fact that it is in this race that by God's free disposing the Church is founded and built up by the operation of this separation which repeatedly means exclusion. The very fact that the κατ' ἐκλογὴν πρόθεσις τοῦ θεοῦ is continued in this race means that its honour and hope continuingly benefit all its members. Even its rejected members (just because of the separation which excludes them) are not forsaken, but after, as before, share in the special care and guidance of the electing God. When Ishmael was menaced by death on the expulsion of Hagar to the wilderness, " God heard the voice of the lad ; and the angel of the Lord called to Hagar out of heaven, and said unto her, What aileth thee, Hagar ? fear not ; for God hath heard the voice of the lad where he is. Arise, lift up the lad, and hold him in thine hand ; for I will make him a great nation. And God opened her eyes, and she saw a well of water. . . . And God was with the lad ; and he grew, and dwelt in the wilderness, and became an archer " (Gen. 21¹⁷ᶠ·). And in the same way the Esau (Edom) of the Old Testament is not one who is forsaken by God but the ancestor of a covenant people who is recognised in his way by God and the people of Jacob and provided with a genealogy of his own which both in Gen. 36 and 1 Chron. 1 is set forth in great detail alongside that of Israel. This should not be forgotten in arriving at the biblical interpretation of what is to be described as " rejection " in contrast or rather in relation to election. But in the first instance it is the first factor which is decisive. It is the free, divine choice within the elected race which founds and builds up the Church. It is the same choice which constitutes this race as such the elected race. It is the choice of grace which is not bound by any natural or moral presuppositions on the part of the elect but the ground of which is to be sought solely in the will of the electing God, in His revelation, in the fact of His call. It is the special choice of grace which as such is to be accepted and affirmed in faith, which can be accepted and affirmed in faith alone. The free divine choice of some excludes others. According to Scripture there was always an Israel excluded by this free divine choice. Israel as such was never identical with the Church. Thus the phenomenon of the refractory Synagogue is no novelty. The Word of God is not proved false by this phenomenon.

But what is God's purpose with the remainder of Israel which is not appointed for the founding and upbuilding of the Church ? What was His purpose with Ishmael ? or with Esau whom, according to v. 13, He " hated " ? What is His

purpose to-day with the refractory Synagogue ? The answer to this question
follows in vv. 14–29.

" What shall we then say ? Is there unrighteousness with God ? " (v. 14).
The question which Paul here holds out for consideration by Paul is not concerning an abstract righteousness but about the concrete righteousness of the God
who elects Israel. Is not this God, the covenant God of Abraham, unjust in
a procedure which excludes from this special election so many of Abraham's race
without regard to the natural and moral presuppositions that they have to commend them ? In the last resort, is it not His will that disposes in this way an act
of arbitrary and unfair preference and prejudice ? We must keep in mind that
along with the question raised by the statement of Scripture Paul is at the same
time faced with the actual question of the majority of Israel remaining outside
the Church. In vv. 6–13 he has explained from the standpoint of Scripture that
from the first God has at all times proceeded in the way in which He manifestly still does to-day, so that there can be no doubt about God's constancy.
But what if it is in relation to the procedure followed from the first by this
constant God, in relation to Ishmael and Esau, that is, from Scripture itself,
that the question of the righteousness of this constant God is raised, and extends
from there to the consideration of what God is also obviously doing in the present ?
In v. 6 f. Scripture was consulted to try to make this consideration of the present
easier, but it only seems to have made it harder. Can it be that the " sorrow "
which, according to v. 2, Paul endures on account of Israel may ultimately be
sorrow that according to His own Word the God of Israel is as wayward to-day
as He always was, that in Him there is unrighteousness ?

Paul opposes to this question the horrified μὴ γένοιτο customary with him in
such cases (cf. Rom. 3[4, 6], 6[2, 15], 7[7], 11[1, 11]). In the consideration of Scripture
as of present-day life he therefore holds fast to the confession of God's righteousness. And this can only mean in the context that it is clear to him that in
the procedure described in vv. 6–13 the God of Israel is not acting in defiance
of but in accordance with the order established by Himself, that is to say, not
arbitrarily but in profoundest harmony with Himself and in a manner supremely
worthy of Himself and therefore in the most objective sense righteously. According to v. 15 the proof of this is the divine name which is revealed to Moses and
which characterises the nature of God. According to Ex. 33[19] it runs : " I will
have mercy on whom I have mercy, yea, I will have compassion on whom I
have compassion." This is obviously a paraphrase of the simpler formula of
Ex. 3[14] : " I will be he that I am." According to this revealed name of His,
God's nature consists in the fact that He renews, establishes and glorifies Himself by His own future ; or materially, that He renews, establishes and glorifies
His being by His future being, or even more materially, His mercy by His future
mercy, His compassion by His future compassion. It is because Paul has clearly
in view this nature of God that to the question whether in this procedure there
is not present some unrighteousness on the part of God he opposes the horrified
μὴ γένοιτο, rejecting the question as absurd. This procedure—and this procedure
alone—corresponds to the revealed name and the nature of God characterised
by this name. It is this nature of God which is His righteousness and therefore
the measure and sum of all righteousness. God's nature is that the One He
now is in freedom He will be again in the same unconditioned, unassailable
freedom to posit and affirm Himself by Himself. In that God will be He who
He is, He is in no way unrighteous, arbitrary or wayward. On the contrary,
His righteousness consists precisely in the fact that He renews, establishes and
glorifies His present by His own future, that as the One He is, but as such positing
and affirming Himself afresh, He advances from each to-day posited in His
freedom into a to-morrow which in its turn will be posited in His freedom. It
is in this way that the eternal God lives in His relationship to time, in His relationship and covenant with the man loved and created by Him. It is in this

way that He lives in the election of Jesus Christ and in the election of the community. But what Ex. 33[19] says here has a still richer content. God's nature consists in the fact that as He freely shows mercy, so He will again show mercy. By doing this and thus maintaining the continuity between His present and His future God does not give man any occasion to complain of an injustice inflicted on him. His righteousness indeed consists in the fact that He not only is but always becomes again the merciful One, that He does not cease to show mercy, but by what He will do in His mercy establishes the truth of what He does and already has done in His mercy. This is how God lives in covenant with man in the election of Jesus Christ and in the election of the community. This is how He renews, establishes and glorifies this covenant. But it is just this nature of God which is the secret of the divine procedure described in vv. 6–13. As God elects Abraham, so among his sons He elects Isaac, and among Isaac's sons Jacob. So, too, He elects Moses. As yesterday He showed mercy, so He does to-day and so He will do to-morrow. All renewal, establishment and glorification of His present (His mercy already shown) by His own future (His mercy yet to be shown), and therefore the life corresponding to His nature in the realm of His creation and in covenant with man, are finally effective and visible in their perfect and at the same time original form, and the day of His future dawns, in the fact that He has mercy on the man Jesus and in Him on all men by becoming man Himself, by taking up and taking away man's burden in order to clothe man with His own glory. In view of the day of this one man in whom God will renew, establish and glorify His righteousness (the righteousness of His mercy) by suffering Himself the judgment which overtakes man, the Israel from which this One will be taken is subject to the order : " I will be he that I am," and the Church is continually separated within Israel. Is there any appropriate standpoint from which we can legitimately complain of this order and accuse it as unrighteous ? God is righteous in the fact that when He shows mercy to Israel—for the sake of all men and all Israel as well—He is concerned with His future act of mercy and therefore with this one man and with His Church. God is righteous in the fact that He causes this electing mercy towards His Church in Israel to follow upon His special electing mercy shown to Abraham and all his race. This sequel, indeed, only renews, establishes and glorifies that beginning. Even in loving Jacob and hating Esau (v. 13), God is supremely righteous—and supremely righteous in the disregard (vv. 10–13) thereby shown with respect to all natural and moral presuppositions of the persons affected. " So then it is not of him that willeth, nor of him that runneth, but of God that sheweth mercy " (v. 16), if (in addition to the fact that as a member of Abraham's race he has a share in the mercy of God) this special mercy falls on anyone, if he is called to the Church. This is true of Moses, true of Isaac and Jacob. If it were of anyone's willing and running, then God would be unrighteous, He would not be consistent with Himself, because He would be letting another attitude, one conditioned by the willing and running of man, follow upon the free mercy in which He elects Abraham. God is righteous when He elects Isaac and Jacob and Moses with the very same disregard of all prior considerations, in the very same free mercy, in which He had already elected Abraham.

But the answer has not yet been given to the question : What is it that God wills and does with Ishmael, with Esau, with all Israel that is not called to the Church ? What is the meaning of : " Esau have I hated " (v. 13) ? Does what was said in vv. 15–16 about the righteousness of the divine mercy apply to him too, and to all the rest as well ? This is, in fact, what Paul is trying to say in the following section. While vv. 15–16 speak of Moses and, retrospectively, of Isaac and Jacob, they form at the same time the major premise for what is to be said in v. 17 f. in relation to Ishmael, Esau and all others rejected within elected Israel. In relation to them, too, the righteousness of God's conduct is exalted far above all doubt because God's name is : " I will be he that I am," or, " I will have mercy on whom I have mercy," and because His conduct with regard to them also accords with this name or with the nature expressed by this name.

The word of God to Pharaoh quoted in v. 17 is not, as one might expect, opposed to that given to Moses by the use of δέ, but set alongside it by the use of a confirmatory γάρ. What follows confirms the insight expressed in vv. 15-16. The figure now used as an example is none other than the mighty opposite of Moses, the Pharaoh of the Exodus. What has he to do with the Israel who is the theme of the whole passage ? Obviously it is only that as its worst enemy and persecutor he is a proper prefiguration of what Paul, as Saul the persecutor of Christians, had himself once been, and what the Synagogue of the present time still is in relation to the apostolic community. But it is this indirectness which makes so very impressive his appearance on this scene as a representative of reprobate and rebellious Israel. In the place where Pharaoh once stood the remainder of Israel now stands. But the context says that Israel necessarily stands there without regard to its running and willing, its purpose and achievement. The God who is righteous in the spirit of v. 15 has placed it there. And what God wills and does by this is to be interpreted with reference to the Pharoah of the Exodus. Not every act of God's mercy is necessarily followed by a further one—for in that case how would it be mercy, how would it be the mercy of God ? That one act of mercy should follow another is a matter for the free decision of Him who is merciful, which might equally well cause a failure in this sequence. This is the negative side of the truth of v. 15. And it is on its negative side that it affects Ishmael, Esau and Pharaoh. But in the first place this has the following positive significance. In the relation of his history to that of Israel, there is an original act of God's mercy towards Pharaoh also. This is how it is represented by the Old Testament itself. The context of the words quoted in v. 17 is indeed : " I could by now have stretched forth my hand and smitten thee and thy people with pestilence ; and thou wouldst have been cut off from the earth ; but in very deed for this cause have I upheld thee (Paul read in his Greek text —I have ' raised thee up ') that thou mightest know my power (LXX and Paul : 'that I might show my power in thee') and that my name might be declared throughout all the earth " (Ex. 9¹⁵ᶠ·). God lets one warning miracle after another take place before his eyes. Pharaoh does not fail to acknowledge on occasion his sin and guilt (Ex. 9²⁷, 10¹⁶). Neither does he fail to appeal to Moses to intercede on his behalf (8⁸, ²⁸, 9²⁸, 10¹⁷). And Moses does in fact repeatedly pray for him (8¹², ³⁰, 9³³, 10¹⁸) ; repeatedly his punishment is, in fact, stopped before it gets the length of his annihilation. In the last resort all this is hardly less than what appears in Israel's own history in the shape of manifest traces of the original divine mercy. What does not befall Pharaoh (unlike Isaac, Jacob and Moses), corresponding to the negative side of the truth of v. 15, is the renewal, establishment and glorification of this original act of mercy by the event of a further one. God makes use of His freedom to refuse him this future. But, of course, even in this use it is the freedom of His mercy. Even while he is refused what is given to Moses, because both acts occur in the same freedom, Pharaoh is still in the same sphere as Moses. The original mercy of God is not turned in vain even towards him, but with a very definite and positive purpose. He, too, has a function in the service of the God who bears this name, and he, too, participates in the honour and hope associated with it. God " upholds," " raises him up," in order to make him a witness to His power, in order by his destiny to proclaim His name over all the earth. It is to be considered that even this dark prototype of all the rejected in Israel serves to show forth the δύναμις τοῦ θεοῦ which in Rom. 1¹⁶ is identified with the Gospel, in 1 Cor. 1¹⁸ with the Word of the cross, in 1 Cor. 1²⁴ with Christ Himself—and to proclaim the ὄνομα τοῦ θεοῦ, i.e., the self-manifestation, self-interpretation and self-affirmation of God that is achieved in God's revelation. God's purpose in the election of His community is executed through Pharaoh too, and not through Moses only. In the way marked by His deeds, which leads on to the day of His future, to the day of Jesus Christ, God finds and uses even him, and not Moses only. He stands fittingly beside Moses because he makes it clear that in respect of its fulfilment God's purpose in the election of His community is not bound up with (v. 16) the willing and running of any man (not even with that of Moses), that in one way or another it has to be carried out by the person concerned. He stands fittingly beside Moses because in his own very different way he bears witness to the righteousness of God and indeed to the righteousness of His mercy. In the same sense, too, Ishmael stands fittingly beside Isaac, Esau beside Jacob, and to-day the refractory Synagogue beside the Church.

" Therefore hath he mercy on whom he will have mercy, and whom he will he hardeneth " (v. 18). The saying obviously looks back on the one hand to Isaac, Jacob and Moses, and on the other to Ishmael, Esau and Pharaoh. Before expounding it in the sense of the classical doctrine of predestination attention should have been paid to the fact that here the twofold $\theta\acute{\epsilon}\lambda\epsilon\iota$ cannot possibly be regarded neutrally, i.e., as an indeterminately free willing which now takes the one direction and now the other. To be sure, this willing of God is free. But it is not for that reason indeterminate. It is determined in the sense given by God's name (v. 15). And it is determined in this sense that it has this twofold direction. On both sides, although in different forms, God wills one and the same thing. The contradiction of $\dot{\epsilon}\lambda\epsilon\epsilon\hat{\iota}$ and $\sigma\kappa\lambda\eta\rho\acute{\upsilon}\nu\epsilon\iota$ is bracketed by this $\theta\acute{\epsilon}\lambda\epsilon\iota$, the one purpose of God in the election of His community. As will be stated in Rom. 11^{32} with complete unambiguity, this purpose is the purpose of His mercy. It is just this purpose which, according to vv. 15–17, both Moses and also Pharaoh must carry out. They do so in different ways and to this extent the single will of God has a differentiated form. He chooses Moses as a witness of His mercy and Pharaoh as a witness of the judgment that in and with this mercy becomes necessary and is executed. Thus He determines Moses as the voluntary, Pharaoh as the involuntary servant of His power and His name. He renews His mercy with regard to Moses. He refuses this renewal to Pharaoh. If it is self-evident that for the men concerned it means personally something very different to be dealt with and used by God in these different ways, there is no mention of that here. It was perhaps the decisive exegetical error of the classical doctrine of predestination that—being more concerned about the things of men (although not to their advantage) than the things of God—it thought to see the scope of Rom. 9^{18} in the personal situation and destiny of Moses and Pharaoh (as of Rom. $9^{6f.}$ in that of the different sons of Abraham and Isaac). But the point at issue here is precisely how the diversity of the personal situation and destiny of Israelite man, which, conditioned by the divine predetermination, is so characteristic of the history and life of the chosen people Israel, does not contradict but corresponds to the election of Israel and the righteousness of the mercy of its God. We are told that there must repeatedly be this division in the sphere of Israel's history and life because its history is in fact the history of the expectation of its crucified Messiah and at the same time the pre-history of the Church of the risen Lord, because it is in this sphere that God intends to justify both Himself and man, and will, in fact, do so. $'E\lambda\epsilon\epsilon\hat{\iota}\nu$ describes in v. 18 the special act of mercy, the renewal of mercy, in which God's purpose with Israel is revealed and becomes effective in its positive aspect, the founding in its midst of the Church and the mercy shown to it, the prefiguration of the mercy in which God will take man's part on the day of His future, in the resurrection of Jesus Christ from the dead. $\Sigma\kappa\lambda\eta\rho\acute{\upsilon}\nu\epsilon\iota\nu$ means to stiffen, harden, make obdurate, petrify (Vulg.: *indurare*), and describes the isolation of the original and the withholding of the special new act of mercy as a result of which the same purpose of God with Israel takes effect in its negative aspect, in the constitution of Israel for itself and as such, the prefiguration of the judgment which God, on the same day of His future—

in the course of showing mercy—will send forth upon man, to which He will on this day submit Himself on man's behalf. V. 18 is, therefore, to be paraphrased as follows: Whomsoever God's merciful purpose in the election of His community determines for the prefiguration and reflection of His mercy, for the unveiling of the goodness of His sovereign dealing, of the grace of His freedom, to him He reveals and gives Himself as He who has and executes this purpose, so that he may serve His will like Moses, as God's friend, voluntarily, in thankfulness and therefore in obedience and under God's blessing. Whomsoever God's merciful purpose in the election of the community determines for the prefiguration and reflection of His judgment, for the unveiling of the impotence, unworthiness and hopelessness of all man's will and achievement as opposed to God's, for the unveiling of the severity of His sovereign dealing, of the freedom of His grace, to him He refuses fellowship and denies Himself, so that like Pharaoh he must serve Him as God's enemy, involuntarily, with an unthankful heart and therefore through the medium of his sin and guilt and under the curse and punishment of God.

The question which Paul voices in v. 19 and which he answers in vv. 20–22 is a challenge. " Thou wilt say then unto me, Why doth he yet find fault ? For who hath resisted his will ? " In order to interpret this we must also quote the formulation which it is taken up again in v. 20 : " Why hast thou made me thus ? " It is such an obvious question that it is superfluous to settle whether it was actually put to Paul and by whom, or whether he discusses it here just because he reckons that it might be raised at this point. Clearly it records the defence of a man who, according to the exposition in vv. 17–18, when he looks at his willing and running (v. 16), sees himself put by God Himself among His enemies, indeed determined as one of these enemies, without regard to what he can advance in favour of the right, the worth and the usefulness of his efforts What, then, can God have against him, if all his willing and running receive no consideration at all, if he is made a Pharaoh by God's will and work whatever course his willing and running may take ? How can he still be responsible, chargeable, punishable ? What occasion is there for him to repent, to make use of God's offer of His grace ? Is he expected, even with his best efforts, to be able to offer resistance to the will and work of God ? And if this is beyond him, what is wrong about being Pharaoh ? There would be some point in this question if in v. 18, as the classical doctrine of predestination will have it, Paul had been speaking of an absolute power of disposal belonging to God. It was not for nothing that on the basis of this presupposition all the arguments in answer to this question and in refutation of this defence were so feeble that about 1700, after 150 years of discussion, it was still or again possible to introduce this *scrupulus de praedestinatione hominis irregeniti* (S. Werenfels, *Opusc.* II, p. 135 f.) with the same lachyrmose assurance as formerly the opponents of Calvin and earlier still those of Augustine and Gottschalk had done. If it is the *decretum absolutum* that Paul proclaims in v. 18, even his own answer to this question in v. 20 is no real answer. But in v. 18 Paul does not proclaim the *decretum absolutum*. On the contrary, he speaks of the merciful will of the free God. In view of this, the challenge in v. 19 is irrelevant. It is irrelevant because if the God who is free in the exercise of His mercy determines man to be the witness of His judgment no man can be in a position to oppose Him with the question why He finds fault, or why He has made him thus. " O man, who art thou that repliest against God ? " (v. 20a). The tenor of the answer which Paul has in mind with this counter-question is not as has so often been assumed : " After all you are only a creature with which God as its Creator has power to deal as seems good to Him." Of course, God " has power " to do this. Of course, man is therefore a being with whom God " has power " to deal in this way. But it is not in respect of an indeterminate power of God that Paul's counter-question puts man in his place. This would only give fresh vigour and a new pretext for the question of v. 19. On the contrary, the " power " of God in His dealing with man, in face of which it becomes man to be humble, is something wholly determinate ; it is settled by the determined purpose on which God has decided with respect to man in Jesus Christ. The tenor of the answer hidden in the counter-question of v. 20 is : " In any case, whether you are a friend of God like Moses or an enemy like Pharaoh, whether your name is Isaac or Ishmael, Jacob or Esau, you are the man on account of whose sin and for whose sin Jesus Christ has died on the cross for the justification of God, and for whose salvation and bliss, and for whose justification, He has been raised from the dead " (Rom. 4²⁵). This man—the man who is concerned in this twofold justification achieved in Jesus Christ, who is confronted with this twofold justification—cannot possibly make the challenge of v. 19. The defence of the man appointed as a witness to the divine judgment will surely wither away on his lips, if he can ever conceive of it at all. Not only the friend but also the enemy of God, not only His voluntary but also His involuntary servant, must be told : " You are this man, and as this man you cannot possibly wish to dispute with God. As this man, whoever and whatever else you may be, you are who you are and what you are by the merciful will of the free God. In every case you have occasion for thankfulness, in every case occasion to recognise your ingratitude, in every case occasion to be aware of your responsibility for it, in every case occasion to repent, in every case occasion to put your hope in God and God alone. Whatever God makes of you, whether you stand in the light or the shadow of His merciful purpose, whether you have to witness to God's goodness as such or to the weakness and unworthiness of man in relation to Him and therefore to the seriousness of the divine judgment—this is what you have occasion for, and therefore you have no occasion to make this challenge." Paul meets it—the sequel will show that this is how he wants to be understood—by preaching and urging the claim of the Gospel of the justification of God and man achieved in Jesus Christ. Man justified in Jesus Christ cannot oppose this challenge to the God justified in Jesus Christ. He accepts this divine reproof. He does not will to resist God. For whatever purpose he may be determined and created he glorifies the hand of God that is upon him. (The *scrupulus de praedestinatione* was the punishment for the way in which the classical doctrine of predestination opposed an indeterminate God and an indeterminate man. Paul did not do that. Therefore he did not need to fear this *scrupulus*.)

The parable of the potter follows in vv. 20–21. This is the focal point of the whole exposition as we can see if we keep in mind the evangelical spirit of the preceding rejection of the question of v. 19, if we interpret the parable itself as it is used in its Old Testament prototypes, especially Jer. 18¹⁻¹⁰, and finally if we pay attention to the interpretation of it which is given afterwards in vv. 22–24 and introduced by an in no sense unimportant δέ. The parable of the potter is, in the first place, a repetition and confirmation of v. 18. God is in His mercy free to disclose Himself here and withhold Himself there. He is free to let His power and His name be shown forth and proclaimed in one way by Moses and in another by Pharaoh. He who in Jesus Christ will have mercy upon sinners uses for the revelation of His way to this goal witnesses to His merciful purpose as such, His Church in Israel, " vessels of honour "—and also witnesses to His judgment (as the operation of His mercy), Israel in itself and as such, " vessels of dishonour." He uses them both as witnesses to Jesus Christ, each in its own way. This is how the potter, the God of Israel, deals in and with His people—not according to the caprices of His omnipotence but in the determinate purpose, corresponding to His name and nature, of His own justification in the death and man's justification in the resurrection of Christ, in the revelation of the way taken by Him in His advance towards the day of His future. Two things are necessarily revealed on this way, that Israel is the place of His glory, and that this glory is His own and not Israel's. But already in Paul's

Old Testament sources the twofold action of the potter does not by any means take place along parallel lines, in symmetry and equilibrium, so that proceeding from a centre of indifference (on the principle of the see-saw), with the same seriousness and the same meaning, indeed with the same finality—with an eternity before Him to the right and to the left—God will now accept and now reject, now disclose and now withhold Himself, now show mercy and now harden. Rather—while both operations are His—His operation εἰς τιμήν is one thing and His operation εἰς ἀτιμίαν is another, and they stand in an irreversible sequence and order. If to the right He says Yes, He does this for His own sake, expressing His ultimate purpose, declaring what He wills to do among and to men in His mercy operative and revealed in Jesus Christ. If to the left He says No, He does this for the sake of the Yes that is to be spoken to the right, on the way to the execution of His ultimate purpose, declaring that which the operation and revelation of His mercy make necessary because they happen among and to men. Without prejudice to the seriousness of the divine purpose on both sides, the relationship between the two sides of the one divine action is one of supreme incongruity, supreme a-symmetry, supreme disequilibrium. The light of the divine willing and the shadow of the powerful divine non-willing are indeed related at this point, but they are necessarily governed by an irreversible sequence and order. " For his anger endureth but a moment ; his favour a lifetime " (Ps. 30⁵). " For a small moment have I forsaken thee ; but with great mercies will I gather thee. In a little wrath I hid my face from thee for a moment, but with everlasting kindness will I have mercy on thee " (Is. 54⁷ᶠ·). " For as the heaven is high above the earth, so great is his mercy toward them that fear him. . . . As for man, his days are as grass ; as a flower of the field, so he flourisheth. For the wind passeth over it, and it is gone ; and the place thereof shall know it no more. But the mercy of the Lord is from everlasting to everlasting . . . and his righteousness unto children's children " (Ps. 103¹¹ᶠ·). This is the relationship between the two courses of action followed by the potter, the God of Israel. A failure to recognise this relationship is the error of the question of v. 20a. The thing that is fashioned cannot with Is. 29¹⁶ say to Him who fashioned it : " He made me not " ; nor can it ask : " Why hast thou made me thus ? " This is forbidden, not by the power, but by the meaning, the tendency, the right of the power of its fashioner. If the " vessels of dishonour " are appointed to demonstrate the impotence and unworthiness of man, of the " lump " out of which they and the " vessels of honour " are taken, " the vessels of honour," shaped by the same hand, stand in relation to them as a demonstration of what God's will and purpose are with this man. How can man, instead of praising God's work with him, deduce from his impotence and unworthiness attested by the " vessels of wrath " a right and a necessity to absolutise them, to play off the divine No against the divine Yes, when the former is, in fact, spoken only for the sake of the Yes ? What option has the man who is determined as a " vessel of dishonour " except by his witness to the impotence and unworthiness of man—which he must give involuntarily in any case—voluntarily to corroborate the witness of the one who is determined as a " vessel of honour," as he sees God Himself, not cancelling His Yes by His No, but corroborating it ? To provide this corroboration is Israel's appointed task in the elected community of God. Israel in itself and as such is the " vessel of dishonour." It is the witness to the divine judgment. It embodies human impotence and unworthiness. For by Israel its own Messiah is delivered up to be crucified. In its midst, however, there stands in relation to it from the very first the Church with its comprehensive and final commission to proclaim to this man the work of God—the Church which in virtue of its Head, the risen Lord, is the " vessel of honour," the witness to the divine mercy, the embodiment of the divine goodness which has taken the part of this man. Can Israel ask : " Why hast thou made me thus ? Why hast thou not made me an Israel which as such and in itself is already the Church ? " It cannot raise questions like this because as Israel, as a vessel of wrath, as a witness to the divine judgment, it has the Church within it from the very first ; because it is with its proclamation of the divine No that it has been determined for and is called to entrance into the Church— called to serve voluntarily where it must in any case serve involuntarily. This calling which it has to be subordinate to the proclamation of the greater divine Yes is God's prior justification in relation to it and its own prior justification in relation to God. It is this which with a factuality that Israel cannot contest makes this question as impossible as that of v. 19. Ishmael is called by Isaac, Esau by Jacob, Pharaoh by Moses—the Synagogue of the present by Paul. In view of this call, in view of the Gospel so clearly addressed to them, can they dare to repeat this question, the challenge of v. 19 ?

That this interpretation of vv. 19–21 is the only possible one is shown by the exposition of the parable of the potter given in vv. 22–24. It consists of an interrogative sentence in the form of an anacoluthon which stylistically fits vv. 19–21 very well in so far as there no less than five questions in all, not directly answered by Paul, form the content of his exposition. The parable of the potter seems to have set a riddle. " But what if (this is taken to mean that) God, willing to show his wrath, and to make his power known, endured with much long-suffering the vessels of wrath fitted to destruction," in order (namely) " that he might make known the riches of his glory on the vessels of mercy, which he had afore prepared unto glory—as which he hath called even us, not of the Jews only, but also of the Gentiles ? " The whole statement is articulated and the relation between God's action to left and right brought into clear view by the καὶ ἵνα of v. 23 (which is to be understood in both a consecutive and a final sense). The sequence of the ἐλεεῖ and σκληρύνει of v. 18 and the εἰς τιμήν and εἰς ἀτιμίαν of v. 21b, conceived in view of the goal, is now reversed in a genetic development, and the apparently unrelated proximity of the two is clarified. In vv. 22–24 it is quite unambiguous that Paul is not speaking of a content of God's will which is to be interpreted as an abstract duality, but of God's way on which in execution of His one purpose He wills and executes in a determined sequence and order this twofold operation. The harsh appearance that can descend on the preceding passage if vv. 22–24 are not taken into account in advance—as if God's mercy and hardening, the existence of " vessels of honour " and of " dishonour," were the two goals of two different ways of God—is now finally dispelled. The principal verb of the decisive second half of the sentence (v. 23) is γνωρίσῃ. Not that there are " vessels of mercy," but that God reveals in them the riches of His glory, is the goal of the divine way, and it is only for this revelation that the " vessels of mercy " are also needed. Similarly the principal statement of the first half of the sentence (v. 22) does not consist in establishing the fact that there are " vessels of wrath," that God has prepared them as such and therefore for destruction, nor even that He has done so in order to show forth His wrath and reveal His power, but in the fact that God has " endured these vessels of wrath with much long-suffering." This is the principal statement of v. 22, not merely because ἤνεγκεν is the principal verb, but above all because it is with this ἤνεγκεν that the statement of v. 23 is connected. God endured these vessels in order to reveal the riches of His mercy through the others. This is the Pauline interpretation of the parable of the potter. According to v. 22 the one will of God has indeed the form both of the manifestation of wrath and of the revelation of power. In showing mercy God is indeed also wrathful—He has " brought forth the weapons of His indignation," says the passage in Jer. 50²⁵ to which Paul alludes. That is, He is wrathful against the perversity that encounters Him from the side of man. And in showing mercy He is also free in His omnipotence, in contrast to the impotence of man. That which He in His mercy on Israel will execute in Jesus Christ will also be an act of judgment and rejection. He will (Rom. 1¹⁸ᶠ·) pronounce a devastating No upon all the willing and running of man by the very fact that He takes his affairs out of his hands into His own. He will in every way disinherit man and dispossess him. But hidden in this very operation of wrath He will be gracious to him. By the very means of this judgment—the shame and distress of which He will bear Himself—He will save him. The history of Israel leading up to this goal can be nothing but an increasingly close succession of intimations of this judgment. That is why there are " vessels of wrath " throughout the whole course of its history. In them is shown and revealed the divine No, veiled in which the divine Yes to man will be spoken in the suffering and death of Israel's Messiah. For the sake of its election and its hope, Israel— otherwise it would not be Israel—must always have in it as well these " vessels of wrath fitted to destruction." Indeed it must finally become a single " vessel of wrath." In delivering up its Messiah to be put to death, it must become in its totality a witness to the divine judgment. But even according to v. 22 the negation of man has no independent or final significance in the will of God, nor has its demonstration and revelation therefore in God's will and dealing with Israel. Paul has clearly in view that at the goal of Israel's history God will not say No to man but that veiled under the No He will say Yes ; that He will not leave Jesus in the grave after being put to death but will raise Him from the dead. Seen in the light of this goal the decisive statement about these " vessels of wrath " is necessarily to the effect that God has endured them with much long-suffering. He has not only left them their time, and in that time life. He has not only waited, although in vain, for their repentance and conversion. He has indeed done that. But He has done more. In willing and using them as " vessels of wrath " He has, in fact, sustained them, carried them with Him, taken them up into the teleology of His merciful willing and running. He has not endured them in vain. The long-suffering in which He left them time, in which He waited in vain for repentance, was not an empty, meaningless tolerance ending at last in disillusionment, but an act of the divine patience, and as such an act of the divine wisdom. Because He bore in His own Son the rejection which falls on mankind, the fact of Ishmael's rejection, of Esau's, of Pharaoh's, of all Israel's also, is in the end superseded and limited ; it is characterised as a rejection borne by God. " To bear " in this context means more accurately to bear forward, to bear to an expected end. It is for the sake of Him who is to come, for the sake of the Lamb of God who will bear away the sin of the world (Jn. 1^{29}), that the sustaining, long-suffering of God (cf. Rom. 3$^{25f.}$) which befalls the " vessels of wrath " is possible and necessary. This bearing to an expected end is the secret of the history of Israel—and therefore also the secret of the continuing existence of the Synagogue alongside the Church. God not only bears with it. He not only waits for its repentance. But in so doing He wills it as a sign of His wrath and freedom which is also the abiding sign of God's mercy. " No power in the world will be able to extirpate Judaism. Indeed, not even the Jews themselves will be able to extirpate themselves so long as God's long-suffering endures this year also (Lk. 13^8) the vessels of wrath." (E. Peterson, *Die Kirche aus Juden und Heiden*, 1933, p. 34.) It may be asked whether after all the Church does not actually need the intrinsically so incomprehensible counterpart of this Israel which after the fulfilment of its hopes repeats its old obduracy and even in so doing is carried towards its hope. It has in any case repeatedly to learn from the existence of the Synagogue, as a living commentary on the Old Testament, from what sort of " lump " (v. 21) it has itself been taken, how it is with man who is found by God's grace, and in the reflection of this knowledge how it is with the grace of God itself, how deeply God has humiliated Himself on man's behalf in order to exalt him so highly.

The goal of this enduring the " vessels of wrath " is indeed, according to v. 23, the revelation of the riches of the glory of God in the " vessels of mercy " prepared for glory, which are then in v. 24 expressly identified with the Church gathered from Jews and Gentiles. We cannot pay too much attention to the consecutive-final connexion of vv. 22 and 23 if we are to understand properly these two verses and with them the whole context of vv. 13–29 as an answer to the question of the righteousness of God in the election of the community. The *telos* of this election is now expressly indicated. God is wrathful and judges and punishes as He shows mercy, and indeed for His mercy's sake, because without this He would not be really and effectively merciful. We now learn explicitly that God's mercy is His glory (His self-confirming and self-demonstrating essence). In His mercy (and therefore not without the justification of man) God justifies Himself, as in the revelation of His wrath. The revelation of His wrath is therefore followed by that of His mercy. The latter must be preceded by the former because this will also be the order in the fulfilment of Israel's hope, in the confirmation of its election by God's self-humiliation for the purpose of exalting man in Jesus Christ, because Jesus Christ Himself will be this " way." But just because of the fact that Jesus Christ will be this irreversible " way," He is already the secret of Israel's history, which has its goal in Him. For this very reason the bearing with the " vessels of wrath " must be interpreted as a " bearing to an expected end." The meaning of its history cannot, then, be perceived in a juxtaposition of two different purposes of God. The existence of the " vessels of wrath," the existence of Israel standing at last before us as a single " vessel of wrath " embodied in the " traitor " Judas Iscariot, has no end in itself. God's sentence of rejection on Israel is not a final word, not the whole Word of God, but only the foreword to God's promise of His glory later to be revealed on this shadow-Israel. The witnesses of this final and whole Word of God, of the glory of God in its revelation speaking irrefutably for itself, are called in v. 23 the " vessels of mercy " in the same special sense in which in v. 15 and v. 18 Moses was designated an object of the divine mercy. " Vessels unto honour " they are called in v. 21. But we are not told there that the " vessels unto dishonour " proceeding from the hand of the God of Israel have not also in their special position and function to serve the coming glory of God and therefore His mercy. On the contrary, from the connexion between v. 22 and v. 23 we have to conclude that in their way they actually do this. Indirectly the real witnesses of the wrath of God are necessarily also witnesses of His mercy. But they are not its special, proper and direct witnesses—the witnesses of the resurrection and ascension of Christ, the witnesses of the Holy Spirit of whom He is conceived in the Virgin Mary, and whom He communicates to His own, by whom He is the Son of God and by whom men are called and may become sons of God. These witnesses are the " vessels of mercy " after and alongside them, taken from the same " lump " (v. 21), the Israelites who are " of Israel " in the sense that Jesus of Nazareth is, who in and with this One may positively and voluntarily confirm Israel's election. The sign of grace in their existence is also set up in Israel, and under this sign of grace Israel is not only the prefiguration of the Synagogue " prepared for destruction " but is also the prefiguration of the Church prepared for the vision and witness of the glory of God, for the praise of His mercy. Although the Israel determined for this service is reduced at the culmination of its mission to the prototype of the one person of the Son of David prepared beforehand, it already exists before Him (since this prototype proceeds from the midst of Israel itself) in many others, in all the children of Abraham and sons of David, in all the prophets and servants of God, in all the poor and as such righteous who form the steadily diminishing " remnant " of those who not only have Israel's calling and hope, but bear it in their hearts. In these " vessels of mercy " there pre-exists along with the Son of David, Jesus of Nazareth, the Church of those called and gathered by Him, of those who believe in Him. The One who creates in Him the Church is therefore no other than the potter, the God of Israel, who wills and produces not only " vessels of wrath " but also " vessels of mercy "—and even the " vessels of wrath " only in order that among the " vessels of mercy " every mouth may be stopped that would glory in man at the expense of God, in order that among them and by them the glory of God alone may be exalted. It is as Isaac has at his side an Ishmael, Jacob an Esau, Moses a Pharaoh, the Church a Synagogue, that they are the genuine children of the promise and faith of their father Abraham. Thus the Church founded by the elected apostles, even though there is a Judas Iscariot among them too, is the unveiled secret of the election—and of the twofold realisation of the election of Israel.

This, however, is not expressly stated until v. 24. The vessel of mercy (prefigured in the patriarchs, in Moses, in David and in the prophets) is primarily the Lord Jesus Christ risen from the dead, and secondarily the apostolic Church called and gathered by Him through the Gospel, " . . . even us whom he hath called not only of the Jews but also of the Gentiles "—so runs the conclusion of the great anacoluthon of v. 22 f. It is this finding, so unexpected to any who might have interpreted too narrowly the vocabulary between v. 6 and v. 23, which (explained by quotations from Hosea, vv. 25–26, and from Isaiah, vv. 27–29) forms the final and culminating point of the Pauline exposition on the subject of the divine dealing with the elected people Israel. Its pregnant wording obviously says that in God's dealing with the Church too, as the goal towards which His dealing with Israel, as a unique prototype, was directed, and in close correspondence to this dealing, we are concerned with two things. There are called and gathered into the Church not just a few " vessels of mercy," a few Jews who as children of Abraham, as heirs of Israel's distinction and endowment described in vv. 4–5, seem to have the exclusive claim to this and to justify this claim by their faith. No, called and gathered with them and justified by the same faith there is a whole abundance of manifest " vessels of wrath," a horde from among the Gentiles, from the realm of Moab and Ammon, of Egypt and Assyria—the very realm into which the whole of that hardened Israel (beginning with Ishmael and ending with the kings and people of Samaria but ultimately also with the Davidic kings and Jerusalem itself) seems to be thrust out by God's harsh dealing with His elected people. On the ground of the divine calling, says v. 24, the former and the latter together form the Church, vessels of mercy at the end and goal of the history of Israel, witnesses to the resurrection of Jesus Christ, recipients and instruments of the Holy Spirit, possessors of the " riches of the glory " of God (v. 23). The miracle of the Church consists not only in the fact that now when the history of Israel comes to its conclusion with the betrayal of its Messiah and the destruction of Jerusalem a few of this Israel subsequently repent and believe ; that Abraham may again beget an Isaac from the now lifeless womb of Sarah (Rom. 4¹⁹) ; that Jacob and his people, wakened in these few from the dead, receive a new life. The miracle of the Church does consist in this too. Paul himself, as is well known, has with particular, proud thanksgiving made the most of his membership of this Israel (of the lost and yet preserved tribe of the Benjamin who was dear to Jacob above his brethren, Rom. 11¹, Phil. 3⁵) plucked like a brand from the burning. The existence of Christian Jews as a sign of the indestructible continuity of the divine way, as an immediate reminder of the awakening of Lazarus, or rather of the awakening of the man Jesus from the dead, will always remain a special sign of grace. And only a cheerless, unspiritual way of thinking can occasion a Christian Jew to be ashamed of his origin from Israel or a Gentile Christian to hold it against him. It is a mark of supreme and indelible honour to be a Christian Jew. But the miracle of the Church does not consist only in the fact that there were and are Jews who finally come to believe, i.e., to know the God of Israel who has taken away from it all its sins. Over and above this it consists also in the fact that Gentiles, many Gentiles, were and are called to the same faith in the God of Israel, an abundance of men from the nations beside and around Israel, from the nations who as such are not elected, who as such have no part in its promise, distinction and endowment, to whom its Messiah is a complete stranger. They, too, were certainly men living on God's earth, His creation, and in the sphere of His rule. As their history impinged upon Israel's, they had stepped repeatedly into the light of the divine work and at times also of the divine promise. Yet they had, as a rule, served only as the dark foil to Israel's history. Israel's sanctification was always its separation from them. Israel's grace was always its preservation from their might and hostility. Israel's distinction was always its discrimination from them. That God loved Israel always seemed to mean that He did not love the nations as such, but let them go their own ways, let them share in His work for the most part only as instruments of His wrath against Israel. Every exception only confirmed the rule that Israel was elected, the nations were not. They did not seem to have either a positive or negative share in God's mercy even in the shape of that " hardening " (v. 18) as " vessels of dishonour " (v. 21) or of " wrath "—and they certainly did not seem to have any claim to a share in the glory of God. Or must this picture be radically corrected ? Did the juxtaposition of Israel and the nations in the sphere of the Old Testament always have a different meaning ? Had the exceptions signalised the true rule ? Is it not rather the case that God did not really concern Himself incidentally with the nations only for the sake of Israel, but that He concerned Himself in such a special way with Israel for the sake of the nations ? Is it not that the special calling of Israel was only the veiling of the divine calling of man and this veiling only the preparation for its unveiling to all peoples as the calling of God's community affecting the whole cosmos ? Is it not that the promise given to Israel was the promise for every man who believes ? From the standpoint of the end and goal of Israel's history the relationship can obviously be seen and understood in no other way. For here in the Church the few from the elected people are accompanied by the many from the non-elected peoples, called along with the former, and children of Abraham like them by faith in Abraham's promise. How does this come about ? What have the Gentiles to do with Israel's Messiah ? Fundamentally and in complete objectivity only what is revealed in the figure of Pontius Pilate. To them He is delivered up by Israel itself to be put to death and after their miscarriage of justice and by their hands He is, in fact, put to death. They thus execute at one and the same time the decisions both of the evil will of Israel and of the gracious will of God with Israel. It is in this way and this way alone that at the eleventh hour they participate concretely in the fulfilment of Israel's hope. But for all that it is soon enough for one of them to be able to utter immediately after Jesus' death the first unambiguous confession of faith and sin : Ἀληθῶς οὗτος ὁ ἄνθρωπος υἱὸς θεοῦ ἦν (Mk. 15³⁹). The Gentiles have taken the last step on the long road of Israel's history, and with the confession of the Gentiles it now begins anew even before the apostles are awakened to the life of the new and true Israel by the resurrection of Jesus Christ and the outpouring of the Holy Spirit. Thus the death of Jesus unites what was divided, the elected and the rejected. Immediately before this it is said (Mk. 15³⁸) that the veil between the holy of holies and the forecourt of the temple " was rent in twain from the top to the bottom." As Israel's hope is annihilated it is reinstated ; the Church, the secret substance of Israel, is already born ; and what happened on Easter morning can only establish the birth of the Church in the blood of Israel's Messiah, in whom the Gentiles once " without Christ, aliens from the commonwealth of Israel, and strangers from the covenants of promise, having no hope, and without God in the world," (Eph. 2¹²) are " fellow-heirs " and members " of the same body " and " partakers with them " of the promise (Eph. 3⁶). " For he is our peace, who hath made both one, and hath broken down the middle wall of partition, the enmity in his flesh . . . for to make in himself of twain one new man . . . and that he might reconcile both unto God in one body by the cross, having slain the enmity thereby " (Eph. 2¹⁴ᶠ·). " Through him we both—

not only from the Jews but also from the Gentiles—have access by one Spirit unto the Father " (Eph. 2¹⁸). That this is so is (Eph. 3¹⁰) the work of the mystery of the πολυποίκιλος σοφία τοῦ θεοῦ which even the angels have to learn only in view of the Christian Church and which forms the central content of the apostolic, the New Testament message, of the Word of God's mercy realised in judgment.

What is the point of the surprising assertion in v. 24 that the Church is called from both Jews and Gentiles ? The opinion of Peterson (*op. cit.*, p. 36 f.) cannot be sustained, that there lies hidden " behind this insignificant copula the whole tragedy and pathos of the unbelieving Synagogue," and that the Scripture quotations following in v. 25 breathe " something of the divine bitterness." For what does this tell us ? The question at issue in the whole context is surely that of the righteousness of God's mysterious guidance of Israel from the very first and in the present, and therefore of the meaning of the divine bitterness which Israel had and still has to experience, the meaning, too, of the " tragedy and pathos " in which the Synagogue confronts the Church. And this question was answered in vv. 22–24 with the insight that all the wrath of God upon the one Israel is always co-ordinated with His mercy upon another Israel which He was preparing within the first to cause it finally to arise from it in the form of the Church. If according to v. 24 the Church is now called from both Jews *and* Gentiles, this casts over the past and present of Israel, not new shadow, but a new, surpassing light. The sin of Israel, which in past and present stands under the wrath of God, will be discussed separately in 9³⁰ to 10²¹, but only after the question of God's righteousness with respect to Israel has been (independently) met. The answer of 9¹⁴ is that God's righteousness in the history of Israel consists in the fact that He willed to manifest and has actually manifested in this people His mercy (not without His judgment). It is precisely this which is revealed in the miracle of the existence of the Church gathered from Jews and Gentiles as it is asserted in v. 24. Thus the assertion of v. 24, in its connexion with vv. 22–23, is intended to assist the decisive insight that every accusation to be made in the manner of vv. 14, 19, 20 against the God who deals with Israel as the potter with the clay is irrelevant because even in the course of His wrath the God of Israel does not cease to show mercy, because He shows wrath in order all the more fully and decisively to show mercy. Who, then, can dispute with God ? But to what extent does this particular assertion serve this insight ? According to the Old Testament explanation which now follows in vv. 25–29, it does so in a twofold way.

In so far as it speaks of the calling of the Gentiles, v. 24 proves, according to vv. 25–26, the absolute superiority and triumphant power of the mercy towards men revealed in Jesus Christ at the goal and end of Israel's history. The sayings in Hos. 2²⁵ and 2¹ which Paul quotes here speak of a people which once was " not my people " (because it was addressed in this way, because it was, therefore, expressly rejected by God), but was then called " my people " by the same God. They speak of an unloved one whom He calls His beloved. At the very place where the judgment, " Ye are not my people " was declared, they are called " the sons of the living God." In both the Hosea passages the people to which this prophecy refers is the people Israel, and particularly the people of Northern Israel characterised and designated in Hos. 1³⁻⁹ as *Lo' Ruḥama, Lo' 'Ammi*, in contrast to Judah as Jezreel. Of this rejected, major part of Israel it is said in Hos. 1¹⁰⁻²¹ : " Yet the number of the children of Israel shall be as the sand of the sea, which cannot be measured nor numbered ; and it shall come to pass in the place where it was said unto them, Ye are not my people, there it shall be said unto them, Ye are the sons of the living God. Then shall the children of Judah and the children of Israel be gathered together, and appoint themselves one head, and they shall come up out of the land ; for great is the day of Jezreel. Say ye unto your brethren, *'Ammi* ; and to your sisters, *Ruḥama.*" And similarly in Hos. 2²¹⁻³³ : " And it shall come to pass in that day I will hear, saith the Lord, I will hear the heavens, and they shall hear the earth ; and the earth shall hear the corn, and the wine and the oil ; and they shall hear Jezreel. And I will sow her unto me in the earth ; and I will have mercy upon *Lo' Ruḥama* ; and I will say to *Lo' 'Ammi, 'Ammi-atha* ! and they shall say, thou art my God." It is to be noted what Paul does when he quotes these passages. It is undoubtedly in the calling of the Gentiles to the Church that he sees the fulfilment of this prophecy of salvation for rejected Northern Israel, the dawn of the great day of Jezreel. The Gentiles, the believers from the nations, from the great darkness surrounding the people of Yahweh, were *Lo' Ruḥama* and *Lo' 'Ammi* in quite a different way from the rejected Northern tribes, and now even these Gentiles have heard the appeal and summons that makes all things new : My people, the sons of the living God. So wide is the sweep of prophecy! So supreme, so triumphant at the goal and end of Israel's history, is the deed of God's mercy announced by Hosea! So great is the miracle of the revelation of glory towards which all things there were striving! But we must not apply negatively against Israel Paul's indication of this overflowing fulfilment of prophecy in the calling of the Gentiles to the Church, as if the Hosea quotations were meant to say : " What was there prophesied for rejected Israel has now passed into fulfilment, not for it, but in its stead for the believing Gentiles. It no longer applies to them." On the contrary, the tenor of the statement is positive. To it, to rejected Israel there was given there the prophecy of God's repentance fulfilled in the calling of the Gentiles, of His mercy that surpasses His wrath, of His Yes that follows His No. It is the *Lo' Ruḥama* which is one day to be addressed as *Ruḥama*, the *Lo' 'Ammi* which is one day to be addressed, and has already been addressed, as *'Ammi*. When Paul states that he sees the prophecy concerning Northern Israel fulfilled in the calling of the Gentiles we have to do with a conclusion *a maiori ad minus*. If God's mercy is so rich and powerful even upon Gentiles who were standing wholly under His curse and sentence of rejection, how much more so upon those to whom He has already promised it ! Indeed we must even read and understand the Hosea quotations quite simply as a repetition of the prophecy originally—and as established by its comprehensive fulfilment, definitively—addressed to *Israel*, namely to that other, *rejected* Israel. In the course of speaking of the calling of the Gentiles they speak—and now that this has become event, they speak no less but all the more strictly—of the future of this rejected Israel. Admittedly they too, like the passages from Genesis and Exodus quoted earlier, speak of the vessels of wrath and dishonour in which the history of Israel is uncannily rich. Of the twelve tribes, ten are in Hosea already assigned quite summarily to this side. So they, too, speak of the riddle of the Synagogue, of the elected people which can only be called *Lo' Ruḥama, Lo' 'Ammi*. They speak of it, however, in such a way as to keep before it as such the word of grace which applies to it, too, and in it to promise a future that will not be the work of God's wrath but of His mercy which applies to Israel also. This future of the lost people *Israel* already become present in the calling of the Gentiles justifies the God of Israel even as the God of Ishmael and Esau, even as the God of Pharaoh. The God who has given this promise precisely to the rejected among His elected people, and who has fulfilled this promise in the ten times rejected who had never been His elected people, cannot possibly be accused, but in view of the miracle of His mercy can only be praised, for His faithfulness and wisdom. Israel has only to recognise this miracle and hold to it as the consolation given to it, as the picture of its own future, and it will have no more occasion for complaints about the unrighteousness of God.

But the assertion of v. 24 serves the apprehension of the righteousness of God in His mercy in still another way. V. 24 does indeed speak also of the calling of the Jews and thus proves, according to vv. 27–29, that what has been revealed in Jesus Christ at the goal and end of Israel's history is divine mercy and not human merit, grace and not nature, freedom and not necessity. How otherwise can it be the righteousness of God, or any kind of righteousness at all ? How otherwise can we take heart from what has been revealed here ? The quotations from Is. 10²²f· and 1⁹ are meant to prove this aspect of the matter. It is to be noted that these passages also speak of God's steadfastly continuing grace towards Israel. The first passage in its context runs : " And it shall come to pass in that day that the remnant of Israel, and such as are escaped of the house of Jacob, shall no more again stay upon him that smote them ; but shall stay upon the Lord, the Holy One of Israel, in truth. The remnant shall return, even the remnant of Jacob, unto the mighty God. For though thy people Israel be as the sand of the sea, yet a remnant of them shall return : the consumption decreed shall overflow with righteousness. For the Lord God of hosts shall make a consumption, even determined, in the midst of the land. Therefore thus saith the Lord God of hosts, O my people that dwellest in Zion, be not afraid of the Assyrian : he shall smite thee with a rod, and shall lift up his staff against thee, after the manner of Egypt. For yet a very little while, and the indignation shall cease, and mine anger in their destruction " (Is. 10²⁰⁻²⁵). And the second passage forms a reassuring conclusion to the opening complaint and accusation of the book against a people which in spite of every punishment and distress continues in apostasy : " The daughter of Zion is left as a cottage in a vineyard, as a lodge in a garden of cucumbers, as a besieged city. Except the Lord of hosts had left unto us a very small remnant, we should have been as Sodom, and we should have been like unto Gomorrah " (Is. 1⁸⁻⁹). The special point given to this promise of grace is clear. It has less regard than that of Hosea to the future of all Israel and more to its present in individuals. It speaks of the remnant of Israel that remains, of its preservation and its future as such. It is just this remnant as such that Paul has before his eyes in the Jews of whose calling to the Church v. 24 speaks. In them as in the believing Gentiles prophecy has come to its fulfilment. Isaiah has " foretold " (v. 29) their existence as the existence of a " remnant." That it is only a remnant is stressed in neither of the Isaiah passages nor is it to be stressed according to what Paul has in mind. The decisive thing here, too, is the positive aspect. The matter at issue is Israel, which in spite of its apostasy is saved from merited ruin and brought by a miracle to conversion ; which is, in fact, being converted. It is not because it is Israel that it may live on as Israel, but because as Israel it is saved by its God, preserved amid the rising tide of consumption and decision. Otherwise it would almost have become like Sodom and Gomorrah. It was entirely due to God, to His gracious reversal of His purpose, that it did not become like Sodom and Gomorrah, but that, like Lot, it was delivered from destruction, that it was given a place of repentance. Thus the calling of the Jews to the Church is also to be understood as the plucking of a brand from the burning (Amos 4¹¹, Zech. 3²)—how much more so, then, the calling of the Gentiles ! It is obvious that in their case above all it is a case of sheer divine deliverance. Over the whole face of the earth there flows the tide of the divine consumption and decision. The conclusion this time is *a minori ad maius*. If even for the rich Jews, according to the prophecy fulfilled in them, absolutely everything depends on God's wonderful mercy, how much more so for the poor Gentiles ! Even the Jews as they rely on the profoundest consolation promised to them as Jews can recognise in their calling only mercy and not merit, only God's grace and not human nature, only creative freedom and not creaturely necessity. It is their mission in the Church—that of believing Jews—to keep this insight clear. But the juxtaposition of converted and unconverted Jews, the splitting up of Israel into Church and Synagogue, can only underline and deepen the insight to the extent that in this very juxtaposition it is actual and visible that the end and aim of all God's ways, His ways with Jews as with Gentiles, is the act of His free mercy. And retrospectively from this point we have to say that Israel's mission as a preparation for the Church and its prefiguration consists in the fact that it has always to exist as this remnant which is saved and to be saved again, as the spared σπέρμα, as the LXX translated Is. 1⁹, and as it was undoubtedly understood by Paul with concrete reference to the " seed " of Abraham who is also the " root of David " (Rev. 22¹⁶). Israel lives by the grace of God, and living in this way it is identical with the offspring for whose sake it was chosen, and in turn identical with all who believe in this offspring, with the totality of those who will be called to faith in this offspring. In this mission of Israel, and ultimately in this its identity with Jesus Christ and His Church, lies the justification of God with respect to what He has willed and done, and still wills and does, with this people.

3. THE PROMISE OF GOD HEARD AND BELIEVED

In the eternal election of the one man Jesus of Nazareth, God makes Himself a witness to the covenant which He has decided to establish between Himself and man, to the judgment and mercy in which He has turned to man. The purpose of the election of this One is God's will that in and through this One man should come to hear His self-witness as the promise, pledge and assurance which is valid for his own life too, and that in faith he should relate to himself what is spoken to him in the person of this One, accepting its truth and actuality for himself, relying on it, living by the fact that it is said to him.

The elected community of God, as the environment of the elected man Jesus of Nazareth, is the place where God's honour dwells, i.e., where this Jesus is revealed as God's promise in person, where this Jesus is heard, where He is believed, where in Him and by Him it comes about, therefore, that God's self-witness, the declaration of His good-will and work for man, finds a hearing and faith. The community is elected in relation to the whole world (as representatives of Jesus Christ and the deed of divine judgment and mercy accomplished in Him) in order to serve the divine promise that awaits the hearing and faith of man. The whole community—Israel and the Church—is elected in this way and appointed to this service, as certainly as it is elected in Jesus Christ, as certainly as it owes to Him its existence, its unity and the differentiation of its two forms. Wherever it lives, it always lives in the service of the divine self-witness which man is permitted to hear and is called to believe.

The special service of Israel within the totality of the elected community consists, however, in the hearing, the reception and the acceptance of the divine promise. Israel is the community of God in so far as the Word of God's grace reaches it. If Israel becomes obedient to its election by rising to life in the Church, its special contribution to the fulfilment of the mission of the community within the totality will be again and again to make room for pure readiness to accept the

Word spoken by God, for humble attention to the fact that it is spoken to man, for close attention to what is said to him—in distinction from and contrast to all that man can say and would like to say to himself. The Church needs this contribution. The promise certainly does not continue to be God's self-witness where it does not continue to be understood as a Word addressed to man. It cannot be believed without being heard. Faith itself can only be the perfect, obedient and active hearing of the Word of God. Witness cannot be borne to Jesus Christ, which is the Church's task, before He has been heard and is continually heard as the divine self-witness in person. It is for just this reason that the Israelite (Jewish) regard for sentence, word and letter must continue in the Church, that it must not on any account be changed and lost in free speculation. A Church that becomes antisemitic or even only a-semitic sooner or later suffers the loss of its faith by losing the object of it. In the same measure in which it tries to tell itself that it must believe, and what it must believe, it has nothing more to say to the world. In the measure in which it becomes autonomous and self-willed, it ceases to be the Church. The Church has every reason to see that Israel's special service in the community is not interrupted but faithfully continued.

The Israelite form of the community of God reveals that when in His eternal election of grace God elects fellowship with man He has Himself assumed in relation to man the indestructible position of Leader, Disposer and Giver. He does not choose the free, the wise and the rich. On the contrary, it is He who makes those whom He elects free, wise and rich by electing them. He chooses for Himself the existence-form of the *Word* which reaches them, which instructs them from the very roots, which first of all summons and awakens them, which reconciles them to Himself before any co-operation on their part. He chooses to be and to live for them by coming to them in His promise and remaining with them in His promise. He chooses to make Himself heard by them. This is what God elects for Himself when in the most radical accomplishment of His fellowship with man He elects to be man Himself in the person of the Son of Abraham, electing the people of Israel in order to acknowledge its flesh and blood as His own. It is the humanity of the whole community of God which is revealed in its Israelite form—and over and above that the humanity of man in himself and as such with which God has concluded the eternal covenant. Man can only follow God ; but he may follow Him. He can only be subject to Him ; but he may be subject to Him. Above all, then, he can only listen to Him ; but he may listen to Him. Such is his humanity, which also and primarily is the fundamental order for the positing of the community in relation to God. The content of the promise (that it speaks of God's mercy ruling in His judgment) is established by the formal fact that there is no reversal or even dissolution of the relationship between the One from whom it comes and the one to whom it is addressed. This is attested by Israel's crucified Messiah, who has appeared not in the form of a king but of a servant. And this is what the whole elected community of God has now also to attest in His service. It is as such the community which hears God, in virtue of the fact that it is the community of Israel's Messiah, and has accordingly an Israelite form as well, and that even in its Church form it is Israel that reaches its determined goal and may live on. As it believes, the community also indicates to the world and to all men that they are determined for hearing, and therefore that they must first hear, because God is and has and keeps the Word, and because man only becomes man as he hears what God has to say to him. When Israel in faith is obedient to its election it then becomes the pledge in the Church that this formal condition of the community's message is, and will continue to be, fulfilled.

God's aim and purpose with Israel undoubtedly consists, then, in the fact that it takes up and discharges this special service, and there-fore—being merged in the Church—attests the unity of the com-munity in its differentiation. It consists, then, in the fact that it passes from hearing to believing. But while this is true, God does not wait for Israel's faith before claiming it for this service. For this service is determined and effected with Israel's election quite irrespec-tive of the attitude that Israel takes up towards it. The attitudes taken up by elected Israel are as such a fulfilment of its determination which in any case is its determination for this service. Whether it attains to faith in God's promise or not, it cannot in any event deny, but must in every case confess, that it has heard it. There can be no evading the " Hear, O Israel." Israel *is* a hearer of the promise. As such it must and will always bear witness to Jesus Christ, to His election, to its own election, but also to that of the Church.

If it were to believe and therefore to be obedient to its election, this would mean that in and with the Church it could hear properly and perfectly what is said to it. Without encroaching on the Church as such, it could then really be Israel *in* the Church. And it would always be its special honour repeatedly to warn and strengthen the Church by reminding it of the divine address which founds and maintains the community of God. It would then be precisely Israel (the " Jewish " element) in the Church which by its special contribution would see to it that the Church remains the Church. As things are, however, Israel as such and on the whole is not obedient to its election. The promise to which it owes its existence and preservation becomes a fulfilled promise. The Word becomes flesh. God speaks through the death and resurrection of Jesus Christ in confirmation of all that He has said from the first. And there is no doubt that Israel hears ; now less than ever can it shelter behind the pretext of ignorance and inability to understand. But Israel hears—and does not believe. This means, however, that it refuses to hear properly and perfectly and therefore to relate to itself what is said to it, to rely on it, and to be willing to live by the fact that God's mercy is promised to it. Precisely at this decisive point it listens inattentively and inaccurately. It hears the promise and lives with it as if its content were not God's mercy but were still God's judgment upon all men, as if it called on man to provide himself the presuppositions for its fulfilment, as if it assured man of a claim to its fulfilment by requiring this provision. It thinks that it can and ought to put itself into the right relationship to God. Through sheer zealous activity it fails to hear and do the one thing it would have to do if it heard willingly. It thus places itself in a vacuum. It besmirches its honour at the very moment when, if only it would believe, it would at last shine out. It jeopardises by its failure the existence of the one community of God which cannot do without it.

But its stopping short on the way from hearing to believing the promise cannot alter the fact that even in this rigidity it is the people of Jesus Christ. The electing God and the elected community embrace even this Israel which steps into the void. It must carry out the service assigned to it even when it falls a prey to this rigidity. Over against the believing witness of the Church, it can now only represent how things are with hearing man as such—the infertile path, the stones and thistles and thorns of the field on which the seed of the Word falls ; the beginning without continuation, the present without future, the question without answer, the missed opportunity. It brings punishment upon itself. But it cannot give the lie to its God. It cannot evade the service for which it is determined. It cannot make itself sterile for God. Ahasuerus, too, is in his own way a witness of Jesus Christ. Though at the decisive point he hears the promise inattentively and inaccurately and therefore quite perversely, yet he does hear it. Though by it he hears of death for himself, yet he hears also the promise which is spoken over a field full of dead bones. Though he hears without believing, yet he undoubtedly hears Him whom he as well as all other men—and he first of all—*could* believe, the only One in whom one can and must believe. As a hearer of the Word he is, at all events, unbelieving in the right place. Where are the world and the Church to learn by whom and for whom Jesus Christ was crucified, and why He had to be crucified, if not—apart from the risen One Himself—from the Synagogue which hears the Word and yet for and in all its hearing is still unbelieving ? Does not even Jewish obduracy and melancholy, even Jewish caprice and phantasy, even the Jewish cemetery at Prague—because all this is bound up with the sterile hearing but yet with the hearing of God's Word—still contain objectively and effectively more genuine Gospel than all the unbelieving wisdom of the *Goyim* put together, and a good part of what is supposed to be believing Christian theory and practice into the bargain ? If this witness passes unobserved it is so much the worse for the world and for the Church, but no disproof of the fact that witness—witness of Jesus Christ—is actually being given.

And this disobedience of Israel cannot alter in the very least the content and scope of the divine promise itself. Israel suffers under this disobedience. The promise, however, suffers no harm at all because it is only heard and not believed by Israel. Israel cannot by any breach of the covenant annul the covenant of mercy which God has established between himself and man. It cannot by its own unfaithfulness turn God's faithfulness into its opposite. It cannot nullify the eternal benefit offered to it in God's Word ; its credibility, its consolation, its summons or its hope. Even with regard to stubborn Israel the promise remains what it is, God's irrevocable and irrefutable self-witness to which man can, to his hurt, refuse faith, but which he cannot by any unbelief change into a message of woe. Nor can Israel do anything to alter the fact that this promise is given and applies to itself, that in and with the election of Jesus Christ it and no other is God's elected people, and that in and with the man Jesus it is the sphere in which God wills to make His promise true—that God expects faith from it, and again that He is waiting to make its faith fruitful in good works of special obedience and to crown it with peace and joy. It cannot prevent the emergence from its own midst of the One who is at once the author and the object of faith, in whom hearing becomes perfect, and in and with Him of the Church as the people of such as are not only hearers but in faith doers of the Word also. It cannot resign from God's community nor do anything to prevent the sound of its voice reaching not only the ears of all the world but its own ears also in the believing witness of the Church. It can resist the gracious favour of God, but it cannot turn it into disfavour, neither in principle nor in practice, neither in itself, nor with respect to the service it owes it, nor indeed with respect to the fact that this grace is directed to itself. It cannot infringe on God so deeply that He ceases to be God, or even to be its God.

In the perfect form of the one elected community of God the service of the Church consists, quite irrespective of Israel's attitude, in the fact that it secures attention for the promise heard by putting faith in it. The Church is in existence wherever the promise finds faith—among both Jews and Gentiles—by creating faith for itself. Faith means putting one's confidence in God's mercy as it is attested to man— both Jew and Gentile—by God Himself in His promise. It is a question of the essential, absolute and total confidence which no one assumes on his own but which is founded for every one on the fact that in the awakening of Christ from the dead God has revealed and turned to man His own glory. It is thus a question of the confidence awakened by God in which man—whether Jew or Gentile—may rely on God as the One who has made, and does and will make, everything right for him. It is a question of the confidence in which man has

Jesus as Lord. The service of the Church is that as it hears the promise it awakens to this faith, lives in this faith and attests this faith to the whole world as the temporal doing of God's good-will with man that prepares for its eternal fulfilment. The Church discharges this service in so far as it has heard the promise and continues to hear it, in so far, then, as Israel's service is also done and continues in its midst. But to this extent Israel also discharges it, that is, to the extent that the Church also lives in it; that the Church arises from it and remains in need of its special auxiliary service; that it is its own determination which finds its fulfilment in the form of the Church; that it is in and from its midst also that the step from hearing to believing is taken. Israel lives when it accomplishes this step, when its hearing rises to life as faith, when it itself rises to life in the Church as its crucified Messiah rises to life in His resurrection as the Lord of the Church. It has, therefore, a redemptive part in the service of the community, a redemptive part in its appointed task with regard to the world. It should not elect its own destruction by electing in relation to the Church and its own service—which for all its defiance it cannot evade—an impotent self-assertion, a mere hearing that refuses faith.

The Church form of the community of God reveals that when God elects man for communion with Himself in His eternal election of grace He promotes him to the indestructible position of His child and brother, His intimate and friend. What God is, He wills to be for man also. What belongs to Him He wills to communicate to man also. What He can do is meant to benefit man also. No one and nothing is to be so close to man as He. No one and nothing is to separate him from Him. And in fellowship with Him every need of man is to be met; he is to be refreshed, exalted and glorified far beyond all need. This, indeed, is what is allotted to him in the promise fulfilled in the resurrection of Jesus Christ. This is what man—whether Jew or Gentile—may lay hold of and relate to himself by faith in this promise. By this he can nourish himself and live in faith. It is always this inexpressible gift that he expects and receives when he is called and awakened to faith. And it is always this that God's community can reveal in its final and Church form. It reveals that God's promise demands so imperatively to be heard only in order to be believed by men, to their own salvation and peace. As it believes the promise it reveals that God counts it a matter of honour to remember man and be his present help. If we are bidden to hear Him as the Leader, the Disposer and Giver, in that very fact we are all the more bidden to entrust ourselves in faith to His care, to have confidence in what He ordains, to accept and make fruitful His gift. All this is attested by the Lord of the Church risen as the reflection of the divine glory, by the faith of the man Jesus rewarded and crowned according to the promise. And all this is what the whole elected community of God has now to attest in His service. It hears His voice and believes in Him as the fulfilled promise of God. It genuinely and accurately hears what God says when it believes in Jesus Christ. In the fact that it believes it is itself the fulfilled promise of God.

The Church is the perfect form of the community to the extent that the latter's unity and mission are revealed in it. As the Church, the community (the environment of the man Jesus) is the centre and medium of communication between Jesus and the world, having its commission to all who still stand outside. For in faith Jesus wills to be accepted by His own ; through the faith of His own He wills to make Himself heard in the world ; and it is to faith again that those who are still outside are to be called by His own. But this brings us right up against the pre-existent Church in Israel. Faith and therefore the Church is already the goal and ground of Israel's election. And accordingly God's promise has not only been heard in Israel but also from time to time it has been already believed, and all that it promises to man has already been apprehended, experienced and lived within Israel. God has already had His children and brothers, His intimates and friends in Israel. The history of the special mercy of God towards Israel is simultaneously and as such the history of the faith which could encounter this mercy. In this special history occurring in and from it, Israel, too, is a believing witness and a participator in the perfect form of the community, a participator in its function and mission with respect to the world.

The Church of faith in God's promise, as it pre-exists in Israel and ultimately arises from it, is the positive confirmation of its election. In Israel to believe means specifically to become obedient to the election of Israel, a voluntary doer of the word of promise given to Israel. And so, conversely, every specific election in Israel is election to *believe*, to trust in God's mercy in judgment. The determination of Israel as such and as a whole is not, of course, altered by the particular existence of believers in and from it. But it receives from it its light ; its teleology is revealed. The promise wills to be heard in order to be believed. In this sense, in the directing of the obedience required of Israel towards the goal of faith, Israel's contribution to the work of the whole elected community must be and will be maintained.

The exception of the few believers in Israel does not cancel the rule according to which Israel as a whole hears and does not believe and is thus disobedient to its election. Even these few are only partially and temporarily to be claimed as believers, and over against them there stand out with equal prominence and in express confirmation of that rule the great mass of the impenitent in face of whom their number seems steadily to decrease. It is possible, therefore, to call them only the prefiguration of the Church which emerges in and with the resurrection of Jesus Christ ; a prefiguration which can be seen only from the standpoint of this its future. The reality of the pre-existent Church in Israel consists in the repeated occurrence in Israel's history of that hearing of God's Word which from the standpoint of the end and goal of that history in the person of Jesus can be understood only as faith, only as a prevision and prophecy of the proper and exact hearing of the Church—or not at all.

The Church of faith in God's promise as founded on the resurrection of Jesus does not have at this point the choice of understanding or refusing to understand. It believes in God's mercy. It therefore reckons with its efficacy. It therefore has keen eyes for even the most obscure and confused traces of it. It therefore sees the light that is shed on Israel's history. It will therefore recognise its own faith in the special hearing of these few in and from Israel and in them the fellow-elect of God. And it will not evade the insight that the existence of these few establishes positively the election of all Israel and therefore its membership of God's community. It will apply this insight with respect to Jewish Christians in its own midst. And, above all, it will have and keep clearly in mind that its own existence as the Church can be possible and legitimate only on the foundation of Israel, only—Gentiles must take special note of this—on the presupposition of the hearing of the promise. It must be aware that the condition by which it stands or falls is that on this foundation (unlike Israel as such and on the whole) it does not merely make a pretence of believing but really believes what it hears from God, and thus becomes for the world and Israel the living testimony for which it is determined. It waits for Israel's conversion. But it has to precede Israel with the confession of the faith required from it as from Israel and offered to Israel as to it, and therefore with the confession of the unity of the community of God.

It is certainly not by chance that Rom. 9^{30} takes the same form as the question of 9^{14}. " What shall we say then ? Is there unrighteousness with God ? " was the question asked at that point. And we are now given what is so obviously the correct answer in view of the enigmatic dual existence of Israel as Isaac and Ishmael, as Jacob and Esau, as Moses and Pharaoh, as the Church and the Synagogue. This answer follows naturally from the recognition of the goal of the history of Israel as it was described in vv. 22–24 by a reference to the formation and existence of the Church of Jews and Gentiles. In this goal two things have become event and revelation. For one thing the Gentiles who were not pursuing the righteousness of God, whose willing and running was not in any sense directed to the fulfilment and doing of the merciful will of God, who did not know anything at all of this will of God, let alone have any power to assent to it and make it their own, have apprehended this very will of God and can now live precisely by and with this will of God. What is the point at issue ? It is righteousness, i.e., the merciful will of God which is fulfilled in the appearance and the death of the Messiah, Jesus, and has revealed itself in His resurrection in order from and by faith in Him to become so palpable for every man that everyone can live, actually live, by and with Him. No ancestry made the Gentiles worthy of it ; no endowment fitted them for it ; no historical path led to the point at which one day they believed in Jesus and in this faith actually apprehended the righteousness of God. Without being able to perceive, they have perceived ; without being able to assent they have assented ; without being able to trust they have trusted. They have simply done it, without presupposition, without preparation, without pre-history. That " calling " (v. 24) occurred, and they obeyed it in the freedom of the dead who are awakened from their graves. It did not depend on their willing and running ; it depended on God's mercy. This is obviously what we have to say about the history of Isaac, Jacob and Moses, viewing it in retrospect. In this way and this alone did these, too, become the genuine heirs and bearers of the promise. And this is what is to be said to-day about the existence of the whole Church. It is in all its members, together with Isaac and Jacob and Moses, the gathering of those who have received and accepted the call, who, in faith in Him from whom this call goes out and of whom it speaks, have found life. In this gathering all confidence in one's own willing and running, in the power of human pursuit, has collapsed, but just because of this so has every doubt of God's righteousness as well. God's righteousness is indeed His mercy, and it is just this which triumphs in this process. This gathering of the incapable and the unworthy, a gathering from graves, the gathering to faith, is one of the things which has become event and revelation at the goal of Israel's history.

The other thing (v. 31 f.) is, of course, that Israel (it is the overwhelming majority of Israel that is meant, Israel with the exception of a few who attained to faith with the Gentiles just referred to) certainly pursued the law of righteousness. In all its willing and running it was intent on the maintenance and fulfilment of the order of a life under the promise, on the Torah and the temple, on the purity and holiness of the existence of the chosen people, on the preservation, fostering and development of its tradition. But then, after all, it came short not only of the righteousness of God, not only of the merciful will of God Himself which this Law signified, but along with its meaning and content it actually came short of and broke even the Law itself, desecrating the temple, destroying the purity and holiness of Israel and denying the tradition. This Israel described in v. 31 f., unlike the Gentiles mentioned in v. 30, lacked neither the presupposition, preparation nor pre-history of its salvation, nor the willing and running corresponding to all this. It had the Law and was intent on doing justice to it. In so far as this is the case, we cannot accuse it of a " misdirected purpose " (Lietzmann). " They have a zeal of God," Paul will say in 10^2 in express confirmation. If, then, the possession of the Law does not help after all, if after all it comes short of the Law itself, this is due to the fact that all that it has can be its living possession only in relationship to Him who is the meaning of it all, only in the apprehension of the divine mercy that attests itself in it all. It is due to the fact that the Law itself can be kept and fulfilled only in this relationship and apprehension, i.e., only in faith. But this was precisely what this Israel lacked. According to v. 32a it did not lack the works appropriate to its mission and endowment. But it did lack the work of all works, the one work which is fundamentally and decisively required in and with all works required in the Law. It lacked the relevant relationship to the meaning and goal of its special mission and endowment. What it lacked was that it did not want to rely on the promise, on the mercy of God, but on itself, on its own willing and running in the direction of the promised fulfilment ; that it sought by its own willing and running to bring about the fulfilment of what was promised. Therefore, having all, it lacked all. It lacked all just because there was no lack of human purpose at the point where nothing but submissive recognition of the divine purpose could be adequate to what it had, to the Law. The omission of the one work of faith required of it is Israel's transgression of the Law. It was in this that, according to vv. 32b–33 it stumbled, being broken to pieces and destroyed on the stone and rock which, according to Is. 28^{16}, constitutes the centre of Zion, the foundation of all its temple cultus and service of the Law, of the whole life of the holy people as such. All building must be grounded on this if it is not to be demolition. All standing must be on this if it is to be real standing and not mere staggering to a fall. This stone and rock, Israel's foundation and support, is God's free mercy which wills to be apprehended as a promise, the fulfilment of which is according to its content to be looked for from God alone, and towards which, therefore, it is impossible to push on by means of any human willing and running. Israel's foundation and support wills to be believed as such. Even when it is not, it does not cease, of course, to be the stone and rock, the presupposition of Israel's history, laid down by God and therefore unshakeable. But it is turned against Israel. The stone becomes for it an occasion of stumbling and offence. Israel is necessarily destroyed by its sure salvation. According to Ps. 118, the zealous but negligent builders reject this stone. In all its works Israel omits this one work which in the last resort is the only counterpart of its mission and endowment. All its works, therefore, the temple cultus and service of the Law, become sin and guilt. For all its willing and running it must stand without justification, exactly like the Gentiles who have no such mission and endowment, and in painful contrast to those Gentiles who without any such mission and endowment do the one thing needful, the work of faith that in fact corresponds to the Law of Israel (Rom. $2^{14f.}$, $^{26f.}$) ; who, being found by God's free mercy, give the honour to this mercy and to it alone. This, then, is what has befallen the overwhelming and characteristic majority in Israel. With all its zeal to be Israel, to become worthy of and to participate in its promise, by failing to believe it has failed to do the one thing in which it could be active and attest itself as Israel. In its relation to Jesus Christ (the very One in whom the righteousness, the merciful will of God has so effectively encountered these Gentiles) Israel's transgression of the Law has become event and revelation. By its attitude to Jesus Christ it has proved that it wished to rely on itself, to push on to the fulfilment of the promise by its own willing and running. It has despised and neglected faith, and in so doing it has rejected its promise also, and the order of life under the promise. It has denied and compromised its own existence as God's chosen people. Looking back from this point, what are we to say to the history of Ishmael, Esau and Pharaoh ? From this point, too, we must see confirmation of the fact that (9^{16}) nothing depends on human willing and running, but everything on God's mercy. In this case there is no lack of human willing and running. But in this case, and indeed as the final work of human willing and running, it is unbelief which is revealed and therefore a human guilt which would necessarily exclude God's mercy were the latter not greater than human guilt. The perfection of human willing and running under the very best conditions given man by God Himself, under the sign of a unique presupposition, preparation and pre-history of his salvation, proves only that God's mercy alone can bring and keep together God and man, and thus make man participate in salvation. God's right to deal with this Israel as He has, in fact, dealt with Ishmael, Esau and Pharaoh cannot be doubted in view of what this Israel does and leaves undone. But if God's right with regard also to this Israel is to be and is always the right of His mercy, in view of what this Israel does and leaves undone it cannot be doubted that it is by the right of His mercy alone if any benefit comes to it as it turns this mercy to its own undoing, as its guilt is exposed, as all justification is stripped from it.

The whole passage 10^{1-21} is a development of this second part of the programmatic statement of 9^{30-33} ; an exposition, that is, of 9^{31-33}. It is customary, and not without reason, to characterise its content as a presentation of the particular guilt of Israel. But we must not overlook the practical reference of this presentation. It is to and for the Church of both Jews and Gentiles that the apostle speaks of Israel's guilt. He is speaking of Israel's guilt to the gathering of those who by faith in Jesus Christ are elected and called, justified and sanctified. He does so in order to interpret to them their own election and thus to confirm it in this election, attesting that this election does not depend on their willing or running but on God's mercy, and summoning them to faith as the work corresponding to their election. He does so in order to show them by means of Israel's guilt what even their own supreme and final work can alone be without faith. In face of Israel's guilt he reminds them that Christians above all are what they are solely on the ground of the right of the divine mercy. Their solidarity with Israel is not effaced but established by what is now said " against " Israel. What is said here is not said against Israel but against elected man as such. It is said for the electing God and in this way for the *Israel* which is elected and yet so wholly unfaithful to its election.

That Rom. 10 is to be interpreted in this way follows not only from its continuation in Rom. 11 but from the opening words in 10¹, where Paul, repeating his confession of 9¹⁻⁵, declares that his desires and prayers are not turned away from the Israel which continues the history of Ishmael, Esau and Pharaoh but are directed to it all the more ; that as apostle of the Church he means to be and must be all the more the prophet of Israel, the servant of the God of Abraham, Isaac and Jacob, concerned for its deliverance. He attests to the unhappy members of the Synagogue that they do have a " zeal of God." He thus attests to them that their purpose is already set in the right direction, and indirectly that the right goal already lies before them, that they certainly do know the God of Abraham and Isaac and Jacob and in Him the Father of Jesus Christ, and hear His Word. That they are the people of the true God and that the true God is their God is not effaced by their guilt. It cannot be effaced at all because it is based on God's election. In God's covenant with Israel the Church too will recognise the eternal covenant of God with man as it is ratified in Jesus Christ. And thus it cannot fail to recognise in the zeal of the Jews for their Judaism the determination of man for life in this covenant. Even in its perversity Israel's zeal is no empty, pointless zeal. Even in its ignoring of Jesus Christ it still witnesses to Him as the fulfilled promise of this people. Even in its emptiness as the zeal of unbelief it attests the fulness that has, in fact, eluded it. But indeed—and this is the shadow upon Israel's election, this is the human guilt that must be revealed in this form of the divine election to the glory and praise of the sovereignty of God's mercy—it is only in its perversity, only in its ignoring of Jesus Christ, only in this emptiness, that Jewish zeal can bear this witness. And only with this in view and under the corresponding reservation can this testimony be borne to it : " They have a zeal of God, but not according to knowledge." The object is not lacking, the God of Abraham, Isaac and Jacob. He is the true God ; He is the Father of Jesus Christ and as such the sum of all salvation allotted and offered to man. But (v. 3) they do not recognise Him as such. When it is directed to Him their will is a perverted and warped will. They destroy themselves on the rock of their own salvation promised and offered to them. They do not recognise, that is, the righteousness of this God. They do not recognise it as His mercy. They do not accept this God for what He is, namely, the One who wills and acts for them. They fail to recognise that the very presupposition, preparation and pre-history from which they derive should lead them on to accept everything as His gift. They are reluctant to concede to Him His right to accept and receive them on His own initiative. They are not ready simply to submit to that. They seek instead " to establish their own righteousness," i.e., by their own fulfilment of the order of life under the promise (as if this were not the order of grace which can be obeyed only in faith) to conduct and attest themselves as those who can be worthy of and lay a claim to its fulfilment. They suppose that they can will and act for God and that they ought to do so. They suppose that they can benefit Him in order to win His favour. They expect from their offering of a perfect obedience the divine return of the fulfilment of what is promised to them. In doing this, however, they " have not submitted themselves unto the righteousness of God " but are disobedient. In doing this they find themselves in full rebellion against their own

God, the God of Abraham and Isaac and Jacob. For His promise has as its content only His own work, and its fulfilment cannot be looked for as a return for something but only as His free and gracious disposal. It cannot in any sense be demanded, but only received. What this God says can be accepted only in faith, and what He does can again be received only in faith. If faith is lacking, the Law of this God is transgressed and broken at its central point. And it is transgressed and broken all the more terribly, the more zealously it is read and studied, the more zealously all the works it requires in fulfilment of this one work are done. For then all the attention to it is intended only to veil the inattention at this decisive point. All the works are intended only to veil the neglect of this one work. And yet they cannot veil it but must, in fact, establish it. If faith be lacking, man lacks everything at the very point where, as in the case in Israel, everything is told and given him from the side of God. Lack of faith means that those who are, in fact, on the right way to the right destination lose their way. By trying to establish their own righteousness whilst on the right way to the right destination, they themselves become sinners, and human sin becomes an event and revealed in them in a way that is impossible on other roads to other destinations. It needs God's election, it needs Israel, for man's guilt to become event and to be revealed in this way.

By striving after its own righteousness Israel has, then, broken the Law, become disobedient to the righteousness of God, and thus forfeited the divine justification. But the proof of this, the demonstration of the guilt of the chosen people itself (and therefore indirectly the demonstration of the sole sufficiency of God's mercy with regard to elected man), is first adduced in vv. 4–13 in such a way as to show that Israel is the people whose promise from the very beginning had been Jesus Christ, so that from the very beginning the order under which it had to live could only be that of faith. By endeavouring to establish its own righteousness instead of believing it had to reject Jesus Christ. And by its rejection of Jesus Christ it was made clear that in its endeavours to establish its own righteousness it was refusing faith. But by doing this it did not keep but broke the Law as the order of life under the promise that had become its own, as the determination under which it had to live after its election. By doing this it revealed man as the rebel against the God who elects him, and indirectly, therefore, the mercy of God as the sole sufficient power over against man elected by Him. By doing this it showed—and this is the special function of its election —that elected man is referred wholly and completely to the mercy of the God who elects him, and to faith, the faith in this mercy which is continually to be proclaimed, offered and commanded. Vv. 4–13 make the presuppositions of this demonstration plain.

If in contradiction to the position of the sentence v. 4 were really to be translated "Christ is the end of the law," and if this were to be taken to mean that in and with Christ the Law given to the people of Israel by its God was antiquated, superseded, set aside and abrogated, then not only would the phrase εἰς δικαιοσύνην παντὶ τῷ πιστεύοντι be left hanging very strangely in the air, but this sentence would so disrupt the whole context that it would be as well to abandon the attempt to explain its meaning. Was it not expressly said in 9[31] that it was the Law that Israel came short of in its efforts to keep it ? Was not the reproach made against it in 9[32f.] that the rock laid down in Zion has become for it a stumbling stone ? Has not its zeal for the Law been expressly recognised in 10[1] as a zeal of God ? Is not Paul in the following verses about to argue, not in any sense against the Law, but indeed from the Law. Where in all these chapters (but also in all the rest of the Pauline theology) do we find the slightest indication that the apostle of the Church regarded the Law of Israel as a gift of God cancelled and invalidated by Christ ? It was not to the Law but to an ignorant adoption and application of the Law, to its desecration and misuse through unbelief, that according to vv 2–3 Paul opposed the righteousness of faith. According to the unambiguous statement of Rom. 3³¹ (in harmony with Mt. 5¹⁷) he was not seeking to abrogate the Law by his preaching but to establish it. At most Christ might be called, not the end of the Law, but the end of the sin which according to Rom. 7¹¹ was controlling and making use of the Law. But even this thought does not suit our context, so that our only option is to interpret τέλος νόμου in analogy to (and even perhaps as a translation of) the rabbinic concept of the *kelal* as a comprehensive formula for the manifold content of the Law, as a designation of the common denominator, the sum of all its demands, or ontically as the substance, the be all and end all of the Law, or practically, as its meaning in virtue of which it has authority as law and which is immediately also the way to its fulfilment. The *kelal*, the ἀνακεφαλαίωσις of the Law, says the apostle of the Church in his function as a prophet of Israel, is the Messiah who was promised for the justification of everyone who believes in Him and who has now appeared in fulfilment of the promise. It is with Him and Him alone that the Law is concerned as the order of life under the promise. It is He who interprets this order and fulfils it. It is He who guarantees its validity. To live in obedience under this order means to believe in Him. By refusing to do this, Israel transgresses and breaks its own Law. It fails to recognise the *kelal* of it, and with all its zeal for keeping it in its individual parts, according to 9³¹ it comes short of the whole, the Law as such. It becomes guilty with regard to the one manifestation of the will of its own God, the norm and foundation of its whole existence as Israel from the first. It fails, not with regard to a new revelation, but with regard to the one Word of its God spoken to it and heard by it from the first. It fails with regard to the basis of its election. According to 9³²ᶠ· it is actually wrecked on the corner-stone laid in Zion itself. Therefore its lack of knowledge (vv. 2–3) is not only a misfortune befalling it, but its sin. Hence it is quite impossible to understand (with Peterson, p. 43 f.) the relation between v. 5 and v. 6 f. as if the Jewish and the Christian concepts of righteousness were here opposed to one another, as if here the voice of the " righteousness of faith " were polemically played off against the voice of Moses and the latter proved, as it were, to be false. This is out of the question because in this very passage (v. 6 f.) Paul continually and particularly appeals to the written words of Moses in Deut. 30¹⁹ᶠ·, in which, as Peterson himself says, we are summoned to an active fulfilment of the Law. Even the γάρ with which the quotation from Moses is introduced in v. 5 points in another direction. In this context (and probably even in the rather more difficult parallel in Gal. 3¹² as well) Paul understands this statement that the man who does the righteousness of the Law shall live by it from the standpoint of that *kelal* of the Law. The man who accomplishes the righteousness which is of the Law, i.e., the merciful will of God expressed in the Law, is the One to whom the statement basically refers as the One whom God means and wills in His Law, for the sake of whom He has placed Israel under this Law, who from the first has secretly been the meaning, fulfilment and authority of the Law, and who has now been revealed as all this —the *Messiah* of Israel. Since it was with reference to Him that Moses wrote, it is impossible, in spite of the connecting δέ, to interpret the " utterance of personified δικαιοσύνη ἐκ πίστεως " (Lietzmann) in v. 6 f. as a protest against that first saying of Moses. Who is speaking here ? Obviously not a " personified " idea, but the very man of whom Moses has written that He will live as the *kelal* of the Law, namely, as righteousness before God, the divine justification for everyone who believes in Him. Since He is the meaning, the authority, the fulfiller and the way to the fulfilment of the Law, He is Himself the righteousness before God, the divine justification that everyone is to receive and can receive through faith. Whoever reads Moses has no alternative but to hear the living voice coming from the subject of his prophecy, from this one fulfiller of the Law calling him to Himself (not against the Law, but recapitulating and thus establishing the whole Law) in order that in Him, by faith in Him, he may obtain a part in His fulfilment of the Law ; in order that he, too, may through faith become and be a man righteous before God, justified by God.

It is, indeed, a single summons to active fulfilment of the Law which is now uttered in v. 6 f. by the voice of this living righteousness of faith, and therefore it is only natural that, lending words to this voice, treading as it were on the heels of the Israelite hearkening to the Law, Paul continues in the words of Moses himself : " Say not in thine heart, Who shall ascend into heaven ? (that is to bring Christ down from above) or, who shall descend into the deep ? (that is, to bring up Christ again from the dead)." This kind of questioning and the human purpose corresponding to it are forbidden—not by a new revelation, but by the Law of Moses which is only too familiar to Israel and recognised by it. These are the questions and the corresponding life of transgressors of this Law. For the Messiah, the hope of Israel, to which the Law binds the people of God, is not the object of any such assault on heaven or hell, nor the object of any such bringing down or up by human art and endeavour. As the divine justification of every man who believes in Him, He is the manifestation of the divine mercy. He wills neither to be brought down nor up. He wills to find faith in Israel. To understand the Law as if its precepts were given Israel in order to secure for it a right or claim or power with regard to God by observance and fulfilment of them, in order to strengthen its hand to master His secret, to compel Him to fulfil His promise and thus ultimately to make the fulfilment of the divine promise the result of human endeavours and achievement, to reinterpret the law of God for Israel into a law of Israel for God—this is rejected as sin and made impossible by this Law itself. This Law, recapitulated according to its own witness in the person of its fulfiller, forbids to Israel this very wandering into the heights or depths, this will to master the divine majesty, this Messianic activism. In this we have the typical sin of the elect. It is the attitude of which they above all should not make themselves guilty. For it conflicts with the election as such. It means that, obsessed with their election, the elect forget the electing God and in that way compromise their election too. It necessarily passes by the Messiah who is really coming and has come. It rejects Him because He certainly does not will to be One who by the elect is brought down from heaven or up from the abyss. They will not recognise in Him the One whom they intended and sought. And they will fail to recognise Him in His real form. He will be a stranger to them ; He will be for them the irregular and indeed blasphemous bringer of a new revelation. And this will show how estranged from and unworthy of their own election they themselves have become. Forbidding all this, the personal righteousness of faith, the *kelal* of the Law, positively demands something very different. It says (v. 8a) that " the word is nigh thee, even in thy mouth, and in thy heart." It demands ? It obviously does this simply by indicating itself. The real demand addressed to the elect, but also the prohibition under which they are placed, can be derived only from the fact that the Word of God is near to them, that it is put on their lips so that there remains as their own doing only the subsequent act of uttering it as their confession, that it is put into their hearts so that what is expected of them is again only the subsequent act of putting faith in it. This is what the Law in its recapitulation, in Jesus Christ, speaking to them in a living way, requires of them. The righteousness of the divine mercy which has offered itself and bestowed itself on elected man requires him only that he should be, and conduct himself as, one to whom this offer and gift has been made. Whoever and whatever he may be, he has heard the Word of God. The Word of God lives with his very self. Therefore he can and may in turn live with it and by it. This is the meaning and substance of the Law. It demands of man this appropriate action, this response, this subsequent motion of his lips and heart. With this in view, all the individual requirements and commandments of the Law are intended to help and serve him. Just because this is the one thing and the whole of what

God's Law demands of His elect, their endeavour to establish their own righteousness, that wandering in the heights and in the depths, that will to master the divine majesty, can only mean transgression, a breach of the Law. It is, therefore, not merely a superfluous and ineffectual but a positively perverse and harmful activity that contradicts the mercy realised in the nearness of the divine Word, that denies and ignores this nearness, that not only hastens to pass God's mercy bye but offers resistance to it, to the one thing that is needful and helpful to man. The elected man to whom by God's Law this response is commanded and this endeavour forbidden is the Jew who now in his zeal for God has rejected and crucified Jesus Christ, and who even after His resurrection and ascension remains all too faithful to his way of work-righteousness, of storming heaven and hell, and therefore of active unbelief.

Paul does not stop to show that the Law has always spoken to Israel, and how it has done so, as formulated in vv. 6–8a. It is undoubtedly his opinion that it has done this, that to the *kelal* of the Law there has always corresponded this *kelal* of Israel's sin, that in every case transgression of the Law and commandments of God in Israel has definitely involved this sin and guilt, this wrong choice of self-righteous and work-righteous wandering instead of the confessing and believing, in correspondence to the divine mercy, of the Word of God spoken to and heard by Israel. By implication he also means to speak historically when, speaking in the first instance from and for the present, he makes (v. 8b) the following equation. The Word of God, which has come so near to us in the act of the divine mercy, and to confess and believe which in the act of imitation and thanksgiving is the one thing but also the absolutely necessary thing that is demanded in and with the whole Law in all its commandments, is identical with the Word of faith proclaimed by the apostles of the Church, with the message (objectively) about Jesus Christ whom man must and can believe, and (subjectively) about the faith in Jesus Christ in which he can be certain of participating in the divine justification and therefore in his real and entire deliverance. Again, this equation tells us that the apostolic message of God's mercy actualised in Jesus Christ does not speak of any new revelation. And again, the one old revelation of God in which Israel participates is as such the message which is proclaimed by the apostles. The attitude to the Messiah to be achieved on the basis of this message is the work of all works which the Law has required from the very first, just as certainly as the Messiah Himself is the one fulfilled and therefore valid demand of the Law. The Synagogue does not have to choose between the authority to which it knows and declares itself to be responsible and another newly arisen and not in any sense obligatory quantity. It has to choose between fulfilment and non-fulfilment in face of the authority recognised by itself. That it chooses non-fulfilment is its guilt—the guilt of unbelieving Israel.

In vv. 9–13 we have the explanation of this equation, of the τοῦτ᾽ ἔστιν of v. 8 and therefore of the two τοῦτ᾽ ἔστιν of vv. 6–7. It is to be noted that, taken by itself, this explanation can also be and perhaps actually was simply a very short formulation of the Christian baptismal confession. It is in this character that it is introduced here as a description of what God to-day openly demands of Israel, although secretly it was always His will; a description of the action which to-day as formerly Israel refuses to carry out. To what Moses wrote, according to v. 5, about the man who will live in fulfilment of the righteousness required by the Law, there now corresponds what is, according to v. 9, the normal attitude of the discerning reader—to confess with his mouth (this confession being put into his mouth by the word of Moses himself) that Jesus is the Lord, i.e., that this very man whom the Law intends and proclaims, who is set before the chosen people by its Law as the aim and essence of all that God wills from it and with it, has all the attributes of true Godhead, and therefore, since these attributes can belong to no other beside God, is the true God Himself. There can be no doubt that here, as in 1 Cor. 8⁶, Phil. 2¹¹ and elsewhere, this is for Paul the unqualified meaning of the formula Κύριος 'Ιησοῦς. " Jesus is the Lord " means " Jesus is God." "The Lord is Jesus" means "God is Jesus." Let Israel confess this man and His fulfilment of the Law as the gift proclaimed to it by its Law, as the self-giving of God promised to it through its Law, as its God coming to it and already come. Confessing Him, let it confess the kingdom of *God*. Let it confess God and His kingdom, His right and claim to this people made in the Law, by confessing this man Jesus. Let it do this on the ground that it believes in its heart (this very faith being planted in its heart by the word of Moses himself, speaking as indeed it does of the " life " of this man) that God raised Him from the dead. Jesus' life as He who is risen from the dead is His authentication as the Messiah, as the One who has fulfilled and Himself is the righteousness of God proclaimed by the Law. Let Israel, then, put its faith in this self-demonstration of God. Let it put in it the trust which on the ground of its election it owes its God and which is made so easy, so obvious for it by what is promised from the side of God, by what has happened from the side of God. Whoever does this, whoever follows and fulfils the Law according to its tenor, in its obvious meaning and intention, will be saved, reaching the goal of Israel's election. As elected man he is the proper partner of the electing God, and therefore a participator in the salvation intended for elected man by the electing God. On the ground of the Law, elected man (v. 10) can effect and authenticate his righteousness before God, his proper status as one of the elect, only by laying hold, on the ground of the resurrection of Jesus Christ from the dead, of that confidence which finds in the confession of this man as his Lord and God its necessary expression, an expression which also involves for him outward obligations and commitments. Let elected man make his election sure in this twofold performance—by the faith of his heart his dignity as elected man, by the confession of his mouth the salvation that falls to him on the ground of this dignity. Scripture is unambiguous with respect to this twofold performance, its necessity, and its full sufficiency. Every man who believes in Him, in the man Jesus risen from the dead (as it is so clearly suggested to Israel by the word of Moses), will (v. 11) not be " ashamed " (according to Is. 28¹⁶). That is, he will satisfy the righteousness required in the Law. He is a true Israelite. He becomes a participant in this man's fulfilment of the Law which is established by His resurrection. He becomes and is in his faith a man who stands before God and is in covenant with Him as if he had himself carried out this fulfilment of the Law—on the ground that this is actually reckoned to him as one who believes in this man. The one who is " ashamed " is the man who arbitrarily and not obediently asks (v. 7) : " Who shall descend into the deep ? (that is, to bring Christ up again from the dead) "—as if the self-demonstration of God for the establishment and glorifying of His elected man were, after all, only a matter for the elect's art and endeavour ; as if by his efforts he had first to justify the Messiah and could do so ; as if He, the true Messiah, could be the object of such an enterprise. The attitude which confronts the true Messiah, which is therefore worthy of elected man and does justice to the electing God, can only be the faith of the heart in presence of the completed self-demonstration of God. It can only be trust in the pure deed of God (promised and enacted) which consists in the resurrection of Jesus from the dead. According to Scripture, this trust, faith, but faith alone, will cause no one who puts it to the test to be " ashamed." And Scripture is equally unambiguous (vv. 12–13) on the other side, with respect to the confession Κύριος 'Ιησοῦς with which man, on the ground of his faith in Jesus' resurrection from the dead and made worthy of Him by this faith, steps into the ranks of those whose deliverance and salvation are secured by God Himself, who do and can look forward and advance with perfect certainty towards this their future in covenant with the electing God. When the Synagogue hears to-day from the mouth of the Church this confession which is so alien to it, which is condemned and rejected by it as blasphemy against God, it should not take its stand against the Church on its own sacred tradition, which does not permit it to discern and call upon and worship the Creator in a creature, God in a man. Nor should it resist and evade this confession on the pretext that this is a hellenistic invention, an arbitrary acceptance and application of pagan emperor-worship, and therefore not commanded by the Law of God but expressly forbidden. " For there is no difference between the Jew and the Greek." The situation, the problem of both Jews and Greeks in regard to the confession of the Church, is identical. What the Jew now hears from the mouth of so many a Greek concerns him too, and should, by rights, be his confession as well. There is only one Lord over all, and, in fact, the man Jesus is this one Lord. He is rich (cf. 9^{23}), that is, as the executor of the mercy of God and therefore of His righteousness. He is rich as the divine mercy and righteousness in person, as God Himself, the sum and source of all blessing and salvation for all who call upon Him as such. In relation to Him all are poor, all are referred to His riches as sinners in God's sight, the Greeks with their emperor-worship exalting the creature to the Creator no less than the Synagogue Jews with their Yahweh-faith delivering the Creator into the power of the creature, but the latter, too, no less than the former. The same error and the same need are present in both cases. The same truth and the same help can alone secure deliverance. The same promise applies both to the Jews and to the Greeks. In both cases, the honour of the Creator over against the creature, but the salvation also of the creature by his Creator, lie in the recognition and invocation of Jesus as Lord. If what is attested as true by the resurrection of Jesus Christ from the dead, and proclaimed as true by the apostles, is not true, that Jesus is God and God is Jesus, for the Jews as for the Greeks there is nothing but destruction, and this destruction will necessarily rest equally on both Jews and Greeks apart from the confession of this truth. But obviously Paul is not wanting to say only that this confession is the only possibility of deliverance for the Jew as well. In this context he wants to say that it is the only possibility of deliverance precisely and primarily for the Jew. When the Jew hears this confession from the mouth of the Church as the Gentiles also hear it, he above all should not draw back. In no circumstances should there be that parallel between a hellenic emperor-worship which resists this confession and a Yahweh-faith which resists it equally. The Jew should at once and first of all step out of this disastrous equality in order to step into the saving equality of all men in face of their real Creator, His promise and His actualised mercy ; the equality of the confession of God's real Godhead and righteousness. For after all the Jew (v. 12) also has the express witness of Scripture regarding this confession (Joel 2^{32}, which is the concluding saying of the Old Testament passage urged in Peter's sermon on the day of Pentecost, Ac. 2^{21}) : " For whosoever shall call upon the name of the Lord shall be saved." Whosoever gives the faith of his heart to this man who has fulfilled the Law, and has thus made himself worthy of his election as an Israelite, will not in his praise and thanksgiving and prayer, in his calling on this man, be calling on a second God but on the Lord Yahweh, the one true God of Israel. In this invocation his lips will open of themselves to the confession that in this man he has encountered his Creator over whom he has as little power as he has ability to confuse Him, like the Gentiles, with the creature. On Him he can and must rely because He is so merciful, because He has on His own initiative sought and found the one who had sought Him in vain. Whosoever confesses this man as Yahweh Himself, the God of Israel, who is also Lord of the world, will be saved in the last times, in the " great and the terrible day of the Lord." And by the outpouring of the Spirit upon all flesh this is the very thing which will happen, that he will call upon the name of the Lord, i.e., that he will call upon the name of this man as the name of the Lord and the name of the Lord as the name of this man, and will thus participate in His deliverance. He will not be saved who arbitrarily and not obediently asks : " Who shall ascend into heaven ? (that is, to bring Christ down) "—as if the goal to which God's election is meant to lead elected man had now to be and could be striven for and attained as the result and fruit of his own righteousness, as if the true Messiah of God could be found in a nearness to God to be attained by himself instead of in the nearness to himself created by God. The act of elected man corresponding to the true Messiah can consist only in the confession which becomes event in the invocation necessarily arising out of faith. In this act and this alone will elected man be saved. This is what Scripture says especially to the Jew. It is not only to him with others, but to him especially and first of all, that this invocation and therefore the confession of the mouth should apply.

Thus the accusation against the Jews takes on a keener edge in vv. 9–13, although there is no express reference to them. The very Scripture which they themselves read and to which they appeal, when it speaks for the *Church* indicates the way on which man is not " ashamed " but is saved—*for* the Church and therefore automatically against them in so far as they refuse to walk in this way. " Whosoever believeth on him shall not be ashamed " (v. 11). " Whosoever shall call upon the name of the Lord shall be saved " (v. 13). This is what Scripture says to him who reads it. It says, then, that everyone who does not believe will be ashamed, that everyone who neglects this invocation is lost. And the Synagogue Jew does not believe ; he neglects this invocation. Indeed he resists this faith and this confession. This is his evident sin and guilt. Paul might already have drawn the conclusion expressed in v. 16 : " But they have not all obeyed." The Synagogue Jews are not numbered among the obedient. The saying recalled in v. 21, confirmed by the authority recognised and exalted by themselves, applies to them : " All day long I have stretched forth my hands unto a disobedient and gainsaying people."

But this conclusion is expressly drawn only on the ground of a special consideration still to be adduced. Perhaps Paul is putting to himself the question which we can sense in the passage vv. 4–13, and even in the more general exposition 9^{30}–10^3, whether the asserted responsibility and obligation of the Jews to believe and make confession in the sense of vv. 9–13 is really present and given. At any rate this is the question which is exhaustively answered in v. 14 f., and it is only on the ground of this answer that the above conclusion is then actually drawn. The question can obviously be put concretely in terms of v. 13 as related to v. 11, or materially in terms of the problem of confession in relation to that of faith. The demand addressed through the Law to the Jews had found its final point in the demand for confession. What God requires from Israel is that along with the Church, being merged in the Church, and thus by attesting itself as Israel and establishing its election, it should confess Jesus as Lord. But Paul himself knows and has already said that this confession can only be the confession of faith. According to v. 10 the righteousness of faith is the presupposition of the salvation to be obtained in the Church by acceptance of its confession. But, according to v. 9 justifying faith is faith in God's self-demonstration in the resurrection of Jesus from the dead. How can Jesus be confessed as Lord without this faith ? How can anything else but this faith bring man into the Church ? What is the situation with regard to this presupposition ? Can it really be claimed that it is fulfilled in the case of the Jew or that he can fulfil it ? Is it with justice that he is held responsible if he neglects the confession of faith ? " How then shall they call on him (how, that is, are they to confess him as Lord) in whom they have not believed ? " (v. 14a). Paul had had (v. 8) no hesitation in assuming that the Word (and its content, the man Jesus shown to be identical with God by His resurrection from the dead) is equally " near " to the heart and mouth of the Jew, so that the supplementary, subsequent motion of the heart and mouth, faith and confession, was in the same way made easy and obvious for him. This is what he had said in relation to the sayings of Moses quoted in v. 5 and in connexion with the further sayings quoted in

vv. 6-8. But he has (v. 10) just recognised that this one demand of the Law does not stand alone ; that faith must precede confession. Where the faith of the heart in Him whom the Law proclaims as its fulfilment is not attained, there can be no calling upon Him, nor confession of the mouth directed to Him, nor merging, or rather rising to life of Israel in the Church.

Whether the readers of Moses attain to faith (and therefore in turn to confession) depends, however, on whether they can hear Him of whom Moses speaks. " How shall they believe in him of whom they have not heard ? " (v. 14b). How can His presence in the written word of Moses acquire for its readers such power that they read it not only as the word of Moses, but in and with the reading of this word hear the voice of Him—the voice of that living One (v. 5), the risen Jesus Christ—who suggests the act of faith and therefore the confession of Him as Lord as the required response, and makes them as easy and self-evident as foreseen in v. 8 ? Obviously it is one thing, as in v. 5, to read of that man that He will come and fulfil the righteousness of the Law and live in virtue of this righteousness, and another thing to hear from Him that He has actually come and been raised again from the dead and is alive. Scripture as the witness to God's revelation is one thing—God's revelation itself as the fulfilment and content of what is written is another.

Does the Jew lack this second thing ? He obviously cannot lack it if he is to be addressed with an appeal to Scripture as in vv. 4-13. If he does not lack it, if in fact he has not only read but has heard as he read—heard the One who is written of in Scripture—this again presupposes that the object of which he read had a voice, and that this voice made itself heard to him. " How shall they hear without a preacher ? " (v. 14c). How are they to perceive as they read, how is the matter read or the object of which Moses has written to attain that proximity to them which makes necessary their faith and finally their confession, if over and above the presence of the written word and their reading there is not also the further event that what is written encounters and is imparted to them as *kerygma*, as a message which reaches and smites home to them in such a way that they cannot elude it, that they become those who are reached and smitten by what is written, and as such must believe and then also confess their faith ?

But this event by which the written word becomes *kerygma* has, on its part, one decisive presupposition. The word of Moses in itself alone is obviously not sufficient to summon its readers effectively to faith and confession, to signify and create for the reader that nearness of its object which makes this response at once absolutely easy and absolutely imperative. Moses can indeed attest it, and the Jew cannot contest that he does so to him too. But does the ministry of the proclamation of what is attested by Moses really reach him as well ? Is the reality of the truth of Moses called to his attention in such a way that he cannot elude it ? Is it said to him that things are as Moses writes, that that man risen from the dead is alive, so that as he hears this he can believe and therefore confess ? " How shall they preach except they be sent ? " (v. 15a). Mission —this is the cardinal presupposition of that event of proclamation and therefore of hearing and therefore of believing and therefore of confessing what is written in the Bible. Mission is necessary in order that beyond the written character and reading of the witness the culminating point of encounter with the attested revelation may be reached. Scripture must open itself. But this can take place only from its object, only in virtue of the fulfilment of its prophecy. And if it is true that men are claimed, as in vv. 4-13, on the ground that Scripture has opened itself to them, this must mean that the proclamation has encountered these men which does not consist in a mere repetition of the written word, or proceed from human arbitrariness with regard to this word, but which rests in fact on mission. It must be the proclamation which according to the terms of its commission proceeds from the object of the word of Scripture, and therefore does not dominate the word of Scripture, but serves it by calling attention to its fulfilment as such, and therefore interprets it according to its own intended meaning. It must be the proclamation which simply discharges its task of delivering the good news that the coming of this Fulfiller of the Law and His resurrection from the dead have occurred as Scripture prophesied. It is clear that no one can undertake this proclamation on his own initiative. It can rest, indeed, only on the foundation that this has occurred. It can be only a mission which proceeds from this occurrence. This occurrence as such creates for itself its messengers. It creates for itself in them preachers who expound Scripture, not only according to its meaning, but in the power of its meaning, i.e., in the power of its object. They render the scriptural witness the service which it asks as witness. In face of the proclamation resting on this mission there is for the reader of Scripture no excuse for not hearing, and therefore for not believing, and therefore for not confessing. In the proclamation based on mission the Word of God is indeed brought near to the reader of Scripture with the power to make response absolutely easy and absolutely imperative as described in v. 8. By it he is set on the way to faith, and from faith to confession; and he cannot halt on this way.

It is to be noted that so far Paul has only been asking questions—almost, one might say, in an attempt to excuse the Synagogue Jew. Does this presupposition, with all its necessary members, apply in the case of the Jew ? Can he be expected to confess with the Church ? In fact, of course, with this chain of questions Paul has not only asked but answered : " Certainly he can be expected," and therefore : " Certainly in face of this well-founded because just expectation the Jews are in fact responsible, and since they fail to meet it are guilty." That this is his meaning is shown by the quotation (v. 15b) from Is. 52[7] which prepares the way for his later conclusion : " How beautiful are the feet of them that . . . bring glad tidings " (perhaps with Peterson, p. 49, " the good as glad tidings," or " the glad tidings as the good "). According to this passage it is Scripture itself which, as it prophesies the necessity of faith (v. 11) and confession (v. 13), prophesies also the *kerygma* by which it is interpreted and its utterance and hearing are given binding force. Scripture must necessarily have drawn the attention of the Jews to this event of proclamation based on mission, to the proclamation of the fulfilment of what is prophesied. This proclamation based on mission is not only part of the fulfilment that has taken place but is already part of the prophecy of it, and therefore of what the Jews cannot but have known. We cannot (with Lietzmann) regard v. 15b only as " ornamental praise of the evangelist's calling." In this quotation Paul says indirectly something which is quite indispensable—that the last of these presuppositions is also and especially fulfilled and given. Starting from this quotation, the whole series of preceding questions can now be opened up and answered in this way. The proclamation based on mission has, in fact, come to the Synagogue Jews. They can therefore hear. They can therefore believe. They can therefore call upon the name of the Lord. They can therefore confess with the Church. What follows shows that this is, in fact, the opinion of Paul. But it is naturally no accident that he brings forward this decisive proposition only in the form of this quotation from prophecy, and that he apparently leaves the preceding questions as such open and unanswered. In the final and decisive term of his train of thought the reference is to the apostolate of the Church and therefore his own office. At this final and decisive point the proof that he brings becomes, in fact, a simple resumption of his existence as a representative of the proclamation which is based on mission, which derives from the risen Jesus Christ, which is called into being and authorised and legitimated by Him. At this final and decisive point Paul has nothing more to prove but everything to do in the establishment and fulfilment of this part of the prophecy. In answer to the question whether the Jews can really believe and confess, he takes his stand ultimately in his own person, i.e., in his own person as a bearer of his office, acting in exercise of his apostolic office, and not, of course, in his experience as a converted Jew. It is interesting enough that neither at this point nor in the whole context does Paul urge his own experience. The strictness of proof from Scripture does not stop even where what is proved by Scripture, the bringer of good tidings promised to the Jews and now in fact present and effective, is Paul himself in his apostolic office, which for its part can be demonstrated as a reality only in its exercise.

And now the way is open for the proposition of v. 16a, in which the πᾶς of v. 11 and v. 13 is taken up again and the final conclusion of the whole argument is at last disclosed : " But they have not all obeyed the gospel." That they did not obey the word of Scripture and therefore God, as was implicitly stated in vv. 9–13, is the terrible reality within the fact that—excepting themselves from the " all " who were intended to do this—they did not obey the Gospel. The messengers whose feet are beautiful, according to Is. 52[7], have come to them too. The message was delivered to them too, the good news of the reality of the truth of Moses—not merely in the form of insistence on the written word, and still less in the form of arbitrary assertion, but legitimated from the place which alone could legitimate it, and yet which has legitimated it, the εὐαγγέλιον as κήρυγμα borne by the ἀποστολή. This ἀποστολή excludes not only the suspicion that the εὐαγγέλιον may not be genuine but also the excuse that it has not been heard or not understood, thus making quite impossible the pretext that it cannot be believed and therefore not confessed. Thus the refusal to confess that Jesus is Lord—the demand which, according to vv. 9–13 sums up all the demands of the Law, and in which its fulfilment as such is prescribed to a reader—can only be understood and characterised as disobedience. This refusal, unbelief, is not a misfortune. It is an action which is forbidden by the Law, and which for a reader of the Law is conceivable only as transgression.

But Paul does not will that even this point should be established by his own authority. He wills, rather, that this point, made in apostolic authority, should be established only in such a way that the Synagogue Jew must recognise it as legitimate from the standpoint of his own presupposition, and therefore again from the standpoint of Scripture. Thus the quotation from Is. 53[1] and its interpretation in vv. 16b–17 serve to underline the conclusion drawn in v. 16a. Paul's whole purpose is that each individual term of the great indictment with which he intends to put the Synagogue in the wrong (in order to bring out the fact and extent that God in His mercy has put Himself in the right in His election of Israel) should be in itself a repetition of the statement of 9[31] that it is the Law itself which Israel has failed to satisfy, or of the statement of 9[33] that it is the very stone laid in Zion which has become a cause of stumbling and offence to it. That is why, in special proof of the conclusion already drawn in v. 16a, he recalls that even this is not his invention but is expressly drawn in Scripture. It is also a prophecy that the messengers who bring the news of the fulfilment of all prophecy will encounter unbelief, that the proclamation which makes faith unhesitatingly and irresistibly necessary and brings it in its train, will incomprehensibly be confronted with the actual refusal of this faith by the hearers of this proclamation. The horror with which Paul faces this attitude of the Synagogue is as little an innovation as the demand for faith (v. 11) and confession (v. 13), or as its legitimation by the existence of the messengers sent forth (v. 15b). When he comes accusingly before the Synagogue with his un-answered question he is not the bringer of a strange revelation but the interpreter and witness of the prophetic word really known to the Synagogue. It had already been the case—and it had surely had to be so then with a view to the present, to the decisive moment in Israel's history, when it is so again and supremely—that the bringer of the good tidings (of the servant of God suffering for His brethren), legitimated and authorised by his mission, could in the end only turn away from those to whom he brings it; could only turn to the God who had sent him, asking to what end He had really sent him, asking indeed on what He was really squandering these good tidings in charging him with them, asking even whether in reality the good thing of which the message speaks had not happened in vain. " Lord, who hath believed our report ? " (v. 16b).   Who ? The answer implied in this question of the prophet is : No one. With this question the prophet confesses his complete loneliness in relation to his hearers, his loneliness with God, and therefore the loneliness of God Himself and the cause of God over against His people.   His people does not believe at the very point where there is the unhesitating and irresistible occasion and obligation to believe. It not only forgets but rejects the good God who has done it.   This is its relation to the God who elects it.   V. 17 is not (so Peterson, p. 50) " merely an incidental remark leading on to v. 18," nor is it (so Lietzmann) a repetitive resumption of vv. 14–15.   The understanding of it is made somewhat difficult only for two reasons.   On the one hand, in this interpretation of Is. 53[1] Paul derives from the negative content of that passage, from the prophetic complaint and accusation, the positive order whose transgression is made a matter of complaint.   And, on the other hand, he does not expressly return to this transgression as such and therefore to the complaint of the prophet, but leaves it to the reader to supply for himself the necessary conclusion that it was against the positive order that the sin was then committed according to the word of Isaiah, and is now again and supremely committed in the decisive moment of Israel's history.   Once we realise this point, the verse can be readily understood.   What is this positive order ?   We can see in what it consists from the fact that in face of the non-appearance of faith in the report delivered by him the prophet can think only of turning to God with complaints and questions.   This yields the conclusion that God is the One who guarantees the necessary issue of faith from this report, that this association as such is, therefore, a strict and necessary one.   " Faith comes (follows, that is) from the report as certainly as the report is effected by the word of the Messiah " (v. 17).   The report of the prophet (" our " report, as it says in Is. 53[1]) has sovereign vitality and power.   This is not because it is " our " preaching.   It is not because these are lent to it by the prophet.   In relation to his message the prophet is in this respect in exactly the same position as Moses.   They derive from its object.   In virtue of its own power alone the prophetic word cannot bring in its train this necessary awakening of faith.   But in so far as the prophet is one who is sent, in so far as it is not his preaching but the report committed to him, it has the power of its commissioner who is also its object, of its origin which is also its content.   It has the power of the Word of the promised Christ Himself.   As it delivers the good tidings of that servant of God, the Servant of God Himself speaks in it, and for this very reason it is the compelling motive for faith, for that confidence of the heart, for everyone to whom it is spoken.   The proclamation made by the Word of the Messiah Himself and put in the mouth of the prophet, and the unbelief of his hearers, cannot possibly co-exist.   The only thing possible where this proclamation is heard is faith.   And so we have to fill out from the context the opinion which Paul has left unexpressed.   If, in spite of this, the prophet has occasion to turn to God with the complaining and accusing question of v. 16b : " Lord, who hath believed our report ? ", it necessarily means that this discrepancy, this becoming possible of the impossible, can only be, as was said in v. 16a, and as is to be proved by the Isaiah passage and its exposition, the act of disobedience which is directed against God and of which God Himself can alone be Judge. If we keep this order clearly in view it is plain that with the act of unbelief which leads the prophet into this isolation over against his hearers something happens to which no man, but only God as the Founder and Guarantor of this order, can say the final, resolving Word.   With this question the prophet in his painful loneliness has already called upon the mercy of God in face of this unambiguously present guilt of God's chosen people. Who believes ? As far as can be seen and said from man's side, *No one.* He will believe whom God's mercy summons and awakens to faith out of the general unbelief.

Even the final conclusion then, the point that Israel is found in a state of disobedience to its God and to His Word spoken and well-known to it, is meant by Paul to be regarded as the content of this Word itself. Along with the demand for faith and confession, along with the advent of the Gospel which all can hear as a constituent part of the promise, the contradiction and resistance of the Synagogue is also a constituent part of the prophecy well enough known to its own self. In this, too, there is accomplished and comes to fulfilment only what is written. How truly Isaiah spoke in his complaint and accusation is revealed in the fact that in the decisive present, which, looking at the Israel of his own time, Isaiah only prophesied, Paul again and with even greater cause has to bring the same complaint and accusation, and as the bearer of the good tidings has to face the chosen people in as great an isolation. And this is necessarily the case if the Scripture is not to be proved false. As God confirms His election of Israel by the apostolic proclamation of the good tidings sustained by the Word of Christ Himself, so Israel confirms its election, its identity with the people of former times of and to whom Isaiah spoke, by the disobedient act of its unbelief. The converse can and must also be said, that, seen in the light of the prophetic word addressed to the chosen people of former times, Israel confirms the fact that its unbelief, its failure to confess Jesus, has the character of disobedience. It confesses, therefore, that it is still and supremely the people from which the prophet could only turn away in order to turn with his heart full of questioning to God, to cry out for His mercy. But precisely because this is not put into words, but remains latent, we can say that the decisive result of this part of the Pauline proof from Scripture is to be found in the other point, that even the undeniable guilt of Israel as it is mobilised against the Church in the Synagogue belongs in its own way to the fulfilment of prophecy, and in all its dreadfulness is also a confirmation of its election. This very people, disobedient to the Gospel and therefore unfaithful to its own election, was and is, as the natural root of the Church called and awakened to faith by His mercy, God's chosen people.

What follows in this chapter, vv. 18–20, and the second conclusion reached in v. 21, may be regarded as corollaries, as a supplementary elucidation of some of the points of detail arising from the train of thought which found its main conclusion in v. 17. We must note, however, that these elucidations, and especially the second conclusion in v. 21, do not merely repeat or underline but shed a new light on the whole subject which is indispensable for its proper understanding and which we cannot, therefore, afford to overlook.

At first sight, we seem to have a mere repetition when the question is put in v. 18 : " But I say, have they not heard ? " Certainly in vv. 14–15 the point has already been made that hearing is necessary for the faith and confession required of the Jews, and that they could, in fact, hear, seeing they did not lack the proclamation based on mission. But in v. 18, as the answer shows, the problem of the ability to hear is a different one from that of v. 14. In v. 14 the point made was that where there is the proclamation based on mission, hearing is possible. This point rested on the presupposition that the proclamation based on mission had actually reached the Jews too, that the messengers with the good tidings had actually come to them. It is obviously the question of this presupposition which is taken up again in v. 18a. Has it been fulfilled ? Or is there the eleventh hour excuse for the Jews that the living interpretation of the Law by Him of whom the Law speaks, by the Word of Christ which makes faith necessary, had not yet reached them ? The answer given with the quotation from Ps. 19[5] shows in the first place that in elucidation of the concept of mission (v. 15) it was not only possible but necessary to think, not simply in general of the apostolate of the Church, but in particular of the apostolate of Paul himself, and therefore to realise that in that passage Paul was speaking indirectly and tacitly of himself. For the answer of v. 18 does not just say that there is also, as Gal. 2⁸ puts it, an ἀποστολὴ τῆς περιτομῆς committed to Peter and the other original apostles and executed by them, and that by this the Jews have really heard well enough all that they had indeed to hear in order to come to faith and confession. Instead of this Paul quotes : " Their sound went into all the earth, and their words unto the ends of the (inhabited) world." That is, he answers by stating positively that what all have heard, necessarily the Jews also heard. But this means that he consciously ignores the division of labour in missionary activity provided for in Gal. 2. He says that the Jews must have heard the Gospel by reason and in the course of its proclamation to all the nations of the earth. He appeals, that is, to his own particular apostolate, the apostolate to the Gentile world. Does he do this because he has especially in view the Synagogue of the Dispersion outside Palestine, and therefore outside the sphere of the " apostolate of the circumcision " ? We can reckon with this possibility, but even more we have to consider that in spite of this practical division of labour in missionary activity, the apostolate in general and as such has presented itself decisively to him as the completion as such of the relation between the Christ risen and exalted to the right hand of the Father and the nations of the world in the cosmos. Thus the proclamation to the Jews is not an independent action but is necessarily included in this relation of the *Kyrios* to the peoples and its completion. It is the necessary, and from a practical standpoint, as the Book of Acts shows, the first, reaction to this completion. In the course of going here and there among the nations, Paul goes also and in the first place to the Jews dispersed among these nations. They are, therefore, claimed on the ground that they have heard the voice which has gone out over all the earth. But perhaps for the interpretation of this quotation we ought not really to adhere too closely to the idea of the missionary activity of the apostles, although this is, of course, denoted by it. We must also take into account that the latter was for Paul only the consequence and sign of a happening which independently precedes it as its condition and basis. As Paul saw it, the relation between the exalted Christ and the nations of the world, and therefore its realisation, was primarily a direct one, and its completion by the mission effected by men was only in some sense its necessary confirmation in the form of an indirect realisation. By the resurrection of Jesus Christ from the dead, the deliverance determined in His name has, at the first, been objectively declared to the whole world, as in the cross of Golgotha it has, at the first and once for all, objectively happened for the whole world. So, then, what is to be mediated to the world as a " report " by the apostolate has in a sense only the significance of a subsequent indication of something which is not only already real but which has in itself already made itself visible and audible. For all we know, in his reference to the αὐτοί of Ps. 19⁵ Paul may even have been thinking primarily of the angels as the proper and primary messengers of the Gospel. What we do know is that in his desire to traverse the whole world to its farthest limit as a bearer of the Gospel, a desire which finds such striking expression in this very Epistle to the Romans (e.g., 1¹³⁻¹⁶, 15¹⁶⁻²⁴), he does not regard himself as preceding but only as following the Word of God itself. Therefore when he quotes this saying from the Psalm he can be thinking only secondarily of the missionary work done by himself and the other apostles. From the standpoint of the sovereignty of the Word of Christ mentioned in v. 17 he knows that the whole world has heard it, and from this standpoint he tells the Jewish community to their face that they cannot possibly urge in excuse that they have not heard the Word. Before the very eyes of Paul there exists already as a completed reality the Church of Jews and Gentiles, which as the earthly body has in the Christ exalted above all angels and therefore above all the world its heavenly Head. In it the Jewish community are inevitably confronted with Christ, and hear His Word and therefore the message of the fulfilment of the Law.

The second supplementary question raised and answered in vv. 19–20 is given a parallel form to that of v. 18 : " But I say, did not Israel know ? " This question does not appear in the series vv. 14–15. It obviously refers back to vv. 2–3, where the guilt of Israel was characterised as a neglect of the necessary and required knowledge. It is this particular form of the apostolic accusation which is now obviously to be substantiated, clarified and deepened. How do matters stand with the ἀγνωσία of the Jews in relation to the righteousness of God, in which they wish to replace the latter by their own righteousness, and in so doing neglect the one thing which is required of them as fulfilment of the Law ? The question and answer of vv. 19–20 cannot be meant to withdraw the established fact of this ἀγνωσία. Their result is rather to accentuate it. What they did not understand, according to vv. 2–3, they really understood very well. Understanding, they did not understand. They did not want to understand. It is exactly the same as in v. 18, where hearing they did not hear, and therefore did not want to hear. The proof of this assertion in vv. 19–20 again shows that in v. 15 it is necessary to look for the conclusive answer to the preceding series of questions in the existence as such of Paul, the apostle of the Gentiles. For the quotations from Deut. 32²¹ and Is. 65¹ adduced for this purpose obviously direct attention to what has happened in the Gentile world in continuation of the occurrence touched on in v. 18 in connexion with the proclamation of the Gospel. Paul does not, then, allow himself to be drawn into a discussion whether the Gospel is intelligible for man in general or for the Jew in particular, let alone into trying to represent it as specially intelligible, or to make it intelligible. In v. 18, too, he had not made any further enquiry whether it was actually heard by the Jews, but contented himself with establishing the fact that it has become so audible that all those who are willing to hear can do so even if they are Jews. In the answer in vv. 19–20 the presupposition is rather that the Gospel is not at all intelligible for man. In this answer, indeed, we are told of a foolish people which does not seek God or ask for Him. This foolish people God has now preferred to Israel, causing Himself to be found by it through the voice of His Word going through the whole world, and thus making it the object of Israel's jealousy. Paul will return later (11¹¹) to this divine provocation of Israel to jealousy as the meaning of this preference of the Gentiles. Here, of course, the meaning is not yet that Israel is already actually gripped and moved by this jealousy. If that were the case, its election would no longer be confirmed in the shape of unbelief but already in the obedience of faith. That this is Israel's future, Paul is sure. It is not, however, its present. So he only says that the objective basis for this jealousy is given, that there is actually this preference. Those who are without understanding, even in respect of the Word of God, do nevertheless understand. God caused Himself to be found by those who did not seek after Him and was revealed to those who did not ask for Him. This is what takes place in the calling and conversion of the Gentiles to the Church. How could these Gentiles have understood the Gospel ? Whence had they the presuppositions for so doing? What, if any, could be the human presuppositions for understanding the Gospel ? Who on his own initiative can seek and ask for the God of whose mercy the Gospel speaks ? But they have actually understood it. God caused Himself to be found and became revealed. This happened as they were called to faith by the miracle of divine mercy. Their faith, their existence in the Church, is the proof that they have understood. This is what has taken place out among the peoples of the world in the power of the free course of the Gospel. Can the Jew, then, still argue that he has not understood ? Can he trace his ἀγνωσία back to an incapacity and therefore to a mischance— as if this incapacity and mischance were not that of the Gentiles also ? They were found by the Gospel in the same situation as the Jews ; but through the

Gospel they were found by God Himself and made participants in His self-revelation. Through the Gospel they were snatched from that incapacity and mischance. But were not the Jews from the very beginning (through their election and the Law given and held up to them) first determined to participation in this miracle ? Were they not, in virtue of what God had from the very first done among them in preparation for His Church, determined as a people which could be understanding, which could seek God and ask for Him ? If this did not and does not happen, it cannot be due to their inability to understand any more than to their inability to hear. The event of mission, the fact of the Church of Jews and Gentiles, the occurrence of the miracle of Pentecost following upon the resurrection of Jesus Christ, rebuts both of these excuses.

Taking this concrete interpretation of vv. 18 and 19–20 as actually prescribed by the text, we cannot therefore say that they merely repeat what has been said before. It may well be that for Paul himself the message of the chapter is only given a final and conclusive form in these to all appearances superfluously appended verses. If there is any semblance of purely scribal erudition in the preceding section, it is now dispelled. The life of the messenger of Jesus Christ pressing on into the Gentile world under the orders of the Lord who has immediately encountered him, and in this world experiencing and realising all the more fully the power residing in the charge committed to him, is here quite unambiguously the place from which the argument is developed and the thesis of Israel's guilt is proved. The new and distinctive feature in these verses is that the events of the Messianic age, in which Paul plays so great a part as a bearer of the apostolate of the Gentiles, enter as such so powerfully into the sphere of this apostolic indictment and make it so peculiarly impressive. But seeing this we must not overlook the fact that even here Paul remains true to the line of argument which he adopted at the outset and has steadily maintained. The proof from Scripture (and to that extent scribal erudition also) does not cease at this point. How easy it would have been for Paul to prove the ability of the Jews to hear, and also to understand, or at least to augment the proof, with information and illustrations drawn from his missionary experience ! In v. 18, for example, he might have mentioned the pains he had always taken about the Jews, and in v. 19 perhaps some of the facts that he had witnessed and was still witnessing among the Gentiles of Asia Minor and Greece. But he does not do this. On the contrary, he continues to quote the Law and the prophets. The one thing that concerns Paul here, too, is that it is prophesied, first that Israel has heard the *kerygma*, second that it could perfectly well understand it, and third that there should take place the whole course of present events in which he is so intensively involved and which so painfully reveals this ability of the Jews to hear and understand in contrast to their factual disobedience. It is for this reason alone that he allows the present and the part taken by him in it to be heard so decisively in the argument. That he continues to adduce Scripture is no whim ; neither is it to be explained by the theological tradition from which Paul comes. He does not always use the proof from Scripture with quite the same concentration and consistency as he does here, where this proof is, so to speak, everything. He chooses to do so here, and indeed has to, because in the envisaged proof of Israel's guilt he does not mean to contest its election. On the contrary, as the sequel in chapter 11 shows, his aim is really to maintain it : its election as this inexcusable, this really disobedient people ; its election by the God who is therefore wholly and utterly the One who has mercy upon it. Because this is his goal, at this stage he cannot afford even momentarily to lose sight of the Word of God spoken to Israel in the word of Moses and the prophets—and in v. 18 the third part of the Canon is heard as well. It is not by any kind of abstract theological considerations, nor by Church experiences of any kind, but only from Scripture, that the guilt of Israel can really be established and proved in such a way as not to contest but to confirm its election. This can be done only from Scripture, not merely because it is only from Scripture, i.e., from the documents of its particular election and call which are in its own possession, that Israel can be accused in such a way that it is really touched by the accusation, but decisively because the same Scripture which accuses it is also the place from which the unshakeable faithfulness of its God is assured to it with the same definiteness, and because this is the source from which not only the Jew, but every man, is told how great is the divine mercy to guilty man, and how the God who has mercy on guilty man is the electing God, and therefore how the act of His election is always an act of His mercy. If he was to keep this final aim of his statement steadfastly in view, this was no place for Paul to forsake the region of Scripture even down to the final word, and he has not actually done so. It is also surprisingly (and yet very naturally) the case that the apparent rabbinism of this chapter is the very thing which serves to give it the eminently evangelical character which is peculiar to it in spite of its thesis.

It is also hard to see how we can explain v. 21, which we have not so far discussed, if both as a whole and in detail, both in content and form, this chapter is to be interpreted otherwise than in the light of this purpose. This verse is not, as is usually alleged, parallel to the quotations in vv. 19 and 20. Indeed, the question of the Jews' ability to understand is no longer under discussion in Is. 65². The point now at issue, in confirmation of v. 16a, is the disobedience and contradiction of God's people which meet His long-suffering and mercy. As a confirmation of v. 16a, v. 21 is, in fact, the biblical conclusion of the whole matter. Not its failure to hear, not its failure to understand, but only the disobedience of Israel which is incomprehensible in view of its ability to hear and understand, only its transgression of the Law and therefore its guilt before God, is the fact on which we can positively rest in face of the Synagogue's attitude to the Church. But the fact that in the Old Testament text, too, v. 21 forms the immediate continuation of v. 20, and that as far as its content is concerned it repeats and underlines the Pauline conclusion already drawn, is certainly not the only reason why Paul concludes with this particular saying. He obviously does so because this saying does not speak only—indeed, to be exact, it speaks only incidentally—of the disobedience and contradiction of Israel, but because it speaks decisively about what God has done in regard to it. To this very people, that is, God has " stretched forth his hands all day long." To this very people God never was and never grew weary of offering Himself, of condescending to it, and repeatedly proving His loyalty. God is the One who has mercy on this people. Is this a mitigation of the establishment of its guilt ? No, it could not be brought out more distinctly and sharply than in this incidental manner. To be sure, it is in this way characterised (and this is why it is the subject of discussion in this chapter) as an object of the divine mercy, and only as such as an object of His judgment, His warning and His punishment. And in this way—again as the content of prophecy —it is set in the light of the fulfilment accomplished in the present, and thus regarded as a fact which in all its dreadfulness does not speak against but for Israel's election. The meaning of its election is that in the very act of becoming guilty towards God it must genuinely magnify His faithfulness.

4. THE PASSING AND THE COMING MAN

In the eternal election of the one man Jesus of Nazareth, God, merciful in His judgment, appoints for man a gracious end and a new gracious beginning. He makes him die in order that he may truly live. He makes him pass in order that he may acquire a real future. The purpose of the election of this One is God's righteous and saving will to deal with man's need at its very root and to show this man the supreme favour by taking his place in the person of this One, taking away from man and upon Himself the bitterness of man's end, and bringing upon man the whole joy of the new beginning. Thus the election of this One is His election to death and to life, to passing and to new coming.

The elected community of God as the environment of the elected man, Jesus of Nazareth, and therefore as the place where God's honour dwells, must correspond to this twofold determination of its Head by existing itself also in a twofold form, in a passing and a coming form, in a form of death and a form of life. It fulfils its determination grounded in its election by representing in bodily form and attesting to the world both the death taken away by God from man and also the life bestowed on man by God. On the ground of its election (as it is elected in Jesus Christ, is founded and constituted by Him, and is His body) the whole community of God—Israel and the Church— has this twofold determination. Wherever it lives, there, not on the ground of its own capacity but on the ground of the capacity of Him who is in its midst as its Head, it will serve to represent the passing and the coming man, the grace of God which kills and makes alive.

The specific service which within the whole of the elected community is Israel's determination is the praise of the mercy of God in the passing, the death, the setting aside of the old man, of the man who resists his election and therefore God. When Israel becomes obedient to its election by being awakened to faith through the promise of God fulfilled in the resurrection of Jesus Christ, its special contribution to the work of the whole community then consists in the critical reminder that the man who resists God is in process of passing, that he must pass in order to receive incorruptible life in peace with God, and that for his salvation he will not be spared this passing—in and with the passing to which God has subjected Himself in His Son. The Church needs this contribution. Its witness to Jesus Christ and to the living future promised in Him to man cannot be heard without the background and undertone of the message of Israel whose Messiah is the Crucified. Without Israel, without the reminder of the transitoriness, the passing and the past of man, without the apprehension and confession of the grace of the mortal judgment which overtakes man, the Church could speak of the eternal life promised to him only irrelevantly and therefore without power. Even its witness to Jesus' resurrection—if it no longer knows that all flesh is as grass—would become an empty word. Without the salt of that apprehension it cannot continue to exist as the Church for a single moment. Its supreme concern must be to see that this statement is preserved for it ; that Israel's service continues within it.

The community of God in its Israelite form discloses what God elects for Himself when in His eternal election of grace He elects fellowship with man. He chooses for Himself what is not His due, what is not worthy of Him, the frailty of the flesh, suffering, dying, death, in order to take it away from man, in order to clothe man instead with His glory. This is what takes place in the election of Mary's Son and with a view to Him in the election of Israel. In the destiny of this people, in its continual abandonment, extermination and destruction from its suffering in Egypt to the final fall of Jerusalem and beyond that down to the present day, in the weakness, torment and sickness of this Job, this strangest of God's servants among the peoples—it has to pay dearly for being God's chosen people—there is mirrored the radicalism in which God Himself makes real His mercy with man, the enigmatic character of His self-surrender. Matching the depth of this people's need is the depth to which God does not count it too costly to condescend for the sake of His eternal covenant with man. What man's necessary lot is, what it means that sin came into the world and with sin death ; but more than that, who and what God is, who takes the part of man in this condition ; how complete is His turning towards him—this is what the community of God in its Israelite form has to declare. In this form it proclaims man's helplessness without God's help, the vanity of all the illusions of self-sufficiency at which he continually snatches, the sole sufficiency of the divine mercy. This latter is originally attested by Israel's Messiah suffering and dying on the cross. And to attest all this in His disciple-ship is the appointed task of the community in whose execution it needs the continued life of Israel within it. It cannot properly proclaim to the world God's life-giving mercy if the world's misery is not clearly displayed to it. But it is clearly displayed to it only when it knows it as the misery in which it, too, participates. This takes place in so far as it is not only the Church but Israel also. It is when Israel comes to faith and therefore into the Church, to the fulfilment of the purpose for which it was determined in accordance with its election, that provision will be made for continuance of this recognition in the community, and with it the indispensable warning against every confidence save that of faith.

That Israel should come to faith and into the Church, and that in the Church it should perform this special service, is God's purpose for it, the promise given to it with its election. It is not at all the case, however, that God is dependent on Israel's obedience; that Israel can evade this service by persistence in unbelief. For in the purpose deter-mined for it in accordance with election there is also decreed that it must fulfil it just as much in and with its disobedience (to its own perdition) as in and with its obedience (to its own salvation). That is to say, it must perform its special service equally in the Church or in separation from it. Israel, the smitten servant of God, is dependent on God's attitude to it, but God is not dependent on that of this servant of His. In one way or another the latter will have to carry out God's will and thus reveal the depth of human need and therefore the depth of the divine mercy. In one way or another this must benefit the work of God's community laid upon the Church. As a movement of the body of Christ it must in one way or another witness to Him, in one way or another confirming Israel's election, but with it that of the Church as well.

If Israel were obedient to its election, its special witness to the passing of the old man and his world, taken up into the confession by the whole community of God's coming kingdom, would supplement and harmonise with the Church's witness of hope founded on the resurrection of Jesus Christ. The Church could speak with richer content of suffering overcome, of death slain, of life remaining in and after all passing, the more definitely it was reminded by Israel living within it of the way on which this victory was won and this truth became and continually becomes truth. It would then be Israel's peculiar honour to hold the Church fast to the Word of the cross in order that from it it may rightly represent and proclaim the Gospel of hope, in order that in distinction from any mere idea its hope may remain concrete.

Now the coming of the new man has indeed taken place already in the resurrection of Jesus Christ. And Jesus is Israel's Messiah, the promised Son of Abraham. In Him, therefore, Israel has already become new. It has already been translated from death to life. Its hope (with that of the Gentiles) has already become present. Its position and task in the Church have already been appointed for it. Everything has happened that can serve its temporal and eternal peace. What does not happen, however, is that Israel as such and as a whole takes up this position, thus actualising the fact that old things have passed away, and all things are become new. And so it resists the gracious passing from which alone it could now emerge alive, but from which it may really emerge alive. It takes a rigid stand on a carnal loyalty to itself and on a carnal hope corresponding to this loyalty. It refuses to accept the sentence of death under which it has placed itself through the betrayal of its Messiah to the Gentiles and under which it might now stand to its salvation, seeing He died for its sins too. It thinks it should and can secure, defend and preserve its existence against the God who has already lifted it up from ruin and renewed and glorified it. It wants to look steadily backwards instead of forwards. In this way it brings about a most unnatural severance in God's community. It wantonly makes itself guilty of attempting a division in the body of Christ.

But this attempt is doomed to failure even as it is undertaken. If Israel wills and does what is intrinsically impossible, this is in the truest sense of the word its own affair. In so doing it condemns and burdens and troubles itself. It cannot, however, cease to be the people of the risen Jesus Christ and of the Lord of the Church hidden from it but none the less supreme over it. What is decided in Jesus Christ from all eternity and in the midst of time is also and primarily decided about Israel—even about disobedient Israel. Old things have passed away. All things are become new. Thus the result of Jewish unbelief (as the pattern of all other unbelief) is not to be sought outside but only within the results of the divine mercy. Thus Israel's perverse choice means effectively and objectively no more than that where it might have served voluntarily it is now compelled to discharge its service in its very perversity, in the execution of this impotent attempt. Over against the witness of the Church it must now be a typical expression and incorporation of the human need consequent on sin, of man's limitation and pain, of his transiency and the death to which he is subject, in the abstraction in which by the mercy of God these are negated and taken away from man. It must be the personification of a half-venerable, half-gruesome relic, of a miraculously preserved antique, of human whimsicality. It must now live among the nations the pattern of a historical life which has absolutely no future—but without having its appointed time like other nations, being then allowed to take its leave and be merged in others. In this way it punishes itself. In this way it disrupts the community of God. Yet even in this way it cannot effectively resist God, but must serve His will and the work of His community, delivering the testimony required of it. The Synagogue cannot and will not take up the message : " He is risen ! " But it must still pronounce all the more clearly the words : " He is not here ! " It must still put all the more pertinently the question : " Why seek ye the living among the dead ? " Persisting in its cheerless chronology, it can and will know nothing of the fact that all things are become new. But it must still attest all the more stridently that old things are passed away. It speaks of the darkness that fell upon the world in the hour of Jesus' passing. It speaks of the travail of the creature which is the characteristic of the cosmos in which and for which Jesus had to die. Indirectly—in contrast to the message of the Church which is not impeded by any Jewish unbelief—this, too, is a testimony to Christ. This was and is the flesh that God accepted and took upon Him. This is the aspect of the ruin from which it is snatched by God's Word. It is a wretched testimony, but in its very wretchedness it is also a usable and powerful testimony. The Synagogue gives it involuntarily and in that way confirms Israel's election. This is not repealed. No one and nothing can make it powerless.

This also applies, however, to the promise given to Israel with its election, that its God kills only to make alive. It also applies to the blessing of God which is not refused even to Jacob who wrestles with God and is therefore lamed by God. It also applies to the Yes which in the end and after all is not concealed beneath God's No even from long-suffering Job, but revealed specifically to him. In His purpose to seek the supreme good of man without and against man's desert, God does not let Himself be dismayed even by the typical unfaithfulness and ingratitude of Israel. Did He not foresee human unfaithfulness and ingratitude in this typical form when before the foundation of the world He directed His love towards man ? Did it prevent Him even at the outset from purposing the supreme good of this very man ? And what has taken place and been revealed in Jesus' resurrection in favour also and primarily of all the sick and captive and afflicted of His people Israel, the investiture of man with the glory of God, cannot be undone again in Israel. It cannot be changed from future into past by any passage of time. For here man comes instead of passing. And the man who comes is always He who comes to meet all the dead, even the people and the Synagogue of death, who calls to Himself and therefore to life even the dwellers in the ghetto. Israel cannot impede Him in this. In this respect too—as in respect of the service which, whatever happens, it must discharge—Israel is powerless against God's will, decree and government. Israel can certainly condemn and burden and distress itself, but it cannot alter the fact that for it too a Redeemer lives. It can certainly suffer what on the ground of its own choice it must suffer ; but it cannot suffer illimitably. It can certainly glorify death ; but it cannot restore to it the power of which it has been deprived. The *eternal* Jew ? No, to eternalise himself or his destiny is the very thing he cannot do. For indeed to his—and in and with his to all such—" eternity " a term is set by God's mercy in the death and resurrection of the Jewish Messiah Jesus. The Jew can do nothing against the fact that testimony has been introduced to the mercy of God directed in the first instance to him. To be sure, he can repeat again and again the old sins of Israel and suffer again and again their old punishment. But he cannot remove the promise of God which confronts his whole typically carnal being as such. Not by any rabbinic orthodoxy, nor by any liberalism or indifferentism, can he manage to succeed in being no longer the brother of Jesus Christ. He is marked as such—as such more strongly than by anything else, and in such a way that he can no longer live as a people and yet cannot disappear in any other people. He is marked as such for death, but also for life.

Independently of Israel's choice and way, the service of the Church as the perfect form of the one community of God consists in attesting, by faith in the Word heard, by laying hold of the divine mercy, the coming kingdom of God as the end of all human need, the coming new man and his eternal life. The Church exists among Jews and Gentiles because Jesus in His resurrection does not shatter the power of death in vain but with immediate effect ; because as the witness to eternal life He cannot remain alone but at once awakens, gathers and sends forth recipients, partners and co-witnesses of this life. The Church thus proclaims Jesus' exaltation as the goal of His humiliation, His kingdom as the goal of His suffering, His coming as the goal of His passing. It proclaims what in God's hands is to become and can become of man taken up and accepted by Him. Its message is, therefore, the final and decisive word of the charge committed to the whole community of God, in which the special word given to Israel has its appointed place, and which it has to assist as a foreword. It is referred to this assistance and therefore to the continuing existence of Israel in its midst. On the other hand, its existence is the fulfilment of Israel's determined purpose with which Israel is always forced to reckon, either to its woe as the people that would like to live at all costs and yet cannot, that can only lead an outcast, despised, dispersed, unreal life among other nations, or to its salvation as the people that had to and could die, for that very reason and in that very way becoming immortal among the other nations as they rise and perish. It could and would live to its salvation if it would live in the Church to render that auxiliary service, if it would believe in its Messiah.

The Church form of the community reveals the scope of what God wills for man when in His eternal election of grace He elects him for fellowship with Himself. In electing him from all eternity He elects him for eternity. In electing him in grace He elects him for his salvation. In electing him for fellowship with Himself He makes Himself the Guarantor and Giver of the eternal salvation offered to man. Without ceasing to be God, and without man ceasing to be man, He really invests him with His own glory. This is what is at stake when He espouses Israel's cause, and in Israel the cause of the man Jesus, and in Jesus that of the many from among Jews and Gentiles. Man elected by God is man made participant by God in eternal salvation. It is this man whom God's community in its perfect, its Church form can reveal. It reveals that even death is surrounded by life, even hell (in all its terrible reality) by the kingdom of the beloved Son of God. If it is futile (according to Israel's commission) to refuse to see and suffer death as a sign of the divine judgment, it is even more futile (according to that of the Church) to reverence and fear death itself instead of rejoicing in the hope of eternal life which is the gracious gift of God's mercy. All this is imperatively attested by the risen Lord of the Church, behind whose revelation it is impossible to penetrate in faith, but whose revelation it is now impossible to ignore because it is the revelation of what comes and abides. To attest all this is the task which the Church for its part has to discharge—in virtue of the fact that it is now awakened and gathered by Him. In face of death it confesses life, life from and in and above death. In face of the man who passes it confesses the man who comes. Even the passing of man it attests only in attesting his coming and abiding, in attesting the living Christ. It is indeed aware of death, but of death finally deprived of its power, subordinated to life and made to serve it.

The Church is the perfect form of the community because the message which the community (the environment of the man Jesus) has to transmit to the world acquires its true and essential form as the message of the Church, the form of the Gospel, of glad tidings for all who are defrauded and deprived of their rights, for all captives and sick persons, for all who are astray and in distress. With such a message Jesus Himself stands in the midst of His own, and proclaimed by the service of His own wills to go out into the world. This is what has to happen continually and at every point between the inner circle of the community and the outer one of the rest of men. The Gospel is to be preached on this frontier. But if this—the shining of the light of the divine mercy—is the goal of God's community, what else can have been the principle of its beginning? The Church of the Gospel is in fact the first and final determination of Israel. Therefore the consolation and blessing and saving power of the Word and will of God have been alive even in the midst of Israel from the very first, and on the basis of special illumination and guidance they have been discerned and tasted by many individuals within all the judgments and visitations. In their special charge and way and work the Gospel pre-exists—as the true and essential form of the charge committed to the whole elected community—even in the realm of the Law, even in the shadow of its sentence and warning. In so far as this pre-history too is enacted within the history of Israel, Israel participates with the Church in the perfect form of the community, in the body of Christ, and it too has this universal mission.

By the Church of the coming man pre-existing in Israel, Israel's election is also confirmed positively. It does not alter Israel's special determination, but illumines and interprets it. It shows that God's fatherly disposition to this people is the prime and ultimate meaning of its history ; that even the intention of the divine warning and punishment that dominate so powerfully the portrait presented by this history is fatherly ; that even the purpose of the obscure dispensation of suffering falling blow after blow upon Job is fatherly. As the crucifixion of Jesus is a divine benefit in its association with His resurrection, so also is Israel's history of suffering in its association with the pre-history of the Gospel enacted within it. It is always in this association that the portrait of man who passes must be present even to the Church.

There cannot be anything more than a prefiguration in the case of the pre-existent Church in Israel. Its reality is revealed when Jews and Gentiles together, called by the risen Christ, receive the consolation and blessing of the Gospel. Those formerly consoled and blessed are indeed a small and dispersed minority within Israel as such and on the whole. The fact that they are consoled and blessed seems without exception to be a passing, fragmentary moment of their existence. In contrast to their preservation and refreshing there stands at least as expressively the hopeless ruin of others. Ultimately they seem to disappear completely in the melancholy total aspect of the issue of Israel's history. As genuinely consoled and blessed there remains finally only the one Jesus of Nazareth. In the strict sense, therefore, only the problem of the new man passing from death into life is posed or rather left open by their existence. We should have to characterise the history of Israel as incomprehensible if it did not issue in the positive solution of this problem, and were not to be interpreted in the light of it.

But in the Church founded on the resurrection of Jesus from the dead this problem cannot possibly be overlooked. It does not itself believe the Gospel if it does not recognise its faith in that of the preserved and redeemed in Israel; if it does not see that the very hope that sustained them is also its own. In so doing it will welcome the positive confirmation of the election of all Israel, and it cannot refuse for its part to make the hope for all Israel its most intimate concern. In grateful recognition of the ties and obligations binding it to Israel, it will be glad to have in its midst Christians from the Jews also. It will itself desire to be no more than Israel fulfilling its determined purpose, to live by nothing else but the grace of God directed towards Israel. Though waiting for Israel's conversion, it cannot and will not hesitate to precede Israel with the confession of the unity of God's community, the unity of the man who, according to the will of the divine mercy, both passes and comes in the person of Him who has suffered death for all and brought life to light for all.

For the exegesis of Rom. 11 E. F. Ströter's pamphlet, *Die Judenfrage und ihre göttliche Lösung nach Römer Kapitel 11* (Bremen, undated) is extremely useful in spite of its glaring mistakes.

The question of Rom. 11^1: "I say then, Hath God cast away his people?" may well be regarded as a continuation of the series of questions in 10^{18-19}. There the question whether the reason for the Jewish failure to believe and confess is to be sought in the fact that the Jews cannot hear or understand was answered with a clear No which in 10^{16} and 10^{21} led back to the finding that they were and are disobedient. But this very finding could evoke a further question. There can, of course, be no doubt that (by the form in which he establishes that finding in 10^{21}) Paul has already answered this question too in the negative. The whole day long God has indeed stretched out His hands to this same disobedient people. In the sphere of Paul's thinking the idea is quite an impossible one that God might have done this in vain and abandoned the attempt, that His faithfulness might finally be to no purpose, and at some point reach its end. This is proved by the μὴ γένοιτο which is immediately inserted in 11^1. Nevertheless the question can arise, and for the sake of complete clarity it must be heard. Does it not follow from this disobedience, from Israel's rewarding the faithfulness of God with the rejection of the Christ Jesus, with His betrayal to the Gentiles to be crucified, that He now belongs wholly to these Gentiles and no more at all to Israel, that Israel itself is therefore rejected, that it is eliminated as a useless and even harmful instrument from the fulfilment of the divine decree, and that to this extent the divine decree itself has been altered? Must not the proved disobedience of Israel be traced back ultimately to such a change in the divine will with respect to it? Though it hears and understands very well, does it perhaps fail to obey because God is finished with it, because He has ceased really and seriously to require obedience from it, because it no longer has any future with God?

What ground is there for the " Impossible" with which Paul interrupts these questions ? Paul provides it by referring—explicitly, in contrast to chapter 10—to himself : " For I also am an Israelite, of the seed of Abraham, of the tribe of Benjamin. God hath not cast away his people which he foreknew " (vv. 1b–2a). I do not think that the force of this proof is to be sought in its unspoken continuation : " As such an Israelite I myself have actually become a Christian (Lietzmann), and attest as such that Israel is not rejected." This is also true, admittedly. But in the Scripture proof that follows it is not a pious Israelite as such, but the prophet Elijah whose voice is heard—an indication, perhaps, that in the reference to his own person Paul is again thinking, not so much of his personal conversion and Christianity, as of his office as an apostle. To be sure, he does not think of this latter without a recollection of the supra-personal, typical significance of his conversion (cf. 1 Tim. 1^16), to the extent that, unlike most other conversions, this was mediated through his direct encounter with the risen Jesus Christ. We can agree with Ströter in supposing that on this ground Paul regarded it as prophecy, prefiguration and pledge of the conversion of unbelieving Israel coincident with the second coming of Jesus Christ, and to this extent as a proof that God has not cast off His people. It is also not without significance, surely, that emphasis is laid on the further fact that the man converted in this way is a Benjaminite (and thus a member of the tribe which, according to Jud. 20–21, at one time almost incurred extermination, but was not allowed to incur it—a fellow-clansman of the rejected and yet elected king Saul). Yet, according to the context, we must not look at these reminiscences, important though they are in themselves, for the emphasis of Rom. 11^1f.. The decisive meaning of this existential proof, of this " Impossible," is that the apostolate itself, the office of proclamation based on mission, the message of the risen Jesus Christ, has as its bearer Paul, an Israelite, a descendant of Abraham, a Benjaminite like many others—and he is conscious, surely, that without exception all the other apostles are also Jews. To admit that God has rejected His people would mean the annulment, not only of Paul himself, but above all (and this alone is absolutely " impossible ") of his office, his commission, and its whole content. In his own person as the bearer of the apostolic office Paul does indeed see his people, Israel, associated not only passively but actively in the saving events in the presence and work of the risen Jesus Christ. He himself has this descent and was and is particularly conscious of it. He had been himself an Israelite, a Synagogue Jew, a hopeful Rabbi. Like the Jews who now oppose the Church, in the name of his Judaism he had been the avowed and active enemy of Jesus Christ even after His crucifixion and resurrection. He had been fully participant in the disobedience of Israel described in chapter 10. Yet in spite of this, has he not seen and heard the Lord ? Has he not been made by the Lord the apostle of the Gentiles ? And in this union of Jew and apostle to the Gentiles effected in him, do we not have clear proof of the fact that God has not rejected His people, that the day in which God stretches forth His hands to the disobedient people has not yet drawn to a close. In this union has not the Church come to Israel, even to the Israel which for its part was so very unwilling to come to the Church ? Has not the new, living shoot made a little progress in the direction of new life for the dead stump as well ? Has not God made a tiny start in realising His purpose with the people whom He foreknew, even in this people itself, so that in view of this bit of genuine Israel we have to say that, through God's mercy in Jesus Christ, Israel itself and as such is not rejected but held fast, being not only the preparatory and first stage of the Church but itself the Church of God, itself the voluntary and conscious witness of the fulfilment of His promises and the recipient of the entire salvation that has become present in this fulfilment ? It is to be noted that in the question of v. 1a, as in the negative answer of v. 2a, Paul uses the words from Ps. 94^14 : " For the Lord will not cast off his people, neither will he forsake his inheritance. But judgment shall return unto righteousness ; and all the upright in heart shall follow it "— to put the verse in its context. The μὴ γένοιτο of v. 1a is obviously demanded on the basis of this passage. A positive answer would be in literal contradiction to this quotation. Thus the proof that Paul advances in v. 1b with the reference to his, the Benjaminite's apostolic office is not meant to stand alone even here, but the underlying reason for adducing it as a proof is rather that, like everything which is to-day decisive for Israel's future, it is a fulfilment of the prophecy given to Israel. Between the divine foreknowledge of Israel and the separation from his mother's womb which, according to his declaration in Gal. 1[15], was the lot of Paul (as of that other Benjaminite Jeremiah), there stands the confirmatory word of Scripture. It is for this reason that Paul can so confidently prove the permanence of Israel's election by the fact of his apostolate.

But what follows shows that he considers his repudiation of the question, or his positive assertion of the faithfulness of God, to need further proof just because of the reason given in v. 1b. What follows in v. 2b–4 is obviously the answer to what is in this case an unspoken question : " Can then the existence of an individual, even assuming that as such he really does reveal the election of Israel in contradiction to the existence and attitude of the majority, really be cogent proof with regard to the election of Israel ? Is not the isolation of the apostle among the people of his origin a distinct repetition of the fate which this people prepared for all its prophets, and ultimately a confirmation of its rejection of Jesus Christ, whose messenger he is ? Did not Paul himself in 10[16] quote Is. 53[1] : " Lord, who hath believed our report ? " Himself sharing the isolation of God, is he not, therefore, in relation to his people the living dis-proof of its election ? How can he, or the union of Jew and apostle to the Gentiles admittedly consummated in him, have for his people any more than the significance of an exception which can only prove the rule that God has rejected this people ? Questions of this kind had perhaps already been asked in Gentile Christian circles in relation to the Jews. Later, and right up to the present time, this has certainly been the case. The question which Paul faces is the question asked by Christian anti-semitism, whether the crucifixion of Jesus Christ does not settle the fact that the Jews are now to be regarded and treated only as the people accursed by God. Is not the Jewish origin of the apostles and the whole Church a *pudendum*, or at any rate an irrelevancy ? In answer to this question Paul recalls the story of Elijah in vv. 2b–4. And in so doing he answers this question too in the negative. It is, after all, the case—this is what the story teaches us—that the actual existence in Israel of an individual sent by God and His faithful servant does actually prove that even for Israel itself, not only for the sake of the Gentiles but also for the sake of the Jews— it is not in vain, not unsuccessfully, not without result, not merely an isolated fact, that until and with and even since the appearance of its Messiah God has been and still is the God of this people, and that therefore this people has been and still is His people. The recollection of the isolated Elijah proves the exist-ence of the Church in Israel itself. The isolated Elijah legitimates the isolated Paul and therefore his reference to his apostolic office as a proof that God has not rejected His people. To what extent is this achieved by this recollection ? " Wot ye not (ye Gentile Christians who raise such a question) what the scrip-ture saith of Elias ? how he maketh intercession to God against Israel, saying Lord, they have killed thy prophets, and digged down thine altars ; and I am left alone, and they seek my life. But what saith the answer of God unto him ? I have reserved to myself seven thousand men, who have not bowed the knee to the image of Baal." It is an episode from the history of the Northern Kingdom which here concerns us. In its separation from the house of David it represented from the very first and as such the principle of apostasy from Israel's God, and under the regime of Ahab and Jezebel it reached the culmin-ating point of the corresponding evolution. The complaint of Elijah in this situation is obviously parallel to that of Is. 53¹, and at the same time it is only too close a paraphrase of the complaint that Paul too has to bring against his people. All that can be done after this complaint, it would seem, is simply to state the exception that proves the rule. The prophet is alone at the heart of his people, assailed and persecuted by it even to the point of death. In this way the repudiation of God Himself is carried to its conclusion, and Israel's rejection is necessarily decided. But the Elijah story is instructive because at this decisive point, when the prophet has already desired his own death, when he has lain down to sleep under the juniper bush, and therefore when he has already obviously drawn the conclusion which the question treated by Paul obviously wishes to draw, it opposes to the complaint a divine oracle which says something totally different. This is God's communication : " Yet I have left me seven thousand in Israel, all the knees which have not bowed unto Baal, and every mouth which hath not kissed him " (1 K. 19¹⁸). The first point to be noted from the context of this saying is that it is the final word, pointing in this different direction, of a divine utterance the main content of which is to confirm the judgment of the prophet on his people by commissioning him (1 K. 19¹⁵ᶠ·) to anoint Hazael king over Syria, Jehu king over Israel and Elisha his own prophetic successor, in order that these might execute the judgment which is to fall on God's people. " And it shall come to pass, that him that escapeth the sword of Hazael shall Jehu slay ; and him that escapeth from the sword of Jehu shall Elisha slay." In this text, therefore, it is not denied but asserted that the majority of Israel, and in this majority Israel as such and as a whole, stands under the wrath and punishment of God. But then it goes on to speak of the seven thousand whom God has left for Himself, who have not conformed, who have not joined in the great apostasy, and therefore of a minority in Israel who are to be brought safely through the fire of God's wrath and punishment. Now in the first instance this settles the point that at any rate the prophet is not the only exception, as he himself thinks ; that he is not entirely alone with God. God has seen to it that where he stands others also stand. But all the same we might ask what do even these seven thousand prove for the whole, for Israel as such ? May it not be that these seven thousand, too, only confirm the fact that Israel as such is rejected ? If we read further, however, we see that these seven thousand with whom the prophet has to console himself as a persistent minority do for their part, strangely enough, represent the whole, Israel as such. For seven thousand is the number of " all the people, even all the children of Israel " (1 K. 20¹⁵) in the story which immediately follows of the war between Ahab of Israel and Benhadad of Syria. And much later (2 K. 24¹⁶) seven thousand is also given as the number of the men of might in Jerusalem who were carried into captivity by Nebuchadnezzar. Thus the minority of seven thousand men in 1 K. 19¹⁸ certainly cannot be regarded as an irrelevant minority. It is these seven thousand men, and not the unfaithful majority, who represent Israel as such. By " leaving them " God holds fast to Israel as such, and it is decided that He has not rejected His people. When therefore (in the same breath with which judgment is announced on the majority) the solitary Elijah is consoled by a reference to these seven thousand men, he does not stand alone, but as the holder of his commission he is invisibly surrounded by these seven thousand proved men. Even in his loneliness he stands effectively before God for the whole of Israel, for Israel as such. In just the same way Paul does not stand alone. In just the same way he is not a private person of no evidential value. He can and must, therefore, appeal to his existence as a Jew and as a Gentile missionary as a valid proof that God has not rejected His people. The work of the risen Jesus Christ which made of the foe and persecutor His ambassador to the Gentiles does actually reveal the faithfulness of God with respect to the whole of disobedient Israel, with respect to the Israel which has crucified its Lord, and which after His resurrection has failed to recognise and has rejected Him.

But by this time Paul has carried the recollection of the seven thousand men of the Elijah story a stage further. Provisionally—for the theme will recur in v. 13—he no longer relates himself to his apostolate in particular, but now sees himself as an apostle invisibly surrounded by the seven thousand who must surely be present in his day too (since this is the fulfilment of prophecy). He therefore proceeds : " Even so then at this present time also there is a remnant according to the election of grace. And if by grace, then is it no more of works : otherwise grace is no more grace " (vv. 5–6). It is obvious that this continuation does not merely contain an application of the divine oracle to the seven thousand of Paul's own day. Admittedly it does bring out this application too. There can be no doubt that Paul is now thinking not only of the apostles who with him came out of and still belong to Israel, but also of the Jews in Jerusalem effectively called to the faith of the Church by their word—of the three thousand of the day of Pentecost (Ac. 2⁴¹) who later (Ac. 4⁴) became five thousand, the number of their further increase (Ac. 5¹⁴), intentionally perhaps, being concealed. And, of course, his thoughts go beyond that to all the named and unnamed figures from the Synagogue to whom he himself had proclaimed the Word of God and not in vain. This is the fulfilment of the prophecy of the reserved seven thousand ἐν τῷ νῦν καιρῷ, in the Messianic present. But what Paul says passes beyond the compass of this application. He gives us a definite interpretation and exposition of this oracle of God, and particularly of the word κατέλιπον, to which he had already given peculiar emphasis in the quotation (v. 4) by the addition of ἐμαυτῷ. The effect of this was to lay the stress distinctly on what God has purposed and done with these seven thousand men in some sense for His own sake and in His own cause. The picture that Paul has in his mind's eye when he recalls this text is not that of seven thousand upright men who did not bow the knee to Baal, and whom for this reason, in recognition of and reward for this resolute attitude, God preserved from judgment. On the contrary, it was for Himself, for His own purpose as the God of Israel, that He willed to see seven thousand men left, and He separated them, so that—we might as well say it right out, as a consequence of and in completion of this act of separation—they then displayed that resolution. The existence of this minority was already achieved by God's decision and determination. And again, on the ground of this divine decision and determination it represents in His sight all Israel as such. It is the witness of the faithfulness of His election of all Israel. The elect in Israel witness to the election of Israel itself. And that is why in place of the concept of the seven thousand men of the Elijah story the concept of the λεῖμμα κατ' ἐκλογὴν χάριτος is introduced as its present-day counterpart. The degree of logical difficulty in this concept is apparent. " Election of grace " does not seem to be a concept we can well relate to the " remnant " of a people which is in any case elected by grace. And again, it does not seem that this " remnant " of the people elected in any case can very well owe the fact that it is left to a special " election of grace." " Remnant " of the chosen people—this makes one think rather of a remaining portion of this people which by action and conduct corresponding to the election of the whole people has made itself worthy to be left, to be withdrawn from the judgment which passes over the whole. But Paul knows nothing whatever of any such worthiness on the part of some in Israel. On the contrary, what he actually says about the Christ-believing Jews of the present, and therefore indirectly about the seven thousand at the time of Elijah, is that it is by the election of grace and therefore not by their own worthiness that they are determined as this " remnant." The meaning is obviously as follows. It is, of course, already grace that Israel as such is elected. And God's grace with regard to Israel consisted from the very first in its election. But this eternal and basic determination of Israel's existence does not lurk somewhere in the background before time was. In time itself it is again and again the basic determination of the existence of this people. Again and again God's relation to it is choice which is grace, grace which is consummated in choice. If God's relation to Israel is from time to time realised concretely by His " leaving " again and again in Israel His representative seven thousand (apart from His individual special servants and agents like Moses and Elijah), this " leaving " is obviously the repetition and confirmation of the election of grace which founded Israel as such and as a whole. Primarily, then, it is not that there is a remnant of men who are loyal, obedient and steadfast, etc., although loyalty, obedience and steadfastness, etc., will certainly distinguish this remnant on each particular occasion. Primarily, it is that there is a remnant of those whom God for His own sake has in free grace selected from among all others and set aside for the confirmation of His election of Israel. That the one Elijah and the seven thousand, the one Paul and other Christ-believing Jews with him are " left " is something they do not owe to themselves. It is something to which they have no right or claim. Nothing that they have achieved or brought, no work of theirs, can make of them this remnant. On the contrary, that they are so is the initial election of Israel itself. It is utterly and exclusively the work of the decision and determination of their God, who to-day as formerly confirms Himself as the God of Israel—and therefore the election of Israel as such—by acting in this way and not otherwise. If from God's side, in spite of Israel's disobedience and guilt, nothing is lost in respect of its election (for again and again this remnant stands in His sight for the whole), this is not because the apostasy of Israel was not, after all, so bad. Nor was it because in individual cases on Israel's side this or that work might be offered which would justify Israel and thus necessitate God's faithfulness to Israel. It is plain that Paul will not tolerate that the courageous attitude of the seven thousand, or even the faithfulness of Elijah himself, or the faith of the Jews converted in his own day, or even his own faith and obedience as apostle, should in any sense be regarded as a justifying work which imposes an obligation upon God. For this reason, whatever " trustworthiness " there may and must be among the seven thousand as the necessary fruit of the election of grace cannot be taken into consideration as the content of a claim which renders the " election of grace " superfluous. That God leaves for Himself this remnant in Israel, and that with this remnant after all He also keeps hold of Israel as such, does not mean that in this remnant at least He finds a worthiness on the ground of which His relation to it can and must be other than that of the election of grace. If the grace of God directed towards this remnant, and with this remnant towards all Israel, were to be related to the work and worthiness of the seven thousand, it would not be grace at all. The really precious thing in which the remnant, and with it all Israel, can glory, would then be of absolutely no value—the free, unmerited and therefore unconditioned favour guaranteed by the goodness and omnipotence of God Himself, the pure mercy of God efficacious in its very purity. Its God would no longer be He who of old appeared to Abraham, He who awakens the dead and calls what is not into being. Requiting human favour with His own, He would no longer be the God who lives from and by Himself, who as such is Israel's consolation and hope. The promise given to Israel would also be of no value (cf. Rom. 4^{14}), and faith in it void. For the content of the promise is the revelation of the righteousness of God through Him who is to come forth from Israel, and faith is the confidence that dares to wait for the fulfilment of this promise. If the grace of God were related to the works of His elect, it would not be grace, because it would be conditioned and restricted by the achievement of human righteousness, and in effect it could only be disfavour. The precious thing in which the elect can glory is the God who lives from and by Himself—the unconditional and therefore the unrestricted nature of His grace directed towards them. It consists in the fact that there is repeated in them the beginning of the relation of God to Israel, the founding of the divine covenant exactly as it once took place between God and Abraham. It is for this very reason and in this very way that these elect stand also for the whole of Israel, and that in and with them God adheres to Israel as such and to everything that He has at any time promised it. The nature of the election of grace and therefore of the consolation and hope of Israel, the meaning of the miraculous derivation of the Son of God and Man from this natural stock, of the divine work of fulfilment corresponding so exactly to the promise and to faith, is all supremely revealed in the seven thousand. Thus they are the very last who can be quoted to prove that there is a work of man which justifies Israel and thus necessitates God's faithfulness to Israel. This is the very last way in which it would ever occur to them to regard their work. It is by God's mercy that again and again there is, in fact, an Israel in Israel, a remnant which by its work, by its trustworthiness, by what the seven thousand of former and latter times and Elijah and Paul are and do and refrain from doing, attests and confirms in and with its own election the election of all Israel. The remnant does this, not because of the fact that after all it is still Israel, but because of the fact that it is already the Church in Israel, already the work of the creative mercy of God which does not fail even in relation to Israel itself, to which no limit is set even by Israel's disobedience and guilt. This remnant does not attest its own and therefore Israel's worthiness. On the contrary, in its own unworthiness which is also that of all Israel it attests the glory of God and of His miraculous work in fulfilment of the promise. For Paul the force of the recollection of the story of Elijah in vv. 2b–4 as a proof that God has not rejected His people undoubtedly resides in this interpretation in vv. 5–6 of the κατέλιπον ἐμαυτῷ of v. 4. Of His own free grace, without any regard to man's work or worthiness, God has left to Himself both this former and latter remnant. Paul himself (the whole proof had indeed begun with a reference to his identity as a Jew and the apostle to the Gentiles), though he is not worthy to be called an apostle because he has persecuted God's community, is what he is by the grace of God (1 Cor. 15⁹ᶠ·). This remnant is, therefore, a clear proof that God has not rejected His people. It is this because it is already the Church in Israel, pre-existing in the seven thousand of olden times, existing in the community of God now called together from among the Jews also, the community of which Paul himself was formerly a persecutor and has now been made an apostle. The remnant in Israel proves that God has not rejected His people because it attests the miraculous work of the derivation from Israel of the Son of God and Man, and therefore itself participates in this miraculous work. The fact that this is possible—as it must be, since in virtue of the divine mercy it is real—proves that the mercy of God is no less directed towards Israel than formerly. The anti-semitic question of v. 1 is, therefore, a question of unbelief, and those who put this question can only be called to repentance with the utmost urgency. Speaking as they do of the election of grace (in the unconditional sense of this concept as made clear in v. 6), the story of Elijah and, against the background of it, the story of Paul speak of the divine mercy which challenges the disobedience and guilt of Israel because it is superior to them. They therefore speak of the constancy of God in the election of this people.

That Paul sees in this the force of his proof is shown by the conclusion of the section in vv. 7–10, which stands out at once by reason of its relentlessness. Its decisive content is summed up in v. 7, but again the Scripture proof of this, and especially of v. 7c, in vv. 8–10 obviously could not be omitted. Τί οὖν does not in any sense signify a new question arising, but means : What further ? What then ? What is the decisive content of what has just been said, the comprehensive deduction to be drawn ? The answer begins as follows. We learn " what Israel seeks for " from 9³¹ and 10³. It seeks to fulfil the law of righteousness with an attempt to establish its own righteousness. It regards the commandment given to it, which certainly expresses the order of life under the given promise, as a summons to make itself worthy of its election, and a possibility of doing so, thus necessitating the fulfilment of the promise, bringing Christ down from heaven or up from hell. Its desire is to establish its election by its own strength and endeavour, by the earnestness and value of the work performed by it. It wishes to be what it is by and through itself. But this is just what " it did not obtain." The extent of its failure had been shown in chapter 10 : how, when Israel took this way, it incurred the guilt of transgressing its Law and compromising its election ; how it involved itself in a disobedience which in the end became irreparably manifest in the refusal of faith and confession when confronted with the fulfilment of all its promises, with the Messiah sent to it from God as the one content, the *kelal* of its Law. Paul does not return to this. On the contrary, in relation to the corresponding verses of chapter 10 the continuation is quite new : " But the election hath obtained it." In 9^{30} we saw that the Gentiles who did not pursue righteousness received righteousness, namely, the righteousness of faith, and in 10^{20} that God caused Himself to be found of those who did not seek Him and was revealed to those who did not ask for Him. But in relation to Israel, the establishment of the guilt which resulted from its unenlightened zeal for God seemed to be the last word. Now however, according to the proof in 11^{1-6} that God has not rejected His people, this cannot possibly be the last word in relation to Israel, even in the form of the dictum in v. 7a. That is why this is at once followed by v. 7b. According to vv. 1–6 the reference in chapter 10 to the astonishing fact that God finds and is found by the Gentiles is matched by the assertion that the election in Israel has actually obtained what Israel in general was seeking without obtaining. The concept ἐκλογὴ is, of course, used here for the earlier and more recent seven thousand, or for the λεῖμμα κατ' ἐκλογὴν χάριτος of v. 5. To that extent it is an abbreviation. But in relation to the theme it is not unimportant that Paul chooses this particular abbreviation. Who has actually obtained what Israel sought and did not obtain ? In effect, no one, not even the men of that remnant, nor even the trustworthy . seven thousand in themselves and as such, but the election, the ἐκλογὴ χάριτος of v. 5, and therefore God Himself in virtue of His willing and doing, has obtained it, and the seven thousand only in virtue of this election, as created and constituted by it, and gathered, defended and kept by God. That the worth and glory of any man is neither the ground nor the consequence of this attainment is already very impressively stated by this abbreviation. If under this sign it is now to be said of the remnant in Israel that it obtained what Israel sought and did not obtain, then, according to the account given in chapter 10 about what the Gentiles obtained without seeking, the immediate significance of this must be that this remnant obtained righteousness before God, namely, the righteousness imparted to man in faith. Its obtaining means that it was reached by God, that God revealed Himself to it. But according to what was said in chapter 10 about Israel's seeking, it must also mean that this remnant obtained the position of the true Israel. It was and is what Israel endeavoured vainly, because perversely, to be—the " Israel of God " (Gal. 6^{16}), the " wrestler with God " who corresponds and is adequate to his election and designation by God. In this remnant God's election of Israel has found its human reflection. There is revealed in it the fact that God's election is not simply transferred to the Gentiles. Israel is not abandoned as its original object. Even less is there any reason to suppose that the election had never been seriously intended as an election of Israel but that it had only the Gentiles as its object from the very first. No, in the existence of the seven thousand God's election is established as an election of Israel. In the light of the existence of these seven thousand we can regard the calling of the Gentiles only as a revelation of the wonderful depth and extent of the election of Israel. In other words, Israel is vindicated in the seven thousand. There shines out in them the unique calling and situation of Israel, its absolute distinction from all other peoples. In the light of this remnant to be a Jew is a necessary joy and justifiable pride. If possible, it is this even more so after the appearance of Christ than before. For this remnant attests that God's election was and is also the election of Israel. Indeed, it attests that it was and is properly and primarily the election of Israel—its election as the Church, but really *its* election. Yet, as we have said, it is the company of the elect, or more accurately the election of God's grace, which obtains this goal sought in vain by Israel in general. And the elect obtain it in just the same way as according to chapter 10 the Gentiles obtain it, as the people that was found without having sought, to whom God was revealed without its having asked for Him. There is thus no trace of a success of man's willing and running ; it is a unique triumph of the mercy of God which is the content of this occurrence, the power and truth of this attainment. It is not a case of Israel coming to the Church, but of the Church coming to Israel. It is not Israel itself but God who in this remnant has made it what it is. There can be no question of any other attainment of this goal than the work and word of grace. In the light of this work and this work alone the seven thousand are proof of the fact that God has not rejected His people. It is because this proposition and therefore its proof, that is, the continuity between Israel and the Church represented in this remnant, are vital for Paul, that its reality and therefore the exclusiveness of the mercy that creates and maintains this continuity are also vital. This, then, is why the continuation is in such sharp contrast : " And the rest were blinded " (v. 7c), and is based on a reference (vv. 8–10) to what is written about this divine hardening of Israel. A glance at the continuation in v. 11 f. is necessary to show us what is meant and not meant by these statements about the hardening of the λοιποί. If we begin there, there can be no doubt about one thing, that Paul sees this divine hardening too in the context of the salvation-history occurring in and with the chosen people Israel. This history is not, therefore, interrupted by what befalls the λοιποί. Even in this occurrence it takes its course. As a salvation-history it also embraces perdition. It is salvation-history even in the history of the perdition of this " rest." According to v. 11 it is through their transgression, as it arises out of this hardening, that there comes salvation to the Gentiles. Moreover, salvation comes to the Gentiles in order to provoke this " rest " to salutary jealousy ; in order that (v. 12 f.) with their conversion there may dawn the concluding, consummating glory of God, which is still awaited even by the Gentiles, by the whole Church. Since this is so, according to v. 12 their stumbling, their transgression as it arises from this hardening, cannot mean their fall. It cannot mean that they had been forsaken by God, or that they too were not elected Israel, or that they had ceased to be so. These advance considerations must control the interpretation of vv. 7–10.

What is said here about the divine blinding of Israel does not of itself seem to bring out clearly the supreme divine control even in this blinding. In contrast with what was said about the " remnant "—that they obtained the righteousness of God by the coming to them of grace, of the Church, so that they themselves could already be the Church and therefore Israel realising its election—there seems to stand in hard finality the statement that the only reference of the " rest "—and this means, of course, the overwhelming majority of Israelites—was to be " hardened " against His promises, to be made deaf to all His speaking with Israel and insensible to all His benefits ; and that all this necessarily proved their undoing (as it did Pharaoh's in 9[17]) according to the will of God. This is what the word hardening says, and it is expressly enough interpreted in this way by the Old Testament quotations in vv. 8–10. There really seems to be good reason for the question of v. 11, whether in this respect, at least in relation to the majority, the election of Israel is not characterised as null, as invalid or no longer valid for this majority ; whether we should not say at least in relation to this majority that God has rejected His people in favour of the Church ? And even if, after all, the seven thousand from Israel belong to the Church, must we not say of Israel as such what is to be said of the majority ? Must we not say of Israel as such that God has forsaken it ? On closer inspection, however, the μὴ γένοιτο with which Paul (v. 11) repudiates this conclusion from vv. 7–10 is seen to be well founded already in these verses themselves. One reason for this is that when read in the context of and in immediate connexion with vv. 5–6 they are obviously meant to corroborate the statement that God's election of grace has brought a remnant out of Israel to the Church and thus to the realisation of Israel's election itself. The corroboration is provided by a reference to what in the same freedom God has done with all the rest in Israel. That Israel has no merit with regard to its election, that it is God's mercy alone which makes possible and necessary the existence of this remnant, emerges clearly from the fact that God can also reject people in Israel, i.e., that in the same freedom with which on the one side He assigns a share in the realisation of Israel's election, on the other He can also refuse it; that He can also exclude from entrance to the Church ; and that this has actually befallen the majority of Israelites. It is against the background of this severity of God towards some, and in fact towards the majority, that the truth of v. 6 shines out—that His grace is grace. But this, too, is obviously what brings to light the consolation and hope, the ground and ultimate certainty, of the election of Israel, to which even they too belong. This, too, is obviously the strongest word that can be spoken even for them, even for their future. If with the making of this contrast between the elect and the hardened in the chosen people there vanishes even the last semblance of the idea that God's elect owe it to themselves that they are such; if this contrast brings all the more clearly into view the nature of the free goodness of the electing God, this obviously means that some light necessarily falls even upon the darkness of the hardened. As Israelites, are not they too at least the chosen possession of the God who elects in this way, on the ground of His grace and not of human works ? Even in their hardening is not God the God of Israel in relation to them too ? If it becomes plain in the elect that it is because He is the merciful One that God has not forsaken His people, does not this apply also and perhaps above all to those in whose case He has not actually made this plain or willed to make it plain, just because and as He willed to make it plain in the others, the remnant as such ? The fact is that only a remnant as such, only an election among the chosen people, could make this plain. Is not what He reveals in this way, and can reveal only in this way, the truth of Israel's election ? But if this is the case, how can it fail to benefit even those whom He causes to serve this revelation by their hardening ? At this point, again, we must pay further attention to the form of the statement, namely, to the fact that in proof of this statement about the λοιποί in v. 7c Paul adduces Scripture (again the whole Canon), Isaiah, Moses and David. This certainly accentuates at first the seriousness of the statement that God has hardened the majority of Israel, that their existence in contradiction and revolt is just as much His work as that of the seven thousand. These quotations heighten the contrast in which it becomes plain that grace is grace. But Paul does not refer to Scripture in order to draw from it particularly pregnant formulations of his own insights and in that way to secure confirmation for his own statements. Indeed, we cannot even say that in order to prove the statement that God has not rejected His people these particular Old Testament passages are the obvious ones to select. He obviously does so because he reads the whole of the Old Testament as a prophecy of the day of salvation that has now dawned in Jesus Christ. And in these chapters especially he reads it as a prophecy of the relation between Israel and the Church ; not only with respect to the seven thousand, amongst whom he counts himself ; but also with respect to the rest who now confront him as the unbelieving Synagogue. Scripture itself tells him what his own statement in v. 7c is meant to reproduce—that God has not rejected His people. Scripture would surely be guilty of self-contradiction if when it spoke of the divine hardening it suddenly tried to evade Ps. 94[14]. Surely this verse affirms even of the hardening, in its own way, that God has not rejected His people. Surely there is no point in *not* remembering this verse.

Surely it *must* be remembered, seeing that it speaks with such special plainness about what still seems to be an unsolved problem after all that has been said of the gracious election of the seven thousand, seeing that it refers to the others, the majority of Israel, those who are Israelites and yet do not belong to the seven thousand representatives. How does it stand with those who are only represented by these seven thousand ? What is their position and role ? What becomes of them ? The answer to this question is given in v. 7c in a formulation of Paul's own : " And the rest were blinded." But Paul means this statement to be interpreted, and we can try to interpret it, only " according as it is written." Scripture as such, namely, as a prophecy of Christ and His time, sets this statement in the light to which it belongs and in which it is to be interpreted, and no matter what it says this light prevents it from being able to stand in contradiction to v. 1 or Ps. 94^{14}. Brought into this light, it too proves that God has not rejected His people, and it proves it on behalf of the hardened of whom it speaks.

Finally, it is an illusion that, viewed as such and in themselves, vv. 7-10 run counter to the plain drift of chapter 11, and require subsequent refutation by the μὴ γένοιτο of v. 11 and the ensuing explanation. In general terms, our first point must be that, as far as their content goes, these verses are only a paraphrase of what was said earlier in 9$^{32f.}$ about Israel's stumbling and falling on the stone laid in Zion. They confirm this stumbling and falling. They describe it as meaning that the disqualified " rest " emphatically referred to in 9^{32} are blinded and stupefied, that they have fallen into a snare and trap, that offence and chastisement are ascribed to them. They also confirm that it was the very rock of their salvation that became their ruin. The present passage is more trenchant only because it says more unambiguously that this is the will of God with them. " *God* hath given them a spirit of slumber " (v. 8). And it is a prayer of David, the royal ancestor of Jesus Christ, against his enemies which in vv. 9-10 is turned against the " rest " of Israel in what seems to be so devastating a way. It must not be overlooked, however, that the presupposition here, as of course in 9$^{31f.}$ and in the whole of the tenth chapter, is always that the Word of God is objectively spoken and to be heard even amongst them ; that the " table " is set up and remains even amongst them as an epitome of all the divine benefits. The fact that they are hardened, and the power with which this befalls them, witnesses to the divinity of the God of Israel. They, too, are in His hand, and they, too, remain in His hand. The kind of stumbling and falling brought up for discussion by the question of v. 11a would necessarily have had a very different appearance. There is no question at all of this in vv. 7-10. The very thing that has not happened is that the God who deals so hardly with this rest has in any sense ceased at least to deal with them. What, then, has happened ? V. 8 is a combination of Is. 29^{10} and Deut. 29^3. In its context the saying about deep sleep is as follows : " Stay yourselves and wonder ; blind yourselves and be blind : be drunken but not with wine ; stagger but not with strong drink. For the Lord hath poured out upon you the spirit of deep sleep, and hath closed your eyes : the prophets, and your heads, the seers hath he covered. And the vision of all is become unto you as the words of a book that is sealed, which men deliver to one that is learned, saying, Read this, I pray thee : and he saith, I cannot ; for it is sealed. And the book is delivered to him that is not learned, saying, Read this, I pray thee : and he saith, I am not learned " (Is. 29$^{9-12}$). Here it can be seen clearly that everything is ready even for the " rest " of v. 7c, the book, the prophets, the seers, the prophecies and their fulfilment, but that all this is closed, covered and sealed for them, so that (whether they are wise or foolish, learned or unlearned) they, on their side, are not ready for what is ready for them. Moreover, it is by the will and decree of Yahweh that they are not ready. What has befallen them is that this readiness is refused them by Yahweh Himself ; that it is He who has put them into that deep sleep with regard to Himself. We must also consider the context of the words of the other text quoted in v. 8 : " And Moses called unto all Israel, and said unto them, Ye have seen all that the Lord did before your eyes in the land of Egypt unto Pharaoh, and unto all his servants, and unto all his land ; the great temptations which thine eyes have seen, the signs, and those great miracles. Yet the Lord hath not given you an heart to perceive, and eyes to see, and ears to hear, unto this day. And I have led you forty years in the wilderness : your clothes are not waxen old upon you, and thy shoe is not waxen old upon thy foot " (Deut. 29$^{1-4}$). Again, the objective element, Yahweh's faithfulness to and care for Israel, is contrasted with the subjective. The heart to perceive, the eye to see, the ear to hear this objective element is lacking in Israel. God has so far refused it to them : He " hath not given it them unto this day." When he emphasises this final point Paul hardly means to say that things are still the same to-day. For the relation of prophecy to fulfilment does not imply that what once was the case has persisted and is still the same to-day. Rather, with the words " unto this day " Paul obviously denotes the term which in prophecy is recognisably set to this divine dealing, so that in the fulfilment it will certainly not be His final word. The objective element and the subjective, just because they both have their source in God, cannot in the long run remain balanced in mutual opposition. Finally, in vv. 9–10 the strong statement from Ps. 69$^{22-23}$ has to be adduced that it is the special favour of God which has necessarily become for this " rest " a special source of illusion, error and humiliation, although it cannot fail to be recognised that the Psalm as a whole is a cry for help from oppressed Israel itself, and that it ends with the words : " The humble shall see this, and be glad : and your heart shall live that seek the Lord. For the Lord heareth the poor, and despiseth not his prisoners. Let the heaven and earth praise him, the seas, and everything that moveth therein. For God will save Zion, and will build the cities of Judah : that they may dwell there, and have it in possession. The seed also of his servants shall inherit it : and they that love his name shall dwell therein " (Ps. 69$^{32-36}$). That God can and actually does harden is said by all these passages. But they all say it in the light of what God makes plain where He does not harden but illumines, where He does not hide Himself but causes Himself to be known. They all say it in such a way that the seriousness of this hardening is displayed and yet the provisional nature of this divine measure is not denied. The last word has not yet been spoken even on the subject of the hardened by the fact that this prophecy characterises them as such. Indeed, in adducing this prophecy, Paul himself cannot yet have spoken a last word about them.

The question answered in v. 11, like that of v. 1, had perhaps actually been raised by Gentile Christians in the Pauline Churches : " Have they stumbled that they should fall ? " Is it according to God's design and intention that they have been hardened and thus made to fall—according to vv. 9–10 by the very table of grace set up amongst them—so that they should finally be excluded from that " obtaining " (v. 7), and therefore from the realisation of Israel's divine election, thus forfeiting in some sense the election itself, and being forsaken by the God of Israel ? If Paul's answer is again : μὴ γένοιτο, this means that a conceptual possibility is repudiated by him as not merely inadmissible in substance and in logic, but absolutely absurd and even blasphemous. A positive answer to this question is something not even remotely intended by him in the preceding passage. We have already taken this " Impossible " into account in the exposition of the preceding passage. That God has not rejected His people is something which for Paul stands even above the statement that the rest were blinded. And even in the apparently so conflicting statements of the Old Testament Paul finds only a confirmation of this major premise. Paul now describes in a twofold dialectic the actual design and intention of God in this hardening and its necessary consequence. By the transgression of these blinded rest, salvation was meant to come to the Gentiles, and this occurrence was in turn meant to provoke to jealousy the hardened rest themselves. Their transgression has brought salvation to the Gentiles. As the Jews delivered up their rejected Messiah to the Gentiles for crucifixion, the latter became with them the instruments of the divine work of atonement completed by the death of Jesus Christ. Stirred up with and by the Jews, they were also made participants in the fruit of this work, in deliverance by the grace of God and therefore in the fulfilment of Israel's promises. It was not the seven thousand elect but the blinded rest, Judas Iscariot to be precise, who managed to break open in this way the door between the Israelite and non-Israelite world, to effect the solidarity both of sin and of grace between Israel and the Gentiles. As rejected by the Jews, and therefore delivered up by them to the Gentiles, Jesus is not only the Christ of the Jews, but the Saviour of the world. It is unmistakeably the case that when Paul bases his own approach to the Gentiles on his repulse by the Jews, which is so much emphasised in Acts (13^{46}, 18^6, 28^{28}), he sees a parallel and illustration of the greater event which came on Jesus Christ Himself. The Gentile Christians must consider that the very thing which they have against the unbelieving Jews, their attitude to Jesus repeated in their attitude to Paul and the Christian Church, in a most remarkable fulfilment of Is. 2^{2-4}, 25^6; Jer. 3^{17}; Zech. 2^{11}, $8^{20f.}$, has become the presupposition of their own salvation. If Jesus had not been delivered up by the Jews, He would not have become the Saviour of the Gentiles. If Paul had not been repulsed by the Jews, he would not have become the apostle of the Gentiles. God needed the Jews for the sake of the Gentiles. He needed their transgression. In order to bring about this transgression, He hardened them. Thus their hardening has become an integral part of salvation-history in a way that is decisive even for the Gentiles. There falls, therefore, on their hardening, as Ströter rightly says, a reflection of the glory of the divine act of love which did not spare the only-begotten Son but delivered Him up for us all. The Gentile Christians are not, then, to ask whether God has now forsaken these hardened Jews. On the contrary, it is patent, and ought to be seen especially by the Gentile Christians, how very securely He holds these hardened Jews as such in His hand. But Paul now turns the tables in the same sentence. He does not let the fact that salvation has come to the Gentiles through the transgressions of the Jews stand for a moment as the supreme end of the divine purpose with these hardened Jews. On the contrary, in the final clause εἰς τὸ παραζηλῶσαι αὐτούς he explains that the salvation which has come to the Gentiles is a means to make the Jews " jealous." Thus we have here (so Peterson) a new and surprising application of the Old Testament illustration of the marriage between Yahweh the husband and Israel His wife, in which Israel's infidelity had so often given Yahweh cause for rightful jealousy. Does Paul mean that the relationship has now been reversed, that Yahweh has now turned to the *ecclesia*, not in infidelity to Israel, but to stir up Israel on its part to jealousy, and thus to recall it to fidelity ? Be that as it may, the meaning is that by the coming of salvation to the Gentiles Israel itself is to be shown what is intended for and still awaits it, although for the moment it has foolishly trifled away its share in it. Israel is to recognise in the Saviour of the world the Messiah who had as such been concealed from it. It is to perceive in God's mercy to the ignorant and lost outside who its own God is, and what He is also and primarily for Israel. This is God's purpose in bringing salvation to the Gentiles, in causing the Jews to commit that transgression, in giving them occasion for that transgression by hardening. In so doing, He has not then forsaken them. On the contrary, in this very hardening He has really made them more than ever His main concern. This must be noted by Gentile Christians, too, who would like to regard the hardened as forsaken. God has so little forsaken them that it is for their sake that He has stretched out His hand to the Gentiles. The existence of Gentiles as recipients of salvation has the meaning and purpose of a summons to these hardened Jews and therefore of a confirmation of their eternal election.

The content of the verses which follow (vv. 12–15) is clear in itself. On the other hand, it is not easy to understand the sequence of the individual sentences as they lie before us in the text. V. 12 and v. 15 obviously belong together in substance, v. 12 being more clearly defined and interpreted by the rhetorical question of v. 15. Again, vv. 13–14 obviously belong in substance to v. 11, so that v. 12 should not precede but follow vv. 13–14. Since there can be no question of a change of meaning in the passage, it is permissible to read them in the sequence vv. 13, 14, 12, 15.

The beginning of v. 13 shows that in v. 11 Paul had actually had in mind a question raised by the ἔθνη. In the first instance, of course, the reference is to the Christians among Paul's Gentile hearers. Yet Paul certainly regards these Gentiles as representative of the whole Gentile world, just as alternately in the λεῖμμα of v. 5 and the λοιποί of v. 7 he sees the whole of Israel. Regarded christologically and eschatologically the Church is always both *all* Israel—not only the seven thousand but also the hardened rest—and *all* the Gentile world, those who have already become believers and those who are yet to become so. But in the foreground there now stand in v. 13, in sharp contrast to the Synagogue which persists in unbelief, the Gentiles already gathered to the Church, and obviously raising questions in the spirit of v. 11. They know Paul as their own apostle, the apostle of the Gentiles. Paul, too, acknowledges this, and therefore them. This is inevitable. More radically than all other apostles Paul has recognised and stated that in Christ there is no difference between Jews and Gentiles, that Christ's community is the Church of Jews and Gentiles. More relentlessly than all the rest he has drawn the conclusion following from this. He has recognised and taken in hand the mission to the Gentiles as the task given to the Church with the resurrection of Jesus Christ and the miracle of Pentecost. In direct and indirect opposition to the others he has striven for the freedom of Gentile Christians—not from the Law but from obligation to its detailed demands (which are no longer binding in and with the fulfilment of its promise)—against a Christian misinterpretation of the relationship between Israel and the Church according to which Gentiles entering the Church ought first to become Jews. But just because he is and means to be this apostle of the Gentiles, it is quite out of the question—he had said so even more sharply in 9¹⁻⁵—that he should forget that obdurate rest in Israel and leave them on the wrong side. On the contrary, he sees the true glory of his service as an apostle of the Gentiles in the task and necessity laid upon him of provoking " his flesh," i.e., his " kinsmen according to the flesh " (9³), of stirring them up to jealousy, so that they also might desire to enter the Church. He neither can nor will give up " his flesh." This has nothing whatever to do with loyalty to blood and race, or even with " warm-hearted patriotism " (Lietzmann). Even less, of course, is it to be confused with anything in the nature of the injured religious pride of a Jew who by way of the Jewish mission and Jewish Christianity aims to bring out more clearly than ever the old special position of his people in the form of a gathering of his " kinsmen according to the flesh " round the " Christ according to the flesh " (2 Cor. 5¹⁶)— a position which, as it is attained in Christ, is also, in fact, abolished in Him. Paul has elsewhere (e.g., Phil. 2³ᶠ·) expressed himself quite clearly against a Christian Neo-Messianism of this kind, and here too what he says about his relation to " his flesh" takes a course directly opposed to it. The δοξάζειν of his apostolate to the Gentiles obviously cannot consist in the glorification of a natural Gentile grouping in place of the Jewish. " On a purely national basis our justifiable expectations are simply non-existent compared with those given to Israel as a people " (Ströter). As regards the natural foundation of Gentile Christianity, the only possible witness is that of Eph. 2¹¹ᶠ·, that it is obscure and hopeless. Even less can the δοξάζειν of the apostle consist—and Ströter is guilty of aberration and misdirection in this respect—in a direct or indirect renewal of Jewish nationalism (which is the prototype of all bad nationalisms).

It can consist only in calling his fellow-Jews to give up their sin against the Law of their nation which is also the Law of the divine election, and therefore in calling them to repentance. But it is in this precisely that the δόξα of his Gentile apostolate does consist. And it is this precisely that the Church of the Gentiles must now know. The Gentile mission and the Gentile Church have as such no δόξα of their own. They share in the δόξα of Israel by serving it. The Lord of the Gentile mission and the Gentile Church is indeed the Messiah of Israel, and it is by Israel, through Israel's transgression, that He is delivered up to the Gentiles and thus bestowed on them by God. The human bearer of this gift is Paul the apostle of the Gentiles, himself an Israelite, and more than that, an Israelite fully associated with Israel's transgression. Admittedly, the delivery of this gift to the Gentiles means that in the first instance it is carried *away* from Israel. But since this is done by this messenger, what else can it ultimately mean but that more than ever it is really being carried *to* Israel ? Provoked and allured by seeing the Gentiles in possession of this gift, Israel is summoned anew to the conversion previously refused, recognising the value of what is most properly its own possession in the very moment that it passes into the hands of others. That it now belongs to others does not mean that it has ceased to be most properly Israel's own possession. He who is proclaimed and believed as the Saviour of the world is not for this reason any less but more than ever the Messiah of Israel, revealed now in overwhelming fulness. Will not Israel have to recognise and finally acknowledge its Messiah precisely in the Jesus who comes to meet it from the cosmos, returning from the wide world into its narrowness ? For Paul the glory of his service to the Gentiles is that it involves this new offer to Israel. It is, therefore, in Israel's glory—not in a subsequently established glory of Judaism, but in Israel's future glory to be attained by way of its conversion—that he sees the glory of the Gentile mission and the Gentile Church.

For this reason, too, he can now present as the real aim of his activity as a missionary to the Gentiles, as a founder of the Gentile Church, the conversion and deliverance of " some of them " (v. 14) as he has experienced it here and there among the Jews of the Dispersion, as exceptions to the general rule. The Church acquires its proper lustre only as these " some " are added to it, only as it becomes the Church of Jews and Gentiles. That the goal of the election of Israel is the Church works itself out, therefore, in the fact that the Church can be what it is only on the absolute condition that it is together with Israel, only as it is absolutely referred to Israel's future glory, and therefore to the presence in it of witnesses to that glory in the persons of these " some of them." The Gentile Christians must accept this. They must not object to being in some degree only a means to the end of Israel's conversion. The apostle to the Gentiles stakes his whole work on this card ; he sees the whole meaning and purpose of his own conversion and calling in this end. Those who from among the Gentiles have come to faith through his word cannot fail to follow him in this. Their existence as Gentile Christians has to serve this new offer of God to Israel. This is the meaning of their baptism and their faith. This is their function in salvation-history. It is as they have this function assigned to them that they are taken seriously by God, and only as they accept it that they can take themselves seriously. For the whole Church, living as it does by hope in the future towards which this offer points, lives only as the bearer of this offer. Its own hope, the goal of its faith, stands or falls with the acceptance of this offer. To be sure, it is complete in itself. But it is constituted only in a provisional form so long as the Synagogue persists in its resistance, so long as there is still an Israel outside the Church. In so far as this is the case, its own election is indeed to some extent foreign to it, so long and in so far it is still to some extent cut off from its foundation. All the progress of the Gentile mission and all the glory of ever so many and ever so large Gentile Churches can in themselves only establish this separation and therefore this incompleteness of the Church. The Church waits for Israel's conversion in order that one day in unity with Israel it may not only believe its own election, but see it in its actuality. This is what Paul says in v. 12 and v. 15 with increasing definiteness of expression. In these verses he contrasts the present state of affairs, which has already its own positive significance for the Church and especially for the Gentile Church, and a coming state of affairs, which will bring for the Church of the Gentiles divine blessing in a totally different way, which only then will bring it the full revelation of the wisdom and goodness of the ways of God, with which at last the final goal of the whole history of God's community will be reached. He has already said in v. 11 that it is by the transgression of the Jews that salvation has come to the Gentiles. All Gentile presumption in face of this transgression is therefore silenced. The hardening of the rest from Israel does not mean that God has rejected His people. How can this be the case when the transgression which follows the hardening is the foundation of the Church of Jews and Gentiles ? This insight is now taken up in v. 12 and v. 15 (in the form of drastically abbreviated sentences) : " The fall of them is the riches of the world. The diminishing of them is the riches of the Gentiles " (v. 12). " The casting away of them is the reconciling of the world " (v. 15). This is the present state of affairs in Israel and between Israel and the Church. And it is to be noted that in the expressions fall, diminishing and casting away the whole complaint and accusation of the tenth chapter are again repeated and recapitulated. Israel has sinned and still sins against its God ; and it has to bear the consequence of this action by having no immediate part now in the fulfilment of the promise given to it, but standing there as an enemy of the God who.has chosen it for His possession. But Israel's election is already authenticated by the fact that even its sin (which it commits because God has not yet given it the understanding heart, the seeing eye, the hearing ear, because even as He was present to it in His goodness He shut Himself off from it) turns into a fulfilment of the work of God's mercy. Indeed, by perpetrating this sin, it throws open the sluice through which the riches of God pour into the world for the Gentiles. Through Israel's promise there is accomplished the reconciliation of the cosmos, i.e., the putting to death of the Son of God become man in place of the cosmos which really deserved this death and which through this death is legitimately absolved from its guilt. Through Israel's sin the forgiveness promised to it, in virtue of this exchange between God and man, is revealed as the promise under which the whole world is placed. The divine electing, hitherto confined to the form of the election of this one people, is revealed as the election which every man by faith in Jesus Christ may recognise as his own election, as the election of the Church of Jews and Gentiles. It was the sin of Israel indeed that was lifted by its Messiah and borne and borne away on the cross, and in it the sin of the whole world. In it ! For what He had to lift and bear and bear away as the sin of the Gentiles was only accessory to the sin of Israel. For, after all, in their sin against Him, the Gentiles had only that dependent share in the crucifixion as it may be clearly enough discerned in the four Gospels. They carried out only what as a decision was the sin of the chosen people. It was this decision of Israel, this betrayal of Judas Iscariot, which, along with the solidarity of the Jews and Gentiles in strife against God's grace, underlay also their solidarity in face of its triumph in the resurrection of Him whom they had delivered up and put to death. It was by this decision that God made Jesus the salvation of all who believe in Him. How could He have rejected there His people Israel (His Judas), the hardened rest among this people of His (to which, after all, Peter too and all the disciples of Jesus belonged) ? This is what the Gentile Christians must now consider in relation to the Synagogue. In view already of the palpable connexion between Israel's transgression and their own salvation they are not to regard the Synagogue as lost. But Paul also wants to bring out the further and more difficult point that salvation has come from the Jews to them, the Gentiles, in order that the Jews in turn may be made " jealous," in order that the Synagogue may be confronted with this new offer. They are to grasp the hard thought that they themselves are in the Church only as a means to this end, to the extent that the wealth in which they are allowed to participate through the wrong decision of the Jews has not ceased to be the original possession of these very Jews, so that it will necessarily revert to them, and the Gentiles can only regard themselves and act in relation to it as in some sense their trustees. But they have to grasp this hard thought in the light of the fact that the end which they are to serve in this way as a means, the home-coming of the Synagogue to the Church, will mean for them too, not only even greater wealth, but the ultimate positive goal of their existence in the Church, the transition from faith to sight, from reconciliation to redemption, from temporal to eternal life. In contrast to the present παράπτωμα of the Jews there stands (v. 12) their future πλήρωμα, their full participation in the grace of God effective through their own sin, although it is not explained what will be the future counterpart of the wealth which has already come to the Gentile world. " How much greater will be the riches which come from their πλήρωμα ? " On the other hand, the statement of v. 15 is quite explicit : " For if the casting away of them be the reconciling of the world, what shall the receiving of them be but life from the dead ? " If, then, the exclamation of v. 12 is indefinite at the decisive point, it is interpreted by the rhetorical question of v. 15. The participation of all Israel as such (in the faith and salvation of the Church) will coincide with the revelation of the eschatological character of the Messianic present, of the whole time which follows the resurrection of Christ from the dead. In that day, when all Israel is gathered together in faith in Jesus as its Messiah, hidden things will be revealed, Jesus Christ will come again in His glory with all His angels, the dead will rise again, Christ's kingdom in the Church will reach its goal in the eternal kingdom of God on a new earth under new heavens. In that day ! This is the greater riches which will succeed the riches of the reconciliation in the death of Jesus Christ on the cross now achieved and already believed by the Church of Jews and Gentiles. This is the glory of which even the Church has now only a foretaste, because, although it lives indeed in the Messianic age, it does not yet live in the revelation of the already present end and new beginning of all things, but still lives by faith—which means that it still lives in tears and suffering and crying and pain, in the realm of death, and not yet by sight, not yet in eternal joy. But in that day Jesus Christ will be manifest as He who has overcome. In that day He who is the mercy of God in person (and therefore His righteousness) will execute the judgment which belongs to Him. In that day all the dead will live through Him as that which they have been through Him and in relation to Him in their time. In that day ! The whole Church waits for " that day." But that day coincides with Israel's πλήρωμα and therefore with the future conversion of the Synagogue, with its πρόσλημψις, its acceptance and reception, its admission to its Messiah and introduction to His community, to the faith of this community. The coincidence is not fortuitous. From the very first " life from the dead " has been the sign under which the history of Israel has stood. We think of Israel's birth and sacrifice, of the deliverance of the Israelite first-born in Egypt, of the passage of the Red Sea, of the blooming and fruit-bearing rod of Aaron (Num. 17[8f.]), of the experience of Jonah the unwilling prophet, of the well-known vision of the revivified bones in Ezek. 37. What is promised to it will in that day pass into fulfilment in the Church, indeed in the cosmos— in that day when all Israel believes in Jesus. But this will itself be the divine miracle of a resurrection from the dead, the revelation of the end of all things in the beginning of a new world. It is quite impossible, therefore, that it should be made apprehensible as an expectation within history. In view of this divine miracle it is the duty of the apostle to the Gentiles, even by means of the Gentile mission—and it is the duty of the Church even as a Church of Jews and Gentiles—to make the Jews jealous. It is not the case, then, that the apostle or the Church can extort or force through anything in relation to the Synagogue, that they can " do " or " achieve " anything at all in a direct sense. The fanaticism with which the Jewish mission was occasionally carried on at a later date has no support in our passage. Indeed, at this point at any rate there is no express mention of a special Jewish mission at all. On the contrary, from the standpoint of v. 12 and v. 15, looking back to vv. 13–14, we can only say that the Gentile mission and the existence of the Church of Jews and Gentiles is, as such, the true Jewish mission. It is this as such which effects that παραζηλῶσαι, which is the renewed and reinforced offer of God to the original people of His choice. And, after all, if the proper and ultimate meaning of the Gentile mission and the Gentile Church is revealed in the deliverance of some of this people (v. 15), this can only be a by-product of its existence, although an indispensable one. It is not the Church but God Himself in the act of that admission and introduction, Jesus Christ in the glory of His second coming, who will convert the Synagogue, as it is He alone who will awaken the dead. In this respect, too, all that the Church can do is simply to be the Church, and in that very way to effect that παραζηλῶσαι of the Jews. But it would not be the Church if it did not effect this παραζηλῶσαι ; if it did not administer the gift entrusted to it in such a way as to bring about this παραζηλῶσαι ; if it did not believe and confess Jesus Christ in such a way as actually to lead to that divine offer; if in its faith and hope and love the Saviour of the world were perhaps so indiscernible that there could be no question of the Jews being forced to recognise in Him their own Messiah. Let the Church accept its responsibility for the Jews by being true and more and more true to itself ! But let it realise that it has to accept its responsibility for the Jews and their conversion ! If by any chance it does not effect this παραζηλῶσαι, if by any chance the admission and introduction of the Synagogue becomes for it an alien, half forgotten or wholly forgotten concern, no more to be considered by it, if it no longer reckons with this divine wonder, this is a fatal but sure sign that it is also not really looking forward to the second coming of its Lord, to His judgment of the quick and the dead. But this will mean that its faith has been stripped of hope and that therefore (not working through love) it has become vain. According to this passage, hope in the revelation of Jesus Christ, which is the life of faith, stands or falls with hope for Israel. Already, then, vv. 11–15 anticipate the exhortation which will afterwards be developed in vv. 19–22. Let the Church see to it that it really is and remains the Church ! What it has received points forward to something greater that it has still to receive. But the advent of this greater thing coincides with a new thing that God wills to do with Israel too, the new thing in which He intends to confirm all His promises to Israel as well. The Church will not be the Church if it does not await the greater thing and therefore with it the new thing which impends for all Israel. It will not, therefore, be the Church if it does not exist in responsibility for Israel as well. This final point is still to the forefront in vv. 11–15. The verses, as a whole, have given the reason why Gentile Christians are not to think and say that the hardening of the rest in Israel signifies that God has forsaken Israel. The decisive reason why they must not do this is that it is through Israel's transgression that the Church has received what constitutes it as the Church, and that it is with Israel's conversion that it has to expect everything that will complete it as the Church. The Church can understand its own origin and its own goal only as it understands its unity with Israel. Precisely in its Gentile Christian members it must perceive that it would itself be forsaken by God if God had really forsaken Israel.

In vv. 16–18 a second refutation is made of the Gentile Christian opinion rejected in v. 11. It consists of an analysis of the principles of the relation between Israel and the Church carried through in the form of a parable. There has never been anything of this kind before in these chapters. Its decisive result is as follows. However it may be with that hardening of the rest of Israel, however it may be with Israel's transgression (which was the special concern of vv. 11–15), Israel is still the possession and work of God, and as such the presupposition without which there would be no Church, and no Gentile Christians. No matter what may have to be said about those who are hardened, they, too, are part of this possession and work of God to which the Church and its Gentile Christian members also owe everything. The conclusion following from this insight will again be that precisely in its Gentile Christian members the Church would have to regard itself as forsaken if it tried to think and say this of Israel or even of the hardened in Israel.

The plainest words of the parable in relation to this conclusion are at the beginning and end of these verses : " If the root be holy, so are the branches " (v. 16), and : " But if thou boast, thou bearest not the root, but the root thee " (v. 18). The illustration of the " holy root " (Is. 11¹, ¹⁰, 53²) and the prior illustration of the " holy firstfruit " (Ex. 23¹⁶, Num. 15¹⁸ᶠ·) may be regarded as denoting one and the same thing. Exegetes are not agreed whether this is to be identified with the patriarchs or again with the " remnant " of v. 5, the earlier and later seven thousand elect in Israel. It certainly includes these. But the Old Testament sources of these illustrations hardly permit them to be related primarily and exclusively either to the former or the latter or even to both. And on this presupposition the illustration of the root afterwards developed in detail would be far too forcible. Above all, the conclusion drawn from the parable is too weighty to be based on this presupposition. In relation to this root the patriarchs no less than the later seven thousand are obviously branches like other branches, although branches which, unlike others, are not cut off but remain in the pruned stem which grows out of this root. To this extent they themselves admittedly belong to the root, or, according to the illustration of v. 16, to the first fruit. The root which communicates its character to all the branches of the stem growing out of it, or the firstfruit whose quality as a sacrificial gift benefits all bread taken from the same dough, can surely signify primarily only that which makes all its members Israel ; that by which in all its members it is and remains the chosen people of God. But this is the promise given to Abraham of a seed by whom all the peoples of the world are to be blessed, and the fulfilment of this promise. All Israelites as such are the ancestors or at least the kinsmen of this seed who is the meaning and goal of the whole, the one thing common to all the members, the constituent ground of their right to exist as Israelites. This being the case, although in order of time He is the last Israelite, He can also be regarded and designated as the first, as the seed, and therefore as the root from which they have all come and grown, or (the first illustration is clearer in this respect) as the firstfruit which being taken from the lump of this whole and offered to God makes all the remaining bread acceptable and eatable. The root of Israel, its last member, who even as such is also its first member, is the " root of Jesse " (Is. 11¹⁰), the " root of David " (Rev. 5⁵, 22¹⁶), the Son of Man, Jesus, who as such is the Word and Son of God, the man beloved of God, in whom His love to every man was decreed from all eternity and became an event in time. It is (only) when the illustration is understood in this way that we can understand the weighty and twice repeated " holy " ascribed (v. 16) both to the firstfruit and to the root. The reason why the firstfruit and the root are holy is because what constitutes the holiness of the God of Israel, i.e., the distinctive characteristic over which He watches with unceasing zeal and which He confirms in all His dealings with Israel, is that He brings forth from this people the one Jesus, and therefore makes the whole history of this people a single annunciation of this Jesus, namely, a single annunciation of the existence and history of His Church. It is only when we understand the illustration in this way that we further understand how it is that without any special proof Paul could begin with the statement that the firstfruit or the root is holy, and use it as premise for the weighty conclusions which are afterwards drawn. Obviously he is speaking of something common to all Israel as such, the holiness of which was at once self-evident to the Gentile Christians, and especially to those who put such questions as those of vv. 1 and 11. The Church was, of course, convinced from the very outset of the special dignity of the patriarchs and the seven thousand. But it could hardly be a matter of course—for its non-Jewish members at any rate—to hear the latter summarily described as the holy root by which all the branches are sanctified and they themselves are all sustained. This kind of statement was possible for the Church of Jews and Gentiles only if Jesus Christ was meant by the root. And it is only if we understand the illustration in this way that finally and above all we understand as such the two minor statements in v. 16. From the fact that the patriarchs or the seven thousand are holy it does not follow by any means that the whole lump without distinction, every branch, Israel as such, is holy. For Isaac is accompanied by Ishmael, Jacob by Esau, the seven thousand by the λοιποί. Even assuming that the adjective " holy " applies to the former, how can it apply to the latter ? But the latter are the persons concerned. To prove that they are not forsaken by God, is it enough to assert that they are holy because their very differently disposed brethren are holy ? For although in vv. 1–11 the former have been said to represent the latter, this can hardly be said again when the issue is the special problem of the latter, of the hardened. On the contrary, the proof must now have special reference to the latter. This is effected when the " holy root " does not mean this or that group of differently disposed brethren, but their last-born, or in reality their first-born Brother. In His holiness they, too, genuinely participate. His distinctive characteristic, the mercy in which God in His person made man His own concern and gave Himself to man, is the distinctive characteristic of the God of Israel, of His election of Israel, of the promise given to this whole people as such ; the distinctive characteristic therefore, the holiness, of each individual member of this people, even of the hardened in this people, even of that rest who always clung to strange gods, who always stoned the prophets and finally took the Son of God Himself and delivered Him up to be crucified, even of Judas Iscariot. His distinctive characteristic is not lost even for the Israel which has so completely failed to recognise it, which has met it with such complete disobedience. The few enlightened are necessarily accompanied by the many hardened, Isaac by Ishmael, Jacob by Esau, Moses by Pharaoh and the company of Korah, David by Saul, Elijah by Ahab, the true by the false prophets, the good kings by those who did evil in the sight of the Lord—they are all indispensable figures in that annunciation of Jesus and His Church. Therefore in every part of the Old Testament the reflection of holiness cannot fail to fall on all these who seem only to be unholy ones, an indirect light of grace on all these who seem only to be judged, to be smitten by God's wrath, just as the aversion almost which we see the elect display towards the rejected (David) tells us plainly enough that the latter are not simply non-Israel, a vacuum, but that they too are God's holy people. Their holiness does not derive, however, from the others, the elect, but from the root of Israel, from the ground and goal of Israel's election, from the source of Israel's being, who is common to the elect and the reprobate, and who last and therefore first is called Jesus. Because this root is holy, the branches are also holy.

And now we can and must understand the meaning of v. 17. It is to be interpreted in retrospect from the conclusion : " Boast not against the branches." In no circumstance has the Gentile Christian to allow his membership of the Church to make him presumptuous in relation to even one of those who belong to Israel : no matter who may be that past or future member of the people of Israel, not even if his name is Judas Iscariot ; and no matter what may have happened or may yet happen among the people of Israel. For it is incontestable that this people as such is the holy people of God : the people with whom God has dealt in His grace and in His wrath ; in the midst of whom He has blessed and judged, enlightened and hardened, accepted and rejected ; whose cause either way He has made His own, and has not ceased to make His own, and will not cease to make His own. They are all of them by nature sanctified by Him, sanctified as ancestors and kinsmen of the one Holy One in Israel, in a sense that Gentiles are not by nature, not even the best of Gentiles, not even the Gentile Christians, not even the best of Gentile Christians, in spite of their membership of the Church, in spite of the fact that they too are now sanctified by the Holy One of Israel and have become Israel. Each member of the people of Israel as such still continues to participate in the holiness which can be that of no other people, in the holiness of the natural root who because He is the Last and therefore also the First is called Jesus. This holiness the Gentile Christian has to respect in every Jew as such without exception. He will, therefore, cease to show presumption towards him even if, in view of the latter's peculiar existence and behaviour and of his own position as a member of the Church of Jesus Christ, he seems to have most just occasion to do so. Such occasion he does admittedly seem to have. For, on the one hand, there are among the holy branches those which have been cut off. They once grew out of this root, and they have sprung from it. They had the nature of this root, and they have it yet. They undoubtedly belonged and still belong to the stem that is borne by this root. Now, however, they are no longer in this root. They have been cut off and lie beside it. Now they no longer grow out of this root. They have now only the transient life of a severed branch, and the sure and immediate prospect of withering away. This is the existence of all those in Israel who, from Ishmael up to the present-day Synagogue, although they were and are Israelites, have proved unserviceable in relation to what God willed with Israel and finally brought forth from it, so that in their totality they can only form that dark and monstrous side of Israel's history. This is the disobedient, idolatrous Israel of every age : its false prophets and godless kings ; the scribes and Pharisees ; the high-priest Caiaphas at the time of Jesus ; Judas Iscariot among the apostles. This is the whole of Israel on the left hand, sanctified only by God's wrath. The Gentile Christian sees this Israel and seems to have every occasion for a presumptuous attitude towards it. But, again, on the other hand, there are living branches which grow out of this holy root, undoubtedly sharing its nature, certainly belonging to the stem which grows out of it. And they do not merely belong to it as can also be said of those severed branches. They live in and with the growing stem, and therefore themselves continue to grow. They have their future from it, and therefore from the root, because they have recognised as such the Holy One of Israel, because they have put their faith in Him, because they have received through Him righteousness before God, and therefore hope of their deliverance. This is the position in which the Gentile Christian finds himself, and so from this aspect he seems to have occasion to assume a superior attitude towards that Israel on the left. But Paul dispels the illusion on which this rests (v. 17). For he now develops the general illustration of the root and the branches. The cutting off of some of the branches is the pruning of a cultivated olive tree ; the existence of those other branches in this tree means that young shoots of a wild olive have been grafted into the cultivated olive in place of the pruned. Exegetes from Origen to Lietzmann have criticised the image on the ground that it is horticulturally impossible. A gardener does not usually graft wild shoots into a cultivated tree, but cultivated into a wild. " Paul is after all city bred—Jesus was of the country," is how Lietzmann explains and excuses this supposed blunder of the apostle. The question remains, however, whether Paul did not intentionally choose the impossible comparison, in order to show that, as there is no analogy of any kind for what is signified, there is no horticultural. Only a reversal of normal gardening practice can describe what God has done to Israel in the founding of the Church of Jews and Gentiles. The cutting-out of those branches and their consequent removal from the stem that bore them and gave them life is itself not a normal process, for, according to v. 16, they are holy—holy by derivation from their root. How can the existence of this other Israel, this dark side of its history, be normal or even possible ? Why does not everything move unambiguously to its goal under the divine blessing and with constant divine illumination ? Why are not all Israelites like Abraham, Isaac and Jacob ? How is it that Judas is numbered with the apostles ? How can there be room to-day, according to the will of God, for such a thing as the Synagogue ? Again and above all, it is highly abnormal that Gentiles suddenly obey and believe and thus enter into full enjoyment of all the promises of Israel, that in this way they may and must call Abraham their father and are therefore living Israel in contrast to countless thousands who by descent and name seem to have the prior right, to have the sole claim to do this ? The wild plant is, in fact, out of place on the cultivated olive tree. What will become of it there ? And what will become of the olive tree ? But it is the incomprehensible with which we have to do, and therefore in defiance of all horticulture the " city-bred " Paul speaks of it in this way—just as it could be shown with respect to the parables of Jesus that verisimilitude in the sense of pragmatic probability is a compliment they are better spared. What Paul means to say with this very surprising development of the illustration of the root and the branches is as follows. It is true that in Israel there has taken place, and still takes place, a fearful separation and severance of many from Israel. It is also true that the Gentile Christians not only belong now to Israel but are, in fact, the true Israel. It is true that many in Israel are not, and do not have, what they really should be and have. And it is true, in turn, that many of the Gentiles are and have what they could neither be nor have at all as Gentiles because it can be theirs only if they are not Gentiles but Israelites. But this does not signify for the Gentiles—Paul has this aspect in view in vv. 11–22—that they can take up a superior attitude towards those lost ones in Israel, that they can turn their backs on them as lost in the sight of God, that they can abandon them and try to be the Church without them. This is quite out of the question because—as is also implied in the illustration of this remarkable treatment of the olive tree—they have entered into the place of those which were taken out. The thought is that of vv. 11–15, of the salvation which has come to the Gentiles through Israel's transgression, but now a new turn is given to it. In the first instance, Israel is diminished through this transgression. It is robbed of all the lost members. But the full complement of its members is restored at once by the addition of Gentile believers. Thus the Gentile Christians are, in a sense, locum-tenens for those who have dropped out. They dwell in their houses, use their utensils and administer their possessions. But, all the same, they are only locum-tenens ; they are only transplanted aliens. And those who are no longer there are not yet dead ; their relation to the newcomers has still to be definitively fixed. If the latter are now where the others used to be, they owe it only to this insertion and therefore indirectly to the others into whose place they have been put. The real emphasis of the thought rests, however, on the point that this exchange involves two incomprehensible events. Those who are Israel originally and by nature no longer live as Israel, because they no longer live by the root of Israel, but only in the separation which death inevitably follows. And those who were outside—not cut off, but outside from the very start, the branches of a wild olive-tree—are the very ones who are now inside : " Thou partakest of the root and fatness of the olive tree." This incomprehensible fact the Gentile Christians owe to the position from which they would like to boast in relation to that other Israel. The inclination to do this must surely be nipped in the bud. For what ground for boasting or judging is afforded by a position into which one has come in this incomprehensible way, the naturally unholy into the place of the naturally holy people ? Apart from thankfulness, what place is left for anything but supreme and most intent interest in the future of those from whom everything has been taken in the same wholly surprising way ? But the reasons given for this warning and exhortation go deeper yet as the argument of v. 16 is resumed. What possible ground has the Gentile Christian for legitimate boasting in relation to that other Israel ? What advantage does he actually have over it ? None whatever, says v. 17, in respect of the fact that he is now within whereas that Israel is without. For the humiliation of the former and his own exaltation are both equally incomprehensible. Paul will return later (vv. 19–22) to the positive significance of this incomprehensible exchange for the Gentile Christian, for the whole Church. But it is certainly not that the Gentile Christians might have occasion to be presumptuous. Only one thing can the Gentile Christian now boast of having which that other Israel does not have. But this is the very thing to prevent him from being presumptuous. It is that he is borne by the holy root from which that other Israel is now cut off, by which it is now no longer borne. He has the Messiah Jesus by faith, and therefore to his own righteousness in God's sight and his eternal deliverance. He is borne by Him. He lives by this faith of his. In the One in whom he believes he has hope and a future in face of all mortal fears and perils. Already in Him he has his citizenship in heaven. Now that Israel on the left has this Messiah Jesus too. He is its Messiah by origin. He continues to be its Messiah. He is proclaimed to it by the Law and the prophets. He was born a Jew, and in Israel's midst in Jerusalem He was crucified and rose again from the dead. But Israel is hardened by God, and therefore it does not believe, and because it does not believe it stands in complete unrighteousness before its God and therefore hopeless and inconsolable before the death which inexorably approaches. It is not borne by the holy root of Israel. In the glory of being borne by this root the Gentile Christians do actually have the advantage over that Israel on the left. But this glory is obviously something which they cannot ascribe to themselves. In this matter they can glory only in the Lord. However else it may be with that great change to their advantage and to the disadvantage of the others, one thing is sure, and that is that they are borne by the root of Israel, and are not in any sense its bearers. It is only if they were bearers and not borne, restorers of life and not restored, givers and not receivers, that they would have occasion to magnify themselves and disparage the others. In fact, however, they are such as are borne, and therefore this is quite out of the question. Moreover, it is by the root of Israel that they are borne, by the holy origin that makes even the others holy even though they are separated from it, and holy in a way in which they as Gentiles will never be holy. How can Gentile Christians be borne by this root, live and themselves be made holy, without recognising the holiness of this root even in the others as well, as David always recognised and honoured even in the Saul who was rejected by God and persecuted himself the elected and anointed one of Yahweh ? " Unto them (the Jews) were (and still are) committed the oracles of God " (Rom. 3²). Even the New Testament " oracles of God " are, without exception, Jewish oracles. Whoever has Jesus Christ in faith cannot wish not to have the Jews. He must have them along with Jesus Christ as His ancestors and kinsmen. Otherwise he cannot have even the Jew Jesus. Otherwise with the Jews he rejects Jesus Himself. This is what is at stake, and therefore, in fact, the very basis of the Church, when it has to be demanded of Gentile Christians that they should not approach any Israelite without the greatest attention and sympathy.

The whole train of thought closes (vv. 19–22) with an exposition of the practical necessity which, when Gentiles become believers, follows from the relationship between unbelieving Jews and themselves. The exposition automatically becomes an exhortation, a summons: " Be not highminded, but fear"

(v. 20). " Behold therefore the goodness and severity of God " (v. 22a). There is also an unmistakeable note of irony (e.g., in the καλῶς of v. 19) and menace (vv. 21, 22b) in the course of this exhortation. Let us again anticipate the result. By the coming of salvation to the Gentiles through the transgression of the Jews, by the founding of the Church as the Church of Jews and Gentiles, a quite definite function is assigned to these Gentiles in the Church, the execution of which by its very nature makes it impossible for them to regard and treat the unbelieving Jews as forsaken by God. The future of the Church which is inseparably bound up with the hope of Israel excludes this, as has been said already in vv. 11–15. So, too, in vv. 16–18, does the origin of the Church, the obtaining and assuming by Gentile Christians of the rights of Israel. The conclusion of vv. 19–22 (in the appropriate form of direct exhortation) is that such an attitude towards the unbelieving Jews is also made impossible by the present existence of the Church, and especially by the existence of Gentile Christians in the Church. The Church exists in the faith and only in the faith of its members, precisely, that is, in the decision which the unbelieving Jews have refused and still refuse to make. It is in faith and in faith alone that Gentile Christians are participants in the salvation which was promised to Israel and has been provisionally withdrawn from that unbelieving Israel and given to them by reason of that unbelief. The mere fact that they may believe is a demonstration in their favour of the goodness of the same God whose severity has overtaken Israel. In faith, therefore, they are bound to this God, and indeed to His goodness. That His severity has not overtaken them as well is the incomprehensible fact of His mercy, and they cannot omit to fear His severity as they contemplate the others overtaken by it. On the contrary, the sight of these others means necessarily that they have to fear God's severity. But they are bound to the goodness of God directed towards them, so that they can only persevere in believing and therefore in relying on the goodness of God and therefore—the continuation (vv. 23–26) will show irrefutably that this is the point—in confronting even unbelieving Judaism in the expectation that the same God can and will direct towards this unbelieving Judaism the same incomprehensible goodness that now benefits them. Existing as they do in the Church, and therefore believing, they can look in that direction with no other expectation and therefore only in the attitude corresponding to this expectation. They cannot believe against but only for that Israel on the left. In this expectation and attitude (together with the Jewish Christians in their midst) they must believe vicariously for all Israel.

V. 19 makes it quite plain what Paul had in mind when in vv. 17–18 he spoke of that presumption and self-glorification of Gentile Christians, and what he was countering with his analysis of the basic principles of the relationship between Israel and the Church of Jews and Gentiles. Behind the question vv. 1 and 11 stands a Gentile Christian theory. " The branches were broken off, that I might be grafted in." Peterson (p. 61) rightly calls this proposition " the typical answer of the Gentile who does not discern in the Church the mystery of the Church of Jews and Gentiles, for whom there is only the ' historical ' succession of Judaism and Christianity." It is, in fact, the main argument of Christian anti-semitism right up to our own time. The Jews crucified Jesus Christ. Therefore this people has ceased to be the chosen, the holy people of God. Into its place there has now stepped the people of Christians from among Jews and Gentiles. The Church is the historical successor of Israel. With the foundation and existence of the Church Israel as such has become a thing of the past. As for those rebellious ones who in past and present make up the majority of Israel, of them it remains only to be said that they are outside, that they are forsaken by God.

The irony of the καλῶς of v. 20 does not exclude but includes Paul's admission of the force of the objective content of this argument and his acceptance of it.

He has said himself in v. 17 that those branches were cut off and that in their place wild shoots from among the Gentiles were incorporated into the stem. With the crucifixion of Jesus Christ, Israel, as Israel, has become a thing of the past to the extent that the chosen, the holy people now continues to live uniquely in the Church. But the mystery of the Church itself is grossly misunderstood if this argument is used as a proof of the assertion that God has rejected His people Israel, that even if only with the unbelieving majority of this people He has dealt in this way in order to forsake them, because He is no longer their God and they are no longer to be His people. What is completely overlooked in this use of the argument—as completely as by the Synagogue itself—is the resurrection of Jesus Christ. For with this the meaning of His death for Jews and Gentiles is set in a light that makes it quite impossible for the Church to apply the argument in this way. In the resurrection of Jesus Christ God Himself has cancelled both the *finis* of the Jewish rejection of Christ and also that of the rejection of the Jews, acknowledging, against the will of Israel, His own will with Israel, the Messiah of Israel as the Saviour of the world, and therefore also and all the more fully of Israel itself. To exist in the Church means to exist by and in the power of the resurrection of Jesus Christ. For the resurrection, the omnipotent cancellation of the definitive rejection by and of the Jews, the self-acknowledgment by God of His will with Israel, has created the Church. To exist in the Church is to believe. If the majority in Israel falls it is because it does not believe, because it does not see and accept this divine cancellation and self-acknowledgment, because it is blind and deaf in face of the fulfilment of all divine promises accomplished in defiance of all the sin, all the past, present and future unbelief of Israel, because it persists in unbelief as though nothing had happened. For this reason and in this way these branches are now cut off. For in and with the resurrection of Jesus Christ what Moses and the prophets have always attested to this people is publicly decided—that to be Israel means to live and grow in union with the root of Israel, to believe. Now this is the very thing which does not happen in the case of these branches from Ishmael right up to the present-day Synagogue. For this reason and in this way they are cut off although they are holy branches. On the other hand, this is the very thing which does happen in the case of Christians from the Gentiles. They believe. For this reason and in this way they are grafted into the root although they are wild shoots. For this reason and in this way they are now holy by and with the holy root of Israel. In this way they exist in the Church. In this way they " stand." But do they really believe ? The use they make of this argument makes it necessary to put very seriously before them this decisive Christian question.

In vv. 20b–21 it is first developed negatively. If they believe, then it is in and by the power of the resurrection of Jesus Christ from the dead. For with the divine refutation of Jewish unbelief, with God's acknowledgment of Israel's Messiah as the Saviour of the world accomplished in the resurrection of Jesus, there took place their calling and awakening to faith in Him who was delivered up by the Jews and put to death by themselves. It is on this deed of God that they rely if and when they believe. But this same deed of God is also a necessary warning : " Be not highminded, but fear." The *finis* arbitrarily written by the unbelieving will of Israel in the betrayal and crucifixion of Jesus has been finally cancelled by a higher hand in His resurrection from the dead. Israel had indulged in presumptuous thoughts when it thought it could be God's people without its God and in a continual ignoring of His promise and His Law, when at last it thought it could repulse the final grasp of its God. It was ruined by its attempt to defy the mercy of the God who had chosen it. This is what has been revealed in the resurrection of Jesus Christ. This, then, is what must necessarily be present to the faith of the Christian Church, even to the faith of Gentile Christians. God gave the lie to the arrogance of the Jews. He caused those branches to be cut off, and thus opened the way effectively for the Gentiles. In so doing He revealed once and for all both to Jews and Gentiles that He is both capable of this radical refutation of human unbelief and arrogance in relation to Himself, and at the same time resolved on it. "If God spared not the natural branches, take heed lest he also spare not thee." If He has dealt in this way with the natural stem of the Church, with His people Israel, He will be powerful and willing enough to deal in the same way with the Church if Israel's unbelief reappears in the Church. If He has exposed in this way the complete impotence of all human revolt against Him, if His judgment has been so thorough just where He has promised His grace, how much more will this be true in relation to a similar revolt where there is no such prior promise, where grace has come without any pre-history and prior contact, as in the case of the Gentiles gathered into the Church. In view of this ground of their faith, it is inevitable that they should fear God, that they should be apprehensive lest they betray themselves into a similar situation with regard to Him as did the Jews with their rejection of Jesus Christ. But they will betray themselves into this situation, they will themselves immediately incur the fate of Ahasuerus—which now confronts them as a gracious divine warning—if in their relation to unbelieving Israel they try to indulge in presumptuous thoughts, if ostensibly along with God, in reality in revolt against Him, namely, against God's mercy, they try to take up a hostile attitude to this Israel. If they do this they will automatically come under the same judgment under which they now see Israel standing. Indeed, they will come under a worse, for they will not only be in a sorry plight like the Jews, but because they do not have their promise, because they do not belong by nature to that root, they will be worse off than the Jews. "Christian peoples which lose their faith relapse into a degree of degeneration and insubstantiality to which the Jew can never attain" (Peterson, p. 62). They relapse into that remoteness from God which is natural to paganism but from which even unbelieving Jews are, as Jews, preserved. But Gentile Christians do lose their faith when they become presumptuous in their thinking with regard to the Jews. Not being Jews, and for that very reason outdoing them in Jewishness, they surrender to the very illusion in which the Jews rejected Jesus Christ. They reject Him again by rejecting His ancestors and kinsmen the Jews, by refusing in effect to accept all the implications of the truth that it is the Messiah of the Jews who is the Saviour of the world. "Do you really believe?" is Paul's question to the Gentile Christians. In faith in the risen Jesus Christ, you will have to fear God who in the raising up of Jesus Christ has overthrown not only Jewish but all presumption against Him. With the same power which he exercised against theirs He will overthrow yours, too, if you become presumptuous and therefore no longer believe.

The same decisive Christian question is then put positively in v. 22. In the resurrection of Jesus Christ God has cancelled the *finis* written by the evil, unbelieving will of Israel with regard to Jesus, and in this way shown that severity towards those who disobeyed Him. He has completed the severance which left behind unbelieving Israel as such and at the same time founded the Church. But this being the case, the wholly other *finis* is also cancelled, namely, that of Israel's rejection. It is the Messiah of Israel whom God has acknowledged by the raising up of Jesus. Against Israel He has acknowledged Him as the Saviour of the world, but in so doing He has obviously acknowledged Him more than ever and completely afresh for Israel. It is not only the severity of God, but much more the goodness of God, the goodness of the God of Israel and therefore His goodness towards Israel, which is the revelation of Easter Day. Does it not reveal that in the death of Jesus God has sealed and kept the covenant made with its fathers, that in the sacrifice of His own Son He has taken away Israel's sin and comforted and blessed Israel? To be sure, neither before nor after is this goodness of God towards Israel perceived and recognised and appropriated in faith by the majority of Israelites. This majority, then, does not make any use of this goodness, and can experience only the severity of His judgment. On the other hand, men from the Gentile world do perceive, recognise, believe and appropriate this revelation of the goodness of God, thus obtaining a portion in the fulfilment of Israel's promises and themselves becoming Israel. Events all take the inconceivably strange form that the very goodness of Israel's God towards His people avails only, apart from a small minority of this people, for those who cannot look back on any special divine election and promise, who have hitherto known nothing of the name and Law of Israel's God, but have naturally been in both faith and life adherents and followers of the gods of this world and therefore without God in the world. In the power of the resurrection of Jesus Christ they now believe in the forgiveness of sins completed in His death by God ; they now stand under God's comfort and blessing. They are now grafted into the stem growing out of the holy root, and as holy branches they draw their nourishment from that holy root, whilst through the same event this nourishment is cut off from the many Israelites for whom it was destined. This is the incomprehensible thing which they must consider, says Paul to the Gentile Christians. And with what result ? Quite simply that they are to abide by the goodness of God so incomprehensibly directed towards them, that they are to hold fast to the revelation as it comes to themselves. No more is required of them, but this *is* required of them. That which, in a way that passes understanding, has actually come to them through the resurrection of Jesus Christ, they are to take seriously as such. They are to continue in the reception of the goodness of God that benefits them. Without looking to the left hand or to the right they are to be thankful for it. They are simply to believe. In and with faith they stand fast (v. 20) in the Church, and therefore as newcomers in Israel. Without faith they can only fall. The severity of God against the Israel on the left concerns them only in so far as the sight of these severed branches should remind them how their God, who is the God of Israel, deals with His enemies, how terrible it is to fall into the hands of this, the living God, how terrible it must be for them too—and for them above all as newcomers—no longer to believe. But they do believe. Do they really believe ? If they do, they praise the mercy of Him who elected Israel. They live by the goodness of God which is His goodness towards Israel. From what standpoint can they pretend to judge that God had left and forsaken His people ? From what source can they pretend to know that their installation must mean the final removal of those into whose rights and duties they are installed ? How can they arrive at the obscure distinction between " Judaism " and " Christianity " as between two separate religions and worlds succeeding one another ? They can do so only as they themselves fail in the decision in which they see the Synagogue failing ; only as they themselves become the Synagogue ; only if they themselves are cut off and the same things happen in the Church as have happened in Israel. If they believe and therefore persevere in living by the goodness of the God of Israel, they can do nothing save hope the best for Israel in all its members and therefore with their faith really take and occupy before God the place which is now lost to Israel.

The material division of chapter 11 does not coincide exactly with its literary division, for the final turn given to the interpretation of Israel's future and hope occurs within the context characterised from a literary standpoint by the illustration of the cultivated and wild olives (vv. 16–25), with its exhortation to Gentile Christians. This illustration does, of course, control vv. 23–24 as well. The exhortation is also continued in v. 23 f. It recurs expressly in v. 25, ἵνα μὴ ἦτε ἐν ἑαυτοῖς φρόνιμοι. The statements of vv. 30–31 are also in the form of direct speech. Nevertheless there is an obvious change in the outlook and content of the statement from v. 23 onwards. What follows is clearly a further answer to the question that dominates the whole chapter, whether God has by any chance rejected His people Israel. But it really is a further, a new answer, in so far as it no longer looks from Israel to the Church, as in vv. 11–22, but from the Church to Israel. The emphasis of the answer is now transferred from the insight that only in its divinely founded and ordered relation to Israel can the Church be the Church of God to the further insight that Israel is and will continue to be the Israel of God in its divinely founded and still to be ordered relation to the Church.

We are told (v. 23) that although the cutting off of those holy branches from the holy stem is for the immediate present a bitter fact, as the existence of the Synagogue shows, it does not involve a final decision. The relation between Israel and the Church has not yet been given definitive form. Therefore in the Church we are not after all to discern in this event the revelation of the goal and end of God's purpose with Israel. Admittedly this is the ugly picture which we see to-day (foretold by everything which happened from the very outset in Israel's history as expressly interpreted by Moses and the prophets). On the one hand, we have the holy root of Israel, its Messiah as the proper object of its election, and with Him the people of those who believe in Him, many from the Gentiles and a few from the people of Israel, who as the exception seem only to prove the rule that this people as such is fundamentally not the people of God's election and therefore has no positive share in God's mercy. On the other hand, we have Israel's majority, the Israel that was elected and served—and has now finished its service—only to reveal the divine mercy in its freedom in face of all human willing and running and the claims to which it gives rise. But this present situation does not in any sense have the character of immutability. It has already been said (vv. 20–22) that we must not entertain wrong ideas about the duration of our own status in the Church. We stand fast in it as we believe. But we believe as we fear God. And we fear God as we renounce every other support and rely on God's goodness. If this support is thrown aside we no longer stand fast, and even in the Church a change, and moreover a decided change for the worse, is both possible and real. Christians who lose this one support are necessarily " cut off " from Jesus Christ as the essence and basis of the Church in just the same way as the Jews are from the meaning and ground of Israel's election. And, strange to say, according to vv. 20–22 it is actually the case that this change for the worse on the part of the Church will take place concretely if by any chance Christians become arrogant in relation to the unbelieving Jews, if they presume to think that the situation between them and the Jews has become unalterable, that it has been decided once and for all in their favour and against the Jews. If anyone in the Church thinks he can take his stand on finalities of this kind he is rebelling against the free power of decision belonging to God's mercy and therefore stepping out into the void outside and alongside the Church. He is no longer relying on the goodness of God. Therefore he is no longer fearing God. Therefore he no longer believes. Therefore he can no longer stand fast. Therefore he has ceased to stand fast precisely in the Church. With this supposed finality he has already left the Church secretly, and it is inevitable that sooner or later this fact will emerge. Particular attention must be paid to this point by mere newcomers like the Gentile Christians. They have everything to lose if they surrender to the illusion of the immutability of the present situation, if they intend to confront the Synagogue on the ground of this revolutionary and highly dangerous finality. No fact or situation is genuinely immutable in the creaturely world as long as time lasts. Only the faithfulness and permanence of the eternal God who is its Creator and Lord are genuinely immutable. It is on Him and on nothing else that the Church must rely if it is to stand on firm ground. But for this reason it must have and keep an open mind for every change and renewal still to be undertaken by this God in the world of His creation, in the fulfilment of His purpose in time. God has not ceased to dispose but is free to dispose again and further—this is the supreme warning and consoling truth in relation to every contemporary situation. And it is this truth, too, which stands as a bond of peace even over the disastrous discord between the Church and the Synagogue : a restraint to the genuine Israel of Jews and Gentiles gathered in the Church ; and a promise even to the debased Israel of the Synagogue. The very God who has cut off can also graft in. He has, in fact, cut off original branches from the holy stem and grafted in wild shoots in their place. The present situation between the Church and Israel corresponds to this. But He can also graft in again what He has already cut off. This is the promise that stands even over the Synagogue. No matter how final its unbelief is intended to be, and may profess to be, and may appear to be when seen from the Church, in His sight it is not an eternal fact, but one which is temporally limited. How can unbelief be or create an eternal fact ? Its essential nature forbids this. Are we not forced to say that unbelief is actually the temporally limited fact κατ᾽ ἐξοχήν beyond which the eternal God as such necessarily looks, and the end of which He sees even though it may be completely hidden from all human sight ? The eternal God as such cannot cease to negate that final persistence in unbelief as He does unbelief itself. For this reason, then, faith in this eternal God must also reckon with the end of this evil persistence and therefore with a change for the better even where from a human viewpoint we think we see an invincible pertinacity of evil. Therefore Paul reckons with the possibility that the branches already cut off will be grafted in again. He has in mind what befell the wild olive shoots, how inconceivably but actually it happened that Gentiles came out of darkness to light, how they came to have a share in nourishment by the holy root of Israel, how they were suddenly revealed as the genuine object of the genuine election of Israel. In the power of the resurrection of Jesus Christ from the dead this has been made real and manifest. In view of this lesson it is quite impossible for him to believe in the pertinacity of Jewish unbelief and therefore in the finality of the divine decision made on this side. Because their unbelief cannot be allowed to have its own way even those who seem to have dropped out of the genuine election of Israel will be gathered again to the elected Israel, and therefore the ultimate reason for doubting the genuineness of the election of Israel as Israel will be set aside. It is to be noted that Paul does not base this prospect for the future of all Israel on any optimistic view of the Israelites with whom we are here concerned, but on a reference to the omnipotence of God. " For God is able to graft them in again." Again, however, this reference to the omnipotence of God in Paul, as in the other witnesses of the Old and New Testaments, is not to be understood as an appeal to or a reliance on the infinite potentiality of the divine being in general. He does not build vaguely and arbitrarily on the postulate that with God everything and all things must finally be possible. It is from an optimistic estimate of man in conjunction with this postulate of the infinite potentiality of the divine being that the assertion of a final redemption of each and all, known as the doctrine of the *apokatastasis*, usually draws its inspiration and power. Paul does not start from this point and therefore he does not get the length of this assertion. He speaks on the one hand of the really lost man whom he sees before him in the Synagogue and whom he has not really tried to interpret optimistically, to judge by Rom. 10. He speaks, on the other hand, of the concrete omnipotence of the God who in Jesus Christ has taken the part and place of man, the omnipotence which has been revealed in the resurrection of Jesus Christ, which is present in the miracle of the Church's faith, and which will finally be unveiled in the expected second coming of Jesus Christ. Both at this point and in what follows the thought of the future of this man and of the omnipotence of this God is, therefore, a thought of faith, a concrete thought of hope which neither over-estimates man nor infringes the freedom of God. But in this very concreteness it has force and precision ; it can and must be thought and expressed. In view of the relation of this God to man it is impossible to expect too much from God, to fail to recognise the supremacy of this God and therefore the promise resting upon this man, to despair of man and therefore to believe in a pertinacity of human unbelief. We can never believe in unbelief ; we can believe only in the future faith of those who at present do not believe.

That this concrete Christian thought of hope is the matter at issue is shown by the development of the statement about God's omnipotence in v. 24. What Paul has in view and what is therefore normative for him for the future is the result of the Messianic present—the calling of the Gentiles to be genuine Israel and the fact of their participation in Israel's election as revealed in it.

A doubly inconceivable thing has happened in the case of these Gentiles before the very eyes of Paul. They belonged by nature to an entirely different stem growing out of an entirely different root. They not only belonged there, but there they grew and lived. They were branches of the wild olive. They were members of a collection of populations and nationalities without promise and, as such, members of the cosmos which never was as such an object of the divine election, and cannot, in fact, become or be so. Apart from Israel, no people as such is God's people. For from no people except Israel has the Son of God come forth as man. No people was determined for this, and none can be subsequently determined. And because man's salvation lies in having a share in the Son of God made man, in being His younger brother, and in and with Him the object of the divine election, therefore no man outside Israel can be determined for salvation, for communion with the eternal living God. Therefore salvation in covenant with God is determined for the Jews and for the Jews only. Therefore " Christ was a minister of the circumcision for the truth of God, to confirm the promises made unto the fathers " (Rom. 15⁸). But these Gentiles were not Jews. They belonged by nature to a situation where no promise and no salvation is to be expected because there is no election. Yet now against all nature they have been removed from their place. They have been cut out of the wild olive to which they belonged and in which they lived. They have been taken out of the hopeless state of their paganism, out of the absolute emptiness and destitution of their non-Israelite existence. Already as such and in itself this negation of negation is a miracle. For how can they have ceased to be what they were of themselves ? How, then, can man cease being a Gentile of himself ? It was not of himself, but only by God's choice and Word, that even Abraham, and in and with him Israel, was taken out of the peoples of the world and exalted to be the people of the Son of God and Man. In the existence of the natural root, holy in its naturalness, we do not have an act of evolution but of creation. It is not nature which reigns, but grace. And now this separation, this severance from the wild olive is repeated. It is not that in place of or beside Israel another of the world's peoples had now become the elected people and is revealed as such. This is in itself impossible. For the election of Israel occurred for the sake of the Son of God and Man who is unique, and it cannot, therefore, be surpassed, supplanted or supplemented by any other. On the contrary, a new separation is now made among the peoples of the earth as such, in the midst of this whole unelected world—and therefore precisely in confirmation of the fact that as the world it is certainly not elected, that there are no other elected people besides Israel. The law of nature is broken. The negation is cancelled. A term is set to the lost condition in which men exist. Suddenly men from many peoples are no longer determined by what was the necessary determining factor for them as members of these peoples and therefore as members of the peoples of the world. Men who belonged there, who lived in the lost condition, in the godlessness which is natural and inevitable there, are now there no longer, but have been taken out of the emptiness and destitution natural there. The story of Abraham and his departure from Haran is repeated a thousand times over. This is one way in which the event is, in fact, understood. And we must consider in and for itself this first side of what Paul clearly has in view when he appeals (v. 23) to the omnipotence of God. It is already inconceivable and awe-inspiring enough that Gentiles have suddenly ceased to be Gentiles, that they have been taken out of the natural and necessary context of their paganism, that they have been crucified, dead and buried with Jesus Christ in respect of what had hitherto been the basic determination of their existence.

But that is, of course, only one side of the miracle. The point that thou " wast cut out of the olive tree of which thou wast by nature the branch " is immediately followed by the other (with which it is in fact identical), that thou " wast contrary to nature (not ' to thy nature '—so Lietzmann—but to the nature of the good olive tree) grafted into a good olive tree." There on the other side was Israel, by God's election and grace created and preserved as the natural stem for bringing forth the Son of God and Man, growing out of the holy root and as such the people of the covenant to whom God's love is directed as it can be directed to no people, because the love of God is, in fact, the communion of the Father with the Son and therefore with the elected man Jesus and therefore with His people, and not in any sense a general divine love for man. There, in and with the one Elect of God, was the promise of future salvation and the present blessing corresponding to this promise. And it was nature too—nature created and preserved by grace but still nature—that all this was just here and only here. This is the reason for the segregation of Israel from all peoples. This is the reason for all the commandments of its Law aiming to achieve and maintain this segregation. This is the reason for circumcision as the sign of the covenant, establishing of every male member of this people that he did not belong to those outside, but to those from whom the one man of God was to come. This is the reason for all the zeal of the prophets against every outward and inward intermingling with those outside. How could the grace which had become nature be protected zealously enough from contamination ? And now the event of the Messianic time consists—quite " contrary to the nature " of this good olive tree—in the fact that these Gentiles, having been removed for their part from what is their nature, actually come to Israel, namely, to Israel's Messiah, and therefore become Israel, participants in all the advantages and privileges of Israel; that they move right into the position which, in fact, can be the portion only of Israelites. Nor was this in any sense effected by the old familiar way of proselytism. They did not themselves have to become Jews. They did not have to be circumcised. They did not have to submit to the practices of the Jewish Law. In relation to the Jews they remained the Gentiles they had always been. They did not give up their Gentile existence for the Jewish. But they were united to the Messiah of Israel by faith alone, and in that very way they really became Israel and entered into possession of all its promises. More than that, they already acquired a part in the fulfilment of all its promises—in the presence of the salvation promised to all Israel, a salvation which has still to be manifested in the future, but is already realised and at hand. How did they attain and obtain this ? Undoubtedly it was παρὰ φύσιν—not against the nature of the holy root of Israel, but against the nature of the stem growing out of it as constituted in what had hitherto been regarded, and had actually been, the only possible way. What was needed to make this possible was the realisation of the goal and end of Israel's history. What was needed was that the promised forgiveness of all the sins of Israel should be accomplished in Jesus Christ. What was also needed was that Israel should be hardened against this final fulfilment of the covenant and deliver up its Messiah to the Gentiles to be put to death. What was needed finally was the great, divine refutation of Israel, and simultaneously the great, divine illumination of the Gentiles, through the raising of Jesus from the dead. The incomprehensible wisdom of the divine omnipotence was therefore needed in order that it should actually be the case : " Thou wast grafted into the good olive tree." This is the other side of the miracle. This is what has befallen the Gentiles. " The Gentiles glorify God for his mercy " (Rom. 15⁹). This, too, Paul has in view when he says in v. 23 : " They also shall be grafted in."

He now explains this : " How much more shall these, which be the natural branches, be grafted into their own olive tree." The force of this future is not that of a supposition or forecast based on the observation or logical analysis of an evolution already begun. He does not hazard this future on the ground that he considers the Jewish mission to which he is so deeply committed to be full of good prospects, nor because he himself perhaps knows of some hopeful new tendencies within the Synagogue. He later calls the content of this future a mystery (v. 25) and it accords with this that he bases it (v. 24) solely on the πόσῳ μᾶλλον. As he sees it, the miracle of the conversion of the Gentiles is obviously the *great* miracle beside which the conversion of the Jews is a smaller, so that he can count on its occurrence as one who was and still is a witness of the first and greater. Indeed, he has to count on its occurrence and therefore risk this future because the great miracle of the conversion of the Gentiles is the event of the Messianic time inaugurated with the resurrection of Jesus Christ, i.e., the event of the fulfilment of every promise of Israel, the miracle in which Israel's own election has finally been disclosed. If the Gentiles come from all parts of the earth to Mount Zion to worship with Israel, constituting with it the one people of the one God, this is, after all, the fulfilment of all the promises of God given to Israel ; it is the revelation of its election. If this has happened in all its incomprehensibility, is it such a great thing that Israel should be included in it as well, the people which is Israel by nature, which belongs therefore to the place where the Gentiles now are, which already dwells on Mount Zion to which the Gentiles now come ? How can even its partial absence be final ? How can there fail soon to be there a gathering of *all* Israel and therefore an ingrafting of the branches now severed ? Now that the great miracle has already taken place, there can be no question of anything but an inevitable consequence which is incomprehensible not so much by nature as in the fact that it has not yet taken place.

This is indeed the point at which Paul began in 9¹⁻⁵. It is incomprehensible that Israel in its totality is not yet gathered to the Church. It is the Church which lives from the very outset in the holy root from which it has come forth. By the special guidance and endowment which it has enjoyed from the very outset, Israel is foreordained to be the Church, and finally to be revealed as the Church, with the revelation of its Messiah, being merged in the Church as its proper and final form. Therefore v. 24 expressly says that when this happens, it is the natural thing which will happen, οἱ κατὰ φύσιν ἐνκεντρισθήσονται, i.e., an incomprehensible disturbance of the natural course will be removed. The great miracle of the Messianic time, the calling and conversion of the Gentiles, will ultimately serve the purpose of announcing and preparing the restoration of the natural order with regard to Israel. Indeed, even now the election of the Gentiles reveals the election of Israel. Therefore the incomprehensible thing now is that this natural thing, the establishment of its own election, is not yet a visible event ; that although announced and prepared by the miracle of the present which has already happened, it has not yet taken place ; that its election is as yet concealed and compromised by its unbelief. This enigma has been thoroughly discussed by Paul in these chapters. He is himself most profoundly disquieted and perplexed by the contradiction of the situation. In sentence after sentence he wrestles with its hard actuality. But at the same time he also endeavours with all his might to restrain the Church from an arbitrary dismissal of this enigma. For the sake of its own election, for its preservation as the Church of Jesus Christ, he seeks to confirm it in thanksgiving and hope, to urge it to humility and loyalty even in relation to this unbelieving Israel.

Paul speaks in v. 25a of a *mysterium* which the Church, especially in its Gentile

Christian members, must know and recognise as such. Οὐ γὰρ θέλω ὑμᾶς ἀγνοεῖν, ἀδελφοί, τὸ μυστήριον τοῦτο. . . . The "mystery" does not in any sense consist in a change which we can one day expect in relation to Israel ; in the reingrafting, according to the nature of Israel and in establishment of its election, of the branches which are now severed, in the future merging of the Synagogue in the Church. The latter will indeed be the natural event already announced and prepared by the calling and conversion of the Gentiles, and in a twofold sense definitely to be expected along with it in two respects. The mystery, on the other hand, consists in the hiddenness of the meaning of the fact that this event has not yet taken place, that Paul, and with him the whole Church, has still to wrestle with this enigma. When Paul describes this hiddenness, this in every respect disturbing "not yet" or "still," as mystery, it is because in this way he means to distinguish it again from a scandal of world history, which is merely contingent and can therefore be judged and treated arbitrarily, and to have it regarded as a dispensation of the divine decree which has absolute precedence and superiority over all human wisdom and enquiry, as based on the one eternal election which embraces both Israel and the Church. It is as a mystery in this sense that from the very first he has actually treated the enigma of the Synagogue with which he and the Church are occupied. From the very first he has traced back this "not yet," or "still" to the gracious will of God. For in 9¹⁻¹⁶ he shows how God had always intended and chosen the Church in Israel and therefore differentiated between Israel and Israel. In 9¹⁴⁻²⁰ he shows how in this differentiating treatment the righteousness of the divine mercy is revealed and in 9³⁰-10²¹ the sole sufficiency. In 11¹⁻¹⁰ he shows how the Church lived already in Israel. In 11¹¹⁻²² he shows how even the Church would not be what it is without unbelieving Israel. What else is all this but a single indication of the divine decree which—well known in its content to the Church, because Jesus Christ is its content—stands everywhere concealed behind even this offending fact ? Concealed, i.e., nowhere present in the form of a simple solution of the enigma proposed to human vision and thought ; nowhere in such a way that man is spared from wondering and adoring in dread, thankfulness and hope ; nowhere in such a way that man can apprehend the mystery otherwise than in the form of faith—but still the well-known divine decree to which faith does have ready access, which excludes every arbitrary solution and dismissal, which rather necessitates dread, thankfulness and hope, wonder and adoration. Although the term "mystery" is finally introduced with reference to the enigmatic delay in the conversion of Israel, it embraces the three chapters in their entirety, and the whole problem posed by them. The aim is to prevent them from becoming ἐν ἑαυτοῖς φρόνιμοι, i.e., from being wise with a wisdom of their own devising, from building on their own wisdom and in that way grounding themselves in themselves. In the words of v. 33 f. it is to make them stand still before the depths of the riches of the wisdom and knowledge of God. That is why Paul wants Christians to know that in this matter they are confronted with the mystery of God. We have seen how in v. 24 the enigma was again put into its most trenchant terms. The incomprehensible thing, the calling and conversion of the Gentiles to the Church and therefore to Israel, has taken place ; the comprehensible, natural and necessary thing, the conversion of Israel itself, has not yet taken place, but is still future. What is the reason for this inversion ?

Paul's answer in v. 25b is that it is the will and decree of God that hardening should overtake that greater part of Israel embodied in the Synagogue of the present ; that this should be kept at a distance from the Church and therefore from the fruits of Israel's election ; that its participation in the fulfilment of the promises given to Israel should be suspended until what is now in its initial stage has been brought to complete fulfilment, namely, until the "fulness of the Gentiles" has come into the Church, until the election of these Gentiles has reached its temporal goal with their calling and conversion. The "fulness of the Gentiles " does not mean the sum total of all Gentile individuals—the Bible nowhere reckons with unqualified totalities of this kind—but the sum total of elected members in the body of Christ from the Gentile world. In Jesus Christ there dwells, indeed according to Col. 1¹⁹ there exists, the πλήρωμα. As the sum and measure of all fulness, wholeness and totality He is also the sum and measure of the totality of the elect ; in faith in Him it is decided both for Jews and Gentiles who belongs to the fulness that enters into the Church. But the fulness of the Gentiles—and this is the mystery of the divine decree—is to be the first to enter. That which, according to Rom. 1¹⁶, naturally belongs " to the Jew first and also to the Greeks " will and must actually accrue (apart from the remnant of Israel) to the Greek first and only then to the Jew. The first are to be last and the last first (Mk. 10³¹). The children of the household are to be thrust out and to be made to wait whilst strangers gathered from the four corners of the earth already sit down in the kingdom of God with Abraham, Isaac and Jacob (Lk. 13²⁸ᶠ·). And it corresponds to this on the political level that " Jerusalem shall be trodden down of the Gentiles, until the times of the Gentiles be fulfilled " (Lk. 21²⁴).

According to v. 26a, God's whole attitude to Israel, the painful separation of the Church in and from its midst, all the dark and grievous side of its calling and determination, the divine hardening and the human unbelief which characterise its history, are not in any sense an accident. They do not rest on divine caprice or arbitrariness. And although they are explained by, they are not grounded in, Israel's guilt and sin. On the contrary, they are grounded in the fact that, according to God's good, gracious and merciful will, the restraining and delaying of the first of His elect to be called, and therefore the mysterious closing of their eyes, ears and hearts, is proper and necessary. The continuing existence of the Synagogue is grounded in the fact that God's election of Israel is its election in Jesus Christ and therefore the election of His mercy, and that even the way in which this election is realised must necessarily correspond to this. " So (in this way) all Israel shall be saved." " All Israel," again, does not mean the totality of all Jewish individuals. It is also improbable, however, that " all Israel " is a simple parallel to " the fulness of the Gentiles," denoting the totality of the elect members of Jesus Christ from the Jews. The whole continuation shows rather that the emphasis of the statement must rest on the οὕτως, on the fact that the incomprehensible inversion of the sequence is the proper and necessary way of the divine deliverance, in which the elect from Israel (in the narrower sense of the word) also obtain a share, thus attesting and establishing the genuineness of the election of the people of Israel as such by the restoration of the natural order. " All Israel " is the community of those elected by God in and with Jesus Christ both from Jews and also from Gentiles, the whole Church which together with the holy root of Israel will consist in the totality of all the branches finally united with and drawing sustenance from it, in the totality constituted by the remnant continuing in and with the original stem Jesus Christ, by the wild shoots added later from the Gentiles, and by the branches which were cut off and are finally grafted in again. This " all Israel " will be saved in the way which is now disclosed in the relationship of the Church and the Synagogue, that is, in such a way that the first will be last and the last first. Why in this way ? The reason is as follows. It is in this way and only in this way that this deliverance of all Israel occurs as an act of the divine mercy and is characterised as such : the act by which the lowly are exalted and the exalted are brought low ; the act in which there is the forgiveness of sins and not the recognition and satisfaction of human claims. Only as it occurs in this inversion can this deliverance be the effect and fruit of the divine election which is itself that of God's mercy.

In the quotation in vv. 26b–27 we must not overlook v. 27. This is a distinctive contraction of Jer. 31³³⁻³⁴. It says emphatically that *this* (αὕτη) is my

(God's) final dispensation for them (God's people) which comes into force with the remission of their sins. The " this " refers back to the quotation from Is. 59[20] in v. 26b : " Then shall come out of Zion the Deliverer, and shall turn away ungodliness from Jacob." The divine dispensation with respect to the sanctification and therefore the deliverance of Israel consists, then, in the promised appearance of a Deliverer coming out of Zion whose function will be to turn away from it its ungodliness. In this alone will the covenant between God and His people be fulfilled. But this decides both that the last will be first and the first last. The last will be first because the Deliverer obviously takes the part of those who are lost, doing for them just what will help them. Those who are exalted by Him are Israel ! But the first will be last because what this Deliverer does characterises those for whom He does it as lost, as those who can be helped only by what He does for them and by absolutely nothing else. Those who are brought low by Him are Israel ! This, then, is God's *modus procedendi* with all Israel " in Jesus Christ," and it finds its necessary expression in that inversion of the natural order, in that incomprehensible sequence : first the Gentiles, then the Jews. The Gentiles can take precedence because in their natural humiliation in relation to the Jews they are the given object for exaltation by the Deliverer coming out of Zion. The Jews must follow after because in their natural exaltation in relation to the Gentiles they are the given object for humiliation by the same Deliverer. In this difference God's mercy directed to both is actual and revealed. Therefore this difference is the will of God, and this is the mystery which is to be believed, wondered at and adored in the enigma of the present relation between the Church and the Synagogue. All those who see the way which God has taken here—the way which as such cannot be hidden from the Church—will certainly be amazed. Yet they will not be shocked beyond recovery, but will confess that everything must be and happen in this way. The chief of all God's ways as known by the Church, God's decree in its origin and revelation, is Jesus Christ. The fact that He comes from Zion means that for Israel, too, He cannot have come in vain. The fact that He goes out from Zion means that He has come into all the world, as we are told in Is. 59[10] immediately before the saying quoted in v. 26 : " So shall they fear the name of the Lord from the west, and his majesty from the rising of the sun ; for he shall come in like a flood, which the breath of the Lord shall drive." But the fact that He is the ῥυόμενος, that it is His kingly office and work to take away sin, means that this inversion must take place, that before Him (because through Him God has mercy upon all, because through faith all are to obtain a share in Him) the rich must be as the poor and the poor as the rich, the elect as the reprobate and the reprobate as the elect. Thus the hope of Israel (the future of the Synagogue in the Church) is taken away from the beginning where it seems to belong and put at the end of all things. It is to be noted, however, that in this way it is really established. And the right of the Jews as the first-born, the original relation of God's election to Israel, is itself obviously confirmed by this inversion. The Jews would not be the last unless they were really the first. Of course, they are not yet even the last, but seem to wish to withdraw altogether from entrance into the Church. But how can they alter the fact that with the Church they live already on the basis of the economy of God's mercy, not yet in faith, but opposed to the faith for which they were first elected in order that they may finally exercise it ? It is in the hope of the Church, therefore, that Israel has its own hope. For even if the Church does believe, yet for it too only the all-embracing economy of the divine mercy can make its faith a sure hope.

This is what vv. 28–36 again express in conclusion. It is best to look first at v. 29 : " For the gifts and calling of God are irrevocable " (literally " not to be repented of "). This statement explains the preceding v. 28b which on its side provides the contrapuntal explanation of v. 28a. And again the statement of v. 29 is the axiom which is afterwards developed and specified in vv. 30–32.

What does this statement say? It reminds us distinctly of 9⁶: "The word of God cannot fail of its effect." We must certainly understand that more general statement, and indeed the whole of chapters 9 and 10, from the point of view of this saying in 11²⁹. The promises given to the people of Israel, nay more, the active love of God bestowed on it (this is the reference of χαρίσματα and κλῆσις), nay more, the foundation of its election, is unshakeable. We anticipate already the famous closing verses of Rom. 11. The promises and love and election of God participate in the constancy of God. The judgments (κρίματα) of God are indeed incomprehensible and His ways of grace (ὁδοί) inscrutable, we are told in v. 33, where "incomprehensible" and "inscrutable" mean that they cannot be judged from a higher vantage point, but are to be discerned as right only in subjection to them as the affairs and ways of God. And they are incomprehensible and inscrutable because God (according to vv. 34–35) is He who has no adviser and no rival, because He precedes with His will all that is and occurs, so that (according to v. 36) all things can have their being and occur only from Him and through Him and to Him. But this magnifying of the divine sovereignty and sole responsibility is unequivocally interpreted in vv. 30–32 to mean that it is because God is He who so incomprehensibly and inscrutably shows mercy that He is unfathomable to us. His mercy is His will that precedes all things; His mercy the beginning and goal and medium of all things. This is the reason why there is no arbitrariness, no chance, no caprice and therefore no unfaithfulness and unreliability in His decisions and ways, however incomprehensible and inscrutable they may appear to us, and actually are. In all that He wills God cannot and will not cease to will one and the same thing. In all that He does, therefore, He cannot and will not cease to do one and the same thing. For He cannot and will not cease to be Himself, One and the Same, He who incomprehensibly and inscrutably shows mercy. As this merciful One He has in His own Son elected the man Jesus, and for His sake He has elected and blessed and called His people Israel. He has not done this futilely or merely temporarily. He will not withdraw from it, either as a whole or in detail. Otherwise He would necessarily give Himself the lie. Otherwise He would be uncertain of Himself in His Godhead. As surely as He is God, He must and will be true to Himself. The statement of v. 29 is not that of an arbitrary philosophy of the *immutabilitas* of the supreme being, just as its counterpart in the doxology of vv. 33–36 has nothing to do with the *incomprehensibilitas* and *independentia* of the same supreme being. But neither is the statement of v. 29 that of a desperate Jewish challenge to a loyalty which God owes to His people because of their special blood or their fidelity to the Law. It is a confession of the Christian hope which clearly has in mind, as its object, the unshakeableness of the divine mercy in the resurrection of Jesus from the dead; which has encountered God in this deed of His as the eternally faithful God, and takes account of Him as such. The χαρίσματα are the essence of the atonement made in the death of Christ and the κλῆσις is the essence of the revelation of this occurrence which has taken place in the resurrection of Jesus Christ from the dead. But this is the fulfilment of all the promises and all the love that God has addressed to Israel, the realisation of its election. Whoever confesses, as the Christian Church does, the faithfulness of God as it is operative and manifest at this point confesses the faithfulness of God in relation to His own people Israel, perceiving and thankfully accepting what is given by God to the people Israel. And whoever with this faithfulness of God confesses, as the Christian Church does, the ground of its hope; whoever sees his whole future rising from the creation by God's mercy of this irrevocable fact, hopes also by this very fact for the future of Israel, i.e., that what God has given Israel must in the last resort benefit not only others but also Israel itself. God is not uncertain about Himself, namely, about His mercy. And the Church on its side is not uncertain about this God. For the second uncertainty is excluded by the first. But so, too, is the third uncertainty about Israel's future. Whatever the continued existence of the Synagogue may mean in itself and for the Church, it is quite certain that it cannot be a reason for this uncertainty (which would necessarily include in itself an uncertainty of the Church about God and an uncertainty of God about Himself).

On the contrary, in v. 29 irrefutable proof is given for the insight of v. 28b, that in accordance with the election that has happened to Israel (as branches from the holy root, cut off indeed but still holy, v. 16), even the Jews who do not now believe are beloved of God for their fathers' sake. If this were not so, the promise given to the fathers would have been left unfulfilled and the faith of the fathers would have been vain—the fathers, too, would then have been unconsoled because in truth unloved. Beloved ! This is the last word which in every present and in respect of every member of this people has to be taken into account in relation to Israel's history from its beginnings into every conceivable or inconceivable future. Not the first, but definitely the last word ! It is from this standpoint, then, that the future of the Jews has to be viewed and judged, no matter what we may have to think or say about their present. And it is from the very same standpoint that the Church looks to its own future. But this is also the last word even in relation to the present state of the unbelieving Jews. It is not for their own being and doing—but then even the Church could not legitimately urge this for its own present—that they are beloved of God, but because of the faithfulness of God who always loves *first*, who loves even where He is not loved in return, who in His own Son has delivered Himself up for His enemies. This cannot be altered even by the truth of v. 28a, that in their relation to the proclamation of the Gospel these Jews are now enemies of God (in view of the parallel ἀγαπητοί in v. 28b we are almost forced to translate this : '' Hated of God ''). For although this judgment is right, it can be valid only in the framework and context of the situation that their election is irrevocable. Therefore in all its seriousness and importance it cannot say more than that in the present situation between the Church and the Synagogue they certainly confirm and attest the sentence of death passed on sinful man in the cross of Christ, the necessary abasement of everything which seeks to exalt itself in the sight of God, the utter pitiableness of the creature as such. This judgment certainly cannot be meant to prejudice the future even in respect of the Jews. If the Church pronounces it in this way, or if it makes it a final judgment on the Synagogue even in respect only of its present state, this means that after all it is uncertain about the God who has no uncertainty in Himself, and it is therefore self-abandoned. It is also self-abandoned because, according to the exposition of vv. 11–22, the unbelieving Jews are still left behind, still hated of God, δι' ὑμᾶς, for your sakes, in order to free the Gospel for the Gentile world, to send out salvation into this world (v. 11), to yield precedence to the Gentiles (v. 25). Ought it not to occur to the Church, and especially to its Gentile Christian members, that those who have this function are moving towards a wholly different future which is still concealed, and indeed that in this function, as those who are hated by God, they are already those who are really beloved of God ?

What, then, is the significance of the Christian axiom of v. 29 that the gifts and calling of God are irrevocable ? According to the development of its meaning in vv. 30–32 it contains the consolation which the Church and the Synagogue have in common, but which also they can hear and receive only in common.

In the first instance, if we look at man, we find human disobedience everywhere. The Gentiles who have now leapt ahead of the unbelieving Jews with their gathering to the Church must remember this. '' Ye in times past have not obeyed God '' (v. 30a). It is not, then, to their obedience that they owe this forward leap and the place which they now occupy. It is not as a result of their obedience that they have reached a point where they now have a future and a hope. It is not their obedience which is the unshakeable thing to which they can look back in order to look forward. What lies behind them, looking at man, is in substance exactly the same as lies behind the unbelieving Jews, their disobedience to God, a disobedience which was far more horrible than that of the Jews to the extent that it was for them a matter of course, the natural thing; that it was not even in the slightest degree interrupted or restrained by any promise or Law of God, but consisted in the perpetual confirmation of the vacuum in which they were situated before God. This disobedience of theirs was brought to an end by their gathering into the Church. Yet it is not stated that they have now become obedient. This might well have been stated, for now they have, in fact, become obedient. But this is only the consequence of their finding mercy, the mercy of the very God to whom they had previously been only disobedient. It was not that they set out and came to Zion but that the ῥυόμενος from Zion came as such to them. He drew them from their " vain conversation received by tradition from their fathers " (1 Pet. 1¹⁸), in order to draw them to Himself and make them His possession. He has set them in the place where they now stand. And the instrument of this mercy which has undeservedly come to them (v. 30b) is the very unbelief of the Jews which now confronts them so enigmatically in the Synagogue. Again, they would not be what they are if salvation had not come to them from the Jews, and indeed through the transgression of the Jews, through the very thing which now makes the Jews the hated of God. How else can they regard themselves except as the object, and how else can they regard the Jews except as the instrument, of the divine mercy ? What can they perceive in both themselves and the Jews but the revelation of this mercy, the revelation of its unfathomableness and unshakeableness ? How can they choose any other point than this from which to look forward both into their own future and into that of the Jews ?

Now admittedly (v. 31) there is in the first instance disobedience among the unbelieving Jews too. It differs in their case from that of the Gentiles gathered into the Church. With them it is not past but present. It is not covered and cancelled by the divine mercy. It is open and flagrant. It is revealed in them as the original and proper attitude of man to God. And the disobedience of the Jews is far more horrible than that of the Gentiles because it was and is exercised amid the revelation of their election, the fulfilment of the covenant between God and them; because it consists indeed in the rejection of their Messiah who appeared to and was crucified for them, so that it has the appearance of the unforgivable sin against the Holy Spirit. Yet there is obviously no point in playing off the triviality of the Gentile against the gravity of the Jewish disobedience, endeavouring to present the former as slighter and the latter as more serious. In the wellknown passage in Rom. 1–2 Paul has already equated Gentile and Jewish sin, for all their difference. Disobedience is disobedience, and as disobedience to God it can be cancelled only by the mercy of God. But the very unfathomableness and unshakeableness of the mercy which has come to the Gentiles, a mercy which, after all, is simply the fulfilment of all the promises of Israel, make it absolutely necessary to see in the revealed sequence of disobedience and mercy a law for the as yet invisible future, and therefore to look beyond the indisputable fact of the present unbelief of the Jews : " These also have now not obeyed, that they also may obtain mercy." Not only, then, that through their disobedience salvation may come to the Gentiles, but also that they themselves may share in the salvation ! They, too, through God's mercy, and not in any other way. Certainly their wrong decision has been made, and as such it cannot be cancelled, just as the past of the Gentiles cannot be undone. But God's mercy would not be the present of the Gentiles if it were not the future of the Jews also. And in this case, too, an instrument has to be and is, in fact, used. The disobedience of the Gentiles cannot be this instrument. On the contrary, according to v. 11 f., it is their obedience which is to provoke the Jews to that jealousy. But now there is no further mention either of that obedience of the Gentiles or of that jealousy. On the contrary, it is by the mercy of God which has come on the Gentiles that mercy is to be and will be the portion of the Jews also. It is their existence, not as a pattern of human being and doing but as a copy of the goodness of God, which is to be and will be the means by which the same divine goodness may benefit those also towards whom it was originally directed ; the means by which God will show mercy on the Jews also. The second νῦν in v. 31, which is well established critically, seems to be rather out of place because the demonstration of the divine mercy towards the Jews, of which the verse speaks, is after all still future. What is not future but present is the mercy shown to the Gentiles. But this is the means of divine mercy for the Jews too, so that in this sense the latter is already present. The mercy of God is already secretly operative in relation to the Jews. What this striking second νῦν makes quite impossible for Christian anti-semitism (he that has ears to hear, let him hear) is the relegation of the Jewish question into the realm of eschatology. That Israel's hope is really the *hope* of Israel and the Church, and is therefore *future*, makes no difference to the fact that in relation to Israel the responsibility of the Church, which itself lives by God's mercy, is already a wholly present reality.

So they are (v. 32) all together. Again, there is no question of an unqualified totality but of the πᾶς Ἰσραήλ of v. 26. Common to it is the state of human disobedience and the determination for divine mercy. The Gentiles had been shut up in the natural disobedience in which God had previously left them. And the Jews are shut up in the unnatural disobedience into which God has now plunged them by hardening their hearts. Both are shut up by God in the same prison. But the prison opens and again they are all together. For God has determined the Gentiles for the mercy in which they now participate, and the Jews for future participation in the same mercy. Everywhere we begin with human disobedience and everywhere we end with the divine mercy—everywhere and for all, i.e., for " all Israel," in the whole sphere of the election of the God whose majesty consists in the fact that He is merciful.

THE ELECTION OF THE INDIVIDUAL

The man who is isolated over against God is as such rejected by God. But to be this man can only be by the godless man's own choice. The witness of the community of God to every individual man consists in this : that this choice of the godless man is void ; that he belongs eternally to Jesus Christ and therefore is not rejected, but elected by God in Jesus Christ ; that the rejection which he deserves on account of his perverse choice is borne and cancelled by Jesus Christ ; and that he is appointed to eternal life with God on the basis of the righteous, divine decision. The promise of his election determines that as a member of the community he himself shall be a bearer of its witness to the whole world. And the revelation of his rejection can only determine him to believe in Jesus Christ as the One by whom it has been borne and cancelled.

1. JESUS CHRIST, THE PROMISE AND ITS RECIPIENT

We shall now seek finally to do justice to the conception of the divine election in its relation to individual human beings.

The traditional doctrine of predestination of every school and shade has always begun with this problem, and has made no essential progress beyond it. It has dealt with everything that has so far occupied us under the heading of the election of Jesus Christ, and the election of the community of God, if at all, merely as it relates to or expands the question which constitutes for it *the* problem of the election of grace : the question of the eternal (positively or negatively determined) order of the private relationship which exists between God and all individual human beings. The haste with which this problem has been attacked, and the way in which it has been self-evidently regarded as that with which predestination is finally and exclusively concerned, are astounding. But they are facts, and indeed such old and commonly accepted facts that they have almost gained the weight and value of inner necessities.

In the development leading to this situation there is mirrored that movement of the general spiritual history of the West which, beginning in the last days of antiquity and breaking through in the Renaissance, led to the discovery and estimation of the individual which has dominated the so-called modern age. To-day as we stand under the sign of so violent a collapse of this movement, it is again high time that we recall and accept anew the norm of truth which was and is here at stake ; and we for our part shall have to do so in this context. However, this need not prevent us from first of all affirming that this general movement of spiritual history has undoubtedly been a questionable contributing factor in the erection of the axiom that in the last resort the doctrine of predestination has to do exclusively with the eternal establishment of the relationship between God and the " individual."

It is not mere chance that Augustine, the father of classical predestinarian doctrine, is also the man to whom we owe the discovery of the literary form of Christian autobiography. The passion and the value of his predestinarian doctrine are certainly not due merely to that ; but they are just as certainly not to be understood without any reference at all to this alignment, this *Deus et anima* of the *Confessions*, which later gained such tremendous significance both in Christian and in secular form. The Augustinian doctrine of predestination as we have already seen, answers the question why, among those who hear the Word of God, some believe and others do not believe. His answer refers us to the *valde remota a sensibus carnis schola, in qua Pater auditur et docet, ut veniatur ad Filium* (*De praed.* 8, 13), where, according to His good-pleasure, God speaks to some, but does not speak to others. This secret " school " is the divine pre-determination in so far as this is the secret of individual human personalities in their variety. Of course, the actual content of Augustine's definition of pre-destination was still objective : it is *gratiae praeparatio* (*De praed.* 10, 19) or *praeparatio beneficiorum Dei* (*De dono persev.* 14, 35). He could also relate it, not to individuals, but to the two kingdoms, the *duae civitates h.e. societates hominum, quarum est una, quae praedestinata est in aeternum regnare cum Deo, altera aeternum supplicium subire cum diabolo* (*De civ. Dei* XV, 1). And we also remember the important contributions to, or rather suggestions of, a christological understanding of predestination, which are not lacking in Augustine.

In common with Augustine, Thomas Aquinas does not define predestination personally but objectively as *quaedam divina praeordinatio ab aeterno de his, quae per gratiam Dei sunt fienda in tempore* (*S. th.* III, qu. 24, art. 1c). And in Calvin the situation is still sufficiently fluid for him to refer election primarily to the Church, at least in the first edition of the *Institutes* and in the *Catechism* of 1542. And in some measure at least he could adopt the Augustinian suggestion of a christological evaluation of the problem. But it is precisely in Calvin that the decisive change is now noticeable. If he describes predestination more comprehensively in the work *De aeterna Dei praed.* (1552, *C.R.* 8, 313) with the words : *qua* (*Deus*) *de toto genere humano et de singulis hominibus quid futurum esset statuit,* it is also true that the idea has been limited, in the final edition of the *Institutes* (III, 21, 5), to the *decretum aeternum, quo apud se constitutum habuit, quid de unoquoque homine fieri vellet. Non enim pari conditione creantur omnes, sed aliis vita aeterna, aliis damnatio aeterna praeordinatur. Itaque prout in alter-utrum finem quisque conditus est, ita vel ad vitam vel ad mortem praedestinatum dicimus.* This established the fashion which is now taken for granted alike by Reformed and Lutheran, orthodox and heterodox, Supra- and Infralapsarians, the " Federal " theologians and their opponents. It is true that both Calvin (for example in his sermons on Deuteronomy, *C.R.* 26, 521 f. ; 27, 46) and the dogmaticians of the 17th century know and speak of an *electio generalis,* i.e., of the election of an entire nation, of the Israelite nation. It is already noticeable, however, that they regard this exceptional phenomenon as a separate genus which, in fact, comprehends only this one species. It is even more noticeable that they do not know what theological use to make of this genus, this exceptional phenomenon of the election of Israel, but without any connexion or explanation (e.g., W. Bucanus, *Instit. theol.,* 1605, *Loc* 36, 1, 5 f. ; A. Polanus, *Synt. Theol chr.,* 1609, *col.* 1572 f.) hurry on to deal with the *electio specialis* and *praedestinatio sanctorum* (*de hac iam nobis agendum*), and can never subsequently free them-selves from this or from the corresponding *reprobatio.* Even a man like

J. Coccejus, who otherwise rendered a great service in the development of doctrine, saw the content of predestination (which for him meant the same thing as the eternal *testamentum*) as follows : *Deum elegisse haeredes vitae . . . alios item reiecisse et odio habuisse* (*Summa Theol.*, 1662, *cap.* 37, 2). The confessional writings also show themselves to be unanimously and unambiguously interested in these individuals on the right and on the left as the real object of predestination— the one exception being the *Confessio Scotica*. The orthodox certainly tried to make use of the idea of predestination in the doctrine of the Church ; but they outlined and developed the concept itself as though there were no such thing as Israel or the Church, as though only the individual man as such could come into consideration as the object of predestination. Moreover, in spite of the teachings received through Augustine and later through Coccejus, the thought that Jesus Christ is primary in this connexion became continually more remote. A certain deepening of insight came about only as they sought to connect the doctrine of predestination more or less closely with the doctrine of universal divine provid- ence ; but if—as was indeed inevitable—they allowed the latter to find its con- summation in the doctrine of the elective grace of God as the predestination of the individual human person, obviously the weight of their individualism, nour- ished by the very idea of the eternity of God, was inevitably increased by this connexion. And in practice contemplation of the predestination of the good and evil angels—an exposition of which was the usual introduction to the doctrine of the object of predestination—could only serve to emphasise more sharply than ever the picture of the *alii-alii* on the right and on the left, opening up as it did a background of the same picture in the realm of higher spirits.

If it is the case that this orientation of the Church's doctrine of predestination certainly did not arise apart from the earlier way of secular individualism, it is equally certain that as orientated in this way the doctrine is not merely one of those factors which have paved the way for Pietism and Rationalism within the Church itself, but is also one of the presuppositions without which the further development of secular individualism would have been inconceivable (the de- velopment from J. J. Rousseau and the younger Schleiermacher through Max Stirner and Kierkegaard to Ibsen and Nietzsche). And in spite of the serious objections to it in the so-called modern age, no one has ever thought of attacking it from this side, and no one could think of doing so. For on this side far too much depended on what it had brought to the notice of the West in so particu- larly impressive a way—far more pointedly than all the ancient mystics and long before the secular prophets of the 18th and 19th centuries—i.e., on the conviction that the beginning and end of all the ways of God, and even the essence of all divine truth, are to be recognised and honoured in individual human beings.

In this matter, again, we have broken with dogmatic tradition. The problem of the divine election is not exhausted in the problem of the election of individual human beings. On the contrary, the former embraces the latter. The latter can be appraised only in its connexion with the former. But its connexion with the former consists in its relation to the problem of the election of Jesus Christ and with this the election of Israel and the Church. The real problem of election includes the problem which was of such pressing and exclusive import- ance for the traditional doctrine. It is concerned with the free decision of the love of God for His covenant with mankind, apart from which —as the Father and the Son will to manifest their inexpressible unity in the Holy Ghost—He does not will to be God. For the revelation of the Father in the Son by the Holy Spirit, and therefore the revelation of the profundity of the Godhead, is identical with the revelation of the covenant, the revelation in Jesus Christ. It is a matter of the eternal self-giving of God in Jesus Christ and of its attestation by His community, which as Israel must represent and proclaim God's abasement to man and as the Church man's exaltation to God; as Israel God's condemnation of sin and as the Church God's acceptance of the faith of man; as Israel the promise and as the Church the fulfilment of the covenant of grace, and therefore the justification and salvation of this whole people. And since this self-giving of God in Jesus Christ constitutes the content of the decree of God, which precedes not only all actualisations but also all His other decrees, comprising within itself all others as the beginning of all the ways and works of God, we may discern in it the eternal double predestination, the divine election of grace. Thus although custom justifies the claim that the essence of the doctrine of predestination is the thesis that God has foreordained some to blessedness and others to damnation, it is extremely vulnerable from this standpoint. For, according to the biblical facts which the doctrine is supposed to express, this thesis says too little. And, indeed, every other description of the election of individuals would also say too little to be at all adequate as the main theme of predestination. This special subject is just one form of the true theme of predestination doctrine. There are others beside it—the election of Jesus Christ and the election of the community. It cannot, therefore, be treated *in abstracto* but only in line with the others, and the correct thesis in this matter is to be sought in a more scrupulous consideration of what we must say concerning the election of Jesus Christ and the election of the community.

The question of the order of treatment of the individual areas of the problem is not of fundamental importance. The selection of this particular order assists the clarification of the antithesis. It would also have been much more difficult to execute and bring out the correction which is necessary in this respect if in agreement with tradition we had begun at the point where we now end. But it cannot be denied that a reversal of the order is intrinsically possible. Indeed, once the correction has been made, it might even be advisable. Following tradition, we could then begin with the election of the individual, proceed in continually ascending circles to the election of Israel and the Church, and conclude with the election of Jesus Christ. The only correction which is basically important is the recognition that the election of the individual must be discussed in the closest possible relation to the election of Jesus Christ and the election of the community of God.

When we say that the problem of the divine election includes that of the election of individual human beings, we recognise that this latter belongs actually and necessarily to the sphere of the former, and must therefore be seriously examined and discussed in this relationship. That which has been eternally determined in Jesus Christ is concretely determined for every individual man to the extent that in the form of the witness of Israel and of the Church it is also addressed to him and applies to him and comes to him, to the extent that in His Word the electing God enters with him into the relationship of Elector to elected, and by His Word makes him an elected man. This is the predestined man of whom the doctrine of predestination must necessarily speak. This is the man who has been seen and known and intended and willed—predestined—by God from all eternity in the election of Jesus Christ and in the election of the witnessing community. It is for him that this self-giving is effective. It is upon him that God passes judgment. It is upon him that God bestows His loving-kindness. He is the object of the divine election of grace. The classical doctrine certainly did not err in speaking so emphatically and assiduously of the predestination of individual human beings. Apart from a consideration of this relationship, there can be no true expression or understanding of all that Church doctrine has to say about God, or its doctrine of the election of grace about the primal history between God and man. We cannot and must not isolate the relationship from the divine election of grace and in some sense hypostatise it, as was done by the traditional doctrine—to the detriment of a correct understanding of the relationship itself. We must everywhere understand and express the divine election of grace in this relationship also.

The " also " does not involve any restriction or diminution of the significance of this third and final area of the problem. It is not merely figuratively or incidentally that predestination is the predestination of individual human beings. Certainly the election of Jesus Christ relativises the election of individuals, but it also establishes their election alongside and apart from Him. Their election is not void because it can be real or significant only when included in the election of Jesus Christ. It is, indeed, their election which is at issue in the election of Jesus Christ. It is in order that every man may understand that he has been elected in his authentic individuality that the election of Jesus Christ must be attested and proclaimed to him. The individual who as the original object of divine election is for all the rest Another does not deprive them by that in which He precedes them, but preceding them in everything—He is indeed the original object of election—He is everything for them and gives them all things. In this Other that which each man is and should be for himself is presupposed and maintained, whereas without Him it could only emerge from nothing and proceed to nothing. It is exactly because of the original election of Jesus Christ that the *particula veri* of " individualism," so far from being eliminated, is given a lasting validity. This same is true of the election of the community. This, too, has a relativising, but at the same time a confirmatory, significance in relation to the election of the individual man, both inside and outside its confines. The latter does not become pointless because it is mediated, conditioned and limited by the election of the community.

It is their own election that it proclaims to men when it attests Jesus Christ to them and calls them to faith in Him. As He lives who comes forth from Israel and from whom the Church comes forth, there live with Him and in Him those whom the community calls, and to whom it may commit its call. It is in their election alone that election can really be visible and effective for the community. This fellowship does not lead any independent life in relation to its members. It lives in them. It does not rob those to whom it mediates the election of Jesus Christ. It, too, precedes them in all things, and yet it has all that it does have for them, and is all that it is only in them. The *particula veri* of " individualism " is not curtailed but genuinely assured and honoured when we understand the election of the " individual " as the *telos* of the election of the community.

To-day especially two distinct delimitations have to be made and maintained at this point.

There is a modern concept which during the last two centuries has shown itself with increasing clarity to be a kind of secular imitation of the concept of the election of Jesus Christ—the concept of the leader. At first in a limited, but then necessarily in a limitlessly expanding sphere, in an area which must finally be nothing less than world-wide, the leader is the individual who in some fashion unites in himself the fulness of the election of grace, so that he is the elect, not on behalf of, but in place of others ; he is the other, besides whom there are finally no individuals, or at least no elect individuals. The whole mystery of human existence in his sphere is his mystery. All freedom and all responsibility, all authority and power in this sphere, belong to him. He is the other, by whom is taken from the many beside him both their election and everything else with it—the mystery of their individuality and solitude, freedom and responsibility, all authority and power—and from whom they hold everything only in fee, to carry out his decisions. Emerging from the ranks of the many and elevated over them as the other who alone may be an individual, the leader is an absolute usurper in relation to other individuals. Election in the sense of the modern leader-concept has nothing whatever to do with the election of Jesus Christ except that it is its utter reversal and caricature. The individualism of the West obviously cannot evade responsibility for the formulation of this concept. All the brutality, all the murderous insolence of the usurper have been involved in it from the very outset. Mastered, as it were, by its own logic and reduced *ad absurdum*, it has brought down upon itself an inevitable and most terrible reaction. But this has simply disclosed the antithesis to the Christian concept of election in which it found itself even at its inception. The Christian concept of election does not involve this despoiling of the many for the sake of the one. On the contrary, when Jesus Christ is the elected One, the election and the accompanying mystery of individuality and solitude, and with it the freedom and responsibility and the authority and the power of the many, are not abrogated, but definitively confirmed in this Other. He is not the object of the divine election of grace instead of them, but on their behalf. He does not retain for Himself or withhold what He is and possesses as the Elect of God. He does not deal with it as with spoil. But He is what He is, and has what He has, in His revelation and imparting of it to the many. His kingdom is neither a barracks nor a prison, but the home of those who in, with and by Him are free. He is the Master of all as the Servant of all. Secular individualism may have reached its goal and end in the contemporary leader-concept, but in the Christian concept of election its own barely understood desire has always been defended against it, and even in face of the catastrophe which has overtaken it, it will continue to be preserved.

There is, however, another modern concept which is important in this connexion, constituting as it does an unmistakeable secular imitation of the election of the community. A feature of its imitativeness is that it stands in as intimate a relation with the first as can be said of the Christian prototype. It is found in two varieties, which were for a long time in opposition, but which in the latest developments have shown a tendency to unite and merge into one another. On the one hand, there is the idea of the social mass, and on the other hand that of the national people. Elected man, according to Communism, is the mass, created as such through the general proletarianisation which is a product of capitalism—while according to Fascism it is the nation as constituted by race, language and history. Both ideas merge in the totalitarian state. In this the mass on the one side and the nation on the other do not merely find their union, but their very being and existence. It becomes the proper bearer of election. In virtue of the totalitarian state, the individual member of the mass can lay claim only to the existence and function of a component part which can be replaced at any time and with no value of its own. For this state the individual is only of interest in respect of what he does or does not do in his specific function. He is of absolutely no interest at all for his own sake, or for what might or could become of him as an individual. In this sense the individual and his will to live, his conscience and understanding, his casual opinions and necessary convictions, and ultimately even his body, have all to die in order that the whole, the mass or the nation as organised in the state, may live. It is not the individual who is elected, but the mass is elected in his place. And therefore from this side, too, it follows that the individual has no mystery, no freedom or responsibility, no authority or power of his own. Everything that he may possess he possesses as a vassal of the whole. And the latter has no obligation to him such as he owes to it. Nor is he under any necessity or duty to give expression in the whole to his inward self as such, his uniqueness and individuality. The duty of doing this is taken from him, together with the right. He lives only as he is subjected and fulfils his subjection, as he is used and lets himself be used. A concept like this has nothing whatever to do with the election of God's community except that it is its absolute opposite. If the leader-concept is to be described as the final logical conclusion of western individualism, the concept of the total mass or national state manifests the fact that in the last resort this individualism has simply wearied of itself, and that it was able to do so. It reveals the profound inner uncertainty and impotence which were inherent in it from the start. Surely it has had time and opportunity fully to express and commend itself—and most of all in the place where it is now most vilely betrayed. Yet we can evidently become so tired of it as to try to exchange it for the total state! But the Christian concept of election, with its reference to the community of the people of God, is no such product of exhaustion. The divine election is indeed to be understood as the election of an entire nation of men as such, and that of the individual as a member of this nation. But this election of the individual is just as authentic and original as that of any whole. Nor is the one consummated without the other. The individual can and does also recognise in his own personal election that of the entire people of God. His own mystery and all that it involves are not taken away from him because he is a member of the whole. On the contrary, they are given and received. He is no mere delegate, but in his own right a bearer of this people's responsibility. He is no vassal, but a free citizen. He receives and gives and works not merely as a transmitting or driving wheel in a machine (or as a cell in an organism) but by his own initiative. He does not stand merely in or under the whole, but in his own place he is himself the whole. And whatever proceeds from the whole proceeds from himself. As each is for all, so all are also for each. On the basis

of the divine election, there can be no possible tension between the " individual "
and the " community." There need, therefore, be no compromise between them,
no continual reacting on the one side or the other, no abdication of individualism
and renewal of collectivism even in our own day. On this basis the " individual "
is constantly honoured just because he is established as such by the " community "—or, rather, he is established with the community in the one Elect,
Jesus Christ, whose promise he has.

These are the delimitations which are necessary at this point. If from the
very start secular individualism could appeal to the Christian concept of election
only on the basis of a misunderstanding, the misunderstanding will only be
increased if the triumphant secular authoritarianism and collectivism of our own
day try to do the same. They can only meet opposition from this quarter.

But the term " individual human being " which we have so far
provisionally used is ambiguous in this context, and must now be
clarified by a definition of those who, in and through the community,
are the object of divine predestination.

Men have an " individuality " in relation to the human group :
the family, the nation, the state, society, the total complex of human
nature and history—in short, humanity as a whole. The event that
stands under the sign of divine predestination does not take place
between God and one of these groups, but between God and individual
human beings. The " sign " itself—the divine election of grace—
already refers to them. This election has been made in Jesus Christ.
The community is its necessary medium. But its object (in Jesus
Christ, and by way of the community) is individual men : certainly,
these individual men in their group relationships, in the callings,
obligations, duties, restrictions and potentialities which are given in
such relationships ; but individuals who are actively responsible in
these relationships, and not the groups themselves or any single group.
There are no predestined families and no predestined nations—even
the Israelite nation is simply the first (transitory) form of the community—nor is there a predestined humanity. There are only predestined men—predestined in Jesus Christ and by way of the community. It is individuals who are chosen and not the totality of men.
And God seeks, calls, blesses and sanctifies the many, the totality,
the natural and historical groups and humanity itself, in and through
the individual. It is in individual men that, from the beginning of
His ways and works, God has loved, regarded, known and marked out
the many and the totality, bestowing upon them the benefit of His
covenant and the grace of His choice. It is they who—as a promise
for the many and the totality—compose the race elected in Jesus Christ,
and by means of the community ; that race which is constituted of
authentic " individuals " in their distinctiveness and particularity, and
is therefore a new phenomenon, distinct from all the other groups of
human nature and history. All this is not in any sense based on the
idea that a man's particular properties make him a greater, better or
more authentic man than do the properties which he shares with the

many or the totality. Nor is it based on the idea that the individual as such is closer, dearer or more pleasing to God than the many or the totality. On the contrary, the affinity of the individual to God which makes him the object of His election of grace is based solely on the nature and activity of God as such. Because God is One ; because His eternal Son, the only-begotten, the beginning of all His ways and works, is the One on whom God wholly (*individua*) bestows His love ; because in this One He has made Himself the God of mankind ; because in this One He has called man His son—therefore it is the individual (that is, this or that single man) to whom God's deity for men and God's condescension to men (in time and from all eternity) refer ; and it is only in this individual that they also refer to the many and the totality. The fact that God is One, both in Himself and from the beginning of all His ways and works in Jesus Christ, means that the man who hears God's Word (or does not hear it), who believes in Him (or does not believe), who is grateful to Him (or ungrateful), is to be one, this or that one, the bearer of a definite personal name. Families, nations, social groups and so on, are not called ; neither is humanity as such. But from all these groups—and as a witness to them— " individuals " are reached and encountered by the Word of God, summoned to faith and confession, baptised and gathered into the Church. These " individuals " recognise the election of Jesus Christ as their own election. The election of the community, moreover, reaches its consummation in the authority and operation of the Holy Spirit in their hearts and in their free personal decisions. From this point of view, then, the idea of the " individual " has a positive meaning in the present context. From this point of view, the Christian concept of election is more fundamentally " individualistic " than anything produced by secular individualism. From this point of view, it is that which guarantees the concern of secular individualism, even though secularism itself is pleased to abandon it.

But this definition of the " individual " is inadequate to characterise man as the object of divine predestination. If a man is predestined as an individual and not merely as a member of a group, he is not predestined in this individuality, as if this itself characterised him as predestinate. Certainly, this is the *conditio sine qua non*, but it is not the *ratio praedestinationis*. Predestination necessarily includes in itself the fact that each one is directly envisaged and intended by God as such, and cannot, therefore, be confused or exchanged. But to say this is not of itself to describe predestination as the gracious election of man. For in what sense is this the election of *grace*—seen with man as its object—as we have it in its original occurrence in Jesus Christ and the witness of the community to this event ? In what sense is this the decision of the free, unmerited and unsought goodness and condescension of God to man ? Quite obviously from this point of view the individuality of the predestinate is something very different

from the particularity in which he stands out above his membership
of the group as this or that person. It has not only to transcend this
particularity, but it has to be of such a kind that on the basis of it
the fact that God regards and intends, wills and loves and elects him
is to be understood, on the analogy of the election of Jesus Christ and
the community of God, as *grace* alone. Thus the concept of the
" individual," if it is to be a fitting characterisation of the predestinate,
must be understood in an entirely new dimension. It must be carried
beyond its immediate, positive meaning to a negative meaning, in
which it is genuinely perceived that predestined man is simply forgiven
man. Predestined man (according to the election of Jesus Christ and
the community) is he who, in and with God's choice, is not met by
honour and approval, but by justification by grace alone, by forgiveness ; who is not the object of divine election in virtue of a life which
is acceptable and welcome to God, but because God covers, transforms
and renews his unworthy and rebellious life ; whom the sovereign God
(in the sovereignty of His omnipotence and loving-kindness, His constancy and patience) encounters, not with a natural Therefore, but
with a miraculous Nevertheless ; whom He chooses absolutely for
the sake of His own will ; whom He makes a partner of His covenant
quite apart from and even contrary to his own merit or ability. Predestined man is man made usable to God by the Holy Spirit. This
makes it necessary for us to examine the further and deeper negative
meaning of the concept of the " individual." It is another matter
that in its relationship to the groups as well the individuality of man
may also be and actually is negatively burdened, bearing the character
of unworthiness and opposition to God, and standing in absolute need
of forgiveness, transformation and renewal by the grace of God. The
point is, however, that this is not necessarily the case. Individuality
in this primary sense is not itself sin which can be answered only by
the grace of God (as the forgiveness of the sinner), and which therefore
characterises the predestination of man *per se* as an election of grace.
If predestination really is this, how does it come about ? How is it
that the individual needs forgiveness and renewal ? How is it that
he can be elect only in the form of forgiveness ?

The witness of the community is to this effect. There is another
individuality of man which is negated in Jesus Christ. It has basically
nothing to do with his individuality in that first sense. On the contrary, it can be understood only as its caricature and perversion. As
such it certainly does most radically involve his individuality in that
first sense. It consists in the fact that the " individual " does not
accept as grace, and gratefully correspond to, the distinction and
dignity conferred on him by the one and only God. Instead, he
desires and attempts to make and vindicate them as his natural possession, as a right which is inherent in his human existence, and therefore
as his claim upon God : as if the fact that God regards, intends, wills,

loves and chooses him rested upon his own abilities and merits ; as if God did not do this for His own will's sake ; as if the covenant—the covenant of grace—which God has made with him were one of those groups ; as if he could therefore exist on his own account in relation to God, as a partner in God's covenant, in the same way as he is able—by the goodness of God—to do so in relation to the many and even the totality of his fellow-men, with all his obligations and duties towards them. This is the individuality of man which is negated by Jesus Christ, and which is therefore only to be understood and judged negatively. It means his sinful and fatal isolation. It is the essence of man's godlessness. It is just because man may genuinely and legitimately be an " individual " before God that if he wills to be this apart from and against God it can only be *per nefas* and to his own ruin. The " individual " man who desires and undertakes this posits and conducts himself as the man who is rejected by God from all eternity. It can only be man's own godless choice that wills to be this " individual," the man who is isolated in relation to God. He therefore chooses the possibility which is excluded by the divine election of grace. For this isolation is not intended for man in the divine election of grace (in Jesus Christ). On the contrary, it is a satanic possibility which is excluded and destroyed. And because the divine election of grace, because Jesus Christ, is the beginning of all the ways and works of God, man chooses that which is in itself nothing when he returns to this satanic possibility, when he chooses isolation in relation to God. His choice itself and as such is, therefore, null. He chooses as and what he cannot choose. He chooses as if he were able to choose otherwise than in correspondence to his election. He chooses the possibility which God has excluded by his election. To that extent he chooses godlessly. He desires and undertakes to go into the void. In the negative act of this void choice of nothing, he is vanquished and overtaken even before he begins by that which God has eternally decreed for him and done for him in the election of Jesus Christ. The testimony of the community is addressed to this godless man, this man engaged in this negative act. It does not deny that he does this act ; on the contrary, it asserts this. Nor can it reverse it. It knows and confronts man—every man—as one who is isolated over against God by his own choice, and who in and with this isolation must be rejected by God. It can do nothing else but testify to him the nullity of this choice and the futility of his desire and undertaking. It testifies to him, in opposition to his own choice, the gracious choice of God in Jesus Christ as the beginning of all God's ways and works, and therefore the futility of his own desire and undertaking. In defiance of God and to his own destruction he may indeed behave and conduct himself as isolated man, and therefore as the man who is rejected by God. He may represent this man. But he has no right to *be* this man, for in Jesus Christ God has ascribed this to Himself with all that it involves and therefore taken it away from man. What man can do with his negative act can only be the admittedly real and evil and fatal recollection and reproduction of that which has been removed from him ; but for all its wickedness and disastrous results this negative act as such can never be other than impotent. Man can do it and persist in it. He can become a sinner and place himself within the shadow of divine judgment which his powerless representation of the man rejected by God is unable to escape. He does all this. But he cannot reverse or change the eternal decision of God—by which He regards, considers and wills man, not in his isolation over against Him, but in His Son Jesus. Man can certainly keep on lying (and does so) ; but he cannot make truth falsehood. He can certainly rebel (he does so) ; but he can accomplish nothing which abolishes the choice of God. He can certainly flee from God (he does so) ; but he cannot escape Him. He can certainly hate God and be hateful to God (he does and is so) ; but he cannot change into its opposite the eternal love of God which triumphs even in His hate. He can certainly give himself to isolation (he does so—he thinks, wills and behaves godlessly, and is godless) ; but even in his isolation he must demonstrate that which he wishes to controvert—the impossibility of playing the " individual " over against God. He may let go of God, but God does not let go of him. It is to the man who does not yet know it—and every man continually unlearns and forgets it !—it is to the man living in the darkness of his own negative act, always sure of himself in his error, always hopeful in his rebellion, for ever renewing his flight from God, for ever applying himself anew to his hatred for God, taking himself seriously in his godlessness—it is to this man, representing the rejected and to that extent suffering the divine rejection, that the witness of the community to the election of Jesus Christ is addressed. It tells him that he is erring, rebelling, fleeing and hating, when everything points to the fact they he should not do so. It tells him also that he does it all in vain, because the choice which he thus makes is eternally denied and annulled in Jesus Christ, and because he for his part may deny and annul everything else by his own choice, but cannot possibly deny or annul the gracious choice of God. It is this very man, godless in his negative act, wantonly representing the rejected man, who is the predestinate. The decision about the nothingness of his negative act has been eternally made in Jesus Christ. It is precisely to him that God's choice has given that which was inaccessible to him and undeserved by him—and more, that which he has positively rejected—the grace of God. This grace is for him, the enemy of God, in spite of his enmity and in spite of his negative act, rejecting his representation of himself as rejected, forgiving his sins, as the justification of the godless. From eternity God knows every man to be this enemy. And—so runs the testimony of the community—in Jesus Christ God has known and loved and chosen and drawn eternally to Himself this very man, in his shameful and wretched isolation, implicated in the sinful fall of Adam and enslaved to Adam's nature. We have said, this very individual. We now say, more precisely, this godless man in his isolation, wantonly rushing into the arms of divine rejection, and therefore suffering it, the very one whose rejection is borne and annulled by Jesus Christ. It is clear that the idea of the " individual," in this decidedly negative sense of our context, involves the crisis and the limit of all " individualism." Let the " individual " take warning ! He has the power to be isolated and godless. According to the testimony of the community he is even destined to be this. He has gambled away and forfeited the dignity of his individuality, and his title to it, by staking it against God from whom he received it. As the " individual " of his own intention and judgment, he now belongs, indeed, to the mass, to the *massa perditionis*. This is the mass of men isolated over against God, who as such neither discharge their duties and obligations towards the groups, nor are able to maintain or vindicate their own properties within the groups. The godless man is ripe for every kind of authoritarianism and collectivism, as for every other dishonouring, perversion and destruction of his human existence. All that remains is for him to confess that this is the case, and to look for the restoration of his dignity and title solely in the fact that his isolation is void in Jesus Christ, that grace is vouchsafed to him, the rejected man, in the same Jesus Christ, according to the higher and original decision of God, and that in Him he may know himself as God's elect.

This, then, is the message with which the elect community (as the circumference of the elect man, Jesus of Nazareth) has to approach every man—the promise, that he, too, is an elect man. It is fully aware of his perverted choice. It is fully aware of his godlessness. It consists itself of godless men who were enabled to hear and believe this promise, and who still need to hear and believe it. It must and does reckon continually with the original godlessness of its members. It is fully aware, too, of the eternal condemnation of the man who is isolated over against God, which is unfailingly exhibited by the godlessness of every such man. It knows what his perverse choice must cost him. It knows of the threat under which he stands. It knows of the wrath and judgment and punishment of God in which the rejection of the man isolated over against God takes its course. And it also knows of the shadow into which every man does actually move because he desires and undertakes at all costs to be a man isolated, and therefore rejected, in relation to God ; because he behaves and conducts himself at all costs as though he were this rejected man. But it knows, above all, about Jesus Christ. It is the community founded by His death and resurrection. It belongs to Him as His property. Its existence is defined by witness to Him. It proclaims Him and nobody and nothing else. It knows men, therefore, only to the extent that it knows Jesus Christ. And so it knows the full extent of their godlessness, and the rejection that accompanies it. But it knows something greater than that. And it knows even that only in relation to this greater thing. It knows what has become of this threat, how and where it has been executed. It knows that God, by the decree He made in the beginning of all His works and ways, has taken upon Himself the rejection merited by the man isolated in relation to Him ; that on the basis of this decree of His the only truly rejected man is His own Son ; that God's rejection has taken its course and been fulfilled and reached its goal, with all that that involves, against this One, so that it can no longer fall on other men or be their concern. The concern of all other men is still the sin and guilt of their. godlessness—and it is serious and severe enough. Their concern is still the suffering of the existence which they have prepared for themselves by their godlessness (in the shadow of that which the One has suffered for them)—and it is bitter enough to have to suffer this existence. Their concern is still to be aware of the threat of their rejection. But it cannot now be their concern to suffer the execution of this threat, to suffer the eternal damnation which their godlessness deserves. Their desire and their undertaking are pointless in so far as their only end can be to make them rejected. And this is the very goal which the godless cannot reach, because it has already been taken away by the eternally decreed offering of the Son of God to suffer in place of the godless, and cannot any longer be their goal. This is the contradiction with which the community opposes the godless, who do not know all this. It testifies to them that the way in which they find themselves was aimless even before they entered upon it ; that their desire and undertaking were nullified before the world began. They may choose as they do. They may proceed as far as they are able. But the situation and reward of the rejected for which they stretch out their hands in their folly when they reject God, will assuredly not be secured by them. God does not deal with them as they deal with Him, and as therefore they might have " deserved." The revelation of this contradiction is the basis of the community itself. How can it meet any other man otherwise than with this contradiction ? But it knows more than this. It knows that God has removed the merited rejection of man, and has laid it upon His own Son, so that He might draw man to Himself and clothe him with His own glory. It knows that God is gracious to man, not only in a negative sense, not only by the removal of his rejection, but positively, in that He elects him. Indeed, the first and essential thing that He has decreed for him in His Son is his election to covenant with Him. He loves His enemies, the godless : not because they are godless ; not because they seek to be free of Him ; but because He will not let them break away ; because in consequence they cannot really break away from Him. What is laid up for man is eternal life in fellowship with God.

This is his situation according to the revelation of the crucified Jesus Christ in His resurrection from the dead. This is what the elect community knows about man. The community itself cannot elect him, and therefore make him one of the elect. The community cannot even make it clear to him that he is elected. Both these concerns belong to God alone. It is only by God's own choice, only by God's own revelation of this His own act, that the community itself came into existence and remains in existence. The elect are what they are through God's offering of Himself, and they know what they are through God's self-communication. The community can only testify to the act and revelation of the divine election of grace. But it cannot possibly withdraw from this testimony. It cannot possibly deliver the message of Jesus Christ without delivering to every man to whom it turns the promise of his election. It must certainly recall the threat of his rejection. But it will do so only for the sake of declaring and stressing the promise. The community has no control over the outcome of this. It cannot determine what man will make of it. But it has just as little competence to distinguish between those who are worthy of this promise and those who are not worthy, loudly proclaiming it in the one case and muffling it in the other. Those who hear and believe it live as God's elect. The community of God, however, can only proclaim it loudly so that it may be heard and believed. It must be loud indeed, and it must be brought to the ears of those who do not know it yet or any longer, or who do so only in part, in order that they may hear and believe it. To do this is the task of the community in relation to the world and its children. It must not let itself be frightened or shocked by their godlessness. It must not be restrained by any " experiences " from repeatedly bringing the promise of his election to every man, in and with the message of Jesus Christ. It has no right to reverse the relationship ordained in Jesus Christ between election and rejection, between promise and threat. Nor has it the right to fence the promise with reservations. It knows perfectly well the original godlessness of every man. But it knows supremely that according to the eternal decree of God Jesus Christ died and rose for him also. And because of this it must address him without reserve—with the summons to hearing and faith, and in anticipation of his hearing and believing and therefore his election. Were not its own hearing and faith anticipated when in the self-revelation of Jesus Christ it, too, was constituted the elect community by the same promise ? As God confronted the community itself in the man Jesus Christ, so is it to confront the *massa perditionis*, the lost children of this world—who yet are not lost, according to the promise. It is to say to each of them that he is the actual object of the divine election of grace.

It is men isolated in relation to God, the godless, who, hearing and believing the promise of their election in and with the message of Jesus Christ, live as the elect of God.

The fact that they *are* elect does not transcend only their hearing and faith, or the promise addressed to them as such, or the existence of the community which brings it to them. Transcending their own being, it also transcends the being of everything which God has created and which is distinct from Himself, with the exception of the one man, Jesus of Nazareth. They are elected by the will and decree of the triune God. They are therefore elected on the far side of their life, and hearing, and faith, and the community, and the promise delivered by it, in the origin and object of the promise, in the Word of God which willed to become and did actually become flesh, and only in Him. Election is the eternal basis, the eternal anterior reality, the eternal presupposition of the existence of those who may live as elect. It is identical with the fact that the elect Jesus Christ elected them also, and that this happened *to* and not *in* their human nature and its possibilities, *to* and not *in* their human history and its developments (as is correspondingly true, of course, also of their rejection).

Between the being of the elect and his life as such there lies the event and the decision of the reception of the promise. It is not for his being but for his life as elect that he needs to hear and believe the promise. Not every one who is elected lives as an elect man. Perhaps he does not yet do so. Perhaps he does so no longer. Perhaps he does so only partially. Perhaps he never does so. In so far as he does not do so yet or any longer, or does so only in part or never, he lives as one rejected in spite of his election. These are possibilities of the godless man as such. And it is the godless man with his negative act and in his distress who is the object of God's gracious choice. The fact that he possesses and realises all these possibilities, and that he lives (preliminarily, subsequently, partially or wholly) the life of a rejected man and under the threat of his actual rejection—this fact does indeed conflict with his election, but it cannot annul it, because it is not to be sought or found in him, but is grounded in Jesus Christ. His rejection may be attributed to him (in view of these possibilities) only as a threat hanging over him, just as his election can be ascribed to him only as the promise given to him. The being of man is on both sides in God's hand alone, as it is seen by God alone. The community recognises and attests the being of man—every man—in Jesus Christ. It recognises and attests, therefore, in regard to every man the threat of his rejection, the promise of his election : the threat which is rendered powerless by Jesus Christ ; the promise which is empowered by Jesus Christ. The community does not disguise the (impotent) threat of man's rejection, but it confronts him with the (powerful) promise of his election. It is only as it observes this order of grace and judgment, acquittal and arraignment, blessedness and perdition, that the community can testify to the crucified and risen Jesus Christ in conformity with its task. But a new possibility appears in the sphere of the godless man with the promise of his election ; the possibility of transition from his mistakenly chosen and intrinsically impossible life as a rejected man to his proper life, the life determined for him by God's prevenient choice, his life as an elect man. The content of the promise when it is rightly delivered in and with the message of Jesus Christ is as follows : In Jesus Christ thou, too, art not rejected—for He has borne thy rejection—but elected. A decision has been made, in Jesus Christ, concerning the futility of thy desire and attempt to live that life ; and it has been decided that thou canst live only this other life. This is the promise which the community has to deliver to the godless man, and which he may receive and hear and believe. To hear means to be aware that in Jesus Christ this decision has been made concerning him. To believe means to accept the situation which has been created by this decision. The godless man makes that transition as and to the extent that he hears and believes the promise. He turns his back on his life as a rejected man and turns to his proper life as an elect man. It is now disclosed that not only is his void life as a rejected man at variance with his election in Jesus Christ, but much more—and supremely and triumphantly—that his election in Jesus Christ is at variance with his void life as a rejected man. This is genuinely disclosed. Secretly and objectively, unwittingly and unwillingly, this conflict always has taken place and will take place and does take place ; for the divine pre-decision, by which he is elected and not rejected, never has been or is or will be ineffective. But now, when the man hears and believes the promise of his election, when it thus becomes a concrete content of his life, immediately and as long and as far as this has happened and is a fact, the conflict will be disclosed ; it will be real subjectively ; it will be desired and willed by the man himself ; it will be committed to his hands and in its manifestations visible to his eyes also—a matter for his own discernment, decision, attitude and act. He now lives— since, of course, and as long as and as far as he possesses and believes the promise—the life of the elect, in opposition to and in spite of his own godlessness and his own void life as a rejected man. As the individual human person that he is in distinction from the person of Jesus Christ, he now lives that which he is in Jesus Christ independently of his own will and conduct and apart from all his own or other desire. He now lives by the fact that in Jesus Christ his rejection, too, is rejected, and his election consummated. He now lives—the futile beneath him ; the significant and true above him ; his arrogant isolation of himself from God with all its consequences behind him as an eternal past ; his justification before God as an eternal future before him. If he hears and believes the promise of his election as it has taken place in Jesus Christ, then he can and will live this life and this life only. For in the election of Jesus Christ Himself, and also in the message of the community, this life and this life only is ascribed to him.

So much for our survey of the third and final area of the problem which occupies us in this chapter. We have described " the election of the individual " more precisely as the election in Jesus Christ of the godless man who is shown to be elect in the fact that as a hearing and believing recipient of the promise of his election he may live the life of the elect. But in this definition we must still point to a final intensification which it certainly needs, but which can be given only as we abandon not merely the language and style but also the intention and attitude of definitive investigation and exposition, and pass over directly to what is, in any case, indirectly unavoidable in dogmatics, the *genre* of preaching and pastoral admonition.

Necessarily we can speak of the " individual human person " as the object of divine election only with what is in the last resort a gentle but sentimental vagueness, so long as the reference is merely to a third person, and it is left open to the hearer or reader to suppose that someone else, and not he himself, is concerned. But the object of predestination in this final connexion is properly and exactly to be understood as " the individual," " the godless," " the one " who hears and believes the promise, " the one " who lives the life of the elect, only in so far as the one characterised in this way is the same and not a different person from the one who hears or reads the description. The hearer or reader can fully realise what we are talking about only when he observes that in this final connexion the whole definitive investigation and exposition of the object of predestination transcends all definition and is transformed into a direct summons to himself : Thou art the man ! Thou art the object of predestination in this its final connexion ! We are talking about thee, nay—we are actually talking *to* thee when we talk about the individual human person in relationship to the election of Jesus Christ and the community ! That which is said merely about and concerning this person suffers from obvious abstractness to the extent that this person is not a subject at all with a being of his own, so that it is possible to view and consider and discuss him in detachment. The being of the elected person is indeed in the being of Jesus Christ, " hid with Christ in God " (Col. 3³) ; and only as constituted through the promise delivered by the community in and with the message of Jesus Christ is it also the being of this other person. But this promise that establishes the elect person is not a theory about an object, but an address to a subject. Certainly it is " teaching," but in the old, authentic sense of " *doctrina* " : instruction, schooling, which claims the hearing and belief of this subject. And in the listening (or not listening), the belief (or unbelief), the gratitude (or ingratitude) of this subject, the decision must and will be taken in what sense the truth is spoken to him through it. In any event it tells him the truth as it assures him (on the basis of the election of Jesus Christ, and as the task of the chosen community of God) that he, too, is one of God's elect. He may refuse to listen or believe—in which case it will merely confirm that in spite of his election he lives the life of one rejected by God and is threatened by his actual rejection. On the other hand, he may listen and believe—in which case it will show him that he now lives the life of an elect man, corresponding to his election. But this is something which is not decided in the word of promise. It is decided in the adoption of the attitude which this subject adopts to the address made to him, and in which he shows whether he is instructed or uninstructed by the promise, that is, whether he is converted or unconverted. All that the promise has to say about man—that he is this individual, that like all individuals he is involved in isolation in relation to God and is therefore godless, that the threat of his actual rejection hangs over him, that this very threat of tribulation and distress is in itself enough to enable him to hear and believe that in Jesus Christ he, too, is elected and not rejected, and that in hearing and believing this he may live the life of an elect man—all this is very different from any mere " statement," and has its specific weight and true meaning in the fact that it is a summons (originating in Jesus Christ, the eternal Word of God, and as the message of the elect community) which has as its aim the decision which each one of those summoned makes himself—or rather, himself is. The promise says to those who hear or read it : Thou mayest not hear or read at this point something said about another. Thou art not in the audience, but in the centre of the stage. This is meant for thee. Thou art " this " individual. Thou art isolated from God, and therefore a godless man. Thou art threatened. And yet thou standest indeed under a wholly new determination. It was for thee that Jesus Christ Himself bore the divine rejection in its real and terrible consequences. Thou art the one who has been spared from enduring it. And it is for thee that Jesus Christ is the elect man of God and arrayed in the divine glory. Eternal life and fellowship with God await thee. Jesus Christ died and rose for thee. It is thou who art elect with Him and through Him. And now that all this has been said to thee, it is the event of what thou for thy part shalt say and do (or not say, and not do) which decides whether the ancient curse will again be laid on thee with what is said, or the eternal blessing will come on thee in utter newness. In and with that which thou dost now say or do (or not say and not do), thou must and shalt give answer to that which has been said to thee, and either way (persisting in thy ungodliness or turning thy back upon it, for thy salvation or thy destruction) confirm its truth.

The community does not perform its task properly if it does not perform it in this manner—speaking implicitly or explicitly in the second person. And its task—the bringing of the promise to an individual man in and with the message of Jesus Christ—is not understood if it is not understood in this way ; if thou dost not understand it as the promise which concerns thyself and in one way or another demonstrates truth to thyself. Where this is not the case, the election of the "individual" or the "ungodly," and the election of Jesus Christ Himself, is most certainly not understood. Dogmatics as such —which of itself is neither preaching nor pastoral admonition—can only indicate this final intensification of the doctrine of God's election of grace. But this indication is absolutely necessary. When we speak in the third person about the "elect" (or about the "rejected"), it is always the second person who is the final meaning and elucidation of what is said.

Hominum praedestinatio est, qua Deus ex humano genere ad imaginem suam creato, sed sua sponte in peccatum prolapsuro alios quidem per Christum aeternum servare, alios vero sibi in miseria sua aeternum damnare constituit, ad patefaciendum gloriam misericordiae et iustitiae suae (Wolleb, *Theol. chr. comp.*, 1626, 1 *cap.* 4, § 2, 3).

This definition must surely make it clear how very far we now stand from the " classical " doctrine of predestination at this point which interests it most. We have departed from it at the very outset by placing the divine *constituere* in a relationship of equality to the *servatio per Christum* instead of one of foreordination or superordination. We have interpreted the concept of the divine decree—according to the rule that God is no other than the One who reveals Himself—by the main articles of Christology : the unity and difference of the divine and human nature, the humiliation and the exaltation, the prophetic, highpriestly and kingly office of Jesus Christ. We have understood Jesus Christ as the one Elector and Elect (in whom the many are elect), and again as the one Rejector and Rejected (in whom the many are not rejected). And we have understood predestination as the election of the community to be the witness of this determination and non-determination of the many decided in the election of Jesus Christ. These are the essentially different presuppositions with which we have approached the specific problem which has always been *the* problem for classical doctrine : the problem of the election of the many (the individual, the ungodly, " thy " election). The concept of a divine decree independent of the election of Jesus Christ carries with it at once the idea of a community whose task, as it would appear from these definitions, is to proclaim to the many another absolute will of God apart from that fulfilled *in Christo* and *per Christum*. If the divine decree is identical with the election of Jesus Christ, then the task of the chosen community in respect of the many is exclusively that of proclaiming the Gospel in which each one is promised his election in Jesus Christ. But with the concept of a divine decree independent of the election of Jesus Christ, there arises also the possibility that the many (the individual, the ungodly, each one) may regard themselves as neutral, i.e., that the election of Jesus Christ may possibly mean something for them, but it may equally well mean nothing. The consequence is that the statement of predestination divides into two sections (*alios . . . alios . . .*). The first deals with the " elect " (for whom Jesus Christ was elected and died and rose again). The second deals with the " rejected " (for whom in actual fact He means nothing). If Jesus Christ is the beginning of all the ways and works of God, the many cannot be neutral in relation to Him, and it is not possible that there should be a different summons to each group, nor can there be any such division into these two groups. This is also ruled out by the concept of the elect community and its witness. If its witness is solely the Gospel, this cannot be an exclusive Gospel, to be withheld from this or that one, and having a serious reference and application only to this or that other one. The community is not entitled to prejudice against one or preference for another if it knows and considers that the *gloria misericordiae et iustitiae Dei* is no more anonymous than the *aeternum beneplacitum Dei*, but is called Jesus Christ. As witness to Him (and therefore to God's eternal decree), it is necessarily concentrated into one statement with which the community must equally necessarily address itself to each and every one. The substance of this statement is that (in accordance with the election of Jesus Christ) the free grace of election is the mighty divine determination of man, but that (in accordance with the rejection of Jesus Christ) the merited rejection of all is the equally mighty non-determination of man : the kingdom of heaven opened and hell closed ; God vindicated and Satan overcome ; life triumphant and death destroyed ; belief in the promise the only possibility and disbelief in it the excluded possibility. Because predestination is the election of Jesus Christ, it can be proclaimed in its relation to the many only in this one statement, only in the disequilibrium of the antitheses which it certainly contains. It must therefore be proclaimed to each and every one as this wholly disproportionately formulated and accentuated statement. It is only as this one statement, only in this ordering of its inner antitheses, only as a statement which concerns everybody, that it can and will be seriously believed—or, again, that it will and can be seriously disbelieved. It is only in this way that it can truly encounter thee and me. Certainly when it is made and received, it can and will actually divide between hearers and non-hearers, believers and unbelievers, grateful and ungrateful. But it cannot foresee this division. It cannot endow it with programmatic necessity. It cannot elevate it to the level of a principle, or make it eternal, as did the classical doctrine with its opposing categories of " elect " and " reprobate." On the contrary, it must continually protest against it, and deny it in view of Jesus Christ. It will continually call the divided together by proclaiming to believers their merited rejection and to unbelievers their unmerited election, and to both the One in whom they are elect and not rejected. It necessarily cancels itself out if in any circumstances, even among the " many " in hell, it ceases to be the statement of the divine election of *grace*.

While making it clear that in this exposition of the " election " of the individual we diverge from representatives of the classical doctrine, we must not fail to notice certain points in their thinking in which they reached positions that point beyond their own context and towards the understanding of the dogma which we are about to attempt in relation to this third and final question.

1. Even in the presentation of this other conception of predestination we are told continually that the election of the elect is realised in their faith, and, indeed, in their faith in Jesus Christ. *Ut credamus, elegit nos* (Augustine, *De praed.* 19, 38). *Elegit eos, quos voluit, gratuita misericordia . . . ut fideles essent eisque gratiam dedit . . . ut fierent fideles* (Peter Lombard, *Sent.* 1, dist. 41 D). *Unde probamus, gratuito electos esse ex hominibus aliquos, nisi quia Spiritu suo Deus quos vult illuminat, ut fide inserantur in Christi corpus ? . . . Prior quidem fide est electio, sed ex fide discitur* (Calvin, *De aet. Dei praed.*, 1552, *C.R.* 8, 318). *Fides electionem consequitur. . . . Electio est causa efficiens fidei. . . . Fides est medium exsequendo proposito electionis destinatum* (Polanus, *Synt. Theol. chr.*, 1609, *col.* 1580). All these statements are polemically opposed to opinions which would make faith in some form the cause, or—as with Melanchthon (*Loci*, 1559, *C.R.* 21, 912 f.)—a co-efficient cause of election. But they express the positive statement that the elect are those who (in the temporal realisation of their election produced by their calling) believe. The meaning of election is visible in the act and event of faith. *Est igitur specialis quaedam vocatio, quae aeternam Dei electionem sic obsignat et sancit, ut patefaciat quod prius fuit in Deo absconditum* (Calvin, *De aet. Dei praed. C.R.* 8, 272).

Faith, however, although it is actual and visible as a distinctive attitude in acts of recognition and love, obedience and trust, is essentially faith in God (*in Deum . . .*), a determination of the believing man by the God who deals with him according to His eternal will, and the orientation of man to Him. Without this foundation and object it would be futile even in its finest actual and visible form. It rests on Jesus Christ as the promise of divine compassion towards the ungodly, and it does so as a work and gift of the Holy Spirit. Faith is the opening of man for God as brought about by God Himself. In faith man is the new subject which can no longer compete with God but can live only by Him and with Him and in conformity with Him—torn away from godlessness by His grace and set in this different status, the status of the knowledge of God, of love for Him, of obedience and of trust. It is correct, therefore, that the election of the elect is concretely actual and visible in his faith. But if the essence of faith (without which he would be nothing even in his best actual and visible form) consists in the fact that man is awakened by the grace of God and born a new subject, it is not on that account possible to oppose absolutely to him the one who, unlike himself, does not actualise and reveal the attitude and form of faith, understanding the latter as reprobate in contrast to the former who is elect. If the former as elect is this new subject, he can as such (this is possible only in Jesus Christ) find himself in some sense high above both himself in his own best attitude and others in their worst. From this standpoint the contrast to them is only a relative contrast which is not identical with that of elected and rejected. For it is the grace of God which has awakened and empowered him for the attitude of faith. And how can the grace of God mean that he is absolutely preferred and others are absolutely passed over ? He believes in the One in whom the others do not believe, but in whom they, too, are objectively called to believe (by the same promise in which alone he can maintain his own faith), in whom not to believe is objectively just as absurd and untenable for them as it showed itself to be untenable and absurd for him when he came to faith. In faith he realises the possibility which objectively is the only one for them too. The believer cannot possibly recognise in the unbelief of others a final fact. How can he even establish it with any certainty as their unbelief ? To be sure, he cannot deny the possibility of it ; for he knows it as a possibility of his own which is now behind him. And he cannot possibly overcome it ; for he knows that faith is awakened, and unbelief overcome, only by the basis and object of faith. But the believer cannot possibly confront the unbeliever with the suspicion that the latter is perhaps rejected. For he knows who has borne the merited and inevitable rejection of the godless, his own above all. How can he possibly regard others as perhaps rejected merely because he thinks he knows their unbelief and therefore their godlessness ? If he does, what becomes of his own faith ? What of his own election ? We cannot—essentially—believe against unbelievers but only for them ; in their place, and as we address to them the promise which is to them also. Even Calvin could occasionally (e.g., *Comm. on* 1 *Cor.* 1⁹, *C.R.* 49, 312) speak of a *iudicium caritatis* according to which, if there is an external *sana vocatio* of others, we can also reckon with a *vocatio ad salutem*, and therefore their election. He could even say of those who had been excommunicated by the Church : *non nostrum est, tales . . . expungere ex electorum numero, aut desperare quasi iam perditos.* Even in the worst cases we are to commend them to God, *meliora de iis in posterum sperantes quam videmus in praesens : nec propterea desinamus pro iis Deum precari* (*Instit.* IV, 12, 9). In the *Articles of Dort* (III–IV, 15) we read : *De iis, qui externe fidem profitentur et vitam emendant, optime secundum exemplum apostolorum iudicandum et loquendum est ; penetralia enim cordium nobis sunt incomperta. Pro aliis autem, qui nondum sunt vocati, orandus est Deus, qui quae non sunt, vocat tanquam sint. Neutiquam vero adversus eos est superbiendum, ac si nosmetipsos discrevissemus.* More generally, it is said in Bullinger's *Conf. Helv. post.* 18 : *Bene sperandum est de omnibus,* and in the *Confessio Sigismundi* (1614, K. Mueller, p. 841, 49) " that we are not to doubt the blessedness of any so long as the means of grace are used, for no man knows when God will effectually call his own, who will or will not in future believe, since God is not bound by time, and everything is ordained according to His good-pleasure." When statements like this are made, not with illogical sentimentality but from material necessity, there is no doubt that even more fundamental and important things of the same kind are to be predicated of the nature of the faith which proceeds from election. If there is a *iudicium caritatis* on the one hand, why should there not be a *iudicium spei* on the other ?

2. A further basic element in the classical doctrine of predestination is the proposition that the elect alone are, by the grace of God, delivered from the human impotence and depravity to which they were originally subject, and which are the misery of the rejected. *Quod in tanta naturae nostrae corruptela et pravitate aliqui tamen evangelio credunt, eorum bonitati adscribere sacrilegium est, sed potius gratiae semper Deo agendae* (Calvin, *De aet. Dei praed. C.R.* 8, 300). For : *Sola gratia redemptos discernit a perditis, quos in unam perditionis concreverat massam ab origine ducta causa communis* (Augustine, *Enchir.* 99) . . . *non eos iam meritis (quandoquidem universa massa tanquam in vitiata radice damnata est) sed gratia discernens* (*De civ. Dei* XIV, 26). It is also said of the elect, with reference to their status before their call : *Extranei censentur. . . . Quum in Dei corde abscondita esset gentium vocatio, quid aliud in illis quam damnata immundities apparuit ?* (Calvin, *De aet. Dei praed. C.R.* 8, 337). *In ipsos si respicias, videbis Adae progeniem, quae communem massae corruptionem redoleat. Quod non in extremam et desperatam usque impietatem feruntur, id non fit aliqua illis ingenita bonitate, sed quia in ipsorum salutem excubat Dei oculus, et manus extenta est.* There is in them no inborn *semen electionis* disposing them for their calling—this was directed against M. Bucer (Calvin, *Instit.* III, 24, 10). No, they were *nec meliores, nec digniores, sed in communi miseria cum aliis iacentes* (*Articles of Dort* I, 7). The authentic object of election is the *homo miser inter multos miseros, quemque absque gratia ad vitam pervenire impossibile est* (Coccejus, *S. Theol.,* 1662, *cap.* 39, 7). In short, apart from the grace of their election, although the elect are not actually rejected, they are among the rejected as if rejected, continually participating in their sin and guilt, and standing with them under the threat of the rejection which they also merit. Only in their call is it revealed to them that from eternity they have been elected and not rejected. *Qui ad Christum accedunt, iam filii Dei erant in eius corde, quum in se hostes essent, et quia praeordinati essent in vitam, Christo dati sunt* (Calvin, *De aet. Dei praed. C.R.* 8, 292). Accordingly—and as Calvin himself emphasised strongly (cf. *Instit.* III, 14, 9 f., 19 ; 19, 14 ; *Comm. on Ez.* 11[20], *C.R.* 40, 249, etc.)—even in their new state they cannot possibly forget the very real and continuing memory of that state of utter ungodliness and merited rejection which even in faith continues in the weakness and perversity of their life and conduct. There is certainly nothing to prevent them from sinking back into that state, apart always from the grace that calls and elects them. *Neque enim electos fingimus continua Spiritus directione semper tenere rectum cursum : quin saepe labi, errare, impingere et fere alienari a salutis via dicimus* (Calvin, *De aet. Dei praed. C.R.* 8, 340). *Enormibus peccatis Deum valde offendunt, reatum mortis incurrunt, Spiritum sanctum contristant, fidei exercitium interrumpunt, conscientiam gravissime vulnerant, sensum gratiae nonnunquam ad tempus amittunt* (*Articles of Dort* V, 5).

But if this is so, what can break the mutual solidarity between the elect and others ? Can the fact that the eye and the hand of God watched over their salvation before they were called ? But is not this just as needful for them afterwards as before ? And how can we know that the same is not true of others too ? Again, can the fact that before their call they were preserved from " extreme and desperate " ungodliness ? But if this does not involve an absolute distinction from others, how can we know that the relative sense which it bears does not apply to others as well as to themselves ? Again, can the new thing which has become visible to them in and since their calling ? But this new thing is itself so burdened by the real memory of the old that it scarcely suffices as an absolute distinction from others. No—all predestinationists affirm—finally and essentially and uniquely only the grace which is always free grace distinguishes the elect from the rejected. But the question is whether grace (the grace that elects and calls, that is eternal and that manifests itself in time) does make this distinction between the elect and the rejected, and not the very different distinction between the godless and the believing. Do we not really have both a continuing distinction and a continuing connexion, since believers have every reason to know that apart from the grace of God they not only were but are and always will be ungodly, and as such threatened by the divine rejection, and the ungodly can be regarded only as those who, standing under the same threat, do not, or do not any longer, hear or believe the promise of their election, and are therefore to be summoned to do so ? We should have thought that in the realm of the older predestinarian teaching everything was making for this conclusion and not for that which was actually reached. Why did not the tremendous seriousness with which it regarded the plight of man lead it to a recognition how bitter is the rejection (only palely reflected in the plight of man) that Jesus Christ took upon Himself in order that suffering man might not be rejected and perish— to a recognition how high and deep is the grace in which God has addressed Himself to the godless, how impossible is their ungodliness, how imperatively necessary and how precious, but also how responsible is the faith of those who may recognise and receive this grace, who rejoice in it and treasure it ? Why is it that in the very desire to glorify this grace they were so intent on opening up the gulf of this absolute contrast between the " elect " and the " rejected " ungodly ? The only reason we can see is that they were not seriously prepared with childlike consistency to understand the grace of God as " the grace of our Lord Jesus Christ." It is for this reason that we are compelled at this point to arrive at a different conclusion.

3. The proposition which has become most important for the ecclesiastical and practical form and outworking of the doctrine is that the election of the elected man and the grace bound up with it are preserved to him under all circumstances, even the most contradictory. This is the assertion of the *perseverantia* (the perseverance, constancy, divine preservation) *sanctorum*. Weighty scriptural passages such as Lk. 22[32], Jn. 10[28f.], Rom. 8[28-39], 1 Cor. 1[8], Phil. 1[6], 1 Jn. 3[9, 24], 5[18], and the ideas of divine μακροθυμία and πίστις and Christian ὑπομονή all point undeniably in this direction. To be sure, in the work of Augustine whose title proclaims this thesis—*De dono perseverantiae*—we find it propounded only to the extent that in the course of a general recapitulation of the anti-pelagian position (as one of a series which includes chastity, obedience, etc.), the special virtue of faithfulness unto death is described as a pure gift of God, and therefore as a concern of divine predestination. But the definition of predestination given in this work is that it is the *praescientia sc. et praeparatio beneficiorum Dei, quibus certissime liberantur, quicumque liberantur* (14, 35). This shows how important was the thesis for Augustine. But the decisive passage in Augustine is to be found in the rather older work, *De corruptione et gratia* : *Quicumque in Dei providentissima dispositione praesciti, praedestinati, vocati, iustificati, glorificati sunt, non dico etiam nondum renati, sed etiam nondum nati, iam filii Dei sunt, et omnino perire non passunt* (9, 23). According to Augustine, no one may presume to include himself in this number (13, 40, cf. *De dono persev.* 1, 1). But it is indisputably true of those who do actually belong to it : *Horum fides, quae per dilectionem operatur, profecto aut omnino non deficit, aut si qui sunt, quorum deficit, reparatur antequam vita ista finiatur et deleta quae intercurreret iniquitate usque in finem perseverantia deputatur* (7, 16). *Horum si*

quisquam perit, fallitur Deus : sed nemo eorum perit, quia non fallitur Deus. Horum si quisquam perit, vitio humano vincitur Deus : sed nemo eorum perit, quia nulla re vincitur Deus (7, 14). It was in line with the definition of Augustine that Thomas Aquinas wrote : *Praedestinatio certissime et infallibiter consequitur suum effectum* (*S. th.* 1, *qu.* 23, *art.* 6c). *Illi qui sunt ordinati ad habendum vitam aeternam ex praedestinatione divina sunt simpliciter scripti in libro vitae. . . . Et isti nunquam delentur de libro vitae* (*ib.*, *qu.* 24, *art.* 3c). One who is predestinated cannot actually die in mortal sin and therefore be eternally lost (*ib.*, *qu.* 23, *art.* 6, *ad* 2).

A new factor in Calvin, who particularly emphasised this fact, was the practical accentuation with which he maintained it—less in relation to the death than to the life of the elect. I quote only two of many references : *Inter tam violentos insultus, tam varia descrimina, tantas procellas et agitationes, in eo tamen consistit status nostri perpetuitas, quod Deus, quod de salute nostra apud se decrevit, brachii sui virtute constanter tuebitur. Si quisque nostrum se aspiciat, quid potest aliud quam trepidare ? Nam circa nos omnia nutant et nihil nobis imbecillius. Sed quia coelestis pater, quos filio donavit, perire non sinet, quantum habet hic potentiae, tam certa est nobis fiducia et gloriatio : quia ideo fortis est, ut constans et invictus appareat suae donationis assertor* (*De aet. Dei praed. C.R.* 8, 275). *Omnibus electis certa est vita aeterna, excidere nemo potest, nulla violentia, nullove impetu quisquam rapitur ; invicta Dei potentia nititur eorum salus. . . . Video me assidue fluctuari, nullum momentum praeteriet, quo non obruendus videar. At, quia electos suos Deus sustinet, ne unquam mergeantur, staturum me inter innumeras procellas certo confido* (*ib.*, 321). The Lutherans also confessed with Calvin : *Meam salutem adeo firmis praesidiis munire voluit, ut eam in aeternum suum propositum (quod falli aut everti nunquam potest) tanquam in arcem munitissimam collocaret atque adeo in omnipotenti manu Domini nostri Jesu Christi (unde nemo rapere nos potest) conservandam poneret* (*Form. Conc., Sol. decl.* XI, 45). And, again, a more doubtful formulation in the 17th century : *Electio Dei constans est et immutabilis, facta secundum immotum Dei propositum ac praevisionem fidei ad vitae finem perseveraturae, adeo ut aeternam salutem electi electione sua excidere ac perire nequeant* (Quenstedt, *Theol. did. pol.*, 1685, III, *cap.* 2 *sect.* 2, *qu.* 8 *th*). Also new in Calvin was the comprehensively asserted presupposition that the elect can be assured by faith of their election, and also of the constancy of the divine grace vouchsafed to them—we shall return to this under 4 below. New again in Calvin was the explicit affirmation of the indestructibility of the faith of the elect once it has been awakened on the basis of their call. *Tenendum est, quantumvis exigua sit et debilis in electis fides, quia tamen Spiritus Dei certa illis arrha est ac sigillum suae adoptionis, nunquam ex eorum cordibus deleri posse eius sculpturam* (*Instit.* III, 2, 12). It is not, of course, that they do not have to wrestle with doubt and anxiety and even unbelief— *et tamen, quod mirabile est, inter istas concussiones piorum corda fides sustentat . . . sicuti David, quum obrutus videri posset, se tamen increpando, ad Deum surgere non destitit. Qui vero cum propria infirmitate certans ad fidem in suis anxietatibus contendit, iam magna ex parte victor est* (*ib.*, 2, 17). This affirmation brought down on Calvin and the Calvinists (cf. Quenstedt, *ib.*, *qu.* 7) the opposition of the Lutherans, who, although they confidently expected for the elect a *status fidelitatis in ultimo vitae puncto seu momento*, that is, at the point of death, and therefore disputed the possibility of a final loss of grace, they could still reckon with a total, if transitory, loss of faith and grace even on the part of the elect. As triply expanded by Calvin, the doctrine of the *perseverentia sanctorum* became a main tenet in several Reformed confessions (*Consensus Bremensis*, 1595, *cap* IX, *Articles of Dort.*, 1619, V, *Westminster Confession*, 1647, *cap.* 17), and in the *Heidelberg Catechism* (*Qu.* 1, 52 and 54) and the *Irish Articles of Religion,* 1615 (*Art.* 38) there are at any rate unequivocal references to it.

To understand the doctrine it is as well to grasp the most developed form in which it was proclaimed at the Synod of Dort, with the criticisms which were then levelled against it. The Remonstrants (in their *Articles* of 1610, and definitively in their explanation to the Synod) expressed themselves on the point as follows. God makes believers so strong by His grace, when He stretches out His hand to them in Christ, that they need not be concerned whether they should fall again. If this happens, as it does, they may perish eternally, but they may also, of course, be recalled to penitence. It is " prejudicial to piety and good morals " to teach that believers can sin only through ignorance and weakness, that they cannot forfeit God's grace by any sin, that their sins are already forgiven. This is simply to " open the windows to a carnal certainty." By all means let us be sure of our faith and good conscience now. But for the future the only assurance is that we should persevere in faith through watching and prayer and pious exercises, and that the grace of God will never leave those who do these things. But how we can know, or how far we need to know, whether we will persevere in faith, as required, with piety and works of love, it is difficult to see. The Synod replied (in the *Reiecto errorum* V) with the following counter-criticism. The constancy in question is in no sense a concern of the free will. It is given to the elect on the basis of their election through the power of Christ's death, resurrection and eternal mediation. God does not help us, therefore, only that we may then be left to continue by helping ourselves. Genuine believers as such are unable to fall into mortal sin, to sin against the Holy Ghost, to perish *totaliter et finaliter*. The assurance and constancy of the grace applied to them results from the constancy of the divine promises. It is not true that this assurance is a soporific for the flesh. A faith easily consoled by it is not justifying and sanctifying faith. There is no repetition of regeneration, nor does there need to be, and it was not for nothing that Christ prayed that Peter's faith " should not fail." The positive statement of the Synod (*Art*. V) runs as follows. It is true that the elect also, even after their call to faith, and even the best of them, live in the flesh, in " the body of sin," and have reason to humble themselves before God until death, to seek refuge in the cross of Christ and to put the flesh to death through the Holy Spirit and His works. But in their own strength they are unable to do this properly, and therefore to remain in grace. But God is faithful ; He Himself upholds them in His grace. This does not mean that they have no need to watch and pray that they should not fall into temptation, that what happened to David and Peter should not happen to them. Nor does it mean that they may not actually trespass most grievously and dangerously against God and against their own conscience, and in so doing lose all perception (*sensus*) of grace. It does mean, however, that God does not remove His Holy Spirit from His own, or allow them to fall into eternal destruction. The eternal seed, of which they were reborn, remains in them. It remains true for them that God does not cease so to renew them by His Word and Spirit that they are penitent, seek and find forgiveness, experience grace again, adore His compassion and all the more zealously seek their salvation with fear and trembling. Thus (not because of their merits and abilities, but because of the grace of God) they are not in a position *finaliter* nor *totaliter* to remain among the fallen and perish. *Quoad ipsos* this would be quite possible, but not *respectu Dei*, whose purpose and promise can neither yield nor deceive. And, each according to the proportion of faith, they may know all this from God's Word, not always fully, not with a carnal certainty, but in childlike reverence, in prayer, bearing their cross, steadfast in confession, observant of the ways of God, fearing the abuse of His goodness and rightly using preaching and the sacraments—and therefore rejoicing in God, who has begun and will also complete His work in them. " This is," the statement concludes, and it is in keeping that these are the final words of the whole *Confession*, " the doctrine of the perseverance of true believers and saints, and their assurance, which God has fully revealed in His Word and impressed upon the hearts of believers, to the glory of His name and for the comfort of pious souls. The flesh does not conceive it ; Satan hates it ; the world mocks it ; the inexperienced and the hypocrite abuse it ; erring spirits assail it. But the bride of Christ loves it most tenderly as a treasure of infinite worth, and resolutely defends it. That she shall continue to do so God Himself will provide, against whom no purpose may prevail, or power rebel. Unto Him, the only God, Father, Son and Holy Ghost, be honour and glory eternally. Amen."

Now obviously we can only affirm and adopt this interpretation of the matter. It is palpable that what the Remonstrants brought against it was unspiritual, impotent and negligible—a feeble postlude to the Catholicism of the late Middle Ages, and a feeble prelude to rationalist-pietistic Neo-Protestantism. Since God—" the Father of mercies, and the God of all comfort " (2 Cor. 1³)—cannot deceive Himself, cannot be conjured, and cannot be unfaithful either to Himself or to us, it is of the essence of election that there can be no fundamental, eternal reversal. The Yes of God to His elect cannot be transformed into an absolute No. Because, then, they have the absolute divine Yes in their ears and in their hearts, they both may and should be assured in faith of their election, and therefore of eternal salvation—not in harmony with their evil human No to God, but in spite of it, and in this way in genuine and successful conflict with it. Even the objection of the Lutherans is valueless, and hardly worthy of Luther himself. If the faith of the elect lives with Jesus Christ as its basis and with Jesus Christ as its goal, it is impossible to see how it can be absolutely lost. A faith that can be lost is as little comfort *in ultimo vitae puncto* as it is relevant in the rest of life. Does not faith, both in life and death, consist in the fact that— *non quoad nos* but *respectu Dei*, trusting in His Word, His decision behind and before us, and armed on this account for the good warfare of faith—we know continually, and not merely occasionally, that our case is sure. Can we more effectively cheapen faith than by denying its constancy ? We cannot be sufficiently grateful to Calvin for presenting the statement of *perseverentia* in this manner, and advancing beyond both Augustine and Thomas Aquinas.

And yet we can hardly be surprised that this statement did not win the general approval which in itself it deserved, nor that even in the Reformed theology and Church it quickly became an incomprehensible and even doubtful requirement of old-fashioned orthodoxy. Think of the agonising anxiety about the salvation of his soul which, a hundred years after Dort, was a lifelong burden to a man like S. Werenfels, even to the point at times of incapacitating him for his work. When the tenet is referred abstractly to this man (the " elect ") as contrasted to that man (the " rejected ")—as was unfortunately the case in the context of the Calvinistic system—is it not necessarily far too logical, arbitrary and dangerous, in spite of all the safeguards and precautions made at Dort, and previously by Calvin himself ? Who can really support, without giving way to arrogance, frivolity or despair, the exacting demands involved in being a Christian who knows his election as described in the 5th Article of Dort ? And who can face, without a hardheartedness that is scarcely imaginable, the thought of others who by reason of their rejection are necessarily excluded from this Christian status—the only status in which a normal life is possible ? Clearly we cannot trifle with the thought that God perseveres *totaliter et finaliter* or that man (in spite of sin, death and the devil) perseveres *totaliter et finaliter*—for of all true thoughts this is the truest. But it is a thought which has to be thought through to a finish if it is not to seem—quite apart from any consideration of " piety " or " good morals "—sheer blasphemy or at least a wholly sterile piece of theologising. The fathers of the Reformation did not think it through like this. And the reason for this may be sought in the fact that although they knew how to make it genuinely fruitful in their own day, it could not continue fruitful beyond their day. It is indeed remarkable how, in the elucidation of this supreme statement of predestination, the argument hardly ever turns on the *decretum absolutum*, but almost exclusively on the basis of the knowledge of predestination, and therefore on the reference to Jesus Christ, the Word of God and His promises, and so forth. It is for this reason that, considered in isolation, the 5th Article of Dort is almost unassailable, and within its limits a quite outstanding evangelical witness. But the further step was not taken—the obvious step which would have saved the day—of recognising that the basis for the knowledge of predestination is also the basis of predestination itself; that this electing God who perseveres *totaliter et finaliter* in His gracious will is again Jesus Christ. They did not state the major premise which cuts at the root of all presumption, nor did they assume it—the premise that His election is ours, and that the grace of our election and our faith in it have stability in time and eternity because He Himself is both Elector and Elect. What they assumed to be the major premise was simply the *decretum absolutum*, in which we do not have a decision about election and rejection according to the grace of God, but the distinction between " elected " and " rejected " according to an inscrutable principle. It is clear that the former premise destroys any possibility of an absolute ascription of the *donum perseverentiae* to some, and an equally absolute denial of it to others. It destroys the apparently heroic but actually decadent and profoundly incredible picture of a people of God inflexibly but also irresponsibly and unconcernedly hastening on to heaven in the midst of the lost children of this world. It is also clear that it involves the necessity of presenting as a promise to those who had not yet recognised it the whole seriousness and power of the faithfulness of God and the constancy of faith in which those who have recognised their election in the election of Jesus Christ may rejoice. The promise which also concerns them ! Is it only for those who have recognised their election, and not also for those who have not yet recognised it, that the lordship of Satan was broken by the divine-human perseverance which took place in Jesus Christ as decreed at the beginning of all God's ways and works ? Was this to be effectual for some, and not for others ? Did Jesus Christ bear the shame of rejected man and put on the glory of the elect man only for some, and not for others ? Is He the kingdom of God in person, the αὐτοβασιλεία, only for some and not for others ? Who may dare to speak in this way about election when election is absolutely the election of Jesus Christ, with no *decretum absolutum* either before or after ? And can those who see in Him the real basis of their election see any others otherwise than as those who do not yet or any longer believe, and who therefore do not yet or any longer find comfort in the divine-human perseverance which took place for them too, who may not yet or any longer live under its ordering, but to whom believers are absolutely responsible for transmitting all this in order that the invitation to faith may truly and effectually come to them too ? The Reformation fathers were quite unable to draw conclusions of this kind from their major premise. It really was a *thesaurus inaestimabilis pretii* that the *sponsa Christi* received in the doctrine of the *perseverentia sanctorum*. No word of praise can be too high for it. The full Gospel can shine out only with this doctrine. But compressed by the paltry view that from the very outset it means everything for some and nothing at all for others, it could shine only dimly, and soon not at all. *This* " from the very outset " has nothing whatever to do with the divine election of grace.

4. We have now to recall again the answer given by the older theology to the question how far individuals may have knowledge and assurance of their own salvation (cf. for the following : W. Niesel, " Syllogismus practicus ? " in *Aus Theologie und Geschichte, Festgabe für E. F. K. Mueller*, 1933, p. 158 f. ; Heinz Otten, *Calvins theol. Anschauung von der Praedestination*, 1938, p. 54 f.).

In this matter the Reformation faced the following objection of the Council of Trent (*Sess.* VI, 1547, *Decr. de iustificatione, cap.* 12–13, *can.* 15–17, *Denz.* No. 805 f., 825 f.). No man can know with absolute and infallible certainty—except on the basis of special revelation—who is elect and will thus persevere to the end. Therefore it cannot under any circumstances be described as a necessity of faith to know one's own election. Calvin replied to this (*Acta Syn. Trid.*, 1547, *C.R.* 7, 463 f.) as follows. When Paul spoke so expressly in Eph. 1 and Rom. 8, can he really have meant otherwise than that his readers both could and should know of their election ? What more *revelatio specialis* is needed than that which all true children of God receive according to 1 Cor. 2[10, 12, 16] ? Augustine and Thomas Aquinas themselves had obviously intended. that the election of each individual should be taught and preached and believed—although in principle the question of the election of individuals generally was to be left open.

The Reformation doctrine gave only one reason in explanation of its positive answer to this question, but this was stated with an important differentiation. As we have already seen, according to Calvin Christ was the *speculum electionis. Unde me electum esse cognoscam ? Si Pighius rogat—Christus mihi pro mille testimoniis sufficit ; nam ubi nos in corpore eius reperimus, in secura tranquillaque statione salus nostra, tanquam locata iam in coelis, quiescit* (*De aet. Dei praed. C.R.* 8, 321). The *tuta et pacata, addo et iucunda navigatio* over the *exitialis abyssus* of the eternal divine counsel, the place where we live (with Bernard of Clairvaux, *In cant. serm.* 23, 16) by the fact that *tranquillus Deus tranquillat omnia et quietum aspicere quiescere est,* is attained when we keep to this one *testimonium* (*Instit.* III, 24, 4), to the "channel" (*ib.*, 24, 3) fed by this hidden spring, to the given copy of the original which God Himself retains (*Sermon on Eph.* 1[4f.], *C.R.* 51, 281). Only *postquam in Christo fundata est fides, possunt quaedam accidere, quae illam iuvent : in sola tamen Christi gratia interim ac quiescit* (*Comm. on* 1 *Jn.* 3[14], *C.R.* 55, 339). *Etsi enim omnibus Dei gratis tanquam adminiculis confirmatur fides, non tamen suum in una Dei misericordia fundamentum habere desinit* (*ib.*). We have here a relationship similar to that which exists, according to Calvin, in the question of the authority of Holy Scripture, between the inner witness of the Holy Spirit speaking in it and the different moments of its outward credibility. But in neither case does Calvin consider it mistaken or superfluous to refer to these *adminicula.* Note how in all these and similar situations he also spoke of faith in Christ as the foundation of the assurance of election, certainly not as a reason distinct from Christ, but rather as the human act and attitude in which it happens that the man comes to rest in Christ as the one foundation. As Christ is certainly the source and object of faith, so Christ Himself assuredly (*Instit.* III, 1, 1 ; 2, 24, etc.) lives and works in the believer through faith, and is one with him. But this being the case, it is inevitable that we should understand faith itself (as a human deed and attitude) and the believer as such and his human life (his life in *faith,* but his *life* in faith) as an incidental, but certainly not on that account superfluous, confirmation of the one, decisive witness. A man is sure that this is established in itself, and is true, by its own weight, and therefore in the power of the witness of Jesus Christ and the Holy Spirit. But he is so only in the form of his own decision, his own faith and confession, his own corresponding being. Christ cannot be to him a witness of his election without his receiving His witness, and therefore himself—even in opposition to himself—becoming a bearer of this witness. Believers recognise in Christ *quae percipiunt quotidie beneficia ex Dei manu* (*Instit.* III, 24, 4). " Forget not all his benefits " (Ps. 103[2]). Calvin spoke with unusual caution about this aspect of the problem. He did not wish to ascribe it any independent significance. He certainly did not want the *certitudo salutis* to be grounded on it (*Comm. on* 1 *Jn.* 3[19], *C.R.* 55, 341). But he undoubtedly did speak of it. He did not merely concede but contended that contemplation of the work of the electing God on man, included in faith in Jesus Christ, is not merely permissible but also necessary. *Vocatio* (*et electio*) *ex vitae sanctitate firma apparet* (*Comm. on* 2 *Pet.* 1[10], *C.R.* 55, 450). If the witness to this *sanctitas* of men offers no basis upon which he may take his stand as a believer, it does at least offer him an *accessio vel adminiculum inferius ad fidei fulturam (C.R.* 55, 341 f.), a *signum,* a *specimen,* a *documentum (C.R.* 55, 450). *Summa est, discerni hac nota filios Dei a reprobis, dum pie et sancte vivunt, quia hic electionis scopus est (ib.).* When it is a matter of the basis of their salvation, the saints will look past that which is evidenced by their works, and solely to the goodness of God Himself. But *sic fundata, erecta, stabilita conscientia operum quoque consideratione stabilitur, quatenus sc. testimonia sunt Dei in nobis habitantis et regnantis.* The faith of the Christian is trust in God's loving-kindness and in that alone. *Non vetamus autem ne divinae erga nos benevolentiae signis hanc fidem fulciat et confirmet. Nam si dum memoria repetuntur quaecunque in nos dona Deus contulit, sunt nobis quodammodo instar radiorum divini vultus, quibus illuminemur ad summam illam bonitatis lucem contemplandam : multo magis bonorum operum gratia, quae Spiritum adoptionis nobis datum commonstrat (Instit.* III, 14, 18).

I do not think it possible to deny—as do H. Otten and W. Niesel—that in this problem what was later called the *syllogismus practicus* did constitute one element in the theology of Calvin himself, nor can I see that it is any reproach against him, in view of the reserve with which he sought to work out the statement, and with which he thought he could work it out in the context of his total conception. The problem which he here sought to answer was and is a genuine problem. The final witness of Jesus Christ to each individual, the least independent and least worthy of a hearing, yet the most indispensable in this situation and function, is the individual himself (in and with that which he is by faith in Jesus Christ). While his witness in and by itself does not give him the slightest assurance, he cannot receive the witness of Jesus Christ and the Holy Spirit—which gives real and complete assurance—unless he receives it from himself, unless he himself gives it in his faith and life and " works." It is as I live as an elect man that I am and shall be assured of my election. This is perhaps the meaning of the well-known section in the *Heidelberg Catechism,* Qu. 86, when the question why we should perform good works is answered in the third paragraph as follows : " that we may ourselves be assured of our faith by its fruits." And in view of this no objection can be taken if in the *Catechism* of Leo Jud (1541)—which was one of the sources of the *Heidelberg Catechism*— the same question is answered : " Sixthly, our election, call to faith and salvation, are known through good works. Thence proceed a right joyful conscience and a certain lively hope, in which we may gladly and cheerfully await the return of Christ, who will reward every believer according to his works. For as I help my neighbour, do good unto him and love him, so will I thereby be inwardly assured that my faith is true, and not false or imaginary, and that I am a real Christian—wherefore Peter saith (2 Pet. 1[10]) . . .'"

How was it that an insight which is not merely useful but in its place essential could be conceived and stated, and actually was stated, in a manner calculated so visibly to damage the matter of faith in God's gracious election that when this was seen further attempts to exploit it were abandoned ?

Calvin's suggestion must obviously have dangerous consequences the moment we fail to take seriously or to understand his affirmation that the testimony in question can consist only in the witness of Jesus Christ Himself or that of the Holy Spirit ; that the testimony of *gratia bonorum operum* is only to be understood as an *adminiculum inferius* and its function as a *commonstrare ;* that it is to be understood, therefore, merely as a relative and not an independent testimony, to be heard only secondarily and subordinately ; that it too, then, is to be understood as a testimony of faith. There were three things which— in the context of his total conception—Calvin tried to ensure, and they certainly need to be ensured. First, the testimony of " works " must not take the first place and assume the role of a crown witness. But this happened when Beza (*Quaestionum et responsionum christianus libellus,* 1580, *qu.* 1, 124, *cit.* A. Schweizer, *Glaubenslehre der ev. ref. Kirche,* Vol. 2, 1847, p. 529) answered the question : *In illa perniciosissima particularis electionis tentatione quo tandem confugiam ?* with : *Ad effecta, ex quibus spiritualis vita certo dignoscitur et nostra electio sicut corporis vita sensu percipitur. Electum igitur me esse primum ex sanctificatione mea inchoata i.e. odio peccati et amore iustitiae intelligam ; huic adiiciam (!) testimonium spiritus meam conscientiam vigentis.* It happened at Dort (in the *Reiectio errorum*, V, 5, unlike *Art.* V, 10) when first the *propria filiorum Dei signa*, and then the sure promises of God, were named. It happened when F. Gomarus in his exposition of 2 Pet. 1[10] expressed himself : *Ex bonis operibus tanquam ex fructibus et effectis propriis dignoscimus ac demonstramus fidem nostram tanquam causam propinquam. . . . Eoque modo a vocationis efficacis confirmatione gradatim ad electionem (a qua vocatio illa tanquam a causa necessario dependet) ascendimus (Opera*, 1644, II, p. 439). And it happened also when Wolleb explained : *In exploranda electione nostra methodo analytica progrediendum a mediis exequutionis ad decretum, facto initio a sanctificatione nostra (Chr. Theol. comp.*, 1624, I, *cap.* 4, *can.* 15). Secondly, the testimony of " works " must not be separated from faith—as if *this* " fruit " could detach itself from *that* tree and be considered by itself. It is not to be treated as a self-supporting (in some sense " existential ") decision of empirical self-examination and self-evaluation, distinguishable from the testimony of faith (and from Jesus Christ Himself), or from the testimony of the Holy Spirit. But this happened when Beza, as we have seen, remarked of the *spiritualis vita* that it is established *sicut corporis vita sensu.* It happened when Wolleb (elsewhere) formulated the syllogism as follows : *Quicunque in se sentit donum sanctificationis, qua peccato morimur et vivimus iustitiae, is iustificatus, vocatus seu vera fide donatus et electus est. Atqui per Dei gratiam hoc sentio, ergo iustificatus, vocatus et electus sum.* And thirdly, the testimony of " works " must not be detached from the self-testimony of Christ, from the promise of the forgiveness of sins, or in general from the objective Word of God, as if it had power in itself to penetrate its mystery, or as if there were a kind of pipeline between God's decree on the one hand, and human piety and morals on the other. But this is what makes the presentation of Dort (Art. I, 12) so hard to stomach. It is not at all self-evident that in this direct confrontation believers will regard the fruits of their election *cum spirituali gaudio* and *sancta voluptate*, as it says there. If we believe that the assurance of election referred to will be finally and conclusively established in this way— in palpable divergence from Calvin—where then do we stand *vis-à-vis* Tridentine Catholicism ? Was not this more reformed than the Reformers when it stated that it would rather renounce an assurance of election that has to be established in this manner ?

It is clear (1) that Beza, Gomarus, the men of Dort and Wolleb recognised the importance of the problem stated by Leo Jud and treated by Calvin (with the caution observable at those three points), and that they were ready to take it up again. It is also clear (2) that they attempted to think the matter systematically through to a conclusion (and therefore for the sake of lucidity to put it in the form of the well-known syllogism). But it is clearest of all (3) that in so doing they concluded that the caution of Calvin could be abandoned ; that the self-testimony of the life of the elect could be moved up to the first place ; that it could be understood as the vote cast by empirical self-examination and self-evaluation ; and that it could actually be given an independent place alongside the testimony of Jesus Christ. The question obviously presses whether by taking this course they merely fell victim to an accidental error, or whether this was a necessary aberration within the framework of the basic view common both to Calvin and themselves. In other word, was it perhaps inevitable that within this framework the attempted safeguard of Calvin should be ignored because it could not be understood ?

The development which threatened from this handling of the problem encountered opposition. It already sounds like a preliminary protest when the *Consensus*

Bremensis (1595) very energetically declares—in the section (VII, 5) which deals with our question—that in face of " great temptation " in respect of our own predestination, we are " not to look to that which we experience or discover in ourselves, but rather to the certain and unfailing promises of the divine Word, which we are to commit to our inward hearts and weigh and ponder, standing firm against all doubts, and struggling and warring against our own feelings, hearts and opinions, until the comfort of the Holy Ghost is recovered, which assuredly is powerful through the contemplation of the Word. . . . In medicine, and the common life of man, experience and feeling come first, and what we believe to be true follows thereafter. But in the conversion and trust of the heart in God we must give place and consent first of all to the Word of the Lord, resisting sins against the conscience, and all doubt and faintheartedness, in and .through the Word of God, and seeking help as did the afflicted father in Mk. 9[24], when he cried : ' O Lord, I believe, help thou mine unbelief.' Then as the comfort and joy of the heart more and more are recovered, with the saving motion and impulse of the Holy Ghost, as David shows in Ps. 130[5], and again in Ps. 119[50, 92]. And the Spirit of God admonishes all distressed and tempted Christians in the well-known Christian hymn :

> And tho' it seemeth God saith naught,
> Let courage fill thy being,
> For where He is most truly thine
> Is hidden from thy seeing.
> Be thou but certain of His Word,
> And tho' thy heart with doubts be stirred,
> Still yield not in the battle.'

The golden saying of Luther is to the same effect : *Qui vere Christianus est, eum opportet credere invisibilia, sperare dilata, diligere Deum ostendentem se contrarium, atque ita in finem usque perseverare in verbo nobis ab ipso tradito."* In this way the position maintained by Calvin's reservations could actually be restored. Yet the truth and beauty of what was said at Bremen, or of the quotations from Luther and Paul Speratus (the extract is from the twelfth verse of " Now hath salvation to us come "), must not be allowed to obscure the fact that the genuine problem of Calvin was itself abandoned as well as the doubtful features of the syllogism as it was understood by Beza and others. The same thing evidently happened when Polanus (*Synt. chr. Theol.*, 1609, col. 1602 f.), and later F. Turrettini (*Instit. Theol. el.*, 1679, *L.* IV, *qu.* 13), do not mention at all the witness of the Christian life, which is at issue, but for the most part deal only with the *testimonium Spiritus sancti internum.* Indeed, the majority of other Reformed dogmaticians (e.g., B. Bucan, Walaeus, the Leyden Synopsis, Heidan, Burmann, van Mastricht) either conceal the existence of the problem altogether or accord it only the most cursory treatment.

M. F. Wendelin (*Chr. Theol.*, 1634, I, 3, 19) attempts a compromise when he states the syllogism as follows : *Quicunque per verbum est ad ecclesiam et vitam aeternam vocatus et fide in Jesum Christum donatus, hoc est, credit, sibi remissa esse peccata sua propter Christi θεανθρώπου meritum, insuperque sincero et minime fucato studio Deum colit secundum verbi praescriptum et proximum diligit, is ad vitam aeternam est electus. Atqui ego . . . vocatus et . . . donatus sum . . . hoc est credo . . . insuperque . . . Deum colo. Ergo ego sum . . . electus.* Notice how for Wolleb's *sentit* and *sentio* he substitutes *est* and *sum*, explaining this by the *credit* and *credo*, attaching the *colere Deum* to the *credere*, and relating the whole to the objective *vocatio* and *donatio per verbum.* But although Wendelin expressed himself more carefully, and also more equivocally, than Beza and the others, did he really mean anything different ? Could he mean anything different in the context of the total view ? He certainly said explicitly that the decisive *minor* of the syllogism, in the sense he understood it, rests on an *examen conscientiae* and its conclusion on a judgment of the conscience. But according to the work of W. Amesius (*De conscientia*, 1643, I, 1, 2), which was authoritative for contemporary Reformed theology, " conscience " has to be understood as the judicial opinion of man, considered as *habitus naturalis*, about his own status in the judgment of God—a *habitus* in which man is in direct touch with God. " Searching of the conscience " (I, 8) is the *actus reflexus intellectus, quo homo intelligit et cum iudicio perpendit suos proprios actus cum eorum circumstantiis.* And the conclusion grounded on the *minor* obtained in this way, and fulfilled by conscience (I, 10), is the *actus conscientiae, quo homo sibimetipsi applicat ius illud Dei, quod factum vel statum suum attingit.* From this act there results (I, 10) either his *excusatio, absolutio* and ultimately *approbatio* (the *actus conscientiae, quo pronuntiat hominem in suo facto Deo placuisse*), or his *accusatio* and *condemnatio.* In the first more favourable case (I, 11) the upshot is the *gaudium, quo in benefacto suo, ut in vero bono sibi coniuncto acquiescit.* If we bear these definitions in mind, we are forced to the conclusion that Wendelin's attempt at a compromise is a failure. In spite of all the care with which he tried to avoid the road taken by Beza and the others, he clearly belongs to those who for their part were aware of the importance of the problem, but could not help throwing off the caution of Calvin when they proceeded to its detailed elucidation.

Unquestionably, they were in a dilemma. They had either to remain faithful to the basis of Calvin's teaching on assurance (*Christus mihi pro mille testimoniis sufficit*) or to follow up the problem it indicated (*bonorum operum gratia . . . commonstrat*). In other words, they had to abandon either the problem of Calvin or the caution with which he had handled it. Calvin, for his part, did not find himself in this dilemma merely because it escaped him. A happy inconsistency led him to believe that he could unify the christological beginning and the anthropological conclusion of his thinking, not ignoring a question which was actually necessary, but avoiding the relapse into a primitive doctrine of self-justification. The followers of Calvin, however, obviously did not share this belief—and rightly so. They therefore had to choose either one way or the other. And either way it was a bad and unpleasant choice. The historical and psychological enigma which will always confront us at this point is that it could escape the perspicacity of the master that a choice had to be made here, and that it was a bad choice.

The dilemma is actually unavoidable in the context of the common basic view which they all shared. Calvin and all his followers were concerned with the question how the man who has been elected by the absolute divine decree, and separated from the rejected, can become and be assured of his election. More particularly, there was the further question how far this man can himself be a witness in the matter with his Christian existence—*this* man, the man who with his " rejected " fellow stands face to face with the mere good-pleasure of the absolute God, and is elected in this way. What will it mean if this man is given permission and the ability to make sure of his election *operum quoque consideratione ?* First, can we really expect this man to put this consideration last, and to hold primarily to Christ ? If Christ is only the means of grace of the God who secretly elects or rejects, then how can He be the crown witness for his election ? If he himself is the one elected by the hidden God, why cannot he himself rather be the crown witness, and the *consideratio operum* be no mere *adminiculum inferius*, but the first and decisive stage of his assurance of election ? But if he is not, how can he possibly be helped by the advice to hold to Christ ? As a man rejected by the hidden God, what can he possibly have to do with Christ ? Second, how can we really say of this man that the *consideratio* which leads to his assurance must be accomplished in faith ? If he is sure of his election in faith, this must mean that he is sure of his being in Jesus Christ, and therefore of Jesus Christ Himself. But how can he be assured of his election in this way when he is actually chosen by an absolute decree ? If he is elect, what else can he do to be assured of the fact except to reach back to a *sentire* quite apart from faith, to enter on the way of an " examination of conscience " with its resultant self-righteousness ? Third, how can we really expect this man to renounce the idea of a mysterious correspondence (and ultimate identity) between the secret counsel of God and his own status of grace, the status of his own piety and morality, which may be established empirically ? How can we really restrain him from " sanctified joy " that he is such an excellent, and for him, gratifying disclosure of what has taken place in the darkness of God's secret counsel ? These are the questions which Calvin, remarkably, did not perceive as such. Beza and the others did perceive them, and since they did not wish to ignore Calvin's problem, they thought it the lesser evil—at this point, perhaps, not fully aware of the results—to set up a *theologoumenon*, the crass humanism of which threatened to compromise almost everything that the Reformers thought they had discerned about the relationship between Christ, grace, faith and works. The typical majority of Reformed theologians also perceived the problem, but chose as the lesser evil—in order to avoid this *theologoumenon*—not to engage in Calvin's problem as such. Either way, however, the choice was enforced by an inescapable necessity.

The need for a total revision of the dogma is plainly shown by the history of this subsidiary problem. If Jesus Christ, rather than the absolute decree, is regarded as the real basis of the election of each elected individual, and the community of God as the medium through which there are elected individuals, then Calvin—and also Beza and the rest—are justified to the extent that the question of the personal assurance of the individual is actually put and must be answered. Individuals as such are godless ; elect only in Jesus Christ and through the medium of the community, and therefore directed continually to grasp their election in faith (" to make sure," 2 Pet. 1[10]), as they hear and receive the testimony of Jesus Christ, holding it before them as their own testimony. They have need of assurance. And if that about which they have to assure themselves can only be the election of Jesus Christ, and the power with which they do so can only be the power of that Christian faith and life which is mediated to them on the basis of His election, then they are not merely permitted but commanded continually to assure themselves of their election, as it has taken place in Jesus Christ, by themselves being its witnesses—living as the elect by their faith. From this point of view, to be elect means to be oneself a witness of one's election, living by one's faith. This must be said even more emphatically than it was said by Calvin. But if Jesus Christ is the real basis of election, the following points must be made in opposition to the interpretation of Beza and the rest, and in answer to the scruples of other Calvinist theologians, as a foolproof version of the reservation of Calvin.

First, the fact that the elect is himself a witness to his election means that he himself may witness to the election of Jesus Christ, and to his own election in and with it. Similarly, the *consideratio operum* in which he himself accepts this testimony can be understood only as the *consideratio operum Christi* ; the consideration of the grace which for the sake of Christ, and through Him, is vouchsafed to him as one of the godless threatened with rejection ; of the re-demptive act of Christ of which he is the subject as His elect. It is obvious, then, that although he participates in this witness as a bearer as well as a recipient, he does so simply as *adminiculum inferius* of the testimony itself, and even as such only by its own inner power, in the inexpressible wonder of the grace of Jesus Christ. And it is also obvious that this participant, the godless man threatened with rejection, who through grace alone has become a bearer and recipient of this witness, cannot possibly understand the difference between his situation and that of the godless alongside him as one of absolute antithesis.

Second, his participation in this witness and therefore his assurance about himself, can have absolutely nothing to do with self-examination and self-evaluation. What can self-examination mean except that the godless considers the godless, and how can this in itself be adequate even for self-condemnation, not to mention the self-justification which is presupposed as possible in the *minor* of the syllogism ? It is not in self-examination or self-evaluation, but exclusively in faith, that he may be and is active as the bearer and recipient of this witness : as he is in fact the elect of Jesus Christ ; as he leaves his godlessness behind him in faith, and therefore lives in acknowledgment of the grace of Jesus Christ vouchsafed to him as a godless man ; as his works are the works of this faith ; as he actually witnesses to the election of Jesus Christ by what he is. It is obvious that the syllogism is not a form which we can use to describe this process. But above all it is obvious that the elect man cannot possibly receive this witness if he gives it only to himself, if as he gives it to himself he does not also give it to his " rejected " neighbour, if he does not permit the contradiction of the rejection that threatens him to benefit this other man as it has benefited him. How can he be the elect of Jesus Christ if the operation of faith by which he is assured that he is elect is not immediately and primarily a work of hope and proclamation to his neighbour also, a participation in the work of the community of God in the world ?

Third, as the elect man is in this way assured of his election, he is indeed aware of a mysterious correspondence (even identity), not between the hidden counsel of God and the condition of his own piety and morality, but between the election of Jesus Christ and the miracle of the actual fulfilment of his faith ; between the inner power of the witness, whose bearer and recipient (and messenger) he may be, and the miracle of the fact that he actually finds himself enabled to be the bearer and recipient (and messenger) of this witness. It is obvious that he will not rejoice in himself because of this correspondence (even identity), but solely " in the Lord," solely in the grace that encounters him in this relationship. It is also obvious—in consequence—that he will manifest this joy of his as a promise and hope, especially to his " rejected " neighbour, the godless one. The *sancta voluptas* of the individual assurance of the elect is that he may hand on the Word by which he himself lives to those who do not yet, or any longer, live by it.

Our conclusion is, then, that Calvin's problem of the self-assurance of the elect can and actually must be tackled, but that the caution with which Calvin dealt with it can and actually must be maintained. In the setting of the classical doctrine the one could take place only at the expense of the other. But in a setting of the doctrine of predestination which has a christological basis there is room for both and both are needed.

2. THE ELECT AND THE REJECTED

What is it that makes individuals elect men (in Jesus Christ, and by means of His community) ?

We begin with a general answer. They are made this by a distinction of God's relationship to them and their relationship to God which is in fact peculiar to themselves (though independent of their personal peculiarities and independent of their conduct and actions). It is on the basis and assumption of this distinction that the guidance granted them, and their own conduct and actions and ultimately their role and task in the world about them, find their appointed, decisive character in relation to those of others. The elect, then, do not first become this either with reference to their person or in recognition of any attributes or achievements, or even through their divine calling. Their special calling simply discloses and confirms the fact that they already are the elect. And the same is true of their awareness of this, and of that which others may know about it. They demonstrate to themselves and others that they are elect by entering upon and continuing along the road that corresponds to their election. It is the consistency in which they are led and act on this way, the fulfilment of the role and task intended for them, that reveal their election. This cannot, then, be considered even for a single moment *in abstracto*, either by themselves or others. It can only be lived by them, and seen by others as it is lived by them. If their life is only the fulfilment of their election, it is equally true that its fulfilment alone can be their life. They are what they are. No creature has given them their distinction. As it consists in the actual relationship of God to them, and their actual relationship to God, so it has its basis in God alone : they, too, are elected in and with the election of Jesus Christ and by means of His community.

It is based on this secret of theirs that if we look for elect individuals in the Bible—and, of course, we do not have to look far for them—we do not need to confine ourselves to passages or contexts where there is explicit mention of election ; where the terms *baḥar* or ἐκλέγεσθαι are therefore used. Just because the idea is so fundamentally important, it need not be always stated explicitly, although sometimes, of course, it may be. It belongs to the very air, so to speak, which is breathed in the Old and New Testaments. Just because the elect are elect in so far as they are what they are, i.e., specifically determined for their specific being, life and acts, it is natural to be silent rather than explicit about their election, and it is readily explicable that these terms are the very ones which do not appear so frequently in the Bible as one might naturally expect. We must therefore pay the greater attention to the matter itself, which, in the implicit fashion which is almost the rule in this case, is apparent on almost every page of the Bible. For the Bible is, in fact, everywhere concerned with the election of individual men. A human name mysteriously appears and occupies the stage for a time, whose peculiar human life, doings and sufferings in relation-ship with those of others form for a time the secondary subject and content of the biblical witness, and therefore themselves become a witness to that which is the primary subject and content of this witness. The enigmatic fact that this one or that one—in many cases significantly characterised by his name—is actually present, and that he is present in this or that way, is the fundamental determination of his election.

When we read in Gen. 4[4] that the Lord looked favourably upon Abel and his sacrifice, we may well ask : Why Abel ? And when we go on to read (Gen. 4[15f.]) about the special protection under which the same Lord places the murderer Cain, we may equally well ask : Why in his own way Cain ? Why in the long succession of the patriarchs from Adam to Noah is it Enoch who, according to Gen. 5[24], is described as the man who walked with God, " and he was not, for God took him " ? How is it that in the midst of a perverse generation, whose creation God repented, Noah is singled out : " a just man and perfect in his generations, walking with God " (Gen. 6[9]) ? Why is God blessed (Gen. 9[26]) by Noah specifically as the " God of Shem," and then the genealogy of Shem is wholly unhonoured and unsung until the name of Abram appears (Gen. 11[26]), dominating the scene until his time is past, and then yielding place to the mysteriously introduced persons and the significant names of Isaac and Jacob ? Why the important stress laid upon the name of Judah among the sons of Jacob, but similarly on the name of Benjamin, and in a totally different way on the name of Joseph ? How does it come about that in Ex. $2^{1f.}$ a new aspect opens up, Moses suddenly appearing " of the house of Levi," and with him Aaron and Joshua, and after them the Judges, each with his special qualities, and then Samuel, Saul, David, the better and lesser known prophets, each one with the same mysterious endowment of the " spirit " and the same peculiar burden of the Word of God ? It is, then, only a confirmation of the facts if Abraham (Neh. 9^7), Moses (Ps. 106^{23}), Aaron (Ps. 105^{26}), David (1 K. 8^{16}, 11^{39} ; 2 Chr. 6^6, Ps. 78^{70}, 89^3), Zerubbabel (Hag. 2^{23}), Jeremiah, the unknown prophet of the exile (Is. 49^7), and the last, shadow king Jeconiah are explicitly described as the elect of God. In these passages the terminology simply denotes that which is self-evident for the Bible even when it does not appear on the surface. This is the utterly mysterious freedom in which these individuals are present, and complete their course, more or less in the light—some in the brightest light and some like Pharaoh of the Exodus or Saul in heavy shadow. It is the freedom in which all of them in their own place are necessarily and yet fortuitously—we might almost say in the necessity of their fortuitousness—subjects of the biblical witness and themselves witnesses. This mysterious freedom is the most general determination of the election of the individual in the Old Testament.

In the New Testament the picture is rather different. The history of Israel is not continued after the crucifixion of Christ, while the Church has no history in the strict sense, but only (in the time that has still to be patiently endured until the revelation of the already consummated end of all time) a status of continual self-renewal. The series of patriarchs, judges, kings, priests and prophets is not, therefore, continued in any corresponding series of Christian men of God, for the simple reason that the Church, originally consisting of and represented by the twelve apostles, is as such the assembly of individual ἐκλεκτοί. But the election of all who are united in the Church, of each individual Christian, like that of the elect in the Old Testament, is the mystery of freedom in which they simply are what they are. This is shown already in the fact that in the twelve named apostles the Church is established by the Word of God addressed to them and proclaimed by them. In particular the figure of the apostle Paul, the prominence given to his personal conversion and his personal commission by the risen Jesus Christ, the completely unique central position which he assumes between Jesus Christ and the Christians united in the congregations, certainly has in the New Testament the function of making clear that the history of Israel does not continue beyond the crucifixion of Jesus Christ. There is no longer any need of special men of God, of special revelations and therefore of special vocation and special election. On the contrary, it is now a matter of the special mystery of these special men of God in the Old Testament for each and all who believe in Him. Just as Christians have their being as a whole elected race of priests and kings, a holy and peculiar people (1 Pet. 2^9), similarly every one of them has his being on the basis of his personal election. Each individual Christian as such is what he is no less definitely than Abel, Abraham, Moses, David and all the prophets, i.e., he lives and manifests the very presupposition and distinction peculiar to his being ; he fulfils his personal predestination. The fact that in the Church *all* are ἐκλεκτοί, elect individuals, constitutes its difference from Israel. But the fact that they are ἐκλεκτοί is something which the Church has in common with Israel. And in this it shows itself to be the fulfilment of that of which Israel had been a prophecy.

But when we have made this first affirmation the question : What makes men elect ? must be probed much more deeply. We have equated with their election the fact that they have to fulfil their distinctive determination as such and such persons. We must now stress what has necessarily been indicated already, that neither the idea of chance nor the idea of necessity is adequate to explain this fact. God Himself is the mystery of the elect. It is a peculiar determination for the service of God, for the work of divine reconciliation and revelation, with which we are concerned in the special course which they have to complete as elect persons, in the historical period or sphere where their specific appearance and being have been determined. This is something which is determined by God, and its peculiarity is therefore His good will and pleasure. The fact that they appear as this or that person is in conformity with—indeed, it is directed by God's good will and pleasure. The enigma of the freedom in which they are what they are consists and is solved in the fact that God has determined it in His freedom. We must immediately add, of course, that this very fact turns what was previously an enigma into a genuine mystery. When we reduce the being and existence of elect individuals to the formula that " they are what they are," we bring them instantly into a remarkable proximity to the being and existence of God Himself. For " I am that I AM," or " I am that I WILL BE," is the very name by which God Himself made Himself known to Moses, according to Ex. 3[14]. Who can authentically bear this name except God Himself—or the man who, according to God's will, and within the limits of creatureliness and his own particular created being, may and must bear this name because he has been chosen by God, i.e., loved from all eternity, received into covenant with Him, and destined for life in this covenant ? Thus, the divine election of individuals does not consist in the enigma of their individuality and solitude, nor in that which distinguishes them as this or that person. On the contrary, the mystery of the special name, of the individuality and the solitude of any one person, consists in his divine election. It is the individuality and solitude of God which constitutes the elect individual, and to which he owes the particularity of his name. Because and as God is this One, they—the elect—are this or that person.

Abel and Cain, Abraham, Isaac and Jacob, Moses and David and all the prophets, with their individual names and persons, do not stand for themselves, but for God. They live and speak and work " in the name of God." It is for this reason that they are God's elect, and that they are who they are in their own place and fashion. For it is the nature of God to confirm Himself in all that He is and does, to be faithful to Himself, and to repeat His own being, with all its glory, in all His attributes as in all His works. And if it is the case that this also characterises elect individual men, that from the outset they have a peculiar distinction which is displayed and consummated consistently in their whole life, it is also made clear in what relationship, on what basis and in what direction they acquire this characteristic : they are *God's* elect, elected by *God*. The elect man in his place and fashion is, in his being, a copy of the divine being.

The life which corresponds to his election, and the manifestation and consummation of the distinction which from the outset is peculiar to him, do indeed develop within very definite limits and conditions. On the basis of his election—the elect man, Jesus Christ, is the only exception—he lives a life that is marked and bounded by his creatureliness, and is therefore utterly different from the life of God. And consequently his election is always different from the election in which God makes sovereign disposition concerning Himself, so that by the might of this inner sovereignty He is outwardly sovereign also, the Lord of all lords. But, again, we cannot overlook in this connexion how valuable and significant it is that the elect are encouraged, especially in the New Testament, to recognise God as their Father, and themselves as His children. The closest relationship is indeed involved between the being of God and the being of the elected man (cf. Ac. 17²⁸). This helps us to understand the restrained expression in Ps. 127² which describes the inhabitants of the city protected by God as " His " (Luther : " His friends "), or, again, 2 Tim. 2¹⁹ : " The Lord knoweth them that are his." And Ex. 33¹¹ says expressly : " The Lord spake unto Moses face to face, as a man speaketh unto his friend." And the term " friend of God " is used of Abraham in Is. 41⁸, 2 Chron. 20⁷, Jas. 2²³. In Jn. 15¹⁴ᶠ· Jesus calls His disciples " friends," in so far as they do that which He commands them, not as mere slaves, but as those who through Him have learned what their Lord, His Father, is doing. In Ps. 45⁶ᶠ·, the king who celebrates his marriage is addressed in the words : " Thy throne, O divine one (Luther, A.V. : " God "), is for ever and ever : the sceptre of thy kingdom is a right sceptre. Thou lovest righteousness, and hatest wickedness : therefore God, thy God, hath anointed thee " ; and in Ps. 2⁷ : " Thou art my Son ; this day have I begotten thee. Ask of me, and I shall give thee the heathen for thine inheritance, and the uttermost parts of the earth for thy possession." In the portrayal of the coming day of judgment upon human judges (Ps. 82) the latter are expressly called " gods " and are addressed as such in v. 6 : " I have said, Ye are gods ; and all of you are children of the most High." To be sure, v. 7 then continues : " But ye shall die like men, and fall like one of the princes." Yet it is to be noted that in Jn. 10³⁴ᶠ· Jesus stated quite definitely of this saying : " The Scripture cannot be broken," and He expressly used these words as evidence of His own divine sonship in the form of a conclusion *a minori ad majus.* We must also remember Rom. 5¹⁷, where Paul opposes to the rule of death, introduced by Adam's sin, the lordship over death assured by Jesus Christ in the future life of those who by Him have become partakers of the grace of God. We also recall 2 Tim. 2¹² : " If we suffer, we shall also reign with Him " ; and in Rev. 20⁴ : " And I saw thrones, and they sat upon them, and judgement was given unto them "—namely, to the souls of those " who were beheaded for the witness of Jesus, and for the word of God, and which had not worshipped the beast, neither his image, neither had received his mark upon their foreheads, or in their hands ; and they lived and reigned with Christ a thousand years." There is also Paul's statement in 1 Cor. 6³ that one day Christians will judge even the angels. From all this it at least follows that as both the Old and New Testament conceive their nature the elect do not stand in a merely external and formal but in an inner and actual relationship to God. As created beings they are completely and utterly other than God, completely and utterly dependent upon Him, and therefore made by Him alone into what they are ; but as the elect of God they are not strangers to Him, but possess a definite affinity with Him and a definite share in His kingship. The elect of God, in fact, gives us a picture of God in the midst of creation. Not of himself, but in and with the choice that has befallen him, he is marked by constancy. In virtue of this constancy he is just as necessarily this or that person, completing the corresponding course of action, as God Himself is always the same and faithful to Himself in all His attributes and works. In him therefore, and what he represents, and what happens through him, what he suffers, his succour and salvation, the peculiar continuity of his existence, a legitimate testimony can be given to the constancy and therefore to the sovereignty and therefore to the will of God. Not of himself, but as an elect man, the elect is an authentic witness of God. It is not by chance that it is just he who is active in the ministry of reconciliation between God and man, as an instrument of God's revelation. Nor is it a contradiction if he, a member and citizen of the lost world, " flesh " like all other men, is actually enabled for this ministry and function, so that this ministry is actually executed, this function discharged by him. He is enabled for it in virtue of his election, and as an elect person. His election as such is an equipment for this end because it is the conformity which he has been given with God Himself, the reflection of the divine countenance. The enigma of his human existence is in reality the mystery of the divine existence. The elect are, therefore, those who walk before God and find His good-pleasure. How can it be otherwise when they are His, when they are His friends, His children ? His good-pleasure towards them is grounded in the fact that in them He recognises Himself.

To the distinction, peculiar to the elect, of God's relationship to them and their relationship to God, there corresponds objectively their difference from other men. This difference is their calling. But their calling—the work of the Holy Spirit—is that by means of the community the election of Jesus Christ may be proclaimed to them as their own election, and that they may be assured of their election by faith in Jesus Christ, in whom it was brought about. This twofold possibility is the objective difference between the elect and other men. By the free event of proclamation and of faith they are placed in a special situation in relation to others, and in a ministry in which the latter do not stand. This is revealed by the fact that they are silent when others speak ; they confess when others deny ; they stand when others falter ; they adore when others blaspheme ; they are joyful when others are sad, and sad when others are joyful ; at peace when others are restless, and restless when others are at peace. They are different because of their calling. In and with the whole community of God, they are strangers among others. In different ways they repeat and reproduce the solitude of Jesus Christ. They are lights in the world because He is the Light of the world. They are His witnesses—for they are elect in Him and called by Him and to Him in that twofold possibility, the work of the Holy Spirit. The difference between the elect and other men, and therefore their calling, is the execution, the objectively necessary expression of their election. What other expression could there possibly be ? How could those whom God has chosen in His Son lack the gift of His Holy Spirit, and thus the twofold possibility of proclamation and faith ? Because the election of Jesus Christ is the truth, then the difference of those who are chosen in Him (their calling) is *the* witness to the truth besides which there is no other. There and there alone the truth is testified—there and there alone it finds expression—where in and with the election of Jesus Christ the election of man is proclaimed to him, and where he may have assurance of it through faith in Him. Thus the difference of the elect from others, their isolation and foreignness among them, is *the* witness to the truth.

But we cannot put this the other way round and say it of what distinguishes other men from the elect. They lack this twofold possibility. They do not possess the Holy Spirit. They do not stand in the area of proclamation and faith. They even refuse this whole offer with hostility. But their explicit or implicit godlessness is not the objectively necessary expression of a real mystery of human existence, as is the life of the elect. The godless life expresses no real mystery of human existence to which testimony can be given. If this is a man's life-witness, it is *ipso facto* false witness. To be without the Holy Spirit, and therefore to live uncalled and godlessly, signifies an evil, perilous, but futile attempt to live the life of one rejected by God. The man rejected by God is the man who, because of his sin and guilt, is denied and repudiated by the righteous judgment and sentence of God, and transferred to the utterly untenable condition of Satan and his kingdom. He is the man abandoned to eternal perdition. He is the man whom this befits, and who has to suffer that which befits him, because he has challenged and drawn upon himself the destructive hostility of God. To be the rejected of God is the threat whose fulfilment would be the inevitable lot of every single human life. And it is this threat which in the election of Jesus Christ is diverted to Him, the One, and in that way averted from all others. By permitting the life of a rejected man to be the life of His own Son, God has made such a life objectively impossible for all others. The life of the uncalled, the godless, is a grasping back at this objective impossibility, an attempt to expose oneself again to the threat which has already been executed and consequently removed. The attempt is evil, perilous and futile for the following reasons. It is evil because it denies that God has taken sinful and guilty man to Himself in eternal love. It is perilous because it conjures up anew the shadow of the withdrawal, the disapproval, the aversion—yes, the hate—of God which inevitably menaces every man. It is futile because while it may indeed demonstrate and confirm the sin and guilt of man, and the wretchedness of his ensuing punishment, it cannot alter the fact that there is only one Rejected, the Bearer of all man's sin and guilt and their ensuing punishment, and this One is Jesus Christ. Those who undertake the attempt may indeed lie—but can only lie—against the divine election of grace.

This, then, is how the elect and others differ from one another : the former by witnessing in their lives to the truth, the latter by lying against the same truth. It ought to be clear that to this extent they belong together. The elect are obviously to be found in the sphere of the divine election of grace, in the hand of the one God, under the reign whose beginning and principle are called Jesus Christ. But the others are also to be found there. The former are there in obedience, the latter in disobedience ; the former as free children of the household, the latter as forced and refractory slaves ; the former under God's blessing, the latter under His curse. If the former testify by their truthful witness to what God wills, the latter no less expressively testify by their lying witness to what God does not will. Thus both serve the revelation of the divine will and decree which by nature are wholly light, but which cannot be revealed or recognised except as light and shade. Believers " are " the elect in this service so far as they bear witness to the truth, that is, to the elect man, Jesus Christ, and manifest and reproduce and reflect the life of this one Elect. The godless " are " the rejected in the same service so far as by their false witness to man's rejection they manifest and reproduce and reflect the death of the one Rejected, Jesus Christ. Because this One is the Elect and the Rejected, He is—attested by both—the Lord and Head both of the elect and also of the rejected. Thus not only the former, but no less indispensably, in their own place and after their own totally different fashion, the latter, are His representatives, just as originally and properly He is theirs.

It is from this solidarity of the elect and the rejected in the One Jesus Christ that there arises a very definite recollection for the elect and an equally definite expectation for others.

The recollection for the elect is this. The distinction of God's relationship to them, and of their relationship to God, is originally and properly the distinction of Jesus Christ. It is He who is the Son and Friend of God. It is with Him that God is well pleased because He recognises His own countenance in Him. It is He who is the secret of God, which is the basis of the fact that there is such a distinction for others also. Apart from Him the elect cannot be elect, but they and all men are inevitably rejected. The sins which make God the enemy of man are their sins also. To suffer that which sinful man justly deserves—repudiation by God and eternal perdition—is the threat whose execution they also must incur. Apart from Jesus Christ they have no advantage over the rejected whose existence the godless undertake to manifest and repeat and reproduce with their false witness. They will, in fact, recognise themselves only too clearly in the false witness of the picture of mankind presented by the godless— namely, that which they necessarily are apart from Jesus Christ. They owe their election to the fact that in Jesus Christ God has from all eternity loved and summoned mankind, and therefore themselves also ; even the mankind which of and by itself could only be rejected (which is what the godless continually undertake to represent). And the way in which God has loved and summoned them from all eternity, in which He has annulled their threatened rejection, is by making Jesus Christ its bearer. Thus, as they work out their election, in faith in Jesus Christ, they can never think of the basis of their election without thinking simultaneously of the rejection which has been diverted from them in their election as it took place in Jesus Christ. As men potentially rejected—in Jesus Christ alone not rejected—they must know and confess themselves to be in solidarity with the godless, although separated from them because of their unbelief. They, too, have neither earned nor may they claim in the slightest degree anything other than the wrath of God. The grace of Jesus Christ is the sole ground of their distinction as the children and friends of God. But their solidarity with others extends also to that which distinguishes them from them. It is only by their calling, by the twofold work of the Holy Spirit, that their election is accomplished in their life. This actualisation, this objectively necessary expression of their election, their very existence as witnesses to the truth (to the election of Jesus Christ), is not at all self-evident. It is not a *datum* of their natural existence. It is not to be found in its disposition or inner potentiality. They are unable either to proclaim to themselves their election as it took place in Jesus Christ, or to determine themselves to believe in this proclamation. Proclamation and faith, and therefore everything that distinguishes them from others, are possible and actual by the Holy Spirit. Without the Holy Spirit, and therefore without their calling, they would necessarily be the same as others in all respects in which they are distinguished from them. Apart from their calling they, too, would be godless, and the witness of their lives could only be the false witness by which the divine election of grace is denied and blasphemed. And this is actually the case. There is no called man who was not once uncalled ; there is no hearer of the proclamation for whom it was not once strange and unknown ; and there is no believer who was not once an unbeliever. Nor is there any whose actualisation of his election has been uninterrupted, and who has not found himself for long stretches of his life far away from the realms of proclamation and of faith. There is none, indeed, who has not continually shown traces of his original uncalled condition, who has not been only too like the godless in specific respects, who has not denied his election. And so there is none who has any reason at any time to see anything other than the expiating grace of Jesus Christ even in his calling and in the gift of the Holy Spirit. But if this is the case, then in this respect, too, the elect will know and confess themselves to be in solidarity with the godless. The cross of Jesus Christ stands between them, and it is the only hope of both. In the godless, the elect see what they themselves were and are and will be apart from this hope. They see the darkness of the great falsehood fall more broadly and deeply across their own lives than across the lives of others ; the lie which Jesus Christ exposes as such, and whose punishment He has borne for us. In the very moment in which, thanks to their calling, they can hear and receive their acquittal, they see themselves as charged with their own as the greatest guilt of all. How else will believers recognise themselves in others if not in that which distinguishes these others from them—in damnation and distress? How can the man who denies this recognition possess the Holy Spirit? He and he alone possesses the Holy Spirit who knows continually that the grace of Jesus Christ is the only basis, not only of his election, but also of his calling.

The expectation for others is this. The original and proper distinction of Jesus Christ, which alone makes possible and actual the distinction of the elect, is the truth which also transcends, comprehends and illumines their existence, but which does not appear to be theirs because their life gives this false witness, because they are obviously involved in the evil, perilous and futile manifestation, repetition and reproduction of the life of men rejected by God. In this respect we must not forget that the distinction of the elect, which originally and properly is that of Jesus Christ alone, is also valid for these others; that they do not possess it only in so far as they do not recognise and accept it as their own distinction. They are unable, however, to oppose any true alternative portrait of man to the portrait which God first introduces in the person of His beloved Son, and then in all His elect. On the contrary, all that they can produce is a denial of the one and only true portrait. They can, of course, dishonour the divine election of grace; but they cannot overthrow or overturn it. They cannot prevent God from regarding them as from all eternity He has willed to regard and has actually regarded sinful men in His own Son. The fact that, in all its wickedness and deadliness, their attempt is powerless in the face of God's will and decree means that it is only conditionally and not unconditionally that it can lack this distinction, or, stated positively, that they can be "rejected." A limit is fixed by the fact that the rejected man, who alone and truly takes and bears and bears away the wrath of God, is called Jesus Christ. They can be only potentially rejected. They may indeed conduct themselves as rejected, but even if they deserved it a thousand times they have no power to bring down on themselves a second time the sword of God's wrath now that it has fallen. They are godless, liars; and they will not escape the rod of divine wrath. But this is also true, in its own way, of the elect. If the latter are not rejected, because of their election as it took place in Jesus Christ; if, although they incur the rod, they do not incur the sword of God; if they are not lost but saved so as by fire, then it is not to be expected of these others, again in view of the election as it has taken place in Jesus Christ, that truly and in the sight of God they are necessarily excluded from this distinction as by their lives they appear to be. We cannot say more than that this is not to be expected. But it would be to ignore Jesus Christ if we were not to say this of any others. It is just the elect who, in view of their own election and in view of the rejected One who has taken all their sins to Himself, have no option but to expect of others too that this distinction may also become theirs, no matter who they are or wish to be. The necessity of this expectation is clear as crystal when we consider what it is that differentiates the elect from others—their calling, the twofold work of the Holy Spirit. Like the election itself, this differentiating factor, the fulfilment of the election, is the will and work of God. But it is to the truth that witness is given when the elect are called. And the existence of the uncalled, the godless, is false witness. It is quite inconceivable that this false witness should have the permanence of the true witness. Where can it find the necessary strength in a world in which it has been objectively overcome by the death and resurrection of Jesus Christ ? The very fact that the calling of the elect is the mystery and miracle of God clearly means, with reference to others, that the barrier between their respective callings is not objectively insurmountable. It is certainly insurmountable for them, but not insurmountable for the act of God attested by the elect and called themselves. No man who has himself received the testimony of Jesus Christ will agree that it is in principle inaccessible to any other man. Nor will any man who has himself come to believe consider that the possibility of belief is ruled out for any other man. Even if he could accept their rejection—and this is quite impossible because he knows too well who is the rejected One—he could not under any circumstances accept their godlessness. How can he accept the idea that Jesus Christ has died and risen in vain for any other man ? So far as their godlessness is concerned—and Jesus Christ died and rose again for the godless—he can only await their calling. Here again we cannot say more, for the calling of others is as much an act of God as the calling of the elect. Here, again, however, it would be to ignore Jesus Christ if we were to attempt to deny to others the hope upon which the elect themselves are also exclusively dependent—and even more, if we were not prepared to regard them wholly in the light of this hope.

Both the necessary recollection for the elect and the necessary expectation for others mean, then, that we have every reason to consider the elect and others together for all their opposition. We cannot, at any rate, regard their opposition as absolute. For all its distinctive sharpness, the opposition between them can only be relative, because both are in the one absolute hand of God.

It is the election of Jesus Christ, as the beginning of all the ways and works of God, that necessitates both the recollection and the expectation, and therefore reveals the relativity of the opposition between the elect and others. But in the light of the election of Jesus Christ the opposition can also be more precisely stated. We began by assuming that there is a number of individuals who as such are elect, designated and distinguished by God, and differentiated by their calling from the others ; and in contrast to them there is a number of other individuals whose election seems to be called in question by the lack of its corresponding expression in life, or indeed to be directly denied by a contradictory expression in life, and in view of this we have described them as " rejected." This assumption is correct. There are, in fact, these two classes of men, the called and the uncalled, the believing and the godless, and therefore the elect and apparently rejected, the community of God and the world. According to the testimony of the Scriptures, both these lines are followed in human history, both as a whole and in detail. It is the history of the continually renewed consolidation, separation and encounter of these two peoples. But we must also observe that according to the same testimony of the Scriptures, the peculiar and primary history of these two peoples, and the peculiar and primary contrast between them, is not to be sought and recognised where the two peoples face one another as such, the " elect " and the " rejected." That which separates one from the other, and connects them both, is properly and primarily realised and revealed, not in the peoples, but where the elect and the rejected face one another in one and the same person—against one another, yet also for one another.

It is strictly and narrowly only in the humanity of the one Jesus Christ that we can see who and what an elect person is. It is He who is the man distinguished by this special relationship to God. It is His life which is the genuine fulfilment of genuine election. It is to Him that it is truly and essentially said : " I have called thee by thy name ; thou art mine." It is He who, in the midst of many others and in the same depths with them, is placed in a special situation and upon a special road. It is He whom God has called His Son and Friend, before and in distinction from all others. It is He who is the elect individual. If there are others who are also elect, it is as a result of and in virtue of the fact that He is originally and properly elect, and that they are included in His election. And if there are others who are also called, then it is in the fellowship of the Holy Spirit, who primarily and properly called Him, who primarily and properly is His God alone. The elect as such are His community : Israel and the Church ; the race of those who share in His election and who by their faith may execute, attest and confirm His election and calling. If we could or would disregard His election, we could understand and characterise all others only as rejected. Indeed, every " individual " in himself and as such would be rejected if it were not that his own election is incorporated in that of Jesus Christ, if it were not that Jesus Christ was elected for the very purpose of taking his rejection upon Himself, and therefore of removing it from him. This is what Jesus Christ willed to do and has done for him in the consummation of His own (and therefore the proper and primary) election. For the one who in himself and as such could only be rejected, He has secured and gained the status and right of an elect man, a child and friend of God. He has done it by taking upon

Himself the rejection which he had deserved. He could not be anything other than a rejected man if this had not been the will and act of God in the election and calling of Jesus Christ. And if his life were not the consummation, attestation and confirmation of the election and calling of Jesus Christ, if he were necessarily excluded from the fellowship of the Holy Spirit who is the Spirit of Jesus Christ, and therefore from the communion of saints—an uncalled man, godless man—what alternative could there be but the false life of a rejected man? It is to this extent that Jesus Christ is not merely one elect but *the* Elect, beside and apart from whom are no others but only the rejected. And He is this, the one and only object of the divine election of grace, in distinction from all others, in order that all others may not be rejected, and therefore for them.

But, again, it is strictly and narrowly only in the portrait of the one Jesus Christ that we may perceive who and what a rejected man is. It is He who—just because of His election—is cast out from the presence of God by His righteous law and judgment, and delivered to eternal death. In the genuine fulfilment of genuine election it is His life which is truly the life of the man who must suffer the destructive hostility of God. The peculiarity of the position which He occupies among all others is that He took it upon Himself to be this man. God has made Him who is uniquely His Son and Friend " to be sin." It is He who is the rejected individual. If there are others who are also rejected, then it is only in the evil, perilous and futile misunderstanding and disregard of the fact that He alone is truly this ; only in the godlessness which will not accept as a right the right which He has secured for them all. And if there are others who must also suffer in their own fashion—namely, the suffering which the wrath of God, wantonly and deceitfully conjured up, betokens for such as will not have it otherwise—the curse lying upon them can only be the echo of the curse which has fallen, not upon them, but upon Him in their place. Rejected individuals as such (those who live the life of the rejected) are the evidence of the sin for which He has made Himself responsible, of the punishment which He has borne. In the last resort, in so far as it seems to indicate their own perdition and abandonment by God, their witness can only be false. For to be genuinely and actually abandoned by God, to be genuinely and actually lost, cannot be their concern, since it is the concern of Jesus Christ. Therefore even this false witness cannot help pointing to Jesus Christ as the One who properly and actually was the lost and abandoned sinner, whose shadow lies upon them. Thus, for all their godlessness, they are unable to restore the perversity for whose removal He surrendered Himself, and so to rekindle the fire of divine wrath which He has borne in this self-sacrifice. In their sinning, and in their suffering as sinners, they can only be arrogant and yet reluctant participants in the rejection which He has averted from them by taking it upon Himself in the consummation of His election. They cannot help the fact that objectively and actually they are themselves witnesses to His election. It is not without Him that they, too, are what they are. It is only figuratively and secondarily that they can be what He alone is primarily and properly. He is *the* Rejected, as and because He is *the* Elect. In view of His election, there is no other rejected but Himself. It is just for the sake of the election of all the rejected that He stands in solitude over against them all. It is just for them that He is *the* rejected One (in His rejection making room for them as the elect of God), and therefore the one and only object of the divine election of grace. Thus Jesus Christ is the Lord and Head and Subject of the witness both of " the elect " and also of " the rejected." For all the great difference between them, both have their true existence solely in Him. It is in Him, who originally is both the Elect and the Rejected, that their mutual opposition finds its necessity. But it is not simply the relativity of their opposition which is established in Him, but also the fact that in all their opposition they are brothers, mutually related in their being and function, forming an inalienable and indissoluble unity. As the election of Jesus Christ finds its scope and completion in His representative rejection, and as conversely this very representative rejection confirms His election, so the elect and the rejected do not stand only against one another, but also alongside and for one another. Because they are not themselves Jesus Christ, but can only testify to Him, they stand both alongside and for one another without prejudice to their opposing character. They are mutually attached to one another. We can no more consider and understand the elect apart from the rejected than we can consider and understand the rejected apart from the elect. Neither on the one side nor the other can we overlook or ignore the hand of the One who is Lord and Head of both. And in spite of every difference, on both sides it is manifest who and what this One is. The elect are always those whose task it is to attest the positive decree, the *telos* of the divine will, the loving-kindness of God. And the rejected must always accompany them to attest the negative decree, that which God in His omnipotence and holiness and love does not will, and therefore His judgment. But it is always the one will of the one God which both attest. Both attest always the covenant which comprehends both, whose power is neither based upon the faithfulness of the elect nor to be destroyed by the faithlessness of the rejected, whose fulfilment is indeed proclaimed by the blessing heaped upon the elect but also announced, and therefore not denied but made the subject of a new promise, by the curse heaped upon the rejected. It is for this reason that the relationship between faithfulness and faithlessness, blessing and curse, life and death, cannot be measured as if some were simply bearers of the first and others simply bearers of the second. It is for this reason that the functions and directions and ways of the complementary figures intersect, as do also the figures themselves. It is for this reason that in their own way the elect are to be censured, while in their own way the rejected are to be commended ; that the former are not free from the judgments of God, and the latter do not lack signs of His goodness and patience. It is for this reason that the elect and the rejected, in spite of the greatest dissimilarities, can see that in many respects they are only too similar. It is not merely that in spite of the variety of their functions they operate together. On the contrary, they can exchange their functions. They are so closely attached to one another, and condition one another so intimately, that in the opposition of the two figures of the elect and the rejected the one figure of Jesus Christ is often more clearly discernible than the opposition itself. As it is the electing and calling God who distinguishes between them, the only possible distinction is that in which He alone is always the One who maintains His faithfulness towards both and for the benefit of both. It is quite impossible that anyone should escape either his responsibility to Him or God's responsibility for him and therefore in some sense be excluded from His election and His grace. Assuredly God is no respecter of persons. If He is present to His elect, this means that they must wrestle with Him as an enemy to be partakers of His blessing. It does not in any sense mean that He is not, in another way, with the rejected also. And if God hides His face from the rejected, He does not on that account cease to be their last and true refuge. If He is their enemy, that is only His characteristic form of presence among them. Where He exalts, there is also humiliation. And where He still strikes, He has not yet cast aside. Even where He is inscrutable in His severity and rigour, the divinely drawn difference between the elect and the rejected is the confirmation of the covenant which is the divine beginning of all things, the instrument of the work in which He embodies this covenant, the prophecy and the announcement of the difference between Himself and all men which He both set up and overcame in His Word made flesh, the grace in which He both vindicates Himself against every sinner and at the same time vindicates every sinner before Himself. God loves as He makes this distinction. This is how He loves His only Son. This is how He loves us in Him. If the proper object of His love is no other " individual " than this One, then apart from this One there is none who can be consumed by the fire of His love which is the wrath of God. It is the function of the many elect and the many rejected to indicate this love of God in its twofold nature. And the authorisation under which the latter stand as well as the former is to live—in their differing functions— by the fact that God has loved and loves and will love this One, and them also in Him.

In this connexion we have to consider in greater detail the witness to Christ in its first and basic form as prophecy and announcement ; the witness to Christ in the Old Testament.

We may again begin in Gen. 4, where the statement that God had regard to Abel and his offering is immediately balanced (v. 5) by the further statement : " unto Cain, and to his offering he had not respect." The difference between the two is not based on any previous mark of distinction between them, but clearly and from the outset it rests on a decision of God concerning them. But this first clear reference to the election by God of one individual man in distinction from another ought to warn us against concluding from vv. 4–5, where Abel is elect and Cain is not elect, that there is an absolutely negative statement concerning the latter. It is true that, according to v. 6, Cain and his offering are not accepted by God. To that extent he is not elect. And he becomes his brother's murderer, who as such must hide himself from God's presence (v. 14), as his parents had already done in Paradise according to Gen. 3⁸. Yet he is not abandoned by God because of this. A special mark and destiny seem to be peculiar to his existence too. He has the promise that God will protect his life. Singularly enough, the determination of Abel, of the offering which is well-pleasing to God, is a determination to death (the first human death mentioned in the Bible). It is that of Cain, of the man who is his brother's murderer and who, according to v. 13, knows that the punishment which he has earned must be greater than he can bear, which is a determination to life. For all the fact that their situations are so different and non-interchangeable, Abel and Cain do very largely enough stand for one another in their own place and fashion. We must remember this in some sense " classical " example when we proceed to examine the biblical situations in which the election of one man as distinct from another is concerned. Noah finds grace before the Lord (Gen. 6⁸) and " was found righteous before him in this generation " (Gen. 7¹). Then midway in the genealogy of Shem, the name Abram is made a word of blessing : " I will bless them that bless thee, and curse him that curseth thee ; and in thee shall all families of the earth be blessed," but on that very account he must also leave his country and relatives and his father's house (Gen. 12¹). This initiates a whole series, or rather a double series, of mutually intersecting differences. God will establish His eternal covenant with Isaac (Gen. 17¹⁹, ²¹) and not with Ishmael the first-born. Yet Abraham's prayer for Ishmael is heard, so that he is to live and be blessed and made fruitful (Gen. 17¹⁸, ²⁰). And although Esau is the older and favourite son of Isaac (Gen. 25²⁴ᶠ·), it is Jacob, the younger, who (by methods better not examined) must receive the birthright and the paternal blessing. But, again, this does not mean that the father has not also a blessing for Esau (Gen. 27³⁸ᶠ·) which in its own way is just as real, although its indication is rather to darkness. And although Jacob himself loves Rachel more than Leah, it is the " despised " Leah whom the Lord makes fruitful (and it is among her sons that we find Levi, the ancestor of the priestly family, and Judah, the ancestor of the royal family, Gen. 29³⁰ᶠ·). Yet Rachel does not continue barren. The disgrace is taken from her and she is the mother of Joseph (Gen. 30²³ᶠ·), who is dearer to his father than are his other sons (Gen. 37³). And the story of Joseph—his hidden superiority over his brethren, his betrayal to the heathen, his reunion with the brothers who had cast him down, the overwhelming kindness with which he makes use of his wealth and power in his dealing with them —is actually far more prophetic of Israel's future, far more Messianic, than the story of any of Leah's sons. And, again, there is in the case of Joseph's sons, Ephraim and Manasseh, who are adopted by their grandfather Jacob, a strange choice and distinction which is fully described in Gen. 48 : " And Joseph took them both, Ephraim in his right hand towards Israel's left hand, and Manasseh in his left hand towards Israel's right hand, and brought them near unto him. And Israel stretched out his right hand, and laid it upon Ephraim's head, who was the younger, and his left hand upon Manasseh's head, guiding his hands wittingly ; for Manasseh was the firstborn," v. 13 f. Jacob is blind ; so Joseph thinks he must correct his mistake : " And when Joseph saw that his father laid his right hand upon the head of Ephraim, it displeased him ; and he held up his father's hand, to remove it from Ephraim's head unto Manasseh's head. And Joseph said unto his father, Not so, my father : for this is the firstborn ; put thy right hand upon his head. And his father refused, and said, I know it, my son, I know it ; he also shall become a people, and he also shall be great : but truly his younger brother shall be greater than he, and his seed shall become a multitude of nations," v. 17 f. In the meantime, however, a completely different kind of distinction has arisen among the sons of Leah. Reuben " my firstborn, my might, and the beginning of my strength, the excellency of dignity, and the excellency of power " (Gen. 35[22], 49[2f.]), is not to be first, but " Judah, thou art he whom thy brethren shall praise ; thy hand shall be in the neck of thine enemies : thy father's children shall bow down before thee. Judah is a lion's whelp ; from the prey, my son, thou art gone up . . . the sceptre shall not depart from Judah, nor a lawgiver from between his feet, until Shiloh come ; and unto him shall the gathering of the people be." Yet we are told of Judah in Gen. 38 that his marriage to the Canaanite woman Shuah is in a real sense fruitless. For his son Er is displeasing to the Lord and dies before he can consummate his marriage with Tamar. The second son Onan then refuses to consummate a levirate marriage with Tamar ; and he, too, is displeasing to God and dies. Yet Tamar then becomes a mother in the most astonishing manner by her father-in-law Judah, and when finally her two sons, the twins Perez and Serah, are born, the second-born Perez takes precedence over his brother and is actually the first-born—the ancestor of David, and mentioned in Mt. 1[3] and Lk. 3[33] as the ancestor of Jesus Christ. The tradition could not be clearer as to the continually operative principle of the distinguishing choice ; the freedom with which this choice cuts across and contradicts all distinctions that are humanly regulated or planned on the basis of human predilections, and the relativity of the distinctions actually made ; the fact that those who are cut off, who are not distinguished by actual choice, are not on that account utterly rejected, but do in their own way remain in a positive relation to the covenant of God. The nearest approach to total rejection is in the case of Judah's sons, Er and Onan ; otherwise it is clear throughout that those who are first condemned are also blessed in their own way, and that in their situation on the left they, too, fulfil a divinely ordained destiny.

Yet strange to relate the divine election ceases to be an open differentiation between individuals with the end of the patriarchal tales of Genesis. The double series with its intersections does not continue into the historical sections of the rest of the Pentateuch and Joshua and Judges. Israel as a whole is now " separated from all the people that are upon the face of the earth " (Ex. 33[16]). Already during the plagues it is cut off by a " wall of partition " (Ex. 8[23]) from the Egyptians. Even here, of course, we still find traces of the relativity of the distinction between Israel and other nations. The Israelites must declare war against the Moabites and Ammonites, the most illegitimate descendants of Lot (Jud. 11[15], cf. Deut. 2[9, 19]). And it is from Moab that there comes the reluctant blessing of Israel by the lips of Balaam (Num. 22 f.), and even, according to Ru. 1[4, 16], 2[11], the great-grandmother of David. Even less does a positive relationship seem to be excluded in the case of the Edomite and the Egyptians : " Thou shalt not abhor an Edomite ; for he is thy brother : thou shalt not abhor an Egyptian, because thou wast a stranger in his land. The children that are begotten of them shall enter into the congregation of the Lord in their third generation." And in the person of Jethro (Ex. 2[15f.], 3[1f.], 18[1f.] ; Num. 10[29f.]), Moses' father-in-law, the race of the Midianites, which is otherwise described as completely hostile, appears in a strikingly close relationship to the way and destiny and even to the God of Israel. Finally, even among the native Canaanites, who were otherwise doomed to destruction, at least Rahab the harlot of Jericho (Josh. 2[1f.], 6[23]—and according to Mt. 1[5] she, too, is a forbear of Jesus) " did not perish with them that were disobedient, when she had received the spies with peace " (Heb. 11³¹), while through their craftiness the Gibeonites also escaped their fate : " And Joshua made them that day hewers of wood and drawers of water for the congregation, and for the altar of the Lord, even unto this day, in the place which he would choose."

If this is all that may be gathered on the question from the historical stories of this part of the Canon, it is all the more striking that in the ritual laws of Leviticus we are confronted by an unusually eloquent reminiscence of the conspicuously differing choices of Genesis. This is to be found in two sets of ritual instructions which are very different but obviously related in general structure. The first has to do with the ceremony for pronouncing a leper clean as described in Lev. 14⁴⁻⁷. In this regulation it is said that the priest has two clean and living birds brought to him, together with cedar-wood and scarlet and hyssop. One bird is killed over running water and its blood is caught in an earthen vessel. The other bird, however, is dipped in the blood of the first, together with the materials mentioned. Then the leper who is to be cleansed is sprinkled seven times with this blood, and the second, living bird is allowed to fly away. The second involves the ritual of the great Day of Atonement (Lev. 16⁵ᶠ·) in which two goats are treated as follows. To begin with, they are both placed " before the Lord," that is, at the entrance to the holy tabernacle. " And Aaron shall cast lots upon the two goats ; one lot for the Lord, and the other lot for the scapegoat. And Aaron shall bring the goat upon which the Lord's lot fell, and offer him for a sin offering : but the goat, on which the lot fell to be the scapegoat, shall be presented alive before the Lord, to make an atonement with him, and to let him go for a scapegoat into the wilderness " (v. 8). According to v. 15 f., the blood of the first goat—when this has first been done with the blood of a bullock—is sprinkled seven times within the sanctuary upon and before the slab that covers the ark (Luther : the mercy-seat, the ἱλαστήριον), and then upon the altar outside. And in this way expiation, or a covering, is made for the uncleanness and trespasses of the people. According to v. 21 f., the second goat, however, is dealt with as follows : " And Aaron shall lay both his hands upon the head of the live goat, and confess over him all the iniquities of the children of Israel, and all their transgressions in all their sins, putting them upon the head of the goat, and shall send him away by the hand of a fit man into the wilderness. And the goat shall bear upon him all their iniquities unto a land not inhabited : and he shall let go the goat in the wilderness."

We can understand the law for both these rites (and the sacrificial law of the Old Testament generally) when we perceive that sacrifice accompanies the history of Israel (as does prophecy in its own manner) as a sign and testimony of the divine intention which underlies it and guides it to its goal, and therefore of the meaning of the events and sequences of events in which this history proceeds. The law and the detailed regulations governing the performance of sacrifice have the function of exhibiting and guaranteeing the character of sacrifice as a sign and testimony by the most precise systematisation possible of the legal form which is appropriate to the sacrifice of this people.

At any rate as they are systematised in Lev. 14 and 16 it is obvious that the following form is common to both. Two creatures which are exactly alike in species and value are dealt with in completely different ways. The selection of the one for this and of the other for that treatment, seems to be a matter for the priest in Lev. 14¹⁵ᶠ·, while lots are cast in Lev. 16⁸. In both cases it is obvious that the selection is inscrutable, and that it is really made by God Himself. It is also obvious with what special purpose and meaning these two acts accompany the history of Israel, and to which special moment of this history they refer as sign and testimony of the divine intention. We obviously face the special aspect of this history according to which it is the history of the divisive divine election of this and of that man. What these choices mean, or what it is to which the whole history of Israel points as a history of such choices, is attested by these particular rites, the witness being given a fixed and permanent form by the detailed legal regulations.

The actual treatment of the two creatures makes this even clearer. Both Lev. 14 and 16 say that one creature is to be used, and that the other is not to be used—or only used to the extent that it is, so to speak, solemnly and necessarily not used. One creature is slain, that is, and the other is allowed to go free. It is too soon to ask what is really meant by using and not using, by slaying and releasing. It is also too soon to ask who is meant by the creature which suffers the first fate, and who by that which suffers the second. But if we study the transaction as such in its general nature, we can hardly fail to recall the Genesis stories of Abel and Cain, Isaac and Ishmael, Jacob and Esau, Leah and Rachel and so on. The ceremonies are obviously a comment on the history of Israel as a history of the differing choices, and its character as witness is fixed in the legal instructions which relate to these actions.

Lev. 14 and 16 also have this in common—that the ceremonies both attest a purification. The purification of Lev. 14 consists in the confirmation by the priest, in his capacity as a medical expert, of the cure of the leper. In Lev. 16 it consists in the removal of sin from the entire nation, to be verified by Aaron or the high priest. Note that the rites as such do not complete but attest a purification which has already taken place, is still taking place, and takes place again. Neither the priest nor Aaron, but God, is its author. *Solius Dei est peccata remittere. Quid igitur homini restat, nisi ut testis sit ac praeco gratiae divinitus collatae ? . . . Interea tamen hoc non obstat, quominus suo quodam modo sordes populi abluant, qui vocati sunt ad docendi munus. Nam quum sola fides corda purificet, quatenus recipit quod ex ore hominis profert Deus testimonium, minister, qui nos Deo reconciliatos esse testatur, merito censetur abolere nostras sordes* (Calvin, on Lev. 14, C.R. 24, 325). We must take account of the fact that not only in respect of the rites themselves, but also in respect of that which they attest and therefore in respect of those stories of election, their occurrence as the acts or sufferings of certain men denotes and attests the purposes and acts of God towards the people of Israel. That this is so emerges already from the fact that the Israelite who as an individual or as the whole nation is the particular object of the purification in question is both here and according to the whole sacrificial legislation no more than a spectator, as it were, of the actions which represent this purification. These actions ignore him as the principal and are concerned exclusively with the creatures. They are addressed to him in that there is shown him in the treatment of the creatures the nature of the treatment which God intends for him and to which He has already in fact subjected him and will subject him ; and what will eventually and finally emerge as the meaning and result of his history, educed and manifested by God. They confirm for him, as simple pictures, that he is himself, with his pictorially explained history, called and intended to be a witness to that which will become true and benefit him, not as his own work, but in the objectivity of the mighty acts of God.

The common content of the rites prescribed in Lev. 14 and 16 is only to be understood, however, if we observe their inner differences ; the differing emphasis with which the two sets of laws testify to the same facts, or comment upon and clarify the same witness (the history of Israel, as the history of this divisive choice). The use and non-use, the slaying and releasing of the two creatures are common to both rites, but they possess a different meaning in each case.

In Lev. 16 the purification of the nation as represented in the treatment of the two animals is understood from the standpoint of the presupposition essential to it, the way leading up to it, and the means employed to attain it. What is important is not so much the nation's new status of reconciliation to God as the fact that a reconciliation is necessary if the nation is to be transferred to this new status, and that there is in fact this reconciliation. It is not the purpose for which the death and blood of the first goat are used, and which they serve, but the fact that they actually are used, and must and may serve. The intended and promised purification presupposes — and it is this presupposition which is fulfilled by the grace and loving-kindness of God, and for which He Himself and by Himself has provided as the wise and omnipotent Judge—that man as the sinner, man in his impurity and therefore as the object of His wrath, must and may die. It is this redemptive endurance of death as such, ordained and accomplished by God in His love for him, which is brought before his eyes in the slaughtering of the different animals on the Day of Atonement, and therefore in the slaying of the first goat, and then in the blood-sprinkling of the ark of the covenant and the tabernacle, in the sanctification of the sanctuary by the slaying of the first goat, by the total outpouring of its life as accomplished in the shedding of its blood. Man is chosen for the Lord, and not for Azazel, not for the wilderness ; and God has made it His own concern that there should be visited on him the redemptive suffering and death by which the presupposition of his purification and renewed life is secured. He may—and this is God's great love— totally surrender his blood, that is, his impure life. The redemptive method by which God leads him is that he is placed under the utter graciousness and terror of this law of death. In the first goat, destined by lot for the Lord, he who as an elect man is distinguished from others can and does recognise himself, namely, that God wants and requires him, for the surrender of his blood, but that for this very reason and in this very way he wants and requires himself. Himself ? We may and indeed must ask : How does this come about ? For man is flesh. He is impure and a transgressor. The whole nation and all the elect stand before God as those who have forfeited their relationship to Him by their sin. But the power of the grace of God which is portrayed here reposes exactly in the fact that the man who is lost before God is actually acceptable for the presentation of this offering as the man he is ; that God truly sees him in all his lost condition, and in his relationship not to Him but to Azazel, to the wilderness, and that He places him as such under His judgment and on the way to life. But here, of course, we have an identity which the picture itself cannot reproduce, and which is also not to be seen in its historical counterpart, that is, in the history of the distinguishing choices as such. On the contrary, both in the picture and the fact indicated by the picture a duality is demanded. There have to be two creatures and two men, to whom the one thing intended and to be represented by both distributes itself as a duality. Therefore in the picture, the ritual of the Day of Atonement, the one usable creature is accompanied by a second and unusable. Or rather it is accompanied by a creature that is solemnly used in its very unusability. The death of the one, which is, in fact, full of grace and salvation, is accompanied by the life of the other, which is, in fact, the essence of desolation, indeed of death itself. The fact that man is of himself unfitted for the service of God, and his blood valueless, is revealed in the treatment of the second animal. His life cannot make good that which is evil by any judgment which follows him, or even by his death. It is not, indeed, a joyful release into freedom which is the lot of this man, but a flight into the realm of Azazel, the demon of the wilderness ; his surrender to an utterly distressful non-existence, to a life which is as such no life. That is where you properly belong !—is said to the nation in the treatment of this second goat, with its banishment to the wilderness. It is from thence that you have been taken and called, and apart from the grace of God you could never find yourself elsewhere, nor know any other life than this life in the shadow of death. But the grace of God has now led you forth from that place. That which was promised you in your elect ancestors, and is now revealed in the picture of the first goat used for sacrifice, is that God leads from darkness into light, from the wilderness into the land of promise. This certainly does not contradict the fact that those who are not chosen must also be regarded as witnessing that the wilderness and the darkness are the regions from which the grace of God leads forth His own. Those who are not chosen do not testify in their existence only and primarily to their own sin, but to the sin and punishment of every man ; and it is therefore laid upon the head of the second goat, the one not used for sacrifice, so that he may take and bear it away before all eyes to the place where it belongs, and where it is its own punishment, far from the community, into the wretchedness of the wilderness. Incapable of purification ! Unworthy of sanctification ! Useless for the redemptive sacrifical death that wins the reconciliation and opens the way to a new life ! Useful only for a life that is no life at all ! That is the sentence which is pronounced upon the second goat, and which is carried out by his banishment. It is the image of the non-elect as they (Cain, Ishmael, Esau) stand apart from the elect ; the embodiment of man as he is in and of himself, as he is even now without the grace of election ; the demonstration of what is the sole possibility and future of this man. Yet we must observe that the second goat is also " placed before the Lord," that the treatment meted out to him and the tragic record of his unusability also form an integral part of the sign and testimony set up on the Day of Atonement. Cain is just as indispensable as Abel, and Ishmael as Isaac. For the grace which makes an elect man of the first can be seen only from the second, because the first, the elect, must see in the second, the non-elect, as in a mirror, that from which he was taken, and who and what the God is who has delivered him from it. It is only as one who properly belongs to that place that God has transferred him from it. Because election is grace, the unused belongs to the used, the sacrificed goat to the goat driven into the wilderness, the non-elect to the elect. We have to remember that they are both of them " placed before the Lord." We have not to remember this only in the case of the first goat, the man chosen for the Lord.

The ceremony described in Lev. 14 obviously runs in exactly the opposite direction. That which is of importance in the purification based on the divine election of man is not manifested here in the first bird which is slain but in the second which is released. In order that he may become pure and therefore a new man, that he may be free from the terrible limitations of the existence of the leper branded by the wrath of God, that he may be exonerated from his expulsion from the congregation, that grace may descend upon the sentenced, and that he who was repulsed by the wrath of God may be accepted, it is, of course, necessary—for, according to this picture, renewal can take place no less radically—that man should die, that his blood should be shed to the last drop. His pure new life can be born only through such a total surrender of his previous impure life. The treatment of the first bird speaks of this necessary presupposition of his purification. The bird is slain, its blood is shed and then made ready for what follows, as in the case of the first goat in Lev. 16. But this time everything really depends on what follows, i.e., the purpose for which this death and blood shedding are used and which they serve, namely, that the second, surviving bird is dipped in the blood of the first, together with the pre-scribed articles of which at least the cedar-wood and the hyssop, signifying the largest and the smallest things, together exhibit the totality of the object purified. The healed leper is sprinkled seven times with this blood, while simultaneously the second bird is allowed to fly away " into the open field," i.e., across the surface of the field, to freedom. Thanks to the fact that the first bird has yielded its life and blood for the purification of the second bird, the latter is actually pure, and freedom may and must be given it—and when the healed leper is sprinkled with the same blood, he is told that he is now removed from the realm of the divine wrath, and is once more a free member of the congregation. " The bird, that feared greatly for itself in the hand of the priest, now flies joyfully out of it " (C. Starke, *Synopsis Biblioth. exeg. in Vet. Test.*, 1763, Vol. I, p. 1605). If E. Geibel had been referring to this bird in his song,

" The lark arose on Easter morn," much of the criticism that we can level against it would certainly have to be modified. This bird undoubtedly signifies the resurrection, the grace of God directed to man, the freedom given to him, the life restored to him, his radical purification and renewal, for the sake of which he himself must first and inexorably die. He himself ? We have no real picture here, or analogy in Israel's history, for this identification of the slain and the living, any more than we have of the identification intended in Lev. 16 between the sacrificed creature and that which is not sacrificed because it is unusable. But in the picture given in the ritual of Lev. 14, as also in the stories to which the picture is related, there have to be two (two animals and therefore two men) to which the one thing which both signify and represent imparts itself as a duality : the *use* which is made of the death of the one ; and the *purpose* for which it is used—the life of the other. The one has necessarily to die in order that the other may live. And this is the real point of the differentiation in the stories of election. The purpose, and the only purpose, in the death of the one bird, the separation and reservation of the one man, is that the other may live. But how comforting it is for all who are separated and reserved that, according to Lev. 14, it is to the second bird, which has no part in the accomplishment of the decisive action, and which is unusable in the sense of Lev. 16, that the benefit of the sacrifice of the first and usable bird accrues. That which was done to the first turns to the advantage of the second. Dipped in the blood of the first bird and therefore itself unhurt, partaking in the salvation accomplished by its death, it is transferred to freedom as a confirmatory sign that the purification of the leper has been achieved and his new life in the congregation has begun. The former is clearly used for the benefit of the unusable. The recipient of the fruit of election is obviously the non-elect. How can we fail to see that Cain and Ishmael and Esau are now given yet another right than that which is remotely visible in Lev. 16 ? They are witnesses to the resurrection reflected in Lev. 14. The promise addressed to the men on the right hand is manifestly fulfilled in those on the left. The one exalted by God through his election is humbled unto death in order that the one humbled by God through his rejection may be exalted. The humbled is not there merely as a dark shadow to emphasise the light in which the exalted stands. He is not related to him merely as poor Lazarus to the rich man, for the sake of the crumbs that fall from his table. For just what is the wealth of the one exalted by his election ? In what does it consist, except that he gives it away, that he pours forth his life and blood in his sacrifice, that he becomes poor ? It is for this purpose and this purpose alone that he is used. This is the greatness and glory of his election. He becomes poor that the other, the poor, may become rich through his poverty. He dies that the other may rise and live. Where then, in the mirror of Lev. 14, in the picture of the second bird springing to freedom from the blood of the first, is there even the remotest appearance of any unrighteousness of God towards the non-elect ? If, according to Lev. 16, the non-elect, those who are separated and rejected, stand in the shadows in order that the grace of God may illumine and continue to illumine the elect, we are also taught by Lev. 14 that it is into the realm of Azazel that the light of God's grace is poured and streams abroad. Let us gratefully know ourselves to be elect in the picture of the first goat of Lev. 16— grateful that we are accepted to sacrifice ourselves, grateful that we may suffer the saving judgment of the wrath of God, which is the wrath of His love, as only the elect can and may do ! But let us with equal gratitude recognise ourselves as the non-elect in the picture of the second bird of Lev. 14—grateful because there is ordained for us the life for whose painful birth the other is elected, the resurrection for whose sake the elect must go to his death !

After this analysis of the differences in the two passages in their differing features, we now return to their relationship and common content. Both are concerned with the will and way of God with men, and both affirm that death and life are decreed by God for man ; first death, then life. Death is the saving judgment of God, which is necessary in the operation of His grace towards man and therefore exhibits His love for him, and through which he is cleansed and led into life. Death is the sacrifice willed and ordained and accepted by God in His goodness to man. The life of which these two passages speak has two possible meanings in contrast to the unequivocal meaning of death. It may be the wretched life of man that does not deserve this death and does not partake of the salvation secured by it. But it may also be the new liberated life of the man who has merited this death, and by means of it passed through to his salvation. In these passages, moreover, both death and life always refer to the one complete man, and that which fellowship with God means for him as such. We can see at once the whole inscrutability of the reality which is attested by both passages. It consists first in the fact that we obviously do not know the death which is here spoken of as a work of the divine love for man, as an honour and distinction which by it are conferred on him, as a purification out of which a new and better life issues for him. We do not know the man of whose death it can be said that it is this saving sacrifice, and who can on that account be described as the elect of God. The predicates which are here applied to the death of man, and therefore to man himself, make of the death, as well as of the man who dies, a reality which wholly and utterly transcends the realities of death or man as known to us. And the same is true of the life described in our passages. We know neither the man who is now really and finally cast out into the wretched realm of Azazel, nor the one who is really and finally transferred to freedom. What we know as life is a reality limited in both its negative and positive aspects. Just as no Israelite could recognise himself directly in the slaying of the first creature, so none could recognise himself directly in the expulsion or release of the second. In the latter aspect, too, what the picture portrays transcends the human reality known to us in this aspect as well.

From this inscrutability of the matter it follows at once that it cannot actually happen to man. This death and life are too superhumanly great to be exhibited to the Israelites otherwise than in the picture of this sacrificial ritual. They are too great to be expected of the Israelites themselves or enjoined on them. And the biblical stories of the elect and the rejected do not exhaust the matter in any of its aspects. What is depicted as the destiny of these elect and rejected persons is never congruous with the death and life described in these passages. On the contrary, their destiny too obviously points beyond itself to a reality which is in no way fulfilled by the elect or rejected persons as such or in themselves. This reality can only be attested by these stories, as by the ritual described in the passages. It can be addressed to man only in the form of a picture. It can be spoken to him—and the stories serve this purpose as well as the ceremonies—as a word of truth, as a revelation of the reality hidden from him. It is in the Word of God, and only in this Word, and then in faith in this Word, but also only in this faith, that that death and life become man's own experience.

But there is another inscrutability here, namely, that of the unity of what is attested. Let it be supposed that we knew the death which is the judgment of God's grace, which is a saving sacrifice, to suffer which is pure honour and hope, the meaning of which is the election of this slain man. Let it also be supposed that we knew the man whose life is now truly purified from leprosy, who was in the realm of Azazel and who will be in the realm of freedom. The question still remains how we are to recognise ourselves simultaneously in both the one and the other. If man may die by the grace of God, how then can he still live, whether in the realm of Azazel or in the realm of freedom ? And if by the grace of God he may live, first in the darkness and then in the light, first a wretched life and then a joyful life, why then must he still die ? What Israelite could think of the ritual of the purification of the leper at the very moment when the atonement ritual was administered, or *vice versa* ? Obviously the fact that we have here a single reality, the one grace of God which has decreed life and death for man, is no less hidden than the grace of the death and life themselves and as such. This shows us again how the matter attested transcends the reality known to us. But from the inscrutability of the unity of this fact it also follows necessarily that it should be attested to us in at least two, or more exactly four, pictures. We cannot see either the death or the life simultaneously, even in the picture. We have to listen to two words in all the distinction which is peculiar to our two passages and their obviously conflicting standpoints. The one looks back from the saving death to the lost life which is annulled by it, the other forward from the same death to the new life created and won by it. And each of these pictures has to speak of two aspects, one of which must attest the saving death, and the other the old lost life and the new life that has been won. The stories of the elect and the rejected, to which these sacrificial rituals are primarily related, do not escape the same duality. Hence it is clear enough that the stories themselves are only witnesses—confirmed by the counter-witness of the ceremonies; repeated, as it were, in the ceremonies—and that they, too, point beyond themselves. Always in these stories the one figure represents only the elect of God, used by Him, and the other only the rejected of God, not used by Him. But then there are, of course, the intersections, in virtue of which the relationship seems suddenly to be reversed, and suddenly and in spite of everything God reveals Himself to the rejected and unused. This shows how inherently fluid are the testimonies of these stories, so that we are prohibited from too hastily identifying the elect with certain persons, or too hastily identifying the rejected with other persons in the stories. But all the same, even in this fluidity, they are always the stories of two figures, and speak with just the same emphasis as the present passages of what is always the completely different divine treatment of these characters. Cain is not also Abel, nor Jacob Esau, nor Rachel Leah. Yet always in one of the characters God's election is manifest, as an election which genuinely divides. The stories to which the ceremonies of our passages are related have, therefore, the same provisional character as the ceremonies themselves. And in this way the Old Testament as a whole, in this matter at least, is determined as the witness to a reality of which, even in the Old Testament itself, we can only say positively that it is that which it attests, its true and proper subject.

We are faced, therefore, by a twofold enigma in connexion with the subject of the Old Testament witness. On the one hand, it consists of the inscrutability of the death and life of the man to whom both the sacrificial rituals, and the election stories of Genesis upon which they comment, refer. On the other hand, it consists of the inscrutability of the unity of this man. Since the commentary in the sacrificial rituals makes it clear that in the election stories we are concerned with this one slain and living man, it cannot and does not try to set aside the riddle either of his death and life, or of his unity. On the contrary, the fact that this twofold riddle is present in the election stories is only brought out with any force by the commentary given in the sacrificial rituals.

These data confront us with the following choice. On the one hand, this subject of the Old Testament witness may be regarded as an unknown quantity. This might mean that for some reason it is not yet known to us, whether because it has not yet made itself known, or has in fact taken place but has somehow escaped us. But it might also mean that the Old Testament has no subject at all, that its testimony points into the void, and that in the place to which its stories and sacrificial pictures (and the prophetic announcements of salvation or doom) all point, there is, in fact, nothing, so that there is nothing to see, and never will be anything to see. On the other hand, the subject of the Old Testament witness may be accepted as identical with the person of Jesus Christ as it is seen and interpreted and proclaimed by the apostles because He had Himself revealed and represented Himself to them in this way. The choice between these two possibilities is not an exegetical question ; it is a question of faith. It is, therefore, to be distinguished from exegesis. But it is inescapably posed by it ; and in the answer to this question, whatever it may be, exegesis is forced (even in the form of a *non liquet*) to speak its final word.

If we assume that the question is to be answered positively, the older Christian investigation of the Bible was quite right to see both in Lev. 14 and 16 and also in the election stories of Genesis prophecies of Jesus Christ, pictures and stories which find their meaning and fulfilment in Him. So far we ourselves have not followed the example of this older exegesis. For we have kept the name of Jesus Christ in the background, preferring to let the Old Testament text, which could not utter His name, speak by and for itself. But this very method has led us to the conclusion that in the last resort the text leaves us with an enigma ; that the subject of which it obviously speaks is inscrutable ; i.e., that it is not to be met with in the human realm of Old Testament events and ideas ; and indeed that it wholly transcends human reality in every dimension, although it offers itself as a human reality. Of course we cannot say that these passages are prophecies of Jesus Christ merely because we are left with an enigma and we happen to know about Jesus Christ, who, according to the New Testament witness, is precisely that which is so puzzling here, the riddle itself, and in His being its solution. It is not enough that as the open secret He fits in at the very place where the exegesis of the Old Testament text can only halt with a penultimate word as it encounters the subject of the text, which as such does not stand in the text but, so to speak, over against it. On the contrary, we have to recognise that a conclusion of this kind is not conclusive as such, because the unknown quantity, whose emergence can be the only sure result of Old Testament exegesis as such, can still be explained quite differently, in spite of what we think we know about Jesus Christ. Indeed, it may not be a real subject at all, but—simply nothing. Only the positive decision of faith in Jesus Christ (as the only way really to know Him as the One He is) can vindicate the older Christian exegesis of these texts as prophecies of Christ. But by the positive decision of faith that excludes unbelief, this exegesis is rendered not merely possible but even necessary. How can we believe in Jesus Christ and not of necessity recognise Him in these passages ? How can we believe in Him and ignore the subject of which they speak, or suppress the final word of their exegesis, namely, the designation of their subject, and therefore the naming of the name of Jesus Christ ? In the decision of faith, then, we have an advantage over the exegesis which does not know this decision, or which thinks to be non-committal in the matter. For we speak the final word, i.e., we are able to specify the theme of the passages. We need not stop short, therefore, with the conclusion that they are enigmatic or an indication of the unknown quantity confronting us, but can conclude with its solution. We must know what we are doing in this—it is just a question whether this was always understood in the ancient Church—but we may also do it in accordance with what we know.

We will proceed, then, on this presupposition. The elect individual in the Old Testament, so impressively and yet in so many different ways distinguished, set apart and differentiated in the Old Testament stories and pictures, is always a witness to Jesus Christ, and is indeed a type of Christ Himself. It is He, Jesus Christ, who is originally and properly the elect individual. All others can be this only as types of Him, only as His prototypes or copies, only as those who belong to Him, only as considerable or inconsiderable, strong or weak members of His body, only as chastised or blessed, humiliated or exalted citizens of His community, only as in different ways His witnesses. In this sense, Jesus Christ is each of the four creatures in Lev. 14 and 16. We have seen how each of them in its own way is equally important and indispensable for the denotation of the reality described in these rituals. The fact that there are more than one in the passages, that the passages speak of two creatures, and necessarily speak of them, as has been shown, in such differing ways in Lev. 14 and 16, is simply because they are prophecy, which as such cannot yet speak of the fulfilment and therefore of the one Jesus Christ. And in the same sense, Jesus Christ is the open secret of the reality of the slain and living man which so utterly transcends the reality of Old Testament man or of man in general. The fact that this is not visible in the passages is simply because they are prophecy, and cannot as such attest the fulfilment as is done in the New Testament witness.

Calvin's exegesis of Lev. 16 is therefore correct: *Utriusque figuræ veritas in Christo fuit exhibita, quia et agnus Dei fuit (cuius immolatio delevit peccata mundi) et, ut κάθαρμα esset, exstinctus fuit in eo decor et reiectus fuit ab hominibus (C.R. 24, 502).* The meaning and the purpose of the election of Jesus Christ consists, indeed, in His honour and glory as the blameless and spotless lamb, foreordained before the foundation of the world to the shedding of His precious blood (1 Pet. 1[19f.]), to the offering of His life in place of many, to become poor that they might become rich. According to His divine nature, Jesus Christ is the eternal Son who reposed in the bosom of the eternal Father, and who coming thence took our flesh upon Him to be and to offer this sacrifice, for the glory of God and for our salvation, and by taking our place to accomplish our reconciliation to God. But as such and in the accomplishment of this reconciliation He is, necessarily, the Rejected. Like that second goat, He must suffer the sin of many to be laid upon Him (and it is the faith of His Church that it can and should lay all its sin upon Him), in order that He may bear it away : out from the camp into the greatest shame (Heb. 13[12f.]) ; out into the darkness, the nothingness from which it came and to which alone it belongs ; and just as radically away from the many, that it may no longer and never again be to them a burden. For this, in our flesh, according to His human nature, as the Son of David, He must be the Rejected. He must be delivered up by His people to the heathen, descending into hell, where He can only cry : " My God, my God, why hast thou forsaken me ? " There is, indeed, no man who partakes of the glory of the Lamb foreordained of God. There is no man who partakes of the shame and abandonment of the one abandoned by men according to the will of God. For how could any man partake of both at the same time ? But in Him, who was very God and very man, in perfect unity, the glory and the shame and abandonment were reality, one reality.

In the same way, the older exegesis was quite right to find in Lev. 14 the prediction of that which is fulfilled, according to Rom. 4[25], in the fact that Jesus Christ " was delivered for our offences, and was raised again for our justification." " Delivered "—that is the amazing, the deeply hidden honour which is given to the first bird, but which properly belongs to the man Jesus Christ, not because He is impure—it is the leper who is this, and the many on whose behalf he is delivered up—but just because in His obedience He is so pure and consequently so usable an offering. In this very purity of His, in His humanity which is sinless in virtue of His obedience, He now steps into the place of the leper. He Himself now is the leper, and He dies the death without which the latter cannot be purified. But it is He and He alone who is also the cured leper, the second bird lifting itself into freedom. For—slain and bathed in His own shed blood—He leaves death behind Him in the revelation and proclamation of the complete righteousness and purity of those for whom He has died ; as in virtue of His divinity, distinguished as the Son of God from all others, He rises from the dead (Rom. 1[4]), so that with Him they may walk in newness of life (Rom. 6[4]). Here, again, there is no man who is delivered up as He is. Of what value would it be to deliver up any other ? Nor has any risen as He has done. For where would he find the power to rise ? And how could any man have been or become at one and the same time both the humiliated and the exalted ? But in Him, who was at the same time very God and very Man, the humiliation and the exaltation were reality, one reality.

Those who think they must reject this as the final word in exegesis of Lev. 14 and 16 must either undertake to prove another and better final word in explanation of these passages, or they must admit that they do not know of any, and therefore that ultimately they do not know to what or to whom these passages refer. The same has necessarily to be said about the election stories on which these passages are simply a commentary. If, according to this commentary, the stories deal with a reality, and indeed a single reality, then the man who in these stories is inscrutable, who transcends all humanity as we know it, who is beyond the always twofold form in which he is revealed in them, is the one man Jesus Christ, who as such is the Son of God. It cannot easily be denied that according to the witness of the New Testament Jesus Christ both came down from heaven and ascended into heaven. And descended, He both lives by the grace of God and is branded by the wrath of God. He both claims the world as His own and is rejected by His own. And, since all this is the will of God, He is both the Elect of God and the Rejected of God, rejected because He is elect and elect in His rejection. But if this is so according to the exegesis of the New Testament, then we must understand the election stories of the Old Testament, if at all, as a prophecy of Christ even in their striking duality. In other words, we have to recognise Jesus Christ not only in the type of Abel but also in the very different type of Cain ; not only in the type of Isaac and his sacrifice but also in the very different type of Ishmael and his expulsion and miraculous protection ; not only in the type of the chosen stock of Leah but also in the very different chosen stock of Rachel ; not only in the type of the Israelite nation but also in the very different type of the excluded and yet not utterly excluded heathen nations. When we say " but also," this does not exclude but involves the fact that we do not recognise Him in any of these types in exactly the same way as in the others, but that in all of them we have to recognise Him as He is. None of the types gives quite the same witness as the others. None simply repeats the witness of the others. The historical multiformity of individual elect and non-elect, of those placed on the right and those on the left, cannot be ignored, and no sound exegesis can afford to ignore it. It cannot be glossed over. It cannot be reduced to a formula. It cannot be simplified. But this multiformity of historical appearances is best observed and maintained if here too the final word in exegesis is actually the name of Jesus Christ, if He is understood as the individual in whom we recover both the unity of that which they all commonly attest, and that which is the peculiar individuality of each.

We can clarify the problem and solution of the differentiating choice of God in that section of the Old Testament where it re-emerges historically with a distinctness which in contrast gives all the corresponding material in the patriarchal narratives of Genesis the appearance of mere intimation—namely, in the opposition of the figures of Saul and David which constitutes the theme of both Books of Samuel.

The key to what the Old Testament is trying to say and attest in the story of these first two kings of Israel is found in the consultations described in 1 Sam. 8 between God and Samuel on the one hand and between Samuel and the people on the other hand. From the First Book of Samuel onwards the decisive concern of Old Testament history is with kings, that is, with the king of Israel. Admittedly, there is a continuing concern for the totality, the twelve tribes of Israel and all their families and individual members, whose entry into the promised land and whose first experiences and deeds there had been described in the books of Joshua and Judges. But already there are indications of a division of this totality into two Israelite kingdoms. For according to Jud. 19-21 the tribe of Benjamin is isolated from all the others when it is threatened with total annihilation and then preserved. Later, of course, it is Judah (2 Sam. 2[1f.] ; 1 K. 11[13], 12[20]) which replaces it in this special situation. But, again, from now on it is no longer the case, as in the earlier stories (despite the leadership of Moses, Joshua, the Judges or Samuel himself), that the congregation of the people as such is the real partner of God in His dealings with Israel. It is now the king who steps into the foreground as the representative and head of the people. And it is the special task of the last of the older ("charismatic") leaders, Samuel, to proclaim and inaugurate this new order. It is by his hand that the first two kings are anointed, that they become χριστοί. This explains the peculiar prominence given to the figure of Samuel by the account of his antecedents. It also underlies the contrast between him and the figure of Eli the priest, and the downfall of the house of Eli (1 Sam. 1–4), which obviously brings the old epoch to an end, as is confirmed by the fact that, according to 1 Sam. 7$^{1f.}$, the sons of Samuel himself are not the judges whom Israel needs. Since the exodus from Egypt there has been no event so climactic as this, that Samuel must anoint the first king, and shortly afterwards the second. This is epoch-making. The way in which this crisis and this event becomes possible and necessary is described in 1 Sam. 8.

In studying this chapter, we must not be misled by any impression that the creation of a human monarchy in Israel was in itself contrary to the will of God ; that it was, so to speak, forced through by the foolish people, or reluctantly conceded by God. This is certainly not the view of the tradition at this point, for with the greatest consistency and clarity it takes its stand on the insight that everything decisive, that is, everything which has now to be recorded about the events and relationships between God and His people, happens between God and the king. This new order does not originate in an interruption or hindering but in a revelation of the hitherto concealed will of God. It is with this revelation that 1 Sam. 8 deals. Certainly the means and the mouthpiece of this revelation are at first wholly and exclusively the folly of the nation, which wants a *melek* of the same kind as all other nations (8$^{5,\ 20}$), who will judge and lead them and fight their battles (8^{20}). Samuel is certainly justified when this demand displeases him (8^6)—more justified than he himself realises, indeed—for it is not himself, as he thinks, but God whom the Israelites have rejected by their demand, in the same way as they have repeatedly rejected God since the exodus from Egypt (8$^{7f.}$, 10^{19}, 12$^{17,\ 19}$). It is certainly a judgment, therefore, which is decreed and executed upon them when God bids Samuel comply with their demand (8$^{7,\ 22}$, 11^1) : " Now therefore behold the king whom ye have chosen, and whom ye have desired ! and, behold, the Lord hath set a king over you " (12^{13}), with all the dangerous rights possessed by such a king (8$^{10f.}$). " Ye shall cry out in that day because of your king which ye shall have chosen you ; and the Lord will not hear you in that day " (8^{18}). Against his judgment, Samuel will give them the king chosen and desired by them, according to their godlessness, but also—be it noted—according to the command and ordinance of God. And, according to 1 Sam. 9–10, it is the choice of God and not in any sense of the nation which introduces this king, the choice which falls on Saul, the son of Kish, of the tribe of Benjamin. It is, of course, significant even at the outset that Samuel is not led to seek and find Saul in his father's house, as in the later case of David, but that Saul meets Samuel, almost coming to hand as it were. He himself does not know what he is doing. He is simply looking for his father's asses. He is then chosen as future king by lot at the national assembly of Mizpah, and " when they sought him, he could not be found," but has first to be dragged forth from a hiding-place that he himself has chosen (10$^{20f.}$). " Hath not the Lord anointed thee to be captain over his inheritance ? Thou shalt reign over the Lord's people and save them out of the hand of their enemies round about " (10^1). " He shall save my people out of the hand of the Philistines, for I have looked upon my people, because their cry is come unto me " (9^{16}). This is manifestly the positive will of God for Saul. This is God's plan for him, and it cannot fail. It will be scrupulously fulfilled. There is neither irony nor reserve in the statement that God changed Saul's heart (10⁹), that the Spirit of God came upon him (10¹⁰, 11⁶, 19²³), and the saying, " Is Saul also among the prophets ? " (10¹², 19²³) certainly does not have any suggestion of the ludicrous according to the tradition—Saul is, in fact, one of the prophets. Those who despise him and bring no gifts on the day of his election really are good-for-nothings (10²⁷) who are spared only by his magnanimity (11¹²). He does, in fact, defeat the Ammonites, the Amalekites and the Philistines. He does, in fact, accomplish everything that Israel could expect of its king, according to the will of God. And nowhere does he conduct or exhibit himself as a godless man. As he sees it, it is only too urgently necessary that the proper sacrifices should be offered to God (11¹⁵, 13⁹, 15²¹). He shows indeed a tendency towards too great a ritual severity, which almost leads him to cause his own son Jonathan to make atonement by death (14²⁴, ³⁸ᶠ·). He extirpates the soothsayers and wizards from the land (28⁹). And after he has sinned he is no less sincere than David shows himself to be later on in the same situation, making confession and imploring forgiveness (15²⁴, 24¹⁷ᶠ·, 26²¹ᶠ·). " And Saul worshipped the Lord "—the account of his fateful sin closes with these words (15³¹). Furthermore, let us remember that Saul also knows full well of David's future righteous rule. Just because he pursues him with the resolve to slay him, he is all the more —involuntarily but in fact—a testimony to it, and therefore a prophet of the final intention of God (18⁸, 23¹⁷, 24²¹, 26²⁵). Nor does Samuel omit to honour him as king before the people even at the very moment when he must tell him that God has withdrawn His hand from him, and is going to take his kingdom from him (15³⁰ᶠ·). He is not David, and therefore he is not the true king, but David above all, even when he is persecuted and threatened by him, does not fail to recognise him as the Lord's anointed as long as he lives, always regarding and treating him with honour, refusing to harm him and strictly preventing his companions from doing so (24⁷, 26⁹ᶠ·). And after his death, Saul is still treated by David as sacrosanct. Vengeance is executed at once on his ostensible murderer (2 Sam. 1¹⁴), and a solemn lament is made for Saul and his son Jonathan : " Ye mountains of Gilboa, let there be no dew, neither let there be rain upon you, nor fields of offerings : for there the shield of the mighty is vilely cast away, the shield of Saul the anointed ! " (2 Sam. 1²¹). " Ye daughters of Israel, weep over Saul, who clothed you in scarlet, with other delights ; who put on ornaments of gold upon your apparel ! " (2 Sam. 1²⁴). And for his sake the death of his son Ishbaal has to be avenged by David (2 Sam. 4). If we look back from this to 1 Sam. 8, where it all begins, where it is already shown how the existence of this first king of Israel is brought about, we certainly cannot deny that the grace of God, concealed of course under the judgment of the divine concession, is the significance and intention of this concession, the purpose which the nation must serve in all its folly and godlessness. What the nation itself desires and intends—to have a ruler and helper to judge it and lead it in war—is, in a way very different from what it intends or desires, the desire and intention of God long before the nation has grasped or expressed this thought. This is only confirmed by the outcry which so rightly displeased Samuel on that day in Ramah—confirmed as man in his folly always confirms the desire and intention of God, and (even involuntarily) is compelled to do so. The folly of the Israelites and their rejection of God at Ramah do not consist in the fact that they demand a king—in this the voice of the people is the voice of God to which the prophet must submit—but in the fact that they demand a king who is so totally different from the one God wills them to have and has already decreed for them. What they demanded and desired was a human kingship in distinction from the kingship of God, opposing and in a sense complementing it. They wanted a hero and leader from amongst themselves, an exponent of their national power, a symbol of their national unity, a personal guarantor of their national security and hope, a man of their own choice. It is, of course, to be noted that they did not simply get this man at Ramah. This is decisively contradicted by the whole story of Saul. Saul is very different from the kings of the nations. He is different from the ideal king who was the theme of Ramah. He goes his way expressly as one who is elect and marked by God, who is truly and authentically anointed by the authentic prophet of God, who is consecrated and sanctified for God, who seeks to meet God and seeks His word, who voluntarily or involuntarily carries out His will at every point, and who is marked like Cain before him so that none may touch him until the end decreed for him by God, whose death is to be avenged sevenfold. Saul unmistakeably bears the character of the king whom God has decreed for His people, against their will and intention, but for their salvation. If we read 1 Sam. 8 as it relates to all that follows, we cannot possibly overlook the fact that the exercise of the right of kings over their subjects, so formidably summarised in vv. 11-17, played no notable part in the story of Saul, nor did the people complain, as predicted in v. 18, about the burden of the monarchy. If this happened at all—as was possibly the case later on under Rehoboam (1 K. 12)—it had no interest for the Old Testament writers at this point. They seem to have understood Saul's reign throughout, not as a mere failure, but, in its non-fulfilment of that threat, as a proof in its own way of the grace of God to His people. The people had indeed committed " a great wrong "—as is sharply reiterated in Samuel's farewell speech (12$^{10 \cdot 23}$)—with their desire for a king after their heart. But as the Lord does not reject them for His name's sake, Samuel would consider it to be a sin against the Lord if he were to cease to pray for the nation. This, then, is the sign under which the kingship of Saul also stands. Already in the figure of this its first king, Israel has received something other and much better than it had wished for itself. In king Saul God has not returned Israel evil for evil, but instead of the evil which it sought and which it thereby did, He has given good. The goodness of the kingship announced and foreshadowed in the old stories, through Moses, Joshua and the Judges, is now revealed in accordance with the forgiving thoughts of God and not the arrogant thoughts of man.

But of course—in view of 1 Sam. 8, and especially of all that follows—it certainly cannot be denied that the figure of Saul stands in shadow, and more in shadow than in the light which is also there. He is not yet the true king of Israel. True, there seems to be a moment when the opportunity and the possibility are given for him to show himself as such. Although formally originating in that " great wrong," the reign of Saul does not exclude the possibility that the king and the nation may fear the Lord, and serve Him faithfully and wholeheartedly. " For consider how great things he hath done for you " (12^{24}). Among these great things the text obviously means to include the divine choice and appointment of Saul. Thanks to the grace which is already the significance of his kingship, there had now to be a new and genuine fear and service of God. " If ye shall still do wickedly, you shall be consumed, both ye and your king " (12^{25}). It is obviously excluded in fact that Saul makes proper use of the opportunity and possibility given. The fact that his kingship actually brings about the threatened evil, that Saul can only be the representative and regent for the true king, David, that he must ultimately fall and himself prepare this fall from the beginning—all this is just as obvious and necessary for the Old Testament presentation, which understands it to be just as God-intended and God-ordained, as the earlier institution of the monarchy itself through the " great wrong " of the whole nation. The holiness of God requires that the revelation of His grace, victorious over all human sin, should not take place without the revelation of His judgment upon sin ; in this case, upon that " great wrong." The instrument of this aspect of God's revelation of His grace is the person of Saul the Benjamite. Throughout, there is no disguising the fact that the sins personally committed by Saul—which bring from Samuel, on divine authority, the immediate and irrevocable rejoinder that he has forfeited his kingship—are actually microscopic sins. To this very day we find it difficult to stifle the sympathy and approval which are more readily felt than their opposite in relation to what Saul does. The first occasion has to do with a burnt-offering which has to be presented at the beginning of the Philistine war, and which Saul himself offers and performs because Samuel's arrival is delayed and the enemy is already advancing. The reply is : " Now thy kingdom shall not continue : the Lord hath sought him a man after his own heart, and the Lord hath commanded him to be a captain over his people, because thou hast not kept that which the Lord commanded thee " (13^{14}). And the second occasion has to do with the incomplete execution of the ban on the Amalekites. Saul has spared king Agag, and he and the people have also spared the better part of the cattle captured from the Amalekites. We then read how this Agag died : " Then said Samuel, Bring ye hither to me Agag the king of the Amalekites : and Agag came unto him delicately. And Agag said, Surely the bitterness of death is past. And Samuel said, As thy sword hath made women childless, so shall thy mother be childless among women. And Samuel hewed Agag in pieces before the Lord in Gilgal " ($15^{32f.}$). May it not be that even this Agag, standing in twofold shadow, does momentarily proclaim the conquest of death, that he is a witness to the resurrection—in a very different way from his prophetic opponent ? But how does this help him ? And how do all the reasons and excuses, even all the confessions of guilt and prayers, help king Saul, who had not himself at the right moment done the difficult thing which Samuel now does ? The reply of Samuel, the reply of God, to Saul's conduct, is as follows (and not one iota is to be retracted) : " Hath the Lord as great delight in burnt offerings and sacrifices, as in obeying the voice of the Lord ? Behold, to obey is better than sacrifice, and to hearken than the fat of rams. For rebellion is as the sin of witchcraft, and stubbornness is as iniquity and idolatry. Because thou hast rejected the word of the Lord, he hath also rejected thee from being king " ($15^{22f.}$) ; " And Samuel came no more to see Saul until the day of his death ; nevertheless Samuel mourned for Saul " (15^{35}). This grief of Samuel's is the last gleam of light on the figure of Saul. Now we have to remember that everything that can really be said against Saul emerges in these two sins. For when it is subsequently said of him that the Spirit of the Lord abandoned him, that an evil spirit from the Lord troubled him (16^{15}, 18^{10}), which made him hate and envy David and more than once come near to murdering him, and which made him become the actual murderer of the priests at Nob ($22^{6f.}$), we have to remember that all that is not regarded by the tradition as part of the sin on whose account Saul is rejected, but is itself the outworking of this rejection. It is because the Spirit of the Lord abandons him, because an evil spirit from the Lord torments him, that he raves to his end, more than once recoiling from his own actions against David ($24^{17f.}$, $26^{21f.}$), and most passionately longing to hear again, through the dead Samuel, the word of God that has been denied him (28^{15})—until finally by his suicide, a dark prototype of Judas Iscariot, he necessarily fulfils his course in his own downfall and that of his son, and has to confirm it after his death in the inevitable collapse of his house (2 Sam. $3^{1f.}$), even to the delayed vengeance of the Gibeonites upon his descendants (2 Sam. $21^{1f.}$). Why this particular career ? How utterly different in its grossness and flagrancy is the later sin of David as compared with these sins of Saul ! But the contrast between the microscopic sins of Saul and his rejection as king emerges just as surely and deliberately in the tradition as does that between the crimson sins of David and the immutability of his election. Quite apart from everything that must be said for or against Saul, it is clear that the monarchy revealed in the decision of God at Ramah (1 Sam. 8) can have (only) the appearance which it has in Saul. For it does not manifest God's grace apart from His judgment. It manifests the judgment and wrath of God against all man's ungodliness and unrighteousness in the midst of grace. It manifest the judgment of the grace of God. Saul was " a choice young man, and a goodly : and there was not among the children of

Israel a goodlier person than he : from his shoulders and upward he was higher than any of the people " (9²). In this respect he expresses what the nation expected of its king. He can thus fulfil the nation's ideal. But exactly as such he is a sinner and must fall and die. This very ideal can only be destroyed, because and as God's peaceful intentions for this people are revealed, because and as the true king is to be given to it. In order to live and die as this ideal, Saul must first become king. For that which is intended and desired by this national monarchy is from the outset and intrinsically not merely different from, but contrary and hostile to, the one and only monarchy of God. " Ye said unto me, Nay ; but a king shall reign over us : when the Lord your God was your king " (12¹²). This No must be broken with the revelation of the divine Yes of the kingdom instituted by God, which does not compete with God's own kingdom. And in order to represent this Israelite No and at the same time the fact that it is broken by the divine Yes, Saul must first become king. No gross, no blatant personal sin of Saul is needed to exhibit this negative aspect of the grace of the kingdom willed and created by God. All that needs to be seen is that he is just the person and ideal which the nation has foolishly imagined, and can only imagine, as its king. And it is this which is made evident in the double sinning which is microscopic to human eyes, but gigantic and absolutely decisive in God's·eyes. Saul himself will sacrifice. Saul himself will represent the reconciliation between God and His people. Saul himself will furnish the conditions for a prosperous national existence in the presence of its enemies, and therefore for its peaceful life in the promised land. And according to the command of God he ought to have stood back before another, and, in the person of that other, before God Himself. But what Israel expected of its king was that he should be head and shoulders taller than themselves, that he should lead them in active competition with the kingdom of God. And this is what Saul did and revealed in the innocent impatience of 1 Sam. 13. Again, when he has carried out 99 per cent. of the will of God in relation to them, Saul attempts a partial compromise, a modest *modus vivendi*, with the world of other kings and nations and gods that surrounds him and Israel, even though they confront him in their worst form in the Amalekite king, and according to the command of God the sanctification of the promised land can be accomplished only with the complete extirpation of the alien. But that the king should be head and shoulders taller than them, and that he should lead them in this second, passive competition with the kingdom of God, in the small adjustments and accommodations (*adaptation intellectuelle*) to the foreign world which seemed alone to make physical or spiritual life possible in Canaan—that is what Israel desired of its king, and what was actualised and expressed in Saul according to 1 Sam. 15. Saul personally did both these things in what may be described as an almost or totally innocent manner. He did both with what was humanly a thoroughly respectable conviction and method. But in both he is an exact portrayal of the monarchy which has made itself independent of the kingdom of God, which is in competition with the latter both in what it does and what it does not do. He is a portrayal of the national kingdom which must be destroyed as such at the very point where God had resolved and was about to inaugurate and reveal the kingdom by His grace and not the grace of man. It is because Saul is the representative of Israel in both this activity and this passivity in relation to God's command, not because of the magnitude or scale of what he does but because he actually does it, and as Israel's king does it representatively, that his rejection for these sins comes on him as a just punishment, and the Spirit of God must leave him and make way for an evil spirit, as it had earlier come on him and changed his heart. These personal sins, the microscopic sins which he commits, suffice to make it clear that Saul shares the guilt of Israel's " great wrong." But it is his royal dignity, his royal office, that God should lay on him the sin and guilt and punishment of that great wrong, that they should become his personal concern, and that it is not between God and the people, but rather between God and himself, that they are fought out and decided. Saul is absolutely indispensable to the Old Testament as the person of the sinful, guilty and punished king of Israel. He is necessary because of the holiness of God's grace. If there were no Saul, with his evil spirit sent from the Lord, delivered up to an insanity which inevitably makes him David's enemy and persecutor, and therefore the embodiment of the whole rebellion of Israel as such, as of its inner impossibility, its destruction by God's wrath, then there could be no David either, no true king of Israel given by the grace of God—the king who does not compete against the Lord as the one and only King, but who keeps His commandments and is therefore a human witness to this one and only King.

When we turn now to the remarkable figure of David, as presented in the Old Testament, we must observe no less than in Saul's case two differing sets of traits, a dual character, a determination which in his case, too, points in differing directions. David is no more unambiguously a figure of light than Saul is unambiguously the offspring of darkness. There is something of Saul in David, just as there is something of David in Saul. We must undoubtedly see both in each, and therefore in the total picture of these so sharply distinguished individual portraits we have to see twice two and therefore four figures in order to see what the Old Testament seeks to show us in this total picture. But in David's case, the emphasis is quite different from, indeed the very reverse of what it is in Saul's. If the story of Saul is the real story of the actual establishment of the Israelite kingdom, if in any sense it can stand automatically and independently before and beside the story of David, we could and should have serious reason to doubt whether the divine sanction of a human kingdom in Israel, described in 1 Sam. 8, really has the meaning of what is in the first instance, of course, a supremely hidden divine act of grace, and not merely that of a *derelictio* (although it is that also), or whether the interpretation of it given in 1 Sam. 12²² is correct : " The Lord will not forsake his people for his great name's sake ; because it hath pleased the Lord to make you his people." But we cannot entertain any such doubts in view of the fact that while the beginning of Saul's story is indeed conceivable without the story of David, its continuation is conceivable, and is in fact transmitted, only in its relation to the latter—while the story of David, in its beginning and right up to the death of Saul, is quite inconceivable apart from that of Saul, to which it is still firmly connected far beyond the latter's death. Even if the traditions about both characters may at one time have existed separately, the meaning of both was properly understood when they were interwoven and worked in the whole in our present texts. According to the total picture, David was, as it were, ready behind Saul from the very first : " The Lord hath sought him a man after his own heart, and the Lord hath commanded him to be captain over his people, because thou hast not kept that which the Lord commanded thee " (1 Sam. 13¹⁴). " In time past, when Saul was king over us, thou wast he that leddest out and broughtest in Israel : and the Lord said to thee, Thou shalt feed my people Israel, and thou shalt be a captain over Israel "—this is how he is addressed at Hebron (2 Sam. 5²ᶠ·) on the occasion of his elevation to be king over all Israel. But at the outset and for a long time it does not really look like this. David is not this ideal, not the most handsome man in Israel, head and shoulders taller than the rest, whom the people scarcely need to see before they break out in jubilation and shouts of Long live the king ! —as is recorded of Saul (1 Sam. 10²⁴). The fact that the women in their dances sing the song about him : " Saul hath slain his thousands, and David his ten thousands," certainly testifies to his popular celebrity as a guerilla leader, but not to his coming kingship. The signs of this kingship as such are at first, and for a long time, concealed from the nation. The man who recommends him to Saul as one who can comfort him by his music in those demonic attacks : " Behold, I have seen a son of Jesse the Beth-lehemite, that is cunning in playing, and a mighty valiant man, and a man of war, and prudent in matters, and a comely person, and the Lord is with him " (1 Sam. 16¹⁸)—does not know that in this way, and especially in the closing words, he is describing the marks of the king chosen by God. And though there are, so to speak, moments, inspirations and utterances of a prophetic nature, when he is spoken of as the future king by Jonathan (1 Sam. 23¹⁷), Abigail (25²⁸), Saul himself (24²¹) and—not without treachery to Saul's family—Abner (2 Sam. 3¹⁷), it is far more significant for his kingship that at first and for a long time it is hidden from all human eyes. In this concealment, in the fact that at first David may and must be wholly obscured by Saul, we have a repetition of Jacob's preference for Rachel over Leah, and the whole subsequent ascendancy of Benjamin, the Rachel tribe, over Judah, the Leah tribe. It is only before God—but actually and effectively, of course, as seen by God—that Bethlehem suddenly emerges and Judah comes to the forefront in the person of David. For this purpose a special mission is necessary (1 Sam. 16¹ᶠ·). For in the first instance, according to the will of God, the lot had actually fallen on the tribe of Benjamin, and within this tribe on Saul, and Samuel himself had said to the nation in accordance with the principle of this first choice : " See ye him whom the Lord hath chosen, that there is none like him among all the people ? " (10²⁴). And even when he stands among the sons of Jesse in Bethlehem, as he sees Eliab, the eldest, his thoughts run again in the accustomed direction, the direction of Saul : " Surely the Lord's anointed is before him." And he has to be admonished : " Look not on his countenance, or on the height of his stature ; because I have refused him : for the Lord seeth not as man seeth ; for man looketh on the outward appearance, but the Lord looketh on the heart." So it continues with all seven sons of Jesse, until it is clear that " the Lord hath not chosen these." But when David, the youngest, is recalled from the sheep-run, the words follow at once : " Arise, anoint him : for this is he " (16⁶⁻¹²). This is confirmed to David himself in the prophet Nathan's great speech of institution and promise (2 Sam. 7⁸) : " I took thee from the sheepcote, from following the sheep, to be ruler over my people, over Israel." And it may also be seen in the fact that David does not overcome Goliath in Saul's armour (1 Sam. 17)—in which he could not even move—but with the shepherd's equipment, the staff, the pouch, the sling. This is he. But why ? We can only answer with the tradition : Just because he, Jesse's youngest, the little shepherd, is definitely not suitable to be the mighty king of Israel ; just because he so completely does not express the ideal picture which Israel had seen at Ramah, and the fulfilment of which had actually been given them in the person of Saul ; just because he was so utterly incapable of doing justice to the necessary intentions of the human choice of a human king. But this means : Just because he was definitely not the king by whose idea and actuality the rule of God over Israel was denied and rejected. Or positively : Just because he was the one whose heart—not his disposition or character, but his real status before Him—God had seen, or rather perceived, and recreated by the omnipotence of His vision, of His divine eye ; the shepherd who as such, i.e., in virtue of the lowliness of this his human status and employment, who in pursuance of this most dependent, most humble, most menial shepherd rule, alone could be the shepherd of Israel as well. This one, a shepherd like this, was the gracious thought of God when He sanctioned the fulfilment of the foolish wish of the nation.

It is from that point of view, then, that we must understand the whole course and status of David as the true king of Israel, first secretly and then openly elected. It is necessary that he should first go through that long period of concealment. It is necessary that he himself should not lift a finger to shorten that period ; that he should prefer to let himself be driven to the southern heathen ; that he should prefer to serve the Philistines (21¹¹ᶠ·, 27¹ᶠ·, 28¹ᶠ·, 29¹ᶠ·), rather than to tread the path of rebellion against Saul's government; that he should prefer to expose himself to constant perils of death rather than shed Saul's blood. It is necessary that he should show absolute reverence for Saul as the Lord's anointed, not only throughout his whole life, but even after his death. All this is necessary because he is the elect of God as distinct from the elect of man or from any self-election ; because he cannot seek its confirmation through men, but can only in fact find and receive it—at the moment of its divine confirmation. Further, it is necessary that he should be persecuted unto death by Saul as the (divinely instituted) bearer of the kingship by Israel's grace, and be continually saved only as by a miracle from the fate planned for him. " There is but a step between me and death " (20³). " The king of Israel is come out to seek a flea, as when one doth hunt a partridge in the mountains " (26²⁰). This is as necessary as the condemnation of Jesus at the hands of Pilate, who himself did not act without the power given him from above. For only as one harried unto death and delivered from such distress by God does David seal with his being the decree of God that he shall become the prince of a people which is itself continually harried but also continually delivered. And it is further necessary that not only in respect of Saul, but in general, David should not be bloodguilty, as is visible in his remarkable last instructions (1 K. 2). In his own person he is again to manifest the divinely elected king in the fact that it is really left to God to avenge him fittingly upon his enemies. The fact that for this reason David orders the eventual removal of his most loyal, but bloody assistant Joab, and that this Joab is buried in the wilderness (1 K. 2³⁴), is of a piece with this. In short, it is necessary that the being of David should exhibit a series of features which, as far as any palpable likeness is concerned, make him absolutely and consistently dissimilar to the typical figure of the oriental *melek* of the period.

If we are to penetrate to the heart of that which makes David an elect figure of light in the sense in which the tradition seeks to portray him as such, we have only to think of the continuing intercourse which he has with God, of the questions which he puts to God (e.g., 1 Sam. 23²ᶠ·, 30⁸, 2 Sam. 1⁵, ¹⁹, etc.), and to which, in distinction from Saul, he always receives a helpful divine reply. The simplest and at the same time the fullest statement of his selection to be king is that the Lord is with him, as is stated in the first characterisation (1 Sam. 16¹⁸) and frequently thereafter—an anticipation of the Messianic name " Emmanuel " of Is. 7¹⁴. Directly related to this is the wild procession (described in 2 Sam. 6) when the ark was carried into Jerusalem and David—" with all manner of instruments made of fir wood, even on harps, and on psalteries, and on timbrels, and on cornets, and on cymbals "—" danced before the Lord with all his might ; and David was girded with a linen ephod," at the head of the whole house of Israel. Also related to it is the record that his wife Michal, Saul's daughter, is punished by barrenness because she despised the spectacle of David. " I will dance before the Lord, which chose me before thy father, and before all his house to appoint me ruler over the people of the Lord, over Israel ; therefore will I play before the Lord. And I will yet be more vile than thus, and will be base in mine own sight : and of the maidservants which thou hast spoken of, of them shall I be had in honour " (6²¹ᶠ·). It is to be noted that this frenzied outburst on the part of the elect is quite unrestrainable and has its justification wholly in itself. But it is also to be noted that we can see here the law which controls the whole life of David : humiliation and exaltation even as he abases himself more, even as he does not let himself be restrained in his course—which in its own way is just as irresistible as the course that led Saul to his death—but only incited to it afresh and more wholeheartedly by the mockery. But this helps us to see why everything else is so obviously necessary that makes David a radiant and even more radiant figure rising out of the darkness. There are certain moral traits which we have to consider in this connexion. In the first description of his character it is already affirmed that he is " a valiant and warlike man " (1 Sam. 16¹⁸). But he could also play the lyre. He was a kind of minstrel of God, as is also seen in the dance of 2 Sam. 6. Both here and elsewhere this is probably more important for the tradition than his military valour or his eloquence, to which little special reference is subsequently made. The superiority of David over Saul, the fact that he is the true king by God's grace as contrasted with his predecessor and regent, is summed up in the picture of 1 Sam. 16²³ : " When the evil spirit from God was upon Saul, David took an harp, and played with his hand : so Saul was refreshed, and was well, and the evil spirit departed from him," to which we have to add at once the second, sinister picture of 18¹⁰ᶠ·, when on just such an occasion Saul takes his spear with which to pin David to the wall. " But David avoided out of his presence twice . . . because the Lord was with him, and was departed from Saul." Notice how beautiful and comforting is the contrast of the first picture, how grimly humorous that of the second, and how both are complementary. It is not, then, with the sword but with the harp in his hand that the tradition sees the elect justified before the rejected, the king by God's grace victorious over the king by Israel's grace—in the one case embodying the loving-kindness of God towards him, in the other exposing his sin and its impotence, but in both cases David the music-maker. For this reason the fact that no less than seventy-three (according to the LXX, eighty-five) hymns in the canonical psalter were ascribed to David is much more interesting than the critical problem of the historical justification for this ascription in individual instances. Even if we calmly accept the possi-bility that hardly half our psalms are even pre-exilic, and that only very few of them could originate as early as David—indeed, even if we calmly accept the possibility that perhaps in none of these do we have a text fashioned by David himself, the fact is all the more emphatic and expressive that from the age of David, and increasingly as this age receded, the cultic community in Israel associated and even identified itself more and more consciously and deliberately with this second, the true king of Israel, when in its singing and playing it sought to adore and worship the beauty of God in its own distinctive, non-plastic way. Now it is this minstrel of God who is also the warrior *par excellence*, sent and equipped by God. The classical illustration is in the meeting with the giant Goliath : " Thou comest to me with a sword, and with a spear, and with a shield : but I come to thee in the name of the Lord of hosts, the God of the armies of Israel, whom thou hast defied " (1 Sam. 17⁴⁵) : " And he slew him ; but there was no sword in the hand of David " (17⁵⁰). We have to remember this when we read the further account of David's military successes : first in the service of God (18⁵) ; then as the leader of a volunteer corps or mercenary group under the direction of the Philistine prince Achish (27⁸ᶠ·) ; then on his own account as a vassal prince of Ziklag—against the Amalekites, whom according to the tradition he apparently defeats so crushingly that the Old Testament never mentions them again, and this at the very time when Saul, who had spared the Amalekites, meets his fate in the lost battle against the Philistines on Mount Gilboa (30¹ᶠ·) ; then, after he has himself become king, as the conqueror of Jerusalem (2 Sam. 5⁶ᶠ·) ; and finally as the victor not only over the Philistines (5¹⁷ᶠ·) but also, according to the glowingly imperialistic chapter 2 Sam. 8, the Moabites, the Edomites and other surrounding nations. As we can see already from the older historical records from Ex. 17⁸ᶠ· on, there is no contradiction in the fact that it is God who fights for the Israelites, and that the Israelite bravely grips and wields his sword in obedience to His command and implicit trust in Him. These two things are so unified in the figure of David that in fact we can only see them together. Yet both are so related in the tradition that the whole light does not proceed from the sword of David, nor does it fall on him as the daring commander and royal general of Israel, but it proceeds from God and therefore shines on God as the One whose wars David is conducting for the salvation of the nation, which is not his people but God's. Equally significant for this aspect of his fame, as significant as his previous active warfare, is the fact that after 2 Sam. 10 David, as commander-in-chief, withdraws behind the figure of Joab, and that he really plays only a passive role in the war against the Ammonites (2 Sam. 10), which provides the background for the story of his sin (2 Sam. 11–12), and in the overthrow of the rebellions under Absalom and Sheba (2 Sam. 15–19, 20). The tradition evidently predicates of David both that he was the mightiest warrior, and again that he was no warrior at all but only the spectator of Yahweh's wars, so that in the last resort he is just as inconceivable and useless for worldly militarism as for worldly pacifism, and has as little to do with the preaching of a passive trust in God as with the preaching of a self-confidence in which man takes his "rights" into his own hands and seeks to defend them in his own strength. Finally, it is to be noted that his most significant military achievement is apparently the least important—namely, the capture of Jerusalem. Jerusalem was an old city-state marked out neither by geography nor by its previous history to play any particularly important role. It lay off the main highway, and was politically decadent. So far it had escaped the general appropriation of territory, almost as if it had been forgotten. And according to 2 Sam. 5[6f.], it was taken by David neither for Judah nor for Israel but for David himself, acting again and for the last time at the head of the free corps whose captain he had been until his elevation. It was to be his own city, the city of David. And it was only now—not after the death of Saul (2 Sam. 1[1f.]), nor after his election by the tribe of Judah (2 Sam. 2[4f.]), nor again after his election and anointment by all Israel (5[1f.]), but only after the conquest and occupation of this mountain lair, Jerusalem—that David perceived that "the Lord had established him king over Israel, and that he had exalted his kingdom for his people Israel's sake" (5[12]). And it was from this relatively neutral third place, as the king dwelling and enthroned in his city of Jerusalem, that he became at the same time the king of Judah and of Israel. And in this connexion there occurs, in the further development of the story, what is indeed a remarkable shift of emphasis, in so far as 1 K. 11[13, 32, 36], 14[21] and 2 K. 23[27] expressly name Jerusalem and not David as the actual object of divine election ; the place where the name of God is to abide. In 1 K. 8[16] the relationship is described in this way : "I have chosen Jerusalem, that my name might be therein : and I have chosen David to be over my people Israel." Clearly the choice of Jerusalem and David's own election are related to one another in just the same way as the dwelling-place of God's name in the midst of Israel is related to David's rule as a human king over the same Israel. He is elected because of God's choice of His own dwelling-place in the midst of Israel. He, on his throne, can only be and is the sentry before the throne of God Himself. That is why he has to capture Jerusalem, and make it his city, the city of the king, and therefore the city of God ; for the human king is there in order to attest that God Himself possesses and has moved into His dwelling in Israel—one chosen by Himself, and not by any geopolitician. Therefore even in this relatively imperialistic aspect the peculiar lustre of the Davidic kingdom is characterised as the lustre which the God of Israel, and not he himself, possesses and sheds about Him. The tradition can also glorify David because he "executed judgement and justice unto all his people" (2 Sam. 8[15]). "The God of Israel said, the Rock of Israel spake to me, He that ruleth over men must be just, ruling in the fear of God : and he shall be as the light of the morning, when the sun riseth, even a morning without clouds : as the tender grass springing out of the earth by clear shining after rain" (23[3f.]). It is said in praise of him by the mouth of the woman of Tekoa : "As an angel of God, so is my lord the king to discern good and bad" (2 Sam. 14[17]), and : "My lord is wise, according to the wisdom of an angel of God, to know all things that are in the earth" (14[20], cf. 19[28f.]). In a presumably later layer of the tradition (2 Sam. 23[13f.]), there is attributed to him the trait of magnanimity towards those who are loyal and valiant on his behalf which we know to be paralleled almost verbally in the story of Alexander the Great. And it is frequently emphasised that his good fortune (1 Sam. 18[5, 14, 30]), his continually increasing prosperity (2 Sam. 5[10]) and his fame (2 Sam. 8[13]) are bound up with the fact that God was with him. The builders of Hiram, king of Tyre, are already working for him (5[11]). But it is to be noted that this whole aspect of David—righteous government, wisdom, good fortune and wealth—is only a dim prototype of the glory with which his son Solomon is (one-sidedly and conspicuously) resplendent. The kingdom of David is the kingdom of the Lord, not of the triumphant but of the militant and suffering Church. It is not devoid of elements of triumph. In particular, it is not devoid of the lustre of the climax of 2 Sam. 5–8, which commences with the capture of Jerusalem and the bringing up of the ark. And to this climax there is attached, most fittingly, and with profound inner meaning, David's loyal and merciful action towards the crippled son of his dead friend Jonathan, as described in 2 Sam. 9. The lustre of David is now reflected upon the family of Saul and therefore upon Saul himself, the unfortunate representative of the kingdom by Israel's grace, and therefore also upon the whole people itself in its great wrong against God. For if we may see in this climax a correspondence to the transfiguration narrative of the Gospels, then even more definitely may it be seen and said that the radiant figure of David, though it is this from the beginning and as it is manifested as such, is always related to Saul, his opponent in life and in death, as his son Solomon is not ; that it is only to be understood together with this other figure, and therefore only in the shadow which this casts upon it. We never see in David a portrayal of the direct and unambiguous human glory which is found in the case of Solomon, unless, of course, we read it into the story.

David has something of the aspect of Saul too. Even in this aspect he is always David, and as such completely distinct from Saul. God is with him—as from first to last He was not, and could not possibly be, with Saul—because of that which the latter had to represent. This emerges in his Saul-aspect even more clearly, if possible, than in the aspect facing away from Saul, which has so far been our concern. But in David, too, we must also see that the divine grace of the monarchy, which took shape in his person, is the grace addressed and given to a sinful nation, which of itself is always ensnared in that great wrong and in itself utterly lost.

We begin with the most impressive feature if we consider first the friendship, or rather the covenant, between David and Jonathan. It is no accident that in the tradition this relationship is viewed and described from the solemn standpoint of a covenant. The question is one of a " covenant of God " (1 Sam. 20[8]), i.e., of an agreement in which God Himself stands continually as a witness between the two parties (20[23, 42]), and which binds them under this condition to mutual loyalty. It is this covenant of God which is concluded between David and Jonathan. And like a promise in respect of the other between Yahweh and Israel, which is continually broken by one partner, it is actually kept and fulfilled by both until and beyond death. " The soul of Jonathan was knit with the soul of David ; and Jonathan loved him as his own soul " (1 Sam. 18[1], cf. 20[17]). And " I am distressed for thee, my brother Jonathan : very pleasant hast thou been unto me : thy love for me was wonderful, passing the love of women " (2 Sam. 1[26]). It is to be noted that in this relationship Jonathan is the one who loves first, and David is the one who is first loved ; Jonathan is expressly named in 1 Sam. 18[3], 20[8] as the one who concluded the covenant, i.e., as the one who took the initiative and who made the resolve and accepted responsibility for it. As Saul the father hates and persecutes David, so Jonathan the son of this father loves and rescues him. If Jonathan, as the son of this father, shares all his destiny and finally perishes with him, it is also remarkable that in his relationship to David he cannot only passively be the accepted friend of the future true king, but he is actively and prominently his comforter and helper in the bitter period of his concealment and persecution, so that later on he receives in his own son the reward of his loyalty. Could the tradition testify more clearly to the forgiveness of sins, under which it also saw and understood the rejected Saul, than by seeing and understanding that his son and heir to the throne—the one whom David actually superseded, and therefore whose existence was necessarily the most serious and dangerous threat to the future Davidic kingdom—was in this relationship given the very position of God in His relationship to Israel, that he precisely was the ex-ponent of the grace bestowed upon David ? And could it testify more clearly to the vital power of this forgiveness of sins than in the account given in 2 Sam. 8–9 how David for his part kept and fulfilled the agreement with Jonathan, in favour of Meribaal, the crippled son of Jonathan, in whom he had before him the living and dangerous blood of Saul ? Even the special mention of his " young son named Micha " is certainly not accidental, for it expressly reflects—in its own way—the reference to " the third and fourth generation of them that hate me " in Ex. 20⁵. David, then, is elected together with Saul. David represents the Divine Yes where Saul can exhibit only the divine No. David is the bearer of the divine blessing where Saul bears the divine curse. And inevitably there falls on David something of the shadow that lies on Saul. When Jonathan says to him : " The Lord be with thee, as he hath been with my father " (1 Sam. 20¹³), the saying is not without significance from this standpoint too.

It is to be noted above all that, according to the whole tenor of the tradition, and a series of important individual indications, David, too, stands under the " Not yet " which is more generally descriptive of the kingdom of Saul. If Saul is only David's regent and representative *in malam partem*, then David himself —*in bonam partem*, to be sure—is ultimately only the regent and representative of another. Together with Saul he is only a symbol and copy of the kingdom of God's grace attested through him. The blasphemous image which the nation had already made for itself in the wilderness of " a god, which shall go before us " in Moses' place (Ex. 32¹¹·)—the image of a bull which had again found its fulfilment in the figure of Saul, and not without the divinely ordained collabora-tion of Samuel, just as there had been no lack of co-operation on the part of Aaron !—was indeed erased by the figure of David, and another and better one substituted. Yet we have no need to think especially of Amos 6⁵, where David with his harp and his songs seems already to the prophet to have become a kind of unfortunate idol of the nation ; it is apparent even in the historical tradi-tion itself that under no circumstances will it see in the figure of David anything more than an image of the true king by God's grace. In the very place where the tradition speaks most clearly and fully of his character, namely, in the prophet Nathan's speech of institution and promise (2 Sam. 7), the figure of David is objec-tively limited, i.e., limited by his commission and its possibilities. David is not unique. Not only Samuel, who anointed Saul as well as David to the kingship, but also Saul himself and his son Jonathan, are indispensable both before and with him. The same is true of Joab, who wields the sword for him, and therefore eventually dies and has to be buried in the wilderness. Above all, however, it is a fact that nothing which David himself is and does, experiences and receives, as the one with whom the Lord is, forms the content of the promise given him at this climax of his life—that God will build a house for him, that He will establish and make glorious the throne of his son—but the very opposite. The limit for David, and the decisive delineation of the provisional and figurative quality of his being, are clear in this climax, in the promise which points away from David himself, and points beyond him. According to 2 Sam. 7², he finds it a problem that he himself dwells in a house of cedar, but that the ark of God stands in a tent. The prophet Nathan seems to be aware of his unspoken thoughts and answers him : " Go, do all that is in thine heart ; for the Lord is with thee " (7³). But then the Lord Himself intervenes, and teaches Nathan, and through him David also, something better : that He, the Lord, is with David even though—for this was the unexpressed idea—David does not build a house for Him ; and that it will be expressed rather in the fact that the Lord makes for him, David, a name " like unto the name of the great men that are in the earth," and through him prepares an abode of peace for His people Israel. But, then, supremely, and this is all future : " The Lord will make thee an house. And when thy days be fulfilled, and thou shalt sleep with thy fathers, I will set up thy seed after thee, which shall proceed out of thy bowels, and I will establish his kingdom. He shall build an house for my name, and I will stablish the throne of his kingdom for ever. I will be his father, and he shall be my son. If he commit iniquity, I will chasten him with the rod of men, and with the stripes of the children of men : but my mercy shall not depart away from him, as I took it from Saul, whom I put away before thee. And thine house and thy kingdom shall be established for ever before thee : thy throne shall be established for ever " (7^{4-13}). It is to be noted that in his prayer at the conclusion of this communication made through Nathan, David accepts absolutely the promise as such. Because of it he calls God the One to whom none is equal, and besides whom there is none other. He asks of Him only the fulfilment of this promise, and even then he recognises openly the limit fixed for himself (7^{18-29}). The tradition has scrupulously adhered to this contrast between himself and the promised son. It is the Lord who builds David's house, and therefore David may not and will not build the temple, the house of the Lord. The contrast is sometimes explained (1 K. 5^{17}) by the fact that David did not find the peace for this task because of the wars which he had to wage. David is sometimes praised because at least he intended to carry out the task : " whereas it was in thine heart to build an house unto my name, thou didst well that it was in thy heart " (1 K. 8^{18}). It is even reported, in the later form of the tradition, that David had prepared for his son all the necessary money and material and even the personnel required for the work : " A hundred thousand talents of gold, and a thousand thousand talents of silver ; and of brass and iron without weight ; for it is in abundance : timber also and stone have I prepared ; and thou mayest add thereto. Moreover, there are workmen with thee in abundance, hewers and workers of stone and timber, and all manner of cunning men for every manner of work. Of the gold, the silver, and the brass, and the iron, there is no number. Arise, therefore, and be doing, and the Lord be with thee " (1 Chron. $22^{14f.}$). Indeed, according to this later account, David had even transmitted to his son a model of the temple and the most exact plans and proposals for all the details of its structure, erection and fittings " on the basis of a writing by the hand of the Lord " (1 Chron. 28^{11-19}). But no account goes even a hairsbreadth beyond the objective limit. Indeed, the explanations and minutiæ only confirm the fact that the task is not David's, but that of the one who comes after him—his son. He himself can only be the forerunner, to whom the successor, who will complete the task, is promised. He, the son, will also be wise, upright and glorious, the king of the Church triumphant, which David is not yet. The greatness of David lies in the fact that he has the promise, and is therefore the forerunner of this successor and the father of this son. The fact and extent that his son Solomon, although and as he completes the building of the temple in all the lustre of his wisdom, splendour and justice, is still not the fulfilment of the promise, but for his part finds himself in a newly drawn objective limitation —a mere symbol pointing beyond himself—is a separate question which need not be discussed at this point. At all events, as seen from the standpoint of David, the figure of David's son, of Solomon, is indispensable to complete and surpass his own ; more essential than all the other figures by whom he is surrounded. It is not David himself, but David's son, who releases him finally and decisively from the bull-image of his predecessor. And it is not David, but David's son, who performs the great and necessary work which is the opposite of the construction of that Israelite wilderness-idol. It is not by David, but by

David's son, that in answer to the fact that the Lord will first build a house for David the work of gratitude is accomplished and a house is also built for the Lord. We have to consider that even in carrying out the act of due repayment, or rather of gratitude, king David is not the representative of his people, but only the representative of his son. It is his son who in carrying out this act becomes the true king of this nation—although he too, of course, only in a figurative sense.

It is also of a piece with this that twice in the story of David it seems as if his life might be sacrificed for that of the nation, as if by his death he might defend his people from evil. On neither occasion does it come to pass, nor is he accepted as such an offering. The advice of Ahithophel to Absalom is that he should surprise the fugitive king with a flying column, and kill him alone : for " I will bring back all the people unto thee : the man whom thou seekest is as if all returned : so all the people shall be in peace " (2 Sam. 17³¹·). But Absalom does not accept this advice, and it is not followed. Again, on the occasion of divine punishment for the census ordered by David, he himself protests : " Lo, I have sinned, and I have done wickedly : but these sheep, what have they done ? Let thine hand, I pray thee, be against me, and against my father's house " (2 Sam. 24¹⁷). But then the angel who smote the people with pestilence halts, and David builds an altar to the Lord on the threshing-floor of Araunah the Jebusite. Yet his offer is not even accepted, and a widespread disaster has already occurred, for 70,000 are dead. Indeed, had not David himself already chosen this punishment of the nation in place of his own ? All that he is finally able to do is to buy the threshing-floor from Araunah. On this occasion, too, his own sacrifice was not willed by God. Similarly, David's cry after the death of Absalom (2 Sam. 23³³) is in vain : " O my son Absalom ! my son, my son Absalom ! would God I had died for thee, O Absalom, my son, my son ! " It is not the natural love of a father which grieves in this way, and for the sake of which David would rather have died himself ; but for David it is the promise itself which is at stake and therefore everything, for the loss of his son means the loss of everything which constituted his mission. But it is all too late ; neither David's grief, nor his wish that he had died in his son's place, in any way alters the fact that this substitution, the sacrifice of David in his place, was not intended. Yet strangely enough the very opposite had taken place some years earlier, for his son, the son by adultery with Bathsheba, had actually died for him, as a punishment for his sin. In this case David himself had pronounced the death sentence upon himself : " The man that hath done this thing is a son of death " (2 Sam. 12⁵). But in answer to his confession of sin (12¹³·), Nathan says : " The Lord also hath put away thy sin ; thou shalt not die. Howbeit, because by this deed thou hast given great occasion to the enemies of the Lord to blaspheme, the child also that is born unto thee shall surely die." David prays and weeps and fasts. For again the promise is at stake. Yet it happens. The child dies. But the strange conduct of David in this bereavement shows that the tradition interpreted this death not only as a punishment but also as *the* great pardon extended to David. For as soon as David heard that the child had actually died, he " arose from the earth, and washed, and anointed himself, and changed his apparel, and came into the house of the Lord, and worshipped." And when he is asked what this strange behaviour means, he replies : " While the child was yet alive, I fasted and wept : for I said, Who can tell whether God will be gracious to me, that the child may live ? But now he is dead, wherefore should I fast ? can I bring him back again ? I shall go to him, but he shall not return to me. And David comforted Bathsheba his wife, and went in unto her, and lay with her : and she bare a son, and he called his name Solomon : and the Lord loved him " (2 Sam. 12²⁰·). It is to be noted that the begetting and birth of this son, who is the loved of the Lord, the promised one, takes place immediately after the death of the other, who seems to have lived only to make possible by his death the punishment of David, and therefore his survival, and therefore the begetting and birth of the promised one. David himself has certainly a great deal to suffer in his life, first because of his mission, then because of his sin. But a vicarious suffering or death is no more his concern than it was Saul's. It is prohibited and made impossible from the very outset that he should be a sacrifice for his people or for his son. We see him grieve for Absalom and grieve for the first son of Bathsheba, but he still survives, and in the end he simply " goes the way of all the earth " (1 K. 2¹), lying with his fathers and being buried in the city of David (1 K. 2¹¹). In this respect—as a sacrifice which is apparently demanded, but then not accepted— he finds himself subject to the same law as Isaac in Gen. 22¹², and king Jehoshaphat in 1 K. 22²³. He also resembles Joseph, who was certainly sent into Egypt by God " to preserve you a posterity in the earth, and to save your lives by a great deliverance " (Gen. 45⁷ᶠ·), but whose own life was not exacted for this purpose or accepted as its price. He also resembles his friend Jonathan (1 Sam. 14⁴³ᶠ·), who had unwittingly sinned and was sentenced to death by Saul, and was himself ready to die, but was begged free by the people, and so did not need to die at that time. The limit which David cannot overstep is clearly the absolute limit which is fixed for Old Testament man in general, and for all these characters. But this helps us the better to understand both the fact and extent that the special role destined for his son is necessarily barred to him—both the fact and extent that the son of David, as the content of the promise given him, is at the same time his own personal limit.

It is in this light that we can appreciate what the tradition has to say to us about David's sin. We have already indicated that it is flagrant and crimson when compared with that of Saul. We have, of course, to read 2 Sam. 11–12 very carefully in its context to see what was the concrete nature of this sin as understood by the tradition. The headings in the Zurich Bible and Luther's Bible, " David's Adultery " and " David's Adultery and Bloodguiltiness," are not really an accurate description. For in Nathan's denunciation in 2 Sam. 12 the special emphasis is not laid upon the adultery. We might have expected this, because David's sin does actually have this primary character, and there seems to have been so close a connexion between it and the original sin of Israel in its relation to Yahweh, as described by Hosea and others. Again, although his bloodguiltiness in relation to Uriah is brought home to David, it is to be noted that he attempts to evade this by the curious stratagem initiated by him, and that he has not murdered Uriah in any direct sense. Even Nathan modifies the first statement : " Thou hast killed Uriah the Hittite with the sword," by the second : " Thou hast slain him with the sword of the children of Ammon " (12⁹). We must concentrate upon Nathan's parable of the rich man who took the poor man's lamb, and upon the decisive antithesis with which " Thou art the man ! " is elucidated : " I anointed thee king over Israel, and I delivered thee out of the hand of Saul : and I gave thee thy master's house, and thy master's wives into thy bosom, and gave thee the house of Israel and of Judah ; and if that had been too little, I would, moreover, have given unto thee such and such things. Wherefore hast thou despised the commandment of the Lord, to do evil in his sight ? " (12⁷). From this it can be seen that the sin of David is that now he has arrived at the summit of his life he has forgotten the Lord who made him king and led him to this height. In this exalted position he is no less blind than Ahab was to be (1 K. 21) in his treatment of Naboth. He is worse than his grandson Rehoboam as described in 1 K. 12, worse even than he himself was in the census described in 2 Sam. 24, which was reckoned to him as a terrible sin. His attitude and conduct have been those of the bull-kings of the heathen, the great or petty tyrants whose law is what is " useful " to themselves and within their power to execute. It is not Saul, but David, who has here realised the possibilities of all human kingship indicated in the threatened " right of kings " of 1 Sam. 8—the grasping by the king at that which belongs to his people, and which he ought to defend. It is David's unexpected and startling and visible transformation into such a bull-king, corresponding to the ideal of the nation and wreaking havoc in the same nation, which is his contempt for the Lord, and his guilt in this respect means inevitably that at once and in a single action he commits the things which God has forbidden—adultery, robbery, murder and deceit. What would be natural for those bull-kings is absolutely unnatural for him. For he is not at all a king of this kind. He is king by the grace of God, and not by that of men. The Lord is with him. It is for him to witness to God's kingdom, and from his throne to defend God's throne. He is the very one who cannot pretend to any " right of kings." David of all men can have no reply to the Wherefore ? addressed to him by the same mouth which only a short time before had imparted the divine promise. He can only say : " I have sinned against the Lord." He can only pronounce sentence of death upon the rich man in the parable, who is himself. For every step that he took along the road described in 2 Sam. 11 was an absolutely impossible step, deserving of death. There can be no doubt that what Saul had once done along the same lines is far exceeded by what David has done here. If we had to do with a mere difference between more or less serious, grosser or more refined sins, David would surely be the rejected and Saul the elect. The very least that could be asked from that standpoint is that they should both stand in the same position before God and be treated as essentially the same before Him. If the tradition which so candidly exposes the disproportion between the sins of these two men judges so entirely differently, and if we are told of David that his sin was indeed punished but was also forgiven, then there must be a reason for this. It is plain enough, at least, that here we see David at his nearest to Saul ; so near, in fact, that we might well ask if here he is not more of a Saul than Saul himself had ever been. The inner solidarity of the two figures is at this point an incontrovertible fact— especially when we see what is decisively involved in David's sin, the abandon- ment of the kingship which distinguishes him from Saul in favour of the heathen kingship which was rejected in the person of Saul. How serious is this solidarity emerges in the judgment which actually follows the sin of David, as inexorably as the end of Saul succeeds his beginning. The death of the child was only the begin- ning of the punishment that was to fall on David. Nathan warns him that the Lord will bring distress upon his own family, that there will be meted out publicly to the women of his harem that which he had secretly done to Uriah, and that the sword will never leave his family. And in the story of Absalom, and sub- sequently in the story of his royal successor in Jerusalem, this is fulfilled to the letter. For David and his whole house everything follows the pattern of the transformation of which he has made himself guilty. From now on his story and that of his house conform to the usual picture of the history of the greater and lesser dynasties of the place and period which *mutatis mutandis* is the history of all such dynasties and potentates. The affair with Bathsheba and Uriah sharply exposed the fact that if David was chosen in the place of Saul, and the Lord was with him, it was certainly not because he was hewn from another kind of wood. In consequence, although his story and that of his house take a different form, they are not absolutely or fundamentally different from that of Saul. Therefore they stand under what are at least similar signs. What secular historian would see any basic difference between the catastrophe of Saul and the catastrophe of the house of David, which was longer drawn out, but in the long run just as evident, for all the differences ? The punishment for David's sin is that from the moment of its outbreak it is clear that he, too, is a figure of secular history, and that for all the light proper to him he shares in the much greater shadow which none of its figures can escape.

Yet while the Old Testament tradition speaks with absolute candour of David's sin and specifically names its punishment, it still regards him as no less different from Saul than night from day. This being the case, we have again to ask ourselves what is and is not to be understood by divine election in this tradition. Clearly there is not to be understood by it the distinction of one man in preference to another on the basis that he has had no share, or at any rate a relatively smaller share, in human sin. Benjamin and Judah, and later the ten tribes of Israel and Judah, were exactly the same as those who already in the wilderness, and again on the day of Ramah, had demanded the bull-image as the god and king who would go before them. And Saul and David were therefore hewn from the same wood. In fact, they were sinful types of the same sinful people. And their gross or refined sins could only make this plain. Again, according to the Old Testament tradition the election of one man in preference to another does not seem to mean that God at once protects His elect from the refined or even the gross outbursts of the sinfulness which is natural to them too, so that they can at least be immune to such flagrant sins as adultery, robbery, murder and deceit. The grace given to David seems to have nothing whatever to do with any such moral immunisation. And the election of one man in preference to another obviously does not mean that he is delivered from the law under which the whole world stands, or that he does not have to suffer —through his own guilt—that which in history is, sooner or later, in one way or another, necessarily suffered by everyone. The Old Testament version of the election of a man is rather that it is the distinction of one who is a sinner with all others—and especially with the one to whom he is preferred by his election —who shows himself to be a sinner and is punished as such. As it is depicted in the Old Testament, the election of a man is that in spite of himself God makes this kind of man a witness to His will, the will of His grace. Election stands or falls with that which *God* purposes and will effect and accomplish with him, and on this very account it can only stand and not fall. It stands or falls with his testimony, and for this reason it can only stand and not fall. It does not stand because of his virtues, nor does it fall because of his failures. It does not stand because he commits only refined sins, nor does it fall because he sins grossly. It does not in any sense stand because he conforms to the testimony laid upon him, nor does it fall because he contradicts it. Who or what he may be, for good or evil, is God's concern, and only to that extent his own concern. If we understand this, we can also understand that the story of David's sin—no matter whether we find it with 2 Samuel in the Bathsheba story, or with the Chronicler in the census—far from being in contradiction to the presentation of him as a figure of light in contrast with Saul, is absolutely indispensable to this presentation. The king by God's grace has the bull-king within him, not merely a minute trace, not merely in harmless intimations, but as completely and devastatingly as is described in 2 Sam. 11. And yet it is as this man that he is the king by God's grace—as the man who in this sinfulness is utterly dependent upon the mercy and forgiveness of God, who is enabled to stand only because God stands and supports him, who has nothing to offer God except his need. The fact that he is a man like this is not, of course, a confirmation of David's election or kingship or office as a witness to the kingdom of God. Saul is a man like this, too. But it is confirmed by the fact that God does not allow His concern with him, a man like this, to waver because he is like this, but rather He intensifies His concern with him as a man like this. That which the " I " who so startlingly encounters David in 12[7] has in His grace determined and disposed concerning him is irrevocable, and it cannot be called in question, but can only be confirmed, by the annihilating Wherefore ? addressed to David. The faithfulness in which God glorifies Himself in David's kingship remains, and for this reason and to this extent the election of David remains. This is why David is always the figure of light in contrast to Saul in spite of the fact that he is a man like this— and we might almost say far more so Saul, in view of this disclosure of his sin. This is why David not only confesses his sin—for Saul had done the same to

Samuel in the corresponding situation—but his sin is forgiven him. This is why all the judgment on himself and his house cannot annul the promise given to him. This is why the Lord is with him to the end, and with his son, and with his house also, although without exception it has to bear the curse upon all flesh which is evidenced by the sin of David. The great confusion into which the witness falls only makes it clearer that God alone is king, and the human king is only the witness. He, the witness, cannot obscure that which God wills to make clear through and to him. He is not released from the service which he had denied, and of which he was obviously incapable. Why not ? Because he is not a bull-king ; No : but because there is no release from God's service even for those who deny it, and those who are incapable of it—not even for bull-kings. Because in this service David bears a character which is indelible, which cannot be taken from him, of which he cannot divest himself. This is the power of his election as it emerges specifically in the story of his sin.

Let us pause and look back. The content of the two Books of Samuel is the story of the foundation and beginning of the Israelite monarchy as accomplished and directed by the will and work of God. More concretely, it is the story of the appointment and reign of the first two and mutually alternating Israelite kings, Saul and David, as rooted in the divine election. We have noted already that this involves a complete shift of theme and interest in the historical presentation of the Old Testament. If the earlier survey was that of the people of Israel as a whole, which did, of course, include leaders and chieftains from Moses to Samuel, attention is now focussed on these leaders and chieftains in the figure of the king. The record thus becomes quite explicitly a history of the kings, which now includes the history of the nation itself, and with which this history is completely bound up, and apart from which it no longer has any independent existence or meaning. From now on the history of the nation proceeds, and consists, in the story of its successive kings : first Saul, then David, and then the kings in Jerusalem and Samaria. This shift is paralleled by the fact that whereas the earlier historical writing had considered the Israelite nation as a whole, first in its wilderness unity, then in its concerted conquest of Palestine (" from Dan to Beersheba "), there is now a vigorous reorientation away from Shiloh towards the south, or to be precise, towards the area between Bethel and Hebron on the one hand, and the mouth of the Jordan and the eastern frontier of the Philistine state on the other. Although this area is subsequently enlarged, it still continues to be the centre of the wider circle of the picture and the record. And if, within this region, attention is primarily focussed on the tribe of Benjamin, it quickly moves away (almost like the star of the wise men from the east) towards Bethlehem in Judah, until eventually it is concentrated upon Jerusalem. The monarchy with which the Old Testament record is concerned is that of the king of Judah, and it is located in Jerusalem. It is only because of the wrath of God, and only in defection from this legitimate monarchy, that there takes place later the division of the state and the constitution of the kingdom which paradoxically, of course, bears the name of the one sacred whole—the kingdom of Israel in Samaria. The monarchy of Saul had looked in this direction from the beginning, and in so doing it defeated itself. But the monarchy of David which God put in its place, and which corresponds positively to the will of God, is that of the kings of Judah in Jerusalem.

If the intention of the record is to this extent clear, we can only describe it as profoundly dark and contradictory in another respect. And as in the passages Lev. 14 and 16, and the patriarchal narratives of Genesis, the obscurity is an obscurity both of the matter itself and also of its unity.

First, of the matter. When we consider the purpose of this first story of the kings, which happily culminates in David's reign in Jerusalem, we must not forget its beginning. We must not forget, that is, the day of Ramah. We must nor forget that the desire which the nation put before Samuel for a monarchy exercised over Israel by a man is described not only by Samuel but also by God as an illegitimate desire, as a rejection of His own kingship. We must not forget that the subsequent election and appointment of Saul carries from that time forward the quality of a divine act of judgment ; and that we are not told—at any rate explicitly—that this is cancelled even when Saul is replaced by David. Indeed in the Bathsheba story it is in David that we see what is meant by the " right of kings " referred to in 1 Sam. 8. And why is it that the whole emphasis of the grace of God vouchsafed to David in 2 Sam. 7 is ultimately the emphasis of a promise given him for the future, and not that of a present fulfilment of the true monarchy ? Why is the content of the promise not related to David, but to his son, as the one to whom God will be a father and who will himself be the son of God in his kingdom ? Nor is this ambiguity in any way removed in the presentation of the later history of the monarchy. It is still there in the portrait of Solomon. And it persists in his successors on the throne in Jerusalem, of whom only a bare half are described as men who walked in the ways of their father David, doing what was pleasing to God and thus giving concrete form to the difference between their legitimate monarchy and the illegitimate rule of Samaria, the difference between the election of David and that of Saul. And does not this whole historical presentation conclude with the account of the catastrophe that finally overwhelmed first Samaria and then Jerusalem, and brought to an end even the legitimate monarchy, even the house of David as such ? According to 2 K. 25$^{27f.}$, does not Jeconiah, the last of the Davidic kings, eventually occupy the role of a pardoned and tolerated guest of honour at the royal table of Evil-merodach the Babylonian, just as the last descendant of Saul —Meribaal—sat at David's table, according to 2 Sam. 9$^{10f.}$? Is it not worse to have to sit finally at the former rather than at the latter table ? The tradition as to the later period was careful to avoid characterising the function of Zerub-babel, the descendant of David, as a restoration or continuation of the Davidic monarchy. During the centuries in which the Old Testament text and Canon reached their eventual form, there was no king in Jerusalem ; no authority other than the more or less outspokenly foreign governor or vassal of the great foreign powers, whose rule has no significance for the theme of the Old Testament, which either ignores it or gives it only a passing and negative attention, in any case not relating it to the monarchy of the Books of Samuel. There is no suggestion of any attempt within the canonical writings of the Old Testament to deny or minimise the significance of the fact that after 586 B.C. there was no further king in Jerusalem. Its portrayal of the older monarchy is perplexing for this reason too. For how could the content of the Books of Samuel, which in the story of Saul and David is set out without any possibility of misunderstanding, be in any way edifying to the post-exilic community ? How is it that they did not find it a stumbling-block in view of the material ambiguity which had become inescapable in the light of the historical development ? In the story everything depended on the difference between Saul and David, but had not this been completely ironed out in the interim ? Had the monarchy in Jerusalem ever really been the will of God ? Had not the act of judgment at Ramah, by which it was introduced, been a warning of what had emerged clearly since the 6th century—that God does not will the Jerusalem monarchy, and wants no earthly king at all in Israel ? Had not the whole history of the Israelite monarchy been the history of a single mistake ? Had not the promise of the everlasting continuance of the house and monarchy of David (cf. 2 Sam. 7) been proved illusory ? It would be difficult to substantiate the idea that it was a purely historical interest, or æsthetic and romantic delight in a great past, which led them to honour these passages and to receive them into the Canon and read them as the text of revelation. Similarly, the supposition that the value attached to them is based on the fact that they could use them as a collection of valuable religio-ethical illustrations of the Law, although it may correspond to the use actually

made of them at that time and in later Judaism—and not only in Judaism !—
is quite inadequate to explain how they were formed and came unaltered into
the Canon. What, then, was the sacral interest with which these texts were
read ? The problem is obviously that of the Old Testament itself. It is the riddle
of the fact of a religious community which is gathered and remains gathered for
centuries about a text whose content is necessarily a riddle for them, in itself
as well as in its relation to their contemporary situation. For in it they can
find only the story of a mistake—and of a mistake which in the text itself is
actually, though not explicitly, admitted. They can find only the story of a
beginning (of a beginning, moreover, which is full of internal contradictions)
without the corresponding development, a broken column pointing senselessly
upwards, or, at any rate, a prophecy so far unfulfilled. They cannot with
certainty derive from this text the idea that the existence of a human king in
Israel is the will of God. Nor can they derive it from the continuation of the
story in the Books of Kings, and definitely not in the later historical experiences
of the Israelite nation, to which the Old Testament scarcely alludes. It is only
eschatologically and therefore only as prophecy that they can read and understand these texts, if at all, as the texts of revelation which for them they
certainly were. But prophecy of whom or what ? That is the great obscurity
which confronts us in relation to the matter of these texts.

But the obscurity is also in respect of the unity of the matter. We may
agree that the matter itself is clarified if the event of Ramah is understood as a
genuine act of judgment, and undoubtedly not merely as an act of judgment,
but at the same time as an act of grace on the part of God, as illustrated and
confirmed by the election of David, by the fact that the Lord is with him, by his
rise to power and finally by the promise given to him. But the question still
remains : Why and how far is his unhappy predecessor also described as elected
by God, and in his own way sanctified for God ? How is it that Saul—explicitly
the king by the favour of men—is placed before and alongside David as a legitimate king, not by an usurpation, like Abimelech at Shechem (Jud. $9^{1f.}$), whose
actions are so critically elucidated in Jotham's fable of the thornbush, nor by
the raising of a revolutionary standard, like Absalom (2 Sam. $15^{7f.}$), but with the
utmost regularity, being called and anointed king by Samuel, acting on the
express instructions of God ? Whence and for what purpose does the Spirit of
God also fall on him, even although it later abandons him ? How is it that he
also is one of the prophets ? We have seen that this aspect and destiny are
inseparable from his whole existence. How is it that we are prepared for the
worst by the way in which he comes to the kingdom, and the worst is actually
realised in the story of what follows, yet all the time we are astounded that
so much light rests on his figure and that there is so little palpable basis for
accusation against him ? In the same way we might go on to ask : How is it
that Jeroboam, the first king of Northern Israel, in whom Saul's monarchy is,
so to speak, resurrected, is not unsympathetically introduced in 1 K. $11^{26f.}$ as
" a mighty man of valour " among Solomon's builders, and " a widow's son,"
while the tradition goes on to relate that the prophet Ahijah the Shilonite (the
parallel to Saul is almost too obvious) speaks to him about his future kingship
in the following terms : " If thou wilt hearken unto all that I command thee,
and wilt walk in my ways, and do that is right in my sight, to keep my statutes
and my commandments, as David my servant did ; that I will be with thee, and
build thee a sure house, as I built for David, and will give Israel unto thee "
(1 K. $11^{38f.}$) ? How is it that the tradition distinguishes this Jeroboam by letting
him follow such a significant road to the throne, relating that he fled from Solomon
into Egypt, and that he returned from Egypt and entered into his kingdom after
the death of Solomon ? We have to remember that it is Solomon's son Rehoboam,
the son of the promise given to David, who in the words of the prophet is given
a rival by God Himself, and alongside whom there is placed a non-Davidic king

over all the tribes of Israel, with one exception. It is a study in itself that
Jeroboam does not fulfil the conditions of this assurance and that as far as the
tradition is concerned there never seems to be any question of a king in northern
Israel who did what was pleasing to God. Why is it, then, that there is this
promise and assurance to the one on the left—explicitly, compared to that given
to David ? How far—and the text offers us no reason to suppose otherwise—
can this really be meant seriously ? Why is it that although the legitimacy of
the Samarian kings is implicitly—if not explicitly—denied by the tradition, its
existence is treated as self-evident under the irritating title of " kings of Israel,"
far from the city of David and from the temple, and often in open war with the
consecrated descendants of David, while the reigns of the kings of Judah are
synchronised with those of the kings of Israel just as unquestioningly as the
reverse ? In a word : What is meant by the divine election of the Israelite
king, that even as one who is in his own way rejected, following his perverse
and fatal course, and under the wrath of God, he is no less seriously elected,
and indeed a divinely elected king ? Is the will of God for this monarchy—
assuming that He has a will at all—a single will or a twofold ? And what is
His true and proper will when in this twofoldness He apparently wills that which
is self-contradictory ? The same question is posed when we look at David himself. Why, if he is God's elect, is he not unmistakeably differentiated from Saul ?
For all the beauty of the story, it is confusing and disturbing that Saul's son
has the leading role in their covenant before God. And it is still more confusing
that the position of the king who is also the son of God is not awarded to David,
but to his son. It is again confusing that for no very clear reason David is
debarred from building the temple. Above all, how confusing it is that in his
sin he actually realises in a much harsher fashion than Saul in his sins the picture
of the heathen king rejected by God. And just what are we to think of the
choice of God when in Solomon, although we have the unequivocal picture of
a *rex gloriae* and the memory of Saul is wholly obliterated, yet immediately
after a detailed description of his building of the temple, his wisdom, justice
and glory, we are quietly told in 1 K. 11 that in his old age his heart no longer
belonged wholly to the Lord his God, as did the heart of his father David, but
that he became a follower of Ashtoreth, the Sidonian goddess, and Milcom, the
abomination of Ammon, and erected a high-place for Chemosh, the abomination
of Moab, on the hill to the east of Jerusalem (the Mount of Olives). And " likewise did he for all his strange wives, which burnt incense, and sacrificed unto
their gods " (1 K. 11⁸ᶠ·). Truly—not an utterly undivided heart ! What has
happened, too, to all his wisdom ? Where is the understanding heart for which
he prayed (1 K. 3¹⁹ᶠ·), and which was promised him with other things as well ?
Where is his sonship of God, according to the promise given to his father ? The
quest for the divinely elected king obviously does not end here. And the same
is true of the later descendants of David. To be sure, after the bad beginning
with Rehoboam we meet an Asa and a Jehoshaphat and later a Joash. After
Amaziah, Azariah, and Jotham, we meet a Hezekiah and later still a Josiah.
And most of these are significantly contrasted with the others by their long reigns.
Yet although they are kings after God's own heart, of none of them is this so
unequivocally true as it was of David, and the series terminates once and for
all with Josiah. And although we may find more or less edification in the characters and deeds of these good kings so far as they have been handed down,
yet we cannot ignore the fact that the kingdom of the elect king of Israel has
not yet appeared in any one of them—quite apart from the fact that they all
have contemporaries and opponents in the troublesome " kings of Israel " in
Samaria. Then the question arises from this side too : What is meant by the
divine election of the Israelite king, if the one whom the tradition presents as
such, and his whole house, which the tradition so clearly describes as elect above
the house of Saul and in distinction from the continually interrupted succession

to the Samarian throne, obviously does not correspond in the very least to this determination ? Is the will of God for this monarchy—assuming that He has a will at all—a single will or a twofold ? And what is His true and proper will when in this twofoldness He apparently wills that which is self-contradictory ?

These are the difficulties of the text with regard to the unity of that which it attests. As they are additional to the difficulties inherent in the matter itself, the question must now be faced in real earnest : How was it even possible for the post-exilic community to read these records as a revelation text and receive them into the Canon when in the last resort it had no historic, æsthetic or pedagogic reasons for doing so ? Is there any other possibility than that they are to be read and understood as prophecy ? They are, in fact, classified under the *nebiim* in the Canon. These "historical books" were estimated as prophetic and symbolic words, and they could be estimated only in this way in view of their total content. But whom or what could be found prophesied in them ? Who or what could be the subject which the community glimpsed or tried to glimpse as it read them ?

Our only remaining task, in conclusion, is briefly to recapitulate our discussion of Lev. 14 and 16 in relation to these.passages. Do these passages have a subject which is still unknown to us, as to the Jewish reader ? Or are they void in themselves because they have no subject at all ? Or is the New Testament answer to the question both authoritative and valid ? What this answer is can be seen from Ac. 2²⁵ᶠ· Peter is introducing a quotation from Ps. 16¹⁰ᶠ· (the words : "Thou wilt not leave my soul in hell ; neither wilt thou suffer thine Holy One to see corruption. Thou wilt show me the path of life . . ."). He prefaces the citation with the observation that David said this εἰς αὐτόν, namely, with reference to the dead and risen Jesus of Nazareth. He then substantiates the observation as follows : "Men and brethren, let me freely speak unto you of the patriarch David, that he is both dead and buried, and his sepulchre is with us until this day. Therefore being a prophet, and knowing that God had sworn with an oath to him, that of the fruit of his loins, according to the flesh, he would raise up Christ to sit on his throne ; he, seeing this before, spake of the resurrection of Christ, that his soul was not left in hell, neither his flesh did see corruption" (Ac. 2²⁹ᶠ·). We find the same exposition of the same section of the Psalm in Paul's speech in the synagogue at Pisidian Antioch (Ac. 13³⁵ᶠ·). In this case it is introduced by some words from Is. 55³ : δώσω ὑμῖν τὰ ὅσια Δαυὶδ τὰ πιστά (Ac. 13³⁴ : "I will give you the sure mercies of David," i.e., the fulfilment of the prophecy given to David in the death and resurrection of Christ). And the brief survey of the history of Israel given in the address closes with the recollection : "And afterward they desired a king : and God gave unto them Saul the son of Cis, a man of the tribe of Benjamin, by the space of forty years. And when he had removed him, he raised up unto them David to be their king ; to whom also he gave testimony, and said, I have found David the son of Jesse, a man after mine own heart, which shall fulfil all my will. Of this man's seed hath God, according to his promise, raised unto Israel a Saviour, Jesus" (13²¹ᶠ·) ; "And we declare unto you glad tidings, how that the promise which was made unto the fathers, God hath fulfilled the same unto us their children, in that he hath raised up Jesus again" (13³²ᶠ·). The Old Testament history of the kings did have a subject, then, according to the apostles Peter and Paul.

But when they say that this subject is Jesus Christ, who according to the will of God was slain under Pontius Pilate and who was raised from the dead by the power of God, we can only say again that the ultimate exegetical question in relation to these passages—the question of their subject—is identical with the question of faith : whether with the apostles we recognise this subject in the person of Jesus Christ, or whether with the Synagogue both then and now we do not recognise Christ. This question obviously cannot be settled by the

Old Testament passages as such. The final result of the passages as such is the difficulty. Again, it is naturally impermissible to accept the reply of the apostles solely because we cannot solve these difficulties in the exegesis of the text itself, or because, on the other hand, we share with them an idea that Jesus Christ is supremely fitted to occupy the place where we are pulled up short. The apostles themselves did not reach their answer as a possibility discovered and selected by themselves, or as a final triumph of Jewish biblical scholarship. They did so because the Old Testament (Lk. 24²⁷ᶠ·) was opened up to them by its fulfilment in the resurrection of Jesus Christ, and because in the light of this fulfilment Old Testament prophecy could no longer be read by them in any other way than as an account of this subject. If we accept the decision of the apostles—for the same reasons as they did, compelled by the revelation of God in Jesus Christ, and therefore as a decision of faith in Him—then the affirmation that the elect king, of whom they speak, is Jesus of Nazareth, will be not merely possible but necessary as the last word in the exegesis of these passages. The *last* word ! So far we have not mentioned His name in our investigation of these passages. We have remained within the Old Testament world and its possibilities. We have tried in this world to bring out and think through what is said there about the elect king. But we have been forced to the conclusion that the entity in question cannot be brought out or apprehended within the Old Testament world : whether we think of it in terms of the monarchy as willed by God, or of the person of the elect king ; whether we think of the matter itself or of its unity. Therefore the decisive question : What is the will of God in this matter ? and whom does He will for this purpose ? is not a question which can be unambiguously answered from the passages themselves.

On the assumption that the last word which the apostles clearly believed they had to say here (as the first word of the Gospel, the first word of the faith which they had to proclaim) may and necessarily must be our last word, because it is also our first word, a light is naturally flung upon our exegesis and its result which is impossible for a Jewish exegesis (or for any exegesis which for different reasons is Jewish in fact). We shall now proceed on this assumption. The elect king of the Books of Samuel (as a special modification of the elect individual) is, in all his potentialities and in every aspect of his widely divergent appearance, a witness of Jesus Christ. In himself he is never more than His prototype and copy ; but in type always He Himself. The fact that this king takes several forms—at least two, or more precisely four in this case too—and that these forms cannot be reduced to any common denominator, and are full of inner contradictions, characterises them as prophetic figures in distinction from the fulfilment actualised in the person of Jesus Christ. And if, lacking in unity, they do not attest the thing itself, the Israelite monarchy, in such a way that it is brought out and can be understood as a divinely willed order, this is simply a confirmation of the fact that they are prophecy. The fulfilment is not to be found in them. The kingship of Jesus Christ is the actuality, the subject which they attest—but which they can only attest. We will now try to reconsider the whole problem of our texts from this standpoint.

The Israelite monarchy set up on the day of Ramah is the prototype or copy of the kingship of Jesus Christ. But if this is so, the fact that the act of God's grace which then took place possesses and retains the character of an act of judgment is just as dark (no darker) and also just as clear as the fact that the king of the Jews, the man in whom God has entered upon His kingdom as a kingdom of grace for all His people is always the very One whom God has rejected for the sin of His whole people, whom He has delivered to death in the fire of His righteous wrath against their rebellion. This man is rejected and afflicted by Him as the Representative and Bearer of all human sin, of all the bull-kingship of man. He is the sacrificial offering required for all the unrighteousness and godlessness of men, for the Saul-like nature which in the long run is surpassed even by David. But as such, and regarded by God as such, He has been placed at the right hand of God. He has been lifted up even to the divine throne. He has been made the King in whose realm, for His own sake and in virtue of the power of His government which He exercises in pure forgiveness of sins, there is none unrighteous and none impure.

The Israelite monarchy is the type, the prototype or copy of the kingship of Jesus Christ. But if this is so, its distinctive transitoriness or evanescence (in which after each apparently present fulfilment there is immediately a new promise for the future, which is always future as seen by Saul in David, by David in his son, by his son in his sons and grandsons, to end at last, significantly, in that final one, Jeconiah, sitting as a guest at the table of the king of Babylon) is just as dark but also just as clear as the fact that in time the kingdom of Jesus Christ, as the kingdom of reconciliation, is a matter of promise and of faith, an object of hope, concealed in the visible appearance of the Church, which in every age and manifestation can reveal the glory of this kingdom in transitory flashes, and which—although representing the rule of Him who made heaven and earth, who is above all men and all things—is at best tolerated and treated as a guest by the powers of this world, and therefore at best can be a sign—but only a sign.

The Israelite kingdom is the prototype and copy of the kingdom of Jesus Christ. But if this is so, the fact that it came to an end, that ultimately the community could only look back on it as a historical phenomenon, is also just as dark (no darker), but also just as clear, as the fact that the kingdom of Jesus Christ, the kingdom of reconciliation, has a limit and a goal like time itself and the present order of creation. "When all things shall be subdued unto him, then shall the Son also himself be subject unto him that put all things under him, that God may be all in all" (1 Cor. 15²⁸). It is only in this eternal being of God as the All-in-All that the kingdom of Jesus Christ, which as the historical phenomenon, κατ' ἐξοχήν, is self-enclosed with time, will be an eternal kingdom.

The king of Israel rejected by God, whether he be called Saul or Jeroboam, is the prototype and copy of Jesus Christ. But if this is so, it is not at any rate an absolute riddle if the rejected one too, in his own way, bears the marks of one elected and sanctified by God; if he, too, receives and holds his throne in virtue of divine law; if he, too, does not appear without grandeur, even in his misdeeds and downfall—an object of awe and not of contempt, and his end a serious and necessary act of judgment, but not a triumphant *coup de grâce*. Saul is therefore legitimately and in all seriousness among the prophets. He and the Samarian kings who follow him, even while they are allowed to fall, do not fall out of the hand of God. In all the frightful blossoming of their sin, which is much more the sin of their people than their personal sin, and in all the terrible darkness of the divine wrath under which their government stands, they prophesy and exhibit the King who, himself innocent, has interposed himself as a Leader and Representative at the head of all sinful men, and between them and God— at the very place where transgressors and therefore the lost stand, where the rebellion breaks out, and therefore the lightning of divine wrath must strike. Who but the King by the grace of God can stand in this way before God in place of the unhallowed king by the grace of men, and be stricken and consumed in this way by the judgment of God? Who but the Son of God can be the King of men in this terrible function? Clearly a King of men like this cannot be deprived of the honour which in the Old Testament presentation of history is peculiar to Saul and the other rejected kings of Israel. Nor, when we consider this King, may we ask whether the will of God was twofold, a self-contradiction, when before and alongside and after David He gave and granted to Saul and all the kings like him their own sphere and their own peculiar lustre. A reflection of the splendour of God's grace lies and is to be seen on them too. For He who died a criminal's death on Golgotha is as such, overtaken by the divine rejection, the legitimate bearer of this glory, and the King of grace. Pilate was quite right to insist on " Jesus of Nazareth, the king of the Jews " (" What I have written I have written," Jn. 19^{22}). In this way even the blind heathen Pilate necessarily confirms that there can be no alteration in what is written concerning the Old Testament prototype and copy of this King.

Conversely, the king of Israel elected by God, David himself and David's son and in his own way every king of Jerusalem, is the prototype and copy of Jesus Christ. But if this is so, again it is not at any rate an absolute riddle if we utterly fail to find in the prototype an unambiguous and directly recognisable and therefore satisfying picture of this King ; if Jonathan and later the promised son of David take peculiar precedence of David himself ; if David is not allowed to build the temple, if he seems to sin more grievously than Saul ; if his promised son brings in the realm of glory only himself at once to make it impossible ; and if this kingdom has no more durability under his successors either. If we look at this picture from the standpoint of Jesus Christ, i.e., of its proper subject, we immediately understand why the Old Testament record itself expressly brings out all these reservations and does not take any real offence at them ; why its picture of the elect king accepts and indeed emphasises so strongly the negative aspect, not attempting to balance it with the positive, or to offer the reader a composite picture made up equally of light and shade. Just as the rejected king is always rejected in spite of all the light that falls upon him, so the elect king is always what he is ; and if the negative side is not suppressed or silenced, what is said and indicated is certainly not negative. On the contrary, it tells how God was with David in all that he undertook, how David conquered and rose to rule, how he danced before the Lord in the streets of Jerusalem, how God forbade him to build a house and built it Himself, how Solomon, on the other hand, did build a house for the Lord, and how great were his wisdom and wealth, and finally, in the case of his successors, how there were always kings like David, obedient to the commandments of God and under His blessing. If the other side is also put, it is only marginal and has no independent value.

The King Jesus Christ is the true subject and hero of these stories of the kings. But if this is so, necessarily there can be no equation or counter-balancing of the divine grace and human sin, of the miracles and blessings of God and their necessary limitation, of the present reality of His goodness and faithfulness and the provisional quality of their historical presentation. The latter will be continually overshadowed and crowded into the margin by the former, as in the Old Testament picture of the elect king. What we see in that picture when we look at it from this standpoint is the resurrection and exaltation of Jesus Christ, the revelation of His eternal divinity in the now glorified weakness of our human nature. Because Jesus Christ is the divinely elected King of Israel, it is necessary that the victory and rule of David, the wisdom and wealth of Solomon, the praise given to the good kings, should be almost unambiguously expressed in that picture. Yet not altogether unambiguously. Not without that margin. The margin is there. And it is confusingly wide. We cannot, therefore, ignore it. We may find its existence a real stumbling-block. Continually, the picture of the elect king merges into that of the rejected. We have to keep very close to the main drift of the historical presentation if we are not to misunderstand what is said and indicated. And this is not merely because in it we are dealing with the picture, and not with the reality itself (or, with the reality itself only in so far as it here confronts us in the picture). On the contrary, it is because of the reality itself. For it is intrinsic to the reality that its portrayal should take this form, that it should have this margin and have it unmistakeably. For if the proper and positive character of this picture—as seen from its subject Jesus Christ—unquestionably places before our eyes the meaning and power of the divine election itself, and the glory of God's grace in the person of the King of God's people introduced by Himself, we are reminded by the negative aspect—

which, although it is crowded out by the positive, is not denied but is specifically mentioned and can still be seen—who it is that God has chosen, and what kind of a people it is whose King is so great and glorious. We are reminded that it is composed of lost sinners who are justified and saved by Him. We are reminded that for the sake of their justification and salvation He had to accept their nature, had to become like them in all things. We are reminded what it cost Him to be the King of grace at the head of this people, and as such to reign over them. We cannot forget the rejected king in the elect. We cannot forget Saul in David and Solomon. We are to see them together in the appointed order in which they are related, but we are still to see them together. David and Solomon necessarily appear as on the edge of an abyss, rescued from death. In what other way can we understand their victory and glory for what they really are ? For how can the One who rose for our justification be seen or understood if He is not seen and understood as the One who was delivered up for our transgressions ? If Saul's portrait does not lack the reflection of the glory of grace, neither do the portraits of David and Solomon lack the shadows of the divine judgment of wrath. It is just because the will of God is one in the establishment of the kingdom of His incarnate Son that the former cannot be lacking in the one case any more than the latter in the other. For the one will of God is grace for lost sinners in the person of His Son, as the Son of Man delivered up on their behalf. How can He lack glory even in the hell of His humiliation unto death on the cross, and how can He lack shame and contempt even in the radiance of His divinity and His exaltation to the right hand of the Father ? His kingdom is complete in both aspects, and that is the secret both of the intrusively positive element in the portrait of Saul and of the intrusively negative element in the portrait of David. They are both one in Him, as in the One who is the subject to whom their stories points—the one true King of Israel in the same peculiar sequence, in the same internal contradiction which characterises each, and in the same relationship of the overcoming of the one by the other in which they stand to one another in the Old Testament.

It is to be noted that if the Israelite kingdom is the prototype and copy of the kingdom of Jesus Christ, and if the individual Israelite king on the right hand or on the left is the prototype and copy of Jesus Christ, this does not really mean that the scandal of the Old Testament history is set aside. On the contrary, it means that it is exposed in all its seriousness. But it is also transformed into a fruitful scandal. It dislodges us, that is, from all the historical remoteness and relative innocuousness, but also from all the strangeness in which it can certainly amaze us, but can say nothing personal to compel us to decision. We can no longer avoid the fact that on the day of Ramah God said both Yes and No to the request with which He was confronted by Israel. Nor can we avoid the fact that the true kingdom instituted then was always to be so hidden, nor the fact that eventually it came to an end. We cannot avoid either the rejection of Saul or the fact that he is not altogether abandoned by God ; either the election of David or the fact that he does not seem unambiguously or definitely to be God's true king. Every easy solution of these difficulties is rendered impossible for us if we follow the example of the apostolic witnesses and assume that all this had to take place as it did because Jesus Christ is the King of Israel elected by God. For then He, and the grace of God for lost sinners manifested in Him, is the riddle of all riddles. Then we are unable to overcome the stumbling-blocks of the Old Testament because they are the stumbling-blocks presented by the operation of divine revelation and reconciliation itself, and we cannot put them on one side, but can only know that they are set aside for our salvation by the operation itself. What is our perplexity then, as we read these passages, compared to that which they must have afforded to the post-exilic community ? And what is that, again, compared to the amazement with which they were obviously read by the apostolic Church, in the light of their fulfilment, as it had taken place in Jesus Christ ? God is really like this. He is the One who is both gracious and wrathful, who both makes alive and kills, who both elects and rejects in this way. And this has been actualised in a single person, so that we cannot deny either aspect, or separate them, but can and must understand the one by the other, and see in the whole, i.e., in the one human figure, the kingship of God as it has drawn near. It is only in a Christian astonishment at its contents—when the final exegetical word provided by the New Testament is actually ventured—that we can see and grasp the fact that the Old Testament history is not merely enigmatic but miraculous, that it is a record of the miracle of the grace of God. And if we read these texts with the apostles, in this Christian astonishment, we shall have no desire to study and describe the perplexity with which they were perhaps conceived and written by the lesser known pre-exilic prophetic circles to which they owe their origin, and later compiled and edited after the exile. " Perplexity " is much too weak a word for the authors and editors of texts like these. It is clear that they were trying to depict the foundation of the ancient Israelite monarchy, and to depict it as they found it. It is difficult to imagine that they did not realise as such the riddle which obviously faced them and which at any rate they placed in all its sharpness before their readers by what they wrote. It can hardly be disputed that their writing is in fact perplexing. That it is necessarily so is best explained if we concede that the fact of which they wrote was itself perplexing, and if we are ready to learn from the New Testament what the riddle in these data was, and at the same time how profoundly they were filled with hidden and revealed divine truth.

And if there are those who for any reason cannot accept our "if," i.e., the presupposition of the apostolic exegesis of these passages—very well, then, let them show us a better key to the problem of the elect king of the Books of Samuel !

For a third illustration of the differentiating election of God, we turn to an investigation of the self-contained chapter, 1 K. 13—the story of the man of God from Judah, and the old prophet of Bethel, in the days of Jeroboam I. The passage appears to be drawn from another source than its context. This can hardly be the same, but it is perhaps similar to the Elisha-cycle at the beginning of 2 Kings. It certainly reflects thought and judgment about the connexion between the authentic man of God and the professional prophets, and the parallels to the Book of Amos are so remarkable and distinctive that it is not impossible that what we have here—not in form, but in substance—is a fragment of ancient tradition concerning the nature of the Israelite prophet and the relationship between the two Israelite kingdoms. And the content of the passage, from whatever period it may have originated, is so meaningful and so instructive for our particular question that it is well worth considering. The story is that of the highly dramatic and complex confrontation between a nameless man of God from Judah (the land of the city of David and Solomon's temple, and the worship established there in accordance with the divine will) and a prophet in Bethel, where Jeroboam, the first leader of the larger Israel, divided from the house of David, had just instituted a national pseudo-cult which he was about to inaugurate. The peculiar theme of the chapter is the manner in which the man of God and the prophet belong together, do not belong together, and eventually and finally do belong together ; and how the same is true of Judah and Israel.

The first section (vv. 1–5) describes how the man of God from Judah, who like Amos (7^{14}) is not a member of the prophetic guild, visits the sanctuary at Bethel by the command of God (cf. Amos 7^{15}), in order to announce his prophecy of judgment against the cult. The Word of God is laid upon him in the form of an address to the altar erected by Jeroboam. A son of David's house, Josiah, will one day publicly and definitively profane and dishonour this altar by slaying its priests and then burning human bones upon it. It is inconceivable that there could be a harsher denial of the legality of the worship practised at Bethel, a harsher threat regarding its future, a harsher expression of the irreconcilability of what takes place there with the cult at Jerusalem, a harsher emphasis on the fact that cleansing and vengeance will come from Jerusalem because God is there and not here, and says Yes there and No here, a more complete exclusiveness in favour of David's kingdom as opposed to the separated North, than are expressed in this divine utterance. A directly imminent divine sign will confirm the truth of this word; the altar will be reft and the ashes lying upon it will be scattered. But King Jeroboam himself is standing at the altar addressed in this way, at the head of his unlawful priesthood, in the presence of the people of Israel, whom he has summoned to a festival planned by himself ($12^{32f.}$). He stretches forth his hand from the altar against the man of God: Seize him! Then his hand stiffens so that he cannot draw it back, and instantly the sign announced actually takes place; the altar cracks, and the ashes are scattered. Up to this point, we could almost think that we are dealing with a rather more circumstantial variant of the encounter which took place at the same place between Amos and Amaziah, the priest of Jeroboam II (Am. 7^{10}).

But in 1 K. 13 the encounter between the bearer of this divine utterance and the Cæsaro-papism of Northern Israel is only the material and presupposition for the real subject. In a second section we hear of a temporary softening of the contrast, although this does not actually alter the harshness with which it was previously revealed, except that now it seems to be momentarily veiled. Jeroboam, that is, shows that he is shocked by what has happened, and begs the man of God to intercede for his paralysed hand: "Entreat now the face of the Lord thy God, and pray for me, that my hand may be restored me again." This duly takes place, and the miraculous punishment of his hand is in fact cancelled. The result is a friendly invitation by the king to the man of God. He calls him to his house. He wants to offer him food and drink. He wants to send him away with a gift. Has he forgotten the threat against the altar, the radical questioning of the whole Bethel cult, and therefore of the legality of his whole monarchy and kingdom, by the word of the man of God, and the confirmatory sign of the rent altar? Or can he think that this sign of the patience of God is accompanied by a cancellation of the threat of judgment that had been pronounced, that the crack in the altar will close itself again, and the even worse future never come to pass? The invitation to share food and drink seems, as a matter of fact, to suggest this. What Jeroboam would like is reconciliation, tolerance, amicable compromise between himself and the divinely commissioned bearer of the word from Judah. For his own part he sees no reason why they could not shake hands, or why Jerusalem and Bethel could not settle down alongside one another. It is precisely that which the man of God refuses to concede by refusing the invitation. It is precisely that which God has forbidden him to do, and to which he could not agree even were Jeroboam to offer him the half of his royal possessions. He is commissioned to lodge that protest at Bethel, and is therefore debarred from accepting even a crust of bread in Bethel, or even the smallest gesture of fellowship between Bethel and Jerusalem. On the contrary, he is to return home by a different route from that by which he had come. He is evidently not to tarry anywhere in this realm except in passing, nor is he to set foot again on any portion of it, as though he had any other interest than to lodge this protest. Even his intercession for the king was clearly not a sign of this kind of fellowship, but was simply to show the king that what had happened to him was actually a miracle of punishment, just as the miracle itself was only to prevent him from seizing the man of God. The contrast was veiled by this mitigating incident. But the attitude which the man of God had still to adopt shows that it was not cancelled.

But the real subject of the passage does not emerge even at this turning-point in the episode. Jeroboam is no more than an introductory figure in the conflict which is to be depicted. The conflict itself emerges in the third section (vv. 11–19). A new figure is now introduced. This is an old prophet, dwelling in Bethel. Unlike the man of God from Judah, he is one of the professional prophets. The existence of these prophets is one of the self-evident presuppositions of the older history of Israel. It is vindicated but at the same time threatened by the existence of these men of God, authentically and directly called, to whom their name was later transferred. It is vindicated because on occasion they could become bearers and announcers of authentic divine oracles. It is threatened because this did not happen necessarily, nor was their function and calling as prophets constituted by the commissioning of such divine oracles. Often enough they might have nothing at all to say ; indeed, they might even be false prophets. One such prophet, about the rest of whose life we are not informed, now intervenes in the story of the man of God from Judah, the bearer and announcer of the divine oracle. He now takes the place of the king in relation to the stranger's word. He himself did not take part in the scene at the altar ; he was only informed about it by his sons. But we are now told that he inquires about the route which the other had taken to return to his homeland, that he saddles his ass and rides after him, that he finds him sitting under a terebinth and urges him to return and eat and drink with him under his own roof. This obviously means neither more nor less than that he has perceived the importance of the refusal given to Jeroboam in vv. 6–10, and that he is determined to reverse it at any price. He has grasped the fact that for the greater Israel everything depends upon ending this emphatic refusal by Judah in the name of God, and upon bringing about the fellowship between Jerusalem and Bethel, the toleration and compromise, which had been the goal of Jeroboam's invitation. He for his part cannot accept the refusal that has been given to the king. At any cost he must and will help him. The man of God from Judah must still eat and drink in Bethel. And in this way he must still demonstrate that the matter is no more ended by the crack in the altar, by the threat of judgment upon it and upon the whole northern kingdom, than it was ended by the king's paralysed hand. This is the reason for his hurried departure and his urgent invitation : " Come home with me and eat bread." And we are now told that the other answers him as he had previously answered the king : " I cannot." He cannot, because he is not permitted to do so : " For it was said to me by the word of the Lord, Thou shalt eat no bread nor drink water there, nor turn again to go by the way that thou camest." At first the prophet of Bethel is also faced by the same insurmountable argument as was Jeroboam. And he would fail in his purpose, like the latter, if it were not that he is a prophet. He may not have much personal experience of divine oracles, but all the same he is a specialist in such questions. Theoretically, at least, he is aware of the possibility of countering this argument with an argument of equal authority and power. His desire to avert the threatened danger to his king and people, and therefore to arrange this meal, prevails —and so he ventures the ambiguous statement : " I am a prophet also as thou art." The ambiguity of his existence as a professional prophet permits him to make this ambiguous statement. There then follows the lie (" he lied unto him ") : " An angel spake unto me by the word of the Lord, saying, Bring him back with thee into thine house, that he may eat bread and drink water." The first crisis in the story is thus reached. The whole issue now rests on a razor's edge. One Word of the Lord asseverated by its recipient is balanced against the other, a later against an earlier. The man of God from Judah has to decide whether what he has received has to be revised and corrected by what the prophet asserts that he has received. Was the threat against the altar, and therefore against the whole of greater Israel, and therefore the sole sovereignty of the God of David and his house, only a provisional truth and revelation ? When God heard his prayer for the king's paralysed hand, had He also had in mind the separation of the two realms which was really at issue? Were grace and judgment, after all, not so apportioned to the two that a friendly agreement between them must be excluded ? Was not the God of David, after all, more tolerant, in reality, than He had at first appeared or shown Himself to be ? Was it not, then, quite in order to give that sign of fellowship ? A " word of the Lord " from the mouth of the prophet of Bethel gave clear support to this view—and the man of God from Judah accepted it as such : " He went back with him, and did eat bread in his house, and drank water." Notice that no moral is drawn. Even the old prophet's lie appears in the text to be culpable only because it was integral to the rejection of Jeroboam, Bethel and the whole northern state that the prophet's intervention on their behalf was possible only by means of a lie. The decision of God had already been taken against this whole kingdom, and even with the best of human intentions it could be denied only in empty words. Nor does the prophet from Judah succumb to a defect in his own character, but to the curious fact that there really were prophets in this rejected kingdom as well. The possibility that a new divine oracle would meet him there was a very real one and could not be *a priori* excluded. It was not to a strange god, but— even under a restoration of the ancient bull-worship—to the God of Israel that sacrifice was made on that altar. In this obscurity between election and rejection the man of God from Judah wavers and falls.

But now the fourth section (vv. 20–26) brings a tremendous surprise, and then the second crisis of the story. For the truth suddenly emerges from the lie : " As they sat at the table, the word of the Lord came unto the prophet that brought him back." The possibility latent in his strange calling is realised. God can use him, too, in the delivery of His Word. He can do so regardless of the fact that of himself this prophet would rather say and represent something totally different. He can do so regardless of the fact that by his lie he had, as it were, slandered the possibility of his speaking the Word of God and forfeited from the very outset his role as a divinely commissioned messenger. On the contrary, it is now as if he is to be nailed down to his lie, to the empty claim with which he had previously spoken. The roles are reversed. He who had previously spoken the truth must now hear the Word of the Lord from the mouth of the liar. He must hear that he has disobeyed the command of the Lord, that in so doing he has incurred punishment, that the judgment of God prophesied by him against Jeroboam and his altar remains in force and is now directed against himself, that the next stroke of divine wrath will fall upon him, the previously faithful but now unfaithful messenger of God : " Thy carcase shall not come unto the sepulchre of thy fathers." The other, the liar, now speaks the truth. He now cries out against the man of God the commandment of the Lord which he had earlier tried to deny and disown. He himself, there-fore, undoes the peace-making in whose interest he had thought he should do it. He denies expressly that the gesture of fellowship fraudulently secured by the meal has any significance. How can it have any significance when it has taken place contrary to the will of God ? The advocate of the compromise must him-self tear it to pieces, and denounce the one whom he had just convinced of its necessity and legitimacy. And it is along the lines of his prophecy that the incident now develops. The man of God from Judah starts a second time on his homeward journey. A lion meets him and kills him, and " his carcase was cast in the way, and the ass stood by it, the lion also stood by the carcase." A singular scene ! Why did the lion kill him but leave him unmauled beside the ass ? Then the old prophet learns that this strange sight has been seen by travellers, and he knows immediately whom and what it concerns : " It is the man of God, who was disobedient unto the word of the Lord ; therefore the Lord hath delivered him unto the lion, which hath torn him, and slain him, according to the word of the Lord, which he spake unto him." He who speaks in this way is the very one who led the dead man into his error, and who, by a wicked abuse of his calling, caused his disobedience ! But that again is of no importance for the record. In it he exists at this moment solely as the witness who knows and who must confirm that the affair with the lion was no accident. Because this man actually did resist the decision of God, he is actually implicated in this same decision—His decision against Jeroboam, against Bethel and its altar, against the whole of Northern Israel, being incidentally struck down like someone touching a high-voltage transmission cable. He is put to death because he made a peace which God did not will and had not made. The disavowal which this signified for the prophet of Bethel himself, for his king, and for the whole cause which he represented, did not require expression. There lay the corpse and there stood the lion which had killed the man. It had all turned out as the man of God had originally said, and as the prophet had been forced to confirm against him and against his own wish and intention. God did not intend peace between Jerusalem and Bethel. The man from Judah had gone against this will, and therefore against his own election and calling ; and so he could only die in the foreign land where he had done that which was not his commission and which was opposed to his commission. Nor is it without significance in the light of Gen. 49[9], or Am. 1[2] and 3[8], that it was a lion which had to execute the judgment upon him.

The story does not end here, however, but hastens towards a third crisis in the fifth section (vv. 27–32). The prophetic expert of Bethel who has now become an authentic prophet, the liar who has now spoken the Word of God against the true man of God, and therefore against himself and the cause which he represents, does not let the matter rest with this reversal of roles. He, too, sets out a second time, and hurries to the scene of the calamity. He finds everything as it had been described to him, and brings the body back with him to Bethel to mourn and bury the man of God. " He laid his carcase in his own grave ; and they mourned over him, saying, Alas, my brother." He then arranges that he himself should eventually be buried next to the dead man. " Bury me in the sepulchre wherein the man of God is buried : lay my bones beside his bones : for the saying which he cried by the word of the Lord against the altar in Bethel, and against all the houses of the high places which are in the cities of Samaria, shall surely come to pass." Evidently the roles are exchanged once more. Just as the sin and punishment of the man of God from Judah have in no way altered his mission, so they have not altered his value or his superiority over the prophet of Bethel. For it is not merely to honour him that the latter conveys him to his own grave, and buries him. It is in order in this way to create a refuge for himself. It is in order that he may actually be secure in his own grave when the threat which has only been reinforced by the sin and punishment of the dead man, and which the prophet of Bethel now solemnly expresses in his own name, is actually fulfilled.

The provisional epilogue (vv. 33–34) which again links the record to the story of Jeroboam tells us that this experience does not cause him to desist from " his evil way " : " This thing became sin unto the house of Jeroboam, even to cut it off, and to destroy it from off the face of the earth." But the real epilogue to the story is only found in 2 K. 23[15-20]. There we read how Josiah carries out the threat of the defamation of the Bethel altar and the other Samarian sanctuaries. He has a burial-ground opened up in order to find the human bones required for this act. In so doing he comes across the grave of the man of God of Jeroboam's time, and when his story is related to him he orders that the grave is to be left undisturbed : " So they let his bones alone, with the bones of the prophet that came out of Samaria."

When we consider the complex nature of this story we may well ask, but cannot decide, what the real problem is. Is it the contrast between the real man of God and the man of the prophetic guild, or is it that between the realms of Judah and Israel ?—for both problems are so interwoven in the story that we obviously have to consider both in order to understand it. Unmistakeably, the prophetic problem is in the foreground. But the problem of the two kingdoms is undeniably more than merely accessory to it. In view of the context of 1 K. 13, we are almost tempted to say the opposite, that the prophetic problem is raised only in order to illustrate the problem of the kingdoms, and therefore that it is only a background to that problem. And if we postpone a decision on this question, it is also difficult to decide which of the figures, representing the two sides, stands, as it were, in the centre as the victorious hero of the story: the man of Judah or the man of Bethel; or behind them the royal sinner Jeroboam, or the prophesied royal reformer and avenger Josiah, who appeared later. For if neither of the two kings can be left out of the picture, each presupposing and completing the other, even more so the ways of the two prophets who occupy the foreground are so involved in their manifold intersections that they are unmistakeably meant to be taken together. If in spite of this we try to understand the whole, while keeping the intertwined threads apart, two double-pictures emerge at once ; one on the right hand and one on the left.

The double-picture on the right is that of the man of Judah, with the figure of Josiah at a distance behind him : authentic, divinely commissioned prophecy, as a representative of the authentic Davidic monarchy and kingdom ; or, conversely, the Davidic monarchy and kingdom as the abode and bearer of authentic divine prophecy.

We see the positive aspect in the first drastic approach of the man of God from Judah to the altar of Jeroboam, and in the confession with which he subsequently refuses the king's invitation, and which he later repeats and maintains in the presence of the prophet of Bethel. What we have here is obviously the divine commission, the divine legitimacy and authority, the divine grace, which elected David and Jerusalem, and called them to the execution of His will. And concretely (as the reverse side of the gracious will) it is the judgment of God, according to which He does not will the worship paid Him in Bethel, or the whole nation which is assembled with its king about that altar, even although this people is called (with particular emphasis) " Israel," even although its king did not reach his throne apart from God and the call of a prophet of God. For their apostasy from the house of David is simply a concealed or flagrant apostasy from Himself. His people have ceased here to be His people. The man of God from Judah is the herald of this divine displeasure. So, too, is the whole being of Judah in its contrast to that of Israel. And so, too, at a later date is the reformer and avenger, Josiah. It is for this reason that the hand of Jeroboam must stiffen in the moment when it is threateningly raised against the man of God. It is for this reason that the altar at Bethel cracks, as a sign of the even worse fate which one day will befall it. It is for this reason that there ultimately follows this worse fate itself. The progress of the cause which the man of God from Judah represents is irresistible. Like the cause of David before it, it is the cause of God Himself. The strict obedience with which the man of Judah at first follows his commission, and the intransigence with which he refuses any compromise, testify to this majestic irresistibility. So, too, does the fact that scarcely has the commission of God been betrayed by its legitimate bearer than it straightway finds a new representative in its opponent, the prophet of Bethel. So, too, does the fact that the lion of Judah immediately appears and strikes when the man of Judah ceases to will to be that which he still is, and shall be, and cannot possibly cease to be. One thing does not happen. He is killed but he is not devoured by the lion. His body is preserved, and also buried. Admittedly, it is buried in a foreign grave. But it is buried properly, securely and with honour. And even later, when judgment breaks on Bethel, the remains of this man of Judah are providentially spared—only his bones, but still his genuine remains. The consistency of the cause which he represented has stood the test, not only of his sin but also of his punishment, and even of his death and what followed. His remains are preserved. The grace of God towards Jerusalem, the faithfulness of the God of Israel, constant to itself, does not finally abandon even this representative of His cause who has proved unworthy. His bones at least are preserved from destruction. No genuine man of God, however serious his trespass, stands finally under any other sign. Neither Jerusalem, nor Judah—in spite of all their sins! His remains are preserved. The stock of David, hewn down to the ground, is preserved. For the grace of God cannot weaken, the covenant of peace cannot fail. That grave in Bethel is the powerful sign of this grace and this covenant.

The negative aspect of this picture on the right naturally consists in the fact that the representative of the cause of God, who is its subject, does at a fateful moment prove unworthy, actually betraying the cause by his mistaken decision about the invitation of the prophet of Bethel. The secret of this mistaken decision is not lack of character, but an astonishing deafness to the Word of God which he has himself already loudly proclaimed and confessed. Is it really possible that he can hear the Word of God and himself obediently execute it, and fail to do that which he ought to be expressing by deeds as well as words, by intransigent opposition to the compromise? Is it really possible that he can take the Word of God, which he himself has heard and uttered, and balance it against a contradictory, supposed word of God from the lips of another? Is it really possible that this second word should tip the scales? According to the story, it is not merely possible but true. The same man of God who executed his commission before the altar at Bethel, who made his good confession before the king and then before the prophet—this same man now denies and betrays the whole cause by what he does, as though nothing had happened. He? Yes, he shows the abyss on whose edge, as is clear from this passage, every man of God and every genuine prophet walks. The Word of God may be denied and betrayed in this way by the very man who is called to bear it. And it is not only the genuine prophet who here becomes a traitor and denier, but in him and like him Jerusalem, the city of David and of God; in him and like him the kingdom in whose midst stands the house which Solomon built for God, and within which the true God has not disdained to dwell. All Jerusalem and all Judah will do as this man of Judah has done. They will weigh the commission entrusted to them, and heard and clearly proclaimed by them, against the alleged commission of another. They will listen to supposed angelic voices from far and near. And their decision, too, will be false. They will become tolerant and then disobedient. They will eventually fall into every form of apostasy. They will become almost or altogether indistinguishable from the northern kingdom, at least in that which they desire and do. Has not all this begun already, under Rehoboam—yes, under Solomon himself, and even further back, in David's time? And in spite of every attempt to check it, in spite of Josiah and his reformation, it will work itself out to the letter. True, Jerusalem and Judah will continue to be what they are. Their commission is not withdrawn, whether they execute it well or badly or not at all. It is not in any sense taken from them. But in the person of so many of their kings, and finally and decisively in the person of the last king, they will do that which displeases the Lord in monstrous contradiction of their commission, just as this man of God did in a first and hardly noticeable step. And the inevitable result is that the lion of Judah turns upon Judah itself, that the voice of judgment that roars from Zion shakes the house of God itself, and finally shatters it. The man of God himself must die for the truth of the Word which he has heard and executed. And Jerusalem itself, even the kingdom of David, must perish because of the power of the truth which its prophets—Isaiah, Micah and Jeremiah—have now to proclaim as judgment upon it. And all that remains in this kingdom is graves—honourable graves, graves of kings and graves of prophets, but graves. It is a city proud with memories such as Samaria never had, but it is still a ruined city which can never again be that which once it was. And the grave of the last descendant of David will not be the burial-ground of his forefathers, but a grave in a foreign land. That is the negative aspect of the picture to the right.

The double-picture on the left naturally displays quite different features. In this case the negative side must be studied first because it is dominant. Jeroboam first occupies the centre of the stage. He is the king who as such also wants to be a priest, the *summus episcopus*, and who obviously has the makings and stature of the author of a new political and religious creation. And we see him on the day proclaimed by him as a festival of the national cult which he has inaugurated, not lacking a genuine dæmonism as he bears the first censer before the altar. Here we have the State-Church and the Church-State in one person. Here the sin of Israel, rejected by God, is unmasked in all its nakedness —the image of the bull is not necessary and is not specifically mentioned in the text. In Jeroboam it is immediately apparent why God says No to this altar and this throne, to this religion and this politics. Jeroboam is *Saul redivivus*, and the people who adhere to him are by this very fact the people who have rejected God as their king—and therefore the house of David. But in the story it is the prophet of Bethel, and not the king, who is the real representative of this dark kingdom ; the prophetic profession in contrast to the prophetic confession of the man from Judah. It is naturally no accident that the roles are allotted exactly as in Amos : on the one hand the institution, the bare possibility ; and on the other the reality of prophecy rooted in the freedom of God. The legitimacy of the institution is not itself denied by this contrast. Prophets of this type were also found in Judah, and conversely there were real men of God in Israel. But confession is shown to be characteristic of the south, and profession of the north, and the light naturally falls upon the former, and the shadow upon the latter. The shadow which lies upon the professional *Nabi*-ism is that which it has in common with the national kingdom of the north. Like it—if we disregard the divine election which is also possible in this kingdom, but immediately signifies its judgment—it is in itself and as such a representative of the Israelite form of the Canaanite vitalism, the religion of blood and soil, which, according to the will of the God of Sinai and Jerusalem, is the very opposite of the life and worship demanded of His people Israel. It is thus no accident that this prophetic order has to the northern kingdom—and later, of course, to the corresponding kings of Judah as well—the affinity which is proper to it in the story. The prophet simply reiterates to the man of God the desire of his king that he should eat and drink in Bethel and thus offer a gesture of fellowship between Jerusalem and Bethel, between Judah and Israel. This kingdom, the Israel separated from David's house, does not wish to stand outside but inside the divine covenant. Jeroboam aims in a special way to be the king of the divinely elected nation Israel, and it is the one God of Israel who is to be worshipped in Bethel. This is also the aim of the *nabi* of our story. It was inevitable that this monarchy and this prophetic order should degenerate openly into undisguised Canaanitism, as happened in the case of King Ahab and the " priests of Baal " who stood at his side. But that was merely its degenerate form. Here we have its purer form, in which, as in our passage, it claims nothing except tolerance for this Israelite, Yahweh-believing variety of Canaanite vitalism, of a religiously determined nationalism. It is because this man is a prophet that he is more aware than the king of the need for a theological justification of the North-Israelite kingdom and cult which are challenged at the altar by the word of the man of God from Judah, and which would be rehabilitated by his eating and drinking at Bethel. Again, it is because he is a prophet that he knows a better method of reaching this objective than the simple man-to-man talk by which the king had sought it—the divine communication which is to be expected of him because of his profession, and which he is now actually able to introduce in virtue of the authority of his profession. Thus the professional prophet becomes that which was impossible for the king of Israel—the true and successful tempter and destroyer of the man of God. That is why he is the real and the worse representative of the kingdom of darkness in this story. That is why what Jeroboam does looks only grey compared with what this professional does. For worse than the fact that Israel is Israel, and as such hastens to meet the judgment which inevitably comes and has been clearly enough announced by Jerusalem, and worse even than the abomination of Jeroboam and all his successors, is the fact that Jerusalem and Judah are led into temptation by Samaria. At first it is only the desire for mutual forbearance and friendship, for such a loyal relationship as later existed between Ahab and Jehoshaphat, for example. But in and with this desire there is the wholly devilish temptation to accept the Israelite form of Canaanitism (" I am a prophet also as thou art ") as the Israelite way of life, as a possible and legitimate form—within the divine covenant—of the life of the one people of God. In agreement with his king, but more effectively, the *nabi* of Bethel takes up this cause and carries it through to victory. He dares to use a divine oracle of his own free invention, suggesting that fellowship between the two is not merely permissible but is commanded by God. And this divine oracle—for, after all, he is the legitimate representative of the legitimate agency dealing with divine oracles—smacks of truth although it is definitely a lie, so that the man of God yields to him (as Jerusalem and Judah were later to succumb to the temptation to tolerance, and eventually to end as Samaria ended). In view of this, there can be no doubt the professional is the real Satan of our story. The peculiar sinful element in the sins of Jeroboam and of the northern Israelites as a whole is not that they question the divine judgment and render themselves liable to it, but that in so doing they compromise the house of David, and his people, and the temple in Jerusalem and therefore the promise and hope of Israel. In this way they attack the very substance of all life in covenant with God. Formally, the attack seems harmless enough to begin with, but in fact it is fatal from the very outset. And according to 1 K. 13 the instrument of this attack is the prophet of Bethel, the very experienced and therefore all the more dangerous representative of the evil cause of Samaria. That is why the prophet is the main character on this negative side of the picture to the left.

But this, too, is a double-picture ; and as that on the right has a negative aspect, so this on the left has also a positive. For one thing, we must observe the patience of God, which is not lacking even in the severe word of judgment against the altar at Bethel. For this judgment has still a future reference so that time is given to Jeroboam and his people. This is still the case even in its subsequent repetition in the mouth of the prophet of Bethel, when it is accentuated by what has happened in the meantime. It is another question that according to the epilogue in vv. 33–34 it was not understood as a warning, and therefore the time afforded elapsed without being used. The time itself is still given. Jeroboam and his kingdom have time. In the first instance God judges only in the form of the word which the man of Judah has to utter against the altar, and in the form of the sign which befalls the altar. The Word of God can still be heard and obeyed. Here, too, there is a divine repentance like that which benefited the people of Nineveh according to the book of Jonah. Bethel, and later Samaria, also stand under this sign of God's patience. It is for this reason that while there are no good kings there, there are genuine men of God, like Elijah and Hosea, and also authentic witnesses to Yahweh in the prophetic guilds or communities as they appear in the time of Ahab and Jezebel, enduring persecution and martyrdom. It is also for this reason that the Old Testament history does not omit to record the events which transpired in this realm right up to the fatal year 722 B.C., as well as the events which took place in the realm of Zion, even ascribing to the figures of Elijah and Elisha a grandeur and a significance unparalleled by the royal and prophetic figures of the Davidic kingdom.

It is as if God Himself willed to wait patiently from century to century. The healing of the king's paralysed hand is also relevant in this connexion. Certainly he had to be prevented from using violence against the man of God. But he can be forgiven for trying to do so if only he will hear what is so impressively said to him in the accompanying miracle of punishment. But what happens in the case of the prophet of Bethel is again far more important. For this old sinner, the real Satan of the story, is the very one who from being a theologian of the worst type later becomes the bearer of the real Word of God. After he has lied, he must and may give himself the lie. He can now see that the one whom he had sought to persuade, and had in fact persuaded with fatal consequences, was in the right. What did it matter if this was against himself ? He was in the right. And he can now act on behalf of the right which the other no longer represents. He, the mere professional, now takes over the office of the genuine man of God. He, the Israelite, now answers for the affairs of Judah and Jerusalem. He is a forerunner of Elijah and Hosea ; and, like them, he is now clearly opposed to his king and nation and country. For how can he utter the Word of God without having to stand in this opposition, without dissolving the affinity between *Nabi*-ism and national-monarchism, without putting to the flames that which formerly he worshipped ? But the very fact that this is possible and actual, even in the form of a contradiction which is all that it can have, is not just a sign but a concrete part of the reality of the grace of Israel's God, which has not destroyed him but now claims and uses him, which is not simply lost and forfeited by the whole realm of Bethel and Samaria, for all the tremendous sins of that realm and the menacing approach of the year 722 (and the day of Josiah). The God of David has neither forgotten nor abandoned the lost sheep of the house of Israel. There is no occasion for the men of Jerusalem to disdain Israel ; and for Israel itself there is no reason for despair. There is an election and calling of the ungodly also. Is there any other ? Was not the faith of Abraham faith in Him who justifies the ungodly ? Was not the elect king David himself, according to the story of his sin, a brand snatched from the burning ? Was there in Jerusalem or in Judah another or better consolation than that of the God who so freely and so wondrously receives a lost people to Himself ? It is the consolation of this God which now overflows and falls to the share of the wretched *nabi* of Bethel ; and in such abundance that perhaps in that hour there was no such confident, no such genuine prophet even in Jerusalem and Judah, as this old sinner of a professional, who now, because he must place the man of God and his own king and people, and above all his own self, under the judgment of God's Word, becomes the mouthpiece of that grace of David which cannot be shaken or annulled by any human folly or wickedness. If we have noted everything which is against him, we must also seriously recognise who and what is far more emphatically for him in this situation which God has so radically altered : for him, and therefore implicitly for Jeroboam and all his sinful kingdom hastening to its downfall ; for him, and therefore for Israel, in spite of its impenitence, in spite of its neglect of the time afforded, in spite of the judgment whose execution will not tarry nor delay for ever. One thing at least is made perfectly clear in the figure of this prophet : that the one true God of Israel, even if He is completely misunderstood and even if He is revered in a way which is quite false and illegitimate, has not ceased to be its God ; that His Law and also His promise continue to stand even in relation to Israel. He, God, is the substance of the covenant of grace between Himself and His people. Therefore this substance is indestructible, however much it may be attacked by seducers and seduced, by Israel and then by Judah itself. Finally and above all there belongs to this positive aspect of the picture on the left the conclusion. For if the necessary punishment of the human trespass in this story does not fall on Jeroboam, in whom the sin of Israel found its true representative and who sought to seduce the man of God from Judah, neither does it fall on the prophet as the theologian who justified Jeroboam's sin and successfully carried this seduction to its goal. But it falls on the one who in fact participates in the guilt of this sin only to the extent that—contrary to the will of God—he does not finally refuse the fellowship of food and drink requested by the sinners. It falls on the one who is here only the seduced. It is this alien figure, and he alone, who is struck by the lightning of divine wrath. The lion slays the man of God from Judah, while Jeroboam survives with his healed hand, and the prophet is at least able to meet his end in peace. He, the most guilty, goes free. He is even preserved beyond his death ; for together with the bones of the man of God from Judah, his bones are spared and preserved on the day of judgment. That is the strange light which falls on the picture to the left, the positive aspect which it obviously does not lack.

Finally, we must consider the peculiar interconnexion and blending of the two pictures to left and right. They are indeed to be seen and understood together. The meaning of both consists precisely in the fact that they mutually complement and confirm one another in the positive as well as in the negative aspects peculiar to both. The very significant position which is assigned, even externally, to the story of 1 K. 13 in relation to the historical record of the Old Testament must not pass unobserved. It comes directly after the account of the disruption under Rehoboam and Jeroboam, and in some sense explains it. But it also constitutes a kind of heading, not only for the whole ensuing history of the two separated kingdoms of Israel, but at the same time for the history of the conflict which now begins between professional and original prophets on the one hand, and false and true prophets on the other. All that follows is already announced and prefigured in this story. For what is the real subject of the whole ensuing history ? For one thing, it is obviously the unity of the will of God for the whole people whom He led out of Egypt, through the wilderness and into the land of Canaan. To this extent it is also the unity of the people itself, of the relatedness of its whole history, of all its tribes and kings and prophets. Then, of course, it is the internal distinction made by the one will of God. He does indeed will this whole nation. That is, He wills them for Himself ; for His service and blessing. He wills, therefore, to sanctify them. But that means that He does not will this sin, but excludes and cuts it off. In other words, in this people He loves His own Son, and therefore hates everything that means faithlessness to this promise, every expectation of salvation from their own skill and power instead of from the fulfilment of this promise. The disintegration of Israel results inevitably from this distinction of the will of God itself, as do the separation of the kingdom into David's kingdom and the national monarchy of Samaria, and the related twofold separation of prophecy into original and professional, true and false. But the will of God—and this is the third fact which emerges in the later history—does not cease to be one and the same for all Israel ; His faithfulness is unshaken, His promise continues open. If the separation and opposition in Israel's course and destiny are necessary, they can exist only in such a way that they point beyond themselves. They must still witness to the unity of God's will, and therefore also to the unity of Israel ; to the truth which is now eschatological, but which is all the more true for that very reason. And they must do so with a force which was impossible for the undivided kingdom, monarchy and prophecy. For the human division speaks much more loudly than any human solidarity could ever do of God Himself as the real basis of Israel, and not its own kings and prophets. Just because of the division there are now authentic relations in the history of Israel. Just because these men—the peoples, kings and prophets—on both sides of this relation show themselves to be so incomplete and so helpless on their own account, they become completely authentic occasions for authentic revelations of God, and as such reveal the authentic meaning of the existence of Israel. The fulness of these relations and occasions already emerges, in title-form, in 1 K. 13. We therefore go on to ask how far these two double-pictures belong to one another, and how far they are opposed, not merely mutely but eloquently—speaking of what in all its distinction is in itself the one will of God for Israel, of that which makes divided Israel more than ever His people.

If we begin again with the picture on the right, whose chief character is the man of God from Judah, his mission to Israel already attests that the true Israel in the south has no right to an existence which is tranquil and settled in itself. It cannot possibly rejoice or boast in its election to the derogation of the false Israel in the north. Nor can it come to terms with it and accept it without at once addressing itself afresh to this Israel. There is, therefore, no possibility of self-sufficiently leaving this false Israel to its error and destruction. On the contrary, it is under obligation to Israel. It has the commission of the divine Word in respect of Israel. The desire for tolerance and fellowship, by which the man of God from Judah is ensnared in Bethel, is therefore misdirected from the very outset. The disruption did not mean that the north was released and expelled from the sphere of the Word of God, and therefore from the scope of His grace. The disruption was hardly completed before salvation began to appear more than ever in the place where grace had been repudiated—and from that place where it had been received as grace, from the Jews. And the right to existence of these Jews was their message, the Word of God given them for themselves—yet not for themselves alone, but for all Israel. It is only by going to the north with this Word that the man of the south can confirm and justify his own election. Thus the cause of Jeroboam and his prophet was vindicated even before it was expressed and executed in its folly. Long before and in a very different way God Himself had provided a common table for His whole people. Nothing could come, therefore, from that arbitrary table fellowship. Genuine fellowship between the true and the false Israel cannot and will not consist in the conclusion of any peace between them, but in the addressing of the Word of God by the former, as the messenger of God, to the latter. Speech and hearing are the mode of the real love which is to rule and conquer here. What is necessary and redemptive is that there should be an utterance and hearing of the Word of God. Certainly this involves disruption. The only thing that matters is that it must be said and heard. But it is also the grace of God in the disruption that His Word is present, that the utterance and the hearing of His Word are not ended but now have a new beginning. The true Israel must converse with the false Israel just because it is not a stranger to the latter's guilt, because everything that separates Israel as a whole from God has simply been made explicit in the northern people, sundered from the house of David and the temple in Jerusalem. It is not from a secure elevation, but from the depths of the same distress, sustained by the unmerited grace of God alone, that Judah addresses and necessarily must address Israel by the mouth of its prophets, and must speak to it the one Word, i.e., the Word of God, which is its own support. From this point of view, the fellowship sought in Bethel has existed long before in a very different way from that imagined. It is just because this other and better fellowship, which is based upon the Word of God and continues in their common guilt, is already present, that the existence of the false Israel now means the serious jeopardising of the true Israel. Everything now depends upon the realisation of this fellowship between the two and not another : not any other ; not one in which the Word of God is stifled and the common need denied. The Word of God must be spoken and heard. There must be no tacit agreement by which both sides quietly come to terms with one another. And the common need must remain exposed. Here, again, there must be no tacit agreement on the basis of which both sides try to reach a mutual understanding, rather than maintaining their relation of speaker and hearer. The false Israel creates for the true Israel the acute danger of an invitation to yield to this suppression and denial which not only allow the false Israel to continue to be what it is but cause the true Israel automatically to become false. The special right to existence of the true Israel consists solely in the fact that it is given and that it assumes the responsibility and initiative with respect to the false Israel. If it does not use them, it immediately surrenders fellowship with the other and with itself also. It has repulsed the grace which made it an elect and called people in preference to the other. Its only remaining option is the guilt which certainly binds it to the other, the sin of David which of itself has no power to unite all Israel—this power belongs to the Word of God alone—but which can only tear David apart. Persisting in their guilt and repelling the grace of God, both sides cannot and do not come together, but of necessity can only fall apart. Only the love commanded by God has unifying power. If this fails, then enmity alone remains. The existence of the false Israel means for the true Israel the danger that it can fall away from this love. And now our story shows that this is more than a danger, that the false Israel is, in fact, the tempter and destroyer of the true. It tells us how the man of God from Judah actually accepts the invitation, and thus becomes unworthy of the service ordained for him and the blessing bestowed upon him—so unworthy that he can only be put to death. He does the very thing which distinguishes the false Israel from the true. He, too, repels the grace of God. And because he does this, he has to reveal in his own person that which was not yet revealed to the false Israel—that where there is only guilt without grace, there is nothing left but death, and Israel returns to the nothingness from which it was created. And the guilt of the false Israel avenges itself upon the true Israel because the guilt is that of the true Israel as well. Only the grace of God holds it above the abyss of this common guilt. And the grace of God is the only hope of the false Israel. The true Israel ought to have lifted high this one hope which it has now surrendered. Much is required of him to whom much is given. Much was given to the man of Judah, infinitely more than to Jeroboam or the prophet of Bethel. Therefore nothing less than his life can now be required of him. He staked everything, and he must now forfeit everything. But this fact—the fact that the false Israel becomes the tempter and destroyer of the true—is still far from being the end of the story. On the contrary, the story now moves on to its sequel, that the very tempter and destroyer must now take up the flag which the other had let fall. The fact that the false Israel as such had not ceased to be the Israel of God is now revealed, to the terrible shame but also to the supreme consolation, of the true Israel. For the Word of God cannot be silenced, nor can the common need be denied, even though Israel as a whole now seems to have chosen the false possibility, the rejection of the grace of God. That which cannot be executed by the true Israel, to its shame and destruction, is now executed by the false, and against the true, but obviously on behalf of all Israel. The professional, the false prophet of Bethel, may and must now stand up against the true prophet, and in this way maintain their mutual cause and Judah's commission as well, in order that the destroyed fellowship, and the love commanded by God, may be re-established between the two sides, and that—in a very different way from what he had intended or desired —the sign of hope may be raised again for the false Israel. So the prophet of Bethel now stands alongside the man of God from Judah. He is his judge, but he is also and supremely his saviour. For if the lion must and does kill him, he is also saved by the fact that the Word of God is not actually silenced, nor the common guilt denied. It is not by his service but by the grace of God that that which makes a people of God out of all Israel, and therefore out of Judah, is actually maintained and revived even in the midst of Judah's treachery. This was and still is—in spite of the lion—the grace of David, the promise made to Judah and Jerusalem. This is the faithfulness of God to which Judah owes its distinction. To be sure, it does not live by its distinction, but by the ongoing work of God, the power of the divine preservation and vivification which it ought to serve in accordance with its distinction. But if it now proves unworthy of this distinction, if it has now to die and pass, the fact that the work of God does actually continue confirms and saves its life in the midst of death. If the saying of the prophet of Bethel : " I am a prophet also as thou art," was at first only a presumption and a lie, and if this saying, whose falsehood the man of Judah could not discern, echoed mockingly in his ears upon the fatal road which he now had to travel, yet the same word was filled with consolation and promise in view of the grace of God that triumphed in his weakness. I am a prophet also as thou art. That which upholds both thee and me is independent of thy standing or falling. It is not whether thou and I are prophets that saves us, but this—that God does not cease to give prophets to His people. And if the cry of mourning uttered in Bethel over the man from Judah : " Alas, my brother ! ", could only be a cry of mourning, yet it did express an objective truth. Even in the false Israel he did have one who called him brother. And this one was his brother. And in his word and activity—because it was the Word and work of God—his own lived on, and therefore he himself lived on. To be sure, this brother had nothing more than a grave to offer him. Both here and in the whole sphere of the Old Testament history of kings and prophets there can be no visible consummation of the restored fellowship other than this common grave. It is Israel's grave into which Judah itself is first laid, and then Israel. The historical conclusion brings a reversal in the actual sequence of events. But either way, it is in this grave that the reunion of the separated brothers is completed. And this grave as such, and the remains of each united within it, will outlast the judgment— the remains of Israel for the sake of those of Judah. An undestroyed element of both is to be the provisional evidence of the faithfulness of God towards His whole people Israel. It should be noted in this conclusion of the story that the superiority of the one side over the other is never abolished, and that there is no retraction of the qualification that the one is the false and the other the true Israel. The man of Judah has not ceased to be the elect, nor has the prophet of Bethel ceased to be the rejected. But in their union as elect and rejected they form together the whole Israel from which the grace of God is not turned away. For the rejected acts on behalf of the elect when he takes over the latter's mission. And the elect acts on behalf of the rejected when he suffers the latter's punishment. Similarly, at the end, the rejected acts for the elect by making his own grave a resting-place for the latter. While again the elect acts for the rejected in that the bones of the latter are kept and preserved for his sake, and together with his own bones. It is exactly the same with the distinction and mission of the true Israel. It is betrayed in this way by itself, and yet also honoured in this way by God. What better thing can overtake the true Israel than this humiliation and this exaltation ?

And now, as in a mirror, we see it all again in the very different picture to the left, whose chief character is the prophet of Bethel. From the very outset now we are in the sphere of rejection. Here dwells the Israel which has forfeited that name and its very right to existence, which is already, so to speak, cast out among the heathen and to be reckoned among them. The guilt of all Israel has erupted here, and as lepers expelled from the congregation must form a wretched community for themselves, so does this Samarian Israel exist, cut off from the throne of David and the temple of God, without right or claim—it has itself flung them away—to membership in the covenant of God, without a share in its promise : an object of horror and a source of danger for the real people of God, as it is an object of wrath and a source of offence to God Himself. What can a king of Israel in Samaria be other than a usurper, a miserable and blasphemous imitation of the promised son of David ? And what can a prophet be in this realm but a mere functionary, a presumptuous liar and a false prophet ? All that can be seen from here, as we look towards Jerusalem, is that which is lost : the lost status of grace from which they have fallen ; the lost home to which they have become strangers. And all that can be expected from that point forward is the confirmation of the judgment under which they have fallen and to which they must now be subject. The beginning of the story corresponds to this. That which the king and people of Israel have to hear through the man of God from Judah is their own rejection *a limine* in and with the threat against the Bethel altar. And the rejection is underlined by the strict refusal of the requested table fellowship ; the most absolute intolerance. Yet even this event itself has its other side. We have already seen that precisely in this harsh form there is a resumption of contact between Jerusalem and sinful, separated Northern Israel, almost before the latter is aware of its separation. It is not indifference at all events, that encounters Israel from this quarter. At least in the form of judgment the grace of God is not removed from Israel the moment it sins. On the contrary, it has hardly left this kingdom before it returns. The guilt which lies upon it is the common guilt of all Israel. But the Word of God which Judah has and Israel does not have is addressed to all Israel, and is, therefore, to be directed by hearing Judah to unhearing Israel. This twofold solidarity is the secret of the beginning of the story, which does not possess for nothing the character of a revelation of the patience of God even in His wrath, which already at the very outset—even though it is a dark and unsatisfactory, tragic beginning —does not speak of an ending, but, on the contrary, of a genuine new beginning of God with this lost people. God chastises, certainly, but He does not destroy ; He chastises with the severity of a rod, not of a sword. He chastises with fatherly severity, as was promised to David concerning his son in 2 Sam. 7[14]. God is always God ; the God who on His side does not abandon the covenant, not even in face of the covenant-breakers. He is always the God even of the lepers. It is even the case that at this moment He is favourably disposed to the pure only in order that they may be at His disposal for service to the lepers. The true nature of the sin of Israel—that it is not rejected unjustly, but with justice— is certainly disclosed at once by the fact that it does not respond to the mission of the man of Judah with repentance, but seeks to evade his summons by the sentimental trick of that invitation. It will not continue in the salutary distance at which it was placed to hear the Word of God from that distance, but it tries to bridge the distance as fast as possible, to conclude an arbitrary peace, when all the time God is really the enemy with whom it must wrestle like Jacob to be blessed anew by Him. Because it does not do this, it confirms that it is not the true but the false Israel. And because its effort at first succeeds, its sin is blood-red, and it does not merely thrust away the blessing itself which the strong hand of God obviously willed to hold out to it, but it becomes a successful tempter and destroyer both of Judah and its mission. The point now seems to have been reached when all Israel must sink into the abyss of its common guilt ; an abyss into which the grace of Judah also falls, and with it every hope for the whole. But it is in this very situation that the miracle happens to Israel itself and its lying prophet. The evil and ungrateful man, addressed by the Word of God, becomes himself its bearer and messenger. This is not, of course, because he has any merit or worth. It is apart from and even against his own intention. It is simply because God is always God, because He has not cast away His people, His whole people Israel. Now, in the person of the lying prophet of Bethel, the sinful kingdom and people of Samaria, which so flagrantly discloses the guilt of all Israel, both may and must appear in the saving service of this God, whom His elect have denied. In the very moment when the wrath of God does actually break forth (as it did not before), when the lion of Judah slays and kills—this whole dark kingdom can let itself be represented by the elect of God in the bearing of the punishment of the sin which is indeed the common sin, but *in concreto* is primarily its own, the seducer's sin. It is he who now lies prone upon the road. It is he who must now be buried in a foreign grave. But they go free. And in the case of the prophet of Bethel his own ambiguous word is fulfilled : "I am a prophet also as thou art." He, the unworthy, can now represent the worthy in the proclamation of the Word of God. Is he no longer unworthy ? Obviously he still is. He is this primarily in relation to God. No worth is imparted to him by this commission. But God has put forth His own worth, and to this end He has used his voice, the voice of the unworthy. He is also unworthy in relation to the man of Judah, whom he well knows to be, in spite of his trespass, a true and righteous man of God in distinction from himself, and over whose death he cannot rejoice as one rejoices over the downfall of a godless man, but for whom he mourns—"Alas, my brother ! "—as David mourned the death of Saul and Jonathan, with the deepest sincerity. The fact that the word entrusted to him was fulfilled against this righteous one, and that he is no longer alive, does not mean any gain for himself now that, in all his unworthiness, he has become a messenger of the Word of God like the other. Nor does it mean a confirmation of his own mission. On the contrary, it means the loss of the most necessary guarantee of the office which has now fallen to him, the unworthy. For what is a prophet in Bethel to do, even though he bears on his lips the most authentic Word of God, apart from the man of God from Judah, who himself is the original and genuine bearer and proclaimer of the Word of God ? What is Israel, apart from Judah ? Samaria, apart from Jerusalem ? The election, the covenant and the promise are in the latter, not the former. What is the former if there is no latter ? What happens to the strangers in a city if the citizens are exterminated ? If in spite of his rejection the rejected is elected by the incomprehensible grace of God, to what is he to cling if the sight of the elect is taken from him because, in spite of his election, the elect stands as rejected in the judgment of God ? To what is he to cling if the herald of the patience and grace of God is snatched away because he has dishonoured the worth of God by his unworthiness ? There can be no question, then, of a victory for the prophet of Bethel, or of any kind of vindication either before God or man. On the contrary, he must make a refuge for himself in his own grave (Mt. 27 59, 60), first laying the dead man of God from Judah in it, in order that he may later rest beside him—bones beside bones, remains beside remains. But here, too, in the appointed order : the remains of the rejected are to be laid alongside the remains of the elect, Israel alongside Judah, and not the reverse ; just as, when judgment falls, the remains of Israel are to be preserved and protected for the sake of the remains of Judah, and not the reverse.

Here, too, we are forced to the conclusion that it is in this unity, in the irrevocable and irreversible order which is confirmed in and in spite of the whole dialectic of the conclusion of the story, that they are together the one whole Israel from which the grace of God is not turned away ; the bearer of the divine promise to all nations, to the whole world ; the attestation of the one true prophet of God. This is in full correspondence with the way in which the figures of David and Saul, as it were, belong together, and together attest the one true king of Israel, and yet cannot be interchanged, and in all their relatedness are not identical at any point. And it is also in full correspondence with the fact that the creatures of the sacrificial liturgy, the two goats and the two birds, certainly attest together the sacrifice and priestly ministry entrusted to Israel, and yet remain two figures ; not just two numerical units, which as such are interchangeable, but two sharply and antithetically differentiated individuals.

We shall not develop again in detail the two questions of the reality and the unity of what is attested in this passage, but must be content with a very brief indication. The two questions are both raised, of course, and they are both, if anything, even more difficult to answer if we keep to the confines of Old Testament history. The grave stands only too eloquently at the end of the story of these prophets. And it is not an empty grave, but a grave " which indeed appears beautiful outward, but is within full of dead men's bones, and all uncleanness " (Mt. 23 27). Certainly it is a grave of prophets, which as such ·could be built and garnished (Mt. 23 29), and which obviously was built and garnished, so that much later it was recognised for what it was by Josiah and his people. Yet it is only a grave. And in it the elect and the rejected, the worthy and the unworthy, the confessional and the professional prophet, Judah and Israel, Jerusalem and Samaria, in all their unity, diversity and relatedness, lie finally together in that corruption and decay which is our last human possibility and expectation ; buried, and on the third day—forgotten, finished, because our time is over. It is surely remarkable that this story, perhaps the most expressive and at any rate the richest and most comprehensive prophetic story in the Old Testament, should end with this grave, and that the only positive thing which is finally unambiguous in both the double-pictures of the story is merely the preservation of their common grave in the judgment which does not spare even the gravedigger. This does not mean, of course, that they are any less dead and done with than any other buried people. Is it not as true of them as of all others that " all flesh is grass," and that " the grass fadeth " ? When our story lays both prophets eventually in the same grave, there can be no doubt that it is saying that this is true of them also. But it obviously means to say something in addition when it speaks of the preservation of the grave and therefore of the remains of the two prophets. According to Is. 40[8], this addition can only be : " But the word of our God endureth for ever." It may well be said that this is in fact the beginning and end, the sum and substance of 1 K. 13—that the Word of God endures through every human standing and falling, falling and standing on the left hand and on the right. But the story itself cannot tell what happens beyond this to the men who have to hear and proclaim this Word, to receive its grace and endure its judgment, on the right hand and on the left. Nor can it tell whether or how far they share in this permanence of the Word of God. The story as such, as an account of Old Testament prophets, cannot tell this within its own Old Testament sphere. Or it can do so only by speaking of the preservation of that grave and therefore of the enduring remains of the two prophets. The eternal duration of the Word of God, and the lengthened but still temporal duration of these remains, are obviously two very different things, just as the remains themselves lie side by side, but are two different things ; the remains of these two so utterly different prophets, and of the two so utterly different Israelite kingdoms they represented. But since they do not continue for ever, it is clear that the question of the eternal duration of the Word of God is raised and—left open. In the same way, the problem of the reality and unity of what is attested by the story is also raised and unresolved. But this story, too, does point to one real subject if Jesus Christ is also seen in it, if at the exact point where this story of the prophets breaks off a continuation is found in the Easter story. The Word of God, which abides for ever, in our flesh ; the man from Bethlehem in Judah who was also the prophet of Nazareth ; the Son of David who was also the king of the lost and lawless people of the north ; the Elect of God who is also the bearer of the divine rejection ; the One who was slain for the sins of others, which He took upon Himself, yet to whom there arose a witness, many witnesses, from the midst of sinners ; the One lifted up in whose death all was lost, but who in His death was the consolation and refuge of all the lost—this One truly died and was buried, yet He was not forgotten and finished on the third day, but was raised from the dead by the power of God. In this one prophet the two prophets obviously live. And so, too, do the two Israels—the Israels which in our story can finally only die, only be buried, only persist for a time in their bones. They live in the reality and unity in which they never lived in the Old Testament, but could only be attested. They remain in Him, and in Him the Word of God proclaimed by them remains to all eternity.

Where else do they remain ? What else is chapter 1 K. 13 if it is not prophecy ? Where else is its fulfilment to be found if not in Jesus Christ ? These are the questions which must be answered by those for whom the suggested result of our investigation may for any reason be unacceptable.

3. THE DETERMINATION OF THE ELECT

The election of a man, the distinction of his relationship to God, operative and visible in his differentiation from other men, takes place with a very definite purpose. It means that his life is given a definite goal and content. As his election is fulfilled in his calling, it is seen that in and with his election itself and as such a determinate expression and fulfilment of his being are planned and executed ; that its determinate meaning and order are not due to chance or to his own caprice, but that all these things are the concern of the divine good-pleasure which elects him. What is this determination of the elect ? To what is he elected ? We must now consider this question further.

The comprehensive and in every respect decisive answer to the question is given in the fact that an elect man is in any case elect in and with and by and for Jesus Christ. To this determination from Him and to Him everything which might otherwise be regarded as his natural and historical determination is subject. In Him he is who he is, and will be who he will be. His fulfilment and his limitation are in Him. The Yes and No of his life are eternally spoken in Him. And who he is or may be in Him (and also who he is not or may not be), his individuality or personality as given him by God, is revealed in the fact that he is called by the Holy Spirit in accordance with his election. The particular meaning and order of his being are based upon and will also be actualised and revealed in the fact that Jesus Christ is for him. As Jesus Christ is for him, the goal and content of his own life are foreordained. The purpose for which he is chosen is to be the kind of man for whom Jesus Christ is.

Included in this first answer, the second is given in the fact that an elect man is in any case elect in and with the community of Jesus Christ ; elect through its mediacy and elect to its membership. The people of Israel is elect in its Messiah, Jesus, and the Church in its Lord, Jesus. Thus every election of individuals is an election in the sphere of the community—on the basis of the fact that this sphere is both established and marked out in the election of Jesus Christ. It is an election which in one way or another is mediated by the ministry of the community instituted by Jesus Christ—an election to participation in the ministry of the community. Because Jesus Christ lives in His community as in His body, the determination of the individual by and for Jesus Christ, as it takes place in and with His election, is his determination by and for Israel, by and for the Church. The elect individual, elect in and with the community of God, is what he is, and has what he has, directly from and for Jesus Christ. But because it is from Him and for Him, it is in the fellowship of the saints, in the acceptance and continuation of the service of His own, who are so inseparable from Him, Jesus Christ, that no individual can be His unless he is also theirs, unless he has the special determinatipn of his own life by and with and among them, in accordance with the fact that Jesus Christ is for him.

The fact that Jesus Christ and His community form the determination, goal and content of the life of the elect, is not to be understood as a merely formal answer to our question, which must be followed by the true and material answer. On the contrary, we must say that the very uniqueness of the determination of the elect consists in the fact that he is a man who has his being in the closed circle described by Jesus Christ above and Israel and the Church below. The being of one who lives in this circle is the being expressed and ordered according to the divine election of grace. His determination cannot be described more factually or concretely than by the reference to this circle. Whatever else we may have to say in explanation of this description can consist fundamentally only in the repetition and confirmation of this supremely material reference. But just because this material reference as such may be repeated and confirmed, this does not mean that the further answers which have to be given along the same line as the first two can only be formal. On the contrary, the true and essential fact that the elect man is determined by and for Jesus Christ, through and for His community, is both capable of and indeed demands a no less true and essential explanation.

We reach back to the basis and root of the true doctrine of predestination if we begin with the statement that the determination of the elect consists in the fact that he allows himself to be loved by God—to live as one whom from all eternity God in His incomprehensible and unmerited goodness did not will to renounce, and therefore will not renounce. This is indeed the determination of Jesus Christ Himself—in our flesh to be the One loved of God from and to all eternity. This is the determination of Israel and of the Church: they are the people and congregation of those who are loved by God in Jesus Christ. Obviously no man can be anything other or better than this—one who is loved by God. This is what God wills with him—to love him. And this is what He wills from him—to allow himself to be loved by Him. It is for this purpose that He elects him. He may and shall live as a partner in the covenant which God of Himself willed and established, of which God Himself is the Lord and Guarantor, the continuance of which is ensured by the omnipotent faithfulness of God. Whatever else this may signify, it signifies love. Severe, wrathful, burning love—but love ; and love that is eternal, not bounded by the limitations of creatureliness, forgiving his sin, giving the creature a share in the glory of the Creator. This participation, provided and executed in free grace, as present promise and hoped for fulfilment, is the goal and content, the expression and fulness, the meaning and order of the existence of the elect. It is the one thing which he really needs, but which also fully satisfies him. He cannot be or become anything greater, nor can he at any point be or become anything other than again and continually the one who is loved by God, loved in His own Son who bears the nature even of his flesh, loved as a member of His body, in the fellowship of the many who also have it as their determination to be loved by God in Him.

The determination of the elect to be the object of the love of God is undoubtedly his determination to blessedness. The glory of God, to share in which is the intention and purpose of His love for the creature, is the overflowing of the inner perfection and joy of God. God chooses the elect from eternity and for eternity, that he may catch up a beam or a drop of His own blessedness and live as its possessor, that he may rejoice in Him and with Him. It is for blessedness that God has determined man, as He determines Himself in His own Son for unity with man, as in Him He offered up no less than Himself. And the resurrection of Jesus Christ from the dead, His ascension, even the " signs and wonders " of His life (as revelations of His glory), disclose Him to us in its full possession. And again, God has determined man for blessedness in that in and with the election of Jesus Christ He chose Israel and the Church as the people and congregation of those who are grateful to Him for His self-offering, who because of it may love and praise Him as those to whom the ascribed and promised salvation has come. Each elect individual as such is, therefore, blessed—whether or not he recognises and enjoys and answers it as is fitting. He cannot and will not lack anything. As the elect of God he has nothing to bring except his thanks. If we ask after the divinely determined purpose and content of his life, we can and must reduce everything to the simple formula that he is elect simply in order that he for his part may be joyful in time and eternity as the beloved of God, and as a partner in the covenant. We should be ill-advised if for any kind of rigorism we tried to abstract from this. On the contrary, whatever further answers we may have to give to the question, this answer must always be included.

It is evident, though, that the blessedness of the elect, as his participation in God's own blessedness, is badly understood if it is understood only as receiving, acceptance and possession ; if his condition of blessedness as such and in itself is understood, so to speak, as a blind alley, in which the overflowing of the inner perfection and joy of God comes to a standstill ; if it is thought that the electing God is satisfied with the achievement of this blessedness for the elect. Certainly God's own glory is the essence of this love in which He never ceases and never tires of revealing and declaring Himself, of expressing and communicating Himself, of securing for Himself recognition. Yet, even as the glory of Jesus Christ, it is anything but an end in itself. On the contrary, even as it is given to this one Elect and received by Him, even as it is wholly His possession, it is the outgoing act both of God and of Himself. And in the same way, as the glory of Israel and the Church, it is not a possession which exhausts its goodness in the enjoyment which it produces for this people. But the enjoyment which this people can derive from it is necessarily bound up with the fact that it is effective and revealed in the work of this people. And it is exactly the same with the glory of each elect individual. It is not as an immanent but as a transitional blessedness, as a reason and occasion for gratitude, that he may receive and accept and possess it. How can it be a participation in His life, a fulfilment of the covenant fellowship secured for men by Him, if it is not active participation in His love, His act, His work, if man remains only an object of the glory of God, and does not become subject ? The fact that the elect man may use God as the ground of perfect joy in time and eternity is one with the other fact that God actively draws him into the event of His own life and act and work— that God wills to use him also, and that he allows himself to be used by God in the service of His self-glorification. This service, and therefore the blessedness of the elect, consists in gratitude for the self-offering of God. God chooses him in order that there may be gratitude in his life (and therefore life in and by grace). God chooses him in order that his existence may become simply gratitude. That he may achieve this gratitude and be this gratitude in his whole person is the determination of the elect. It is for this that God gives Himself to him in the election of Jesus Christ, in the election of Israel and the Church, in his personal election. He may be grateful. That is the secret of the gracious election of the individual.

But what is meant by gratitude, and therefore blessedness, and therefore being loved by God ? Clearly, participation in the life of God in a human existence and action in which there is a representation and illustration of the glory of God Himself and its work. There can be no question of anything more. Gratitude is the response to a kindness which cannot itself be repeated or returned, which therefore can only be recognised and confirmed as such by an answer that corresponds to it and reflects it. Gratitude is the establishment of this correspondence. The gratitude of the elect for the grace of God cannot be anything more than the establishment of this correspondence. But it can and must be this. The elect man is chosen in order to respond to the gracious God, to be His creaturely image, His imitator. Not that of a self-devised picture of God-and-man, but that of the gracious, electing God Himself and as such the elect under obligation to Him. He owes himself to Him. God has chosen him for Himself before he came into being. He determines him far beyond and above all self-determination. He can possess his own life only in imitation of Him, of the gracious God. What else is the elect Jesus Christ, the incarnate gratitude of the creature, but the original of this representation and illustration of the gracious God which is free of all self-will and therefore joyful, the true imitator of His work ? And what else can His community be but the people and assembly which, as they are created by the grace of God, declare this their creation, exhibiting and glorifying their Creator, not according to their own imagination or invention, but as He is and as He wills, as the One He has shown Himself to be in relation to them ? So, too, it is with the elect individual. He is what he is by the divine election of grace. The election of Jesus Christ is his own election through the mediacy of His community. His determination is to be its witness, and this is the purpose which God has for him, and in the execution of which the meaning and order of his being consist. The gracious good-pleasure of God is ñot merely achieved in him but through him, and it is in this way that it is effectively achieved in him. He is its real object as he is its witness, and therefore its subject.

The elect is, therefore, one who stands in the service and commission of the gracious God. As a result of his election, he is summoned by the operation of the Holy Spirit. His election as it has taken place in Jesus Christ can be declared to him. By faith he can appropriate the promise given. But if this is the case, it is not merely his private calling but also and as such his official calling. Not only are his salvation and blessedness disclosed and promised to him, but at the same time he is introduced to his service and commission as a witness. Just as Jesus Christ has His office as the elect bearer of the glory of God, just as the existence of the whole community reflects the existence of His divine office, so, too, does the life of each elect individual. Inwardly and inseparably bound up with that which God is for him, is that which he may be for God ; with his deliverance, his employment ; with his faith in the promise of God, his responsibility for its further proclamation ; with his blessedness, his obedience in his service and commission as a witness of the divine election of grace. For that which is the basis of his blessedness is also the goal and content of his office—his election, to the extent that this has happened in and with the election of Jesus Christ and His community. He is elected in order to provide in his own place the demonstration of the Spirit and of power for his own election and the election of Jesus Christ and His community, in order to confirm and reveal in his own participation this beginning of all the ways and works of God, showing that it is the decision of the Lord who is above all, the truth beside which there is no other. He is elected in order to break forth with his weak voice, but with all his voice, into the rejoicing which has its source in the divine election of grace, and courses through all God's creation, accompanying all His works and ways. This is his determination, and it is his duty and obligation to do this. If he does not, he necessarily compromises and denies his election. As God is gracious to him, too, He wills that he should praise the grace in which He addressed the

world before it was created, and still addresses it even when He causes
its form to change and pass.

Each elect individual is as such a messenger of God. This is his
service and commission. It is for this purpose that he may represent
and portray the glory of the grace of God. It is in this that he may be
grateful and blessed. He is sent. He is an apostle. The reason for
this is the election of Jesus Christ to be an apostle of grace. Its context is the apostolate of grace which is the meaning and order of the
life of His whole community. The determination of the elect is to
allow the light which has kindled within himself to shine ; to pass
on the good news of God's love for man which he himself has received ;
and to make the calling, in which he has been given a share, his own
concern in respect of all others. The dark antithesis of his distinction
from others and theirs from him is now set against the light of his
task for them. He must make known to them that which they do
not know as it was also unknown to him ; that which can be known
to him, too, only on the basis of his calling, but which—because it is
known to him on this basis—he cannot possibly fail to confess. He
possesses a contradiction to set against the lie in which they are
trapped, in which he himself would still be hopelessly trapped if the
truth had not been revealed to him, against which it is therefore a
matter of vital necessity that he protest. When he thinks of them,
he has to reckon with the recollection that their lost life outside the
circle of proclamation and faith displays the rejection which would
necessarily have fallen on him, too, apart from Jesus Christ ; and with
the expectation that the work of the Holy Spirit is the result of the
decision which has also been made about their human life. And in
this recollection and expectation he has to address them. And just
as he himself—when he realised the divine election of grace as it took
place in Jesus Christ—was not summoned by human eloquence,
although this was also used, so he is to seek to win others, laying
before them the offer which is made to them also, inviting them to
share the hope by which he himself is enabled to live. We are not
forgetting that everything is primarily and actually the work of Jesus
Christ Himself, and that the mediating work of Israel and the Church
is in His service. But when a man is elected in Jesus Christ, and to
His community, he thereby becomes a witness to that work, sharing
the office of Jesus Christ and His community. He cannot and will
not attempt to undertake more than the service of a messenger. But
he cannot evade his determination to this service. It will be his
honour and his delight to accept it, and to make way for the expression
and fulness of his being through this task.

The distinction between the electing God and elected man remains
clear. It cannot be the business of elected man to choose or to reject
others. All he can do is to attest, represent and portray that which
God really is and does in Jesus Christ alone. It is his determination

to point to the divine decision. But this divine decision is perfectly clear. It is to the effect that, in order to elect men to share His own glory, God willed to elect and actually has elected for Himself the necessary rejection of sinful men. But this means that the testimony which the elect man has to present to others has necessarily a very definite order. He cannot place before them the divine electing and the divine rejecting as two possibilities which are equally open. He can only show them God's election as the possibility which is basically open, and God's rejection as the possibility which is basically excluded —because it is excluded by God's offering of Himself. He can only call upon them to recognise their election, as one calls for recognition of the truth. He can call upon them to recognise their rejection only by warning them against the temptation to involve themselves in the possibility which God's offering of Himself has excluded ; against the temptation to give the lie to God, who has destroyed this possibility. It is, therefore, impossible for him to regard any of them as if they were not elect, as if God's love for men did not apply to them too, as if His covenant of grace had not been sealed for them, as if the godlessness in which they deny their real status were to be seriously taken as conclusive, as if it were therefore senseless and futile to witness to them too of the divine election of grace that has taken place in Jesus Christ. He will certainly meet them with the recognition that they too (just as little as the elect, just as little as the whole community of God) cannot presume of themselves to be elect, the object of the love of God, members of His covenant, and sharing as such the summons of the Holy Spirit. Yet, on the other hand, he cannot refuse the obligation to attest to them by word and deed and attitude that which God wills and has decided eternally for them too in the election of Jesus Christ ; and to proclaim the Gospel to them too, without any restraint or limitation, urging them with all earnestness and love to believe it. He will do all this without any reservation, in the confidence that there is in God's grace no ungraciousness in virtue of which any man is fundamentally debarred by God—as if he were rejected, as if Jesus Christ were not the One rejected on his behalf— from being His elect, and from receiving the corresponding calling. In this recognition, obligation and confidence every elect man will show himself to be such in his dealings with other men. He will be a messenger and apostle of the gracious God. And in this service and task, in this representation and reflection of the glory of God, and therefore in the fulfilment of his determination, he will himself be blessed.

It is not within the power of the elect to elect others, or to call others. He has not even called or elected himself. But it certainly is within his power—for all its total difference from the power of God —to be a faithful, joyful and earnest witness to the election and calling of these others. It is a modest task. He does not need to inquire as to the worthiness or unworthiness of the recipient of his message ; and while he is responsible for delivering it, he is not responsible for its success. It is a task, however, which is possible precisely within this limitation. It is not a titanic undertaking, and therefore not an undertaking which is foredoomed to failure. It is not an undertaking at all, but a commission, whose primary and proper burden he does not have to bear. And if it lays a total claim upon human possi-bilities, it does not overstrain or shatter them. If it demands all that man can give, it certainly does not demand more than this. If it assuredly does not allow him to be satisfied with himself, yet it is filled with the comforting knowledge that God is satisfied with him— that is, that God accepts what he has to offer, if only it is his all. Thus the task of the witness to God's gracious choice is a human task. In its fulfilment the elect certainly cannot take the place of God or speak the Word of God or do anything which God alone does. But in its fulfilment he shares in God's work as far as it is possible for him to do so, as the creature of God, loved and elected by Him. God does not make him a fellow-god when He gives him this determina-tion. Both the glory and the power of his service are always those of his Lord. But just because of that they are also his concern. It is the glory and power of the elect man in this matter that he may live by the grace of God as he stands in this service.

And now, if we may venture a final word, the determination of the elect consists in the fact that in and with his election and calling, in and with the service for which he is intended and which he has to perform, the ongoing of the reconciling work of the living God in the world is included and takes place. The election of each individual involves, and his calling completes, an opening up and enlargement of the (in itself) closed circle of the election of Jesus Christ and His com-munity in relation to the world—or (from the standpoint of the world) an invasion of the dark kingdom of the lies which rule in the world, a retreat and shrinkage of its godless self-glorification. The existence of each elect means a hidden but real crossing of frontiers, to the gain of the kingdom of God as the kingdom of grace. It is the concern of God that there should be these frontier-crossings. It is also His con-cern how and when they should take place. Again, it is His concern what should be the end of these frontier-crossings, which are many (in relation to the unworthiness of all men), or few (in relation to the great numbers of mankind). It is His concern what is to be the final extent of the circle. If we are to respect the freedom of divine grace, we cannot venture the statement that it must and will finally be coincident with the world of man as such (as in the doctrine of the so-called *apokatastasis*). No such right or necessity can legitimately be deduced. Just as the gracious God does not need to elect or call any single man, so He does not need to elect or call all mankind. His election and calling do not give rise to any historical metaphysics, but only to the necessity of attesting them on the ground that they have taken place in Jesus Christ and His community. But, again, in grateful recognition of the grace of the divine freedom we cannot venture the opposite statement that there cannot and will not be this final opening up and enlargement of the circle of election and calling. Neither as the election of Jesus Christ, the election of His community, nor the election of the individual do we know the divine election of grace as anything other than a decision of His loving-kindness. We would be developing an opposing historical metaphysics if we were to try to attribute any limits—and therefore an end of these frontier-crossings—to the loving-kindness of God. We avoid both these statements, for they are both abstract and therefore cannot be any part of the message of Christ, but only formal conclusions without any actual substance. We keep rather to the clear recognition that whenever an individual is elected and called, a new man is created out of the old, the reconciled world is fashioned out of the unreconciled, and to that extent, in secret, it becomes the kingdom of God and at the same time a new witness and messenger of the truth of the divine election of grace. This is the determination of every elect individual in salvation-history, and it cannot be treasured too highly. Independently of all that it means for himself, a victorious step is taken. For although (like the whole community of God, and even the man Jesus Christ Himself) he belonged and still belongs to the world of men, elected now in Jesus Christ he is taken from it and put in that service and commission. In this way the truth is repeated and confirmed, and a new sign erected in face of the whole world of men. This sign points unambiguously in one direction, that the gracious God is in the right and the man who denies Him is in the wrong. The free decision of God alone can lead further, but this step is one which gives us every reason and confidence to believe and hope that there will be further steps of the same kind, further confirmations and repetitions of the same truth, further signs pointing in the same direction. It gives us every reason and confidence to suppose that the people of God concealed in this world of men, which does not yet recognise the love of God for men, and its Lord Jesus Christ, and therefore its own true self, may be greater than was previously visible. It gives us every reason and confidence to go after this concealed and dormant people of God in the world. Clearly, his part in its awakening is the determination of every elect person. He is called in order that he himself may be one who calls within the world. It is not for him to know or to decide the result of his call. The actual opening up and enlargement of that circle will always take place exactly in the area which corresponds to the eternal free will of God. There will always be those who hear the proclamation of their election, always those who believe it, whom God has chosen in Jesus Christ and therefore determined for this faith and hearing. Those who are really this people by the grace of God will always recognise and confess Jesus Christ, emerging, therefore, as His people, as the communion of saints, recognising and confessing Him. That will always happen by the power and grace of God (of Jesus Christ and the Holy Spirit). It will always happen at His time (the time determined by Him). He Himself directs His own affairs. That is what makes those two statements impossible. But one thing is sure. The elect man is chosen in order that the circle of election—that is, the circle of those who recognise and confess Jesus Christ in the world—should not remain stationary or fixed, but open up and enlarge itself, and therefore grow and expand and extend. What is given him in his election and calling is undoubtedly the task not to shut but to open, not to exclude but to include, not to say No but Yes to the surrounding world ; just as he himself is undoubtedly one to whom it was opened, who was included, to whom Yes was said—the Yes of the unmerited, free and eternal grace and love of God. It is by and in this Yes that he must live with others. He represents and reflects the gracious God, and Jesus Christ and His people, as he causes them to hear this Yes. If he says No he also says Yes ; even when he closes he opens ; even when he excludes he includes. He will face others wrathfully but never contemptuously, with indignation but never with malice, angered but never embittered, a guest and a stranger but never an enemy. He will never renounce the recognition of their (and his own) lost condition. But he will also never renounce the obligation by which he is bound to them, as a lost soul to whom the grace of God has been revealed and come. Nor will he renounce the confidence that the same grace is addressed to them too. He will not weary in his service towards them, nor will he ever be disloyal to it, because of any self-made judgments of his own concerning them. It belongs to God Himself to determine and to know what it means that God was reconciling the world unto Himself (2 Cor. 5[19]). The concern of the elect is always the " ministry of reconciliation " (2 Cor. 5[18]), and no other. This is the determination under which he has to live.

We shall now pose and answer this question of the direction and aim of the life of the elect man in its biblical context. In this case we must be instructed by the witness to Christ in the New Testament.

In the Old Testament, of course, as well as in the New, election certainly does not mean merely the distinction or differentiation of the elect, but his concurrent determination to a life-content which corresponds to this distinction and differentiation. Yet if we confine ourselves to the Old Testament, we cannot characterise this life-content precisely. The question of the Whither ? of the election of the individual cannot be answered more clearly than by the affirmation—which is, of course, valuable, but needs further elucidation—that every such man is elected in his own way and place in order that God Himself, the God of Israel, the Founder and Ruler of the special history of this people, and therefore the will of God for this people in any particular modification of the course of its history, should be the direction and aim of his life. But the Old Testament itself does not disclose the intention of Israel's God in Israel's history. On the contrary, by its witness it envelops it in renewed darkness, by reason of the seeming contradiction in which it continually speaks of the love of God and the wrath of God, of future salvation and future judgment, of the life and the death of this people of God—with the emphasis, all in all, more on the latter than on the former. It is because of this that it is difficult, if not impossible, to derive from the Old Testament itself the answer to the question of the meaning of the election of the individual to be a friend and servant and child of God, sanctified by and for Him in distinction from those who are not so. According to the witness of the Old Testament, the wrath of God apparently opposes His love as an independent and apparently even the definitive direction of the divine will for the people of Israel. Every promise stands from the outset in the shadow of the much more impressive menace, every consolation in the shadow of the much more powerful judgment. And as the purpose of God can be affirmed only as we acknowledge its twofold direction, so the Old Testament elect and the meaning and function of their existence are inconceivable without the opposing fact of the non-elect, indeed the rejected. Yet these, too, are in their own way sanctified by and for God. They, too, must serve His will of judgment and grace towards Israel. They, too, are in their own way exponents of the election of all Israel, and therefore elect also. If, then, we are to see and understand the elect, we must always see and understand these others as well, the non-elect and indeed the rejected. This means, however, that we cannot see in the Old Testament any unambiguous picture of the life-content of the man elected by God. That there actually is this man in the Old Testament sphere, we can gather from its witness only when we come to know it—as is right—in the light of its revealed fulfilment in Jesus Christ, and in the reality of His Church. Necessarily then—but only then ! The will of God for His people Israel, from the beginning and at every stage of its history, is revealed in the fact that according to the New Testament Jesus Christ is born, suffers, dies, rises from the dead and takes His place at the right hand of God, assuming His earthly form in His Church for the time that remains. As the witness of the Old Testament is proved true in this fulfilment, it is comprehensible, emerging from the obscurity which lay upon it and in which we should still have to see it if we could separate it from Jesus Christ. But in view of the frontier set to this sphere, we can no longer say that according to the Old Testament the will of God is really a will which in its love and wrath, grace and judgment, life-giving and destruction, is self-contradictory and self-cancelling, and therefore not unambiguously recognisable or definable. On the contrary, in view of the frontier set to this sphere, we see and understand that what we have in the Old Testament is a wrathful love which burns even in its wrath ; the necessary judgment of the grace of God ; a death which does not take place on its own account, but for the sake of the life-giving ; a will of God for Israel which is the will of almighty loving-kindness. On the one hand we are not surprised, nor on the other hand are we confused, by the fact that light and shadow are so unevenly distributed in this sphere, that the faint light seems to be no more than the fringe of an immense realm of shadow. This is inevitable. For in this whole area Jesus Christ has to be indicated as the One in whom the whole concentrated darkness of the world is to be overcome by the light of its Creator and Lord. And, again, He can be only intimated and not yet named. What we have called the aim and direction of the life of the elect man, and the clear reply to the question of the purpose of his election, is disclosed only in the revelation of the will of the God of Israel as we have it in the New Testament, only in the bordering of the Old Testament sphere by this revelation. The blurred double-picture of the love and wrath, the grace and judgment of God is brought into focus when it is seen from this frontier. And because of this the corresponding and equally blurred double-picture of the elect and the rejected is also brought into focus. The fence is removed which, according to the Old Testament, seemed to separate the one from the other—Israel from the heathen, accepted from rejected Israel, Abel from Cain, Isaac from Ishmael, Jacob from Esau, David from Saul, Jerusalem from Samaria. Their connexion, which is so puzzling in the Old Testament, is now explained as the damnation of all mankind is now revealed in all its unbounded severity, but in subordination to the almighty loving-kindness of God towards this same mankind.

This is how it stands with the one Elect, Jesus Christ, who, according to the New Testament witness, sets a frontier to the Old Testament sphere, and lifts the veil which lay over its witness as such.

1. Jesus Christ is not accompanied by any Cain, Ishmael, Esau or Saul. He does not need any such opponents. God's will for His elect, the purpose of a man's election, the direction and aim of his life as an elect, are all real and recognisable in Him without such opponents, and therefore unambiguously.

2. Jesus Christ does not need them because it is His own concern as the Elect to bear the necessary divine rejection, the suffering of eternal damnation which is God's answer to human sin. No one outside or alongside Him is elected. All who are elected are elected in Him. And similarly—since no one outside or alongside Him is elected as the bearer of divine rejection—no one outside or alongside Him is rejected. Where else can we seek and find the rejection which others have merited except in the rejection which has come on Him and which He has borne for them ? This rejection cannot, then, fall on others or be their concern. There is, therefore, no place outside or alongside Him for Cain, Ishmael, Esau or Saul.

3. Jesus Christ is in His person the reality and revelation of the reconciliation of the world rejected by God because of its sin. But this means that in His person He is the utter superiority of the electing will of God over His rejecting will, the absolute subordination of the rejecting to the electing will. It is to be noted that it is a matter of superiority and subordination. The fact that the will of God is also the will which rejects the world because of its sin cannot possibly be ignored or denied by Jesus Christ. On the contrary, it is only in Him that it is taken seriously, that it is genuinely real and revealed as God in His humanity makes Himself the object and sacrifice of this rejection. But this is not the end in Jesus Christ. On the contrary, in the same man who bears His rejection God has glorified Himself and this man with Him. God has willed to awaken from the dead the very One who on the cross atones for the sins of the whole world. The will of God triumphs in Jesus Christ because He is the way from the heights to the depths, and back again to the heights ; the fulfilment but also the limitation of the divine No by the divine Yes. God presents this man in omnipotent loving-kindness as His Elect, and Himself as the God who elects this man. Jesus Christ is this irreversible way ; and therefore He is also the truth and the life.

4. Jesus Christ in His person—and this brings us to the particular purpose of our discussion—is the reality and revelation of the life-content of the elect man. For everything that He is—in His humiliation as in His exaltation, in the execution of divine rejection as in its limitation and subordination—He is not for Himself, or for His own sake, but as the reality and the revelation of the will of God on behalf of an unlimited number of other men. He is elected as the reality and revelation of the omnipotent loving-kindness of God towards these many. He is elected to bear their rejection, but also to overcome and therefore to complete in Himself their own eternal election in time. He is elected, therefore, to be for them the promise and proclamation of their own election. Jesus Christ is, therefore, what He is—the Elect—for these many.

For what many ? If we cannot simply say for all, but can speak only of an unlimited many, this is not because of any weakness or limitation of the real and revealed divine will in Jesus Christ. This will of God, as is continually and rightly said in harmony with 1 Tim. 2⁴, is directed to the salvation of all men in intention, and sufficient for the salvation of all men in power. It agrees with 1 Cor. 5^{19} that Jesus Christ is called the light of the world in Jn. 8^{12}, 9^5, 11^9, 12^{46} ; " the Lamb of God, which taketh away the sin of the world " in Jn. 1^{29} ; the Son in whose offering God " loved the world " in Jn. 3^{16}, and who was sent " that the world through him might be saved " in Jn. 3^{17} ; " the Saviour of the world " in Jn. 4^{42} ; " the bread of God which cometh down from heaven, and giveth life unto the world " in Jn. 6^{33} (cf. v. 51) ; " the propitiation for our sins : and not for our's only, but also for the sins of the whole world " in 1 Jn. 2^2 ; and the light " which lighteth every man " in Jn. 1^9. When we remember this, we cannot follow the classical doctrine and make the open number of those who are elect in Jesus Christ into a closed number to which all other men are opposed as if they were rejected. Such an assumption is shattered by the unity of the real and revealed will of God in Jesus Christ. It is shattered by the impossibility of reckoning with another divine rejection than the rejection whose subject was Jesus Christ, who bore it and triumphantly bore it away. It is shattered by the fact that Jesus Christ is the irreversible way from the depths to the heights, from death to life ; and that as this way He is also the truth, the declaration of the heart of God, beside which there is no other and beside which we have no right to ask for any other. It is shattered by the fact that Jesus Christ will not reject any who come to Him, according to Jn. 6^{37}. And yet it is not legitimate to make the limitless many of the elect in Jesus Christ the totality of all men. For in Jesus Christ we have to do with the living and personal and therefore the free will of God in relation to the world and every man. In Him we must not and may not take account of any freedom of God which is not that of His real and revealed love in Jesus Christ. But, again, we must not and may not take account of any love of God other than that which is a concern of the freedom realised and revealed in Jesus Christ, which, according to John's Gospel, finds expression in the fact that only those who are given to the Son by the Father, and drawn to the Son by the Father, come to Jesus Christ and are received by Him. This means, however, that the intention and power of God in relation to the whole world and all men are always His intention and power—an intention and power which we cannot control and the limits of which we cannot arbitrarily restrict or enlarge. It is always the concern of God to decide what is the world and the human totality for which the man Jesus Christ is elected, and which is itself elected in and with Him. It is enough for us to know and remember that at all events it is the omnipotent loving-kindness of God which continually decides this. For the fact that Jesus Christ is the reality and revelation of the omnipotent loving-kindness of God towards the whole world and every man is an enduring event which is continually fulfilled in new encounters and transactions, in which God the Father lives and works through the Son, in which the Son of God Himself, and the Holy Spirit of the Father and the Son, lives and works at this or that place or time, in which He rouses and finds faith in this or that man, in which He is recognised and apprehended by this and that man in the promise and in their election—by one here and one there, and therefore by many men ! We cannot consider their number as closed, for we can never find any reason for such a limitation in Jesus Christ. As the reality and revelation of the omnipotent loving-kindness of God, He is not dead, but lives and reigns to all eternity. This event in and for the world, and therefore its movement and direction at any given moment, its dimension and the number of those whom the event affects at any moment, are all matters of His sovereign control. For the very same reason, however, we cannot equate their number with the totality of all men. With the most important of those Johannine texts (3^{16}), we must be content to say that " God so loved the world, that he gave his only begotten Son, that whosoever believeth in him should not perish, but have everlasting life." This event always concerns those who believe in Him. It is always they who are the actual object of the sovereign control of God, of Father,

Son and Holy Spirit, over the world. The reality and revelation of the omnipotent loving-kindness of God in Jesus Christ is always so directed to them that they may recognise, apprehend and receive the promise of their own election in Him. Those who believe in Him, however, are not all men, nor mankind as such in its totality. They are always distinct from this totality. They live in the world as elected ἐκ τοῦ κόσμου (Jn. 15¹⁰). They are the many, the πολλοί, for whom He gives His life as λύτρον (Mt. 20²⁸), And as the many they are always, in fact, few, ὀλίγοι, according to Mt. 22¹⁴—few in relation to the total number of the rest, few also in relation to those who could believe, to whom He is also sent, for whom His call is also objectively valid, and whom He still does not reach, who do not yet believe. Nowhere does the New Testament say that the world is saved, nor can we say that it is without doing violence to the New Testament. We can say only that the election of Jesus Christ has taken place on behalf of the world, i.e., in order that there may be this event in and to the world through Him. And this, of course, we do have to say with the strongest possible emphasis and with no qualifications. If we ask about the meaning and direction of the life of the elect, in the light of this centre of all the reality and revelation of election, in the light of the person of Jesus Christ, the Son of God and the Son of Man, promised according to the Old Testament in Israel's history, and actually born, crucified and risen according to the New Testament, we have to reply that the elect lives as such in so far as he is there on behalf of others, i.e., in so far as it is grounded in him and happens through him that the omnipotent loving-kindness of God is at all events directed and opened up to the world, i.e., to others among those who do not yet recognise it and are not yet grateful for it. If the person of Jesus Christ had been consistently and decisively kept in mind when this aspect of predestination was under consideration, it would necessarily have been perceived that the content of the life of the individual elect cannot possibly be exhausted by the regulation of his personal salvation and blessedness, and everything belonging to it, understood as a private matter. On the contrary, he is saved and blessed on the basis of his election, and is therefore already elected, in order that he may share actively, and not merely passively, in the work and way of the omnipotent loving-kindness of God. This loving-kindness, which saves and blesses man, is so great and good that it wills to use him. He can serve it. He himself can help to direct and reveal it to others. and therefore to these others. That is what the elect man Jesus Christ did and does. How can any elect man—for they are all elect in Him—do otherwise ? This is the difference between the biblical view of elect men and the view which has unfortunately been basic to the Church's doctrine of predestination from its first beginnings. The New Testament does, of course, also know and describe the life of this man as that of one who is saved and sanctified, expecting and ultimately receiving eternal life. But whereas the Church's doctrine of predestination ends and halts with this definition as in a *cul-de-sac*, and whereas its last word is to the effect that the elect finally " go to heaven " as distinct from the rejected, the biblical view—in a deeper understanding of what is meant by the clothing of men with God's eternal glory—opens at this point another door. For as those who expect and finally receive eternal life, as the heirs in faith of eternal glory, the elect are accepted for this employment and placed in this service. They are made witnesses.

To take last things first, let us think of the description in the Apocalypse of the congregation of the coming age as it is integrated into the choir of angels and all creation restored to its true purpose. The twenty-four " elders " of Rev. 4 are distinguished by white clothing and golden crowns (v. 4). Similarly the innumerable throng which according to Rev. 7 is composed of all nations and tribes and peoples and tongues, and which stands before the throne of God and of the Lamb, is again adorned with white raiment and carries palms (v. 9). " They shall hunger no more, neither thirst any more ; neither shall the sun light on them, nor any heat. For the Lamb, which is in the midst of the throne, shall feed them, and shall lead them unto living fountains of water : and God shall wipe away all tears from their eyes" (v. 16 f.). According to Rev. 14 they are the virgins " redeemed from among men, being the firstfruits unto God and to the Lamb. And in their mouth was found no guile : for they are without fault . . ." (v. 4 f.). But the concern of those who have reached their goal in the coming age does not seem to be a passive, functionless enjoyment of their eternal innocence, justification and blessedness. On the contrary, we read of the twenty-four elders (Rev. 4[10]) that they fall down before Him who sits on the throne and worship Him, and cast their crowns before Him, raising the song of praise : " Thou art worthy, O Lord, to receive glory and honour and power : for thou hast created all things, and for thy pleasure they are and were created." In Rev. 5[9f.] we read that they sing " a new song " about Him who is worthy to open the book of judgment, because He was slain and has redeemed men for God—the song which is then taken up with variations by millions and milliards of angels and finally by the whole creation in heaven and on earth, and under the earth, and in the sea. Finally, Rev. 7[10] says : " They cried with a loud voice, saying, Salvation to our God which sitteth upon the throne, and unto the Lamb." And because they have come out of great tribulation and have washed their garments and made them white in the blood of the Lamb, " therefore are they before the throne of God, and serve him day and night in his temple " (Rev. 7[15]). Again, in Rev. 14[2], with the new song which they alone are privileged to learn, they are the bearers of that voice from heaven which is like the sound of many waters, like the sound of mighty thunder, and yet like harpists playing on harps. As we see clearly from all these references, there is given to them, with their innocence, righteousness and blessedness (and, so to speak, as the scope of their personal endowment), a word and a voice, and the task of using this voice and uttering this word, so that it may be heard in the wholly renewed world of God. How can it be otherwise if it is true that " these are they which follow the Lamb whithersoever he goeth " (Rev. 14[4]) ? And if this is their future and enduring determination, how can their present and temporary determination, their eternal predetermination, their predestination, be taken to mean anything else but that they are elect in order to be witnesses, God having predestinated them " to be conformed to the image of his Son, that he might be the firstborn among many brethren " (Rom. 8[29]) ? If only we hold clearly before us the fact that we are to recognise both the electing God and elected man wholly and exclusively in Jesus Christ, we are forced to look in this direction to see the life-content of the elect—that he is elected to be a witness. It will then be clear that the New Testament answer to our question is actually and necessarily very different from that which it has to be in the Church's doctrine of predestination. The fact which constitutes this obvious difference is that both in this world and according to the New Testament, the elect are not merely saved and blessed, but as such they are the bearers of that mighty voice from heaven.

It is presupposed, of course, that the elect—we refer to those who are elect in and with the man Jesus Christ—are only secondary bearers of this voice, only witnesses at second-hand. The true witness to the omnipotent loving-kindness of God, and therefore the reality and revelation of His will, is Jesus Christ alone. It is their function to take up and transmit the voice which they have heard in Him. But what they have heard is not this or that particular ; all that they have heard is decisively comprised and comprehended in the fact that they have heard Him. For the heavenly voice which they hear in Him is Himself, and not a higher thing above or behind Him which is merely transmitted through Him and comes to Him from heaven. He is Himself the reality and revelation of the will of God. He is Himself the kingdom of God which He proclaims. Therefore He is also the good news of that kingdom. As the Son of the Father, He can and may witness to the whole truth, the totality of that which God has to say to man about Himself. Accordingly, those who are elect in and with Him do not have to attest any abstract will or abstract kingdom of God, or to proclaim any abstract Gospel which He has first known, and then communicated to them, detaching them from Himself as independent representatives of this concern. On the contrary, their function is bound to His person. " Ye shall be witnesses unto me " (Ac. 1^8) : witnesses to the witness, who simply witnessed to Himself; witnesses to " the Lamb that was slain " and to nothing else. Whatever goes beyond or past this, or even contradicts it, cannot possibly be part of their life-content as elect persons, but can only compromise their election. How can they proclaim the omnipotent loving-kindness of God other than as the basis of their election, as a proclamation of the One in whom it is vitally real and manifest ? How can they proclaim the innocence, righteousness and blessedness in which they participate, and of which they are assured on the basis of their election, except as a proclamation of the One in whom it is promised and upon whom they believe, to find their participation and assurance in this faith ? " Abide in me, and I in you. As the branch cannot bear fruit of itself, except it abide in the vine ; no more can ye, except ye abide in me . . . without me ye can do nothing. If a man abide not in me, he is cast forth as a branch, and is withered ; and men gather them, and cast them into the fire, and they are burned " (Jn. $15^{4f.}$). It is of a piece with this that the Prologue to the Fourth Gospel says of John the Baptist, and through him of John the Evangelist, and through him of the New Testament witness as such : " The same came for a witness, to bear witness of the Light, that all men through him might believe. He was not that Light, but was sent to bear witness of that Light " (Jn. $1^{7f.}$). " And of his fulness have all we received, and grace for grace " (Jn. 1^{16}). It is also of a piece with it that in contrast to the many different forms of far too opulent and self-conscious Christianity emerging amongst them Paul tells the Corinthians of his decision " not to know any thing among you save Jesus Christ, and him crucified " (1 Cor. 2^2). And his earlier reminder has undoubtedly to be understood decisively in this light : " For ye see your calling, brethren, how that not many wise men after the flesh, not many mighty, not many noble, are called : but God hath chosen the foolish things of the world, to confound the wise ; and God hath chosen the weak things of the world, to confound the things which are mighty ; and base things of the world, and things which are despised, hath God chosen, yea, and things which are not, to bring to nought things that are ; that no flesh should glory in his presence " (1 Cor. 1^{26}, cf. Jas. 2^5). It is because they are poor as those who are elect in and with Jesus Christ and therefore alive wholly and utterly in and by Him, that they are also poor in the world, and in this way, and only in this way, victoriously superior to the world in virtue of their hidden wealth in Jesus Christ. Their function as the elect stands or falls with the fact that it is exclusively this function of service to Jesus Christ. It depends upon the recognition, and its continual confirmation, that " he is of God made unto us wisdom, and righteousness, and sanctification, and redemption " (1 Cor. 1^{30}). This is a necessary assumption in relation to the witness of the elect, and the secondary character of their function. If our definition of the word with which they are charged is to be in harmony with the New Testament, it can be described only as the word about Jesus Christ. Apart from Him it has no content.

It is also to be noted at this point that this opens up the way to an understanding of the direction and aim of the life of the elect of the Old Testament in their strange solidarity with the rejected. It gives fulness and concretion to the general proposition that the God of Israel is the meaning and direction of their life. What else can this mean but that they, too, are already to be understood, if at all, simply as witnesses to Jesus Christ, as witnesses to the limit which He sets to the history of Israel, as His regents, agents and deputies ? The One in whom God reconciled the world unto Himself, in whom the barrier was lowered and the hostility ended, has not yet appeared and is not yet named in the Old Testament sphere. That is why the elect and the rejected, like the love and wrath of God, confront one another in that strange antithesis yet no less strange solidarity. But the coming of this One, and His name, constitute the frontier of this realm, and therefore the goal and direction of all the history that takes place in it. This means that the appearance of accident and contradiction in these historical pictures is dissolved, so that the existence of these figures does not point to nothingness, but with that of the New Testament elect points to the one Mediator in whom the electing will of God has borne witness to itself. They, too, become and are clear in the light in which they stand when seen from that frontier. And they, too, become and are witnesses to this light. But only in this light! Only as He, whom they attest, first and of His own accord gives them His witness! Only as " he that cometh after me is preferred before me " ὅτι πρῶτός μου ἦν (Jn. 1¹⁵)! In the light of this πρῶτός μου, however, they too do become and are clear. They, too, are really His witnesses. It is not, of course, accidental that in the formulation of this affirmation we look at the final figure of the Old Testament sphere, who is also the first of the New Testament —John the Baptist. We owe it to the teaching of the New Testament that in this respect, too, we can understand the Old. Our question can be answered indirectly from the Old Testament because it is answered directly in the New.

It is, therefore, to the New Testament that we must turn for confirmation that, according to the Bible, the elect individual in analogy to the Elect, Jesus Christ, is determined to be a messenger of faith to the world, a witness to the omnipotent loving-kindness of God which in Jesus Christ is the basis and the gift of his own election.

When the relatively few New Testament passages in which there is explicit mention of the ἐκλογή or πρόθεσις or προορισμός of God in relation to the individual, are read in conjunction with the question as to the object of this divine decision and action, the general conclusion is that election or predetermination in the New Testament means election or predetermination to being in the community or Church of Jesus Christ ; that is, to being among and with those who have entered into fellowship with one another in virtue of their fellowship with Jesus Christ as fulfilled in their calling, by the work of the Holy Spirit. As God, according to Eph. 3¹¹, makes this eternal decision (πρόθεσις) in Jesus Christ, " in whom we have boldness and access with confidence by the faith of him," He creates (v. 9) a household (οἰκονομία) whose visible reality and manifestation is the ἐκκλησία (v. 10), in which those who have this boldness and access are as such gathered and held together. This is clearly the subject of Eph. 1³ᶠ·, which speaks of those whom God has blessed in the heavenly places with every divine blessing in Christ ; those whom He has chosen in Him before the foundation of the world, that they might be holy and blameless before Him. And the ἐκκλησία is equally clearly the content of the " they " or " we " whose life of obedience, in hope and inno-cence, under the law of the Spirit, is described in Rom. 8 ; the essence of those " foreknown " and " predestinated " to conformity to the image of His Son, who as such are called and justified and glorified by Him (v. 28 f.), the elect of God, whom nobody and nothing can separate from His love (v. 33 f.). According to 1 Thess. 1⁴, Paul knows of the ἐκλογή of the totality of the Christians addressed by him. And knowing this, he also knows that the Gospel did not come to them merely in word but in power, in the Holy Ghost and great fulness (v. 5). He can, therefore, thank God continually for them all, for their faith and love and hope (v. 2 f.). The various declarations that they are elect, beloved of God, reached by the Gospel, awakened and blessed by the Spirit of God, the Christian community of Thessalonica—all these are synonymous. The admonition of Col. 3¹² that the reader should " put on " bowels of compassion, goodness, meekness, gentleness, patience and so on, rests upon the fact that they are summoned ὡς ἐκλεκτοὶ τοῦ θεοῦ ἅγιοι καὶ ἠγαπημένοι. And this admonition, according to v. 10 f., is equivalent to " putting on " the new man who is renewed in knowledge after the image of his Creator : " where there is neither Greek nor Jew, circumcision nor uncircumcision, Barbarian, Scythian, bond nor free : but Christ is all, and in all." Election, the decision of God in respect of these men, their sanctification as the power of His love, the community of Jesus Christ, the life of those who are united in it by and in the direction determined through it—these, too, are all synonymous expressions. The same is obviously the case when in Rev. 17¹⁴ those who as companions of the Lamb, the Lord of lords, wage war against the beast or against the ten kings are also called κλητοὶ καὶ ἐκλεκτοὶ καὶ πιστοί. It is also the case when in 2 Pet. 1¹⁰ Christians are advised to " assure " their calling and election, i.e., to confirm it by everything which is necessarily concluded in their faith as grounded upon the promises of God. In Tit. 1¹ and 2 Tim. 2¹⁰ the ἐκλεκτοί are clearly and unreservedly identified with the community. In the first passage Paul characterised his office as the apostolate of their faith and knowledge of the truth, while in the second he says that he perseveres on their behalf. But the First Epistle of Peter is the chief passage to be considered in this connexion. At the very beginning the dispersed strangers of Asia Minor (1¹⁻²) are commonly addressed as ἐκλεκτοί. The following expansive definitions of their election are given. They derive from the πρόγνωσις of the Father ; they stand in the sanctifying power of the Spirit ; and they are destined for obedience and cleansing through the blood of Jesus Christ. All that they are, they are in virtue of this election. We learn explicitly in 1¹⁷ᶠ· what is the nature of that πρόγνωσις of the Father. Its object before the foundation of the world was the spotless and sinless Lamb, Christ, by whose precious blood His own are redeemed from the vain conversation received by tradition from their fathers, so that they are now called with the utmost earnestness to " be holy, for I am holy " (v. 16). According to 2⁴ᶠ·, they have come to that living stone which is rejected by men and denied by unbelief, but still chosen by God and precious. They themselves, built upon Him, have become living stones in a spiritual house, " a chosen generation, a royal priesthood, an holy nation, a peculiar people." All this honour is theirs as they believe, and in distinction from those who do not believe. All the admonition and comfort of the letter point back to this : You stand as Christians on this foundation ; and, conversely, because you stand on this foundation you are necessarily Christians, with all the consequences of suffering and action and hope which this involves. There is a kind of indirect confirmation of this identification of election and the Church when, in the greetings which conclude the letter (5¹³), the community from within which it is written (probably the Roman community) is called ἡ ἐν Βαβυλῶνι συνεκλεκτή. In the same way 2 Jn. 1 and 13 speak explicitly of one community as ἐκλεκτὴ κυρία, and another as ἀδελφὴ ἐκλεκτή, and Christians as the τέκνα of these elect persons. When we survey the teaching as a whole, it is unquestionable that, where the New Testament speaks of God's ἐκλογή, πρόθεσις or προορισμός, it always means—not apart from the election of Jesus Christ Himself, but as established in and with His election—the election of those who are called to Him and therefore believe in Him. The election of Israel, as we have seen in a previous connexion, is not for this reason denied or invalidated. But the election of Israel itself, as its election for the sake of Jesus Christ, is the election of those who believe in Him, the election of the Church. Election means faith. And since those who believe are the Church, election means to be in the Church. We have here a closed circle which cannot be penetrated. There is no election to anything else or to any other situation. There is no election of an individual man on the basis of which he is not led by the Word into faith, and therefore into the fellowship of believers, and therefore into the Church. What is promised him as an elect person, what is expected of him as such, what he receives from God and what under God he will become, is never a special gift or task or destiny peculiar to himself. All the predicates of the elect individual are predicates which apply originally to Jesus

Christ, and then, in and by Him, to His own, to those who believe in Him, but to all believers in the same way, with no basic difference. It may be noted that the idea of election or its equivalent is used only once by Paul (Rom. 16¹³) about an individual Christian. Elsewhere it always refers to the totality of Christian " we " or " you." The elect individual, as an individual, secures his own right and growth because that which is ascribed to and expected of the community of Jesus Christ, on the basis of revelation and the reconciliation of believers as it has taken place in Him, is ascribed to and expected of him in his own particular way, but in a way which does not differ basically from that of all others in this community. Yet the circle is also closed in the sense that there can be no question of a distinction between the elect and the non-elect within the community of those who believe in Jesus Christ. Election and the Church are coinciding circles. According to the New Testament the elect gathered into the community are very seriously threatened and endangered. But " there is never any talk in the New Testament of a selection (élite) within the Christian community itself " (Schrenk, *TWB z. N.T.*, IV, 185, 6). No qualification is ever made to the effect that one of the Christian " you " or " we " might not belong either secretly or openly to the ἐκλεκτοί. If, like Calvin, we see election and rejection cutting clean through the Christian community, we should realise that the notion of community presupposed is not the same as that of the New Testament. Wilfully or otherwise, we are confusing it with the picture of the people of Israel as it is not illuminated by the New Testament and therefore characterised by the differentiation between the elect and the rejected. The reality and revelation of the New Testament ἐκκλησία are the correction of this picture. The differentiation is not found in the New Testament community. By the election of the One who has taken all rejection upon Himself in His death, and left it behind in His resurrection, it is obviously constituted for participation in His election and His triumph, through faith in Him, in which rejection is taken from men, and the community is authorised and commanded to hold fast to its election. The man who is still rejected would not believe. And he who believes is as such no longer rejected. A rejected person in the New Testament community is " wooden iron." It may well be that everyone in the community has to see to it that he does not hazard his κλῆσις and ἐκλογή with his πίστις. It may well be that the question of πίστις, and therefore of κλῆσις, may and must be continuously raised and answered. But it is still the case that where there is πίστις there are also κλῆσις and ἐκλογή. It is still the case that the circle cannot be broken on this side either.

But we must obviously pursue the question further. If the circle of election is coincident with that of the community or Church of Jesus Christ, what does it mean to be in this community ? What is the inner nature of this community ? Again, the only finding which we can give as an answer to this further question in view of the text is as follows. The last word about the Christian community and life in it, and therefore, inclusively, the meaning and purpose of the election of the individual Christian, is not in any sense that those united in it are as such saved from the world, sin and death, justified, sanctified and made heirs of eternal life. The goal of the admonition and comfort given them is not in any sense the all-round fulfilment of their personal aims. The Church is not in any sense to be understood as the divine institution for the satisfaction of needs related to this fulfilment, or the provision and employment of the means necessary and available for it. It is true, of course, that all this is also the experience, reality, gift and task of the community. We may and must say that election to life in the Church includes this as well. But on a closer examination all this will be seen to be subordinate. The Church has its true meaning, and therefore the man elected to life in the Church has his true personal determination, in the fact that, equipped and empowered by these benefits, instructed by this admonition and comfort, he is made serviceable to the Lord of the Church, and therefore, in the omnipotent loving-kindness of God realised and revealed in Him, to the rest of the world. That is to say, the Church as such, and every individual in the Church in his own place and manner, becomes a bearer and proclaimer of this name and this fact. If the *catena aurea* of Rom. 8²⁹ᶠ· culminates in the ἐδόξασεν, we must remember that the necessary connexion of the concept of δόξα with the display of radiance excludes any idea that the final purpose of election is attained with the coincident exaltation, glorification and quickening of those to whom δόξα is communicated. But as God Himself is glorious in His power to declare Himself and the act in which He does so—He, the uncreated source of light, He, the irresistible radiance of His own perfection—so inevitably the up-lifting, honouring and quickening which He communicates to His only-begotten Son, and therefore to His brothers elected in and with Him, will become a pro-clamation to others. Those glorified by Him may and must glorify Him again. This is the true scope of their own glorification. The most appropriate passage in this connexion is Mt. 5¹⁴ᶠ·, where in unmistakeable relationship to Jn. 8¹² it is said : " Ye are the light of the world. A city that is set on an hill cannot be hid. Neither do men light a candle, and put it under a bushel, but on a candle-stick ; and it giveth light unto all that are in the house. Let your light so shine before men, that they may see your good works, and glorify your Father which is in heaven." Again, we are told in Eph. 1⁹ of our heavenly blessing in Jesus Christ, in v. 4 of our election in Him before the foundation of the world, and in v. 5 (as also in Rom. 8²⁹) : προορίσας ἡμᾶς εἰς υἱοθεσίαν διὰ Ἰησοῦ Χριστοῦ εἰς αὐτὸν κατὰ τὴν εὐδοκίαν τοῦ θελήματος αὐτοῦ. But we must not overlook the conclusion of this passage, which, apart from First Peter, is perhaps the strongest presenta-tion of predestination in the New Testament. All this happened—for your sake ? Assuredly ! It is the beginning of the work of grace that encounters us. But just because of that εἰς ἔπαινον τῆς χάριτος αὐτοῦ (v. 6). Again, in Eph. 1¹¹ we read that in Him we are made heirs, predestinated according to the purpose of Him who operates all things according to the counsel of His will. But the continuation in v. 12 is to be noted, in which it is stated even more plainly than in v. 6, obviously in relation to the work of the completed community of the last day : εἰς τὸ εἶναι ἡμᾶς εἰς ἔπαινον δόξης αὐτοῦ τοὺς προηλπικότας ἐν τῷ Χριστῷ Ἰησοῦ. Again, we have in Eph 3¹¹ an impressive saying about the existence of the com-munity as it rests on the eternal predetermination of God. But it is to be noted that the community does not exist as an end in itself, but as the instrument by which the manifold wisdom of God is to be proclaimed to heavenly powers and authorities. In 2 Ti. 1⁹ the reference to the πρόθεσις and χάρις of God, which we have from eternity in Jesus Christ, is used by Paul as a basis for his admonition to Timothy that he should not be ashamed of the testimony of the Lord, nor of the testimony of the imprisoned Paul, but should endure hardship with him for the sake of the Gospel. In Rev. 17⁴, which deals with the eschatological war of Christ and His elect, the same relationship is quite clear. And if it seems not to be so prominent in Col. 3¹² and 2 Pet. 1¹⁰, it is outstanding in 1 Thess. 1⁴ᶠ· For in this passage Paul sees that the purpose of the equipment of the community with the Word and Spirit, on the basis of the divine election, is that they should be followers (μιμηταί) both of himself and of the Lord. By joyfully receiving the Word in much tribulation—and transmitting it—they have become a τύπος of faith in Macedonia, Achaia and beyond (v. 6 f.). The same is true of the great passage in 1 Pet. 2⁴ᶠ·, where the portrayal of the glory of believers as the elect nation (v. 9) culminates in the definition of its purpose : ὅπως τὰς ἀρετὰς ἐξαγγείλητε τοῦ ἐκ σκότους ὑμᾶς καλέσαντος εἰς τὸ θαυμαστὸν αὐτοῦ φῶς. Nor is it by chance that in this letter (2¹², 3¹ᶠ·, 3¹⁶, 4¹⁶) such emphasis is laid upon the outward demon-stration of Christian faith to the heathen. We do not know, perhaps, why a certain Rufus is described in the greetings of Rom. 16 (v. 13) as ὁ ἐκλεκτὸς ἐν κυρίῳ. But we can see all the more clearly why there is what seems to be the only other apparent exception to the rule that the plural ἐκλεκτοί corresponds to the ἐκλογή—

namely, the elect apostle, Paul. It is immediately apparent what his election and all that resulted from it meant for him personally. If he proclaims the Gospel as the power of God to save all believers, and therefore as something of which he has no real need to be ashamed (Rom. 1¹⁶), it is because he himself has experienced it as such. And we learn from 1 Cor. 9²⁷ᶠ· that he knew the fear that while acting as a herald to others he himself might be rejected. Yet especially in the case of Paul—think again of Rom. 9⁵—there can be no real question of his conversion and being as a Christian, and therefore the election on which they are based, finding their goal and fulfilment in the fact that he himself shares both here and hereafter in the predetermined and therefore unalterable divine benefits. On the contrary, what Ananias (Ac. 9¹⁵) is told about Saul, the one-time persecutor, is that he must go to him, " for this man is a σκεῦος ἐκλογῆς to bear my name before the heathen and before kings and before the children of Israel." According to Ac. 22¹⁴ᶠ·, Ananias performed his commission with the words : " The God of our fathers hath chosen (προεχειρίσατο) thee, that thou shouldest know his will, and see that Just One, and shouldest hear the voice of his mouth. For thou shalt be his witness unto all men, of what thou hast seen and heard." And according to Ac. 26¹⁶ᶠ·, Jesus Himself, whom he had persecuted while he was still Saul, said to him : " Rise, and stand upon thy feet : for I have appeared unto thee for this purpose, to make thee (προχειρίσασθαί σε) a minister and a witness both of these things which thou hast seen, and of those things in the which I will appear unto thee ; delivering thee from the people, and from the Gentiles, unto whom now I send thee, to open their eyes, and to turn them from darkness to light, and from the power of Satan unto God, that they may receive forgiveness of sins, and inheritance among them which are sanctified by faith that is in me." Similarly, Paul writes of himself that he is ἀφωρισμένος εἰς εὐαγγέλιον θεοῦ . . . περὶ τοῦ υἱοῦ αὐτοῦ (Rom. 1¹ᶠ·), and more fully (Gal. 1¹⁵) that it pleased God, who set him apart from his mother's womb, and called him by His grace, to reveal His Son in him, that he " might preach him among the heathen." In the same way, according to 1 Ti. 1¹⁶ he received mercy in order that Jesus Christ should show His all longsuffering to him as the first—the first of sinners, he calls himself in v. 15—for a pattern (ὑποτύπωσις) to them which should hereafter believe on Him to life everlasting. If Paul glories (as in 1 Cor. 15¹⁰ᶠ· or 2 Cor. 12⁹ᶠ·) in the divine χάρις in relation to his own person, we may be sure that the final and decisive reference is to the grace of his apostolic office, just as his εὐχαριστεῖν (1 Cor. 1⁴ᶠ·, Phil. 1³ᶠ·, Col. 1³ᶠ·, 1 Thess. 1²ᶠ·, 2 Thess 1³ᶠ·) occurs always in connexion with the Christian community and his work as an apostle. This relationship, which is so clear in Paul's writings, between election, grace and apostleship, shows that the striking connexion of election with his own person does not actually involve any breach of the New Testament rule that election is the election of the Church, or to being in the Church.

What it means to be in the Church, and even what the Church itself truly is, may be seen typically in what is described in the New Testament as the reality of the apostolate, and particularly in what Paul describes as the reality of his apostolate. On the one hand, of course, the Church is the elect man, Jesus Christ, and in Him His people, that is, all who believe in Him and are therefore the object of divine election. But, on the other hand (and here we are concerned to explain how Jesus Christ comes to His own, and they to Him), it is the group of twelve apostles (completed after the defection of Judas by Paul, not by Matthias), and with them all those who are called to faith and drawn to Jesus Christ by their appointment and work, and who in this form are the chosen twelve tribes of Israel scattered abroad (Jas. 1¹). This is the teaching which we receive about this matter in the first section of the Canon, and it confirms and clarifies everything that we have said already concerning the content and task of the life of the elect. In and with the grace which comes to it, the Church (and therefore the *congregatio electorum*) has its essential direction outwards to mission, to the world, because it is not merely based upon the apostolate but is identical with it. By its very origin and in indissoluble connexion with it, it is the city set on a hill, the light placed upon a candlestick, not hidden but visible. It is of its essence to reveal, to be the bearer of revelation. It seems to me to be lacking in clarity, to say the least, when Schrenk (*op. cit.* p. 179, 20 f.) says that in the Gospels the twelve are " an indication of what is true of the whole community. The meaning of election finds a living example for the whole at its source, in the apostolic group." This reads as if in the relationship between election and the apostolate we merely have an illustration and interpretation of the reality of the community by that of the apostolic group which was subsequently discovered by the Evangelists. If the apostolic group is really " the source " of what the New Testament calls election, the very opposite is true, that everything which may be said about the elect community, and which is said about it in the New Testament Epistles, can only be an indication and living example of what originally and always and primarily may be said and is said of the apostolic group. It is in this group that the Church originally exists, and it is from the Pauline apostolate itself that we see clearly that this does not simply mean at the beginning, but that the Church cannot cease to exist in the work and word of the apostle without self-surrender or self-betrayal ; that the predicates of the unity, holiness and catholicity of the Church stand or fall with the inclusive predicate that it is the apostolic Church. On the one hand, " apostolic " means that it exists by the ongoing work and word of the apostles, and, on the other hand, that it exists by itself doing what the apostles did and are still doing, in virtue of the nature of their own works and words. There is no life of or in the Church which can comprehend more or less than what appeared as " life " (1 Jn. 1²) to the apostles, and was communicated, transmitted, commanded, presented and committed to them. To live in the Church means, in this twofold sense, to live with the apostles. It is because the Church stands under this norm that the relationship between election and the Church can only be described as it is described in the New Testament Epistles.

When we consider the sections of the Synoptic Gospels which deal with the apostolate, we see at once that there are three groups which are interrelated but plainly distinguishable both in form and substance. At every point, of course, we have to do with the mission of the twelve, or eleven, who are given prominence over the other disciples as the essence and representation of discipleship. To begin with, however, the emphasis is on the calling of these twelve, in the context of the description of Jesus' own Galilean activity. Prominence is next given to their function as visible representatives of the basis and norm of the discipleship or community of Jesus, in the context of the description of Jesus' last journey to Jerusalem. Finally, there is their commission to speak to the world, which is again the commission of the discipleship or community of Jesus as such, in the context of the resurrection and ascension. The three circles overlap, for the mission of the apostles, of those sent by Jesus, is the content of all these statements. But we cannot ignore the varying emphasis with which this content is brought out in the three circles. It is immediately apparent, of course, that in this differentiated unity of the apostolate, and therefore of the community, we have a correspondence to what was later called the threefold office of Christ. The prophetic office at the first (Galilean) stage, the priestly at the second (the passion) and the kingly at the third (the exaltation) all find their secondary continuation in those who are sent by Him. The answer to *Question* 32 of the *Heidelberg Catechism* : " Why art thou called a Christian ? Because by faith I am a member of Christ and therefore participate in His appointment, that I may likewise confess His name, offer myself as a living sacrifice, and in this life resist sin and the devil with a good conscience, and in the life hereafter reign with Him over all creatures," would be a good definition of the New Testament apostolate according to the Synoptic Gospels. The apostolate is the active participation of the members of Christ in His unction, His Messianic office. This participation is wholly by grace. It rests entirely on election and takes place only in faith. By its very nature, therefore, it can only be an active participation. For the Messianic office itself, as is also true of its members, is supremely the office of One who is sent, sent by God the Father ; the Son, who comes from Him, and in His almighty power, into the world which He created, and which stands in need of His love. Hence Jesus Himself is called ἀπόστολος in Heb. 3¹, and in St. John's Gospel (especially in cc. 5–8) the fact that He is " sent by the Father " is the dominant description which Jesus uses of Himself to declare Himself to His disciples and the Jews. And it is here that we find the explicit interconnexion and transmission : " As thou hast sent me into the world, even so have I sent them into the world. And for their sakes I sanctify myself, that they also might be sanctified through the truth " (Jn. 17¹⁸ᶠ·) ; or, again, in the resurrection narrative : " Peace be unto you : as my Father hath sent me, even so send I you. And when he had said this, he breathed on them, and saith unto them, Receive ye the Holy Ghost " (Jn. 20²¹ᶠ·). The apostolate consists of this sharing in Jesus' own mission. Those who possess it are to do what He Himself does : not because of their own will or choice, but because Jesus wills it and has chosen it for them ; not in their own power, but in that might which is given them for the purpose by Jesus ; not by their own decision, but both formally and in fact according to the strict instruction which they have received for the purpose from Jesus. Or conversely, His own action goes on into the world in the secondary form of the action to which the apostles are appointed, empowered and guided by Him. In this sense it may certainly be said of them that " participant in His anointment " they (and through and with them the whole Church, all Christians) are not merely χριστιανοί but χριστοί. They have " the unction (χρίσμα) from him who is holy " (1 Jn. 2²⁰, cf. 2²⁷). They are themselves prophets, priests and kings (1 Pet. 2⁹) because He is this, and has made them His own.

It would hardly be possible to analyse and exhibit historico-pragmatically the structure of the apostolate as it appears in the Synoptic Gospels. The picture given in the Gospels certainly covers these three stages, both in Jesus Himself and then in the apostles. But it is not to be understood as the picture of a historical development which would enable or compel us to see and understand the reality it describes in three independent parts, connected only by their sequence and therefore to be interrelated only in a consideration of the whole. The structure of the apostolate is a material differentiation of one and the same reality. We shall best understand it, therefore, if we take as our point of departure the final and all-inclusive form in which it meets us at the end of the Gospels in the story of the resurrection. This does not exclude, but includes, the two previous forms, and it is in this way, as comprehended within the final form, that the Evangelists themselves certainly saw and understood the earlier forms. We are thinking of the so-called great commission which in Luke, the spurious conclusion of Mark, and Acts, immediately precedes the story of the ascension. As is explicitly emphasised in its reiteration in Ac. 1⁸, this constitutes the transition from the first to the second part of the New Testament Canon, in which the words and works of the apostles are in the foreground. It is worth noting that Matthew (28¹⁶) transfers the event to Galilee, thus closing, as it were, both the circle of Jesus' own activity and also that of the foundation of the apostolate. But according to Lk. 24³⁶ᶠ· the same event obviously takes place in Jerusalem, opening up the way for the story of Pentecost and the subsequent commencement of the departure of the apostles (or, more exactly, of the apostle Paul) from Jerusalem to the heathen world. It is also worth noting that according to Mt. 28¹⁸ " the commission " is a direct word of Jesus Himself, whereas in Lk. 24¹⁶ᶠ· it is found in the context of the explanation that everything which

Jesus told His disciples while He was with them consisted in, and meant, that the things written concerning Him in the Books of Moses, the Prophets and the Psalms must be fulfilled. The risen One has revealed their meaning. They now understand the Scriptures. They see that the whole event of His death and resurrection is written in the Old Testament. There is now added to what is written the fact that repentance for the forgiveness of sins is to be proclaimed in His name to all nations, " beginning in Jerusalem." The disciples are witnesses to this fulfilment of the Scriptures, and therefore in this sense they are " my " witnesses (Ac. 1[8]). The actual teaching given us by these variants is obviously more important than the historical difficulty which we may legitimately feel, especially in relation to the first of them. The two aspects are both true and have both to be considered : the commission of the risen One—as is the obvious meaning of Matthew when he transfers it to Galilee—is exactly the same as that which Jesus gave to His disciples before His death for proclamation to Israel, and in virtue of His resurrection it is the commission in whose execution the Word of God goes forth from Zion into the whole world. Again, the two aspects are both true, and have both to be considered : it is the commission which only Jesus Himself could give, and has given, and yet as such it is also fulfilled Scripture, the content of the whole Old Testament. The common content of the Matthean and Lukan accounts consists in the following elements. At the decisive point, in their relationship to Jesus, the attitude of the disciples—this may seem strange at the end of the Gospels, but obviously it must have been the case—is twofold. It is said in Lk. 24[37] that when He appeared in their midst they were confused and frightened because they thought they were seeing a spirit. And in Mt. 28[17] we read that they fell down before him—" but some doubted." This account corresponds only too exactly to that of the attitude of the disciples before the death and resurrection of Jesus. Of themselves, they are not in any sense suitable instruments for the carrying-out of their appointment. The person of Jesus Himself was still necessary to create for them the relationship to Him which enabled them, as sent by Him, to perform what He performed. It is clear that even at this supreme moment—after the resurrection, in the solemn moment of this transference of the apostolate from its original possessor and bearer, to them—the Evangelists did not regard or understand the apostles in any other way. If it is true that a royal office has really been given to these men, it is certainly not because they are in any way regal, or bear the stamp of kingliness upon them. Jesus the King must make them kings, or they can never be kings. And it is as King—as Himself the bearer and giver of the fulness of their future office—that He now appears to them. According to Mt. 28[18], He begins His commission with the affirmation that He is the One who has the right to command : " All power (ἐξουσία, *potestas*) is given unto me in heaven and in earth." He addresses them in this power and they are commanded to share in this power. At first sight there seems to be no parallel to this in the Lukan text. But we can actually see one in the fact that for Luke, Jesus—who is Himself the fulfilment of Scripture—is also and alone its expositor, confirming and demonstrating that He is the bearer of God's power and glory. This emerges in the preceding Emmaus story of Lk. 24[13-35]. It is because Jesus is Himself both the content and proclamation of Scripture that He makes the disciples what they could not be of themselves—witnesses to the content of Scripture, and therefore His witnesses. In Mt. 28[19a] we are then given the simple commission which they are to execute as those whom He has enabled for the purpose : μαθητεύσατε πάντα τὰ ἔθνη. The clauses which follow : πορευθέντες, βαπτίζοντες . . . διδάσκοντες are all dependent upon this main clause. Μαθητεύσατε : make of them what you yourselves are, my disciples. Let them learn what you yourselves have learned. Πάντα τὰ ἔθνη : men of all nations, men of the whole world. It is to be noted that the μαθητεύσατε revives, continues and confirms the first prophetic stage of the activity of Jesus and also of His relationship to the apostles. But conversely, the teacher-scholar relationship which previously dominated the picture is deepened by the fact that it is repeated, being raised and set against the light of the relationship between a king and his subjects. In its connexion with πάντα τὰ ἔθνη the μαθητεύσατε tells us that the prophetic Word which Jesus uttered as a Teacher to His pupils in Galilee raises and vindicates a claim to become the Teacher of all men, of all the world, in the mouth of these pupils : " What I tell you in darkness, that speak ye in light : and what ye hear in the ear, that preach ye upon the housetops " (Mt. 10²⁷). This prior order obviously discloses the power immanent from the outset. The twelve were called to be disciples of Jesus in order that they themselves should be in a position to make disciples (πορεύεσθαι) as He did, going out to all nations, going before all nations, and therefore themselves summoning them to follow Jesus. In Lk. 24⁴⁷ the content of the Word which they had heard, and which they are now to proclaim to the world, is made explicit. Through them repentance for the forgiveness of sins is to be proclaimed and demanded of all nations in His name. Repentance for the remission of sins is the practical content of the name of Jesus which they are to proclaim. But it cannot be separated from the proclamation of His name. It is only in His name, in the revelation and reality of His person, that it becomes practical and meaningful proclamation. The world, then, is to be summoned to faith in Him, to the recognition and acknowledgment of the repentance which He has completed for it, and therefore to the repentance in which the bearing away of sin which He has accomplished becomes recognisable and real for the world. This is clear in Mt. 28¹⁹ᵇ, where the μαθητεύσατε—rather surprisingly at first sight—is explained in the first instance by the βαπτίζοντες αὐτοὺς εἰς τὸ ὄνομα τοῦ πατρὸς καὶ τοῦ υἱοῦ καὶ τοῦ ἁγίου πνεύματος. That which the world has to learn from the apostles is defined, therefore, as the way opened by baptism into the revelation and reality of the mercy of the triune God. The world has to learn from the apostles, and they are to teach the world, the recognition and acknowledgment of the free grace which God has already prepared for them in all fulness and with compelling might. The command given to the apostles is simply the command to preach the Gospel. But they are to preach it—for it is not arbitrary to recognise the approach of the Pauline Epistles in Mt. 28¹⁹ᵇ⁻²⁰ᵃ—not in a vacuum, or without form, but in the specific form of its application to those who listen to it in the world. Where it is a matter of baptism in the name of the triune God, of the recognition and acknowledgment of the divine gift of grace, we have to do necessarily and originally with a τηρεῖν, the maintaining, proving, guarding, defending, maintaining intact, of a form which cannot be controlled either by men or by the apostles, but is given with the thing itself, with the Gospel, and therefore by Jesus Christ ; by the One who has taken away their sin by the repentance which He has completed on their behalf. We have to do, therefore, with the τηρεῖν of that which He has committed to the apostles as the rule of faith, with the application which is not an accidental but a necessary form as an explication of the Gospel. Thus Mt. 28²⁰ᵃ goes beyond the διδάσκοντες and approaches the βαπτίζοντες of 19b. Concrete direction is also given to the repentance which, according to Lk. 24⁴⁷, is certainly required of those outside as well. If we are still doubtful whether the command given to the apostles to baptise and teach is directly connected, in substance, with the One who issues it, whether it consists simply in proclaiming that He who commands is Himself the gracious command of God, and seeing to it that He Himself is heard throughout the world as the gracious command of God, then the concluding words of Mt. 28²⁰ᵇ must surely be instructive in this direction : " Lo, I am with you alway, even unto the end of the world." To Me—who give you this commission and this office with it—to Me is given all power in heaven and on earth. You may rely in every age on the power of My authority in which I send you forth. This conclusion also marks out the apostles as those who really are to perform this commission in virtue of His authority. " He that heareth you, heareth me " (Lk. 10¹⁶). But this also binds their whole μαθητεύειν finally to Him, both in form and substance, so that there can be for them no question of any other content than that βαπτίζειν in the name of the triune God, or of any other form than that διδάσκειν, that direction to protect that which He has entrusted to them, or of any other Gospel or Law than that of His name. His being with them to the end of the world means both that He will always confess them if they confess Him before men, and that He will always deny them if they deny Him before men in favour of another revelation which they themselves have discovered (Mt. 10³²ᶠ·). The conclusion of Luke's account (24⁴⁹) is to the same effect when with a distinctively Lukan connexion with Pentecost He says : " I send the promise of my Father upon you : but tarry ye in the city of Jerusalem, until ye be endued with power from on high." This power from above, the Holy Spirit, is the firm guarantee, the authorisation and legitimisation, and yet also the necessary judge of the apostolate, through the presence of Jesus Christ, immanent in its word and work. He, Jesus Christ, gives them this power, which is, of course, originally His. According to Jn. 20²¹, the fulfilment of this promise, and therefore the Pentecostal event, coincides with the command to missionary action. According to the Synoptic Gospels, and with particular definiteness in Luke (cf. also Ac. 1⁸), even when the apostles are commissioned they have still to wait a given time for the fulfilment of this promise which is decisive for the completion of their task. But the " without me ye can do nothing," the *ubi et quando vult*, which is so clear in the Synoptic presentation, is also the Johannine teaching. And, again, the latter simply underlines that which is the Alpha and Omega of the Synoptic account when it speaks of that " breathing upon." The apostles are what they are and have what they have because and as Jesus wills that it should be so and fashions them accordingly, constituting Himself the substance of their commission, and the power for its execution, as well as its criterion. It is because of the fact that He is King, and always in the realisation and proclamation of His kingship, and with the power of His kingship, that they for their part are also kings. Their election to this is in Him and Him alone—because and as He is the elect King of Israel, and of the whole world. But in Him it is their election—and the election of the whole Church in them—to *this*, to be rulers with Him, in the power of the Word for the world which they have learned from Him and have to teach about Him.

We now move back to the second stage of the Gospel account of the apostolate. Externally, it is to be distinguished by the turning of Jesus Christ from Galilee to Jerusalem ; and concretely by three related predictions of suffering. It is linked with the picture which we have just considered by the fact that the predictions of suffering all culminate with the words : " and on the third day he will rise again." It is not in spite of the road to death upon which He now enters, but on this road, that He who gives the apostles their office and commission is the King of the whole world which He is revealed to be in His exaltation, entering on His rule with the sending out of His apostles to proclaim the bearing away of sin which He has accomplished, and continuing to exercise it to the world's end by this proclamation. And on the part of the apostles it is a matter of recognising this kingship of His, and even of recognising their own function in the kingdom. Their institution to this function is specifically reported and confirmed—especially in the saying to Peter in Mt. 16. To this period there also belongs the story how Jesus led Peter, James and John to a high mountain, " and was transfigured before them : and his face did shine as the sun, and his raiment was white as the light. And, behold, there appeared unto them Moses and Elias, talking with him." And they heard " a voice out of the cloud " which said : " This is my beloved Son, in whom I am well pleased ; hear ye him " (Mt. 17¹ᶠ·). According to Lk. 10²¹ᶠ·, it was also in this period that Jesus " rejoiced in spirit, and said, I thank thee, O Father, Lord of heaven and earth, that thou hast hid these things from the wise and prudent, and hast revealed them unto babes : even so, Father, for so it seemed good in thy sight. All things are delivered to me of my Father : and no man knoweth who the Son is, but the Father ; and who the Father is, but the Son, and he to whom the Son will reveal him. And he turned him unto his disciples, and said privately, Blessed are the eyes which see the things that ye see : for I tell you, that many prophets and kings have desired to see those things which ye see, and have not seen them ; and to hear those things which ye hear, and have not heard them." Luke also groups in this period (12²ᶠ·) the sayings about the necessary revelation of that which is hidden and preaching from the housetops ; the promise that His messengers need fear nobody except God, because every hair of their heads is numbered ; the sayings about the confessing and denying of Jesus and the assistance of the Holy Spirit in the hour of persecution, both of which speak so clearly of His continuing presence ; and in 11³³ the saying about the candle and the candlestick. Again, according to Luke (11²⁷) it is in this context that Jesus' reply to the woman who sought to bless His mother is found : " Blessed are they that hear the word of God, and keep it." And in connexion with the institution of the Last Supper, in sublime forbearance and transcendence of the quarrel about status which, according to Luke, had flared up at that very moment, there are the words : " Ye are they which have continued with me in my temptations. And I appoint unto you a kingdom, as my Father hath appointed unto me ; that ye may eat and drink at my table in my kingdom, and sit on thrones, judging the twelve tribes of Israel " (Lk. 22²⁸ᶠ·). For when the sun and the moon are darkened, and the stars fall from heaven, when finally the Son of Man, coming on the clouds of heaven, is His own witness and His own sign, then at His command His angels will go forth with a mighty peal of trumpets, to gather the elect from the four winds and the four corners of the earth (Mt. 24²⁹ᶠ·). Here, again, we see the apostolate in the light whose origin is revealed only in the resurrection narratives, but which falls on them already in this second stage when not only Easter, but Good Friday, Peter's denial, the flight of all the disciples, and even more darkly, darkening even the present, the treachery of Judas, are still future. This light is supremely to be seen in the great passage, Mt. 16¹³ᶠ·, the account of the conversation near Cæsarea Philippi. According to this passage, Jesus has asked His disciples, with obvious reference to all His own and their earlier activity : " Whom do men say that I, the Son of man, am ? " And He receives the naive replies that He is one of God's prophets : " Elias, Jeremias, or one of the prophets." These replies are not absolute errors if we take into account the specific nature of the preceding first stage in the activity of Jesus. They repeat what was surely a sound recognition in the first, Galilean period : " There came a fear on all : and they glorified God, saying, That a great prophet is risen up among us ; and, That God hath visited his people " (Lk. 7¹⁶ᶠ·). Again, when, according to Mt. 21¹¹, ⁴⁶, Jesus is conducted into Jerusalem by the accompanying crowd of people as " the prophet of Nazareth," the multitude was not making a mistake according to the Synoptists. The only thing is that when Peter makes his confession in the name of the twelve as we have it in Mt. 16¹⁶, he simply goes further. To what point ? Obviously to the point at which even Jesus' disciples really stand only after His resurrection, on the basis of His special will and command, of the imparting of the Holy Spirit which has already partly taken place in them, enabling them publicly to proclaim their confession and declare its content. The confession itself—and this is why it can only be whispered here and only really proclaimed when the third stage is reached—is this : " Thou art the Christ, the Son of the living God." The opening words of Jesus' reply to Peter (v. 17) show that what we have here is an anticipation : " Blessed art thou, Simon Bar-jona : for flesh and blood hath not revealed it unto thee, but my Father which is in heaven." Now that the confession that Jesus is the Messiah is both possible and actual, the revelation of the One who was raised from the dead by the power of the Father, and the impartation of His Holy Spirit, have—secretly—taken place. The command to silence with which Jesus concludes His reply in v. 20 is a further indication of the anticipatory nature of Peter's confession, of what is still the secret character of its content. And this command is even more sharply emphasised by the other Evangelists (ἐπετίμησεν, Mk. 8³⁰). If Jesus is the Messiah, He is the King. As the Son of the living God He is *the* King of Israel, and as such the King of the *world*. He is not merely a prophet, but—*the* Prophet, *the* Teacher, as He will later confront His disciples in the resurrection narrative, to make teachers, royal teachers, of them. This is the radicalising of the other answers implicit in Peter's confession, and it is because of this that Jesus calls the one who makes it blessed, Peter, the spokesman of the twelve. Yet at this stage of His career He will not permit it to be published. Why not ? Clearly, because this publication of the secret of His Messianic identity, as it is already known to the twelve, is still a matter of the special revelation of the Father and the Son. And the stage has not yet been reached for this special revelation. There must first be completed a second, intermediate stage of His work, and therefore of the calling and appointment of the apostles. When this has been done—but only then and not before—He Himself will see to it that the twelve shall actually preach from the housetops what has already been spoken in their ears. They and the words which needs the revelation of His secret must wait for His disposing. Jn. 6¹⁴⁻¹⁵ is a most instructive parallel : " Then those men, when they had seen the miracle that Jesus did, said, This is of a truth that prophet that should come into the world. When Jesus therefore perceived that they would come and take him by force (ἁρπάζειν), to make him a king, he departed again into a mountain himself alone." This is the kind of violence that none can or may offer Him. A Jesus who was made king by men, or arbitrarily proclaimed king by the apostles, would not be that Prophet who is to come into the world, nor would he be the King of Israel and the world. Such a Jesus would not be Jesus at all. And apostles who acted in this manner, without His special authorisation, would not be His apostles, for all the completeness of their recognition and confession. Or else they would be treacherous apostles, turning against Him. In this connexion it is to be noted how strangely Jesus answers Peter's confession in Jn. 6⁷⁰ : " Have not I chosen you twelve—and one of you is a διάβολος " ; and to this the Evangelist adds the note : " He spake of Judas Iscariot the son of Simon : for he it was that should betray him, being one of the twelve." He, Jesus, who chose the twelve, will empower them for the proclamation of the secret of His Messianic identity which they have recognised and confessed. Otherwise they will never be empowered at all. They will belie their calling as His apostles, and in spite of their election, recognition and confession they will only be διάβολοι, only able to betray Jesus, as Judas actually did. It is not for nothing that the whole of the well-known saying to Peter in Mt. 16¹⁸⁻¹⁹, from which Romanist exegesis, or rather Romanist theory, has drawn its authorisation for a Church independent of its Lord in the proclamation of His name, is given in the future tense : οἰκοδομήσω . . . οὐ κατισχύσουσιν . . . δώσω. It is a promise, and between it and its fulfilment there stands always the cross of Jesus Christ which He is preparing to approach at the very moment when He answers Peter's confession with this promise. Between this promise and its fulfilment there stands always, with the suffering and death of Jesus, the temptation and sifting of His disciples, including the apostolic group and Peter in particular ; the disclosure of the fact that in human frailty the apostles are really indistinguishable from the world to which they are to proclaim the mystery of Jesus ; and that for this proclamation they always need the special authorisation of Jesus if what they do is not to be its opposite, namely, betrayal. This aspect of the situation, which obviously meets us again in the third stage, the resurrection narratives, is the particular mark of this second, middle stage of the calling and appointment of the apostles. As it stands wholly and utterly under the sign of the suffering and death of Jesus, so it stands under the sign of their temptation. Immediate and extraordinarily sharp expression is given to this in Mt. 16²¹ᶠ· The first prediction of suffering succeeds at once the promise and the command to silence. In response to it the same Peter, who had just uttered the Messianic secret and received the promise, reveals his complete inadequacy by taking Jesus on one side, reproaching Him and attempting to restrain Him from the course He has announced : " This shall not be unto thee." He then receives the terrible reply which reminds us only too clearly of what is said about Judas in Jn. 6⁷⁰ : " Get thee behind me, Satan ; thou art an offence unto me ; for thou savourest not the things that be of God, but those that be of men." This is followed directly by the saying to the disciples : " If any man will come after me, let him deny himself, and take up his cross, and follow me " (16²⁴ᶠ·). Only he who loses his life for My sake shall save it. Only when this crisis is past will the Son of Man come in the glory of His Father to reward every man according to his πρᾶξις. Only then will it be true that some standing here will in their own lifetime see this coming of the Son of Man in His royal glory. It is of a piece with this that the transfiguration story emphasises (17⁴) the folly of Peter, who wanted to build booths on the mountain, "one for thee, and one for Moses, and one for Elias," and also (17⁶) the fear of all the apostles present—as in the resurrection story—at the sight of Jesus' transfigured appearance, and the powerlessness of all the rest (in the story of the healing of the epileptic boy, 17¹⁴ᶠ·) because of their ὀλιγοπιστία (17²⁰). Shortly after the second prediction of suffering (17²²ᶠ·), there follows (18¹ᶠ·) the disciples' question : " Who is the greatest in the kingdom of heaven ? " and its answer, that he who humbles himself like a child, i.e., who begins his life all over again in the sense of Jn. 3³, is the greatest. Also relevant are the sayings in Lk. 9⁵⁷ᶠ· about the homelessness of the Son of Man, the threat which this means for His followers, and the necessity laid upon them to let the dead bury their dead and not to look back once their hand has been laid to the plough. So, too, is the saying to the seventy disciples on their return to Jesus (Lk. 10²⁰) : " In this rejoice not, that the spirits are subject unto you ; but rather rejoice, because your names are written in heaven ; " and the saying to Mary and Martha (Lk. 10⁴¹) about the one or the small thing that is necessary rather than the many things which His own want to do for Him according to their own ideas. Relevant, too, are the saying about the servants who await their lord and prepare for him (Mt. 24⁴³ᶠ· ; Lk. 12³⁵ᶠ·, 17⁷ᶠ·), and the parable of the ten virgins (Mt. 25¹ᶠ·). If these are not given a first place here it is impossible to understand their relationship to the second coming. Also relevant are the parables about the man who sought to build a tower, and the king who planned to make war (Lk. 14²⁵ᶠ·). The third prediction of suffering is then followed in Mt. 20¹⁷ᶠ·, as if this were the most appropriate reply, by the request of the mother of the sons of Zebedee (Mt. 20²⁰ᶠ·, cf. Mk. 10³⁵ᶠ·). And when these disciples have vigorously asserted that they also could drink the cup that Jesus is to drink and be baptised with the baptism with which He is to be baptised, the answer is given that this will assuredly take place : " But to sit on my right hand, and on my left, is not mine to give, but it shall be given to them for whom it is prepared of my Father." Then, when the others are angered by the assurance of the two brothers, they all have to learn (Mt. 20²⁴ᶠ·) that their questioning is in terms of the values and functions of a worldly kingdom, not of the kingdom of Jesus : " Whosoever will be great among you, let him be your minister ; and whosoever will be chief among you, let him be your servant : even as the Son of man came not to be ministered unto, but to minister, and to give his life a ransom for many." Then the great discourse about the end of the world and the second coming (Mk. 13 and parallels) stands as an admonition and warning to the disciples. They are not to let themselves be impressed by the splendour of the Jerusalem temple, for not one stone of it will remain on the other (Mk. 13¹ᶠ·). They are to beware lest any mislead them by professing to be the Christ (Mt. 24⁵). Such pseudo-Christs will be so tempting that if it were possible even the elect would be deceived (Mt. 24²³ᶠ·). They will be subject to persecution by Jews and Gentiles in the great darkness and distress that will descend upon Jerusalem at Jesus' death : " And except those days should be shortened, there should no flesh be saved : but for the elect's sake those days shall be shortened" (Mt. 24²²). This is something which is already " at the doors " (Mt. 24³³), and will take place in the lifetime of this generation (24³⁴). When ? Neither man nor angel knows, and Jesus says that He Himself does not know. Only the Father knows ; but He does know. This is the crisis which approaches for the disciples. So, once more : " Watch and be vigilant ! "—for you do not know when it will happen. " What I say unto you, I say unto all, Watch ! " (Mk. 13³⁷). Or, as Lk. 21³⁶ has it : " Watch ye therefore, and pray always, that ye may be accounted worthy to escape all these things that shall come to pass, and to stand before the Son of man." Luke places his account of the disciples' quarrel immediately after the institution of the Lord's Supper. It is resolved by the saying about greatness in service which, as Luke has it, passes over and melts into the promise of the future glory of the apostolate. But this does not prevent him from recording (22³¹ᶠ·) what Jesus says to Peter : " Simon, Simon, behold, Satan hath desired to have you, that he may sift you as wheat : but I have prayed for thee, that thy faith fail not : and when thou art converted, strengthen thy brethren." Luke also records that Peter declares himself ready to be imprisoned and to suffer death with Jesus. But the latter can only reply : " Peter, the cock shall not crow this day, before that thou shalt thrice deny that thou knowest me." A fuller description of the same incident is given in Mt. 26³⁰ᶠ· After they have sung the Hallel, Jesus utters the devastating words : " All ye shall be offended because of me this night." The truth of this is shown at once by the fact that during His agony in Gethsemane they are unable to watch with Him even for one hour (Mt. 26⁴⁰). Is it not as if He were addressing a void when He again summons them : " Why sleep ye ? rise and pray, lest ye enter into temptation " (Lk. 22⁴⁶). Then, when He actually is arrested, " all the disciples forsook him and fled " (Mt. 26⁵⁶), and Peter actually denies Him, as Judas had already betrayed Him. This is the picture of the apostles in this second, middle stage. It is one of absolute blindness in face of the way which Jesus has chosen for Himself, and in face of the fact that He will and must follow it to the end. Again, it is one of absolute misunderstanding about the manner in which they may follow and serve Him. Again, it is one of absolute error about their own power and capacity to follow Him. Again, it is one of absolutely wrong ideas about that which they may anticipate for themselves in following Him. Finally, it is one of absolute denial in practice at the moment when they ought to make good their insights and resolves, and actually follow Him. In fact, they do *not* follow Him. They are presumptuous, they quarrel, they fall asleep, they run away, they disown and betray Him. This is the commentary which the apostles themselves give on Peter's confession at Cæsarea Philippi. If the statement in Lk. 22²⁸ : " Ye are they which have continued with me in my temptations," is justifiable, we can only understand it to mean that although the apostles and their recognition and confession and perseverance and loyalty are not exempt from the passing of heaven and earth referred to in Mt. 24²⁵, in them and above them the truth remains : " My word shall not pass away." What endures and remains is the continual call of Jesus to watchfulness and prayer, to humility and service. But this call is not made into the void. For Jesus Himself remains, interceding for them now with the wholly sufficient work of His person—interceding Himself for the apostles who at every point deny Him. The positive aspect of the picture seen in this second, middle stage of their calling and appointment is that He is for them, watching for them, praying, humbling Himself, serving, accepting the cross in His death and passion. " As they were eating, Jesus took bread, and blessed it, and brake it, and gave it to the disciples, and said, Take, eat ; this is my body. And he took the cup, and gave thanks, and gave it to them, saying, Drink ye all of it : for this is my blood of the new testament, which is shed for many for the remission of sins " (Mt. 26²⁶).

Does it not seem as if the apostolate which Jesus conferred upon the twelve in the first stage is now taken from them at the supreme point of the second stage and restored to Himself as the true apostle ? The truth is, however, that the apostolate, as the meaning and power of the election of the twelve (and in them as the meaning and power of the election of all Israel and of the Church) is nowhere so clear as in this contrast, in which only the " I for you " appears to have genuine validity, but this gives to the " You for me " the solidity which is revealed and active in the πορευθέντες . . . μαθητεύσατε . . . βαπτίζοντες . . . διδάσκοντες of Mt. 28¹⁸. The revelation and activity are those of Jesus' death on the cross : the death on the cross which He suffers alone—not with the sons of Zebedee, but with two criminals, on the right hand and the left. It is He, in whom alone God has reconciled the world to Himself, that has power to transfer to men the ministry of reconciliation in this world—to men reconciled to God through Him, whom He has chosen out of the world. The non-imputation of sins, as God causes this to come into force and to be revealed by Him and for His sake, is necessary in order that this may be " the word of reconciliation " (2 Cor. 5¹⁸⁻¹⁹) on the lips of these men. Because this necessary thing takes place at this second stage of the Evangelists' account of the apostles, because at this point the apostles themselves cannot be reconcilers, redeemers or revealers of God, because they can only withdraw behind Jesus and let Him go forward alone, it is obvious that here we have the very core of the mystery of their calling and appointment as His witnesses. Yet it is to be noted that the apostles are not said to be abandoned. Interpreted by the continual call and admonition and command of Jesus, interpreted by the way in which Peter in particular is repeatedly warned and punished but also upheld, interpreted by the whole series of assurances and promises which, accompanying the continuing defection of the apostles, point to the glory which is to follow the sufferings of Jesus, and to their own share in that glory, the institution of the Lord's Supper speaks of the strongest possible affirmation and confirmation of the fellowship between Jesus and the apostles. It reiterates in a way which the " I for you " makes quite unmistakeable the " You for me " of their calling and mission in Galilee. And it affirms, as is possible and necessary, that their lips will later be opened to proclaim the mystery of the Messiah to the whole world, and that they will in truth preach from the housetops that which was spoken in their ears.

We can now return to the main passage, Mt. 16, and attempt to understand the decisive import of the reply given to Peter when he made the confession as the spokesman of the twelve. We ought never to explain the " Thou art Peter . . ." (v. 15) independently, separating it from the context which we have just sketched, or from its relationship to the second part of the Gospel record which culminates in the passion story. Plainly everything depends here upon who or what this Peter is. There can be no doubt that the Evangelists gave him a prominence over the rest of the apostles as their spokesman, for this is repeatedly evidenced by the text. Exegetically, however, the question does not even arise whether this is also true of his successors on the Roman episcopal throne in their relation to the bishops of other communities, for there is no passage in the New Testament which even hints at such an interpretation. At any rate, even according to Mt. 16 he was never anything more than a spokesman for the whole apostolic group. " Whom say ye that I am ? " is the question to which his confession is the explicit reply. The decisive point, however, is that this same Peter continues to be distinguished as their spokesman in their subsequent, satanically inspired defection, which degenerates finally into a wild flight and denial. Even his true and authentic confession is at once placed under the restriction of Mt. 16²⁰, being provisionally taken from him until a new direction is given. And when he takes the initiative (v. 22 f.) over against Jesus, what he says is characterised and rejected as a satanic word. If we want to make a " prince of apostles " out of this spokesman—in the starkest contrast to what Jesus Himself said about the use of such categories—then in view of what we are told about him from Mt. 16 to the passion we have to say that he is this only as their leader and representative in this defection, in their misunderstandings and mistakes, in their weakness and disloyalty. And as the " prince of the apostles " in this sense he—and the others with him—are led through temptation by the faithfulness of Jesus which never fails. What is Peter apart from Jesus, apart from His continual Word, apart from His intercession, apart from His vicarious suffering and death, apart from the glory which was not the goal of his own way but of Jesus' way ? What is Peter apart from what Jesus makes of him as He wills and expects it from him ? If there is any warning at all against an ecclesiasticism which makes itself independent of the person and Word and work of Jesus, which transforms Jesus' authority into its own authority ; if there is any underlining of the " without me ye can do nothing," it is provided in the Gospels by the figure of Peter himself. If he is a " prince " among the apostles, it is as a living demonstration that there is no apostle who is not a brand snatched from the burning, that the basis of the authority and glory of the apostolate is simply that an apostle—not merely Paul (1 Cor. 15¹⁰) but every apostle—is what he is by the grace of God. It is to this objectively and finally subjectively humbled Peter, and to this man as the representative and spokesman of all the others, that the words of Mt. 16¹⁸ are spoken : " Upon this rock I will build my church ; and the gates of hell shall not prevail against it." Self-evidently it is not the special integrity or loyalty to principle of the man Peter and his companions which constitutes the foundation and invincibility of the Church. We know what they were like. If these men continued with Jesus in His temptations they did so according to the whole tenor of the Gospels, only to the extent that the one Victor over temptation, Jesus Himself, actually continues with them in their temptations. Again, it is only with reserve that we can say that the foundation and invincibility of the Church is the faith of Peter and the other apostles. Certainly, this is true to the extent that flesh and blood did not reveal to Peter the object of his faith, namely, the kingship of Jesus Christ, but the heavenly Father of Jesus by the Holy Spirit, the God who raised Jesus from the dead. It is also true, of course, to the extent that Jesus prays for Peter that his faith should not fail. It is also true to the extent that when we use the word " faith " we think of its object and source, and therefore of Jesus Himself, crucified and risen, who was first for Peter, and then Peter for Him. Similarly, the confession of Peter and the other apostles is the foundation and invincibility of the Church only because Jesus went to the end of the true Messiah's road, the road of the Son of the living God ; because in His death He established and entered into His kingdom, in this way validating Peter's confession, making it the subject of proclamation to the whole world, and therefore putting it properly and legitimately on the lips of the apostles. If Peter and the twelve are indeed the foundation and invincibility of the Church, it is in virtue of their determination by Jesus in spite of and in their human unfitness, in virtue of what He Himself makes of them without and even against their co-operation. If the faith of Peter and the twelve is this, it is in virtue of the fact that Jesus was its object and origin, and that He did not cease to be this. If the confession of Peter and the twelve is this, it is in virtue of the fact that Jesus is the One of whom it speaks, in virtue of the fact that it is audible by His command, and not because of the initiative of those who recognise it. This Peter and these twelve—gathered and invited by Jesus to the Lord's Supper to partake of His body and blood—are indeed, according to the clear statement of Mt. 16¹⁸, the foundation and invincibility of the Church of Jesus Christ. It is through the men called, authorised and equipped in this way that Jesus Christ is proclaimed. But this is true only because, in this relationship of the superior and inferior, of giving and receiving, of ruling and obeying, as He is both for and with them, He also proclaims Himself, and builds His community through them. According to v. 19, what they say and do—accompanied by the power of Jesus, for what other power could do it ?—has the power on earth, in the world, to bind and loose (according to Jn. 20²³, to remit and retain sins), to open and close the doors of the kingdom of heaven. What they say and do always has the divine power of the keys in virtue of the fact that Jesus wills it, Himself acting and deciding in it. Clerical pride and arrogance in the exercise of this power are essentially impossible by reason of the contrast and fellowship between Jesus and the Peter, the apostolic group, in which it is established and conferred. Clerical pride and arrogance mean that the contrast and fellowship are lacking, and therefore that the power is neither established nor conferred. There can be no " misuse " of this power. For the clericalism which appears to misuse it merely demonstrates that it has already lost it, or never possessed it. When we do have it, as it was given to Peter and through him to the apostolic group and therefore to the whole Church, it is rightly used. And it consists in the fulfilment of the proclamation of Jesus Christ. When this takes place, it is the loosing and remitting of sins. When it does not take place, it is the binding and retaining of sins. But either way, whether it takes place or not, it means a crisis for the world. It effects a continuous separation corresponding to what is decreed in heaven and not on earth, by the counsel of God and not by the apostles or the Church, that is, by the everlasting decree for the world, in Jesus Christ. The apostles are the executors of this decree. They are this as those whom Jesus has won for Himself by giving Himself for them. It is in virtue of His priestly office and ministry that they are priests. They are established as those who are objectively and subjectively humbled, and therefore bound to Jesus, dependent wholly upon Him and living by and with Him. They are givers because they are receivers of the Lord's Supper, of His body and His blood. The power of the keys is the power of their mission. To this extent v. 19 anticipates Mt. 28¹⁸, where the missionary command becomes explicit, the missionary power first promised being actually given to the disciples through the outpouring of the Holy Spirit. The emphasis in Mt. 16¹⁸⁻¹⁹, however, is placed upon the fact that Peter and the apostolic group, in the sense given by the connexion with the passion story, serves Jesus in the establishment and guaranteeing of the Church, which as such is the bearer of the missionary power. Verse 18 says that it will serve Him as the rock, as an indestructible guarantee. It must indeed be established and guaranteed in this way to become (v. 19) the bearer of this power in face of the world ; to make resistance to its proclamation, or recoil from it, basically impossible ; to make itself absolutely sure of its cause. The apostles are this foundation and guarantee as they are both humbled and strengthened on the path of Jesus' suffering. This is the meaning and purpose of their appointment to the apostolate in the second and middle stage of the Gospel record.

It is in its first form (corresponding to the Galilean period of Jesus' activity) that we have what is relatively the simplest aspect of the matter. The connexions between the apostolate and the kingship and high-priesthood of Jesus Christ, as we have them at the third and second stages, are also to be seen here. But now, corresponding to the second stage, we hear explicitly of the appointment of the apostles as such, and we shall see how the characterisation of the apostles in respect of their appointment corresponds to what we found there concerning their position in relation to Jesus. The subject now is much more prominently even than at the second stage that of their mission, and the extensive nature of their office in its reference to the world ; an anticipation of what at the third stage is to be the final word of commission with which they are released (or, rather, are not released) by Jesus. But in the first stage all this is still veiled, to the extent that it is not yet unfolded, not yet visible in the definite words and sharp contours and contrasts which are typical of the second and third stages. It is all there already, and in a way not to be ignored—just as the cross and resurrection are there already, and are quite unavoidable and indispensable if there is to be a proper understanding of what we are told at this stage. But His coming sufferings and death, His Messianic nature and His exaltation are still concealed. They are not yet the subject of direct expression and statement. And it is exactly the same with the critical purifying and confirming of the apostolate, and its exaltation, as they are actualised and revealed at the second and third stages. Jesus Himself is for the moment just the Teacher and Prophet of Nazareth—although in an extraordinary way which shatters all existing concepts. In the same way the apostles are simply those who are called by this Prophet to be His disciples and followers, those who are enrolled by this Teacher in his school. It is only in the light of this calling that their appointment to special office, and the exercise of this office in the form of their preliminary mission, which ends and is provisionally terminated with their return to Jesus, have any real substance or importance (in contrast to the second and third stages, when their calling seems to gain its peculiar power only from the fulfilment of this appointment in that critical purifying and confirming, and finally from their commissioning and sending).

How necessary is the part of the apostolate in the whole record is shown at once by the fact that, according to all three Synoptists and also to John, the call of the disciples is one of the very first reported actions of Jesus. Matthew makes it quite clear that it is only at His baptism in the Jordan, and during the temptation (corresponding to His later solitude on Good Friday) that Jesus is alone. This is also how it appears in John. But we also find the same in Mark, for although the first calling of the disciples is preceded by the statement (1^{14}) that Jesus came into Galilee and proclaimed the good news of God : " The time is fulfilled, and the kingdom of God is at hand : repent ye, and believe the gospel," this is to be understood as a preface to all that follows rather than as the condensation of a proclamation by Jesus prior to the call of the disciples. The only divergence is in the Lukan account, in which the temptation narrative is followed by a preaching visit of Jesus to Nazareth and a number of healings in Capernaum, and only then—in the story of Peter's draught of fishes—by the first calling of the disciples. But the prefatory character of these previous stories is undeniable in Luke as well, so that one may venture the statement that the existence of the apostolate opens with the activity of Jesus itself. Of the apostolate—for that is how we must at once describe it in view of what we are told by all three Synoptists about the first calling of the disciples. We certainly cannot separate the words δεῦτε ὀπίσω μου (Mk. 1^{17}) from the further words καὶ ποιήσω ὑμᾶς γενέσθαι ἁλεεῖς ἀνθρώπων. Jesus calls them to come to Him, and to follow Him, in order that He may make something specific of them. What they already are on their own account has nothing to do with the situation. The only thing related of them is that they were fishermen and cast their nets. And, remarkably enough, a special light is thrown even on this fact by Lk. $5^{4f.}$, where we are told that they did it at His special command and were miraculously blessed by Him. Thus even in the transition from this former occupation to the following of Jesus they do not come from a different situation. Already, as it were, they come from Jesus Himself, from His activity, and from the revelation of His miraculous aid, which they seem first to encounter in this transition. Again, it is made quite plain in Lk. 5^8 that they are worthy to come to Jesus only because they already come from Jesus : " Depart from me ; for I am a sinful man, O Lord." The basis and presupposition of their calling cannot, on their side, be anything other than election, and election as it has taken place through Jesus Himself. This recognition is clearly underlined and strengthened by the fact that the disciple whose later calling is explicitly related like those of Peter and

Andrew and the two sons of Zebedee is deliberately and of set purpose a tax-gatherer, Matthew (Mt. 9⁹ᶠ·), or Levi (Mark and Luke). When Jesus calls them to Him, He does not promise that He will make them Christians, or even that He will first make them Christians and then as such apostles ; but He immediately promises that He will make them fishers of men—that is, apostles, bearers to men of a commission that will be given them, the commission to seek and gather men as a fisherman seeks and gathers fish in his net. If from this moment and on the basis of this calling they are called His μαθηταί, what He has to teach them and they have to learn from Him is not to be understood as being from the outset a kind of private route to their own salvation and blessedness, but as the message which they are to proclaim to men in order, through this message, to seek and gather them. What is involved is calling in the fullest meaning of the term. Jesus takes them from their previous calling, or more precisely He transforms their previous calling, so that they now have their new calling in this seeking and gathering. It is described in very general terms as the seeking and gathering of men. Already, then, we have to find the sphere of their calling both in the Church as concerns gathering, and in the world as concerns seeking. In order to learn this new and proper calling they leave their nets and ships, and follow Him. It is for this that Jesus has called them to this discipleship. It is for this that He has elected them. What the New Testament has to say about the meaning and purpose of the election of individuals could not be clearer than it is here. It is their election through Jesus. It is their election to belong to Him. And it is their election for the purpose for which He Himself is elected, for the proclamation to many, for the creation of the Church with its task in relation to the world, that the candle placed on the candlestick should illumine all that are in the house. To be precise, this call to the apostolate, resting upon election, is all that this first section of the evangelical record has to say about the matter. For everything else that we find in it is strictly speaking only an elucidation of the basic fact that Jesus does not will to be alone in the consummation of His own election and calling ; that He does not will merely to have objects of His work. The apostles are, of course, objects of His work. They are this primarily. But He wills them as those who, as He elects and calls them, are actively to work with Him, to share with Him His own office. And this office is His prophetic office. They cannot share this prophetic office with Him without sharing His suffering and glory. For His own office is not merely that of the Prophet, but also of the Priest and King. This will emerge, of course, only in the later sections of the evangelical record. Already, however, in this first section, in the elucidation of their calling to the prophetic office, there are developments which point to these later stages and in some sense anticipate them.

Our main attention must be given to the actual " appointment " of the twelve apostles, of which relatively independent accounts are given by all the Evangelists. According to the record of the call, what they received was an express promise. And the status into which they were transferred and entered at the time of their calling was that of the disciple or pupil, as the presupposition of the fulfilment of this promise. It is to be noted that they do not completely lose this status even later. The Evangelists make only the most sparing use of the title ἀπόστολοι. Those who have been specifically made this and have apparently graduated as such, are still called μαθηταί, just as if nothing had happened. This is the case in all three sections of the evangelical record. It is this very fact, however, that enables us to conclude that obviously the calling itself already includes in itself institution to that to which it seems as calling only to lead, that the institution is to be understood as an element of the calling itself, and not at all as a promotion that leads them beyond the calling and the status of disciples and pupils which it confers, beyond their status as receivers of the promise. The status into which the fishermen and the tax-gatherer were received and entered at the Lake of Gennesareth needed no such enhancement. We can only accept that the status itself already includes this enhancement—their appointment as apostles. This is clear from the fact that the appointment of the apostles is recorded as a special event. And we must add at once that it is obviously an anticipation of what will be described at the second stage as the critical purifying and confirming of the apostolate. The institution of the Lord's Supper, with everything that precedes it, is clearly the real institution of the apostolate. But the institution of the Lord's Supper, and the whole picture of the apostolate offered in that context, emerge already at the first stage of the portrayal, in this first and undeveloped form of its reality. We read in Mk. 3^{13} that Jesus went up into a mountain, and Luke explains that He went up to pray, and that He spent the whole night there. And it is significant and instructive that in Mt. $9^{35f.}$ the story is introduced very differently. For we are told that Jesus went about teaching, preaching and healing through the villages, and that He was moved with compassion for the crowds He saw because they were scattered and exhausted like sheep without a shepherd. It was this spectacle which led Him to say to His disciples : " The harvest truly is plenteous, but the labourers are few ; pray ye therefore the Lord of the harvest, that he will send forth labourers into his harvest." We can see at once how this disagreement regarding the situation and the occasion illuminates what follows in all three accounts—the appointment of the twelve apostles. On the one hand we have Jesus in His solitude with God ; on the other we have Him in His solitude over against man and his need. The question which account is correct is again a pointless one. We would actually have to complete and explain the one by the other even if we had only the one or the other and therefore an unambiguous report. For what necessarily follows from this twofold solitude of the praying Jesus and the Jesus who addresses Himself to the people as a teacher, preacher and miraculous healer, is the reality of the apostolate as the human co-operation with Jesus which already exists, but now emerges and is to be proclaimed openly. The One who both prays to God and is grieved as He beholds the people is utterly alone ; He has no fellow. He is the One who uniquely and in isolation represents man to God, and God to man. But neither in His uniqueness nor in His isolation, His twofold solitude, can His presence be in any sense futile and ineffective. For as such He is not merely the prophet and proclaimer of the good news of God's covenant with man, nor does He merely call men to hear and receive this news, but in so doing He calls them to active co-operation in its proclamation. It is to this fact that all three Evangelists testify when they tell us that Jesus called His disciples to Him (according to Lk. 6^{13}, on the day following that night of solitude). " Whom he would," says Mk. 3^{13} : He chose them, says Lk. 6^{13}— and the meaning of both is obviously that it was again His decision and decree if His disciples became or revealed and confirmed themselves to be what they were destined to be as His disciples. But what He wills and chooses in virtue of His decision and decree is the existence of the twelve apostles. The number " twelve " is not to be understood arithmetically but symbolically. Both in the Old and New Testaments it describes the people of Israel, its election, its summoning out from the other nations, its peculiar character and function as the people of the coming Messiah and Saviour of the world. The fact that Jesus " ordained twelve " of the disciples who were called means that He again set up among His disciples the office and calling of the people of Israel with respect to all other nations. He transferred this office and calling to His disciples. He ordained ($\dot{\epsilon}\pi o \iota \eta \sigma \epsilon \nu$) the twelve, we are very emphatically told in Mk. $3^{14,\ 16}$—corresponding to the promise of Mk. 1^{17}. The fact that the One of whom it is said that He " makes," creates or founds the people of Israel, is Israel's Messiah, is perhaps involved in this expression without being stated specifically. What now emerges is the work of the One who called these fishermen and tax-gatherers to Him. At the very heart of Galilee of the Gentiles, the classical sphere of Israel's apostasy and rejection, we now have a new Israel, or rather the old Israel of God, now arrived at its goal and entering upon its mission. We now have the twelve, whose decisive destiny, according to Mk. 3^{13}, is ἵνα ὦσιν μετ' αὐτοῦ, that they might be with Him. How indispensable it is to consider already all that subsequently transpires between Mt. 16 and Mt. 26 emerges clearly from this first and comprehensive description of the apostolate (Mk. 3^{14-15}). The new Israel, or rather the old Israel which has now reached its goal, in the form of the group of twelve men who are later named, has and fulfils its destiny in the fact that it may be with Him, with Jesus, sharing His office with Him and performing His work. This is brought out by the two other specific features of their existence as the twelve according to Mk. 3^{14-15}: καὶ ἵνα ἀποστέλλῃ αὐτοὺς κηρύσσειν καὶ ἔχειν ἐξουσίαν ἐκβάλλειν τὰ δαιμόνια. Mt. 10^1 mentions only the second of these features, the power over demons which is given to the twelve. Jesus has called them out from that tormented and exhausted people, that unshepherded flock scattered upon the hills, to be with them the new Israel. And they are now to walk with Him among this people — with Him, and therefore possessing and using His power, renewing the old, purifying the unclean, healing the sick, breaking the rule of Satan, as is the intention and power of the divine compassion present, real and manifest in Jesus. When Matthew places the great charge of $10^{6f.}$, directly after the account of the appointment of the apostles, he expresses all the more forcefully that this is what is to happen in the execution of their mission as heralds of the message of God's kingdom. No parallel content is given to the idea of the apostolate in Lk. 6^{13}. Here it is apparently enough that Jesus gave the name " apostles " to the twelve. But the missing element emerges in Luke as well, for in $6^{17f.}$ we go on to read that Jesus came down with them from the mountain to the crowds from " all Judæa and Jerusalem, and from the sea coast of Tyre and Sidon, which came to hear him, and to be healed of their diseases ; and they that were vexed with unclean spirits : and they were healed." Because He goes with them, and because they are with Him, they are and will be themselves the new Israel, with its task of proclamation, its power to purify and to heal, and to fight victoriously against Satan. The connexion with what will follow at the two succeeding stages of the account, the standing and falling of the apostles with Jesus, is obvious.

The sense in which they actually go with Him, and how far Jesus relies on them, may be seen in what Jesus says and does (Mt. $12^{46f.}$) when His mother and brothers stand outside and ask to speak with Him : " Who is my mother ? and who are my brethren ? And he stretched forth his hand toward his disciples (and he looked round about on them which sat about him, Mk. 3^{34}) and said, Behold my mother, and my brethren ! For whosoever shall do the will of my Father which is in heaven, the same is my brother and sister, and mother." It is also clear from the explanation of the parable of the sower in Mt. $13^{10f.}$: " Because it is given unto you to know the mysteries of the kingdom of heaven, but to them it is not given (unto them that are without, all these things are done in parables, Mk. 4^{11}). For whosoever hath, to him shall be given, and he shall have more abundance : but to whosoever hath not, from him shall be taken away even that he hath." Jesus speaks to them in parables in fulfilment of the word of the prophet Isaiah about seeing and not perceiving, hearing and not understanding—the unalterable law that of himself man does not have the ability to turn to God, but that this is taken from him when God actually converts him to Himself. This law is the secret of the kingdom of heaven which they learn from Jesus as His disciples, and therefore actually know with Him. He has thus drawn them into His solitude before God and over against the whole world. It is, therefore, strange but logical that according to Mk. 4^{13} Jesus went on to say to them : " Know ye not this parable ? and how then will ye know all parables ? ", and that He has to explain to them even this parable —the parable of the mystery of man's encounter with the Word of God. But He does explain it to them, that is, He places them alongside Himself in this knowledge. In this knowledge, and therefore from His own position between God and man, they are to be His heralds and the bearers of His power. They continue to depend wholly upon Him. We may refer to the account of the feeding of the five thousand in Mk. 6³⁰ᶠ·. The apostles who had been sent forth have returned to Jesus, telling Him of all that they have done and learned. It can hardly have been intended as a mere expression of human concern that Jesus then says to them : " Come ye yourselves apart into a desert place, and rest a while : for there were many coming and going, and they had no leisure so much as to eat," and that He then takes them by ship to a place of this kind. For the people follow them there—it is here that Mark introduces the saying about Jesus' compassion for those who were like sheep without a shepherd. And when the question of feeding is raised and Jesus commands the apostles : " Give ye them to eat," they stand helplessly looking at the five thousand with their five loaves and two fishes. And it is perfectly clear what is the ἀναπαύεσθαι which they themselves need, and which Jesus has intended for them. It is He Himself who must and does cause the crowd to group itself into units (συμπόσια) of a hundred and fifty on the green grass. And what He does is even formally an obvious anticipation of the institution of the Lord's Supper. He took the five loaves and the two fishes, looked up to heaven and gave thanks, broke the bread and gave it to His disciples, that they might distribute it; and He divided the two fishes among them all. " And they did all eat, and were filled." That is the " rest " promised to the apostles as the beginning and end of their work ; the work of Jesus Himself. He feeds the five thousand with the little that the apostles themselves have to offer them, and all that truly remains for them is to deliver and offer the much that He gives in the form of the little that they have to give. We find the same relationship between Him and them in the story of the calming of the storm in Mk. 4³⁵ᶠ·, and more clearly in that of Jesus walking on the lake, and the sinking of Peter (Mt. 14²²ᶠ·). If the One who slept among them in the midst of the terrifying storm had not awakened ; if the One who for a time was separated from them had not returned to them over the raging waters, inevitably they would have perished. And they are even vexed that He sleeps among them : " Master, carest thou not that we perish ? " (Mk. 4³⁸) ; " Master, Master, we perish ! " (Lk. 8²⁴) ; " And when the disciples saw him walking on the sea, they were troubled, saying, It is a spirit ; and they cried out for fear " (Mt. 14²⁶). In both cases His Word is needed to restore them : " Be not afraid." In both cases His presence and Word are needed if the storm is not actually to overwhelm them. And if, according to Mt. 14²⁸, Peter not only ventures more than the others, but does actually take a step such as he sees Jesus Himself taking, he takes only a single step, and then he again looks at the wind rather than the Lord, so that immediately he begins to sink, and is saved only by the Lord's hand which catches him—" O thou of little faith, wherefore didst thou doubt ? " It is also worth noting that Mark's briefer account of this episode (6⁵¹ᶠ·) closes with the words : " They were sore amazed in themselves beyond measure, and wondered. For they considered not the miracle of the loaves : for their heart was hardened." It is always in this way, therefore—but, let it be understood, in this way with power—that there is fulfilled in them the fundamental determination of the apostolate to which they were appointed : " that they might be with him." They are with Him as and because He is with them.

It is in the same first stage that the Evangelists also tell us, not only of the calling and appointment, but also explicitly and specifically of the sending forth of the apostles. Matthew alone links this directly with the appointment (10⁵ᶠ·), but he, too, describes it as an independent action. When Luke reports a special mission of seventy other disciples (10¹ᶠ·) in addition to that of the twelve (9¹ᶠ·), he brings out the connexion, or unity, of the apostolic twelve with the Church as a whole. The directions which he says were given to the seventy are exactly the same as those given to the twelve according to the other Evangelists, so that the address to the twelve and that to the disciples or the Church as a whole merge into one another. We can only briefly recall at this point that in this case the mission of the apostles, as distinct from that in the resurrection story, is not the mission to the nations, but to the lost sheep of the house of Israel (Mt. 10[5]), for Jesus has not yet traversed His whole path as the servant of God rejected by Israel, nor has He yet entered upon or manifested His kingship over Israel and the world to which this leads. The apostles cannot rush on ahead, but can only follow Him in this. Hence the express prohibition against travelling " the ways of the Gentiles, and into any city of the Samaritans." There are, however, two things which they are to do, and these correspond to the instructions given them at the time of their appointment : " He sent them to preach the kingdom of God, and to heal the sick " (Lk. 9[2]). The fact that " healing " constitutes an essential part of the apostolic task belongs necessarily to the form peculiar to this task in this first context. That is, healing by the disciples, like the miracles of Jesus Himself, is the sign, the indication of that overcoming of demons and death which takes place once and for all in the resurrection of Jesus. It is a sign of His Messiahship and His kingdom. It is the differentiation of this prophet and His disciples from the prophets of the Old Testament. Accordingly and necessarily, this part of their task does not reappear in the missionary command of Mt. 28, just as Jesus Himself does not perform any miracles after His resurrection. The fact that mention is again made of the healing work of the apostles in the presentation of the missionary command given in Mk. 16[17f.] is a significant internal sign that the whole passage, Mk. 16[9-20], does not belong to the original content of the Gospel, but to a period when this difference was no longer understood. The fact that after Jesus' resurrection healing no longer formed part of the Church's task does not mean—as is shown in the Acts of the Apostles—that all such healings were in future excluded. Even less does it mean that the power over demons and death, given to the apostles, was withdrawn from them and from the Church. But it does at least mean that once the resurrection of Jesus has happened it no longer requires to be particularly indicated. All healing, all cleansing, all victory over death and the devil, are now to be regarded and believed and proclaimed as accomplished in Him. With reference to Mt. 28[18f.], we have probably to say that the healing commanded of the apostles in the first stage of the account found its legitimate and complete continuation and fulfilment later in the baptism which they were commissioned to give in the name of the triune God.

The instructions given to the disciples by Jesus as He sends them forth are relatively scattered in Mark and Luke, but to some degree codified in Mt. 10. When we consider them, three main groups appear. A first expresses all the things which characterise the apostles as such, and with them those who are in the Church, as they may go their way as such among men, receiving neither support nor help from men because they do not need it, but borne by the message itself as bearers of the message, and therefore free in respect of men. " Freely have ye received, freely give " (Mt. 10[8f.]). A second group (Mt. 10[17f.]) speaks— partly in the same words as the address on the second coming—of the temptations and persecutions which are to be expected by the apostles and the Church, but in which they are not to allow themselves to be oppressed by anxiety or fear. Why not ? " The disciple is not above his master, nor the servant above his lord. It is enough for the disciple that he be as his master, and the servant as his lord. If they have called the master of the house Beelzebub, how much more shall they call them of this household ? " (Mt. 10[24f.]). The company in which they find themselves makes them invincible. A third group (Mt. 10[26f.]) states positively that it is in this fearlessness, which is for them self-evident, that that which is necessary will take place, and that which is hidden (but not from them) will be made manifest. Because God wills that this shall happen, every hair of their heads is numbered. When they carry out the will of God and confess Jesus before men, He will Himself confess them before God. Because the will of God must take place, they will not be afraid in face of the discord which they will provoke by the revelation of what is hidden, and which they will suffer in their own immediate environment. But as the will of God takes place, all the willing reception that they find from men, and all the goodness that men show them, will be rendered to Him, Jesus Himself, and appropriately rewarded. " He that receiveth you receiveth me, and he that receiveth me receiveth him that sent me." No reader of Mt. 10 can fail to see how the bond between the apostles and the One who sends them forth becomes increasingly intense in the middle of this " address," and how everything that is said about the apostles themselves, from their deeds and sufferings to their admonition and comfort, finds its meaning and support in the fact that they must and may be His emissaries. It may well be asked why there is in this speech so little mention—basically none at all—of their actual achievements as apostles. What is meant is evidently that there is nothing more explicit or impressive to be said about their achievements than by the reference to their " rest," to the centre and support of all their functions. They are to proclaim the kingdom of God— and that means that they are to proclaim Him. It is the secret of their mission that He is Himself with them, and therefore they are able to be with Him ; but that even this is not on their own behalf, but on behalf of the men to whom they are sent. This is the whole secret of their apostolate, the secret of the determination of the elect according to the teaching of the New Testament.

To what does God elect a man ? The New Testament answers this question with its portrayal of the existence of the apostles ; their calling, appointment and mission. It is in them, in their being and their deeds, that the Church can and should recognise itself as the assembly of the elect for all time. It is in them that each individual member of the Church can and should recognise the meaning and purpose of his own election. He who is elect of God is elect in Jesus Christ. For Jesus Christ is the original object of divine election. He is the one Elect, apart from whom there can be no others. He who is elect of God is elect through Jesus Christ. For Jesus Christ is also the original instrument of divine election. It is through Him, as the object of His election, and through Him alone, that others are also elected. It is in this way, in and through Him, that the apostles and those gathered into the apostolic Church are elect. But what is their determination ? According to the New Testament it is simply the transmission of the assurance and promise which have come upon themselves. It is therefore the attestation, the proclamation of Jesus Christ in the sphere of the world and among the men who have not yet heard His name, who have not yet come to believe in Him, who have not yet been benefited by the work which as God's Prophet, Priest and King He performed for them too, who certainly stand under His lordship, but have not yet recognised and confessed Him as Lord, or given thanks to Him as Lord. The determination of the apostles is to go into this world with the task of baptising it. Through the apostles this is the determination of the Church, and in the Church it is the determination of all its members, of the elect. If God elects a man, it is that he may be a witness to Jesus Christ, and therefore a proclaimer of His own glory.

4. THE DETERMINATION OF THE REJECTED

A " rejected " man is one who isolates himself from God by resisting his election as it has taken place in Jesus Christ. God is for him ; but he is against God. God is gracious to him ; but he is ungrateful to God. God receives him ; but he withdraws himself from God.

C.D.—15

God forgives him his sins ; but he repeats them as though they were not forgiven. God releases him from the guilt and punishment of his defection ; but he goes on living as Satan's prisoner. God determines him for blessedness, and His service ; but he chooses the joylessness of an existence that accords with his own pride and aims at his own honour. The rejected man does exist in his own way alongside the elect. We do not fully understand the answer to the question concerning the determination of the elect if we refuse to consider the situation of these others, the rejected. What is God's will for them ? What is the purpose, the goal and content, the planned outworking and fulfilment, the meaning and order of their existence as itself also an object of the divine predetermination ?

The proposition from which we must start is that in the determination of the rejected we have to do with the will of God in what is by definition a wholly different sense than in the determination of the elect. The one will of God which determines both is here the almighty, holy and compassionate non-willing of God. No eternal covenant of wrath corresponds on the one side to the eternal covenant of grace on the other. Nor does an established or tolerated kingdom of Satan correspond in scope or duration, in dignity or authority, to the kingdom of Jesus Christ. On the contrary, just because God does not will always to chide with man, He has initiated the covenant of grace as the beginning of all His works and ways and to destroy the rule of Satan over mankind, thus opposing the kingdom of Jesus Christ to Satan in triumphant superiority. The rejection of mankind is the rejection borne eternally and therefore for all time by Jesus Christ in the power of divine self-giving. It is, therefore, the rejection which is " rejected." Because this is so, the rejected man is from the very outset and in all circumstances quite other than the elect. He is the man who is *not* willed by the almighty, holy and compassionate God. Because God is wise and patient in His non-willing also, he still exists and is not simply annihilated. But although —as the object of the divine non-willing—he exists with the elect, he has no autonomous existence alongside or apart from him. He is not a second person whose nature and determination may be fixed and weighed and explained on their own account, in isolation from the nature and determination of the elect. The most negative possible statement against him is also the great positive statement for him. How can he possibly have a life of his own over against the elect ? It is only as the object of the divine non-willing that he exists as a rejected man. Only as such does he share as a rejected man in the grace of creation and providence. And as such he also stands—to the extent that he does not cease to be the man created and sustained by God—in the sphere of the eternal covenant of divine grace ; he is as such surrounded by the election and kingdom of Jesus Christ, and as such confronted by the superiority of the love of God. This love may burn and consume him as a rejected man, as is fitting, but even so it is still to him the almighty, holy and compassionate love of God. And this very love does not permit but debars him from any independent life of his own alongside or apart from the life of the elect. This very love, against which he maliciously and perilously transgresses, reduces him to the weakness and insubstantiality, the shadowy existence, of a life that wills to challenge the truth, yet cannot actually do so, but can only bear reluctant witness to the truth. Man may be possessed and ruled by Satan. He may be devilish. The rejected is this. But he can no more raise himself than Satan can to the dignity of the being created and sustained by God, to a positive and independent existence of his own. It is only improperly and incidentally (by the wisdom and patience of God) that he can be, as and because the elect genuinely *is* on the basis of the election of Jesus Christ as the beginning of all God's ways and works.

It is because the elect is that the rejected is also. Only the elect knows the rejected. He cannot know himself as such, or his election, without at the same time knowing the rejected. He knows him in all his improper and shadowy character as an object of the divine non-willing. But he does actually know him in his distinctive reality. He knows him decisively and supremely in his prototype Jesus Christ ; in the person of the One who, Himself blameless, fulfilled His election by taking the place of all the rejected, bearing their rejection. There he stands—the man who is hostile to God, ungrateful to God, withdrawing from God, repeating sins already forgiven, and therefore enslaved and cursed. There we see the sin and death of the man who is overpowered by Satan, and has himself become devilish. What this man does and is in revolt against the love of his Creator, how he stands before God, what is his just reward in the righteous judgment of God, is revealed in all its truth at this place where it is stripped of its truth and exposed and destroyed as a lie, where the Elect both willed to be and was the Rejected as well, where the rejection merited by all others was His—the only One who did not merit rejection—and therefore no longer theirs. It is here and in this way and therefore in and with the basis of his own election that the elect recognises and knows the rejected. Who other than the elect knows the One in whom he is elected ? Who other than the elect, therefore, knows also the Rejected ? And as he knows Him in this place and in this way, the conclusion is unavoidable that the existence of the elect involves that of the rejected, with him, but not apart from or alongside him. It is in Jesus Christ, and therefore on the basis of His election, that the elect has the rejected, not in himself, nor yet apart from nor alongside himself, but with himself ; taken up with him into his own existence which is not reprobate, but eternally loved and justified and sanctified by God. Where and how else can the rejected be but in this being with the elect, the beloved ? It is in this way and only in this way that the elect knows him, just because and as he himself is elected in Jesus Christ. And in this way he will surely then recognise him supremely in himself, that is, in his own godlessness as it lies behind him, and yet is always present and always future. He is himself the man whose place was taken by Jesus Christ when He became the Rejected for him. He himself ought to have been the rejected. And more than that, he himself is the man who—as if Jesus Christ had died in vain—continually attempts to occupy the place of the rejected, to do his works, to assume his sentence and fate, and to revive all the evil, fatal and futile rebellion against God's grace which is the essence of sin, as if it were not settled and ended by the forgiveness of sins resolved and executed in the divine self-offering. Therefore he recognises and knows the rejected a second time—in the light of the rejection of Jesus Christ as the plight from which he himself has been saved and which he himself continually conjures up. Who but the elect knows the One who was rejected for his sake, and in His light the shadow which accompanies him ? Believing in Him, he faces the old man, the body of death from which he has come, and also the godlessness with which he has repeatedly to contend. If he did not believe, if he were not elected, this shadow would not accompany him. In regard to the elect, and the elect alone, is it the case that as the one whom God loves he has with him the one whom God hates : again, not in himself, yet not apart from or alongside himself, but with himself ; taken up into his election, borne and covered by the grace of Jesus Christ. It is for this reason that finally—not primarily or supremely, as the older doctrine of predestination would have it—he will recognise the rejected in the godlessness of others : in all the blatant and refined examples of dreadful corruption ; in the brutality and sophistry, the stupidity and weakness, the self-will and frivolity, the superstition, heresy and unbelief by which he sees himself surrounded on every hand in ever widening circles. It is useless to conceal all this. But it must be realised that all this is a sign or recollection of the rejection which Jesus Christ has borne for us all to take away from us all—even from these others. It is also very much to the point to consider that the mote in our neighbour's eye (quite apart from the beam in our own eye) grieves and repels us because it is undoubtedly part of the sheer incompatability, the rebellion against his election and against the grace of God, in which he too is implicated. We are quite right : this is supreme, intolerable disorder ; the disorder which is remedied by Jesus Christ, and the guilt of which we continually incur. Therefore the elect knows and recognises the rejected a third time—in the dark shadow by which he sees that the other is similarly accompanied. But the more sharply he sees this, the more clearly must he see the light in which the other also stands, and against which he casts this shadow. It is for the elect that the neighbour too—and he, too, in the realm of Jesus Christ's election—

has the rejected, not in himself, nor yet apart from nor alongside himself, but with himself, mysteriously and paradoxically enough included in his election as it is decided in Jesus Christ. What other kind of reality can the elect predicate of the rejected in the form of his neighbour than the peculiar reality of this " beingwith " ?

In answering the question of the determination of the rejected, it is crucial that no other existence should be ascribed to the rejected than this improper and dependent " beingwith " ; that no other existence should be conceded than existence in relationship to the elect (to Jesus Christ and to the man elected in Him). We can take his existence seriously only as it is taken seriously by God Himself. We certainly do not take it seriously if we understand it other than as a shadow which yields and dissolves and dissipates. The shadow is itself sinister and threatening and dangerous and deadly enough. Yet it is this within the limit set for it by God. It is more important, urgent and serious to see its divinely imposed limit than the horror which is peculiar to it within this limit. And this is its divinely imposed limit, and therefore its shadow-quality—that the rejected man exists in the person of Jesus Christ only in such a way that he is assumed into His being as the elect and beloved of God ; only in refutation, conquest and removal by Him ; only in such sort that as he is accepted and received by Him he is transformed, being put to death as the rejected and raised to his proper life as the elect, holy, justified and blessed. Because Jesus Christ takes his place, He takes from him the right and possibility of his own independent being and gives him His own being. With Jesus Christ the rejected can only *have been* rejected. He cannot *be* rejected any more. Between him and an independent existence of his own as rejected, there stands the death which Jesus Christ has suffered in his place, and the resurrection by which Jesus Christ has opened up for him His own place as elect. It is only as one who has been, but is no longer, that he may again proclaim or assert himself. It is bad enough that even this is not yet taken from him. But in any case, it takes place only within the divinely appointed limit and not with the absolute force of that which is properly and autonomously present. This power is taken from it by what took place in the death and resurrection of Jesus Christ, as willed and decided from all eternity in the resolve and decree of God. Therefore even in the past, present and future godlessness of the elect the rejected himself exists only as the object of that evil, dangerous, but powerless representation—in such a way that he is denied from the very outset by his election (the election of Jesus Christ), and is now denied in practice too by his faith in Jesus Christ, being exposed and discredited as a liar. He is permitted neither respite, peace nor consolation. He may be able to query the election of the elect, to obscure or jeopardise it, but he cannot reverse it. He can lie, but he can lie only against the Gospel. He has no truth of his own to assert against it. He can do nothing against the one truth. Even although it is no greater than a grain of mustard-seed, faith refutes and overcomes him. He can reproduce, but he cannot again perpetrate, the sins for which Jesus Christ died. He can endure a likeness of the punishment of death that Jesus Christ has suffered in his place, but he cannot—even remotely—endure death itself. He may deny and blaspheme the transformation, the renewal of life, which has come to him also in the resurrection of Jesus Christ, but he cannot now evade the sign under which his own life is placed by it. The faith of the elect is the recognition of the supremacy of the elect Jesus Christ in face of the rejected—the very rejected to whom the godlessness even of the elect seems daily to give substance and actuality. The faith of the elect (his faith in the election of Jesus Christ) denies the actuality and asserts the passing of the existence of the rejected. It is faith therefore—together with Jesus Christ—which marks the limit of the shadow. And even in the godlessness of others, the rejected cannot exist except in this shadow-form. The elect—and only the elect knows the rejected—cannot give more credence to the imitation in which he sees both others and himself involved than to the promise by which he himself lives in spite of his godlessness. He can and must, of course, take it seriously as participation in the unholy attempt to oppose the grace conferred on men by Jesus Christ. But he cannot reckon with any final validity or power of this opposition, or success of this attempt, even on the part of his neighbour. As he believes that the supremacy of the elect Jesus Christ in face of the rejected is true for himself, he must and will believe that it is true for the other. He will oppose his godlessness. He will confess, and not remain silent, in face of it. He will oppose his assertions, and not yield. He will not fear, but defy them. But however he may do this, it is only with his faith in the Gospel that he will in fact oppose them. His weapon will be the assurance that Jesus Christ died and rose again for others too. His defiance of others will mean that he does not grant them any final competence to play the role of the rejected. He will testify to them, too, that the election of Jesus Christ is the beginning of all the ways and works of God which controls even their life. If he cannot release or absolve them, any more than he can himself, from the gloomy accompanying shadow—for only God can do this—he can and must attest to them the freedom which has been created and really exists for them. In the light of the Gospel (and only the proclamation of the Gospel is the determination of the elect) the rejected, even as he appears in others, is a shadow which yields and dissolves and dissipates, being clearly limited by God.

His distinctive determination is rooted in his distinctive nature. He does not have it apart from or alongside, but with that of the elect. It indicates the meaning and purpose of the determination of the elect. It is the necessary reverse side of this determination, which must not be overlooked or forgotten. And in its ultimate range it points to the very spot at which the proper and positive determination of the elect begins.

(1) In the reality of the existence peculiar to him, it is the determination of the rejected to manifest the recipients of the Gospel whose proclamation is the determination of the elect. The rejected has not simply vanished or been destroyed. Thanks to the divine wisdom and patience, he can take different forms within the appointed limit. And in this capacity he represents the world and the individual in so far as they are in need of the divine election. As a sinner against God, he is the lost man who in spite of his election, and the salvation and preservation which it includes, necessarily confirms this fact by his godlessness. He is the man whose salvation and preservation made necessary the self-giving of God in His own Son, and for whose salvation and preservation only this divine self-giving could avail. He is the man whose offence is so great that there neither is nor can there be conceived anything greater—except the compassion of God. The life of the rejected is the representation of this man. It is another matter that it is only a representation, that as such it is a lie, because this man—the truly rejected—cannot be any other than Jesus Christ. This lying representation is itself the distinctive reality of the existence of the rejected. It is in this lying representation that he witnesses— and he " is " the rejected in this witness—to the man who is in need of divine election ; the man for whom there is no grace because he has wantonly withdrawn himself from it, and from whom God has turned away because he himself has turned his back upon God ; the man who has chosen the curse instead of the blessing, and death instead of life, and who must now live under the presupposition of this perverse choice. This man is obviously the man who is in need of the divine election, the election of Jesus Christ, the election of grace that took place in Him. It is for this man, for his replacement and transformation, that Jesus Christ died and rose. It is this man whom the elect confronts in himself and in others. It is to this man that the Gospel is addressed as the Word of truth. It is to this man that the elect is to address it. It is to him that the good news is to be told. It is for his benefit that the election of Jesus Christ must be represented and depicted by the elect. His calling must be served by all those who are themselves called. But as the one who is only addressed, as the rejected who so far does not participate, or participates only involuntarily, in the chorus of praise which goes out through all creation from the election of Jesus Christ, he embodies the fact that this chorus does not lose itself in the void. He represents the ears which wait to hear it because they must hear. He represents creation sighing in its utterly objective longing. He embodies, therefore, the meaning and goal of this chorus. And just because he embodies a mere *ecclesia audiens*, which cannot possibly be a true *ecclesia*

in this abstraction, over against the *ecclesia docens* he embodies the totality of the *ecclesia* of which the neediness of the listener is as much a part as is the fulness of the proclaimer. Just because he embodies the pure object of election—the elect " before " and without his election, the elect without his appropriate determination—he shows openly and unmistakeably what grace and election and the election of grace really are. This might easily be overlooked or forgotten without the rejected. But it must not be overlooked or forgotten, either in time or eternity. The real existence of the rejected is a guarantee that this will not happen. The memory of the crucified and risen Jesus Christ ensures that His election and the revelation of His election in His resurrection are to be understood and grasped as the divine election of grace. The presence of the rejected in the continual eruption of godlessness in the elect ensures that his election will continually present itself for him as the choice of God. And therefore his presence in another provides that the elect can never forget that for the attestation of the grace which he has received he is indebted to those who have not yet realised it, or who do so no longer, and that it is open and ready for them too. As the rejected does this, he has a part in the determination of the elect. And in this very fact he has his own determination.

(2) In the distinctive character of his existence, the rejected has the determination constantly to manifest that which is denied and overcome by the Gospel. In word and voice he has to raise a *Gloria Deo ex profundis* in face of, and yet also in concert with, the *Gloria Deo in excelsis*. The rejected is the man whose only witness—and most powerfully in his false picture of God—is to himself and his false choice as the man isolated over against God, the man who at the deepest level and in the deepest sense has nothing at all to say. He is the man who lives in a false service as well as in a false liberty. He is the man who is deceived because he deceives himself. He is the man who has a part in the truth only in so far as he demonstrates the fact and extent that he is utterly and finally unadapted for life in God's presence apart from the self-offering of God, because there is nothing in him which could make such a life either actual or even possible. He is the man who is ungrateful and therefore unblessed. But it is just this man who, according to the Gospel, is denied and overcome by the divine election of grace in the establishment of the eternal covenant between God and man. God has made this man's rejection His own. It is for him that the Word of God is eternally intended and eternally valid. It is the true emancipation of this man, and his enrolment into service, which is the act of God's love towards man, decreed before time began and realised at the heart of time. The Gospel is that it is just for him that there is communion in holy things and therefore the communion of saints, the forgiveness of sins, the resurrection of the body and life everlasting, for the sake of Jesus

Christ, and in the power of His election. But how can the Gospel be clear and explicit and concrete if it does not have this margin or background (which can only be seen in the light of it but in that light is actually seen in all its singularity), namely, the judgment which is lifted from man by the divine election of grace or man under judgment, as is necessarily true of every one who bears the name of man, but cannot be true of any because of the divine election of grace ? This man under judgment must not be denied or forgotten if the Gospel is to be rightly preached and heard and believed. The existence depicted by the rejected ensures that this cannot happen. The Rejected on Golgotha sees to it that there can never be any doubt what man it was who was raised on Easter Day to the glory of God the Father ; that He truly died and truly rose again. And the sharp outlines of the rejected, which every man can see in his own mirror, and therefore in the figure of his neighbour, are a guarantee that communion with God and the brethren, the forgiveness of sins, the resurrection and life everlasting—whether these words are applied to ourselves or to others —can never be empty words. The rejected—the negative apostle, the man with nothing to say—sees to this in all his different forms. And in so doing, he does have something to say. He has a part in the determination of the elect. He is not, therefore, without a divine determination. And his *ex profundis*—even if they are the *profunda* of hell—becomes *Gloria Deo ex profundis*. What would become of the determination of the elect if the rejected were not with him with his own distinctive determination ?

(3) The rejected has the determination, in the distinctive limitation of his existence, to manifest the purpose of the Gospel. We have now reached the point at which the determination of the rejected indicates the beginning of the determination of the elect. The form of the rejected is in every respect one which yields and dissolves and dissipates. He is condemned to impotence and insubstantiality by the way in which disposition is made concerning him in the election of Jesus Christ, being only an object of the victory of actuality and truth as it was decreed concerning him from all eternity, and as it has been achieved for him in the midst of time. The rejected has no future. As the man who wills to be his own master, he can only achieve his own destruction. But the purpose of the divine election of grace is to grant to this man who in and of himself has no future, a future in covenant with God. It is with this in view that the Gospel speaks. It is with this purpose that God turns to man, and that His Word is addressed to man. It is addressed to the man who in and of himself is rejected, who has fallen a prey and is delivered up to absolute destruction. But the concrete form of the purpose of the Gospel is its proclamation and faith in it, the work of the Holy Spirit in the summoning of the elect man, in which his whole determination to blessedness, thanksgiving and witness has its basis and origin. And it is this purpose of

the Gospel in its concrete form which is manifested by the existence of the rejected to the extent that only this shadow-reality is proper to it. It is manifested indirectly—like the manifestation of light and grace and life by death and judgment and shadow—as the limit beyond which there can take place either nothing at all or the purpose of the Gospel. For the rejected, the only alternatives are nothing or proclamation and faith. Just as the only alternatives for the Rejected on Golgotha were nothing or (the real alternative) the resurrection, so, in view of the awful possibility that he might be rejected, the only alternatives for the elect are either nothing or the Word of proclamation and of faith, the work of the Holy Spirit. Necessarily, therefore, he has to regard and address all others as those for whom the only alternatives are nothing or the Word and faith. He knows that for himself and all others the real alternative is the Word and faith, as the beginning that opens up beyond the end of every other possibility. He knows this as he knows of the resurrection of the Rejected on Golgotha. Hence he knows decisively what God wills for the rejected. He does not will him as rejected. Only in His non-willing does He will him as such. But in virtue of what was determined in the election of Jesus Christ and what took place in His death and resurrection, this non-willing is enclosed and surpassed and excelled by, and subordinated and made subservient to, that which (even in His non-willing) He positively wills—His loving-kindness, the loving-kindness of His election. The positive will of God is that this loving-kindness should be revealed to us in proclamation and faith, that we might live by and with it. This must not be forgotten. The rejected in all his transitoriness and hopelessness cannot forget it. But is it only where there is no hope—and the Rejected on Golgotha, and the rejected in ourselves and in all others, has no hope—that there is real hope, for it is only there that the work of the Holy Spirit can intervene and proclamation can become really comprehensible and faith really alive. The rejected causes the elect to consider this —reminding us again of the service of Israel to the Church, and the relationship of the Church to Israel. But because he does this, he has a part in the determination of the elect, and in this participation he has his own determination. His determination is that, as the rejected man which he is, he should hear the proclamation of the truth and come to faith. It is that from being a reluctant and indirect witness he should become a willing and direct witness to the election of Jesus Christ and His community.

The character in which the problem of the rejected is concentrated and developed in the New Testament is that of Judas Iscariot, the disciple and apostle who "betrayed" Jesus. We observe at once that—like the Old Testament, but much more unequivocally—the New Testament does not seek or find the rejected at a distance, but in the closest conceivable proximity to Jesus Christ Himself, and so not in the alien, hostile world to which Jesus Christ came and to which the witness of His apostles, the Church and the elect is to be addressed. The counterpart of the elect is not really an opponent who confronts and opposes the kingdom of God from outside. Certainly, the existence of this counterpart stands in the closest relationship to the power and effectiveness of what St. John's Gospel calls " the prince of this world." But, according to his manifestation in Judas Iscariot, " the prince of this world " obviously cannot be so easily and simply recognised and engaged as would be the case if he were to oppose Jesus Christ and His Church at a distance as one who is wholly foreign to the kingdom of God, if he were to oppose Jesus Christ and the testimony to Him from outside, representing, as it were, the " malice of the object." Again, however, he obviously does not possess the authority, value and the power of this kind of objective opponent. But just as the existence of the rejected of God, the " son of perdition " (Jn. 17^{12}), betrays by its sinister proximity to Jesus Christ and His apostles all the intimacy of the dangerous power and effectiveness of the devil, it also reveals its relativity, and the fact that it can express itself only under the direct supervision and control, as it were, of the overruling power and effectiveness of the Lord Himself, only in the work of a disciple and apostle.

Judas Iscariot is undoubtedly a disciple and apostle : no more so, but also no less so, than Peter and John ; sharing as they do the same calling, institution and mission ; more so rather than less so, to the extent that he alone among the twelve belongs like Jesus to the tribe of Judah, the seed of David. In all the various lists of the twelve there is a final specific mention of his name. When the three Synoptists record his treacherous agreement with the high-priests (Mk. 14^{10} and parallels), and its later execution (Mk. 14^{43} and parallels), they all lay special emphasis again on his discipleship : " Judas, one of the twelve." And as if to obviate any misunderstanding, Jn. 6^{70} carefully states : " Have not I chosen you twelve ; and one of you is a διάβολος ? He spake of Judas Iscariot : for he it was that should betray him, being one of the twelve." No matter what the Gospels record about what Jesus said concerning His disciples, what He said and did for them, and what He did through them, we have to realise that Judas Iscariot was also present ; and he played a full part in it all both passively and actively. " He was numbered with us, and had obtained part of this ministry " (Ac. 1^{17}). " One of you which eateth with me " is particularly underlined in Mk. 14$^{18f.}$, or in Lk. 22^{21} : " the hand of him that betrayeth me is with me on the table." And in Jn. 13$^{18f.}$ the saying of Ps. 41^{10}, to which there is an allusion in Mk. 14^{18} as well, is even more strongly emphasised : " I know whom I have chosen : but that the scripture may be fulfilled, he that eateth bread with me hath lifted up his heel against me." None of the Synoptists denied that Judas also received that which Jesus gave to the apostles at the institution of the Lord's Supper. It would, therefore, be a plain misunderstanding of the closing verses of Jn. 6 if we were to infer from them that Jesus was disputing the actuality and sincerity of Judas' confession with Peter : " Thou hast the words of eternal life. And we believe and are sure that thou art that Christ, the Son of the living God " (Jn. 6$^{68f.}$). According to v. 64, what Jesus denies is that this subjectively true confession was also objectively true in the mouth of Judas. The New Testament account of Judas does not say that among the genuine apostles there was one who was an apostle only in appearance, or that among the presumed and supposed elect there was one who was actually rejected. What it does say is that it was one of the genuine apostles, one of the genuinely elect, who was at the same time rejected as the betrayer of Jesus.

Particular attention must be paid to the remarkable calm with which the New Testament speaks of Judas Iscariot. The unavoidable assertion concerning him is made quite openly from the very outset : " Which also betrayed him " (Mk. 3^{19}) ; " Who also betrayed him " (Mt. 10^{4}) ; " Which also was the traitor " (Lk. 6^{16}). The necessary depositions are also made about the agreement, the execution of the betrayal and the traitor's end. In Ac. 1¹⁵ᶠ· we are told what the disappearance of the traitor involved for the rest of the apostles, that is, in terms of practical necessity. Strictly speaking, however, not a single stone is thrown at Judas. It is characteristic that apart from an allusion in the Johannine presentation of the anointing at Bethany no attempt is made to single out the traitor in advance by the mention of other features or peculiarities in his character and conduct. On the contrary, with this act of his he is more like a planned figure with a planned role, which as such does, of course, fall under the anathema as Peter's confession falls under the corresponding beatitude, but from which there seems as little reason specially to condemn Judas as to give special honour to Peter. The dominating truth that, according to Jn. 6⁶⁴, Jesus " knew from the beginning . . . who should betray him," stands over the whole being and behaviour of Judas as he was chosen and called with the others. And in the end Jesus gave him the express command : " That thou doest, do quickly " (Jn. 13²⁷). The word which is always used to describe Judas' act (παραδοῦναι), and which we have so far translated in the usual way as " to betray," really has the much weaker meaning of " to hand over." And if we carefully consider what Judas did, we can only say that even technically the use of the word " treachery " raises ideas far too complicated to account for the transaction in question. During the week before the passover (as is shown explicitly by Mk. 14¹⁸ and Mt. 26⁵⁵) there was no secret hiding-place of Jesus whose disclosure required a " traitor." What the high-priests required was simply an opportunity to arrest Him with the least possible disturbance : " Not on the feast day, lest there be an uproar among the people " (Mt. 26⁵). And Judas really came into the picture only as the one who informed them of such a suitable opportunity. He " only " handed Jesus over. In relation to Jesus he was not guilty of a maximum but only of a minimum of hostile activity—we think of Saul as he appears in the Books of Samuel. According to Jn. 18³ᶠ·, he was merely a spectator of the arrest of Jesus, and if in the Synoptic account he identified Him for the officers with the famous kiss, this simply shows us again the proximity to Jesus from which he had taken the fateful step of this " handing over." The only essential thing is that Jesus was handed over by one of His own, by one of His disciples and apostles, from within the Church. That is, He was torn from His own sphere, the divine sphere of God, which He Himself had created and ruled, the sphere of His free utterance and work, and—as the prophecy of suffering had long since foretold—delivered into " the hands of men," into the hands of the high-priests, into the hands of the Gentiles, and into these hands for crucifixion. This is the stone which Judas Iscariot starts rolling—but only starts rolling. He hands Jesus over to the high-priests. These hand Him over (Mk. 15¹, Mt. 27², ¹⁸, Jn. 18³⁰, ³⁵, ³⁶) to the Gentiles, to Pontius Pilate. And Pilate hands Him over to be crucified (Mk. 15¹⁵, Mt. 27²⁶, Jn. 19¹⁶). All the subsequent links in the chain are obviously much more important than the first. But this almost incidental denunciation by Judas is the first link in the chain ; the smallest, but one which involves and controls all those which follow. And at this first and decisive place that the Church stands and acts in identity with the Israel which rejected its Messiah, together with the heathen world which allied itself with this Israel, and made itself a partner in its guilt. At this point it is a disciple and apostle of Jesus who makes the decisive movement. It is quite a small movement, trifling as compared with everything that follows once it has taken place. It is carried out by the kiss, which, in point of fact, attests and seals again the fellowship of the perpetrator with Jesus. Judas delivers Jesus, and in so doing he initiates the decisive movement which Jesus had to perform for the accomplishment of His work—His suffering and death. We must see both the paltriness and the tremendous consequences of this event properly to understand the Judas of the Evangelists. It is the two together which give to the story of Judas its extraordinary calm. Judas Iscariot is certainly not an accidental figure. He is an essential one in the totality of the evangelical record. Even in the prophecies of suffering the decisive word tells us of what he did in the first instance : μέλλει ὁ υἱὸς τοῦ ἀνθρώπου παραδίδοσθαι εἰς χεῖρας ἀνθρώπων (Mt. 17²²). Between the sphere of Jesus Christ (as God's sphere), between the twelve apostles and the world there has to be this relation too, and it takes precedence over all others. At one point—and at the decisive point—the apostles have to share the guilt of Israel and the Gentile world towards Jesus, in order that Jesus may carry out the will of God, not only in relation to them, but also to Israel and the world. The Son of Man has to be handed over into the hands of men (" into the hands of sinful men," Lk. 24⁷; " of sinners," Mt. 26⁴⁵). Otherwise they would not and could not possess Him, as they actually may and do possess Him, nor receive from Him that which God has determined for them through Him. The whole significance of the apostolate, of the election of the twelve apostles, depends upon the fact that this happened. And the apostle Judas Iscariot is the special agent and exponent of this handing-over as it was decreed to be necessary in the counsel of God.

We cannot explore the vista which opens up at this point before verifying the fact that—for all the calm with which it considers it—the New Testament unquestionably regarded and judged the action of this man as sin and guilt of the most atrocious character. " The Son of man indeed goeth, as it is written of him (as it was determined, Lk. 22²²) : but woe unto that man by whom he is betrayed ! Good were it for that man if he had never been born " (Mk. 14²¹). If the saying of Jesus to Pilate in Jn. 19¹¹ : " He that delivered me unto thee hath the greater sin (than thou)," has immediate reference to the high-priests of Israel, and the Jews generally, it obviously refers primarily and in the first instance to the one who is the first link in this chain of handing-over— Judas. Judas is *the* great sinner of the New Testament. Jesus was " troubled in spirit " when He bore witness to this and said : " Verily, verily, I say unto you, that one of you shall betray me " (Jn. 13²¹). It was the devil who planned in his heart that Judas Iscariot, the son of Simon, should hand over Jesus (Jn. 13²). It was Satan who led him as he actually went about the deed (Lk. 22³ Jn. 13²⁷). Therefore Judas himself, the " son of perdition " of Jn. 17¹², can be called " a devil " in Jn. 6⁷⁰. " He then having received the sop went immediately out : and it was *night* " (Jn. 13³⁰). Even in Paul it is surely not just a chrono-logical observation : " The Lord Jesus the same *night* in which he was betrayed . . ." (1 Cor. 11²³). What the Johannine Prologue announced is now manifestly realised and fulfilled : " The light shineth in darkness " (Jn. 1⁵). " He came unto his own, and his own received him not " (Jn. 1¹¹). On the contrary, their reaction to Jesus is παραδοῦναι instead of παραλαμβάνειν. We are also told, of course, that this work of darkness does not mean an overpowering (a καταλαμβάνειν) of the light. But the work of darkness is certainly that of His own—of His own in the strictest meaning of the term, of His own in the figure of the apostle Judas. But what is the sin of the apostle Judas ? We first note the saying of Jesus in Jn. 17¹² : " While I was with them in the world, I kept them in thy name : those that thou gavest me I have kept, and none of them is lost, but the son of perdition ; that the Scripture might be fulfilled." In very general terms this means that among the elect of Jesus Judas is the one for whom the presence and protection and vigilance of Jesus were in vain. Jesus had already said to Peter, when He washed the disciples' feet : " He that is washed needeth not save to wash his feet, but is clean every whit : and ye are clean, but not all. For he knew who should betray him ; therefore said he, Ye are not all clean " (Jn. 13¹⁰). Thus, the apostles as such are wholly clean, for Jesus has chosen them to be so, and He has given them His presence, and protected and kept them. Therefore Jesus must and will wash their feet : " If I wash thee not, thou hast no part with me " (Jn. 13⁸). The feet are the unclean part even of the wholly clean. This uncleanness of the wholly clean, the unclean feet of the apostles, is represented by Judas Iscariot. It is to be noted that he represents it ; for the feet of all the apostles must be specially washed. It is also to be noted that this remaining uncleanness of all the apostles, even the uncleanness of their feet, is actually washed away by Jesus. In spite of Peter's protest, He devotes Himself to it. Even more, Jesus says explicitly to them (Jn. 13[14]) that it is their duty to wash one another's feet, mutually to wash away this remaining uncleanness. But it is Judas who is in a special sense the bearer and representative of this remaining uncleanness of theirs. He is the one in whom we see both the fact and extent that the presence and protection and vigilance of Jesus could be in vain, even for His elect. What is the nature of this uncleanness of his, in which the uncleanness of all the apostles is evident, even though they were washed and quite clean, but still needed to have their feet washed ?

The answer may be found in principle in John's account of the anointing of Jesus in Bethany (Jn. 12[1-8]), in the contrast there drawn between Judas and Mary, the sister of Lazarus. " Mary took a pound of ointment of spikenard, very costly, and anointed the feet of Jesus, and wiped his feet with her hair ; and the house was filled with the odour of the ointment " (v. 3). It is an utterly prodigal, a wholly generous and selfless, and at the same time an absolutely humble action, and Jesus later says (v. 7) that it honours His dead body in anticipation, and will therefore glorify His death. It is not for nothing that the subject is again that of the feet—this time the feet of Jesus upon which Mary lavishes this extravagance. This total offering, this gift of the most costly of her possessions, is to Jesus, who goes about on this earth of ours as a man, and to that extent Himself shares its uncleanness, to Jesus in all His condescension, which reaches its final point in His death. It is clear that this deed of Mary's describes the life of the apostles so far as they are wholly clean, so far as the presence and protection and vigilance of Jesus have not been in vain for them. And this is what is to take place in the world through their life—the whole house is to be filled with the odour of the ointment. But it is precisely this, this prodigality, which Judas—as seen by his protest (v. 4)—cannot and will not understand or accept. He is not opposed to the surrender of Mary's costly ointment. But he wants something for it—namely 300 denarii—not for himself, as he explains, but to give to the poor. He is not willing that the complete devotion, which by her deed Mary had in a sense given the apostles as a pattern for their own life, should be an absolute offering to Jesus. For him it is too little a thing that the death of Jesus should be glorified by it. If there is to be an offering, he wants to exploit it. A good and profitable work is to be carried out in the strength and exercise of this devotion. It is to be for the benefit of the poor, of those who are injured or needy, to help improve their lot and that of others, and in that way it will be a meaningful devotion. This view, this attitude of Judas, is what makes him unclean. It finds relatively innocuous expression. It is not really evil. To correct it would be comparatively easy. But it was because of it that Judas " handed over " Jesus. If a man does not devote himself prodigally to Jesus, if he considers something too good to be offered to Him, if he thinks another purpose more important than the glorifying of His condescension, of His death, that man is as such unclean and opposes his election. He makes himself impossible as an apostle. He must and will hand Jesus over— hand Him over to men, to be crucified. He has virtually done so already in and with this attitude towards Jesus. Already, by this attitude, he has acted as one of the men at whose hands Jesus can only be slain. Already he has made himself an accomplice. If he is an apostle, he is already the apostle " who will deliver Him up," as is said of Judas in the apostolic lists from the outset, and on almost every subsequent mention of his name. He cannot be other than the representative and bearer of the uncleanness of all the apostles. The Evangelist has relentlessly expressed these facts in the comment of v. 6 : " This he said, not that he cared for the poor ; but because he was a thief, and had the bag, and bare what was put therein." Here he is undoubtedly accused of avarice for money, and downright dishonesty. But it is still to be inferred from the whole manner of the Johannine presentation that (like Mary's deed) this outward mark of the attitude of Judas points beyond itself. It is an indication that his nature and function are those of the apostle who ultimately regrets his own devotion and the devotion of others to Jesus, who would prefer ultimately to use the power of this devotion for something which his own judgment considers to be better ; for whom Jesus is finally less important and indispensable than this better thing. He is not opposed to Jesus. He even wishes to be for Him. But he is for Him in such a way—not totally, that is to say—that actually he is against Him. He reserves to himself the right to decide for himself, in face of Jesus, what the way of apostolic discipleship really involves. For him this is not an end in itself, but a means to some other end, which is perhaps not yet clear to him, but about which he believes that he can in any event decide and dispose, and in view of which he permits himself continual interruptions in his relationship to Jesus. This freedom of his own decision and disposal in face of Jesus, this freedom to " interrupt," is what he really intends and wills at bottom, and not in itself and as such the other purpose which he envisages (" not that he cared for the poor ") ; not the good work, but his *own* work ; not the help that he will bring to others, but his own initiative in this work. It is in this way that he robs Jesus and the other apostles. It is in this way that he makes himself impossible as an apostle. It is in this way that he is from the very first the apostle who will hand Jesus over. If he were to " receive " Him (Jn. 1[11]), he would acknowledge that He is right, surrendering this reservation of his own freedom of disposal, and renouncing these interruptions. But he does not see himself as being in a position to do this. He cannot and will not acknowledge that Jesus is right. Therefore he has already decided against Him and made himself an accomplice of His enemies. For what stands between Jesus and His enemies except the claim of Jesus to total faith, absolute humility and unceasing prodigality ? From the position which he has taken up, Judas can only hand Jesus over to be crucified, to the radical elimination of this claim.

The Synoptists obviously try to understand the sin of Judas in the same way as John, for they tell us that he decided upon this handing-over for a payment of money (Mk. 14[10f.], Lk. 22[3f.]). According to Mt. 16[15] this was thirty pieces of silver. This obviously means that for Judas Jesus was for sale. He had his own freedom in face of Him which he was resolved to maintain. He had indeed turned to Him. But he had not bound himself to Him. He had not yielded himself to Him. He could surrender Him for something else which appeared better to him. Because he could do this, because he reserved for himself this judgment of his as to what was better, because he did not hand himself over to Jesus, he for his part was able to hand Jesus over. In fact he had already done so in principle. The reward offered by the high-priests, or the suggestion of a reward with which he himself approached them according to Mt. 26[15], was merely the external occasion which, as the Synoptists saw it, revealed this basic fact. But if Mt. 26[15] speaks more exactly of thirty pieces of silver, this opens the way to a further consideration. For we are referred to Zech. 11[4-17]. The relationship between the two passages is certainly a very peculiar one. There the prophet (as the embodiment of Yahweh Himself) receives thirty pieces of silver. He receives it as wages from the sheep-dealers, that is, from the selfish leaders of the people of Israel, in whose service he has for a time tended the poor sheep of this people (whom they had marked for sale and slaughter). He has given up keeping them : " For my soul loathed them, and their soul also abhorred me " (v. 8). He says to the shepherds : " If ye think good, give me my price : and if not, forbear : so they weighed for my price, thirty pieces of silver. And the Lord said unto me, Cast it into the treasury : a goodly price that I was prised at of them. And I took the thirty pieces of silver, and cast them into the treasury in the house of the Lord." Formally, it is Judas who, according to Mt. 26¹⁶ᶠ·, takes the place of the prophet (and therefore of Yahweh Himself). He, too, enters the service of these sheep-dealers, the leaders of the people of Israel. He, too, asks and receives payment from them—thirty pieces of silver. But, in fact, the whole situation is reversed. The service for which he receives this payment does not consist in his tending the sheep that are ready for slaughter, but in his handing over the Good Shepherd Himself for slaughter— a feature which is quite alien to the original context of Zech. 11. He occupies the place of Yahweh Himself in the impossible way that in this very situation he does that which causes Yahweh to lose patience with the sheep of His people, to give up His guardianship over them and leave them to themselves. Judas himself—obviously representing the whole flock—is the sheep which withdraws itself from the Good Shepherd, and make all His care nugatory. There is also brought out by him—and this is the new light which is thrown on his sin by the passage in Matthew—a point which is perfectly clear in Zech. 11 as well, that the poor sheep of Israel are not simply the sacrifice, and they are not in any sense the innocent sacrifice of the sheep-dealers, but that the people have the leaders they deserve, and stand in solidarity with them over against the Good Shepherd. Who is this Judas, the man who will maintain his freedom in face of Jesus for the sake of something better, the man for whom Jesus is for sale, who can also deliver Him up and surrender Him, and who has already done so in principle? Obviously he does not bear this name for nothing. Within the apostolic group—and this shows us what is meant by the uncleanness of the feet of all the apostles—he obviously represents the Jews, the tribe from which both David himself and his promised Son sprang. When he reserves something for himself, and therefore in principle everything, in face of Jesus in this characteristic fashion, he merely does that which Israel has always done in relation to Yahweh. He merely does that which has always made Yahweh's rejection of His chosen people inevitable. There never was a time when Israel encountered its God as Mary encountered Jesus, when it was willing to trust Him and therefore to dedicate itself wholeheartedly and unreservedly to Him. Israel always retained the possibility of serving other gods as well as Yahweh. Israel always tried to buy off Yahweh with thirty pieces of silver. It gave Him a modicum of Yahweh-religion which it made as similar as possible to the religion of all other peoples. It gave Him a minimum of sacrificial and legal observance—just enough to maintain the cultus formally throughout the centuries, much as the thirty pieces of silver were eventually good enough to be put in the treasury whose contents were earmarked for the current upkeep of the temple. Israel was never prepared to give Him the full offering of thanksgiving for His faithfulness as the Shepherd, and it therefore refused to give Him the one thing which it owed. The paltry and wholly inadequate payment which Israel dared to offer its God for His faithfulness as the Shepherd, the thirty pieces of silver, are themselves returned to Judas and therefore to the people of Israel as a payment for his faithlessness, for his freedom to behave so differently from Mary, for the handing over of Jesus. This is his contribution, his work. This, then, must be his reward. In the person of Judas there is, so to speak, handed back—and from the hand of his own leaders—that which he had dared to offer to God in place of what he owed Him. The rejection of Israel by its Good Shepherd, to which that passage in Zechariah refers, is now inexorably executed, but in a way which is certainly not foreseen in that passage, for it is not the flock sold by the sheep-dealers that is led to the slaughter, but the Good Shepherd Himself. This is how His non-willing, His wrath, is worked out against them. This is what is meant by the destruction of the two staves " grace " and " covenant " as described in Zechariah. He Himself, the Shepherd, is now to be broken. He Himself is broken. And Israel itself delivers Him up to slaughter, to His destruction. What does it receive for this? What does it gain by it?—this Israel which rejected the protection of the Good Shepherd. What is left when it has refused this protection? The thirty pieces of silver, and therefore the modicum of religion with which it tried to buy off its God, a good enough contribution towards repairing over and over again the dilapidated temple ! And these thirty pieces of silver are not a surprise, a kind of unexpected fate. They are just what Israel willed and intended all along. According to Mt. 26[15], Judas asked what would be the payment for the handing-over of Jesus, and this exact sum was immediately weighed and counted before him. With a full awareness of the reward, he then began to look for an opportunity to hand Jesus over. So the thirty pieces of silver were really the better thing for which Judas wanted to maintain his independence of Jesus. They were not too little for him, although to his way of thinking the three hundred denarii of Mary were too much to be offered so simply and unrestrainedly to Jesus. This was the measure of the greatness of the wisdom of Judas' own decision and choice, in which he willed to persist in opposition to Jesus. This .was what he got for Him, what he made out of it, what he really wanted from it—thirty pieces of silver ! Judas and all Israel, Judas and in and with him the Jews as such ! Like Esau, the rejected of God, they sold their birthright for a mess of pottage. They did not do so with closed but with open eyes. Yet these were obviously the eyes of the blind. And now—this is the direct result of the handing-over of Jesus, of the slaying of the Good Shepherd willed and executed by them—they are left intact to the consumption of this mess of pottage. They can now live and die in their Judaism, their Yahweh-religion without Yahweh. They can make the best of it. They can call it a gain—and enjoy it as such—that they are the people of God, and yet do not have to believe in God or obey Him. " I will not feed you : that that dieth, let it die ; and that that is to be cut off, let it be cut off ; and let the rest eat every one the flesh of another." This is what the good shepherd says in Zech. 11[9], as he leaves the stubborn flock which deserves only bad shepherds. And He still says the same as He takes it upon Himself to be led to the slaughter on their behalf, because of their guilt and according to their will. They have the reward which they wanted and earned. And it is with this reward that their punishment secretly begins. The sin of Judas is that, with all Israel, he wants this reward with which the punishment already begins ; that for him Jesus can be bartered for this evil reward. This sin makes it clear that as far as he was concerned Jesus was present with the disciples in vain. He protected and watched over them in vain. In it there is exposed an uncleanness which was the uncleanness of all the apostles and needed a special cleansing.

Before continuing this line of thought, however, we must follow to its end the particular road taken by Judas as described in the New Testament. The end of this road shows, in the first place, how terrible was that which Judas had done in the eyes of the New Testament. Again, it is Matthew (27[3]) who, still thinking about Zech. 11, provides information which is, of course, partially contradicted by that given in Ac. 1[18f.]

We are first told in Mt. 27[3] that Judas repented when he saw the direct result of his deed ; when he saw Jesus condemned by the High Council, and handed over to Pilate. What he personally wanted was only the first small step and not this result. His interest and intention were satisfied by the manifestation of his freedom in face of Jesus, and what he derived from it. We have seen that he was not opposed to Jesus, just as the people of Israel was never absolutely against Yahweh. It was just that he was not for Jesus in the way that we must be for Him if we are not actually to be against Him. He had no wish to bear responsibility for the further links in the chain ; nor, in view of what immediately followed, for the first link either. He did not want any part in the delivery of Jesus to Pilate. And when he saw that this took place, he regretted his own handing-over of Jesus, and wished to withdraw it at least to the extent of returning the reward to those from whom he had received it. " He brought again the thirty pieces of silver to the chief priests and elders, saying, I have sinned in that I have betrayed the innocent blood." There is no reason not to take seriously this repentance, this confession, this attempt of Judas to make restitution. In what respect does it fail to be perfect penitence ? *Contritio cordis, confessio oris, satisfactio operis*—all the things which were later said to constitute true repentance are there. Is it not in its way more complete than that of Peter, of whom we are told in Mt. 26^75 only that after his threefold denial he went out " and wept bitterly " ? We need to keep this in mind if we are to avoid a too hasty moral judgment of the person of Judas. In the light of it we cannot see, even in the kiss, the absolute deceit which has so often been seen. How else can an apostle carry out even the handing-over of Jesus but under this sign—in the form of a final testimony to his fellowship with Him ? How can an apostle fail, then, to repent at once of what he has done ? How can an apostle be incapable of genuine penitence for this deed ? It is obvious that Judas can only affirm again the nature of his person as that of an apostle, both in the form of his evil deed and also in his repentance. But the Evangelists are not so much concerned with the person of this apostle as with his deed, with that which objectively and irrevocably transpired between Jesus and himself. What did actually happen ? We have seen that in its externals it was something of relative insignificance. Does not the treachery of Judas compare with Peter's denial in the same way as Saul's ritual offences compare with David's adultery ? Here, again, does not the rejected seem to be a lesser sinner than the elect ? Judas led the officers of the high-priests to the spot where they could arrest Jesus without a disturbance. Now this could obviously have happened at some other spot and in some other way. But in fact it happened at this spot and in this way. And through what Judas was able to do and actually did do here, there began the movement which concluded with the death of Jesus. At this point it was not the high-priests, or Pilate and his soldiers, or Peter the denier and the fleeing disciples, who put their hands to the lever. It was Judas the apostle. And it was in *his* act that Israel finally showed itself to be the people of God which would not wholly serve its God, and would not therefore serve Him at all. By *his* act the sheep themselves sold the Good Shepherd to be slaughtered for thirty pieces of silver. By *his* act the tribe of Judah testified that it rejected the promised Messiah who has now been given. By *his* act even the apostolic group made itself guilty of this rejection. The transaction between Jesus and Judas was insignificant in itself, but this was the irrevocable event which took place in it ; just as the sins of Saul as recorded in 1 Sam. were trivial in themselves and yet gave the irrevocable testimony to the fact that Saul's kingdom was the rejection of Yahweh's kingdom. Because it was an act of this nature, no sincerity of repentance such as Judas later experienced could in any way alter the fact that Jesus' saying about this act was still valid : " Woe to the man, by whom the Son of man is betrayed ! " Thus, for all the earnestness of his intention, he could not really repent, or make restitution for this deed by another and better deed. Saul, too, did not fail to repent sincerely, confessing his sins and attempting amendment. And in the same way Judas could indeed repent of what he had done, acknowledging that he had sinned, and trying to make restitution. But he was no more able to make real restitution than Saul. The high-priests and elders were perfectly right when they could give only this answer to his penitence, confession and attempt at restitution : " What is that to us ? see thou to that." They could help him as little as he could help himself. They could not undo his deed, for by this time its consequences were already out of their own hands. The whole movement, which led to this conclusion, had now begun, and whoever else was involved, the fact that it had begun was the fault of Judas. And so, according to the New Testament account, his repentance is left an open question which is not met or heard or answered by a promise of grace. How can it be, when Judas' repentance cannot be perfect as his own work, but—if at all—only in virtue of the goal of that movement, the restitution which Jesus perfected by His death for the sin of the whole world, and therefore for Israel's sin, and therefore for the sin of Judas as well ? But this restitution, and with it the opening-up of the possibility of a full and true and acceptable repentance by faith in the atonement which Jesus accomplished for the sin of the whole world, this actualisation of the grace of God through the handing-over of His Son into the hands of sinners for their own blessing, and the revelation of its actualisation in the resurrection of Jesus, had not yet taken place, but could do so only as this movement ran its course. Judas, and his penitence, stood on this side of the event—dependent on his own work, his own freedom of choice and decision, which in contrast to Mary he had kept for himself in face of Jesus. He had refused to accept Jesus unreservedly as his Lord, wholly to surrender himself to the glorifying of his death. He wanted to be an apostle with this reservation. The incompleteness and therefore the unreality of his repentance correspond necessarily to this incompleteness of his surrender, to this inward duplicity in his confirmation of his apostleship. With this reservation his work was bound to result in the handing-over of Jesus. But with this reservation it was also impossible for him to make restitution for this deed. Judas, then, is guilty only at the beginning of the movement which reached its conclusion in the death of Jesus. He does not participate in the promise which reaches out from that conclusion to him also. He stands at the cross of Jesus simply as the one who brought Him there, who has " shed innocent blood," who is accused and condemned. And in him his tribe, the Davidic family of Judah, and all Israel, stands just as he does, at the cross of Jesus—like Saul the Benjamite before David, and like Israel before Yahweh as described in so many interminably long chapters of prophetic accusation. How can there be grace for him when he will not live wholly by grace, when he has completely rejected grace ? How can the repentance of one who has made this rejection be other than a rejected repentance ?

This explains very well why the other account of the end of Judas, in Ac. 1, not only fails to mention his repentance, which Matthew describes so impressively, but seems not even to know about it. According to v. 18 of this account, Judas bought a field " with the reward of iniquity." It does not appear that he felt any remorse at what had happened to Jesus in the meantime. We certainly cannot seek to remove by harmonising the contradiction between the two stories on this point, but it does at least show us that, according to the New Testament view, no promise of grace could be held out for Judas, and no genuine penitence was possible. That which, according to Matthew, he had so earnestly desired and done in this respect, can with equally good reason be ignored by the Acts of the Apostles. It can only be recorded that he personally paid for his deed (without being able to make restitution for it). It can only be said that he and his apostleship perished. The only account can be that of his horrible downfall. Anything else is on the far side of his deed. Because this deed took place on this side of the death and resurrection of Jesus, because, unlike Mary, he had renounced a share in this future atonement, nothing else could be expected, or at any point detected, as in the case of Jerusalem, which could look forward only to destruction when, in the words of Jesus (Mt. 23[27]), it " would not." What happened to Judas' reward, according to the two contradictory accounts, is like a gloomy parallel to the utter absence of any future ascribed to Judas himself.

According to Mt. 27[5], in the fervour of his attempt at restitution Judas tried in a sense to do with his thirty pieces of silver what had been done with those of the prophet of Zech. 11 : " He cast down the pieces of silver in the temple, and departed." But it was obviously too late for this use to be made of them. The time had passed when anything could be done with the modicum of Judaism with which Israel had so long tried to buy off Yahweh, and for which, conversely,

Jesus could now be bartered in Judas' eyes. The time had passed when anything could be done with the thirty pieces of silver, at least as a contribution to the current costs of repairing the temple, the maintenance of the ongoing worship of Israel. For the time of the temple itself, of Jerusalem itself, of the special worship of this city and of the existence of Israel as the special people of God, had passed. When Judas handed Jesus over, this era drew to its close. The further restoration of the temple, and further contributions to the treasury, into which the widow of Mk. 12⁴² had cast her mite, had now become meaningless. Nothing more could be made of the Judaism that Judas had chosen as his portion in place of the promised and manifested Messiah of Israel. After the rejection of this Messiah as initiated by Judas, no more could be done for the continuance of the temple and Jerusalem and Israel as the special people of God. Naturally, this was not the argument of the high-priests and elders when they were left with the money flung down in the temple. On the contrary, " they took the silver pieces, and said, It is not lawful for to put them into the treasury, because it is the price of blood." In this way they themselves confirm that the deed for which they had given the money to Judas was an unclean deed, a deed of blood. In this way they indirectly accuse themselves. And in this way they themselves necessarily prevent the spoils of this deed from assisting the purposes of the temple treasury, a kind of analogy to what happened in Zech. 11. But what is their solution ? They buy the " potter's field " with the money, as a " burial place for strangers," that is, for Jews of the Diaspora who might die during their residence in Jerusalem while guests at the passover. Matthew comments (v. 9b) that this fulfilled the word : " And they took the thirty pieces of silver τὴν τιμὴν τοῦ τετιμημένου ὃν ἐτιμήσαντο ἀπὸ υἱῶν Ἰσραήλ and gave them for the potter's field, as the Lord appointed me." In Matthew this word of Zechariah is said to be from Jeremiah. And if this is not a mistake but intentional, the intention is in relation to just that element of the passage (that is, the " potter's field ") which already in the Hebrew rests on a scribal error—for Zech. 11¹³ certainly refers to the temple treasury and not to a " potter's field." But as Matthew saw it, the " potter's field " was connected with the " potter's house " of Jer. 18¹ on the one hand, and the purchase of the field of Anathoth in Jer. 32⁶ᶠ· on the other. We have here another example how even in its misunderstandings and confusions the Bible is usually more instructive than other books in their accuracy. For all these points have their own meaning and reference. The introduction of Jeremiah gives to the whole incident a general reference and brings out the connexion between the acts of Judas and the high-priests and the impending fall of Jerusalem. That the account of the potter's house in Jer. 18 belongs to this sequence means that we have to consider what is said in v. 4 : " And the vessel that he made of clay was marred in the hand of the potter : so he made it again another vessel, as seemed good to the potter to make it," referring it to Israel as a whole as well as the apostleship of Judas in particular. But there is also undoubtedly a reference to Jer. 32. Here the subject is not a prophet, but the purchase of a field by the prophet. This purchase is a sign of promise just before the fall of Jerusalem : " Houses and fields and vineyards shall be possessed again in this land." As Matthew sees it, however, the completed purchase of this burial ground by the high-priests is obviously a terrible reversal of this promise. After the act of Judas, after the rejection of the Son of David as the awful outcome of this act, its fulfilment can consist only in the existence of a burial ground for strangers in Jerusalem, that is, for children of Israel who have become visitors in their own homeland. Instead of a temple filled with life there will now be room only for graves. All this takes us well past Zech. 11, but this does not alter the fact that it sheds a most terrifying light on the final sentence in Zech. 11 (v. 17), in relation not only to Judas, but also to the high-priests and elders. " Woe to the useless shepherd that leaveth the flock ! the sword shall be upon his arm and upon his right eye : his arm shall be clean dried up, and his right eye shall be utterly darkened." By disposing of Judas' reward in this way, the high-priests and elders sign not only the sentence on Judas, but their own sentence of rejection, and the sentence on Israel itself.

According to the divergent account in Ac. 1, it was not the high-priests who bought this field, but Judas himself—we are not told anything about his repentance. And if it is here called " the field of blood," in the popular speech of the period when this New Testament writing was composed or copied, the reference is not—as in Mt. 27⁸—to the blood money with which it was bought, but to the fact that Judas could not enjoy his acquisition and possession for a single day, but was doomed at once to die a sudden and horrible death. The Acts of the Apostles sees in this a fulfilment of Ps. 69²⁵ : " Let their habitation be desolate ; and let none dwell in their tents," and also of Ps. 109⁸ : " Let another take his ἐπισκοπή." We must refer both passages both to Judas and to the people of Israel, as does the Acts of the Apostles. At one and the same time Judas loses what he has foolishly earned by handing over Jesus (the field), and also what Jesus had given him with his apostolic calling (his ἐπισκοπή). And in exactly the same way Israel loses both what it tries foolishly to ensure at the price of rejecting its Messiah (the undestroyed continuance of its exclusive national-religious life, and the prospect of its future world-domination), and what was on the point of being realised with the appearance in its midst of the Messiah (its existence as the true people of God and the performance of its true mission to the nations of the world). What is left ? On the one hand, there is left only a field without an owner,. an office without a person, which can only be transferred to someone else ; and on the other a city and a country which are desolate, a holiness and a mission which are no longer Israel's, but necessarily become those of an entirely different people. We can see at once how this account coincides with that of Matthew, not perhaps in externals, but certainly in material content. Both accounts of what happened to the reward of Judas confirm the fact that both Judas and Judah—Judas as the embodiment of Judah, and Judah as embodied in Judas—have, in fact, no future as such and in and for themselves.

According to Mt. 27⁵, this lack of any possible future is sealed by Judas' suicide : " He went out and hanged himself." This climax is undeniably a reminiscence of 2 Sam. 17²³, where the same is told of Ahithophel, the former friend and counsellor of David. This man had gone over to the side of Absalom when the latter plotted and rebelled, and had given him wise advice which might have brought David into mortal peril. Indeed, he had offered his services in the execution of the plan. Through the opposing influence of Hushai, the whole remained loyal to David and was only ostensibly on Absalom's side, the whole plan was frustrated. " And when Ahithophel saw that his counsel was not followed, he saddled his ass, and arose, and put his household in order, and hanged himself, and died, and was buried in the sepulchre of his father." The figure of Judas is obviously different from that of this Old Testament counterpart to the extent that Judas hangs himself because he succeeded where Ahithophel failed, while Ahithophel hanged himself because he failed where Judas succeeded. But we may say equally well that Judas hangs himself because, like Ahithophel, he faces the fact that he has played the wrong card, identifying himself with a lost cause which is destined to perish. Even when he has succeeded where Ahithophel failed, even when he has actually handed over the Son of David to death, Judas faces the utter nothingness of what he has gained in so doing. And as the suicide of Ahithophel is a clear testimony that with the miscarriage of his proposal he is certain of the victory of David, we must seriously ask ourselves whether this reminiscence does not mean that as Matthew sees it the suicide of Judas after the success of his evil deed has also to be understood (and not merely incidentally) as an anticipatory testimony to the coming resurrection of the Son of David. Primarily and in itself, of course, it is simply the judgment which necessarily had to follow the act for which he could not repent—

even although he wished to do so. It is the final word concerning him in the fulfilment of Jesus' saying : "Woe to the man !" It is the liquidation of the person who had done this deed. It is the closing of the absolute gap in the apostolic group which had necessarily appeared at the point where the group was itself guilty of Jesus' death. It is the marking off of that place in the apostolic group and in the Church as such where only a completely new creation, only the replacing of this person by another, can guarantee its continuance and the realisation of its mission. Judas has no future as an apostle, or in the Church. Only Mary has any future in the Church, the Mary from whom he so distinctively separated himself. Only an apostleship accepted and exercised in the manner of Mary has any future. Judas can only be that which is past in the Church. And Judas means Judah—the Judah which delivered the Son of David to the Gentiles. Judas means Jerusalem—the Jerusalem that "would not." This Judah and Jerusalem can only perish and disappear, to make way for another. Its lost and forfeited life can only continue in this other, being raised again from the dead—literally from the dead. This is the judgment which is carried out in the death of Judas. According to Matthew this judgment has the distinctive form of a self-judgment. Judas dies, as Saul had done, by his own hand. Obviously it is the consistent pursuit of a free choice and decision in face of Jesus—the same as led him to hand Jesus over—which now that his repentance is rejected drives him to this end, to suicide. Had he not wanted all the time to be his own judge ? Well, that is what he is in this definitive way, in his death. Defying even the rejection of his repentance, he wills to take to himself that which in any case could only be given him : the final judgment, the judgment of God on his act, and therefore the restoration of the order that his act had destroyed. He expects this restoration to follow from the fact that he himself declares his life to be forfeit, and that as his own executioner he hangs himself on a tree. He could not confirm more terribly the fact that he stands and acts on this side of the reconciliation of the world to God which took place in the death of Jesus and was revealed in His resurrection. He will not accept and await from the hand of God, as the free grace of God, the judgment of God which he incurred by his act. But he wills to take even the judgment of God into his own hands, and himself executes it upon himself. It is in this light of a usurped self-judgment crowning all previous offences that Matthew evidently sees the corresponding downfall of Jerusalem and the whole national and religious life of the Jews. With the killing of its Messiah, Israel has entered a road on which not only is God's judgment upon its whole existence inevitable, but in sheer self-consistency it must end by committing suicide. That is what Israel finally did in the revolt against the Romans and particularly in the defence of Jerusalem against Titus in A.D. 70. Unable to live any longer, it gave itself up willingly and wittingly—we have only to think of the account of the end of the last high-priests—to the death which in itself could not be an expiation for its sins, but only their consummation.

The version given in Ac. 1 makes no mention of a suicide of Judas, but speaks darkly of his meeting his end by an accident after purchasing the field : "Falling headlong, he burst asunder in the midst, and all his bowels gushed out" (v. 18). The frightfulness of this description defies all the explanations by which later legends and secular learning sometimes soften and sometimes enhance it. But it obviously suggests that Judas perished from within himself. It was because of an inward impossibility—in the New Testament the σπλάγχνα means the inmost part of a man as this is revealed—that he came to destruction. His creaturely being could no longer endure the monstrousness of the contradiction in which he had enmeshed himself, and so it had to explode like a released hand-grenade. He could only die therefore—Ac. 1 does not say by his own hand, but of himself. Here too, then, the judgment on him is in this way understood as a self-judgment. And here, too, we can again see Jerusalem and Israel. Whoever does what

Judas did, does more than the deed itself. He does that which makes him insupportable to himself. He passes judgment upon himself. His inmost being moves irresistibly to this explosion of his whole existence. The man who kills Jesus also kills himself, even though he may not technically be a suicide. In this respect, too, the material agreement and mutual affirmation of the two accounts is much greater than the formal discrepancy would at first seem to suggest.

This, then, is the sin of Judas. And no matter how we look at it, we cannot say that the universal expressions of horror with which the New Testament surrounds his figure and accompanies his way are inappropriate to their subject. What was done here, as the work of Israel from within the apostolic group, the Church, was really work which belonged to the night. As the representative of Israel within the apostolic group, within the Church, Judas is indeed the " son of perdition," the man into whom the Satan has entered, himself a devil. The New Testament, then, can only reject his repentance, however sincerely he may undertake it. The New Testament can only record with horror that he came to this miserable end. There can be no doubt that here at the very heart of the New Testament we are confronted by the problem of the rejected, by the question : What is the will of God for him ? what has God determined concerning him ? And we meet this question at the same central place where the New Testament also raises and answers the question of the elect.

We must insist as definitely as we can that it is at the same central place. We recall that Judas is always " one of the twelve." " He was numbered with us " (Ac. 1¹⁷). This is not merely a formal statement. None of the other apostles handed Jesus over. But for all that Judas and the other apostles belong together as closely as possible—with all the closeness with which Jesus chose and called them together (the others with Judas, and Judas with them). What Judas did affects them also. To be sure, they have not actually done it or co-operated with him. But the point is that they obviously could have done it. The possibility of doing it was their possibility too. How else are we to explain the extraordinary fact that when Jesus declared : " One of you shall betray me " (Mk. 14¹⁸, Mt. 26²¹), they were all " exceeding sorrowful " and asked about each other (εἷς καθ' εἷς), and about themselves (εἷς ἕκαστος) : " Lord, is it I ? " According to Lk. 22²³ they asked among themselves " which of them it was that should do this thing," and in Jn. 13²²ᶠ· the disciples looked at one another, " doubting of whom he spake." Peter questions the disciple who lay on Jesus' breast. And Jesus Himself replies on his behalf : " He it is, to whom I shall give a sop, when I have dipped it," and at once He dipped the sop and gave it to Judas. The tension of this scene, emphasised by all the Evangelists, clearly arises from the fact that although it was actually this one disciple, any of the others might equally well have been the one. This emerges clearly from the peculiar form of the tradition of the anointing at Bethany. Who did actually protest against this act of prodigality, expressing the pious idea that the three hundred denarii, for which the ointment might have been sold, could have been given to the poor? According to Jn. 12 the question and idea are those of Judas, and in the sequel the Evangelist places the worst possible construction on his words and describes him as a thief. As we have seen, it is this story of the anointing, as given in Jn. 12, and the contrast between Judas and Mary, which gives us the key to the question of Judas' sin. But it is very striking that in the parallel account of Mk. 14⁴ it is not Judas who raises the protest, but " some had indignation within themselves, and said, Why was this waste of the ointment made ? " and that in Mt. 26⁸ these " some " are quite simply and explicitly " the disciples." This, be it noted, is at the very point where John singles out Judas, and subjects him to that analysis. But again, the historical complications in which we may find ourselves because of this discrepancy are of little consequence compared with the instruction which is yielded by the inconsistency. The literary process which we see here may consist in the interaction of different traditions, but it may also consist in the fact that Matthew's statement is a conscious clarification of Mark's (or Mark's a conscious blurring of Matthew's ?), while John's is a conscious concentration into one person, Judas, of the many persons referred to by Mark and Matthew. Or could it be that John's statement is the original, and that it has been generalised by Matthew and Mark ? However that may be, the New Testament does actually give these varying accounts of the matter. and in so doing it says something which no reader of the New Testament Canon can any longer disguise from himself : that what Judas said on this occasion could have been said by others of Jesus' company ; indeed, that it could have been said by His disciples as such, those who did not betray Him ; or, conversely, that what was actually said by some or all the disciples could also have been an utterance of Judas on this occasion. The New Testament does not see Judas and the other apostles apart, but together, even at the point where it gives us a key to the question of Judas' sin. In Jn. 12 we are shown the decisive contrast between Judas and Mary. We are shown the fraudulent, thieving refusal of a total devotion in response to Jesus' claim, concealed under the pious intention of apostolic discipleship according to an individual pattern and judgment. But we see from the Synoptic Gospels that all the disciples are implicated in this same refusal. They all stand in the same contrast to Mary. They are all in need of the same reprimand : " Ye have the poor with you always (and whensoever ye will ye may do them good) ; but me ye have not always " (Mk. 14⁷, Mt. 26¹¹). They are involved with Judas in just the situation from which they might have betrayed Jesus as he did. Indeed, to all intents and purposes they have already betrayed Him. We can understand, therefore, the sincerity and the necessity of the question : " Lord, is it I ? " They were all questioned when Jesus said that one of them would betray Him. We can also understand the washing of the feet in Jn. 13. This had really to be done by Jesus to all His disciples, His disciples as such. For although the others were distinguished from Judas by their clean hands and heads, they were no less unclean than Judas as to their feet. Without a special cleansing, their feet shared the same uncleanness as his. So far as the feet are concerned they are all guilty and accused and in need of cleansing, as Judas was. And if Judas is in need in a special sense, it is only to the extent that he embodies and manifests the unclean feet of all the apostles, that is, what the Church has in common, in its origins, with obstinate, rejected Israel, and therefore with the world. In Judas—and not only in Judas, but in all the apostles as children of Abraham according to the flesh—Ishmael lives on in spite of Isaac, Esau in spite of Jacob, Pharaoh in spite of Moses, Saul in spite of David. How can it be otherwise ? How else can it be true that the Word of God Himself has taken this flesh of Abraham's children, that the Church in its original apostolic form is chosen and gathered from these children of Abraham according to the flesh ? To be sure, an objective cleansing, the washing of their hands and heads, is provided for all the apostles, including Judas, in the fact that Jesus chose and called them, and was present with them (Jn. 17¹²), protecting them and watching over them. It consists in Jesus' calling them to Himself, gathering them to Himself, and making them witnesses of His acts and hearers of His Word. It consists in the overpowering might with which the light of the world shone upon them while they were in the world. It consists in the fact that Jesus called them His own, and was with them as His own. It consists in the fact that Jesus established the relationship between them and Himself which He describes categorically in Jn. 15⁵ : " I am the vine, ye are the branches." And " ye are clean through the word which I have spoken unto you " (Jn. 15³). This relationship was not nullified, and the objective cleansing that met them was not given the lie, because according to Jn. 13¹⁰ and 17¹² it was ineffective for one of them—namely, for Judas—and because he actually remained unclean in head and hand. And it was a mistake when Peter (Jn. 13⁹) demanded that Jesus should also wash his head and his hands, for that had already happened : " He that is washed needeth not save to wash his feet, but is clean every whit : and ye are clean . . ." (Jn. 13¹⁰). The objective counteraction against their uncleanness is always there in the person of Jesus. It is to be recognised and acknowledged as such, and as such is not to be questioned. It is not, therefore, of any final importance whether the (textually uncertain) qualification of Jn. 13¹⁰ : εἰ μὴ τοὺς πόδας, is an explanatory addition by a later editor, or whether it dropped out through a misunderstanding on the part of the editor (who thought he saw in it incompatibility with the καθαρὸς ὅλος). The latter is probable. But even in the first case the context would inevitably demand this explanation of the saying that he needs no further washing. John 15² also speaks of a special cleansing of those who objectively are already clean as branches of the vine. And it depicts the danger that those branches which do not remain in the vine, and therefore bear no fruit, will be removed. The washing of the feet as the special subjective cleansing of those who already are objectively clean cannot be overlooked or minimised, any more than the objective cleansing which they have already experienced ; and this is particularly the case if, according to the illuminating hypothesis of more recent exegesis, the function of this account in John's Gospel is to replace the omitted institution of the Lord's Supper. What is said to Peter in Jn. 13¹⁸ cannot be misunderstood : " If I wash thee not, thou hast no part with me." The special washing of the feet is a *conditio sine qua non* for fellowship with Jesus. Apart from it, even Peter would be in the fellowship of Judas, the fellowship of the devil. Peter must be specially cleansed from that which he has in common with Judas. In order fully to understand this, we must pay particular attention to the opening verses of the chapter. In v. 1, it is said that " when Jesus knew that his hour was come, that he should depart out of this world unto the Father, having loved his own which were in the world, he loved them εἰς τέλος, unto the end," and at the same time " with supreme fulness," with a love that unceasingly and wholly embraced them. In v. 3 it is then said that Jesus knew that " the Father had given all things into his hands, and that he was come from God, and went to God." And (according to v. 2) it was at the very moment of His loving disposition towards His own, and His conviction about Himself and about God, that the devil had already conceived the plan in his heart, or had put the plan into the heart of Judas, that the latter should betray Him. In John's Gospel there is an all-embracing concentration at this critical moment. From above, there is the approach of His death, but also the ascent to the Father which corresponds to His departure. From beneath, the actualisation of the satanic possibility of Judas has already begun. In Jesus Himself, there is an awareness of His absolute power, and the will to make the last perfect use of it in His relationship to His own, and on their behalf. It is at this critical moment that Jesus proceeds to wash the feet of His own. The parallel to the institution of the Lord's Supper emerges from the act. But what is the decisive parallel ? We must start with Jesus' answer to Peter's first question : " Peter saith unto him, Lord, dost thou wash my feet ? Jesus answered and said unto him, What I do thou knowest not now ; but thou shalt know hereafter " (v. 7). Not now : before Jesus died, Peter knows neither the need of what happened to him in the feet-washing, nor its power and effect. But hereafter : after the death of Jesus, what is now hidden will be revealed to him, and he will experience the power and effect of that which is now necessarily obscure even in the sign of it, thus perceiving how much he needed the power and effect of what is signified in the feet-washing. The feet-washing, like the Lord's Supper, obviously anticipates what is mediated and given to the apostles and the whole Church not merely by the presence and life of Jesus but by His death ; the perfection of the love which He always gave them in the power of His divine omnipotence as exercised in His death, and revealed and disclosed in His resurrection. He will give them more by His death than He had given them by His presence in this hitherto objective relationship. As anticipated and represented in the Lord's Supper, He will give them His body to eat and His blood to drink. He will give them Himself at the cost of His death. He Himself will be in them. They will live by Him Himself ; by His sacrifice of His life. He is not giving it in the void when He gives it in death. He is giving it to them. This is the love with which He loves to the end His own who are in the world ; with which He loves them perfectly. There can be no doubt that this is what is signified in the foot-washing too. It has primarily the character of an act of humility on the part of Him into whose hands the Father has given all things, and as such it is utterly amazing to His disciples. In the Lord's Supper Jesus is the Host who shares bread and wine with His own. In the feet-washing He makes Himself their slave. It is to humble Himself completely before them and for them that He uses the fulness of power placed by the Father in His hands, just as in the Lord's Supper, strangely enough, the Host uses the bread and wine only to signify Himself, in His self-offering, as the One whose body is to be broken and whose blood is to be shed. Thus the feet-washing has definitely to be understood in the light of Phil. $2^{7f.}$: " He took upon him the form of a servant . . . and humbled himself." And it is to be noted that Jesus Himself is here seen to be the prototype of the Mary of Bethany who lavishes her best upon Him. Within the uncompromising saying to Peter that he has no part with Jesus if he is not washed by Him, there is thus a concealed recollection that fellowship with Him necessarily involves the attitude of Mary—not as a *conditio* but as a *consequens sine qua non*. Indeed, the disciples are later required explicitly to wash one another's feet as a demonstration of their confession of Him as their Lord and Master. The foot-washing, then, characterises the death of Jesus as the service, performed in inconceivable condescension, which Jesus offers them as their Lord. But it must not be overlooked that this is not just any menial service, but a foot-washing. It is, therefore, a service of this Lord who has become a slave, the nature and content of which are determined. It is a service which only this slave, who is indeed the Lord, can perform for them. It is a service of which they all stand in the greatest need. Jesus looks, then, to His immediate death. He is conscious of the fulness of the power received from His Father. And He uses it (now clearly in anticipation) to " love His own to the end " and to become their slave. But as He does so, Judas already walks inwardly the road that is to lead him to deliver Jesus. Therefore, even as He undertakes and performs this servant's task, Jesus sees the open wound in the body of His own. He sees that although they are clean for the Word's sake which He has spoken to them, although they are branches of Him who is the vine, although already their hands and heads are washed by Him " in the world " (v. 1), they have an intimate part in the being of Israel and its rejection. For Judas, whom He chose like the rest, is among them. The feet-washing as such shows what is meant by this " loving to the end " (ἀγαπᾶν εἰς τέλος), this love in the revelation and disclosure of His divine omnipotence. It shows what they lack apart from His death, and what can be given them only by His death. It shows what the need is which can be satisfied only as He gives Himself to them. It is because Judas is among them, because the presence and act of this apostle show what is involved in the fact that all the apostles are " in the world," that Jesus must die for the sake of this uncleanness and its removal. And in view of Judas—indeed, of what they all have in common with him—the representation of His death is a feet-washing, which is indispensable even for those whose heads and hands are already washed. The apostle Peter, elect and called, is just as much in need of the death of Jesus, of this perfecting of His love in the slave-service of the Lord's utter and final devotion to His own, as is the apostle Judas, also elect and called. For the nature of Ishmael and Esau, of Pharaoh and Saul, whose rebellion breaks out in the person and act of Judas, is no less the nature of Peter than it is of Judas. If Judas fell into the danger of being cut off as an unfruitful branch of the vine, Peter was inescapably confronted by the same danger. Peter no less than Judas was inclined to be independent in face of Jesus, as is shown in the story of his denial, although Peter did not hand Him over but only—and how emphatically !—denied Him. The symbolic act of Mary of Bethany was as new and strange to Peter as it was to Judas. The basic flaw was revealed in Judas, but it was that of the apostolate as a whole. At this decisive point the apostolate was also Israel, and Israel was the world and therefore of the night. The elect were also rejected and as such elected. This was why Jesus had to " love them unto the end," to die for them, and as the One who died for them to be theirs. Jesus had to die because of the sin for which none of them could make restitution but could only be forgiven ; for the sake of God's righteousness and on the condition of the judgment executed upon Him. Their rejection required judgment upon them—notwithstanding the cleansing which had already taken place, which objectively had excluded and prohibited the act of Judas, but which had not made it subjectively impossible, which could, in fact, take place in vain, as the case of Judas showed. And this judgment which they had all incurred with Judas was taken upon Himself by Jesus in His death. Even the cleansing which was only possible in the form of enduring of judgment, in the form of the completion of the divine rejection of those who rejected God, even this Jesus accepted as His own responsibility when, in line with His election, He gave Himself to this service of the rejected even to the final point of self-offering. This is what is signified in the feet-washing. On the basis and in the power of His service, the apostles are enabled to live as those for whom He intercedes, for whose uncleanness He repents, and to whom He gives His purity. It is in this office as the Reconciler of the world to God, as the King and Prophet who also is the High-priest sacrificing Himself, that Jesus is the Head of the Church. And it is before this Head of the Church that Peter and Judas now stand side by side and on the same footing, at least in respect of their need. All His own, including Peter, would be lost if the subjective side of the relationship between Jesus and His own were not controlled by His death ; if in defiance of their own nature they were not born again as new subjects by the substitutionary death of Jesus ; if they were not given the freedom to live a new life in the world by the power of the life which He sacrificed for them. " Without me ye can do nothing " (Jn. 15⁵)—this is as true for Peter and the rest as it is for Judas. C. Starke (*Syn. Bibl. Exeg. in N.T.*, Vol. 2, 1735) has this apt comment on Ac. 1¹⁵ᶠ· : " If Peter had not had assured forgiveness of his sins, he would not have made this speech. For he would have had to be careful lest One should come and say : Peter, thou art also a brother of Judas." And in the account of this final gift of Jesus to His own, to His Church, without which all others would be futile, which is only intimated in all others, Jesus washed the feet of *all* His disciples, and the Synoptists say that it was to *all* His disciples that typically in the Lord's Supper, under the signs of bread and wine, He offered and distributed His body as broken for them and His blood as shed for them.

When we say *all* His disciples, the question arises whether and how far this took place effectively for Judas as well. In other words, is there a redemptive significance even for Judas in the death of Jesus as portrayed in the Lord's Supper and the feet-washing ? The question is not easy to answer. For, on the one hand, according to all the Evangelists he is still an elect and called apostle of Jesus Christ, and all the Evangelists concede that he took part in the Lord's Supper, or in the feet-washing. And it would be an unspeakably hard affirmation that there was no forgiveness of sins for Judas, that what was symbolised in those actions had no positive meaning for him, that Jesus died in vain for him, when his act only revealed what was concealed in Peter as well and all the apostles. Can it be that the " loving unto the end " of Jesus does not reach him, the very one who in his person and act simply makes manifest the fact and extent that without His death Jesus had not yet loved His own unto the end ? Can it be that the prayer of Lk. 23³⁴ excludes him, or is ineffective in his case ? But, again, all the Evangelists tell us that he broke away from this final decisive and definitive attestation of the care of Jesus to the execution of his evil act ; and the saying about the protective activity of Jesus over His own (Jn. 17¹²), which was in vain in his case, seems necessarily to be connected with this final attestation made to him too. According to Matthew and Acts, is he not excluded already from the positive realisation of what was attested to him too, by the fact that his road ends on this side of the death of Jesus, and is to be placed wholly in the sphere and under the sign of the old covenant broken by Israel, so that even his sincere repentance is necessarily futile ? And, according to Jn. 13²⁷, at the very time when he receives this final attestation is he not driven on to the execution of his act : " and after the morsel Satan entered into him. Then said Jesus unto him, That thou doest, do quickly."

If we follow the Evangelists, then, it would be both hasty and illegitimate to give a final answer one way or the other. In the form, at least, in which we have put it, the question can only be left unanswered. The better course is clearly to consider the unresolved contrast : Jesus, on the one side, in the full sweep of His absolute care for His Church and therefore for the world, to which He addresses Himself through the service of His Church, in the full sweep of the radical restitution of the basic corruption of the world, and of Israel and of His Church, and therefore of the completion of His own election, His whole mission as the Son of God and Man ; and Judas on the other side, for his part only the object of this care, only the bearer and representative of this basic corruption, only the rejected whom God has taken to Himself in the election of Jesus Christ, to whom God has turned Himself in the mission of Jesus Christ. On the one side, Jesus *for* Judas too, indeed for Judas especially ; and on the other side Judas *against* Jesus, against the very Jesus who is for him, who gives Himself wholly and utterly for him, who washes his feet, who offers him His broken body and shed blood, who makes Himself his. The New Testament gives us no direct information about the outcome of this extraordinary " for and against." Really none ! It does not describe Judas' repentance in such a way that we may draw an irresistible or even a probable conclusion as to a final and conclusive conversion of Judas in this life. It does not open up for us any prospect of the completion of such a conversion in the hereafter. Nor does it say anything about the inadmissibility of such a conversion. It strikingly fails to make use of the tempting possibility of making Judas a plain and specific example of hopeless rejection and perdition, an embodiment of the temporal and eternal rejection of certain men. It emphasises the unambiguous contrast on both sides. On the one hand, it places no limits to the grace of Jesus Christ even with regard to Judas. It sets Judas against the brightest radiance of this grace. And on the other hand, it does not use even a single word to suggest that Judas is an example of *apokatastasis*. The situation between Jesus and Judas which is only a heightened form of the situation between Jesus and all other men—between God's election of man, and his necessary rejection—is obviously described, therefore, as the open one of proclamation. The full and unrestricted promise of his election, of the eternal love of God aimed at him too, and seeking and finding him, has reference to Judas too, as we can see from the Lord's Supper and the feet-washing as signs of the fact that Jesus " loves His own unto the end." Yes, it has reference to him, the rejected, who in face of it can only confess his unworthiness of it ; to him, whose rejection rests on and works itself out in the fact that he has no wish to be loved in this way, that he is an enemy even of the grace of God. What can and will be the upshot ? What will be the outcome of this situation ? " When the Son of man cometh, shall he find faith on the earth ? " (Lk. 18⁸). Judas, in his contrast to Jesus, shows how burning this question is, how extremely open it is on both sides in the situation of proclamation. But he also shows—for there is also the contrast of Jesus to Judas—what it means that the question is comprehended within the situation of proclamation, which is created not by the promise in competition with the men to whom it is addressed, but solely by the fact that the promise addresses men and that men are addressed by the promise. It is in this situation, but only in this situation, that the divine determination of the rejected is decided. And therefore this situation is not merely an open one. It is this specific situation. It is the situation which is determined so absolutely differently above and below. It is the situation which involves a " for and against " which is not merely unusual but completely unique. It is the situation which involves the contrast between the irresistible divine grace of Jesus Christ and a hostility of man towards this grace which humanly speaking—but only humanly speaking— is absolutely immovable. This contrast remains in the situation of proclamation. Judas is placed in this contrast, and it is in this contrast that the rejected will recognise himself, and that Peter knew himself to be in solidarity with Judas. This is the open contrast of which the Church and every member of the Church must think when the question of the final and definitive rejection of men is raised. The Church will not then preach an *apokatastasis*, nor will it preach a powerless grace of Jesus Christ or a wickedness of men which is too powerful for it. But without any weakening of the contrast, and also without any arbitrary dualism, it will preach the overwhelming power of grace and the weakness of human wickedness in face of it. For this is how the " for " of Jesus and the " against " of Judas undoubtedly confront one another. We may not know whether it led to the conversion of Judas or not, but this is how it always is in the situation of proclamation. The rejected cannot escape this situation and its relation of opposites. He cannot extricate himself from this order. He will necessarily confirm it and even in his own way be active in it. And in the New Testament this divine determination of the rejected is unambiguously clear even, and especially, in the person and act of Judas.

Whatever may or may not be the positive significance of death for him, there can be no shadow of doubt that by the act which revealed the basic flaw concealed in all the apostles he could not in any sense reverse or invalidate the institution of the apostleship for the proclamation of the election and grace of Jesus Christ. He could not do this even in part, even with respect to a single member of that tribe of Israel which refused its Messiah and was now wakened to new life in the apostles on the basis of the election of Jesus Christ. He could not do so in such a way that any final breach could be made in the basis of the Church by his defection, by the suicide with which he withdrew from the exercise of his office at the very moment when he should have entered upon it ; nor in such a way that the apostolate and the Church built upon it ceased to be " all Israel " (Rom. 11[26]) because of what he had done. However powerful we may esteem that disobedience, it has no power to bring about a destruction or even a disturbance of this kind. The grace of Jesus Christ is too powerful. It may be noted that in 1 Cor. 15[5] Paul does not hesitate to say that the risen Jesus appeared to " the twelve " even when Judas could no longer complete the number, and there could be no question of Matthias or Paul himself. The disobedience of Judas is only strong enough later to degrade him (not as a denial but as a confirmation of his election and calling) to the status of a mere *locum tenens* of his special apostolic office, who, when he had done his work as such, must be replaced by another, but who had to take up his work in its essential and genuine meaning, and carry it out with the other apostles. The account in Acts. 1[15f.] is again relevant at this point. It tells us how Matthias was elected, by lot, to be a witness of the resurrection, the occupier in Judas' place of the κλῆρος τῆς διακονίας ταύτης which had originally been given to Judas. About 120 persons are assembled. Peter explains to them how Scripture has been fulfilled not only in the act but also in the fate of Judas, and how it is now necessary to replace him by one of those who had accompanied Jesus from the beginning with the apostles. Two men, Joseph-Barsabbas-Justus and Matthias, are proposed (evidently by the assembly as a whole). A prayer is then offered that God Himself, who knows men's hearts, will reveal which of the two He has chosen to receive " the place of this ministry and apostleship," " from which Judas by transgression fell that he might go to his place." They then cast lots for them both, " and the lot fell upon Matthias; and he was numbered with the eleven apostles " (συγκατεψηφίσθη). The account is striking, but perfectly straightforward. The really remarkable feature is that this same Acts of the Apostles, which begins with this story of the apostles, becomes the history of the apostle Paul in a way which begins progressively to emerge after the story of the first martyr Stephen (ch. 7), and is quite unequivocal after ch. 13, so that we can hardly deny that it is really Paul who took over Judas' place and the work abandoned by him. Whether the Acts of the Apostles really intended to say this implicitly, is another question. But we cannot deny that the man in whose person and work the original apostolic group, now numerically complete, finds its proper and essential completion—a form which corresponds to the situation following Jesus' death and resurrection and to the forgiveness received for sins—is Saul the Benjaminite. Already before his conversion he was like a ghost of Judas, working with a zeal which is specifically mentioned by all the accounts (Ac. 9[1f.], 22[4f.], 26[10f.]) to arrest members of the Christian assemblies, men and women, and to bring them to Jerusalem. As the Benjaminite Saul of the Old Testament persecutes David, so he of the New Testament persecutes the people of God (Gal. 1[13], 1 Cor. 15[9]), and at the very heart of this activity—twice described specifically as a παραδοῦναι (Ac. 8[3], 22[4])— he is overtaken by the appearance and word of Jesus : " Saul, Saul, why persecutest thou me ? " and commissioned to a special apostleship. Because of this he describes himself as the ἔκτρωμα (1 Cor. 15[8]), as the least of the apostles (1 Cor. 15[9], Eph. 3[8]), as the first of the sinners to save whom Jesus came into the world (1 Tim. 1[15]). Those of his readers who knew the Gospel stories must have been reminded of the Judæan, Judas ! Paul as Saul embodied the evil eye of Israel in relation to the newly existent Church as Judas had embodied it in relation to Jesus. But now, in Paul, this evil eye is, as it were, temporarily stricken with blindness, and then reconstituted as a sound eye for the truth. This very man now finds inconceivable compassion, and becomes the object of the boundless grace of the Lord (1 Tim. 1[13f.]). Having become what he is by the grace of God, but as such working more than all the others (1 Cor. 15[10]), Paul—no longer the ghost of Judas, but a regenerate man, freed from his sin and shame, and clothed with another life—is the embodiment of a new Israel, obedient and fulfilling its destiny. For what is Israel's destiny, according to the Old Testament, if not to be a light to the Gentiles, to the world ? But the light of Israel is its promise in the person of its promised Messiah. And according to the Acts of the Apostles and the Epistles of Paul, the special office of the apostles is to bring Israel's Messiah to the Gentiles. This then—in a radical reversal of his own beginning, as of the badly begun work of Judas—is the peculiar and essential continuation of his work. Paul sets out from the very place where the penitent Judas had tried to turn back and reverse what had already happened. He begins by doing what to Judas' horror the high-priests and elders had done as the second links in that chain of evil. He fulfils the handing-over of Jesus to the Gentiles: not this time in unfaithfulness, but in faithfulness to Israel's calling and mission; not now aiming at the slaying of Jesus, but at establishing in the whole world the lordship of this One who was slain but is risen. Judas had been so little able to nullify the appointment and establishment of the apostleship, to destroy or even to disturb it, that when he fell and vanished, not only did the group of twelve re-form at once, but even outside it, in the figure of this supernumerary, there begins the true story of the apostles in the sense of Mt. 28[19], the genuine handing-over of Jesus to the Gentiles.

And now we hardly venture to think further, but we cannot refrain from taking at least one step if we are to realise what it means that, although Judas was *de iure* replaced by Matthias, he was *de facto* replaced by Paul, so that his later degradation was to be the *locum tenens* for this supernumerary among the twelve. According to what we might term the hesitant, almost reluctant, but eventually clearly stated picture of the Acts of the Apostles, it is Paul who, although he is only added to the twelve, from a supremely alien background, emerges not only as an apostle, but as *the* apostle in the period between the resurrection of Jesus and the unrecorded death of the twelve. And the total picture presented by the New Testament Canon is of a piece with this, for its second part is dominated by the word of Paul in a way which must at least remind us of the domination of its first part by the Word of Jesus Himself. It amounts to this, that from no other apostles do we have anything like so many or such vital and intimate testimonies of the way in which there was fulfilled in this existence what Jesus promised them in the words of the Lord's Supper, or what was also promised them in another form according to the account of the outpouring of the Holy Spirit : the direct provision of food and drink; the sustaining and guiding of their human life by the presence of the divine-human life of Jesus as it was offered up for them, for the forgiveness of their sins. From what we know of them, no apostle spoke so boldly and consistently of his personal fellowship with Jesus Christ, or so confidently—for all the necessary distance—of the direct correspondence of his office to that of Jesus Christ Himself, as did the Paul whose place prior to Jesus' death had been occupied by Judas. How, then, does it stand with Judas, even though, of course, his picture can only negatively reproduce that of Paul ? Is not Judas also, in his own place and after his own fashion, *the* outstanding apostle ? Is he not the holy one among them—"holy" in the old meaning of the term, the one who is marked, branded, banned, the one who is burdened with the divine curse and thrust out, the one who is thus brought into remarkably close proximity to Jesus Himself ? What does it mean that, according to the clear portrayal of the Evangelists, the rejection of Judas can only be regarded—without any diminution of his guilt—as the revelation of the rejection of all the apostles, of all Israel, that Satan seized on him, impelling him to his deed and reaching his goal in his terrible end, while all the rest, although they were no different in themselves and did not deserve anything different, went free ? For all the dissimilarities, is it possible to overlook the likeness in which Judas alone of the apostles stands face to face and side by side with Jesus ? or the more than chronological proximity of his very different death to the death of Jesus ? *Mutatis mutandis*, could not the famous utterance of the high-priest in Jn. 11⁵⁰ : " It is expedient for us, that one man should die for the people, and that the whole nation perish not," be said of Judas too in his relationship to the other apostles ? *Mutatis mutandis*, for, like the crucified thieves and even more so (Lk.23⁴¹), he receives his deserts—death as the wages of sin (Rom. 6²³). He does not really die an atoning death, but the utterly hopeless and fruitless death of one who is not obedient but disobedient even in death, who in death still regarded himself as his own judge ; the death which has no justification and therefore cannot create or accomplish justification ; the death which is not a sacrifice but only a punishment, and which therefore has no power either to illuminate or to quicken. There remains only the similarity that he too, like Jesus, suffered his death in the place of others ; that Jesus actually did not go alone to the death which the sin of all the apostles made necessary. Although lacking the power of His death, there went with Him this one apostle, and represented in the person of this one there went all the dead of the old covenant which Israel had continually broken, those whose death could only be a punishment, Ishmael and Esau and Pharaoh, Saul and Ahithophel and all their kind. All that the utter darkness of the death of this one apostle can do is to emphasise the light and life of the death of Jesus. But it can do this. This is the proximity of Judas to Jesus, the resemblance to Him, which he alone knows of all the apostles. The utter wickedness of his deed and the utter frightfulness of his fate do not alter the fact that it is he who finds himself and is to be seen in this direct confrontation with the grace of God as it appeared in Jesus Christ. This confrontation cannot be annulled. To be sure, it cannot be transformed into a positive relationship as the " Cainites " of the 2nd century thought. The " Gospel according to Judas," which has not come down to us, but which was used by this sect, can hardly contain anything other than what is grossly offensive. But it is a part of the New Testament Gospel of Jesus Christ that before His death Jesus had an apostle beside Him as a witness to the divine rejection of men which He bore and bore away, just as after His resurrection He had an apostle beside Him as a witness to the divine election of men which was bestowed upon Him and which He Himself fulfilled. The fact that Judas had the former function, as Paul subsequently had the latter, is something which remains to Judas, whatever else may be involved in his determination. And in any case, when we consider the question of the determination of the rejected, in view of Judas and Paul we have to bear in mind that the elect always occupies what was originally the place of a rejected, and that the work of the elect can only be the amazing reversal of the work of the rejected. Between them both, between Judas and Paul, stands Jesus Christ—as, according to Lk. 23³³, He hung on the cross between the two malefactors who were crucified with Him ; and the rejection of Judas is the rejection which Jesus Christ has borne, just as the election of Paul is in the first place His election. Apart from Him Judas would not be Judas, just as apart from Him Paul would not be Paul. But if it is Jesus Christ who stands dominatingly in the midst, as the unattainable but mighty prototype of both, then the situation between the elect and the rejected is the open situation of proclamation. If the elect cannot create it, neither can the rejected destroy it. In this situation the rejected cannot be awarded any other position than that of a *locum tenens* for the elect who is predetermined to disappear. But nothing else may be expected or conjectured of any rejected than that in his place, by God's wonderful reversal as it was accomplished in Jesus Christ, an elect will one day stand.

Yet this cannot be our last word about Judas. He is powerless to defy or destroy the determination and institution of the apostleship. It is too strong for him, as is shown by the Acts of the Apostles and the whole New Testament witness to the apostolate after the resurrection of Jesus. It is so strong that he himself—by his subsequent degradation to the status of a mere *locum tenens* for another—is made an outstanding bearer of the apostleship in all the negativity of his figure and work. This is primary, but it is not everything. On the contrary, beyond it there is also—always on the basis of the overwhelming power of the grace of Jesus Christ, and certainly not because of any merit in Judas, but against his will and deserts—a co-operation for which the apostle Judas was obviously responsible, and which he actually executed by his wicked act, in the task of the apostolate and the Church as it is based on the election of Jesus Christ.

In order to see this we must return to the basic term which the New Testament uses to describe his deed, the " handing-over," παραδοῦναι, of which he made himself guilty. It has a decidedly negative, and only a negative, character as applied to the act of Judas. It says that Judas was the man who, from within the apostolic group and the Church of Jesus Christ as it was now being assembled, not merely denied and renounced the Lord for himself, but gave Him over to His enemies, putting Him at their mercy, to deal with Him according to their own hostile discretion. However Judas came to do it, this was what he objectively did. He was the first in a whole series, as we have seen, but he—the apostle Judas—was the first. There is a definition of the technical meaning of handing over in Mt. 5²⁵. A man has an adversary, and if he cannot be reconciled to him " so long as thou art with him in the way," then there is a risk that this adversary will deliver him to the judge (μήποτέ σε παραδῶ), and the judge deliver him to the officers, who will imprison him. Or again in Mt. 18³⁴, the master was angry at the servant whose enormous debt had been all forgiven but who treated a fellow-servant very differently, and he delivered him (παρέδωκε) to the tormentors, until he should pay everything which he owed. Formally, it is exactly like this adversary or master that Judas treats Jesus. Or again, when John the Baptist was imprisoned, it is described as a " delivery " in Mk. 1¹⁴ and Mt. 4¹². Judas prepared for Jesus the fate of John the Baptist. Again, in Mt. 24¹⁰ Jesus foresaw and foretold that things would reach the stage when Christians would " deliver " one another in times of persecution. Judas is the first to do so, and to do it against Jesus Himself. The unconverted Saul " delivered " those Christians on whom he could lay his hands, and when he had become Paul he was himself " delivered " by the Jews to the Gentiles (Ac. 21¹¹, 28¹⁷), and by one Gentile to another (Ac. 27¹, 28¹⁶), just as Peter had previously been " delivered " by Herod to his soldiers (Ac. 12⁴). In all these contexts " delivery " is the handing-over or transfer of a free or relatively free person to the confining power of those who wish him harm, and from whom he must expect harm. And it is the sin of Judas that he delivered Jesus in this way. It is this act of Judas which ends the freedom with which Jesus had previously moved, the spontaneity with which He was previously able to speak and act, with which He was able to preach the kingdom of God, to call to faith and repentance, and to perform signs and wonders as manifestations of His message. All the power of Jesus is now limited by the power of those to whom He was delivered by Judas. He must now be satisfied with the restricted power which remains, and which may at any moment be reduced to zero. He is in their hands and can offer no opposition. He can only endure what they inflict upon Him. If He is still to defeat them, it can only be on the far side of what He must suffer at their hands because of the handing-over by Judas, and not in virtue of the power of which He is robbed by His delivery. The proclamation of the kingdom of God, from which He is now completely debarred, must be taken up afresh from what is relatively a third side—from a height which is above the power of His enemies and His own weakness. He must be justified in His very powerlessness before the might of His enemies. He must be clothed with a completely new power. This is the situation into which Jesus is brought by Judas, the entirely new road along which He is driven by Judas. With the act of Judas the relationship between Jesus and His human environment ceases to be a free trial of strength, an open struggle for its attention and understanding and conviction and goodwill. He is now immobilised in respect of everything that could help Him in this struggle, and every hour increases the threat—the threat intended from the outset in His delivery—that He will be wholly immobilised and decisively eliminated, as has always been the case with unwelcome human power when men wish to be quite safe against it. And this threat is carried out. When the handing-over begun by Judas reaches its goal, Jesus must die at the hands of those to whom He is handed over. And if there is no decision from that third side, Jesus will have lived for nothing and the preaching of the kingdom of God will have been futile, just as it had notoriously been futile so far as Judas himself was concerned. This is what Judas has taken upon his conscience—to bring Jesus into the situation where apart from God no one can help Him, to place into the hands of men a power over Jesus which can and must render Him utterly powerless and finally kill Him, and from which He can only call upon the power of God. In doing this, Judas seems indeed to have perverted his office as an apostle into its exact opposite. For he was chosen and called to be an apostle, not to bring Jesus under the power of men, but men under the power of Jesus ; not to deliver Jesus to sinners, but sinners to Jesus ; " to bring into captivity every thought to the obedience of Christ " (2 Cor 10⁵) ; and therefore to confirm and glorify the freedom of Jesus Christ in the world, and to prepare an open road for the proclamation of the kingdom of God. " All power is given unto me in heaven and in earth " (Mt. 28¹⁸)—the kingship of Jesus Christ is indeed the presupposition of the apostleship of the Church, to be revealed after the death of Jesus and Judas. But what Judas does with his παραδοῦναι seems to be a dark parallel to the very different presupposition about which the devil can boast in Lk. 4⁶—that all the ἐξουσία and δόξα of this world are delivered (παραδέδοται) to him and to whom he wills to give them. This παράδοσις and therefore the lordship of the devil seems not merely to have been confirmed by the παραδοῦναι of Judas, but once and for all—because it is the ἐξουσία and δόξα of the Son of God Himself that are involved—to have been verified. It is not for nothing, therefore, that in Lk. 22³, Jn. 6⁷⁰, 13², ²⁷, his act is described as that of one possessed by Satan. Could he more effectually disown his apostolic office than by what he had done ? It was obviously not his own will or work if his act had another meaning and content than the " delivery " which was to serve the monstrous lie of the devil. But there can be no doubt that it did in fact have another meaning. Judas did share actively even in the positive task of the apostleship by his very παραδοῦναι.

It is no mere semantic accident that the word " delivery " (παράδοσις), which has this purely negative meaning when applied to the act of Judas, is elsewhere used positively to define and describe the apostolic ministry, as this consists in the faithful and complete transmission into a second set of hands—the hands of others in space or time who had not originally received it—of the unchanged and undiminished message of Jesus, the record of His words and deeds and death and resurrection, the knowledge of the will of God manifest in Him for the being and ordering of the Church. The New Testament does not disguise the fact that when the apostles became bearers of this παράδοσις they entered formally upon the activity which, as the activity of the Jewish scribes, had become simply a particular form of their disobedience, a final form of the complete faithlessness of Israel to its God. It is as the scribes held fast to the " tradition of the elders " that according to Mk. 7⁶ᶠ· the saying about hypocrites in Is. 29¹³ is fulfilled : " This people honoureth me with their lips, but their heart is far from me. Howbeit, in vain do they worship me, teaching for doctrines the commandments of men." This is the accusation : " For laying aside (ἀφέντες) the commandment of God, ye hold the traditions of men . . . full well ye reject (ἀθετεῖτε) the commandment of God, that ye may keep your own tradition " (Mk. 7⁸ᶠ·). " Ye make the word of God of none effect (ἀκυροῦντες) through your tradition which ye have delivered (τῇ παραδόσει ὑμῶν ᾗ παρεδώκατε, Mk. 7¹³). It is, therefore, most strange, and in its strangeness must not be overlooked, that the very thing which, as the act of the Jews, Jesus Himself called a material ἀφιέναι, an ἀθετεῖν, an ἀκυροῦν of the Word and commandment of God, later becomes the form of His apostles' distinctive function, as in 2 Thess. 2¹⁵, where in phrases which necessarily can only be reminiscent of Mk. 7, Paul does not hesitate to write : " Therefore, brethren, stand fast, and hold the traditions which ye have been taught, whether by word, or our epistle." The danger in which the apostles are thus placed is obvious. But they have no option but to take the risk. It is necessary that Jesus Himself should now become the subject of the " tradition of the men," that His Church should be built by His delivery from one human hand to another. He does not fear the delivery by Judas and the Jews. In spite and in the midst of the dangers into which He again ventures, He wills to be handed over. On this side of His resurrection the danger of Mk. 7 is obviously now a neutralised danger. That Christ henceforth dies no more (Rom. 6⁹) is true even in the sense that He has nothing more to fear from His new delivery into the hands of sinful men. He will now triumph by means of this delivery. And after the woe has been pronounced and executed upon Judas who delivers, and upon the Jews and their delivery, there is a new, authentic, redemptive delivery of Jesus in the power of the resurrection of the One who was delivered by Judas and the Jews. That is why Lk. 1¹ defines the Gospel as a " declaration " (διήγησις) of the things which have been fulfilled among us, as they " delivered them unto us (καθὼς παρέδοσαν ἡμῖν) which from the beginning were eyewitnesses, and ministers of the word." That is why, corresponding to the παραλαμβάνειν of the Lord which distinguishes the faithful apostle from Judas (Jn. 1¹¹), there is the παραδοῦναι of that which he has received to other men (1 Cor. 11²³, 15³) ; and this very παραλαμβάνειν is the way in which the apostolic παράδοσις encounters these others (2 Thess. 3⁶). According to Rom. 6¹⁷, after they have been servants of sin and as they are so no longer, they become those who, determined by the tradition mediated to them in the form of the apostolic teaching, are characterised as those who are now altogether its objects (παρεδόθητε) and to that extent obedient.

Paul made special reference to his peculiar position as the bearer of the tradition in three passages which are clearly decisive for him. The first is 1 Cor. 11², where the subject is the inferior status of women to men, which at bottom is obviously that of the relationship between Christ and the community. The second is 1 Cor. 11²³ which treats of the Lord's Supper. And the third is 1 Cor. 15³, which has to do with the witness to Jesus Christ's resurrection. What Paul is representing in these passages, and what he has done for his readers as this representative, was tradition itself, the act of the transmission of the information he had originally received from his hands into their hands. It was because he laid it in their hands, and they received it from his hands into their own, in the unavoidable but obviously no longer formidable danger of this event, that there was a Church in Corinth, and that in the words of Rom. 6¹⁷, from being servants of sin, they became obedient. They had been made this by the act of delivery which had taken place between him and them. That is why Paul can and must look back and refer to this act in the further transactions between himself and them. That is why everything further that he has to say to them can consist only in a sharper repetition of this act, in an explanation and application of what he has delivered to them as an apostle. It is striking enough that except in Lk. 1¹ and the Pauline passages this use of παραδοῦναι occurs only in Jude 3, where Christians in general are urged to " contend for the faith which was once delivered to the saints." Notice that it is primarily the apostle Paul who applied this concept to his apostolic office, and that he once did so, namely, in 1 Cor. 11²³, in such a way that in the same verse he also applied it to Judas' treachery : " I have received of the Lord that which also I delivered unto you, that the Lord Jesus, the same night in which he was betrayed (delivered), took bread : and when he had given thanks, he brake it. . . ." The two " deliveries " are obviously mutually determinative, so that Paul is set in the shadow of Judas, as Judas is set in the light of Paul. There is no apostolic παραδοῦναι which does not have behind it the judgment of Judas' παραδοῦναι : the handing-over, of which Judas and the Jews have made themselves guilty by their rejection, evasion and nullifying of the Word and commandment of God. The disobedient, faithless action, of which Judas and the Jews made themselves guilty by their handing-over, is taken up again, on the basis of the death and resurrection of Jesus, in the delivery which calls the Church into life in all the world—the delivery of the apostles, of whom Paul is the least, and the one who worked more than they all.

In view of the context, are we not forced to ascribe a positive meaning to the act of Judas, to the extent that in all its faithlessness it foreshadows the act of faithful apostolic tradition ? Was it *only* an attempt on the royal freedom of Jesus ? Was it only a service of the devil, the transference of the Son of God to powerlessness, to the power of sinful men ? In view of the character, conduct and deed of Judas we cannot subtract from this definition, nor can it be weakened, or transformed into a positive definition. His disobedience was certainly not obedience. On the contrary, it was total disobedience. What he did was a rejection, evasion and nullifying of the Word of God, like the tradition of the

Jews in Mk. 7. The rejection of this elect apostle was certainly rejection, and cannot be transformed into mysterious election. It is arbitrary and futile to try to credit him with hidden ideas and intentions on the basis of which he can be understood at the last moment as a man who was fundamentally righteous. Neither the sin of Israel, nor the sin of the other apostles which appeared in that of Judas, nor human sin in general, has any such mysterious justification concealed within itself. That which justifies Judas' delivery falls far short of achieving his personal justification. But we are not asked to answer the question of Judas' personal justification in relation to any ideas or intentions of his own. On the contrary, we are asked to leave this question as one which can be answered only by the Judge who is competent in the matter. It is the question which is put to the thief who was crucified on Jesus' left hand by the saying of the thief on the right, and the promise which he received. But no answer is given to it. We can only leave it standing in the light in which nevertheless it does stand. For although the act of Judas cannot be justified in itself, it does actually have the form which found its positive disclosure in the acts of the faithful apostles, and in the transmission of his successor Paul. What justifies Judas is the fact that Paul, too, is what he is by the grace of God in the activity of handing-over. This is the positive significance of his handing-over. This is what characterises his act as an apostolic function corresponding to his election. This is what marks the victory of the election of this rejected man over his rejection—although it prevents us and will continue to prevent us from making any subtraction from his rejection as such. What justifies him is only his character as a *locum tenens* for the one who will so differently occupy the role which he so wickedly filled. But this does justify him. And what alone justifies the Jewish tradition, the utterly disobedient Israel which rejects the fulfilment of its promises and the grace of God manifested towards it, is that it has always the role of the chosen people of God which finds its true fulfilment in the Church. It is always the root out of which the Church has grown, with Jesus Christ Himself. It is always the foreshadowing of the reality to come in Jesus Christ and His Church. This alone justifies it, and it cannot be taken from it by its sin and rejection, by the crucifixion of Jesus and the downfall of Jerusalem. It is therefore true that although the Jews " hand over " the Word and commandment of God—as they reject and evade and nullify it—nevertheless they do not and cannot and obviously must not cease to hand it over. This justifies Israel even as it confirms its condemnation. This is the eternal light which illuminates even the " eternal " Jew, as it reveals the full darkness of his way. This is the proclamation which remains open for him too. This is the invitation and warning and plea addressed to him too. He can cease to be a mere *locum tenens*. Like Paul, he can turn from emptiness to fulness. For even apart from his conversion and in all his negativity, he is not merely a negative but a positive figure—indeed, in a very definite sense he is a uniquely positive figure.

But all this can only become fully clear when we observe that according to the New Testament, apart from the παραδοῦναι of Judas and the apostolic παραδοῦναι and as a prototype of both, there is above all a divine παραδοῦναι, in which we can hardly fail to see the interrelation of both, the characterisation of the one by the other, even though we may be profoundly horrified by its inner paradox, and in which we are clearly shown that the formal correspondence between them cannot depend upon a semantic accident. It is actually the prototype of both. There is the mysterious and terrible divine " delivery " according to which God in His burning wrath (cf. Rom. 1^18f.) does to men what Judas did to Jesus. He takes their freedom from them. He makes them so powerless that He gives them over to the authority of a power which is too great for them—the power, in fact, of their enemy—that he may rule them. Who is this enemy ? We read in Ac. 7^42 that God turned away from the Israelites and gave them over (παρέδωκεν) to worship the host of heaven, and therefore to the worship of strange, false gods.

And in Rom. 1 we read in three different places that God " gave them up (παρέδωκεν) to uncleanness through the lusts of their own hearts " (v. 24), " gave them up unto vile affections " (v. 26), and " gave them over to a reprobate mind, to do those things which are not convenient " (v. 28). Therefore, according to these passages, the mighty enemy to whose power God delivered men is their own work, which begins within them and then breaks out in evil deeds. God abandons them to themselves, and therefore to their destruction. This is the operation of His wrath against them. This is what is meant by παραδοῦναι in this context. And this handing-over includes what we read in Eph. 4[19] : " They have given themselves over unto lasciviousness," and also what 2 Pet. 2[4] describes as God's handing-over of the sinful angels for judgment.

With this divine " handing-over " to destruction, which is revealed " from heaven " according to Rom. 1[8], there is certainly connected, as its earthly counterpart, the technically obscure event which is twice described in the Pauline letters as the handing-over of certain men to Satan. On both occasions it appears to involve a kind of excommunication as the final act of Church discipline. On both occasions it is the apostle Paul himself—naturally acting in the name and by the order of God—who decides that it should be executed. There is, first, the case of the incestuous man in 1 Cor. 5[1f.] Paul is astonished that the one who did this has not yet been dismissed from the congregation. He explains that he himself, bodily absent but spiritually present, has already decided that when he is among them (" when ye are gathered together, and my spirit, with the power of our Lord Jesus Christ "), the person in question is " to be delivered unto Satan for the destruction of the flesh, that the spirit may be saved in the day of the Lord Jesus." Again, in 1 Tim. 1[19f.], Timothy is to hold the faith and a good conscience " which some having put away, concerning faith have made shipwreck : of whom is Hymenæus and Alexander ; whom I have delivered unto Satan, that they may learn not to blaspheme." The men who are punished in this way—and it certainly means their eviction from the community—are in the first instance to be left to themselves, which is here characterised more sharply as their delivery to Satan. They are left alone, under the authority of the one whom they have tried to serve and have actually served with their actions. We note that this use of the concept of " delivery " in its primary sense is borne out by the Pauline passages. We therefore find ourselves in what is essentially the same sphere as that which we have just left. God in heaven, and the apostles on earth, " deliver." Those who are " delivered " are specific men. According to Ac. 7[39f.], they are the Israelite fathers, to whom God had spoken but who disobeyed Him, who returned in their hearts to Egypt, who made a calf for themselves and " rejoiced in the work of their hands." According to Rom. 1[18], they are the Gentiles who know God indeed but neither honour nor thank Him as God. According to 1 Cor. 5[1f.], it is a Christian whose offence showed that he was an evil remnant of the old leaven and quite unfit for the celebration of the Easter festival. According to 1 Tim. 1[19f.], it is two Christians who have suffered a shipwreck of faith and become blasphemers. The punishment in each case is that they are " delivered " to all the consequences of the existence which they have chosen themselves by their deeds. They can only fall where they have put themselves : the Israelites, with their Egyptian delight in the work of their own hands, into unrestrained idolatry ; the Gentiles, with their arbitrary wisdom, into the folly of unrestrained immorality ; the Christians, from the freedom of the children of God, back under the power and lordship of Satan. This is the work of the wrath of God. It is a stern, burning, destroying wrath. It is again impossible, as in the case of Judas' sinful " handing-over," to make a single reservation or in any way to soften or diminish the severity of the event. Rejection—for that is what God visits on these men—is rejection. Abandonment is abandonment ; abandonment to Satan, as Paul does not hesitate to describe his action in relation to Christians. The imprisonment into which man is flung by God, according to these passages, is of itself and as such unconditional and unlimited. There is indeed no more utter powerlessness than that of the man who has severed himself from God, no more absolute tyranny than that to which he is delivered when God leaves him to himself. And there is no doubt at all about the justice of the sentence executed in this way. Has not God, in perfect justice, given him just the existence which he merits ? Nor can there be any question of a possibility that this sentence may subsequently be altered, or of an appeal from it to that of a higher judge. God's dealing with men in the execution of this judgment has this much in common with Judas' dealing with Jesus. The only possibility which it leaves to the one handed over is that from the necessary and irresistible consummation of his delivery, the unlimited powerlessness in which he is placed and the hopelessly overwhelming might to which he is subject, he should appeal to God, not to try to change His mind about that which must necessarily befall him in his powerlessness and beneath that overwhelming might, nor to move Him to alter His sentence or to halt the execution of His judgment, but to implore Him (*ex profundis*, from the depths of the irretrievably delivered) that even as the Judge He will not cease to be his God and to show Himself as his God, that even in His rejecting His might should still be mighty over and to him, the rejected, that he, too, might still see and hold to it in his rejection, that the last word for him might still be His Word and the last work upon him His work. It is quite clear in these passages that the divine handing-over of men has actually the force to put man in the situation where he has no other possibility than this final one. Consider again Mt. 5[26] : " Verily I say unto thee, Thou shalt by no means come out thence, till thou hast paid the uttermost farthing." Or think of the threat of Mt. 25[41] and Rev. 19[9], 20[15], 21[8], 22[15]. A final possibility—or, rather, an entirely new possibility beyond the completed judgment, beyond the payment of the last farthing—is not absolutely cut off by these passages from those handed over by God. There is still the prospect of it, even if in endless remoteness and depth. This is certainly true of the two passages which deal with the delivery of Christians to Satan. For while in 1 Cor. 5 Paul does indeed say of the man delivered up that " the flesh must be destroyed," that the judgment on his human existence must take its course, as must the final outcome of the fact that he was lost, he does not say this without adding : " so that the spirit may be saved in the day of the Lord." In Pauline anthropology the πνεῦμα (not to be confused with the ψυχή, the invisible spiritual principle of life in human existence) is the fellowship with Jesus Christ which is given to the Christian at baptism and on the basis of which he has become a new and therefore for the first time a real subject. The " flesh " (as the totality of body and soul) of those delivered up is forfeited to the result of the delivery. But Paul did not say that the spirit of this man is forfeited by this handing-over. On the contrary, he said that just because of the handing-over it partakes in future salvation. Paul carried out the handing-over of this man with the express purpose that while his flesh should be destroyed, by the necessary destruction of his flesh his spirit should be saved. Paul does not know of any other method, not merely to deal with the immediate task of purifying the community, but also to save the spirit of this lost Christian, than that of detaching him from the community and handing him over to Satan, so that his flesh may be destroyed, but that by and beyond destruction, truly *ex profundis*, his spirit may be preserved in the day of the Lord. The same is said in a rather less emphatic manner of Hymenæus and Alexander in 1 Tim. 1[19f.]. Their punishment of being handed over to Satan is not an end in itself, but it is executed in all rigour and without restriction " so that they may learn not to blaspheme," so that on the basis of their punishment they have no option but to cease to blaspheme. What is meant is obviously the eschatological possibility, salvation on the day of the Lord. This does not remove nor weaken the punishment, but it gives it a limit which encloses even that which is boundless in itself, eternal fire. For the power of Satan, against which man has no power, is certainly limited by the might of the Lord.

There is substantial reason why it is in the case of Christians delivered up in this way that the limitation is revealed. In the reference to the Israelite fathers in Ac. 7 there is no such limitation. The whole of Stephen's speech is in the form of an indictment and it concludes on this note in v. 53. And the indignation with which the hearers receive it shows pitilessly that the delivery of the fathers is still justified in the case of their children's children. Similarly, in Rom. 1 it is not immediately visible what other turn could be given to the delivery of the Gentiles to the lusts of their hearts. In reality, the silence of Ac. 7 and Rom. 1 about this limit—which they do not expressly deny—speaks even more impressively, if possible, than what is said in the other passages. We have only to study the contexts carefully. In Ac. 7, we must consider the real conclusion. Stephen's speech is interrupted by the rage of the listeners. But while this rage necessarily gives terrible emphasis and confirmation to the words about the tradition of the fathers, it is said of Stephen (v. 55) : " But he, being full of the Holy Ghost, looked up steadfastly into heaven, and saw the glory of God, and Jesus standing on the right hand of God, and said, Behold, I see the heavens opened, and the Son of man standing on the right hand of God." According to Ac. 7 that is obviously the limit of Israel's punishment, the eschatological possibility which lies beyond the completion of its rejection. Admittedly those who are delivered up do not themselves see it—this is also true of 1 Cor. 5 and 1 Tim. 1—but Stephen sees it : not merely for his own person as the promise with which he goes at once to martyrdom ; and not merely as the confirmation of his previous indictment as such ; but genuinely for those who are called traitors and murderers in v. 52, and who now become his murderers too, as the hope by which their hopelessly sealed rejection is still enclosed. The goal of their divinely executed rejection, the necessary end of its endlessness, is the fact that Jesus stands at the right hand of God, and all that this means for them and offers to them. And Stephen's last words are : " Lord, lay not this sin to their charge " (v. 60, cf. Lk. 22[34]). Again, in Rom. 1 we do not read of any diminution or softening of the wrath of God as it flames forth against the heathen. But it is also solidly established that in the context of v. 17, and the continuation of the whole passage to Rom. 3[20], for all its burning severity this wrath of God revealed from heaven is not an isolated or, as it were, self-enclosed manifestation of the divine life, but the reverse side of His righteousness, of the judicial sentence by which those Gentiles and Jews who believe in Jesus Christ are acquitted and justified. This sentence is itself annihilating in its action. It excludes mankind, both Jew and Gentile, from any freedom or justification except those that come by faith. It judges men absolutely. It utterly abandons them. It burns them right down to faith, as it were, that there it may promise and give them as believers both freedom and justification. That is why it has the reverse side of wrath. That is why it cannot be revealed apart from a simultaneous revelation of wrath. It is of this aspect that the whole passage Rom. 1[18]–3[20] speaks. What is revealed in the revelation of wrath is that God has delivered up the Gentile, that He has abandoned him, that He has handed him over to himself. But what this involves is not foreign to the love of God. On the contrary, it is His love which burns in this way, burning away in men that which opposes and defies it, in order that they really live by faith in Jesus Christ—" so that his spirit may be saved," " so that they may learn not to blaspheme." The fact that He delivers them, that He abandons and hands them over to themselves, means that in their madness they are no longer present to Him, that they are, as it were, swept out of His presence (apart from the one possibility of faith), and that God will no longer acknowledge them (apart from this one possibility). Because He wills to know them in faith as those who are free and righteous, He wills not to know them any longer in any other way. Therefore, παρέδωκεν.

It would not be the love of God which dealt with them in any other way, or spared them this sweeping away. But it really is the love of God which deals with them in this way. From this end He wills to make a fresh beginning with them. He will awaken them from this death which they must die. He will speedily deliver them from this distress, from which there is no escape, which they can only increase, the inevitability of which they can only confirm. The fact and way that the revelation of God's wrath does as such aim at this eschatological possibility of faith, the fact and way that even in His stern handing-over He actually means well to Jews and Gentiles, is the subject of the rest of the Epistle to the Romans from 3²¹ onwards. We must bear this clearly in mind even to understand the παρέδωκεν of Rom. 1.

But we can really discern this strict connexion only when we turn to the other and positive sense in which the New Testament (and here again the apostle Paul is decisive) speaks of a παραδοῦναι executed by God Himself.

We have seen that the savage and sinful handing-over of Jesus by Judas, in itself absolutely without justification, corresponds objectively to the handing-over of Jesus into the hands of men which is the meaning and content of the apostolic ministry, by which the Church on earth is established and maintained. The latter handing-over rectifies the mischief done by the former. Jesus is glorified as He was once blasphemed. Witness is now given to the lordship of the One who was once robbed of His freedom and delivered into the power of His enemies. But it is also a continuation—in a very different way—of what the other began. In both cases—even that of Judas— we have to do with the objective justification of the sinner. The activity of Paul—himself a converted Saul, himself once a deliverer like Judas—shows that an active participation in the positive task of the apostolate cannot be denied even to the apostle Judas and his handing-over.

But this deduction is too daring if we cannot show that it rests on the fact that there is a similar correspondence in the concept of the divine παραδοῦναι as well. Here again, however, the New Testament does not speak only of the wrathful delivery in which God abandons man and leaves him to himself, indeed to Satan. If it said no more than that, we could not so boldly emphasise that definite limits also emerge, and that in the last resort we can find in every major passage that deals with this handing-over one form or another of the eschatological possibility, the possibility of the salvation of those who are handed over and therefore utterly lost. We would not know how properly to handle this eschatological possibility, just as earlier we would not have known how to handle the παραδοῦναι of the apostle Judas and his election and calling, if there had not been set against him the apostolic παραδοῦναι and the apostle Judas himself had not stood in the light of the apostle Paul. But as we cannot escape the factual correspondence in the one case, we cannot do so in the other. In the concept of the divine παραδοῦναι, we can see clearly from the text itself that God's delivery of wrath has also a positive connexion. This is quite inescapable when we note that as such it is confronted by a very different delivery of God, whose meaning and content are quite unambiguously the eschatological possibility. We must therefore be prepared to speak of this, and to establish and refer to as a reality, in view of these passages. We must be prepared to bring out in all its fulness the light which we cannot deny to the delivery of wrath. But if here there is a divine Yes, by which the divine No is to be understood, it is not merely not too daring but quite essential that we should find on this other plane the connexion in the relationship between the delivery of Paul and that of Judas ; and in view of this connexion to speak of an objective justification of Judas. But the other divine delivery of which the New Testament speaks, apart from the delivery of wrath, is the one in which God Himself is the One who hands over Jesus (Rom. 4²⁵, 8³²), or in which Jesus as the Son of God is Himself the One who hands Himself over (Gal. 2²⁰, Eph. 5², ²⁵). According to this mode of expression, too, God has acted as Judas acted, but in a much more direct similarity. Previously it was men that God delivered up, as Judas delivered up Jesus. Now He delivers up Jesus ; Jesus hands over Himself. At this point we obviously have to do with the handing-over which takes precedence over all others in value, importance and meaning. Before Judas had handed over Jesus, God had handed Him over, and Jesus had handed over Himself. Before Jesus was the object of the apostolic delivery, God had delivered Him, and He had delivered Himself. Before the wrath of God handed over Jews and Gentiles, abandoning and yielding them to themselves, He had not spared His only Son, but had delivered Him up for us all (Rom. 8³²). Clearly the necessity and power and meaning of all delivery are established in this first and radical delivery, in which God, in the person of Jesus, or Jesus as the Son of God, made Himself the object of delivery. It is not permissible to understand any other delivery except with reference to this one (without prejudice to its special meaning). All other delivery looks either to or from this. It has its reality in what happened here. It is impossible to interpret it apart from its connexion with this event.

Attention must be paid to the importance of the contexts in which the subject is this divine handing-over. In Rom. 4²⁵ it comes at the climax of the elucidation of faith and the divine justification ascribed to it, as illustrated by the example of Abraham. The faith of which Paul says that it justifies the believer is faith in Him who raised our Lord Jesus Christ from the dead. This God of Abraham has ascribed justification to us in the fact that Jesus was delivered by Him for the removal of our trespasses, and then raised from the grave that we might be clothed with His righteousness. The handing-over of Jesus by God creates the indispensable preliminary condition for the positive thing which we receive in faith. For it removes the obstacle which prevents God from acquitting us as a just Judge. With the handing-over of Jesus our trespasses are taken away. Rom. 8³² confirms this meaning of the event. It is found at the climax of the exposition, which occupies the whole of chapter 8, of the life of Christians under the law of the spirit of life given to them, and in particular of the exposition in 8²⁹⁻³⁹ of the guiltlessness in which they may stand before God. If God is for them, who can be against them ? But God is for them. And how shall He not give them everything that can prove and demonstrate this guiltlessness, when He has done the most radical thing for them ? For He did not spare His own Son. He delivered Him up for them all—the παρέδωκεν of Rom. 1 reappears here. And in the delivery (in which God does violence to Himself as once—but very differently—He had done to Abraham at the time of Isaac's sacrifice) there is accomplished by the One who alone can be their Judge that which purifies them from every accusation, and makes any future accusation irrelevant from the very outset. Therefore (v. 33 f.) who can or will accuse them—the elect of God ? Who is to condemn or judge or reject them ? The answer is that only One, Jesus Christ, the Son of God, who was delivered up both does and has done all these things as He died, but also rose again, and is now at God's right hand, not to plead against them but for them—in a love for them from which no one and nothing can separate them. In Gal. 2²⁰ there is another climactic point at which Paul shows the fact and extent that he " through the law was dead to the law " ; that is, that he was liberated from the accusation and sentence of the Law, and could now " live unto God," because of the fulfilment of the Law as it took place on Golgotha. He, too, was crucified there with Christ to the extent that in the death of Christ the Law was fulfilled for him too, and at the same time his life as one accused by the Law was ended and done away. His present life is nothing but the life of Christ in him, that is, his life in faith in the Son of God (perhaps more directly : on the basis of the faith shown by the Son of God) " who loved me and gave himself for me." With this self-giving there took place that which brought Paul fundamentally and finally into liberty, not merely forbidding but making it quite impossible for him to return to bondage under the Law's accusation. For there, on the other side of the self-giving of Jesus and the death which followed it, his new life—the only life which is now possible for him—had its beginning. Finally, the two passages in Eph. 5 are obviously parallels to Phil. 2 ⁶ᶠ· to the extent that the paragraphs which again treat of the self-giving of Christ are connected with specific exhortations. According to v. 1 f., Christians are to be " followers " of God as " dear children," taking the dealings of God as their model and therefore walking in love, " as Christ also hath loved us, and hath given himself for us, an offering and a sacrifice to God for a sweet smelling savour." And in v. 25 f., husbands are specially urged to love their wives " even as Christ loved the church, and gave himself for it ; that he might sanctify and cleanse it with the washing of water by the word, that he might present it to himself a glorious church, not having spot, or wrinkle, or any such thing ; but that it should be holy and without blemish." We can see that even in the very different world of thought and speech of Ephesians the primary statement is christological and ecclesiological, and this is identical in substance with that of Romans and Galatians.

It is a matter of the reconciliation of man to God to the extent that this must basically subsist in his cleansing from sin. Only the guiltless can stand before God, and be righteous in His presence, and be treated as righteous by Him, and serve Him in righteousness. But man is not guiltless. He is guilty. Therefore he needs to be cleansed. Yet he cannot cleanse himself. If it is to happen at all, this cleansing must be accomplished by God. His sins must be forgiven him. And this is just what happened when God delivered up Christ and Christ delivered up Himself. In this way the pre-condition was created for what is positively to become of Christians and the Church : for the birthright and freedom and hope of believers ; for the glory of the congregation which consists in its power to glorify God in time and eternity. In this way the pre-condition was created for those who are reconciled to God, who are therefore acquitted and justified by God, to belong to Him here and now, to be represented before Him by Christ who is at God's right hand, to have their citizenship and future with Him in heaven. Apart from the forgiveness of their sins, their exaltation would be impossible. And as they owe their exaltation to the exaltation of Christ in His resurrection, so the pre-condition of their exaltation, the forgiveness of their sins, made it necessary for Christ to be humiliated, to humiliate Himself. The forgiveness of their sins must have its basis in the fact that God " gave up " His Son, that Jesus " gave up " Himself for them. We must emphasise again the technical meaning of the concept. To be " handed over " is to be delivered up in powerlessness to strange and hostile overwhelming power. To " hand over " is to deprive a powerful person of his freedom, so that his power is not merely damaged but is as such destroyed, and he has no option but to submit to that which is inflicted on him, for the rest looking only to the higher power of God. The freedom of which Jesus was robbed by Judas is clearly only a pale reflection of the divine freedom of which God robbed Him, of which He robbed Himself. The Son of God, whom neither His Father nor He Himself spared, is not merely one powerful being with others, but the all-powerful. " All things were made by him ; and without him was not any thing made that was made " (Jn. 1³). He existed in " the form of God " (Phil. 2⁶). It is in this light that we must consider what this delivery involves. It was the divine omnipotence, and freedom of which Jesus let Himself be robbed—by means of Judas, yet not by Judas in the first instance, but originally in that He humbled Himself and took the form of a servant and was found in fashion as a man. The real and original handing-over of Jesus is clearly the fact that the Word became flesh (Jn. 1¹⁴). This was only revealed in its ultimate results by what Judas did or began to do—and who is really the agent in the account given in Jn. 18¹⁻¹² ? The fact that in the sense of this ultimate result the Son of God had to be delivered into the hands of sinful men has its basis in this original and authentic handing-over whose author and subject is God Himself or Jesus Himself, just as the fact that Jesus humbled Himself in obedience unto death, the death of·the cross (Phil. 2⁸), is based on the fact that primarily and decisively He had emptied Himself of that divine form and taken the form of man. The first took place for the sake of the second, and the second was the outcome and revelation of the first. We cannot understand the positive divine παραδοῦναι, which is the basis of all others and in the light of which even that of Judas ultimately stands, unless we hold to the original and authentic παραδοῦναι. And to know this we cannot begin at a lower level than that of the decree of God's eternal love, in which the Father sent the Son and the Son obeyed the Father, by which the will of God turned towards man even before he was created—his creation itself being dependent upon this decree—with the inconceivably merciful intention of enabling him, and all creation through him and in him, to participate in fellowship with Him and eternal life, by giving Himself to be his Covenant-partner. The kingdom of God is the fulfilment of this decree. It is as God shows this love to man, and as He shows it in this way, as the grace of God overflows (He does not need this but He willed it out of the fulness of His glory) and as it overflows in this way (it could have done so differently, but He willed that it should happen in this way), that He establishes His lordship. The positive divine παραδοῦναι is included in the decree of God's eternal love. Concretely, the sending by the Father and the obedience of the Son are simply this divine παραδοῦναι. It is not for nothing, therefore, that Rom. 8³⁵, Gal. 2²⁰ and Eph. 5²⁵ relate it so emphatically to the divine ἀγαπᾶν. It does not enter into this relationship. The relationship is not merely in history. It is from the very beginning, from all eternity, and therefore necessarily in history. Delivery, handing-over, abandonment by God are themselves included in and necessarily result from the fact that God wills to make man participant in eternal life by giving Himself to be his Covenant-partner. For man of himself is neither worthy nor capable of giving himself in this manner, of acquiring God as a Covenant-partner. The fact that this takes place is included in the condescension of God, in which God resigns His divine glory to the extent that He conceals it, that He does not assert it, that He even allows its opposite to triumph over Him. If it is truly the will of the Father to send His eternal Son, and the will of the Son to obey His eternal Father in the execution of this mission ; if it is truly the will of God to give Himself to man in such seriousness and fulness that He Himself becomes what man is—flesh, a bearer of human unworthiness and incapacity—then this means that it is the will of God to deliver Himself into the situation of impotence in face of the power by which man is overborne, giving Himself not merely to the constraint of the limitations of creaturely life, but to the curse of human guilt, to the rejection of the life of man as it is ruled and determined by his sin, abandoning Himself to the utter opposite of His own divine form of existence. It is to this man, whose existence is so diametrically opposite from His own, that He directs His eternal love. It is this man whom He wills to make participant in eternal life. It is he whom He intends and seeks and desires. He is the one with whom He has determined to ally Himself. And if this is what He wills—in all the seriousness and fulness in which He actually wills it—then He wills His own handing-over. He wills to deal with Himself as Judas dealt with Jesus. And it is His utter love for us actually to have done this. " He loved me, and gave himself for me " (Gal. 2²⁰). Regardless of Himself, He has taken our place, not sparing His own Son (Rom. 8³²). He has taken upon Himself all that existence in our situation brings with it. He has made it His own. He did not think His divinity too precious to disguise and eclipse it, even to cast it in the mire, by Himself taking on humanity and becoming one among men, one of the people of the Jews, and as this One the promise for all, for the men of all nations. He brought this offering and presented this sacrifice (Eph. 5²) ; the offering of His freedom to His love. So great is His love that He regarded it as worthy of this offering. And, of course, we can and must also say that His freedom is so great that He was able freely to subject it to this disguise and eclipse and soiling, because it is the freedom of His love. God is so faithful, so constant in the freedom of His love, that for the sake of it, while remaining unchanged, He could also become as unlike Himself as He did in the act of His delivery. But however that may be, as God gave Himself up in His Son to our situation, as He took our place, as there took place this unequalled deprivation of freedom—the deprivation of the freedom of God Himself—the forgiveness of our sins was established, apart from which we would never have eternal life, nor could the kingdom of God's loving-kindness be set up. For the effect and meaning of this handing-over is that when God entered into our situation and took our place, He made Himself responsible for us, to cleanse us from sin and liberate us from its guilt and punishment. He gave Himself up " for us," " for me," as it says in all these passages. In Gal. 2[20] this is quite clear when Paul speaks explicitly of the new life which is freed from the accusation and bonds of the Law, and is his own life, as the life of Christ Himself within him. But to stand in his place in this way, as the One who establishes and maintains this freedom, as the Lord of this new life, to assume responsibility for the life of Paul and for its cleansing, He must first stand in his place in a very different way to which Paul makes reference when he says that the Son of God has given Himself up, sacrificed Himself, for him. And Eph. 5[25] is equally clear, speaking of the glory of the Church as it is completely free from every shadow and blemish, its form again being Christ, because Christ loved the Church and gave Himself for it. Everything positive that Christ does for man, so that it is a reality for man in Him, and effective by faith in Him, is rooted and grounded in the fact that Christ first gave Himself for man, or, as in Rom. 8, was handed over by God for man.

This handing-over is, however, His voluntary entry into the place of man as a sinner rejected by God. What does He do in this place ? A first general and provisional answer must be that He sanctifies this place and its environment by His presence and by what can be His work in this place, as that of one individual man among others (in the setting of a human work which is limited as such). He proclaims the kingdom of God by words and signs as other prophets had done. He again consecrates and blesses and enlightens Israel as time and again this had been done in the past by prophets, priests and kings. This is itself a handing-over, a delivery, a self-offering, because it is the Son of God who does it. It means already the inconceivable and intolerable limitation of His glory. The whole miracle of the divine condescension and self-abasement is that God puts Himself in the place of an individual man, that in it, and therefore in all the limitation and conditioning of an individual human existence in relation to its environment, and amidst milliards of others, He represents His own cause which at bottom is really ours—which is just what Jesus did in the form of His life up to His arrest and crucifixion. But the real nature of this miracle only emerges when we observe how from the very beginning the life of Jesus moves towards His arrest and crucifixion, how from the very beginning it stands under the shadow which will finally be utter darkness when He has to be arrested, and to suffer and die. What happens to Him in our place, in the place of man which He takes, is that His prophesying and the work He began are taken out of His hands and shattered. The performance of the one necessary thing which He began has as its answer His rejection by the Israel which He consecrated and blessed and enlightened. And for His work's sake He is punished by death at the demand of Israel. Absolutely nothing is left to Him except recourse to that glory of His Father which has now been completely obscured. He can look forward only to His return from the darkness which has engulfed Him. As a man He is blotted out with all death's finality. This is what happened to Him in our place, in His existence and function as a man like ourselves. This is what happened to Him who is the Son of the living God, who could command legions of angels (Mt. 26⁵³) but made no use of them. It was for this that He gave Himself up for us.

This " for us," which is so strongly emphasised by Paul, obviously shows us in what sense this handing-over is the eternal will of God, in what sense it has to be said that it did not happen by chance, that it has nothing whatever to do with human tragedy or the like, but that it had to happen, as the will of God—and not the will of fate—has to happen. As there was inflicted on Jesus what we see beginning in His life and fulfilling itself in His arrest and suffering and death, there happened that which had to happen between God and man, if the love of God for man was to reach its goal, if man was to participate in fellowship and eternal life. In and with this handing-over of Jesus, God took the step which was necessary in view of man's unworthiness and incapacity to become His covenant-partner and to receive eternal life. For in and with this handing-over, God judged, condemned and punished man. Before it can be positively made good, that which stands between God and us must first be removed, and removed according to justice and righteousness. The handing-over of Jesus shows how great and serious is that which must be removed. It shows that it can be removed only when God takes upon Himself its necessary condemnation and punishment, so that they can no longer fall on us, so that we no longer have to bear them, so that we may be set free for that which God wills to give us. This is what God resolved to do in the person of Jesus Christ. God *could* do it because in His omnipotence He is capable of this handing-over, because in His self-abasement—far from committing any breach against His own nature—He causes His omnipotence to conquer, and because the concealment and darkness and mire to which He gave Himself are quite unable to diminish His divinity. God acted divinely when He did this. For not only did He show Himself to be faithful to man, but He also remained faithful to Himself. The mercy which He manifested was an act of His righteousness, and the righteousness which He exercised was an act of His mercy. He—who in this situation is both the offended and the accuser, both judge and law—is free to order it according to His good-pleasure, and He employed this freedom of His in such a way that in its ordering He willed to suffer that which we ought to have suffered. For this reason God really acted helpfully, " for us," and for our advantage, when He did this. For in the person of this one, individual man (though He was His own Son) His self-offering was in the dignity and power of the Lord of all men, who enabled all to receive the benefit of the release from guilt and punishment which took place in the handing-over of this One—for all belong to Him. And more than that—He loved them all eternally in this One, in respect of Him, when He elected Him. The handing-over of Jesus is, therefore, the cleansing from sin which is indispensable for the reconciliation of the world to God. It is its definitive removal from the world, its forgiveness and therefore the opening of the gates of the kingdom of God, accomplished in the righteous mercy and the merciful righteousness of God, accomplished by God's intervention for us when we could only perish before Him, when it would have been all up with us if He had not done this. That is why in Rom. 8³¹ Paul asks with that truly reverent defiance : " If God is for us, who can be against us ? " He has no other reason for this defiance than the consolation of Jesus. But it is the consolation of Jesus which makes this defiance necessary. For here, in the delivering up of Jesus, in the distress of Gethsemane and Golgotha of which He was wholly undeserving and we ourselves wholly deserving, here in the result of Judas' act, God is indeed for us. It is a genuine reverence—the reverence of faith in Jesus who was handed over—which flings out the question of Paul in Rom. 8, which clings so unconditionally to the fact that, with this handing-over, we are not merely provided with the forgiveness of our sins, but we receive and take and possess it in virtue of this handing-over, that we may live before God on the basis of this handing-over. It is the decree of the eternal love of God itself, and man would be disobedient to it if he were to struggle against it or to seek to live elsewhere than on its basis. He would then, as Paul says (Gal. 2²¹), frustrate the grace of God. Christ would then have died in vain to the extent that the gift of freedom which He obtained for us by His death would, as it were, remain suspended in mid-air. In view of this gift, the only legitimate possibility is that we accept as something which has happened for us what has happened for us, so that it may indeed happen for us again, and this time truly, that in Christ God stands in our place and is for us, as the owner and Lord of our life, as the Head of His Church, ruling and determining us. If we want it otherwise, we can only be against ourselves, working against ourselves and at the same time resisting God. It is decisively an act of reverent and godly fear to recognise that this has happened. God Himself is checked and disturbed in His ordering of the relationship between Himself and creation where it is not realised that the first and decisive step in His activity is that in Jesus Christ He has delivered up Himself for the world's cleansing from sin, for the removal of man's unworthiness and incapacity before Him. This obstacle to the covenant between God and man is actually removed. The way to the realisation of this covenant, God's way to the establishment of the kingdom of His mercy, and man's way to eternal life, is actually opened up. Everything necessary for this opening up is accomplished in that God delivers up Himself in Jesus Christ. He does not merely execute judgment upon sin. He takes it upon Himself and suffers so that there can be no further question of suffering it ourselves. There can be no going behind this regulation of the order between God and the world He created. This is what makes absolutely necessary Paul's defiance in Rom. 8, and also his passionate earnestness in Galatians. With the handing-over of God Himself in Jesus Christ there is spoken, not indeed the last word, but certainly the penultimate word which necessarily precedes the last word, and which we cannot in any circumstances ignore, or on any pretext undermine.

From this position, which Paul so strongly advocates, we will now look back to the observations which we made regarding the other use of παραδοῦναι, and see what new light is thrown upon them.

To begin with, it is obvious that no worse fate overtakes the Jews and Gentiles " handed over " by God in His wrath, or those Christians whose delivery to Satan is occasionally mentioned, than that which God visited on Himself in the handing-over of His Son. On the contrary, what is the freedom of which they are deprived, compared to the majesty of which God emptied Himself in His Son ? What does their bondage mean compared with the bondage which God caused to fall on Himself ? What have they lost in comparison with that which God Himself surrendered when His Word became flesh and accepted that suffering at the hands of evil powers to which all flesh is subject ? If they, too, must undoubtedly suffer punishment, this punishment of theirs, however severe it may be, is surpassed even before it begins, and overshadowed at once, by that which the delivered Jesus Christ had to endure " for the sake of our trespasses." The severity and hardship of a punishment are not decisively measured by the punishment itself, but by the one who has to suffer it. What might affect one as severe, but still bearable, can have a frightful and even a fatal effect on another. There is, therefore, all the difference of heaven and earth when, on the one hand, the Son of God is left to Himself, indeed to the power of Satan, and, on the other, the same thing happens to Jews and Gentiles, or to the incestuous man of Corinth, or Hymenæus and Alexander. Even if it does truly fall on them and affect them with all severity, there does not fall on them anything that God has not decreed from all eternity to fall on Himself, and has actually caused to fall on Himself, although He is incomparably more severely affected than they are. Their suffering is, as it were, only a prelude and postlude to the suffering of Jesus Christ. It is in His and not in their delivery that there took place the true and proper handing-over of man in weakness to a strange and overwhelming and hostile authority. Compared with the condemnation of Jesus Christ their condemnation is only like the sighing of creation in Rom. 8²²ᶠ· as compared with the sigh of Jesus on the cross. In view of this we can understand why it is that this handing-over of wrath is never mentioned without direct or indirect reference to the eschatological possibility of a saving aim and meaning even of the wrathful action of God against man. In particular, we can understand that the subject of Rom. 1, the revelation of God's wrath against all the ungodliness and unrighteousness of men, is, in fact, the inevitable complement of the revelation of the righteous decision which He executed in Jesus Christ for the benefit of all believers. The handing-over of these men, and their punishment, however real and severe it is, cannot have any independent significance alongside that of Jesus. It may, of course, be said that the suffering of these men who are delivered by God in His wrath is quite different from that of Jesus Christ to the extent that, according to the relevant passages, it consists in their delivery to themselves, to Satan. The wicked are made captive in such a way that they are remorselessly left to continue in evil (Rev. 22¹¹). The hell into which the rejected are cast, with all its eternal fire and wailing and gnashing of teeth, consists in the fact that every one finds, and necessarily is and has, that which he looked for in his folly and wickedness, that every one has to lie on the bed which he has made himself. This as such is the eternal torment which they must suffer, the eternal death which they have incurred. And at a first glance we may say that Jesus Christ did not suffer this, since it was in obedience that He humbled Himself unto death. But what follows from this obvious incongruity between His action and His suffering ? It is certainly not that He suffered something different from the torment and death, the fate, which the rejected have earned and prepared for themselves. It is rather that He suffered this torment and death, this fate, which by His obedience He had not earned or prepared for Himself, for them, in the place of these rejected. If we are to find any significance at all in the handing-over of Jesus in face of this incongruity, we have no alternative but to accept the witness that He was delivered to suffering and death on our behalf. " For us " —who when we believe and confess it must consider ourselves to be in solidarity with those rejected Jews and Gentiles, with the incestuous Corinthian, with Hymenæus and Alexander, to the extent that we must recognise that we, too, have merited the wrath of God which Scripture tells us has broken out against them. What Jesus Christ suffered innocently was undoubtedly the punishment of the man handed over to himself by the wrath of God, the judgment which man brings upon himself, and, like Judas, must execute upon himself, in his freedom to continue in evil. Although He Himself was not evil, Jesus had to suffer just what has to be suffered in the freedom to continue in evil : the suffering of Israel given up to idolatry ; the suffering of the Gentiles given up to the lusts of their own hearts ; the suffering of Christians given up to Satan. In Gethsemane and on Golgotha Jesus reaches the very place of the man who is given up in this way, and the inescapable distress which he necessarily prepares for himself in consequence. He Himself drinks this cup, after praying that it might pass from Him, but also repeatedly recognising and affirming that it is God's will that He should drink it. And we must add at once that He alone drinks this cup—not Peter and not Judas, and not those who are delivered up by the wrath of God —none of us who have also deserved to be delivered up in this way. He alone is delivered up in this way and to this end. How else could it be seriously said or maintained that He was delivered up " for us," in our place ? It follows that whatever those who were delivered up have suffered, and whatever all who have deserved the same handing-over may still have to suffer, they do not have to suffer that which Jesus Christ suffered, but Jesus Christ has suffered for them that which they are spared by His suffering, that which God has therefore spared them by not sparing His own Son. We must certainly take their punishment and suffering in all seriousness. The judgments which fall on them and us are not merely merited, but are, in fact, hard and severe. It is a serious matter to be a Pharaoh, a Saul, a Judas, an Alexander or a Hymenæus. It is a serious matter to be threatened by hell, sentenced to hell, worthy of hell, and already on the road to hell. On the other hand, we must not minimise the fact that we actually know of only one certain triumph of hell—the handing-over of Jesus —and that this triumph of hell took place in order that it would never again be able to triumph over anyone. We must not deny that Jesus gave Himself up into the depths of hell not only with many others but on their behalf, in their place, in the place of all who believe in Him. And it is to Him who humbled Himself to a criminal's death, to the Son of God hanged in spite of His innocence, that God has given the name which is above every name : ὑπὲρ πᾶν ὄνομα (Phil. 2⁹). That which He has done has absolute precedence over everything else that has been done or can be done, whether good or evil, actively or passively. It has precedence, therefore, over all the torment, the death, that others might have to suffer as rejected by God. Jesus Christ is *the* Rejected of God, for God makes Himself rejected in Him, and has Himself alone tasted to the depths all that rejection means and necessarily involves. From this standpoint, therefore, we cannot regard as an independent reality the status and fate of those who are handed over by the wrath of God. We certainly cannot deny its reality. But we can ascribe to it only a reality which is limited by the status and fate of Jesus Christ in His humiliation, His descent into hell, on the basis of the handing-over which fell on Him. We can thus ascribe to it only a reality which is necessarily limited by faith in Jesus Christ. In this faith we shall never cease to leave wholly and utterly to Him the decision about us and all other men. In faith in Jesus Christ we cannot consider any of those who are handed over by God as lost. We know of none whom God has wholly and exclusively abandoned to himself. We know only of One who was abandoned in this way, only of One who was lost. This One is Jesus Christ. And He was lost (and found again) in order that none should be lost apart from Him. From this standpoint, therefore, we can understand what Scripture tells us happened to those who were handed over by the wrath of God and abandoned to themselves, to Satan, only as an approximation to the suffering of Christ, fulfilled to their own salvation and at an infinite distance from this suffering. We can understand it only as a kind of terrible warning or reminiscence, as a sign of the death of Christ, and therefore indeed as a sign of the damnation which man has deserved, but above all as a sign of the grace by which he is saved from this damnation. It ought now to be clearer, perhaps, why it is that the eschatological possibility of a limit to this delivery of wrath plays so important a part in all the relevant passages. It is clear that it can be considered only as an eschatological possibility. The rejection of the rejected, the sentence and judgment under which they stand, are in themselves a quite firm and established fact which as such is unalterable. In fact, and not for nothing, they stand in the shadows, and of themselves they cannot escape from these shadows. Scripture speaks of countless men, as it does of Judas, in such a way that we must assume that they have lived and died without even the possibility, let alone the fulfilment, of any saving repentance. If there is also light for them, and hope, it can only be because and if there is an *eschaton*, a limit, by which even their inescapable bondage is hemmed in from outside. This *eschaton*, which confronts the status and fate of the rejected absolutely externally, and encounters them as an absolutely new factor, is the handing-over of Jesus, and all that this involved for the world and for them too—their cleansing from sin. Whatever God may inflict on them, He certainly does not inflict what He inflicted on Himself by delivering up Jesus Christ. For He has done it for them, in order that they should not suffer the judgment which accompanies the cleansing of the world's sin, and therefore should not be lost. It cannot be our concern to know and decide what has or will perhaps become of them, for they also stand in the light of what God has done for the world. As the forgiveness of sins is established in Jesus Christ alone, and as He alone has risen from the dead, so we have Him alone, both for ourselves and others, as a pledge of hope. There is all the less reason for us to deny that the rejected also stand in this light. For if in faith we can confess this for ourselves, we can do so seriously only as we recognise that we no less than they have deserved to be handed over to bondage by the wrath of God. We can confess it seriously only when we are in solidarity with them. If we are to make Paul's defiant question our own : " If God be for us, who can be against us ? ", the genuineness of our use of Paul's words can be tested by whether, thinking and speaking in faith, we can go on to say even in respect of apparent or obviously real Judases : " If God be for them, who can be against them ? " The fact that God is for them, too, is all the more striking, the more plainly we see that they are delivered to themselves, or to Satan. For to this extent—in all the distance of their sphere from that of Jesus Christ—the similarity of their fate and status to His increases. The recollection of what God has done for the world—He delivered His own Son for us—is not weakened, but strengthened, the more clearly we see what rejection means for others—or, better still, for ourselves—and what judgment it involves to be a man rejected by God. Therefore because this becomes clear to us we are all the more urgently required, in respect both of ourselves and others, to accept the eschatological reality of the delivery of Jesus Christ in the place of sinners. And in view of the efficacy of this event, we must not lose sight of the hope of the future deliverance of the rejected at the very frontier of perdition.

From the positive divine παραδοῦναι we now look back at the concept of the apostolic παράδοσις, and we see at once that when the news of Jesus passes from the hands of the apostles into a second and third set of hands, when the Church is established by this saving delivery, this action undoubtedly has its origin in the act of God Himself. The action of the apostles is obvious plenipotentiary in character because it is not in any sense original, but has its prototype and example in the delivery in which God delivered up His Son, in which the Son delivered up Himself into the hands of sinful men. If all the darkness of the divine judgment and rejection of sinful men is only the inevitable shadow of the judgment and rejection which God decreed from all eternity and executed in time when He did not spare His only Son, it is also clear that all the gracious light of the commission and ministry in which sinful man may proclaim the Gospel to other sinful men is only the reflection of the radiance of the eternal mercy in which God willed to take sinful man to Himself, and actually did take him to Himself by the handing-over of His Son. As the bondage and torment of the rejected is not a new or strange thing, an independent reality, in relation to what Jesus Christ suffered, and suffered on their behalf, so also the saving apostolic tradition is not a new or strange thing, an independent reality. It is simply the human transmission of that which God has divinely given. It is not a productive, but only a reproductive, activity. The apostle is not himself a master, but a servant of the one and only Lord. He has neither invented nor found in himself what he proclaims. It exists as it is created and posited by God. And it found him, the apostle, even before he sought it. It found him quite apart from his seeking, or even perhaps when he was seeking something very different. Even the fact that he proclaims it to us is only a human repetition and imitation of the divine original. He hands over Jesus Christ because originally and properly He was handed over by God Himself. In his existence as an apostle he is simply a witness to the fact that God has decreed this handing-over and its execution. Here, again, we must say that there is all the difference of heaven from earth between what happened to Jesus Christ originally at the hands of God Himself, and what now happens to Him as a result, through the ministry of the apostles. It is only in this difference that the two belong together. If, in both cases, He is given into the hands of men and passed from one human hand to the other, this is true now only because God Himself willed it from all eternity and accomplished it once and for all. What would the apostolic word be apart from the incarnation of the Word of God ? What would the grace of the apostolic proclamation be without the grace of the divine act from which it derives and in which it has its content ? As the praise of God by creation is related to the praise which God Himself has prepared for His Son in the glory of His resurrection, so that which the apostles will and do is related by their παραδοῦναι to that which God Himself has decreed from all eternity, and accomplished in time, with His delivering up of Jesus Christ. This is the true and proper παράδοσις. This is where the omnipotent love of God addressed itself effectually to men. This is where the bridges were built across the abyss between God and man. This is where God sought and found man. This is where it was made possible for man to stand in God's presence, and to live with Him. This is where the stumbling-block was removed which stood in the way of man, necessarily excluding him as an enemy of God from covenant with Him. This is where, by the cleansing of man from sin, there was opened up his entrance to the kingdom of God, the foundation of his sure hope of eternal life. This is where the Church was and is established before any human hand raised a single finger. This is where God gave Himself into danger on our behalf—for how could it not be dangerous and compromising for God, a threat to His glory, to enter so far into relationship with men that He Himself became man, mixing as a man with other men, and prosecuting His cause among them ? This is where God allowed Himself actually to succumb to this danger, to be rendered powerless as a man by other men, and to be rejected and slain. But this is where He also perfected His good-will towards man by exposing Himself to this danger, and in this exposure taking the decisive step on man's behalf, for man's benefit and deliverance, and for the establishment of the hope of eternal life. It is this divine handing-over that now finds its repetition and reproduction in the acts of the apostles. Because God is in earnest about that which He willed and did in this handing-over of Himself, because this could not happen in vain, it necessarily finds this repetition and reproduction. Because God has spoken in this παράδοσις, the echo cannot be absent in the sphere of His creation. The apostolic tradition is this echo. It can only be an echo, not an independent voice. But, according to the New Testament, in all its range and quality, it is undoubtedly the echo of this divine handing-over. In it, in the act of the apostolic tradition, men dare to place before other men, in their own human words, the fact that the omnipotent love of God is available for them too, and for them specifically ; that the bridge is built ; that God has sought and found them ; that they may stand in God's presence and live with Him ; that there is nothing between God and themselves which necessarily prevents this or necessarily excludes them from the covenant and kingdom of God ; that for them, too, the door is open ; that they may hope—hope for eternal life. But the content of their human words cannot be regarded as merely the abstract truth of all these statements. It can certainly be pronounced abstractly, but it is not then truth or revelation. It is simply a myth or a speculation on their lips, impotent and insubstantial. What the apostles place before men is not in this case a fact at all. But it is fact. For the content of their message, the subject of their tradition, is quite simply the name of Jesus Christ, the " account of the things which have been fulfilled among us." They do not speak as thinkers, but as eye-witnesses and servants of the Word which has encountered them in Jesus Christ, and to the claim of which they are subject. Enclosed in His name, as the declaration of His name, as the record of His story and work—these statements declare the truth, not abstractly, but as a fact and therefore as revelation. The substance and power of what the apostles have to say to other men in human words is in the name of Jesus Christ. Their message is surpassed but also borne and enlightened by the Word of Him of whom they speak. Their human word lives wholly and entirely by this subject. The apostolic " tradition " takes place because there has taken place once and for all this divine " tradition," and it has now found its echo in these particular human words. And if the Church is established by the human word of the apostles, it is obviously not they themselves who do this. They call only those whom God has already called, and who are reached by His call through the medium of their call. They are only the workers who are called to the ripened harvest to gather where they have not sown ; to the harvest which grew apart from them and before they arose. They point to the foundation of the Church as it has already taken place, both eternally and in time, in virtue of the divine handing-over. And in so doing they must and will, of course, place themselves in danger. In this respect, too, the divine handing-over necessarily finds its repetition and reproduction in their handing-over. The threat to which God exposed Himself, the suffering and even the death which God Himself drew upon Himself in His Son, are repeated. Everything which is said about this along the lines of Mt. 10²⁴ᶠ·—that the disciple cannot be above his master, or the servant above his lord—shows indirectly that matters of extremely hard fact are involved between the apostles and other men as they proclaim to them the name of Jesus Christ. The man who in all its divine substance and power hands over the name of the One who was handed over by God must allow himself to be handed over, and therefore himself experience in his own way the utter severity of that which God inflicted upon Himself in His Son. It is not for nothing that on at least one occasion (2 Cor. 4¹¹) Paul related the idea of being delivered to himself, and therefore to the bearer of the apostolic office in general : " For we which live are alway delivered unto death for Jesus' sake (εἰς θάνατον παραδιδόμεθα διὰ 'Ιησοῦν), that the life also of Jesus might be made manifest in our mortal flesh." And it is surely from this point of view that Col. 1²⁴ is to be understood : " I rejoice in my sufferings for you, and fill up that which is behind of the afflictions of Christ (τὰ ὑστερήματα τῶν θλίψεων τοῦ Χριστοῦ)." What is still lacking to the afflictions of Christ as such can only be their echo in creation, their repetition and reproduction in the ministry of His apostles, to the extent that this could not manifest the life of Christ if they themselves were not men who were delivered up, who in the execution of their human commission had to suffer for those to whom it was addressed. But we can and must also ask what is the danger, in which they placed themselves and to which they had actually to be exposed in fellowship with the One whom they proclaimed, compared to the danger in which God again placed Himself when He gave them their commission and they accepted it. The danger which seems to threaten is that of the tradition of Mk. 7⁶ᶠ·—the danger that in the act of human transmission the Word of God may be evaded, rejected and invalidated by its human subject. What becomes of the divine " tradition " when as apostolic matter it becomes human tradition ? What happened to it in the hands of the scribes ? Who is to guarantee that Jesus Christ might not be betrayed again by the eleven apostles, or by Paul himself, or that in their person Christian scribes might not fall under the same judgment as that under which Mk. 7 tells us that the Jewish scribes stood and still stand ? One must face this question in all its harshness if we are to realise that when the New Testament speaks about the apostolic tradition it obviously regards this danger as one which has been banished and overcome, as one which is in practice non-existent. The New Testament does not draw a parallel between the apostles and the scribes of Mk. 7, but presupposes as obvious, and accordingly proceeds on the assumption, that the precedent of Mk. 7 has not and cannot be repeated in the case of the apostles. It certainly describes the activity of the apostles as a continuation of the activity of the scribes. And it undoubtedly does not intend to place the apostles, as men, on a higher plane than the scribes. But between them there stands the death of Jesus by which God defied this threatening danger before it could assume a new form. It previously had its form in the apostle Judas, in the Jewish scribes, in the whole tradition of Israel. But after the death of Jesus it can no longer have this form, nor can it take on any new form. It has been made formless by the death of Jesus, and it is therefore disarmed. For God gave Himself up to danger in the death of Jesus, voluntarily submitting to it, in order that sinful man might be cleansed and freed from his sin, and therefore disarmed, as He Himself executed the sentence upon him and took it to Himself. Sinful man cannot resist this disarmament in relation to God. He can certainly delay to recognise it. But he cannot undo it. He has made a captive once of the Son of God delivered up for him. But he cannot and will not do so a second time. The story of God's faithfulness and Israel's faithlessness, the story of Judas Iscariot and what follows at Gethsemane and Golgotha, will not be repeated. All apparent repetitions of these stories are only formless phantasmagoria. What cannot be reversed is the fact that Jesus is the Victor. And this emerges decisively at the point where the news of Him, of the divine self-surrender, is met by faith and is proclaimed and by proclamation awakens new faith, that is, in the act of apostolic tradition. It is true that in this repetition and reproduction Jesus and the divine " tradition " fall into the hands of sinful men. But if it is the divine " tradition " which is humanly repeated and reproduced by men, if their human word lives by this subject, there can be no question of any new form of the danger in the apostolic tradition, once the old has been overcome. It necessarily ceases to be the apostolic tradition, and the human word which lives by that subject, if it even appears to reintroduce this danger. And this can happen only in appearance. For the cause of God, as God Himself prosecuted and vindicated it when He delivered up His Son, cannot again be jeopardised objectively as it was once exposed to this peril. Nor can it be jeopardised subjectively—not even in appearance—when as the cause which God has vindicated by this delivering-up it is placed in the hands of sinful men, as happens in the apostolic tradition. Of itself and as such, it cleanses these hands, however foul they may be. In itself and as such, it cannot be misrepresented or falsified by the hands of sinful men as they receive or transmit it. In itself and as such, as the accomplished death of Jesus, it cannot be evaded, rejected or invalidated by any other scribes. It certifies and confirms and defends itself as such in the hands of sinners in which it is placed and which grasp it. The only thing is that it must always itself and as such be the content and subject of human activity, that it must always itself and as such be firmly held and not allowed to fall from the hands of sinners. The apostolic tradition is the human repetition and reproduction of the divine " tradition," in which the hands of sinners hold and transmit the divine tradition itself as such, as they have received it. That is why the New Testament speaks so urgently of the need for faithfulness and purity in the apostolic tradition. Its faithfulness and purity consist in its correspondence to the situation objectively created by the death of Jesus. They consist in the fact that the apostolic tradition can have neither content nor subject apart from the accomplished death of Jesus ; that all its contents and subjects must always be included in this single one. If it takes place in faithfulness and purity, then the act of apostolic tradition is, in fact, protected and safeguarded against the possibility of becoming what the tradition of the Jewish scribes became and was according to Mk. 7. If it takes place in faithfulness and purity, the correspondence of this activity to the divine tradition cannot be more than this : that on the one hand the apostles can repeat and portray by their proclamation the action of the divine grace addressed to man ; and that on the other hand they can repeat and portray by their sufferings the act of the self-humiliation of God for the fulfilment of this grace—the second being a confirmation and attestation of the first. What Judas did cannot be repeated or copied in the act of apostolic tradition. Otherwise it necessarily ceases to be apostolic—the human proclamation which lives by the divine tradition. It makes no difference that its bearers are sinful men like Judas. Because they hand on the accomplished death of Jesus, their activity can only be the exact opposite of that of Judas. The accomplished death of Jesus which is the content and subject of their tradition makes it quite impossible for their activity to be another betrayal of Jesus. In correspondence to the positive meaning of apostleship, it can only be His glorification, the glorification of His accomplished death as represented by the act of Mary of Bethany in Jn. 12. At the very point where Judas says No, Paul says Yes. And Paul does this after he himself had previously, in the same situation, said No with Judas. The fact that it is the same situation —the death of Jesus—binds him and all the other apostles to Judas. But it is by the death of Jesus that the Judas in Paul dies, and Paul is cleansed and liberated from his own past, so that he is no longer capable of what Judas inflicted upon Jesus, of his own previous παραδοῦναι. The possibility of again saying No is taken from him, together with the possibility of again seeking to make Jesus powerless in face of the superior power of men. " Old things are passed away ; behold, all things are become new " (2 Cor. 5^{17}). It is man who is now made powerless in face of the overwhelming power of Jesus. To make man powerless is the whole point of the act of apostolic tradition. The danger of the scribes of Mk. 7 has now been completely routed by the accomplished death of Jesus, by the divine " tradition," which it is now the task of Paul and all the apostles to repeat and reproduce.

And now finally we must ask concerning the specific relationship of the handing-over by Judas to this central and decisive handing-over.

We have seen what was involved in the case of Judas. He brought Jesus into the situation where nobody but God could help Him. He seems to have perverted his apostolic function into its opposite by this act. He seems to have served the devil. And not only seems—for if we look at his act as such, its intention, execution, and consequence in the sphere of the human history of Jesus and his own history, we must undoubtedly say that he actually did this. He revealed and willingly and wittingly executed the final consequences of the fact that the Word of God became flesh, willing to have and actually having a human history, the history of one man among others. By his action he completed the reaction of these other men to the man who was the Son of God. He condemned this very man, and in that way revealed the justice of the condemnation which lies on all other men. He decisively confirmed that the world of men into which God sent His Son is the kingdom of Satan : the kingdom of misused creaturely freedom ; the kingdom of enmity to the will and resistance to the work of its Creator. Everything which others, apart from and after Judas, inflicted upon Jesus, up to and including the act of His final murder, followed from that which Judas did, just as the insignificant seed already contains and represents the entire growth which emerges from it.

But the more profoundly and comprehensively we attempt to formulate the sin and guilt of Judas, the more nearly his will and deed approach what neither he himself willed and did, nor the people of Israel, nor the Gentiles at whose head he finally appears—the more nearly his will and deed approach what God willed and did in this matter, the divine handing-over which here took place, the humiliation to which God Himself willed to give Himself, and did give Himself, intervening for man and against the rule of Satan in the world of men, to cleanse them from the sin against Him of which they are guilty and of which it is Judas who now, at their head, incurs the guilt. Consider the sin of Judas in its ultimate, most terrible meaning. The Adam who, listening to the suggestion of the serpent, only wished to be like God, a divine man alongside God, unlimited and undisturbed by his mere creatureliness in its distinction from God, has now gone on to an open assault upon God. To make sure of his pretensions, Adam has now raised his hand against God Himself, as did Cain against his brother Abel, to rid himself of Him, and therefore to be quite unmolested in his divine humanity. But supposing that from all eternity God willed to let this assault be made upon Him, and did actually let it be made in time, in order by enduring this assault to cleanse and liberate man from the sin of pretension, from the evil delusion and fearful curse of his usurped likeness to God, in order to restore man to His own image, the image of His own Son ? Is not Paul right even in relation to Judas—indeed primarily and specifically in relation to Judas—when he says (Rom. 5[20]) that it is at the very point where sin reaches its fulness that grace overflows, at the very point where the Law definitively condemns man that the Gospel is heard with its disclosure of what God has determined for the man whom it definitively condemned ? It is impossible for us to ignore the fact that if and as God willed to endure this assault on the part of man, and because He has actually endured it for man in accordance with His omnipotent will, if and as He willed to cleanse and liberate man in this way from the delusion and curse of his usurped likeness to God, and restore him to the image of His Son, and because He has actually done this, this assault on Him had to be planned and executed, and the Son of Man had to be betrayed. The act of Judas cannot, therefore, be considered as an unfortunate episode, much less as the manifestation of a dark realm beyond the will and work of God, but in every respect (and at a particularly conspicuous place) as one element of the divine will and work. In what he himself wills and carries out, Judas does what God wills to be done. He and not Pilate is the *executor Novi Testamenti*. But with his vile betrayal of Jesus to His enemies he is also the executor of the surrender which God has resolved to make and is now making for the benefit of hostile man, and therefore for his benefit. For all its futility, the empty bargain which Judas makes with the high-priests in relation to this surrender is a reflection of the eternal decree in which God Himself has resolved that His own Son shall not be spared. For all its insincerity, the treacherous kiss by which Judas distinguishes Jesus from the surrounding disciples at the arrest is the sign of the gratitude of lost man for the existence of Him who now wills to intervene for him. For this reason, although the earlier saying of Jesus to Judas : " That thou doest, do quickly," is the bitter judgment upon him, it is also the clear command with which Jesus, as it were, takes from his hand that which he is planning, Himself deciding that what Judas intends to do with Him shall actually be done. It could not remain undone. In one sense Judas is the most important figure in the New Testament apart from Jesus. For he, and he alone of the apostles, was actively at work in this decisive situation, in the accomplishment of what was God's will and what became the content of the Gospel. Yet he is the very one who is most explicitly condemned by the Law of God. He is the very one who might cause us to stray completely from the insight that in the New Testament no one is merely rejected —because he seems so unequivocally to act as one who is rejected and only as such among the elect apostles. If we consider the indispensability of Judas from the point of view of the divine delivering-up of Jesus, we can almost understand for a moment what inspired the ancient sect which gave special veneration to this man. In itself, it is no more foolish than the considerations which at a very different point led to the veneration of Mary, the mother of Jesus. At any rate, we have to say that the usual horror at this " arch-villain " (as Abraham a Sta. Clara puts it) is quite unjustifiable in its over-simplication of Judas' actual function. And when a man like Carl Daub (*Judas Ischarioth oder das Böse im Verhältnis zum Guten*, 1816 f.) could make no more of Judas than repeatedly to condemn and decry him as a " sinner without equal," he only showed the blindness and impotence of German Idealism in relation to the central truth of the New Testament.

But veneration is just as misplaced as contempt. The paradox in the figure of Judas is that, although his action as the executor of the New Testament is so absolutely sinful, yet as such, in all its sinfulness, it is still the action of that executor. The divine and human παραδοῦναι cannot be distinguished in what Judas did, as in the genuine apostolic tradition, where the human is related to the divine παραδοῦναι as to its content and subject. In the case of Judas, the apostle who perverted his apostleship and served Satan, the two coincide. As the human παραδοῦναι takes place, the divine takes place directly, and the divine takes place directly as the human takes place. It is to be noted that there is this coincidence where the human παραδοῦναι can only be regarded, and is undoubtedly regarded by the New Testament, as conscious and deliberate sin, as sin with a high hand. In this case sin is made righteousness, and evil good. The Yes does not follow the No as in the case of Paul, or the other apostles, but the No itself and as such is the Yes, because it pleased God to make it the Yes which He Himself wills to say and does say in this matter. God wills this final consequence of the incarnation of His Word, and it is He Himself who now actually brings it to pass. God wills this conclusion to His history as the history of the man Jesus, and He Himself reaches this conclusion in Him. God has here condescended to man absolutely, even to the point of allowing Himself to be reduced to utter impotence by a man like Judas, i.e., by the revealing and unfolding of the final consequences of what Adam had willed and done, and by allowing Himself to be completely overwhelmed by the superior power of Satan ruling in the world of men. Was it not Judas, the sinner without equal, who offered himself at the decisive moment to carry out the will of God, not in spite of his unparalleled sin, but in it ? There is nothing here to venerate, nor is there anything to despise. There is place only for the recognition and adoration and magnifying of God. In face of this the man Judas with his act is so clearly abandoned that no defence is possible and all praise would be folly. But censure and condemnation are also folly, because what was done here by the One who was so very differently abandoned—namely, God Himself—makes them superfluous and irrelevant. For when God abandoned Himself, it pleased Him so to confront this man who was also abandoned that he of all men became His servant, not indirectly but directly and in his blatant rejection, as not even Paul and Peter were His servants. That is, he became the servant of the work of reconciliation itself, in which these others shared only later and as witnesses. This is what we must keep primarily and decisively before us in relation to the handing-over by Judas. And it is true irrespective of the consequences to himself. This is the participation of Judas in the positive task of the apostolate. It is an outstanding participation because it is participation in its very basis, in the divine handing-over. Because the divine handing-over is the content and subject of the apostolic tradition, this would not exist apart from Judas and his act. Therefore there can be no doubt that—in a way which is basic—he co-operated positively, against his will and deserts, in the task of the apostolate and the Church as it is grounded on the election of Jesus Christ. So great is the over-whelming power of the matter entrusted to the apostles, and of their election to the service of this matter ! It draws into this service even the man who would refuse and betray it and deny his election as an apostle. Its power is not only so great that he is quite unable to prevent the execution of this service, that when he is seduced by Satan he cannot degrade himself lower than to be a *locum tenens* for the true bearer of the New Testament apostolate, a negative type of Paul. It is not only so great that although he is rejected it still holds him in the circle of election to the extent that he has to stand on the left where the elect apostle Paul stands on the right, i.e., where Jesus Christ is in the centre, as the prototype of both. It is not only so great that it firmly holds this one on the left in confrontation and similarity with Jesus Himself, to the extent that he alone of all the apostles must die with Him : no saving or atoning death, to be sure ; but the death of the disobedient which they all merited, and for that reason the death which none of them could let themselves forget when they thought of Jesus' death ; the death of the sinner, which Jesus suffered for them all. It is not only great enough for all this. But as we have learned from the context of the linguistic use of παραδοῦναι, it is so great that for the divine delivery (apart from which the apostolic tradition would have neither theme nor content) it can employ as its human instrument even Judas, the παραδιδούς, who with his delivery carried the fall of Adam to its final consequence as man's revolt against God, and who because of his delivery can only die the death of a sinner, and be degraded as an apostle to the status of a mere *locum tenens*. It does not merely defy his handing-over. Nor does it merely overcome it. But it accepts and uses it. It does not give it only an incidental function, but this distinctive and decisive function.

We must not draw from these considerations any deductions to extenuate or justify what Judas did. If we are not to dissociate ourselves from the clear statement of the New Testament, we have no reason to judge his act otherwise than as one of sin and guilt. And since we can only accept this judgment, we must be careful not to draw from the relationship between his handing-over and the divine handing-over the conclusion that his determination is ultimately positive. All that we may affirm is that the power of the matter entrusted to the apostles is so great that even Judas is not exempt from its positive service, but subject to it ; and that an outstanding function is indeed allotted to him in this service. But this is something that we must affirm, because, according to the New Testament, it is just as undeniable as his sin and guilt.

But this is obviously the final explanation of the remarkable circumstance which we took as our starting-point—that in the New Testament Judas is always described as " one of the twelve," and that the concept of election is expressly applied to him. The power of the apostolic cause which can be seen in him to the ultimate degree that he must serve it even in his sin and guilt, is the power of the divine election which has fallen on him too. His election excels and out-shines and controls and directs his rejection : not just partly, but wholly ; not just relatively, but absolutely. And this is not because it was not really a serious rejection. It is just because it is so serious. It is just because in this figure if in any biblical figure one perceives nothing at all except divine rejection. This very man, who is wholly rejected, is elect. He is " one of the twelve." And in the decisive situation he more clearly than all the rest must demonstrate and confirm that he is this—that this is the service for which God elects those whom He elects. We began by emphasising that it is of decisive importance for the New Testament teaching on predestination that the man rejected by God, the counterpart of the elect, should not be shown at a distance but in the most intimate and direct proximity to Jesus Himself. This helps to bring out the sinister threat which results for the elect from the fact that the rejected is among them, and sits at table with Jesus. " Lord is it I ? "—each individual can and must ask himself this, even in the closest proximity to Jesus, even among the elect. But it also brings out even more clearly that the rejected man, who finds himself in this proximity to Jesus, cannot have the authority, dignity or power of an objective opponent of Jesus. On the contrary, although his whole being and activity are evil, and nothing less than the authority, dignity and power of Satan stands behind them and works through them, they can operate and develop only under the dwarfing excellence and superiority and domination which Jesus exercises upon him. His area is limited, and on every side this limited area is enclosed by the greater sphere of Jesus. His evil action is always relative to the saving action of Jesus. Indeed, it must submit to the fact that in this relationship, and against its own intention, it does ultimately acquire a positive significance. In the New Testament counterpart of the man rejected by God he does not have an independent but only a dependent position and role. This counterpart exists, but only as a shadow. In its relationship to the elect it exists only as the dead Judas exists in Paul, only as the old things that are past continue as the past after the new has come, only as the flesh exists after the spirit is given to man, and has become mightier than his flesh. The human παραδιδόντες exist under the power of the divine παραδοῦναι accomplished in the death of Jesus Christ, under the power of the proclamation proceeding from it.

They exist, as described in 1 Pet. 3¹⁹, like the spirits in prison to whom Christ descended to bring them the *kerygma*. It is true that they are rejected, spirits in prison, but it is even more true that Christ has entered their prison, that they have become the object of His *kerygma*, that it is said of them too : " God did not spare his own Son, but delivered him up for us all." Whatever their future may be, it will take place under the power of the proclamation of this handing-over, in the situation which is not merely kept open by this proclamation, but is kept open in the wholly disparate relationship of the two powers.

In this doctrine of predestination, or more precisely in this doctrine of divine rejection and the rejected, the New Testament understood itself to be the fulfilment and explanation of the Old Testament, and in particular of the Old Testament picture of the shadow cast by the divine election. We remember how carefully it is indicated, and especially in the most important passages relating to Judas, that everything had to take place in just this way in fulfilment of Old Testament prophecy. Judas, the παραδιδούς, in his concentrated attack upon Israel's Messiah, does only what the elect people of Israel had always done towards its God, thus finally showing itself in its totality to be the nation rejected by God. In Judas there live again (as it were in compendium) all the great rejected of the Old Testament who had already had to testify that this elect people is in truth rejected, that it is elect in and from its rejection, that it is elect only in the form of the divine promise given to it in the beginning and never taken away, that it is elect finally only in the person of the One for whose sake this people could and must have its special existence. In view of the act of Judas there can be no further doubt about the rejection of this people and the seriousness of the typical rejection of all these individuals within it. For it has delivered up to the Gentiles for death the very One in whom it is elect. This Judas must die, as he did die ; and this Jerusalem must be destroyed, as it was destroyed. Israel's right to existence is extinguished, and therefore its existence can only be extinguished. But if the power of the divine delivering-up over the human is true for Judas, it is also true for Israel ; and it is retrospectively true for the whole divine rejection of the elect people, as it becomes progressively clearer in the Old Testament. This rejection, as the prophets continually testified, is absolutely serious, and has all the unqualified severity of the divine wrath, but all the same, it has no meaning independent of God's election. And if the individual rejected of the Old Testament are always unquestionably rejected, this in no way alters the fact that Israel's promise is valid and relevant for them too, that they too have a share in it even in their rejection, just as in the Old Testament itself they are always confronted by the elect, in whom this promise lives on, and who as elect are witnesses to the One in whom Israel is always elect even in and in spite of all its rejection. As Judas could do nothing against the cause of the apostolate, but in his treachery and rejection could only become a *locum tenens* for the genuine apostle, so Israel could not destroy the God-given promise by its unfaithfulness, or reverse or nullify the mission to all people which had been entrusted to it. Israel has fulfilled and vindicated the meaning of its existence by giving rise to Jesus Christ. If it must pass because it has rejected the promise in its fulfilment, it still has the promise as it has been fulfilled, and its mission as it has been discharged. Again, as in his handing-over and rejection Judas had to co-operate actively in the execution of the divinely determined handing-over of Jesus, so in the repudiation and handing-over of Jesus to the Gentiles Israel too—as Paul showed in Rom. 11—has had to play an active part in its mission. The grace of God to Israel was, in fact, all-powerful in and above the faithlessness in which it sinned against Him, and the judgment which in so doing it drew down upon itself, and which must now be executed upon it. This event is the final justification of the Old Testament in its constancy to it through all the wanderings of its historical and prophetic narratives, in spite of all appearances, and futilely, as it would seem, in view of the innumerable threats which it places alongside it, and the execution of which it records. It is also the justification of the Old Testament in its refusal to depict the rejected without also awarding them the characteristics of election, or in its reference, contrary to the picture of the general rejection of the whole nation, to elect individuals, who, although not free from the marks of rejection, bear open witness in their distinctiveness as elect to the promise given to all Israel. If Israel had eventually to pass, it did so only in such a way that in the Church of Jesus Christ, gathered from Jews and Gentiles, it experienced a first resurrection as the pledge of resurrections to come, and as it already participated to that extent in the grace of the divine delivering-up. And if, after what it has done to Jesus Christ, it is always a past and rejected people, as the people of God, to the extent that it has not arisen to new life in the Church, it is still true that with its evil human " tradition " it was the instrument by which the Church of Jesus Christ was built, by which even for Israel itself the light of hope was placed on the candlestick. The divine " tradition " which the Church of Jesus Christ proclaims in its confession is the hope of Israel, the promise of its election, which always outlasts and excels and surpasses its rejection. The proclamation of this delivering-up is addressed to Israel too. It declares that Jesus Christ died also for rejected Israel. What the result will be is in the hand of God. If we cannot answer this question, we have still to maintain that even rejected Israel is always in the open and at the same time so very unequally determined situation of proclamation, and that the question of its future can never be put except in this situation.

But to say this is to say all that we need to say about the general question of the divine will and intention for the rejected, the non-elect. The answer can only be as follows. He wills that he too should hear the Gospel, and with it the promise of his election. He wills, then, that this Gospel should be proclaimed to him. He wills that he should appropriate and live by the hope which is given him in the Gospel. He wills that the rejected should believe, and that as a believer he should become a rejected man elected. The rejected as such has no independent existence in the presence of God. He is not determined by God merely to be rejected. He is determined to hear and say that he is a rejected man elected. This is what the elect of the New Testament are—rejected men elected in and from their rejection, men in whom Judas lived, but was also slain, as in the case of Paul. They are rejected who as such are summoned to faith. They are rejected who on the basis of the election of Jesus Christ, and looking to the fact that He delivered Himself up for them, believe in their election.

CHAPTER VIII

THE COMMAND OF GOD

CHAPTER VIII

THE COMMAND OF GOD

§ 36

ETHICS AS A TASK OF THE DOCTRINE OF GOD

As the doctrine of God's command, ethics interprets the Law as the form of the Gospel, i.e., as the sanctification which comes to man through the electing God. Because Jesus Christ is the holy God and sanctified man in One, it has its basis in the knowledge of Jesus Christ. Because the God who claims man for Himself makes Himself originally responsible for him, it forms part of the doctrine of God. Its function is to bear primary witness to the grace of God in so far as this is the saving engagement and commitment of man.

1. THE COMMAND OF GOD AND THE ETHICAL PROBLEM

In the true Christian concept of the covenant of God with man the doctrine of the divine election of grace is the first element, and the doctrine of the divine command is the second. It is only in this concept of the covenant that the concept of God can itself find completion. For God is not known and is not knowable except in Jesus Christ. He does not exist in His divine being and perfections without Jesus Christ, in whom He is both very God and very man. He does not exist, therefore, without the covenant with man which was made and executed in this name. God is not known completely—and therefore not at all—if He is not known as the Maker and Lord of this covenant between Himself and man. The Christian doctrine of God cannot have " only " God for its content, but since its object is *this* God it must also have man, to the extent that in Jesus Christ man is made a partner in the covenant decreed and founded by God. We dare not encroach on the freedom of God by asserting that this relationship of His with man is essential, indispensable, and inalienable. But we cannot avoid the free decision of His love in which God has actually put Himself into this relationship, turning towards man in all the compassion of His being, actually associating Himself with man in all the faithfulness of His being. We cannot try to go behind that. Of course man in himself and as such has no place in the doctrine of

God. But Jesus Christ has a place. God's compassion and faithfulness towards man have a place. A God without Jesus Christ, without this compassion and faithfulness towards man, would be another God, a strange God. By the Christian standard He would not be God at all. The God of Christian knowledge, the only true and real God, is as surely the Lord of the covenant between Himself and man as He is " the God and Father of our Lord Jesus Christ."

The first element in the concept of this covenant is the doctrine of the election of grace, of predestination. God elects Himself to be gracious toward man, to be his Lord and Helper, and in so doing He elects man to be the witness to His glory. This election, decreed from all eternity in Jesus Christ and executed in Him in time, is the mystery of the will of God. Preceding all other resolutions and actions of God, it is His basic mystery, which He reveals in His Word, and which may be known and grasped in faith in His Word. To say divine election, to say predestination, is to name in one word the whole content of the Gospel, its sum. For that reason the doctrine of election belongs to the doctrine of God. For how can we really speak about God, without speaking directly, if only summarily, about the Gospel?

But the concept of the covenant is not exhausted by the doctrine of election. The partner in this covenant is man. What does it mean —looked at from God's side—for man to be a partner in the covenant, to be placed in this relationship to God ? Already, at the conclusion of the doctrine of election, it was necessary for us to ask : What is the purpose of the electing God for the man whom He has elected ? And the answer we found was that in all circumstances God wills to rule over man. He wills to take him into His service, to commission him for a share in His own work. He wills to make him a witness of Jesus Christ and therefore a witness of His own glory. But obviously we must now go on to ask what it is that God wants *from* man. What does He expect, what does He demand of him ? The divine election is, in the last resort, the determination of man—his determination to this service, this commission, this office of witness. It is man who is determined in this way. Therefore—whatever else he may be—he is certainly not a mere thing, a neuter, but a *person*. And as a person he is a partner in the covenant which God has made and established between Himself and him. If this is the case, then obviously another problem opens up from the doctrine of election. To be sure, it can only be legitimately put in the light of this doctrine. But it has an independent content as compared with the doctrine of election, and therefore it must have a special answer. As election is ultimately the determination of man, the question arises as to the human self-determination which corresponds to this determination. The question ? For the moment we cannot say more than this, and in saying it, we do not make it into an answer—least of all an answer which would limit or perhaps even destroy the truth that the election and determination of man are by God's grace alone. The good news that in Jesus Christ God has decided in favour of man, and given him this determination in His omnipotent wisdom, must not be reversed even by a single iota. It is obvious, however, that this determination confronts man with the question as to his attitude to it. How is he going to exist under this determination ? As the one who is determined in this way, what sort of a man will he be and what will he do ? It would not be his determination if he were not asked these questions, if to the divine decision there did not correspond a human one in which the partner in the covenant has to give his answer to what is said to him by the fact that God has concluded it. That God wills to rule over him clearly means that He wants his obedience, and the question of obedience is therefore put to him. That God has determined him for service clearly means that He claims him for Himself, and he is therefore asked whether he will satisfy this claim. When God becomes his Partner, as the Lord of the covenant who determines its meaning, content and fulfilment, He necessarily becomes the Judge of man, the Law of his existence. Man is judged as he is measured against God. And as he measures himself against God he necessarily judges himself. Unless he accepts this question—however it is to be answered—he obviously cannot be elect. He cannot be in this covenant with God. God cannot draw him to Himself without involving him in responsibility. It may be noted that when we come to this second question we do not leave the circle of our consideration of the being and essence and activity of God. It is within this circle, within the doctrine of God, that the question arises. It is in and with man's determination by God as this takes place in predestination that the question arises of man's self-determination, his responsibility and decision, his obedience and action. To answer this question cannot, then, impose any limitation upon the knowledge of the absolute authority of God's grace. There can be no question, therefore, of having to speak of anything other than the Gospel. What we have to establish is that the being and essence and activity of God as the Lord of the covenant between Himself and man include a relationship to the being and essence and activity of man. It is as He makes Himself responsible for man that God makes man, too, responsible. Ruling grace is commanding grace. The Gospel itself has the form and fashion of the Law. The one Word of God is both Gospel *and* Law. It is not Law by itself and independent of the Gospel. But it is also not Gospel without Law. In its content, it is Gospel ; in its form and fashion, it is Law. It is first Gospel and then Law. It is the Gospel which contains and encloses the Law as the ark of the covenant the tables of Sinai. But it is both Gospel *and* Law. The one Word of God which is the revelation and work of His grace is also Law. That is, it is a prior decision concerning man's self-determination. It is the claiming of his freedom. It regulates and judges the use that is made of this freedom. As the

one Word of God, which is the revelation and work of His grace,
disposes of man, it is also the impulse directing him to a future that
is in keeping with this " disposing." As the one Word of God which
is the revelation and work of His grace reaches us, its aim is that
our being and action should be conformed to His. " Be ye (literally,
ye shall be) therefore perfect (literally, directed to your objective),
even as (i.e., corresponding to it in creaturely-human fashion as) your
Father which is in heaven is perfect (directed to His objective) " (Mt.
5⁴⁸). The truth of the evangelical indicative means that the full stop
with which it concludes becomes an exclamation mark. It becomes
itself an imperative. The concept of the covenant between God and
man concluded in Jesus Christ is not exhausted in the doctrine of the
divine election of grace. The election itself and as such demands that
it be understood as God's command directed to man ; as the sanctification or claiming which comes to elected man from the electing God in
the fact that when God turns to Him and gives Himself to him He
becomes his Commander.

Election in Jesus Christ means separation for the purpose of subjection to
the lordship of Him who gave Himself for us " that we which live should not
henceforth live unto ourselves, but unto him which died for us, and rose again "
(2 Cor. 5¹⁵). It is made sure (βεβαία), confirmed and proved by the fact that this
subjection takes place, that the elect accept this subjection. Its aim is this confirmation and proof—" salvation through sanctification of the Spirit " (2 Thess.
2¹³). We may refer (although not without reservation) to Thomas Aquinas :
Deus adjuvatur per nos, inquantum exequimur suam ordinationem, secundum illud
(1 Cor. 3⁹) : *Dei enim adjutores sumus. Neque hoc est propter defectum divinae
virtutis : sed quia utitur causis mediis, ut ordinis pulchritudo servetur in rebus, et ut
etiam creaturis dignitatem causalitatis communicet* (*S. theol.* 1, qu. 23, art. 8, ad. 2).
If this can be understood in accordance with Mt. 5⁴⁸, we may rightly put it in this
way. The summons of the divine predecision, the sanctification which comes on
man from all eternity and therefore once and for all in the election of Jesus Christ,
is that in all its human questionableness and frailty the life of the elect should
become its image and repetition and attestation and acknowledgment. In this
sense Calvin again and again urged : *Electionis scopus est vitae sanctimonia*
(*Instit.* III, 23, 12). *Quae in electis futura erat sanctitas, ab electione habuit exordium*
(*ib.*, 22, 3). Election is the sun, sanctification its shining—who is to separate the
two ? (*Congrég. sur l'élect ét.*, 1551, *C.R.* 8, 107). *Ce sont choses conjointes et
inséparables, que Dieu nous ait eleu et que maintenant il nous appelle à la saincteté.
. . . il ne faut point séparer ce qu'il a conjoint et uni . . . il faut, que l'élection soit
comme une racine, qui jette de bons fruits* (*Sermon on Eph.* 1⁴⁻⁶, *C.R.* 51, 270 f.).

This makes it plain that ethics belongs not only to dogmatics in
general but to the doctrine of God. This is something which ought to
have been apparent for some time. For who can possibly see what is
meant by the knowledge of God, His divine being, His divine perfections, the election of His grace, without an awareness at every point
of the demand which is put to man by the fact that this God is his
God, the God of man ? How can God be understood as the Lord if
that does not involve the problem of human obedience ? But what
is implicit must now be made explicit. What is self-evident must now

be brought out specifically. The doctrine of God must be expressly defined and developed and interpreted as that which it also is at every point, that is to say, *ethics*. Otherwise, human carelessness and forgetfulness may only too easily skim over the fact that it actually is this, and that all that we have so far said as the doctrine of God has also this further sense—the sense of basically ethical reflection and explanation.

If we adopt here the term ethics to describe the special task of dogmatics which the Law as the form of the Gospel has imposed on us, we do it in the freedom—which is so very necessary and is always enjoyed in dogmatics—to take such terms as are to hand, not allowing ourselves to be bound and fettered by the meaning which they may have acquired from their use elsewhere, but using them in the sense which, when they are applied to the object with which we are concerned, they must derive from this object itself. No term has as such an absolutely universal and therefore binding sense. This is equally true of " ethics." At any rate the dogmatics of the Christian Church cannot make use of any terms (not even those of mathematics!) without examination, without reserving the right to give them a sense of its own, and to apply them in its own way. And this is also true of the term " ethics." But—granted this reservation—there is no reason not to make use of the term in dogmatics. A relatively general conception of ethics which we might take as our point of departure γυμναστικῶς is as follows. The ethical question is the question as to the basis and possibility of the fact that in the multitude and multiplicity of human actions there are certain modes of action, i.e., certain constants, certain laws, rules, usages or continuities. It is the question as to the rightness of these constants, the fitness of these laws. It is the question as to the value which gives any action the claim to be the true expression of a mode of action, the fulfilment of a law—the right to be repeated and in virtue of its normative character to serve as an example for the actions of others. What is the true and genuine continuity in all the so-called continuities of human action ? What is it that really gives force to all these recognised laws ? What is the good in and over every so-called good of human action ? This is— roughly—the ethical question, and—roughly again—the answering of it is what is generally called " ethics."

" Ethics " comes from ἦθος (orig. dwelling, stable), is synonymous with " morals " (from *mos*), and means the doctrine of custom or habit. Τὸ ἠθικὸν τῆς φιλοσοφίας (*Diogenes Laertius*) is the part of philosophy which deals with the principles of the moral. To correspond to the true meaning a general definition would have to be as follows. Ethics is the science or knowledge or doctrine of the modes of human behaviour, of the constants or laws of human behaviour. But obviously this definition which derives from the meaning is not enough. There are all sorts of questions about modes of human behaviour, about the law and rule and continuity of human action, which do not so far, or any longer, have anything to do with the ethical question in itself. " Will-psychology " investigates the constants of human behaviour within the sphere of natural law. The science of moral statistics, the study of customs and in a wider compass the morphology of cultures all ask about the constants of human behaviour which have freely arisen and which perist in history. The science of positive law investigates the continuity of human behaviour which is guaranteed and sanctioned by national communities. The philosophy of history investigates the constant of human behaviour in the common temporal change and development of human aims and achievements. But where the task of ethics has been undertaken, it has always been understood as a different one from the task of these sciences.

Morality in the sense of the ethical question is something other than the congruence of an action with a demonstrable natural law of human volition and action. Even if the moral action is subject to such a law of nature, this dependence and agreement does not make it moral action. Surprisingly enough, even the naive identification of the moral law with natural law, as variously represented by J. J. Rousseau, L. Feuerbach, M. Stirner, Friedrich Nietzsche and E. Haeckel, was not carried out in the form of mere descriptions, but always in the form of definite imperative claims upon human volition and action. With Rousseau and Nietzsche it actually has something of the character of a passionate proclamation. If the moral law is no more than natural law, all it needs is to be stated as that—the more objectively the better. There is no need to preach it. When natural law is preached, the alleged identification of moral law and natural law is revealed as a mere predication, and the fundamental difference between the two is disclosed. Therefore, whatever be the position with regard to the possible congruence of the moral action with a natural event, we cannot evade the question of a specific moral law as distinguished from natural law.

Again, morality in the sense of the ethical problem is not merely the conformity of human behaviour with a more or less widespread and prevalent usage, custom, culture or civilisation. Here, too, a congruence may well occur, and moral philosophers like H. Hœffding and Friedrich Paulsen have been able to approximate very closely to an " identification " of the ethical with these concepts. But so far no one has seriously attempted to merge moral philosophy completely in the science of custom. Indeed, it could never be seriously contested that immoral customs on the one side and moral breaches of custom on the other side are possibilities with which ethics has inevitably to reckon. But this means that even for the law of human behaviour as this is ascertained by the historico-morphological method, the question of a specific ethical law remains.

And morality in the sense of the ethical question is not at all the same as the congruence of human behaviour with the existing laws of the state. It is far more than legality. State law with its obvious generality may of course, as Jeremy Bentham maintained, be understood as the most pregnant expression of the constant of human behaviour which ethics has to investigate. And, conversely, morality may be understood, as in the teaching of H. Cohen, as the immanent power of all legality. There can be little doubt that in one form or another many positivist and idealistic moral philosophers have had dreams or visions of a mutual approximation of morality and law and their meeting in infinity. But it has never yet occurred to anyone seriously to assert a simple equation of ethics and politics, of ethics and jurisprudence. The ethical question is still a specific one even alongside that of the law of the just state. It is only after the former that the latter question, and that of the connexion between the two, can be put.

Finally, in the sense of the ethical question a particular human action is not moral just because it agrees with what is perhaps a demonstrable law of general development or of a specific historical development. There may well be a philosophy of history, and therefore a law of historical development, e.g., that which was proclaimed by Karl Marx in application of Hegelian theory, or that which was more recently proclaimed in words and acts by Neo-German Nationalism. But obviously the establishment of these laws is one thing, and the active affirmation which is so stormily demanded another. History may stand under this or that law ; but if this is the case, why are we assured by those who maintain these laws that history must be *made* by men with much toil and sacrifice, with many conflicts and tribulations. Why is this claim raised ? A different law of human volition and action obviously intervenes, and it is only if this other law is sure and valid that the same can be said of the so-called law of history, and the demand that this law should be obeyed can have authority and force. The question of the validity of this other law, the ethical question, is still open—and the more so, the more violently people try to ignore it, the more wildly they anticipate the answer to it.

If we try to equate the ethical question unequivocally and consistently with the psychological, or historico-morphological, or politico-juridical, or philosophico-historical question—to which the actuality of human behaviour may also be subject—this means that we have not yet put to ourselves the ethical question, or have ceased to put it. And the strange thing is that while there is apparently a desire to make this equation, no one is able to do it. The strange thing is that in all these identifications the fact is only too apparent that they are actually only predications. The ethical question can no doubt be translated into all sorts of other questions. But this does not stop it from being put in its original language. To declare that any one of these laws is valid in the sense of daring to demand subjection to this law is consciously or unconsciously to work with a presupposed ethic. The only thing is that it has obviously been decided to avoid the scrutiny of ethics by not putting the question of its law, the question of the moral law, and therefore the question of the authority and force of the demands made in its name. What cannot be avoided, however, is that the ethical question remains open in face of every arbitrary ethic and its demands and the corresponding human actions, and that one day it will claim to be posed and answered again specifically and for itself. For to put the ethical question, the question of the moral law, is to put it specifically and for itself, irrespective of the question of those other laws. The ethical question transcends those other questions. For it asks concerning the genuineness and rightness and value of the constants which are at issue in those other questions, and to which genuineness and rightness and value are all too uncritically attributed. The ethical question asks concerning the validity of the laws of human behaviour ascertained on the basis of these other questions. It asks concerning the law of the good, and the connexion between this law and those other laws and the human behaviour which is in conformity with them. It raises, then, the fundamental question. Only an answer to this question makes it possible to regard the conformity of human behaviour with those other laws as good, and nonconformity as evil. But, conversely, the answer to it may make it necessary to regard the same conformity as evil, and the same nonconformity as good. Therefore in relation to those other questions the ethical question is the supremely critical question. It is supremely critical because it questions not only individual human actions from the standpoint of general modes of action, but also general human modes of action from the standpoint of the good.

Our contention is, however, that the dogmatics of the Christian Church, and basically the Christian doctrine of God, is ethics. This doctrine is, therefore, the answer to the ethical question, the supremely critical question concerning the good in and over every so-called good in human actions and modes of action.

It is the *answer*—this must be our starting-point. But we must be more exact and say that it is the attestation, the " tradition," the repetition of the answer. For the answer is not theology, or the doctrine of God, but their object—the revelation and work of the electing grace of God. But this, the grace of God, *is* the answer to the ethical problem. For it sanctifies man. It claims him for God. It puts him under God's command. It gives predetermination to his self-determination so that he obeys God's command. It makes God's command for him the judgment on what he has done and the order for his future action. The ethical task of the Christian doctrine of God is to attest this answer to the ethical problem. The ethical problem as such, in the sense of that general definition or conception of ethics, is something with which we are not here concerned.

We are not, of course, surprised at the existence of that general conception. We are not surprised that in every age and place—for all the many and varied attempts which have been made—men have never been able to acquiesce in an equation of the good with all the other different continuities in human behaviour. We are not surprised that the question of the good had and has still to crop up as a specific question which transcends the question of these other conformities. And therefore we are not surprised at the different attempts made by man to give himself a human answer to this specific question —with varying degrees of insight into its special nature and in greater or less correspondence to its actual openness compared with all other questions. We are not surprised because by revelation and the work of God's grace this question is actually put as the inescapable question of human existence which is quite incomparable with other questions in weight and urgency and which the answers to others are quite unable to silence. For it is as he acts that man exists as a person. Therefore the question of the goodness and value and rightness, of the genuine continuity of his activity, the ethical question, is no more and no less than the question about the goodness, value, rightness and genuine continuity of his existence, of himself. It is his life-question, the question by whose answer he stands or falls. " To be, or not to be, that is the question." Why ? Because with its answer there is put into effect the decision of the power which disposes absolutely of his existence or non-existence, the power of God. For it is the electing grace of *God* which has placed man under His command from all eternity. The command of God is therefore the truth from which—whether he knows and wants to know it or not—man derives, and which he will not evade. By the decree of the divine covenant with man, the ethical question as the question of human existence is put from all eternity as the question to which, on the basis of revelation and the work of grace, man will himself in some way be the answer. That is why it is such a necessary, a burning question. And that is also why all possible attempts to answer it, all forms of ethics, are so pressing.

Man derives from the grace of God, and therefore he is exposed from the very outset to this question. Before he was, before the world was, God drew him to Himself when he destined him to obedience to His command. But, strangely enough, it is just because of this that the impossible—sin—presses so insistently. For man is not content simply to *be* the answer to this question by the grace of God. He wants to be like God. He wants to know of himself (as God does) what is good and evil. He therefore wants to *give* this answer himself and of himself. So, then, as a result and in prolongation of the fall, we have " ethics," or, rather, the multifarious ethical systems, the attempted human answers to the ethical question. But this question can be solved only as it was originally put—by the grace of God, by the fact that this allows man actually to *be* the answer. Revelation and the work of God's grace are just as opposed to these attempts as they are to sin. From all eternity it is not the will of God to acquiesce in man's presumption and therefore to let man fall into the perdition which is the necessary consequence of his presumption. The grace of God protests against all man-made ethics as such. But it protests positively. It does not only say No to man. It also says Yes. But it does so by completing its own answer to the ethical problem in active refutation, conquest and destruction of all human answers to it. It does this by revealing in Jesus Christ the human image with which Adam was created to correspond and could no longer do so when he sinned, when he became ethical man. This human image is at the same time God's own image. The man Jesus, who fulfils the commandment of God, does not *give* the answer, but by God's grace He *is* the answer to the ethical question put by God's grace. The sanctification of man, the fact that he is claimed by God, the fulfil- ment of his predetermination in his self-determination to obedience, the judgment of God on man and His command to him in its actual concrete fulfilment—they all take place here in Jesus Christ. The good is done here—really the good as understood critically—beyond all that merely pretends to be called good. But it is not done because, like Hercules at the cross-roads, this man chooses between good and evil and is good on the basis of His choice of the good. The Son, who is obedient to the Father, could not possibly want to ask and decide what is good and evil. He could not possibly regard as the good that which He had chosen for Himself as such. No, it is as He is elected by the grace of God that the good is done. As this Elect, quite apart from any choice of His own between good and evil, He is concerned only with obedience. He does not crave to be good of and for Himself. And so in all His acts He is subject only to the will and command of the God who alone is good. This is how the good is done here. This is how the ethical question is answered here—in Jesus Christ. What has taken place in this way—in antithesis and contrast to all human ethics—is divine ethics.

To go behind this divine ethics, behind its attestation, is quite impossible. We cannot understand the ethical question as the question of human existence as if it were posed in a vacuum, as if there were an ethical question in itself and for itself, as if it were not first posed by the grace of God—and not only posed but already answered by the grace of God. We cannot act as if the command of God, issued by God's grace to the elect man Jesus Christ, and again by God's grace already fulfilled by this man, were not already known to us as the sum total of the good. We cannot act as if we had to ask and decide of ourselves what the good is and how we can achieve it; as if we were free to make this or that answer as the one that appears to us to be right. Certainly the existence of that general conception of ethics as an answer to the question of the good is an exceedingly instructive fact. It confirms the truth of the grace of God which as it is addressed to man puts the question of the good with such priority over all others that man cannot evade it and no other question can completely hide or replace it. But in so far as this general conception of ethics seems to speak of an answer to the question which is to be worked out by man himself, it confirms also that man tries to escape the grace of God by which the question of the good is put, but by which it is also answered in advance. Strange as it may seem, that general conception of ethics coincides exactly with the conception of sin. So we have every reason to treat it with circumspection. We do take up again the question of the good and we try to answer it. But there can be no more trying to escape the grace of God. On the contrary, we have to try to prevent this escape. When we speak of ethics, the term cannot include anything more than this confirmation of the truth of the grace of God as it is addressed to man. If dogmatics, if the doctrine of God, is ethics, this means necessarily and decisively that it is the attestation of that *divine* ethics, the attestation of the good of the command issued to Jesus Christ and fulfilled by Him. There can be no question of any other good in addition to this. Other apparent goods are good only in dependence on this good. And the acknowledgment of this good must have absolute precedence of its investigation. In the strict sense, all investigation of the good can be only an investigation of its explanation (self-explanation) and confirmation (self-confirmation). The ethical problem which we have to answer can be an open problem only in the sense and to the extent that our human life and will and action áre put in question by the command of God and the revelation of the good which takes place in it, that is, as they are questioned as to their correctness, but also corrected; as they are tested as to their value and genuineness, but also invested with genuineness and value.

We have to realise how far-reaching is this change in the conception of ethics. From the point of view of the general history of ethics, it means an annexation of the kind that took place on the entry of the children of Israel into Palestine. Other peoples had for a long time maintained that they had a very old, if not the oldest, right of domicile in this country. But, according to Josh. 9²⁷, they could now at best exist only as hewers of wood and drawers of water. On no account had the Israelites to adopt or take part in their cultus and culture. Their liveliest resistance, therefore, could be expected, and their existence would necessarily be for the Israelites an almost invincible temptation. Ethics in the sense of that general conception is something entirely different from what alone the Christian doctrine of God can be as a doctrine of God's command. Whatever form the relationship between the two may take, there can be no question either of a positive recognition of Christian ethics by that conception or of an attachment of Christian ethics to it. Christian ethics cannot possibly be its continuation, development and enrichment. It is not one disputant in debate with others. It is the final word of the original chairman—only discussed, of course, in Christian ethics—which puts an end to the discussion and involves necessarily a choice and separation.

When the ethical thinker who starts out from that general conception encounters the attestation of the command of God in the Christian doctrine of God, he finds himself precipitated into a strange world because he is confronted by an enigmatic knowledge of the Whence ? and Whither ? of all ethical enquiry and reply. This violates at its nerve centre what usually passes for ethical reflection and explanation. As we cannot disguise this in relation to the doctrine of God, it is something which we can only have or not have. It presupposes a fundamental decision which, described in the categories of revelation and faith, undoubtedly means an unprecedented demand, if not worse. The problem of ethics generally—the law or good or value which it seeks as a standard by which human action and modes of action are to be measured, and according to which they are to be performed, the problem of the truth and knowledge of the good—is no problem at all in the ethics immanent in the Christian conception of God, in the doctrine of the command of God. For in virtue of the fact that the command of God is the form of His electing grace, it is the starting-point of every ethical question and answer. It is the starting-point which is already given and to that extent presupposed and certain in itself, so that it can never be surpassed or compromised from any quarter. And, conversely, that which is no problem at all to ethical thought generally, or only a problem which can be lightly pushed aside and left open—the actual situation of man in face of the question by which he is confronted when he answers the ethical question, his actual commitment to the good, his actual distance from it and the actual overcoming of this distance (not by himself, but by the actuality of the good itself)—this is the burning problem in Christian ethics, the very aim and content of the whole ethical enquiry and reply. When a doctrine, or science, is dominated by the knowledge of this Whence ? and Whither ?, what can it possibly have to do with what is usually understood as ethics within the framework of that general conception ? Certainly when we proceed from this knowledge we cannot fail to see that here, too, it seems in some way to be a matter of the investigation of the goodness of human action. But this " in some way " is obviously of such a kind that it appears almost impossible to avoid the judgment that the undertaking of ethics, as it is undertaken here, really means the negation of this undertaking. For, when the starting-point is the conception of God as the given and presupposed sum of the good, when it is the truth—conceived as actuality—of a command, directed to man and absolutely supreme and decisive ; or conversely, when man is the sinner who by the grace of God is as absolutely condemned as he is absolutely raised up and righted—the ethical answer is made impossible. This is the opposition which we must expect and face when we subject the conception of ethics to this change. We must stand firm against this opposition. It may easily be forgotten on our side that the Word of God, and in its faithful proclamation the preaching of the Church, and with preaching dogmatics, and at the head of dogmatics the Christian doctrine of God, are always the aggressor in relation to everything else, to general human thinking and language. When they enter the field of ethical reflection and interpretation they must not be surprised at the contradiction of the so-called (but only so-called) original inhabitants of this land. They cannot regard them as an authority before which they have to exculpate themselves, and to whose arrangements they must in some way conform. The temptation to behave as if they were required or even permitted to do this is one which must be recognised for what it is and avoided.

This temptation might perhaps consist in the invitation or challenge to embark upon an apologetic debate with the protest which can and actually will be made by a general conception of ethics. Apologetics in this case would be the attempt to establish and justify the theologico-ethical inquiry within the framework and on the foundation of the presuppositions and methods of non-theological, of wholly human thinking and language.

It is apologetics when Schleiermacher (*Chr. Sitte*, p. 29 and 75) maintains that, not the specifically Christian self-consciousness, but the general religious self-consciousness which is supposed to underlie it, with its moral content or its moral orientation, is a necessary element even in a general philosophico-ethical enquiry, and when in so doing he tries to justify Christian ethics at least indirectly before the forum of philosophical ethics. Similarly, when De Wette (*Lehrb. d. chr. Sittenlehre*, 1833, p. 2) thinks he can glorify the revelation from which Christian ethics derives by characterising it as " the reason which has appeared and been realised . . . or the completed task of the pious life." Similarly, when K. R. Hagenbach (*Enzyklopädie*[12], 1889, p. 436) directs philosophical ethics to the Christian goal at which alone it finds its fulfilment, since faith in God, even regarded from this general standpoint, presents itself as " the highest stage of the moral life." Similarly, when W. Herrmann (*Ethik*[4], 1909, p. 3) declares that every ethics which tries to deal, not only with the conception of the good, but also with the realisation of the good by men, must see to it that the Christian religion is understood as a morally emancipating force, and must therefore itself become Christian ethics at its supreme point. Similarly, when G. Wünsch (*Theol. Ethik*, 1925, p. 59 f.) tries to understand Christian ethics as a possibility of " value-attitude " which is foreseen in general philosophical ethics, i.e., as the affirmation of a definite " value-position "—that the " holy as really known in the form of personality " is the supreme value " anchored in the transcendent " ; and when he recommends it at the same time on the basis of the fact that its formal criteria are identical with those of philosophical ethics.

Our comment is that the super- and subordination of viewpoints with which it is hoped to establish and justify the theologico-ethical enquiry, cannot actually accomplish what it meant to accomplish. The only possible meaning of this apologetic is a sincere conviction that theological ethics must be measured against a general ethics. For the latter is recognised as its judge, as the authority by which even for it the question of truth is raised and decided. It is presupposed that the proper content of theological enquiry and reply (or at any rate a kind of empty place for it) is comprehended in general ethical enquiry and reply, that this is where it has its original and proper place, and that this place has only to be indicated to give the desired legal basis for the existence of a theological ethics. But what can be legitimated in this way, what can be indicated as included in the content of a general ethical enquiry and reply, is certainly not the distinctively theological enquiry and reply in which we have to do with the grace of God in the issuing and fulfilling of His command. The ethical bent of the religious self-consciousness, a " value-attitude " and the like, may be justified in this way, but not the attestation of the commandment of God as the form of His grace. This theme is automatically lost when the apology succeeds. For the man who—as a philosopher perhaps, or even as a politician—thinks that he knows a general principle which is actually superior to the origin and aim of theologico-ethical enquiry and reply, and who in the matter of the doctrine of God thinks that he can actually step forward as judge in the question of truth, a theological ethic with its Whence ? and Whither ? will necessarily be an objectionable undertaking, which he will regard either as insignificant or even perhaps as dangerous. And theological ethics on its part will cease to be what it is, if it dares to free itself from this offensiveness, if it dares to submit to a general principle, to let itself be measured by it and adjusted to it. Here, as elsewhere, we cannot concede to any other authority the competence to decide in a way which is binding even for theology what may or may not be a principle in matters of human knowledge and science. We cannot interpret the distinctive principle of theology in such a way as to win for it the recognition that, judged from some other principle of this sort, it is possible or perhaps even necessary. We

cannot translate the truth and reality of the divine command into a
necessary element of man's spiritual life, or the realisation of human
reason, or the realisation of the good as achieved by man himself, or
a value-position anchored in the transcendent. We can only do that
if we are no longer concerned with the command of God and therefore
if we have not really been treating of theological ethics even from the
outset. For the man who obediently hears the command of God is
not in any position to consider why he must obey it. He is not in any
position, therefore, from the vantage-point of a higher principle to try
to show either himself or others how this law of human volition and
action is reached. He knows that the command of God is not founded
on any other command, and cannot therefore be derived from any
other, or measured by any other, or have its validity tested by any
other. He knows that man cannot say this command to himself, but
can only have it said to him. He has not invented this principle of
theological ethics, and he cannot evade or even so much as conceal
it. He has not given it its offensive character, and he cannot try to
take it away. If he himself is at first surprised at having to come to
terms with this Whence ? and Whither ? of ethical inquiry and reply,
he cannot spare others the surprise of seeing him actually engaged in
this process. Much can be demanded of him, but what is demanded
in the opinion of the adherents of an apologetico-theological ethics is
not actually demanded. On the contrary, this is the very thing which
is forbidden him, for to fulfil this demand is to abandon the ethical
task of the doctrine of God before it is even begun.

The concern of the apologetic school of theological ethics in its
recourse to a general moral enquiry and reply can, of course, be recognised as justifiable upon one condition : that is, if in its annexation
of the realm of general ethical problems theological ethics behaves as
the Israelites did or should have done on their entry into Canaan.
They had to invade Canaan, not as a foreign country which did not
belong to them, but as the land of their fathers. Had it not for a
long time belonged to Yahweh ? Had He not for many years spoken
to Abraham, Isaac and Jacob in this very land ? Was it not, therefore, the land which was promised and actually belonged to them as
the people of Yahweh ? This means that theological ethics has to
accept the fact that it must not believe in the possibility and reality
of a general moral enquiry and reply which are originally and ultimately independent of the grace and command of God, which are not
touched or affected by them and to that extent stand inflexible and
inviolate in themselves. It has to accept the fact that it must believe
in the work and revelation of the grace of God alone and therefore in
the actual overlordship of God's command over the whole realm of
ethical problems. It has not to reckon with man's possession of a
kind of moral nature, with a knowledge of good and evil which is
peculiar to him, and of which he is capable apart from the fact that

he is under the overlordship of the divine command. It has, therefore, to be on its guard against a retrospective reinterpretation of the fall, as though the presumption of man in wishing to know of himself what is good and evil were only a natural inclination to do the will of God. It has to be on its guard against conferring on man the dignity of a judge over God's command. Conversely, it will regard the revelation of the grace of God as so true—so very much the revelation of the actual involvement of man—and the work of grace as so powerful—so very much the decision which God has actually made about man—that, whatever attitude man may take up or however he may act in relation to God's command, it necessarily understands him as actually determined by God's command, as altogether orientated by it objectively. It will not accredit or adjudge to him a moral enquiry and reply which are actually independent of God's command —in spite of and in the presumption which makes him think that out of his own resources, he knows what is good and evil. Itself proclaiming and explaining the command of God, it can and should, on this condition and presupposition, appeal to what F. C. Oetinger called the *sensus communis*, the rule of truth imposed on all men as such by the divine wisdom active and revealed in Jesus Christ—and not, therefore, to a knowledge which belongs to man, which man controls, but to a knowledge addressed to him and controlling him. It will not, then, make the disastrous, traitorous use of " natural " theology, which is the only use that can be made of it. On the contrary, it will assert the theology which derives from God's revelation in that pre-eminence in face of all " natural " theology which belongs to it if revelation is revelation and is believed as such. Therefore, when it turns to this general moral enquiry and reply, it will do so with the understanding that it has its origin and meaning from the divine command which objectively applies to man, whatever attitude man may take to it. It will understand that the ethical question is so urgent because there is no escape from divine grace and its command, not even for those who would like to evade it ; and that it is put so stringently because in the first instance the command of grace is so stringent, because the grace of God itself is so inward and penetrating. When it is understood in this way, why should not the general ethical enquiry and reply be for theological ethics a witness to the ethical knowledge which has itself to present, and which is to be acquired from, the divine command of God ? To that extent, why should it not have a legitimate place in the discussion ? Why should it not give ear at the point where—as it knows and maintains against all protest—the one Word of God is also objectively spoken and prevails even in the midst of human perversity ? Why should it not be ready to receive instruction and correction from the source where the Word of God, although it is so fully concealed, is also in force, knowing so well, as it does, that of itself it can only attest and explain this Word with a human voice and therefore fallibly ? Without detriment to its loyalty to its own task, indeed, in its very loyalty to it in this aspect too, theological ethics can and must establish a continuous relationship of its thinking and speaking with the human ethical problem as a whole. It does this when it believes that finally and properly its own Whence ? and Whither ? are not alien to any philosophic moralist, when it does not take seriously his possible opposition to this Whence ? and Whither ? (because this opposition cannot be maintained, because it cannot be serious), but regards and addresses him unswervingly on the basis that grace, and therefore the command of God, affects him too. But this relationship must not in any circumstances take the form of apologetics. It rests on the assumption and consists in the substantiation that this annexation is right. The counter-position attacked by theological ethics is obviously in a state of disintegration and the opposition offered from it cannot be sustained. The one thing which will not happen in this relationship is that theological ethics will try to eliminate from its own task the alien element which from that point of view necessarily characterises it. Annexation remains annexation, however legal it may be, and there must be no armistice with the peoples of Canaan and their culture and their cultus. Therefore theological ethics must not and will not disarm its distinctive Whence ? and Whither ? in order to assure itself a place in the sun of general ethical discussion. What it must and should disarm is the opposition which confronts it in the discussion—which was disarmed long ago by the death and resurrection of Jesus Christ. But it must not disarm itself, because it cannot do this without destroying itself. It will be absolutely open to all that it can learn from general human ethical enquiry and reply. It can be absolutely open because it has absolutely nothing to fear from this quarter. But it must always be absolutely resolved to stick to its colours and not to allow itself to be hindered in the fulfilment of its own task. The attempt to set up general ethics as a judge, and to prove and justify theological ethics before it, can only disturb and destroy theological ethics. The attempt must, therefore, be broken off. The apologetic orientation of theological ethics is false. The apologetic attitude must be completely abandoned.

But the temptation which comes from the opposition to theological ethics might take a very different form, or one that is apparently very different. The desired adjustment to general ethical thinking and language can be undertaken in the form of a proper isolation of theological ethics from the former, of a suitable allocation of roles to the two. The attempt can be made to show that, whatever may be the interconnexion between them, there is a twofold ethical inquiry, let us say, a " theological " and a " philosophical," which touch and limit but do not abolish each other. By an ultimately friendly demarcation of the difference between the two, the special task of theological ethics can be defined and preserved, and an attempt made to assure its formal compatibility with that of ethics generally.

In spite of all apologetics, theology has never so completely forgotten the peculiar nature of its task and activity as not to recover its self-consciousness at some point. The proof of the basis and justification of its task and activity has always been fulfilled in some way in the proof of its independence, its distinctness, its particular character in contrast to the task and activity of the non-theological moralist. The reckoning which is considered necessary in relation to philosophy succeeds only too well if its result is that theological ethics itself is simply philosophical ethics, a special form of general ethics. That is obviously what must not happen, although it has nearly done so on occasion, e.g., with W. Herrmann. On the contrary, once theology has legitimated itself apologetically, it then has to show, either well or badly, that it is not superfluous, not a mere double of philosophy. Some separate or additional knowledge must now be claimed in face of the general knowledge of good and evil, and the attempt must be made to define this more closely. What is usually said along this line can be comprehended under four heads.

(1) A special source of theological ethics is affirmed. Sometimes, as in E. W. Mayer (*Ethik*, 1922, p. 191) it is termed the so-called Christian religious consciousness and then the task of theological ethics is defined with Schleiermacher (*op. cit.*, p. 33) as "the description of the way of acting which arises from the domination of the Christianly determined self-consciousness." Instead of speaking of this consciousness, De Wette (*op. cit.*, p. 2), O. Kirn (*Grundriss der theologischen Ethik*, 1906, p. 2) and Wünsch (*op. cit.*, p. 64) can speak of "revelation," but they mean the same thing. In contrast to this, De Wette and E. W. Mayer describe reason as the source of philosophical ethics, Kirn experience, and Wünsch reason and experience together. In all cases it is obviously a self-consciousness which is not Christianly determined.

(2) A special subject of theological ethics is affirmed. As Schleiermacher especially (*op. cit.*, p. 33 f.) emphasises so strongly, its locus is the Church, understood as a community of those who share the Christian outlook. According to Wünsch, the subject of theological ethics is "the man who is born again through conversion and to whom the knowledge of God has been imparted through illumination." For this reason, as Schleiermacher expressly states (p. 29), theological ethics lacks "a universal-historical relevance." "What is ordered by Christian morals binds only Christians. Philosophical ethics makes a more general claim, for it would bind everyone who can rise to an insight into the philosophical principles from which it is derived" (*op. cit.*, p. 2). According to Wünsch, it is "the man of reason" who is the subject of philosophical ethics.

(3) A special presupposition of theological ethics is affirmed. According to K. R. Hagenbach (p. 436), it consists in the "Spirit of God or of Christ as the power operating in believers," or, according to Kirn (p. 3), in the "living energy of the personality filled with God's Spirit," although as against this the same writer finds the presupposition of philosophical ethics in man's moral or rational self-determination. According to Wünsch, the question of philosophical ethics is: "What must I do because the categorical imperative orders?", whereas that of theological ethics is: "What must I do because God is?"

And (4) a special content of theological ethics is affirmed. According to Hagenbach, this consists in "historically determined moral views," and, above all, in the "personal divine-human view of life of the Redeemer"; or, according to De Wette, in "positive laws"; or, according to Kirn, in the "idea of the kingdom of God;" while Hagenbach attributes to philosophical ethics "the idea of moral personality which is valid for all who would be rational beings."

But the diastasis attempted in this way is no less suspect than the synthesis of the two spheres which we have already mentioned and discussed. For what really happens? If this procedure is carried out seriously, we have a theological ethics which is concerned only with the human behaviour which originates under the dominion of the Christian self-consciousness as determined by special revelation or religion, and in the sphere of the corresponding historical outlook. The statements of this ethics are binding only for Church members, for believers, although they are, of course, to be fulfilled by them, because the Spirit of God is active in them. And in contrast to this, there is a philosophical ethics which can be traced back just as abstractly to reason or experience or both. This, for its part, is just as content with the " idea " of the moral, and its last word is the self-determination of man, a word which it does, of course, have to speak with the claim to universal validity. What we have to ask in relation to this view is whether theology can seriously contemplate two things. First, can it really be restricted in this way to a sphere which is no doubt remarkably distinguished by the concepts of religion, revelation, Church, grace, Spirit, etc., but which is characterised as a very narrow and rather obscure sphere by its isolation from the sphere of reason, experience and human self-determination? And secondly, can it really ascribe to reason, experience, human self-determination, etc., an independent content of truth, an autonomous dignity and authority, which in its own preoccupation with revelation and the outpourings of Christian self-consciousness it can safely leave on one side? To put the question differently : Is God's revelation revelation of the truth, or is it only the source of certain religious ideas and obligations, alongside which there are very different ones in other spheres? Outside and alongside the kingdom of Jesus Christ are there other respectable kingdoms? Can and should theology of all things be content to speak, not with universal validity, but only esoterically? Is it, or is it not, serious in its alleged knowledge of a Whence? and Whither? of all ethical enquiry and reply which are superior to all reason, experience and self-determination? If it is serious about this, how can it, even if only for a moment, take seriously and accept the validity of an ethics which necessarily lacks or even disavows this knowledge? How can it liberate this ethics, as it were, by entering into an armistice with it ? How can it imagine that it can secure its own right to exist in this way? Does it really believe in its own theme if it concedes that the other ethics has its source and subject in reason, experience and self-determination?—as if all this did not lie from the very outset in its own sphere, the sphere of theological ethics ; as if it could be right to accept all these quantities as self-evident, to concede autonomy to man's knowledge of good and evil ; as if Jesus Christ had not died and risen again ; as if we could salute the grace of God, as it were, and then go our own way ; as if it were the task of theology positively to encourage and invite people to do this by the establishment of this diastasis. If theological ethics has really to do with God's command, this differentiation obviously belongs to the things which cannot be expected of it. This, too, is forbidden. And this, too, is forbidden, because it would mean that the ethical task of the doctrine of God is abandoned before it is even begun.

The differentiation of theological ethics from other ethics can have meaning only if it is understood either as its purely provisional detachment (to be carried out only γυμναστικῶς) from an ethics whose theological basis has not been made explicit, or as its definitive detachment from an ethics which lacks or even denies this theological basis and is therefore wrong and false and perverted. Its starting-point is that all ethical truth is enclosed in the command of the grace of God—no matter whether this is understood as rational or historical, secular or religious, ecclesiastical or universal ethico-social truth. Just because it recognises its task to be the proclamation and exposition of this command, and therefore thinks and speaks on the basis of God's revelation, it has a place which is not less but all the fuller (because, as it were, from the source) for the voice of reason and experience (or whatever else we may call the supposedly contradictory " philosophical " principles). To speak with universally binding force is an obligation from which it cannot possibly seek exemption. It has to take up the legitimate problems and concerns and motives and assertions of every other ethics as such, and therefore after testing them in the light of its own superior principle. It has to listen to all other ethics in so far as it has to receive from them at every point the material for its own deliberations. To that extent its attitude to every other ethics is not negative but comprehensive. But just because it is comprehensive, it is fundamentally critical and decidedly not one of compromise. It is in agreement with every other ethics adduced to the extent that the latter is obviously aware—explicitly or implicitly —of its origin and basis in God's command ; to the extent that it does not seek authorisation before any other court ; to the extent that it actually attests the existence and validity of this principle. But it cannot and will not take it seriously to the extent that it tries to deny or obscure its derivation from God's command, to set up independent principles in face of autonomies and heteronomies which compromise the theonomy of human existence and action, to confront divine ethics with a human view of the world and of life which is supposed to have its own (if anything) superior value, and to undertake the replacement of the command of the grace of God by a sovereign humanism or even barbarism. In the former respect it will meet the other ethics comprehensively. But in the latter it can only meet it exclusively. The exclusion means that in this latter respect it can only address and deal with it as wrong and false and perverted, and therefore not really as ethics at all. On the one side, therefore, it absorbs it into itself, and on the other it opposes it. But either way, it renounces openly the motive which lurks secretly behind that division of roles. It is obviously no longer content to assign separate tasks to itself and other ethics. Either way, it necessarily accepts full responsibility for handling the whole problem of ethics—and not merely of an esoteric ethics which appeals to special sources and proceeds according to a special method, but of ethics generally and as such. In so doing, it also dismisses the last relic of apologetics which underlies this differentiation of tasks. But in view of its principle, and presupposing that it takes this seriously and does not itself abandon it, it obviously has no alternative.

But we have still to take into account a third possible way of defining the relationship between theological ethics and other ethics. This is the Roman Catholic view of the matter, and both historically and materially it merits the closest attention. There is this at least to be said in its favour, that it perceives the doubtful elements in both apologetics and differentiation, and, allowing for the questionableness of the basic Roman Catholic view as such, is not altogether unsuccessful in avoiding or at any rate concealing them. We certainly cannot accuse it directly of either surrender of theology to the authority and judgment of principles alien to it, or escaping into the narrow confines of a special theological task. Universal human morality, the natural morality represented by a wholesome philosophy, is decisively claimed by it (*anima humana naturaliter christiana*), not as theological, but certainly as Christian morality. And it is recognised and treated as an equal partner for theological morality, whose voice the latter must consistently hear, although never granting it real precedence. Two ethical sciences which are to be distinguished but never separated— moral philosophy and moral theology—are mutually co-ordinated, and mutually presuppose and complete each other, in the teaching of Roman Catholic moralists. They are always interconnected in a personal union. Yet the relationship is not one of equilibrium, but of disequilibrium. From the very outset moral theology is the pivot of the eccentric wheel, and it can never lose this position. Moral philosophy has its own natural centre, but it is also caught up in this movement.

Two different, and in themselves equally worthy, problem-complexes are ranged in a necessarily fixed gradation. Moral philosophy is, as it were, the lower, and moral theology the upper storey of one and the same structure. Moral philosophy recognises the principles of moral behaviour as it is taught by experience and history, using the light of the natural reason which is proper to all men as such and which is in a limited way capable of performing this function. It apprehends moral principles as rational principles in the same sense as it apprehends the laws of logic. It knows them as the imperative which has its roots in man's very being, although it is, of course, liable to go very far astray if in its assertions it does not also follow the light of revelation which comes streaming towards it. It sees, then, that the destiny of man is to glorify God the Creator by his existence as creature and in this way to prepare himself for eternal bliss. It sees that the moral good, as it is to be practised in the four philosophical virtues of prudence, justice, fortitude and temperance, is that which corresponds to the rational nature of man. But it knows it as the good which is only relative good : relative, that is, to the absolute good, the highest good, the divine being, which is the idea of the good. Communion with this is at once the source and the sum of the human bliss which constitutes the ultimate aim of human action. As opposed to this, moral theology draws its knowledge directly from the springs of revelation, from Holy Scripture, from tradition and from the assertions of the teaching office of the Church. Its presupposition is the healing and exaltation of fallen man within the order of grace. Its task is to exhibit the supernatural morality by which alone man is in fact led to that goal, to develop the positive Christian moral law, and the universal and particular duties which follow from it, and supremely the three theological virtues of faith, love and hope. But if grace is indeed a higher element of life, completely different from the natural constitution of man, the effect of its administration and impartation is " at once a healing and renewing of nature from the disorder of sin and a raising of nature to mysterious godlikeness and ˙divine sonship " (J. Mausbach, " Chr. Kath. Ethik " in *Kultur der Gegenwart*, I, 4, p. 540). The law of the new covenant regulating this renewal forms " a striking parallel to natural law " (p. 523). On the one hand, " the unfolding of the purposes and laws immanent in creatures includes for the rational being the development of their personal endowments to beatifying God-possession " (p. 534), and, on the other hand, " the universally maintained axiom : *Gratia non destruit, sed supponit et perficit naturam* recognises the persistence of man even after original sin, activates his moral-religious endowment with the attainment of justification, and maintains within the life of grace the moral necessity of natural thinking and willing " (p. 540). This is the construction of the relationship with which we are concerned. There were indications of it in the Early Church ; it was given its characteristic features by Thomas Aquinas ; and in the course of the centuries it went through a process of continual elaboration and extending application by Roman theology. Taken as a whole, it is a bold " combination of Aristotle and Augustine " (p. 527) with all the possibilities of free individual movements to right and left which this involves.

We hardly need compare this construction with the uncertainty and confusion of the corresponding Neo-Protestant proposals to be forced to acknowledge that what we have here is on any count a very imposing, indeed in its way a classical, attempt at a solution. Does it not maintain that the knowledge of God must necessarily be one and the same ultimate and proper presupposition not only of theological but also of all ethics ? Is it not shown that theological ethics—deriving like every other ethics from this ultimate knowledge, but drawing incomparably much more illumination from it—cannot possibly allow this other ethics to put and answer the question of truth, as though it were an exercise set and corrected by it ? Could it not give us the necessary irenic and polemic—the claiming and acknowledging of other ethics in respect of the remnants of that presupposition still to be found in them, and the rejection of all other ethics in so far as they do not know or indeed deny this presupposition ? At a first glance we may even be tempted to regard this solution as ideal. And if we were compelled to choose between the Neo-Protestant and the Roman Catholic solutions, in this as in so many other questions we should have no option but to prefer the latter. Yet in spite of all this we cannot really be satisfied with it. Within this framework the command of the grace of God as the content of theological ethics definitely cannot have the status which properly belongs to it.

For this Roman Catholic co-ordination of moral philosophy and moral theology is based on the basic view of the harmony which is achieved in the concept of being between nature and super-nature, reason and revelation, man and God. And it is quite impossible to see how in this basic view grace can really emerge as grace and the command as command. According to this view, the fall does not alter the fact that man's imitative knowledge is capable and to that extent partakes of true being even without grace, and therefore—*analogia entis*—of communion with the supreme essential being, with God, and therefore with the supreme good, although on account of the fall a special illumination by the grace of revelation is needed actually to prevent it from falling into error. Indeed, the knowledge of God and therefore of the good offered to man has been made so difficult by the fall that as a rule, or at any rate in its whole depth, it does not become real without grace, *gratia sanans et elevans naturam*. Yet the fall has not made this knowledge absolutely impossible. A remnant is left of the adjustment of man to God in creation. In virtue of this, even without grace he can know that God is, and that He is one and spiritual and personal. And to some extent at least he can also know the good which God requires of him. Similarly, his volition in regard to that which he ought to will is no doubt enfeebled, but it is not enslaved to the obedience of sin. And on this basis, on this unimpaired *liberum arbitrium*, Roman doctrine claims that the *anima humana* is *christiana naturaliter* and not *gratuito* ; and on the strength of this, that the light of natural reason is the principle of knowledge in its moral philosophy. The same ordination of man to God, of nature to super-nature, which is not conferred and constituted in spite of the fall, but maintained and continued in spite of the fall, and which is natural, as deriving from creation, is the connecting point by which the moral theology which is ostensibly based on grace alone, and derives from Scripture and dogma, has actually to be orientated. Whatever its superiority may be to moral philosophy, it cannot exist except as super-structure upon that sub-structure. If it is this which legitimates the latter, it is the latter which carries it. And whatever it will have to say of special theological virtues and duties, it will not say it in respect of a subject newly created by the grace of God, but in respect of the subject who is fully capable of knowing and doing the good, and therefore even without the grace of God the subject of the Christian behaviour which is under consideration.

This presupposition of the Roman Catholic construction is in every respect unacceptable. Strong opposition must be made to the idea that the metaphysics of being, the starting-point of this line of thought, is the place from which we can do the work of Christian theology, from which we can see and describe grace and nature, revelation and reason, God and man, both as they are in themselves and in their mutual relationship. The harmony in which they are co-ordinated within this system is surreptitious. For what has that metaphysics of being to do with the God who is the basis and Lord of the Church ? If this God is He who in Jesus Christ became man, revealing Himself and reconciling the world with Himself, it follows that the relationship · between Him and man consists in the event in which God accepted man out of pure, free compassion, in which He drew him to Himself out of pure kindness, but first and last in the eternal decree of the covenant of grace, in God's eternal predestination. It is not with the theory of the relationship between creaturely and creative being, but with the theory of this divine praxis, with the consideration and conception of this divine act, of its eternal decree and its temporal execution, that theology, and therefore theological ethics, must deal. But since it has to deal with this theory, preoccupation with the relationship between creaturely and creative being, the doctrine of the " analogy " subsisting between the two, has necessarily to be condemned as a perilous distraction. From this standpoint we can only issue a warning against the harmony between heaven and earth which is achieved on the basis of this very different theory, and against the falsification of all theological conceptions which is inevitable on the basis of this very different theory. Grace which has from the start to share its power with a force of nature is no longer grace, i.e., it cannot be recognised as what the grace of God is in the consideration and conception of that divine act, as what it is in Jesus Christ. And therefore revelation which has from the very outset a partner in the reason of the creature, and which cannot be revelation without its co-operation, is no longer revelation. At any rate, it is not the revelation which takes place in the act in which God opens Himself to man in pure goodness ; in which He does not find an existing partner in man, but creates a partner ; in which even the fact that God is known and knowable is the work of His freedom. And therefore, when from the very outset man is co-ordinated with God on the basis of this analogy—not in the humanity of Jesus Christ and therefore on the basis of God's own free decree, but simply in his metaphysical being as a rational creature—God is no longer God. At any rate, He is not the God who from all eternity has made all fellowship between Himself and men the content of the will of His love. The concepts of grace and revelation and God as they derive from the knowledge of the will and act of God in Jesus Christ are not adapted to be applied as they are in the Roman Catholic system. They burst through this system. And if this is true, the same is also to be said of the concept of sin. In discussion with Roman Catholic theology it is better not to start from this negative concept, for what we have to say about it can be seen only in the light of these positive concepts. It is because the grace of God, as it is defined in relation to Jesus Christ and therefore to that divine act, is His free gift to man, because revelation includes the creation of the God-knowing subject, because the love of God and that love alone accomplishes and is the co-ordination of man with God, that we have to deny to man the aptitude to co-operate with grace, revelation and God. It is for these reasons that the co-ordination which God effects cannot be interpreted as a disposition which is proper to man. And it is for the same reasons that we cannot accept that merely relative and quantitative scope and significance of the fall, that doctrine of the nature of man which regards it as merely sick, deranged and impotent, that talk of a remnant of the original divine image and likeness which remains in spite of the fall. This explains why we have to object against Roman doctrine that with its doctrine of the surviving *liberum arbitrium* it misunderstands and distorts in the most dangerous way the seriousness of sin and therefore the seriousness of the human situation in relation to God. Accusing it of a misplaced optimism, we have not to oppose to it a corresponding pessimism, but the twofold question : whether Roman doctrine does not see that it is precisely the knowledge of the kindness of God which makes its optimistic judgment of man impossible ; and why it shuts itself off from a knowledge of the kindness of God by finally turning its eyes away from Jesus Christ in the question of grace, revelation and God, and looking to the height or depth of a metaphysics of being in which it thinks it has found that original union between heaven and earth, that far too beautiful harmony, and, as a note in that harmony, the irreducible creaturely disposition of man to God. Only when the mind is distracted is it possible to speak of man in this way.

Thus the central task of the Protestant irenic and polemic in relation to Roman Catholic theology is to recall it from this distraction to its proper business, the Christian theme. For in this distraction it is particularly incapable of establishing the concept of the divine command, and therefore introducing serious theological ethics. The order of obligation built on the order of being cannot as such be a real order of obligation, or at any rate of a divinely imperative obligation, as introduced in Jesus Christ, in the divine act of the world's reconciliation with God as the act of His pure goodness. If obligation is grounded in being, this undoubtedly means that it is not grounded in itself, but ontically subordinated to another, and noetically to be derived from this other. It is imperative only in virtue of that which is over it ; and it becomes imperative for us only in virtue of its derivation from it. But if what is over it is the being in which man participates in his way as God does in His, how can it be and become imperative except with the assistance and co-operation of man, except on the presupposition of his agreement ? But on this presupposition it is quite impossible that it should confront him, his being and his existence with an absolute challenge ; that it should dominate him and claim him with absolute sovereignty ; that it should have for him the character of majesty ;

that it should be able to meet him and concern him as a command of God. From the very outset man is assured of a right of consultation and control in God's command. Whatever else it may be and mean for him, it can never become for him a command that affects him personally and binds him unconditionally. It can certainly never become a command of *God*, in so far as by God is meant the Lord who in Jesus Christ controls man absolutely and beyond all question by the decree of His mercy. But it is not really this God that Roman theology means when it uses the term. This God is replaced by the divine image of being, the god-concept of ancient philosophy. Now admittedly this divine image can do many things, as is the case with such demon-figures. But it cannot in the true sense of the word command. It can never become an inexorable and indisputable necessity for human action. It cannot place man before the question of his existence or non-existence. Indeed, this is the very question which is expressly excluded. For man exists, and even exists in analogy to God Himself, whether he keeps the command or not. It is no doubt good for him to keep it. It may go ill with him if he does not keep it. But it cannot possibly be for him a matter of life or death. For the command does not have behind it the eternal power and severity of predestination, of the free goodness of God. The binding force of the reconciliation which has taken place between the world and God is something which it cannot have.

But all this applies as much to the moral theology of Romanism as to its moral philosophy, to its Aristotelian teaching on virtue as to its Pauline. For the decisive misunderstanding of God and man is not confined to the sub-structure but affects the whole edifice of this moral doctrine. It is no help to the moral philosophy that it tries to pay attention not only to the natural light of reason, but also to the light of revelation, and therefore from the very outset to give the desired theological shape and finish to the determination of man. Nor, again, is it any help to the moral theology that it tries to focus attention on the light of revelation and only incidentally attends also to the natural light of reason. For in both cases, first in the foreground and then in the background, everything is compromised by the fact that revelation is not really accepted as revelation, but is constantly set against the light of reason with its independent, if limited, illumination. Neither in the one case nor the other can there be any attestation or explanation of the divine command (or, if there is, it can only be the result of a happy inconsistency in relation to the whole system). The enterprise of theological ethics is not one with which to trifle. It must be taken up properly—and this can mean only on the assumption that the command of the grace of God is its sole content—or it is better left alone. The complaint which we have to make against the Roman construction of the relationship between theological ethics and general human ethics is that it is dominated by this great distraction, and therefore it only plays at theological ethics. It thinks it can combine and co-ordinate the Christian and the human far too easily. To achieve this combination and co-ordination it has emptied out what is Christian. Therefore in spite of its inherent advantages we cannot accept it.

The remarkable thing is that here as elsewhere these inherent advantages—we have mentioned them—cannot be denied to the Roman doctrine. The gross blunders of apologetics and isolationism which are so evident in the theological ethics of Neo-Protestantism have been avoided, or at least they remain invisible. In fact, however, they are avoided or invisible only because they are in some sense committed in principle, and therefore do not need to be committed in particular. Roman theological ethics is the wisest of all mediating systems because it is apologetic from the very outset in its understanding of grace and revelation and God, i.e., because it is an establishment and justification of the Christian position before the forum of general human thought, and accomplishes the fatal assimilation of the Christian to the human. But it is also the wisest because, without any inner conflict, it works with that division of roles, and in this way safeguards its task as theological ethics, although obviously rendering it innocuous. It does not need to expose itself on both sides as in the apologetic and differentiating movements of the theological ethics of Neo-Protestantism, because from the very first, and officially, it finds itself on the very tracks which in Neo-Protestantism are so pitifully revealed to be emergency exits. But this being the case, there is no real reason to prefer it to the theological ethics of Neo-Protestantism.

From the Roman standpoint it is possible to look down on the Neo-Protestant position with such sovereign superiority because it does, in fact, do classically what in the latter is only epigonous. It displays the skill of the master where in the latter we have only a palpable dilettantism. It knows what it is about where the latter does not—where the latter has no intention whatever of being catholic, but thinks that it is administering the heritage of the Reformation in a particularly consistent way. This is the abiding superiority of Roman Catholicism to Neo-Protestantism as it emerges in this matter too. But it is characteristic in both cases that in this matter they do exactly the same thing.

To avoid the appearance of malicious calumny on both sides, let us quote in conclusion what G. Wünsch has to say at the end of his *Theol. Ethik.* (1925, p. 122 f.) on the theme, " Christian and natural Morality."

" 1. As everything has the origin of its being in God and no creature can disown the Creator, there is no opposition in kind between natural, i.e., this-worldly, immanent morality as directed by naturalistic and human criteria, and, on the other hand, Christian morality as determined by the being of God. Only the pure being of the world and man, as these are in themselves apart from sin, must in its pure essentiality determine the laws of the moral. This pure being, which lies at the base of all empirical existence and can be disengaged from it, is the obligating being in the sense of the pure law of nature ; it is the means of the primal revelation which is accessible to every man.

" 2. But Christian morality is directed to the God of the *revelatio specialis* which has taken place in Jesus Christ. It includes natural morality, which, with the help of an overbracketing of values, will always be an idealistic morality, and in content it shoots out beyond it. Its particularity is to give divine sanction to natural morality, to recognise its commands as expressions of God's will effected by creation, and to demand reverence not only for the essence of the world, but also for the being of God. It demands an attitude on the part of man to God which corresponds to the distinctive relationship to Him; the relationship of creature to Creator, or rather, of pardoned sinner to gracious God, a relationship of absolute reverence, love and gratitude."

In Marburg, where this was written, it was not appreciated that that very same thing could be written in Münster, Paderborn or Freiburg—only better.

Now that we have made these delimitations, we can give the following outline of the ethical enquiry of a Church dogmatics and its relationship to other ethical enquiries.

When God is understood as the Lord of man, by this very fact the problem of human obedience is also posited. But the problem of obedience is the problem of human behaviour. To that extent dogmatics coincides with the ethical problem. But the latter is not merely a concern of dogmatics. It is not merely a Church problem. It is a general human problem; a problem of philosophy, politics and pedagogy. It may be put and answered consciously or unconsciously, superficially or profoundly, but it is the problem of every man, the problem of human existence. To exist as a man means to act. And action means choosing, deciding. What is the right choice? What ought I to do? What ought we to do? This is the question before which every man is objectively placed. And whatever may be the results of his examination of the question as a question, it is the question to which he never ceases even for a moment objectively to give an answer. When we take up this problem from our starting-point in a knowledge of the God who elects man, it is inevitable that right at the outset it should undergo a change of form by which it is immediately differentiated from what is usually regarded elsewhere as the ethical problem, and in such a way as to exclude in practice any return to the ethical questions and answers that arise from other starting-points. As compared with all ethical enquiry and reply which is differently orientated, that which has its source in God's predestination must always be and become something distinctive both as a whole and in detail. Certainly, the question taken up is still that of human action, of human existence as such. But for us this question is at once the question of human obedience. Starting out from the knowledge of the divine election of man, we can know of no human action which does not stand under God's command, of no human existence which does not respond in one way or another to God's command, which has not the character of obedience or disobedience to God's command. We do not know any human action which is free, i.e., exempted from decision in relation to God's command, or neutral in regard to it. And for just the same reason we do not know any free investigation of good and evil. We cannot take up the ethical question in this sense. All that we can say of a theological ethics which tries to take up the ethical question in this sense—as a free question of good and evil—is that at the very first step it has dropped its own theme, its own problem. There is no ethical problem in this sense. Or there is so only *per nefas*, only in virtue of the misunderstanding of unbelief, which does not know or does not want to know about the lordship of God over men. Theological ethics must not fall back into this misunderstanding. This is the frontier at which it must halt. For the question of good and evil has been decided and settled once and for all in the decree of God, by the cross and the resurrection of Jesus Christ. Now that this decision has been made, theological ethics cannot go back on it. It can only accept it as a decision that has been made actually and effectively. It can only attest and confirm and copy it. Like theology in general, it is not concerned to penetrate to the foundation of things. It can only bear witness to the foundation which all things actually have, and which has actually been revealed as such. It can only be as receptive and open as possible to this revealed foundation of all things, as true and complete as possible in its attestation of it. But it cannot act as if it had first to be discovered and disclosed. It cannot put itself on the same footing as an ethics which first tries to investigate this foundation, to make it the content of its own answers. It cannot adopt the questions and answers of this ethics : not even if the latter later returns to its own line ; not even if it later asks and answers in almost or altogether the same words as itself ; not even if it later acts as an ostensibly Christian ethics. We can only move along this line when we have started on it. Theological ethics has to move along this line from the very outset.

But this means, first, that the reality of the good as such, the reality of the command of God as the sum of the good, cannot be treated as a mere possibility. We cannot first make a problem of the reality of the good in the command of God, or of the reality of the command of God as the sum of the good, and then come back to the affirmation of them in the form of a solution of the problem. We cannot even incidentally reckon with the possibility that there is no good, or that it consists in something other than the command of God. We cannot even incidentally make it the object of our choice. For if we do, it is no longer this good, not even if we do finally approve it. This good is chosen only in obedience, i.e., in the choice in whose making we have no choice, because we are chosen ourselves and can only make this one choice. Its possibility demands our recognition and apprehension as it is included in its reality as the reality of God, which either includes all possibility or excludes it as an impossible possibility. Even when it takes up the ethical problem, theological thinking is always bound to this reality. It apprehends only one possibility—that which is affirmed and determined in this reality. It cannot, therefore, wander around in the field of other possibilities. And since this possibility is a reality, it cannot treat it as a mere possibility. It cannot—even incidentally—abstract from it. It cannot bracket it under something higher. There is nothing higher from which it can survey, test, estimate, and as a result affirm and adopt it. It cannot act as if there were no God, or as if God were not what He has revealed Himself to be in Jesus Christ, or as if it had first to investigate whether He has really done this and what He has really achieved by it. When it takes up the ethical problem, and so for a moment falls into line with all man's ethical thinking, and with it poses and answers the question of right conduct, it presupposes that even this general question has its basis in the fact that man (objectively each man as such) is confronted with the command of God, that the command of God is objectively valid for him, and that only for this reason (but for this reason necessarily) he is in a position to ask about right conduct. But if from the very first—before the discussion even begins—it understands man and the ethical problem from this standpoint, and regulates its own enquiry and reply in accordance with it, it immediately leaves the general series. In all its solidarity with this series, it confronts it as question and summons. In an irenico-polemical contrast to it, it represents the insight that " what is good " has been " said " to man (Mic. 6⁸), so that man has been forbidden to try to say it to himself, and bidden simply and faithfully to repeat what has been said to him. This is what theological thinking calls ethical reflection and discussion. It is to be noted that it has not sought this out for itself. It has not capriciously chosen and assigned to itself this special task. It only intervenes with its distinctive method because, long before it arose, the subject proclaimed itself. And, among other things, the subject demands that its nature should be scientifically noted, and that therefore a scientific procedure should be employed which is adapted to its special nature and to that extent distinctive. Theological thinking cannot possibly evade this subject. It cannot cease from being a positive science of this subject, and therefore from being bound to its nature. But the nature of this subject demands, above all, that the reality of the good as such, and the reality of the command of God as the sum of the good, should not be for it a problem. It demands a recognition of the ethical problem as put by this reality.

This orientation of theological ethics means, secondly, that while it, too, enquires concerning the right conduct of man, it cannot cease to attest and interpret the reality of God, and therefore His Word and work. It cannot change either its direction or its theme. When it asks about right conduct, it cannot stealthily become an indicative or imperative representation of the Christian ; an empirical or ideal depiction of Christian existence. It cannot turn its back on the Word of God in order, for a change, to see what has become of the man who hears the Word of God, or what will perhaps become of him. Even as ethics, theology is wholly and utterly the knowledge and representation of the Word and work of God. What is the true Christian way of speaking about right conduct? In this respect, too, we cannot go roaming around. We cannot cling to a man, perhaps someone whom we regard as an exemplary Christian, or to a human type, perhaps a representation of Christian living that we find particularly instructive in a historical or contemporary group or school. If obedience to God's command is right conduct, what incontrovertible reason have we to pass off any individual or general human model as obedience? What authority have we to make it a norm? And what are we to think if in the portrayal of this obedience the spokesman is something in the nature of a Christian self-consciousness, even if this is ever so sure of its case and objectively ever so purified? Again, it is difficult to see in what sense and with what right we can undertake to sketch an ideal picture of the Christian life which can then be proclaimed as the realisation of the good, as the norm of Christian obedience. Where are we to derive this ideal picture? And what authority have we for maintaining that this is the form of living that corresponds to divine election? In this way a more or less imposing law can no doubt be found or excogitated. Often enough, Christian ethics—in analogy with all sorts of other ethics—has been surprised at law-making of this kind. But in this case it is definitely not speaking about God's command. In this case the task of ethics has definitely not been understood as a task of the doctrine of God. What emerges as law can have just as much or as little authority as those who have found or excogitated the ideal pictures, or as the ideal pictures themselves. They cannot possibly have any more. Therefore they cannot possibly have any theological authority, any ultimately binding and obligating authority, even if in themselves they are ever so beautiful and impressive. We cannot deal with the command of God, and therefore with the realisation of the good, with right conduct, in a way which is unattached and vagabond. We can speak only as we ourselves are bound by the command of God. But ethics is always in bondage to God's command when it directs its cognition to the Word and work of God and when it persists in doing so, when it begins as a cognition of the grace of God and never ceases to be this. If it accepts the prohibition to develop an arbitrary knowledge of good and evil, how can it try to cling to any pictures which it may find or excogitate of Christian obedience, as if this were not again that arbitrary knowledge in a new and ostensibly Christian form? If it starts off from the fact that what is good is said to man, what else can or will it do but cling to what is said? But what is said to man is the Word and work of divine election which has taken place and been revealed in Jesus Christ. This Word and work of God as such is also the sanctification of man, the establishment and revelation of the divine law. What right conduct is for man is determined absolutely in the right conduct of God. It is determined in Jesus Christ. He is the electing

God and elected man in One. But He is also the sanctifying God and sanctified man in One. In His person God has acted rightly towards us. And in the same person man has also acted rightly for us. In His person God has judged man and restored him to His image. And in His person again man has reconstituted himself in the divine likeness. We do not need any other image but this: neither another image of God nor another image of man and his right conduct; neither another Gospel nor another Law. In the one image of Jesus Christ we have both the Gospel which reconciles us with God and illumines us and consoles us, and the Law which in contradistinction to all the laws which we ourselves find or fabricate really binds and obligates us. This is the Law to which theological ethics clings. It is ethics of grace or it is not theological ethics. For it is in grace—the grace of God in Jesus Christ—that even the command of God is established and fulfilled and revealed as such. Therefore " to become obedient," " to act rightly," " to realise the good," never means anything other than to become obedient to the revelation of the grace of God; to live as a man to whom grace has come in Jesus Christ. But this is the very reason why there can be no change of standpoint or theme when dogmatics becomes ethics, or, rather, when it reveals its ethical content. It cannot live less, but must live wholly and utterly, by the knowledge of the Word and work of God, by the knowledge of Jesus Christ. It cannot, then, proceed to divide its attention between Jesus Christ and the man who is received and accepted into favour in Jesus Christ. It cannot enquire first about Jesus Christ, and then specifically about this man. The light of Jesus Christ is itself and as such the light " which lighteth every man " (Jn. 1⁹), the light which falls on man, irradiating and illuminating him. The grace of Jesus Christ itself and alone is the reality in which from the very start man himself has his reality. The man to whom the Word of God is directed and for whom the work of God was done—it is all one whether we are thinking of the Christian who has grasped it in faith and related it to himself, or the man in the cosmos who has not yet done so—this man, in virtue of this Word and work, does not exist by himself. He is not an independent subject, to be considered independently. In virtue of the death and resurrection of Jesus Christ—whether he knows and believes it or not—it is simply not true that he belongs to himself and is left to himself, that he is thrown back on himself. He belongs to the Head, Jesus Christ, of whose body he is or is to become a member, the Lord of the Church who is also the Lord of the cosmos, and therefore the Lord of those who so far do not believe in Him, or do so no longer. He exists because Jesus Christ exists. He exists as a predicate of this Subject, i.e., that which has been decided and is real for man in this Subject is true for him. Therefore the divine command as it is directed to him, as it applies to him, consists in his relationship to this Subject. Therefore the action of this Subject for him is the right action or conduct which we have to investigate. In relation to the individual what we have to investigate is his participation in the righteousness of this Subject and not his own abstract immanent righteousness. We have to investigate the sanctification that God effects in this Subject, Jesus Christ, and the self-sanctification of man which is accomplished by this Subject, Jesus Christ, not a sanctity of our own which we have to practise and demonstrate to others. When we say : What ought we to do ? we are asking about Him, for it is in Him that this question of ours is answered. In Him the obedience demanded of us men has already been rendered. In Him the realisation of the good corresponding to divine election has already taken place—and so completely that we, for our part, have actually nothing to add, but have only to endorse this event by our action. The ethical problem of Church dogmatics can consist only in the question whether and to what extent human action is a glorification of the grace of Jesus Christ. Theological ethics cannot consider a view of man that is severed from this life-centre, from the decision made in Jesus Christ. It cannot consider a question of good and evil that is abstracted from the question of this glorification. It asks to what extent the sanctification of man in Jesus Christ has taken place. It asks, therefore, concerning the glorification which necessarily corresponds to this occurrence. Otherwise it is not theological ethics. It asks about the action of the man who is actually placed in the light of grace. Obviously, when it has and maintains this orientation, it takes a distinctive way in comparison with all other ethics. It must not be ashamed of this distinctiveness. It must not be diverted from going this way from the beginning to the end. The nature of its object requires this way. It does its work well or less well as it is true or less true to this way.

At this point the question arises whether and to what extent another ethics, a non-theological ethics, can be recognised as legitimate and possible alongside the theological.

If this question is to be understood strictly, it must read : Is there, as the supreme and final imperative, a γνῶθι σεαυτόν which man can and should address to himself, as was presumably the intention of this catchword of late antiquity ? Is there a self-reflection, a self-understanding and a self-responsibility, in which man has to tell himself what is good ? Is, therefore, the doing of the good something which in itself is quite different from obedience to God's command, or concretely, from the glorifying of the grace of Jesus Christ ? Can it be said, perhaps, that obedience to God's command is good only because and in so far as it is possibly included in the concept of that doing of the good about whose meaning and necessity man himself can and should pronounce ? When it is understood in this way the question is obviously to be answered in the negative. Theological ethics can only oppose the most resolute disbelief to faith in the right and power of this self-reflection, self-understanding and self-responsibility, to faith in a doing of the good in itself which is not obedience to God's command, although at best it includes this obedience. It has to disarm it right away by not treating it seriously. In other words, it can accept it only on the presupposition which it ignores or denies, that voluntarily or involuntarily it, too, derives from the validity of the command of God and has necessarily to attest it. The right and power with which it tries to assert itself have been borrowed from the very place where theological ethics itself has found the right and power to answer the ethical problem, and will never cease to seek it. In so far as a non-theological ethics has for its content a humanity which is grounded in itself and discovers and proclaims itself, theological ethics will have to deny the character of this humanity as humanity and consequently the character of this ethics as ethics. It will still have to do this even when the latter includes a more or less friendly and appreciative regard for religious and ostensibly even for Christian interests and positions. There is no humanity outside the humanity of Jesus Christ or the voluntary or involuntary glorifying of the grace of God which has manifested itself in this humanity. There is no realisation of the good which is not identical with the grace of Jesus Christ and its voluntary or involuntary confirmation. For there is no good which is not obedience to God's command. And there is no obedience to God's command which is not the obedience of Jesus Christ or His positive or negative glorification. But in its true and strict historical sense γνῶθι σεαυτόν does not lead to the obedience of Jesus Christ and His glorification. In its true and strict historical sense it can be understood only as a summons to rebellion against the grace of God. This rebellion does not become less heinous if later, perhaps, it proceeds to make the grace of God an object of human self-reflection, self-understanding and self-responsibility, to make it a special content of human self-consciousness, and therefore to give to this self-consciousness, among other things, a religious or even a supposedly Christian content, as in the classical attempt of Schleiermacher, the Christian apologist among the Idealists. What begins with the human self cannot end with the knowledge of God and of His command. Nor can it end with the knowledge of the real man in his real situation. In its true and strict historical sense, the γνῶθι σεαυτόν, and an ethics conceived and developed in the practice of this imperative, is shown—*post Christum natum*—to be illegitimate and impossible by the death and resurrection of Jesus Christ. In so far as an ethics derives from this source, in so far as it carries out in the background an apotheosis of the self or the self-given answer or the self-undertaken enquiry, in so far as it tries at best (if it does not prefer to be atheistic) to understand God decisively from man instead of man decisively from God, it cannot be regarded by theological ethics as legitimate or possible. Only that well-meaning interpretation *in meliorem partem* can be expected of the latter. It must be content to be understood by it differently (we say better) than it understands itself.

The case would naturally be rather different with an ethics whose self-reflection, self-understanding and self-responsibility were from the outset over-shadowed, determined and guided by a prior, even if more or less inexplicit, knowledge of the Word of God. An ethics of this kind would renounce all claim to try to speak a final word in solution of the problem of right conduct. Now an ethics is certainly conceivable which, although not theological ethics in the direct sense, would open up the whole problem of the uncertain and questionable nature of human life and conduct, without being guilty of that apotheosis in the background, without asserting that there is an ultimate reality either from or within the human self as such, without seeking or exhibiting in man the principle and the reality of the good. It would be an ethics that knew the limits of humanity, and would not therefore treat humanity as an absolute, but would for that very reason do justice to it and serve it. Indirectly, it too would find the goodness of human action in the fact that it is obedience. Indirectly, it too would call man away from himself ; from the attempt to become master of the claim which is made upon him ; from the attempt to translate it into a claim which he makes—the final and highest triumph of all heathen ethics. Indirectly, it too would be a summons to the responsibility in which man must acknowledge and confess that a demand is made on him because a gift has been conferred upon him, and that he always owes what is demanded, that he therefore stands in constant need of forgiveness, that even as he is sanctified he cannot dream or boast that he is a saint. Indirectly, it too could easily be a proclamation and glorification of the grace of Jesus Christ, and could therefore give the glory to God alone. And therefore already it would itself have tacitly interpreted and practised the γνῶθι σεαυτόν in a Christian sense. In the face of an ethics of this kind the question would obviously have to be answered in the affirmative. It is a " Christian " ethics in a loose sense, and it has, in fact, a place alongside theological ethics. It has its starting-point, basis and aim in common with the latter. The difference is that these do not emerge directly— or do so only occasionally. It does not attempt to draw up expressly and specific- ally any basic principles. It is content to show by its actual handling of the problems of human life that the Christian knowledge of God is its presupposition and that it does, in fact, derive from this. It stands in a sense half-way between theology and the Christian life itself. For it has heard the Word of God attested in Scripture and in the preaching of the Christian Church, or it shows actual traces of the dominion of that Word over all men. It is, therefore, occupied with it. But its own concern is to put this understanding into effect in a definite interpretation and representation of human life. It cannot be expected, there- fore, that this type of ethics will be encountered in an academic form. To be academic, it would have to be based on principle. It would have to expose and expound its presupposition. And if it did, it would become theological ethics. It is no part of our present task to mention a particular instance of an ethics which is " Christian " although not theological. With the necessary qualifica- tions we might think of phenomena like the life-work of H. Pestalozzi. It might be contended that this type of ethics has been presented more or less clearly and consistently, although in very different ways, in the novels of Jeremias Gotthelf, H. de Balzac, Charles Dickens, Dostoievski, Tolstoi, Theodor Fontane or John Galsworthy. Traces of it might be found—and not only within historical Christi- anity—in certain old and new political and social conceptions, and also, it goes without saying, in the studies of the philosophical moralists. But the touch- stone of non-theological ethics of this kind will always be whether and to what extent it can stand an examination of its fundamental principles ; whether and to what extent its implicit presuppositions, if they were made explicit, would prove to be identical with those of theological ethics. In practice, how- ever, it is impossible to apply this touchstone to any great extent, for explicit theological principle is not everybody's concern. We can and must accept the fact, therefore, that this is not actually necessary. Thanks to the wisdom and patience of God, and the inconsequence of men, it is quite possible in practice that Christian insights and deductions may actually exist where their Christian presuppositions are wholly concealed, or where a closer investigation would reveal all kinds of presuppositions that are only to a small extent Christian. There are many people who live by Christian presuppositions, who even represent and proclaim them, and yet if they were questioned, could only tell us something very far from satisfactory or quite unsatisfactory, something which we might have to dismiss as heathenism or Jewish doctrine. The wise course, then, is to keep to what they actually know and not to what they unfortunately seem not to know or even in their folly to deny. The business of the reader or hearer of this type of ethics is tacitly to supplement and correct its more doubtful—implicit or explicit—presuppositions (as Paul did in Ac. 17[28]), and for the rest to learn from it what it actually has to teach. But this does not in the least alter, but rather confirms, the fact that *in thesi*, in principle—and this is what concerns us here—correct ethics can only be Christian ethics, and Christian ethics, if it speaks scientifically, cannot be differentiated from theological ethics. In the last analysis, therefore, the only strict answer to our question is to say that in a scientific form there is only one ethics, theological ethics.

2. THE WAY OF THEOLOGICAL ETHICS

It is the Christian doctrine of God, or, more exactly, the knowledge of the electing grace of God in Jesus Christ, which decides the nature and aim of theological ethics, of ethics as an element of Church dogmatics. It has its basis, therefore, in the doctrine of God Himself. For the God who claims man makes Himself originally responsible for man. The fact that He gives man His command, that He subjects man to His command, means that He makes Himself responsible not only for its authority but also for its fulfilment. Therefore we do not speak completely about God Himself if we do not go on at once to speak also about His command. But it is the Christian doctrine of God, or, more exactly, the knowledge of the electing grace of God in Jesus Christ, which also decides the special way of theological ethics, the special form of its enquiry and reply, the attainment of its fundamental principles. Here, as everywhere, the rightness of these is decided by the matter to which they must be related—the matter which is to be presented by them. Now the matter of theological ethics is the responsibility which God has assumed for us in the fact that He has made us accountable through His command. Its matter is the Word and work of God in Jesus Christ, in which the right action of man has already been performed and therefore waits only to be confirmed by our action.

In view of this matter, we must first refuse to follow all those attempts at theological ethics which start from the assumption that it is to be built on, or to proceed from, a general human ethics, a " philosophical " ethics. In the relationship between the command of God and the ethical problem, as we have defined it in its main features, there is not a universal moral element autonomously confronting the Christian. It is, therefore, quite out of the question methodically to subordinate the latter to the former, to build it on, or to derive it from, it.

Just as we cannot take the road followed by Roman Catholic ethics, we cannot tread that of Schleiermacher and De Wette, and more recently W. Herrmann [(1) Natural-moral life and moral thinking, (2) The Christian-moral life]; T. Haering [(1) Christian moral teaching and its opponents, (2) Christian moral teaching in its inner context]; O Kirn [(1) Doctrine of ethical principles, (2) Systematic presentation of the Christian moral life]; E. W. Mayer [(1) Moral philosophy, (2) Moral doctrine]; G. Wünsch [(1) The essence of the moral, (2) The essence of the Christian-moral] and others. Thinking which does not reflect about the matter, but from the matter, cannot possibly allow itself to be crowded on to this path.

But again, in view of the matter in mind, we shall have to cut ourselves free from all those deductions and classifications which start from the presupposition that while dogmatics has to do with God and faith in Him, the concern of ethics is with man and his life. This distinction usually avenges itself at once, for the distinctive Whence ? and Whither ? of theological ethics are smothered by the various questions man as such has to put and would like to see answered in relation to the shaping of his life. These questions of human life replace the command of God as the proper theme, the framework of all thinking on the subject. But this being the case, how can the command of God be really stated with its primary and comprehensive questioning of man and his questions ? How can justice be done to this element when in the change of scene between dogmatics and ethics it is suddenly deprived of its natural position as the subject of all statements, and is understood only as the predicate of the man who believes in God ? And if justice is not done to it, how can justice be done to the task of theological ethics ? Because there is no satisfactory answer to this question, we cannot take the customary path of theological ethics, quite apart from its doubtful relationship to ethics in general.

According to Schleiermacher's ingenious conception, theological ethics has to speak of the " purifying " activity of ecclesiastical and domestic as well as legal and political discipline ; of the " disseminating " activity of marriage and again extensively of the Church ; and finally of the " exhibiting " activity of worship, social fellowship, art and sport. According to J. C. v. Hofmann (*Theol. Ethik*, 1878), its concern is with the Christian disposition as expressed in moral action towards God in the different spheres of the Church, the family, the state and society. According to W. Herrmann, it has to do with the question of the origin and development of the Christian life. According to O. Kirn, it deals with the origin and development of Christian personality on the one hand, and, on the other, with the practice of morality in society. According to T. Haering, its theme is the new life of the Christian as a personality and what it means to be a Christian in the sphere of human fellowship. According to E. W. Mayer, it has to do with the moral disposition of the will, the nature of moral action in the different forms of activity and communities, its ordering and structure, and finally its result, the kingdom of God. According to G. Wünsch, whose arrangement is not very clear, its concern is (1) with the being of God, (2) with the consequences for morality of the experience of God, (3) with the Christian character, and (4) with " some residual problems," which include amongst other things the ethics of the Sermon on the Mount. The way of A. Schlatter (*Chr. Ethik*, 1914) is, without doubt, original and powerful. As he sees it, the *schema* of investigation and presentation is provided by the four Platonic virtues of justice, truth, happiness and power as they are related to the community of will, cognition, emotion and life.

The objection to all these classifications is that they do not derive from the matter of theological ethics, but have been foisted on it from outside, and not to its advantage. It is certainly a very fine observation of Schleiermacher's that there are to be distinguished in human activity the three moments of criticism, edification and play. But to what extent is Christian activity as such really grasped and described by this distinction ? In its own place it is certainly right and important that the fact of the Christian life confronts us (as in Herrmann and Kirn) with the problem of its origin and development, or (as in v. Hofmann) with the contrast of reflection and activity. But do these distinctions in any way characterise the Christian life ? Could they not just as well be made in relation to any form of life we choose ? The favourite distinction into individual and social ethics, which we find to a greater or lesser degree in v. Hofmann, Martensen, Haering, Kirn, E. W. Mayer, may be accepted as one which is both possible and meaningful in itself (although Schlatter, *op. cit.*, p. 53 f. has some arguments against it which merit our attention), but in any case it has to be pointed out that it assumes as self-evident that Christian activity is only a particular instance of human activity in general, and that if the correlation of individual and community is constitutive for the latter, it must also be so for Christian conduct.   Schlatter's derivation of the Christian doctrine of virtue from will, cognition, emotion and life has a decidedly refreshing effect alongside the rather drearily formal classifications of the Ritschlians.   But we still have to ask with what higher right this determination of human action is taken from Plato and made a pattern for the portrayal of Christian conduct.   These derivations and classifications are all suspect for the obvious reason that if we accept without question the correctness of the methods we have only to fill out the concepts in a different way and we can equally well derive and classify a Buddhist, or a communist, or an anthroposophical ethics as a Christian.   In the fundamental concepts acquired and presented in this way there is no specific adaptability to the special matter with which theological ethics is concerned.   They presuppose that the form of a theological ethics is left to the mercy or genius of the respective moralist.   And so they do not of themselves make any contribution to the Christian understanding of the goodness of human conduct.   They do so only when they are filled out.   But to explain what is Christian, do we not have to say things which cannot be said in the framework of a concept of human action generally, however deep ?   To reach the Christian understanding of the goodness of human conduct, is it not indispensable that there should be a distinctively Christian way of understanding, and therefore a characteristic form of theological ethics as such ?   Is it not inevitable that the Christian understanding of this matter will be severely curtailed if, through taking things for granted (as was surprisingly the case from Schleiermacher to Schlatter), ways are entered and trodden which in themselves can plainly lead to very different destinations ? The distinction in principle between dogmatics and ethics obviously does not bear good fruit at this point.   It normally involves a change of direction and theme which, if it is maintained, necessarily means that the problem of human conduct is the measure of all things, and forms the framework of every investigation and presentation.   The situation is then necessarily as it is assumed to be in those derivations and classifications, in the arbitrary self-assurance with which those different ways are taken.   Man himself has to ask certain questions : How he can become and be a Christian man ?   What does it mean to be this, not only in disposition, but in conduct ?   What is meant by Christian volition, cognition, emotion and living ?   Assuming that his conduct is Christian, what will be the result of his vitality and cultural striving, his economy, the state and the Church, marriage and the family, art and science, his work and his recreation ?   And theological ethics has to answer these questions which are not posed in decision before the revealed command of God, in the act of responsibility.   It has to say something to man in answer to his questions.   But in reality it is man himself who is questioned.   The one thing which can really be said is to be said by man himself with the act of his decision in face of the revealed command of God. Theological ethics can consist only in a sharpening of the recollection that man has always to give answer with his conduct, and that his answer is to the revealed command of God.   This is where the fault lies.   To be sure, even in the framework of an ethics which gives man an answer to his own questions many profound and true and serious and fruitful things are said, things which we do well to ponder. This is particularly the case in the authors cited.   But the fact remains that an ethics of this kind spreads a veil over its relationship, and man's relationship, to the revealed command of God, and that this veil has only to be seen to be recognised as intolerable.   For, after all, why should theological ethics act as a kind of information bureau, inviting questions from outside, instead of putting its own questions in order that man may be called in question by the divine command ? Is it not obvious that even the most profound and true and serious and fruitful things that it can say in this character are from the very outset said in a corner, that is, with no relationship to real human conduct, and that they cannot, therefore, be heard as a call to decision, or can be so only in spite of their untheological beginning ? If theology, and therefore theological ethics, is in principle the science of the Word of God as it is attested in revelation, in Holy Scripture and in the proclamation of the Church, it is man who must be the questioned in face of these statements, and not ethics itself which must answer the questions of man with its statements. Its subject is not the Word of God as it is claimed by man, but the Word of God as it claims man. It is not man as he is going to make something of the Word of God, but the Word of God as it is going to make something of man. Of man—yes, with all the problems of his behaviour and therefore in the whole range of his activities. But this does not mean that its theme is these activities, or what Christianity can contribute to their fulfilment. It is not from them that it can learn its prescribed task, or derive and classify what it has to say, or win its fundamental concepts. It cannot achieve in this way what it has to achieve in relation to the problem of human behaviour. It can do this only as it sees it from the very outset in the light in which it actually stands. It can do it, that is, only when it no longer adopts a new standpoint and method in the transition from dogmatics to ethics, when it makes and keeps as its central concept, as its starting-point and destination, not the action of man in itself and as such, but the claiming of man by the command of God, his sanctification as it is accomplished in Jesus Christ, and therefore the action of God for man and in man. It can do it, then, when it directs its course by the Word of God, and not the Word of God by its own self-chosen course.

If we ask first concerning the basis of ethics, the first task which obviously confronts us is to understand and present the Word of God as the subject which claims us. It is to understand and present the Word of God in its character as the command which sanctifies man. This basis will be our particular concern in this final chapter of the doctrine of God.

The goodness of human action consists in the goodness with which God acts toward man. But God deals with man through His Word. His Word is the sum and plenitude of all good, because God Himself is good. Therefore man does good in so far as he hears the Word of God and acts as a hearer of this Word. In this action as a hearer he is obedient. Why is obedience good ? Because it derives from hearing, because it is the action of a hearer, namely, of the hearer of the Word of God. It is good because the divine address is good, because God Himself is good.

We can also put it in this way. Man does good in so far as he acts as one who is called by God to responsibility. To act in and from responsibility to God means to act in commitment. Our action is free in so far as it is our own answer, the answer which we ourselves give to what is said to us by God. But as an answer, it is bound. It is a good action when it takes place in this commitment. Therefore its good consists always in its responsibility. Responsible action is good because the divine address is good, because God Himself is good.

We can also put it in this way. Man does good in so far as his action is Christian. A Christian is one who knows that God has accepted him in Jesus Christ, that a decision has been made concerning him in Jesus Christ as the eternal Word of God, and that he has been called into covenant with Him by Jesus Christ as the Word of God spoken in time. When he knows this, when he is " judged " by God through confrontation and fellowship with Jesus Christ, his action, too, becomes a " judged " action. It is in the fact that it is " judged " that its goodness consists. Therefore its goodness derives from this confrontation and fellowship. His action is good because the divine address which is an eternal and temporal event in Jesus Christ is good, because God Himself is good.

In its simplest and most basic expression this is the theological answer to the ethical question. This is the sum and substance of theological ethics. The characteristic feature of the theological answer to the ethical problem is that—although it also answers the question of the goodness of human action—it understands man from the very outset as addressed by God, so that in regard to the goodness of his action it can only point away from man to what God says, to God Himself. " From the very outset " means from the eternal grace of God as it has eventuated in time, from the lordship of His grace as it is resolved and established by God and cannot now be overthrown by any contradiction or any denial. When we understand man from this point of view, we have a positive answer to give in regard to the goodness of his action, but we have to do it by pointing away from man to what God says, to God Himself. To put it concretely, we have to do it by pointing to God's commanding, to God as Commander. The good of human action consists in the fact that it is determined by the divine command. We shall have to consider more closely what is involved in this command and this determination. But we can never seek the good except in this determination of human action and therefore in the divine command which creates this determination, in God the Commander Himself. We cannot in any sense seek it in human action in itself. " There is none good but one, that is God " (Mk. 10[18]). We must remember, of course, that this is a truth of the Gospel. It is not, then, the affirmation of an abstract transcendence of the good. To receive this truth is not to reject and abandon the question of the goodness of human action. It is only with this truth that we take it up. This truth is its positive answer. For this God who alone is good is the God who is gracious to man. He is not a transcendent being, not even a transcendent being of the good. From all eternity He has determined to turn to man, to make Himself responsible for man. He has dealt with man on the basis of this self-determination, and He does so still. And it is in this self-determination and action—not excluding, but including man—that God alone is good. He is this in the eternal-temporal act of His compassion for man. He is this in Jesus Christ. It is not to any god that we point, but to this God, the God of the Gospel, when, in the question of the goodness of human action, we point to the divine command, to God Himself. There is no more positive answer to this question than that which is given when we refer to this God, just because it means that we refer away from man.

The first thing that theological ethics has to show, and to develop as a basic and all-comprehensive truth, is the fact and extent that this command of God is an event. This is the specific ethico-dogmatic task as it now confronts us within the framework of the doctrine of God. We cannot emphasise too strongly the fact that by the ruling principle of theological ethics, by the sanctifying command of God— corresponding to the fact that we do not know God Himself otherwise than as acting God—we have to understand a divine action, and therefore an event—not a reality which is, but a reality which occurs. Not to see it in this way is not to see it at all. It is not seen when we try to see it from the safe shelter of a general theory. It is not seen when we think we see a being and then ask whether and to what extent we can derive from this being this or that obligation. The proposition : " There is a command of God," is quite inadequate as a description of what concerns us. For we should naturally have to weigh against it the denial : No, " there is " no command of God. What " there is " is not as such the command of God. But the core of the matter is that God gives His command, that he gives Himself to be our Commander. God's command, God Himself, gives Himself to be known. And as He does so, He is heard. Man is made responsible. He is brought into that confrontation and fellowship with Jesus Christ. And his action acquires that determination. The command of God is the decision about the goodness of human action. As the divine action it precedes human action. It is only on the basis of this reality, which is not in any sense static but active, not in any sense general but supremely particular, that theological ethics has to make answer to the ethical question. Its theory is simply the theory of this practice. It is because this practice occurs, because theological ethics cannot escape noticing this practice, in the contemplation of this practice, that theological ethics fashions its concepts. The same practice of the Word of God forms the basis of the Christian Church. It is in view of it that there is faith and obedience in the Church. It is in view of it that all theology has its legitimacy and its necessity. It is as God gives man His command, as He gives Himself to man to be his Commander, that God claims him for Himself, that He makes His decision concerning him and executes His judgment upon him. It is as He does this that He sanctifies him, and the good (which is God Himself) enters into the realm of human existence. To understand the command of God as this claim and decision and judgment will therefore be the first task to which we must address ourselves in the present context.

Once this foundation has been laid, in later sections of the *Church Dogmatics* we shall have to show in detail to what extent this divine command is actually directed to man. Even as His command, the Word of God is the Word of His truth and reality in the act of creation, in the act of reconciliation and in the act of redemption. Or we might put it in this way, that it reveals the kingdom of the Lord Jesus Christ as the kingdom of nature, the kingdom of grace and the kingdom of glory. Or we might say that it manifests the pre-temporal, co-temporal and post-temporal eternity of God. Or, alternatively, it speaks to us about our determination for God, our relationship to Him and the goal of our perfection in Him. As the command of God, too, His Word has this threefold meaning and content. The concept of the command of God includes the concepts : the command of God the Creator, the command of God the Reconciler and the command of God the Redeemer. The three concepts are identical with the fundamental concepts of dogmatics which it is the task of theological ethics to explain and recapitulate in their ethical content. They characterise in the shortest possible form the act of the God who in grace has elected man for the covenant with Himself, and in so doing they also characterise the command by which He has sanctified him for Himself. Of course, there can be no question of three parts or even stages of the one Christian truth and knowledge. The position is as in the doctrine of the Trinity. Three times in these three concepts we have to say the one whole, in which Jesus Christ is the presupposition and the epitome of creation and redemption from the dominating centre of reconciliation as it has taken place in Him. As there is only one God, so also there is only one command of God. But as the one God is in Himself rich and multiple, so also His one command is in itself diverse, and yet there is only one way to achieve the knowledge of it. It is of this inner diversity of God's command and the way to achieve a knowledge of it that we are thinking when we stress these three concepts. We are asking who and what is man in the Word of God and according to the Word of God, that is, the man elected, received and accepted by God in Jesus Christ, and therefore, as such, the recipient of the divine command. We find this man in the person of Jesus Christ Himself. He is the Son of David and of Adam who is determined and created to be the image of God. He is the One who is laden with human sin, and condemned because of it, but loved and preserved as the Son of God even in this judgment. And finally, in His resurrection, sitting at the right hand of God, He is the realisation and revelation of the divine image, received into God's eternal glory. In this threefold determination of the humanity of Jesus Christ we recognise the roots of these three concepts. And if we understand man in general from the humanity of Jesus Christ, it automatically follows that we have to understand him as God's creature, as the sinner pardoned by God, and as the heir-expectant of the coming kingdom of God. In these relations we recognise ourselves, not as in the mirror of an idea of man, but as in the mirror of the Word of God which is source of all truth. And it is obviously not in the framework of unguaranteed concepts borrowed from psychology or sociology, but in that of the concepts arising from these relations, that our sanctification, and the significance of the claim and decision and judgment of the divine command, can and must be understood. In these three relations we know that we are placed under the command of God. We are, therefore, taking as our basis, not a general, abstract concept of man, but the concrete Christian concept when we say that this is the sanctified man who is not the subject, but is certainly the predicate of the statements of theological ethics. Man is the creature of God. He is the sinner to whom grace has been shown. He is the heir of the kingdom of God. It is as all these things that he is addressed in God's command. In all these relations the divine command is the principle of the goodness of his actions. The one whole command of God has this threefold relation. As he lives in the Word of God and according to the Word of God, the one whole man stands in this threefold relation. In accordance with the context, the autonomy, but also the totality of the chief concepts of dogmatics, we shall not, in ethics, isolate any one of these relations from the other two. We shall not be guilty either of preference on the one hand or prejudice on the other in our systematic treatment of the three. On the contrary, we shall have to understand each one separately, not only in its connexion with the others, but also in its autonomy and totality.

The history of Christian ethics tells of numerous conflicts between the different schools of thought which derive from creation, reconciliation and redemption, or from nature, grace and eternal glory, with the one-sided orientation corresponding to this derivation. The movement which lies at the basis of these conflicts is necessary ; but the conflicts, the actions and reactions in favour of one or the other of the different relations of sanctification are not necessary. Indeed, although they may often have been important historically, they are fundamentally dangerous. We shall have to understand them as historically meaningful. We shall have to note and consider and estimate their aims and interests. But for our own part we must be careful not to become involved in them. We must avoid the rigidity and the enthusiasm with which one or the other of the equally necessary and possible points of view is constantly seized and more or less absolutised. In this way we must learn from history to do justice to history.

There can be no question even of a systematic combination of the three points of view. The reason for this is that we never at any point know the divine command in itself and as such, but only in its relations. The multiplicity of God Himself obviously resolves itself as little into His unity as His unity can be lost in His multiplicity. God is not dead in a rigid unity. He lives in the multiplicity of His triune essence, of His inner perfections and therefore of His Word and work. This being the case, we have to pursue the knowledge of

His command in such a way that we try to understand and bring out its relations as stations on a road which we have to tread, and the unity of which we shall know only as we tread it. Therefore the later task of a specific theological ethics will not be to contemplate a system—either from this point of view or that, or even from a fourth position superior to it—but to traverse this road of knowledge which corresponds to the inner life of God Himself, to execute this movement of knowledge. In it we shall have to realise the fact and extent that the divine command is actually directed to man, and the divine decision concerning man is made in it. It will be an exact repetition of the same movement which dogmatics itself executes on the road indicated by its basic concepts. There is only one difference—and it is not one of matter or method, but merely of fact and practice. It is simply that in it special attention is given to the question of the character of the Word of God as the command of God, and therefore of the claiming of man. The best place to discuss it is, therefore, in a concluding chapter to each of the different parts of dogmatics. In the present instance, this means that " general " ethics forms the last chapter of the doctrine of God.

§ 37

THE COMMAND AS THE CLAIM OF GOD

As God is gracious to us in Jesus Christ, His command is the claim which, when it is made, has power over us, demanding that in all we do we admit that what God does is right, and requiring that we give our free obedience to this demand.

1. THE BASIS OF THE DIVINE CLAIM

Mihi Deo adhaerere bonum est. " For me the good is to cleave to God." Every ethics which is at least half serious, aims consciously or unconsciously to say this. The divisive question is why this constitutes the good—the question of the basis of the divine claim. Why has God a title to man, and therefore a claim on him ? What is the source of His power over him ? Why has man to obey Him ? Why God, and not any other authority ? That God has a claim, *the* claim, on man, that the command under which man's action stands is, in fact, the command of God, that first and last it orders us to cleave to God, is something which, if it is established as true in itself, is necessarily distinguished epistemologically from all other opposing assertions by the fact that this Why ? is met by an overwhelming Therefore. What is it, then, that directs and binds man, not to any other authority, but to God ?

It might be said that God is the power which is over and in all things, the necessity which rules in all being and occurrence, the existence and activity of which we sense and experience, which we must also recognise as a necessity of thought, to which even man is obviously subject, to submit to which is for him the best course because it is unavoidable, because he cannot evade this submission, because a reluctance to submit can only do harm without altering actual subjection. Now, in addition to all the other things He is, God is, in fact, this power. Obedience to Him does actually include this subjection to His predominance. But this does not give us an ultimate, compelling basis for His claim to our obedience. It is perfectly true that the circling planets, the falling stone, the animal in its living and dying, and within the totality of the cosmos and interwoven in its course the inner and outer destiny of man too, are all subject to God as the power over and in all things, and cannot escape this subjection. But of itself this does not provide us with the basis of the divine claim and the basis of human obedience to this claim. Man may indeed be ruled and determined by a power—even by a power which confronts him as absolute predominance. But this does not mean that he has been reached and affected as man, that he has been compelled to a subjection which really signifies the recognition of a claim made upon him and obedience to it. Man as man is still free in face of power as power. He can sink under it ; he can be annihilated by it. But he does not owe it obedience, and even the most preponderant power cannot as such compel him to obey. Power as power does not have any divine claim, no matter how imposing or effective it might be. To maintain himself against power as power, even to his own undoing, is not merely a possibility for man. It is not merely the assertion of his right and dignity. It is the duty which he has to fulfil with his existence as man. The very man who is claimed by God, for whom God has become too strong, who is overcome by God, is distinguished from the falling stone by the fact that it is in his own most proper freedom that he has been determined for God, in his own most proper freedom that he has decided for God. By deciding for God he has definitely decided not to be obedient to power as power. It is in this way and this way alone that he is subdued and subject to the power of Almighty God. The man who comes from this decision knows freedom. He will " maintain his right against all might." And it is in so doing that he fulfils his foreordination. Power as power cannot possibly be the basis of his obedience. For it is not the basis of the claim made upon him, in spite of the fact that this is the claim of God, the Almighty.

It is because he misunderstands the nature of claim and obedience in this respect that the teaching of Schleiermacher is so profoundly unsatisfactory. As he sees it, all religion, including the Christian, is to be brought under the common denominator of the concept of the " feeling of absolute dependence." It may even be questioned whether all non-Christian religion can actually be brought under this denominator. But if so, it only explains why at this point religion is exposed, as it is, to a denial of its authority and relevance from the standpoint of human dignity and human rights. Indeed, it shows us why, in so far as it rests on this basis and is a modification of the feeling of absolute dependence, all religion is necessarily denied and opposed and rejected from this standpoint. To the extent that it rests on this basis, it is an outrage to the essence of man. It is intolerable, not only from the standpoint of humanism, but even according to Christian insight. It has necessarily to be repelled, for it opens the door to the establishment of every possible kind of caprice and tyranny and therefore to the profoundest disobedience to God. If the Christian faith, too, is only a special determination of the feeling of absolute dependence, this simply proves, not only that it is at the mercy of a deeply founded scepticism of man in relation to all religion, but that this scepticism is basically justified even in relation to itself; that a protest has necessarily to be made against it, too, in the name of humanity. It is curious enough that the humanism of Schleiermacher ultimately culminates in this inhuman view of the relationship of man to God, it being necessary in the last resort to protest against his doctrine of religion in the name of humanity itself. But so it is. Prometheus is justified against Zeus. The Stoa was right when it opposed to its own doctrine of *heimarmene* the doctrine of the freely and defiantly maintained *ataraxia* of the human mind and spirit : *Si fractus illabatur orbis, impavidum ferient ruinae.*

And Goethe was right when he opposed to all kinds of musty and in no sense Christian Christianity, and to all kinds of other secular imbecilities, the confession (which was a special favourite of A. v. Harnack) :

> Come ! For we will promise you
> Rescue from the deepest smart—
> Pillars, columns can be broken,
> Never a free heart :
>
> For it lives a life eternal,
> 'Tis itself the man complete,
> In it surge desire and striving
> Nothing can defeat.

This is all true. How true it is, and why it has to be proclaimed more loudly to-day than ever, we do not realise, of course, until we find the real basis of the real, the divine, claim on man. But then we do realise it. It is not in spite of Christian faith, but because of it, that we have to say that this is all true, and must be maintained in opposition to all deisidæmony not with less but with far more definiteness than by these pagans. The basis of the divine claim does not consist in the fact that God can overcome and smash and annihilate man. By doing this God cannot and will not compel man to obedience ; and He never has. He could certainly compel him—but only to something which falls far short of man's obedience. If He were to compel him in this way, His claim on him would still be without foundation. Even in the depths of hell it could still be flouted and despised.

Again, it might be said that God is the essence of the good, the eternal good itself. He therefore claims man for Himself to the extent that man as man participates in God from the very first. In some sense and degree he is ready of himself to will and do the good. He is, therefore, on the way to God, and he thus finds himself from the very outset directed to cleave to God. In point of fact, God is, of course, the eternally good, and when He claims man, He shows Himself as such, and confers on man a participation in Himself. But our present enquiry concerns the basis of the claim in which this takes place, the dignity and authority with which God places Himself in this relationship with man, and man in this relationship with Himself. The fact that He is the eternally good is not a compelling basis for this claim and for man's obedience in this relationship. For unless we understand by it what takes place only in this claim, the participation of man in God and therefore in the good is a mere assertion, and against it we have to set the fact that man does not find the divine good in himself, that he is not at all ready on his side to will and do this good within the limits of his creatureliness, that in no sense, therefore, is he from the very outset on the way to God, or driven and compelled for his own sake to cleave to God. What is proper to him from the very outset is the desire (the longing) to be equal to God. And with this desire he not only does not participate in the essentially good of God, but he fences himself off from it. How, then, can this be the basis of the divine claim on him ?   His willing and doing in this desire is a reaching out beyond the limits of his creatureliness.   And so the way on which he finds himself is the war-path on which he has entered in opposition to God.   Between God, the eternally good, and man, the relationship might easily be one of scorn on the part of God and envy on the part of man.   But it cannot be one of claim on the part of God and obedience on the part of man.

The question arises whether the Greek tragedians did not see deeper than Plato and all the Platonists. Their characters are all portrayed in an impotent desire for godlikeness and attempt to attain it. And they are coldly directed back to their own limits by the gods. But this opposition of man to the absolute superiority of the eternally good and his desire to master it on the one side, and the wrath of God against this undertaking on the other, are changed by Plato and his followers into a mutual *methexis* (or participation), in which the originally existent good is as clearly reflected and recognised in the finite as the finitely good in the infinite. That the harmony of this transformation has been attained fraudulently is betrayed by the fact that within the framework of this transformation it is quite impossible to show any basis for a real divine claim or real human obedience. These categories are alien, and always will be alien, to this transformation. We can only return from this position to the world of the tragedians if we are again to see clearly the real proportions, or rather disproportions, and therefore to see that a recognition of God as the eternally good cannot form a basis for the divine claim.

Finally, it might be said that God is simply the all-sufficient being " whom I have selected as my supreme good."   Is it not true : " Thou sufficest solely, Pure within and wholly, Soul and heart and mind " ? Is the enmity of man to God really a phenomenon of final, invincible magnitude ?   In spite of this enmity and in this enmity, is it not true that " our heart is restless till it find rest in Thee " ?   Does not the enmity itself, even the fall of Adam, attest this ?   Is it not possible, and even necessary, that in the last resort it will be transformed into a human " selection " of God " as my supreme good " ?   Since, objectively (and even at times subjectively), God alone can suffice man, is not the claim of God really based on man ?   Man must obey God because without Him, except in obedience to Him, he cannot live ? Well, he certainly cannot.   For God and God alone—above and in spite of all enmity to Him—is all-sufficient.   When He claims us for Himself God does give us complete satisfaction by and in Himself. But it is necessary to guard against the idea that this is the basis of His claim on us.   For if the relationship between God and man finally consists in the fact that God is the One who gives man satisfaction, that He can be revealed and known to him as such, and that man on his side is able (on the strength of desiring this satisfaction and finding it in God) to choose God, then in this relationship there can be a divine claim only in the setting and on the basis of the claim which man has first made on the God whom he has chosen.   Every divine claim is ultimately only a confirmation, a condition, of the fulfilment of this human claim. It has the character only of an invitation. It is certainly not a claim which is grounded in itself. We hold to God because and to the extent that finally we want to uphold ourselves.

The same man who to-day selects God as his supreme good may to-morrow wish to select a very different good. Where, then, is the claim of God ? Of course, the command of God is also a promise. Its fulfilment produces fruit. It yields a reward. That is something which we must not, of course, overlook or deny. But we cannot and must not seek the basis of its claim in the fact that its fulfilment has this consequence, that along with blessedness, the fellowship of man with God, it brings with it the answer to the problem of human life—the only possible answer to it. The divine command, whose fulfilment has this promise, must be known and understood as grounded in itself, as having a divine basis, if there is to be any understanding of the justice and force of this claim.

It is the God in whom we may believe, and He alone, who calls us in such a way that we must not only hear but obey; who orders us in such a way that in all freedom we must recognise the force of His order; who claims us in such a way that the claim is valid and we necessarily find ourselves claimed. The power of the imperative about which we enquire is to be found in the fact that we may believe.

Let there be no mistake : this imperative and therefore the justice and the real basis of the divine claim do not begin merely with our believing, nor are they conditioned or limited by it. There is obviously a circle—Luther often used to speak of it. God and faith, and faith and God, are two things which belong together. In this circle God becomes the One He is for man, and man the one he is for God. The deity of God enters for man into the light and power of the specific, direct and personal encounter and movement of actual faith in God, and the humanity of man enters for God into the same light and power. To this circle there belongs the fact that the claim of God is made on this or that man in particular and accepted by him. But our present enquiry concerns the basis and justice of this claim, the majesty with which the command of God is proclaimed and heard in this circle. This majesty as such is certainly operative in this circle, but it is not included in it—as though it were majesty, and the command of God had to wait to acquire this majesty, only by God's encounter with this or that man in particular, and His claiming of that man. The basis of the faith which shows itself strong in this circle lies as such outside this circle. And God Himself is already God, and God for us, before this becomes a particular event for any man, before it is actualised in a particular relationship between God and a man. The light and power of this specific, direct and personal encounter and movement fall into this circle from above. They are light and power in this circle because they are always light and power in themselves. That is why the light is so clear, and the power so irresistible. But they are not bound to what happens here or limited to it. It is exactly the same with the majesty of the divine command. It is majesty even when the awakening of faith has not yet taken place. If it is only recognised for what it is with this awakening, it is there and valid even when it is not recognised. Yet we describe it best if we define it as the majesty of the God in whom we may believe.

This is what distinguishes it from the majesty which is no majesty. Godhead as power, godhead as the essentially good, the godhead in which we find our satisfaction—these are not the God in whom we may believe, and it is for this reason that they are not the God who really claims us. The being of the true God is determined and characterised generally by the fact that He is the God in whom we may believe. And the same is true of the superiority and authority, the basis and justice of His claim. It is as we may believe in God that His claim confronts us in the loftiness and dignity of the obligation which derives automatically from the gift that He has made us, a gift as incomprehensible as it is unfathomable. God has given us Himself. He is not only mighty over us. He is not only the essentially good. He is not only our complete satisfaction. He has given Himself to us. He has graciously turned to us. He has made Himself ours. With His divine goodness He has taken our place and taken up our cause. He is for us in all His deity. Although He could be without us—He did not and does not will to be without us. Although He has every right to be against us—He did not and does not will to be against us. This is the God in whom we may believe. He is this God even if we do not yet or no longer believe in Him. It is as this God that we know Him when we may believe, when the opportunity presents itself, when we make use of it. But He is this God before and above this event, before and high above all the knowing imparted to us in this event. He is this God as the one true God beside whom there is no other, beside whom all gods are nothing. And it is from the fact that He is this God that there derives the superiority and authority, basis and justice of His claim, the validity of His command, the vanity of all other commands, the freedom in which we are bound to Him, to His command, the absolutely distinctive imperative of obedience to His will.

All this is actual in Jesus Christ. The Law is completely enclosed in the Gospel. It is not a second thing alongside and beyond the Gospel. It is not a foreign element which precedes or only follows it. It is the claim which is addressed to us by the Gospel itself and as such, the Gospel in so far as it has the form of a claim addressed to us, the Gospel which we cannot really hear except as we obey it. For Jesus Christ is the basis on which we may believe in God, the Word in which dwell the light and force to move us to this event. He Himself is the Gospel. He Himself is the resolve and the execution of the essential will in which God willed to give Himself to us. The grace of God, of the God in whom we may believe, is this. In Jesus Christ the eternal Word became flesh. Without ceasing to be who

He is in Himself, God became as one of us. He assumed our humanity
into His deity. Although it was darkened and destroyed by our sins,
and under sentence of death, He took it up into Himself in an indissoluble unconfused unity. He did not do this because of its strength
or dignity or any other qualification. He did it only because of His
own good-pleasure, His incomprehensible compassion. Or again, the
grace of this God is this. Our human existence is no longer alone. It
is no longer left to itself. But in Jesus Christ it is received and adopted
into the deity of God. In Him it has already been raised and cleansed
and transfigured into the divine likeness. Or again, the grace of this
God is this. The human existence of all of us is not really enacted at
an undefined point in empty space, but in proximity, fellowship, even
brotherhood with the human existence of Jesus Christ and therefore
with God's own human existence. In Jesus Christ we can see our
human existence wide open to heaven, irradiated, purified, held and
sustained from above, not rejected by God, but in a love that inter-
penetrates all things affirmed by Him in the way in which He affirms
Himself. And this view is not a mere theory, or vision, or moral ideal,
but the unlimited and unconditional truth of our human existence,
irrespective of what we deserve or achieve in our behaviour or attitude
to this love. The grace of this God is this. When He took our flesh
in Jesus Christ, God Himself undertook in our place to subject Himself
to the judgment and punishment that must be executed if we are to
be raised up to Him. He Himself renounced and confessed our self-
will and godlessness. He Himself maintained His cause against us.
He Himself executed and suffered Himself the necessary slaying of
our obstinacy. He Himself accomplished the great work of faith, so
that it no longer requires to be accomplished for us, but we with our
faith have only to look up to His, to approve and follow it, to endorse
it with our own faith. Again, the grace of this God is this. The
promise of the true repentance which He has performed for us is not
something which has still to be fulfilled, something outstanding. It
has already been fulfilled. It was not in vain that in Jesus Christ
God adopted and assumed this flesh of ours which was under sentence
of death. In so doing, He really accomplished both His own and our
justification and glorification. In the resurrection of Jesus Christ from
the dead as it has already been accomplished, we sinners are already
revealed as the righteous who may live by their faith. Death could
not hold Him, and therefore it cannot hold us. His life (and His life
is our life) had necessarily to swallow up death, and it did swallow it
up. In the midst of death we have in Him no future but that of
resurrection and eternal life. The grace of this God decides and has
already decided concerning our human existence. What does it mean
to be a man now that this decision has been reached by the grace of
God ? It obviously means to be one who stands and walks and lives
and dies within the fact that God is gracious to him, that He has

made him His own. It obviously means to be one for whom God has intervened in this way, with whom He has dealt in this way. It obviously means to be one for whose human existence Jesus Christ Himself stands before God according to the will, in the name, and by the commission of God, in all the wisdom and the fulness of the might of God—so stands before God that he is completely covered by Him, completely destroyed both in his weakness and in his self-will, completely offered as a living sacrifice, but in this way made completely holy and completely glorious.

" I am crucified with Christ : nevertheless I live, yet not I, but Christ liveth in me : and the life which I now live in the flesh, I live by the faith of the Son of God, who loved me, and gave himself for me " (Gal. 2¹⁹ᶠ·). The fact that I live in the faith of the Son of God, in my faith in Him, has its basis in the fact that He Himself, the Son of God, first believed for me, and so believed that all that remains for me to do is to let my eyes rest on Him, which really means to let my eyes follow Him. This following is my faith. But the great work of faith has already been done by the One whom I follow in my faith, even before I believe, even if I no longer believe, in such a way that He is always, as Heb. 12² puts it, the originator and completer (ἀρχηγὸς καὶ τελειωτής) of our faith, in such a way, therefore, that every beginning and fresh beginning of our faith has its only starting-point in Him, indeed, the only basis of its awakening. It is the only basis, but it is also the overwhelming and compelling basis. It is " he that dwelleth in the secret place of the most High," and abides " under the shadow of the Almighty," who says to the Lord : " My refuge and my fortress : my God, in whom I will trust " (Ps. 91¹ᶠ·). It is he who believes, he who may believe, and does so. It is he who, believing, stands in the communion of saints ; who has received, receives and will receive the forgiveness of sins ; who hastens towards the resurrection of the flesh and eternal life. His faith is the victory which has overcome the world. But that it is this victory does not rest with him, but solely with Him in whom he believes, in whose faith he believes. It rests upon the fact that the Lord Jesus Christ—born a man for us, dying for us, risen for us, reigning for us in the glory of God—is also his refuge, his fortress, his God : the secret place in which he dwells ; the shadow under which he abides. Yet all the same he may believe, and it is this which makes his faith mighty, immovable and invincible.

And now we can answer the question of the basis and justice of the claim which is addressed to us and objectively to all men. It is the claim of the God in whom we may believe, of the God who is constituted our Lord and demands our obedience in and with the fact that He is gracious to us in Jesus Christ. That is the majesty of His command, from which we in our self-will, our pride, our anxiety, our foolishness and wickedness, can certainly flee, but which we cannot evade. We must seek the command of God only where it has itself torn off the veil of all human opinions and theories about the will of God and manifested itself unequivocally. We must seek it only where He has revealed Himself as grace and therefore in His truth. We must seek it only in what happened in Bethelehem, at Capernaum and Tiberias, in Gethsemane and on Golgotha, and in the garden of Joseph of Arimathea. In this event God uttered His command. If we hear it here, it stands before us, well founded and legitimate. It is from what God has done for us that we must learn to read what God wants with us and of us. And then there is revealed to us the majesty of His will—the majesty with which His command stands for us, and not for us only but also for those who do not seek it here, for those who apparently do not seek it at all, for all the poor souls who mistakenly think that they have found it elsewhere. God calls us and orders us and claims us by being gracious to us in Jesus Christ. It is because of this that all other claims but His founder, or, if they are to stand, can only be forms of His claim.

For the grace of God in Jesus Christ is the proclamation and establishment of His authority over man. Where and how does it find him ? It finds him in the position of Adam. This means, on the one hand, that he is the creature whom amid the rest of creation He has determined to be His image, i.e., the mirror and therefore the reflection of His own being. And, on the other hand, it means that he is the sinner who perverted this determination of man by trying to determine himself for equality with God. The grace of God in Jesus Christ is the restoration of the first status and the negation of the second. In it God maintains Himself as the Creator of man aiming at his completion, i.e., the fulfilment of that determination. But He maintains Himself by reconciling him with Himself, in this way leading him, in spite of everything, to that completion, which now acquires necessarily the character of redemption. It is the infinite divine favour to man, as decided from all eternity, which is actualised in this way— incomprehensibly, but certainly not contrary to plan. At the same time however—and it is to this that our attention must now be directed—what God maintains in this way in relation to man is His own glory, His authority and majesty. God could not demonstrate and proclaim more clearly than with His grace in Jesus Christ that He is not mocked, that He will not give His glory to another, that " all that He proposes to do and wills to have will finally achieve its goal and end." The fact that God is gracious to us does not mean that He becomes soft, but that He remains absolutely hard, that there is no escaping His sovereignty and therefore His purpose for man. To know His grace is to know this sovereignty. And obviously to accept His grace can only be to acknowledge this sovereignty, and therefore the duty of obedience to Him, or, briefly, to become obedient to Him. No conception of His power, no thought of Him as the idea of the good or the all-sufficient being, can lead us to this. But the knowledge of His grace does so. It obviously does so because here we have to do with His original self-declaration. God cannot at this point be confounded with something else which we have excogitated about Him, and which we can just as easily evade. As against all our ideas about Him, all our arbitrariness and self-will in face of Him, He actually comes as the Almighty, as goodness in person, as the One without whom there is no satisfaction, binding us so strongly that any evasion or flight is rendered impossible, and we are really brought to a reckoning and responsibility.

That this is the case we see at once and above all in the person of Jesus Christ Himself, in which the grace of God has eventuated in a way which is primary and original and exemplary for all other men. There is nothing which more strongly characterises the human person of Jesus than its tie with God. It has about it nothing of the magical tie of man to a *numen*, to a higher being in whose service he either becomes a slave of the cosmos, or, on the other hand (and often indeed at the same time), sets himself up as a thaumaturgic lord of the cosmos. It is an entirely free tie, but even so complete. What establishes it is that this man has known and possesses in God the One who is " our Father in heaven." It is in this way that God is " perfect " for Him. And it is precisely this God who has authority for Jesus. It is His claim which He does not evade, but to which He is wholly subject. It is to Him that He is obedient. It is not a matter of any kind of subjection to a power of fate, nor of any kind of subordination to a self-imposed rule. It is a matter of the obedience of the One who is received and accepted by God in free grace, and who for that very reason is terrified to the depths at the majesty of God and placed completely at His disposal. It is a matter of the obedience of the free man to the free God. And for that very reason it is a matter of real obedience. At this point the basis and justice of the divine claim emerge quite clearly, and so, too, do man's situation in relation to it, the validity of the claim, and the necessity of meeting it.

Everything, therefore, that we read in the New Testament about the relationship of Jesus to the will of God is to be understood from the point of view that it is the grace of God which has acquired human form in this person, and that in this relationship Jesus only, as it were, responds to the fact that God is so kind. It is in this sense that " Thy will be done " stands in the Lord's Prayer, and is heard again in the prayer at Gethsemane in the moment before the actualisation of the " given for you." It is because God is gracious, and His grace is His sovereignty, that Jesus knows that He has " come down from heaven, not to do mine own will, but the will of Him that sent me " (Jn. 6^{38}, cf. 5^{30}), and it is really His meat to do the will of him that sent Him (Jn. 4^{34}). This is " the will of him that sent me, that of all which he hath given me I should lose nothing, but should raise it up again at the last day " (Jn. 6^{39}). The will of God which He fulfils is to be read, from what He does, as the will " to deliver us from this present evil world " (Gal. 1^{4}). It consists in our " adoption to sonship to himself . . . to the praise of the glory of his grace " (Eph. 1$^{5f.}$). It consists in our " sanctification " (1 Thess. 4^{3}, cf. Heb. 10^{10}). It consists in our being thankful in everything (1 Thess. 5^{18}). But it is the same will of God which is also reflected in the " obedience unto death " (Phil. 2^{8}) accomplished by Jesus. Through His obedience, the obedience of the one, " many shall be made righteous " (Rom. 5^{19}). As " a priest for ever after the order of Melchisedec," He has " in the days of his flesh, offered up prayers and supplications with strong crying and tears unto him that was able to save him from death, and was heard in that he feared," and " though he were the Son, yet learned he obedience by the things which he suffered ; and being made perfect, he became the author of eternal salvation unto all them that obey him, called of God an high priest after the order of Melchisedec " (Heb. 5[6f.]).

What we find in the case of the man Jesus is a valid model for the general relationship of man to the will of God. When God wills something from and for man, when man's will is claimed by God, there can be no question of an arbitrary and purposeless control which God can exercise just because He is God and therefore superior to man. On the contrary, what God wills from and for man stands or falls with, and is revealed and revealed only in, what the same God will do and has already done for us and in us. Jesus is obedient to God as the Father in heaven, as the One who wills our salvation and in and with our salvation His own glory. And as the Father in heaven, as the One who wills our salvation, God is the Lord of all of us in His Son Jesus Christ, and He wills that we should be obedient to Him. The grace of God had to be resolved upon in heaven, and actualised and declared on earth, in order that we should be summoned from the irreverence and rebelliousness of Adam to respect towards God, attention to His Word, and fulfilment of His will. When grace is actualised and revealed, it always means that the Law is established.

This is the basis even of the Old Testament legislation, especially as we have it in Deuteronomy. " Take heed, and hearken, O Israel ; this day thou art become the people of the Lord thy God. Thou shalt therefore obey the voice of the Lord thy God, and do his commandments and his statutes, which I command thee this day " (Deut. 27[9]). " Thou hast avouched the Lord this day to be thy God, and to make thee high above all nations which he hath made, in praise, and in name, and in honour. But the Lord hath avouched thee this day to be his peculiar people, as he hath promised thee, and that thou shouldst keep all his commandments, and walk in his ways, and keep his statutes, and his commandments, and his judgments, and hearken unto his voice, and that thou' mayest be an holy people unto the Lord thy God, as he hath spoken." (Deut. 26[17f.]). " When thy son asketh thee in time to come, saying, What mean the testimonies, and the statutes, and the judgments, which the Lord our God hath commanded you ? Then thou shalt say unto thy son, We were Pharaoh's bondmen in Egypt ; and the Lord brought us out of Egypt with a mighty hand : and the Lord shewed signs and wonders, great and sore, upon Egypt, upon Pharaoh, and upon all his house, before our eyes ; and he brought us out from thence, that he might bring us in, to give us the land which he sware unto our fathers. And the Lord commanded us to do all these statutes, to fear the Lord our God, for our good always, that he might preserve us alive, as it is at this day. And it shall be our righteousness, if we observe to do all these commandments before the Lord our God, as he hath commanded us " (Deut. 6[20f.]). It can be said confidently that this is *the* basis of biblical ethics, *the* answer of the Bible to the question of the legitimacy of the divine claim. Openly or secretly (but, as a rule, openly), its imperatives stand on its indicative : " that I am not my own, but belong to my faithful Saviour Jesus Christ." When this indicative holds, when there is this background of the covenant made between God and man, when God saves and helps and emancipates and redeems, when He magnifies His glory (by conferring salvation on man), by the weight of the demand which this involves man is always called and summoned to be obedient to God, and the Law is proclaimed. This is no less true of the Old Testament *Torah* than of the directions of the apostolic letters. It is no less true of the Ten Commandments of Moses than the exposition of them in Jesus' Sermon on the Mount. The divine claim never stands alone. It is never uttered *in abstracto*, either as that which in some way precedes the occurrence and proclamation of the grace of God, and is therefore primary, or as that which can only follow it, and is therefore secondary. On the contrary, it is always the form, or shape, or garment of grace. As may be seen from these passages in Deuteronomy, it is always a concealed repetition of the reality of grace and the promise of grace. Conversely, the grace of God never stands alone. It is never unveiled. At once and as such it is the summons which draws man's attention to the fact that when God is gracious to him, he himself is meant, and therefore what he is and does. The gracious God wills to be respected and loved and feared as the Lord of man. Not only in the mouth of the forerunner John (Mk. 1⁴), but also in the mouth of Jesus Himself (Mk. 1¹⁵), to believe in the Gospel means to repent. And therefore even the apostolic message (Rom. 1⁵) asks not only about the faith of the Gentiles, but about their obedience to the faith ; and rejection of this message (Rom. 10²¹, 11³⁰, 15³¹) is definitely described as disobedience. " And why call ye me, Lord, Lord, and do not the things which I say ? " (Lk. 6⁴⁶). In the disturbing parable of the house built on the rock and that built on the sand (Mt. 7²⁴ᶠ·), the decision as to a man's election or rejection depends on whether Jesus' word is done or not done. It is not possible rightly to understand the mystery of Christmas, or the cross and resurrection of Jesus Christ, if from the very outset they are not also understood as command. " And hereby we do know that we know him, if we keep his commandments. He that saith, I know him, and keepeth not his commandments, is a liar, and the truth is not in him " (1 Jn. 2³ᶠ·). Jesus Christ Himself as the Gospel, revealed, proclaimed, offered to man and affecting him, is always clothed in the Law, hidden in the manger and the swaddling clothes of the commandments, His divine commanding. We cannot believe or have Him except in this form. It is in this form, and only in this form, that He is powerful and true. That is why Paul can say in all seriousness that " the law is holy, and the commandment holy, and just and good " (Rom. 7¹²). That is why he protests that it is not opposed to the promises (Gal. 3²¹). That is why he says that it was given to us unto life (Rom. 7¹⁰). That is why (in harmony with the familiar words of the Sermon on the Mount, Mt. 5¹⁷ᶠ·) he declares that to proclaim faith does not lead to the abolition of the Law, but rather subserves its establishment (Rom. 3³¹). That is why he describes himself —obviously in his capacity as an apostle to the Gentiles—as ἔννομος Χριστοῦ (1 Cor. 9²¹). That is why he can say in plain words and not in any sense hypothetically that only the doers of the Law shall be justified (Rom. 2¹³). What is so characteristic of the message of Christ in the Old Testament—the praise of God's Law, the seriousness with which it is enjoined—does not come to a sudden end in the New. Why should it ? The Law which really binds is the Law which was fulfilled once and for all in Jesus Christ. It is obvious, therefore, that the Church is not the Church of Jesus Christ if it does not make the Law of God, His commands and questions and admonitions and accusations, visible and palpable in its own existence and life and conduct. And, of course, it has to do this, not only in its own place and sphere, but also outside it, for the world, for the state and society, which are also claimed objectively by the Law of God. According to the three articles of the Creed, the message of the grace of the triune God, whose proclamation is the sole task of the Church, is as such the prophetic witness to the will of God which requires to be done by men, the witness against all presumption and disorder, against all irreverence and lawlessness of man. If it is not this, it is certainly not this message, and the Church itself is certainly not the Church. But, of course, the Church cannot possibly proclaim the Law of God except as the form and fashion of this message. Except as the proclamation of the Gospel pointed and applied, even the most serious talk about the will and command of God can only be idle chatter, for which a Church is not needed, which can be much better done outside the Church.

It is where the grace of God is proclaimed as the resolve and act of God, in which at one and the same time He has come with mercy to help our distress, maintained His own glory, and in both these things shown and proved Himself to be the Lord who has the power to order us and to whom we owe obedience, that the Law is validly established, and that this is done with authority and emphasis, and therefore impressively and effectively. It is not at all the case that the establishment of the Law and the call to obedience are adversely affected when this side of the revelation and proclamation of the Word of God is not allowed to become an independent theme. On the contrary, it is only when it is not allowed, as in the Bible, that it has the importance and authority proper to it. When the claim or Law of God is considered and treated as an independent divine reality and truth, this side of the Word of God can be spoken only in a way which is hollow and weak and cannot command our credence. There then has to be substituted for the seriousness which belongs to God's Law as such an arbitrarily introduced seriousness of man. But this definitely means that the way is opened up even in content for all kinds of misleading self-will or self-opinion in its proclamation and interpretation. What is discussed is certainly not the free God who claims the obedience of the free man. At every point there is the great lack that the alleged claim of God has no divine basis, no divine right in relation to man, and is not therefore the real claim of God at all. A divine basis and divine right for this claim exist only in Jesus Christ, only in the grace in which God is the Lord of man.

There are many answers to the question of the good, the question what man should do. If an answer to this question is to be effective, if it is really to call and win and convince, if it is not merely to instruct and interest man but to move him actually to do the good, this does not depend on the earnestness or weight or decisiveness with which it is given. On the contrary, it is only when it has a solid basis that it can be given with earnestness, weight and decisiveness. It is only when it is grounded in such a way that man cannot take up an attitude of reserve towards it—either by appealing to his freedom, or by appealing to his weakness, or above all by finally understanding himself as this answer, in which case the question of the good is certainly solved but no less certainly extinguished. That is why at some point and in some sense every ethics which is at least half-serious usually points to God as the basis of the ethical claim, representing and describing as a divine claim the ethical demand which it formulates But the general reference to God and even the special reference to a definite conception of God are not enough. The God who is the basis of the ethical claim— the basis that summons man, that wins and convinces him, that moves to the doing of the good—must have authority over man, and therefore the power to deprive him of recourse to his own freedom or weakness, to his own alleged identity with the good. He must have the power really to claim him for Himself, and therefore for the doing of the good. He must have the power to claim him in such a way that he does the good demanded of him really as something demanded, and does it really gladly. But a general or special conception of God does not establish this authority. This takes place only when we understand the God who is the basis of the ethical claim as the God in whom we may believe, the God who is gracious to us in Jesus Christ. He is the God who, without ceasing to be God, has made Himself man's own and has made man His own. He is the God who Himself has done good to man, and therefore has brought the good into man's sphere. He is the God who has summoned man by Himself becoming man and as such not only demanding obedience but rendering it. He has spoken of the good by doing it ; He has spoken of Himself by delivering Himself up for us. It is in this that He is God. This is His majesty. This is how He maintains and proves His authority over man. The Law is valid because God Himself is the doer of the Law, because God orders and only orders on the basis of the fact that He Himself has given and realised and fulfilled what He orders. The Law is valid because in Jesus Christ God encompasses us on all sides and holds His hand over us. It is valid because, in becoming man in Jesus Christ, God has claimed for Himself our human freedom. It is valid because, once God has Himself become man for us in Jesus Christ, there is no longer any excuse for our human weakness. It is valid because we can no longer confuse the divine good manifested in Jesus Christ with the good which we fancy we ourselves are and have. That is why the God to whom we may refer has authority in contrast to all other gods. That is why He is the real basis of the ethical claim made by Him. That is why He has the right to claim man for Himself.

The peculiarity of theological ethics does not consist in the fact that it is " theonomous " ethics, that it understands the command of the good as God's command. The same thing is done elsewhere with seriousness and emphasis. But its peculiarity and advantage consist in the name of Jesus Christ with which it can state the basis and right of the divine claim. It cannot guard this advantage too zealously. If it ever forfeits this advantage, it can never make good what is lost, even if it speaks for the command of God with all the earnestness, the weight, the decisiveness in the world. We had to begin by putting and clarifying the question of the basis and right of the divine claim because this is the touchstone of all that follows. We cannot possibly proceed to think or say anything more except with the basis and right of the gracious God, the basis and right of the name of Jesus Christ. Every deviation from this path is *per se* a step into the unfounded. We cannot take such steps. We submit in advance to the criterion that, whatever else may have to be said about God's command in general and in particular, what must always be and remain visible in all that is said is the Gospel as the power of the Law.

2. THE CONTENT OF THE DIVINE CLAIM

" He hath shewed thee, O man, what is good ; and what the Lord doth require of thee, to do justly, and to love mercy, and to walk humbly with thy God " (Mic. 6⁸). This is the truth which we have now to recognise and develop as such. We now ask what it is that God wills from and for us when He claims us ? We cannot stop at the affirmation that God claims us for Himself. This is quite true. But as the basis and right of this truth had first to be clarified, it must now be explained what is meant by saying that God claims us, that we should live as those who are claimed by God. For what would it mean to " be claimed by God " if man could decide and control according to his own calculation and opinion where and in what he was to find the divine claim ?

According to what has been said above, it is the God in whom we may believe, the gracious God, God in Jesus Christ, who controls the content of the claim addressed to us. From first to last the content of the divine claim follows from the fact that this God has every basis for His claim and every right to it. As His command has no other basis and no other right, so also it has no other content than that which is given with this basis and right. The content of the divine claim which derives from this source, and is already present there, is secure against our caprice.

We have seen that the Law is the form of grace. As the grace of God is actualised and revealed, He claims men. His love commands. But the Law is not a casual form of grace. Grace could not equally well wear other garments. God's love could not equally well command something else. As the authority of the commanding God does not consist merely in the fact that He is God, that as such He stands formally over us, and is therefore formally justified in issuing orders to us, so the content of His command is not chosen arbitrarily or haphazardly. His commanding is not the empty positivity of commanding that this or that should be done. And that is why it cannot be left to our whim how we are to fill it out, in what special way we are to obey God. There is no divine claim in itself. There are only concrete divine claims. For it is the grace of God which expresses itself in these claims. It is always God in Jesus Christ who, as He puts these claims, wills to have us for Himself, to call us to Himself.

Therefore the grace of God—wherever it is actualised and revealed—has teleological power. It is not exhausted by the fact that God is good to us. As He is good to us, He is well-disposed towards us. And as such, He wills our good. The aim of the grace actualised and revealed in God's covenant with man, is the restoration of man to the divine likeness and therefore to fellowship with God in eternal life.

It cannot possibly, then, be self-circumscribing and self-exhausting. This would mean that God had resolved from all eternity to send His Son into flesh, but that in time He had actually omitted to do so. Docetically understood in this way, Christ would eternally hover over the world, and He would therefore be unfruitful for the world in His divine-human glory. In the same way, grace would eternally hover over man, and would never be the grace actually bestowed on him. It would never be his grace. But the Son of God has, in fact, entered into flesh, and in Him the grace of God has become the grace of the real man. This is what we mean when we say that it has been actualised and revealed, that the covenant between God and man has been established. But if it is established, this means that man is jolted and impelled by the aim and goal of a future determined for him. Grace is the movement and direction of man in accordance with his determination. It does not, therefore, find man in vain, but in order to act on him in its determined way. It is when a man is found in this way by the grace of God that he comes under the claim of God. And this claim of God can only be the judgment upon him that His grace will and must have its right in relation to him, its course in his life. It is this τέλος which prevails. The τέλος which man himself has set for himself as a child of Adam is invalid, and all other τέλη of his existence can only be subordinated to this. His behaviour must be a behaviour actuated and directed by this impulsion. Starting out from this basic divine decision about him, he is not his own master in any of his own decisions. Every single thing which he will do or omit to do is predetermined by this basic divine decision. In its very singularity it will always bear the character of a human confirmation of this basic divine decision.

The well-known passage at the close of Mt. 5 shows us almost word for word what we have to say about the teleological character of grace. In it the τελειότης of the heavenly Father (the τελειότης of grace) is revealed in the fact that He vouchsafes rain and sunshine to all men, and therefore loves even his enemies. This shows that the peculiarity of those who know and receive His grace, in contrast to what the publicans do, must and will consist (ἔσεσθε) in the fact that they, too, love their enemies, and are therefore τέλειοι like their Father in heaven.

The concrete form of this teleological power of grace is the person of Jesus Christ Himself. We have seen how the basis and right of the divine claim are revealed in the obedience of the man Jesus Christ —the will of the heavenly Father who has turned to man in pure kindness. But as He is obedient to this will of God, Jesus also shows what it is that God rightly wills of us. The basic divine decision concerning man is embodied in Jesus. The determination in which man is directed to his promised future, and set in motion towards this future, is given in Him. Jesus Himself is the impulsion of all men to eternal life. He Himself is the claim which God has made and continually makes upon all men. What is good, and what the Lord requires of him, is told to man because and as Jesus Himself lives and reigns and conquers.

It is told to every man, and therefore to those who believe in Him, but also to those who do not yet or no longer believe in Him. For as Jesus is both the grace of God itself and also its form, both the Gospel and also the Law, there is no divine claim that is not included in this claim which is embodied in Jesus. Paul knew what he was saying when he wrote that it was his office " to bring every thought into captivity to the obedience of Christ " (2 Cor. 10⁵). First and last there is for every thought only this obedience. In the last resort this Law stands over all thinking, and Christians are distinguished from others only by the fact that they know this, that they recognise and observe this Law, and keep His, Jesus', commandments (Jn. 15¹⁵, ²¹, 15¹⁰ ; 1 Jn. 3²²).

We have to keep what is demanded of us by the fact that Jesus lives and reigns and conquers. But everyone is bound to this first and last. Submission to all other demands, even if made in the name of God, can only be provisional and not binding, and it always involves the risk of error. The criterion by which all other demands are to be measured is whether they, too, proclaim indirectly the life and rule and victory of Jesus. If they fail to do this, if they do the very opposite, they are definitely wrong, and when we know this, it is only with a violated conscience that we can submit to them. What God wills of us is the same as He wills and has done for us. God wills Jesus. This is how He directs His demand to us. This is how He claims us for Himself. It is as well to consider the matter in this simplest possible formulation. All explanations of what it means in detail can only return continually to this simplest formula. They need the light which streams from this simplest form of the truth. The name of Jesus is itself the designation of the divine content of the divine claim, of the substance of God's Law. We cannot hurry past Him. We cannot treat Him as though He Himself were not this substance. We cannot think of Him as a mere container, or a husk which we have to open in order to reach this substance, but can then discard. If we do, it means that we have definitely not heard what has been told to man as the good. Obedience to God always means that we become and are continually obedient to Jesus.

The concentration and intensity with which this was continually said by Nicolas von Zinzendorf was amply justified. He said it in opposition not only to a secularised orthodoxy, and not only to the Enlightenment, but also to the moral and mystical ambiguities of the Pietism of his time. In so doing, he re-established not merely a Reformation but a New Testament insight. We may be astonished at baroque features in the way in which he said it. And we may argue that, entangled in certain Lutheran ideas, he did not say it universally enough. But we must give him credit that he was one of the few not only of his own time but of all times who have said it so definitely and loudly and impressively.

To become obedient to Jesus is actually to become obedient to God, not a conceived and imaginary God, but to God as He is in His inmost essence, the gracious God, the God in whom we may believe. Jesus Himself is the divine demand which confronts us as a genuinely compelling demand and which is also rigorous in the sense that it can be fulfilled only willingly or not at all ; the demand upon us ourselves, which claims our heart, and therefore the fulfilment of which really brings us ourselves into harmony with the will of God. Nothing that we can do in fulfilment of the will of God is higher and deeper than to love Jesus and therefore to keep His commandments—just because they are His, just because we cannot love Him without keeping His commandments. We definitely fulfil the will of God when we do this. And whatever is done in line with and in the sense of this action even where Jesus is no longer or is not yet known ; whatever bears in itself something in the nature of this action and is therefore an actual witness to the fact that Jesus lives and reigns and conquers, is definitely a fulfilment of the will of God. In all ages the will of God has been fulfilled outside the Church as well. Indeed, to the shame of the Church it has often been better fulfilled outside the Church than in it. This is not in virtue of a natural goodness of man. It is because Jesus, as the One who has risen from the dead and sits at the right hand of God, is in fact the Lord of the whole world, who has His servants even where His name is not yet or no longer known and praised. The Church can know and praise Him. The Church can live in the consciousness of what is said to us. The Church can call all men to the consciousness of what has force and truth for all men. How great, then, is its primary task and obligation to realise for itself that the only thing which has truth and force is that it is in the fact that Jesus lives and reigns and conquers that man is claimed by God !

The decisive New Testament term in this connexion is that of following. " Christ also suffered for us, leaving us an example ($\dot{v}\pi o\gamma\rho a\mu\mu\dot{o}s$), that ye should follow his steps " (1 Pet. 2²¹). " If any man serve me, let him follow me ; and where I am, there shall also my servant be " (Jn. 12²⁶). The term is filled out in certain passages. According to Mt. 10³⁸, to follow Jesus is to " take up one's cross " ; according to Mt. 16²⁴, it is to " deny oneself " ; according to Mt. 19²⁷, " to leave all " ; according to the account (in Lk. 9⁵⁷ᶠ·) of the three who wanted to follow Jesus, and evidently could not, and therefore did not genuinely want to do so, the radicalism of the necessary turning to Him and away from everything else ; according to the context of 1 Pet. 2²¹ᶠ·, to suffer persecution without returning evil for evil but rather requiting evil with good. In Jn. 8¹² to follow Jesus has the promise that those who do so will not walk in darkness, but will have the light of life. But the decisive passages even for these more concrete formulations are those where the term is used absolutely, where the meaning of " following " is obviously only to be explained by the fact that it is the following of Jesus. The concretions all speak of demands which are made in this way only by Jesus and which have little or nothing at all to do with the generalities they seem to suggest—escapism, asceticism, ethical rigorism and the like. A realisation of what is meant by taking up one's cross, denying oneself, leaving all, loving one's enemies, etc., cannot lead us to the realisation of what is meant by following Jesus. On the contrary, it is only as we realise what following Jesus means that we can go on to realise the meaning of these concretions as well.

When the disciples of Jesus are constituted His disciples by the command : Follow Me, the simple but incommensurable meaning is that they are to be with Him, to abide with Him, to accompany Him on His ways wherever they may lead. Why ? Well, obviously in the first instance only to be there, to hear what He says and see what He does, and therefore to be His ear-witnesses and eye-witnesses. No other meaning is possible even where, as in Mt. 4²⁵ and many other places, it is applied even to those whose attachment to Jesus is more occasional and transitory. In every case " following " means simply to be there, to be with Jesus, in His proximity. This simple " being there " has for their existence all the consequences which are given in the more concrete explanations. There is assumed in it an obligation which loosens and limits and disturbs all the other relationships in which they might otherwise stand, all their ties with men, things and circumstances. By it they are tested and sifted. Not all who would like to be there really desire it. And those who do not really desire it, are not able to do it ; their following ceases when it has appeared to begin or before it has even appeared to begin. According to Lk. 14²⁸ᶠ·, to want to be where Jesus is, involves a resolution comparable to that of a man who desires to build a tower, or a king who desires to go to war. To want to be where Jesus is, is to abandon oneself to this total claim : to take one's cross, to deny oneself, to leave all, to love one's enemies. Why all this ? Only because Jesus is there as the One by whom this claim is issued ; only because He Himself is the Lord as the One who is subject to this claim, the obedient servant who in accordance with the will of His heavenly Father does all that these demands indicate. " And where I am, there will my servant be also." It is not possible to be with Jesus without necessarily being called and drawn into the occurrence indicated by these demands. What Jesus says cannot be heard, and what He does cannot be seen, without coming under the lordship which consists in the fact that He is subject to this servitude, to these demands in the obedience which He renders to the will of His Father. His servitude is His lordship because in it He lives and proclaims the grace of God by His obedience. That is why He has " authority " (ἐξουσία), why He does not speak as the scribes (Mt. 7²⁹), why His doctrine is not a way of life or programme of world-betterment, or His life a pattern for its execution, but wholly and utterly the event of God's dealing with man. We cannot, then, be with Him merely to learn and accept this or that and leave on one side what we find inconvenient. Being with Him means at once the separation of those who do not desire and are not able really to be with Him, and the acceptance of those who desire it and can do it because they belong to Him. But the claim which His existence implies—just because it is God's own claim—is still addressed to the former and valid for them. Perhaps to-morrow they will have the desire and the capacity that they do not have to-day. And perhaps those who have it to-day will no longer have it to-morrow. The command : Follow Me, is issued and is there and valid quite independently of what is done or not done. In relation to it something will always be done and something not be done. But in face of this command there is no neutrality : no hopelessness for those who as yet have no desire or capacity ; but also no security for those who have. The important thing is that it is issued and that it is there and valid—and that is something which cannot be altered. It is issued and is there and valid like the bronze tablet from which the will of God could be read, even though it had never been fulfilled by any man nor ever would be. In the fact that it is issued and is there and valid, Jesus lives and reigns and conquers, and whatever the relationship of man may be to it, he is told what is good. It is good to be with Jesus and not elsewhere. This is good because it is there that God Himself is good for us. We can certainly try to be elsewhere and to be good for God of ourselves. But how far astray we shall go on such independent ways ! How ineluctably we shall fail, even when we imagine we are doing well, if we deviate from the sure way which God Himself trod for us and still treads ! We do not possess the teleological power to adjust our action to that goal of our determination. As sinful men we have our own perverted τέλος with which all the detailed τέλη of our existence can only be perverted. The very thing which we try to do for God of ourselves will be the most perverted of all, as has happened again and again in the history of religions. But Jesus has this teleological power. There is a walk outside the darkness, in the light of life, and it is this walk which is meant when the New Testament speaks of the following of Jesus.

We are not saying anything different, but only the same thing over again, when we say that the form of the teleological power of grace is the existence of the people of God : of Israel, according to the Old Testament promise ; of the Church, according to the New Testament proclamation. Thanks to the wisdom and omnipotence of divine grace, Jesus never exists alone and for Himself, but always as the first-born among many brethren, as the prophesied King of Israel, as the revealed Head of His community. It is not of their own means and merit, but by Him and from Him, as His people, that those who belong to Him are bearers of the grace of God for all men and therefore of the divine claim on all men. They are this in so far as among them the name of Jesus may be confessed, as He may be believed and proclaimed and magnified as the sum of the Law, as the fulness of the good, which God has done for us and wills to have done by us. The kingdom of Christ is greater than the sphere of Israel and the Church. But it is in this sphere, and in it alone, that it is believed and known that the kingdom of the world is His, and not the devil's. From this sphere all men may and must be told who it is to whom they and their activity are properly subject, whom alone they and their activity can serve. By giving His Son to rule and live and reign and conquer by His obedience, God has created this sphere too : the sphere where His name is the object of the promise and proclamation by which all its inhabitants live ; the historical sphere which is created among all others by His coming and the fact that He has come, in order that the grace of God, and with it the claim of God on men, may have a continuing abode in space and time, in order that in it the omnipresent God may have also His specific, concrete presence. The sphere itself is nothing, and those who live in it are nothing and can do nothing, without Jesus, who constitutes its origin and its centre. But as Jesus is its origin and centre, this sphere exists in Him and this people lives with Him. And when we ask what is the good which is told to man, and what it is that the Lord requires of him, in a fitting subordination, but quite definitely, we shall answer that we have to keep to what is demanded from us by the fact that this people has been founded and may exist. The law of this people's life is the Law of God. In the fact that He wills and creates this people, God says what He wants of it and what He wants of all other men. God's command is the command which He has given to Israel and which He has given to the Church.

The man who, according to Mic. 6[8], has been told what is good, is not man as such and in general, but Israelite man, the people of Israel. That which is required of him—to do justly, and love mercy, and walk humbly before his God —is not, therefore, the compendium of a natural duty incumbent on men generally, but, as in the case of the Ten Commandments, a condensation of the demand which is proclaimed and established and enforced by the fact that God has chosen this people of Israel to be His people, and Himself to be the God of this people. Compare with this Deut. 10[12f.] : " And now, O Israel, what doth the Lord thy God require of thee, but to fear the Lord thy God, to walk in all his ways, and to love him, and to serve the Lord thy God with all thy heart and with all thy soul, to keep the commandments of the Lord, and his statutes, which I command thee this day for thy good ? Behold, the heaven and the heaven of heavens is the Lord's thy God, the earth also, with all that therein is. Only the Lord had a delight in thy fathers to love them, and he chose their seed after them, even you above all people, as it is this day. Circumcise therefore the foreskin of your heart and be no more stiffnecked. For the Lord your God is God of gods, and Lord of lords, a great God, a mighty and a terrible, which regardeth not persons, nor taketh reward : he doth execute the judgment of the fatherless and widow, and loveth the stranger, in giving him food and raiment. Love ye therefore the stranger : for ye were strangers in the land of Egypt. Thou shalt fear the Lord thy God ; him shalt thou serve ; to him shalt thou cleave, and swear by his name. He is thy praise, and he is thy God, that hath done for thee these great and terrible things, which thine eyes have seen. Thy fathers went down into Egypt with three-score and ten persons ; and now the Lord thy God hath made thee as the stars of heaven for multitude." Yahweh has called Israel His son, His first born (Ex. 4[22], Jer. 31[9], Hos. 11[1])—therefore " consider in thine heart that, as a man chasteneth his son, so the Lord thy God chasteneth thee " (Deut. 8[5]). Yahweh is holy in Israel, and the demand that Israel is to be holy unto Him has its basis, in the fact that when He created this people He created it to be His people and dealt with it accordingly. What He demands is not, therefore, a generality. It is all the special paternal ordering of its life in the relationship to which it owes its existence. There is, therefore, nothing accidental or arbitrary which a man might equally well demand of himself, or another god of another people. There is no abstract cult-regulation, no abstract legal norm, no abstract moral law. Everything that God wills is an exact expression of the fact that those of whom He wills it are His own—an exact counterpart of the " great and terrible things " which God had already done for these men. " I am the Lord thy God, which have brought thee out of the land of Egypt, out of the house of bondage " (Ex. 20[2], Deut. 5[6]). The Ten Commandments and the various ceremonial, legal and moral enactments, are not independent and cannot be separated from this antecedent. They receive and have from it their specific content. They are merely part of the law of the life of the people led by God out of Egypt and into Palestine. It is because it is this people, because it would not exist without these " great and terrible things " done by God, because it owes its existence to these acts of God, that it is bound and obliged to keep the commands of its God. And in content each of the commands reflects and confirms the fact that Israel is this people, the people created and maintained by these acts of God. *Thou* shalt ! means, *Israel* shall ! and everything that Israel shall is only an imperative transcription of what Israel *is*, repeating in some sense only what Israel has become by God, and what it must always be with God. But Israel is the people of promise, and therefore from the very outset it is the people of the promised Son, in whose name all generations shall be blessed. In view and for the sake of Him as its future and yet already present King, Israel is itself called the son of God, and chosen and created and ruled by God as this special people. For His sake it exists and with its existence it has received the Law of God, being claimed by God in this special way. For

His sake this Law, which is given only to it, and the fulfilment of which is demanded only from it, has objective and universal significance in all its parts, to the extent that He, this coming Son and King, will keep and fulfil it, when everything that Israel did to keep and fulfil it has finally shown itself to be disobedience. That in relation to the God who claims him man is continually not only in arrears, but in the wrong—is what has to emerge unequivocally in the man, the people, which, like Israel, is told what is good. This is what makes it so clear that it is this man who lives by the promise made to him, by the promised One who alone will keep and fulfil the Law. And it is on this account that he is really claimed. The meaning of all those great acts of God towards Israel was to shadow forth the fact that it can have a share in what this promised One will be and do as divine Deliverer of man, that it can live in His sphere, in the sphere of " the great and terrible things " which the exodus from Egypt and the entry into Palestine only herald. The grace in which Israel may rejoice is this : that expecting and grasping the promise made to it in spite and in the midst of all its disobedience, it can have a part in the action of the divine faithfulness which will be revealed in Jesus, and which now already has its sphere, its circle of light and power, in its whole history, although the centre is so far hidden. And in the light of this we can understand how it is that the divine claim in regard to Israel is so distinct and is maintained in and through all the disobedience that it encounters, with all the judgments threatened and executed, but also the continual renewals of the promise, and the actual demonstrations of help and blessing. As certainly as the divine promise will be fulfilled, so certainly the divine faithfulness persists in regard to this people. And as certainly as this faithfulness, as the Law of God persists, so certainly it must be there on tables and in books, and be solemnly read and heard, from generation to generation (Deut. 31¹⁰ᶠ·, Josh. 8³⁴ᶠ·, 2 K. 23²ᶠ·, Neh. 8¹ᶠ·). But although blessing rests on human loyalty towards it, and a curse on human disloyalty, in the long run and as a whole, human disobedience preponderates and therefore the curse must be fulfilled. Yet the faithful One is still the end and goal of the whole history of Israel. It is clear, therefore, that what Israel does and fails to do under God's claim is one thing, but the fact that it is always the people claimed by God, that God does not cease to declare His will to it, is another. And this other holds whatever has to be thought and said about this people's answer to what God says. Its disobedience may be exposed and it may be convicted of its unfaithfulness, but it still has the Law. The Law has been given. It is characterised and maintained by its unshakeable validity. It is reminded again and again of God's will. It is never released from the obligation which this imposes. It is allowed no escape from this obligation. It may set little or no store at all by the fact that it is characterised in this way. Yet it always has the honour done it by the fact that it stands under this obligation. It bears it always, and therefore against all its deserts, in and in spite of its utter unworthiness, it also bears the grace which is the secret of this claim. In all its foolishness and perversity, there has always been a basis for the self-glorification of the Jewish people as the people of the Law. For " it shall come to pass in the last days, that the mountain of the Lord's house shall be established in the top of the mountains, and shall be exalted above the hills ; and all nations shall flow unto it. And many people shall go and say, Come ye, and let us go up to the mountain of the Lord, to the house of the God of Jacob ; and he will teach us of his ways, and we will walk in his paths ; for out of Zion shall go forth the law, and the word of the Lord from Jerusalem. And he shall judge among the nations, and shall rebuke many people " (Is. 2²ᶠ·). What the Lord demands of Israel : to do justly, and love mercy and walk humbly before its God—this counterpart to the " great and terrible things " which God has done for this people—has secretly from the very first an objective and universal significance, the significance of the divine claim on all men which it acquires openly with Jesus' call to follow

Him. That this cannot be disproved and cancelled by the sin of man emerges typically in the history of the people of Israel, which was always unfaithful and disobedient, but always confirmed and characterised as the bearer of the divine Law. Just as the promise and command of God are present and valid among the sinful people of Israel, so the claim of God (which is only the form of His grace) has its permanent place in space and time. In this place an unholy people, a people utterly in need of divine sanctification, will always be found confronting its holy and merciful God in the most radical unworthiness. In this place there can only be thanksgiving to God because He is friendly and eternally maintains His kindness. The divine claim will always be directed to a man, a people, which on account of its disloyalty and disobedience can only give thanks. It will be directed to this people to shame it, but also to characterise it; to expose its wrong before God, but also to instruct it in all its wrongness; to attest that it can live only by grace, but also to attest that it may really live by God's grace. And because the claim of God has this place, it will also be heard in the world around as the claim of God on all men. Those who bear and proclaim it can only be those who are sanctified by their presence at the great acts of God, instructed and punished, disciplined and confined, disquieted in their quiet and quieted in their disquiet, and thus continually brought into the right way by the promised One of Israel. By the existence of a people like this, God speaks to all men, telling all men what He will have of them. For this to happen, for this people really to be the light and the salt that it was intended to be, what is needed is that Jesus should be among it.

But Jesus *is* among this people. This is what has been brought to light in the New Testament Church, with the fulfilment of the promise of Israel, in contrast to the existence of Israel as such. The biblical portrayal of the Church as the spatio-temporal locus of the divine claim, as the Zion from which the Law goes forth, is distinguished from that of Israel by the fact that the divine accusation of man's disloyalty and disobedience, which had almost completely dominated the Old Testament, has now been reduced to silence, and is only a warning recollection. This is not because it has become objectless. It is because it has found its proper object in Jesus Christ. The judgment which necessarily followed has found its fulfilment in Him. The command of God can be understood and proclaimed only as the command kept and fulfilled by Him. It is as such that it is now valid and authoritative. And its content is that we should take up the right attitude to Him, Jesus Christ, with the faith and love and hope which all have in Him as their ground and content. The secret of the Old Testament, that it can only be a matter of thanksgiving, has now been publicly declared in the Church as the people of Jesus Christ. That those who give thanks are unfaithful and disobedient is a fact on which it is no longer necessary to lay particular emphasis. In view of Jesus' death on the cross, it is the obvious presupposition of their thanks. The new feature of the order of life in the New Testament is that these men who are unfaithful and disobedient, together with all the lost people of the old covenant, really do give thanks, that they for their part may really keep and fulfil the command of God—always in their relationship to Jesus, always in following Him. But even this order of life, and this order in particular, can be understood only as the Law of the life of God's people. It cannot have a materially new content in contrast to Mic. 6⁸ or Deut. 10¹²ᶠ· or the Ten Commandments. It only clarifies and defines the relationship in which everything that the Old Testament Law demanded had always stood, but in which it has now been revealed with the appearance of Jesus, His death and resurrection. " Beloved, I write no new commandment unto you, but an old commandment which ye had from the beginning. The old commandment is the word which ye have heard from the beginning. Again, a new commandment I write unto you, which thing is true in him and in you : because the darkness is past, and the true light now shineth " (1 Jn. 2⁷ᶠ·). As the new Law it is " that ye love one another ;

as I have loved you (with the purpose) that ye also love one another " (Jn. 13³⁴).
The new thing is Jesus Himself. But Jesus Himself is also the old. For He is
the promised One for whose sake the Law was given to Israel. Always when He
wills and creates a people for Him, God also explains what He wants of man.
He establishes His law. Not, then, in spite of its weakness, but in the very
midst of it, this people may and must be the witness to the divine claim upon
all men.

But what is meant and expressed by the divine claim made in
and with the person of Jesus Christ, in and with the existence of His
people ? What is the aim of God's grace when it becomes a command
for man ? If we look steadfastly at the place where the divine claim
is revealed, that is, at Jesus and His people, we can hardly avoid the
following comprehensive answer. The concern in the divine claim is
that man's action should become and be always that of those who
accept God's action as right.

It is the grace of God which is attested to us by the claim of God.
The grace of God wills and creates the covenant between God and
man. It therefore determines man to existence in this covenant. It
determines him to be the partner of God. It therefore determines his
action to correspondence, conformity, uniformity with God's action.
How can God will and create this covenant, or man exist in this
covenant, or God be gracious to man, without this determination of
man ? What is involved is that man and man's action should become
the image of God : the reflection which represents, although in itself
it is completely different from, God and His action ; the reflection in
which God recognises Himself and His action. It is in this determination of man that his peace with God consists, his righteousness before
Him, his holiness. And this is the eternal life which he is promised.
Eternal life is God's own life, and the life of the creature when it is
uniform with God's own life. What God wills of man when He establishes the covenant between Himself and man, when He is gracious
to him, is that his creaturely life and being and action, his thoughts
and words and works, should acquire this uniformity. But He wills
this only as He is gracious to us. He wills it only as He wills Jesus
and the people among whom Jesus is King. God's action is that He
sent Jesus, that He offered Him up for us, that, again for us, He
exalted and glorified Him, and that in and with Him He also elected
and created His people, that He elected and created Israel and the
Church to be the place of faith in Jesus and a witness to Him. It
is to this, therefore, that the required uniformity of our action with
God's action must always be related. The determination of man is
always to reflect this. The covenant of grace alone constitutes the
real relationship between God and man. Man is determined only to
be the partner of the gracious God. What other claim can be considered in relation to this partner, indeed what other claim can be
known by man at all, except that he must be one to whom God is

gracious, and think and speak and act as such ? God's action is that He is gracious, and man in his action is committed to correspondence to this action. He is the image of God and His action when his own action reflects and to that extent copies the grace of God. Man is righteous and holy before God and on the way to eternal life to the degree that he lives *by* the grace of God and therefore *for* the grace of God, for its glorification in his creaturely existence. Sin, on the other hand, can obviously be only the surrender of this righteousness and holiness, a deviation from this way which is the open but also the only way to eternal life. But the grace of God is the existence of Jesus Christ and His people.

What are we to do ? We are to do what corresponds to this grace. We are to respond to the existence of Jesus Christ and His people. With our action we are to render an account to this grace. By it and by it alone we are challenged. To it and to it alone we are responsible.

This is brought out very clearly by the context of the bold saying of Paul in Eph. 5¹: γίνεσθε οὖν μιμηταὶ τοῦ θεοῦ ὡς τέκνα ἀγαπητά. In other passages (1 Cor. 4¹⁶, 11¹; 1 Thess. 1⁶) Paul urged Christians to become "imitators" of himself, the apostle. In 1 Thess. 2¹⁴ he spoke of the Church of Thessalonica "imitating" the way of suffering of the Church of Jerusalem. He described himself in 1 Cor. 11¹ as an "imitator" of Christ. The even stronger saying in Eph. 5¹ shows us plainly what is meant. He had (Eph. 4³¹ᶠ·) summoned Christians to put away all bitterness, all wrath, anger and clamour, all railing and malice ; and to exercise mutual kindness, tenderheartedness and forgiveness, corresponding to the forgiveness which had come to them from God through Jesus Christ. They were to be "imitators" of this God, and therefore to walk in love "as Christ also hath loved us, and hath given himself for us, an offering and a sacrifice to God for a sweet-smelling savour." This "imitation"—and there can be no question of any other—is obviously related in the strictest possible way to the gracious attitude of God to us men revealed and operative in Christ. This attitude is the Law which is given to us. It is to this attitude that we and all our activity are bound, and by it that we are measured, and must orientate ourselves. *Ne devrions nous pas et soir et matin, et iour et nuict penser à la grace qui nous est faite en nostre Seigneur Jesus Christ, qui est le soleil pour nous esclairer ? Faut-il que nous soyons abrutis et que nous ne cognoissions point qu'il fait luire sa clairté spirituelle sur nous, à fin de nous conduire à salut ? Et comment cela se fait-il, sinon par la miséricorde de Dieu ? Apres, quand nous voyons la grace que Dieu nous fait de nous maintenir en ceste vie presente, sommes-nous dignes d'estre nourris à ses despens ? Non : mais le tout nous vient par nostre Seigneur Jesus Christ. Il faudroit donc et en nostre dormir et en nos veilles et en nostre boire et en nostre manger et en nostre repos et en nostre labeur et en tout et par tout, que nous cognoissions tousiours la miséricorde de laquelle Die a usé envers nous et qu'elle fust reduite en memoire et que ce fust notre exercice continuel. Et aussi en priant Dieu il faut tousiours que ceste grace nous vienne devant les yeux. Car quel acces aurons-nous pour parler privément à luy et pour descharner toutes nos sollicitudes et angoisses comme en son giron et le nommer mesmes nostre pere, sinon d'autant que nous sommes convoyez par sa bonté gratuite en nostre Seigneur Jesus Christ et qu'il nous a par-donnés nos transgressions ? Si nous ne pensons à tout cela nous sommes par trop stupides et abrutis* (Calvin, *Sermon on Eph.* 4³¹ᶠ·, *C.R.* 51, 664). It is clear that even where Paul describes himself as an imitator of Christ or the Thessalonians as imitators of those of Jerusalem, or where he summons to an imitation of himself, he is thinking only of this gracious attitude of God in Jesus Christ.

The same is true of 1 Pet. 3¹³ where, instead of rendering evil for evil, or reviling for reviling, Christians under persecution are invited (3⁸ᶠ·) to bless, as those who are called to inherit a blessing. " Who is he that will harm you, if ye be ζηλωταί (or μιμηταί) of the good " (probably masculine, therefore of Christ or God) ? If only you sanctify the Κύριος Χριστός in your heart, you need not fear anything or any man (3¹⁴ᶠ·). " It is better, if the will of God be so, that ye suffer, than that ye do evil. For Christ also hath once suffered for sins, the just for the unjust, that he might bring us to God " (3¹⁷ᶠ·). The need to imitate Christ even in His passion, which plays such a decisive role in the first Epistle of Peter (cf. 2²¹), is plainly rooted in the fact that the passion of Christ took place for us, that it is the great revelation and reality of the grace of God to us, and that as such it demands uniformity from us, since it is to us that this grace is shown. Gal. 6¹ is also relevant in this connexion : " Bear ye one another's burdens, and so fulfil the law of Christ." So, too, is Rom. 15² : " Let everyone of us please his neighbour for his good to edification. For even Christ pleased not himself, but, as it is written, The reproaches of them that reproached thee fell on me.'' So, too, does Col. 3¹³ : " Forbearing one another, and forgiving one another, if any man have a quarrel against any : even as Christ forgave you, so also do ye." Finally and above all, we may refer to the whole passage Phil. 2³ᶠ· The basis of this exhortation to unity, and to the lowliness which puts the things of others above one's own things, is an appeal to Christians to live in the mind " which is in Christ Jesus," and which must as such be normative for them. This is the mind in which He did not maintain Himself in His Godhead, but emptied Himself of its glory and assumed the servant-form of a man, being obedient to God in this form even to the death of the cross. It is in this way, on the basis of this gracious condescension, that He has been genuinely exalted and glorified anew. And it is to this One who became a servant for us that every knee must bow, and every tongue confess that He is the Lord. What is required of us is that our action should be brought into conformity with His action.

But what is meant by demanding conformity with divine grace, and to that extent conformity with Jesus Christ and His people ? In what does our responsibility to God consist if God is its object and measure in this His concrete action ?

We must first be clear that there can be no question of a conformity which means equality, of anything in the nature of a deification of man, of making him a second Christ. The correspondence which alone can be considered in this connexion cannot and will not mean abolition of " the infinite qualitative difference " between God and man. It is a question of responsibility and therefore of a correspondence in which God and man are in clear and inflexible antithesis. It is a question of displaying the image of God, and not of the creation of a second God in human form, or of a mixing or changing of the human form into the one divine form. It is a question of the eternal life of the creature as such. Whatever the action demanded of us may be, it will be our action, a human action. It will have to attest and confirm the great acts of God ; but it will not be able to continue or repeat them. The covenant, the partnership remains, but there is no development of an identity between God and man. In face of the action of man the great acts of God will always be what they and they alone are. Jesus Christ will reign and man will be subject to Him, and they will always be different in and in spite of the closest fellowship between Him and His imitators. There will be no more Christs. No second or third person will be able to come with the promise and claim : " I am he ! " According to Mk. 13^5 and Mt. 24^5, only " deceivers " will be able to say this of themselves. Again, the people of God, as the exemplary form of the kingdom of grace, will always be a special people in relation to the rest of the world. No other chosen people will ever stand alongside Israel. No state or group or class will ever become the Church. The unique will always be unique and the distances will remain. It will always be the case that even for the best men the good is a matter of command and prohibition, of exhortation, warning, precept and direction. Even in the kingdom of perfection this relationship will be maintained. Then we shall " see face to face." What constitutes the contradiction and the pain of this opposition will be taken away. Tears and suffering and crying and death will be no more. But even then we shall not be gods, let alone God Himself. There can certainly be no question of our being or becoming this now.

All the New Testament passages so far adduced speak of definite acts and attitudes in which this imitation of God and Christ must take shape. They are all in line with Mt. 5^{48}. Our aim must correspond to the distinctive aim of our Father in heaven, who meets both the good and the evil with the same beneficence. It must be a readiness to forgive one other, to be compassionate, to bear one another's burdens and to live and help one another. It must be persistent kindness even towards persecutors of the faith. It must be a humility in which we do not look at our own things, but at the things of others. It must be a love which is directed even—and especially—to our enemies. But the very definiteness of these demands shows their limitation. These demands obviously do not mean that man is invited to usurp the prerogative of God and to meddle in His affairs. The fulfilment of all these commands does not in any sense mean that he becomes a " gracious Lord " to his neighbours. Neither for himself nor for others can he or will he do what Jesus Christ did. For what Jesus did, the satisfaction for our sins, was done ἐφ' ἅπαξ. This is emphasised not only by the Epistle to the Hebrews, but also by the first Epistle of Peter (3^{18}). And it is certainly not overlooked or obscured by Paul, the very one who proclaims the perfect community and imitation of Christ. Neither for ourselves nor for others can we do the good which God does for us. What we should and can do is correspond to this good. We can and should seek and find in it the pattern of what we have to do. But what we now do will always be something different. It will be our creaturely action, and here and now it will always be an action conditioned, and indeed perverted, by our sin. That is, in so far as it is done out of respect for that pattern, in so far as that pattern is given to it, it will be righteous and holy ; but in so far as it is regarded alone, in so far as it is questioned and investigated according to its own inner content, it will be unrighteous and unholy. This action is a good action only in virtue of its correspondence with God's grace. In so far as it is good in this correspondence, it will not wish to be freed from this correspondence, or to claim for itself any immanent goodness. Just because Rom. 8^{33} tells us that there is no accusation against the elect of God, and Rom. 8^1 that there is no condemnation to those who are in Christ Jesus, the latter will be particularly on their guard against losing the freedom and therefore the real goodness of their works by claiming it as a goodness of their own which they themselves have produced and accomplished, and by playing it off even to the slightest extent, even only for a moment, against the goodness of God. It is just for this reason that this goodness cannot acquire the character of a " merit." The content of the divine demand on man is that he should do in *his* circle, and therefore with an obedience which makes no claim, that which God does by Christ in His circle. The demand is serious, penetrating and inescapable, just because it is so simple, just because it requires and expects of man no more than he can do, just because it is always the demand of grace. It does not demand that man should himself become a creator, reconciler and redeemer, that he should possess, control and dispense grace. It demands only that he should attest it, but attest in definite deeds and attitudes which correspond to it. Its commands are " not grievous " (1 Jn. 5³). They are rigorously directed to men. But they do not actually exceed the measure of human power. On the contrary, they stir human power to action—only human power, but really to action. " My yoke is easy, and my burden is light " (Mt. 11³⁰). It cannot be sufficiently pondered that the summons to take up this yoke is identical with the invitation : " Come unto me, all ye that labour and are heavy laden, and I will refresh you." The claim which fails to speak of this divine refreshment, or which summons man to create this divine refreshment for himself, is definitely not the divine claim.

But the required conformity with the grace of God is this. His action must be determined by the fact that he accepts the gracious action of God as right. This, or something just as simple and apparently sterile and non-committal, is the best possible expression to describe the content of the divine claim. We might perhaps substitute for " accept as right " some such phrase as " acquiesce in " or " respect " or " allow to stand " or " adhere to." The crux of the matter is that we should understand the Law as " spiritual " (Rom. 7¹⁴), or as " the law of the Spirit of life " (Rom. 8²), that is, as the form of grace and the Gospel, and therefore in the simplicity, indeed the " lightness," of its demand and fulfilment. We do the right when we accept as right what the gracious God does for us, and acquiesce in it. When man is summoned to do the right, primarily and decisively he is summoned only to adhere to the fact that the gracious God does the right. Whatever he himself does, it will be the right if only he is satisfied that the gracious God does the right. And it will never be the right, even to the slightest degree, if he is not satisfied with that. All the sublimity but also the intimacy, all the harshness but also the sweetness, all the rigours but also the compelling gentleness of the divine Law are contained in what is, after all, its only requirement : that what we do, we should do as those who accept as right what God in His grace does for us.

" To accept as right " means to lay aside all hostility to God's action—as if we were injured or humiliated by it, as if we had to guard and defend ourselves against it, as if there were some important interests which inclination or even duty compelled us to defend against it. " To accept as right " means again to lay aside all indifference to what God does, or non-participation in it—as if we knew nothing of it, as if it were no concern of ours, as if He did it for Himself, or for all kinds of others, as if He did not do it for us, for me, as if we, I, were not affected and determined by what He does. " To accept as right " means finally to lay aside all one's superiority and self-will in regard to God's action—as if alongside and apart from it we could acquiesce in and accept all kinds of other things as right, as if in our action we could choose again between orientation by this or that authority, as if acceptance of God's gracious action as right did not mean that we were bound to this authority, to this norm, and free only in obedience to it. " To accept God's action as right," and to live and act as those who have done and do and will do this in and above everything, is to confront God's action in a spirit of contentment, or better, with joyful participation, or better, with the burning and exclusive desire to be obedient to it. " To accept God's action as right " is to love God in this His action, to love Him with all our heart, and soul, and strength. That it demands so much makes no difference to the simplicity, indeed the lightness of God's command. On the contrary it is the lightness and simplicity of His command that, when it claims us in this way as God's command, it binds us to the God whom we may love, but who wills actually and wholly and utterly to be loved in what He does.

It is unfortunate that the saying : " My son, give me thine heart, and let thine eyes observe my ways," can be adduced only as a dictum of the translators and not as a correct rendering of Prov. 23²⁶. But Paul says materially the same thing in Col. 3¹f· when he exhorts those who are risen with Christ to seek what is above, where Christ is, sitting at the right hand of God : " Set your affection on things above, not on things on the earth." For there, above, hidden with Christ in God, is their true life. There God acts for them. There, consequently, is the norm and the principle of their own action, in the sense that what is done there is to be seen, discovered, considered, observed and valued by us, and then confirmed contentedly, joyfully and willingly in and by what we do. All other things which might try to claim us elsewhere—such as the δόγματα of the false teachers at Colossæ—are an earthly authority which does not deserve to be considered and valued and confirmed by us and therefore cannot really become normative, because it can never be divinely normative, because God does not stand behind these claims. The claim behind which God stands, and which is therefore binding, is " above." But it is not a heavenly power or spiritual force which is " above." It is Christ as the outstretched and active right arm of God Himself, as God's gracious dealing and gracious work in person. " To seek " and " to set the affection on " what is " above " is, therefore, to seek and set the affection on Christ, and then to live as one who does this, who from his heart accepts as right the gracious dealing and gracious work of God which he has experienced and is experiencing, who takes pleasure in these ways of God.

What are we to do ? We are to accept as right, and to live as those who accept as right the fact that they do not belong to them- selves, that they therefore do not have their life in their own hands and at their own disposal, that they are made a divine possession in Jesus Christ. Against this alienation, against this objective assign- ment of our existence to the very different hand of the gracious God, there will always be raised the hostility of those who would rather belong to themselves, who have no desire to be dispossessed and deprived of their most primitive possession, namely, themselves, who think they see a robber and enemy in the One who does this to them. There is also raised the indifference of those who do not see the hand which holds them, who do not recognise the kindness which is done to them, who do not understand the importance which this must have for their own action. There is also raised the wilfulness of those who, alongside the sphere to which they are directed, always see other spheres open into which they may move and desire to do so. But in contrast to all this, we have to accept it as right that we are God's possession. Why and how ? For this reason and in this way—that it is not possible for us to see God's gracious dealing and work in Jesus Christ without recognising that it is good for man, that it is the best thing possible for man, simply to be God's possession. However deep may be the ocean of that opposition within us, it is already drained to the depths in Jesus Christ. With Him our life, however we may regard Him or whatever we may wish to make of it, is already " hidden in God," hidden and secured against all the danger-ous folly of our opposition. In Him that alienation and assignation of man has already taken place, and the glory of God with which man is invested is already a revealed reality. What we have to do is to accept and maintain what He regards as true of our life against our own opposition and to let our action be illumined and ruled by this acceptance. This is the required conformity of our action with that of the gracious God.

What are we to do ? We are to accept it as right that God never meets us except compassionately, except as the One who comes to the help of our misery, except apart from and against our deserts, except in such a way as to disclose that what we have deserved is death. Here again hostility is provoked in those who would prefer—if at all— to stand and treat with God on the same footing, who want to co-operate in His counsel and participate in His acts, who regard it as too belittling and even hurtful a thing to have to live by mercy alone. Again, there is aroused the indifference of those whose heart has not been penetrated by God's mercy, who do not yet or any longer con-sider what it costs God to be merciful to them, who do not yet or any longer estimate what it means to be really saved from death by God's mercy. And, again, there is stirred up the wilfulness which wants to divide its attention and purposes between God's mercy and the value and rights of its own or others' claims and interests. In contrast to all this, we have to accept it as right to dare to live by the unfathomable mercy of God which has its basis—but an unshakeable basis—only in Himself. Why and how ? For this reason and in this way—that in Jesus Christ, as God's gracious dealing and work in person, we shall find and unveil only sinful and lost man—ourselves (for it was our sins and our lost estate which He took upon Himself and bore)—but this man, ourselves, awakened from the death which he had deserved, not by human power, but by God's power, not in the course of a natural development, but by the miraculous act of the free God. In face of these ways of God what is the significance of all the solid opposition which we might and actually do raise against them, of all our displeasure at having to live by mercy alone ? Certainly let it be voiced ! But let it be confronted with the opposition which God Himself has long since brought against it ! The required conformity of our action with the gracious action of God is that we accept the fact that our opposition is already met, that a term has already been set to it, that it has already been liquidated by what God has done. It is required that we should accept what has been done, even in the noisy opposition which we always make to it. It is required that there should not be lacking in our action the sign of this acceptance.

What are we to do ? We are to accept it as right that God is our righteousness. Beyond our physical and spiritual delights and desires, beyond our bondage to earth and titanic strivings, beyond our faults and virtues, beyond our good and evil works, He is always our righteousness. Against this " He " and against this " beyond," there again arises the hostility which would like to say " I " instead of " He," the indifference which does not see that we are left groping in a fog until this inversion is made, the wilfulness which would continually like to reverse it, at any rate temporarily and partially. All the opposition which man carries in his heart to the fact that he is not his own possession, but God's, and that he has not to live by his own merit but by God's mercy, finds a definite focus in the point that he cannot and will not realise that in fact " Yahweh is our righteousness " (Jer. 23[6], 33[16]), and that we have no righteousness of our own to set against this. There never has been and never will be a Christianity which is free from this opposition. The Phariseeism of a publican trying to boast that he is free from this opposition would be the worst of all the forms which this opposition can assume. But, in defiance of our opposition, we are summoned to accept as right what God does, and on this basis (and not for a moment apart from it) to do what we do, and therefore to do the right. No matter what may be our opposition to it, we are to accept it as right that God is our righteousness. Why and how ? Again for this reason and in this way—that this is the very thing which has taken place in God's gracious dealing and work, in Jesus Christ. In Him God has executed His judgment by making Him a sinner for us, but also by exalting Him before us to His glory. In Him we are acquitted and justified. In Him " He," God, has stepped into our place, suffering punishment, but also receiving a reward—my punishment and my reward. In Him God's righteousness has become my " beyond," actually mine. Of what avail will all our grumbling and murmuring be against this decision ? Of what avail will all our devices be to make an " I " again of the " He," and a " here " of the " beyond " ? What can we and shall we contrive against what has been done for us by God ? We were not asked whether it suited us so, nor are we asked what we want to make of it. What was done with us in Jesus Christ was that God made Himself our righteousness : in defiance of our defiance, in opposition to our opposition. Our required conformity with the action of divine grace is that we accept it as right, as the upper part of the Yes and No in which we move ; that our action be played out under and within the frame of this divine action. This is the content of the divine claim upon all men.

We can sum it all up by saying that what God wants of us and all men is that we should believe in Jesus Christ. Not that we should believe *like* Jesus Christ—that aspect is better left on one side seeing that He is God and we are only men—but that we should believe in Jesus Christ, in the gracious action of God actualised and revealed in Him. The essence of faith is simply to accept as right what God does, to do everything and all things on the presupposition that God's action is accepted as right. That is why it can and must be said of faith that in and by it we are righteous before God. In the last resort, the apostles had only one answer to the question : " What are men to do ? " This was simply that they should believe, believe in Jesus Christ. All the answers of theological ethics to the same question can only paraphrase and confirm the imperative : " Seek those things which are above, where Christ is."

3. THE FORM OF THE DIVINE CLAIM

By the form of the divine claim we understand the form and manner in which the command of God meets man, in which it imparts itself to him, in which it becomes—and it is this special concept which must now be elucidated and explained—a claim upon him. Our present question is how man—corresponding to the basis and content of the command of God—becomes its addressee and recipient. We ask concerning the distinctive mode of its revelation or, in relation to man as its addressee and recipient, concerning the particular hearing which it demands and creates for itself in him as it claims his obedience. What is it that distinguishes the command of God in this respect from other commands ?

There are other commands as well as that of God which, in their own way, approach man with a demand for hearing and obedience.

It can be said of every object in the natural and historical world that it contains and expresses a command to the extent that in its existence and essence it demands our attention, observation, consideration, investigation and understanding—purely for its own sake, because in its special existence and mode of existence it is our object, i.e., it confronts us, and as such asks us a question—perhaps many questions—which await our answer, i.e., our cognition, recognition and acknowledgment of it in its special existence and essence. Even of the axioms of mathematics and logic as the presuppositions of all investigation and understanding of the objective world it can be said that. they are commands. And from time to time, certain results of human knowledge can assume the character and role of intellectual commands of this kind : some of the pictures of nature and history, of the essence and structure and morphological change of creaturely existence, which we reach by way of intuitive conception or conceptual intuition ; some of the concrete hypotheses and conventions in regard to the bases and interconnexions of creaturely things which stamp themselves so deeply on whole centuries or even millenia that those who belong to these periods are scarcely conscious of their relativity. Constructs of this type usually demand our acceptance with almost or exactly the same categorical seriousness as if they themselves belonged—which they certainly do not—to the order of the objects or even to the order of the inner elements of human knowledge, as if we could not possibly escape them without showing ourselves to be perfect fools, as if respect for them were the criterion of intellectual honesty. But there are commands which are even more clearly related to the decisions of the human will than those mentioned. There are obviously the compelling necessities of life—from that of food and drink and warmth and sleep to that of seeing that our life always has such qualities as dignity and honour. There are commands of utility and comfort which seem to exist for us all and which can speak to us in the most urgent way, drowning all other commands. There are commands of circumspection, foresight and discretion which have been forced upon us by education or custom on the basis of tacit agreements in the greater or smaller circles within which we live, or which we have imposed on ourselves on the basis of our own insight. There is what is called the " command of the hour " which a man thinks he has discovered for himself and others, even for whole nations, or for all his contemporaries—a discovery which certainly requires a kind of inspiration, and in any case a very loud voice for its effective proclamation. There are commands to do this and not to do that which become commands simply because they are promulgated by someone who in his circle has the authority to do this, like the pregnant command which issued from Cæsar Augustus. There are others which no one issues but which in a definite situation are just as solid and lasting as if they had been promulgated by Augustus Cæsar. And there are others which are not lasting but which are so evident to you or me in a definite situation at a definite time that for the moment at least they seem to be eternal commands. Man, and the race, in every possible grouping and historical circumstance, stands under a plethora of commands. They may not all be equally pressing or urgent. They may not be received and experienced with the same clarity. But in their own way they are all peremptory. At a greater or lesser distance they all claim attention and conformity. In some form they all aim at the corresponding decisions of our will. And they are all obviously different in themselves from God's command, whose special manner of claiming man is the subject of our present enquiry.

Nothing seems easier than to regard one of these other commands as God's command and to pass it off as such, to see it invested with His authority and dignity, or pretend to others that it is invested in this way, and thus to give it additional weight both in our own eyes and those of others. It is indeed the case that—without prejudice to its particular form—the claim of God's command always wears the garment of another claim of this kind. An object with its question, the compulsion of a necessity of thought, one of those hypotheses or conventions, a higher necessity of life and particularly a more primitive, a necessity which in itself seems to be that of a very human wish or very human cleverness, a summons coming from this or that quarter, a call which a man directs to himself—all these can actually be the command of God veiled in this form, and therefore genuinely participate in the corresponding authority and dignity. But what is the proper form of the divine commands under and in all these garments ? What is its mark and characteristic among the many other commands under which man and humanity continually stand, without being able to say off-hand that they stand under the command of God ?

If we follow the lines along which we were led in our investigation of the basis and content of the divine command, there can be only one answer. The form by which the command of God is distinguished from all other commands, the special form which is its secret even in the guise of another command, consists in the fact that it is permission—the granting of a very definite freedom. We know who it is that orders here, and what it is that makes this ordering peremptory. It is the God in whom we may believe as the Lord who is gracious to us—gracious in the sense that He gave Himself for us in order that we might live before Him and with Him in peace and joy. And we know what it is that is ordered. We have to live as those who accept as right what God does for us. We have not to do that which contradicts but that which corresponds to His grace as it is directed to us. We have to believe in Jesus Christ, and in and with the fact that we live in this faith to do the right. The command of this Commander is a permission, and in this it is fundamentally and finally differentiated from all other commands.

It cannot be said of any other commands in themselves and as such that they are permissions, releases, liberations ; that they give us freedom. On the contrary, their commanding is in every respect a holding fast, a binding, a fettering. Each of them constitutes one of the many powers and dominions and authorities which restrict the freedom of man, which, under the pretext of their own divinity and in the supposed best interests of man, are not at all willing to allow him to go his own ways happily and peacefully. They all mean that at some point man is interrupted and even jostled ; that at some point—and worst of all when he begins to command himself—he is vexed and tormented. In one form or another they all express to man the suspicion that it might be dangerous to free him, that he would certainly misuse his liberty, that once liberated, he would only create trouble for himself and others. From the most varied angles they fill him with anxious fears : the intellectual fear of spiritual isolation ; fear of the possibility of a world food shortage ; a moral fear of his own possibilities ; political fear in face of his own weakness. They use these fears to appeal to him, instilling them into him and holding him in their grip. In essence, their bidding is a forbidding ; the refusal of all possible permissions. This is what distinguishes the sphere of these commands very sharply from that of the command of God. Commands which are only ostensibly and allegedly divine, and misunderstandings of the real command of God, always betray themselves by the fact that they create and restore and maintain this sphere of distrust and fear.

The command of God sets man free. The command of God permits. It is only in this way that it commands. It permits even though it always has *in concreto* the form of one of the other commands, even though it, too, says, " Thou shalt " and " Thou shalt not," even though it stands before man, warning, disturbing, restraining, binding and committing. The command of God and other commands do the same thing, but it is not really the same. No matter in what guise the command of God meets us, in accordance with its basis and context, it will always set us free along a definite line. It will not compel man, but burst open the door of the compulsion under which he has been living. It will not meet him with mistrust but with trust. It will not appeal to his fear but to his courage. It will instil courage, and not fear into him. This is the case because the command, as we have seen, is itself the form of the grace of God, the intervention of the God who has taken the curse from us to draw us to Himself—the easy yoke and the light burden of Christ, which as such are not to be exchanged for any other yoke or burden, and the assumption of which is in every sense our quickening and refreshing. This is what God prepares for us when He gives us His command. The man who stands under the jurisdiction of all those other commands of God and is not refreshed is not the obedient man but the man who disobeys God, who, instead of living according to his determination to be the image of God, and therefore in conformity with the grace of God, has succumbed and succumbs to the temptation to eat of the tree of the knowledge of good and evil, which is forbidden him for his own good, and in this way to exalt himself to a spurious divine likeness.

This act of godlessness, sin, is man's undoing. For it is this which leads him at once and directly into the uncomfortable sphere of all those commands. He now knows how to distinguish between good and evil. He is the one who not only can do this, but must do it. In all his cosmos, wherever he goes or stays, the line is drawn between good and evil. He is confronted on all sides by *sic et non*, motives and quietives, commands and prohibitions—all contradicting one another, but all in their time and place subjecting him to the highest possible degree of unsettlement, assaulting him, grasping at him, forcing him in different directions and detaining him at different points. His eyes are now open but only like those of a victim of insomnia. He now has to choose and decide and judge on all sides. He has to try to hew a track for himself through the unending primeval forest of claims. He has to establish his preference. With the help of a classification of values, he has to set up a little system of the commands which he thinks he can and should satisfy first. But he cannot ignore the fact that he cannot even satisfy those which he has selected with their constant and voracious demands for more. He cannot ignore or prevent the fact that even those which he has set aside and neglected continue to exist, and secretly and openly clutch at him and claim him. He will never satisfy all claims, and he will not really satisfy even one. This is the divine likeness of the godless—of Adam, the man who would not first satisfy God because he was not content with the grace of God. When man sins—sins against God (which is the only real sin, the sin in all sins)—he is delivered up, like a hunted beast to the hounds, to what the world and life and men want of him, to what, above all, he himself must continually want of himself. To play at being the Creator and Lord is something which he can do quite successfully. But actually to be the Creator and Lord is something which he cannot do, and therefore, when he is severed from the real Creator and Lord, his only alternative is to become the slave of the created world and above all his own slave. Compared with this assault of commands that harass the sinner, the command of God is indeed seen to be a different, a totally different command. It is not the sum and superlative of this infernal assault. It does not mean that the intensity of this assault is infinitely multiplied. How, then, did man come to be exposed to this assault according to the story of the fall? It was not because he obeyed the command of God—which was designed to spare him this ordeal—but because he fell, fell from obedience to this command, and therefore—attaining divine likeness to his own destruction—fell into the sphere of the many commands which necessarily have authority and power over the man who for his part, in his relationship to God, refuses to live of and by His grace, but tries to invest himself with an authority and power of his own.

The command of the gracious God, however, will summon man out of this sphere of harassment.

It is true, of course, that this command also says : Do this and do not do that. But in the mouth of God this means something different. Do this—not because an outer or inner voice now requires this of you, not because it must be so in virtue of any necessity rooted in the nature and structure of the cosmos or of man, but : Do this, because in so doing you may and will again live of and by My grace. Do this, because in so doing you may make it true that your rejection has been rejected in the death of Jesus on the cross, that for His sake your sin has been forgiven. Do this, because in Jesus Christ you have been born anew in the image of God. Do it in the freedom to which you have been chosen and called, because in this freedom you may do this, and can do only this. For this, and not for any other reason, do it. You may do it. And : Do not do this—not because you again hear an outer or inner voice which seeks to make it doubtful or dreadful for you, not because there is any power in heaven or on earth to prevent or spoil or for some reason forbid it. No, but : Do not do this, because it would be a continuation of the fall of Adam, because it would not correspond to the grace addressed to you but contradict it, because you would have to do it as the captive which you certainly are not, because you, the free man, are exempted from the necessity of doing it—really exempted by the fact that you have been made righteous and glorious in the resurrection of Jesus Christ, that you have actually been cut off by Him from this very possibility. This is how the command of God speaks.

It always speaks concretely. It did that already according to the story of the fall. As long as time lasts and with it this form of the divinely created world and our own existence, it will always speak concretely like other commands. But it is not for this reason to be confused with any of them. It is distinguished from all of them by the fact that it is permission, that it sets us free, that with it the Sabbath always dawns—our discharge from the usurped office of judging good and evil, in the exercise of which there can be revealed only the judgment of ourselves. The command of God wills only that we, for our part, accept that God in Jesus Christ is so kind that He accepts us just as we are. It wills only that we make use of the given permission by the grace of God to be what we are, and therefore that we do not leave again the shelter which the faithfulness of God has given us against the infernal tempest of all other outward and inward claims, that we do not do again what Adam did, that we do not play the lord and therefore become masterless and therefore helpless and defenceless. The command of God orders us to be free. How can it be otherwise ? The command is only the form of the Gospel of God, in virtue of which —not in and by ourselves, but in and by Jesus Christ—we are free. This is what characterises the command of God, distinguishing it from all other commands, not just relatively but absolutely, with the distinction of heaven over earth.

In Mt. 22[1-14] we are told about the great and urgent invitation to the kingdom of heaven which is so badly received by those who are invited, which is finally answered with the maltreatment and death of its bearers, and which after their punishment is passed on to those at the street-corners, both bad and good (v. 10). It belongs not only to the parable but to the matter itself that it is an invitation, and indeed the invitation to a feast, to a marriage feast : " My oxen and my fatlings are killed and all things are ready " (v. 4). The epilogue (which is wrongly conjured away by many exegetes) tells us about the individual who certainly came, but came without a wedding-garment (v. 11 f.), and it shows that in the last resort it all boils down to the fact that the invitation is to a feast, and that he who does not obey and come accordingly, and therefore festively, declines and spurns the invitation no less than those who are unwilling to obey and appear at all. Reluctant obedience to God's command is not obedience, and decisively for this reason, that in itself and as such the command of God is a festive invitation. It is for this reason that the wedding guests—the disciples of Jesus in contrast to those of John and the Pharisees—cannot fast when the Bridegroom is with them (Mk. 2[19]). It is for this reason that when John the Baptist subordinates himself to Jesus in Jn. 3[29] he confesses that although he does not have the bride he is a friend of the Bridegroom and rejoices at his voice. It is for this reason that the χαίρετε of 2 Cor. 13[11], and especially of the Epistle to the Philippians (2[18], 3[1], 4[4]), seems to epitomise, as it were, all apostolic exhortation. How can any part of what Paul demands of Christians be rightly done if in the first instance it is not done with joy, as an " ought " whose seriousness lies at bottom in the fact that it is a " may," something permitted ?

There is no New Testament writing which presents the Gospel to men so emphatically and unwaveringly, so consistently from the standpoint of the divine claim, as the Epistle of James. But it is here (1[22f.]) that the controlling demand not to be a forgetful hearer of the Word, but a real hearer, and therefore a doer, the doer of the work which forms the content of this Word, is explained as follows. We are not to be like a man who sees " his natural face " in a mirror but then goes away and forgets how he looks. On the contrary, we are to " look into the perfect law of liberty," and to persist in looking, in order that we may become doers of the Word and therefore " blessed in our doing." The expression παρακύπτειν is the same as that which is used in Lk. 24[12] (?) and Jn. 20[5, 11] of those who, stooping, looked into the grave of Jesus and found it empty, and in 1 Pet. 1[12] of the angels who long to look into that which has been declared to the Church by the prophets and apostles. And if the "perfect law," which is that of freedom, is contrasted to the mirror in which we behold our natural face, this obviously means that in the Word of God, which we have to hear and as right hearers to do, we find our other, proper face ; we find ourselves as those who may and must do what they do in freedom ; we find ourselves as those who are willing and ready, but also able, in the last resort to live our own lives. It is as the Word of God holds before us this picture—which is unforgettable for those who have once seen it—that it is the "perfect" law ; the law which we cannot hear and not immediately do it. And action in obedience to this law is the action of a free man, and to that extent a blessed action. That is why we read in Jas. 2¹² (immediately before the well-known saying that there can be no faith without works) : "So speak ye, and so do, as they that shall be judged by the law of liberty," that have to give an account to God, as the free men they are in virtue of the Word of God. The directions of the Epistle of James cannot be understood if it is not seen that they all stand upon this denominator.

And for the same reason we can and must leap across from the Epistle of James to what seems to be the very different lines of thought of Galatians and Romans and the Gospel of John, although in reality these only bring out in a broader and more forcible way what is said in James about the command of God as the "law of freedom." They are best regarded in their inner connexion. Here, too, the thesis is quite clear : "If the Son therefore shall make you free, ye shall be free indeed, i.e., essentially (ὄντως, Jn. 8³⁶). "For liberty Christ hath made us free" (Gal. 5¹, cf. 2⁴). "For, brethren, you have been called unto liberty" (Gal. 5¹³). "The law of the Spirit of life in Christ Jesus hath made you free" (Rom. 8²). "If ye continue in my word, then are ye my disciples indeed (ἀληθῶς) ; and ye shall know the truth, and the truth shall make you free" (Jn. 8³¹ᶠ·).

According to v. 33, this summons to the obedience which sets man in freedom, and which as obedience consists in the use of his freedom, is not understood by the Jews because they think that they are already free, and not in bondage, as the descendants of Abraham. Jesus replies in v. 34 with the statement that to commit sin always means to be a slave and not free. That a sinner is a slave of sin is also maintained in Rom. 6¹⁷, ²⁰. What we do as sinners is not done in freedom, but in the greatest unfreedom. We will it, certainly, but what we do is not what we may or essentially will, but what we must do. "It is no more I that do it, but sin that dwelleth in me" (Rom. 7¹⁷, ²⁰). "I do not know it" ; indeed, "I do not will it," says Paul again and again in Rom. 7¹⁵ᶠ·. If I still do it, it is because my will is not basically free. This is the state of the man who is not obedient to the call of Jesus to continue in His Word, to be His disciple in truth, and therefore to know the truth. This is the state of insubordination to the divine command. "Now I say, That the heir, as long as he is a child, differeth nothing from a servant, though he be lord of all" (Gal. 4¹). The sinful man as such is, in fact, "in bondage under the elements of the world" (the στοιχεῖα τοῦ κόσμου, Gal. 4³). And the reward which he receives as this slave is shame and death (Rom. 6²¹ᶠ·). "He abideth not in the house for ever"—these words of Jn. 8³⁵ give us a comprehensive description of this condition. He is in it. He belongs to it. But he can never be more than an outsider, a stranger. He has no part whatever in the goods of the house. And Paul expressly describes this servile state and service of sinful man as a subjection to a law which confronts him with the claim to be the Law of God, which undoubtedly is this Law in its inmost concealed substance, but which is also "the law of sin and death" (Rom. 8²) in its form and effect. Apart from the Gospel and faith, and therefore apart from the summons to obedience issued by Jesus, there is for man only this Law, and therefore only this servile state and service with all its consequences. The heir who is a minor stands docilely under the "tutors and governors" (Gal. 4²), under the divinely appointed "schoolmaster" (Gal. 3²⁴ᶠ·), although the latter does not educate him "unto Christ," as in the customary and much too pragmatic interpretation, but represents the reaction of the divine wrath—the shutting up, the arrest (Gal. 3²³, Rom. 11³²) which man suffers "until Christ," i.e., until the heir is declared of age and therefore freed by the summons of Christ and in obedience to it. Apart from this, before it happens, or in abstraction from it, the Law, the command of God, which is holy and righteous and good (Rom. 7¹²) in itself, is for man the harmful thing described in Rom 7⁷ᶠ· Of course, even apart from the Gospel and faith, and therefore under this Law, man has to do with God. But it is with the God who according to Gal. 6⁷ᶠ· is not mocked, who inexorably causes a man to reap what he has sown. Sin is man's action in the misunderstanding and misuse of the Law. In face of the command of God, which, when it is encountered, requires only that we be satisfied with the grace of God, sin consists in our yielding to the prompting of the desire (ἐπιθυμία) to be like God, to cleanse and justify and sanctify ourselves before God, to lord it against Him. When we listen to this desire and obey it, the sin which is dead in itself wakens to life—and man is already dead, as we are told with gruesome clarity in Rom. 7⁹ᶠ·. He becomes a sinner. He becomes guilty before God. He has fallen under His judgment. What God has forbidden is forbidden because in its root and essence it is always this one forbidden thing. It is the act of our desire for self-glorification against God. It is the act of our hatred of the all-sufficiency of God's grace. All evil consists in the fact that we do what we do under the impulsion of this desire. And when it is misused in this way, the Law itself can only prepare death for us. It can only execute and confirm that shutting up, that arrest, that exclusion from the house of our Father and from all His goods. This misused Law certainly does not become ineffective in this misuse. It is fatally effective. And its message and revelation to us (Rom. 7¹⁴ᶠ·) is that sin dwells in us, so that we continually do what we really do not want to do, and (Rom. 7¹⁸ᶠ·) that the good does not dwell in us, so that we never do what we really want to do, and always do what we really do not want to do. The Law, then, can only tear us in two. This contradiction is death as the wages of sin (Rom. 6²³). This means dying in a living body. This is what life is in the tempestuous assault of commands which we cannot escape, and which we can satisfy neither as a whole nor in detail. It is from God the Creator of all things, and therefore from our legitimate Commander, that they derive their authority and force. But the form which they now take—corresponding to our severance from the gracious divine command which is their source and truth—is the disintegrated, dismembered and individually distorted form of the στοιχεῖα τοῦ κόσμου, against whose rule and operation, which in the last resort are so utterly harmful, Paul tried to warn the Galatians, exhorting them so urgently and sharply to abandon this fresh attempt to improve justification by faith in Jesus Christ by linking it with the self-justification of an effort to fulfil the works of the Law. " O wretched man that I am ! who shall deliver me (ῥύεσθαι) from the body of this death ? " (Rom. 7²⁴).

There can be no doubt about one thing. By his own efforts man will never deliver himself from this body of death, from existence under the Law of sin and death. There is only one deliverance, and life only on the basis of what this really is. The crucial thing is that in view of this reality we should drop the question what we are and what is to become of us. The way leads forwards from the body of this death. It is not a way which we have trodden or ever will. It is the way which Jesus Christ has trodden once and for all. But because there is this way, we must not look back. This is the inner necessity of the great polemic of the Epistle to the Galatians. For this deliverance is the " freedom " for which Christ has made us free. It is freedom from sin, or more exactly, from the servile state and service of sin (Rom. 6¹⁸, ²²). And from what we have said, this can only mean—and in Paul it does mean this as clearly as possible—liberation from the Law, the Law which for sinful man can only be the Law of sin (i.e., the Law which is misused by his sin, but at the same time unmasks him as a sinner), and the Law of death (i.e., the Law which punishes him as sinner). The negative meaning of freedom is undoubtedly liberation from this Law (Rom. 8²). " Ye are not under law, but under grace " (Rom. 6¹⁴). The positive side has to be added at once if this freedom is to be properly described. It is the new freedom for the state and service from which man has alienated himself. Exactly into the place of that Law there steps grace. It is itself " the law of the Spirit of life " (Rom. 8²). But it steps into the place of the Law and therefore it radically excludes it. In Jesus Christ both the negative and the positive have already taken place, and in Jesus Christ we shall always find that they have taken place and are true. " When the fulness of the time was come, God sent forth his Son, born of a woman, made under the law, to redeem them that were under the law, that we might receive the adoption of sons (υἱοθεσία) " (Gal. 4⁴ᶠ·).

Paul developed the same idea in greater detail and with a different comparison in Rom. 7¹⁻⁶. (It is not always given sufficient weight that this is the controlling statement of the chapter and all the rest is only an illustrative counterpart.) The aim of these verses, and therefore of the whole chapter, is to show that we are snatched and lifted right out of the Law—this Law of sin and death—that it has been completely done away. There is an anticipation in Rom. 6¹⁴. It is not the case that, in spite of the death and resurrection of Jesus Christ, in spite of our baptism in His name, in spite of our faith in Him, this Law can continually call sin to life and keep it alive, accusing us as sinners, i.e., branding and punishing us as its slaves, destroying our sanctification and therefore our reconciliation with God, and finally giving the lie to God's decision and work as they have already taken place in our favour. As we are shown in Rom. 6, there is no going back on the road which God has trodden with us. For the Law—this is what has to be specifically shown in Rom. 7—this peculiar " power " of sin (1 Cor. 15⁵⁶), has been deprived of its power by what God has done for us upon this way of His. The Law rules over man—attention should be paid to the depiction of its rule in v. 5: it arouses the motions (or passions) of sin (corresponding to vv. 7–13), and what it brings forth is fruit unto death (corresponding to vv. 14–23)—as long as the sinful man (" the old man " of 6⁶) lives. In terms of the parable which begins in v. 2, I am bound to this sinful man and the Law that governs him as a wife is bound to her husband as long as he is alive. The wife is freed, however, by the death of her husband, and in the same way I am freed by the death of this sinful man—freed also from the Law that governs him. There is no freedom (v. 3) without the death of this sinful man. Every attempt to escape the sin and death, to which I am manacled by the life of this sinful man, can only bind me the more strongly to them, leading to the idolatry and self-righteousness which the Old Testament describes as the aggravated adultery of Israel against its God. But I can be made free legitimately, I can be removed altogether from the Law of sin and death, by the death of this sinful man. Another man can then step into his place, as a widow can legally become the wife of another. This, says St. Paul in v. 4, is exactly how it is with those who are baptised into Christ. They are those whose " old man " has been killed (6²ᶠ·) ; killed in and with the killing of Jesus Christ on Golgotha. This killing took place in order that freedom should be won for them : not only negatively, but positively ; the freedom to belong to the Other who died for them but also rose and lives for them. Released from that old connexion and placed in this new, they are no longer subject to the Law that ruled the old man. Life in the sphere of that rule has become a thing of the past with the death of Jesus Christ (v. 5). The subject Adam, arrested and shut up and unable legitimately even to attempt to escape, is eliminated. The subject Jesus Christ has replaced and excluded this subject. But this means also (v. 6) the replacement and exclusion of the misused and distorted Law which had become a temptation and destruction, to which Adam was subject and had to remain subject as long as he lived, to which we, too, can only remain subject in and with Adam and his life. And exactly into the place of that Law there came and is now executed " service " in newness of spirit " (v. 6)—in the existence which begins where the " oldness of the letter," i.e., the rule and the validity and operation of that Law, ceases. This is what is meant by deliverance from the " body of this death " (7²⁴), " being under grace " (6¹⁴), the real emancipation of man realised in the Liberation effected by the Son of God (Jn. 8³⁶) as an emancipation from the Law. If those who are freed in this way still live " in the flesh," this can only mean (Rom. 8⁵ᶠ·) that they are still confronted with the flesh and therefore with that old sinful man in his subjection to the Law. But it does not mean (Rom. 8⁵, ⁸, ⁹) that they still are in the flesh, for in virtue of their liberation their being is no longer their being in Adam, but their being in Jesus Christ their Liberator. In relation to Him the will of the flesh can only be the unauthoritative and ineffective will of a dead person. In relation to Him, the power of the Law which governs this dead person can have no more power.

For the liberated person, therefore, the decisive consequence of this liberation consists in the fact that there is for him (Rom. 8¹) no κατάκριμα, no condemnation. He may live as one who is not condemned. And, according to Rom. 8, the fact that he may do this is the sum of what he ought to do, of what is required and demanded of him. It is the Son of God, sent " in the likeness of sinful flesh " (Rom. 8³), who is condemned. And in and with Him there is also condemned the flesh of those who are His, the nature in which sin dwells, the religious, the moral flesh, which tries to bend and break the Law of God by repudiating the grace to which the Law orders it to adhere. It is Adam, the sinner himself, who perverts the Law to a rule of human self-purification, self-justification and self-sanctification, that is condemned. But in virtue of that condemnation of Jesus Christ, there is no condemnation but acquittal for the man who (Rom. 8²), belonging to the risen Jesus Christ, stands under the " law of the Spirit of life," i.e., under the true Law of God, revealed again in its proper substance as Law of grace, and made effective again in spite of its perversion by sin. " Ye shall know the truth, and the truth shall make you free." When the Law of God frees itself from that misused, corrupt and pernicious form of the Law of sin and death, the man who is liberated in and with this event, who belongs to Jesus Christ, is cut loose from the distress which this Law necessarily causes him and to which he himself cannot put an end. He has broken through to the life which according to Rom. 8¹²ᶠ· will be a life in obedience, according to Rom. 8¹⁷ᶠ· a life in hope, and according to Rom 8²⁸ᶠ· a life in innocence. The break-through to this life, which results from what took place at Golgotha, is described by Paul in Rom. 8¹⁴ as the work, the ἄγειν of the Spirit, who, according to Gal 4⁶, is the Spirit of His own Son, and therefore, according to Rom. 8¹⁵, the Spirit of the sonship—and therefore not the spirit of the bondage (δουλεία)—of those who belong to Him. That the Spirit cries—or that we ourselves cry in the spirit : Abba, Father ! (Gal. 4⁶, Rom. 8¹⁵)—is the absolutely basic and primal form of the service for which, according to Rom. 7⁶, we are freed. Obviously, therefore, it is the basic and primal form of the command of God. This is what God's command wants of us—the crying of the child, of the children, who have at last found their father again, have at last been found by him, have at last been freed from all the " tutors and governors," at last been freed from the " schoolmaster," at last been freed—self-evidently—from the real power of disobedience, at last been freed from the nerve or lever of sin. It should be noted that the conclusion of Rom. 8 (vv. 28–29) refers back to the beginning of the chapter and therefore to the problem of Rom. 7 and therefore to that of Rom. 6. That God is for us, and therefore no one and nothing is against us (v. 31), is the reason why it is quite impossible for us to remain in sin (6¹), and so necessary for us to transfer from its service to the obedience of righteousness (6¹²ᶠ·). And if no one and nothing is against us in consequence of the fact that God is for us, this means simply that we are not condemned ; that the Law of sin and death is repealed ; that the lordship of the world-elements is broken. It is not a case of " must," but " may." Our " may " is our " must." Therefore, not only according to the whole tenor of the Epistle to the Galatians, but according to the clear and systematic context of Rom. 6–8, freedom from the Law is for Paul not merely an incidental qualification of the obedience claimed by God, much less the peculiar and rather dangerous qualification of a higher, more advanced stage of this obedience, which in itself necessarily begins elsewhere, in a legality, with a " must." On the contrary, as both Paul and also James formulated it, the Law itself is the " law of liberty " and its τέλος, its intention, its general sum and substance, can be understood only when it is understood as the law of liberty. In the plain statement of James, those who hear it differently will never do it —not merely in part, but as a whole. If it does not confront us as the Law of liberty, so that we for our part are forced to stop in front of it as such, if it is not our " may " which is claimed, if what is demanded is not the crying of children to the father whom they have at last found again, if the appeal is not to our innocence, if we are not stirred to action as those who are righteous, as those whom God is for and therefore nobody and nothing can be against—then it is not the command of God, or, rather, it is only that Law of the divine wrath which corresponds to our sin, the corrupt and pernicious Law, and with all our attempts to be obedient, we can only make ourselves guilty of that adultery (Rom. 7³), only entangle ourselves more and more deeply in disobedience. According to Jas. 1²² a doer of the Law is only a free and happy doer. For the content of this Word, the meaning of the divine claim, consists in the fact that, promising us freedom and joy as the Gospel, it requires of us the same freedom and joy as the Law. All our knowledge of the character of the divine command as such, and therefore all our obedience to it, stands or falls with our knowledge of the connexion between the indicative and the imperative in Gal. 5¹ : " For liberty Christ hath made us free : stand fast, therefore, and be not entangled again with the yoke of bondage."

It is precisely and only this distinction of the command of God from all other commands, precisely and only its characterisation as permission, which reveals its seriousness and rigour. The command of God is imperative. When it orders us to be free, it orders with authority. And it enforces itself. It secures obedience by itself setting us free. As the divine permission given to us, it is not the confirmation of a permission that we have given ourselves, or obtained or secured elsewhere, although there are, of course, other permissions, just as there are other commands, and in the most intimate connexion with these commands.

We are continually " permitting " ourselves all possible things, decisions and attitudes, thoughts and words and works, in which we regard ourselves as free, which we apparently do gladly, in which we think that we are happy. There is none of those other commands which, when it imposes its yoke upon us, has not a way of recommending itself to us. Its fulfilment is perhaps a particular confirmation of our freedom, or it is perhaps bound up for us with a particular desire, or the avoidance of a dislike, so that at bottom we want to do the thing which it would have us do. And so in the fulfilling of these other commands there is, in fact, no human action which is not in some measure bound up with the consciousness, experience and and feeling of apparent freedom and joy. " And the woman saw that the tree was good for food, and that it was pleasant to the eyes, and a tree to be desired " (Gen 3⁶). And so the man permits himself to make use of the permission of his wife, who on her part had accepted it from the serpent : ' The man said, The woman whom thou gavest to be with me, she gave me of the tree, and I did eat. And the Lord God said unto the woman, What is this that thou has done ? And the woman said, The serpent beguiled me, and I did eat " (Gen. 3^{12f.}). It is apparently pure permission that rules. The man permits himself to renounce the grace of God. He permits himself to be set up as one who knows good and evil and therefore as judge over both. He permits himself therefore to be established in the divine likeness. Man obviously thinks that he is particularly free and happy even in his fall.

The permission of the command of God cancels all this, not by opposing His prohibition to a real permission, freedom and joy, but by revealing the truth, by unmasking the supposed permission, freedom and joy as the deception of a strange lord and tyrant, who under its semblance has made man a slave. The command of God is the renewed offer of the grace of God that man has repelled. The command of God wants man to be genuinely free. It wants him to make use of the real permission at his disposal, to return to his true freedom, to rejoice not merely in appearance but in truth in what he does. The free will of man has nothing to do with permission, freedom and joy. It is in his free will that he is tricked and tricks himself out of all this, reducing himself to that servile state and service, however free and happy he thinks himself to be. He is then oppressed and tormented by the law of that foreign lord and tyrant, to whom he does not belong, who has not created him, with whom his destiny has nothing to do, who has nothing that he can command him to do and therefore nothing that he can permit him to do, in whose service he can never be free and happy (whatever his consciousness, experiences and feelings may be), in whose service he can only be deceived even in this consciousness. The command of God rends this veil, and it does it by being and expressing the real permission given to man. It is in this that it is serious and rigorous, binding and committing us with a seriousness and rigour beyond the power of all other commands. The command of God sets itself against human free will, not because it does not wish man to be really free and happy, but on the contrary, because God does want this, because he cannot really be free and happy in his self-will. The command of God protests against what man permits himself, or knows how to create or find elsewhere by way of permission. The reason for this protest is that these permissions are really only the disguises of the servitude to which he is subjected. The form which it takes is that, in opposition to the foreign dominion to which he has yielded, it gives him again the permission which is really proper and belongs to him.

It is in this profound and radical way that it unsettles and terrifies and assaults and seizes him. It does not do this like an enemy, who can certainly attack him from outside, but from whom he can flee, from whom he can wring concessions, with whom he can make agreements, with whom he can ultimately come to a peaceful understanding, as happens in view of the fact that in the last resort he thinks that he can freely and gladly gratify its wishes. The unsettlement and terror, the assault and seizure, which the command of God means for man, are radical just because the command of God is the command of our true, best friend ; because it comes up alongside us from behind as it were ; because even in its majesty it addresses us absolutely from within in opposition to all that we allow ourselves, putting an end to our supposed freedom and joy ; because it is just permission, and it wills only that we do what we are permitted to do ; because everything else is not permitted and can therefore be only the fulfilment of a compulsion. We are not under this compulsion. We are not bound and obliged to obey it. And obeying it in freedom and joy is the most miserable of all self-deceptions. Just because it is real permission the command of God separates us from the domination of all other commands and therefore from our desires and lusts. It does so by taking our part, by engaging that we may begin to live at last in real freedom and joy, and therefore turn our backs on the foreign domination under which we have placed ourselves. Expressing God's decision concerning us, that we belong to Him, that the claim which He has on us as the Creator cannot be broken, it demands of us that we finally act on our own decision—our very own, the one which corresponds to our determination. This is how it affects us. It sets us on our feet. It is against us only in so far as we are against ourselves. Under the domination of all other commands, and therefore under the domination of our own desires and lusts, in the self-will in which we subject ourselves to that foreign domination, in the permission which we believe we can and should give ourselves, we are really against ourselves. And it is certainly against this self-hostility and self-destruction that the command of God sets itself. This is what gives it its uniquely distinctive sharpness and necessity. This is what makes it impossible for us to withdraw in face of it to a place to which we can withdraw in face of all other commands—to ourselves. No other demand or order can be so serious and rigorous. No other command can engage man at such close quarters that he is cut off from retreat upon himself. No object and no axiom, none of the hypotheses or conventions that can become a command to us, no biological necessity or social law, not even a command of conscience, has the power to press us so closely that we cannot keep our distance from it, remaining within ourselves, or constantly returning to ourselves, behind and in all that we think and say and do in submission to its claim. It belongs to the nature of all other commands that in face of them we necessarily have to come back again and again to ourselves, to our function of judging between good and evil, either conceding obedience to them from this position, or perhaps in the future confronting them with partial or complete disobedience. In the servile state and service which are our only possibility outside the command of God, there is only the servile

obedience which is distinguished from real obedience by the fact that
it is qualified obedience, obedience with a sidelong glance at the opportunity which may be within reach or present itself, and is perhaps
always conceivable, of acting and behaving quite independently of
what is commanded. Where the course of human life and the system
of human relations are not regulated by the command of God, they
are based on this servile obedience and imbued with the qualification
that we might also be disobedient. No command but God's command
can prevent man from making this qualification, at least inwardly.
No wonder that under these presuppositions the structure and trap-
pings of individual and social life are never lasting, but necessarily
suffer continual disintegration through their inner contradictions,
which, on the basis of this qualification, can never lose actuality.
But the command of God makes this qualification impossible. For it
proceeds from the only possible source of this qualification—ourselves.
In its core it always consists in the deposition of man as the judge of
good and evil. In the teeth of all the spurious permissions which he
has given and might give himself, it permits him to live by the grace
of God. In face of this permission, how can there be any further
place for this qualification ? When God has so radically espoused his
cause—and this is the meaning of His command—how can man take
up his own cause again ? How can he give himself a permission when
he actually receives and may enjoy and use the true and comprehensive
and effective permission ? How can he hanker after freedom and joy
when he is promised real joy and freedom ? There is no escaping the
command of God because, when it confronts us, it immediately and
at the same time places itself behind us. Pursuing the cause of God,
it immediately and at the same time takes up also our most proper
cause. Executing the decision of God, it immediately and at the same
time claims also our own decision—in which alone there could be that
flight. This is its seriousness and rigour, and in this respect no other
commands, however solemn and inexorable, can approach it. Its
seriousness and rigour are unconditional just because it imposes freedom on man, just because it sets man free with the obedience which
it requires of him, just because it is the command of the grace of God.
As the command of the grace of God, it circumvents the person who
would save and purify and justify and sanctify himself. It circumvents all the submissions to other commands which he would make to
this end. More than that, it circumvents all the permissions which
he would give himself to this end. Above all and decisively, it circumvents his retreat into himself, the further exercise of his office as the
judge of good and evil. He is to know and accept the fact that God
is for him. He is to live as one whom God is for. Whatever the
concrete content of the command of God may be, this is what God
will have of man. It is just because He wills this of him that He calls
him in question so absolutely—not merely this or that which he has

done and does in fulfilling other commands or in using the various permissions which he has given and created for himself, but the man himself in his attempt to try to act without God's grace, to try to be himself the judge of good and evil and therefore to be like God. And willing this of him, He wills to have him absolutely—not merely this and that act of obedience, as imposed on him by other commands, not merely the renunciation of this or that arbitrarily granted permission, but the man himself as one who is obedient, and therefore his renunciation of free will itself and as such. It is the fact that God is for him which binds and commits man himself, and that unconditionally. It is this which completely excludes, therefore, everything which would in any way mean that he for his part wanted to be for himself. Since God is for him, he is relieved from the post of being for himself by the One who alone can be actually and effectively for him. He is relieved of all the care and all the fear of being for himself. The basis of the " must " which corresponds to the command of God is, then, the fact that what comes from the command of God can only be the deepest and most radical " may " of the man who sees that God is not against him, but for him.

We can realise the absoluteness of the seriousness and rigour of the divine command, as rooted in its freedom, if we remember the commands which occupy so dominating a position in the New Testament—that we are not to be anxious and that we are not to fear. " Take no thought for your life " (Mt. 6²⁵). " Take therefore no thought for the morrow " (Mt. 6³⁴). " Take no thought how or what ye shall speak " (Mt. 10¹⁹). " Be careful for nothing, but in every thing by prayer and supplication with thanksgiving let your requests be made known unto God " (Phil. 4⁶, cf. 1 Cor. 7³²). " Casting all your care upon him ; for he careth for you " (1 Pet. 5⁷). The other command meets us even more frequently and urgently : " Fear not." Zacharias (Lk. 1¹³), Joseph (Mt. 1²⁰), Mary (Lk. 1³⁰) and the shepherds in the field (Lk. 2¹⁰) are not to be afraid when the birth oft he Messiah is announced to them in such extraordinary circumstances. Simon Peter is not to be afraid when the Messiah is revealed to him in the miraculous draught of fishes (Lk. 5¹⁰). The disciples are not to be afraid when He appears in the midst of the storm at sea (Mk. 6⁵⁰), or when He is transfigured on the mountain (Mt. 17⁷). The women at the empty grave are not to be afraid at His resurrection (Mt. 28⁵, ¹⁰), or the seer John on Patmos when He appears in glory (Rev. 1¹⁷). Again, the apostles are not to be afraid when He tells them of His departure (Jn. 14¹, ²⁷). The little flock is not to be afraid because it is small (Lk. 12³²). The Church is not to be afraid of persecutors who can kill only the body (Mt. 10²⁶ᶠ·), or of the terrors of the end (Mk. 13⁷). Jairus is not to be afraid of triumphant death (Mk. 5³⁶), or Paul of his task in Corinth (Ac. 18⁹) or the mortal danger of his voyage (Ac. 27²⁴), or Christians of the representatives of temporal authority (Rom. 13³). For " God has not given us the spirit of fear ; but of power, and of love, and of a sound mind " (2 Tim. 1⁷). God " swore an oath to our father Abraham, that we being delivered out of the hand of our enemies might serve him without fear, in holiness and righteousness " (Lk. 1⁷³). " Ye have not received a spirit of bondage again to fear ; but ye have received the Spirit of adoption, whereby we cry, Abba, Father " (Rom. 8¹⁵). " There is no fear in love ; but perfect (τελεία) love casteth out fear : because fear hath torment. He that feareth is not yet made perfect in love " (οὐ τετελείωται ἐν ἀγάπῃ, 1 Jn. 4¹⁸).

The anxiety and fear which are so strongly forbidden in this way obviously meet in the fact that when man is anxious and afraid, instead of going his way in confidence and hope, he lets himself be burdened and arrested (or burdens and arrests himself) by looking at a threat which confronts him, and by the considerations which he lets this threat obtrude on him—as if he knew that it might, or necessarily would, involve a catastrophe. The way in which the two conceptions are related is that anxiety is in a sense the term for a little fear, and fear the term for a great anxiety. Anxiety has to do expressly with penultimate things which we can more or less envisage. It has to do with questions of the future external form of life. The anxious man wants security in face of the uncertainty of his future before he goes further and decides to live for that for which he should properly live. The anxious man argues : *primum vivere, deinde philosophari*. He, too, is really afraid. He has already withdrawn his hand from the plough. He has postponed that which really ought to happen. He is not genuinely and seriously moved and claimed by it. He is moved and claimed by the non-essentials of which he believes and maintains that they must first be thoroughly regulated before that which is properly essential can come into its own. But he will never admit that he is afraid. He will " only " postpone the real essential. He will say that *philosophari* is a good thing in itself, but is for the moment untimely, because *vivere* is more pressing. When he is anxious, he creates a small fear, and conceals from himself the fact that he is no less afraid because his fear takes this shape. In fear itself, the contrast is more serious. In the New Testament the object of fear is primarily Jesus Himself—Jesus in the glory of His miracles and His resurrection. Then, in a strange inner relationship to this, it is certain phenomena of, so to speak, a definitive character—the absolute predominance of the world in relation to the Church, and, conversely, the insignificance and weakness of the Church, the constant threat of the Law, and death. Fear is the shock caused by the supposed knowledge that I shall not be able either to be or to do what I should be and do in face of that which gloriously and fearfully confronts me ; I shall not endure, but perish. That which comes will simply be too great for me (positively or negatively). Fear is the anticipation of a supposedly certain defeat. And therefore to be afraid is to be anxious. It is to decide the future, and, appealing to the future, ourselves, in the sense of condemning ourselves not to be or to do what really ought to take place in our existence. It is again to postpone what ought to take place. But in fear the absolute capitulation which is what anxiety already means in secret is open and operative as such. Fear is a magnified, acute and definitive form of anxiety. Fear is the resignation from which there can obviously be no road forwards. To fear is to give up all thoughts of a victorious encounter with what impends. It is to know it so well, its predominance and our own impotence, that, if we are still capable of any purpose at all, our one thought is to avoid meeting that which impends.

In what they have in common, anxiety and fear, both in their difference and in their inner connexion, are obviously the direct opposite of what the New Testament describes as freedom and of what we have described as the permission given to man by the command of God. When we see ourselves threatened by the possibility of a coming catastrophe in such a way that we either postpone the continuance of our course until better days in order first to deal with this possibility, or we think it necessary to abandon it altogether, we are not free, and permission is not the basis of our life. What we see in the future means for us that we are not free in the present—and in practice it is almost always in the present that we are and live. This is the case whether our eyes are concerned with to-morrow's bread when we look forward, or with Jesus Christ Himself, or with any middle term of the series marked out by these extremes. It is the case whether we regard ourselves as only provisionally held up by what we see in the future or as definitively halted. Provisionally or definitively, we are not facing the true essential. We have not advanced to that real love. In our little fear or great anxiety we are actually doing what can be understood only as the result of an experienced compulsion and pressure, but never as the result of a given permission. If we had permission, we would not be anxious or afraid. To be sure, the causes of our anxiety and fear would not be eliminated. When it forbids anxiety and fear, the New Testament does not think of denying the existence of the object of human anxiety and fear—the actual insecurity of our future, the majesty of Jesus Christ on the one hand, and, as its counterpart, the complete abandonment of those who are His. But when man is not a prisoner, when he is not a slave, when he has permission, he does not in any sense confront what lies before him with anxiety and fear. On the contrary, he lets the actual conflict with it develop without regarding it as impossible, but also without wasting time in anticipating it, without trying to assure his position in advance. If he takes up a different attitude, he is not free. Whether he admits it or not, his being and thought and speech and action are those of a slave. It is this slavery of anxiety and fear which the command of God in the New Testament opposes when it orders : Be not anxious ! Be not afraid ! In these two imperatives any separation between Gospel and Law is absolutely impossible.

On the other hand, it is obvious that an order is issued. In contrast to what may seem natural and obvious to man, in contrast to what he again and again desires, and must necessarily desire in continuation of his attempt to be a judge of good and evil, he is summoned away from a disposition and attitude which are forbidden by God and unworthy of himself. The two imperatives are gravely misunderstood if the seriousness and rigour in which God turns to man are not seen in their absoluteness, if they are regarded merely as a kind of advice or offer, in regard to which man can reserve his attitude. The axe is now laid at the root of the tree. It is obviously the very man who wilfully plans for his own future and himself—for that is what the anxious and the fearful do—who is put in question. A most radical conversion is now demanded. In face of this : Be not anxious !—Be not afraid !—the only possibility is either utter obedience or utter disobedience.

On the other hand, it is just as obvious in content what is commanded is simply the liberation of man. This is seen unambiguously in all the passages in which these imperatives are used. The place from which man is summoned is not really a beautiful and desirable one. The prohibitions are not of something sweet and pleasant. He cannot complain that what is required of him is worse instead of better, heavier instead of lighter, alien and strange instead of familiar. What can be worse or harder or stranger than a life in anxiety and fear, a present determined by these attitudes ? And what is better and lighter and more familiar than a life without care and fear, a present characterised by liberation from these attitudes ? Is not a present passed in anxiety the very *philosophari* in face of which a decided preference is to be given to the *vivere* ? And if the preference is really given to this, is it not itself a *philosophari* in face of which a *vivere* in anxiety is properly a *mori* ? When we fear, do we not really fear fear itself more than the anticipated defeat, the present possibility of future evil more than the evil itself ? And this being the case, is it not better not to fear ? Whatever the threat of the future may be, is not freedom itself the first and most pressing concern, the one which always demands our attention ? Do we not stand to lose all the evil, and win all the good, if, obedient to the command, we are not anxious and do not fear ? The desire to be for ourselves is not salvation but perdition, and it is from this that the command frees us. It is, therefore, full of the Gospel, full of grace, full of God's friendship for man. It is unconditional, and there is no alternative to obedience or disobedience, but it is also a single invitation to do what, in contrast to the achievements of our anxious and fearful self-will, we can and shall do gladly. This is the tree which is really pleasant to the eyes and to be desired.

And it is from this source that the command of God derives its absoluteness. For in contrast to what we ourselves think and will, it orders us to do what we can and, in fact, will do gladly. And for that reason any pretexts or excuses we make can only be implausible and ineffectual. If we transgress it, if we persist in wanting to be anxious and afraid, we have obviously failed to see that it is permission, and as such command. We have obviously failed to see that God is for us, and that therefore no one and nothing can be against us, and that we should not be anxious, since our heavenly Father knows what we need, but should cast our care upon Him, because He cares for us. We have obviously failed to see that Jesus, the only One whom we have to fear as our Judge, is the very One who raises and restores us, and that there can be no temptation or catastrophe now or in the future which is excluded from the rule of Rom. 8[28], that to those who love God, all things necessarily work together for good. How can those who really do see the permission which this gives escape the command ? From what place can they hold the command at a distance ? How else but in obedience to the command can they find the consolation and shelter which they vainly seek when they are disobedient and in their disobedience to the command they necessarily reject ? But conceited opposition and revolt against the command can only cease, of course, when the command comes to us like this, when it is revealed to us in its character as the Gospel, and therefore as permission, therefore as God's command : Be not anxious ! Be not afraid !

It may be instructive to bring out the same truth by means of another pair of expressly ethical concepts from the New Testament—a pair which in this case have a clearly positive content. If God's claim on man is to be comprehended in a word, on the one side (predominantly in the Johannine writings) it is that we should abide, and on the other (predominantly in Paul) that we should stand.

In the most concentrated expression of Jn. 6[56] and 15[4] we read of an abiding " in me," or, according to 1 Jn. 2[6], 3[24] and 4[13], " in him," i.e., in Jesus Christ, in whom we have to abide like the branches in a vine if we are to bear fruit. Similarly, we read of an " abiding in the light " (1 Jn. 2[10]), " in eternity " (1 Jn. 2[17]), " in God Himself " (1 Jn. 4[15f.]). This abiding is concretely fulfilled, however, as an abiding " in the grace of God " (Ac. 13[43]), " in his goodness " (Rom. 11[22]), in the faith (Ac. 14[22], Col. 1[23], 1 Tim. 2[15]), in the doctrine of Christ (2 Jn. 9), in the doctrine of the apostles (Ac. 2[42]), in the special calling in which each is called (1 Cor. 7[20]), and in brotherly love (Heb. 13[1]). In the same way, we also read of a standing—" in the Lord " (1 Thess. 3[8]), " in grace " (Rom. 5[2], 1 Pet. 5[12]), " in the Gospel " (1 Cor. 15[1]), " in the faith " (1 Cor. 16[13]) or " through faith " (Rom. 11[20]), in the unity of the Spirit (Phil. 1[27]), in the apostolic tradition (2 Thess. 2[15]), in the armour in which a Christian is able to encounter the assaults of the last time (Eph. 6[14]).

The essential unity of the two conceptions is clear. Christians who are summoned to an " abiding " and a " standing " have a possibility in what is given them in Jesus Christ and through life with Him and in His Church ; and the sum of all that is demanded of them is to make use of this possibility, or rather to let it realise itself. The anxiety and fear forbidden to them are definitely excluded as this possible becomes actual. And the achievement of everything that is positively to be demanded of them is definitely guaranteed. At the place and on the ground on which they are set, it is already decided in advance what they will and will not do, and therefore what they will decide. In what they will do or not do, they will be obedient to the command of God, accepting His claim as right. The place of their abiding and the ground of their standing are identical. In both cases the reference is to the Lord, grace, faith, the apostolic proclamation. The concern, and the only concern, is that they should abide at this place and not leave it, that they stand on this ground and not stumble or stoop or fall or be brought down because they exchange it for another.

The seriousness and rigour, the absoluteness and radicalism of the demand are unmistakeable in both forms of the summons. Both pictorially and conceptually, the "standing" (as, for example, in the passages 1 Cor. 16¹³ᶠ· and Eph. 6¹⁴ᶠ·) undoubtedly demands an active and virile determination, perseverance and restraint. And although at a first glance the "abiding" seems to be merely passive in contrast to a vagabond and vacillating caprice, it, too, impresses the hearer in such a way that there can be no mistaking the fact that it demands obedience and is therefore a command. The possibility presented with this place and ground is a law for those who are set in it. It is presented to them. It is to be realised in their existence. Its glory will necessarily be revealed in what they do and do not do. The fact that it is presented in this way makes them responsible that this should happen. But if it leaves them no choice but obedience, it is the choice of their *obedience*, in which they themselves are to realise it, they themselves are to be the active witnesses of its realisation. Humility and love and selflessness and every other act of Christian virtue, the confession and the loyalty and perseverance of faith, the joyousness of hope—all these are for Christians a simple duty, a fulfilment of the injunction to let their light shine, not in any sense extraordinary, but the ordinary rule of life. Yet they are an obligation which they have to meet, a debt which they are required to pay. To allow to happen what at this place and on this ground has to happen with unavoidable necessity is something which can take place only through the Yes and No of their own will and determined act. There is repeated in this "abide" and "stand" the assault and disturbance of the wholly alien majesty of the new being which with their calling and baptism has burst in once and for all on their old man, and by which the latter has been once and for all vanquished and superseded.

But again it is the case that the disturbance and assault of this demand, its character as divine Law, is grounded in the fact that in content it speaks no less than the warning against anxiety and fear of a liberation which man is to give himself and in which he is to acquiesce. Those who are to "abide" are told openly that they are already in the native sphere to which they belong, in which they can breathe freely, in which everything they need comes flowing in to them from all sides, so that they can quietly renounce all seeking and hunting after other possibilities. Experimenting with other possibilities is a necessity for those who have not yet found the reality of life. But those who are told to "abide" have found this reality. To be "in Christ" is not one of the many stages on the way of life from which we may be ordered, and it may be good to look farther afield and to go on because they are only stages. It is not a standpoint which it is advisable to compare with other standpoints and then perhaps to exchange with them on account of the relativity of all standpoints (out of regard for that truth which, according to Lessing, is for God alone). Those who are "in Christ" are already, even in the time when there is nothing abiding, in that which does abide and in which it is self-evident to abide. If we want to press on and look farther, we shall only come back to this place if the search is successful. The only alternatives are the madness of a seeking for seeking's sake, or the misery of a seeking which can never lead to a finding. The obligation to abide at the place where we may abide because that which is abiding is there spares us not only all superfluous flights and detours, but also that madness and misery. This is obviously an invitation and permission even as a command ; a liberation as a commitment. It obviously engages us by freeing us in the depths of our being. It puts us under an obligation by giving us the freedom which we can only jeopardise and lose at once by trying to be disobedient ; the freedom which can be won and kept only by obedience to this command. And those who are to "stand" are evidently told that they are on ground on which they can stand—not on marsh or on a *trottoir roulant*, but on solid earth. Is it possible that we prefer to stumble and stoop and fall and lie, or at best crawl ? If we cannot prefer this, and if we are given the presupposition that we may stand, how can we fail to rejoice when we are told that we are to realise this presupposition and therefore to stand ? Falling and lying have a fatal similarity to sickness and death. For this reason we must beware of that favourite word of philosophers and humanists—*die Lage* (the lie of things). Strictly speaking, it ought to be applied to human relationships and conditions only *sensu malo*, only when there is a desire expressly to characterise them as fatal, as a suspicious " lying around " of men and social groups and whole nations who ought properly to be standing on their feet. To be healthy and to live is to stand. And the honest man who would rather stand than lie must surely hail as particularly good news the imperative : Stand ! Stand because you are able and are permitted to do so ! There can be no doubt that the New Testament στήκετε or στῆτε (cf. Eph. 5¹⁴) is directly connected with the sound of the trumpet (1 Cor. 15⁵²) in the ἀνάστασις νεκρῶν. It commands both the later standing which the Christian is allowed and commanded in and with the resurrection of Jesus Christ, and the preliminary standing which he is allowed and commanded in anticipation of his own resurrection. This is commanded because it is permitted. It is a liberation and loosing because it comes to him as an alien and imperious law. It is a genuine consolation because it is so diametrically opposed to the foolish wishes of the old man. These terms, then, do not give us any grounds for supposing that the Law can be dissevered from the Gospel, or that it can be explained and proclaimed with pith and power unless it is interpreted on the basis of the Gospel. What makes the demand so majestic and unconditional when we are told to " abide " and " stand " is not in the first instance that God wills or does not will something of us, but primarily that God is for us and not against us.

Obligation—the obligation of the real command—means permission. That was the first point. But the second is that permission— the permission which is the proper inmost form of the divine command —also means obligation. The New Testament passages in which this emerges have all led us close to the point where we can see the decisive reason for this, and for having to state it in this way and not differently. We must now consider this point if our two propositions are to stand.

What we have to describe as the form of the divine claim and to defend against a legalism which as such would rather amount to lawlessness is not an ethical principle which is distinguished from others by its attempt to identify authority with freedom. If equal justice is to be done on both sides, the propositions that the right obligation is the true permission, and the right permission the true obligation, cannot possibly be deduced from a general concept of command, even of God's command. If the two propositions are to be brought together and related, as it were, in a vacuum, and something intelligible is to result, then necessarily either the conception of obligation or that of permission will become so flabby that either the one or the other loses its proper seriousness, the result being either an obligation limited by the permission or inversely a permission limited by the obligation. To identify authority and freedom is impossible as such. The reality of the form of the divine command, in which it demands as permission and is the Law as Gospel, is something which is in principle incomprehensible. Definition and construction in principle lead inevitably either to *legalism* on the one hand or to *lawlessness* on the other.

In the knowledge of the form of the divine claim it is no more possible than in that of its basis and content to abstract from the fact that grace—the sanctifying grace of the command of God—is grace. The fact that God gives us His command, that He puts us under His command, is grace ; for in this way he testifies and proves that He wills to have us for Himself. A first result of this is the two propositions that the obligation of this command is at bottom a permission and that this permission is its proper obligation. A further result, however, is that the unity of authority and freedom which characterises the form of the divine command as opposed to all others, is revealed and present to us as a promise and only as such, and therefore only in faith. The propositions of Christian ethics are propositions of Christian dogmatics. This means that as with all the other propositions of dogmatics the truth in them is contained and lies in the Word of God, that it can be known only in the Word of God, and must again and again be sought and caught in the Word of God and therefore in faith. Their truth is spiritual truth, i.e., truth which is revealed and operative in the presence and work of the Holy Spirit. This is true of the knowledge of the basis of the divine command in God's mercy. It is true of the knowledge of its content as the demand that we accept God's merciful action as right for us. It is also and particularly true of the knowledge of the command of God formulated by these two propositions. We cannot see and understand that the matter is as these two propositions express it, if we are not willing to listen to the Word of God or to see the basis and object of His promise, if we do not turn to Him with the trust and obedience, the humble love, which are those of faith. Apart from faith and therefore from the Word of God, in ourselves therefore — in our conscience, thought, volition or emotion, or in some kind of special experiences—we cannot expect to find a point or points where we are in such agreement with the command of God that what we ought to do according to this command is for us a direct permission and the great permission of this command a direct obligation. Apart from faith, i.e., apart from the Word of God Himself, we shall always find necessarily that we are either on the right hand in a condition of legalism (under an obligation which is not a permission), or on the left in some condition of lawlessness (in a permission which is not an obligation). The concrete truth of the unity of the two, by which we are preserved from the abyss on both sides, is the truth of the grace of God Himself, which wills always to be known and grasped as such in its promise and which is our sanctification as the promise made to us. If we let go the promise, if in any sense we lean on ourselves instead of it, if we no longer seek and accept the sanctifying grace of the command of God as is appropriate to the grace of God, we can only fabricate illusions about our permission as well as our obligation, illusions which openly or secretly will be quickly enough revealed in their character as such and which can issue only in disillusionment or in worse and worse illusions. To live at all it is essential that we should never cease to hear the Word of God and see the ground and object of the promise, nor grow weary in faith, nor fail to recollect the spiritual nature of the command (Rom 7[14], 8[2]).

Who is the man who can take to himself the words of Ps. 40[8f.] : " Then said I, Lo, I am come : in the roll of the book it is written what I must do. I delight to do thy will, O my God : yea, thy law is within my heart " ? To be sure, this was said by a member of the later Jewish Church, but in what dimension was he thinking, in what hidden sense—pointing up and away from himself— was he speaking, unless we are to take it that he was most strangely puffed up and self-deceived ? And the latter assumption is impossible in view of the later verses : " Withhold not thy tender mercies from me, O Lord ; let thy loving kindness and thy truth continually preserve me. . . . Mine iniquities have taken hold upon me, so that I am not able to look up ; they are more than the hairs of mine head ; therefore my heart faileth me " (v. 11 f.), and the conclusion in v. 17 : " I am poor and needy : thou art my help and my deliverer ; make no tarrying, O my God." The Psalmist was no doubt speaking of himself, but in so doing he obviously did not focus his gaze upon himself but upon the place to which he finally addressed that prayer. In these verses we have an almost verbal reminiscence of the well-known promise of Jer. 31[31ff.] concerning the new covenant of the last day. When and as God establishes this new covenant, it will come to pass that " I will put my law in their inward parts and in their heart will I write it." The subject is obviously what Jer. 32[39] speaks of as " another heart," and Ezek. 11[19], 36[26] as the promised " new spirit "—the future I that lives and works only by the grace of God and that is promised to the Israelite by the grace and Word of God. The one who speaks as a member of that people of the last time which will be a people of doers of the Law, in the words used by Paul in Rom. 2[13f.] to describe this people as the fulfilment of all these promises. He speaks, therefore, in the person of one of the Gentiles (as ἐν τῷ κρυπτῷ Ἰουδαῖος, circumcised in the heart, in the spirit, Rom. 2[29], cf. Deut. 30[6], Jer. 4[4]) who are a law to themselves because and in so far as the work of the Law is written in their heart, and who for this reason—as those who have this other heart, this new spirit—fulfil it of themselves (φύσει), and therefore rightly, so that they are justified in the sight of God as its doers. When the Psalmist looks in this direction, and comes to speak of himself, as it were, from this standpoint, he can speak only in this way. According to Ps. 110[3] (if the translation is correct), a willing people is one of the predicates of the priestly King of the last day, and therefore some of the passages which stress the willingness with which the Israelites made their contributions—first for the ark and then for the temple : " Every one whose heart stirred him up, and every one whom his spirit made willing " (Ex. 35[21]), " with perfect heart they offered willingly to the Lord " (1 Chron. 29[5f.])—are to be understood eschatologically in essence, although without prejudice to their concrete content. Of a piece with this is the fact that the free life of the children of God is expressly described in Rom. 8[15] and Gal. 4[6] as the work of the Spirit sent into their hearts, or in content as a crying Abba, Father. In this crying they are not slaves but children, and they may live as such before and with their father. Those who cry in this way—it is not arbitrarily that we think of the conclusion of Ps. 40—are obviously freed from all illusions as to what they find in themselves apart from the work of the Spirit. They obviously look away from themselves elsewhere. Their sanctification by the command obviously does not take place in the power of experiences and accomplishments which they are in the position to claim as their own.

The spiritual nature of the command, in which its obligation and permission are one, consists in its fulfilment as it has taken place in Jesus Christ. It is His Spirit which drives the children of God into the freedom which as such is real obedience. It is from His obedience that we have to discern what distinguishes the command of God from other commands. It is in and with His obedience that the decision is made as to what the command of God means for us in contrast to other commands. It is not only possible but necessary to describe His obedience in these two propositions. This and this alone is the effective ground for the rightness of these propositions. In what Jesus does, everything is permission, freedom, spontaneity. The will of God is His own will. To do it is the meat by which He lives. For He is *the* Son of the Father. It is as we look at Him and only at Him, on the basis of the privilege gained and confirmed by Him and only by Him, that others—we ourselves—may be called and be children of the same Father. He is therefore genuinely free, the One who is subject to the Law by His own volition. And again, it is only as we look at Him, and under the protection of the right to freedom which He has established, that others—we ourselves—can also be called and be free. Jesus is free as God Himself is free, because and as He executes the resolve and will of the free love of God. It is in freedom that God has turned and covenanted Himself to man, and it is in the same freedom that the act of the covenant has been completed by Jesus. It is in this freedom that He lives the life of the first and basic and normative covenant-partner of God. As surely as God is serious in His pity to man, as surely as He wills to have man himself, the whole man and therefore his heart, to the salvation of man and His own glory, so surely is this One, in whom God's hand is laid on all others, *the* willing doer, the cheerfully and happily obedient doer of His command, the lowly " in heart " (Mt. 11²⁹). All that Jesus does is, therefore, suffused and irradiated by the way in which He does it. He does it in the ἐξουσία of Him who is permitted to do what He is commanded, and commanded only what He is permitted. And this obedience of Jesus is the clear reflection of the unity of the Father and the Son by the bond of the Spirit in the being of the eternal God Himself, who is the fulness of all freedom.

If the subject of Ps. 40⁸ᶠ·—however we may explain it historically and conceptually—does not speak in His name, we can only say that the verses have no conceivable subject at all. But in what Jesus does everything is genuine obedience, real subordination, even subjection—not at all the self-exaltation of man to the throne of God, but very definitely the work of a servant, indeed a slave of God, which takes place in a relationship to God in which God gives the orders and man submits, a position which cannot therefore be reversed. The Early Church knew what it was about when in the monothelite controversy it insisted on the distinction and confrontation of the divine and human will in the person of Jesus. It did this in the light of the temptation story and Gethsemane, where it emerges clearly enough that the freedom in which Jesus obeys

is real obedience. He " learned obedience " (Heb. 5⁸). Permission with Him
was not caprice, but the permission of the One who is under discipline because
He has disciplined Himself. His freedom did not correspond to the meaningless
idea of a divine *potentia inordinata*, but to the *potentia ordinata* which is the real
freedom and omnipotence of God. Like God, He lived in the freedom of the
One who is law to Himself. Indeed, He lived out the freedom in which God
from all eternity has bound and tied Himself for His own sake and for our good.
He lived in an ἐξουσία which was legitimate and not tyrannical, and therefore
beneficial and not destructive. And He did this as the One who executed the
covenant made and established by God, His course being regulated by this first
and in the true sense only sacred contract. He revealed and confirmed the fact
that God is not a God of confusion but the God of peace (1 Cor. 14³³). He fulfilled
the command—both permission and obligation " undivided and unconfounded."
And it is as He fulfils the command that He is the ground and object of the
promise of divine grace, the Word of God Himself, to which we must keep strictly
when we investigate the form of this command, its differentiation from other
commands and superiority to them.

That the nature of the command of God is spiritual means that it
does not confront us as an ideal, whether that of an obligation, that
of a permission, or that of a combination of the two, but as the reality
fulfilled in the person of Jesus Christ. This person as such is not only
the ground and content but also the form of the divine claim. And it
is in this person and only in Him that the identity of authority and
freedom is accomplished. Deriving from this person, in His relationship to us and in our relationship to Him, this identity becomes normative for what is demanded of us. What makes it so is that it is to us
that God turns in this person. We are those whom He accepts. It is
with us that He has concluded and sealed the eternal covenant. What
makes it so is that it is in this person that the divine claim is made
and proved and executed. If it did not meet us in this person, it
would have no authority, because it would have no reality. It would
be a construction that does not reach our actual life, and is of no use
to it. But actually meeting us in this person, it does affects us. It
is the form of the command of God as it is directed to us. For this
person is not a private person representing only himself and standing
over against us. His commission and work do not extend only to the
sphere of His own existence, but to the existence of all men. This
person is appointed and stands before God for the person of all other
men. We all have to recognise in the commission and work of this
person the accomplishment of the will of God in our own stead. Root
and branch, we all belong to this person and not to ourselves. Our
commission and work can consist only in the fact that in and with
our own lives we acknowledge and approve what this person has
accomplished, showing in this way that we belong to that person.

The strong passage Tit. 2¹¹ᶠ· is relevant in this connexion. " The grace of
God hath appeared "—the reference is to this person in whom God has concluded
the eternal covenant with man ; this text was rightly used by the Early Church
as the Epistle for Christmas day—" bringing salvation (σωτήριος) to all men) "—
the universal character ascribed to this person is to be noted : there is salvation

for every man in this person !—" instructing us (παιδεύουσα ἡμᾶς) "—it is therefore grace itself and as such (incorporated in this person), and not a factor which precedes or only follows grace (and therefore this person), that carries out our instruction, as the ethical principle which controls us and by which we must direct ourselves, as the command which sanctifies us—" that, denying ungodliness and worldly lusts "—there need be no fear that this instruction will not be radical and incisive ; such anxiety would be in place only if we were entirely dependent on ourselves, and had to do with an abstract principle instead of the principle which encounters us in this all-powerful person and controls us in virtue of His authority ; here, in Him, we have a true and overmastering *principium,* and therefore the effect of His παιδεύειν is a fundamental denial, renunciation and separation in face of the interposing false *principium* of the fall in its original form as our estrangement from God's grace and in its development as our domination by our own self-will ; here in this *principium* there can be peace between God and us by the death of Adam on the cross of Golgotha—" we should live soberly, righteously and godly, in this present world "—grace, or this person, instructs us to do this, not only by taking from us what is ours, all the falsehood in which Adam tried to be free and succeeded only in becoming a captive, but by giving us what belongs to God, all the wisdom and righteousness and holiness of the Son of God, everything, as He is for us and represents us, everything, as we belong to Him and He treats us as His own, His members—" looking for that blessed hope, and the glorious appearing of our great God and our Saviour Jesus Christ ; who gave himself for us, that he might redeem us from all iniquity, and purify unto himself a peculiar people, zealous of good works." It is surely clear that this conclusion does not speak of a further aim to which the grace that has appeared directs its instruction. Strictly, the passage speaks of only one such aim : ἵνα . . . ζήσωμεν, that we should be what we may and therefore ought to be in its sphere and under its order and authority. This is what it wills for us. This is what it accomplishes in us. In relation to this positive aim the preceding negative (ἀρνησάμενοι) can have only a preliminary and subordinate position. And the conclusion in vv. 13–14 describes explicitly what makes up this sober, righteous and godly life in which we are instructed by grace against the background of the negation executed by it. It is life in expectation, in a strained looking forward and upward, with this person, Jesus Christ, as the object. And about Him (and therefore about the grace itself that instructs us) there is then the decisive thing which has to be kept in mind in all that precedes : He " gave Himself for us," i.e., with His commission and work, with His obedience, He stepped into our place. His obedience was that He suffered in our place the death of the godless who is surrendered to worldly desires, the death of Adam, and that in His resurrection, again in our place, He was clothed with the wisdom, righteousness and holiness which God intended for us. It was to mediate what God intended for us, and to take away what He refused, that He gave Himself for us. According to God's eternal will and in virtue of its execution in time He is the public person to whose existence and life ours is adjusted and subordinated, whose justice displaces and replaces ours (the evil justice of our injustice)—displaces it by His death and replaces it by His resurrection. By Him we are " redeemed from all iniquity," and, by Him again, we are positively " purified a peculiar people." As we wait for Him as " our great God and Saviour," as we let Him be " our blessed hope," we live that right life which is the aim of grace's instruction, a life in sanctification by the divine command. This life is a " waiting " and hoping because the glory of the unity of Jesus Christ with us, and of our unity with Him, is hidden and not manifest, present and certain to faith but withdrawn from sight, as long as we live here and now, as long as " this world " (v. 12) forms the sphere of our obedience. Our instruction for that life still proceeds and is not, therefore, completed. Grace has still to be continually given and received by us. Therefore this life has still to be continually learned and exercised of and with grace. There is no one who can yet dispense with sanctification on the score that he is holy otherwise than by the fact that the command is holy and as such sanctifies him. The epiphany of Jesus Christ—the appearing of what has been done for us through Him, the disclosure of our life with Him as eternal life, the appearing of what we are (1 Jn. 3²)—has not yet taken place. In the words of 1 Cor. 13, we still see " through a mirror in a riddle." For that reason and to that extent our life under instructing grace is a waiting. But its reality is not diminished by the fact that we wait for the epiphany of Jesus Christ and of our life with Him. We wait for the disclosure of that which here and now is veiled. But even here and now, in the concealment in which we now live it, this life does not lack anything of reality, and therefore of significance and power, of truth and force. What has happened—happened for us—has really happened. What is demanded of us is really demanded, and what is given us is really given. We cannot be more strictly, more intimately, more completely subject to a demand than when we stand in this expectation. Nor, again, can we be more lavishly endowed than we are already in this expectation. This expectation, in which already Jesus Christ is for us everything which He is in Himself, is the form in which there is to be realised here and now, i.e., practically acknowledged in its reality, not only His being-for-us, but our being-for-Him, our existence as His " peculiar people." It is precisely in waiting for His appearing that we shall " be zealous unto good works." That the sober, righteous and godly life in this world is our life in *faith* is decided by the fact that it is a waiting for the epiphany of Jesus Christ. What is also thereby decided is that it is our life determined and ruled by Him and therefore really claimed by Him.

The problem of distinguishing the command of God from other commands narrows down accordingly to that of distinguishing Jesus Christ from all other lords and ultimately and decisively from the lord that each of us would like to be over himself. His person is the fulness of the divine command. God wills that we should live in Him, and accept and use the grace which has appeared in Him for all men. God wills that we should be His possession. God wills that we should believe in Him. All distinction between the divine command and other commands has only provisional and in itself uncertain truth and power, if it does not finally issue in the distinguishing of this person, outside and alongside whom we have no other lord, whom especially we cannot confront as lords over ourselves, outside and alongside whom we cannot trust anyone or anything else. All permission is empty— indeed in the last resort it is only our own ultimately fatal lawlessness —and all obligation is really empty—again it is our own and ulti- mately no less fatal legalism—if it is not the permission and obligation of Jesus Christ, the permission and obligation which are proper to Him and which may be learned and exercised in His school. And so if it is not His call that summons us to do this, we cannot abandon either anxiety or fear. We cannot either abide or stand, and therefore we cannot be free and obedient. In contrast to all other claims, the claim of God is that by which we are claimed as the possession of Jesus Christ, by which we are claimed for faith in Him. Whether this takes place or not, whether we accept it or not, is what decides whether our permission is the permission of the divine command and our obligation its obligation, whether we have to do with the command of God or with some other.

The obedience which the command of God demands of man is his decision for Jesus Christ. In each individual decision it is a special form, a repetition and confirmation of this decision. The command of God is therefore distinguished from all other commands by the fact that it makes this very definite obligation which cannot be confounded with any other. It may bind us in other ways. It may seem to be in harmony with other commands. It may seem to be identical with them, or at least similar., It may seem open to confusion with them. But in all these obligations its aim and intention is always the same. It seeks to bind us to Jesus Christ in order that in this bond our life may be liberated and free. Every bond which claims us is, therefore, to be recognised as a binding to the Word of God by the fact that, in and with the specific thing in which it binds us, simultaneously and primarily it binds us to Jesus, obligating us to Him, and, as an obligation to Him, making us free. If it does this, we have to do with God's command. If it fails to do this, it fights against God's command. If it does this, we owe it our obedience. But if it fails to do it, we owe it our resolute disobedience.

The command of God is " personal " because it claims our obedience in relation to this definite person, Jesus Christ. There are other commands which have a personal character in so far as they direct us to be obedient in our relationship to definite persons. And even the command of God itself no doubt contains within itself demands for obedience in relation to other human persons. But it is distinguished from other commands by the fact that, whatever other persons it directs us to, properly and finally it refers always to obedience to this one person. Even as it claims our obedience to others, it demands our obedience " in the Lord." If we are not obedient to them " in the Lord," in all our obedience to them, we are not at all obedient to the command of God which demands this obedience. And if we cannot furnish the required obedience to other persons " in the Lord," and therefore in obedience to this person, we do not furnish it in obedience to God's command. There then necessarily comes into force the well-known rule of Ac. 5^{29} that we " must obey God rather than man " in the form of a resolute disobedience to them. The personal character of the divine command is bound to the name of this one, single person. When it claims us, the command of God puts this name above not only our own but all other names, and its law above not only our own but all other law—not to destroy all other names and law, but to kill them and make them alive by this one name and its exclusive law, as is demanded by the seriousness of the divine judgment and the depth of the divine compassion.

But in virtue of its personal character, understood in this way, the divine command demands a genuine decision. No other command can do this. All other commands claim us in definite relationships, for definite attitudes and actions. In other respects they leave us neutral. It is only with this limitation that even other persons can claim us for themselves. Of course, the command of God itself challenges me with a limitation of this kind. The command of God requires that I should do this and not do that. But within this limitation it is distinguished from other commands by the fact that in itself it is unlimited, that in and with all its individual demands it demands myself—myself for Jesus, my subordination to this name and its law. That I may live in subordination to this name and its law is the great permission which it gives me, the great liberation which it accomplishes. It binds me to this one name and its law. And this obligation reaches out over all attitudes and actions as such to myself. In its specific requirements and prohibitions, it demands everything, the totality of my life. It demands my active acknowledgment " that I am not my own, but the property of my faithful Saviour Jesus Christ." It demands my life as that of a limb of His body, of which He is the Head. With the specific question of obedience it places me before the question of my existence as He has already answered it. It reminds me that I am dead and risen with Jesus Christ. It speaks to me about this death of His and this life of His as if about my own. Demanding my obedience to Jesus Christ, it assumes that I belong to Jesus. It does not, therefore, give me the choice between obedience and disobedience as if they were two possibilities. The disobedience to it which is open to me can only be utterly unnatural. It can only be the impossible which is excluded by my own experience (namely, by the answer to the question of my existence which has been given by Jesus Christ). Just as the obedience which God's command demands can only be wholehearted and essential obedience, the obedience which determines from within everything that I am and do, so, too, it is with disobedience to it. There is no neutrality in relation to God's command—least of all a neutral mind. On the contrary, the command of God requires decisively—to use the apostolic formulation—that we should be " minded " in a certain way. It excludes all other ways of thinking, characterising them as enmity and disobedience. There is no option : we can only affirm that name and its law or deny them. We can only will to be what we are in Jesus Christ or will not to be. The decision which has been made concerning us in Him is much too radical and comprehensive for us to be able to evade it with our decision. In our decision we cannot say both Yes and No, or simply say nothing at all. Where can we possibly escape when that decision is the eternal predestination, when it is our election resolved at the beginning of all God's ways and works, and therefore our only real possibility, over against which there can, of course, be the real impossibility of disobedience, but not a third course. How can there be a third course between what God wills and what He does not will, between what

He has elected as our being and existence in and with the election of Jesus Christ and what He has in so doing rejected from all eternity? No other command confronts us with this Either-Or. The command of God alone confronts us in this way, and it is distinguished by its genuine character as decision from all other commands. Even where it resembles these other commands or sounds like them, it bears this character as decision. When it meets us, it allows us only the blessedness of complete obedience or the disobedience which in its totality is as monstrous as obedience is blessed. This disobedience is not a second possibility, but the impossibility of the sin of Adam, who in Jesus Christ is already killed and made alive for the service of righteousness.

But again in virtue of its personal character, the decision demanded by God's command cannot be other than a joyous one. No other command can be exclusive in this regard. In respect of all other commands, the question whether we obey them with or without joy is indifferent or at least secondary. If they do not preclude joyous obedience, they certainly cannot demand it. Now even God's command does demand many things apparently without touching this question. But let there be no mistake. Ultimately and decisively it touches just this question. In large matters as in small we obey it only when we obey it joyously, and every time we obey it without joy, we have not obeyed it at all. For reminding us, as it does, that we do not belong to ourselves or to anybody else but Jesus Christ, and demanding, as it does, the witness of our deeds and life as a confirmation of this fact, it proclaims great joy to us, the best and brightest and most comforting thing that we can possibly hear. We do not decide for Jesus in the way that it demands if we do not hear it in this way and obey it accordingly. The correspondence in our obedience may to all appearances be deeply hidden, as even in the command itself it is to all appearances deeply hidden. But just as it does not really lack in the command, it cannot and must not lack in our obedience. Anything that in itself is really dark and accursed cannot possibly be the cross that we are ordered to carry, and if in the last resort we really carry it sullenly and unwillingly, we are not carrying it at all. Here, too, the inexorable Either-Or, the genuineness of the decision demanded by God's command, enforces itself. And, again, this is inevitable from the point of view of the divine decision that precedes ours. The act of the eternal predestination and election of Jesus Christ, to which God's command ultimately reaches back, this beginning of all the ways and works of God both generally and therefore in our life, is the act of His " good-pleasure " and therefore of His joy, and it is in keeping with this that its fulfilment in time was surrounded by the jubilation of the heavenly hosts. In and with the decision to which we are summoned by God's command there has simply to be an echo of this good-pleasure of God Himself, of this jubilation of the angels. If this is wanting, what is there in common between our decision and the divine decision to which it is related, to which it should be obedient ? Where is the permission without which no obligation is a divine obligation ? If no one can be compelled to give cheerfully what is demanded of him, God Himself cannot be compelled to love an uncheerful giver. The character of His command can only be such that it is done gladly or it is not done at all.

Yet again in virtue of the personal character of the decision demanded by God's command, in all its distinctive genuineness and joyousness, it can and must be continually repeated and confirmed. To some extent, of course, the same is true of other commands. But the repetition and confirmation of all other commands is limited : partly because, so far as content is concerned, they aim only at individual temporally limited achievements; partly because they aim at attitudes and therefore at usages which once they are established need no new decision. But the necessity as well as the possibility of the repetition and confirmation of the command of God is without limit. Even if it aims at definite achievements and attitudes and actions and usages it always aims beyond them at our decision for Jesus, and just in this its substance the decision demanded by God's command is of such a kind that it can and must be repeated and confirmed. Just because the command is eternal—the proclamation of the will and resolve of God, in force before all time and beyond all time—there is no moment in time which can be empty of it, which it cannot fill, which we do not have to consider capable and in need of this fulfilment. Every moment that lacks this fulfilment is in the strictest sense a moment of lost time, given to us by the patience of God, but not used by us for the purpose for which that patience gave it. It is a piece of lost life because it is not a life in all that makes life worth living. The command of God is eternal because its demand binds us to Jesus, and, doing that, it secretly fills every moment of our life. There is no end to the question as to our relation to this person. It is always being put to us afresh. When did we not live in the illusion that we belong to ourselves ? When was it not necessary for us to be called out of this illusion and to be reminded that we belong to Jesus ? As well for us that the demand of the command of God does actually have the force of this summons, and that it does not actually come to a full stop ! If it did not continually re-emerge there would really be for us only lost time, lost life. For in face of it, when and where would we not find ourselves failing, retreating, deviating from the straight course of repeating and confirming the decision that it demands ? But the command does not fail. It continually puts itself to us in this form. In this form it binds us to the eternal will of God and therefore to His saving grace. It has all the constancy of the divine faithfulness in contrast to our unfaithfulness. We never dare lose sight of this mark of the form which the divine command takes—

that as our bond to the person of Jesus it spans the whole of the time granted to us in a continual present.

It will serve to stress this final and decisive christological determination of the form of the divine command if we conclude with a consideration of the story of the rich young man in Mk. 10$^{17-31}$ and par.

The narrative describes very fully the form of the divine claim. It shows that the demand of the living divine command made in the person of Jesus aims at the genuine, joyous and sustained decision of man for this person and therefore at the fulfilment of the one entire will of God. It shows this negatively in the figure of the rich man who was unequal to this demand, and positively in the disciples of Jesus who have become obedient to it.

Both the rich man and the disciples, the disobedient and the obedient, are within the sphere of the judicial authority and power, the *regnum Jesu Christi*, being subject to the living command of God embodied and established in Him. Even the rich man, the disobedient ! That this is the case, he himself shows in a particularly ostentatious way. " He ran up and fell on his knees before him " (Mk. 10^{17}). We cannot say why or for what reason or with what mind and intention, but the fact remains that he does it. And in so doing he adjusts himself to the order which is still order even where we are disobedient to it. He ranges himself with the disciples. He bears testimony to what the command is which has force for him as well as them. He cannot and will not reverse or nullify this testimony by his later withdrawal (Mk. 10^{22}). No one can withdraw from the kingdom of Christ. It embraces even the kingdoms of disobedience and all their inhabitants. " He went away sorrowful." By his sorrow in disobedience, he again testifies what the command of God is which has force even for him ; he again testifies that even he, even in his disobedience, is in the kingdom of Christ and not elsewhere. It is quite possible to leave or be expelled from a society, but never from the kingdom of Christ, from the community in which that order is established and obtains. This does not imply any mitigation of the sin and guilt of his disobedience. On the contrary, it makes it manifest. It clearly points again to the hope of which he is not deprived even in and with his disobedience. Even as one who is disobedient he is still at the place where another time he can obey, although he has failed to do so this time. " Good teacher, what shall I do that I may inherit eternal life ? " This is the question which he had put to Jesus as we have it in Mk. 10^{17}. He was sure, therefore, that beyond the insecure possession and enjoyment of the present temporal and therefore fleeting life it is necessary for man to attain eternal life, the true life that persists in contrast to the problematical character of this present life as it is revealed in death. He was also sure that in this present fleeting life man has to be and do something definite in order to attain this eternal life. Who can secure the inheritance if he is not the heir ? What must I do to act and prove myself as such ?—is what he asks, therefore. And, finally, he was sure that it was to Jesus that he had to come with this question. He could not answer it himself, and he did not expect anyone but Jesus to answer it. All this confirms at once the witness which he has already borne by his running to Jesus and kneeling before Him. With all this he confirms the validity of the order under which he, too, stands. It is in Jesus that man has this future, and therefore this present task. And it is Jesus who has to tell him about this task. For it is in Jesus that there has been concluded between God and man the covenant which forms the beginning of all the ways and works of God, and therefore the objective law under which the existence of all living creatures runs its course. But what will be the relationship to Jesus into which he enters as one upon whom and for whom all this is necessarily valid and binding objectively ? Will that which is objectively valid for him become true or not true in this relationship ? Will it be realised as obedience or as disobedience ? Will he conduct himself as one to whom eternal life is so necessary that, to obtain it, he will do what is necessary, i.e., exactly what Jesus commands him? This is the judicial question to which he exposed himself when with his question he testified to his objective membership of the kingdom of Christ.

That this question is now a burning one emerges in Jesus' first answer in Mk. 10[18] : "Why callest thou me good? None is good except the one God." Calvin's interpretation (*Comm. ad loc.*, *C.R.* 45, 537) is probably right : *Tu me falso bonum vocas magistrum, nisi a Deo profectum agnoscis. . . . Iam quidem aliquo obediendi affectu imbutus erat, sed eum vult Christus altius conscendere, ut Deum loquentem audiat.* The man who desires His, Jesus', judgment upon his life asks for nothing other or less than *God's* judgment. Is he conscious of this? Is he prepared to listen to this judgment? Has he come to Him for it? Is he willing and ready to listen not to the instruction of a good human teacher, but to that of the divine Teacher Himself? It is possible to listen to the instruction of a human teacher—even the best—and still find it possible and necessary to test whether the case is as he says, and only to make up our mind and act after this test, and therefore ultimately on the basis of our own judgment (even if it is stimulated and enriched by that of the teacher). But this cannot be done with Jesus. Jesus is not a "good teacher" of this kind. And although the man has certainly come to the right person, he has not come in the right way to this right person if his question is meant only as it can be directed to a human teacher, perhaps the best imaginable. The Word that he will hear from Jesus will be the Word that closes all further questioning and excludes all scrutiny, and it is by his obedience or disobedience to it that he will stand or fall. This is the way in which Jesus Christ is Lord in His kingdom, i.e., in the whole sphere of the man with whom God has made His covenant in Him. When He calls, God calls, and when man encounters Him, he encounters God—the one God, outside and alongside whom there is no other. Therefore the question put to man in this, His kingdom, the decisive question which is secret, but from time to time suddenly revealed, is whether he will or will not meet Him with the obedience which the one God demands and which he owes the one God. That this decisive question has been revealed for him is proved by the fact that this man honours the objective order under which he stands, and comes to Jesus with his question. How will it fare with him and how will he stand in the light into which he has stepped and in which he now actually stands?

According to Mt. 19[16], his question was somewhat different : "Teacher, what good thing must I do that I may inherit eternal life?" The presupposed objective certainty of the questioner in regard to the aim, the way and right information about this way, is clearly the same as according to the Markan account. The only difference is that here the idea of good is not connected with the addressed "teacher" but with the action concerning the right form of which he would like the latter to instruct him. Jesus' answer is (Mt. 19[17]) correspondingly different : "Why do you ask me concerning that which is good? One there is who is good." But the point of the answer is the same : If you ask me about what is good, then you must know that you are asking about what is good in the sight of God—in the sight of the One who is the good. When you ask me about the good, you step before the seat of the Judge from whose verdict there is no appeal to a higher court. And when I give you an answer to this question, you are answered in such a way that there can be no further question either to yourself or to others about the good that you ought to do. Will you listen to this verdict? Are you prepared to listen to that which, once it is uttered and heard by you, means that you cannot possibly shelter behind any test or scrutiny or decision of your own? Do you know that with your question about the good you have demanded this Word, and therefore decided in advance your righteousness or unrighteousness before God?

What follows next, the reference to the commandments and the rich man's answer that he had observed them all from his youth, is at once a preparation and postponement of the communication of the inexorable Word which—in the light into which he has now entered—he must now accept. It is a preparation in so far as the reference to the commandments does in fact make the communication, and the rich man's reaction to the reference is a proof that he is actually in a position of disobedience, and therefore through this reference is condemned by Jesus and therefore by God. It is a postponement in so far as the communication of this Word occurs only in a concealed form in this reference, as does also the actual disobedience of the rich man in his reaction to it. Jesus does not appear to have said anything new to him with this reference, and he for his part does not see any reason, on the basis of this reference, to confess his disobedience and go away, as he did later. The divine judgment already made is still hidden under the form of a continuing conversation between the rich man and Jesus—continuing apparently to his advantage. Now that he has stated that he has done, and does, everything that Jesus with His reference to the commandments has described as the action in question, what is to prevent his being told : You will obtain eternal life ; for you are on the right road to it ; you are living as one must live who has the prospect, claim and hope of it ? Why can he not be told this ? Why is the apparently so promising conversation about the commandments nothing more than a preparation for the disclosing of the divine judgment, to the proclamation of which the rich man has exposed himself, and which secretly already—and very much to his disadvantage—has been pronounced over him ?

According to Mk. 10[19], Jesus strengthened the warning as to the Judge before whom he stands with the statement : " You know the commandments "—therefore you know the Law by which the Judge to whom you have appealed will judge you, according as your actions correspond or do not correspond to it. According to Mt. 19[17], this part of the answer of Jesus runs : " If you would enter into life, keep the commandments." The point is the same, for the man who has to do with God, as we have seen, has only to be reminded of what God wills of him—the God of Israel, the God of grace and pity, the God in whose sphere he has shown himself to be with his question. He is to do what this God wills of him according to His commandments. When he does this, and does not do what they forbid, he is on the road to life, eternal life. The reference, therefore, establishes a twofold fact. First, the questioner is within hearing of the command of God. When he comes to Jesus with his question, he has actually heard already what he asks. And, second, this range of the hearing of God's command is the sphere of the authority and power of the One whom he questions. The One who is questioned and the One God who is so well known to the questioner are not two but One. Therefore when He answers the questioner, in principle and substance He can only repeat what He has already said to him. That is just what He does when He refers him to the commands. He has already told him what he should do to inherit eternal life. Therefore the questioner knows very well what should be the form of life of one who has this prospect, claim and hope. It is not for nothing that he was in the kingdom of Jesus Christ even before he came to Him.

In Mt. 19[18] the rich man interposes a question : " Which (commandments) ? " This draws attention to the fact that the command of God is an ordered quantity. The Law has both an external and an internal side, a $\mu o \rho \phi \eta$ and a $\tau \epsilon \lambda o s$ (Rom. 10[4]). In the different commandments, i.e., in the different proclamations of the one command of God, it may sometimes be the one and sometimes the other which is more or less visible, or even hidden. It is not the Decalogue in its entirety, nor is it even the comprehensive double command of love to God and one's neighbour (Mk. 12[29f.]), which is adduced by Jesus when He refers the rich man to " the commandments." What Mk. 10[19] enumerates are the commandments of the so-called " second table," somewhat rearranged, reduced and enlarged : Do not commit adultery ; Do not kill ; Do not steal ; Do not bear false witness ;

Do not rob ; Honour your father and mother. And Mt. 19[19] adds from Lev. 19[18] : " Love your neighbour as yourself." The selection and combination is clear. The well-known command of God is set before the rich man in its external aspect—the aspect from which it can be seen that it involves a concrete doing or not doing. It is not as if there were not included in these forms the command to love and fear God above all things, the prohibition of making or worshipping images of God, the command to keep holy His name and His sabbath—just as the commandments of the " first table " do not exclude but include the concrete forms of the God of the " second." In the New Testament sense it is not possible either to love one's neighbour without first loving God, or to love God without then loving one's neighbour. We can and must say, indeed, that in this unity of the command of God there is reflected the mystery of the person of Jesus Christ—the unity of the eternal Word with our flesh, of the Son of God with the Son of David and the Son of Mary. At any rate the genuineness with which the command is heard and kept on the one side is always a test whether it is also done on the other, and therefore as a whole. We have a test of this kind in the present passage. How this man is related to God, whether he loves and fears God above all things, is what decides—and has already decided—whether or not he is on the road to eternal life. And the concrete form of the test to which he has exposed himself is whether he will hear in the voice of the human teacher, Jesus of Nazareth, the voice of the one God and obey it accordingly ? That is what he must do to inherit eternal life. But it is for this very reason that he is presented with the commandments of the second table, the external side of the divine command, the side that relates to life with one's neighbour. " You know the commandments "—how they are given you in the sphere of the most concrete doing or not doing, in dealings with your fellow-man. It is in this sphere that you meet them again, now that you confront your neighbour in Me and in My person. Be and do now what you must be and do in accordance with them, and you will prove that you give God the glory and that you will therefore be an heir of eternal life. The answer of the rich man in v. 20, that he has observed all these things from his youth, naturally implies : I expect and am willing to observe them in the same way in the future as well. If Jesus has no more to say than merely to repeat these commandments, the questioner's answer means that he is fortified and confirmed in the way which he has always gone and intends to continue. He will now tread it to the end in the certainty that this is the way to eternal life.

According to the sequel, this is undoubtedly a misunderstanding of the answer which Jesus gives. But again according to the sequel, the mistake which trips him is not to be sought in the fact that he has subjectively deceived himself and Jesus with that assertion of v. 20, hypocritically or foolishly making himself out to be a saint when in fact he is a transgressor of all these commandments.. This may well have been the case. It will in fact turn out to be so. But Jesus Himself is not interested in it according to the text. That he has observed everything that he had to do according to these commandments, that he has not been guilty of adultery, murder, stealing, robbery, calumny or disrespect to his parents, and that he will not be guilty of them in the future, is at once accepted without question, as in the case of the servant in Lk. 17[10]. He has had the commandments of God before him. To the best of his knowledge and conscience he has done what they command, and not done what they forbid. Regarded from his own point of view and with respect to the external form of the command, his relation to the command of God is in order. He meets his neighbour as required by the command of God. No accusation can fairly be brought against him either by himself or others. He has good cause indeed to ask (Mt. 19[21]) : " What lack I yet ? " If it is a matter of keeping the commandments, what more can be required of me, what more can be done by me ? Has he not put his confident answer to the final and supreme test by coming to Jesus Himself and throwing himself down on his knees before Him ? Yet this is all a misunderstanding and delusion. Indeed, it is a demonstration of the disobedience in which he stands, in which he has come to Jesus, and in which he will also leave Him. The commandments which he knows—he does not really know. Observing them, he has not really observed them. And coming to Jesus, he has really passed Him by. He lives in His kingdom. He knows its order and the respect he owes this order. He has no choice but to observe this respect. He has done this from his youth, and formally and at the decisive point face to face with Jesus he has now done so again. So far nothing can be said against him. He can have the clearest conscience—but only the clearest conscience of the disobedient man who, although he stands objectively under God's order, and necessarily and willingly acknowledges this subjectively, is still a rebel, determined to go his own way even under this order, allowing the command of God to determine his action but not himself, not subjecting himself to it. For it is himself that all the commandments demand —even the external commandments of the second table with all their reference to his life with his neighbour. Binding him externally, they aim to do it internally. Directing him to his neighbour, they aim to send him to God. That he should *be* something—the covenant-partner of God—is what all the commandments demand when they claim both what he does and what he does not do. That he should *love* his neighbour is what God wills when He tests him with all these directions regarding his relationship with his neighbour. That he should *belong* to Jesus— as King of the kingdom in which he lives—is the necessary meaning and truth of the obedience which he is now so willing and ready to give to Jesus. That he is very far from this being, loving and belonging will emerge later. And since he is so far from it, it is clear that even his action in fulfilling the commandments, of which he can justifiably boast from his own point of view and in respect of the external form, is not what he takes it to be—the action which God demands of an heir of eternal life. His mistake is that he looks at the external form of the command. And he does this from his own point of view, so that judging himself along these lines he naturally acquits and justifies himself. He thinks that the external form of the command is the whole command, the command itself. He thinks that when he has heard the whole command, the command itself, he has a position from which he can judge and acquit and justify himself. According to the best of his knowledge and conscience, he clings to its external form, to what it tells him either to do or not do. But in so doing, he alienates himself from the imperious will of God in the commandments of the second table. He does not encounter this imperious will of God in Jesus' solemn repetition of the commandments. This is the mistake which is still hidden—but secretly unveiled— in the intervening conversation about the commandments in vv. 19–20. And it is this mistake which will now emerge.

What follows in v. 21 is certainly astonishing. For it does not bring the expected unmasking of the fallacy of which the questioner was guilty when he regarded himself as a doer of the Law. On the contrary, there is the unexpected statement : " Jesus looked upon him and loved him." At this point, we cannot agree with Calvin (*Comm. ad loc., l.c.*, p. 540 f.), who softens the important ἠγάπησεν αὐτόν to mean that Jesus loved him as God loved Aristides and Fabricius on account of their civil virtues and therefore on account of the *commune bonum* of the world : *quia illi grata est humani generis conservatio, quae iustitia, aequitate, moderatione, prudentia, fide, temperantia constat.* Nor can we agree with the exposition of C. Starke (*Syn. Bibl. Ex. in N.T.*, Vol. I, 1733, p. 912) : " At least there was this in him to love and praise, that he had not defiled his youth with gross vices, but had led an honourable life, and displayed a zeal to learn how to attain blessedness." There is more to be said for the conjecture of the same author : " And it may be, too, that Jesus saw many things in him which would be revealed later, as we read of Nicodemus." But why should ἀγαπᾶν have a special meaning in this case ? In relation to the disobedient man, Jesus does the very thing which, for all his so-called keeping of the commandments, this man does not do in relation to Jesus : He loves him, i.e., He reckons him as His ; He does not will to be without him ; He wills to be there just for him. For whom else is Jesus there but for the disobedient ? Whom else has God loved from eternity ? Necessarily He will pronounce the divine judgment by which he is declared disobedient, and on the basis of which he must prove that this is the case by going away from Jesus. But He does not do this because He hates him. He does not do it because He is indifferent to him. He does it because He loves him. In this ἠγάπησεν αὐτόν, which is to be followed by a no less emphatic unmasking of the sinner, the Law is obviously the form of the Gospel ; the judgment declared by the Law is the shape taken by the grace of God. When Jesus now goes on to tell him what he lacks, He loves him and wills him for Himself. But the very thing that the questioner lacks is that he will not see this. He will not lay hold of it. He respects and measures himself by a law, the reference and concern of which is only for what he does and does not do, and not for himself in what he does and does not do. This law is not the Law of God, the living Law established and confronting him in the person of Jesus, the reference and concern of which is for himself, because the Lawgiver, the one God Himself, with whom he has to do, does not will to be without him, because He has made His covenant with him, because He has made him His covenant-partner and therefore demands that he should live as such. It is required that he should let himself be loved. This is the demand to which he is not equal, to which he is disobedient, of which he will be unmasked as a transgressor. But even so, the demand does not cease to be the form of the good tidings addressed to him that his Judge is his Friend and Helper. He can certainly reject what Jesus wills of him. He can certainly go away, as he later did. But he cannot overthrow or leave the kingdom of Jesus Christ. And, similarly, he cannot destroy the inalienable, decisive element in the light into which he has now entered—the fact that Jesus loved him, loved him the obdurate and evasive rebel, who would later return to the darkness without the Gospels having any reason to tell us how far Jesus did perhaps see " many things " in him. The fact that Jesus loved him is the one thing to which we can cling in his favour— quite apart from what he does or does not do. But who, strictly, can cling to anything better in his own or anyone else's favour ?

Yet the form of the love of Jesus is the command, the declaration of what he lacks, of what he has not done in and with all that he has done : " There is one thing you lack " (v. 21b). What follows is the long-expected sentence upon the questioner. Having failed to do this one thing, and not being willing to do it, he characterises himself as unrighteous before the judgment seat of God, as one who goes another way than that which leads to eternal life. For he has not penetrated to the τέλος of the Law as it is brought out in Mt. 19²¹. Yet this accusation, too, must in the first instance be understood positively. The Word of God which is now uttered condemns the man who resists it, but it is also the justification of the man who accepts it. It is the command, but at the same time it is also the divine offer, and it is still this even for the man who will not obey it. What the questioner lacks is the fulness of what Jesus has, and has for him, the fulness with which Jesus loves him and is therefore willing to be responsible for him. And if he is, as it were, invited to remedy this lack, the remedying consists only in a readiness to let the fulness of Jesus, and therefore the fulness of God which is ready even for him, stream over him and benefit him. His sin is that he is not ready for that which is ready for him in Jesus. But more is to be gained from noting the opportunity offered than how badly he let it slip.

What he lacks is now revealed (v. 21c). He is not the covenant-partner of God. He does not love his neighbour. He does not belong to Jesus. This is what he lacks. But it is not described in an abstract and academic way. It is aimed concretely at his specific existence and condition. We see it as that which he personally lacks. It is only now that we learn—indirectly—that the man is rich. And this is not stated explicitly until v. 22b : " He had great possessions." " Go, sell all you have and give it to the poor—so you will have a treasure in heaven—and come, follow me." This is the sentence. This is what the man lacks for the life of an heir of eternal life. This is the substance and the aim of all the commandments which he has not recognised as such, and to which he has not done justice with all his so-called observance of the commandments. This is what he has not done even in his coming to Jesus and falling on his knees before Him. Woe to him, the transgressor of the Law ! But we do not overlook the fact that the sentence has the form of an invitation and direction. Formulating what the man lacks, it opens for him the door to the fulness which is there even for him : Go ! Sell ! Give ! Follow Me ! This is all an opportunity and possibility. It is not only offered, but it will remain open even when it has been let slip. It will follow him even when he is disobedient to all these imperatives. He can never complain that the saving Word—even in the form of the command of God, interpreted, revealed in its substance and its aim, and therefore unmasking and annihilating him—is not near him, that it is (Rom. 10[8]) not laid on his heart and lips. Grace has met him as he is placed under God's judgment. Above all, therefore, let us not forget that it is as Jesus loved him that He uttered this judgment on him and gave him finally this saving direction on the way. He does not condemn him without seeking him, without willing to have him for Himself ; and He does this by interposing Himself and making Himself responsible for him. And for the man who ought to be living but is not living as an heir of eternal life, the direction which He also gives is saving, and genuinely consoling, because as a direction it is always the indication according to which what God has already done for him belongs to him and will accrue to his benefit if he will only make use of it. The essential content of this Word of Jesus is obviously threefold : Sell what you have ! Give to the poor ! Follow Me ! The three Evangelists all agree on these three elements. In Lk. 18[22] the first is accentuated by the addition of πάντα, but this only expresses the undoubted meaning contained in the wording of Mark and Matthew. None of the three elements must be overlooked, or allowed to slip into the background in favour of the other two. But each of them must be understood as a characterisation of that one thing, that whole, which Jesus has said to the man in answer to his question.

That he should sell what he has, that he should therefore part with what belongs to him, indicates what he lacks as the freedom in which he could and should live as the covenant-partner of God. What the commandments of the second table, which he thinks that he knows and has kept, require of him from this first standpoint is, therefore, the total obligation to the gracious and compassionate God who has chosen and called him into covenant with Himself, an obligation which has to be implemented in the sphere of his relationship to his neighbour. What he lacks is, therefore, obedience in the special sense of the commandments of the first table. The commandments of the second table require that he should confront his neighbour as one who is utterly bound to this God and who lives by nothing but His grace and compassion—if he lives in this way he will not kill, or commit adultery, or steal. They require that he should be wholly and genuinely free in relation to his neighbour : freed by his absolute obligation to God ; freed from all other divine or quasi-divine masters ; and therefore freed for an action which will really do justice to his neighbour. If he does not stand in this freedom, he will strive in vain to keep these commandments. He knows them quite well, but he does not know them at all. He does what belongs to their fulfilment, but how can he fulfil them when he neglects what they really require of him, when he is captive and bound by a regard for other lords and powers besides God ? The man who is a captive in this way is a murderer even if he does not harm a fly, an adulterer even if he never looks on a woman, a thief even if he never appropriates a straw that does not belong to him. The man who is a captive in this way is impure even if he is never so pure. Demanding that he should sell what he has, Jesus wills that he should be bound to God and therefore freed from all other lords. He is not this. He is a captive of his " great possessions." What he has really has him—in the very way in which God would have him, and alone should have him. He is ruled by the life proper to his great possessions with their immanent urge to preservation, exploitation and augmentation. The grip of mammon—of the life proper to what he has, to what really has him—makes him inaccessible and useless as far as the command of God is concerned. It does this in a very simple way. It, too, instils into him fear and love, and trust and hope. It, too, demands obedience, because it, too, is his lord. And if the commands of all other gods might tolerate man's subjection to the commands of mammon or similar lords as well as to themselves, the command of the gracious and compassionate God who has chosen and called man to covenant with Himself does not tolerate a division of this kind. For this God is not prepared to be a lord alongside other lords. The reason for this is that He is not a lord alongside other lords, but the Lord of all lords, the only Lord. We can live by His grace and compassion, in covenant with Him, only completely or not at all. His commands are kept only by the man who does not accept any command but His, because apart from Him he has, in fact, no lord whom he must honour and respect. The man who honours and respects another lord apart from Him transgresses all His commands, as a captive of this other lord, even if he does every thing that belongs to their fulfilment. The aim of Jesus' requirement that the rich man should divest himself of his wealth is plain to see. In accordance with the truth, he may and must be free from his other lord, from mammon, from the life proper to his great possessions, in order that, freed in this way, he may fulfil God's commands. As long as he has great possessions, they have him, and as long as they have him, God cannot and will not have him. He can only transgress His commands. He can never be an heir of eternal life. He must die—as the rich man he is, he must really die and pass—he must become poor if he is to tread the way of life. Because he is not willing to do this, it is in vain that he asks about this way even when he comes with his question to Jesus. Or is it in vain ? He is certainly told what he wants to know. He now knows what is involved. He has only to act. Even if he is still a prisoner, he is no longer a helpless prisoner. The door of his prison is wide open. Jesus loved him when He put to him the absolute demand : Sell what you have. He would not have loved him if He had spared him this demand. He proclaimed great joy to him when He did not spare his hearing this demand, when He did not withhold from him the saving Word of God.

The second element is that the proceeds of the sale should be given to the poor. This tells us positively that what he lacks is that love to the neighbour which is the meaning of the commandments of the second table. What they require of him is that he should not only not do what they forbid, but do something definite. That is, as a covenant-partner of the gracious and compassionate God and therefore as a free man, he should meet his neighbour as God meets him. But God meets him as the infinitely rich—what are his own " great possessions " compared with the possessions in God's house ?—and in His covenant with him this God has really given him what He has, placing it at the disposal of him, the poor man. This is how God acts in contrast to all the other so-called lords of man, in contrast particularly to mammon, whose dazzling gifts are distributed only to make man more and more subservient to himself. God is rich in the sense that He gives away what belongs to Him without return, without making man subservient, but free. And it is in this that man may and should become His imitator in relation to his neighbour. What has he to give his neighbour in proportion to what God has given him and still gives him ? But let him give this little as a small acknowledgment of what he has himself received. Anything less than all this little will be totally inadequate. What is the love which man can show to his neighbour in comparison with the love with which he is himself loved ? But let him give this little love to his neighbour and let him give it all. More is not possible, therefore more is not demanded—but all this little cannot be too much. It is when he gives what he has—not more, but also not less—that he fulfils God's commands. The aim of all of them is that, as the man who has been freed from strange lords, within the modest limits of his existence but within these limits unlimitedly, man should be free to be for his neighbour what God is for him—to be there for him, to be at his disposal, as God is there for him and stands at his disposal. " Give it to the poor." And in that way prove that you really have it, that it does not have you. In that way prove your freedom. Prove that God is your Liberator and that you are a witness to this Liberator. Note the addition : " So you will have a treasure in heaven." The dying of the rich man is not, then, a futile and meaningless dying ; his becoming poor does not mean his destitution, but his true and genuine enrichment. At bottom, therefore, it is not required of him that he should not have what he now has. On the contrary, he is shown that he may really have it, and how he may really have it. Giving it away, and so proving that freedom, he will change it into a possession which—in contrast to the false show with which mammon deceives—he may really have as his own. If with the little that is his he does what God does with the infinite wealth of His goodness, he enters into fellowship with this God. He receives the confirmation that his inheritance is sure, that eternal life already belongs to him even as he waits for it. He is not only the possessor, but the genuine owner of what he has. When he gives it to the poor—it cannot be taken from him. But to become its owner, he must subject it to this transformation. He must give it away. He must not hesitate to die as a rich man, to become poor. And it is because he is not ready to do this that he is disobedient and therefore off the way to eternal life, and it is in vain that he asks about it or even brings his question to Jesus. Not being willing to give what he has, he is not the child of God. But there is now displayed to him the invitation to give—to give not only something but all that he has to the poor. And in this invitation he sees the substance and the aim of all the commandments. If he has not known and not observed the commandments and therefore the saving Word of God, there can be no doubt that that Word now confronts him so plainly and has attacked him so sharply that his question is answered. He has been instructed. He has only to look at his life with his neighbour, and the goods which lie freely in his own hand, to know at once what he has to do to inherit eternal life. And Jesus loved him when He gave him this instruction. He did not want to take from him what belonged to him. On the contrary, what He wanted was to give to him what did not belong to him, and yet did belong to him as the child of God. He wanted him really to have this. He wanted him to have treasure in heaven. He wanted to help him to his rights against all strange lords. It was to this end that He demanded so sternly that he should sell all he had and give to the poor. He would not have loved him if He had pressed him less sternly. He brought him good tidings even as He pressed him so sternly.

The third demand of Jesus, or the third form of the one demand, is that he should come and follow Him. It is only in this third form that the two first, although they do not lose their own inherent force, are brought clearly into focus. What is required of this man if he is to inherit eternal life ? It is required that he should belong to Jesus. He has run to Him and fallen on his knees before Him. But he has obviously not come near enough. He has not really come close. He must come to Him—this is what the third form of the demand says— in order that he may stay with Him, not going away any more but directing his future course in accordance with that of Jesus. In place of his self-movement he may and must enter this new movement : Follow Me. This is again, and decisively, the interpretation of the commandments of the second table as they are supposed to be known to the questioner and fulfilled by him. The freedom for God which they demand from man is freedom for Jesus. And the freedom for one's neighbour which they demand is again freedom for Jesus. They aim at the true God and true man when they aim at God and man. And here in the person of Jesus the true God and true man stand face to face with the addressee and hearer of the commandments of God. With God, and as the Son of God, Jesus waits for our acknowledgment that He alone is the Lord, and as the Brother of the poor who are our neighbours He waits for our attestation that this Lord is so kind. The two obligations—that this man should sell what he has and therefore become free for God, and that he should give it to the poor and therefore become free for his neighbour—both derive their meaning and force from this final demand, that he should come and follow Jesus. To follow Jesus is the practice of this twofold freedom to the extent that life in the following of Jesus is the life of that covenant-partner of God who as such is so completely bound to his neighbour. To follow Jesus is to acknowledge the justice of the command of God in both these aspects. And to acknowledge the justice of the command of God in both these aspects is necessarily to follow Jesus. It is precisely at this point that the man comes short. Captivated by the claims of his great possessions, occupied with the maintenance, exploitation and augmentation which they demand of him, and kept back by these claims from the attestation of freedom with which he would have to meet his neighbour, he wants to continue in his own way. He does not see or realise that in this self-movement he is not free on either side. He does not want even Jesus to disturb him in the unfreedom which he regards as freedom. When the Word of Jesus discloses this state of affairs, it shows him that he is excluded from eternal life. It is a Word of judgment. But it is a Word of judgment which—decisively in this third form—reveals the direction in which eternal life is present and is to be sought and found by him. In this third form especially it is a command which is also an offer. When Jesus summons the man to follow Him, He offers him nothing less than Himself. He offers him nothing less than that he should belong to those at whose head and in whose place He has set Himself. He offers him nothing less than that He Himself assumes responsibility for his temporal and eternal future. He offers him nothing less, therefore, than participation in His own freedom.

But in v. 22 we are told that the rich man was horrified by this saying, this explanation of the commandments, and went away sorrowful. This definitely confirms the fact that what was said to him was the communication of his condemnation from the throne of God. He was not equal to the command of God in the form in which it was now completely and unequivocally revealed and authentically interpreted. He did not even dare to contemplate doing what was required. Much less did he proceed to do it. And so he stood confronting it, unworthy, impotent and lost. What was required was incommensurably too much, too great for him. He could not sell what he had—he could not free himself from the lordship and the commands of mammon. He could not give his possessions to the poor—he could not make himself a witness to the goodness of the eternally rich God. He could not follow Jesus—he could not stop the self-movement of his life, turning it into the movement of thankfulness. He was not the man for this. He could not do it. He was disobedient. How could he obey or even want to obey? He was not free for the freedom commanded and proffered. And so the opportunity with which he was presented to become an heir of eternal life could, in fact, only be the opportunity by which it was revealed that this was something which he could not become, since he lacked the being which was the presupposition of this becoming. He could only be horrified at this. He could only go away by the same road as he had come—a different road from that which leads to eternal life. And he could only go away sorrowful: sorrowful at the unattainable remoteness and strangeness of the glory of God which he had encountered, and sorrowful at his own incompetence and insufficiency in relation to it; sorrowful in face of the contrast between God's will and his own. And all the sadness which he might feel and express could only be a shadow of the real and infinite sadness of this contrast. What opened up at his feet was the abyss of the absolute impossibility of the relationship between God and the man who has committed sin and who as sinner sets himself in opposition to God.

But although that is the last that we are told about the man, it would again be a mistake to see and understand the incident only negatively. We recall what was stated at the very outset: that it is within the sphere of the kingdom of Jesus Christ that the incident is enacted. The sovereignty and majesty of Jesus are no less attested by the fact that the rich man sorrowfully goes away than by the fact that he came with his question. It is with Him that he has still to deal even in the state of disobedience out of which he came and to which we now see him returning. It was on Him and therefore on the command of God that he was shattered. It was His fulness that he lacked, and to the lack of which he had now to confess. Jesus is the man who is free from all other forces and lords because He is completely bound to God. Jesus is the man who stands at the disposal of the poor with all that He is and has, as a witness to the goodness of the rich God. It is only in and through Jesus Himself that another man can and will become and be a follower of Jesus. It is in relation to Jesus that he is the poor rich man—the man who is determined and ruled from elsewhere, the man who has great possessions. He has all possessions except the one—the fulness of Jesus. And this is what condemns him. This is what excludes him from eternal life. This is the abyss of the inner impossibility at his feet. This is what makes him disobedient to God's command, and therefore sorrowful. God's command is: " Rejoice." It is the one that has the fulness of Jesus who fulfils God's command, who may and must rejoice. But how can this be done by one who does not have the fulness of Jesus even if he has ever so great possessions? What else can they mean for him but the confirmation of what he lacks and therefore the confirmation of his disobedience and therefore an intensification of his sorrow? But just because he has this lack, the fact that he is now unmasked as disobedient, and can only go away sorrowful, cannot in any sense mean that he is abandoned. We do not know what happened to him later. But we do know that what he lacked, the fulness of Jesus, was still there even for him, even for poor rich like himself—and for them especially. We remember that Jesus loved him as He proclaimed that sentence. What else does this mean but that even as He condemned him He willed always to be totally there for him, the condemned, that even as his Judge, He willed always to be his Friend and Helper? His kingdom—the kingdom of this One who loves—embraces the evil contrast between the will of God and human will, between God and sinners, between God's glory and the unworthiness, impotence and lostness in which man confronts Him. His kingdom embraces the abyss of the inner impossibility of human existence, in which His fulness—the fulness of the love with which God loved the world before it was—is misunderstood, derided and resisted. Where else but in the depths of this abyss has He established His kingdom? Sinking into this abyss man will continually encounter Him and in Him will continually find and have One who does not desire his loss in this abyss and who, in spite of all the power of his impotence, will not tolerate or accept it.

The unmasking of human disobedience in the story of the rich man, the sorrow with which he went away, show that, in virtue of the totality in which it confronts man in the person of Jesus, the command of God kills. But the continuation in v. 23 f., in which Jesus confronts His disciples as the Commander of those who are obedient to His commands, shows that, in virtue of the same totality, even as it kills, it does not cease to make alive. The saying of Peter in v. 28 is not contradicted. They have indeed left all and followed Him. They have therefore done what the rich man was incapable of doing. They have satisfied the total demand by whose proclamation he was unmasked and condemned as disobedient. They are, therefore, on the way to eternal life, as they are assured in v. 30. Twice (in v. 23 and v. 27) it is stated emphatically that Jesus " looked on " them. He is looking at His own. It is the look of the One who knows that they are His own, and also how and why they are. But for this very reason it is not an exclusive look. He does not turn away his eyes from the one who has gone away sorrowful. On the contrary, according to all that follows, He looks right past and through them after or towards the one who has gone away. If the one Word of God has made a separation between the obedient and the disobedient, it is not that the Word of God itself has disintegrated into two parts. It remains a Word of judgment even to the obedient, and a Word of promise even to the disobedient. And it is in this indivisible totality that it is now imparted and presented by Jesus to His own. What Jesus has to say to His disciples after what has taken place between Himself and the rich man is certainly not that a man like this with his great possessions is as such excluded from the kingdom of God—that he cannot possibly enter this kingdom. But what they are twice emphatically given to consider in Mk. 10^{23-25} is that it is " hard " for men like this to do so—harder than for a camel to go through the eye of a needle. A veritable hill of difficulty stands in the way of what they have admittedly done—the keeping of the commands. It is on this hill that the rich man has been broken before them. According to his own decision and according to the confirmatory word of Jesus, he was not the man to conquer or remove it. Were they then, the disciples, the men to do it ? It is remarkable that this obvious conclusion is drawn neither by Jesus nor by the disciples themselves, and that the statement of Jesus does not create for them the joy and satisfaction of having left this hill behind by doing what the man did not do. Why is it that they, too, are " amazed " (v. 24) and " more astounded than ever " (v. 26) ? Where is that peace of a good conscience which they can surely enjoy if in the words of v. 26 they even have to ask : " Who then can be saved ? " They surely know that everyone can be saved, and how. They have surely done what is necessary, and therefore can do it. To be sure, it is a hard and thankless matter. To be sure, it needs a very radical resolve and a very free will to do what was required of the rich man and what they themselves in their way have done. But where is the so terribly difficult thing, the downright impossibility, which seems to loom before their eyes, and in face of which, although they are in fact obedient, they are so astounded, so full of questions, and even compelled to accept solidarity with the disobedient in a concern for salvation ? There can be no doubt that even according to the view of the Evangelist their astonishment and question are strictly appropriate. It is quite right that, even though they have fulfilled the commands of God, they should be surprised by the demand addressed to the rich man, his refusal and the statement of Jesus about the great difficulty of this fulfilment—just as if they had heard all this for the first time, just as if all that they had left to follow Jesus still towered before them in all its value and necessity, and could still hold and hinder them from being obedient to Him. As the Evangelist saw it, what took place between Jesus and the rich man had obviously shown them—the obedient—in a completely new and surprising way what obedience is, how great a step obedience involves, and that even when this step has been taken once, it has to be taken again and again in all its difficulty. Standing as the obedient alongside the disobedient, they are made to realise plainly that even the obedient are always standing on the edge of the abyss of disobedience, and that this abyss yawns even at their feet. And this is the significance of the story according to vv. 23–31. The disciples themselves have been made to realise it. In face of the command of God they have had to confess their solidarity with the disobedient. That is why they ask : " Who then can be saved ? " That they have done what this man did not do cannot prevent the revelation of this fact and must not prevent them confessing it. In relation to

Jesus, in relation to the command of God, they are in exactly the same position as this man. Even their own entry into the kingdom of God seems to be harder to them than the passage of a camel through the eye of a needle. According to the saying of Jesus in v. 27, even that they—the obedient—should be saved is impossible with men. And their only hope is the same as that of the disobedient —the fact that with God all things are possible, and therefore even their salvation, and, as the way to their salvation, their obedience. This saying in v. 27 is obviously the hinge on which the whole narrative turns. The saving of anyone is something which is not in the power of man, but only of God. No one can be saved—in virtue of what he can do. Everyone can be saved—in virtue of what God can do. The divine claim takes the form that it puts both the obedient and the disobedient together and compels them to realise this, to recognise their common status in face of the commanding God. What it requires, and what it invariably achieves when it is proclaimed, is that we come to stand on the spot where—whether we are obedient or disobedient—we cannot be helped at all by ourselves, but only by the power of God, the power of His pity. The claim is as radical as that, and it grips and binds us as radically as that. According to the text we are studying, it demands of the rich man something that is quite impossible on the strength of what he can do. We have seen that what he lacks in the matter of the fulfilment of the substance of the commands is life in the fulness of Jesus, His freedom for God and for His neighbour. It is only in this freedom that he can be obedient. But it is just this freedom which he lacks. He is not Jesus. He is only the man with great possessions and as such not capable of this freedom. He can only be disobedient to the commands of God. He cannot even enter the way to eternal life, much less travel it. To do this he would have to be another man than he is. As the man he is, he is excluded from it. And who can make himself to be another than he is ? With men, in virtue of human capacity, it is impossible. Human capacity does not include within it this ability. It is easier for a camel to pass through the eye of a needle than for a man to do what is necessary for entry into the kingdom of God—to make himself another man than he actually is. But this is also true of the disciples of Jesus who inconceivably confront this rich man as those who have done what he has not done, what he could not do, and who are to be blessed as those who are on the way to eternal life. From the point of view of their own ability, they, too, lack everything that he lacked. They, too, do not possess the fulness of Jesus, His freedom for God and for His neighbour. They, too, have no organ, no aptitude, no power to apprehend this. They, too, are not Jesus. They, too, being what they are, can only be disobedient to the command of God, and miss the way to eternal life. They, too, are unable to make themselves into other men than they are. The hill of difficulty which confronts him also confronts them. This is the discovery with which they are faced according to our text. Who can be saved ? Nobody can. Even they cannot. The judgment upon the rich man, the affirmation of the one thing which he lacks, has a direct reference to them too. Without the omnipotence of the pity of God they, too, could only give themselves up for lost. But we do not fully describe what God's command requires of man if we characterise it as what is impossible with man. On the strength of what God, not man, can do, what is impossible with men is possible with God. In this way, therefore, it is really possible with man too, not in virtue of his own, but in virtue of divine power. And what distinguishes the disciples of Jesus from the rich man, and gives them the advantage over him, what differentiates the obedient from the disobedient, is the fact that they may be witnesses to this divine possibility. They have actually left all and followed Jesus. How did this happen ? It happened as they made use of that which they possessed as little as he, but which was at their disposal as the gift and present of God. It happened as they recognised, claimed and appropriated that which they lacked no less than he, but which was available for them in Jesus.

It happened as—without regard to their own inability to apprehend, which was no less than that of the rich man—they accepted the fulness of Jesus as their own. It happened as they let His freedom—which was not theirs—count as theirs. It happened as they put it into effect. It happened as at the Word of Jesus they held to Jesus without being Jesus. It happened, therefore, as they accepted Jesus' different existence as determinate for themselves and therefore lived as other men without actually being other men. In this humility or boldness—or, rather, in virtue of the grace which allowed and commanded this humility or boldness—the impossible became possible to them. To them ? No, it was never possible to them. It was still possible only to God. But in the knowledge that what is possible only to God has become possible *for* them, in this confidence, in this humility or boldness—we can now say simply in *faith*—they became obedient. They accepted it as true that Jesus was obedient for them. They became obedient with Him, as those who on the strength of their own ability can be only the disobedient—obedient in following His obedience. They believed, i.e., they were pleased to have His ability attributed to them, to have their own inability covered over by His ability. They undertook to live in the shade and shelter of His ability. This life in the shade and shelter of His ability was their obedience—their willingness and readiness to leave all and follow Him. It is just because they are in this way obedient and on the way to eternal life that the judgment upon the disobedient must obviously fall upon them too. In this humility or boldness they have grasped at the freedom of Jesus attributed to them. They have placed themselves in the shade and shelter of His ability. But this being the case, how can they help being frightened when—in the light of the disobedience of another —they again see how they themselves would be situated without this freedom, without this shade and shelter. How impossible it would then be even for them to be obedient ! How disobedient they themselves would be outside this shade and shelter ! How could they possibly imagine that they had turned themselves into other men, that of themselves and by their own efforts they were other men than their true selves, and therefore, on the strength of their ability and accomplishment, secure in face of the judgment that falls on him ? If they do not lack the one thing that is needful for the fulfilment of the divine command, it is certainly not because they themselves possess it and achieve it. It is only because it is there for them in Jesus. It is only because they are pleased to accept it by faith in Him. And it is just because they are in this way—and only in this way—obedient and on the way to eternal life that they must obviously not apply only to themselves the acquittal which they have received in contrast to the rich man, the disobedient, and the hope and confidence in which they are permitted to live in contrast to him ; not keeping these things to themselves in face of him. If they stand with him under the judgment which is passed upon all that is possible with men, he on his side is united with them under the promise of that which is possible with God. To what is possible with God there obviously belong both their present obedience and also the future obedience of the rich man, both their own prospect of eternal life and his also. If they really live by the fact that the fulness of Jesus is there for them, the disobedient, they can only view and address this other disobedient on the basis of the fact that the same fulness is there for him too. If their own fulfilment of the command consists simply in the fact that they live as those who make use of the freedom of Jesus attributed to them, and therefore of the ability of God which is greater than their ability, how else can they judge this or any other transgressor of this command except as one for whom also this freedom is there, but who has not yet made of it the use which he may ? If there was and is grace for them—the grace of the divine ability that covers their own inability—how can there fail to be grace for this man or for any others who like themselves lack the ability ? No disobedient man can evade the all-prevailing authority and validity of the divine command which demands that man should be committed to the compassion of God. And no obedient man can conceal this fact from others, or use it for his own advantage to the disadvantage of others. On the contrary, those who know it must attest and tell it to those who do not yet know it. It is for this end and only for this end that they are better off than they, and distinguished from them. As it emerges in the incident of which they were witnesses, the significance of what marks off the disciples, the significance of their differentiation from the rich man, is simply that these disciples, who are what they are and are permitted to do what they do by the grace of God, become apostles, i.e., men who proclaim what is impossible with men, but possible with God. (There is unmistakeable reflected and repeated in the relationship between the disciples and the rich man of this story the relationship between the Church and Israel, and not only this, but the relationship between the whole community of God and the surrounding world.) Made obedient and set on the way to eternal life, in relation to all other men they are witnesses to the fact that what they are permitted to be and do is the will of God for them too, and that the possibility by which they themselves live is given to them too, and may be used by them. Saved by faith alone, they may and must say to all who are not yet distinguished in this way, that this distinction is their determination too, and that even in the deepest depth of their disobedience they cannot cease to be determined for it. To that extent, when Jesus looks on the disciples as His own, as the obedient, He also looks after and towards the rich man, the disobedient, and all those like him, as those who are within the range of the divine command and cannot possibly be removed from it.

The interchange between Jesus and Peter in Mk. 10^{28-31}, which brings the whole story to a conclusion, ends in v. 31 with the significant saying : " Many that are first shall be last, and the last first." These final words seem to make it unmistakeable that everything that has taken place between Jesus and the rich man on the one side and the disciples on the other involves a threat of judgment even for the disciples and a promise even for the rich man. It is to be noted that the basic presupposition is again predominant that the kingdom of Christ is the sphere in which the whole action is played out and to which it all bears witness. We do not hear of the saved and the lost, or of those who are within and those who are without, or of participants and non-participants, but of a serious, and yet for all its seriousness not an absolute, difference within the same sphere. We hear of the first and the last, and this means of the possibility of a very radical change within this sphere in the status and estimation of different people, the obedient and the disobedient, who are its citizens and inhabitants. The disciples with their obedience, which they do not owe to themselves, but to the divine ability bestowed on them, are now first, and the rich man, in virtue of his human inability, is one of the last. The former are distinguished, and the latter is disdained. Yet both participate in both presuppositions. The relationship between the former and the latter is reversible in virtue of the presuppositions that are true for both. The rich man, who is now the last, could become a first on the strength of the divine ability, which is not withdrawn even from him, but available even for his use. And the disciples, who are now the first, could become the last in virtue of their own human inability which resists the divine ability. We remember Rom. $11^{14f.}$ The visible situation which has developed between these men and that man is not fixed or absolute. Only the command of God is fixed. Only Jesus is absolute as King of the sphere in which both exist, as the rule of the divine pity to which both are accountable, and before which both stand in need of help.

The interchange between Jesus and Peter in vv. 28–30, to which this final statement belongs, reveals at once both the high distinction and also the great peril of the disciples themselves. It shows that their position is first, but it also shows that from being first they may actually become last. " We have left all and have followed thee," is what Peter said in v. 28 in reply to the saying about what is not possible with men but is possible with God. His words are appropriate in one sense. For on the strength of what is possible with God, the disciples had, in fact, done what is impossible with men. But they are also highly inappropriate, for—as Matthew has rightly understood it—the announcement expresses a jarring concern : " What becomes of us ? " This concern does not derive from faith in what is possible with God and therefore from the obedience which distinguishes the disciples from the rich man, but, if at all, only from what they unfortunately have in common with the rich man—the disobedience which was theirs too, and which was unmasked and condemned with that of the rich man. To judge by this concern, the obedience in which they had left all and followed Jesus had not been a joyous obedience. To judge by this concern, they had no doubt looked forwards in faith, but they had also looked back at all they had left behind to follow Jesus. But how, then, had they really left it ? How, then, had they—in contrast to the rich man—really followed Jesus and really done justice to the substance of the divine commands ? Was it not inevitable that, in spite of what they had done, they must see themselves seriously and totally called in question along with the rich man ? How, then, could they fail to be threatened by the possibility which he now realised—the possibility of being last instead of first ? He had gone away sorrowful. But what had they done when, to judge by the concern in their question, they had come sorrowful ? In this question, what is possible and impossible with men in regard to the command of God emerges no less evidently in the case of the disciples than it had done in the case of the rich man, and, along with it, the danger in which they, too, stood. Jesus tells them consolingly in v. 29 f.—to some extent quietening and dissipating their concern—that there is no man that has left house, brothers, sisters, mother, father, children or lands for His and the Gospel's sake who will not receive a hundredfold for what has been surrendered, even now in this world in the midst of persecution, and in the world to come eternal life (and, according to Mt. 19[28], He strengthened this promise by a reference to their apostolic office, in virtue of which they are destined to be judges of the twelve tribes of the people of God). But while this is true, we must not overlook the inherent reference to the danger that faces them, the threat of judgment that is addressed against them too. Those who, following Him, have for His sake left everything, are those who are not only certain of eternal life in the world to come, but have not really lost anything in this world, since they will receive again all that they have lost, not merely as they lost it, but a hundredfold, what they had never had before and could never have attained. They are those who already in this world proceed to the richest and truest reward. They will have to the full everything that man can have or desire in human and material values and goods. They are the meek who, according to Mt. 11[29], will find rest for their souls, and, according to Mt. 5[5], will inherit not only eternal life but also the earth. But is this really the case ? That is the very critical question which lurks in the promise. Are they those who have this promise and live with it ? When they leave all and follow Him, have they heard and accepted the Gospel as good news for life and death, body and soul ? When they choose obedience to God's command instead of disobedience, have they really chosen the better, the best, which is what this obedience surely is ? If they have done this, how then can they put the plaintive question : " What becomes of us ? " How then can they look back ruefully, as it were, at what they have given up ? How can the man who is capable of looking back be obedient, if obedience means to gain by surrendering, to lose a little and be given infinitely more ? If they are capable of this backward look, are they even a single step in advance of the rich man who went away sorrowful ? Do they not stand with him already among the last in the kingdom of Christ ? Is it not possible that they may have at any moment the experience of being outstripped by him and seeing him in their place among the first ? But, of course, it is not by accident that this question, and with it the threat of judgment addressed to the disciples and revealing their serious peril, is so completely covered and clothed by the dazzling promise which Jesus gives them. And the seriousness and weight of the threat lie in the fact that it meets them in this concealment—indirectly. Between the word of Peter in v. 28 and the answer of Jesus in v. 29 f. there is a supremely indirect relationship. A great gulf obviously opens up between the being which the disciples (within the limits of what is possible and impossible with men) have represented as theirs, and that other being, based on what is possible in God's free compassion, which is ascribed to them by Jesus as their new and proper life; the being which He sees in them and does not cease to see in spite of their representation of themselves. When Peter and the other disciples look back in concern and half-regret at what they have lost they are obviously not the same as those whom Jesus—as if nothing had happened—addresses as men who have left all for His sake and the Gospel's, and who as such are worthy and certain not only of this hundredfold temporal but also of the eternal requital and reward. Does Jesus not know that, as the saying of Peter shows, they are still these others, and that by this same saying they have unmistakeably denied what they are through Him ? He obviously knows it well. The saying determines His answer. But in His answer He steps, as it were, over that abyss for them and with them—again making them, from what they are by themselves, into what they are permitted to be by and with Him. This silent action is a repetition of the act of creative goodness, in which He called, indeed " made," them out of nothing to be apostles (Mk. $3^{14, 16}$). And on the strength of this act they are now addressed as what they are not according to that anxious question. They have now ascribed to them an existence which is so contradictory of the presuppositions of the question. They are now described as those who are sure of all these temporal and eternal benefits just because they have lost all and followed Him, and can therefore be certain, and cannot therefore be anxious. It is to be noted that this is how they are comforted. In face of their scarcely concealed defection, Jesus becomes and is again, and this time truly, Jesus the Saviour. He steps in again with His freedom to supply their deficiency. And in so doing He assuages and dissipates their concern. This would obviously not be possible in any other way. For in any other way they would be left standing on the other side of that abyss. Now that they had lost all, their concern would not only be natural, but necessarily it would be limitless and invincible. And how could they ever move away from this position ? They are relieved of their concern by the fact that Jesus takes it on Himself. And it is as He intervenes for them that the promise He gives them becomes powerful and decisive. It shines out for them and over them, because it is the reflection of His own glory, of His hidden but real kingship. As He Himself lays down His life in His great freedom for God and men, in order by this very means—risen from the dead, sitting at the right hand of God—to win it again in incomparable divine splendour, they will have the same experience, for all that He does is done for them. And as He Himself is already, here and now, in the secrecy of His existence in the flesh, really in possession of all the rights and joys of His kingdom, the same is true of them, i.e., in and with Him, through the fact that all that is His belongs also to them. If it meant anything else but this, the promise of v. 29 f. could hardly be more than a strange *fata morgana* not very appropriate to the existence of the Church " in the midst of persecutions " (v. 30). It is because what Jesus says to His disciples is filled with the dynamic of what He Himself is and does—is and does for His own— that His promise is full of reality, clarity and truth, and is therefore a consoling promise, not only contradicting concern, but destroying it. But as such, it is obviously directed not only to the disciples, but also to the rich man who went away sorrowful. From the Markan (and Lukan) account it is quite clear that this is the meaning of the text. To the saying of Peter : " *We* have left all and

have followed thee," the answer of Jesus stands only in an indirect relationship
with its general declaration : " *No one* that has left house, brothers, sisters . . .
who shall not receive again a hundredfold." This is the general answer which
holds for all the anxious, all who are not free, all who still stand on the other
side of that abyss, all who are bound by what is possible and impossible with
men. The decisive element in this answer is what Jesus is and does for those
bound people. But this being the case, it is obviously true for the rich man who
went away no less than for the disciples. No matter what attitude he assumes,
even if he runs to the very depths of hell, he cannot evade either the command
of God or the divine promise which is its meaning. What has been said and
done in their favour by Jesus, the disciples cannot refrain from repeating in
favour of him and those like him, and with the same indefatigability as Jesus
devoted to them.

There remains for the rich man the explicitly stated hope : " The last shall
be first." But we now understand the fact and extent that what Jesus said
must really affect the disciples, too, as a Word of judgment—not in spite of the
fact, but just because of the fact that it is so completely covered and clothed
with the promise. If they were not still at the place where they were, according
to the saying of Peter, how could they be accessible to God's accusation, or
be held responsible as transgressors of His command ? If it is not possible
with men to be other than they are, is there not justification and even excuse
for their anxieties ? But they are accused and condemned because they are
addressed on the basis of their new existence, as those who benefit by what is
possible with God ; because, indeed, this new existence is again and rightly
adjudged and assigned to them. This, the grace of Christ, is the attack upon
the old being to which, according to that anxious saying, they again wished to
return or had already returned. It is this that makes them responsible, guilty,
inexcusable and, of course—for otherwise the story would not be in the Gospels—
ready to confess their guilt and repent. This is the demand—that they should
turn and draw back, regretting their regret. They are told who they are, and
at the same time who they cannot be ; where they belong, and at the same
time where it is impossible for them to belong. Thus the story of the rich young
man shows us in all its aspects the constancy of the divine faithfulness in the
divine command, so far as its substance consists in the fact that it binds the man
who hears it (protesting against his unfaithfulness, but also victorious over the
evil into which that unfaithfulness plunges him) to the person of Jesus.

THE COMMAND AS THE DECISION OF GOD

As God is gracious to us in Jesus Christ, His command is the sovereign, definite and good decision concerning the character of our actions—the decision from which we derive, under which we stand and to which we continually move.

1. THE SOVEREIGNTY OF THE DIVINE DECISION

The command of God is more than what may be connoted by the idea of a claim. We could not describe it in terms of a claim without exceeding the boundaries of the term. A claim confronts man from without. Of course, the command of God does this too. It must even be said that in the strict sense man cannot be moved and claimed from without except by God's command. But if it is characteristic of every other claim that it leaves man unmoved and unchanged in his innermost self, it must be said of the divine command that in virtue of its distinctive validity it so concerns man that by this claim he in some way becomes a different man from what he would be without it. A claim which is not that of the Word of God may be justified or not, possible or impossible, binding or the reverse. And the subject of it is himself more or less competent to decide whether it is so or not. But the claim of the divine command does not leave any place for this freedom. By its very nature it is a justified, possible and necessary claim, by which the one whom it concerns and encounters is arrested, so that however he may react towards it he cannot possibly evade it as though he were not claimed. Other claims are limited by the fact that they can be satisfied either by obedience or disobedience. But the claim of God cannot be satisfied in this way, either by obedience or disobedience. For both obedient and disobedient it means, when they are claimed, that they belong to it, that they are marked by it, that it qualifies them ineluctably. Above and beyond whatever else might be described as a claim on men, the divine command is a statement about him. It not only subjects him to a requirement, but in so doing, places him under a conclusion. It not only demands that he should make a decision in conformity with it, but as it does so, and as man decides in conformity or contradiction to it, it expresses a decision about man. And as a statement, conclusion and decision concerning him, it moves and changes, marks and qualifies him. We must now examine this aspect of the matter in detail.

That God is gracious to us in Jesus Christ is the divine decision about our whole being, what we do and do not do. This is the will of God for us. In virtue of this will He has taken the initiative from all eternity and in the heart of time, making Himself responsible for our relationship to Him and participation in His glory. This is His will for us at every moment of our lives. The divine command is the witness to this will. It requires our obedience, i.e., that we should live in this surrender to God which He both wills and effects. It requires the witness of our will and actions as the praise of His great love. Our obedience, will and actions do not create the relationship through which we belong to God. Therefore the command of God does not require that we should create this relationship. But as this command bears witness to what God wills with us and does for us, it demands from us the witness of our will and actions as the confirmation of His grace directed towards us, our active acknowledgment of the fact that we are what we are by this grace, the response of our witness to what He has given us. To this extent the command of God is a claim. As we have seen, the grace of God in Jesus Christ is not only the foundation but the content, the decisive form, of the claim addressed to us in the divine command. But it is not only this, and therefore the command of God is not just a claim. For what does it mean when we say that *we* belong to God in virtue of the divine will and the divine action corresponding to it ? " We " are the men who stand before God as creatures, who for their part exist in willing and acting, in the venture of a series of decisions which is as long or short as our temporal life. The claim of the divine command is concerned with these decisions both as a whole and in detail. It is in these decisions that we give our witness to the fact that we belong to God. If they are subject to God's claim, this includes the further and greater fact that they are measured by the will and act of God, that the will and act of God is in some sense the prior decision by which they are all asked whether or not they attest and praise His great love. Because the will of God expressed in His Law is the good which as such requires our active recognition, it is also the criterion of the good or evil nature of our conduct. The latter is made accountable by it (from eternity and at the heart of time and at every moment of our life in time). We either conform to it or not in what we will and do. We either give or refuse it the testimony of our will and act. We either praise or blaspheme God's great love. This is what differentiates between the good and evil in our lives. And the differentiation is made in the fact that God is gracious to us in Jesus Christ. This His will with us and His act for us is the law of our lives both as a whole and in each detailed moment. It is this because He is the Lord of our lives, because we belong to Him, because we belonged to

Him before we existed and will always belong to Him—to no one else, and certainly not to ourselves. What we were and are and will be stands or falls by whether it is righteous or not in His sight. And the conclusion that we are righteous or not in His sight, and therefore stand or fall, is not for us to make but for Him. It is a matter of the primal decision made and expressed in the will of God from eternity and the act of God at the heart of time, and continually made and expressed again at every moment of our life in time. What we will and do is exposed to this decision of God and awaits the disclosure of it. " For we must all appear before the judgment seat of Christ ; that every one may receive . . . according to that he hath done, whether it be good or bad " (2 Cor. 5^{10}). The judgment seat of Christ, before which we obviously do not stand here and now, has already been set up, and whether we have done, do or will do good or evil has already been decided from it. We have been, are and will be observed and weighed. This is established by the fact that God is gracious to us in Jesus Christ. This fact is the starting-point of all the ways and works of God and our own starting-point. Because this is God's decision for us, it is also God's decision concerning us—the primal decision to which all our own decisions are subjected. And the command of God, which is the witness to His grace, is as such a witness to the infallible criterion whether we walk in light or darkness, whether we stand or fall. Because God wills to have us as His own, and already has us in virtue of His command, He also knows how He will have us and already has us. As He is our Lord by reason of His command, He is also the Law by which we stand or fall. Whether we remember or forget His Law, whether we study it or neglect to do so, whether we recognise and regard it or it remains distant and alien to us, whether we are compliant or refractory to it in the form in which we imagine we recognise and observe it, we must always recollect that it is a question of the presence of the One who does not merely require certain things of us—things great or small—but who even as He requires them has already decided how we stand before Him, as good or evil ; how we have come to Him and taken up a position with regard to His will. The Law of God as the divine demand, order, direction and commission is the crisis of our life both as a whole and in each individual moment. Whatever may be our attitude to Him, because it is our attitude to Him, it always includes in itself a definite attitude on the part of God to us. In some sense it is itself the realisation of this divine attitude. In our attitude and conduct we emerge always as those who are known by God as He gives us His command.

This is the sovereignty of the divine decision to which the command bears witness. It does not really affect the freedom of our own decisions. It is our own free decisions whose character God decides even as we ourselves make them. It is they which are claimed and measured by His command. It is the use of our freedom which is subjected to the prior divine decision—the decision of the question whether it is right or not, whether it consists or not in the witness required of us. It is in the use of our freedom that we give an account how we stand in the sight of God, and are pierced to the depths by the searching glance of God. It is in the use of our freedom that we have to embody God's righteous judgment upon us. The sovereign decision of God by which we are confronted in the presence of His Law relates to our own free decisions.

It is, therefore, a genuinely serious and relevant question which faces us when, in the light of the presence of the divine command, we are confronted by the fact that our life consists in a continuous series of decisions which we have to make and execute. This is why we have necessarily to examine the direction of our way both as a whole and in its particular turns and sections, to scrutinise the nature of the choice which is now before us in its integral connexion with past and future choices. How will it be with us in this choice of ours, if, as we make it, God too will choose, deciding the character of our choice, whether it is good or bad, obedience or disobedience ? The command is there. It is always according to its relationship to this that our choice will be good or bad, that we shall be obedient or disobedient. God will decide this. He has decided it from all eternity, and at the heart of time, in the person of Jesus Christ. He will, therefore, do so in our own life also and at every moment of it ; and therefore in the moment of decision which we now approach. But it is *our* decision that He will judge. And it is in His command that His decision waits for ours, as it is there that it waited for us on our earlier path, and there that it will wait for us again on our later path. How, then, can and shall we encounter His judgment ? With what understanding of the divinely given command ? With what readiness for God's judgment, for His differentiation between good and evil ? In what condition in view of the criterion by which we shall be measured ? We obviously do not do justice to the sovereignty of the divine decision if we try to evade this testing, if at every moment of our willing and acting we are not occupied with the question of our readiness for willing and acting at the next moment, if our willing and acting at the present moment are not sustained and inspired by this question, by our knowledge of the accountability of our life in its sequence of yesterday, to-day and to-morrow. The sovereignty of the divine decision is obviously ignored from the outset if it is not regarded at every point as the criterion under which we stood and stand and will stand, as the seat of judgment from which we are already seen here and now as good or bad, even though it is not apparent here and now what we are there seen to be in the totality of our life decision. Our submission to this decision, and therefore our obedience to God's command, begins always with the fact that we look towards it as those who know that it is our own free decision which will there be judged. From the very outset, then, this our own free decision is there called in question, and therefore in need of preparatory testing as we approach it. We cannot attempt to make it without submitting it to this preliminary testing. Standing under God's judgment to-day, as we stood under it yesterday, we are claimed by the fact that we will always be exposed to it again to-morrow. That what we will and do should take place in this self-examination— with a glance backward at what we willed and did formerly, and forward to what we shall will and do in the path that is now to be pursued or not, and therefore with a readiness for the next thing, or rather for the judgment which we approach in and with it—this is our proper attitude to the divine decision which awaits our own decision in God's command. It has nothing whatever to do with theory or contemplation. It does not form an empty moment between one choice and decision and another. On the contrary, it belongs to every choice and decision and therefore to the practice of every moment. It is the bearing of every moment on both past and future moments, and on the totality of our life in so far as it is lived, not merely in our own decisions, but both as a whole and in detail under the divine decision, and its approaching disclosure. It is not made superfluous by the fact that the divine attitude and decision stands in sovereign independence of it. The latter is genuinely independent. It cannot be forestalled or compelled by any of our attitudes and decisions. No readiness in which we undertake a step can be a prescription for the divine judgment that will wait for us at the moment of each step, or rather that we ourselves will execute by means of this step. To be sure, the decision of God is always as superior to ours—whatever this may be—as eternity is to time, as His holy and righteous knowing and willing is to our sinful and perverse willing and knowing. To be sure, we will not be our own judges when we make our decision, but will stand under the judgment of God, executing it ourselves. And the same is true of the self-examination in which we approach our next decision. But again and again, it is to our own free decisions that the divine decision about good and evil refers. It is they as such which are pleasing or displeasing to God, which are a praising or blaspheming of His love, and by which we ourselves are the executors of this divine decision. The divine person reacts to our person, and is not unknown to us but well known in Jesus Christ. In this person known to us, He is always the Law which will pass judgment upon us, upon our willing and doing and upon our decision. If He is utterly superior to us, if He knows infinitely more about us than we will ever know ourselves, and if He knows infinitely better what He wills from us than we could ever come to appreciate even in the most searching self-examination, yet it is He—and not a blind fate or capricious demon— whose judgment we continually approach, under whose judgment we always stood and stand even now, when with the step which we now take we are in some way implicated in preparation for the next. Do we not make a mock of Him, and ourselves also, if we try to persuade ourselves, and act accordingly, that this sequence of our conduct is a matter of indifference to us, that we can carry it through without any real personal concern, that we are ignorant and incapable, that it is not worth while to take seriously this question of preparation ? If, in our willing and doing, in our personal decisions, we have to do with the person of the omnipotent and omniscient God, this is obviously not in any sense an obstacle, but a cause and summons that we should reflect and prepare an account. It is an urgent and compelling reason why—in and with what we now will and do and with a view to the next step—we should consider the question what we ought to do, and then answer the question with what we next will and do, not forcing the divine judgment on the one hand, but also prepared to submit to it, to be condemned and judged by it. Between the arrogance of those who regard themselves as judges of what they will and do, and the false humility of those who take no notice of God's judgment because they cannot change it, there is the third possibility—the sense of responsibility of those who know that God alone is their Judge and not they themselves, and that because God is their Judge they have every reason to remember Him in all their willing and doing, to keep Him before their minds' eye, and in their own self-examination continually to move towards their examination by Him.

We propose to elucidate this matter by a consideration of the New Testament use of the group of words, δόκιμος, δοκιμή, δοκιμάζειν. Assuming always the basic presupposition that God is gracious to us in Jesus Christ, this illuminates (1) the sovereignty of the divine testing, judging and deciding over human being, willing and doing ; (2) the fact that it is precisely our own decisions which are subject to this sovereign divine decision of God ; and (3) the necessity of making it always in preparation for our approaching encounter with this supreme divine decision.

In the LXX δοκιμάζειν is the translation of *bachan*, and therefore recalls particularly the process of testing, searching, knowing and concluding which God carries out in regard to man, which, according to Jer. 11[20], 17[10], 20[12], reaches to the heart and reins, which, according to Ps. 139[1f.], we cannot escape in our downsitting or uprising, our going or lying down, in any of our ways or thoughts or words—" whither shall I go from thy Spirit ? " or " whither shall I flee from thy presence ? " (v. 7)—a process in which the righteous man who knows that he stands in a covenantal relationship with God does not see a burden but, on the contrary, the proof and confirmation of divine grace, and for which he therefore prays : " Search me, O God, and know my heart : try me, and know my thoughts : and see if there be any wicked way in me, and lead me in the way everlasting " (Ps. 139[23f.], cf. Ps. 26[2]). It is not so much the fact that we cannot escape it, but rather that we cannot wish to escape it, which makes the divine δοκιμάζειν, the decision of the divine command, into the two-edged sword which pierces " even to the dividing asunder of soul and spirit, and of the joints and marrow," the " discerner of the thoughts and intents of the heart," as it is described in Heb. 4[12], or the fire by which the work of every man shall be basically tested according to 1 Cor. 3[13]. For God tests our works, says Paul in 1 Thess. 2[4] (with a glance at his own preaching of the Gospel), by trying our hearts—an obvious agreement with the Old Testament view. Those who stand the test, who are therefore δόκιμοι in His eyes, and as such receive the crown of life, are, as Jas. 1¹² puts it, those who love Him in what they are and will and do. When the divine δοκιμάζειν has a positive result, and the divine test is passed, its object is a human δοκιμή or δοκίμιον, i.e., the authentication of man as one to whom God is gracious and who is God's covenant-partner. The authentication consists in the fact that man proves himself to be such by his conduct, that his willing and doing proceed from a heart which is really in this matter and not in something else. Absolutely and properly, only the divine Judge is capable of this proving and testing of our works. He sees both our actions and also ourselves, the heart from which they proceed, τὰ κρυπτὰ τῶν ἀνθρώπων (Rom. 2⁵, ¹⁶). And therefore Paul is well aware that even though the work which he does may be good to himself and others—even though he is a preacher to others in the sight of God he may still be an ἀδόκιμος (1 Cor. 9²⁷). We cannot be approved of ourselves and therefore we cannot ourselves claim to be such. Otherwise we exalt ourselves as judges of ourselves—which we cannot be : οὐ γὰρ ὁ ἑαυτὸν συνιστάνων, ἐκεῖνός ἐστιν δόκιμος, ἀλλὰ ὃν ὁ κύριος συνίστησιν (2 Cor. 10¹⁸). And so, according to 2 Cor. 13³ᶠ·, Paul must be content to be questioned by the Corinthians about the δοκιμή of the Christ who presumably speaks in him, without being in a position to demonstrate it to them, since only God sees it and knows it. His answer is to remind them that Christ Himself was crucified in weakness—His δοκιμή, too, was hidden from the eyes of all except those of God Himself—and that He now lives in the power of God and is powerfully at work among the Corinthians themselves. Although he, Paul, now stands before them in weakness, unable to demonstrate to them the δοκιμή of his works and words, yet he hopes that in and with Christ, trusting in the divine δοκιμάζειν, in virtue of the power of God thus imparted to him, he will finally stand before them as δόκιμος. Meanwhile, they are to prove themselves, that is, to test their faith. If they themselves are not ἀδόκιμοι, they will not try to regard and treat him as ἀδόκιμος when he stands before them in all his weakness. " Now I pray to God that ye do no evil ; not that we should appear approved, but that ye should do that which is honest, though we be as reprobates."

Man cannot be approved of himself. And as this passage shows, he cannot claim to be such either to others or even to himself. But this does not exclude the fact that he is approved by God, i.e., that the righteous vindication of God is pronounced over him in such a way that he himself must fulfil it in his will and actions, approving himself in his work and all the details of his work. δοκιμή is, therefore, at every point an object of Christian exhortation, the content of the imperative which is always implied in the Christian indicative. That the heart of a man is right—and God's concern is only with the heart—is to be shown in his work, in his conduct as a believer in this world in which we must walk by faith and not by sight, and therefore the life of faith means affliction— θλῖψις—in the most comprehensive sense of the term. How is it that Christians may prove themselves, i.e., fulfil the secret judgment of God under whose sovereignty they stand, in their will and action ? In 2 Cor. 8², Paul congratulates the Macedonians that their joy has abounded even ἐν πολλῇ δοκιμῇ θλίψεως, that even their deep poverty has been overwhelmed by the richness of their sincerity (ἁπλότης). What, then, is the meaning of δοκιμὴ θλίψεως ? According to Rom. 5³ᶠ·, it is not merely vindication in face of, and in conflict with, affliction as the assault of Satan, but, as is shown by the phrase of 2 Cor. 8² concerning the poverty which overflows in riches, the vindication resulting from affliction, evoked and produced by it. Christians are to congratulate themselves and consider themselves fortunate when they fall into trial and affliction, because they know that affliction results in steadfastness (ὑπομονή), steadfastness in experience and experience in hope ; and that hope does not make ashamed, because those who hope as the approved are necessarily those in whose hearts the love of God has been shed abroad by the Holy Ghost, and who therefore cannot be afraid but only hope. According to this passage, the testing which those who hope in this way have experienced leads to steadfastness; to the patient, persevering holding of the faith, to stability in face of the ground and object of faith, to fellowship with Jesus Christ. And Christians owe this steadfastness and stability to the fact that they are plunged into affliction and poverty—a copy of the situation of Jesus Christ Himself. The call of Jesus means that He places them in this situation and that they must suffer it for His sake. That they prove themselves in this situation by the steadfastness of their faith is their necessary and necessarily grateful answer to this call. As they give this answer, they may and must make progress as those who unfailingly hope. Only the unstable and therefore the untested can and must fear—those who do not obey the call of Jesus Christ which goes out to them in their position of affliction and who therefore show that the love of God has not been shed abroad in their hearts. It is worth noting that on the same presupposition and to the same effect the matter can be seen and expressed in reverse in Jas. 1²ᶠ·. That Christians should count it all joy when they fall into divers temptations is now based upon the insight that τὸ δοκίμιον ὑμῶν τῆς πίστεως works patience, by the practice of which the work of man grows into a right-minded obedience corresponding to the meaning of the divine Law. ὑπομονή is obviously understood here as more than the continuity and sequence of the action which springs from faith and reveals faith. As such, it is just as much a consequence of the testing of faith as in Rom. 5⁴—as the ὑπομονή of faith—it is the presupposition and the mode of this testing. δοκιμή or δοκίμιον is grounded in the ὑπομονή of faith or reveals itself in the ὑπομονή of works. It is the power to persevere in the status of one to whom God is gracious, who has become His covenant-partner in Jesus Christ and who is confirmed in this status by the affliction, the manifold temptations, to which as such he is exposed. Thus, according to 1 Pet. 1⁶ᶠ·, Christians are to rejoice in the adversities which fall on them because what awaits them in this situation, and must come to them from its inmost meaning, can only be " the trial of your faith," which as such—because it is the human fulfilment of the divine judgment pronounced in their favour—is " much more precious than of gold that perisheth, though it be tried with fire." A relative manifestation of the proving which is required of us, and to be fulfilled by us in certain definite modes of conduct and situations, is not excluded by the fact that its recognition is ultimately and properly a matter of the divine knowledge and judgment. Paul tells the Corinthians in 2 Cor. 2⁹ that he has written to them in order to have proof of their obedience. In 2 Cor. 8⁸ he calls their attention to the question of alms for the Church at Jerusalem in order to subject the genuineness of their love to the necessary test. And by the proof they furnish in this ministry (of alms) they are to praise God (2 Cor. 9¹³). He can tell the Corinthians that there must needs be heresies amongst them ἵνα οἱ δόκιμοι φανεροὶ γένωνται ἐν ὑμῖν (1 Cor. 11¹⁹). He can invite Timothy to be zealous to show himself δόκιμον παραστῆσαι τῷ θεῷ, a good workman who can rightly distribute the word of truth (2 Tim. 2¹⁵). And he can say of Timothy to the Philippians τὴν δὲ δοκιμὴν αὐτοῦ γινώσκετε in view of the fact that as a son with the father he has served with him in the ministry of the Gospel (Phil. 2²²). He can exhort the Roman Christians to greet Apelles as δόκιμος ἐν Χριστῷ (Rom. 16¹⁰). He can say of the man who serves Christ truly that he is well pleasing to God and δόκιμος τοῖς ἀνθρώποις (Rom. 14¹⁸), while the heathen show by their ungodly deeds that God has given them up to εἰς ἀδόκιμον νοῦν (Rom. 1²⁸).

In the same passage, however, the fact that the heathen do not pass the test of God's judgment, but are rejected, is brought into connexion with the fact that they themselves οὐκ ἐδοκίμασαν τὸν θεὸν ἔχειν ἐν ἐπιγνώσει. Their judgment was that of men who did not know God, so that God was not before them in their actions and in consequence their conduct was inevitably corrupt. This brings us to the use of the verb δοκιμάζειν to connote the Christian's testing of his actions in the presence of God and in the light of God's own examination of them. To the testing to which he is subjected by God, and the proof which he is invited to furnish by his own conduct, there corresponds in the third instance the testing which he has to undergo in relation to his future action (because it is subject to the scrutiny of God, and must be the proof which he himself must furnish). If, in our conduct, we are to pass the test of the approaching divine judgment, if our conduct is to be that of those who are approved and manifested as such, then it must consist in the doing of the will of God. Whether it will be this, God, and only God, will decide in His own good time. But it is still the case that our deeds will have been a doing of the will of God or not. Necessarily, therefore, our present deeds must be accompanied by a searching question as to the will of God in regard to our future deeds. Are we in any position to put this question? From what we are told in Rom. 1²⁸, this obviously cannot be said of the heathen. But of Christians it is said : μεταμορφοῦσθε τῇ ἀνακαινώσει τοῦ νοός, εἰς τὸ δοκιμάζειν ὑμᾶς τί τὸ θέλημα τοῦ θεοῦ, τὸ ἀγαθὸν καὶ εὐάρεστον καὶ τέλειον (Rom. 12²). As surely as they believe in Jesus Christ and have received the Holy Ghost, they know God, and He is before them as the One who commands, and therefore His command is not unknown to them—in spite of the gulf which it discloses as a declaration of His will over against theirs—and they can therefore ask themselves in what relation it stands to their future conduct and their future conduct to it. The consideration of this twofold question is δοκιμάζειν in this third specific connotation. It is just as possible as it is necessary to the one to whom God is gracious in Jesus Christ. Already Paul has explicitly ascribed both possibilities to the Jew : δοκιμάζων τὰ διαφέροντα κατηχούμενος ἐκ τοῦ νόμου (Rom. 2¹⁸). Being instructed by the Law—the τέλος of which is Christ (Rom. 10⁴)—he can sift the various alternatives open to him. There can be no doubt that, unlike the heathen, he can in fact do this. The only question is whether he does not leave out of account the true τέλος of the Law and therefore fail to practise a true δοκιμάζειν. And we have to admit that this is the case. But Paul can pray confidently for Christians : εἰς τὸ δοκιμάζειν ὑμᾶς τὰ διαφέροντα, ἵνα ἦτε εἰλικρινεῖς καὶ ἀπρόσκοποι εἰς ἡμέραν Χριστοῦ, filled with the fruits of righteousness which are by Jesus Christ unto the glory and praise of God (Phil. 1¹⁰). What is the meaning of τὰ διαφέροντα? Obviously, " that which is relevant in the existing situation." (W. Grundmann, *ThWB z. N.T.*, II, 263, 13). But what is, in fact, relevant in the existing situation? It is certainly not a kind of necessity immanent in the situation, a kind of " law of the hour," so that the capacity for δοκιμάζειν and its exercise consist in a kind of divination, an uncanny sense of the demands of the time. Quite apart from the inclinations of our own fleshly nature, the existing situation as such is always ruled by all sorts of demons, and sensitiveness to it can have very little to do with sensitiveness to the will of God. The passage speaks expressly of testing the διαφέροντα, and not of an instinctive feeling for their greater or lesser necessity. The sovereign decision of God in His command stands absolutely supreme above the existing situation, although absolutely related to it. And the point at issue is the mutual relationship between this, that or the other possible line of action in this situation and the divine command. τὰ διαφέροντα are, then, the various possibilities of action open to us in the existing situation, and the relevant question is whether we can (and so should) adopt this or that particular possibility in the confidence that the relation between it and the divine command will be positive and therefore the action will be " good, and acceptable, and according to the purpose of God " (Rom. 12²). " Walk as children of light : (for the fruit of the Spirit is in all goodness and righteousness and truth ") ; δοκιμάζοντες τί ἐστιν εὐάρεστον τῷ κυρίῳ (Eph. 5⁸ᶠ·). The positive divine significance of the existent situation is that those who have the light—as Christians have—should effect in and with their actions that which is the necessary operation of the light. So then, in face of our situation, we have to ask what is appropriate to us because it is pleasing to the Lord who is the Judge of goodness, righteousness and truth, and their opposite.

This enquiry cannot be replaced by even the most penetrating systematic or intuitive analysis of the situation as such and the objective and subjective factors which condition it. For, obviously, this enquiry only begins where an analysis of that kind leaves off. It presupposes that the διαφέροντα are spread out before us in their immanent value or lack of value. 1 Thess. 5²¹ even goes so far as to say πάντα—and only then does it add πάντα δὲ δοκιμάζετε, τὸ καλὸν δὲ κατέχετε. Only then, in contradistinction to every mere analysis of the situation, does the enquiry begin in which it is a question of the will of God (whose judgment is not discoverable in the various possibilities open to us, but stands in sovereign transcendence over them). Only then do we begin to consider the goal of the κατέχειν, the holding fast of what is well pleasing to the Lord, according to our prior decision—in face of which the prior decision of God is, of course, reserved and has to be remembered in all humility. 1 Jn. 4¹ carries a warning against the demonism of the existing situation and an allusion to the difference between ethical reflection and every mere analysis of this situation : " Beloved, believe not every spirit, ἀλλὰ δοκιμάζετε τὰ πνεύματα εἰ ἐκ θεοῦ ἐστιν ; because many false prophets are gone out into the world." Even in the saying of Jesus to the Pharisees (Lk. 12⁵⁶) : τὸ πρόσωπον τῆς γῆς καὶ τοῦ οὐρανοῦ οἴδατε δοκιμάζειν, τὸν καιρὸν δὲ τοῦτον πῶς οὐ δοκιμάζετε, the accusation does not really consist in the fact (so Grundmann, *op. cit.*, 263, 23) that they do not discern the course of divinely controlled history, as though Jesus was trying to train them in a historical sense in contrast to their much too one-sided observation of nature. For the καιρὸς οὗτος which they cannot perceive, the σημεῖα τῶν καιρῶν which they cannot distinguish according to the parallel in Mt. 16³, naturally denote the Messianic epoch in its absolute difference from all other epochs. And the accusation which they incur is that while they are adept at analysing all kinds of different situations, although they have been instructed in the Law (Rom. 2¹⁸), they do not devote to the question of the will of God, as it is now manifest in the Messianic age, the attention which it deserves, and they therefore neglect the possible and demanded δοκιμάζειν. The reverse side of this failure will emerge in the positive evil that, as indicated in the woes of Mk. 8³¹ and Lk. 9²² and 17²⁵, the priests and scribes and elders of this generation (represented in the previous passage by the Pharisees) will reject the Christ (ἀποδοκιμάζειν). The prophecy of Ps. 118²² will be fulfilled (Mt. 21⁴²) : " The stone which the builders rejected (ἀπεδοκίμασαν) is become the head of the corner." In this ἀποδοκιμάζειν we have a clear warning about the limitation of all human δοκιμάζειν, the danger of overestimating it, and the necessity that it should be transcended by the divine judgment which has made this very stone the chief cornerstone. That the δοκιμάζειν required of Christians is twofold or has a twofold aspect—the two-sided question of the relationship between the Law of God and our action—emerges in the fact that Paul can say in 2 Cor. 13⁵ : δοκιμάζετε ἑαυτούς, and again in Gal 6⁴ : τὸ δὲ ἔργον ἑαυτοῦ δοκιμαζέτω ἕκαστος. The demand is made with particular and noteworthy insistence in relation to participation in the Lord's Supper : δοκιμαζέτω δὲ ἄνθρωπος ἑαυτόν, and so let him eat of that bread, and drink of that cup (1 Cor. 11²⁸). It is not a matter of an essentially different testing from that of the divine will or the διαφέροντα if the reference is now specifically to a self-examination. The διαφέροντα themselves are the various courses of action open to man in existing situations, and the object of the enquiry is to fix the mutual relationship between one or other of them, between the man himself in their realisation, and the will of God. To examine ourselves means, therefore, to prepare ourselves for the encounter with our Judge. And it is not merely a warning against undisciplined and disorderly administration of the sacrament, but it has the deepest intrinsic significance, that we are invited to undertake this self-examination in relation to the Lord's Supper. What is involved in the readiness engendered by the δοκιμάζειν, emerges typically in our readiness for this action of actions, for our public and solemn participation in the communion of the body and blood of

Christ. " Know ye not your own selves (the Pharisees of Lk. 12⁵⁶ certainly did not know, although as Israelites, instructed by the Law, they ought to have known) how that Jesus Christ is in you ? " we read in 2 Cor. 13⁵. The goal of all δοκιμάζειν is finally and properly this self-knowledge correspondent to the action of the Lord's Supper, which is the good will of God to man, inviting him to partake in this sacrament and expecting him at the table of the Lord. To be prepared for our Judge is to be those who worthily partake in the communion of the body and blood of Christ, who expect their spiritual nourishment from this communion and find in it their life, who can say of Jesus Christ : " I am His, and He is mine." In this readiness, the Lord's Supper is rightly observed, and is the constant renewal of the communing as the body of Christ, and of each of its members as such. In this readiness for the Lord's Supper all readiness for the Judge of our actions finds typical expression and therefore all δοκιμάζειν in this δοκιμάζειν ἑαυτόν. If we examine ourselves at this point, we examine ourselves always and everywhere. If we fail to examine ourselves at this point, we do not examine ourselves at all. And all examination of ourselves and our works, of the divine will and the διαφέροντα and the time and its signs, can only be a repetition and modification of the self-examination in which we ask ourselves how it stands between Jesus Christ and us, whether we are such as may live in the strength of His life, death and resurrection, of His Word and the power of His Spirit, whether we are " in the faith," as Paul puts it very simply in 2 Cor. 13⁵. If we " are in the faith," God will find our heart and works pure, and we shall not fail to hear the δοκιμή of our walking which He will pronounce upon us. But are we in the faith ? Or will we be found amongst those who have rejected the stone which was to become the chief cornerstone ? This is the question which is the true theme of all ethical enquiry.

It is the idea of responsibility which gives us the most exact definition of the human situation in face of the absolute transcendence of the divine judgment. We live in responsibility, which means that our being and willing, what we do and what we do not do, is a continuous answer to the Word of God spoken to us as a command. It takes place always in a relationship to the norm which confronts and transcends us in the divine command. It is continually subject to an enquiry concerning its correspondence with this norm. It is always an answer to this enquiry. Man does not belong to himself. He does not exist in a vacuum. He is not given over to the caprice of an alien power, nor to his own self-will. He may or may not know and will it, but because Jesus Christ as very God and very man is the beginning of all the ways and works of God, man is inseparably linked with God and confronted by Him. He is subjected to the divine will, Word and command, and called to realise the true purpose of his existence as a covenant-partner with God. As a man, he is objectively tested by this determination and objectively questioned as to its fulfilment. This is the essence of his responsibility. And with what he is and wills, does and does not do, he is ineluctably caught up in one continuing responsibility, in the constant need to render an account. How far is he really God's covenant-partner ? How far does he actualise his original and proper status ? How far does he honour or dishonour it ? That he is conscious of this, that his being and willing, what he does and does not do, are accompanied by the corresponding

C.D.—21

reflection, that, called to faith in Jesus Christ and obeying this call, he gives an account to himself and is answerable to himself—all this is secondary. The primary and decisive thing is that, consciously or not, he continuously gives God an answer, that, objectively and constantly, and in the last resort with reference to the totality of his existence, his being and willing, what he does and does not do, are questioned by God and render an account to Him. The seriousness of the human situation consists in the fact that it is always lived in responsibility, both as a whole and in detail, and whether we understand it or not. We come from pure responsibility. We are caught up in responsibility. And we shall always be responsible. The whole of our life indeed, the filling out of the time allotted to us by our being and willing, by what we do and do not do, is one long responsibility. And because we stand before the transcendent divine decision, it is not at all the case that the full seriousness of our situation will become apparent and operative only with the termination of our life in time, when its responsible character will be expressed as a totality and will also be revealed to us ourselves. On the contrary, each of our decisions and responsibilities as such is an anticipation in miniature of the total responsibility which, with our whole life, we fulfil before God and in which, at the close of our existence in time, we shall stand before God as our Judge. Even in its apparent littleness it is no less important. Even in its temporal limitation, because it is a responsibility to the eternal God, it is here and now a responsibility of eschatological significance.

The idea of responsibility, rightly understood, is known only to Christian ethics. This alone teaches a true and proper confrontation of man. This alone excludes the possibility that in the last resort man is utterly alone and therefore not in a position to give a true and proper answer. This alone knows of man's confrontation by One to whom he must give an answer, because He is the One who confronts him in sovereign transcendence and lays upon him an ineluctable obligation. And, again, this alone knows that the relationship between this Other and man is such that necessarily and in all circumstances— quite apart from man's own insight and judgment—what man is and wills and does and does not do is an actualisation of responsibility and therefore objectively an act of responsibility. Christian ethics alone understands the full seriousness of the human situation which this implies. Every non-Christian view of human life, i.e., every view which does not have a christological basis, will betray itself as such by the fact that while it may perhaps arrive at the idea of a certain claim upon man—although without making clear how or why it is binding—it will not attain to the idea of true and proper responsibility and therefore the conception of the uninterrupted responsibility in which we stand. Without a knowledge of the transcendent divine decision executed in the grace of the covenant between God and man, or an awareness of the Law which God has eternally established in Jesus Christ and revealed in time, we can think and speak of responsibility only in a diluted form which does not do justice to the real significance of the term and which may eventually deny and dissolve it. Christian ethics itself cannot limit its validity to Christians only, i.e., to those who are aware that their life is essentially and objectively a life in responsibility. How can it be Christian ethics if it does not know and take into account the fact that the divine covenant of grace with man is the beginning of all God's ways and works, and that the human situation grounded in this covenant is, therefore, the situation of every single man ? Christian ethics, then, will see every man as responsible, and involved in the dreadful act of responsibility. It cannot believe or accept that he is left to himself, or to mysterious elemental forces, or to his own caprice, that he has no master or another master, that he is responsible only to himself or some other men, that he is only partially responsible or not yet fully responsible— or however else the qualifications may run. It cannot allow anyone to be content with this position, whatever may be the reasons or attitude with which he defends his irresponsibility. Because Christian ethics knows the transcendent divine decision, it knows the secret of all men—both believers and godless—and therefore its peculiar task is to attest the revelation of the secret of their existence, in the name of faith to the godless, and as a warning against godlessness to believers ; to attest, that is, their responsibility and the fact that they are actually involved in responsibility.

The idea of responsibility shows us what is meant by moral reflection, the examination of what we are and will and do and do not do, of the mutual relationship between the command of God and our existence. It consists in our attitude to the fact that we are responsible and are objectively involved in responsibility. It also presupposes that we know this and have therefore been shown our true situation. But we can be shown this only as we hear and apprehend in faith the message of the divine covenant of grace. It is the Christian who really knows man's responsibility, and the frightening fact that he is objectively and continuously involved in responsibility, in the rendering of an account to the sovereign decision of God. Who else really does know it ? Who can know this of himself without that revealed message and faith in it ? It is the Christian therefore, and he alone, who can take up a serious attitude to this fact. But, again, he cannot genuinely receive this message without becoming its witness to all other men. He cannot believe, and in faith adopt a right attitude, without implying by his faith that this attitude is necessarily demanded of all others, that the responsibility in which all are involved is a summons to all to adopt this attitude. To hear and believe this message is the determination of all men. Therefore a knowledge of the situation implied by our responsibility is expected of all men. The attitude demanded by this knowledge is not, then, a private concern of the Christian, but a universal human necessity, and it is to be represented as such by Christians to those who are not yet or no longer Christians. The right attitude to the fact is, of course, to enquire how our being and willing, what we do and do not do, have stood and stand and will stand in the light of the command of God to which they are responsible; how far—in our being and willing, in what we do and do not do—we have acted and act and will act in true responsibility to God's command; under what judgment of this supreme court we have come, and come and will come. This question is the question of moral reflection as demanded by our situation in responsibility. It is put by the fact that what we are and will and do and do not do, and therefore our objective responsibility, is not an alien happening which passes us by at a greater or lesser distance without involving our participation, but that we are ourselves its subjects and it is we who are responsible in it. Therefore—notwithstanding the sovereignty of the divine decision —we ourselves are asked, indeed we are summoned to a prior decision how we are to fulfil this responsibility. Formally, then, it is a question of the rightness and goodness of our choice between the various possibilities of our existence, of its rightness and goodness in the light of the command and decision of God to which we always were and are and will be subject in our whole existence, of the direction of our path in view of the fact that both as a whole and at each of its turnings it is good or bad according to the judgment of God. As we look towards the judgment of God with this question, it is, in fact, the question of our readiness—the readiness of our being and willing, of what we do and do not do—to receive this judgment.

What ought we to do? If our action were to take place in an awareness of what we are asked with this question, the responsibility before God, fulfilled in our action, would mean our justification before Him. It would be the action of those who are holy in the sense in which God is holy. The will of God would then be realised in our lives in the sense that we had made it our own, and, willing what God wills, we fulfilled it of ourselves. Our decisions would then run parallel to God's decision, and to that extent identical with it. But in this case moral reflection would obviously be superfluous. But so, too, would the command of God as such—as distinct from what we say to ourselves. So, too, would Jesus Christ as the Mediator of the covenant between God and man. Of ourselves we would keep this covenant as faithfully as it is kept by God. But we are not at all saints in this sense. And the relation between God and man is not that of a parallelism and harmony of the divine and human wills, but of an explosive encounter, contradiction and reconciliation, in which it is the part of the divine will to precede and the human to follow, of the former to control and the latter to submit. Neither as a whole nor in detail can our action mean our justification before God. It does not spring from a true awareness of what we ought to do. It is simply the self-willed desire of man to know good and evil. It is his craving for the divine likeness of a human existence reconciled with God in and of itself, not needing divine grace. It is itself the fall which separates man from God. And in this way it establishes something that man would prefer to deny—the character of the covenant between God and man as a covenant of grace. But this means that Jesus Christ is indispensable as the Mediator of this covenant, and the Law of God as the expression of the sovereign decision of God in face of man's decisions. They are shown to be such by the presumptuous imagination that they are unnecessary. " Salvation has come to us of grace and pure goodness." It is not intrinsic to ourselves but extrinsic. Our sanctification is God's work, not our own. It is very necessary, therefore, that there should be the encounter, the confrontation of our existence with the command of God. We must ask what the command of God is, and what we are to do, without having an answer ready and being able to furnish it ourselves. The divine work of our sanctification for God, the true preparedness for the responsibility which we must fulfil by our action, consists in this—that we should cleave to the salvation accomplished and prepared for us by the death and resurrection of Jesus Christ, and therefore to His sanctity, so that we for our part may ask in all earnestness : What ought we to do ? When we do ask sincerely in this way, when we persist and progress in our search, when we accompany our deeds with this question, allowing them to be shaped and controlled by it, we adopt the right attitude to the fact of our responsibility and its actual realisation. It is right and proper that we should ask concerning the command of God as the norm which is not in us but over us. When we ask concerning it, we recognise and respect it. When we ask concerning it, we implicitly obey it. To the extent that our action is determined and controlled by this enquiry, it becomes obedient action. But it can never do so in virtue of any supposed knowledge of it. A supposed knowledge of it, and all attempts—in virtue of this knowledge—to impart to our action anything in the nature of a divine likeness, signify at once and automatically apostasy from Jesus Christ, the denial of the divine grace by which we live, and therefore a relapse into disobedience. Moral reflection as a reaction to the fact of our responsibility, as the establishment of a readiness to encounter God our Judge, can only be the result of the most sincere humility which does not know but genuinely and indefatigably asks : What ought we to do ? Our analysis of this question is as follows.

(1) *What* ought we to do ? If the What ? is seriously meant, every answer that we and others may have given is continually questioned again. It is not, of course, dismissed and effaced. We are never *tabula rasa*, and we cannot and must not try to make ourselves such. Integral to the humility in which we must ask what we are to do

according to the divine command is the sober recognition that we always come from the school of the divine command and that we have not been in vain to that school, always bringing with us all kinds of more or less well-founded hypotheses and convictions that the command of God demands from us. To forget all this could not possibly be a good presupposition and basis for ethical reflection. It is not the effacement but the questioning of all our previous answers which takes place when we begin to put seriously the What ? of the ethical question. Our previous answers cannot consist of more than hypothesis and opinion. They cannot be a knowledge of the will and command of God. We are not in any sense already in harmony with God's sovereign decision. This must be prayed and sought for as the grace of God—established and prepared for us in the death and resurrection of Jesus Christ. This is the meaning of the What ? of our question as the necessary presupposition of all further enquiry. It means that the goodness of God—including specifically the goodness of His work for our sanctification—is new every morning. It means that He will again receive and accept us as we are, and therefore with all our hypotheses and convictions as to what is well pleasing to Him, with our *ethos*, i.e., with all that we have made of what His command has meant for us as we have so far sought it—that in His grace (which we shall sorely need) He will receive and accept us again with all this. If we ask seriously : What ought we to do ?, the What ? necessarily means that we are not complacent about ourselves, that we do not anticipate the answer in view of the continuity of our previous works, that under the guise and pretext of the What ? we do not secretly ask : How can I progress further on the right path which I am, of course, already treading ? It necessarily means that even in relation to our best works and the most sacred of our hypotheses and convictions we confess that we are sincerely sorry and repent, not of the grace of God which has hitherto sustained and controlled us, but of the way in which we have treated the grace of God even in our best works and the construction of our most sacred hypotheses and convictions. If we do not regret this, if we look back complacently to our previous progress under the grace and command of God, how can we be honest and sincere when we direct a questioning glance upwards and forwards ? When we honestly ask : *What* ought we to do ?, we approach God as those who are ignorant in and with all that they already know, and stand in dire need of divine instruction and conversion. We are then ready, with a view to our next decision, to bracket and hold in reserve all that we think we know concerning the rightness and goodness of our past and present decisions, all the rules and axioms, however good, all the inner and outer laws and necessities under which we have hitherto placed ourselves and perhaps do so again. None of these has an unlimited claim to be valid again to-day as it was valid yesterday. None of them is identical with the divine command. Even at best none of them is more than a refraction of the divine command in the dim and fallacious prism of our own life and understanding. If we seriously ask : *What* ought we to do ?, a radical attack is already opened on our own life and understanding as such. We have again admitted the great possibility of the grace of God, that our own life and understanding can be made new and different. We have thus already conceded that we again need a complete openness. We have already confessed that we will go forward in this complete openness. This openness to new insights cannot remain somewhere behind us as the past of an instruction and conversion already accomplished. But the very recollection of earlier instruction and conversion, in so far as it is genuine, will be an invitation to us to fulfil the same movement, to accept this new beginning of our life and understanding. We can never look back upon a genuine previous conversion and instruction without its necessarily compelling us to be more serious than ever in our present circumstances, to prepare ourselves for fuller openness to truth, to enquire more searchingly than ever before : *What* ought we to do ?—so that in this conversion even from our best we may make up for what we have surely neglected (even in our best). It is to be noted that the continuity of divine grace in our life, and our obedience to it, will be maintained only in so far as we do not refuse the discipline of the new beginning of our life and understanding brought about by moral reflection. The continuity of a life which steadily affirms itself from one decision to another, developing from within itself, can only be the continuity of disobedience. For the law which governs the life of the Church is repeated in every individual life. The Church is most faithful to its tradition, and realises its unity with the Church of every age, when, linked but not tied by its past, it to-day searches the Scriptures and orientates its life by them as though this had to happen to-day for the first time. And, on the other hand, it sickens and dies when it is enslaved by its past instead of being disciplined by the new beginning which it must always make in the Scriptures. Similarly, the individual is true to himself, and to the history of the act of God from which he derives, when he allows his baptism to be the sign which stands over every new day. And on the other hand he necessarily sickens and dies from the moment he tries to place the new day given him by God's goodness under the sign of a previously experienced instruction and conversion (even the most radical). The principle of necessary repetition and renewal, and not a law of stability, is the law of the spiritual growth and continuity of our life. It is when we observe this law that we practise perseverance (ὑπομονή) in the biblical meaning of the term ; a perseverance corresponding to the steadfastness of God Himself, which does not signify the suspension, but the continuing and indestructible possession and use of His freedom. Inevitably, therefore, all our answers that we think we know are weighed again and thrown into the melting-pot by the What ? of the ethical question. The more truly it derives from previous ethical reflection and testing, the less will this process be injurious to it, the more surely will it again prove its value. But even if it does not stand this test, even if our enquiry as to God's command leads us necessarily to a different answer to-day from that of yesterday, no wrong is done to the former. But supposing an injustice is done to it ? Have we any guarantee that in our enquiry as to the divine command we will not go astray to-day, abandoning and replacing an answer previously affirmed, a hypothesis and conviction previously adopted ? No, we have no guarantee against this. We can make a more serious mistake to-day than we did yesterday. Yet if the law of repetition and renewal is the law of ethical reflection, provision is made that if we err to-day, to-morrow or the next day we shall have the opportunity to retrieve an error of to-day by new instruction and conversion, and so perhaps again to do justice to the answer of yesterday that to-day we have unjustly abandoned. Why should not the sincere confrontation of our life and understanding by the command of God, by the frank question : *What* ought we to do ?, lead often enough to the result (as happens time and again in the life of the Church) that we must know again an answer formerly rejected, a " tradition " formerly repudiated, because it has, in fact, been placed in a fresh light by the command of God ? Those who are concerned about the truth itself need not be concerned about old truth as to-day they relentlessly open their minds to new truth. But again, they need not be concerned about the discovery of new truth, for which some are just as anxious as are others for the maintenance of the old. Our one concern must be with truth itself, and not with the maintenance of old truth or the discovery of new, not with the rights and wrongs of either anxiety. The truth itself demands complete openness. From the standpoint of the truth itself thoroughgoing conservatives are as useless as thoroughgoing modernists. The old will persist and the new will come if they are worthy to do so. And the old will pass and the new be excluded if they are not. The question : *What* ought we to do ? cannot be the question of our anxiety, but only the retention or discovery of what is intrinsically valuable. And what is intrinsically valuable truth is the command of God which always surpasses what we consider worthy either to be retained or to come, which always transcends our hypotheses and convictions of yesterday, to-day and to-morrow. When we ask seriously : *What* ought we to do ?, confessing that in our ignorance we are known by God, that His gaze is eternally fastened on what we are and will and do and do not do, we will leave it confidently in His hand, committing it to Him. If this is what we really mean by our What ?, in the very fact that we ask we will receive the knowledge of God's command ; in the very fact that we desire this knowledge, what we are and will and do and do not do will be directed by the command of God and obedient to it and sanctified by it—and the more profoundly, the more seriously our question implies our realisation of the sovereignty of the divine decision. Everything depends upon how far it does imply this. If this is the case, if our whole *ethos* is called in question in this way, this testifies to the fact that we have not been asking in the void, but in the presence of God's command, and concerning the character of that command as it must affect our actions. It testifies, therefore, to the fact that we know the divine command because it has itself revealed itself to us.

2. What *ought* we to do ? the question continues. It does not ask concerning something that we might or must know merely for the sake of knowing. If it asks after truth, it is not the truth that we seek, but the divine truth that seeks us, the truth of the divine command that desires us and demands us and binds us and commits us, the truth that we must know because it is the rule and norm of our conduct. We ask after something which claims not only that we should consider it but observe it, not only that we should hear it but obey it. If our reflection is serious, we ask concerning what we ought to do. This is the second criterion of the genuineness of our preparation for our encounter with the divine command. His sovereign decision about the good and evil of our conduct, under which we stand to-day as we stood yesterday and will stand again to-morrow, concerns our relationship to what we ought to do in virtue of His claim. We must ask, therefore, what is meant by this *ought*. It certainly means, of course, what we are to will. We ourselves, our will, even our free and joyful will, belong always to what is required of us and to what we ought to do. If we do not will, freely and joyfully, what we are to do in virtue of the claim of the divine command, we shall always be disobedient to it. Therefore the question of our obligation will always be that of what we are freely and joyfully to will. But it is not the mere fact that we should will it that makes it an obligation, the sovereign divine decision. The mere fact that its claim finds true hearing and obedience only when we will it freely and joyfully does not mean that we are responsible to it, and that our action becomes responsible. As we have seen, its requirement of this spontaneous obedience means that the claim of the divine command is different from all other claims. And our meeting of this requirement distinguishes our obedience to it from all other obedience. But our present question is as follows : What makes the divine command the transcendent decision of God over all other decisions ? What distinguishes our (willing, free and joyful) obedience to it from disobedience ? What makes the responsibility which we fulfil by our conduct something that is well-pleasing to God ? When we put this question—which is the question of ethical meditation—we have to remember that what is well-pleasing to God, what makes our obedience obedience, and the command of God a sovereign decision, consists in the fact that our

will is confronted by, and subjected to, an *ought*—and not conversely. Thus the ethical question : What *ought* we to do ?, is not sincerely put if secretly or openly it means : What do we will to do ? What do we will of ourselves, in virtue of the equally objective and indisputable claims of our own will, in responsibility—but not this time genuine responsibility—to the aims which our own promptings lead us to propose ? Aims of this kind—in their various combinations—are usually what appears pleasing and useful and valuable to ourselves. What seems desirable and necessary to us, and even what we think to be true and good and beautiful, can in its own way seem to be obligatory and present itself in the form of an imperative.

There can be no question that these aims of our will are connected and point us to real problems. They are not, therefore, to be summarily discredited and set aside. And when one of the widespread and constantly re-emerging moral systems—hedonism, utilitarianism or eudæmonism, the so-called ethics of value —tries to use these natural aims as a basis for its presentation of the ethical, Christian ethics must be careful not to adopt at once towards this system the well known and purely negative attitude of Kant and the Kantians. Where the obligatory is to be understood as the content of the divine command, we cannot refuse absolutely to interpret it also as that which is supremely pleasing and useful and valuable. That " he shall give thee the desires of thine heart " (Ps. 37[4]), " upholding thee as thou desirest," and that He does this by giving us His command—this is also true in its own place and sense, and it must be stated, and justice must be done to it, in Christian ethics. On the other hand, we have to admit that Kant has expressed the essential concern of Christian ethics by pointing out that of itself the concept of what is pleasing and useful and valuable does not give us the concept of what is obligatory.

Therefore when we ask : What *ought* we to do ?, we must keep this question distinct from that of what seems to us to be desirable or necessary or even good and true and beautiful, from the whole question of even the supreme value of this or that action. However serious and deep our formulation of the latter, it can alter not at all the fact that we are asking about what we will—about what seems to us to be most useful and therefore most real, most real and therefore most useful, and on this basis supremely desirable. But to the extent that our decisions are subject to the sovereign decision of the divine command, we have not to be answerable to ourselves, and therefore to our own ideas of what is supremely real and useful and desirable. With all our ideas and the resultant aims, we are answerable to the divine command, so that the question is whether, as those who entertain these ideas and set themselves these aims, we are good or bad according to God's command. What we consider desirable, useful and valuable may be very important to us as the truth of what we ought to do. But we can understand and claim it as our true obligation only in a conditional sense, i.e., as conditioned by ourselves. For what validity has that which seems desirable and useful and valuable to us but the fact that it is understood and felt and viewed and experienced and therefore asserted and affirmed by us as such ? What authority and power can its imperative have but that with which we ourselves are able to clothe it ? If an imperative, a command, is to have the authority and power to claim nothing less than ourselves, our life—the only one we have to live—and over and above that to be the judge which decides whether our whole existence is good or bad, is it not necessary that this imperative should have far stronger qualifications ? An imperative to which I owe absolute obedience must necessarily come in the most radical sense from within, in order that it may claim me most radically within. A command which transcends our actions cannot in the last analysis be merely a command which I have given myself on the basis of what I myself have seen and experienced and felt and judged of the good and the true and the beautiful. It must come to me as something alien, as the command of another, demanding as such that I should make its content the law of my life. If there is an *ought*, it must not be the product of my own will, but touch from outside the whole area of what I can will of myself. It must lay upon me the obligation of unconditioned truth—truth which is not conditioned by myself. Its authority and power to do so must be intrinsic and objective, and not something which I lend to it. Its validity must consist in the fact that the very question of its validity is quite outside the sphere of my own thinking and feeling ; that I can no longer entertain the idea of making sure of its authority and power by seeking its basis in what I myself have understood or seen or felt or experienced ; that I can no longer consider how it may best be proved and demonstrated. On the contrary, it establishes its own validity by asking concerning my own : whether and how far I can satisfy it and be justified and stand before it. The essence of the idea of obligation is not that I demand something from myself but that, with all that I can demand of myself, I am myself demanded.

It is because it does not do justice to this meaning of obligation that serious reservations are required in our approach to every form of eudæmonism, both ancient and modern. And in this connexion, at least in regard to post-Kantian development, we have to ask whether this idea of obligation is so unequivocally attained in the sharply contrasting Kantian ethics of law, duty and imperative, and also of " freedom," that we can accept its formulations. We do not seriously ask what we ought to do except when we see our duty as the content of a decision which confronts our own will—even when it is supremely free in form—in absolute and inflexible sovereignty, so that, even when we give it our wholehearted, spontaneous approval, it is never the result of our decision, and therefore it never owes its authority and power to our decisions but always to itself. That this is the case is unequivocally clear, and safeguarded against all relapses into eudæmonistic distortions, only when we keep plainly in view—as Kantian ethics very obviously failed to do—the christological foundations of the concept and actuality of obligation.

The true and genuine obligation, law and duty voiced by another than ourselves, emerges and persists, in face of our own will with its conceptions and aims, in and with the fact that, in fulfilment of the divine will, Jesus Christ has died and risen again for us, so that now that He is our Lord and our Head we should not belong to ourselves but to Him, and therefore should not live to ourselves but to Him. This is what makes us ourselves debtors to God ; and we experience obligation—as distinct from desire—in and with the fact that we ourselves become debtors to God. This is the sovereign decision which confronts our decisions. This is unconditioned, self-grounded truth which establishes its validity by requiring that we should vindicate ourselves before it. This is transcendence—a transcendence which is basic, not merely transcendence in thought, but objectively—in face of the self-enclosed circle of our own desires and cravings, but also of our highest sublimations of what seems to us to be desirable and useful and valuable, and even of our conceptions of the good and the true and the beautiful. But it also includes our salvation, namely, what God ascribes to us as desirable and pleasant and true and good and beautiful. In face of it, the justifiable concern of eudæmonism need not be displaced. Here is a demand which is addressed wholly or altogether to *us*, quite beyond what we ourselves find to claim or postulate or desire from ourselves ; addressed to us for our own highest good, so that everything—the lowest as well as the highest—which we might demand of ourselves comes into its own by the fact that it is we ourselves who are demanded. The obligation revealed and grounded in the person and work and lordship of Jesus Christ fulfils the idea in all its strictness. It is a categorical imperative, not merely in name, but in fact. And as such—unlike the Kantian imperative— it reveals the fact that to obey it is not merely the highest duty but also the highest good. It is the moving and illuminating and uplifting of man—inextricably involved in the ideas and aims proper to his own will—by the goodness of the free transcendent divine will. It is the promise which he is given of a new and eternal life of which he is not worthy, but towards which he may already move step by step in this life as he is confronted by the divine command. How could he make such a promise to himself ? It is done by the divine command with its obligation as actualised in the vicarious person and work and lordship of Jesus Christ. To cling to the grace which takes the form of this obligation is the way to eternal life. And again, the position is as follows. When we ask seriously what we *ought* to do, we confess already that, implicated in our own will, caught up in our own ideals and aims, and therefore in so great need of the vindication and justifi- cation of our lives, we are not strangers to God because He obviously did not will to be a stranger to us but to reveal His will to us, because Jesus Christ was our Representative too in His person and work, because we too are in the sphere of His sovereignty. If this were not the case, how could we even so much as ask about our true and proper obliga- tion, about the imperative which we have to obey ? Those who ask after it already know it. And those who know it do not know it of themselves. Of ourselves we may well know what we want to do, but not what we ought to do. When we ask what we ought to do, we confess that obligation is not alien to us, that we are already involved in obligation, that the command of God has already been spoken and received by us. When we ask this seriously, we have already understood our decisions to be subordinated to the sovereign decision of God. We have already recognised ourselves to be those who are known by God. We have confidently committed ourselves into His hand. If our asking is sincere, we receive, as we ask, what is ordered by God's command, and what we are and do and do not do is directed by the command of God which it needs as a matter of our decision. Everything depends upon whether we ask seriously. If we do, if we and our will are confronted by real obligation, the witness that we have to do with God and ask concerning Him is that He Himself has asked concerning us, that He has revealed and given us His command.

3. What ought *we* to do ? The third criterion of the genuineness of moral reflection is whether in this matter we sincerely ask what *we* ought to do. It is, of course, a question of what we are and will and do and do not do in the light of the fact that it is subject to the sovereign decision of God whether this is good or bad. It is a question of the divine judgment on human affairs concealed in the divine command. But the human element referred to is man, and that means ourselves. It is we who are the subject which derives from God's decision, which is now its object, and continually becomes its object. It is we who are and will and do and do not do. The command of God, His infinite promise and terrible threat—all have reference to us. It is we who are the covenant-partners of God. And therefore the question of our readiness for confrontation by the divine command is necessarily : What ought we to do ? Two delimitations are necessary at this point. The first is that the question cannot be put impersonally : What ought *one* to do ? We do not ask concerning the action of others, but concerning our own action and its correspondence with the obligations of the command. We ask concerning ourselves. As the question of grace and election must find its ultimate and decisive answer in the fact that we ourselves, in faith in the election of Jesus Christ, dare to live in correspondence to the divine predestination of man, so the ethical question can be answered only as we make our own the necessary reflection of man on his confrontation by the divine command. As long as we do not do this, but think we can solve the ethical problem by concerning ourselves with human conduct in general, all ethics is ghostly, insubstantial. For if we merely ask what " one " ought to do, or with a false objectivity, what ought to be done, we can always stand aside and at bottom be interested only in what others ought to do or—as spectators of ourselves—in what we ourselves ought to do in a case which has not yet cropped up but may do so in the

future. And the probability is overwhelming that in point of fact we shall remain detached, not realising that our *inter-esse* is an accomplished fact, but idly " interesting " ourselves in this and that—a procedure which has nothing whatever to do with our real *inter-esse*. In ethics it is not a matter of what somebody ought to do in a hypothetical case, but of what we ourselves ought to do in our own given situation. It is a matter of the step which we now take from the past into the future. The question is not whether men in general, or certain men, or even we ourselves in a hypothetical situation, but whether we ourselves in the actuality of our present, as it represents the totality of our life, are adjudged as good or evil by the divine command. And it is to the answering of this question—already answered in God's sovereign decision—that we must always look, and for it that we must always prepare, as we make our decisions. Confronted by this question, and dealing with the problems which it raises, we have no time whatever to look aside—to the character of human life in general, to the conduct of this or that group, or to ourselves in an imaginary situation. It may be right enough if in a historical and psychological study of mankind we look round at those who are in some way different from ourselves. But even here, if the study is to be fruitful, there are certain well-defined limits. And there can be no question of it at all in ethical reflection. We really know good and evil only when it is clear to us that it carries with it the judgment which has been, and is, and will again and again be passed on what we ourselves are and will and do and do not do until we are finally revealed to ourselves in the totality of our life as good or evil, in the way that we are now revealed to God. It is a question of responsibility. And responsibility refuses to be delegated to man in general, to this or that group, or to ourselves in a different situation from our real one. Responsibility cannot be surveyed and studied as though it were not we ourselves who constantly bear and shoulder it, as though it were not to us that the question is now put and we who must answer. No one can take our place in this matter. We ourselves are summoned. We ourselves must step out—even from the conceptual and imaginative shadows of our own existence. We ourselves must give an account. The ethical as opposed to a purely historical or psychological issue is whether in the question : What *ought* we to do ?, we are ready to be open for the answer of the divine command. It is whether we are willing to accept the inevitable relativisation of all our own hypotheses and convictions. It is whether we are prepared to allow our own will and its aims to be confronted by the will of God as we meet it in His command. It is whether we agree to be limited and determined in this twofold way, and what the choice will be that we execute in our own conduct in the light of this divine limitation and determination. The ethical question is our personal question, just as the grace of God concerns us personally, and therefore the command of God is addressed to us personally. This is the first delimitation which is necessary. The second is that the question must actually be : What ought *we* to do ? and not, what ought *I* to do ? The former does not exclude the latter. Indeed, it can seriously be put only if it really includes the latter. But, again, everything depends on whether the second is really understood as included in the first. I am myself the subject of responsibility to the command of God, and therefore the subject of which the question of ethical reflection speaks. But I am this only as included in the " we." I am myself the covenant-partner of God, but my God is our God. I may and must hear His command, but His command applies to us all. It is the act of His will for us all. I have to answer for myself, but before the judgment seat at which the secrets of all our hearts must be disclosed. I go forward to the decision whether I am good or bad, yet I never do so alone, but always in the midst of a great company. Even in the necessary testing of my conduct I cannot overlook or forget the fact that I am never alone, and never will be. And I must remember it—not merely as a kind of prologue or epilogue, but as a constituent element from the very outset—when I make the prior decision from which I move to the divine decision. The one absolute thing which is the object of God's command, and to which we are summoned when it is declared to us, is not something that I am and have alone, but only in the community and solidarity of many, perhaps of all men. It is only as I detach myself as an individual that I can seriously ask : What ought I to do ? But as I do so, I do not really detach myself. I return at once to the ranks from which I step out. For even as I step out in the moment of my decision, and even in the moment of my corresponding reflection, I still belong. In fact, the question can only be : What ought *we* to do ? I am invited and made responsible and enabled to fulfil my responsibility not merely as the specimen of a natural or historical collective, nor as a so-called personality or individual or special case, but as this particular man, i.e., this one beloved by God and therefore a responsible partner in the divine covenant. Even the claim which is addressed to me is not for me alone but of universal validity. And I have to understand the universally valid claim as valid for me too and applying to me. If I refuse to do this, then from the detached standpoint of the individual and peculiar characteristics of my situation, my special case, I can protect myself against the crisis which the existence of God's command signifies for me and brings down on me. And in the last analysis who cannot claim in every respect to be in a highly singular situation ? In the last analysis, whose case cannot be described as a very special case ? Who, then, is not tempted to make of the unconditional truth of the divine command something conditional, to give only partial scope to the required openness to it, by emphasising the exceptional character of his life-situation ? There is an overwhelming probability that those who pose the ethical question only in individual terms will try to use this possibility of affirming the exceptional character of their case over against the claim and judgment of the divine command. And this is the very thing which must not happen. That the universally valid command of God applies to me and affects me in a very definite way cannot be taken to imply that I can treat it as conditioned by the peculiar factors of my personal situation; that I can secure and fortify myself against its universal validity as it certainly applies to me too. At this point, again, we have something to learn from Kant—from his definition of the ethical as that which is adapted to be " the principle for a universal law." If it is put seriously, then in face of all the singularity of my personal situation, my own particular question can only be : What are *we* to do ?—which means that we have thrown off this most efficacious, because most obvious and apparently most honourable covering—the pretext of being so differently placed from others—and exposed ourselves to the crisis of the command. This does, of course, confront me in the singularity of my circumstances, as this particular individual, as this one of all the covenant-partners of God. It reaches and concerns me in and with my particularity, my own particular situation, yet not in such a way that it must adapt itself to it, but rather the reverse. It, and not I, determines the particularity of the practical realities of my life, of the obedience that it demands from me particularly. But we do not rightly understand the *we* of the ethical question, or take it seriously from the two points of view indicated, if we do not bear in mind here, too, the christological basis of the divine command. This *we* of the ethical question is not an unqualified *we* but the highly qualified *we* of those who—whether they know and believe it or not, whether we can appeal to them on this ground, or whether this is not yet or no longer the case—are elected in Jesus Christ to be covenant-partners with God and therefore placed under the divine command. An unqualified *we*—the universal *we* of the human race, or the special *we* of a particular group or collective—would be no safeguard against an escape into irresponsibility along the two lines indicated. For why should we see ourselves determined and confined within a *we* of this kind, and therefore denied all possibility of adopting the attitude of a spectator ? And against what *we* of this kind may not the individual with some show of justification assert the exceptional character of his particular case ? The *we* of those who are in Jesus Christ makes us unconditionally the subject of the ethical question. To be elected, called, justified and sanctified in Jesus Christ is not merely a predicate which is placed in juxtaposition to man, in relation to which he can adopt a reserved and distant attitude, or with which he can concern himself with the leisurely interest of the historical or psychological spectator. To be in Jesus Christ is to be oneself the new creature fashioned by Him, to belong to Him as a member of His body. We ourselves either are this or are not. And so we ourselves can only either believe or not believe. But if we do believe, our responsibility to God's command becomes what it is by its intrinsic nature—our own personal responsibility ; and so our ethical reflection becomes in the strictest sense our intimate personal concern. And the *we* of those who are in Jesus Christ—again according to the intrinsic nature of the term—includes every I as such. In Christ there are no exceptions. There is, indeed, the richness of many particular gifts, the manifoldness of the life of the members of His one body. But there can be no limitation of His lordship in favour of our own special concerns and peculiarities. There can be no competition between the uniqueness of the one Lord and our own unique circumstances—however noteworthy. We can say *Credimus* in Jesus Christ only when and as the I says *Credo*, and when the I says *Credo*, he does so with all the responsibility of the *Credimus*. The unconditioned truth of those who prophesy and speak with tongues is measured by the unconditioned truth of the one Spirit of the community. For if their spirit is the Holy Spirit, it can only be the one Spirit of the community. And so the obedience which I owe to the command is measured by the obedience which it claims from us all. The qualified *we* of those who are in Jesus Christ is safeguarded on both sides. It corresponds to the sovereign decision of God in relation to which we must pose the ethical question. We cannot affirm as much of any other *we*. When the *we* of the ethical question is seriously understood in this way, it is only because the questioners do not evade the order of Christ's kingdom and cannot disown the traces of this qualified *we*. And, again, we conclude with the observation that if in this twofold sense we ask seriously : What ought *we* to do ?, we confess already that we know the divine command, that it is present to us, that it has been disclosed to us, and therefore that the necessary ethical reflection which sets this question cannot be made in vain. If the *we* of the ethical question is seriously meant from both points of view, then it is the qualified *we* of those who are in Jesus Christ. Our question is then in very truth a question about God's sovereign decision. Not knowing but asking what we ought to do, we confess that God knows about us. We subordinate ourselves to what He wills and orders, and our action is directed and·established by His command. Everything depends on how far we ask seriously. But when the *we* of our question is seriously meant in this twofold sense, we ourselves are witnesses that we ask seriously concerning the divine command.

4. What ought we to *do* ? It is not superfluous to be sure that we are really those who are asking what they are to *do*. This is not self-evident. The question : What ought we to do ? might well be prompted by curiosity, by a playful desire for knowledge, by a purely theoretical interest. And, of course, it is not a culpable but in many ways a laudable thing to be curious.

Curiosity is a powerful motive in the pursuit of knowledge. And even human conduct can itself be a legitimate object of highminded curiosity. Practice can be the object of theory. Our *inter-esse* can be the object of our " interest." We again remind ourselves of the task, or, at any rate, the initial task, of history and psychology, which, in the broader sense of the term, include studies like statistics and sociology. This curiosity is misguided only when it refuses to recognise any limits to its investigation, i.e., to admit the independent existence of the ethical question beyond the sphere of its own researches, or—which is far worse —when it tries to identify its own enquiries with ethical questions, to pretend that it is itself ethics. Ethics, too, is theory. But it is a theory which has left even the most highminded curiosity behind. It is theory which—when the questions prompted by mere curiosity about human conduct have been asked and answered, as far as is possible along those various lines—asks and must know what we ought to *do*.

The *we* no less than the *ought* removes this question of the *do* from the sphere of purely detached consideration. What we are commanded is never something that we can merely wish to know. We cannot stand aloof from it with the degree of detachment in which it can be for us a mere óbject of knowledge. An object like this, standing at a distance which allows and requires us to be content with a mere knowledge of it, and critical investigation of this mere knowledge, cannot as such be that which is commanded, no matter how deep an insight or how pure an idea it may express. In this respect it is important that ethical reflection is itself an ethical act, a moment of what we are and will and do and do not do as subjected to the divine command, or rather a special determination of each such aspect. Ethical reflection is the awareness by which each of our decisions is accompanied as it looks back to those which precede and forward to those which are to come. This is what distinguishes human conduct from the actions in which the life of plants and animals and even nature as a whole runs its course. It is accompanied by awareness. This accompaniment can assume many forms ranging from fully reflective consciousness to the various degrees of what is called subconsciousness —which does not cease to come under the category of consciousness. But as long as man lives as man, this awareness cannot be broken off. In virtue of the unceasing accompaniment of our activity by our awareness, we ourselves are its authors and true subjects. In virtue of this awareness, it is responsible. Just as our activity cannot be abstracted from this accompaniment, the latter cannot be abstracted from our activity. The command about which we ask is the command under which we stood and stand and will stand. To ask concerning it is to ask concerning the One who was and is and will be our Judge. We ask, therefore, concerning ourselves, concerning our judgment by the command as it has already been accomplished, is in process of realisation and is still to be developed. We cannot, therefore, want to know about the command in such a way that we survey it detachedly from without, making sure of its contents, forming an opinion about it and finally adopting an attitude towards it. We cannot ask about what is commanded merely to amass material for answering the later question whether we are to perform a certain action or would prefer to do this or that. There are no times, no intervals or neutral points in time, at which we can make this separation and perform this separated action. Even though I apparently ask for the first time concerning God's command, I already behave in a certain relationship towards it, either of obedience or disobedience. And in my present action, I in some sense recapitulate all my past, and anticipate my future conduct. Therefore when I weigh my prior decision in relation to my future decision, I am not involved theoretically, in respect of the future decision that has now to be considered, but practically, in respect of the decision that is now being taken in the full crisis of the command about which I ask. And this present decision stands in unbroken continuity with all my earlier decisions. It is not merely what we do, our action in the narrower sense of the term, which constitutes our action from the point of view of ethics. What we do not do, our omission, is exposed to the command about which we ask. And not merely what we do or fail to do, but also what we will, which is the preparation for what we do or do not do—for what we will or do not will is also something that we do or do not do. And not merely what we will is under the command of God, but primarily and supremely what we are—we ourselves who will and do not will, who do and do not do, yet not abstractly outside but within the circle of what we will and do and do not do. When the ethical problem is posed, we have to do with a completely unbroken circle. This as such is the object of God's sovereign decision, This as such is the subject of our responsibility to Him. This as such is judged in some way by God in that decision. As our life runs its course in this closed circle, as certainly as it is our human life (and not plant or animal life), it is accompanied by the ethical question which at every step necessarily challenges what I do and can never be mere examination and observation, mere explanation. Moral reflection is, of course, explanation. It means a realisation of the critical character of my whole situation, past, present and future, But this realisation is not the goal. The goal is that I may live in this realisation, that in respect of the whole series of my decisions (I now recapitulate the earlier ones and anticipate the future) I may be prepared for the divine decision to which my own are subject and responsible. In my doing or not doing of what *we* (in the twofold sense already explained) *ought* to do (in the precise antithesis of this genuine *ought* to our own will), the unconditioned truth of the good is present in a concealed form—as my pardon or condemnation. It is present here and not in a sphere outside or above what I do or do not do, not at a point where I can merely investigate and conclude without deciding, without making a decision in and with my investigating and concluding. Seriously put, the question : What ought we to do ? makes the presupposition of the testing of our conduct a responsibility. It means that there can be no escape from ethos into ethics, that for good or ill ethics is already ethos. All this can be true, of course, only if it is realised that it is the sovereign decision of God as the norm of all our decisions which makes it necessary to interpret our own life as a closed circle of responsible being, willing, doing and not doing, as an indissoluble nexus of theory and practice, and that the sovereign decision of God is identical with the reality of the covenant which He has set up between Himself and us and sealed in the death and resurrection of Jesus Christ. If it were a question of the mere idea of the will and command of God, a distinction could be drawn between our recognition of the good or evil of our conduct on the one hand, and its practical expression on the other. A neutral sphere could be marked off free from the responsibility of decision and apart from our own real decisions. There could be an ethics which is not itself ethos. Indeed, this would be basically necessary. For we are not responsible to an idea as such. We become so only when we recognise and acknowledge in it an authority which demands responsibility. In regard to an idea, the process by which theory and practice are nicely discriminated is justified. If we think of the divine will and command, the sovereign decision of God, in terms of an idea, then, as far as ethical reflection is concerned, we shall constantly relapse into this process, that is, we shall not be able to engage in genuine ethical reflection at all. But the idea of the sovereign divine decision as the norm of our conduct is not genuinely realised and assimilated by us if we think of it as an abstraction and not as the concrete reality of the covenant between God and man, as the person and the work and lordship of Jesus Christ : His person, in whom the eternal Word has taken our flesh and assumed and accepted human existence in its totality into union with Himself in order that He may be the Head, and also our Head, in His community, but also secretly in the whole cosmos ; His work, by which all human autonomy is delivered up to death and resurrected to a new and different life, as self-dedication to God ; His lordship by which all the places where man might hide from God and arrogantly try to make his own decisions, all the refuges and strongholds of our ethical neutrality, are destroyed and dismantled. We cannot deal evasively with Jesus Christ as one does with an idea. God's decision as it is really embodied in Him is a sovereign decision. ·It characterises not only our conduct but our asking what we ought to do as responsible decision. It drives us from the last of these neutral refuges—an ethics which tries not to be an ethos. It forces us out into the open, exposing us to the divine claim and the radical questioning of our whole being which it involves. When moral reflection is more than the play of what may, perhaps, be a highminded curiosity, when it has the seriousness not only of scholarship but of life itself—and therefore the seriousness of scholarship as well—it can only be from this source. It is not in vain that Jesus Christ is King and Victor. Theory and practice cannot be separated in the human world which God has loved from all eternity in Him and within which He has risen again as King and Victor. The Christian Church alone knows and confesses why it is that they cannot be separated, why it is that the will and command of God cannot consent to be treated as a mere idea, why it is essential, therefore, that ethics should begin where all mere curiosity leaves off. But the recognition of this indissolubility and necessity need not be always explicit. There is always an implicit practical recognition of it when the question : What ought we to *do* ? is put with the particular seriousness characteristic of the concept of action. When this happens, we are not far from the will of God, even though we do not yet or any longer understand it as such, even though we are indeed aliens to its establishment and disclosure in Jesus Christ. When we ask seriously : What ought we to *do* ? we testify that we ourselves are challenged by that supreme authority which makes all escape or neutrality quite impossible, because it is the supreme and in the strict sense the only judicial authority. God knows us, even if we do not know God. And He drives us, therefore, to serious reflection, and in our own limits to the ordering of our way according to His command.

It is as well to remind ourselves, at the conclusion of this analysis, that the question : What ought we to do ?, is the question which was put to Peter and the other apostles (Ac. 2³⁷ᶠ·) by those who heard Peter's sermon on the day of Pentecost. This means that, although we ourselves have to ask it, we must not ask it of ourselves. We must ask it of God, of the God who has revealed Himself to us and has given us the witnesses of His revelation. It is a question which is put by Holy Scripture, and therefore we must put it to Holy Scripture as the witness to God's revelation. That the sovereign decision of God confronts us and our decisions objectively in Jesus Christ is, as we have seen, the supreme criterion of all ethical reflection. But Jesus Christ cannot be separated from His apostles, from the whole witness which underlies the community of God in the form of Israel, and then of the Christian Church. We hear Him as we hear His witnesses. It is in their testimony that the divine command is always to be sought and will always be found as the sovereign divine decision. We must not be surprised, then, if—in very different forms—we are always given what is in fact the one answer : " Repent, and be baptised every one of you in the name of Jesus Christ for the remission of sins, and ye shall receive the gift of the Holy Ghost."

2, THE DEFINITENESS OF THE DIVINE DECISION

We have tried to see that the command of God is the inescapable verdict of the supreme Judge by speaking of its sovereignty—of the sovereignty of the divine decision. But the conception of the divine decision, and the corresponding conception of human responsibility to it, must now be particularly considered from the standpoint that the divine Word is given to us, and that it is concretely filled out, that it is given with a definite and specific content. It is in this way— and this way alone—that it is the inescapable verdict of our supreme

Judge, the divine decision concerning good and evil in our own decisions. It is in this way—and this way alone—that we are responsible to it.

That God is gracious to us in Jesus Christ means a total divine claim to our obedience and a total decision concerning good and evil in the choice of our decisions. It means our total responsibility. For the love of God in Jesus Christ intends and seeks and wills us in our totality. The work of atonement accomplished in Jesus Christ refers to the whole of our lives. And therefore our gratitude for the divine love and its work can only be a wholehearted gratitude. We touched upon this problem of the totality of the divine command and our responsibility to it when we pointed out that in its sovereignty the divine decision confronts all our own decisions and the whole series of actions of which our life is composed, and is Judge of them all. But fully to grasp it, we have to consider an aspect without which our recognition of the totality of the divine command, and therefore that of its sovereignty, and that of our responsibility to it, and finally our appreciation of the essential character of moral reflection, will necessarily be incomplete. This is that the divine command as the judicial divine decision confronting all our own decisions is given to us with a definite and concrete content. It is the particular command which faces each of our decisions, the specially relevant individual command for the decision which we have to make at this moment and in this situation. The radical nature of the decision made concerning us in Jesus Christ, the whole seriousness of the holiness and mercy, the omnipresence and eternity of God, the penetrating energy of the love but also the freedom, the patience but also the omnipotence in which He has turned and is still turned to us in Jesus Christ, do not permit us to understand His command in any other way, any the less intimately and intensively. The divine command to which we have been, are and will be subject, before which we have been, are and will again be responsible, was and is and will be God's *voluntas specialis* and even *specialissima*, His *mandatum concretum* or rather *concretissimum*. In it as such God is near to us, wills to sanctify us for Himself, wills to draw us to Himself, wills to be ours and to have us as His own. In it as such God is our Judge, deciding about the obedience or disobedience, the good or evil of our decisions. In it as such we are asked concerning our faith, our love, our hope. The genuinely particular, the concrete, the individual, the uniquely determined, is not, therefore, as is readily supposed, our moment in time and its inward and outward conditioning in itself and as such.

We remember that it is not time itself which is originally determined as the fulness of times. But God's eternity as such is the fulness of all times and therefore of each of our moments. It is not in and of itself that space has the infinite diversity of its various places, but in God's omnipresence—or, rather, it is because of the original spatiality of God Himself that there are many spaces in His creation, each in its particularity, but all corresponding necessarily in their particularity to the fact that God Himself, the Lord who occupies space, has willed and posited them in their manifoldness. It is not the manifoldness of creation, its nature and history, which is the true manifold; but because the one and only God is Himself the manifold; the eternally rich God, that there is also manifoldness and rich variety—only a drop from the ocean of His plenitude—in His creation. And, again, it is not our human individuality and its vitality in space and time, not the mystery of our personality with its contingent potentialities and decisions, which is the true and original source of vitality and individuality; but what we know and enjoy as such is only the created reflection of the vitality and individuality of God, of the freedom of His personal life, of the contingence of His will and action, of the particularity of His grace and mercy and patience, which would belong to His eternal being even though we and the whole world did not exist, but in which He willed to turn to the world as its Creator and Lord, and in the world to us as His covenant-partners. Therefore even the glory of the special, the concrete, the individual, the uniquely determined is a glory that belongs to God and not to us. It can be our glory only in so far as we may have a part in it as the creatures and children of God, acknowledging and magnifying it as His glory. But it cannot in any circumstances be claimed and asserted as our own glory as distinct from the glory of God.

Here we cannot try to secure for ourselves an advantage as against the command of God by understanding and asserting it as a general rule but regarding its application, i.e., its concrete embodiment, as' a matter for our judgment and action, so that the particular individual expression of what is laid down and prescribed in the command as a universal rule is only actualised in and with our own decisions—like the verdicts of a human judge, which are particular applications in each case, according to his own discretion, of what the law prescribes in general. The Law of God cannot be compared with any human law. For it is not merely a general rule but also a specific prescription and norm for each individual case. At one and the same time it is both the law and the judge who applies it. For as God is not only the God of the general but also of the particular, of the most particular, and the glory of the latter is His, so is it with His command. His command is not at all an empty form to which we have to give specific content (appropriate to this or that moment of our lives) by our action and the accompanying judgment of our ethical reflection. It is not a generalised thing to which particularised expression must accrue from elsewhere. The command of God is an integral whole. For in it form and content, general prescription and concrete application are not two things, but one. The divine decision, in which the sovereign judgment of God is expressed on our decisions, is a very definite decision. This means that in the demand and judgment of His command God always confronts us with a specific meaning and intention, with a will which has foreseen everything and each thing in particular, which has not left the smallest thing to chance or our caprice. The command of God as it is given to us at each moment is always and only one possibility in every conceivable particularity of its inner and outer modality. It is always a single decision, including all the thoughts and words and movements in which we execute it. We encounter it in such a way that absolutely nothing either outward or inward, either in the relative secret of our intention or in the unambiguously observable fulfilment of our actions, is left to chance or to ourselves, or rather in such a way that even in every visible or invisible detail He wills of us precisely the one thing and nothing else, and measures and judges us precisely by whether we do or do not do with the same precision the one thing that He so precisely wills. Our responsibility is a responsibility to the command as it is given us in this way. And ethical reflections means that we render an account in these terms, that we were and are and will be responsible to the command as it is given us in this way— really *given*, and given integrally, concretely filled out, and with a definite and specific content.

It is surely apparent at once that the concept of an unconditional truth of the divine command is incompletely grasped, or not properly grasped at all, if its definiteness is not taken into account. No description of the command can do justice to the concept if it leaves us to understand by the command merely a general norm or rule which has no definite content and the truth and validity of which are to be perceived and recognised apart, so that—on the basis of this perception and recognition—we can choose and make our own application of what it prescribes by our action. For according to this widely held view the case would be as follows. On a way which has still to be more narrowly determined, we must have the knowledge and conviction that our conduct stands under this or that universal rule and must always assume the corresponding form. But it is for ourselves to say exactly what we are commanded to do—not in general but here and now, at this moment with its concrete characteristics—what therefore we ought to do (assuming the general conformity of our action). And granted this conformity, we can count on the fact that what we do will be well done—that it will be what we are commanded. Is it not obvious, however, that according to this conception precisely the decisive thing to which any serious command must relate, namely, the origination of our conduct in the command, is not attained, that it is, in fact, surrendered, that we ourselves are to judge concerning its conformity with the presupposed universal rule ? If the content of our action is not determined by the command, is it not necessarily a doing of what we ourselves wish ? And is it not all the more objectionable because we are justified in regarding it as something that we ought to do ? The best interpretation that can be put on obedience to this command is that we have allowed our will to be limited, in some degree canalised, and to that extent co-determined by the obligation laid on us by the universal rule. A less favourable construction is that we have poured the dictates and pronouncements of our own self-will into the empty container of a formal moral concept, thus giving them the aspect and dignity of an ethical claim (although, in fact, it is we ourselves who will them). We have vindicated ourselves as judges, i.e., as interpreters of that law, justifying our own will in the concrete situation. Strictly speaking, a generally formal abstract command of universal import is not a command at all, for it does not become anything like a command until it is first heard, and understood, and acknowledged in itself, then made a law on the basis of that perception and recognition, and then given the necessary interpretation and application to the case in hand—which is, again, of course, a matter for our own decision. In this conception far too much devolves upon those who, in relation to a real command, do not enter in except as the obedient or disobedient. We cannot, therefore, recognise in this " command " the claim which a real command makes on man or the judgment which it passes. We cannot describe it as a command in the true sense. Whatever else it may be, a command whose truth is conditioned in this way is not a real command. A command—that is, the command in the strictest sense, the command of God—is a claim addressed to man in such a way that it is given integrally, so that he cannot control its content or decide its concrete implication. A command is a demand and not merely a theoretical exposition of the form which it may take. It comes to us, therefore, with a specific content, embracing the whole outer and inner substance of each momentary decision and epitomising the totality of each momentary requirement. It does not need any interpretation, for even to the smallest details it is self-interpreting. Only when the command has this character is it obviously a question addressed to us and demanding the response of our actions—the action of every moment with its concrete characteristics. Only then is the command distinguishable from the answers which we ourselves have continually given and give and will give to ourselves. Only then are our actions distinguishable from mere repetitions and corroborations of the dictates of our self-will. Only then do we stand in a relation of responsibility, of obedience or disobedience, to Another, to a transcendent Commander and Judge. Only then is the question of our responsibility different from that of our agreement or disagreement with ourselves, of our loyalty or disloyalty to the criterion which we ourselves have discovered and established. This is not to deny that the latter can in its own way be a very important and interesting question. But it is certainly not the same thing as the ethical question. The ethical question begins with the fact that even the special, concrete, particular and uniquely determined features of our action are commanded and that in this way our real action is claimed and judged ; that we are, therefore, asked concerning the specific theory which is commanded, and that even in its particularity this is not left to our own discretion, but is a matter for the divine decision.

The " idea of the good " cannot be the same thing as this specific divine decision. It cannot be denied that there is an idea of the good—the concept of the perfect correctness and therefore morality of human will and conduct, which may be identified with that of perfect being, and even of the original transcendent ground of all being, and therefore regarded as the sum of all that is required and commanded. The idea of the good is that of the norm of actuality, or actual norm, which, as it is the unconditional ground of our being, also makes an unconditional claim and passes an unconditional judgment on our will and conduct. Now, undoubtedly, the idea of the divine command is to some extent coincident with this thought. For the idea of God's command, too, includes that of the perfect correctness and morality of human conduct. It, too, understands this supremely correct and moral element as something required of us simply because it is being at its truest and highest, because, indeed, it is the origin of all being, because we can even say that it is God Himself, because our own participation in being and its original depths, our existence as God's creatures, depends on whether we reflect His character, the correctness and morality prescribed to us by the character of His own essence. But the identity of the two ideas is only on the surface. They are distinguished by the fact that the idea of the command is not a norm which we have thought out for ourselves, i.e., acquired and established by the process of dialectically developing and deepening the insights of our own will and conduct, but something which we plainly encounter from without. The idea of the divine command is the idea of something which is incomprehensible to man of himself—that he is not his own master, and that it does not lie in his competence to think out and prescribe for himself the rule under which he lives, to lay down the law which he is to obey, but that he has a Lord whose lordship over him is rooted in His personal will and defined and determined by it, and whose law is not a matter for our own discovery but for His revelation. In contradistinction to the idea of the good, even in its most mature conceivable form, the idea of God's command is that of the good which is proclaimed to man and required of him, which claims him and judges him. This distinction is seen in the fact that God's command is specific and concrete in its living relevance to every moment of human life, whilst the idea of the good can obviously be a command only in so far as he himself, as he has conceived and planned and established it, gives it its concrete embodiment in particular cases according to his private judgment and discretion, so that *in concreto* he is his own lord and master. But the fact is that we always will and act *in concreto*. How, then, in this presupposition, can we be anything else but our own rulers ? In what sense can we be the object of divine decision ?

It is just the same with regard to the so-called " categorical imperative "— the idealistic doctrine of law and freedom. We will assume that it is understood in the formal purity in which Kant himself wished it to be understood as a characterisation of the unconditionally binding nature of the moral law : " Act in such a way that the principles of your mode of action may at any time become those of universally valid legislation." We will also allow that this formula is not purely formal but material to the extent that it seems to make at least human society and its maintenance a genuine obligation, a substantial demand. We will also take it that this Kantian formula—as the followers of Kant have tried to prove with more or less success—is capable of various other material extensions. Yet, however we look at it, whether in the formal thinness originally envisaged or with the greater material fulness which it can be given, it can never be more than a formula for the idea of the imperative abstracted from the actuality of the imperatives which encounter us—" categorical " in so far as it defines, illuminates and describes the category of the imperative, differentiating it from all sorts of suppositions, desires and aspirations which as such cannot constitute an imperative because they do not correspond to the necessary definition of an imperative. But this or any similar formula can never be an imperative in itself and as such, or " categorical " in the current (but not originally Kantian) meaning of the term, i.e., confronting man with an absolutely obligatory demand, in such a way that he must and will obey this formula. The categorical imperative as such will never be a command. It can become this only when we receive, not this formula, but a real imperative—distinguished by the fact that it corresponds to the formula—and we bow or do not bow before this real imperative—but not the formula. It can become a command in the mouth of another only as this other somehow acquires the courage and authority—after concluding a study of the formula as such—to approach his fellows and to tell them—not in a repetition, but in an adequate interpretation and application of the formula—that in certain specific situations or questions they must do this and not do that. In proportion as a demand remains general, formal and abstract, leaving the question of interpretation and application to those to whom it is addressed, it is not yet a command, but at best only a perspicuous discussion and description of the command. It is to the credit of Kant that his imperative was not meant to formulate the command as such but only to show what is always involved in a real command. In his strict formation (even if it was not perhaps so strict in practice as in intention) he was far less inclined than those who thought they could improve on him to imagine that one of his formulæ could take the place of the genuine moral imperative, of the command which is actually addressed to man and claims and judges him. The imperative itself can never take the form : " Act in such a way . . .", but : " Do this, or do not do that, in the unique and unrepeatable situation, the position in which you find yourself at the moment : not because you have discovered that this line of conduct corresponds to the general form of an imperative, not because you are your own judge applying this principle to your own circumstances and concluding after due consideration that with this line of conduct you will be in harmony with the command, that you can claim and vindicate the principles underlying your present mode of action as those of universal legislation ; but do this and do not do that, because I— and in this connexion an ' I ' which is distinct from and confronts my own I is quite indispensable to the concept of the command—command it, and because I have the right and power to order you to do this, because you must respect and obey my command (simply because it is mine), because you stand or fall by whether you do my will or not." If it is a question of the imperative itself, the detailed and concrete determination of what is required of us is none of our business. The command is intrinsically concrete. It is already interpreted and applied to myself and my circumstances, to my position at the moment. There is nothing that I myself can add to it. I am asked only concerning my obedience or disobedience. I am not asked concerning my interpretation, but only my perception and the consequent practical recognition of the form in which it is given me. Formal general conceptions of what is commanded—even those which approach more nearly to the material and concrete than is the case with the Kantian imperative, even those which have the form of material rules (though still generalised and in need of particular application)—can never be more than reminiscences and indications of the command which has been or is actually issued. Understood in any other way, they can only minister to the illusion in which man wills to be good of himself and to impute the good to himself instead of allowing it to be the good in such a way that it comes to him and confronts him as the real command which itself reaches him, demanding his perception and practical recognition and therefore making his decision a decision between obedience and disobedience.

The same is equally true if we try to make conscience the supreme arbiter to which man is responsible and either obedient or disobedient in moral decisions. Conscience is the totality of our self-consciousness in so far as it can receive and proclaim the Word and therefore the command of God as it comes to us, in so far as we can be participants in the divine knowledge (συνειδότες, *conscientes*) because God Himself wills to speak with us. The Word and command of God which comes to us is the promise that we can be this. We have to see, then, that accurately and seriously understood the concept of conscience (like that of the " spirit " in man corresponding to the Holy Spirit and in contradistinction to body and soul) cannot be classed as an anthropological but only as an eschatological concept. It is only in the light of the integral connexion of our existence with that of Jesus Christ, in the light of the future consummation which is our inheritance and possession in Jesus Christ, that conscience or our self-consciousness can be understood and claimed as the organ of the divine and claim and judgment confronting our will, and therefore as the organ of our participation in the good. Above all, the conscience which lives wholly in the strength of this promise, and has it only in this eschatological context, in faith and only in faith, cannot possibly be interpreted as an independent " voice of God," or ranked above or even alongside the Word and command of God, but only subordinated to them. Conscience knows the command of God as it hears it. It gives it authority over us by bearing witness to it. The command is not revealed and given *by* conscience but *to* conscience, so that it cannot first gain through conscience the definiteness which alone makes it an effectual command. That it is both given and given in concrete definiteness derives from its own essential power and dignity. It is not, therefore, the function of conscience to interpret and apply, as though the command in itself were empty and needed concrete filling. In conscience, then, we are not made judges, but witnesses to the judgment to which we are subjected. Conscience can only be a reminder and indication that the command is addressed to us in all conceivable definiteness and that we have to render account to it in this its definite form. Conscience itself—all the more in proportion as it is awakened by the divine command and we allow it to speak definitely—will warn us against every perversion of the divine command into the dictates of our self-will. Conscience guards the frontier between the will of God and our own will. Conscience will see to it that the freedom of the command is maintained to be always a total command to the totality of our life.

Finally, it would be an even worse abuse if we were to understand the ideas of the will and kingdom, or the glory, righteousness or love of God, only formally as normative concepts like the " idea of the good " or the " categorical imperative," which have to be filled out in content by our interpretation, according to our own judgment and discretion. It is not as if these concepts derive from our own mental activities and, in order to constitute them as norms, we have to impart to them fulness and concreteness by our own reflections. It is, in fact, always a matter of the will and kingdom, the glory and righteousness and love of God in the command, and in what we will and do and do not do in subjection to the decision of His command. But all this denotes the concept of the God who has a personal life and therefore acts and speaks directly and concretely. How can we possibly be taking the idea of God seriously if we try to understand by His will and kingdom, His glory and righteousness and love (as a summary of the command which claims us) a mere *schema*, the practical realisation of which God Himself watches only as a spectator encouraging and consoling and finally distributing rewards and punishments—a formula with certain subdivisions, the contents of which can only be supplied by our application of it to our own particular case. How can the command of God be regarded as unconditional truth and confront and bind and claim and judge us as such if what these solemn ideas of God imply for us *in concreto* is subject to our own preference to the light shed by our *liberum arbitrium* ? These concepts which are all of them, in fact, titles for God's command, are, of course, so many names denoting so many different perfections of the essence of the personal and living God who rules all space and time in His creation. How, then, can these concepts coincide with, and justify, the presentation of a synergism in virtue of which there can be no doubt that we ourselves are finally the lords and masters of the divine command ? How can it be that we see portrayed in them only the good in general and not the good in the most detailed particular, and so do not understand the divine command as the requirement to serve and do justice to the will and kingdom, the glory and righteousness and love of God, and therefore as a command which has a concrete content, as a *mandatum concretissimum* ?

It is in this definiteness that the command is unconditional, leaving us no other choice than that between obedience and disobedience. Its unconditional character consists in the fact that, independently of our own views, always and in every relationship in which I find myself placed it has the particular form that God demands from me in all seriousness this or that concrete thing. The divine decision, therefore, in regard to my conduct does not mean that God later approves or disapproves, rewards or punishes, my own choice and decision in the interpretation and application of His command—as though the latter were simply a kind of proposal and programme within the bounds of which I had to find my bearings to the best of my ability and good-will, being pleasing or displeasing to God according to the result. The divine decision over me is already made in the command itself to the extent that it wills and expects from me something quite specific to the exclusion of all other possibilities, so that, as it is given to me and my reaction to it becomes a matter of personal decision, the verdict upon me is already included and expressed : I shall either do or not do what it wills and expects from me, and therefore be pleasing to God or not, deserving His reward or falling under His condemnation. And on the other hand, my human decision in face of the divine command does not consist in a decision of the question whether this or that is the good, whether the command wills this or that of me, whether I am to do this or that—this question would be just about as intelligent and relevant as the question whether there is a God, who and what He is, how and what we ought to think of Him, when all the time He Himself has already decided all this in His Word and revelation, and our task can only be to think precisely about what He affirms in this revelation. No, my decision—the human ethical decision—is whether in my conduct I shall correspond to the command which encounters and confronts me in the most concrete and pointed way, whether I shall be obedient or disobedient to it, whether I, for my part, shall meet it according to my election (the election of Jesus Christ) as a believer or an unbeliever.

The objection is obviously futile that God has not really given, and does not and will not give, His command with such wholeness, clarity and definiteness that it only remains for us to be obedient or disobedient, and not to try to discover what the divine command really is ; that we cannot be unequivocally responsible to it simply because it has not been unequivocally given to us. This objection is futile because it tries to evade the objective fact that God—God in His Word, the God who has sacrificed Himself for us in His Son and who in His Son is King of kings—is present to the world and each individual, and confronts him in the smallest of his steps and thoughts as his Commander and Judge. Because God has given us Himself, and constituted

Himself our Lord, He has also given us His command.   Because He is ours and we are His, He gives us His command.   Because He will not cease to be ours, as we cannot cease to be His, He will not cease to give us His command.   We are able to hear it, as surely as we belong to Him and to no one else.   The question cannot be whether He speaks, but only whether we hear.   And this means that we are already faced again by the question of our obedience or disobedience, our faith or ungodliness.   For obedience and faith begin as we hear, as we recognise what is spoken to us.   And ungodliness begins with our not hearing, and our lack of vision.   We are already involved in the decision which is assessed and judged in God's command, and pleasing or displeasing to God, when God's command either confronts us with the wholeness, clarity and definiteness which are its intrinsic qualities, or seems hidden in a cloud of various possibilities, between which we have to choose and among which we think we can seek and determine that which is for us the divine command.   This supposition is in itself the fruit of our disobedience and unbelief, and, according to Rom. 12^2, there is only one remedy for it, namely, our transformation by the renewing of our minds, by penitence, by a return to the obedience and faith in which we shall certainly attain the right kind of testing, which does not consist in an investigation whether this or that is the will of God, but in the testing of ourselves from the point of view of our readiness to conform in our conduct to what we know well enough to be the will of God.

The objection that the divine will is not known to us, or not sufficiently known, in its definiteness is not only futile but cunning and deceitful because it makes a virtue or an excuse out of our need, because it raises our unwillingness to hear carefully what is precisely spoken to us as those to whom God is present and near, to the status of a necessity on the basis of which we can withdraw into the supposed neutrality of an arbitrary questioning as to the good, so that we are acquitted in advance if in our arbitrary choice between the many possibilities open to us we may not coincide with the will of God.   Our very retirement into this neutral position is in itself the signal of a perverse decision, an act of disobedience and unbelief.

We should not overlook the fact that, according to Gen. 3^1, this apparently well-founded objection was first raised—and raised by the serpent—when man was not at all confronted by a welter of possibilities, and could not evade the divine Law by exegesis and application, but when he was faced by the *mandatum concretum*, or *concretissimum*, that he should not eat of a certain tree, the tree of the knowledge of good and evil.   It will always be the case that when the divine command makes its impact upon us in its most concrete and piercing form we are most disposed to evade it by the suggestion that the divine will is so obscure that we have first to investigate and establish in what it actually consists.

We have to realise both the futility and the deceitfulness of this suggestion, and therefore seriously to reckon with the fact that the divine command is always a command given to us in a concrete embodiment, and not a requirement of a merely general nature to which we have to impart the necessary validity and authority according to the light of our own understanding and judgment.

The fact that the decision of God which claims and judges us in His command is a specific decision is something we must affirm because this is how matters stand according to the witness of Holy Scripture, and therefore the witness of God's revelation of His real relationship to us and our real relationship to Him. It is in this way, concretely, that man is commanded in Holy Scripture, and from this we may infer that it is in this way, concretely, that we ourselves are commanded. Furthermore, in Holy Scripture we have to recognise the witness to the concrete command that encounters us too, and by which we too are confronted. It bears witness, not to an alien and dead, but to our own living Lord and Commander and Judge. As it attests and discloses to us the grace of God as the truth of God which transcends all human godlessness and resignation and despair, as it proclaims aloud what always and everywhere was and is and will be true, namely, that God's faithfulness is greater than our unfaithfulness, it also attests the will and command of God as the order which covers even the unfaithful and disobedient, to which they too are objectively subject and responsible, and which can only seem novel to them because of their futility and cunning.

That all are without excuse in their perverse decision, because God has spoken and speaks and always will speak to all, is made plain by the witness of Scripture. In the sphere of its witness, in the sphere of the elect community of God called by His Holy Spirit to faith and obedience, in the sphere of Israel and Church, of the self-attestation of Jesus Christ and its echo in the prophets and apostles, this objection is unmasked and shown to be invalid. When the witness of Scripture is heard and accepted, it is known that this objection is a deception, and the real situation of man is known : that in truth he is always confronted by the whole and clear and specific command ; that it is his own fault if he supposes himself to be in a fog, and is actually befogged in this opinion ; that in such an error he is disobedient (disobedient to the command of God as it is specifically given) when he becomes his own lawgiver and poses as the interpreter of his own laws. On the basis of the witness of Scripture, which attests its true Master to a supposedly masterless world, it can be known that the supposedly lawless man, who decides and chooses for himself, who is his own lawgiver and judge, is a liar. As he can only play the part of the divinely rejected with a false—if dangerous—theatricality, it is only with the same theatricality—which is bad enough in itself—that he can play the part of the godless. He does both as he is opposed and given the lie in advance by the election of Jesus Christ (to be the Lamb of God which takes away the sins of the world and to be the King of Glory to whom all principalities and powers are subject). That this is so is once for all revealed in the epiphany, in the death and resurrection of Jesus Christ in opposition to the natural but false witness of the whole world. And the witness to this revelation is the Holy Scripture of the Old and New Testaments. By holding to this witness we oppose to the heathen doctrine of the vagueness and uncertainty of the divine command that of its definiteness and concreteness. This is its Christian antithesis. But this does not mean that the doctrine is true and valid only for Christians. It means rather that it is generally true and valid for all men and for each man. It must be steadily opposed under all circumstances to all error and disobedience in this matter.

If we are to assure ourselves of the specific character of the divine command in view of the biblical witness, we must distinguish the following two facts : (1) that the divine law in the Bible is always a concrete command ; and (2) that this concrete commanding to be found in the Bible must be understood as a divine command relevant to ourselves who are not directly addressed by it.

The question to which the first point is an answer is exegetical in the narrower sense.

When it is a matter of the divine command in the Bible we usually think too readily and one-sidedly of certain contexts in which (according to an equally facile and one-sided exegesis) we believe we have to do with lists of universal religious-moral-juridical rules and therefore with legal codes that are valid regardless of space and time. But, however these passages are to be interpreted, it is surely arbitrary to seek the biblical witness to God's command, and therefore what might be called biblical ethics, only or even primarily in these contexts. What God's command is, and what it means even in these particular contexts, is rather to be derived from the greater whole to which they belong. Thus it is certainly not the case that, according to the Bible, God commands only or even primarily where these universally valid rules are thought to be discovered. We should rather consider the fact—putting aside for the moment the question of the interpretation of these particular contexts—that the whole relationship of God with man in the course of the historical unfolding of His covenant of grace, which forms the true content and object of the biblical witness, is continuously realised in the shape of the divine commanding and prohibiting, the divine ordering and directing. We fail to see the wood for the trees if we refuse to recognise that, apart from those particular contexts, the whole remaining content of the Bible is replete with ethics—except, of course, that what is usually understood by " command " and " ethics," namely, universal rules, is not to be found there. For, as the Lord of this history, God seems hardly to be interested at all in general and universally valid rules, but properly only in certain particular actions and achievements and attitudes, and this in the extremely simple and direct way of desiring from man (as a father from his child, or a master from his servant) that this or that must or must not happen. Nothing can be made of these commands if we try to generalise and transform them into universally valid principles (unless, of course, we artificially distort them). Their content is purely concrete and related to this or that particular man in this or that particular situation. It consists in what God wills that he should do or not do in a specific situation. Commands of this sort must be left as they stand. They belong directly to a specific history, and they must be left in all their historical particularity and uniqueness. What God wills and for what purpose He requires the active participation of man, for what purpose He claims his being and willing, what he does and does not do—this is the course of this history, which consists, therefore, in purely individual, concrete and specific events. Thus God's commanding can only be this individual, concrete and specific commanding. We must divest ourselves of the fixed idea that only a universally valid rule can be a command. We must realise that in reality a rule of this kind is not a command. We must be open to the realisation that the biblical witness to God's ruling is this : to attest God as the Father, or Lord, who in the process of the revelation and embodiment of His grace, *hic et nunc*, orders or forbids His child, or servant, something quite specific, and in such a way that there can be no question of an appraisal or judgment by man of what is required (which would be legitimate and necessary if the command consisted in a universally binding rule), but the question put to man can be only that of his hearing and obeying.

By way of factual example we must remember that up to the first edition of the Ten Commandments in Ex. 20[1f.], and the legislation which immediately follows, the Pentateuch does not contain any element that could conceivably be transformed into a universal principle. The very first command in Gen. 1[28] : "Be fruitful, and multiply, and replenish the earth, and subdue it," is specifically and concretely addressed to the first man and woman after creation and before the fall, and it is unique and unrepeatable in its unconditional character. It takes on rather a different form when, later on, after the fall and the flood, it is addressed to Noah (9[1f.]). In 2[16f.] this command is followed by the one already mentioned, which, in truth, embraces and exhausts all ethical disciplines, and yet is not universal but highly particular. This is the prohibition with regard to the eating of the tree. And, significantly enough, the point of this prohibition is that man should not know good and evil for himself, and on the basis of this knowledge become his own judge. But this knowledge and judging are not forbidden as such. To prevent them, what is forbidden is what seems to be the ethically irrelevant eating of the tree. And it is by the transgression of this purely factual prohibition that the fall takes place as a type of all sin. The next plain command of God is the meticulously exact instruction given to Noah regarding the building of the ark (6[14]). The next is the command to Abraham (12[1]) : "Get thee out of thy country, and from thy kindred, and from thy father's house, into a land that I will shew thee." There follows the summons to Abraham to walk through the land of Canaan as a symbol of its future possession (13[14f.]), and in 15[9] we have a detailed prescription concerning sacrifices on the occasion of the setting up of the covenant. It is striking enough that here especially there is no question of any other ordinances, more purely religious and moral our sense. In 16[9] and 21[12, 18] directions are then given concerning the relationship of Isaac and Ishmael. In 17[10] we have the ordinance of circumcision. In 17[15] Sarah is told to change her name. In 19[12] Lot is commanded to leave Sodom ; in 20[7] Abimelech to free Sarah ; in 22[2f.] Abraham to sacrifice Isaac ; in 26[2] Isaac to remain in Canaan ; in 31[3] Jacob to return to Canaan, and in 46[3] to go into Egypt. In Ex. 3[5] Moses is told to remove his shoes before the burning bush ; in 4[3f.] he receives directions about his appearing before Pharaoh ; in 4[19] he is ordered to return to Egypt ; in 4[27] Aaron is told to approach Moses ; in 6[13] they are given their joint commission to Pharaoh, which in cc. 7–10 is repeated in individual commands. In 12[2f., 43f.] and 13[1f.] we have the institution

C.D.—22

of the Passover and the consecration of the firstborn; in 14[1, 15] directions concerning the crossing of the Red Sea; in 16[4] details about the gathering of manna; in 17[5f.] instructions to Moses about the rock in the wilderness; in 19[12f.], 21[f.] warnings against an unauthorised approach to Sinai. The list is remarkable enough. According to the witness of these texts, when God confronts man with His commands, what He wills is purely *ad hoc* actions and attitudes which can only be thought of as historically contingent even in their necessity, acts of obedience to be performed on the spot in a specific way, pure decisions the meaning of which is not open to discussion, because they do not in any sense point to a higher law, but is rather contained in the fact that God has decided in this way and spoken accordingly, so that human decisions can only obey or disobey the divine decision. In these texts there is no such thing as a general rule which can be debated and needs to be filled out in its application. If this vexes us, it cannot be helped. But there is no real reason to be vexed by it. For it does not mean that they tell us nothing about the will of God. Do they not mean just what they say—the supremely specific thing that in contrast to all other commands the command of God is the command of the good and therefore indisputable even in its definiteness? And this series of commands, as could easily be shown, continues throughout the whole of the Old Testament. Apart from the codified laws in Ex. 20 f., God does not cease to demand specific things from Moses, and Aaron and the whole people, and later from all His charismatic leaders and representatives, repeatedly confronting them with the necessity of making the most concrete decisions. And there can be no doubt that the sequence of these concrete ordinances characterise the course of the history of the covenant which it is the aim of all parts of the Old Testament to attest and proclaim.

It is exactly the same in the New Testament. We shall take our examples only from St. Matthew's Gospel, leaving aside for the moment the Sermon on the Mount and other discourses which might seem to justify the usual interpretations that we have to do with the proclamation of universal principles. It is obvious that we are still wholly in the atmosphere of the patriarchal stories when we are told in 1[20] how God uses an angel to tell Joseph to take Mary to wife; and in 2[13] how he is to flee with her into Egypt, and in 2[20] to return from Egypt. From this point onwards the expressions of the will of Jesus are themselves authoritative, and the first is the insistence in 3[15] on the necessity of His baptism in Jordan : " It becometh us to fulfil all righteousness." In 4[19] He orders Peter and Andrew to leave their nets and come to Him. In 8[3f.] His Word to the leper is quite specific : " I will ; be thou clean." So, too, is His Word to the ruler of Capernaum in 8[13] : " Go thy way ; and as thou hast believed, so be it done unto thee "—in exact correspondence to what the latter had said about himself in v. 9 : " For I am a man under authority, having soldiers under me : and I say to this man, Go, and he goeth ; and to another, Come, and he cometh ; and to my servant, Do this, and he doeth it." In 8[22] the man who is called to be a disciple but first wants to go and bury his father is given the very precise direction : " Follow me ; and let the dead bury their dead." In 8[32] Jesus commands the demons to go into the swine. In 21[19] He orders the fig tree never to bear fruit again. In 9[6] the sick of the palsy is commanded to take up his bed and walk ; and in 9[9] Matthew is required to leave the seat of custom and follow Him. In 9[24] He ejects the mourners from the house of Jairus. When the blind man is cured, He forbids him (in 9[30]) to declare what has happened ; and He forbids His disciples to disclose that He is the Christ (16[20]). In 10[5f.], when sending out His disciples, He gives them the most concrete directions concerning those whom they shall meet in the way. In 11[4] He sends a message concerning His deeds to the imprisoned Baptist. In 12[13] He says to the man with the withered hand : " Stretch forth thine hand." In 14[16] He orders His disciples to give them to eat, and in 14[29] Peter is told to come to Him out of the ship. In 17[17] He orders that the lunatic boy should be brought to Him. In 16²³ He tells Peter : " Get thee behind me, Satan." And when Peter, James and John fall on their faces on the mount of transfiguration, He commands them to get up and not to fear (17⁷). In 19²¹ the rich young man is to sell all that he has and give to the poor, and the Pharisees and Herodians are to pay tribute (22²¹ᶠ·) and thus render unto Cæsar the things which are Cæsar's. In 21²ᶠ· it is purely and exclusively a question of the ass and her colt which the disciples are to free and bring to Jesus. The words at the Last Supper are : " Take and eat," and " Drink ye all of it " ; and then in the Garden of Gethsemane : " Sit ye here " (26³⁶), " Watch with me " (v. 38), " Watch and pray " (41), " Rise, let us be going " (v. 46), and finally to Peter (v. 52) : " Put up again thy sword into his place." Last of all, in 28¹⁰ He says with a new authority : " Be not afraid : go tell my brethren that they go into Galilee, and there shall they see me." The list is again remarkable enough. It could easily be extended from the other Gospels, the Acts and in a different way the Epistles. This is how Jesus spoke to command or forbid, in His intercourse with His disciples and other men. What would become of Matthew's Gospel, or the Gospel as such, if we tried to think away this list ? The most important insights and decisions depend on these commands. None of them can be dispensed with. None is irrelevant. We are surprised to see how far they go beyond the sphere of human willing and not willing, the human sphere in general. And yet they are none of them less fortuitous, contingent, unique and involved in time and space than the commands of God in the Pentateuch, each provoking the question : Why has Jesus ordered this ? Why is it that this must be done ? And, again, it is the case that those who want religious ethical principles will find nothing here, but will have to turn to the other words of Jesus which seem to be more pregnant in this respect. Yet if they do they turn away from the living and acting person of Jesus Himself which is the content of the Gospel. They overlook the fact that we can best learn what the commanding of Jesus means at this point where we are so unequivocally confronted by His sovereignty, where He Himself and His will take the place of every universal precept, and where we see Him make this very definite use of His sovereignty. This is what happens when Jesus commands. The essential character of His command is as we see it here.

It can hardly be disputed that in this question of God's command in the Bible the obvious thing is to keep first and primarily to these series of direct commands which abound profusely in all parts of the Old and New Testaments, and in which we see the commanding God and Lord directly at work as it were, and obedient or disobedient man directly involved in the corresponding deed. At this point, do we not have to infer as a decisive principle of biblical ethics the fact that primarily the divine command does not take the form of universal and general rules, but that of individual concrete and specific orders and directions, so that man is not required to assimilate general rules, himself deciding about the good and the bad when he comes to apply them, but rather to keep steadily before him the special and definite thing that God enjoins him to do or not to do ? One thing is clear— that the consideration of these historical pictures, with what seem (in content) to be such fortuitous and contingently historical directions, compels us in a very special way to interest ourselves in the One who issues these directions. Just because it is a question of purely material circumstances and conditions, and we are not given any general ideas and points of view, the one sure thing is thrown so much more clearly into relief : the hand of God which is mighty and disposes in His Word ; the will of God which is revealed as such ; and the person of God in its sovereignty, which stands before us as directly as a human person, but, as distinct from the latter, with a majesty which allows neither contradiction nor reserve. In the command of God we are face to face with the person of God, with the action and revelation of this person, with God Himself. This is the lesson which we have to learn from these historical pictures. And we certainly cannot learn it from the Ten Commandments or the Sermon on the Mount if we consider them in the usual fashion as separate from these historical pictures and not as integral parts of the one great biblical view of history. The decisions of God which are normative for those of man are always made in this personal encounter, as is clear from the issue of these commands. He, God—and in the New Testament, Jesus—precedes us with His transcendent knowledge of what is necessary and right and salutary, declaring and presenting it to man as His resolve, which man must acknowledge and execute as such. And the whole singularity and uniqueness of God as the Lord is reflected in the particularity of what He wills and commands, of what the man who confronts God in this way is ordered to do or not to do. The command is always the particular decision and disposition, and therefore the particular revelation, of this supremely particular Commander. This is the truth which emerges from these historical pictures. Yet this does not mean a dissolution, but an intensification, of the idea of command. An ethics which separates the idea of what is commanded from the person of the commanding God ; an ethics which is more concerned about the erection or discovery of definite human orders than the personal will of the divine Orderer, can hardly be constructed, if at all, on the basis of these historical pictures. But this is an even greater challenge to take them as our primary point of orientation. For the seriousness and value of an ethics of this kind is highly questionable. If there is a genuine and unassailable order, self-grounded and secure, it must be rooted in the living and indisputable presence and counsel of an Orderer who is superior to man. And this is how it is presented in these biblical texts, which seem to be so barren from an ethical standpoint.

But we have not said everything when we have shown that the divine person and its authority and freedom are marks of the command as attested in these texts. The fact that this divine commanding is contingently historical, involved in time and space, concrete and not abstract, does not mean that it is accidental or meaningless. The person of this God is a very definite person, and in its definiteness, in the character of its will and the bent of its purposes, it is not concealed from us, but revealed and known. What this God determines is not a whim, and what He presents to man to do or not do is not the product

of the fickle caprices of a tyrant whose right consists in his might.
We have already pointed out that the dealings of God with man,
which always take the form of this commanding and forbidding, constitute the history of His covenant of grace, the story of the actualisation and fulfilment of the love in which from all eternity He has inclined
to man in the person of His only Son, the application of the predestinarian decree of His election of grace. God is faithful and constant. He is the God of this election of grace. In the event which is
the object of the biblical testimony, and therefore in the divine ordering, there can be no question of a mere play of His almighty pleasure
with all the variety of man's creaturely possibilities. In this connexion
those to whom we owe the biblical text and canon, the biblical witnesses
of the Old and New Testaments, the community in its form both as
Israel and the Church, saw both a way and a plan. As hearers and
readers of this testimony we can and must realise that it is all well
thought out, even where it is not easy or even impossible for us
to follow in detail the way and plan to the framework of which the
individual event belongs, to demonstrate and verify it in detail.
The question of the meaning of the will of God, of His decisions, of
His commanding and forbidding is not, therefore, suppressed and
eliminated in this consideration of these historical pictures. But we
must be concerned to discover the meaning of the will of God in His
commanding and forbidding and not a general human meaning behind
what is commanded and prohibited. We must keep in view and try
to understand His own purpose and action as the true content of what
He commands and forbids. But His purpose and action in the story
of the covenant of grace to which the Bible bears witness is the mercy
for the sake of which and in the strength of which He draws man to
Himself in the person of Jesus Christ, in which He Himself becomes
man in order to execute on man the just judgment of sin, that man
may be pure and free and blessed, to give man over to death that he
may come to a new life which is life indeed. This is the simple and
sufficient meaning and content of the covenant of grace which characterises and inspires all the divine commanding and forbidding to
which the Bible bears witness and which is its true *ratio*. For the sake
of His mercy, and therefore for the sake of Jesus Christ and through
His agency, God wills to bring into being His community in its form
both as Israel and the Church—this one people with its twofold testimony and message which in both respects means the proclamation
of the one Lord Jesus Christ : on the one side His death, on the other
His resurrection ; on the one side the rejection of man which God has
taken upon Himself in Christ, on the other the election in which God
has turned to man in Him. The history of this one and twofold people
as the circumference of the man Jesus of Nazareth, the history of its
preparation and guidance to be the witness of the one Saviour, and
therefore the witness of God's mercy to the whole world, the Bearer

of which both derives from this people and is the origin from which this people springs—this history is the history of God's covenant of grace to which the interest of the whole Bible in both its parts is indissolubly directed. And it is just in the course of this history that there arises the commanding and forbidding which is now our special concern. If we are to understand this, we may as little think of abstracting from this story as from the person of the God who commands. On the contrary, we must continually keep before us and therefore understand the person in the history and the history in the person. If God wills this or that from these men according to the texts, commanding and forbidding so particularly, it is because and to the extent that He wills supremely and uniquely this particular thing—the actualisation of His election of grace, man as the object of His love in His own Son, and therefore the death and resurrection of the One as the end and new beginning for all, and therefore Israel and the Church, and therefore their preparation and equipment for the office of witness. That this is God's will and action is the testimony of the Bible, and it makes this testimony as it testifies to God's commands. Since this history is its essential theme and content, its only possible testimony in relation to the decision of God concerning what man does and does not do is that He wills that it should correspond to this history, that it should be subordinate to its purpose, and adapt itself to its course. God wills that man should be called and gathered to this people of His choice to share in its office of witnessing. God wills that he should be and will and do and not do the unique thing required by the unique thing which God Himself is and wills and does and does not do in Jesus Christ. This particular thing which cannot be reduced to any moral common denominator is the specific meaning and content of the demands which God makes on man as we see from the historical pictures. How strangely would the Bible deviate from its proper theme and content if it presented matters otherwise than it actually does in the shape of this, so to speak, historical ethics, if it were to describe the will of God as the establishment and proclamation of general precepts and rules which can be filled out only on the basis of the reflection and decision of man! It does not do so. It represents God as the Father or Lord who requires always this or that, a particular thing. It would not be the Bible, but the code of a Hammurabi or the law of a Solon or Mohammed, if it put things otherwise, if it knew of any other duty for man but that in his time and place and situation he should take the part allotted to him in this history. It is not in virtue of any intrinsic universal truth, but in virtue of the special truth of its divine foundation and embodiment that this duty signifies the good which man is to perform (co-operating in the course of the history of the covenant of grace).

If we again consider passages already adduced from Genesis and Exodus, it cannot be denied that the divine commanding and forbidding follows a distinct thread—that of the history of the divine covenant of grace. It is not always and everywhere that this commanding and forbidding is specially emphasised. But it certainly is at all the critical points of the story where the presentation aims at making clear both the sovereign initiative of God and also at the same time the fact that God requires the active co-operation of man as a partner in the divine work. This is the case with the command : " Be fruitful and multiply," which does not seem to reckon with the possibility of sin ; and the prohibition concerning the tree of knowledge. The grace of God wills that man should live (as the animal denizens of the sea and air are also told to do in Gen. 1^{22}), but live without question or discussion and not as his own judge. If, in spite of the transgression of this command and its consequences, God remains true to him, then, as we see from the command to Noah about the building of the ark, he may not expect his salvation from any self-discovered technique, but only from the strict observance of a precise divine prescription. The command to live must now be repeated under the sign of the divine patience, and from now on it must be heard under this sign and with this caveat. And if in the covenant with Abraham this faithfulness of God assumes the form which in the opinion of the redactors of Genesis was clearly foreshadowed in the story of Noah's ark, there can be no question at all of man's initiative, but the initiative of the divine election of grace must necessarily be accompanied by all the special commands with which the story of Abraham is so thickly scattered and that of Isaac and Jacob somewhat less thickly. A similar crucial point in the story is obviously to be found in the Exodus and the story of Moses, who is secured from the temptation to interpret himself as a religio-political leader by the fact that all his decisive actions are characterised as fulfilments of direct divine commands. And that the people of Israel itself has not helped itself but received divine help emerges clearly in the fact that its movements, too, are either directly or indirectly (through the mouth of Moses) accompanied by divine commands. God actualises His covenant with man by giving him commands, and man experiences this actualisation by the acceptance of these commands. The people of God from which Jesus Christ will spring is constituted by this immediate and direct guidance.

Similarly, according to the typical material surveyed in St. Matthew's Gospel, the Church is constituted as the second form of the community—that which itself derives from Jesus Christ. If the directions to Joseph, the foster-father of Jesus, form in a certain sense the conclusion and climax to the call of Israel, the commands of Jesus Himself all reflect more or less clearly the two aspects of the Messianic presence, the two poles of Christology : the humiliation and exaltation of Jesus, the hiddenness and manifestation of His election, His suffering to take away the sins of many and His lordship as the Giver of life to these many. When Jesus commands and forbids, it means that He discloses His Messiahship and that He summons men to share either in His priestly or His kingly office, either exclusively as recipients or exclusively as those who are themselves to work and give. It is always a question of His person, but because this is so, it is a question of the imminent coming of God's kingdom, of the revelation of the secret of the election of grace in its twofold form.

It is because the divine person and the divine cause are so specific in both the Old and New Testament that in both the commands and prohibitions of God are so specific and are always filled out so concretely.

But we must not overlook the fact that there are some biblical contexts in which the command assumes the form of general rules which are valid for large numbers of people and are detached from any particular historical circumstances. The question arises how far the command in these passages is to be interpreted differently from the historical sense upon which we have insisted. It cannot be denied that these passages exist and that if we could take them out of their context, or if they had come down to us otherwise than in the larger nexus of the biblical writings and Canon, it would be quite possible to interpret them as if they were a statement of principles and rules and to understand the commands of God to be rules and principles of this kind. And the question certainly arises—and it is an exegetical question of the first importance—whether we have to interpret these special texts in the light of their historical context, or whether, conversely, we have to interpret the historical context in the light of a general ethical understanding of these texts. To a very large extent, both openly and secretly, the Christian Church and theology have taken the latter course. They have viewed these passages in isolation, trying to explain their historical context as a more or less important or unimportant excrescence, or as a mere illustration. They have understood these passages as if they stated ethical principles, definite norms for the determination of good and evil actions and attitudes, the former commanded and the latter forbidden. They have interpreted them as if these principles had a weight of their own, an autonomous significance ; as if the command and will of God, the good which God requires of man, were to be found in these principles as such. This interpretation easily recommended itself by its convenience. It meant that the command of God could at once be understood in formal analogy with what man usually understands in any case as the sum of the good, as law, even apart from God. And on this presupposition there could easily be found in what these texts describe as the good a good deal of what man thinks to be the good in any case, and the rest with a little adaptation. It was thought that the substance of the whole biblical witness could be seen in these passages as interpreted in this way. The rest of the Bible had then to be explained and appraised by them, and it was only a secondary question whether the historical context was despised as a (basically obstructive) scaffolding or honoured as an illustration of the principles which were found here and in which it was considered that the substance of the whole biblical witness was contained. The first attitude was the more natural where the historical difficulties were more keenly felt, the second where it was thought possible to overcome them. But it ought to be said that this solution of the problem is in no sense that of a sound exegesis because it rests from the very outset upon a capricious assumption. For it is capricious to detach these texts from their background and to prefer them hermeneutically to their background simply because it is thought possible to recognise in them something already familiar. It is obvious from the supposedly secondary background of these passages in both Old and New Testaments that the theme of the Bible is something other than the proclamation of ethical principles. This cannot be denied, whatever may be our attitude towards the fact. Therefore those who decide for that solution of the problem must realise that they are taking a disastrous freedom with the Bible, and if they appeal to the Bible they must be reminded that they are appealing to a Bible which they have first adjusted to their own convenience. If we keep in view the theme of the whole Bible—whatever may be our attitude towards it, whether sympathetic or not—there can be only one prior decision in this fundamental exegetical question. It can be expected that this will be the theme of these special contexts, that even the divine commanding and forbidding of which they speak will therefore have the same meaning as in the rest of the Bible, and that in them, too, this theme will have to be understood historically and concretely and not in a general, non-spatial and non-temporal sense.

These texts, too, obviously purport to be witnesses of what God—or in the New Testament Jesus—once addressed as His demand either to one man or to many. In this respect they do not differ from the other passages. Nor do they differ from them in the sense that they, too, point to a historical occasion for the divine communication of the Law, or at least allude to a person who has heard and imparted to others the disclosure of the divine command or the counsels of the divine wisdom. Again, they do not differ from them in the sense that they, too, plainly and exclusively refer to the sphere of the community as it is elected, separated and gathered by the will and Word and act of God. As it is presented in these passages, too, the command is an event which forms a particular step in the nexus of the history of divine grace, and which in fact can be understood only in this context.

The special feature of these texts consists (1) in the fact that, according to their witness, the command appears to be addressed to an indeterminate number of men, and (2) that they therefore appear to be concerned, not with the specific actions of specific men, but generally with certain possibilities of action on the part of all kinds of men. If this twofold appearance is not a mere appearance we are naturally forced to conclude that these passages proclaim something like general principles as the command of God. But the appearance is, in fact, deceptive. It could arise only from the fact that in these texts we have to do with collections or summaries of divine commands. As several beams of light are brought to a focus in a lens, or several threads in a cable, so many particular commands are united and expressed in these comprehensive demands addressed to the people in the Old Testament and the Church in the New. It is certainly not the purpose of these collections either to compromise or weaken the directness and urgency with which God elsewhere turns to the individual man, to exchange here His personal address for a more generalised word by which the individual may feel himself affected or not. There is here no dismissal, but an extremely energetic apprehension of the individual in his capacity as a member of the people or the Church. This is the intention of the comprehensive demands expressed in these passages. They are

not in any sense meant to blur the definiteness with which God elsewhere requires concrete individual decisions, replacing them by abstract rules or general points of view by means of which the individual
has then to decide for himself how he must obey. There is here no
evasion, but in the true and strict sense a strengthening of the concreteness of the divine demand, for everything which God requires
from the individual is proclaimed in these summaries as His will for
His people or Church, and therefore for the individual members of
this people or Church. It is not, then, the intention of these proclamations of law to replace and supersede the special events in which God
addresses the individual as such and wills to be heard by him. But
what takes place in these proclamations is that God declares Himself
to be the Subject of all these special summonses, the One who has the
power and right to confront the individual in these specific addresses
with binding commands and prohibitions because He is the Lord of
the people or community to which the individual belongs, whose
property the individual is, and to whose control and claim the individual is subject. They speak of Himself and His sovereignty, of His
essential nature in contrast to that of other lords, of the constitution
of His people or community and the implied conditions and characteristics of the individual members who belong to it. These summaries
remind us of the obligation which God has undertaken with regard to
each of the individuals who belong to Him and which each of these
individuals must accept in relation to God. They affect in some sense
all the individuals to whom God belongs and who belong to God, who
form this people or community. They concern them because they are
not just any men—as God is not just any being—but these particular
men and women to whom God has specifically bound Himself and who
for their part are specially bound to God by the divine election of the
community whose members they are and who therefore share its divine
election. These summaries of the command concern the true individuality of man in that they claim him for the cause of God. They put
before him, and prepare him for the fact that as the One He is God
will always continually claim man as the one he is in the whole range
of his life. As God speaks in the events of these summaries, He will
always and in all circumstances speak to each individual, and the one
who is now man as the object addressed in these summaries will always
and in all circumstances be face to face with God, whoever he may be.
God will always say to all individuals : " Be ye holy, for I am holy."
But what this holiness is, and the holiness always required of each individual, they are in all circumstances to learn from these proclamations
of law. That is why they must continually hear them and hand them
on from generation to generation, so that they may rightly hear at
all times the God who always speaks to each individual, not confronting
Him as though He were a stranger, or confounding His voice—the
voice of the Good Shepherd—with other voices. These summaries are,

therefore, in some sense the solemnly proclaimed self-qualifications of God, and at the same time, and by the fact that they are revealed, the solemnly proclaimed qualities of His own, of those with whom He has resolved to speak and whom He has called to hearken to His voice. They reveal the background against which the dealings of God with man are always unconditionally transacted with the urgency and immediacy which characterise them ; the presuppositions on both sides ; the series of divine attributes and human obligations which will form the framework of the particular events of divine commanding and forbidding, of the actual encounters between God and man, of the events in the history of the divine covenant of grace. They distinguish these events from events of other kinds. Therefore the passages in which we have to do with such summaries are not concerned with special commands above and beyond those which God give to His own under the conditions and definiteness of time and space. On the contrary, they speak of the commanding God as such and committed man as such. They show how God and man and man and God are bound to one another—bound in exactly the same way as emerges in the other texts with the descriptions of concrete and definite divine-human encounters, of the definite and special divine commanding and forbidding. They proclaim this interlocking as such. They are, therefore, indispensable alongside the other texts. They form with them a single whole. And the command of God which they attest is no less historical than in the latter, even these proclamations of law being described in the express form of definite historical events. Indeed, we can only say that they present us with a kind of concentrated form—the basic historicity—of the divine command.

For an appraisal of the Ten Commandments, which we will take as illustrating our point (for what follows, cf. Alfred de Quervain, *Das Gesetz Gottes*, 1935 and 1936), it must primarily be noted that their proper and original proclamation consists in such an action as takes place between man and man, i.e., in a direct encounter between God and Moses from which the mass of the people are held aloof by the strictest warnings. In both Ex. 19⁵ and Deut. 5 God's speaking with man is represented as a highly particular and dangerous matter, accompanied by thunder, lightning and the blast of the trumpet, phenomena against which the rest of the people can only take fearful precautions. The man who is fitted to meet and speak with God must be marked out for this purpose, and called and equipped by God Himself. Moses is a man of this kind, but he is the only one in these passages. As a representative of the people, he receives the commands appointed for the ordering of their life. He receives them (Ex. 32¹⁵ᶠ·) on two tables of stone inscribed on both sides. " And the tables were the work of God, and the writing was the writing of God, graven upon the tables." As their first and qualified recipient, Moses is then to give them to the people. But even this seems too direct for the people, and is, in fact, frustrated. Before Moses has come down again from the mountain, and before the people have received the commands, they have sinned with the golden calf, and in view of this event " his anger waxed hot, and he cast the tables out of his hands, and brake them beneath the mount " (Ex. 32¹⁹). In the event, the people finally receive two other tables (Ex. 34⁴, ²⁸) hewn out and inscribed by Moses himself.

Thus the command to Moses—he alone was the man to whom Yahweh spake face to face as a man speaks with his friend (Ex. 33[11])—was from the very outset distinct and different from the command which was later given to the people and received by it. The former revelation was an absolutely unique event between God and Moses. The latter—in a quite different sphere—is simply the attestation of that revelation. This is made unambiguously clear by the whole narrative.

It is to be noted further that, according to the accounts in both Exodus and Deuteronomy (Ex. 34[28], Deut. 5[22], 10[4]), the Ten Commandments are only the peak points of a whole series of special decrees and ordinances. " And Moses came and told the people all the words of the Lord, and all the judgments : and all the people answered with one voice, and said, All the words which the Lord hath said will we do " (Ex. 24[3ff.]). This means that the Ten Commandments belong to the whole corpus of ordinances for the common life, law and culture revealed to Moses and declared by him to the people. It is another question that these detailed ordinances are partly (but only partly) to be read as a commentary on the Ten Commandments, which are perhaps their original and oldest form, or to be understood, conversely, as a summarised extract from them. What cannot be disputed is that the former stand with equal seriousness and weight by the side of the latter and that the latter can properly be understood and valued only as constituting with them a single whole. This means again that the Ten Commandments, revealed to Moses and attested to the people of Israel, are to be interpreted as part of the direction given for the concrete shaping of the people's life in the presence of its God. It cannot be said that this particular part of the direction was singled out for special veneration in the other Old Testament writings—historical, prophetic or otherwise—and that we are therefore constrained by them to isolate it from its immediate context. Nor, above all, can we say that it constitutes a blank sheet which has to be filled by interpretation and is thus susceptible of various interpretations. The fact of the matter is that the Ten Commandments are fairly exhaustively interpreted by their immediate context. These apparently formal and general directions, which seem to be open to various applications, have in reality a very precise content. For example, we cannot really understand by " killing " anything but deliberate murder, or by adultery anything but illicit intercourse between one man and the wife of a third party, or by bearing false witness against one's neighbour anything but malicious false testimony before a court of justice. It has also to be remembered that the reference is always to relationships between members of the people. We are not at liberty to understand anything and everything by these things, but must keep to what they intend to say, and do actually say, according to the clear declarations of the context.

The third point to be noted is this that in the strict sense the Ten Commandments do not contain any direct commands, but only prohibitions or rather delimitations. The holiness of God, and the holiness of man conditioned by it means delimitation, separation, setting apart, as befits the divine election and the position of the elect defined by it. In this context even the command with regard to the Sabbath day, as also that concerning the respect due to parents, has the following meaning. A definite sphere is marked out, but not positively and inwardly. No account is given of what must happen within this sphere. Directions to this effect obviously belong to quite a different plane and cannot be discussed in connexion with the Ten Commandments and the related legislation. We are simply told what must not in any circumstances take place in this sphere, what can do so only in definite conflict with the divine will and as an absolutely reprehensible action on the part of man. It is impossible for the member of the community to which these general and juridical and cultic directions are given to have any other god but the Lord who led Israel out of Egypt. It is impossible for him to make images of this God and worship Him in them. It is impossible for him to use the name of this God for profane purposes. It is impossible for him to work on the day when the Lord rested. It is, therefore, impossible for him to treat his parents without respect (to strike them or curse them, as is explained later). It is impossible for him to murder, or to violate the marriages of others and thus to jeopardise the legitimacy of his neighbours' offspring. It is impossible for him to steal, or to slander, or to covet the goods of others. What must happen positively is another question. But whatever it be, it must not violate these prescribed limits. It cannot be what is here declared to be impossible. *In concreto* many other things not excluded by these terms are illegitimate. But what is excluded by them must not be done in any circumstances. How and in what God always wills to be honoured by His people is the theme of the first four laws, and how and in what He wills to see His people protected against fratricidal strife and self-destruction is the subject matter of the last six. Taken together, they mark off the sphere within which the dealings of God with His people and their conduct before Him and towards Him are to run their course. They are the indication of a definite sphere. The legislation which follows is only a fuller and more detailed form of this indication.

It is a very substantial indication. We can infer from it quite enough in relation to the interested parties. They tell us of a God who has shown Himself unique and incomparable by constituting Himself the Lord and Helper of this people and thus claiming it as His own. Just because He is this free and loving God, He is not interchangeable with any creature in heaven or on earth, or with the likeness of any product of human imagination. He is sovereign, and His name is holy above every other name, and not to be named with any other in the the same breath. And as this sovereign God, He gives His people a place on the earth. In the land which He will give them He promises to show them mercy to the thousandth generation, and to cause their history to move to the Sabbath rest of consummation, just as—symbolically—every working week culminates in the Sabbath. And, again, they tell us of this people as a people from whom the worst is always to be expected. They have to be warned and protected against committing the most blatant sins against Himself and one another. They are inclined by nature (*Heid. Cat., qu.* 5) to hate God and their neighbour. But because God has joined Himself to them and adopted them as His sons they are actually warned and protected against these things. They can therefore live with Him and with one another. The weak are protected from the strong. Justice is done especially to the weak. And the people are secured against self-destruction and dissolution. This is the place indicated by the Decalogue as widened and completed by the legislation which follows. Because it is itself an event—in fact the basic event in the story of Israel—it unfolds the programme of the whole history of this people, or rather of God's dealings with it, of this people as controlled by His guidance, and therefore by implication of the whole history of His elect community—of the Church as it is prepared and announced in Israel and finally derives from Israel. It was not, therefore, without justification that the Decalogue was adopted as the basis of the Christian catechism. It is the foundation-statute of the divine covenant of grace and valid for all ages. Everything that the true God, the Founder and Lord of this covenant, has commanded and forbidden, or will command and forbid, is to be found within the framework of the programme of all His decisions and purposes as contained in the Decalogue. In all His commands and prohibitions it will always be a question of the divine glory and the divine protection as revealed to Moses as a type of the Mediator between God and man, and attested by him to the people of Israel in the summary of the Ten Commandments and the more detailed legislation which follows. The action of the true God and the life of men in fellowship with Him will always be distinguished by these limits from the action of all other lords and from all other possibilities of human life. The only thing is that we must not expect to find here something more or other than a framework and programme of the divine action and corresponding human conduct, and therefore of the real history which takes place between God and man. God will command and forbid within these limits and not elsewhere. But His commands and prohibitions will not consist simply in repetitions and applications of the Decalogue. There would be no sense in giving them an artificial interpretation as if they contained already all the directions in which God requires man's obedience and his life or death is decided. The nature of the relationship founded and ordered by God between God and man, and of the concrete divine directions to man which this relationship involves, is another matter. What these directions are, their aspect and character, is something that we cannot infer from the Ten Commandments or the wider associated legislation as such. On the contrary, we can only find it in the other biblical narratives, in those accounts of the living demand for obedience directed to particular men in particular situations, as, for example, in the direct intercourse of God with Moses on the mount (Ex. 19 ff.). The revelation of the Law as such proclaims who it is that deals with His own in these directions, and who they are that can receive these directions as His own. But it is the event of this direction itself only for Moses, who has to attest it to the people, in order that they, for their part, may be prepared for the reception of this direction, for the further development of the covenant history which will take the form of these events. Later this people is expressly told (Ex. 23²⁰ᶠ·) : " Behold, I send an Angel before thee, to keep thee in the way, and to bring thee into the place which I have prepared. Beware of him, and obey his voice, provoke him not ; for he will not pardon your transgressions : for my name is in him. But if thou shalt indeed obey his voice, and do all that I speak ; then I will be an enemy unto thine enemies, and an adversary unto thine adversaries." The whole history of Israel develops, accordingly, within the framework provided by the revelation of the Law, but not as if this framework were itself the picture : for the latter consists in the special concrete events of divine commanding and forbidding, of human obedience or disobedience, not envisaged in the Law as such. The salvation or overthrow of Israel depends upon whether or not it will hearken to the voice of this angel, to the living voice of Moses and later of the prophets (in the broadest sense of this term), and therefore to the living and never utterly silent voice of God Himself. What is the use of Israel's possessing and observing the Law if it does not do this ? How it sins against the Law itself—perhaps even in a literal sense, but at all events against its spirit even though its letter be strictly observed, and therefore against the meaning and the purpose in which and for which it is given—if it is not obedient to the angel, for whose voice it should have been prepared by the Law and to whose authoritative office the Law bears witness ! How the Law is misused, and made an instrument of sin in the sense finally indicated by Paul, if man considers himself obedient and righteous, and himself wants to bring about the fulfilment of the promise, by keeping the Law—as though he could keep the Law in any other way but by being willing and ready to obey the voice of God who has called Him to Himself in the Law, and willing and ready to be the man—the man committed to this Lord—who is marked as such by the Law ! To keep the Ten Commandments is to take up the position which they outline and define, and in this—the only possible—position to wait for the specific commands of God for which the proclamation of the Law prepares us, to be constantly obedient to His call. The man who does this is righteous and will live. The man who does not transgresses all the Ten Commandments and the whole Law, however precisely his conduct keeps within the limits defined by the Ten Commandments. For without living obedience to the living God, he does not in fact stand in the place to which he is directed by the commandments.

All this becomes still clearer when, again by way of illustration, we turn to the so-called Sermon on the Mount as presented by Matthew. (Cf. for what follows the monograph of Eduard Thurneysen, *Die Bergpredigt*, 1936, which is so illuminating in this connexion.) If it is the basic rule of interpretation, which we must apply to this passage too, that a text must be read in the light of its context, i.e., in this case against the background of the rest of St. Matthew's Gospel, then in this instance it is clear that the decisive character of its contents is to be sought in its special connexion with the theme of God's kingdom as it has come in the person of Jesus Christ in fulfilment of Old Testament prophecy. This is true of the Sermon on the Mount as of other great discourses in Matthew. The special feature of this reference in the Sermon on the Mount consists in the fact that now it is Jesus Himself (as once the God of Moses) who defines, in the form of comprehensive positive and negative directions, the sphere in which He is present with His own, with those whom He has called and will call, the sphere of His care for them and lordship over them. It is the sphere where it is proclaimed and heard and authentic that the kingdom of God has come because and as He, Jesus, has come, because the seventh day, the day of days, has now dawned. The Sermon on the Mount outlines the order proper to this Sabbath day. It cuts across the Ten Commandments in a new dimension not yet visible in them —vertically, on the presupposition of an event coming from heaven to earth. It makes clear what is still concealed there in the expectation of this event—that God Himself in His own person not only faithfully upholds the covenant that He has established with man, but Himself completes it in favour of man and fulfils its conditions. The order which constitutes the life of the people of God— for this is what the Sermon on the Mount is, and to this extent it is only a repetition and confirmation of the Ten Commandments and the whole of the Old Testament Law—is now set in the light of the fact that, as it was founded and proclaimed by God, so now is it fulfilled by Him for man's salvation, which means, however, that the life of obedience for which it prepares and summons man, rejected by the people of Israel in its conflict with Moses and the prophets, is now established and fulfilled by Israel's Messiah for the Israel which has always rejected and now definitively rejects Him, and therefore for all men. In the light of this fact what can the life-order of the people of God be but the definition of the sphere within which men cling to this life of obedience lived out on their behalf and use the grace thus shown to them—the sphere in which they may live with Jesus their Lord who has made Himself their servant and who in this service proves Himself their Lord ? It is of the order of life seen in this light (and in substance it is the same as that described in the Law) that the Sermon on the Mount speaks. It is true that it attacks and overthrows the Judaistic understanding of the Law, the understanding of disobedience. But this is only in some sense incidental. The fact that this understanding is the false under-standing of disobedience only confirms the obvious teaching of the whole of Israel's history. Even more true is the further point that the superior righteous-ness of the kingdom of heaven is revealed by which man's disobedience is un-covered, but uncovered only that it may be at once and finally and effectively covered, and by which the air in which this disobedience can breathe and subsist is dispelled. It is also true that the Sermon on the Mount orders the life of man in the light of the fact that the seventh and last day has now dawned, so that the time which mankind now has, the time of the six worldly and working days, is only borrowed and improper time, the end of all things being at hand and men being able to live only as members of the last age. But this again is only in a sense incidental. It does not constitute the substance and meaning of this order of life. For it is not the end of the old and the beginning of the new æon which forms the nerve of the order proclaimed in the Sermon on the Mount, but the fact that Jesus is both end and beginning, that both are fulfilled in Him, in the reality of the kingdom which has drawn near in Him. That He rules in virtue of His ministry as the Mediator between God and men is even more true than the establishment of the dawning of the last age and the implied necessities, and it is this alone which gives to the eschatological assertion its proper weight and characteristic seriousness. It is also true that the directions of the Sermon on the Mount seem to be objectively concerned with certain problems of human life and the false or correct solution of these problems—the maintenance of life and marriage, the question of swearing and justice, the problem of enemies and the matters of almsgiving, prayer and fasting. But it must not be overlooked that this, too, is incidental and only by way of illustration. And, as in the case of the Ten Commandments, the negative far exceeds the positive. For it is essentially a question of delimitation. That is why it has always proved impossible to construct a picture of the Christian life from these directions. The picture that they offer is, in fact, the picture of the One who has given these directions and of the light which He Himself sheds on the problems raised, and not only on these, but on man as a whole as he stands face to face with Jesus. The Sermon on the Mount is intended to draw our attention to the person of Jesus—to the question of this person—which shows itself, of course, to be the original and (necessarily) the final point at issue in all human conduct.

The Sermon on the Mount, too, is primarily and decisively a notification, a proclamation, a description and a programme. Its imperatives, too, have primarily and decisively the character of indicating a position and laying a foundation. The position indicated and the foundation laid are the kingdom, Jesus, the new man. And these are not three things, but one and the same. The kingdom is the new man in Jesus. Jesus Himself is the kingdom of the new humanity. The new Adam is Jesus the Bringer and Herald of the kingdom. Proclaiming this threefold unity, the Sermon on the Mount proclaims the consummation of the covenant of grace, and therefore the *telos* of the Law and the Ten Commandments. It proclaims the position which in the Ten Commandments was determined and promised to Israel, but only determined and promised and not given. The Sermon on the Mount, like the New Testament as a whole, defines and describes it as something now given. If the Ten Commandments state where man may and should stand before and with God, the Sermon on the Mount declares that he has been really placed there by God's own deed. If the Ten Commandments are a preface, the Sermon on the Mount is in a sense a postscript. The history of the covenant of grace has reached its goal and end. It does not continue in the history of the Church at whose beginning there stands the declarations of the Sermon on the Mount. For time does not continue after the death and resurrection of Jesus Christ. It can only move away from this its centre—moving to its already appointed end. For its end is determined by the fact that it has been given this centre. The Church is the community of God in this time which moves away from this centre to its appointed and already visible end. The covenant of grace as such has no further history in this time. The only question now is whether the Church will live or not live in the fulness of life already granted to it, in recognition or non-recognition, gratitude or ingratitude, in face of what God has finally and once for all accomplished for man, in the freedom which God has decisively accorded to man, or the bondage from which he has been finally and conclusively released, and which has now become a complete anachronism. The Sermon on the Mount, as a postscript, as a document of the completed covenant of grace and its concluded history, defines and describes the freedom which is given to the people of God in its new form as the Church, and which is to be proclaimed by the Church to the whole world.

As an announcement of the kingdom of God, the Sermon on the Mount makes the following declaration. Here on this earth and in time, and therefore in the immediate context of all human kingdoms both small and great, and in the sphere of Satan who rules and torments fallen man, God has irrevocably and indissolubly set up the kingdom of His grace, the throne of His glory, the kingdom which as such is superior to all other powers, to which, in spite of their resistance, they belong, and which they cannot help but serve. The concrete existence of the kingdom of God means not only opposition to this resistance, but victory over it, like an offered checkmate, after which the defeated adversary, if he is not sufficiently intelligent to give up the game, may wonder for yet a few minutes whether there is not the possibility of avoiding it. To the extent that this lack of understanding on the part of the defeated adversary is a fact, the conflict seems as if it would and could go further. The kingdom of heaven seems not yet to have come, or merely to have drawn near, or merely to beckon to man as a future possibility. The Sermon on the Mount reckons with this powerful and fatal appearance by saying of those that weep that they *shall* be comforted, of the meek that they *shall* possess the earth, of those who hunger and thirst after righteousness that they *shall* be filled (Mt. 5⁴ᶠ·). That it is only an appearance, it attests by the fact that its overwhelming and decisive emphasis is not on the future but on the present. It says of those who are poor in spirit that theirs *is* the kingdom of heaven, and again of those who are persecuted for righteousness sake that theirs *is* the kingdom of heaven. Those who hear and believe the message, who do not see a future but a present transformation of the whole world situation, and therefore of that of man—the twilight of the gods completed, Satan falling as lightning from heaven—such begin to live on the basis of this change. Because they hope in what is promised to them by this declaration, they already have it. Because they have understood that the kingdom of heaven has drawn near, they are already called to be its citizens and to participate in its rights and duties, in its active proclamation. That is why it is said : " Ye are the salt of the earth " ; " Ye are the light of the world " (5¹³ᶠ·). By the witness of their own experience, they are exponents of the kingdom which comes and has already come. The new man of the Sermon on the Mount is not, therefore, a beautiful dream or only a divine promise. The Israelite man of the Ten Commandments is this—and it is a good deal. But the new man of the Sermon is a present reality. He is this because Jesus is there, not merely for Himself, but as the Herald, Proclaimer and Bringer of the kingdom, the One who speaks of it with ἐξουσία (7²⁹), because this is His right, because He is the One in whom it comes into proximity with all human spheres, and because with this ἐξουσία He speaks to other real men. As He does this, as He is heard and believed by the latter, the kingdom achieves reality and, in spite of all appearances, unmasking it as appearance, there is human life in the kingdom of heaven. " Therefore whosoever heareth these sayings of mine, and doeth them, I will liken him unto a wise man, which built his house upon a rock " (7²⁴). But in and of himself man is not this—nor can he be according to the evidence of the whole of the Old Testament and of the manner in which Israel reacts to the advent of its Messiah. He can be this wise builder, a μακάριος (5³ᶠ·), and then at once also the salt and light of the earth, only as he hears and does the words of Jesus. No human life is constructed as the Sermon on the Mount depicts it. Who can ever find himself achieving that higher righteousness (5²⁰), or really fulfilling the Ten Commandments and the rest of the Law, as indicated in 5²¹ᶠ· ? For whom can the picture of the truly pious man, the man who rightly gives alms and fasts and prays (6¹ᶠ·), or that of the man who is not avaricious and therefore truly carefree (6¹⁹ᶠ·), or that of the man who refrains from judging his neighbours, ever cease to be a novelty, the picture of a new and different man, as compared with his own state of life ? Most certainly, we are not this. And in view of the notorious non-fulfilment of the Ten Commandments by the people of Israel, it would be sheer folly to interpret the imperatives of the Sermon on the Mount as if we should bestir ourselves to actualise these pictures. Yet the whole picture of the new man which seems to be there unfolded is not a fantasy but a reality. It has not been introduced as a reality by us but for us. We hear and do all this as the Word of Jesus. We must be pleased to allow our very different life to be illuminated by Jesus. This is the point of these imperatives. They demand of us that we be pleased to accept the supremely wonderful and unexpected interpretation of the dark text of our lives by the grace of God which has appeared in Jesus. You wretched ones are truly blessed ! You transgressors and evil doers are righteous ! You hypocrites are sincere ! You victims of the lust for gold and possessions, you prisoners of care, you blind judges of your neighbour are free ! How does this come about ? It comes about by the Word which I speak to you—the Word which contradicts your life, and in so doing catches it and holds it and saves it, interpreting it according to the purpose of its Creator. It comes about by the light which, from the fact that I am in your midst, falls from above upon the tangled skein of your life. It is not by yourself, but by Me. Condemning you, I exonerate you. Judging you, I accept you. Slaying you, I make you alive. The life of the new humanity is that which is interpreted by Jesus and lived out in this interpretation. Of course, it is a life in hope to the extent that it can be lived as new life only as we hear the Word of Jesus, to the extent that man has continually to look beyond himself in order, in that moment to be able to live in this moment the life of the new man. But it must also be realised and said that in this moment it is objectively present as new life. Man does not look only to the future as such, but to Jesus as His only and real future. And this future is not a mere future without present actuality, or a mere promise without present fulfilment. His Word is the truth —not to-morrow only but already to-day—for His kingdom, the kingdom of heaven proclaimed by His Word, is the kingdom of the eternal God Himself, and this God is faithful. That is one aspect of the position defined in the Sermon on the Mount.

As a self-disclosure of Jesus its message is as follows. The kingdom, and with it the new man, has now appeared. For the Lord of the covenant, and therefore the Lawgiver Himself, the Ruler and Controller of life in this covenant, has now in His own person become the neighbour of man and of all human spheres. Because this has happened, the covenant is completed, its history is closed, and the time still left has become a mere running out of time to its appointed end. The Law, as it is given to Israel, and within the framework of which the living voice of God was heard through the prophets, is not revoked by this new indication corresponding to the effected transformation of things. This is strongly emphasised in $5^{17f.}$: " Think not that I am come to destroy the law, or the prophets. I am not come to destroy, but to fulfil." Not one jot or tittle of the Law shall pass away until everything is accomplished—everything that is to be accomplished in confirmation of the already realised fulfilment. Therefore there can be no question of the Sermon on the Mount setting up a new Law in place of the old, or taking up a different position from the old in relation to the covenant. The position is not a new one, but the old one differently expressed. The difference is that the Lawgiver on the mount does not keep back His disciples who are to receive His Law, as God once kept back the people, but calls them to Him, and opens His mouth and speaks to them, as God once spoke to Moses like a man to his friend. What Moses brought down from Sinai was not the kingdom and the new man, but the promise of these ; the definition of the sphere in which the history of the covenant will run towards the kingdom and the new man. As against this, what the disciples of Jesus, and in them the Church, take away from this other mount, is the full reality of the kingdom itself and the new man. For what is ascribed to them is not a law of righteousness but righteousness itself : the righteousness of the kingdom (6^{33}) ; the higher righteousness without which (5^{20}) no one can enter into the kingdom of heaven ; to hunger and thirst after which (5^6) is not, therefore, a question of mere inclination, but a real, the most real determination of human life ; to which every man willingly and wittingly or not, is subject ; but in which no one can participate (5^{10}) without being persecuted for it and therefore having to suffer. It is the fulfilling of all commands (6^{33}), and therefore in itself *the* command. But this can be said only if we mean by it that it is itself the Commander who embodies the command. For righteousness in the Bible is not a constitution and state conceived as an idea or decree, but a deed and action, inseparable from the conception of a human person, in which a wrong state of affairs is restored and reconstituted, and by which those who suffered by the wrongness are helped. Or, more precisely, it is the verdict of a judge, expressed and executed with full competence, who as a righteous helper proclaims and secures the right where wrong was triumphant. This is the righteousness with which we have to do in the imperatives of the Sermon on the Mount. They require a life controlled by the right, by the strictest and most real, the divine right. As is well known, they stand at right angles to the Old Testament Law to the extent that with their " But I say unto you " they exalt into something universal all that is there meant and said with supreme particularity as the forbidding of a transgression of definite limits, giving to everything that is there connected with the outward form of human life a new orientation to the inner life of man, and his existence in its totality. God does not merely forbid killing ($5^{21f.}$), but the contemptuous word, the careless connivance in the existing accusation of another. He does not merely forbid adultery ($5^{27f.}$), but the lustful glance at the wife of another. He does not merely forbid the false oath ($5^{33f.}$), but the oath-taking which encourages human falsehood. He requires order ($5^{38f.}$), but an order which does not need to prevail through violence. He commands love of one's neighbour ($5^{43f.}$), but the love which recognises a neighbour in those who are most distant, and therefore also and especially in one's enemy. This is necessarily the state of affairs in human life when it is controlled by divine righteousness. So complete and thoroughgoing is that righteousness ! And the Word of Jesus which blesses those who hear and keep it, comparing them to wise builders, to the salt and light of the world, creates and establishes this righteousness, setting up this order of righteousness in contrast to every other, in contrast to everything which in the affairs of men is considered to be an order of righteousness, and which in this contrast can only be revealed as unrighteousness. The Word of Jesus as such, performed by those who hear it, is righteousness, and therefore a powerful help to all who suffer from unrighteousness, and in such a way that it proclaims the existence of a man which is controlled by the divine command not only in particular things but integrally, not only outwardly but inwardly and therefore in its totality. This man is obviously the Israelite, the man of Jer. 31^{33}, of whom it is said that God has implanted His Law in his inmost being, and written it on his heart. As it is said to a man by Jesus, and he allows it to be said : Thou art this man !, as he accepts the Word of Jesus and dares to live in the strength of it, righteousness is imparted to him, the unrighteousness that Satan and he himself have brought upon himself is dispelled, and he becomes a righteous man. The grace of this Word, the Word of truth, makes him this. In contrast to the promised grace of the Ten Commandments with their reference to the sphere within which God wills to and will deal with His people, it is the real grace in which God in person has fulfilled His promise, sought out His people, and in His own person led His people to that place and established them there. Thus the grace of this Word is itself the righteousness which comes to man and is to be exercised by him—the higher righteousness of the kingdom. It is better than the righteousness of which, even with the best will and knowledge, the scribes and Pharisees can speak (5^{20}), and it is the righteousness of the kingdom (6^{33}), because it consists directly in the deed and gift of the Lawgiver and Judge, because it is powerfully created and imparted by Him, because it is the living righteousness of those to whom He utters it and who allow Him so to utter it. Those who hunger and thirst after it—which means objectively all mankind— will be filled because He creates and imparts it (5^6). For He has come to fulfil the Law (5^{17}). That is why the Law in His mouth stands at right angles to the Law of the Old Testament. That is why the rigour and fulness of the divine right controlling human life emerges only with the " But I say unto you " which He opposes to the Old Testament Law. That is why this emergence of the rigour and preciseness of the divine righteousness is at the same time and as such an act of real grace—not merely promised but consummated. Jesus has come to fulfil the Law. To fulfil, πληρῶσαι, means always in St. Matthew, and therefore here too, to do and achieve those things—as only Jesus can and does—to which the Old Testament pointed as prophecy and promise. In the person of Jesus the people of Israel takes up the position assigned to it by the Ten Commandments and the whole Law. The newness of the new covenant of Jer. 31³¹ consists in the fact that all Israel, small and great, will know the Lord, to know whom it was invited by the covenant made with the fathers and by the Ten Commandments—an invitation which it was the duty of each brother to extend to his brethren. This original knowledge of the Lord, which does not need any such invitation, has become an event and reality for all Israel in Jesus Christ. He has come to fulfil the Law. He has given God the glory which He ought to be given according to the first table of the Law, and He has fulfilled the purpose of the second table and its demands. He has made true the whole prophecy of the Ten Commandments and the rest of the Law by its fulfilment in His own person. And in His own person He has fulfilled it and made it true for all Israel. In the Sermon on the Mount we see the completion of what Jer. 31³⁴ proclaims as the presupposition of the doctrine of the new covenant : " I will forgive their iniquity, and I will remember their sin no more." That is why He dares to pray in His own name as in the name of all His disciples (6⁹), and to place this prayer upon their lips : " Our Father which art in heaven." That is why the request : " Give us this day our daily bread " (6¹¹), is accompanied by the command : " Take no thought for your life, what ye shall eat, or what ye shall drink " (6²⁵) ; and the prayer (6¹²), " Forgive us our debts," by the realistic observation : " Ye cannot serve God and mammon " (6²⁴). That is why Jesus can count on the fact that there are those (7¹⁷) who bring forth good fruit like good trees, those whose light must shine before men (5¹⁶), so that men may see their good works and glorify their Father in heaven—although naturally the goodness of these fruits and works (7²³) depends absolutely upon the fact that He, Jesus, knows those who bring forth such fruits and do such works, and according to the conclusion of the parable (7²⁴ᶠ·) the question whether the house built by men will stand the shock of storms depends absolutely upon whether he does or does not do the Word of Jesus. Thus the righteousness which the Sermon exacts is inseparable from the One who exacts it. It is His righteousness. It does not consist in the greatness and splendour of what man himself achieves. He may speak as a prophet (7²¹), cast out demons, do many mighty works and yet belong to those who do not know Jesus, and therefore do *ex definitione* that which is against the Law. Everything depends on this ἔγνων ὑμᾶς—on Jesus Himself. Everything depends on the fact that the required righteousness does not now consist in a self-assertive grasping at the promise, in a self-willed desire to fulfil the Law, as though this were an independent Law and not the one fulfilled by Him, as though He were a lawgiver like Lycurgus and Solon, as though He were not the Lawgiver in the sense that in Him it is embodied and fulfilled for all, so that there can be no question of any other objection but to Himself, so that no other obligation can supplant this, so that every other obligation is, in fact, utterly at variance with this one essential obligation to the divine Law. Where it is lacking, man is necessarily (7¹⁵ᶠ·) a false prophet, a wolf in sheep's clothing, a corrupt tree which can only bring forth corrupt fruit, however fine it may appear to be. The righteousness of man required by the Sermon on the Mount consists objectively in the fact that Jesus recognises him as His own, and subjectively in the fact that this righteous man belongs to Jesus, to the people which Jesus confesses in the judgment, which will not be condemned in the judgment (7¹) but will receive mercy (5⁷). What decides his righteousness is not his life and work, nor his confession of Jesus, but Jesus' confession of him. Thus his confession of the fact that the decision rests on Jesus' confession of him is a confession of the divine grace revealed and operative in Him. But this genuine confession is itself grace. Those who keep to the content of it will not boast about it (" Lord, Lord, have we not . . . ? "). That is why the Sermon begins with the blessing of the poor in spirit (5³), of those who are convinced as such by the Spirit, who are poor—absolutely needy—and impotent in themselves, but rich and strong only in the One who pronounces them blessed. The single eye which is the light of the whole body (6²²), the " pure heart " which has the promise of seeing God (5⁸), is the realism of those who accept the decision and Word of Jesus, being pleased to live the life conferred on them by this decision : no more, but no less ; nothing above, or below, or alongside. To do this is to pass through the straight gate, to tread the narrow way (7¹³ᶠ·). For many other things seem more inviting than having the single eye and the pure heart. Many things seem more tempting than the realism of those who are prepared to rely on the Word and decision of Jesus, and therefore content to reckon and confess that they are amongst the spiritually poor. The arrogance which would seize the promise on its own initiative, the delusion which would aspire to fulfil the Law in human strength, the mischievous error of the sick who think that they are whole and in no need of the physician, will always lead men past this narrow gate. This is the parting of the ways. This is the crucial point where the righteousness required by the Sermon is attained or not. At this point sinners are righteous, and therefore on the way to life, and the righteous are sinners, and as such on the way to death. The whole promise of the Sermon (already fulfilled), and its whole threat, are concentrated on this one issue, on this straight gate, this narrow way of the poor in spirit. " Few there be that find it," while the wide gate and the broad way are used by many. It is the uniqueness of the One who has fulfilled the Law for all which is reflected in this relationship of the few to the many. This is inevitable. For the required righteousness is His, the righteousness of the One. He, this One, is Himself the embodiment of the righteousness He demands. In essence, therefore, this righteousness is itself highly distinctive. The existence of those for whom this One is can never be anything but that of brands plucked from the burning. It is grace—election—that we are permitted to live this life ; to be new Israelites, the new men of Jer. 31, the men for whom the position in which we may live with God and unto God is not merely indicated, but actually entered and adopted. The Sermon on the Mount proclaims this grace, this election, because it is the Sermon of Jesus, the disclosure of His person as the One who brings the succour of divine righteousness, who bears and brings and heralds the kingdom. That is the second aspect of the definition of position achieved by the Sermon on the Mount.

And as an indication of the new man as such, the Sermon on the Mount tells us that the new man is called into life by the fact that there is addressed to him by Jesus the Word of the higher righteousness, the righteousness of the kingdom, the Word of the grace of God directed to him. The one who is addressed in.this way, and lives as such, is the new man. By the fact that the kingdom has drawn near to him in the person of Jesus Christ, he has become a new creature. It is not a newness of which he can be conscious and boast, except in Jesus, except in the approach of this kingdom. According to the description of the true saint (6⁴, ⁶, ¹⁸) it is a newness that is concealed from all men and even from himself, and yet a real newness of life. The decision and verdict of Jesus do not take place in vain. Those for whom He accomplished it share in the fact that He and He alone has obediently fulfilled the Law to the glory of God and the salvation of mankind. Those who in themselves are disobedient are claimed and absorbed by the act of His obedience. The kingdom which has come to them in all its strangeness is the reality which is so transcendent and efficacious to them that it cannot remain a merely external fact hanging over them. They themselves have to be within it. It is necessarily made their own. It has to be put in their inward parts and written in their hearts (Jer. 31). The step which God has taken towards man in fulfilment of the history of His covenant of grace with him is a step which He has taken into man, and with which He makes Himself the Lord of man. Thus the Sermon on the Mount—although it is still a description of the standing of man in the light of this fulfilment, and, indeed, as it exactly defines this position—is instruction and exhortation, the training and exercise of man. Every " Thou shalt ! " and " Thou shalt not ! " is seriously meant as an intensified indicative which has the force of an intensified imperative. The man who is reached and affected and determined by these imperatives is the new man : Jesus in His own, Jesus in His disciples, Jesus in those who hear and do the Word of grace spoken by Him, Jesus in those who have recognised and assimilated the higher righteousness of the kingdom which He Himself is and proclaims ; *Jesus* in them, but also Jesus in *them*, Jesus who gives them a share in the fulfilment of the Law as He has accomplished it, and from whom they have received this share as a gift. Because they will possess the earth, they are the meek and to be honoured as blessed (5⁵). Because they will obtain mercy, they are the merciful (5⁷). Because they will be called the children of God, they are peace makers (5⁹). Because their trespasses are forgiven them, they forgive the trespasses of others (6¹², ¹⁴). Because they will not be judged, they do not judge others (7¹). They mete out with the measure with which they are themselves measured (7²). The newness of the new creature is not, therefore, a goodness which he has achieved himself, or which has been imparted to him or infused into him, but simply the goodness promised and done to him in the new position of his proximity to the kingdom of God, his confrontation with Jesus. But it is this very newness as such which has the significance and force of an imperative. To this category there definitely belongs the saying which at first sight seems so strongly reminiscent of a general moral principle : " All things whatsoever ye would that men should do to you, do ye even so to them " (7¹²). The addition : " This is the law and the prophets," obviously means that this is the Law and the prophets in the authentic exposition which it receives from the fulfilment of the promise. This is the conduct of the new man to which the Law and the prophets have referred. The saying stands immediately before that concerning the straight gate, and it has nothing whatever to do with Kant's categorical imperative, or with a recommendation to treat one's neighbour with an amiableness that one would like to receive from him. Jesus did not address this saying to men in general, but to His own, to those whom He called. What can the latter will that people should do to them ? They can only will that they should approach them as the vessels and witnesses of the mercy and forgiveness which they themselves have received and which they need constantly as their daily bread. It is what they have received and would always receive that they are to bring to others. They must not withhold from others the witness which they themselves need to receive from others. Not " give and take " but " take and give " is the golden rule of life for the Israel which stands at the goal and end of the covenant history and is regenerated by the presence of its Messiah. The members of this people love their enemies and pray for their persecutors because it is only in so far as they do this that they can continue to grow as what they are : children of their Father in heaven (5⁴⁴). Because their reward is so incomparable they cannot be content like the publicans and heathen to love those who love them and to greet only their brothers (5⁴⁵ᶠ·). Because they have one Father in heaven, who is τέλειος, who has a total concern, who causes His sun to shine on the evil and the good and His rain to fall on the just and the unjust, they, too, can and must be τέλεοι and as the witnesses of grace have a total concern. And because this is rewarded by their Father in heaven who seeth in secret, they do not need to expect or solicit any other reward—the reward of men, nor will they practise almsgiving, prayer and fasting to be seen and praised of men, but for its own sake, or for the sake of the will of God (6¹⁻¹⁸).

Because they are concerned to lay up for themselves lasting treasures in heaven they cannot allow themselves to be consumed with the toil of amassing transient treasures here ($6^{19f.}$). Because they have one Master who is not mammon, but God, they cannot serve two masters, God and mammon (6^{24})—and " therefore ($\delta\iota\grave{a}$ $\tau o\hat{v}\tau o$) I say unto you, Take no thought for your life" (6^{25}). Because God cares more for them than for the sparrows and lilies of the field (and He does really care for these too), because He knows and does not forget what they need, they can seek first the kingdom and its righteousness, and—as they do this—receive other things in addition (6^{26-34}). Properly speaking, it is not the case that all the astonishing things required bear to some extent the character of an obligatory response. It is true, of course, that (with the *Heidelberg Catechism*) we can and must understand the good works of the new man as the fruit of thankfulness. But this thankfulness, this $\epsilon\mathring{v}\chi a\rho\iota\sigma\tau\acute{\iota}a$ itself must be understood as a primary and fundamental God-given $\chi\acute{a}\rho\iota\sigma\mu a$, as a work of the divine $\chi\acute{a}\rho\iota s$. For the demand addressed to the new creature is the gift in itself and as such. It is the divine mercy and forgiveness, the divine sonship, and the comfort which it brings on every side, the rich and generous reward of those who are called to enter the kingdom of heaven. It is not something which only follows upon this gift, and can, in fact, be differentiated from it. This new man does not live at all if he is not subject to the claim of this demand, if he does not recognise it as rightfully addressed to him. It is his own claim to life, which he cannot surrender and disown. It is suicidal for him to reject it, to refuse to obey it. The saying about not casting that which is holy to the dogs (7^6), and pearls before swine, is relevant in this connexion. It stands between the sayings about judging and about tireless asking, seeking and knocking. If it were only a warning against the imprudent publication of the secrets of the kingdom, it would have no meaning in this position, and would be alien not only to the Sermon on the Mount, but to the Gospel as a whole ; for elsewhere Jesus never warned against such publication on the ground that it could be dangerous to the disciples. But the saying becomes intelligible and important if it is a warning against this suicide on the part of the new man—the suicide of judging, for example, when he himself is not judged but receives mercy, or loving only those who love him when he has as his Father this $\tau\acute{\epsilon}\lambda\epsilon\iota os$, or of being anxious like the heathen when God has pledged Himself to care for him. To do this is to cast that which is holy to dogs and pearls before swine. It is to imperil one's own life in the Spirit. It is to surrender again to a different order of life—to the order, or disorder, which stands outside the sphere of grace, which is far from the kingdom of God, and under the wheels of which man can only perish. The one who does this is like the wicked servant of Mt. $18^{32f.}$ And he need not be surprised if the holy loses its virtue and the pearls their value. Grace must be lived out, or it is not grace. The sayings about the city on a hill and the light under a bushel ($5^{14f.}$) are obviously important in this connexion. The new man lives in virtue of the fact that he does what is described in $7^{7f.}$ He has his Father in heaven who, in a way which far transcends that of any earthly father, is ready to give the good to those who ask Him. The position accruing to the man who lives by the mercy of God, the divine fulfilment of his claim to life, is seen in the fact that he makes use of it —asking his Father, knocking, seeking what he needs, i.e., the mercy which he has already received but must receive ever continually to be what he is. When he does this, he does not give that which is holy to dogs, but is definitely maintained and secured in the order of grace under which he is placed, and all the promises linked to these requirements will be fulfilled to the letter. " For every one that asketh receiveth ; and he that seeketh findeth ; and to him that knocketh it shall be opened." The man who does all this can grasp the fact that God never makes a mistake, and that for all his fallibility he himself will not make a mistake. Asking, seeking and knocking, he will definitely do the will of God. He can only fail to do this if he neglects this asking, seeking and knocking. That this asking, seeking and knocking are necessary, that the will of God, the life of grace, the righteousness of God's kingdom can be fulfilled only when this asking, seeking and knocking continually take place, in a clear reminder, of course, that he who is called to follow Jesus is always as much in need of the Master Himself and His accomplished fulfilment of the Law (5^{17}) as he was on the first day—which means that apart from his relationship to Jesus, apart from what the Father is and gives to him in the Son, he would be no more than the Pharisees on the one hand and the heathen and publicans on the other. Left to himself, he would certainly give that which is holy to the dogs in favour of a system of law or lawlessness. His gratitude would immediately be turned into ingratitude. The goodness of his works would disappear at once. " Without me ye can do nothing." It is not for nothing, therefore, that the Sermon on the Mount has its heart and centre in the passage in $6^{9f.}$ where Jesus teaches His disciples to pray. It may well be said that the whole relationship of Jesus to His own, with which the saving presence of the kingdom of God stands or falls for them, works itself out exhaustively in the fact that He prays for them, and that this means at once that He prays with them and bids them pray with Himself. It is impossible that the Sermon on the Mount should place its hearers in a position of independence over against Jesus, that its directions should have in view a work which they are themselves to accomplish in competition with the work of Jesus. Again, we must not conceal from ourselves nor be astonished at the fact that these directions as a whole are so extraordinary. This is inevitable, seeing that their aim is to call upon men to pray with Jesus, and therefore to enter with Him under the order of grace and never to leave it again. The new life which Jesus has promised and given to those who in themselves are sinners like all other men is so new that even in its reflection in their conduct it appears highly unusual and reminds us all too plainly of the strait gate and narrow way. It has occasionally been said too loudly and confidently that in the examples formulated in 5^{21-48} the radical deepening of the Old Testament Law is not meant to be understood in terms of Law, as so many precepts which we are literally to practise. And it is good that there have always been so-called fanatics who have understood these requirements, and all those of the Sermon on the Mount, as a Law which has to be fulfilled literally. For it is true enough that what we have here are only examples. But it is also true that these examples are intended to make clear that the grace of Jesus Christ, the grace of the kingdom which has dawned, claims the whole man absolutely. It is also true that the only One who really fulfils the Law as understood in this way is Jesus Himself. All others are called to obedience only by the fact that Jesus is obedient for them. It is also true that because Jesus has fulfilled them the radicalised demands of the Mosaic Law are declared and established among His disciples and indirectly in the world as a whole. The uneasiness which this fact causes is very real and cannot be argued away. How can a man pray with Jesus if he insulates himself against this uneasiness, or can handle it in such a way that it ceases to disturb him ? These sharpened requirements point—inevitably—to superhuman possibilities. It would be wrong to say that any of them are inapplicable to us—even the plucking out of the eye or the cutting off of the hand (5^{29}), or the smiting on both cheeks (5^{39})—on the plea that they have been fulfilled by Jesus, and therefore we do not need to fulfil them again, but have to learn from them how great is the distance which separates Jesus from our sinfulness. Far too many things in the Sermon on the Mount and the rest of the Gospel would go by the board on this view. To be sure, these demands and those of all the Sermon on the Mount and the rest of the Gospel, do put us in our place over against Jesus. They do hold up a mirror before us. And, of course, we do have to confess our sin and unworthiness for fellowship with Him. But all the same they do not leave us in that place, nor do they allow us to be content with it. On the contrary, they claim us as sinners—but as those for whom Jesus prays and whom He summons to pray with Him. They insist on the obedience of the disobedient, and the latter cannot elude this obedience by referring to the measure and limit of their capacity. The limit of their capacity becomes irrelevant when that which Jesus the Lord accomplishes for them occupies the centre of the picture which is a norm for their own life's picture. We cannot play fast and loose with the grace of God, as if the supernatural life that it confers could suddenly have only what we judge to be natural consequences. Grace itself decides what is natural in its own sphere. And so we must accept the fact that—whether their fulfilment seems possible or impossible to us—these demands denote modes of conduct which can become possible and necessary even in their literal sense for those who will hear and do the words of Jesus. They show very plainly that the impact which is made on man by the mercy of God revealed and operative in Jesus Christ is something radical and revolutionary. If each individual must first decide about the particular thing that this impact means for him and his life, none has the right to insulate himself against it from the very outset by that over-subtle argument. The existence of the new creature depends on the fact that we stand defenceless in face of the impact made by the Sermon on the Mount as recorded not only in the fifth, but also in the sixth and seventh chapters; that we accept the fact that the sphere in which man is claimed for obedience to God—to the God of grace of the New Testament—is always somewhat greater than we would like to think and have it of ourselves (not giving the glory to this God of grace). That is the third aspect of the position indicated in the Sermon on the Mount.

To sum up, the Sermon on the Mount, too, is from every point of view the indication of a position and the laying of foundations. Parallel in form to the Old Testament Law, and not superseding but confirming it in content, it describes the conditions of life of the people of God from the new standpoint, which sheds a new light even on the Law, that God has set up the kingdom of His covenant of grace with man in such a way that He has now finally and efficaciously translated man into this kingdom in the person of His only Son. This is the event of the kingdom, of the person of Jesus, of the new man, which is reflected in the claims of the Sermon on the Mount. Because the Old Testament Law points forward to this event, its requirements, the conditions of life of the people of God laid down in the Ten Commandments, are not superseded or suspended by the new Law of the Sermon. The people of God needs the prophecy of this event as well as the proclamation of its fulfilment. It lives just as much in and with Israel in Advent as it does as the Church in the light of Christmas. But as it can live in the light of Christmas and not merely in Advent—and this is the new thing in the New Testament witness—the divine requirements of the Old Testament witness, although they have not been suppressed or replaced, have acquired for it the new dimension, the radical depth, which characterises the Sermon on the Mount in contrast to the Ten Commandments, and gives to the latter themselves their true force. That the Law of God demands a life lived from and of and with the grace of God is something which the Sermon on the Mount as distinct from the Ten Commandments clearly shows to be not only the omega but also the alpha of the divine demand. Everything that the Sermon seems to require differently and to a fuller extent than the Ten Commandments rests upon this difference, reflecting the revelation of the fact which is also attested in the Ten Commandments, yet not yet openly, but only in a concealed manner—the actuality of the kingdom, of the person of Jesus, of the new man, the objective existence of man in the sphere of the divine covenant of grace. Israel makes shipwreck on the hiddenness of this objective fact to the extent that the Decalogue is given to it but not the Sermon on the Mount. Without the revelation of this fact the decisive claim of the divine demand is exposed to human misunderstanding and distortion, and the divine Law, as the history of Israel shows, can only be transgressed and broken by man, as he replaces the required life in grace by the arbitrariness of his own works by which he aims to seize and obtain grace, and the life of the promise by the attempt to bring about its fulfilment according to his own ideas and resources. It requires not only a reference to the real fulfilment of the promise, but the real fulfilment itself, to overcome and dispel this misunderstanding and distortion, and so to give effect to the divine Law, procuring for it respect and obedience. It is not by the mouth and witness of Moses, but by the mouth and witness of Israel's Messiah, that the Law gains this efficacy. What man receives from the mouth and witness of Moses—not through any defect in the Law which Moses proclaims, but simply because Moses is only Moses and not Jesus Christ, only the witness of the Mediator and not the Mediator Himself—is merely a disclosure of man's opposition to the divine Law, and as the history of Israel shows, although this disclosure will take place objectively, it will remain concealed from those who are guilty of it. They will not themselves contradict their own contradiction. They will continue to regard their transgression and breaking of the Law as its true fulfilment. They will increase their sin against it. They will disown and repudiate the Messiah Himself while always supposing themselves to be obedient to the Law. It is not until the Messiah Himself comes that the Law can be fulfilled by His death and resurrection. It is He who will reveal the Law as an order of life embodied in His own person, thus bringing His people into the right way, and showing how the forgiveness of their sins is the real beginning of their life with God. It is He who will reveal it in such a way that this life acquires substance and meaning as life lived under a Law that is not transgressed and broken, but kept and fulfilled. Martin Buber is more right than he supposes when he accuses the Jesus of the Sermon on the Mount of trying to go back " into the cloud above the mountain from which the voice sounds," of trying " to penetrate into the primal intention of God, into the primal absolute of the Law, as it existed before it was cast into the mould of human material." He is mistaken, of course, in making this a subject of accusation against Jesus, condemning it as cruelty to a " people which is no more able now than formerly to breathe in the atmosphere of primal purity" (qtd. from E. Gaugler, " Das Spätjudentum," in *Der Mensch und die Religion*, 1942, p. 288). This is the inevitable error of the neo-Pharisaic Jew, and of all those who think they should read and understand the requirements of the Sermon on the Mount in abstraction from the fact that they are reflections of the Messianic event. What necessarily appears to them as cruelty, is in reality the mercifulness of the Sermon and its Preacher just because the voice which sounds out of the cloud, and with it the people " who will be able to breathe in primal purity," have been introduced in its requirements. It is just the life of this people that is described in the Sermon on the Mount.

By this, of course, we do not mean—and here we return to the main line of our argument—that the Sermon on the Mount any more than the Ten Commandments replaces the events in which the life of God's people actually takes its course, and God's dealings with man find expression. The individual concrete directions of Jesus to the men who surrounded Him, and the concrete decisions and ordinances which Paul issued to the community of Jesus Christ in His name —what is described in the New Testament as the guidance of the community, of the apostles and its other members by the Holy Spirit—are no more made super-fluous by the Sermon on the Mount than are the voice and leading of the angel by the Ten Commandments and the whole Mosaic Law. It is not the case that the community and its members, now that they possessed the authentically interpreted and effectually operative Law of God. were left to themselves in respect of their obedience and disobedience, their private interpretation and application of this Law. The Sermon on the Mount as little precludes the con-crete actions and attitudes which are decisive for the preaching of the kingdom of God, the person of Jesus Christ and the new man, as does the Law of the Old Testament all the turns and movements which, according to the historical and prophetic records of the Old Testament, it has necessarily to take as it leads up to the appearance of the Messiah. The proclamation of the divine Law in the Sermon on the Mount and in the other comparable parts of the New Testament is clearly one thing, the outpouring of the Holy Spirit and the new life it inspires is quite another. For all the difference between the Sermon on the Mount and the Ten Commandments, what we have in it is obviously the delimitation of the sphere in which the life of the divine community will be fulfilled under the control of the Holy Spirit. The fact that it is the people which is not only called, and under an obligation, to live in the sphere of the divine covenant of grace, but may and will actually live in it, receiving the Holy Spirit and being ruled by it, is something which is certainly affirmed and decided in the Sermon, for it manifests the kingdom, the person of Jesus and the new man as the conditions of life which are not only promised to it, but created and given by God. Yet the life itself and as such which will be subject to these conditions is not yet lived with this proclamation, but what is given in the proclamation is the basis, the immovable framework and the objective order within which this life may and will be lived. The life itself will always involve a series of events in which there will be a repetition and confirmation of the fundamental event attested in the Sermon on the Mount. The group of requirements addressed to the men belonging to this kingdom will certainly not be greater or smaller than is here outlined. They will have to be prepared to render nothing more or less than the obedience of which we have here a positive and negative description. They are here shown why and for what purpose they will be impelled by the Holy Spirit. How sharply and deeply—if He wills it—God's commanding and forbidding will pierce their lives is something for which they have to prepare themselves by a consideration of this collection of commands and prohibitions. They have neither to exceed nor to fall short of this revealed standard of the life of man in the Messianic time between the death and resurrection of Jesus Christ and His return, because the commanding and prohibiting God who is the Lord of this time will always be the One who has here revealed Himself as at once the Law, the Lawgiver and the Fulfiller of the Law. They will have to recognise the voice of the Holy Spirit and to distinguish it from the voices of other spirits by the fact that, in repetition and confirmation, in elucidation and application of the Word of the Sermon on the Mount, He will lead them into all truth and from one truth to another. But this necessary repetition and confirmation, elucidation and application of the Word of the Sermon, and therefore their progress from one truth to another, will not be their own concern but that of the Holy Spirit. Just how the Holy Spirit, and in the Holy Spirit Jesus the Lord, and in Him God, will in fact govern men is as little foreshown in the Sermon as in the Ten Commandments, and as far as the biblical witness is concerned, it will have to be inferred from other parts of the Old and New Testaments. As " the law of the Spirit of life " (Rom. 8²), which is what the Sermon on the Mount undoubtedly sets out to be, it is wrongly understood if it is not understood as a constant direction to new and particular obedience on the lines it lays down. A man can be obedient to the Sermon on the Mount only in so far as he is ready and prepared for acts of the most specific obedience on the lines it indicates and as God demands them from every man in his own hour and situation ; only in so far, that is, as man is content to fill the position it requires and therefore to feel that he has no other choice but to direct his life according to its claims. What happens in this position will be the good in the New Testament sense, and what happens in any other position will be the evil in the New Testament sense. But as we learn to distinguish in it the voice of the Good Shepherd, and to discriminate that voice from others, again and again we shall have to hear that voice itself afresh in order to hear *in concreto* what this good and bad are, and what *in concreto* the will of God is.

If the Ten Commandments and the Sermon on the Mount seem to be well-chosen and even classical examples of biblical texts which may be plausibly interpreted as expressions of a general law without concrete or specific content, we can now see that this appearance is deceptive, and that the biblical witness knows no such thing as universal moral principles. What it *does* know are summaries of divine commands—as the basis and sphere of the kingdom in which God confronts man either to command or to forbid, as self-determinations of God who does this and the determination of man who experiences the divine encounter, as indications of the relationship in which God utters His definite Yes or No to man's action, as ordinances with which a man must be familiar in order to be able to hear, and actually to hear, the decrees of God which concern his actual life. But obviously the requirements of these texts are neither addressed to an indefinite number of men nor, as regards their content, concerned in general with certain possibilities of human conduct. On the contrary, they belong to the history of the covenant of grace and its goal to the extent that they aim at the conduct of man in his relationship to it. They aim, therefore, at the individual and concrete things which God will command and forbid man in regard to his behaviour in the context of this relationship. They point to God as the Subject and man as the object of a most personal election of grace ; to God as the Lord and Head and man as the member of the body of His community, Israel and the Church ; to God as the Father and man as the brother of Jesus Christ. They describe the union as such between God and man and man and God. They prepare the way for that openness of heart which is not an end in itself but which has to be demonstrated and realised in a specific obedience which is always new. Texts like the Ten Commandments or the Sermon on the Mount do not, therefore, contest but confirm the insight elicited from the many other texts that in the Bible the idea of the divine command is inseparable from the realities of history. A place has to be found for them in the biblical picture of God's dealing with man merely because they make clear its underlying character, presuppositions and intentions. The angel of the covenant and the voice of God heard by the prophets in the Old Testament, and the Holy Spirit in the New Testament, are not a nameless and formless *numen*, but the God whose face bears the features which emerge in the Ten Commandments and the Sermon on the Mount. And so we can also see in these texts the distinctive features of the man who is brought into this relationship with God. This is what these texts make clear. How, then, can they obscure the fact that the relationship between this God and this man is one which is constant and alive and continually renewed ? It was only with post-biblical Judaism, and then unfortunately the post-biblical Christian Church, that this was misunderstood, and the idea arose that all the descriptions of the concrete divine commanding and forbidding should be disregarded and zealously replaced by the command and commands of God in the Mosaic Law and the *nova lex* of the Sermon on the Mount as a kind of universal moral code established in complete detachment from the historical process. And then, of course, it was not an accident that it was thought necessary in both cases to give life and relevance to the biblical divine command (understood in this way) by all sorts of elucidatory appendices, so that, in fact, it was increasingly divested of its divine character and authority. The fundamental misunderstanding had already changed the divine command into a human command. In both cases it was inevitable that it should be shrouded and concealed, like every human command, in a cloud of further legislation which is supposed to make it more effective but, in fact, can only weaken it.

We take it that the result of these exegetical considerations is to prove that in the Bible itself the divine command is always a concrete command. But this being the case, we can now turn to the question which we have answered in our second proposition, viz., that the concrete divine commanding which we find in the Bible must be understood as a divine command which concerns us also. A systematic survey must now be added to the exegetical.

In respect of what it says about God's command, the Bible is a witness to the will and work and revelation of God. Other men—the biblical authors—testify to us, their readers and hearers, that God has confronted other men, the persons of biblical history, in these specific ways, commanding one thing and forbidding another. They attest to us that this is the will and work and revelation of God. This is the fact which must form our point of departure. It may be summarised as follows. We understand from the Bible that a very definite God has entered into relations with very definite men at very definite times in such a way that He has commanded and forbidden very definite actions and attitudes with a view to the conclusion and consummation of His covenant of grace, and later on with a reference back to this event and in relation to His own action. The definiteness of this God and these men results from the fact that this God is the Subject and these men are the object of His eternal election of grace, or, more concretely, that this God and these men are linked together in the person of Jesus Christ. The determination of the times of the divine commanding and forbidding and the determination of the commanding and forbidding themselves result from the way which this God willed to take and has, in fact, taken with these men in the historical process which leads up to the goal of the covenant of grace, and in the subsequent development which follows the attainment of this goal. That this is what happened there and then is the testimony of the Bible. Yet it does not give us this testimony merely out of an interest in the facts or a desire to record them, but in the character of a witness before a court of justice, whose statement is made for the sake of our judgment, and therefore claims our acceptance and acknowledgment of its truth with a view to our own decision and reaction to what is said. The Bible speaks of God's command in order to call our attention not merely to what the will and work and self-revelation were there and then, but to what they are here and now for us ourselves. In its capacity as witness it claims not only our recognition of facts but also our faith, not merely our appreciation of the past events which it attests but also our realisation that matters are still the same here and now, and that as and what God commanded and forbade others, He now commands and forbids us. The Bible wills that we should be contemporaneous with and of the same mind as these other men in regard to the divine command, our hearing and understanding of it, and our situation as affected by it. In this connexion we are to be in every sense the contemporaries of these men. Whether or not we comply with this biblical intention is another question. But it cannot well be denied that this is its intention, and that its texts were conceived and written down with the object of exercising this influence upon its readers and hearers. It is of the essence of the situation in which a witness finds himself that he can be accepted or rejected as such, i.e., with his claim to credibility. But it cannot be denied that since he is a witness he does make this a claim. What he says cannot easily be divorced from the fact that he says it with this pretension. The Christian Church as such, without whose existence there can be no dogmatics and therefore no Christian ethics, assumes that this claim will be accepted, and the biblical witness approved as true. It is on this presupposition that our own thinking must proceed. It is on this presupposition, again, that in this matter of the definiteness of the divine decision we had to dissociate ourselves from the very outset from all those ideas which represent the command of God as a general rule of conduct which has to be concretely filled out by man.

We have now to show how from this assumption we arrive at the opposite conclusion that God's command is always for us also a concrete and specific demand. If the Bible is right in regard to the special witness it bears to God's command, we deceive ourselves about God if we think of Him as a Lord of our life, and human life in general, who gives man certain guiding lines and principles on his way, but then leaves him to his own devices, i.e., to his own understanding of this given norm. But we also deceive ourselves about ourselves if we believe that man is left to himself, and that in this abandonment he is compelled and competent to be the interpreter of the divine norm and therefore to be his own judge, although in some way bound to the divine Law. If the will and work and self-revelation of God of which the Bible speaks apply to us too and are normative for us, if the dealings of God with man never take place in any other way but that described in the Bible, if the dealings of God with man are in point of fact summed up in what is for the Bible the focal point in these dealings, namely, the consummation of the covenant of grace, the fulfilment of the divine election of grace in the person of Jesus Christ to which everything else that may be classed under this heading can form only a preparation or an appendix, then the thesis to which we have referred is proved to be impossible on both sides, in respect of God on the one side and of man on the other. For God is not far from us but near—the living Lord of the people who both in eternity and therefore in time is faithful to them both as a whole and in regard to each of its members, not turning to His people only to leave them to themselves, or having mercy on them only to abandon them to the decisions of their own wisdom, but approaching them to go with them truly and wholeheartedly every step of their way. And again, man is not far from this God but near—actually or virtually a member of the community of God, of Israel and the Church, who either has been or will be called as a member of this body, who either has been or will be freed by faith in Him. A God of any other description than this does not exist, the Bible tells us. And it tells us with equal definiteness that a man of any other description than this does not exist. All other gods and men are creatures of our imagination opposed and dispelled by the reality attested in the Bible. And this leads to the further conclusion that a divine command conceived as a general rule of morality does not exist, or exists only in our imagination as a shadow and caricature of the real command of God which is opposed and dispelled by the living reality of the divine command to which the Bible bears witness. The real command of God has the same aspect as it bears in the Bible as an event of commanding and forbidding, obeying and disobeying, between the God and man of the Ten Commandments and the Sermon on the Mount. The good required by the command of God is not a general and intrinsic good, as is presupposed in every moral scheme, but the good of the divinely controlled history of the covenant of peace and its subsequent developments, the good of God's eternal election of grace, the good which bears the name of Jesus Christ. As God and man do not confront each other in empty space, but in a given space-time situation, so the divine decision and judgment about man, and the divine command as its underlying point of reference, are integrally bound up with this history and its sequel. What God wills and works in this history and its sequel—and in both cases for the sake of Jesus Christ—is the good. And the good of the command which He addresses to man, by which He invites him to be a participant, bearer, object and witness of His will and His work— the good of this history and its sequel cannot in any sense be separated from the latter. Whenever God commands according to the witness of Scripture, there can never be any question of the fulfilment of an ideal of human conduct as such, but always of an action which is integrally connected with the establishment and proclamation of His covenant, with His promised kingdom which has now drawn near. There can never be any formal question of the performance of something good in itself, but always the material one of the execution of a commission or partial commission in the service of this cause. According to the command of God as it is understood in Scripture, like Abraham, Moses or David, Peter or Paul, the centurion of Capernaum or the rich young ruler, we constantly experience one of those greater or lesser movements of hope or gratitude, of expectant or fulfilled joy, performing those ministrations of the servant or child which are good because they are necessary as a vital act of the divine community in its members, as an expression of the true Israel and the true Church, and their fulfilment is part of the earthly existence of the divine people and its vocation, and therefore a divinely appointed task. For it is of divine appointment, and can only be of divine appointment, to have a part in this work. This commission, and therefore what is required of each individual in a specific time and situation, whether it be great or small, cannot be undertaken by anyone out of nowhere, nor can it be self-prescribed and self-appointed. There are here no questions of reflective appraisal or arbitrary decision, however wise. The Lawgiver and Judge, who alone is competent in this matter, will Himself dispose and decide. Who He is, and who man is who is subject to Him and has to obey Him, cannot be hidden here, in analogy to the biblical relation and occurrence to which we are called by the witness of the Bible, just as the basic matter at issue—both in small things and great—is not concealed. From God's side nothing is hidden at this point. Man will be and actually is told what is good and what the Lord requires of him—and with absolute definiteness, so that only obedience or disobedience remains, and there is no scope for his free appraisal and will in regard to the shape of his obedience. At the place where God encounters man—according to the witness of Scripture—He will always require of him specific things; and then—also according to the witness of Scripture—man in obedience will always have to do this one thing, while everything else can only be disobedience.

But if the Bible is right in its witness to God's command and we must accept this witness, we are not only in some sense theoretically instructed *how* God commands and forbids us too. This is certainly the case. The Bible gives us a basic orientation concerning the God who commands and forbids us, concerning ourselves, concerning our position with regard to Him, and finally and above all concerning the fact that the divine commanding and forbidding is always a specific concrete decision in which we are confronted by God as Lawgiver and Judge, according to which our own decision has to be directed and by which it is appraised, without our being able to change it one whit. But that is not all. The Bible not only instructs and guides us concerning the command of God, but also attests and mediates its revelation. It tells us, not only that God does demand and how, but also what He demands. Its voice, the voice of the Word and command to which it testifies, is the divine secret, the divine criterion, the divine judgment with which we have to do in all our decisions from one moment to another, in all that we do and do not do.

This does not mean, of course, that we possess in the Bible a kind of supernatural register or arsenal containing all sorts of counsels, directions and commands, each one of which has an even more supernatural connexion with the life situations of men in the most varied circumstances, so that we have to be on the look out for direct hints, and if possible—it has, in fact, been done—to consult it as a kind of box of magic cards. When it is used in this way, the historical uniqueness of its contents is necessarily overlooked ; the unity of its actual connexion is destroyed ; it is itself profaned ; and the specific concrete command of God which it really attests is surely missed. What is undoubtedly the wonderful richness of its real relevance to us men, and our times, and life in the inexhaustible fulness of its development and forms, consists in the unity underlying all the details of its content.

It is the case, then, that both as a continuous whole and in its individual parts the Bible attests the existence of God as the Lord who rules over us, but who discloses this divine existence in the act of His lordship and work, and His work as that of establishing, maintaining and confirming the covenant of grace. This Lord in the fulfilment of His work is the biblical Word. Those who accept the witness of the Bible submit to the truth of the Word which is identical with this work, and those who do not accept this witness—although they do not submit—still stand under the truth of this Word. For the Lord in fulfilment of this work is the Lord of the whole world and—whether He is recognised, loved and honoured or not—the Lord of each individual life, who is present with every man at every time and in every situation in life, and confronts him to judge and recompense not only in the greatest things but also in the smallest, not only openly but also in secret. The voice and witness of the Bible is God the Lord in the fulfilment of His work. In the fact that it proclaims this objectively it declares to us in fact, not only that God's command commands us and how, but what it commands us. This Lord in the fulfilment of His work is Himself the divine command. And by the very fact that He is the divine command, the latter is concrete and specific and relevant to every moment and action of every human life. Therefore the Bible is the source and norm and judge of all ethical disciplines, not as a pack of cards, not as it is divided and dissolved into a multiplicity of timeless revelations of the divine will unrelated to history, but in the historical unity of its content. And its Word is to be understood and valued as a Word of command (and not merely as ethical instruction, as a collection of ethical principles or example). God the Lord in the fulfilment of His work, who constitutes the historical unity of the Bible, is rich over all and for all, abounding in counsels and purposes for all, and working in all things, in the whole space-time multiplicity of their existence. And He is rich as He lives and acts and speaks. If He is present with them, confronting them in life and speech and action, then concrete commands are issued. But if the meaning and substance of the biblical testimony is the revelation of the reality of God in His works, then we cannot avoid the conclusion that the Bible itself is this Word of command. The Bible itself does not only give instruction or formulate rules or furnish examples. It issues decrees. It effects decisions. It makes us responsible by continually commanding this or forbidding that. When we say the Bible, we do not mean, of course, the Bible *in abstracto*. We do not mean the biblical authors—Moses and the prophets, Matthew and Paul—in their own name, but the God to whom they all bear witness. But this God does not speak in this way without their witness. This God speaks in His reality revealed by their witness. This God speaks as the Lord whom they attest in the fulfilment of His work in the establishing and maintaining and preserving of His covenant of grace. The Bible alone of all possible witnesses attests His revelation and therefore His Words and acts. In practice, therefore, this God and the Bible, His commanding and its commanding, are not to be separated. If there is no abstract authority in the Bible, there is no abstract authority in God. If the Bible is the living speech of God only in so far as it attests it, the living speech of God cannot be other than that attested by the Bible. It follows, then, that by the biblical witness we are not only called and set, as already formulated, in an analogous position to the biblical relationship and occurrence between God and man. We are not only invited to be contemporaneous and likeminded with the biblical men. We are not only exhorted to hear the command of God as they heard it. But at once the God who has spoken and acted in relation to them also becomes our God in virtue of their witness. And so the command given to them and heard by them becomes directly the command given to us and to be heard by us. Their task becomes our task. They and we are not identical, nor is their time or situation ours. In so far as everything is different as seen from below, here and now God must speak to us as then and there He spoke to them. But the divine command which can and will be given to us, and heard by us, even though then and there it was uttered once and for all, cannot either formally or materially differ from that which was given to them and heard by them. The Ten Commandments, and the Sermon on the Mount, and the other ordinances of the Bible, and all the specific individual directions in which we hear the God of the Old and New Testaments speak in a specific way to particular men, concern us directly and not merely indirectly. That is, they do not concern us only when we have discovered a translation and application of those commands in which they may seem practicable, but absolutely in their historical concreteness and singularity. They demand that in our own very different external circumstances we should not only act *like* Abraham, Peter, the centurion of Capernaum, the Israelites or the Church at Corinth, but again act as those who then and there were addressed by God, allowing the command given to them to be again, in our very different time and situation, the command given here and now to us, and therefore ranking ourselves with them, and in their divinely addressed person taking our place in the history and sequel of the covenant of grace, accepting and fulfilling our mission, or partial mission, not as something new and special, but as the renewal and confirmation of the task laid upon them. We cannot aspire to get beyond the existence of the Israel, and hidden in it the Church of Jesus Christ, which then and there moved towards and derived from the fulfilment of the covenant of grace. The people of God in *all* its members and in the whole life of its members can only be this people—Abraham and Peter. It can only live out its own history in this utterly unique history and its sequel, and therefore recognise in the wholly concrete commands and prohibitions once given to the people of God the ordinances and commands given to itself. The witness of the Bible does not, therefore, refer to a temporary expression of the divine command which we have to divest of its temporary character if we are to deduce from it an eternal content valid for us. It refers to the divine command which has eternal and valid content for us precisely in its temporary expression, and demands that we should hear and respect it in our very different time and situation. If we take it in this way, the concreteness and definiteness of the divine command need not be our concern. As the Word of the God who is eternally rich, and speaks with living power in His eternal riches, it has these qualities in itself and therefore for us—to be perceived by us if only we will listen to it, if only we will take up the position which it calls us to adopt, if only we will again allow ourselves to be addressed as those to whom it was given then and there, if only we will accept it as also meant for us. The realisation depends, of course, upon whether we do accept this, whether we allow that the biblical witness is right. If we do, then the command certainly confronts us with concrete and specific content.

We have presupposed that we are willing to do this. We have rested our argument on the fact that the Christian Church, and therefore all that we here adduce in understanding of God's command, is founded upon the assumption that the biblical witness speaks the truth. But this presupposition is not self-evident. We can see this from the inferences here drawn from it. It is by no means the case that even what we know as the Christian Church, even those of us who call ourselves Christians, have taken this presupposition so sincerely and unreservedly that we see this insight as an obvious deduction. There can be little doubt that to a very considerable extent the so-called Christian Church and we so-called Christians do live and think as though the biblical witness is not the truth, as though its " Thou art the man ! " is not to be taken quite so seriously, or at any rate quite so literally, as though when we answer the question what the divine will requires of us we have to take into account all possible voices alongside or apart from the biblical commanding and forbidding, with the result that the present inference can only affect us as a very curious paradox. For the present we must be content merely to report, as it were, that if the presupposition is seriously made and accepted, the deduction is also valid that in its biblically attested form the commandment of God is the concrete and specific command which concerns us also, that it is not merely instruction, regulation or example, but is itself the demand with which we ourselves have to do both here and now and always and everywhere. But the truth of this point of view does not depend upon the fact that we realise it when and because we have fully and seriously made the requisite presupposition. We have not only to reckon with the fact that the so-called heathen world unreached by the biblical witness—both outside and inside the sphere of the Church—is not capable of this insight.

We must also and especially remember that it is to a large extent hidden from the Church and Christians too—even from the best of us—because we have not really made the necessary presupposition fully and seriously, or realised radically enough what obedience to Scripture entails. We do, no doubt, regard the Bible as in a specific and perhaps good sense the normative Word of God. But over a large area, and perhaps with only insignificant exceptions, we think and live as though this were not the case. It is no wonder that the sense of our confrontation by God's specific and concrete command, which is always an event, is so rare and superficial. But it is not our awareness of this point, or the awareness of the Church or the world, which decides its truth. For, in the last resort, what is even our keenest awareness of it in comparison with its truth? That God is the immediate Lawgiver and Arbiter of all our actions is true even when we do not know and consider its truth, even in and over the terrible ignorance and thoughtlessness with which we constantly face this truth. We stand under the arbitrament of God's precise and definite command and prohibition, not as and because we realise it and think of it, but as and because He has issued His command once and for all, and therefore for us and our times and all the situations of our lives, in and with the history, and its sequel, of His covenant of grace. For by this covenant we are not only embraced by the fact of the death and resurrection of Jesus Christ, whether as believers or unbelievers, righteous or unrighteous, saved or lost, and always as both in the specific meaning of the election of grace fulfilled in Jesus Christ. We are also embraced (and closely so, without any empty or neutral zones) by His living command through which He wills to sanctify us, attract us to Himself, and therefore awaken us to obedience, as partners in His covenant. However we react to it, we are confronted and claimed by this command, which wholly embraces and accompanies our whole life, not only in accordance but in and with the fact that this happened to biblical man, the original and proper witness of the person and work of God, His severity and His mercy.

3. THE GOODNESS OF THE DIVINE DECISION

We understand by goodness the sum of all that is right and friendly and wholesome : the three taken together. If we subtract two, or even one of the three, we are not speaking truly or seriously of goodness. What is merely right and not also friendly and wholesome is not goodness. What is merely friendly and not also wholesome and right is not goodness. And what is not right and friendly is not wholesome. God and His command are good in the full sense of the term—genuinely and truly good. We are speaking of the One whom the Bible calls God, and of what the Bible calls His command. Any evaluation of the idea of the good to the exclusion of even one of its aspects involves a loss of the idea of this God and His command. On the other hand, every dissolution of the idea of this God and His command entails a dissolution of the idea of the good. This is so because the two conceptions are synonymous. God and His command are good, and the good is God and His command. We must emphasise this because the idea of God and His command are absolutely and unquestionably prior to the idea of the good. The good is a perfection predicated of God and His command. God and His command comprehend all that is right and friendly and wholesome. In this far-reaching sense the command as a divine decision is a kind decision. God establishes the right, doing what is appropriate and creating order, by making a decision about man in His command. But He is moved to do this by His friendliness and goodwill to man. And what He purposes and effects is man's welfare, salvation, life and eternal joy in His presence. When man encounters God's command, he is confronted by the decision of God which is kindly in this broad sense. Without prejudice to its sovereignty and definiteness, or rather in its true sovereignty and definiteness, this divine decision is the decision of God's goodness. When it is rightly declared, its proclamation, like that of the divine election of grace, is *evangelium*, good news. Those who have the task of carrying it out must remember that they have to declare something good—the very best—to others. And those who may hear it, and hear it rightly, have every reason to be grateful because the good—the very best—is announced to them. But however the proclamation of God's command is performed and received, we must remember that the case is always objectively as follows. The command is God's good decision. In it, man does not meet with any injustice, or harshness, or injury. In it, God is not against man, but in all His glory for him. We bear in mind this objective reality when, over and above all the embarrassments and misunderstandings caused by the human element in the proclamation and hearing of the command, we remember that inherently and as such, as it proceeds out of the mouth of God, it is unquestionably the instrument of His election and covenant of grace, that it is called Jesus Christ, that it is nothing but the birth and life and death and resurrection of Jesus Christ, and His revelation as it is attested by Moses and the prophets, the Evangelists and apostles. This essential theme lies behind the command of God even in its most imperfect declaration, and even where it is most imperfectly understood there is always at the back of it the objective fact that this is the decision of the divine goodness. It is, therefore, a challenge to obedience, and the full meaning of disobedience to it can only be established and disclosed in all its frightful impossibility against this background. It is the norm and criterion of what we do and do not do. We must pass judgment on ourselves according to the command of God's goodness, and we shall always be measured and judged by this command.

We have often touched on this element in the idea of the divine command as the divine decision. But we must now emphasise it again because it is adapted to give an indispensable final clarification not only to the idea of the sovereignty but also to that of the definiteness of this decision. When we spoke of the sovereignty and definiteness of the divine command we had to underline the particularity both of God in His relation to man and of man in his relation to God. We had to mark off this element of particularity from the wrong idea of universal truth and validity both in regard to the divine work generally and the divine command in particular—an idea which in itself has nothing to do with the will and command of God. God confronts man in an individual and solitary relationship when He gives him His command and prohibition, and again man stands before God in an individual and solitary relationship when he has to receive this command and prohibition. This is what happens when *God* makes man responsible and therefore when He makes him really responsible. What this means finally became clear to us especially in our consideration of the particularity of the divine decision. God intends and finds and reaches man in the most detailed way when He gives him His command. He does not give us a selection of possibilities between which we must decide according to this or that rule. He confronts us with a concrete necessity in relation to which obedience puts us in the right and disobedience in the wrong. This specific necessity is always at one and the same time the sovereign and definite will of God. At this point, however, it is important to think again and in particular of the goodness of the divine decision. This is the secret and truth of the concrete encounter between God and man. It characterises that element of singularity and solitariness which cannot be sufficiently emphasised. It differentiates the latter from an isolation and fortuitousness which are not at all true of the encounter between God and man, but can only be a caricature of what really takes place. The goodness of the divine command is something universal; the universal truth and validity of God in this specific relationship. That God is kind in His commanding and forbidding is always and everywhere important for every man in every situation because in this truth consists the inalienable and unchangeable substance of all His commanding and forbidding, because His goodness is His very essence. Because God is rich in His goodness, His commanding and forbidding are not uniform, but particular, and therefore so manifold. But because God is rich in His goodness, this universal element persistently lives and works in the particularity, in all the manifoldness of His commanding and forbidding, as a bond of peace, which prevents the particular from becoming the isolated and the fortuitous, not allowing the manifold to split up and disintegrate, but uniting and holding it together as a single whole. Whatever God wills and demands in the sovereignty and definiteness proper only to Him, in the great singularity and solitariness of His decision, it is always the case that He loves the right, that He is friendly, that He wills and effects what is wholesome. He wills what He wills, and demands what He demands, in the process of realising His eternal counsel formed in Jesus Christ. He wills and demands it in the sequence of His acts, which form the history and its sequel of His covenant of grace. As we have at all points interpreted both the sovereignty and the particularity of the divine command in this connexion, we have now to retract nothing of what we have said concerning its particularity. But we have now to clarify further this specific element by saying that though it distinguishes it does not divide, and that it does not distinguish without welding together and uniting. That the command of God has this specific character does not mean that it dissolves itself into a chaos of individual conflicting intimations to individual men in individual situations. And, similarly, the men addressed by the divine command are not split up into a chaos of alien and conflicting individuals, each of whom is placed in a different relationship to the commanding God from his neighbour ; nor is the life of the individual man disintegrated into a chaos of diverse temporal existences in which he stands in different unrelated and conflicting relationships to God. This might well be the case if the real God was a capricious God, capriciously determined, and if the divine commanding and forbidding were simply the execution of His whims. We must constantly be on our guard against this fiction and its evil consequences. We must always make sure, in regard to the revelation of the real God, who and what He is. The real God and His commands are good. This puts an end to all possible errors concerning the sovereignty and particularity of His decision. Because it is the decision of His goodness, it is not disorderly nor does it operate chaotically, but it establishes and creates fellowship : fellowship as the inner connexion of all that God wills and requires yesterday, to-day and to-morrow, from this or that man, in this or that situation ; fellowship as the inner connexion between all those who hear and accept His will, but also as an objective inner connexion between all those who do not do so ; and finally fellowship as the inner connexion binding into an integral whole the life of each individual. Because the goodness of God is the one thing in which He is rich, it is also the one thing in which His command as it addresses the individual is particular and diverse. Again it is the one thing, and the universal thing, which He says to each individual in particular and to all of them in common, and which they all have to hear in common. Again, it is the one thing which is for each individual the constant factor in all that God has to command and forbid him on the various stages of his path.

1. Because God and His command are good in this full sense of

the term, the divine will may not be atomised, as though in the last resort it consisted in, or could be resolved into, the fact that different men in their different times and situations received specific divine intimations; as though it could be related closely, and even identified with the needs and urges and instincts of the individual life. What corresponds so closely with the voice of our inner man, or is indeed identical with it, is not in any case the command of God, for even if we tried to distinguish them conceptually from our own impulses, we could not say of its atomised dictates, addressed exclusively to individuals, that they even remotely fulfill the idea of the good—except, perhaps, that they sound very friendly to us. For the same reason, the divine will cannot be split up into different commands for the men of different epochs, or nations, or social groups, or spheres of life— for example into a multiplicity of religious, moral, economic, scientific, artistic and political dictates. If by divine dictates we understand the νόμοι, rules, maxims and usages, customs and agreements which have emerged and shown themselves useful in these various spheres of life, we cannot deny that these dictates exist, or that there are very considerable contradictions between them. But it is not the case that there are also these discrepancies in God's command, that it, too, contains these inner contradictions, so that it now demands something right which is not also friendly, now something friendly which is inconsistent with what is wholesome, now something wholesome which is in contradiction with the right. We may believe that this technical and departmental wisdom is unavoidable in practice. But if we do it is entirely on our own responsibility. It has no foundation in God's command. On the contrary, it is necessarily limited and relativised by this command. We recognise the divine command in all times and places, nations and spheres of life, by the fact that it is good in the full sense of the term. For this reason, the divine command cannot be split up even in view of the fact that it concerns both our relationship to God and our relationship to other men, our natural being and our being under grace, our outer life and our inner life, our position in the Church and our position in the state. It cannot be divided into the Christian command on one side and natural ordinances on the other. However varied it may be in its concrete content, it is the same in both connexions, and recognisable as the divine command by the fact that nothing can be added to its goodness on the one hand or subtracted from it on the other, just as nothing can either be added to the one God Himself or taken from Him. Either we hear it as the command of His goodness (even though it is a command to shoot) or we do not hear it at all (even though it commissions us to preach). Either we obey it in the unity in which it is always and everywhere true and valid on the various planes which call for consideration, or we do not obey it at all. We love, or we do not love. We are grateful or ungrateful. It is at this point that the fundamental cleavage, the real contradiction, begins. It is not in God Himself or in what is commanded us. What is commanded is always and everywhere that we should allow ourselves to be summoned to penitence by His goodness.

We will first illustrate this unity of the command itself by a study of the paranetic chapters of the Epistle to the Romans (12^{1-15}, 13). Paul seems sometimes to have known, and sometimes not to have known, the congregation at Rome and its members, circumstances and problems. It is difficult, therefore, to be sure whether and to what extent the imperatives and directions in this chapter are to be regarded as comparable with many passages in the Epistles to the Thessalonians, Corinthians and Pastorals and taken as direct exhortations, or whether they are to be thought of like the Sermon on the Mount and interpreted as a general indication of place and order for the outliving of the Christian life by the Christians at Rome. Passages like those about the political responsibility of Christians (13^{1-7}), or the discourse about the attitude of the " strong" towards the " weak " in the congregation, can be properly understood only as very direct and special intimations. But as against that the rest of the material relates it more closely to the indirect formulations of the divine command. The distinction is not important for our problem. There can be no doubt that in these chapters Paul has given a discursive and comprehensive—if not exhaustive—account of what he thought could be more narrowly stated as the will and command of God for the active and passive conduct of the members of a Christian congregation, and of this one in particular. And there can be no doubt that these essentials of Christian living which he tries to bring out in the form of exhortation (παράκλησις) form for him a single and indissoluble unity.

We must first notice the external unity of what Paul has to say. He speaks expressly (12^3) to " every man that is among you," according as God hath dealt to every man the measure of faith. Every man must " be fully persuaded in his own mind " (14^5). Everyone of us must please his neighbour for his good, and that of the whole community, to edification (15^2). Everyone " shall give an account of himself before the judgment seat of God " ($14^{10, 12}$). " The God of patience and consolation grant you to be likeminded one toward another according to Christ Jesus, that ye may with one mind and one mouth glorify God, even the Father of our Lord Jesus Christ " ($15^{5, 6}$). Thus it is not the case that any member of the community can evade what Paul proclaims as the divine command by suggesting that there is for him another law, that in one regard or another he stands under a different order and necessity, and is not, therefore, required to obey what Paul dictates, except perhaps in part or in a particular respect. Diversity there certainly is, but only within the bounds of the one Law which is asserted here. The form of obedience varies, but it is always to this one Law, just as gifts of grace (12^6) are all gifts of the one grace, and members (individual Christians in the distinctiveness of their personal calling and task) are all fellow-members of the one body of the community. Again, it is not at all the case that, apart from what he has to put before the community and Christians, Paul has to reckon further with the existence and relevance of another will and command of God determined and valid for other men and other planes of life. That which is a Law for the community is the Law of God. What Christians, transformed by the renewing of their minds (12^2), are to prove—the bar before which they must stand—is the will of God : what is good, and acceptable to Him, and perfect. It is obvious that neither for them nor for others has the form of this passing world any significance as a source of law and principle. Neither for them nor for others is it their reasonable or relevant service to conform to it. The service of God which is required is *the* reasonable service. There is no good apart from that (12^9) to which they must cleave, no evil apart from that which they must abhor. They have to pay heed to the good (12^{17}) which by its very nature will prove and commend itself as such in the sight of all men. They have to overcome evil with good (12²¹). Without losing sight for a moment of the Christians to whom it is addressed, the demand for political responsibility is expressly directed to every man (πᾶσα ψυχή). Paul does not need to trespass the limits of specifically Christian exhortation to speak also of this matter, nor does he need to refer to any law of nature. And notice that, when he comes back from this apparently generalised human address to the apparently peculiarly Christian command to love (13⁷⁻⁸), he deliberately effaces the distinction which there seems to be between the two very different spheres. Hard on the challenge to owe nothing to state ordinances and their representatives, to give them in every respect what is their due according to their divine institution : " tribute to whom tribute ; custom to whom custom ; fear to whom fear ; honour to whom honour " (13⁷), there comes with an almost confusing change of viewpoint, but obviously for Paul in essential continuity, the summons that Christians should see and fulfil their whole obligation by loving one another, that in reciprocal love they are to build up and maintain the Church and so fulfil the whole Law, thus proving themselves to the world, and accepting their basic responsibility to the divinely instituted order of the state, not out of fear, but because they know the will of God (διὰ τὴν συνείδησιν, 12⁵). Similarly, the insights developed in the passage 14¹–15³ regarding the relationship of the " strong " to the " weak " in the community (14⁹) have their basis in the fact that Christ is the Lord of the living and the dead, and, again (14¹⁰ᶠ·), that we must all appear before His judgment seat, as we read in Is. 49¹⁸ : " As I live, saith the Lord, every knee shall bow to me, and every tongue shall confess to God." And when finally Paul compares the relationship of the strong and the weak in the community to that between Jewish and Gentile Christians, or even between Israel and the heathen world as such, his final peroration is almost lyrical in quality : You must receive one another, because Christ has received you all, because He has made Himself both a minister of the circumcision in fulfilment of the promise to Israel, and the Lord of the Gentile world in virtue of the fact that the mercy of God is the meaning even of the promises made to Israel. Because in Christ all are chosen and called to thank and praise God, there must be reciprocal acceptance in the Church. Even in regard to the outward form of this Pauline exhortation, we cannot say that even the least trace of an atomisation or disintegration of the command may be detected, although there is, of course, an obvious diversity of its expression in particular cases.

That the will of God is one in spite of the diversity of its expression emerges even more clearly when we analyse the inner roots of Paul's exhortation. In this connexion, it must be emphasised that the expression for what Paul does when he proclaims the will and command of God to the community is παρακαλεῖν (12¹), which signifies both exhortation and comfort ((cf. 15⁵). In face of the utter misery of human existence, which is theirs, Paul comforts them by exhorting them. And he exhorts them and invites them to live in faith by comforting them and strengthening their faith. He beseeches them by the mercies of God. He does not appeal, therefore, to their reason, insight and freedom, nor to their own goodness, but to their acknowledgment of the goodness of God. According to Paul, what God wills from them has its foundation and meaning and authority in the fact they are men who have experienced and known the mercy of God ; they have felt and tasted how gracious the Lord is. This is the ground of all exhortation, and it is on the basis and in attestation of it that Paul exhorts them. We certainly ought to notice at this point the connexion between 12¹ and the conclusion of 11, where in v. 30 the thought had been developed that Christians and unbelieving Jews must confess that they are those who because of the steadfastness of God's promises can live by God's mercy alone, and may and should actually live by His mercy. Even in this matter too, as a Christian moralist, Paul speaks as an apostle of Jesus Christ, " through the grace given unto me " (12³), and not therefore as though at this point a new task were taken in hand or a new principle or method used. What Paul is about to proclaim as a divine command is also the Gospel—the one thing which he has to declare in the whole Epistle. Where it is genuinely proclaimed and truly heard it is also exhortation—a proclamation and hearing of the divine command. Only in the Gospel can this command be truly proclaimed and heard. In this respect it is noteworthy that in its ethical aspect as admonition the Epistle to the Romans is nowhere addressed to outsiders—either Jewish or Gentile—although both classes are discussed extensively enough. Its ethic—and we mean this, of course, in its most universal sense—is exclusively addressed to circles where the Gospel has already found obedience. Its intention is to discuss and explain this obedience as a life of obedience. This is confirmed by the striking fact that the special admonition of 14¹–15¹³ does not take the form we might have expected. It is not an equal admonition both to the strong and the weak in faith. But up to 15⁷ it is preponderantly an address to the strong and an exposition of the rules to be observed by them in regard to the weak. Almost everything that the weak have to note in this admonition is said only implicitly and can be elicited from the text itself only indirectly. The command of God can be declared plainly and with binding force only when an appeal to God's mercy is possible. In proportion as this is not possible, or not possible with complete clarity, as seems to be the case with those who are weak in faith, the exhortation dies away, although it obviously remains in force. To hear it is the privilege of believers, and of those who are strong in faith. It is significant that they are the very ones who need it and are bound to observe it. The admonition which the apostle has to give " through the grace given unto me " has as its essential theme that its hearers should present their bodies (i.e., their whole person, including all its elements, possibilities and functions) a living sacrifice, holy, acceptable to God. It is evident that this claim can be recognised and accepted and satisfied as meaningful only where a man realises that his life is a living and sacred gift, a sacrifice well-pleasing to God, and as such desired and claimed by God. This is not at all self-evident. That man is to be understood as a sacrifice devoted to God and welcomed by Him, and that he is authorised and called to bring this sacrifice as a priest, is the truth of human existence as it is realised only in Jesus Christ. He, Jesus Christ, is alone the acting and directing subject (both offering and offered) of the reasonable service of God which corresponds objectively to the real relationship between man and God. To participate in this divine service is not for everyone—although this is the only reasonable service of God there is. To participate in it is only for those who believe in Jesus Christ, i.e., who confess Him as their Lord, who put their trust in His person and work, who are baptised in His name, who share in His Holy Spirit, and are therefore ready and able, in their own sphere, to have a part in His office and mission. Because believers in Jesus Christ know and accept the truth that His righteousness avails for their unrighteousness, His holiness for their sin, His life for their death, because they put on the armour of light (13¹²), or Jesus Christ Himself (13¹⁴), they are the ones to whom this demand applies, to whom its fulfilment is vital, and from whom it can be expected. Their nobility obliges them, not to something which is not binding upon all men, but to a life which, because it is binding upon all men, must at all costs be lived out among all men as a token of its universal obligatoriness. As witnesses to the death and resurrection of Christ, they have to attest by their life that the fashion of this world passes away, because the kingdom of God has drawn near. They have to do this by refusing to conform to this world (12²), asking, in opposition to it, what is the will of God—that which is good and acceptable and perfect. Notice in this connexion how in 13¹¹ there is a reference back to the faith of those whom the admonition concerns as the history from which they come : ἐπιστεύσαμεν—this being succeeded by a forward look to the future as it is shaped by this history : ἀποθώμεθα, ἐνδυσώμεθα, περιπατήσωμεν . . . Between this past and this future they are like those who are awakened in the middle of the night while the rest sleep. They have already slept but (like those who must be astir first on guard duty) they now have to get up. The day has not yet dawned, but they have to walk as in the day (ὡς ἐν ἡμέρᾳ). Now that they are awake the night and its life are behind them. It may lie heavy on their eyes and in all their limbs, but it exists as that which is past. They know that Christ has received them (15⁷) ; and therefore they have no option but to receive one another. They know that they can no longer live and die unto themselves, for whether they live or die they belong to the Lord (14⁷ᶠᶠ·). It follows, therefore, that what they do or do not do as those who are strong in this faith, if it is rightly done or not done, must always be an act of εὐχαριστία, of thanksgiving to God (14⁶). They know that they must always serve Christ in the Holy Spirit, and so be well pleasing to God, and approve themselves in the sight of men (14¹⁸). It follows, therefore, that they must always see and seek the kingdom of God, not in licence to eat and drink as they please, but in righteousness, peace and joy in the Holy Ghost (14¹⁷). The whole admonition of the apostle can be summed up, therefore, in the prayer (15¹³) : " The God of hope fill you with all joy and peace in believing, that ye may abound in hope, through the power of the Holy Ghost." Throughout Paul is concerned about this abounding in hope, about the joy and peace which spring from this hope and which he presumes his readers to have as those who have come to faith in Jesus Christ. That they might not be empty, but full of this hope, that they might always show themselves to be aware of the goodness of God in their conduct—this is what constitutes the inner unity of the admonition and command which he has to set before them. And this inner unity is the root of the outward unity—the fact that, according to this text, there cannot be any other command of God but this.

2. Because the command of God is good, this means that, in spite of all the diversity of its claims on men it unites them. It has never yet appeared that generally recognised principles can produce real unity among men. On the contrary, they require interpretation. Indeed, they require individualistic interpretation. If they are to be applied, this is a downright necessity. Thus their establishment always exercises a secret centrifugal effect. They bring into play self-will, better judgment, particular standpoints, various interests, jealousies, cleavages and parties. Moral fellowship can and will arise where people see and know that they are in the same situation and in the same ground to the extent that they recognise themselves to be placed under the sovereign and definite decision of God. Where the living command of God claims and judges two or three people it may do so in very different ways, but the very fact that in these different ways they are claimed and judged by this command will necessarily bring them and hold them together. It does not always go without saying that they can accord each other mutual respect as true hearers of the command. The question of confidence can be seriously posed among them. Yet this is not an insoluble problem, as it is when we have first to believe in the goodness of the other if we are to have confidence in him and in his interpretation of moral principles. There is here an archimedian point beyond all existing differences. It is always possible and even necessary to enquire about the unity in and beyond all diversity. In every case—both where it is heard, and also objectively where it is

heard only imperfectly or not at all—the command of God is a revelation of the freedom of the Lord of all men. But where this freedom is disclosed, it is objectively quite impossible that those who stand together under the judgment of this Lord should judge one another. On the contrary, the objective possibility or necessity is to be mutually free for this Lord, and in this way, in this freedom, to come together in a true fellowship. The oneness of their Lord can and must obviously find a reflection in the unity of His servants. And where the command is truly heard, this objective possibility and necessity becomes a subjective reality. The reflection of the divine in the human takes historical shape. Men are actually in fellowship one with another, however far apart they may seem to be in consequence of the diversity of the concrete manifestation of the divine command to each individual. Mutual trust and living fellowship are then present. Common responsibility emerges without any mutual encroachment, or usurpation of individual responsibilities. This is the case because God's command is good in the full meaning of the term. The command of God will never allow a man to escape his personal and direct responsibility, to shelter from the divine claim behind the overwhelming force of the opinions and judgments current in his environment, to bow before the dictate of another conscience. The command of God will always place man in the freedom of immediate obedience. Again, the command of God will never allow him any other freedom but a freedom in fellowship. It will never permit him to break off his unity with others, no matter what may be the circumstances of his relation to them. It will never allow him to pass from a relative to an absolute conflict with them. It is never the fault of the command, but only of its hearers, if men think that there is no further place for right and friendliness and wholesomeness in their mutual relations and that they should engage in mutual conflict on the basis of this kind of abstraction. Only a relative conflict is possible and necessary in respect of the hearing of the one command which is good in the fullest sense. We cannot and should not spare either ourselves or others this conflict. But it can and will be rightly conducted only as we recognise that in itself the command of God is the command of absolute peace, and that we can engage in strife only for the sake of peace. To hear and obey the command of God is always to be on the way to fellowship. If we are not, if our feet are on the opposite path, there can be no doubt that—even under the most honourable title—we are in conflict and contradiction with the command. True and radical division amongst men begins only as they oppose or accept the command of God which is the command of His goodness. This division does not consist in God, or in what is required of us. For it is always required of us that we ourselves should become and be good in correspondence with the goodness of God.

From the very first sentence (12¹) Paul addressed those whom he admonished in his Epistle to the Romans as brothers, and the expression is emphatically repeated (14¹⁰) when there is a particular question of differences between the brethren. Here, as elsewhere, the phrase is obviously meant to remind us that the God whose commanding and forbidding we must recall is our Father because Jesus Christ is our eldest Brother. Because they are addressed as brothers, those who are admonished are from the outset brought together on common ground. The exhortation which they are to hear cannot possibly involve divisions or the recognition of divisions between them. There can be no question of the one judging or despising the other when both live by faith (14¹⁰). Brother cannot possibly give offence to brother, i.e., threaten him by his conduct with exclusion from fellowship with God the Father and His Son Jesus Christ (14¹³). He cannot trouble him, i.e., confuse him in his own particular faith, which is the only one he has. Whatever the divine command is focused by the apostolic exhortation may mean for each individual, it is certain that it will signify his share in the sacrificial act (12¹) to be accomplished by a single race of brethren, in the service of God which as such is not the private business of any one individual, and in which none can act in opposition to the others in the name of God, but which can only be rendered in common. They must all together, if in different ways, make that protest against the form of this world, and transform themselves by the renewing of their minds according to the will of God (12²). Therefore the particular admonition of the apostle begins with the warning that none should aim his thoughts more highly (ὑπερφρονεῖν) than he ought, but each should think discreetly and soberly according to the measure of faith which God has given him. It is obviously unfitting, because over-ambitious, if a man accords absolute value to the measure of faith assigned him, and therefore aims at pitting it against the faith of others. Sobriety is the attitude of those who recognise in their own faith, but also in that of others, the one true faith—its ground and object—but in the strength of this faith are prepared to live with those who believe differently. The reality of the difference between them may, of course, rest (14¹ᶠ·) upon the serious difference between strong and weak faith. But even in this case it does not offer any occasion for an absolute division or disintegration of the community. Even then the relative conflict can only be waged for the sake of the absolute peace of the community. But Paul only speaks of this at the end. For the moment, he points out (12⁴ᶠ·) that the one undivided body of Christ, to which all believers (strong as well as weak) belong, has many members, and the one indivisible grace—the same for all, strong as well as weak—is diverse in its operations. Whereas the diversity of human gifts and temperaments and tendencies can only divide, the diversity of the members and the manifold operations of grace can only unite. So certain is Paul of this that in 12⁶ᶠ·, for example, when he had to speak of these human differences, he did not take the expected course and warn men to keep in the background the divisive factors and concentrate on the unifying. On the contrary, he summoned each member not to allow his vitality to be impaired but to make an earnest and consistent effort to use the gifts granted to him. Each one must make full use of what has been given him by the will of God, doing that which is committed to him. It is by the freedom in which he will live on the basis of the freedom of the Lord who thus calls him that he will live soberly (12³) and build up rather than destroy the common life. The gift of grace given him as a member of the body of Christ—the prophetic word or the service of love or teaching or exhortation or liberality or administration or mercy—cannot be a cause of dispute. It is not made in order that he may serve himself (as he would do if he lived according to his impulses and desires), but in order that he may serve the community, and in it all others, and beyond the community and all others the world, to which the community is engaged, as both the community and the world are engaged in the service of Him who is the Lord of both. In and with all this he will definitely take part in the common act of the reasonable service of God. There then follows (12⁹⁻²¹) a chain of loosely linked intimations consisting almost entirely of short adjectival, participle phrases. Notice that not a single one of them relates to the private life of individual Christians. Formally, the whole series is connected with the passage about gifts of grace by what is strictly an imperceptible transition. Materially, it contains directions about the life of Christians in relationship with others : first (12^{9-13}) their fellowship among themselves, and then (12^{14-21}) their contacts with the surrounding non-Christian world. The admonition to accept the political order follows on quite naturally from this (13^{1-7}). The insistence upon the law of love, which sums up the whole Law (13^{8-10}) and by which the Church is built up in the world and therefore the work of God done, brings the sequence to a conclusion which is both meaningful and in harmony with the beginning in 12^9. It is evident that here, too, we have a description of that act of fellowship, with the emphasis on its public aspect. Under the category of ἀγάπη (12^9) the whole conduct which Paul requires of Christians is included—even what is said about their relationship to the state. The love which edifies the Church is without dissimulation and genuine when it is sincere, and it is sincere when it bears witness to the love of God of which each member of the Church may confess himself the object. This love will be full of wisdom towards one's neighbour. It will be able to overcome the evil which it encounters in him and strengthen the good. In this wisdom it will be an inward brotherly love (12^{10})—the affectionateness in which we seek neither ourselves nor others but the common Lord in brotherhood with others, gladly seeing in our brother, although without surrendering our own freedom and responsibility, the representative of our eldest Brother, and therefore the common Father, and thus yielding him the preference and honour. The zeal of this love, awakened by the Holy Ghost and under its control, will not fail. Its flame cannot be quenched (Cant. 8^7). Its service (of the Lord) cannot be interrupted. Its hope (12^{12}) will always rejoice. Its steadfastness in adversity is constant. Its prayer does not cease. It will never neglect the needs of the saints—for that is the life of the whole community directed to the service of the Master. It is in this way, in the form of this full and uninterrupted but, as may be seen, very material claim upon each individual, that love lives in the community. It is in this way that there is fellowship in that reasonable service. Personal inc..nation of the one towards the other is certainly not excluded, but it does not seem to be necessarily demanded by what is here described as love. This Christian love has the meaning and power, the seriousness and freedom, the infinity and limits, of supreme objectivity. And it is in this form that it is genuine and capable of endurance, that it can never fail (1 Cor. 13^8), that it cannot degenerate into sentimentality nor grow weary nor be deflected into indifference, aversion and divisiveness. By claiming all passion, though not itself passion, it acquires permanence, power and authority. Both its movement and its rest are rooted in grace and not in nature, in the office and commission of the community and its Lord and not in the personal needs of the men there assembled, in the fear of God and not the respect of persons—or, conversely, in nature caught up and renewed by grace, in the personal need that sees itself obliged to serve the Church and its Lord, in the respect of persons that flows from the fear of God.

What Christians decidedly owe to the world (13^{8-10}) is just that they should love one another in this way. In so far as this love is alive among Christians, in all its depth and reality, with all the joy and sorrow it brings, with all its fervour that must not be confused with passion, the Church is edified, the good work which God requires takes place, not only in the inner circle of Christians, but with the creation and maintenance of this circle for everyone and for the whole world. In this good work every individual Christian has his share as he, too, is one who loves with this supreme realism. In so doing, he will give what is due to all his neighbours. Thus the special fellowship of the Church, whose formation and preservation is the basic divine purpose, does not mean an absolute separation, but is the basis of a worldwide fellowship. Protesting against the form of this world (12²), the Church cannot be against but only for the men who are still caught up in this world. Therefore the Church and all its individual members cannot meet the persecution directed and threatened against them with curses—as though it were a question of conflicting parties—but only with blessing (12¹⁴). As Christians themselves were reconciled to God when they were still enemies (Rom. 5¹⁶), so now they must undertake and fulfil the ministry of reconciliation (2 Cor. 5¹⁸) while others are still enemies. But they cannot bless them if they let them go their different ways and themselves pursue their own Christian path. They can only bless them as they answer all criticism and opposition by living all the more in fellowship with those that are without, rejoicing with them, weeping with them, acting towards them as brethren (12¹⁵). This will not happen by the surrender and loss but by the confirmation of their own characteristic Christian life—by living according to the way suggested by the unity of the community and its task (τὸ αὐτὸ εἰς ἀλλήλους φρονοῦντες, 12¹⁶). And this way consists in the fact that they will not share in the distinctive desire for prominence (cf. 12³), the impulse to be as gods, which is so characteristic of the form of this world and to which the children of this world are enslaved. On the contrary, they will be found in the world, offering their sympathy in joy and sorrow, at the point where God's grace came to them—in the humility of a humanity which is conscious of owing nothing to their own cleverness and strength, where nothing is to be expected from man and everything from God, where men acknowledge their own frailty in contrast to every presumption of divine likeness (12¹⁶). In this verse we have again the all-important φρονεῖν of 12³, and to it is added : μὴ γίνεσθε φρόνιμοι παρ' ἑαυτοῖς. We are reminded again of the warning as to the impartation and right use of the gifts of grace. Even within their non-Christian environment Christians will always be " brought down " to the ταπεινά, the little things, the less distinguished, less popular possibilities. They will be found at the side of the minority, the humiliated and oppressed. For they are what they are only by grace. Only by grace are they endowed with gifts and held together as a fellowship. It is just in this disposition, as those who are endowed by grace, and therefore humble, and in this way held together in a unity, that they face the surrounding world which contradicts and opposes them, or rather stand as priests at its side. In this disposition they will certainly not pit themselves against their adversaries as one party against another (12¹⁷), requiting evil with evil, answering worldly arrogance and force with Christian. But in the sight of all men—whether the latter perceive it or not—they will work for the objective grace and the common weal of all. Only those can do this who do not consider themselves as wise because they know the wisdom of grace. But these can do it—and they can do it in all circumstances. As those who have received and accepted the divine offer of peace (Rom. 5¹), they are themselves a living and absolutely sincere and in every way irrevocable offer of peace in the sight of all men (12¹⁸), and most of all in the sight of their adversaries. The outcome is not in their control. But within the limits of the possible, so far as in them lies, they cannot wish to be other than this universal and absolute offer of peace. They do not fight in their own cause, and they cannot, therefore, wish to vindicate their right (12¹⁹) when a wrong is done them. They are the beloved of God who as such, as is indicated by their submission to the political order which God has instituted for this purpose, are not concerned to attest the wrath of God. For they know that this will be done in another way. Even as Christians they are responsible, according to 13¹, for seeing that it is done at the right time and in the way which God has ordained. Because they do not evade this responsibility, because they give the wrath of God its due place, they go beyond this place, for they do not only know about the wrath of God, but realise that His wrath is the burning of His love. The mission of the Church and every Christian (12²⁰) does not deny the mission of the state, but includes and transcends it. It consists in the fact that instead of requiting like with like, it requites like with unlike. In this way it resists and overcomes the enemy, the man who refuses to accept the message of reconciliation. For it does not recognise him seriously as an enemy. It does not allow him to persist in his hostility to the extent of provoking retaliation. The Christian will refuse to become his enemy even within the framework of the political order and its necessary fight against disorder. Even within this framework, and in fulfilment of the divine meaning of this order, he will not be against him but for him. He will beat him decisively, heaping "coals of fire on his head," by treating him as one who is in need—hungry and thirsty—and giving him food and drink and all that one in supreme need requires. Christian intransigeance, the Christian resistance to evil, consists in this, that the Christian never allows himself to be seduced from his offer of reconciliation, never lets himself be overcome by evil, is never enticed to requite evil with evil, is never led astray from the overcoming of evil with good, and therefore from the path of fellowship with the enemy. He does not refuse communion to the enemy, but to evil. And for this reason he seeks it even with the enemy.

The famous verses in 13^{1-7} do not form any exception to this fundamental rule concerning the Christian's relationship to the world. They suggest that no one need fear the outbreak of general chaos as a result of following this rule. Provision is really made that God's opposition to the world's evil will be vindicated where the Church's message of reconciliation is not yet or no longer heard and received. That is why Christians do not need to form a party in the struggle against the wicked, but can and must continue undismayed to tread the way of fellowship with the latter, because God has long ago taken sides against their violence, has long since barred their way so that although they may rattle the bolt they cannot open the door. The wicked are objectively controlled by the order which God, the Father of Jesus Christ, has established and confirmed even in the world outside the Church, His Son being the King and Ruler over all powers, and ruling as such in might. Protected by Him, Christians and the Church are free to requite evil with good. " All power is given unto me in heaven and in earth," Mt. 28^{18}. " Thou hast given him power over all flesh " (Jn. 17^2) —even genuine political authority. For this reason the special duty of the Church extends to recognising this true political authority, and its special mission includes sharing the responsibility for the execution of this authority. Everyone—every member of the Church, " because of the mercy of God," must submit himself, not blindly and uncritically (Paul never means that when he speaks of ὑποτάσσεσθαι), but with true self-adaptation to this political authority. The power of the state as such is of God (13^1), and wherever this power is found (not in so far as it may be partially anarchy or tyranny, but in so far as it is legitimate authority) it is ordained of God, so that those who try to evade or oppose it resist the ordinance of God and the kingly rule of His Son. It is God's ordinance for the security of the collective life of man even where the latter provides no scope for grace, where, because the light of grace cannot yet shine, the shadow of divine wrath must be cast. But divine wrath does not really exist apart from grace. That God's grace prevails here in the form of His anger is shown by the fact that the political order is the order of the sword, of compulsion and fear. It reckons with the destructive power of natural human ambition (12^{16}) which is so characteristic of this world, with the aggressive, explosive effect of all thinking which has not yet (12^2) been renewed and which makes man esteem himself wise. It is not God's will that men, in this condition, should mutually devour themselves as would necessarily be the case if they were left to themselves. God has not given up humanity as a prey to its own lusts (cf. Rom. $1^{24, 26, 28}$), for He has restrained men against breaking out in a way which would be the natural consequence of their own lusts. God is patient. God will give men time to recognise His grace. God will also grant His Church time to proclaim His grace. That God wills to give the world and the Church time to receive grace is the secret purpose of the political order. That it must be an order of the sword, compulsion and fear, springs from the essence of this divine intention. Where the grace of God is not yet known and exalted, has not yet found obedience, only the sword and compulsion and fear can reign. Where it is only a question of finding time and freedom for the proclamation and knowledge of grace, of making possible the social life of men under the presupposition that their life is lived apart from and contrary to the grace of God, grace itself must assume and maintain the form of a graceless order. This graceless order, corresponding to the form of this world overcome and abolished in principle by Jesus Christ, is the political order, the rule of law, which is established and protected by threats and the use of physical force. Why may we not evade or oppose it ? Simply because in all its gracelessness it is an expression of the kingdom of grace : of grace in so far as this refers and extends itself to humanity still involved in the form of this world ; of grace in so far as it has the character of a protecting and restraining patience. Christians who are treading their very different path to fellowship, consistently with the fact that the kingdom of God has now dawned, must recognise the grace of God even in this graceless order. They cannot be ungrateful to the God who wills to give them and the world more time and opportunity. They themselves would be such as esteem themselves wise if they refused to recognise this ordinance of God. For this reason the apostle invites them to adapt themselves to this temporal order. This does not mean that they give up their special task, their special way of life in fellowship, which springs from their apprehension of grace. In so doing they are as little compromise with the form of this world as does God Himself who appoints this order for humanity as it is entangled in the form of this world. For He does not do this in order to confirm this form, which has been overcome and abolished in Jesus Christ, but to prepare its final and total dissolution. It is in this sense that Christians must adapt and subordinate themselves to the temporal order. It is in the most literal sense a provisional dispensation, preceding and making ready for that which is ultimately to be revealed. As such it is of God's appointing, declaring itself to be such by the fact that it, too, represents a kingdom, a πολίτευμα and that though it does not itself create and proclaim that which is good and right and friendly and redemptive, it provides and safeguards the external conditions for this proclamation (in so far as it is an order of state and not its opposite) ; for, in spite of every manifestation of the evil which has not yet been identified and abolished, it preserves the common life, keeping it from a destruction which would inevitably make the existence of the Church irrelevant. Because Christians recognise the order of God in the order of the sword, compulsion and fear, they themselves can be neither anti-political nor a-political. They can be neither hostile to this order, nor alien, indifferent and aloof. If they were, it would indicate that they were abandoning their own way of fellowship by themselves ceasing to be hearers, bearers, doers and proclaimers of the divine command, guarantors of the kingdom of Christ, and that they themselves were willing to let go of the grace of God— their sole support—in the delusion that they had no further need of God's patience. If they do not cease to be what they are, they will not become impatient where God Himself is patient. They will then understand, and realise in practice, that their reasonable service, consistently with the will and work of God Himself, must take the form of the service of God in politics, consisting in their participation in the life of that provisional, graceless order of earthly things. In 13[4] the power of the state is expressly described as διάκονος θεοῦ, and its bearers and executives, rulers and their officers, as λειτουργοὶ θεοῦ. But where God is served in these things according to His appointment, Christians can neither make objection, nor stand passively aside. They cannot regard this order, as is explained in 13[5], merely from the point of view of its gracelessness, as the order where the wrath of God finds expression (cf. 12[19]). They cannot subject themselves to it only as they would have to subject themselves to an outbreak of plague or an earthquake—as other tokens of the divine wrath. They cannot be willing merely to suffer under the existence of the state. On the contrary, they are enjoined to adapt themselves to it διὰ τὴν συνείδησιν, and to recognise in this graceless order an expression of the gracious will of God. They are enjoined to offer it, even in this form, a free and willing obedience, to affirm it sincerely, actively and completely. It is just because and as they render to God what is God's that they will also—unreservedly—give to Cæsar what is Cæsar's —every personal service required of them and necessary for the maintenance of the state (13⁶ᶠ·), and therefore a share in the responsibility for the continuance of this dispensation. It is they, above all, who know what they are doing when they think and act as citizens of the state. It is they who are competent and called to do this in all seriousness. For them it is not a matter of chance motives or personal inclinations, but the service of God. But they know, too, the limits and the provisional character of this matter. They therefore bring it the necessary temperance, the candour and the courage necessary to distinguish between a political order and all the forms of disorderliness concealed under the appearance of a political order. They will always understand Cæsar better than he understands himself. They will always be in a position to give him what it is right, to give him better than he himself can demand it. They will rightly obey men within the framework of this order because even here they obey God, who is the Founder and Guarantor of the order, rather than men. They will be citizens in all seriousness because they are not merely or primarily or finally citizens, but citizens as those whose πολίτευμα is in heaven (Phil. 3²⁰). Their service of God is not simply to be equated with political service. It only includes the latter. Their thinking and action as Christians transcends their political thinking and action. Their special way of life as Christians does not break off altogether with their subordination to the state, but is only intersected by it. Even here they still continue to overcome evil by good (12²¹). They still continue to love as God Himself does not cease to love when He establishes and maintains this order, but continues to do so in a special way. The Church with its proclamation of grace lives on within the graceless order of the state : not in contradiction to the latter, but revealing its ultimate meaning and purpose, providing its ultimate vindication and therefore transcending it ; not confined to the immanent purposes of the state but beginning where the possibilities and powers of the state end, and living, therefore, its own characteristic life. It is clear from the context in which Paul introduces the subject—from the preceding verses in 12¹⁴ᶠᶠ· as from the continuation in 13⁸ᶠ· to which we have already referred, from his smooth transitions from the distinctive notes of the Christian life to its political repercussions and then back again to the special Christian way—that he does not intend the incorporation of this central political section to be understood as an intrusion in his admonition. The work of Christian love takes place as the Christian community lives its own life. But the characteristic life of the Christian community has this political dimension. Otherwise it would not be the supreme way to fellowship. Yet even here everything depends upon the fact that it continues to be the life of the Christian community.

The Christian life, Christian love has, therefore, this aspect. It expresses itself in its non-Christian environment as described in 12¹⁴ᶠ·. Aware of God's patience, it demands that Christians should participate in the work of the state. The meaning and power of this admonition are wholly dependent on whether the Church remains the Church, whether there is the common endeavour of Christians in the cause of their Lord as described in 12⁹ᶠᶠ·, and therefore whether they fulfil the whole Law by their mutual love, by a continuation of the act of fellowship described in 12³ᶠᶠ·—an act which is made possible and evoked by the grace revealed to the community and recognised by it, on the basis and within the limits of the gift of grace imparted to each individual Christian. Everything depends upon whether Christians are really the host that is awakened and astir in the midst of many sleepers (13¹⁰ᶠ·). If they are not pursuing the path of fellowship among themselves, how can they be in their relations with the surrounding world, in their participation in the life of the state ? The Christian fellowship is the essence of all fellowship, both of those which Christians have to evangelise with their message of reconciliation (12⁹ᶠ·) and of those toward whom they have to act as Christians (13¹ᶠ·) in a sphere which their Gospel has not yet penetrated and in which the patient will of God demands that there should not be the destruction of human life in community but its preservation. Whether Christians love in these ways, and in so doing fulfil the command of God, depends on whether they love each other. The great concluding passage, which obviously refers to a special difficulty of the Church at Rome, deals with this essence of all fellowship. There is not only, as described in 12³ᶠᶠ·, a diversity of gifts of the one grace, in face of which the command must be that each shall make full use of the gift vouchsafed to him, thus living the life of a holy member of the one holy body of Jesus Christ, representing the whole in his own place and sphere, and therefore deliberately serving all others and the whole. Apart from this diversity of gifts, there is a diversity in the appropriation of the one grace, and therefore a humanly conditioned diversity in the form of the obedience required from all. This flows from the fact that the Church has a provisional character and is conditioned by the form of this world which, although it overcome and abolished in principle, still has power over it. For this reason alone it cannot escape solidarity with the order of the state which rests upon the same presupposition. From the point of view of the grace revealed to it and apprehended by it, of Jesus Christ and His Holy Spirit, it cannot be understood or explained that there are those who are weak in faith (14¹) as opposed to those who are strong (15¹). Paul did not undertake to justify the diversity among the members of the Church. He simply registered it as a fact, just as he did the continuing manifestation of evil in the world as the presupposition of the political order. He did not, therefore, praise the diversity as adding to the richness of the Church's life, nor evaluate it as a sign of vitality. He simply reckoned with it, and gave directions about our attitude to it, seeing it cannot be simply set aside and dissolved. It is clear that he ascribed the dimension of patience to the grace of God in this respect too—in respect of its appropriation by the community, of its effective presence in the prism of this Christian humanity. He therefore required of Christians that in their mutual love they should be patient, and that their forbearance must persist in face of this diversity. It is to be noted that Paul nowhere takes a neutral position in regard to the divergence in question, which is obviously conditioned only on the human level. He does not in any sense adopt a mediating standpoint between the strong and the weak. According to the whole tenor of the argument, there can be no question that as an apostle of the Gospels he regards the activity of the so-called " strong " as intrinsically the better. But as he views the non-Christian world, not outside the kingdom of Christ but within it in the form of the state, he sees that Christians who do not have this better, strong faith are not outside the community, but represent a type of Christian life which we must tolerate and respect. He says that the community, or, concretely, those who are strong in faith, must not recognise the position of the weaker brethren as an equally justifiable possibility, nor must they merely tolerate them. They are to receive them (προσλαμβάνεσθαι), to invite them, to keep company with them and to bear their infirmities (15¹), as Christ has received us all. This is something which—independently of our judgment about the divergence—is better than their higher degree of faith. This is the good required of Christians in face of this divergence. It can only be the good of Jesus Christ Himself who is Lord of the living and the dead (and how much more Lord of the strong and the weak !), who did not live to please Himself but His neighbour, bearing the shame of those who despise God (to whom the strong in faith might also belong), who as He fulfilled the promises made to Israel is also the God whom the heathen magnify (who therefore wills to be magnified by both the strong and the weak together). In subordination to this Law, the community, and especially those in it who are strong in faith, must be prepared to accept the fact of this divergence, being made responsible for the fact that, as the command is one, so also the obedience to be offered by the community must always be one, in spite of all serious differences as to its form. They have received no better grace than the weak. That they have assimilated it better cannot be allowed to separate them from the latter, but only bring them so much the more together. Otherwise their better is the enemy of the good—of the good which is Jesus Christ Himself. This is what must not happen—any more than the resistance or indifference of Christians to the state regarded as the form assumed by the kingdom of Christ in the world outside the Church. In both cases it is a question of obeying the Lord. In both cases the better and the best expression of human obedience is measured by whether we are really obedient to the Lord, and not disobedient, in spite of the appearance of this better or best form. Those who are obedient to Him—and the primary appeal is to the strong in faith—will see to it that no διακρίσεις διαλογισμῶν, no divisions arise in the community through the particular (less sound) opinions of the weak, the special principles and practices with which they think they must maintain their faith. Those who hold these views—the weak—must not judge others. But, above all, the strong who do not hold them must not despise others. Why not ? Because God has received both (14³). Because both are servants, each serving the Lord with their better or less good faith, each finding in the Lord his own Judge and Saviour. They cannot exclude each other when God has accepted both and will judge their faithfulness or unfaithfulness by His mercy. Let each be certain in his own mind whether he can confidently proceed on his chosen course. Each man can do this (14⁶⁻¹²) when he does what he does in gratitude to God and the Lord and not in a spirit of self-seeking. Each and all are to be measured by this standard. By this standard the Christian with the better and freer faith might find himself condemned, and the Christian whose tottering faith needs support might find himself justified. Who can dare to make this the crucial test (and no one can fail to do so, for each is asked whether he does what he does thankfully, for the Lord) and then proceed to judge or to despise ? As we are asked this question, can we do anything but join with those whom we might well have had cause to judge or despise in bowing our knees before the One who is Lord of the whole Church and who alone is right as against all the members of the Church ? As for those who would like to judge or despise, when they do this do they not show that their conduct is not rooted in thankfulness towards God and service of their Master ? And if this is the case, how can they behave with absolute conviction that they are right ? If they behave with complete assurance, in thankfulness towards God and for their Lord, and therefore in a common subservience with those whom they might have had cause to judge or despise, then, according to 14¹³ᶠ·, all pretentious behaviour is excluded by the fact that another positive duty presses upon them, namely, not to be a cause of stumbling or offence to their brother, never to confuse him in his faith (whether it be sound or less sound), never to induce him to do what can only be sin in his case, since he cannot do it in faith (14²³). Each has to be concerned that the other should strictly cleave to the way which his faith (whether more sound or less) dictates to him as the recipient of grace he is. This is the positive concern which replaces the temptation to judge and despise others, and it is a concern which we can none of us attempt to evade. No objective right against others can excuse us if in the exercise of this right we provoke them to disobedience, to do what they can only do through disobedience. No objective right ever permits any of us not to walk in love, to bring to ruin those for whom Christ died. In common with them (14¹⁶ᶠ·), and therefore in a concern for our own faith, we must secure the good of God's kingdom and not the good of our own better faith and better way. Let us show the superior soundness of our faith by unhesitatingly preferring to our own objective right our concern for the peace and the common edification of the Church and therefore for the faith of our neighbour. This is precisely what the strong in faith can do. And they especially are bound to do this when this course is dictated from that higher standpoint. Those who are objectively right are the very ones who must be able to resign all thoughts of asserting and maintaining this right if they cannot do this without forsaking the way of love or the common upbuilding of the Church, without destroying the work of God. The strong in faith do not become weak when they act in this way but evince their strength by the fact that they do not only tolerate the weakness of the weak but genuinely bear it, making it their own, being weak with the weak. It is the strong who owe it to their strength to do this (15¹). They owe it to their strength to live for the sake of their neighbours, not just in a way which pleases their neighbours, but in such a way that what happens to their neighbours necessarily happens for their good, for the upholding of their faith and therefore the edification of the community. The more strongly and consistently faith is directed to Jesus Christ alone, and the life of the believer nourished by Him alone, the more necessary this is. For Jesus Christ (15³) did not live for His own sake. He emptied Himself of His divine majesty, and took the form of a servant, and became like men, and took to Himself the shame of those who dishonour God. The strong in faith are called upon to imitate this His conduct. How can it be strong, how can it be faith at all, if it does not involve this imitation ? By cleaving (15⁴ᶠ·) to the One who, according to the witness of Scripture, humbled Himself for us all in the omnipotent mercy of the living God, it has no option but to affirm the corresponding unity of all who believe in Him and live by Him. On this model the strong and the weak in faith are so bound up with each other that the strong have to carry the weak and care for the weak. Seeing themselves in this mirror, the strong in faith cannot live to please themselves. They cannot live out the strength of their faith. They can live only in the community, and therefore in a fellowship of faith with the weak, and therefore without despising them (even though the latter judge them !), and therefore in a readiness to praise God in consideration for their weakness. In this unity of faith, and with this united faith praising God in the world of which they are appointed to be the light, the strong and the weak (15⁷) in the Christian community will receive each other, as they have both been received, having no existence except in this reception, but in this common reception their one and all. Where would be either the strong or the weak in the Church at Rome if Jesus Christ had not revealed and actualised the faithfulness of God (15⁸⁻¹²) as the Messiah of the Jews and the mercy of God as the Saviour of the world, thus making one body of the elect people and the many non-elect ? What is the antithesis of the strong to the weak in comparison with that of light and darkness which Jesus Christ overcame at the cost of His death on the cross ? It is worth nothing that already in 15⁵⁻⁶ and again in 15¹³ Paul's admonition passes over into prayer and intercession. And in 15¹³ it does this in such a way that the specific content of this concluding section needs no further mention. It obviously needed only this apostolic prayer and its hearing to bring about what was urged particularly in this concluding section—but also from the very outset. The hearing of the divine command will then lead and keep Christians in the way of fellowship even though it is understood that the command is heard well and less well among them.

3. Finally, because the command of God is good, it unifies each individual man in himself. At this point too—and supremely—there is the threat of contradiction, conflict and chaos. It is because man is not at one in himself that we are not at one with each other. It is

because inner consistency and continuity are lacking in the life of the individual that there is no fellowship among men. Yet the fault is not with God's command, but with man himself—not with his obedience but with his disobedience to the command—if he cannot be at harmony with himself and others. In Rom. 7$^{7f.}$, Paul has described how the real work of sin consists in misinterpreting and misapplying the divine command. Sinful man makes of the command a pretext for trying to justify and sanctify himself, instead of allowing himself to be justified and sanctified by the command. He then goes on to show in 7$^{13f.}$ that when man tries to do this he gives himself over to death, i.e., to the disunity of an existence in which he does not will what he does, or do what he wills. The various attempts which he makes along these lines, the various possibilities at which he catches in this enterprise which is so contrary to the command, the various stages on his way as conditioned by the varied forms assumed by this attempt will always necessarily be variations on this one unhappy theme, serving only to demonstrate afresh the reality of his inner conflict. He can never be alone without fighting against himself, without being necessarily locked in inner strife. Therefore he will fear nothing so much as being alone. And driven by this fear he will turn outwards towards others and will have nothing to bring them except himself and his own dispeace. He will try to escape from this condition by giving it the form of conflict between himself and others. And the more he succeeds in doing this, the less will he be able to escape from the toils of his personal conflict. All this is relevant to the divine command only to the extent of making it crystal clear that we cannot trifle with it, that if it is not seen and accepted as the "law of the Spirit of life" it must work itself out as the "law of sin and death" (Rom. 8^2). As the Law presents itself in its self-revelation, and is heard and accepted as such, it does not divide but unite. It unites the individual in himself and then makes him an instrument and messenger of this harmony to others. Only the opposite can be said of all moral principles. These are instruments of the misinterpretation and misapplication of the command, provoking the very desires which are excluded by the command, the very attempt at human self-justification and sanctification which is forbidden by God and absolutely fatal. They may be absolute in appearance, but in fact they are altogether ambiguous and dialectical. They can and must continually be completed and replaced by others. As they are established, recognised and applied, they constantly provoke antitheses. With them man can only give a fresh demonstration that he does not will what he does, and does what he does not will. The result is that they all have their season. They cannot bring consistency or continuity into human life. But the good command of God does do this. From the height which transcends this opposition, it comes down to the man who is shut up in this opposition. It always tells him, of course, that he is not his own master. It always opposes the error and folly of his own attempts at living the fact that God is for him, and that He demands only—but with sovereign power—that he should and must direct his life accordingly. It always advises him that all his attempts at self-justification and self-sanctification are futile ; that so, too, is his consequent inner conflict ; that so, too— and basically and essentially—is the disharmony which in his flight from himself he thinks he must spread around him. The divine command sets him in the truth of the peace in which God has accepted him as one who has no peace in himself, so that in this peace, which passes all understanding (Phi. 4⁷), he may live a life which is maintained and guarded and protected by it. He is commanded to live in this peace, beyond all conflict with himself, by the command of God— the law of the Spirit of life. This law requires that man should be in inward harmony, i.e., that he should leave his dispeace below and behind him and therefore be free. It wills that his life should have a single direction and constitute a single whole. It creates and fixes this direction and wholeness by freeing him from his attempted self-dominion and placing him under the lordship of God.

It will reward us to consider the admonition in Rom. 12–15 from this standpoint. It has also the following fundamental significance. In and with the life of the community it reduces to a common denominator the life of its individual members—Christians—and, prophetically foreshadowed in them, the life of individuals generally. It takes the individual as such in all seriousness by seeing all individuals only in the light of the community, with an apparent unconcern for their private life as such. In this connexion it is of importance to note that it is σώματα ὑμῶν which are expressly claimed as materials of the living sacrifice, holy and well pleasing to God, which is to be offered to Him. These are, of course, the same σώματα of which it is said in Rom. 8¹⁰ that they are dead through sin, but that He who raised Jesus from the dead will also quicken them τὰ θνητὰ σώματα ὑμῶν for the sake of the Spirit who dwells in them. As the mortal is claimed by the divine command it is clearly viewed and treated in the light of this hope. Its destiny (1 Cor. 15⁵³) is to put on immortality. It has not yet done this. We have still to say of it what Paul said of the "body of this death" (7²⁴) in Rom. 7. It is still locked in that inner conflict. But already as a living body it is claimed and evaluated as the material of that sacrifice. Its inner conflict is already overlooked and outmoded. Man is viewed and addressed as a single whole, as if he had already found harmony and peace. Already it can be postulated and expected of the man who has no peace—and this is the interesting light which is shed on him in 12³ᶠ·—that as an independent member of the body of Christ, as the recipient and bearer of a special gift of the Spirit, he will serve the cause of reconciliation both in a narrower and wider sphere, in the Church and in the world. What, then, has happened to his inward dispeace ? That it is simply effaced and overcome is the meaning neither of Rom. 7–8 nor of this passage. The Christians whom he exhorts in Rom. 12–15 are obviously neither angels nor saints—if we understand by saints those for whom the inward conflict has simply ceased. But it is their personalities which—although they are wholly mortal, although they have fallen victim to the death described in Rom. 7, to the fatal contradiction between willing and doing, and therefore to the separation between body and soul (which is death !)—are claimed for this sacrifice. If, in spite of everything, they are living and holy, well pleasing to God, it can only be because the Holy Spirit dwells in them, because He is the Spirit of the One who raised Jesus from the dead, because the resurrection of Jesus from the dead is also their hope. Apart from this, we can only conclude that they are not in any sense released from their dispeace, that the latter is still the most characteristic thing proper to these Christians. It is because this is the case that they need admonition. They must still be exhorted : " Be not conformed to this world ; but be ye transformed by the renewing of your mind " (12²) ; and : " Let us cast off the works of darkness, and let us put on the armour of light " (13¹²) ; and : " Put ye on the Lord Jesus Christ, and make not provision for the flesh, to fulfil the lusts thereof " (13¹⁴). The fact that we are still dealing with the man described in Rom. 7—in his weakness as in his strength—ought to be plain from the sentence (13¹³) which was once so important for St. Augustine, for according to this verse it was apparently not self-evident that " revelling and drunkenness, chambering and wantonness, strife and envying " are not compatible with a walking εὐσχημόνως, ὡς ἐν ἡμέρᾳ. Naive talk about the spiritual reality of the life of the Early Christian Church ought to be sobered by this verse, which is not without parallel. From the point of view of the Christian man, we have here a degree of worldliness no less than that of which the later Church is often so severely accused. We may rather ask whether the worldliness of the Christian man is not to be seen more radically here and given its true name, whereas the true evil of the later Church consists in the fact that the humanity of its members could disguise itself more cleverly. At any rate, admonition is necessary at this point, and it is radical admonition. Its final word, that Christians should put on the Lord Jesus Christ, is obviously the first as well. It amounts to this —that they all have reason first and foremost to become what they are, and that they are invited and challenged to do this. But the amazing thing about this invitation and challenge is the serious way in which account is taken of the reality of the resurrection of Jesus from the dead, of the indwelling of the Holy Spirit among and in even these worldly Christians, of the sure hope given to them as an ever present truth. Their new standing as Christians has still to be assumed. Yet it is not treated as an ideal and distant goal, but as the basic implication of their whole existence. What happens to the dispeace of the Christian as he becomes the object of the apostolic admonition is that it is placed under the presupposition and category of this higher and truer reality. From this higher standpoint it is challenged and attacked and overcome by the victorious transcendence of the ground and origin of absolute peace. In the fact that the Christian is a member of the body of Christ, a recipient of the Holy Ghost, what happens to it as the dispeace of the Christian is not that it is removed but that it is relativised exactly as described by Paul in Rom. 7²⁵. The unity of the body of Christ implies the inner unity of all its members, and the unity of the Spirit implies also the inner unity of all those who receive His gifts. Whatever may be the state of their inner conflict, as they live the life of the members of this body, as they make considered use of the gifts severally imparted to them, according to the command of 12³ᶠ· they find themselves on the far side of this conflict. Those who may prophesy, or minister, or teach, or exhort, or exercise liberality, do not in so doing live within but beyond their personal conflict. From the standpoint of their vocation and mission, their life in conflict is made a thing of the past. And as they exercise this mission, they will be able to treat their life in this inner disunity only as a thing of the past. That they should do this is the point of the apostolic admonition to the extent that it is directly relevant to this inner conflict, as in 13¹²ᶠ· Rom. 8⁸ᶠ· applies here : " So then they that are in the flesh cannot please God. But ye are not in the flesh, but in the Spirit, if so be that the Spirit of God dwell in you." In Rom. 12–15 it is not concealed that this insight must be lived out, that the saving warfare of the Spirit against the flesh must be waged (Gal. 5¹⁷). That life in personal conflict is in truth to be treated as a thing of the past. It is to be demolished and buried. The imperatives of the Epistle to the Galatians ($5^{16, 25}$) are in force : " Walk in the Spirit and ye shall not fulfil the lust of the flesh." " If we live in the Spirit, let us also walk in the Spirit." But it is characteristic and significant that here as elsewhere the apostolic exhortation applies for the most part only indirectly to this conflict, that its primary aim is that this conflict should be daily made a thing of the past; that it urges men, as in Rom. 12^{3f}, to live as members of the body of Christ and recipients of the Spirit, and therefore to be freed in principle from that conflict and on the way to overcoming it in practice. Each man has only to do, in the unity of the Church and the Spirit, that which according to the measure of his faith (12^3) and the faith of the whole community (12^6) he in particular is called upon to do. If he does, then no matter what may be the state of his inner conflict, the unity of the Church and the Spirit will necessarily be reflected and evinced and expressed microcosmically as his own personal unity.

The same attitude to the problem emerges in the sequence which begins in 12^{9f}. It is again presupposed as self-evident that what each individual has to contribute to the life of the Church, and as a member of the Church to manifest to the world, is not the explosion of his own inner disharmony, but love. From what is described in these verses as Christian fellowship in the Church and with the world we can understand to what inner state of mind the apostle appealed in addressing these men, what point of departure he simply ascribed to them in his exhortations. If they do what he here demands, they will always leave their own dispeace behind them, living and acting at peace with themselves. We have already referred to the substance, and the unremitting commitment to it, which is so characteristic of the picture of the Christian life sketched in these verses. This unremitting commitment is obviously of advantage not only to the fellowship of Christians and non-Christians with each other but also to the inner unity of each individual Christian life. Those who obey the challenge to co-operate in responsibility, as is here implied, will necessarily find that the whole matter of their personal disharmonies grows noticeably pale and dim and pointless. They no longer live in the contrast between willing and doing, even if they are not yet freed from it. They are no longer, or only subordinately, occupied with the hopeless task of trying to solve or suppress their problem from one or the other point of view. They have no more time for it. They are otherwise engaged. Conflict or no conflict, they have their call and mission to fulfil. And if this is the case, then, however sick they may be, according to the opinion of the apostle they are on their way to health, and their conflict is indirectly overthrown and buried. The genuinely relevant and important antitheses are now very different from those which threaten their personality as such and characterise it plainly as θνητὰ σώματα. They can now be critical in the spirit of love, distinguishing between good and evil as described in 12^9. They can now move within the pregnant dialectic of hope and affliction and prayer (12^{12}). In Christian solidarity and sympathy with the children of this world, who understand themselves so badly, they can now share their joys and sorrows. Where this takes place seriously, what is their inner agitation compared with it—however distressing ? Is it not at least checked, its importance at least much diminished, by the fact that as Christians they have such very different impulsions. Again, and all the more forcibly because indirectly, the admonitions of 12^{14f} suggest that Christians, as they live outwardly, are caught up as such in an inner process of healing. Their inner peace cannot be more strongly implied and asserted and demonstrated than by the fact that, according to the tenor of these verses, they cannot allow themselves to be overcome by the evil which they encounter objectively as something that assails and pursues them, but that they will overcome it with good (12^{21}). Are they the men to achieve this victory ? Is it not their own enemy whom they must necessarily recognise and resist when they meet it openly in their neighbour ? Is it not inevitable that their unredeemed humanity will now break out again ? Paul seems not to have been aware of the problem as such, although he cannot really have forgotten Rom. 7, and 13[12f.] plainly enough recalls the truth of Rom. 7. But he does not really conceal anything, because the life and mission of Christians as members of the body of Christ and recipients of the Spirit is for him a definite fact by which the inner enemy which each man is to himself is so contained and arrested and disarmed that Christians can be confidently enjoined to give their enemy food and drink, in this way ignoring his hostility, instead of allowing their own inner conflict to boil up again and treating him as what he declares himself to be. According to 12[18] there is a possibility of doing what the man torn by his inner distress cannot do. This is the possibility, as much as in them lies (τὸ ἐξ ὑμῶν), of living at peace with all men, of bringing to all men peace and not war. This possibility is certainly not one which they can have of themselves. Even Christians do not have it of themselves. They have it only as Christians, only as they accept the injunction to be, and continually to become, what they are—and yet only to the extent τὸ ἐξ ὑμῶν, as a work of which they are capable and which can be confidently expected of them. Those who are in a state of inner disquiet can and must be peacemakers.

And how can they be this outwardly if it is not already true inwardly, in spite of their dispeace ? Thus the passage about the state (13[1-7]) has also to be interpreted from the point of view which, as against all schizophrenia, all division of spheres and incompatibility of outlooks, all dualistic mythology and all double standards, reduces Christian and civil responsibility to a common denominator, understanding Christian responsibility in itself and as such as political, and political as Christian. The thesis defeated by the Pauline exhortation (which ascribes to the Christian a kind of dualistic existence in this respect, in which he has to regard as evil from one standpoint what is good from another and *vice versa*) is only a special reflection of the conflict which rages in the inner life of the individual. Paul himself sees this matter very differently. He speaks of it at the very heart of his exposition of the love which Christians must always evince. It is obvious that in so doing he does not see and understand it in the light of the inward malady, but appeals to the inner unity of the Christian life which necessarily permit and command Christians even in these very different spheres to be true to themselves and self-consistent, keeping to the one course and not living a double life or alternating between two contradictory methods. It is rather strange that this passage has been constantly used to justify an outward disunity in human existence, and even to introduce it wherever possible into the idea of God. But this disunity can derive only from man's internal disharmony. And far from approving it in this passage, Paul disputes and denies it in the name of the inner peace of the Christian.

The admonition of chapters 14 and 15 is written on the same presupposition. The dispute between the strong and the weak in the Church cannot, then, be conducted in such a way that the work of God is destroyed (14[20]). For Christians as such are in a position, and are summoned, to seek and to will in common τὰ τῆς εἰρήνης καὶ τὰ τῆς οἰκοδομῆς. And for this purpose they have only to be prepared to accept the challenge that " each should be fully persuaded in his own mind " (14[5]). Their own conviction will necessarily lead them to a grateful service of the Lord and therefore to a maintenance of communion with others. Is this really the case ? Have we not necessarily to reckon with the explosive effects of the common inward conflict in this dispute between the exponents of a stronger and a weaker faith ? It is quite evident that Paul does not do so, or does so only to a limited extent, in respect of what is impossible to the Christian as such. Here, too, those whom he addresses are assumed to be integrated personalities, so that he can confidently appeal to their conviction and therefore to their sense of fellowship. The basis and justification of this striking appraisal of the Christian man are even plainer in chs. 14 and 15 than in 12 and 13. Who and what is the Christian man? According to $14^{7\mathrm{f.}}$, he is the man who does not in fact live to himself, or die to himself, but who—whether he lives or dies—belongs to the Lord. If this involves death, it also means life. If it involves dispeace, it also means peace. Both the past that has gone and the new that is to come are from one and the same hand and stand under the lordship and control of the one Lord. Under the sovereignty of this one Lord the Christian is and becomes the one he is. He finds and possesses the unity which, apart from this sovereignty, he can only lack. In all his dispeace, he is surrounded on all sides by absolute and unshakeable peace. And it is not too much to ask of him, nor is it asked in vain, that even outwardly he should be and become a messenger of peace.

§ 39

THE COMMAND AS THE JUDGMENT OF GOD

As God is gracious to us in Jesus Christ, He judges us. He judges us because it is His will to treat us as His own for the sake of His own Son. He judges us as in His Son's death He condemns all our action as transgression, and by His Son's resurrection pronounces us righteous. He judges us in order that He may make us free for everlasting life under His lordship.

1. THE PRESUPPOSITION OF THE DIVINE JUDGMENT

It is not without purpose that the command of God is at one and the same time God's claim upon us and God's decision concerning us. Defined in this way, the command is not an abstract idea, but a definite event. God's claim and God's decision is God's way of dealing with men. The meaning and character of this event is again God's judgment on man. In God's claim and decision God's sentence on man is prounounced and fulfilled. We have still to speak of this event, of the divine decree and ordinance concerning man, executed by the divine command. In the doctrine of God the concept of the divine judgment brings us, as it were, to the reverse side of the concept of the eternal decree of the election of grace at the beginning of all the ways and works of God. The judgment of God in His command is the sum of every earthly realisation of this decree, its temporal explanation and revelation. What God wills with and for and from man takes place as He judges him in His command. But this event is, in fact, identical with that of the atonement. From this final point in the doctrine of God we thus look forward already to the centre of all Christian truth, and therefore of all Church dogmatics. The concept of God is completed as God is understood to be the One who not only wills the reconciliation of the world with Himself, the judgment on man by His command, but who actually causes it to become a fact. He is God in this act, in His ways and works at this central point. It is obvious that we here reach the outermost frontier of the doctrine of God as such. *How* God is God in His ways and works, and in this their central act, can only be understood and developed independently in the wider contexts of Church dogmatics. For the moment, we can only state that He *is* God in this way, in the form of a very brief anticipatory sketch. The purpose of this sketch is simply to establish

733

the fact, and it is surely indispensable at this point, not only for the sake of completeness, but by reason of the matter itself.

We now understand the divine command, its claim, its sovereign, definite and good decision, expressly and in particular as the temporal, historical event in which God, commanding man, and in vindication of all that He wills to be for him, and to have from him, encounters him as his Lord who deals with him. The meaning and character of this event is necessarily that man is judged by God, that his existence is measured and weighed and assessed, not merely intellectually and verbally but in fact, by God as His absolutely competent and omnipotent Lord. That is to say, his actual standing, which is his standing before God and in relation to Him, is genuinely ordered and controlled by this Lord. The real nature of man is disclosed as God maintains His command against him, and therefore judges him.

The primary and fundamental proposition which we have to make concerning this event—on the basis of the connexion between the divine election of grace and the divine command and in conformity with what we have already said respecting this command—is obviously as follows. However this judgment may turn out, whatever man may show himself to be in it, or whatever he may really be on the basis of it, it is quite incontestable that God receives him in this judgment, that He judges him because He wills to treat him as His own. It may well be the case—as indeed it is—that man cannot stand when measured by God's yardstick, that he is found too light when laid on His balance, that if he is placed under His sentence he will necessarily be condemned. But the positive presupposition which we have always to make and remember is that he does actually lie in God's balance, that he is actually measured by His yardstick, that he is actually subjected to His sentence. Summoned to appear before the judgment-seat of God, forced to receive His enactment and disposition concerning himself, incapable of being or making himself anything other than what he is, as he stands manifest before Him, He is first and foremost invited to the recognition that God counts him as His own, that He has received him into fellowship with Himself, that he belongs, as it were, to the province of God, that he is considered and treated as His possession.

The judgment of God is significant and possible because God does actually make this presupposition. Man is, in fact, a dweller in His household, a member of His people, a citizen of His kingdom. It is as such that God calls him to account when He meets him in His command. It is as such that He makes him responsible. It is as such that He judges him according to the full righteousness of His yardstick, balance and sentence. If man could not be measured or weighed or assessed by Him, how could His command become a judgment on him? If his existence had no connexion with the will of God maintained in His command, what appeal could be made to him in this context. How could he even be judged and rejected and condemned by the will of God? Genuine wrath is obviously possible only on the basis and in the context of original and true love. The judgment pronounced in God's command concerning man—whatever else it may involve—is always the demonstration of His love for man, even if it is only an angry, burning and consuming love. If man were alien and indifferent to Him, how would this encounter come about? How would even its most negative outcome be explicable? The mere fact that it takes place at all, that God stands before man as his Lord, that man's existence can become his confrontation with God's command, always means that God does not will to be without us, but, no matter who and what we may be, to be with us, that He Himself is always " God with us," Emmanuel.

To hear the command of God means then, first and decisively, to hear that God is our God, and that we are His Israel, His Church. For the positive factor first and decisively stated by the command is that the man on whom judgment is passed is God's—a member of His family, of His people, of His kingdom—and therefore whatever this may involve, that he must be assessed and distinguished and loved as one who is subject to God's command, and judged by it. The man who does not hear this original Yes of the command does not hear it at all. But, again, the man who does hear it is already justified in the judgment. The command is fulfilled so far as he is concerned. Even in the midst of the condemnation which had certainly been pronounced upon him, he is already placed on the way of forgiveness and obedience which is the intention of the command. The basis of divine judgment in the command consists in the fact that God has first bound Himself to man, and then and for that reason bound man to Himself, calling him to answer before His judgment seat, and ordering and controlling him as He does when He encounters him as Lord. His love lives and rules before and over and even in His judgment. Thus even as the ineluctable judgment of wrath, which is the form it necessarily takes, His judgment is the instrument of His love. The command is the pledge of this love. And its work is done when it is given to man and fulfilled by him. For as the command of God is spoken to him, he is told that he is loved by God. And as he hears the command of God which is spoken to him, and is obedient to it as such, he acts as one who is loved by God before his own decision, before he shows himself to be God's servant in it, before he betrays himself as God's unprofitable and disloyal and perfidious servant, before he accepts God's forgiveness, and before he hears and embraces His call to a new obedience. With regard to the final and proper meaning of his decision, commission, failure, justification and conversion, a prior decision is made in the command of God as it is given to him. It proves itself as such to be the decision of His love. For even as God orders man He addresses him as one whom He loves. To hear and obey God's commandment is to hear and obey this prior decision. When a man does this, when he acts as the beloved of God, as which he is always addressed in God's command, he will certainly stand as such in the judgment of God, however severely he may be condemned by the divine command, as he undoubtedly will be. He will always act in such a way that the judgment which overtakes him can only confirm that he is God's. But if he will not hear and obey this decision, he imperils everything, and has every reason to fear the judgment of the command. The love of God, and the knowledge of His love, and therefore His command—when it is heard and heeded as it wills to be—do not permit anyone to be afraid of His judgment, even though for his own part he may have everything to fear from God's wrath. The command of God wills the sanctification of man even as it judges him. It tells man that God wills to have him for Himself. Those who hear it cannot possibly hold that they are alien and indifferent to God. Their primary conviction is necessarily that God is presented to them, and that He seriously receives them, so seriously that He may ask concerning the conformity of their will with His, concerning their justification before Him. The severity of judgment which there may be in His answer will not obscure the fact that God is presented to them, and that they are seriously received by God. Their only real fear is that God might cease to do this, that they might become alien and indifferent to Him. The command does not give them any occasion for this fear. The harder they are pressed by His judgment, the less ground they have for this fear. If there is one thing which is made clear to them by the radical No which necessarily affects them in this judgment it is the extent of God's concern for them, and His expectations for them when He asks them so sternly and inexorably concerning this conformity to His will. Can they possibly wish that God should treat them otherwise? Would not every mitigation of His severity mean only that He loved them less? Is there not every reason to rejoice that God does judge them with the severity that He does? This very severity is simply the measure of His love and faithfulness, His grace and heartfelt compassion.

God judges us, and gives us nothing, because He has given us everything in His Son Jesus Christ. He has given us Himself, and direct fellowship with Him. It is in Him that He judges us. In Him He must deal sternly and inexorably with us. In Jesus Christ He has chosen man from all eternity as His own, for life in His kingdom, to be a member of His people, His possession. In Him He has bound Himself to us, before He bound us to Himself, and before we bound ourselves to Him. In Him He has decided Himself for us before all our decisions, before we recognised ourselves as His servants, His unprofitable servants indeed, before ever He forgave us our sins and called us to a new obedience. In Him, the everlasting Son, He has recognised us as His servants from and to all eternity. In Him He has loved us, and we are those who are loved by Him. Because this " in Him " is valid, because it is revealed truth in Jesus Christ that the commanding God is related from the very first to those whom He commands, the love of God is the real presupposition of the divine judgment and not merely an ideal and purely conceptual presupposition. Jesus Christ Himself is the divine pre-decision, made in God's eternal decree and at the heart of time, from which we already come when we approach God's judgment-seat. He is the image to which we have to conform ourselves, the basis, assurance and significance of the relationship between God and man. He Himself is the command which tells us first and foremost that we are to live as the beloved of God, and as such to give account of ourselves before Him. For He Himself in person is the act of love in which God has turned Himself to man, to every man, from all eternity and in time. In Him God deals with us so seriously that He cannot spare us the judgment, that He cannot condone anything, that we must experience the full severity of His measuring, weighing and assessing. We sever ourselves from Him if we wish God to encounter us in any other way than this. We follow Him when we approve and accept the fact that God encounters us in the very way in which He does in fact encounter us. He is the promise that we take with us when we come into God's judgment. He is the reason why we can be without fear in God's judgment. Looking to Jesus Christ, we need not fear that we can ever become alien and indifferent to God. And since this was the only basis of our fear, what need have we to fear ? Indeed, we can go further and say that the only way in which we can approach God's judgment is with real joy in Him. This is the very way that Jesus Christ has trodden before us. God's judgment in His command has been achieved and may be contemplated properly and primarily in His person. Primarily and properly He is man confronted with God's command. Primarily and properly He has taken to Himself that which must overtake man in this confrontation. Primarily and properly He has entered the place where man might be afraid, where he will in fact be afraid when it weighs upon him that he might conceivably become alien and indifferent to God. But this did not happen when Jesus Christ entered this place. Far from treating man as alien and indifferent to Him, God treats him as His beloved Son, as He there allows the judgment of God's command to overtake Him. It was, indeed, the good-pleasure of God in the man who allowed this to overtake Him. Surely all the choirs of angels rejoiced when it happened. This event was, for the man who endured it, the entrance to everlasting glory. The man who is judged by God's command stands even now at the right hand of God the Father, and all the extremity and shame of the judgment are covered over by this glory. If God is a radiant King, so too is the One who is judged. If holiness and peace may be expected, it is only with Him, and in fellowship with Him. And the command of

God summons us to this fellowship. The thing we are to hear as we hear the command is that we may belong to Him. To obey God's command is to accept this invitation to live as those who belong to Him, and therefore to rejoice as we stand in fellowship with this One who has been judged.

We must be very clear about this, for an understanding of the presupposition of divine judgment is absolutely dependent on the understanding of this fact.

Primarily and properly, what God wills with man and to have from man is not decided and executed and revealed in us, but in Jesus Christ. He is the only-begotten Son of the Father, loved from all eternity and in God's eternal decree commissioned for the sake of man, for our sake. And He it is who in God's eternal decree, and by His corresponding Word and work in time, is at once the Son of Man endowed and claimed by the grace of God. It was He who first perceived God's will with man, when He was in the bosom of the Father. It was He alone who in the first instance heard and took to heart the command of God for man. What we learn of this, we learn from His witness and know when we receive His witness. And so it is primarily and properly in Him that man's confrontation with God's command takes the form of God's judgment on man. That is to say, it is in this relationship, between this Lord and this servant, that there takes place the measuring, weighing and assessing which mean that man is asked by God about his righteousness ; asked by the One who has the competence and power to ask, and who has given man the dignity of letting himself be asked concerning this thing which cannot be measured. The fact that the meeting between God and man has this character, the form of an act of judgment, does not follow from any conception of God and man. It is the reality of man's encounter with God, infinitely humbling and at the same time infinitely exalting, as it actually took place in Jesus Christ. This is the content of His witness. When we receive His witness, it becomes an insight for us. But it is in Him that the event actually takes place, and on His witness that the insight depends that in this judgment man is actually lost. This means that, measured by the standard of what God expects and requires and orders in His command, his existence and actions and decisions are shown to be unrighteous, contradicting and opposing God's intention, and therefore provoking the wrath of God. It is to be noted that primarily and properly it is not in his own person, but in that of Jesus Christ, that man stands under the judgment of God's command in such a way that he is threatened with something worse than God's wrath, namely, that he might become alien and indifferent to God, that God might cease to have any concern for him, as one who is completely unusable. Jesus Christ Himself is the man for whom the question : " My God, my God, why hast thou forsaken me ? " could and did for the first time become a genuine question. He is the man whom God in His eternal counsel, giving Him the command, treated as its transgressor, thus rejecting Him in His righteous wrath, and actually threatening Him with that final dereliction. That this was true of Adam, and is true of us, is the case only because in God's counsel, and in the event of Golgotha, it became true first of all in Jesus Christ. In Jesus Christ God has recognised Adam and all of us in our relationship to His will and command, and has uttered and fulfilled over Adam and over all of us the sentence which corresponds to this recognition. In Him, He has sentenced Adam and all of us to death, and has handed us over to death. And yet, in the judgment that overtook Him, this sentence and its execution were not the whole of God's judgment, or the last word of His righteousness. In Him the wrath of God and the condemnation of man do not mean that there is that dereliction of men which does of course threaten, and concerning which Jesus asked that question on the cross. Neither does it mean that man might become alien and indifferent to God.

And it is not merely that the judgment of the command of God which Jesus Christ suffers does not mean this abandonment. The truth is rather that as God fulfils this judgment in Jesus Christ, He treats this One who is judged as His Elect and eternally Beloved. The very condemnation and reprobation here executed on man are the decree and the work of the love in which He has, from all eternity and here and now in time, loved man and drawn him to Himself. Even this judgment is the form of God's eternal predestination and the effectual working out of it in time. Even though conflict between God and man in Jesus Christ is so much to the detriment of man, the reconciliation necessary to man, and desired and fulfilled by God on man's behalf, is resolved and accomplished—his reconciliation, the reconciliation of the world with God. For there takes place in it the sanctification of man for God. The fact that he belongs to God is possible and real as he experiences God's command as God's judgment, and God's judgment as his own condemnation and execution. In this way he is made free for what God wills for him—that he may live with Him for ever. And in this way there is accomplished what God wills from him. It is accomplished in Jesus Christ, as God gave Himself up in His Son to be this man, to be the transgressor and sinner who must bear His wrath and be condemned and die. Between the eternal Father and the eternal Son, and therefore between God and man, there is established in Jesus Christ the order in which man, even though he is a transgressor and sinner, but put to death and destroyed as such, may live before God. This order consists in the judgment which is executed upon man by God's command. Obedience to God's command, the maintaining of this order, consists, therefore, in our submission to this sentence, in a readiness to be put to death and destroyed, because in this way God's good will for us is done. As Jesus Christ renders this obedience, He acts both as the electing and sanctifying

God Himself, and also as elect and sanctified man. As He renders this obedience—which is both the obedience of the Son to the Father, and the genuine obedience of man to God—He acts in the Holy Ghost, the bond of peace between Father and Son, as the Mediator between God and man, making atonement, not between God and man, for this is quite superfluous, but between man and God, which can exist only in the rendering of this obedience. It is to be noted that primarily and properly it is Jesus Christ who has rendered this obedience, for primarily and properly He is the Elect of God, sanctified man. It is He, and not Adam, who is in the state of original innocence. It is He, and not we, who is in the state of eternal innocence, righteousness and holiness ordained for us. Adam's innocence and ours are possible and real only because Jesus Christ, when He was rejected by God and bore His wrath, and was judged and put to death according to His command, was never less abandoned by God than in His self-exposure to that threat and posing of that question. Adam's innocence and ours are possible and real because Jesus Christ was innocent even in His suffering of the divine judgment. Indeed, He was obedient in it. Even as the object of God's wrath, He was also the object of His supreme good-pleasure, the fulfiller of His will and command. It is for this reason that there is for Adam and for us a state of obedience, just as Adam's state of disobedience and ours is not in the first instance his and ours, but in virtue of the inconceivable wisdom and mercy of God has been made that of His own Son.

For it is our place, the place which belongs to us, that is the place which this man has chosen for Himself, and for which He is chosen. It is our election and sanctification which are determined and fulfilled in Him. It is for our sakes that He is the man chosen for rejection, who, by God's judgment of wrath, has become and been sanctified man. It is we whom God has loved and has drawn to Himself in Him. It is we whom He has ordained in Him for life in covenant with Him, to eternal life before Him. It is we whom He has made His children by giving us His Son as our Brother. It is we whom He has created as His Israel, and called to His Church, by instituting Jesus Christ the Messiah of Israel, and the Lord and Head of the Church. It is we whom from all eternity He has seen in Him as unable to stand in face of His command, as able to be sanctified and rescued only by His judgment of wrath, and yet as neither willing nor able to bear this judgment of wrath, as incapable of reconciling ourselves with God, of being our own mediators between Himself and us. And, again, it is we whom He has not abandoned in Him, as we had well deserved. It is we, the rejected, whom He has chosen in Him, and sanctified and rescued by the judgment of wrath which has overtaken Him. Again, it is to us that all the love of God is turned with which God in His counsel, before all worlds, has loved this One in view of the judgment to be fulfilled on Him—and loved Him even as He actually fulfilled this judgment on Him. God's eternal Son in the bosom of the Father did not need this love, for He possessed and enjoyed it already—the same love with which He had loved the Father from all eternity. But we needed it and lacked it. We would not exist if God did not love us, and love us with the whole of that love with which He loves Himself, the Father the Son, and the Son the Father. " For us it is, all this is done." It all has reference to us in Jesus Christ. It is our reconciliation with God, the world's, that is accomplished in the fact that Jesus Christ became obedient to God and was truly guiltless, that He bore the sin of man, that He stood before God burdened with it, and made atonement for it in God's judgment. The presupposition of the divine judgment so far as it actually concerns us is that in the first instance it has fallen on Him and not on us. Our concern is to hold fast to Him, that is, to enter the darkness to which God has sentenced and condemned Him, in which He suffered under Pontius Pilate, was crucified, dead and buried, and descended into hell. Our concern is to submit to the judgment that has fallen on Him, so that in virtue of His rejection we may be the elect and sanctified, consenting to hear and accept the curse which is pronounced on us as it was pronounced on Him, but also to hear and accept the promise of love and the divine good-pleasure, as the object of which He was on the brink of dereliction, because for our sakes God did not will to abandon Him and did not in fact do so. It is our part then to share in His election and sanctification, to recognise ourselves as those who have participated in it, and for the sake of it to accept our condemnation and rejection as fulfilled in Him, our own death as already suffered by Him. In God's command, even as it becomes our judgment, we have first to recognise God's love as it is directed to us in the man who fulfilled His command. We have to hear as His basic imperative : " Be ye reconciled to God." Be those who are reconciled to God in Him, and nothing else. If God's command then judges us too, it cannot judge us except in accordance with itself, and as it has judged Him : to perish, and yet to be saved from perishing ; to death, and yet to life from death ; to rejection, and yet to the saving rejection of the elect. The comforting presupposition on which we go to God's judgment, the sure promise which accompanies us, is that in Jesus Christ we are fellows of the household of God, members of His people and citizens of His kingdom, and that it is as such, and only as such, that we come into judgment at all. Jesus Christ is the basis of judgment, and Jesus Christ is the promise which confirms itself as such in the midst of judgment. For this reason there is no fear, but there is only joy, at the prospect of coming into God's judgment. For this reason we shall stand in the judgment of the command only, but very definitely, when we go to meet it without fear, in the joy of those who belong to Jesus Christ.

2. THE EXECUTION OF THE DIVINE JUDGMENT

The first result of man's confrontation with God's command is that he is proved relentlessly and irrefutably to be its transgressor. The man who has no knowledge either of God's command, or of himself, or of the fact that God's command refers and is given to him and must be kept by him, would like to deny this, to acquit himself of transgressing God's command. It is the essence of every transgression of the command, the decisive proof that man is a sinner, that he continually denies the fact, trying to excuse and acquit himself in face of the accusation and sentence against him. This is the sin that is blacker than any other sin. Of all the things that God hates, the most hateful is that we should not admit ourselves to be the transgressors that we are, but should try to excuse and justify ourselves as what we are. In this we follow (*Heidelberg Catechism, Question* 5) the propensity of our nature, the fallen human nature which we have in common with Adam, hating God and our neighbour when we ought to love them. We can love God and our neighbour only if we recognise and confess ourselves as the transgressors we are without any attempt at excuse or self-vindication. As we are confronted with God's command, we are revealed as those who do not do this, but who permit that bias of human nature to run its course, so that in the effort to excuse and justify ourselves we can only hate God and our neighbour, struggling with might and main to know nothing of God's command, or of ourselves, or especially of the fact that God's command has specific reference to us. But the fact remains that the command of God is in force, and we are what we are, and the command of God is specifically given to us. The fulfilment of the divine judgment cannot, therefore, be arrested. The whole attempt of man to arrest it can only confirm that the sentence which is reached in this judgment is not unrighteous, but righteous. We are in fact transgressors. We are useless for what God wills with us and wills from us. We are lost for Him, and because everything depends on what we are for Him, and before Him, we are really lost.

We may sustain and develop this insight by a retrospective glance at the contents of the last two sections. We are neither those who fulfil and satisfy the *claim* of the divine command, nor those that we ought to be on the basis of the *decision* made concerning us in the divine command. We do not keep or fulfil the command, and therefore in the first instance the judgment in which we stand can consist only in our condemnation.

Yet it is not in the fact that God is gracious to us, and that we ought to believe in Him, that we do actually seek and find the basis of the divine claim. Curiously enough, we would rather have nothing to do with this God who wills and does the very best for us, and whose claim has an actual basis, a real and compelling authority. Instead we re-interpret Him as an aggregate of the supreme power, majesty, and above all worth, whose claim permits us to assert our own claims in face of Him, until finally we understand Him only as the sum of our own claims. Why should we keep God's command if our work and attitude are opposed to the basis of His claim? Again, it is not in the fact that we are required to approve the gracious act of God on our behalf that we do actually seek and find the content of the divine claim. We do not at all respect the Law as the form of His grace and therefore as the demand to conform our life to His grace. We do not live and behave as those who are God's property, to whom He is merciful, of whom He Himself is the righteousness. To this, the clear will of God, we remain in the deepest sense hostile, indifferent, self-willed, loveless. We desire many things—under the plea and excuse that we can and should desire them in virtue of the divine claim—but we do not desire the one thing that is really demanded of us. There is obviously no real thought of keeping and fulfilling God's command if we wish to overlook and hurry through its own proper content. And further, we do not truly seek and find the distinguishing form of the divine claim in the fact that, as distinct from all other commands, it orders us to make use of the freedom accorded to us by the grace of God as those who are loved by Him. We do not obey Him as those who are permitted to obey Him. We do not recognise His sternness and severity in the joy and conscientiousness and fearlessness in which He commands us to live as those who are given permission and freedom to live in this way. We do not keep our allotted place. We do not stand in the order in which we are set. We always think we know better than God does in His command. We keep the freedom to be our own judges of good and evil, always imagining that this is more salutary than the freedom of the children of God. We continually protest and revolt because the command of God pursues us so relentlessly. How can we possibly keep it and fulfil it if we treat it as though it were a feeble, man-made command, dependent on the judgment of ourselves or others? In short, have we ever even heard the claim of the divine command? Do we seriously accept the fact that it raises this claim and has this basis, content and form, and therefore demands a corresponding obedience, not just any obedience, but this particular obedience? When and where have we ever rendered this obedience? When and where do we not fall far short of that which is by nature indivisible and will bear no diminution? When and where, in face of the alternative with which we are here confronted, do we not deny that it is even raised and pressed? Who is righteous in face of this claim? By the fact that it is raised and pressed—and we may doubt this fact but we cannot alter its reality—we are proved to be transgressors against it, and doubly and trebly so in the fact that we do not recognise this proof, that we deny and question it, for this means only that we confirm it in this way, committing fresh transgression, which the claim of the command discloses as it is raised and pressed.

This, then, is the situation in relation to the divine decision executed in and with our encounter with God's command concerning us. Who and what are we in face of the sovereignty of this decision, in face of the fact that, by the command of God, our whole existence and action are revealed as responsible, and as the actual discharge of responsibility, to Him? What have we to bring forward in this encounter, in which we are required to adduce, with our existence and actions, a correspondence to the will of God for us and with us, namely, an obedient prosecution of this will, as it is revealed and must therefore be confessed in His command? All serious preparation for the encounter with the One who here decides concerning us, or radical ethical reflection on the inward questioning of our whole existence which takes place in this meeting, can result only in the knowledge that this inward questioning cannot be avoided, that there is preparation by which we can save and safeguard ourselves in face of it. This is because the will of God, not through its own fault but ours, in consequence of the mistaken and stupid and malicious way in which we ask concerning it, is never so fully known to us that we can arm ourselves in advance with righteousness in face of it, let alone imagine that we can really produce this righteousness on the basis of this preparation. But if we do not do this, who and what are we in God's sovereign judgment? Yet it may well be that, in face of our responsibility and actual response to the divine decision, our only thought has been that of flight, and we have never made any attempt at honest preparation. For when and where were we ever really honest in this matter? When and where have we ever seriously enquired concerning the will of God? But this being the case, how very far we are from fulfilling it! Now we are really at the place where there can be no alteration of the decision made concerning us in the sovereign command of God.

But, again, how do we stand in relation to the fact of the definiteness of the divine decision if it is true that no general principles have anything to do with the command of God and no supposed obedience to them is the obedience which we owe to this command? If it is true that the required good is a matter of our choice between several possibilities laid before us, a matter of our interpretation and application of this or that general rule, we can set our minds at rest. We know that we can fulfil this choice, interpretation and application with the utmost sincerity, the best of good intentions, and a good conscience which we can certainly concede to ourselves if we have this power over God's command. But, amongst all the possibilities, God's command always purposes and wills one thing only, this or that specific thing. Our obedience has to consist in an exact and concrete doing of this or that, as a human correspondence to the specific divine precept. To fulfil the command of God, I must be the kind of person who passes day and night as God's friend, who hangs day and night on His Word, who hearkens day and night to His bidding. We may again doubt, but we cannot alter, the fact that God on His side is so close to us in His grace, that He speaks with us so truly and continuously in His Word, that we are in a position to hear Him with the same truth and exactitude, and to obey Him accordingly. But this is the very thing that we do not do. When and where do we ever hear God's command with any exactitude even when we take the exceptional step of expressly undertaking to do this? And how can we really expect that this will happen in any useful manner when it is so exceptional, when our hearkening to God's command is never more than transitory, when we come running to God only on special occasions to hear His instructions, when we do not spend our lives generally as the friends of God that we ought to be, but in every other possible sphere of friendship? And how shall we fare if in this respect also our direct thought is only of flight from the command of God, namely, from the concrete and specific thing that it wills to have from us here and now, if we refuse basically to have in God's command a real " lamp unto our feet," if we persistently pursue a worldly or even a Christian righteousness of regulations, i.e., an arbitrary self-righteousness? This is just what we do! But where then is our actual righteousness, our righteousness before God, concerning which we are questioned? Can it be anything other than utterly filthy rags? And finally, how do we stand before God's command in view of the fact that it is definitely the command of His goodness, that it requires from each and all of us, in every respect, that which is right and friendly and wholesome? Where do we really find, in correspondence with this one universally valid command, the single-minded orientation of those to whom it is directed, their unity in and among themselves, which obedience to it would necessarily bring in its train? Does it not seem rather that we are subject to a very different command from this, and have to obey it? Does that which we do and do not do, in our own orbit and in relation to others, in the smallest as in the greatest spheres of human existence, produce the evil instead of the good which corresponds to the command, the wrong, the unfriendly, the harmful, and therefore discord in big and outward things and schizophrenia in little and inward as well as big and outward, the one conditioned by the other and calling to the other? This is quite inevitable when we deny the sovereignty and definiteness of the divine decision. But how diversely we stand in relation to this needle point, this simple content—that it is our determination to goodness! We are creatures cast in a very different mould, living according to quite different laws; creatures who do not appear to be able to stand comparison with the being of God given them in the command; creatures who, brought into this light and placed in this atmosphere, can obviously only perish like fish on dry land, dissolving like snow on a hot stove. But here, too, the true and characteristic mark of our conduct may well be flight from the command. We need not waste many words on the subject, because the phenomenon is well known, and has often been described, that we know and easily enough recognise the good as such, thus proving the proximity with which God always honours us in His command whatever may be our attitude to it ; but that we do not really accept it, far less love it ; that its opposite, evil, is always much closer to us than this thing which is closest of all ; that even in its darkness it is always much more illuminating than good, and even in its unnaturalness much more natural. How can we really come to the point where, in accordance with the command, we may treat the good, not as something alien, but as our very own rendering to the command outward and inward obedience, as those who are obedient from their hearts, in fellowship one with another, and in the inward peace which it obviously requires from us ? Who really adapts himself to its decision, according to which we have to confront it in this unity and fellowship ? If it is difficult or impossible to give to all these questions the answer that we are those who can stand before the decision of God's command ; if the recognition is unavoidable that we in our decisions stand opposed to the decision of the command in every kind of incongruity and heterogeneity, and that we show ourselves to be sinners against it, then the execution of the divine judgment can be seen by us, and we can realise quite conclusively that we are lost in this judgment, and unserviceable for God when measured by what He wills from us. The reason why God is angry need not be asked, and the threat that He might turn away His face from us altogether is quite understandable.

But we must not deceive ourselves. It is when and as the judgment of God is executed that these questions are unanswerable, and we are proved by God's command to be transgressors. The road which leads to an establishment and development of the knowledge that we are unrighteous before God is necessarily this. We realise that we are confronted with God's claim and decision. We constantly ask how we really stand in face of this claim and decision. And our answer is to the effect that we obviously stand very badly or not at all in this judgment. It is also very right and necessary to strengthen this answer from the very outset by realising that every other answer, and every contradiction against this one answer, can only confirm and underline its rightness. The command can require nothing higher of us than that we should be willing to be those as whom it addresses us. We cannot transgress more heinously against the command than by not admitting its accusation, for it is the blackest of all sins to try to deny that we are sinners. But at the very moment when we understand the matter in this final sharpness, we must be clear that this answer, and all the way that leads to it, has no real certainty in itself, but only in the fact that God's judgment is actually exercised in His command ; that the fulfilment of the divine judgment is an event that takes place between God and man, and that all that we have said in description of our confrontation with the command, and about the questions to which it gives rise and their tentative answers, may lay claim to be a description of this event, and to be indisputable in the light of it. Apart from this event, it would certainly not be indisputable. The proposition that we are in the wrong before God is proved by the fact that God shows it to be the case, i.e., that He actually puts us in the wrong, so that we actually are those who are put in the wrong by Him. This is not merely because we are aware of that confrontation, or ask those questions, and then more or less definitely admit and confirm that they are unanswerable, or, at least, that they can only be answered negatively. Even where this is the case we do not see that we are those who are put in the wrong by God. If it were not the case that God's judgment is actually executed in His command, we could not possibly ignore the fact that man has the power finally to contradict that proposition, and openly or secretly has quite definitely done so. The mere concept of the divine command as claim and decision cannot of itself force us to accept the verdict that we are its transgressors, and guilty and lost as such. Those who seriously recognise and confess that man is a transgressor of the command must also see that this recognition and confession cannot be occasioned and enforced by any demonstration, however clear, of the situation between God and man, by any posited questions, however pertinent, or by any given answers, however apposite—unless, of course, they are all sustained and verified by the fact that God's own action may be seen as the subject of this demonstration, revealing Himself and speaking for Himself, and thus giving force to the demonstration, questions and answers, and driving us into the position where we are inevitably put in the wrong before God. Without the proof of the divine act, it is always possible to contradict even the best human evidence in this matter. The transgression goes to such lengths, the transgressor uses such crafts, and his transgression is so hopeless, that unless this fact of the divine proof supervenes and prevents him he can listen to everything that must be said concerning his confrontation with the command, and asked in relation to it, and maintained as the obvious answer, and yet not really hear it, but still persuade himself and even assure others that he is not actually conscious of any lack of righteousness before God. Grace is the secret of the command, and except in the light of this secret it cannot be understood how strong and radical its claim and its decision are ; nor can it be known that we are put wholly in the wrong by the command. Except in the light of this secret, men speak of the judgment of God's command in the same way as the blind speak of colours. The contradiction cannot be silenced by the demand that they should recognise themselves as the transgressors of the command or the reproach that it is insincere, flippant and superficial not to be prepared to do this. We must not be deceived. In the last analysis no arguments can overcome it, however cogent. No direct means will suffice. The contradiction can be beaten down only by the divine judgment itself. The blind man would not be blind, but endowed with sight, if he were to talk about colours in any way other than the unfortunate way in which he does. The secret of grace must first have been seen if we are to demand of anybody that he forgo his self-justification. The transgression of the sinner must first have been forgiven and he himself acquitted if he is to recognise and confess that he has no possible hope of standing his ground before the claim and decision of God. No exhortation and no persuasion can create this situation. We can none of us put either ourselves or others in it. It arises only as the judgment of God is executed. It arises only as we come under the fatherly chastisement of God, which consists in the revelation of the secret of His grace, and therefore of the sternness and severity of His judgment. If we really understand that we are transgressors, that we are all apostate and worthless, that the people of God is always and at all points a people of the lost, which cannot of itself receive or pronounce its own justification, which can live only by the justification of God, we shall always remember this, knowing that every demonstration of judgment in which we stood or stand or will stand has validity only when it is actually executed upon us by the Word and work of God, only when it is an actual event. We shall know that this event is, for him and for all others, the act of divine proof. It is of this act of divine proof that we must now speak as giving force to all that we have so far said concerning the divine judgment.

The death of Jesus Christ is this act of divine proof, the execution of the judgment. This is the miracle whose occurrence alone can decide, and has in fact decided, the truth of the statement that we are sinners. In the death of Jesus there occurs visibly, effectively and once and for all the confrontation of God and man, of the divine command and man's existence and conduct. For on the basis of the eternal election of this One, of His personal unity with God, on the basis also of God's will to act with and for us all in the person of this One, His own Son, God stands before man and man before God in a mutual encounter. In God's encounter with this man it is a matter of the decree and the act of love in which He loved and loves and will love us all. And the love of God finds in this One, as the Representative of all the rest, nothing worthy of love, nothing that He can affirm or approve or praise, nothing in which He can have pleasure—no inward, excellent part in man, no higher striving, no imperfect obedience which might constitute even a relative perfection and therefore make him righteous and acceptable to God. If man has a glory, or even an exculpation and vindication to bring forward, where is God more likely to find it than at the point where he stands before the Father in the person of the Son of God Himself ? Will not even the most secret good there may be in us, or at least in a few of us, be disclosed at this point ? But in fact not a single argument is here adduced in our favour. The election of this One, the representation of all by God's own Son, bring a very different truth to light. For in the name of all of us, Jesus Christ can only produce our sins, our transgression of the command. In His person man is shown to be a recreant and rebel, an enemy and opponent of God, whom God can meet only as such. In this person the case is instigated against him. In this person he is impeached and sentenced and condemned. The one Righteous has no righteousness to proclaim in our name or to our credit. This one Righteous can be righteous in our place, can be obedient for our sake, only because He acknowledges our sin, and drinks to the bitter dregs the cup of temporal and eternal destruction which must follow our transgression. The only thing that affords any real plea for the rest of us is the fact that He has done this for us. And be it noted that this is what He has in fact done. He has openly confessed and avowed our apostasy. He has borne our guilt, the suffering of the righteous wrath of God on our behalf. This is what God has done for us by giving us His own Son as our Brother. For the rest of us there remains only the cardinal fact that our sins are forgiven because He Himself has confessed and atoned them in our place. This is the execution of the divine judgment. This is the way in which God actually contradicts our contradiction, silencing the voice which denies our transgression, and which we cannot silence just because we are transgressors. This is God's fatherly chastisement in the revelation of the secret of His grace, a chastisement which takes place and concerns us all and is therefore inescapable. We can, and indeed do, evade every self-judgment that we try to execute on ourselves in the form of a reconstruction of our actual meeting with God, or every theoretical computation of our standing in relationship to the command of God and its claim and decision, unless there stands behind it God's own judgment, the real judgment, giving to our self-judgment a seriousness and force which it cannot have of itself. In defiance of every computation, unless God's own judgment gives it force, we will continually excuse and vindicate ourselves, and that voice of denial, a thousand times contradicted, will continually be raised again. How can a judgment be anything but worthless if the judge is himself the transgressor ? How can we ever expect a man like this to pronounce himself guilty, even if the law and prosecution and hearing of witnesses speak clearly against him, and the speeches in defence are quite empty ? We cannot and we will not escape the real judgment of God which is executed in the death of Jesus Christ, for it is our actual meeting with God, which we can hardly reconstruct in all our self-judgment, even in the best of circumstances. In Jesus Christ God has found us once and for all as the men we are, irrespective of any present or future ideas we might have of ourselves, adjudging ourselves to be more or less sincere and logical. For it was and is God's good-will from all eternity to see us in Jesus Christ, to deal with us as He deals with Him and therefore as the men we are, to find us in Him, to judge us as He judges Him. It was and is His good-will to give us in Him our Head and Advocate ; to establish and ordain our whole relationship to Him in His relationship to His person, and therefore to reveal the truth of our existence in His. As this happens, as from all eternity, and in what God has done in Him at the heart of time, we are those who are loved and known by God in Jesus Christ, all self-judgment to which we might submit ourselves is absolutely subordinated to His judgment. Any reconstruction of our actual meeting with Him can be only a reflection of the meeting with man which He has willed and accomplished in the person of His dear Son. In this meeting we are in truth what we are. And there is no escaping the truth of what we are in this meeting. Before the voice of this reality, the voice of denial, my voice as the voice of the transgressor, is necessarily silenced. In place of every weak theory of our relationship to God and to His command there comes the powerful theory of this practice—the theory of our actual relationship to God. And in place of the weak self-judgment in which we cause ourselves to be exculpated there comes the powerful self-judgment in which we must and will declare that we are guilty, because we ourselves, as the sinners we are, can only repeat the divine sentence, adding to it not at all either for good or evil. There, on the cross of Golgotha, hangs the man who in His own name and person represented me, my name and person, with God ; and who again in His own name and person represented God to me in my name and person. Everything, therefore, that God has to say in His relationship to me is originally and properly said to Him ; everything that I have to say to God in this relationship is originally and properly said by Him. All that I have to do, therefore, is to repeat what is already said in this conversation between God and the Son. But what takes place in this conversation is that in the person of Jesus Christ I am addressed as a sinner, a lost son, and that again in the person of Jesus Christ I confess myself to be a sinner, a lost son. In this conversation the voice of denial is absolutely silenced. For in the death of Jesus Christ, this conversation between Father and Son is conducted with me and about me—with me and about me in His person as my Advocate before God. Even in the soliloquy and self-judgment which I cannot escape in face of the divine colloquy and judgment the voice of denial cannot be raised. I am not one who, as a hearer of this divine conversation, and a participator in this divine judgment, can either hear or make any kind of excuse. At the point where God deals with me, where He has sought and found me, at the cross of Golgotha, I am exposed and addressed as a sinner. Indeed, I have found and confessed myself to be this. I have nothing to add to what is said and confessed there, nor to subtract from it. The transgression in all transgressions, the sin in all sins, namely, that I should refuse the name of a sinner, is made quite impossible. It is literally nailed to the cross with Jesus Christ. It can only die. The only thing that I can do is recognise that my sin is really dead—the sin from which I cannot cleanse myself, the sin which I cannot even recognise and confess, the sin which I could only see awakening, and myself awaken, to constantly new forms of life if it were not already dead in the fact that God has pronounced and executed His sentence on His beloved Son in my place, and that the latter has accepted it in my place. This is the execution of the divine judgment which takes place as God gives us His command ; for He gives it as He is gracious to us in Jesus Christ, as He gives us this His beloved Son to be our Head and Representative, as by Him He speaks to us and causes us to speak to Himself, as by the Holy Spirit He accomplishes our unity with His Son, for which He has destined us from all eternity. In the same Holy Spirit, in which that divine conversation is conducted and divine judgment fulfilled at the cross of Golgotha, it is also true that they both happen in our name and in our place and that we are actually made participators in them, called to faith in Jesus Christ, awakened to the knowledge of our unity with Him, and therefore given a share in the confrontation with God. In this confrontation, there is no escaping, or trying to escape, the recognition and confession that we are transgressors. On the contrary, we are ready to live as those who are in the wrong before God, expecting every good from our continuance in this knowledge and confession, and fearing nothing more than attempts to remove ourselves from this position.

It is clear that even the reference to the actual execution of the divine judgment, to the death of Jesus Christ as the unmistakeable exposure of our transgression, can never be more than a reference. And it, too, is a reference which we can only fill out with human words, not displaying or introducing or exploiting as such the event which it signifies. It is really a matter of the act of divine proof which alone can decide in this question, and which obviously cannot be either created or replaced by this final consideration. If the Holy Spirit does not Himself speak, so that we see what is to be seen in this consideration, the secret of the grace of God will not be revealed even by the most basic deliberation, even by this final reference. The revelation of this secret is really a matter for the Holy Spirit, and not for our spirit. But this does not make our final reference superfluous any more than it did the reflections with which we started. It reminds us that the whole recognition of man's sin and guilt, which is our present concern, cannot be achieved in a self-imposed and self-conducted conversation and judgment ; that it is no less the work of

God in us than everything that we have still to consider as the grace of God in judgment ; indeed, that in itself and as such this recognition is an inalienable constituent of the recognition of the grace of God. In actual fact, it can be achieved only in prayer. It is in prayer that what we have referred to is really true, i.e., that in view of the death of Christ our excuses are all silenced, however obvious they may be or however eager we may be to find them. The man who really prays never attempts to justify himself. In true prayer, he knows that he cannot do so. When we really pray, the voice of denial, which we have no direct power to stifle, definitely cannot be raised or heard. We are in the position where the only thing that we can hear is the divine sentence on man visited on Jesus Christ, and the only thing that we can express is the confession of the transgression and misery of man which Jesus Christ has once for all defeated. When we really pray we believe in Him ; and the work of the Holy Spirit is in process of fulfilment. The meaning and value of the final reference is that it directs us to the point where there takes place radically and irresistibly God's effective contradiction of our contradiction, and the shattering of all self-righteousness. This point is neither remote nor unattainable so long as we pray, and believe as we pray, and in faith participate in the death of Jesus Christ, and in this participation abandon every other life but that of the lost son.

All this, however, is only our first word concerning the execution of the divine judgment and a second must be added if we are to say all that has to be said on this subject. We cannot understand the full truth of the first unless we first think of the second. We can really comprehend that we are in the wrong before God only in the light of the fact that God will put us in the right in His judgment, that He is gracious to us in Jesus Christ, and not the reverse. As He actually addresses His love to us, He condemns us as transgressors and male-factors in the person of His own Son. But we are acquitted and justified because, although this condemnation refers to us, it does so in the person of Jesus Christ, and therefore in such a way that what remains for us is the forgiveness of our sins. It is in this way that it does really affect us. And it is when it is understood in this way that it forces us to recognise that we are sinners. The forgiveness of our sins in Jesus Christ is God's judgment on us, and only the revelation of forgive-ness is the revelation of our sins. It confronts us with ineluctable and incontestable compulsion only when it alone forms the true and final reality. For this reason we must now turn our attention specific-ally to the fact that God's judgment is executed in the forgiveness of our sins, or, positively, in our justification.

As God's command is given to us, what we do and do not do is shown in different ways and to differing degrees, but at bottom in every respect, to be apostasy, treason and revolt. But on a Christian view, although it is true, it is only a penultimate and not an ultimate fact that, measured by God's command, I do the evil and not good, never being in the right but always in the wrong before God in all my thoughts and words and acts. For my whole calling and ability and competence and right to say that which is ultimate, to create eternal facts, to make divine decisions in my acts, is completely abrogated by the fact that the judgment of God is executed on me by His command. Only the man who does not yet know the divine command, who has not yet submitted himself to its judgment, can think it possible to make an eternal choice as though he were a second God. If he does, he really suffers under the curse which actually accompanies our own choice, and he is forced to bear it as an eternal curse. This is precisely the error of unbelief. What is promised man by the judgment of the divine command is a perfectly definite, but as such a strictly limited, self-knowledge. As self-knowledge, the realisation that we are transgressors in all our actions is incontrovertible truth which cannot be abrogated, with which we have to live, for it cannot in any sense serve our peace of mind to renounce it. Only this self-knowledge corresponds to what man is and always will be of himself before God, the state in which he is sought and found by God. To deny this state is nothing less than to deny God's grace. For the grace of God has reference only to those who are transgressors of their own accord, and the revelation of it has reference only to those who acknowledge and confess themselves to be transgressors.

But it is not the will of the gracious God, nor is it the purpose of His command, to enslave man with this state in which He seeks and finds him, or with the corresponding self-knowledge. Nor will He enslave Himself with this antithesis of His own holiness and man's lack of holiness, His own righteousness and man's lack of righteousness. The final end of His judgment is not the disclosure of this state of affairs between Himself and us, so that we are compelled to confess this, and He deals with us accordingly. For in the execution of His righteous wrath, this could mean only that He would drive us from His face, i.e., abandon us to eternal destruction. But when He gives us His commandment, He brings us to judgment as those who are elected and loved and blessed by Him. He takes us so seriously as His covenant-partners that these are the lengths to which He is prepared to go with us. Because His faithfulness is eternal, our unfaithfulness is necessarily revealed and self-endorsed. But He cannot leave it at that. For where is His faithfulness if our unfaithfulness has the last word? How can His right be divine right if our wrong is allowed and able to maintain itself against Him? What Titans we necessarily are if we can posit ourselves absolutely, as it were, in the corresponding self-knowledge, as if we could create and provide it for ourselves, as if it were not inherently the work of God's grace, and to be attained only in prayer! For if on the one side man is obviously the transgressor of the command which he is found to be in God's judgment,

on the other he is the object of God's love which he was before he
became a transgressor, and cannot cease to be even as a transgressor
who is condemned in the divine judgment. If, on the one side, there
is man's self-knowledge as a transgressor, which he cannot avoid and
definitely must not renounce, on the other there is his knowledge by
God. For this certainly confirms the truth of his self-knowledge. Yet
it is not exhausted by this truth, but transcends it. In it, even as
the transgressor he is, man is elected and loved by God, the partner
of His covenant and the possessor of its promise. And he does not
cease to be this. But because there are these two very different
aspects, we can and must regard even the incontrovertible and
relentless proof that man is an evil-doer as only a first result of
the confrontation of man with God's command, and not as its final
outcome.

In this antithesis, we are, in fact, something very different from
what we are in and of ourselves. In it we have an additional quality
which we cannot possibly maintain in any continuation or extension
or intensification of our self-knowledge, and which has nothing to do
with any dignity that we may oppose to God—as if we either possessed
or had obtained it for ourselves. Yet it is a real quality of our own,
and it persists and prevails as such in and in spite of our judgment
by the divine command, and cannot be denied, but only confirmed,
by the necessary self-knowledge that we are transgressors. It is the
quality in which God knows us beyond His knowledge of us as sinners.
It is the quality in which we do not know ourselves but are known
by Him ; our quality as those to whom He has sworn and maintains
fidelity in spite of our infidelity. Because of this quality, we are
justified in the judgment—the very judgment in which, on the basis
of our other qualities, we are shown to be wholly unjustified, in which
we can answer and adduce absolutely nothing in self-justification.
We have neither the power nor the liberty to evade at any price the
sentence on our actions and their value, on our life as we live it of
ourselves. But we cannot and must not evade the further judgment
in which this first sentence is included. It is true enough that our
actions are valueless in the sight of God, and our life forfeit. But we
evade the righteousness of God if we try to refuse to hear His sentence
beyond this conclusion. It may well imply a final and particularly
evil form of self-justification if we insist rigidly in the self-knowledge—
which we cannot resist and definitely must not renounce—that we
are transgressors, placing ourselves as such in absolute antithesis to
God : as though by what we are and do—and therefore by what we
are and do as sinners before God—we had made, or were in a position
to make, an eternal choice ; as though we had in this way introduced
an eternal factor into our relationship with God. At this point what
seems to be the deepest and most sincere humility may obviously be
only the crassest pride, which merely betrays the fact that we have

not yet accepted the sentence executed upon us by the command of God, or attained the corresponding self-knowledge. If we have really done this, we must not resist the fact that God knows us in another way than we know ourselves in this self-knowledge. If we have really attained it, we must not oppose the fact that God will pronounce us free and righteous, forgiving our sins and addressing and treating us as His dear children, on the basis of the one quality which, beyond all our reprehensible qualities, He sees and finds in us, on the basis of His own goodness, in which He wills to see and seek us in this way. The actual and necessary penitence for our sins is obviously fulfilled in the fact that we are ready to accept this, just as the judgment of God is fulfilled in the fact that He addresses us and deals with us. Our penitence is not fulfilled, and we have not accepted our sentence, if we try, as it were, to rivet ourselves to our sins, ignoring the fact that God can see and judge us otherwise than in relation to our sins. He can indeed look beyond our sins even as He sees them, and, in so doing, pronounce upon us the final and decisive Word of His judgment, in face of which we have real cause to humble ourselves. I have not really humbled myself at His first Word if I refuse this final Word. God is righteous in this Word, i.e., He maintains His right to us, and vindicates it against the claim which Satan might make to us, and the false claim which, seduced by Satan, we might think we have to ourselves—thus creating our right before Him in face of the wrong which Satan does us and which, seduced by him, we do ourselves. For in virtue of that quality which is known to ourselves but well known to Him, denied and forfeited by us but indestructible according to His will, God looks upon us as His children and covenant-partners, and acquits and justifies us as such. Our justification takes place in default and defiance of our merit, but even so in true and supreme justice. It does not take place because of a weakness or indifference in relation to our transgression, but as this is expressly perceived and treated as such ; yet not in such a way that, constrained by it, God is forced by our unfaithfulness to abandon His faithfulness, but in final confirmation of His faithfulness. It takes place by way of forgiveness, by the conscious non-imputation and non-assertion of our sin, and yet in all seriousness as the decisive action of God against our sin, as His most forceful protest against our transgression of His command. How indeed could He protest more energetically against it than by the mere fact that He does not lay it to our charge, that although He knows and convicts us as sinners, He does not treat us seriously as such, but in spite of our sin continues to deal with us as He had decided and as He wills ? The objective meaning of our justification in God's judgment is that God does not permit Himself to be hindered and arrested in His course by our sins, but maintains His right against us, not merely in opposition to us— He does this, too, but if this were the whole story it would be a human,

one-sided right and not the right of the supreme Judge over all parties
—but in fellowship with us. It therefore takes the form, not only of
the revealing and chastisement of our wrong, but also of the annulling
of wrong by right. We can be pardoned in the judgment—and our
sins forgiven—because God wills to be in the right, not only for Himself, but in fellowship with us, and because He wills not only to reveal
wrong as such, but also to destroy it. The forgiveness of our sins is
the final and decisive word which the command has to say to us, and
which we have to consider. Forgiven sin does not mean sin connived
at or forgotten or no longer indicated by the command. The statement
that it is forgiven does not mean that there is no longer sin in our self-
knowledge, or that penitence is no longer required. We have not
received forgiveness, nor are we acquitted and justified in God's judgment, if we do not acknowledge and confess our sin, if it does not
grieve us to the heart, if we do not remain under the accusation of
the command, if we do not maintain the responsibility which we owe
to God for what we are and do and which shatters all our assurance.
Our forgiveness means that God does not allow us to fall under the
past, present and future accusation of His command ; that even as
the accused and condemned people we were and are and always will
be before Him, we do not cease to be His children, and to enjoy all
our rights as His children. Forgiven sin means real sin, but sin in
which God does not see or accept our sinfulness, the folly and wickedness of our intentions and actions—far less the doubtful relics of an
accompanying good, or the relative perfecting of an unfulfilled obedience, or anything of that sort—but primarily Himself, His love to
us, His sworn covenant, His faithfulness, and then ourselves as He
knows us, as He has known about us from all eternity. Forgiven sin
is our being and action as—corrupt in itself, and not to be considered
apart from penitence and sorrow—it is received and accepted by Him
as good in virtue of His imposed, unarbitrary, infinitely righteous,
but free and fatherly good-pleasure. It is good, therefore, because
He does not allow our sin, folly and malice to prevail before Him, or
recognise it as our essential being and condition, but cancels it ; because
He sees us as snow-white, and because, in the creative truth of His
being and condition, we are actually snow-white where we have made
and always make ourselves blood-red in His judgment. Forgiven sin
is our being and action in so far as God takes us to Himself, even though
we and our deeds are evil, accepting our being and action as real
obedience and righteousness before Him. The forgiveness of sins, or
justification, is thus the total and radical acceptance of the sinner,
and the total and radical reversal and conversion of the being and
action in which he appears before God's judgment-seat, unable either
to excuse or justify himself. When He justifies us, God does not
interpret evil as good ; for He never allegorises. Nor does He call
evil good when He forgives us ; for He cannot lie. But in virtue of

His omnipotent compassion, and because He is Lord and Judge over good and evil alike, He makes that which is intrinsically evil good, that which is sick whole, that which is feeble glorious, that which is dead alive.

We are totally evil when we enter His judgment and totally cleansed when we leave it. In the one sentence of God we are both *semper peccatores* and *semper iusti*. The forgiveness of sins consists in the fact that these two predicates do not exclude one another, that they stand opposed, not in dialectical equilibrium, but with a preponderance of the second over the first ; in the fact that their sequence is irreversible, that God never creates evil out of good, but good out of evil ; in the fact that *semper iusti* is the second and final word which is to be heard and considered at this point. This is God's grace in judgment. It is just when we are in utter terror for ourselves that we are completely comforted, and in such a way that we can put the whole fear, however serious and settled it may be, behind us, and have all the comfort of the inconceivable divine inversion and transformation of our being and actions before us. The command of God, as it becomes our judgment, places us in this direction. It cannot be otherwise if it is true that the Law is the form of the Gospel.

We must now emphasise and underline the fact that all this is true in the event and execution of the divine judgment—powerfully, compellingly and convincingly true. What we have just completed is again a reconstruction of this event. The execution of the divine judgment itself is another matter. It alone can provide the compelling truth of even the most accurate reconstruction. If we assume that our reconstruction is accurate, God judges us in the true and righteous judgment of His command, according to His own truth, according to the law of His covenant of grace, according to the righteousness of His mercy, and therefore as His own people, as those whom none can pluck out of His hand, and therefore, as He condemns our transgression, as those who are righteous before Him, so that our evil being and action are good, our perverted works are righteousness before Him. Nobody can say that this incredible proposition, the doctrine of the justification of sinners in God's judgment, is either clear or self-evident. It is attested by the event to which it refers and which it reconstructs, but not by the proposition as such. It is proved only by the act of divine proof. As a proposition, it is no less contestable than the prior affirmation that in the divine judgment man is found to be a transgressor. If we realise that both propositions speak only of God's own grace, we shall have to admit this. Only God Himself can speak of His grace in such a way that every contradiction and misunderstanding is excluded. Is any doctrine more contestable than that of the justification of the sinner ? And is there any doctrine which can be more perilously affirmed ? If we try to understand it in abstraction from its reference to the actual execution of the divine judgment, we can only misunderstand it, whether we accept it or reject it. Here, too, the blind eyes must be opened if true statements are to be made about the colours. Here, too, the divine proof of the actual execution of the judgment must first speak for itself—the doctrine of justification does not do this in its own right—if the contradiction and misunderstanding of it are really to be excluded. We have again to consider this act of divine proof, which we can now interpret only as a divine miracle.

This act of divine proof is the resurrection of Jesus Christ. The resurrection alone is decisive for the truth that, as sinners before God, we are pronounced righteous. It silences both the contradiction and the misunderstanding of this proposition. In it, the confrontation of man with God has run its course and reached its end. This end is that the sinful man who was condemned and punished by God on account of his sin is acquitted and justified by the same God, being invested with all the glory of one who is righteous, and therefore rescued from the death into which he had fallen. And this man was sinful in the sense that He was the Bearer of our sin and took our place before God, and therefore accepted God's sentence and punishment for us. As our Head and Representative, He was sinful, and died for sin. And as our Head and Lord He also rose from the dead, and beyond that sentence received God's justification. Having first been humiliated, He was now exalted to the right hand of God. And just as He was our Head and Lord in the first case, so, too, He is in the second. Just as the *Ecce homo*! is true in the first case, excluding every contradiction of the conclusion that we are sinners, so, too, it is in the second, resisting every contradiction of the truth of our justification, and every misunderstanding of this truth. The resurrection of Jesus Christ reveals the fact that God makes no mistake in His faithfulness to His dear Son, and therefore that the latter does not cease to be this because He stands before the Father at Golgotha burdened with all the actual sin and guilt of man and of each individual man, and is treated in accordance with the deserts of man as the transgressor of the divine command. The Father in His faithfulness has set Him there, and the Son in turn evinces a corresponding faithfulness by allowing Himself to be set there. And it is for our sakes that the Father has set Him there and the Son has allowed Himself to be set there. His name, therefore, represents and includes our name, His person our person, both in what He suffers and in what He does, in what He undergoes both as condemnation and as justification. If the resurrection of Jesus Christ is simply the revelation of the faithfulness of the Father and the Son, which persists in the judgment to which He was subjected, it is also the revelation of the faithfulness which persists in our judgment. It is the revelation that even in the judgment which affects us and to which we have to submit we do not cease to be the elect and beloved of God. It is the revelation that God does not maintain and uphold His right against Satan and against ourselves by turning His face away from us and letting us fall as we had deserved, but by turning His countenance to us and safeguarding and honouring our own right to live against Satan and against ourselves. That is how He treated His own Son when He raised Him from the death to which He had been delivered. And that is how He has dealt with us in Him as our Lord and Head. He has " delivered him over for our transgression, and raised him for our justification " (Rom. 4²⁵). The sentence which God has pronounced on His own Son, and on us in Him, has, in fact, the twofold character implied in the doctrine of justification. It speaks both of our transgression and also of our justification. In the light of the original form of this sentence as a sentence on Jesus Christ Himself, it is impossible either to contradict the doctrine of justification or to misunderstand it.

Who is the God of whom the doctrine seems to say such wonderful things ? If He remains true to the transgressor of His command, even to the extent of acquitting and justifying Him, He remains equally true to Himself, because He has promised fidelity to the transgressor in Jesus Christ ; because the sentence and condemnation of the transgressor is executed to the letter in the person of his Head and Advocate ; because, now that this has happened—not for our sakes, but for the sake of our Head and Advocate—He owes it to Himself, and therefore, for the great love with which He has loved us in Him, to us, to receive us as those who are free from every sentence and condemnation and righteous and acceptable to Him. There comes on us in Jesus Christ that which is supremely fitting for us as those who are elect in Him, sinners whose sins He has taken to Himself, justified on the basis of the righteousness of His obedience. That there comes on us that which we have deserved we cannot, of course, say in any meaningful way. Even the reward which Jesus Christ Himself receives for the obedience in which He took up our case—our liberation, justification and atonement—is not really a strict repayment, for He is obedient as a Son to the Father, and it is simply a free gift of the Father from the wealth of His possessions which are those also of the Son. And the fact that we receive this reward certainly cannot be understood in terms of any merit of ours. It is sufficient proof of the righteousness of God that in His judgment we actually receive that which is fitting and proper for us, our right and due : in Jesus Christ the condemnation and rejection corresponding to our transgression ; and by Jesus Christ the justification and adoption corresponding to our election in Him. The forgiveness of our sins is indeed an act of free divine mercy, as is also the whole fact that He has loved and elected us in His own Son, that He appointed Him our Head and Advocate in both evil and good, in relation to our transgression and also to our justification. The rule of this compassion of God is fulfilled in the form of an act which cannot be interrupted or denied as such. It is true that our sin is real sin and unpardonable as such. But as real sin against God, it can be forgiven as in the person of His own Son God Himself intervenes in accordance with the love with which He has loved us from all eternity, taking upon Himself the condemnation and rejection corresponding to the reality of our sin, and finally, in keeping with the power of this vicarious act, taking away its guilt and punishment and forgiving us our sin. When He does this, He does not act as an unjust judge, but as the most just of all. Someone might ask : What kind of knowledge is this, in which God is in a position to see and accept as good, in fact to invert and transform into good, that which we have done from evil motives, and which He Himself has defined and characterised as evil ? The answer is : It is His almighty and holy knowledge of the truth in His everlasting Word which is Jesus Christ ; in the Word at the beginning of all His ways and works by which He sustains all things, which He opposes, pre-eminent and triumphant, to Satan, to evil, to sin, to Adam's fall, and to each individual sin of each individual man from all eternity, in which He says No to all these things from all eternity, but in which, in spite of all these things, He has said Yes to man. That He sees and hates our intrinsic sin, that He sentences and condemns us as sinners, is so true that it led to what took place at Golgotha. But it is also true that He does not allow our sin to prevail, that He defines it as falsehood, and puts His vital and powerful truth in its place. This is indeed the essence of truth, which proclaims itself in that sentence and condemnation, and is directly revealed in the justification of the sinner. For it is what took place in the garden of Joseph of Arimathea that reveals the secret hidden in the event of Golgotha. God has recognised and known us only in His eternal Word, which is Jesus Christ. We hear this one Word of God, and therefore who and what we and our existence and activity are in God's cognition which is the epitome of all truth, when we finally hear His command and judgment as our acquittal.

And who is the man to whom God has simply sworn fidelity, with whom He will keep covenant in all circumstances, in whom God has such interest that He regards him as His under all conditions and in spite of his transgression ? It is the man whom God has recognised and known from all eternity in His own dear Son, whom He has loved and elected in Him, to whom He has given Him as Head and Advocate, and whom He has destined to live in and through and for Him. This man as such is as assuredly the object of the fidelity and unalterable interest of God as is Jesus Christ Himself. That this is the case is the revelation of Easter Day. In relation to this man, there is no right of God against Satan, or evil, or his own sin, which God champions and asserts except in such a way that man's own right of existence is also revealed and vindicated in face of the death to which he has fallen victim. This man's cause is, in fact, God's own cause. He is certainly the man who cannot help himself. But powerful and decisive help is given him in Jesus Christ. Of himself, he has nothing to bring before God but his sin. But in his shame and nakedness he is covered by Jesus Christ, by the righteousness of his Head and Advocate. In it he is righteous and acceptable to God because, over and above the sin which speaks against him, he can allow the forgiveness accorded him to speak for him. In it, God's own Son speaks for him. Where, then, is his sin and guilt? It persists to the extent that he does not live by the forgiveness which he is granted, that he does not allow God's Son to speak for him, but continually tries to conduct his own case, refusing to confess his sin, preferring to excuse and justify himself. This is his continued sin and guilt. We need not look very far for the sin. We shall continually meet ourselves on this way, and in so far as we are on this way our sin and guilt lie on us in all their gravity. And the more eagerly we proceed on this way, the basically evil way of all apostasy, the more heavily they do so. But if we realise again that God's Son is made sin for us, if we hear afresh the annihilating accusation that is raised against us, if we listen anew to the voice of the selfsame Son of God speaking for us, we certainly cannot continue in this way. We are made responsible as we have heard the voice of the risen Lord, and it is our responsibility to continue to hear this voice. It is as hearers of this voice that we are taken seriously in God's judgment, and it is as such that we must take ourselves seriously. As there is no other true responsibility, there is no other true seriousness. All other seriousness is frivolity, a gamble with eternal perdition. It is by this seriousness alone that we can turn our back on the possibility of eternal perdition. This is the seriousness of those who are ready to live only by the forgiveness granted to them. And it is the true and vital seriousness demanded of us. And in it we cannot fail altogether to see the particular attribute in which God considers us in this astonishing judgment—the unknown subject of our life, whose predicates are all so very different from what we must ascribe to ourselves if our self-knowledge is authentic and accurate. If we keep before us the fact that " Jesus lives, and I in Him," this unknown attribute, the new subject of human life may be very hard to see or demonstrate in ourselves, yet it is no mere paradox, but the most obvious and natural truth. This unknown quality consists in the fact that from all eternity we confront God, not in some form of self-will or self-sufficiency, but in His own Son ; that we are what we are, not in our own name or person, but in the name and person of Jesus Christ. The existence of the new man in us, which is so hidden when we try to observe and investigate and confirm it in ourselves ; our existence in eternal membership in God's Son ; our being in Jesus Christ—all the new and inconceivable predicates of our life are real because they are the predicates of Jesus Christ, and they are revealed to us in the fact that in His resurrection, rescued from perdition and death, He is invested with them ; that He is revealed rather as their original and proper Bearer. He is our Head and Representative, so that we have only to look at Him to discover them as our own predicates, and we give Him the lie if we are not willing to admit that we possess this quality, that we are actually the new man with these inconceivable predicates.

Where in truth is the insoluble contradiction between the concepts of God and of man which we might oppose to the doctrine of justification ? Where is the overpowering proximity between the holy God and unholy man, or the obscuring of the command of God, which are laid to its charge ? It is itself justified against all critics, and becomes strong, convincing truth, the moment we understand it, not with anthropological narrowness, but in its proper christological breadth and depth. If it is understood in this way, it certainly does not give any occasion for the misunderstanding of an unwelcome applause. How can we really go to meet the judgment of God without fear for our own persons if we do not continually fear it in face of its fulfilment in the person of Jesus Christ, and of the accusation which He causes to fall on Himself and which is therefore raised against all men ? If we try to seek and find any other freedom than that of the Son of God taken from judgment and raised again from the dead, we are not free—either in a moral or a non-moral sense—but the slaves of sin. We are not free in God if we think we can be free in any other way than by allowing God to make us free. We are not free if we do not know that it is only by the grace of Jesus Christ that we are made free, and that this happens on the brink of the abyss into which our self-will and self-sufficiency can and should hurl us every day and every hour ; if we do not know that we always need the One who is our Head and Advocate in the kingdom of the living God, and by whom we are torn away from every path of self-excuse and self-justification which leads directly to destruction. We are not complete if we do not know that we constantly renounce this path, not trying to find our fulfilment, even in the slightest degree, outside the name and person of Jesus Christ. Man's justification in judgment, as it has taken place in Jesus Christ, is as little exposed to the perfectionist cr libertine misconception in any of its forms as it can be confounded with it in any competent criticism. Always—as the actual execution of divine judgment—it will speak for itself both on the right hand and the left.

But it is salutary and necessary for us to add at this point : Yes, when it does so, when our justification in Jesus Christ itself speaks to us. For the reference to the resurrection of Jesus Christ, which has the decisive word at this point, can only be a reference. We cannot produce the event itself and its attestation. When we speak christologically, we do not leave the sphere of theology and enter that of the divine action to which the whole of theology can only refer. We have considered the secret of Easter Day. But the Holy Spirit is the secret even of that which, in the revelation of the eternal divine purpose, took place between the Father and the Son on Easter Day, at the heart of time. And it is the work of the same Holy Spirit when this secret does not remain dumb but speaks with us, so that the secret is revealed to us and our justification in Jesus Christ does itself speak to us in a way which we can neither contradict nor mistake. This last reference and consideration necessarily remind us again that, however earnestly theology may struggle to achieve breadth and profundity, it is always impotent until it transcends itself, until it becomes the theology of the resurrection, which means concretely, until it becomes prayer. In prayer the work of the Holy Spirit, who is the secret of Easter Day, is done in those who pray. In prayer this secret is disclosed to them. In prayer they live as those who are risen with Jesus Christ. We cannot expect the actual disclosure of the secret of the risen Christ, or the effective dissolution of resistance to the doctrine of the justification of the sinner, or the removal of the possibility of misunderstanding it, merely from a broadening or deepening—however serious—in the understanding of the doctrine as such. To the impure all things are impure. These things can be expected only when the doctrine itself is made a matter for prayer. Then we shall not wait in vain for this disclosure, for the dissolution of all resistance, for the removal of every possibility of misunderstanding. In prayer this tenet becomes true. In prayer no one has ever found any contradiction in the justification of the sinner, or its presuppositions with regard to God and man. As we really pray we are freed from all contradiction and live in the truth that sinful man may stand before his Father as God's dear child, and have familiar intercourse with Him. As we pray we cannot misunderstand or misuse this tenet, or convert it into its opposite. As we genuinely pray we understand it correctly, and make proper use of it, venturing the very thing we can and should venture in the atmosphere of this truth, and refraining from the very things that are made impossible and excluded. The work of the Holy Spirit is really done where there is real prayer, and the work of the Holy Spirit is the power of the resurrection of Jesus Christ from the dead, and therefore the power of the divine justification of sinful man. When we pray, we are engaged in a decision for the truth, not of a doctrine of justification, but of justification itself. When we pray, justification speaks, specifically and conclusively, for itself. To refer to this point where the decision is made by God Himself is the true purpose of the christological explanation of justification. To the extent that the decision is made, justification—and it is only now that we can say this—is our justification by faith, by faith alone. For it is only faith that really understands its truth. It does so because faith in Jesus Christ is itself life in its truth.

3. THE PURPOSE OF THE DIVINE JUDGMENT

The presupposition of the divine judgment is that God wills to have man for himself. The execution of this judgment is that He creates right for the man who is in the wrong before Him, setting him in the right against himself. Its goal and purpose is that man should be the one who passes from this judgment, the one who is judged by His command. It is as such that God wills to have him for Himself. It is as such that man can and should live in covenant with Him. We must now speak more particularly of this purpose of the divine judgment and therefore of the command by which God judges man.

The execution of the divine judgment does not take place in vain. Nor is this true only for God, who as such knows and wills and attains what He wills. It is true of the God who elects man and deals with man and has entered into covenant with him. Therefore, as it is true for God, it is also true for man. The man who comes from the judgment of God is not the same as the one who comes to it. And the judgment of the divine command is the secret of every day and hour of human life. Man is always on the point of coming to the divine judgment and coming from it. To the extent that he comes from it, he is never the same as he was. He is always another man. He is newly orientated. He lives always in a post-judgment epoch in which he is a new being—an epoch which in this life will always be a pre-judgment epoch as well, lived in expectation of the new judgment of the next hour, the following day, to which he moves. Yet he lives always in this post-judgment epoch. The judgment from which he comes has not taken place in vain. The grace of God which is its presupposition was not addressed to him in vain, whatever may be the use he makes of it when he moves forward to fresh judgment. The purpose of God has as such definitely been fulfilled in him. He can never be the same as he was before. The effectiveness of the divine command, and the power of his condemnation and acquittal, have not been for nothing. Whatever he may make of it, he stood before the God who loved him and willed to have him for himself. He stood before Him as a malefactor and enemy, and God stood before him as the One who did not allow Himself to be deflected, who did not suffer any breach of His own right and therefore his right, whose faithfulness persisted. Man may forget or despise this, but the fact remains that it is true and actual, and always true and actual for him, that after this has happened he is different from what he was before. Between God and him a new beginning has been made, and an order has been set up corresponding to this new beginning. The evening and the morning have given rise to a new day. What it will bring is another matter. But it is a new day of grace. Our Church hymns, with their relating of night and day to the death and resurrection of Christ, to the putting off of the old man and the putting on of the new, are an exact description of the true state of affairs : " New every morning like the dew, The grace of God is sure and true, It never ends the livelong day, But is a certain strength and stay." The fulfilled purpose of the judgment from which we come is the decisive law of our future, the given atmosphere of each new day, of each hour we enter. We live after the judgment in which we are accused and condemned, but also pardoned and justified. And the decisive preparation for everything that follows definitely consists in the fact that we accept this, that we allow this law to obtain. If there can and must be a new evening and night, if we must stand again in the judgment as before, this is clearly bound up with the fact that we have either not sung our morning hymn or unfortunately ceased to sing it because we regard other things as more important. But this does not alter the fact that it was morning and that we come from this morning of God. It does not alter the effectiveness of the judgment of God which is behind us. The humiliation and exaltation which have come on us have actually taken place and cannot be reversed. The invitation and permission and exhortation that we receive still hold good. We ourselves are still those in whom the grace of God has acted in the judgment.

No matter what we make of it, no matter what attitude we take to it, it is still the case that we are judged by the command of God. And in the full sense of the term developed in the preceding subsection, this means that we are directed to live by the grace of God. We are unmasked and convicted as those who in their wickedness and folly try to escape the command of God, and thus give themselves up to the destruction to which this desire can only lead us. And yet in spite of this desire we are not allowed to fall, but upheld and carried above the yawning abyss where no power on earth, and least of all our own, can save us from a headlong plunge to destruction. We are sinners before God, but this fact is covered by the high righteousness of the divine forgiveness. That we are judged in this way is the purpose of the divine judgment as it is not merely attempted but actually fulfilled. It is on this basis that God will again see and address us. It is as such that we are sanctified by the command of God. It is as such that God will take us seriously the next hour and the next day. Thus it is not a mere problem and postulate of our existence that we should be this. But the character always given already to our existence, our modification and orientation by the divine judgment, consist in the fact that we actually are this. And the true problems and postulates of our existence only arise from this fact. It is only from this fact that we can ask what the actualised purpose of the divine judgment can mean for us the judged in all the hours and days which are still before us ; what it will mean to live by the grace of God in these coming hours. The moment we forget or depreciate the fact that we live by the grace of God, all questions as to the manner of this life, all the problems and postulates of our existence—however seriously they may be posed and tackled—are quite irrelevant. We have forgotten and depreciated the command of God itself, and therefore broken it. For what we must keep before us is that we are judged by God's command, and therefore directed to it, to the right created by it, and therefore to live by the grace of God. Beside this one thing we cannot know anything else in obedience to the divine command. It is in respect for this one thing that all further questioning necessarily ensues.

As those who are judged by God, and directed to His grace, we are, in fact and objectively, called to faith. " In fact and objectively " means independently of whether faith has already been proclaimed to us by the preaching of the Gospel, or what attitude, if any, we have adopted to this proclamation. Faith is something which is objectively demanded from us by the judgment of God, irrespective of whether we know and receive it or not. The preaching of the Gospel can only proclaim and show that this is how things stand objectively. And when we take up an attitude to the preaching of the Gospel, we can only take up an attitude to the fact that this is how things stand objectively, that our existence as characterised and modified and established by the judgment of God can be lived only in faith. Faith corresponds exactly to the judgment and grace of God. In faith we acknowledge that we are judged, or rather that we are directed to live by God's grace. In faith, and only in faith, we can meaningfully ask what this reality necessarily means for us. In faith, and only in faith, the problems and postulates of our existence can be meaningfully considered and treated. Without faith, and therefore without corresponding to the call which in fact and objectively has come to us by God's judgment, without hearing this one demand from the very outset of each new day, we can never correspond to the reality of this day, but only be betrayed into futility when we ask concerning its significance for us. Whether proclaimed by the preaching of the Gospel or not, whether heard or not, the grace of God in His judgment issues always a call for faith, i.e., for our practical affirmation of the judgment fulfilled in our being and action. Faith is practical acknowledgment that right is done to us by God. Faith is an acceptance of the rightness of this right of God. We believe when we live before God and with God as those who are judged by Him, whom He has made His own, in whom He has glorified Himself by humbling and exalting them as He has done in His judgment. All sin, great or small, conscious or unconscious, flagrant or refined, consists in the fact that we do not do this. It consists in an attitude in which we ignore in practice where we have our origin and what God has done in us and for us. All sin consists in unbelief—and perhaps in error or superstition as particular forms of unbelief. Not merely the sin of the Christian who is expressly called to faith by the preaching of the Gospel, and confesses faith, but the sin of the whole world, which in fact and objectively is continually called to faith by the execution of the divine judgment, consists in unbelief. Unbelief is the denying and obscuring of the purpose of the divine judgment. In itself, therefore, it is an impotent action. It is, of course, deadly enough even in its impotence ; for it calls for new and heavier judgments, and how can unbelief know that these are again the judgments of divine grace when it does not know this, or has forgotten or discounted it, in relation to the judgments from which it has come ? To believe is not to forget or discount the judgment of divine grace from which we come ; not to deny or obscure its purpose. We believe when we consider this judgment in what we do ; or rather, when we attest it in our action (because God has Himself attested it to us in this judgment) ; when we magnify it (because God willed to magnify Himself in us in this judgment) : when we display it in our action before God and men and all angels. In faith man confirms that he is not merely present in the judgment of God's command as a hearer and spectator, but that he is its object, that he is himself the accused and the acquitted in this judgment, and that he has come from it as such. It is at once apparent that the idea of a purely theoretical faith separable from life can only be an absurdity —just as absurd, in fact, as that of a life separable from faith. If the existence of the judged man is the purpose of the divine judgment, the acknowledgment of this fact by man obviously cannot consist in any contemplation or conviction which may be differentiated or separated from the totality of his existence—as though he were only a spectator of the judgment—but only in the total shaping of his existence. Faith, then, can only be a determination of his whole being and action, which is, of course, in the first and decisive instance a determination of his knowledge, but as a determination of his existence —how else can it be genuine ?—a determination of his life, and therefore the obedience of faith. Faith never understands itself as an enterprise undertaken in man's own caprice or capacity or competence. It never understands itself as an original or meritorious achievement of man. It is an answer to the divine call and can only try to reflect and correspond to the fact that we are directed to live by the grace of God. It is the acknowledgment and attestation of the basis of right which is created by the mercy of God and to which every achievement can only be an achievement of thankfulness. But if faith understands itself only as a miraculous gift of the Holy Spirit, this does not alter the fact that it has to be undertaken as a conscious and determined act of the man whose being and essence are condemned and rejected in the divine judgment, and whose whole sinfulness is now forgiven. Man does not try to transcend himself in this act. But he is to give place to the God from whose judgment he comes. And if it is true that even this act as such—faith as our act—is not without sin, but will appear in the judgment as everywhere spotted with sin, this does not mean that we can neglect it. For the grace of God calls for it. When we are referred to the grace of God, we have no option but to give the response of our Yes, and we must not hesitate. Even this action, even our faith, will always need forgiveness when we bring it to God. It is a faith in which we can only cry and pray that God will help our unbelief. But this cannot alter the fact that we are always summoned by the fact of our sanctification in God's judgment to give it to God, irrespective of whether it is good or bad, strong or feeble. That God's forgiveness is and always will be the last word is something that we acknowledge and attest when we are not afraid but confidently dare to give our faith to God even in its need of forgiveness, not withholding it in an affectation of humility. How can we live by God's grace if we refuse to believe because our faith is always weak and poor ? It is not the man who believes, but the God in whom he can and should believe, that makes faith the sacred work of an answer to the judgment which is passed on him.

If we try to clarify the nature of this faith which thankfully responds to the divine judgment and therefore corresponds to its purpose, the simplest and most comprehensive insight is yielded by the fact that in its origin and basic form faith is always the act of repentance, i.e., of the conversion which corresponds to the morning of each new day. The new day which we enter when we come from the judgment of God is characterised by the fact that our sin is recognised as such and forgiven as such. To walk in the light of this day, and therefore to believe, is obviously to affirm in practice that our forgiven sin is recognised as sin and that our recognised sin is forgiven as such. When we do this we repent ; we are converted ; we turn from disobedience to obedience. And this is what God wills of those who are judged by Him.

1. It is only of forgiven sin that we know that it is recognised as sin, that it is sin. What we may more or less know apart from forgiveness is perhaps defect, error or vice. But to know sin as sin, as our rebellion against God, as our transgression of His command, we must know its forgiveness. It is unequivocally from this standpoint that it is spoken of in the Penitential Psalms. Only those who are justified by God are awakened from the sleep of the opinion that their acts can be justified of themselves. And it is (Rom. 2⁴) the goodness of God which leads us to repentance, i.e., when repentance means more than remorse, self-accusation, despair and the like, when it means that man has really come to an end of himself, when it has to be understood as the corresponding knowledge of this fact, and the attitude corresponding to this knowledge. That I do not love God and my neighbour ; that I thus bring mortal guilt on myself ; that I put myself in mortal need ; and more than that, that I am a man who of himself will

always go this way, even in his best efforts ; that, although there is nothing to force me, I can never be anything different ; that, however heavily they oppress me, I can never free myself from my guilt and need because of myself I do not seriously want things changed ; that there is in me no archimedian point from which I can reverse my transgression ; that I do not control any resources by which to escape disquiet in my own strength—these are all things that I learn only when and as I learn the grace of God. The sinner whose sin is not forgiven is always distinguished from the sinner whose sin is forgiven by the fact that he does not know these things, that he does not think of admitting them and living by this admission. He will always be distinguished by the fact that he has still a great deal to say in his own favour. But a confession like that of Paul in Rom. 7 not only shows that the Pharisaism of the one who speaks is overcome, but that this has taken place because the forgiveness of his sins has been revealed, because he has not come in vain into the judgment. Similarly, the fifth petition in the Lord's Prayer—for Jesus Himself is the first to use it—can surely be understood and prayed only out of the fulness of forgiveness. And there can obviously be no better place for the *Kyrie eleis* than at the end of the Christmas hymn " All praise to thee, O Jesus Christ." We can all ask for pardon—and we all prefer a good conscience to a bad. But we can cry for God's mercy and therefore for forgiveness only when we know that although we are lost God has accepted us and redeemed us. How else can we know that we need mercy and forgiveness ? How else can we know to whom we cry ? How else can we know that we can and should cry to Him ? Only from the deep quiet of the knowledge that grace is given does there follow the genuine disquiet of the knowledge that we need it, and not *vice versa*. It is the Gospel, and not a Law abstracted from the Gospel, that compels us to recognise our transgression, to take our guilt seriously, to accept the consequent distress as a just punishment rather than refusing it as an injustice. That we yield to this compulsion, not rejecting that disturbance, not ceasing to pray : " Forgive us our trespasses," not suppressing that Christmas *Kyrie eleison*, always thinking and speaking and acting, just because we are forgiven, as those who need forgiveness—this is the one vital thing in the faith which is demanded from us by the divine judgment from which we come. To believe is to admit that we are at the end of ourselves because God wills to make a new beginning with us and has actually done so. To believe is to take the place which belongs to us as those who are helped, and can still be helped, by the divine mercy. To believe is to act in big and little things alike as those who can expect all the necessary seeing and hearing, insight and experience, power and perseverance, only from the fact that we may continue to pray, and to pray : " Forgive us our trespasses." To believe is to accept and pursue, for the sake of the peace that we are granted with God, the conflict in which we are quite finally alone apart from the fact that God is with us, in which we have finally no weapon apart from that which God supplies, and in which we must daily and hourly receive and accept and pray for the free grace that God is our Friend and not our worst enemy. To believe is to consider the assault that God Himself will immediately and necessarily mount against us if even for a moment or by a hair's breadth we seek our security elsewhere. To believe is to defy our own unfaithfulness with the recollection of God's faithfulness, running through the mist to meet it in the recognition that it is we ourselves who create the mist, who bring the assault on us, who make God the enemy He must always be to those who alienate themselves from Him, but will not be if only they will accept life in correspondence to His judgment, and therefore life in repentance, as is fitting. Faith is this life in repentance to the extent that this is not something odd but our true and natural life at the very deepest level. All transformation or renewal of our life has its basis and mysterious essence in the fact that our life is ready to be lived in this true and natural surrender to the death of all self-centred dignity and power—true and natural to the extent that we always come from the judgment of God, and on the basis of this judgment are always given up to this death in order that we may really live beyond this death. As our being and action, which are sinful in themselves, are placed in this repentance, they are directed to the work of obedience, to good works which are pleasing to God. Good works are always works of repentance, works in which our sin is recognised, works in which we pray for the divine mercy, works in which we are helped because they are not the works of self-help, but a sighing—and finally and inwardly a happy sighing—for the help of God. There can be no question of any other goodness of our being and activity than this. But this goodness of the lost people of those who can see no hope apart from the divine mercy is always and very definitely ascribed to our works. And these good works of the lost sinner are the purpose of the divine judgment. In view of this purpose—already fulfilled, already actualised by God—we can enter with confidence each new hour or day with its own particular problems and cares—" But is a certain strength and stay."

2. Yet it is only of sin which is recognised as such that we know that it is forgiven. Without the knowledge of sin man himself may ignore or forget it as a defect or error or vice. But God does not ignore or forget. God knows. Ignoring and forgetting do not create the order which has always to be set up. Only the forgiveness of God can do this—of the God who knows about our sin. We therefore evade and escape the forgiveness of God if we for our part try to avoid a recognition of our sin. Where God's pardon is heard, the condemnation of God is always heard as well. Thus it is only where the condemnation of God is heard that God's pardon is also heard. That

our transgression is forgiven cannot, therefore, mean that the command of God is no longer set before us. It means, rather, that it is genuinely set before us. Those who are justified by God are those who are awakened from the sleep of the opinion that the corruption of their being and action can be accepted, that it rests on a final necessity, against which nothing can prevail. Has not God set up His right against man ? Has He not put man himself in the right by justifying him without any merit of his own ? Was not his justification in the judgment a divine defiance of that presumed necessity ? In this conclusive word of His judgment, has He not explained that our transgression is not necessary, and that its supposed invincible claim is in every respect a lie ? Is it a real knowledge of sin that tries to appeal to the fact that in the sphere of our self-knowledge we know absolutely nothing of its overcoming, that we undoubtedly find that we are those who, in fact, will what we should not will, thus giving new force to that denied necessity ? Is it denied or not according to what we have heard in God's judgment ? Has God affirmed or negated our sin, accepted or rejected it, as He forgives us ? The question is not what power or weakness we are able to know in ourselves, but what God has said and decided about us in this matter in all our power or weakness. Was God right or wrong to acquit us of our sin ? Is this pardon valid or not ? If we really bow under the verdict passed on us in the divine judgment—under the final and decisive word of this verdict— we obviously bow (and this is the fruitful knowledge of sin demanded of us) under the truth that the good will of God is effective against it and has a superior validity even for our life, that there is allotted to it the power to rule over us, and to us the weakness in which we let ourselves be ruled by it. The justification of a man in God's judgment means the establishment of the lordship of God over this man, fulfilled in majestic defiance of the supposed necessity of our sin and in irresistible contradiction of the claim that we can and must continue in it. If my sin is forgiven, this means that I am subjected to the lordship of God, and concretely that I am recognised and acknowledged by God to be one whom he reckons as His and who is therefore actually and objectively free to do His will. It is a curious repentance if I do not follow God in this recognition and acknowledgment, but oppose His better knowledge of myself on the basis of my own self-knowledge, reserving for myself, as it were, the claim that as a sinner I am not in any position to do His will. This kind of assertion has very little relevance now that I have been told in the divine judgment that my sin is forgiven, that God knows me very differently from what I know myself, and much better, that He has taken me seriously in this hidden quality which is quite inaccessible to my own self-knowledge, ranging Himself at my side, taking up my cause and calling and liberating me in consequence. The knowledge of sin demanded of me is that I should grant that He is right in His Word. If I will not do this, I despise and reject the proffered forgiveness. In my apparent truthfulness I am then quite untruthful. For the truthfulness required of me is that I should accept the Word of God, His Yes, as it is spoken to me, even though I find myself quite powerless to pronounce this Yes of myself. It is that I should not try to rise above the wisdom in which God has recognised and acknowledged me, although I cannot achieve this knowledge of myself. When it is accomplished in this truthfulness, the repentance of faith necessarily leads to conversion. From this standpoint faith is conversion—in the freedom in which we are placed by God's pardon. To believe is to turn from every opinion and conviction which we may have in our own strength about good and evil to the truth in which we stand before God according to the divine verdict. To believe is to turn from the obedience of our own works in the cleverness and power with which we might invest our being and action, to the obedience in which the same works can be done under the lordship of God. To believe is to turn from the sloth which allows the sinfulness of our own works to remain as though it were an eternal necessity, to the joy and readiness which derive from the knowledge that God's good will alone has eternal necessity, and therefore wills to be honoured in our work, too. To believe is to turn to the place which belongs to those who know mercy. Thus faith is the birth and life of the new man who can and will do what is good and well-pleasing to God. For faith is the apprehension and affirmation of the divine justification. It is the truthfulness in which we accept this as something that has really taken place. If we do accept it, the new man is born who as such can only do good works, to whom the desire and love for the will of God are fitting and natural, who as he breathes and eats and drinks and sleeps will definitely do what God approves and this alone, both in the secret recesses of the heart and in every relationship to his neighbour both in Church and state, at every stage and in every situation of life. This new man and his work are the purpose of the divine judgment. We must know that with every step we take into each new time, if we come from the divine judgment, we stand under this purpose ; and that it is always fulfilled and realised already. To believe—to believe in true repentance—is to affirm in practice that God's purpose is fulfilled and realised already as we are those who are judged by Him. The morning has already come. We have only to live as we ought to live in this new day.

The purpose of God in His judgment is the sanctification of man, i.e., his direction, preparation and exercise for the eternal life ordained and promised. Eternal life is a life which, ascribed to man in his creatureliness, is invested with God's own glory, i.e., as an object of the openly revealed love of God in which God has turned to him and in possession of the openly revealed freedom which He has granted to him in fellowship with Himself. It is man's indissoluble, indestructible, unceasing and unlimited life with God, his life in the clarity which is proper to God, in which God sees Himself, in which He has always seen man too, and still sees him, but in which here and now man is so far unable to see either God or himself. It is man's life in the participation in the joy of God which corresponds to this clarity, which was always the purpose of his life, which already waits and is ready for him here and now, but in which here and now he cannot rejoice, or can do so only in the profound disjointedness of human life and its doubtful and transitory joy. Eternal life is man's life in harmony with the life of God and all His angels, but also with that of all the rest of the elect, and, indeed, of all creation : in the harmony in which God saw and willed him when, before the foundation of the world, He knew and willed him in His Word, which is the beginning of all His ways and works ; in the harmony in which He sees and wills him here and now, but in which here and now he is so utterly hidden from himself. It is man's perfect entry into the service of the glorifying of God to which God has drawn him by determining him for His own image, and which here and now is the task, but here and now only the set and unsolved task of his life, to be revealed one day in its perfect solution as the reality of his life. That man should have this eternal life " of him and through him and to him " (Rom. 11^{36}) is the purpose of God in the covenant in which He has bound Himself to man, in the command by which He has bound man to Himself, and especially in the judgment to which He subjects man by giving him His command. Everything that takes place in the history and fulfilment of this covenant, including the establishment of the command, and the judgment which is passed on man in and with the command, is a preliminary temporal stage, or provisional form, of the gift of eternal life. The divine purpose in the command, already fulfilled and realised, is that man, as one who is judged by it, may always enter a new hour and a new day, living actually and literally in the morning glow of eternity. In faith—to the extent that this is an affirmation of this judgment, the acceptance of its outcome—it is actually and literally a matter of grasping and having eternal life in its temporal form. In the twofold sense already described, as a dying of the old man and birth of the new, and to the extent that it consists simply in our acknowledgment of the state of affairs created by the judgment of the divine command, faith is actually and literally our temporal orientation, preparation and exercise, and therefore our sanctification for eternal life. Except in this concealment eternal life is not yet present. But in this concealment, in our sanctification by the command, in God's judgment and the faith which assents to it, our eternal life is present. The revelation of our real status before God, and therefore of our real existence, although it has not yet taken place, has been indicated and is in force. Eternal life is the real secret of this temporal life. We do not yet live eternal life here and now. But we are here and now made free for eternal life. Each act of divine judgment from which we come is the offer and work of this freedom. And each act of faith in which we give ourselves to live as those who are judged by God is the acceptance of this offer, the consequence of this work, our real entry into this freedom, a provisional form of the great final step into eternal glory and clarity and harmony, into the eternal service for which we are selected. Each part of life in the light and in face of that morning glow is as such a part of the promise which is already fulfilled if still concealed in its fulfilment—the promise under which our whole life stands, and which always waits to be recognised and grasped by us as such. We have to remember both when we come afresh into the judgment of God and when we leave it that it is the God who has this purpose for us that commands us and demands us. He does not rule for the sake of ruling, or command for the sake of commanding, or judge for the sake of judging. He has this definite purpose. He sanctifies us for eternal life as He sanctifies us for Himself. He wills the best for us as He seeks His own glory. He is Himself our hope as He is our Lord. He saves us from eternal death, and nourishes us to eternal life, as He causes us daily and hourly to die, and beseeches, allows and commands us to accept this in faith, in the perfect repentance of faith.

But we must now be clear as to the true and only possible basis of this knowledge and therefore its true and essential meaning. We have spoken far too rashly and categorically and confidently about the purpose of the divine judgment if this purpose does not speak for itself like the presupposition and execution of this judgment, if our witness on this matter is not grounded in and cannot be related to the fact that first and last the matter has witnessed and will witness to itself. We have described the sanctification of man, his existence as that of one of those who are judged by God, as a fact which is already completed, which has been factually and objectively created. We have understood faith only as the answer of man demanded by this fact and corresponding to it. We have understood this fact itself as man's temporal liberation and capacitation for eternal life. But is not everything in the air when we investigate this fact ? For where is this man who is directed by God, who is convicted as a sinner and pronounced free and righteous in spite of his sin, who is called as such to repentance, who stands as such in that morning glow in which man can enter each new day with resolution and each new hour with the confidence that in this way and as this man I have come from God's judgment, that I have really set out, and can and should actually live, according to the law of this event ? Can I in some sense believe in myself, in my status as one of those who are judged by God ? But who am I to see myself called of myself to repentance and brought of myself to the death of the old man and life of the new ? And who am I to be to myself the promise of eternal life ? Am I not giving way to the worst of hallucinations if I count on this fact in relation to myself and try of myself to live by it ?

We have only to put this question and we have the answer. As we spoke of our sanctification as the fulfilled and realised purpose of God, we spoke of ourselves, but only in a very definite relationship. To try to abstract from this relationship is to give way to one long hallucination. And everything is then left in the air. To be sure, the purpose of God has to do with us and our life. To be sure, this purpose is not futile, but is fulfilled and realised in us and for us. But we have to remember that as God's purpose it is fulfilled and realised in God's judgment. Therefore, if we are to understand it properly, we have to let it speak to us as God's purpose in God's judgment. We have to let it speak for itself. It is as such that it obtains and is valid. It is as such that it is the truth in contrast to all the hallucinations which we might oppose to it or with which we might try to evade it. And it is as such, and therefore as it speaks for itself, that it must be revealed to us. There can thus be no question of seeking this fact in our own life, among the inner and outer data and conditions and relationships of our existence as we know them. What we live here and now cannot as such—divorced from this one relationship—be our sanctified life, the life which is liberated for eternal life, the life which comes from God's judgment. And therefore that which we live and experience and know in our own sphere, and sphere of observation, cannot as such be this life which is judged, and liberated by judgment. We never see ourselves as those we are before God ; and of and by ourselves we never are those that God Himself has chosen us to be. In all the heights and depths of our life, even our Christian life, we look in vain for our true sanctification for God as it is already impregnably and irrevocably accomplished. What we see in our own life are all kinds of attempts and fragments, all kinds of unfulfilled and therefore very doubtful beginnings, all kinds of half-lights which may equally well be those of sunset or sunrise, which vouch less for our sanctification than for the fact that we have never come from the judgment of God according to the divine purpose, which testify just as much, and even more, against the factuality of our sanctification by God's command. When and where is not that which we know of our sanctification in ourselves merely an attempt at our self-sanctification which as such is again that which is forbidden us—a part of our conflict against the divine command ? When and where have we so fulfilled that repentance of faith that this fact is so evident in what we have lived and experienced or done that we are summoned by it to new faith ? When and where are we such believers of ourselves that we can believe on the basis of our own witness, the witness of our own inner or outer works ? Those who trust in these things, in their conversion and new birth as such, in their walk before God as an element of biography, ascribing credibility and the force of witness to a supposed " pneumatic actuality " in the sphere of experience, and thus trying to live in faith in themselves, building their house upon the sand, are only involved· in a feat of juggling in which they may achieve a sensational but very dangerous interchange of supreme rapture and the most profound disillusionment, but will know nothing of the death of the old man and the life of the new, and therefore of man's direction, preparation and exercise for eternal life. It is not in this way that we can and shall taste and see how good the Lord is. In this way we do not even ask concerning Him. We do not allow the purpose of His judgment to speak for itself. We do not, therefore, understand it. And we are not justified. We do not live in a way which corresponds to the day, the hour, the time, that follows God's judgment and is determined by it. We still live in an " as if "—as if it were not by the purpose of God in the divine judgment that our time is determined, but by a good human purpose in a human judgment passed by ourselves on ourselves.

It is also the case that we cannot and must not investigate the fact of our sanctification by which our time is determined as if it were a fact which has first to be proved, which needs our acceptance and acknowledgment to be a fact and to be significant as such. Our acceptance and acknowledgment can only do justice to this fact because it is a fact, and is significant and powerful as such, and reveals itself as such. How else can our sanctification be a divine fact, and therefore one which is credible in itself and able to attest itself ? We have first to consider creaturely facts—either in themselves or from some other standpoint—before we can be convinced that they are real facts and significant and powerful as such. But we need not and cannot consider divine facts in this way. Factuality, significance and force cannot be conceded to them. We misunderstand and deny them if we treat them in this way. They are there, and they are in force, and we have to acknowledge and accept them and their power as such. But it is with a fact of this kind—or, more precisely, with *the* divine fact, which as such speaks for itself—that we have to do in our sanctification by the command of God. And this fact is beyond any inward or outward discoveries that we may make of ourselves. Where this fact does not speak for itself, or we do not listen to it, we can speak about the purpose of the divine judgment only in surmises and opinions and expectations. We shall then be forced to admit that we do not really know it. At bottom, we shall be in the dark as concerns God's will for us. Even the actual execution of the divine judgment will be doubtful and its presupposition uncertain. For knowledge and certainty in these matters depend upon our certainty that we are those who are judged by God. Again, we shall be in the dark as to the command of God, its claim on us and decision concerning us, if we do not finally have a certainty at this point, and cannot, therefore, speak as boldly and confidently as we have actually done. For at this point it is a matter of seeing and saying who we ourselves really are in the light of the claim, under the decision and in retrospect of the actual work of the divine command. Nor are we left in the lurch at this point, for the divine command does, in fact, speak for itself here with particular force and distinctness.

We do not need to seek the fact of our sanctification. It is the ground on which we stand, the horizon by which we are bounded, the atmosphere in which we breathe. It is the life of our life. It is inaccessible and concealed just because it is so real—with a divine reality over which we have no control, but which controls us with a force with which none of the known and accessible elements of our life can even remotely compete. It is not in the sphere of our knowledge because it is wisdom itself, without whose light our knowledge would not be possible even in its limitation. We have no power over it because it is omnipotence, by which all our power is created, and without which it would be impotence. It does not exist as one of the facts which we seek and can discover because it is we who are searched and discovered in our existence by it. It cannot be grounded because it is itself the basis which is our starting-point for all our demonstrations. The sanctification of man by God's command takes place in the relationship by which his life is constituted, which gives it its reality and essence and continuance. This is how it attests and explains itself. It speaks to us before anything else speaks, even before we can speak to ourselves. It speaks always as the voice from above. That is why we wait in vain for it to speak in any voice from below, even that of our own best and most secret self, even that of our own most genuine Christian experience. That is also why it speaks with a force and penetration incomparably greater than those of any other voice : with force even though it seems to be quiet and easily missed compared with others ; and with penetration even though it seems to come so completely from the far distance compared with others.

It is the voice of the Good Shepherd which speaks to us in this unique way. " I know my sheep, and am known of mine. As the Father knoweth me, even so know I the Father " (Jn. 10$^{14f.}$.). Jesus Christ is the completed fact of our sanctification, the fulfilled and realised purpose of God in God's judgment, just as He is also its presupposition and its execution. We now come for the last time to this basic strand in the whole doctrine of God's command which is also that of the doctrine of the divine election of grace, and of the whole Christian doctrine of God. Ethics as the doctrine of God's command, and therefore as the doctrine of the sanctification given to man by God, is grounded in the knowledge of Jesus Christ. It can be attained and developed only as the knowledge of Jesus Christ. At each point we have been able to present the claim and decision and judgment of the divine command only in such a way that we have been brought back again and again to the point that the command of God is revealed and true and actual and valid as the command which is established and fulfilled in Jesus Christ. For—this was our starting-point—He, Jesus Christ is the holy God and sanctified man in one. In His person God orders and man obeys. In His person, as we have now seen in detail, the command of God becomes the judgment of God ; the claim of God on man, as it is raised in His command, becomes His right ; and His determination of man, as it is implicit in His command, becomes its goal. In His person God's gracious Yes to man, which is the meaning and content of His command, coincides with man's grateful Yes to God ; the command of God with the obedience of man. In His person in which the sin of man is condemned but sinful man justified, in His death and resurrection, God sanctifies man and man is sanctified by God, being liberated and capacitated for eternal life. In His person this hidden thing is already revealed. He lives already the life to which we are directed and for which we are prepared and exercised by sanctification—eternal life in the glory of the Father. But this Jesus Christ is not one person amongst others, so that our sanctification is a new problem as compared with that which He achieves. His person, the person of the Son of God and therefore of God Himself, is by God's gracious and righteous will *the* human person, our common Head and Representative. In Him God has seen each human person from all eternity. As He judges Him, and He is judged by God, judgment is executed on every human person. He is the Word that was in the beginning with God. He is, therefore, the Word that is true of every man. He is our sanctification for God and eternal life as it is unshakeably and irrevocably accomplished. The fact of our sanctification speaks so incontestably, from so great a height and yet so intimately, because it is *His* sanctification. It is for this reason that it has the character of a divinely present and wise and omnipotent reality as distinct from all other facts. This is why it is the *prius* of our existence, to deny which is at once to deny our existence, the fall of which involves our own destruction. Jesus Christ is our sanctification because we are what we are only in relation to Him, because we owe the reality and essence and continuance of our human life to Him, because He is the life of our life.

That this is the case is something that we can only confirm by our faith in Jesus Christ. We cannot create it or even complete it. Our faith in Him can add nothing to the fact that He is our sanctification, that it is fulfilled in Him. It can only confirm and accept the fact that it is so. That this should happen, that we accept this, that we agree to participate in His sanctification without which we are nothing, that we live as those we are, i.e., as His, in that repentance as the death of the old man and birth of the new—this is what is demanded of us by this fact which is self-grounded and speaks for itself, by the voice of the Good Shepherd. For an understanding of this demand it is vital that we should know and discern that it is He who demands,

3. *The Purpose of the Divine Judgment*

His voice by which we are summoned to repentance. It is not the voice of a creature, or a man. It is not our own voice. No other voice ever can or will call us to repentance. No other voice ever can or will make us able and willing to believe. No other voice ever can or will transpose us from a state of disobedience, to one of obedience. No other voice ever can or will win our hearts. And in God's command it is a matter of accepting from the heart the sanctification which has taken place for us. The voice of Jesus Christ is the voice of God Himself, who wills to have us for Himself, to make us free and ready for eternal life. But as the voice of Jesus Christ it is not just the voice of a God who commands and promises, and who therefore confronts us from afar. How could we hear a voice like this? How could we be led by it from an alternation between doubt and despair on the one side and rash certainty on the other? As the voice of the holy God it is also the voice of sanctified man—of the man who was sanctified in our place, for us, as our Head and Representative, who can as such really speak to us in our own name, whom we can hear when we speak to ourselves in His name. This voice demands our faith and calls us to repentance. It is with this authority, from this height, but also in this proximity, that we are here addressed. It is with this overwhelming force that obedience is here required of us and obedience is made so natural and self-evident. It is in this radical way that we are here called to decision, and it is made quite impossible for us to choose disobedience and reject faith and repentance. For in the decision in which we are here placed by the word spoken we have no choice. The demand issued by this fact, the demand of Jesus Christ, is such that every other choice but obedience is cut off. If we hear it, this is definitely the case. Only as we listen to other voices can we think that we can choose between good and evil. If we know and discern that He and no other calls us, we definitely have no choice between obedience and disobedience. The decision has been made even as we are confronted by it. There is absolutely no place for disobedience, unbelief and impenitence. Evil becomes for us the absolutely excluded possibility that it is for God Himself. It is the shame that we can only leave under us and behind us. When we obey we do the only thing that we are free to do; the thing that we can do only in real freedom. We can be disobedient only as we are not free. Disobedience is not a choice, but the incapacity of the man who is no longer or not yet able to choose in real freedom. So majestic and penetrative is the call of Jesus Christ that when it is heard as such, when we know and discern that it is He who calls us, it is irresistible, i.e., it calls us to faith which cannot possibly be unbelief, repentance which cannot possibly be renounced, to faith which is indestructible and quite incapable of changing into its opposite. This faith and its repentance— the faith which is irresistibly awakened and therefore continues indestructibly—is the genuine faith which confirms and accepts the fact of our sanctification. In this faith we are holy ; we are sanctified for God and eternal life. In this faith we live the life of those who are judged by God—that life which is the purpose of the divine judgment. In this faith Jesus Christ Himself lives in us—the Head in His members, the " author of faith " in His followers. We spoke of this faith when we described repentance as the life of the man whose sin is recognised but also forgiven, who is therefore humbled but finally established. We can never speak too boldly or positively or confidently of this faith, of its assurance on both sides, of the goodness of its works, of the pleasure that God finds in it. It is the faith which gives the glory only to its object, to Jesus Christ as man's sanctification ; which wills to live only as an echo of His call, but to live a full life by His call. It is only in relation to Jesus Christ that this true faith—which is irresistibly awakened and therefore continues indestructibly—is either conceivable or possible. We necessarily look away from Jesus Christ, and speak of faith without true faith, if we describe it in any other way than as the confidence in which we who have every reason to fear have no one and nothing to fear.

As Jesus Christ calls us and is heard by us He gives us His Holy Spirit in order that His own relationship to His Father may be re-peated in us. He then knows us, and we know Him, as the Father knows Him and He the Father. Those who live in this repetition live in the Holy Spirit. The gift and work of the Holy Spirit in us is that Jesus Christ should live in us by faith, that He should be in solidarity and unity with us and we with Him, and therefore that our obedience should be necessary and our disobedience excluded. And life in the faith irresistibly awakened and indestructibly granted by the call of Jesus Christ is as such life in the Holy Spirit ; life in possession of the divine " seal," and therefore in the certainty of the resurrection and eternal life ; life in which we are directed to eternal life and prepared and adapted for it. From this standpoint, too, we cannot speak any less boldly or positively or confidently of the purpose of the divine judgment than we have actually done. Since the life of repentance is life in the Holy Spirit, we shall take care not to confuse it with our own spiritual life, putting our trust in things—our own experiences or acts—which do not merit it and cannot justify. We shall be all the more joyfully prepared to live our spiritual life humbly but courageously as those who have the witness of the Spirit that they are the children of God, having received from the one Son of God the status and authority of His brothers in relation to His Father. From this standpoint, too, there can be no possible limitation of the factuality of our sanctification. From this standpoint we can better understand that in Jesus Christ we are accepted as holy by God— only accepted, but really accepted. From this standpoint we can only realise afresh that the required life in repentance, and therefore in conversion, consists in prayer. We are converted when we hear the call of God and respond to it, calling upon it in thankfulness and worship and intercession. It is in this way that we confirm that we are accepted and therefore sanctified. It is in this way that we make use of the filial right that we are given, and at the same time fulfil the filial duty that is laid upon us. It is in this way that we confirm and accept the fact that we are placed before the divine *fait accompli*, acting as those for whom the dawn has come and who have a new day before them. In all its petitions the prayer that is set in our hearts and on our lips in Jesus Christ is the prayer of those who come from this *fait accompli*, the prayer which is prayed by " the communion of saints." And when we join in this prayer in this communion, the One who teaches us to pray in this way Himself intercedes with the Father for us in His Spirit. He Himself is the pledge that we do not pray in vain. The Father who hears and answers His own Son must and will—in Him and for His sake—hear and answer us. There can be no reservation in the magnifying of His grace or the serious acceptance of the factuality of our sanctification. We cannot think or speak too realistically in this matter, or too greatly magnify the grace of God. All threatened boasting in the flesh—the pious flesh— will always be put to shame by the fact that in the prayer which is the Lord's prayer we cannot tire of praying constantly for the grace of prayer itself, and of sighing continually but joyfully, as those who have received the Spirit : *Veni Creator Spiritus* !

INDEXES

I. SCRIPTURE REFERENCES

Genesis

Exodus

II. NAMES

III. SUBJECTS

God, self-offering, 101, 122, 161 ff., 175 f.,
    195, 197, 261, 309, 319, 557.
  unchangeableness, 185.
  uniqueness, 156, 314, 317, 676.
  wealth, 662.
  will, 6, 19, 21, 30, 141, 145 ff., 156,
    161 f., 165, 170 ff., 178, 185,
    205, 211, 225, 260, 266, 277,
    561, 567, 632.
  wisdom, 146, 156 f., 172, 175, 178,
    210, 226, 271, 274.
  work, 5 f., 80, 88 ff., 95, 100, 107,
    135, 148 ff.
  and world, 7 f., 25 f., 44 f., 50 ff., 155 f.
  wrath, 122 f., 164, 171, 211, 216,
    225, 352, 450, 485, 494, 605, 735.
  v. Father, Triunity.
God, Doctrine of, 3 ff., 52, 76, 89, 133,
    146, 197, 509, 515.
Godlessness, 316, 319, 346, 349, 451,
    586, 671
  v. Sin.
Good, The, 169, 513 f., 516, 536, 546 f.,
    564 f., 571, 578, 614, 632, 678,
    703, 708 ff., 744 f.
  idea of the good, 665 f.
Grace, 9 ff., 19, 26, 28, 62 f., 91 ff., 95,
    101, 121, 174 f., 210, 232, 272,
    296 f., 317 f., 558 f., 560, 608,
    646, 692, 765.
  v. Command, Election of Grace.
Gratitude, 166, 168, 186, 223, 413, 695.

Heathendom, 37, 39 ff., 57, 149, 158 f.,
    198 f., 202 f., 215, 228 ff., 249,
    256, 262, 268, 273 f., 279 ff.,
    306, 478, 638, 707.
  nations, 229, 256, 262, 285.
  Pontius Pilate, 229.
Hedonism, 650.
Hell, 27, 92, 164, 265, 496.
Holy Scripture—
  authority, 3, 152, 705 ff.
  command, 671, 704 ff.
  concept of election, 15, 91, 195 f.,
    341 f., 354 ff., 419 ff.
  God, 5, 52 f., 59, 91, 148 f.
  man, 55 ff.
  prophecy, 253 ff., 269 f.
  revelation, 704 f.
  self-revelation of God, 49, 53.
  truth, 707.
  unity, 245, 276, 279, 704 f.
  witness, q.v.
  Word of God, 150, 705.
Holy Spirit, 101 f., 105 f., 118, 159,
    227 f., 249 f., 345, 352, 435, 458,
    699, 728, 751, 763, 780.
  calling, q.v.
  divine sonship, 105 f., 121, 125, 227,
    344, 347 f., 592, 604.
  new man, 427, 688 ff., 761 f., 772.

Holy Spirit, regeneration, q.v.
  repentance, q.v.
Hope, 153, 223, 262, 281, 284, 295.
Humanism, 70.
Humanity, 541.

Imperative, Categorical, 650 ff., 666 f.
Individual, 8, 41 ff., 51 f., 133 f., 136 f.,
    141 ff., 196, 306 ff., 313 f., 351.
  collectives, 313 ff.
  and the community, 310 f., 313, 318 f.,
    410 f., 426 f., 656 f., 728 ff.
  faith, 320 ff.
  individuation, 315 f.
  Jesus Christ, 310 f., 315 ff., 410.
  promise, 319, 321.
  rejection, 316 ff., 321, 351.
Individualism, 306, 310 ff., 318.
Infralapsarianism, 127, 129 ff., 143 f.,
    307.
Israel, 15, 53 ff., 83, 185 f., 195 ff.,
    202 ff., 227, 233 ff., 259 ff., 267,
    308 f., 341 f., 351, 427, 464, 484,
    505, 544, 679.
  Church, 205 ff., 211 f., 224, 233 ff.,
    237 f., 250, 255, 264 f., 268, 276,
    420 f., 506, 574.
  consolation, 231, 266, 272.
  covenant, q.v.
  disobedience, 207 f., 235 f., 255 f.,
    262 f., 268 ff., 273, 292.
  faith, 200, 206, 216, 235, 237, 260.
  guilt, 242, 247, 259.
  holiness, 285 f.
  Jesus Christ, 242, 246 f., 273, 285 f.,
    355 ff.
  Law, 203, 216, 241, 244, 253, 273 f.,
    356 ff.
  ministry, 206 ff., 226.
  obduracy, 275 f., 281 f., 286.
  obedience, 206 ff., 233 f., 261, 573 f.
  promise, 203, 243, 272 f., 285, 295,
    297, 572 f.
  prophecy, 393 ff.
  remnant, 269 ff., 285.
  rejection, q.v.
  repentance, 204, 226.
  sacrifice, 357 ff.
  worship, 203.

Jesus Christ—
  ascension, 173, 412.
  creation, 99, 116, 195.
  cross, 117, 120 ff., 161, 167 f., 172,
    174, 179, 198, 206 ff., 211 f., 261,
    266, 282, 438 ff., 492, 563.
  death, 229, 235, 318, 453, 558 f., 607,
    748 ff.
  deity, 7, 26, 59, 95 f., 103 f., 116 f.,
    125, 157, 165, 176, 247, 490 f.,
    605.

Neo-Protestantism, 67, 69, 111, 332, 534.

Obduracy, *v.* Israel.
Obedience, 30, 168, 177, 199, 511, 535, 538, 560, 567, 576 ff., 589, 592, 608 ff., 624, 634, 704, 707, 717, 724, 744, 767, 779.
abiding and standing, 600 ff.
disobedience, 27 f., 167, 611, 618, 670, 696, 779 f.
fear and care ?, 597 ff.
hearing, 195, 197, 233 f., 255, 539, 670, 745.
joy, 649.
ministry, 591 f.
v. Israel, Jesus Christ.
Order, *v.* Revelation.
Orthodoxy, Older Protestant, 46 f., 67 f., 70 ff., 74, 77 ff., 81, 84 f., 111, 114 f., 127 ff., 135, 307 f.

Pelagianism, 74 f., 111, 119.
Power—
of evil, 141.
of God, 185, 552 f.
impotence, 193.
infinite, 49.
of Jesus Christ, 150.
Prayer, 126, 178 f., 194, 561, 726, 751, 763, 868.
cf. Worship, *v.* Jesus Christ.
Predestination, *v.* Election of Grace.
Predestination, Classical Doctrine of, 13 ff., 36 ff., 40 ff.
assurance of election, 37 f.
Christian theology ?, 24.
Christology, 60 ff., 118 ff., 148 ff.
decretum absolutum, 106 ff., 115, 183, 222 f., 325 ff.
decretum generale, 46.
doctrine of God, 22 f.
dogmatic position, 76 ff.
double predestination, 171, 174 f.
experience, 38 f.
hermeneutics, 152 f.
individualism, 306 ff.
Infralapsarianism, *q.v.*
Jesus Christ *fundamentum electionis*, 67 ff., 113.
Jesus Christ *speculum electionis*, 62, 64 f., 110, 115, 155, 333.
number of elect, 377.
perseverantia sanct., 329 f.
rejection, 167 f.
scrupulus de praedestinatione, 222.
subject and object of, 145 ff.
Supralapsarianism, *q.v.*
syllogismus practicus, *q.v.*
v. Election, Doctrine of.
Proclamation, 5, 34 f., 209 f., 251 ff., 264 ff., 318, 418, 506, 563 f.

Proclamation, mission, 251 f., 255.
unbelief, 254 f.
Promise, 195, 197 ff., 215 f., 227, 233 ff., 235, 238, 243, 318 ff., 628.
v. Israel.
Prophecy, *v.* Revelation,
Providence, 45 ff., 78, 80.

Quietism, 187 f.

Rationalism, 308.
Reconciliation, 80 ff., 88 ff., 101, 123, 149, 163, 173, 208, 282 ff., 417, 489 ff., 739 ff., 759.
Redemption, 80, 89, 149, 283, 295.
Regeneration, 587, 772 f., 775.
Rejected, The—
determination, 449 ff., 454 ff.
existence, 450 ff.
Judas, 458 ff.
limit, 453 ff.
ministry, 346 f.
proclamation, 475 ff., 506.
as witness, 346 f., 352, 455 ff., 479 f.
v. Jesus Christ.
Rejection, 16, 27, 33, 40, 44, 122 ff., 127, 131, 149, 154, 163 ff., 171, 186 f., 200, 220, 225, 227, 231, 276, 291, 306, 318 f., 416, 449 ff., 587, 739.
non-rejection, 167 ff.
v. Individual, Jesus Christ.
Repentance, 223, 466, 563, 670, 755, 768 ff.
Return, *v.* Jesus Christ.
Revelation, 6 f., 53, 66, 76, 91 f., 94 ff., 105, 117, 151, 156 ff., 173, 179, 222, 247, 257, 265, 282, 293, 309, 422, 516 ff., 526, 532.
basis, intra-divine, 97, 108, 175.
history, 8, 94, 136, 141, 175 ff., 200, 239, 342, 677, 690.
incarnation, *v.* Jesus Christ.
miracle, 19, 228, 232, 257 f., 273, 296, 748, 757.
sign, 55, 226, 297.
mystery, 104, 151, 157 f., 185 f., 257, 273, 296 f., 748, 757.
order, 8, 12, 22, 33, 151, 157, 174 f., 193, 219, 223 f., 244, 254, 589, 600, 739.
prophecy, 252, 258 f., 271, 276 ff., 505.
unity in Old and New Testaments, 150 f., 197 f., 200 ff., 419 f.
world history, 7 f., 47, 55, 136, 185.
Righteousness of Works, 236, 273 f.
Roman Catholicism, 528 ff.
analogia entis, 530.
assurance of election, 336.
concept of God, 532 f.
concept of sin, 354.